The WORLD ENCYCLOPEDIA OF CONTEMPORARY THEATRE

VOLUME 1
EUROPE

The WORLD ENCYCLOPEDIA OF CONTEMPORARY THEATRE

VOLUME 1
EUROPE

DON RUBIN

LONDON AND NEW YORK

First published in 1994
by Routledge
11 New Fetter Lane, London EC4P 4EE

Simultaneously published in the USA and Canada
by Routledge, Inc.
29 West 35th Street, New York, NY 10001

© 1994 The World Encyclopedia of Contemporary Theatre Corporation

Typset in 9/10½pt Sabon and Optima by MCS Ltd, Wiltshire
Printed in Great Britain by Biddles Ltd, Guildford and Kings Lynn
Printed on acid-free paper

This encyclopedia is a project implemented with the support of UNESCO and at the request
of four non-governmental organizations. The opinions expressed in the various articles are
those of the authors themselves and do not necessarily reflect the point of view of the
sponsoring organizations.

British Library Cataloguing in Publication Data
A catalogue record for this book is available from the British Library.

Library of Congress Cataloging-in-Publication Data
A catalog record for this book is available on request.

ISBN 0–415–05928–3

INTERNATIONAL EDITORIAL BOARD

The World Encyclopedia of Contemporary Theatre would like to acknowledge with sincere thanks the financial contributions of the following:

REGIONAL SPONSORS

Canadian Department of Communications
Ford Foundation
Ontario Ministry of Citizenship and Culture
Rockefeller Foundation
Routledge, Chapman and Hall
Social Sciences and Humanities Research Council of Canada
UNESCO
York University

NATIONAL SPONSORS

Autonomous National University of Mexico
Cameroon National UNESCO Commission
Canadian National UNESCO Commission
Cultural Ministry of France
German Centre of the ITI
Higher Institute of Dramatic Arts, Damascus
Mexican National UNESCO Commission
Joseph S. Stauffer Foundation
University of Bordeaux
University of Dakar
Herman Voaden
Woodlawn Arts Foundation

STATE SPONSORS

Apotex Foundation
Austrian Ministry of Education and the Arts
Samuel and Saidye Bronfman Family Foundation
Floyd S. Chalmers
Faculty of Fine Arts, York University
Finnish Ministry of Education
FIRT

Georgian Ministry of Culture
Greek Ministry of Culture
Calouste Gulbenkian Foundation
International Theatre Institute (Paris) and National Centres in Bangladesh, Belgium (Flemish Community), Belgium (French Community), Bulgaria, Canada, Czech Republic, Finland, Hungary, India, Netherlands, Poland, Romania, Slovak Republic, United States, Switzerland and Venezuela
Israeli Ministry of Foreign Affairs, Division of Cultural and Scientific Relations
Japan Foundation Cultural Centre, Bangkok
Henry White Kinnear Foundation
Ministry of the Flemish Community (Cultural Affairs)
Moldovan Theatre Union
Organization of American States
Polish Ministry of Culture
Republic of Macedonia Ministry of Culture
K.M. Sarkissian and the Zoryan Institute
Conn Smythe Foundation
Turkish Embassy in Canada

LOCAL SPONSORS

Arts Development and Promotions
Australia Council
Mariellen Black
Lyle B. Blair
Canadian Theatre Review
Centre de Recherches et de Formation Théâtrales en Wallonie
Joy Cohnstaedt
Freda's Originals
John H. Moore, FCA
Erminio G. Neglia
Farouk Ohan
Ontario Ministry of Skills Development
Peter Perina
E. Marshall Pollock
Rodolfo A. Ramos
Calvin G. Rand
Lynton Reed Printing
Don Rubin
St Lawrence Centre for the Arts
Storewal International Inc.
Anton Wagner

Special thanks to:

Margrethe Aaby (Norway), Eric Alexander (Netherlands), Ebrahim Alkhazi (India), Ina Andre (Canada), Gaida Barisone (Latvia), Curtis Barlow (Canada), Alison Barr (United Kingdom), Isabelle Barth (France), Alexei Bartoshevitch (Russia), Shaul Baskind (Israel), Jean Benedetti (United Kingdom), Eric Bentley (United States), Mariellen Black (Canada), Lyle B. Blair (Canada), Gaston Blais (Canada), Monica Brizzi (Italy), Robert Brustein (United States), John Bury (United Kingdom), Judith Cameron (Canada), Richard Cave (United Kingdom), Katarina Ćirić-Petrović (Serbia), Joy Cohnstaedt (Canada), Martha Coigney (United States), Communications Committee (International Theatre Institute), Leonard W. Conolly (Canada), Robert Crew (Canada), Renée L. Czukar (Canada), Gautam Dasgupta (United States), Susan Frances Dobie (Canada), Francis Ebejer (Malta), Krista Ellis (Canada), John Elsom (United Kingdom), Claes Englund (Sweden), Debebe Eshetu (Ethiopia), Martin Esslin (United Kingdom), Alan Filewod (Canada), Stephen Florian (Malta), Mira Friedlander (Canada), Julia Gabor (Hungary), Bibi Gessner (Switzerland), Madeleine Gobeil (UNESCO), Sevelina Gyorova (Bulgaria), René Hainaux (Belgium), Bartold Halle (Norway), Peter Hay (United States), Ian Herbert (United Kingdom), Nick Herne (United Kingdom), Frank Hoff (Canada), Eleanor Hubbard (Canada), Huang Huilin (China), Djuner Ismail (Macedonia), Stephen Johnson, (Canada), Sylvia Karsh (Canada), Naïm Kattan (Canada), Ferenc Kerenyi (Hungary), Myles Kesten (Canada), Valery Khasanov (Russia), William Kilbourn (Canada), Pierre Laville (France), George Lengyel (Hungary), Henri Lopes (UNESCO), Paul Lovejoy (Canada), Margaret Majewska (Poland), Lars af Malmborg (Sweden), Georges Manal (France), Suzanne Marko (Sweden), Bonnie Marranca (New York), Ruth R. Mayleas (United States), Giles R. Meikle (Canada), Paul-Louis Mignon (France), Ian Montagnes (Canada), Mavor Moore (Canada), Richard Mortimer (Canada), Judi Most (United States), Julia Moulden (Canada), Irmeli Niemi (Finland), Farouk Ohan (United Arab Emirates), Louis Patenaude (Canada), Oskar Pausch (Austria), André-Louis Perinetti (International Theatre Institute), Donald S. Rickerd (Canada), Roehampton Hotel (Canada), Mr and Mrs Irving Rubin (United States), Marti Russell (Canada), Raimonda Sadauskienė (Lithuania), Suzanne Sato (United States), Willmar Sauter (Sweden), Richard Schechner (United States), Petar Selem (Croatia), Małgorzata Semil (Poland), Mary Ann Shaw (Canada), Neville Shulman (United Kingdom), Mikhail Shvidkoi (Russia), David Silcox (Canada), Phillip Silver (Canada), Singer Travel (United States), Ron Singer (Canada), Mike Smith (Canada), Prince Subhadradis Diskul (Thailand), Anneli Suur-Kujala (Finland), Péter Szaffkó (Hungary), Carlos Tindemans (Belgium), Indrassen Vencatchellum (UNESCO), Janusz Warminski (Poland), Klaus Wever (Germany), Don B. Willmeth (American Society for Theatre Research), Claudia Woolgar (United Kingdom), Piet Zeeman (Netherlands), Paul Zeleza (Canada).

DEDICATION

This series is dedicated to the memory of Roman Szydłowski of Poland (1918–83), a former President of the International Association of Theatre Critics. His vision for all international theatre organizations was truly worldwide and his tenacity in the service of that vision was genuinely legendary. It was Dr Szydłowski who first proposed the idea for a *World Encyclopedia of Contemporary Theatre.*

CONTENTS

VOLUME ONE • EUROPE

Contents · **The Nations and Their Theatres**

VOLUME ONE

EUROPE

AN INTRODUCTION

OF NATIONS AND THEIR THEATRES

The encyclopedia has been with humankind since the ancient Greeks. Aristotle's works are certainly encyclopedic in nature; that is to say, they encircle particular aspects of knowledge, some extremely specialized, some more general. Pliny the Elder (AD 23–79) compiled a thirty-seven-volume encyclopedia of natural science. The largest encyclopedia seems to have been edited by the Emperor of China, Yung Lo, in the fifteenth century. Called the *Yung Lo Ta Tien*, it required 2,169 scholars to write it and ran to 917,480 pages in 11,100 volumes.

The World Encyclopedia of Contemporary Theatre (*WECT*) is a somewhat less exhaustive encyclopedia than Yung Lo's. When complete, we expect it to run to only 3,000 or so pages in a mere six volumes. However, Yung Lo sought to cover a much wider range of subjects than *WECT*. His goal was to examine nothing less than all of Chinese literature from the beginning of time.

WECT makes no such claims about its comprehensiveness. *WECT* is specifically an encyclopedia of nations and their theatres. The starting point is 1945, the end of World War II, a time of change politically, socially and culturally for much of the world. Sketching out a social and political context for each of the countries being studied, *WECT* seeks to explore in a comparative fashion each country's theatrical history since that time. The assumption from the beginning has been that theatre is an art form which grows from its society and which feeds back into it through reflection, analysis and challenge.

No other international theatre encyclopedia has attempted such a comparative, broad-based, cross-cultural study. The fact that every one of our writers is from the country being written about adds still another level of authority and uniqueness to this work, which is attempting to present each nation's view of itself, a view not of politicians or propagandists but of each country's theatrical scholars and theatre artists.

It should also be made clear here that *WECT* is not intended as a guide to individuals, companies, festivals or forms. One will not find here analyses of Stanislavski, Brecht, Craig, Brook, Grotowski or Artaud. Nor will one find biographies of Soyinka, Fugard or Havel. *WECT* is also not the place to look for a history of the Comédie-Française or the Stratford Festival, Venezuela's Rajatabla or Japan's Tenjo Sajiki. Nor will readers find extensive documentation on the Carthage Festival or Edinburgh, on BITEF or Adelaide, on the Cervantes Festival or even Avignon.

The world of theatre is far too large and has become far too specialized for that. Information on the lives of everyone from playwrights to puppeteers, choreographers to composers, directors to designers can be readily found in a wide range of reference works available in every major language. There are book-length analyses and histories – some critical, some just documentation – of all the major companies and festivals that one could ever want to know about. There are also dictionaries available that focus on virtually every specialized theatrical subject from semiotics to cultural anthropology. Many fine theatre journals around the world maintain a valuable and continuing dialogue and documentation of current issues.

What has not existed before – and what *WECT* has attempted to create – has been a theatrical reference work looking at a wide range of *national* theatrical activity on a country-by-country basis from a specifically *national*

3

standpoint. As we near the end of the twentieth century, as nations in many parts of the world finally shed their colonial pasts, and as new nations emerge in the aftermath of the collapse of the Soviet Union and Yugoslavia, such a gap in our cultural knowledge may seem curious. What, for example, does Romanian theatre look like to a Romanian in this post-modern world? Canadian theatre to a Canadian? What is of import to an Australian about his or her own theatre? To a Senegalese? A Brazilian? A Vietnamese? An Egyptian? And what of all the individual republics that once made up the Soviet Union, Yugoslavia and Czechoslovakia? What is the self-perception of theatre professionals in the new Germany, where two totally different systems were uncomfortably reunited as the 1990s began?

To allow the reader to draw conclusions and to allow comparability, each of *WECT*'s writers was given the challenge of bringing together just such a national impression in a very specifically structured essay which would include not lists of names and dates but rather a context – in some cases, contexts – for international comprehension. That is, each of *WECT*'s extensive national articles – ranging from 3,000 to 30,000 words per country (small books in some instances) – has been written so as to provide theatrical professionals and those concerned with research on the profession with not only the basic material they would need if they were going to work in or visit a particular country for the first time, but also the basic material necessary to identify international trends and movements in the decades since the end of World War II.

Those who already know their own or some other country's theatre very well, no doubt, will find the information contained on those countries useful but probably too basic. Even at 30,000 words, these articles cannot possibly replace the library that would be needed to completely cover the theatre of any one country. In any event, encyclopedias historically have been intended only as introductions. Indeed, it is difficult to imagine them being anything more than that on any given subject. The philosopher and encyclopedist Denis Diderot (1713–84) argued that encyclopedias should be seen as basic libraries in every field but the reader's own. In this case, it is a theatre library for every country but the reader's own. To this end, we have asked writers to think of their ideal reader as a sophisticated professional from abroad.

In this light, we believe that *WECT* will be most important to readers for the breadth of its coverage; in this case, for the distance from home that each reader can travel through these articles. This is not in any way to suggest a lack of depth but rather to honestly recognize given limitations. *WECT* is therefore providing extended and extensive articles on every theatre culture in the world, more than one hundred and fifty countries by the time the project is concluded. Looked at as a whole, they will be more than able to help theatre professionals in every part of the world put plays, companies, policies and productions into a national context, and in our complicated world this seems an important and unique contribution.

WECT material can be accessed in one of two ways: by either reading vertically (from beginning to end in any particular country) or horizontally (focusing on only a single subject such as Puppet Theatre or Dramaturgy across several countries). Having suggested earlier that this is not an encyclopedia of individuals, companies, festivals or forms, the fact is that one *can* identify individuals, companies, festivals and forms by referring to the index at the back of each volume or to the comprehensive multivolume index planned for the final volume. By going to specific pages, the reader will then be able to follow the influence and development of particular figures or groups within their own countries, within regions and ultimately in the world.

Whichever approach one is using, whether professionally focused or casual, it is probably useful at this point to understand the many section headings in each of the national articles and what each section is intended to include.

Each national article in this volume is divided into twelve sections: History, Structure of the National Theatre Community, Artistic Profile, Music Theatre, Dance Theatre, Theatre for Young Audiences, Puppet Theatre, Design, Theatre Space and Architecture, Training, Criticism, Scholarship and Publishing, and Further Reading. These sections are intended to provide the following information.

History: Each national article opens with basic geographical, historical and/or socio-political material. In the cases of countries whose histories may not be well known outside the immediate region, we have encouraged writers to provide a more extensive background than might normally be found. Included as well is a history of the country's major theatrical movements and events since 1945, treated on a decade-by-decade basis or treated thematically.

In each case the intent has been to give the national writer flexibility in interpreting the material being discussed.

Structure of the National Theatre Community: This is essentially a demographic section intended to offer information on the types of theatres (commercial, state supported, regional or municipal) and the numbers of theatres operating in a particular country, their geographical distribution and relative sizes (both in terms of employees and budgets). One will find in this section information on the various infrastructures that have developed (national associations, national and international linkages), unions, as well as information on the major festivals in the country and national awards.

Artistic Profile: Divided into sub-sections, this examination of the major artistic trends in each national theatre since 1945 begins with **Companies**, goes on to **Dramaturgy** and concludes, where writers did not already deal with these areas in previous sections, with a discussion of **Directors, Directing and Production Styles.** Because our intent has been to look at the relationship between theatre and society, readers of this section are urged to look as well at the first two sections. Once again, the intent has been to provide the *foreign* theatre professional with an understanding of which groups, writers and directors are the most significant in the country and to put them into a national perspective. The sub-section designated as 'Dramaturgy' was initially called 'Playwriting' but was changed to 'Dramaturgy' to allow *WECT* to recognize the many companies that have worked collectively during the period being examined and to acknowledge the significant role of the director in script development. In no way is this intended to demean the importance of the playwright whose work, we believe, still remains central to the process of theatrical creation.

Music Theatre and *Dance Theatre*: We start in both these sections with the assumption that there has long been a relationship between music and theatre, and dance and theatre; we have asked our writers to examine those relationships from a theatrical rather than from a musical or dance standpoint. In suggesting such differentiations we have proposed that the writer take into account the kind of training needed to perform the work (music/dance or theatrical) and how the work is professionally assessed (by music/dance or theatre critics). In cases where the answers come down firmly on the side of music or dance, we have proposed not including the material in *WECT* since it might more appropriately be included in a music or dance encyclopedia. In some cases writers have focused exclusively on the line where the forms connect – often in multimedia experiments; in other cases they have written about more traditional opera and important dance or music groups. Those specifically interested in mime will find it discussed – where it has some national artistic significance – in the **Dance Theatre** section.

Theatre for Young Audiences: In many countries – especially in the period since 1945 – theatre for young audiences has developed significantly. By including a separate section in these articles, *WECT* intends to acknowledge the importance of this very special area of contemporary theatre life. The light thrown on such work seems of significance in the long-term development of theatrical art generally since 1945.

Puppet Theatre: Sometimes linked with the **Theatre for Young Audiences** section but most often recognized on its own, puppet theatre is at once one of the oldest of the popular theatrical arts and, where it has been rediscovered by contemporary theatrical practitioners, one of the most avant-garde. Within this section we have asked writers to trace developments in the form from its theatrical mimetic roots (imitation of actors) to what has come to be known as Object Theatre in which things take on a dramatic life of their own thanks, very often, to black light techniques that emerged during this period in eastern Europe. We have asked our writers as well to look at experiments involving the interrelationship between live actors and puppets or live actors and objects. This is a fascinating and important area which theatre professionals ignore at their own imaginative risk.

Design: This section examines the work of each theatre community's visual artists. In some cases this has been done thematically; in other cases, on a decade-by-decade basis since 1945. Again, we have asked our writers to avoid lists. Instead of just naming names, we have asked them to choose a small number of representative designers and discuss their individual work.

Theatre Space and Architecture: When we began, this section was simply titled 'Theatre Architecture'. The words 'Theatre Space' were added as the articles began to arrive. Many of our writers originally interpreted this section as being only about buildings created specifically as theatrical venues. Clearly this would have eliminated many of the experiments relating to theatrical space which began in the 1960s and are still with us today, experiments which seem to have begun in North America out of sheer desperation and which evolved in many parts of the world into the total breakdown of proscenium theatre with its visual accoutrements as an *a priori* requirement for theatrical events.

Training: This section discusses the most important theatre schools and other professional training programmes in each country, their types of curriculum and the traditions they follow.

Criticism, Scholarship and Publishing: The most important theatre research and documentation centres in each country, major performing arts museums and the types of critical approaches being taken by leading critics and theatre scholars are identified in this section. The discussions here range from journalistic reviewing to more analytical philological, anthropological, semiological, and/or other types of structural approaches. In some cases historical context is provided; in others, contemporary developments are emphasized. As well, writers have been asked to identify the most important theatre journals and magazines along with the major theatre publishing houses in their countries.

Further Reading: Each national article concludes with a brief bibliography identifying the major works available within the national language as well as the most important works about the country's theatre that the authors are aware of in other languages. We have tried to follow the bibliographical form recommended by the University of Chicago but in some instances writers followed their own scholarly form leaving us with certain Chicago-style omissions. Though we attempted to fill these gaps it was not always possible. In general, however, enough information has been provided to allow the diligent reader to find the works mentioned.

To some, this structure may seem overly complicated and perhaps even contradictory in terms of allowing each writer or team of writers to identify and define their national theatres. But in every instance, the key was to maintain comparability country-to-country and ultimately region-to-region. It is our belief that as interesting and informative as each national article may be, the real value of *WECT* will ultimately lie in its ability to provide comparability of theatres world-wide, in its ability to allow directors, playwrights, dramaturges, designers, critics, scholars and even those in government to look across a wide range of theatre communities.

Certainly this structure was not arrived at quickly or casually and it continued to be refined almost until publication. When this project was first conceived by the Polish theatre critic Roman Szydłowski (1918–83) in the late 1970s, it was seen simply as an opportunity to provide accurate and up-to-date documentation for theatre critics who were being confronted more regularly than ever before with theatre from all over the world as part of their daily reviewing duties. Visiting groups were no longer rare and exotic events on a critic's schedule. They were appearing with amazing regularity and the best critics simply wanted to do their homework.

But where could a working critic go to find quickly information on Turkish *karagöz*, on Thai *Khon* or South Africa's Market Theatre? Critics just seemed to be expected to know everything and everyone. Even when some information did exist, the sources were too often out of date or existed only in a language not widely spoken.

Most scholars would probably point to the nine-volume *Enciclopedia dello spettacolo* as the standard reference in the field. Available, however, only in Italian, the vast majority of the documentation included there was gathered before World War II and was, to say the least, Eurocentric. Published after the war, this encyclopedia of world theatre history was certainly strong the further one went back in time. But despite the fact that non-European theatre generally and the twentieth century specifically were not especially well served, the *Enciclopedia dello spettacolo* did become a standard. Most libraries found it essential for their reference sections. By the 1970s, however, it was clearly out of date even in its approaches to some of its early material.

Through the years, less ambitious attempts were made. Along with specialized individual volumes, these were very useful but, because of their specificity or, in some cases, their purely academic approach, they were not always useful to theatre professionals. It was at this point in time that Roman Szydłowski proposed a new type of world theatre reference work to the International Association of Theatre Critics, one of many international theatre communications organizations that had sprung up in the wake of two world wars.

At this organization's Congress in Vienna in 1979, Szydłowski, its president, received wide support for the proposal but no clear directions on how to proceed. Within eighteen months, however, he had convinced the International

Theatre Institute's (ITI) Permanent Committee on Theatre Publications – a loose association of editors of theatre magazines and journals – to take up the challenge. The ITI, it was felt, being affiliated with the United Nations Educational, Scientific and Cultural Organization (UNESCO) at a higher level than the other international theatre associations, would be the right agency to bring the idea to fruition on the world stage. At its 1981 Congress, this committee (subsequently to be called the Communications Committee) endorsed the idea and recommended it to the organization as a whole. It was the ITI's new secretary-general, Lars af Malmborg from Sweden, who decided that the project would be a concrete contribution to world theatre communication.

Malmborg, with the support of the ITI Executive Committee, brought the idea forward and in early 1982 called a meeting of interested international theatre organizations and individuals who might be able to help realize the project. It was from this meeting, held under the aegis of the Fine Arts Museum in Copenhagen, that specific plans began to be made. Four organizations – the ITI, the International Association of Theatre Critics (IATC), the International Federation for Theatre Research (FIRT) and the International Society of Libraries and Museums for the Performing Arts (SIBMAS) – agreed to combine efforts towards the realization of what was now being called *The World Encyclopedia of Contemporary Theatre*.

By 1983, with the support of the Faculty of Fine Arts at York University in Toronto and with the initial interest of a major Toronto publishing house, *WECT* was incorporated as an independent not-for-profit project under Canadian law. Initial grants came from York University, UNESCO and, the largest grant to that time, from the American-based Ford Foundation (thanks to a willingness to risk on a project that did not fit neatly into any previously established programme by its Theatre Officer, Ruth Mayleas). During 1984, representatives of the four sponsoring organizations met in Toronto (courtesy of Canadian philanthropist Floyd S. Chalmers) to set up parameters. Without this initial support and all the faith it implied in an unprecedented vision, *WECT* would never have got off the ground.

The year 1945 was established as a starting point though it was agreed that nothing ever really starts or ends neatly in the world of theatre. It was agreed that television and radio would not be dealt with but that music theatre

and dance theatre would be included. It was agreed that a socio-cultural approach would be taken and that the relationship between theatres and the nations from which they grew would be explored. It was agreed that comparability would be emphasized and that writers should be chosen from within each country.

During 1984 an outstanding international team of editors was selected to coordinate the work and to advise in such specialty areas as theatre for young audiences (Wolfgang Wöhlert), music theatre (Horst Seeger), dance theatre (Selma Jeanne Cohen) and puppet theatre (Henryk Jurkowski) among others. Over the years the International Editorial Board would expand and contract as needs appeared or as particular individuals found themselves unable to continue the work. But throughout, the notion of self-identification for each national article was maintained and continued to be the primary reason why *WECT* searched for leading writers, critics, scholars and theatre professionals within each country.

The first full International Editorial Board meeting was held in Toronto in 1985 during the twenty-first World Congress of the ITI. There were five people present from North America, another five from Europe (including *WECT*'s two associate editors, Péter Nagy of Budapest and Philippe Rouyer of Bordeaux) and another six from Latin America, Africa, the Arab countries and Asia/Oceania. It was one of our Asian editors who put the first question to the gathering. 'What exactly do we think *we* mean when we use the word theatre?' he asked. 'I'm really not sure there's a definition we can all agree on. And if we can't come to an agreement on this basic question, how can we possibly agree on anything else?'

The apparently simple question led to an enormously involved discussion about the various types of spoken drama that had evolved in Europe and North America. Objections were quickly raised that we were ignoring musical theatre forms and forms involving movement. Others objected that we were locked into text while our puppet theatre editor was concerned that we were leaving out everything from Wayang Kulang to Punch and Judy. Our African colleagues suggested that our preliminary definition seemed to be ignoring the social relationships in much African theatre, from wedding ceremonies to circumcision rituals. And what of traditional forms in Asia such as *Kathakali, Noh, Kabuki,* Chinese opera, or even the Vietnamese *Hat Boi*? What of folk forms in so many parts of the world? What of contemporary experiments?

What had appeared to be a rather innocent question in the beginning quickly turned into a life-or-death debate on the whole future – not even to mention the international credibility – of the project. During the next few days, we turned to various standard texts on theatre in search of a suitable, internationally acceptable definition. It was a fascinating, though ultimately frustrating, exercise. To our amazement, we couldn't really find such a definition. Examinations of standard dictionaries – including the *Oxford English Dictionary* – were of even less help. Most simply defined 'theatre' as a building.

So we created our own international, intercultural working definition of the word. It is offered here not as a conclusion but rather as a starting point for a continuing consideration of what those of us working in the field mean when 'theatre' is spoken of in a contemporary global context.

> *Theatre*: A created event, usually based on text, executed by live performers and taking place before an audience in a specially defined setting. Theatre uses techniques of voice and/or movement to achieve cognition and/or emotional release through the senses. This event is generally rehearsed and is usually intended for repetition over a period of time.

By the time *WECT*'s International Editorial Board next met, it had become clear from discussions with the various international organizations that *WECT* would have to respect various national differences in approaching this work and would have to take, as the American poet Robert Frost once said, 'the road less travelled by' in seeking its writers; that is, it would go to source for its information and interpretation in every instance. Indeed, *WECT* has through the years taken pride in this unique approach, slow and costly though it has been. But it has also been an approach which has led the project to develop close working relationships with theatre people *in* each of the more than 150 countries now involved in what has become the largest international cooperative venture in the history of world theatre, and certainly the largest international publishing venture in world theatre today.

In focusing the work this way, it was obvious that the *WECT* project was taking many risks. The approach was obviously going to make this a much longer project than anyone had ever dreamed of. By the time this work is concluded,

it will have taken almost fifteen years. The approach would also force us to find significant international funding at a time when economies were just beginning to go into recession in many parts of the world. As this volume goes to press, *WECT* is still seeking national and international partners to fund the subsequent volumes in the series: *The Americas*, *Africa*, *The Arab World*, *Asia/Oceania*, and the concluding *World Theatre Bibliography/Cumulative Index*.

But we believed when we started – and still believe – that our approach was one which would afford the best opportunity to ensure both the long-term goals and the highest standards of international scholarly excellence and accuracy. This approach was also one of the key reasons why UNESCO decided to support the project and why UNESCO ultimately named *WECT* as an official project of its World Decade for Cultural Development (1988–97). Such recognition is unusual for a scholarly work and we feel with some pride that it is an important model for future intercultural, interdisciplinary arts research.

A few words are needed here about world politics and its effect upon our work. For most people, political change is simply interesting newspaper fodder or the stuff to support opinions – pro or con – on particular subjects. The closer that politics gets to home, however, the more directly it impacts on one's reality and the more it affects how one goes about one's daily business. Political change has constantly impacted on *WECT*'s reality and profoundly affected its already complicated work.

To give but one key example, when work began on our European volume, there were only two dozen or so countries to deal with, and those in eastern Europe were guaranteeing they would cover all our writing and translation fees for the region. That was in 1985. By 1990, the two Germanys had become one (requiring a significant restructuring of our German material) while the USSR, Yugoslavia and Czechoslovakia went from three separate national entities to twenty-three separate countries (fifteen individual republics from the Soviet Union, six from Yugoslavia and two from Czechoslovakia). Not only did the already completed major articles on the USSR, Yugoslavia and Czechoslovakia have to be completely revised and turned into what we decided to call 'historical overviews' but also new writers needed to be found and new articles had to be commissioned on each of the republics, republics that were, in many instances, in the midst of social, political or armed revolution. With such changes swirling around us, we read the newspapers each day with genuine trepidation. By the time of publication, the volume had expanded to some forty-seven articles. Suffice it to say here that trying to keep up with this ever-changing political landscape continues to be *WECT*'s greatest challenge, a challenge we are trying to meet through computerization and the establishment of *WECT* as an international theatre database.

It was precisely these political changes which Martha Coigney, president of the ITI, was referring to when she said, perhaps optimistically, at the opening of the ITI's 1993 World Congress in Munich that in the future it would no longer be wars between superpowers that people of peace would have to be concerned about, but rather confrontations between cultures. If this is so then we believe that *WECT* may well be able to make a real contribution in at least introducing those cultures to one another. *WECT*'s goal from the beginning has been nothing less than that.

In helping the project to achieve this end, many organizations, many theatre and government agencies, many foundations and individuals have played important roles. A list of the financial sponsors and those who have worked with us appears elsewhere but we would like to acknowledge specifically the ongoing help of UNESCO, the Ford and Rockefeller Foundations (Rockefeller came to *WECT*'s aid at precisely the moment that recession and the enormous political changes in Europe threatened to kill the project), the Faculty of Fine Arts and the Office of Research Administration at York University, the Canadian and Ontario governments, the German Centre of the International Theatre Institute and particularly Rolf Rohmer, who has long served as president of the project's International Executive Board. This project would not have survived without the help of the Canadian Centre of the ITI (especially Curtis Barlow in the early years of the project) and the various members of the Canadian-based Board of Directors who worked to find funds to realize this work. The support of our two recent Board presidents has been particularly appreciated – Calvin G. Rand (founding president of Canada's Shaw Festival) and Professor Leonard W. Conolly, formerly of the University of Guelph and now president of Trent University in Ontario.

This project could also not have survived without the ongoing support of the Faculty of Fine Arts and the department of theatre at York University, its deans and its chairs (including Lionel Lawrence, Joyce Zemans, Joy Cohnstaedt, Ron Singer and Phillip Silver) and especially the sponsors of the Walter A. Gordon Fellowship, York University's highest research award, which allowed me the time to bring the European volume to fruition.

This project would not have succeeded had *WECT* not had the active support and understanding of all the members of its International Editorial Board, particularly the wisdom and advice of Péter Nagy, whose diplomacy in the face of *WECT*'s own political struggles was never less than brilliant. Nor would it have succeeded without the stubborn belief in this project of its Managing Editor and Director of Research, Anton Wagner, whose work was long funded by the Canadian Social Science and Humanities Research Council, and the project's indefatigable administrator Donna Dawson. Our editors at Routledge – Alison Barr, Michelle Darraugh and Robert Potts – have been most understanding in working with us on what must have appeared to them a mad dream at times. Without their personal commitment and the corporate support behind them, *WECT* would still be in the planning stages.

If I have personally been seen through the many years of this project as its architect, I can only say that the building would never have stood without the strength, determination and belief of my wife and too rarely recognized co-visionary, Patricia Keeney. Against all her writerly instincts and sometimes against all logic, she bravely sat through meeting after meeting of every one of this project's boards, a duty she took on because she believed in the work. Without her faith and goodwill, *WECT* might well have foundered.

There are far too many people to thank here by name. It would be remiss to try, for too many would be left out. But to all of them, particularly to all our editors, writers, national editorial committees, ITI Centres and translators, to all the sponsoring and other organizations which supported this work, thank you for believing with us and in us. We trust that your patience and support will have proven to be worth all the time, the pain and the effort.

DON RUBIN

Toronto, May 1994

THE NEW FRONTIER

AN INTRODUCTION TO THEATRE IN EUROPE SINCE WORLD WAR II

Is it proper to speak of eastern and western European theatre? Theatre with an individual, identifiable point of view representing a regional expression of art? Is eastern European theatre a separate entity or should one more properly speak now of a European theatre, without regional distinctions?

We believe the question valid even given the enormous cultural, political and social changes that have rocked Europe since the late 1980s. As a result, the answering of such questions is more complicated than previously and far too complex to be performed in a strictly political manner.

It's worth pointing out that the United Nations and its cultural affiliate, UNESCO, still recognize an eastern European region to which the former Soviet Union and Warsaw Pact nations belonged. This categorization was established during the Cold War's heyday for practical and political reasons, without philosophical considerations. The sole commonality was their belonging to the bloc of 'existing socialism' regardless of their specific relationship to the Soviet Union.

With Soviet imperialism now history, with political conflict between east and west all but eliminated and with differences now more economic than ideological, is it logical to speak still of a specific region? It might be argued that continuing such a concept simply proves that we cannot leave the past behind even when our best interest lies in looking to the future.

Nevertheless, a region is distinguished by various factors, the most readily identifiable and longest lasting being its culture, that which both connects and defines its boundaries. The three cultural philosophies of Europe – western

Christianity, eastern Christianity and Islam – have long established and influenced everyday behaviour, society, art and belief in this part of the world. Without doubt, various sects within Christianity – Scandinavian Lutheranism, British Presbyterianism or eastern European Catholicism – are far less distinguishable from one another than an Orthodox Christian is from all those, or Islam is, say, from Christianity. Nevertheless, even within these sects, separate cultural and historical traditions subtly interweave seemingly disparate lives. The result is regular and unavoidable interregional and international cultural intercourse.

Looked at this way, it is obvious that we cannot view eastern and western European theatre any more as purely separate entities. Certainly countries like Poland, the Czech Republic and Hungary are more clearly connected to the west, while others like Russia, Serbia, Bulgaria and Romania are much more linked with eastern cultures. Regions of Albania, Bulgaria and the former Yugoslavia, along with several republics that emerged from the collapsed Soviet Union, are also influenced by Muslim traditions.

Yet in spite of the distances and the differences, in spite of the many interactions between these areas, it seems to us that there is still something that can be called specifically eastern European or specifically western European, something which cannot be easily identified, but which can be felt and sensed by everyone.

There is a great divide in Europe which really does split the continent into east and west from Tallinn to Dubrovnik. It is along this line that Byzantine heritage is separated from Roman heritage, a cultural frontier separating, for one, eastern and western Christianity. As a result, most countries bordering or straddling this line position themselves on one side or another of the cultures. Nations are both separated and united by this divide. Those living along it become 'bridge' countries enriched by both cultures and, like everyone else, are seeking answers to their individual problems while assessing their own errors and achievements.

Eastern Europe

Geographically and historically, eastern Europe was influenced by three large empires and their cultures: the Russian, Ottoman and Habsburg empires. All three, even today, maintain an historical influence on architecture and urban development, culture, morals, behaviour and dress. The links to the past are both liabilities and assets at the same time. On the one hand, the inhabitants of this region – as people living at the end of the twentieth century – may feel that they do not belong to any of these groups or that they live between them all the time. As they look to the west, some have had a different kind of spiritual thirst, a wish to assimilate or simply to create something different and independent and self-reflective. Perhaps such thoughts apply only to intellectuals and to those who are involved in politics. The people, on the other hand, those who live on the plains and the mountains, those who are integrated and mixed to the point of no return, have no wish but to exist peacefully under their ever-changing values, to preserve and protect their languages, religions and customs, their traditions, beliefs and tales. For these people, living and working together in the same villages, nothing in their everyday life really separates them; indeed, everything keeps bringing them together.

During the 1930s, many eastern European intellectuals recognized this and voiced it loudly, above all as a protest and as an attempt to balance increasing Nazi influences. After World War II, all eastern European countries came under the direct influence of Stalin's Soviet Union with various degrees of enthusiasm: the only road open to them was the type of socialism or communism which had to be copied from the Soviets. Though their fates became entwined, the various countries moved further from one another than ever before. During the 1950s, as the Cold War reached its peak, borders were impossible to walk through – or even approach – for ordinary people; only officials or members of official delegations were allowed to cross. They all spoke of their eternal friendship to each other but behind the scenes they simply tried to ensure better lives, a bit more breathing room for themselves at the cost of the others.

This relationship, held together by sheer force, started to decline after Stalin's death in 1953 and the process led to complete collapse by the 1980s. Every nation in the region went into shock, as in a national disaster, and has subsequently struggled to revive itself. The real question was whether or not they would recognize their shared fate and similar conditions and cooperate with and support one another, which would certainly get them further than they ever could go alone, certainly further than they would get by fighting one another. Along with their new-found freedoms came the recognition of possibly showing their teeth to one another. Without Big Brother to watch and interfere, these various nations suddenly had the opportunity to fight out their often secular differences, which were violently put under the bushel by the slogan of proletarian internationalism.

Clearly, togetherness is written into the fate and future of eastern Europe and the big winners will be those who first recognize this truth and are able to make it happen.

One of the most effective ways to express the implications of fate is through the theatre. It has long had the ability to point out the value of human cooperation from similar lifestyles – even if lived in separate ways – and that similar problems can develop, and can be mutually solved. This can bring cultures – and especially theatres – closer to one another.

Perhaps the most important common feature is the late awakening of the theatres of eastern Europe. One reason could be that eastern Europe is on the outskirts of Europe's central cultural plateau and is traditionally late to accept invitations or opportunities presented to it; or perhaps it is the influence of religion that was holding development back more than in western Europe. Whatever the reason – and one does not necessarily contradict the other – the fact remains that theatres and the theatre-going public in the region are at least a century, if not more, behind western European theatre customs and achievements. Poland is where the difference is smallest; Albania is where it is largest; this is reflected in the theatre culture of these two nations.

In general, it was during the period of romanticism that theatres became lively cultural forces in the region. This is not to suggest that there were no folkloric roots and traditions of playacting; but there was little or no transition from these types of performances to performances by professionals. Maybe this is one of the reasons why romanticism in these countries remained vivid for such a long time; in some it lasted for over a century, dominating the fate and directions of the theatre and becoming the 'natural' form of national classic works.

What is also similar in the literature of eastern European countries and especially in their theatres is the mixture and joint appearance of art and politics. In more fortunate countries politics and art do not go together nor is it necessary for them to connect. In this part of the world, however, to a great extent because of the lack of democratic traditions and democratic experience, artists seem forced to take over some of the functions which in a normal society belong to politicians. This is why in eastern Europe every other politician seems to be a failed poet and every other poet is a politician who escaped into verse-making. This political dimension has greatly affected the public's appreciation and response to the art, especially during periods of overt or hidden dictatorship. Audiences were captured by the 'message', often accepting a lack of aesthetic value and a disregard for artistic achievement. From an artistic standpoint, the situation was the same: these people usually had more vivid connections with the major nations of the world than with their own neighbours. Thus, if theatre people from Budapest or Belgrade wanted to know the latest developments in their profession, they did not visit each other but rather went to Paris and Berlin.

This changed to some extent after World War II when each nation went through a period of self-discovery. This was rooted in the desire to catch up with achievements of more fortunate nations, but always while keeping an eye on changes in neighbouring countries. To this was added a burgeoning feeling of solidarity and brotherhood, especially among young people, with the hope that the direction was being followed by all the nations in the region. But the political system started to destroy solidarity among social classes and individuals. Various types of massive repression began to occur: ethnic and religious minorities were branded with 'collective guilt', jailed or forced to emigrate under the banner of the growing class struggle; injustice and fabricated accusations against individuals and social groups were the accompaniments of a growing terrorism.

Between 1948 and 1950, the hegemony and dominance of the Communist Party forced all these eastern European nations to turn introspective. The only external influence was from Soviet culture which demanded that all art be socialist-realism in style. From the west, only 'progressive' art – generally critical of its society – was recognized. Exposure to foreign literature was therefore limited to world classics and to other communist artists.

This blinkering, the aesthetics of which were strict and built on the new political theories, lasted only a few years. Almost immediately after Stalin's death, things began to open up once more. Nevertheless, its effects and influences are still felt – sometimes only in a negative way – but they clearly still represent that era and its art. This is one of the key signs which lets us justifiably state that eastern European art, specifically the art of theatre, is identifiable as a special, separate entity in this period.

But were all these changes in the period from 1948 to 1953 negative or not? This is an important question and in fairness one must say that not all the changes were negative. Yes, it was negative to accept the all-permeating influence of daily politics on art, something which made it impossible to look at creativity in the long term or even simply as a diversion. And it was negative to have political institutions actively and regularly, often aggressively, interfering in every theatre's affairs. On the other hand, state ownership of theatres guaranteed incomes, provided social benefits, and eliminated the worry about personal security. It was positive as well that the theatre community had the opportunity to study their art without charge in state schools and especially to become familiar with the Stanislavski method – the use of natural body movements and voice – even though some of them did not go further than a busy lip-service, continuing their trade as before. It was only later on that they felt the drawbacks: that artists became state employees and theatres began to resemble inwardly state bureaucracies.

Eventually, this closed and rigid system began to break up and everywhere a 'thaw' began, opening up the theatrical world to new achievements and new values. As for the timing of these changes, it depended in each country on several contingencies, not least on the rigidity of the political leadership and the flexibility of the artistic milieu. In the world of theatre, one of the most influential in this movement was the German dramatist Bertolt Brecht. Through his art and his theories, communist theatre found a window on the modern and the contemporary. And the window stayed open through Brecht's loyalty to communist ideals. After his death, his influence became even stronger, effectively blending theory and practice in the service of art.

There is neither time nor space to deal with specific details here about how this all occurred in each country but happen it did, though not without difficulties, successes and failures, fights and setbacks. A more detailed picture can be found in the individual national articles in this volume. The essential point is that this process did take place in every country in eastern Europe with more or less similar results. By the 1970s and 1980s, a new sense of nationalism was added to the artistic search, an element that many hoped would strengthen theatre life further in both theory and practice.

As of 1993, it is virtually impossible to know if this new nationalism/individualism will result in a booming new theatre life with an intermingling of national and regional characteristics or whether it will develop into a vague type of homogenized art in which western forms generally and American styles specifically will simply take over from the earlier Soviet way. Each is a possibility and each has its own advantages and disadvantages. But rather than worrying about prophecies, it might be wiser to concentrate on the earlier question of what is and has been specific to eastern European theatre, what is unusual in it, what makes it different from other theatres?

This specificity can be found first of all in playwriting. From the end of the 1950s, a new direction could be seen in several countries – more or less independently – which could be called Eastern European Grotesque. Rooted in the existential notion of the absurd but following the social directions and moods of their time, these plays present their absurd plots as the sheerest banality of everyday life, in this way making the extraordinary banal and through banality discovering the absurdity of contemporary existence. In most cases, these plays have a clear allegorical dimension, an element generally missing from the western European absurd.

Clearly, this movement had various influences.

Mrożek in Poland, Örkény in Hungary and Havel in Czechoslovakia could not have become dramatists without the earlier work of Kafka and Jarry, Roger Vitrac and Bruno Schulz, Beckett and Ionesco. But saying that it could not have happened without them does not mean that it happened through them. They simply made it easier for the Mrożeks, the Örkénys and the Havels to discover their own voices. Obviously, these creators of the Eastern European Grotesque did more than follow examples; they developed their own approaches.

It is also necessary to speak about two other movements which came out of eastern European theatre and theatrical art and which widely influenced many other countries in many parts of the world. The first is the Czech Laterna Magika; the other is the work in Poland of Jerzy Grotowski. Both were rooted in the 1920s avant-garde and both still have many adherents in the region, albeit more or less fading away. Each takes a different direction and uses different methods: the Laterna Magika was looking to create a *Gesamtkunstwerk* while Grotowski experimented to the point where simplicity – poverty in his terms – tried to achieve and create the metaphysical dimension of the theatre. Nevertheless, these movements can be seen as complementary and together gave something to the theatre which simply did not exist before. Both movements helped to create a new and specific face for the eastern European theatre.

Another difference worth noting was the connection between the professional and amateur theatres in the region. The relationship was specific and the exchange worked in both directions. Not only did leading amateurs (mainly students) find their way into the professional theatre but also professional actors, directors and even choreographers worked with amateur groups for varying periods of time during which they experimented with new ideas, renewed their artistic talents or simply experienced the life of a group which lived and worked purely for one another.

Finally, a word about the perception of eastern European theatre in the west and in other parts of the world. It is difficult to speak about this in a critically balanced way. Certain companies, playwrights, directors, actors and other individuals from this region have been recognized in many ways, most noticeably at international festivals. Obviously, the standard has been high during this period and eastern Europeans earned their place among leading theatre cultures. But one still senses that in the eyes of the western public this theatre, taken as a whole, is still looked upon as simply exotic and often recognition is given more for that than for its real artistic achievements. Perhaps this will change in the years ahead.

Certainly what is most important to those who produce theatre in the region and what is most important for all these nations is the hope that even as Europe and the world change they will continue to grow and will not lose their identity either as individual creators or as a group of nationalities which have produced

important work in the period under discussion. Whether this theatre will retain its exoticism and its piquancy as it becomes even more a part of Europe is a question only time will answer. One can only hope that its specific stages and its various colours will add new qualities to the European stage that may not have been seen before.

Péter Nagy
Budapest
Translated by George Hencz

Western Europe

Over 250 years, the idea of a common European culture has had its ups and downs for theological, political, social and aesthetic reasons; at the beginning of the eighteenth century Russia was considered outside the bounds of Europe by Britain, France and the Habsburg Empire. Things change.

With Diderot and the German philosophers, the Enlightenment, which was probably the first truly pan-European movement, gradually accepted into Europe the Russia of Catherine the Great (1729–96). By the beginning of the twentieth century, after the American and French Revolutions and with the effects of British and French imperialism, it had become a model to be exported to the rest of the world. The new frontiers of Barbaria had moved southeast with the rise of the Ottoman Empire.

The forces that shaped the Enlightenment were actually a mixture of acceptance and withdrawal from the previously accepted Christian ideal. With the rise of the individual, the commoner, the rational citizen, came the fight for and against royalty, republican and national ideals, federal and centralized structures.

The romantic movement taken in its broadest sense tried to establish individual and universal values at the same time. Its poets claimed that a new order, founded on merit (and wealth) was simply exchanging royalty for the bourgeoisie and was not enough; poets alone could unite liberal values (liberating them from the weight of reason), religious values (liberating them from theological tenets), thought and feelings in a new social order that accepted both universal and national ideas. Heinrich von Kleist's *The Prince of Homburg* (premièred in 1821) is a good example. It is also interesting to note that

in the early 1850s Victor Hugo had proposed the creation of a United States of Europe.

Against a background of triumphant imperialism, the world changed. World War I was the result of profound changes in Europe from the Atlantic to Moscow; cities like London, Paris, Vienna, Berlin and Moscow – Rome and Madrid to a lesser extent – became symbols of cultural cosmopolitanism. The aftermath of World War I led to the creation of a utopian world structure: the League of Nations (established in 1919), and a Universal Society of Theatre was proposed by Firmin Gémier in 1924. Soviet communism and above all fascism made the dreams difficult to keep alive. At the end of World War II, a new world order was defined at Yalta. Again, plans for a United States of Europe were discussed by people like Churchill, de Gaulle and Stalin but by 1946, the Cold War again put an end to the dream. Eastern Europe came under Soviet influence – the czarist dream come true – while the Council of Europe was founded in 1949 as a loose union of countries which accepted a common identity based on liberal, socio-democratic values in pluralistic societies. Although the Council of Europe has had little power, it has been instrumental in developing a European idea of culture with the creation of the European Cultural Foundation in 1950, the *Tindemans Report* of 1975 and the Oslo Conference of 1976 which all advocated bridges and exchanges between European countries.

At the same time, the European Economic Community (EEC) was born (1950) which led to the Rome Treaty of 1957 and later to the Single Europe Act of 1987; in between, the Copenhagen summit meeting of the EEC in

1978 had published a 'Declaration of European Identity' which led in 1984 to the definition of 'European Culture'.

Jean Monnet (1888–1979), who tried to define the idea of a united Europe (six, later nine, and currently twelve countries), saw Europe (the EEC) as a means of going beyond economic and political issues; in the late 1950s he declared: 'If I had to do it again, I'd start with culture'.

One would obviously need more than an economic union to fight against the rapid globalization of culture occurring through the new communications technologies which were quickly turning the world into a global village. Culture, and more particularly theatre, were eventually looked to as forces to change the world. The rise of the developing countries in the 1950s and the student movements that affected the western world in the 1960s (culminating in the May 1968 events in France) demanded a revision of everyone's image of the world. The blockade of Berlin in 1961 and the Cuban missile crisis in 1962 once again postponed hopes of developing a European culture. Has the dismantling of the Berlin Wall and the reunification of Germany in 1990 given new cause for optimism? A cautious 'maybe' is the only answer.

The European idea of culture has itself long been based on a view which developed out of political and social changes which occurred from the 1750s onwards. The picture frame stage and proscenium arch theatre with its box sets – a far cry from the Greek or Elizabethan models – became the modern European model and found its way to most parts of the world. It was to be illustrative, decorative and illusionistic. It clearly reflected the commercial values of a bourgeois society in which theatre could bring pleasure and entertainment through illusion while producing meaning to master the world at large. This new theatre, though, could also help define and disseminate social values and could become an ideological tool. The unrepenting romantic heroes could be used as negative or dangerous examples. Strangely enough a commonly shared idea emerged in Europe: theatre as a socially relevant art, even though relevant didn't mean the same for conservatives and revolutionaries, reformists and radicals. Against the all-encroaching influence of commercialism and cosmopolitanism, a feeling of revolt developed across western Europe between the 1880s and 1914: Antoine's Théâtre Libre (1887); the Freie Bühne and the Volksbühne movements in Germany; versions of the same idea in Norway and the Netherlands; the Irish Literary Movement. Theatre began to develop new ethical values, European values, which could incorporate new relationships between artists and audiences, European and non-European cultures. Theatre became the place to discuss the fate of humanity, its relationship to its time.

In half a century, however, from 1900 to 1950, the proscenium arch, the decorative box set and the well-made play gave way to experiments in which fragmentation and a whole new approach to stage and theatre design came alive. Theatre became a place where historical/chronological time could take on universal/technological time, where the backlash from various acculturation attempts would welcome other forms of theatre from other parts of the world. Theatre would now help bring down political barriers.

Gémier's idea of a Universal Society of Theatre came true in a sense with the creation of the Theatre of Nations Festival in 1954. For the next fifteen years it was to be one of the only points of contact between eastern European, western European and world theatre cultures.

Beginning in the early 1900s, but mainly from 1945, most European states began devising cultural policies to ensure that theatre was available, as the Dutch say, 'vertically and horizontally', that is, to all classes of society in every part of each country. The French decentralization movement was one among many of the same kind.

The question of state funding also became a major issue: should money come from the central government, from regional or county government sources or from municipalities? The question was asked, in western Europe at least, to make sure that theatre culture did not become state culture. The question of profits from aesthetic activity was also hotly debated. On this question the United Kingdom struck a delicate balance between private and public funding, between artistic and administrative management of the new cultural facilities that would soon be built.

André Malraux, the first French Minister for Cultural Affairs, in a famous speech in 1966 written for the formal opening of the Maison de la Culture in Amiens, said that he regretted that France could not follow the remarkable model of the Soviet Union in its organization of theatre and art, stopping short, of course, of mentioning its indoctrinational and censorship aspects.

A vast movement of theatre reconstruction

and building swept away the ruins of World War II. Multipurpose buildings with more than one stage – discarding the proscenium arch, the velvet curtain and horseshoe auditorium – brought audiences into better contact with the stage. Many were built by architects of fame using the Bauhaus ideal. The result was a series of huge palaces of brutal concrete with state-of-the-art technologies for sound, lighting and moving sets, not basically different from the much derided Soviet Palaces of Culture. Ironically, many of the artists turned to other types of spaces. By the 1970s, new theatre was being performed in such old churches, factories and warehouses (the Théâtre du Soleil in Paris or the Kampnagel site in Hamburg are telling examples).

This new theatre can be traced back to the intimate theatre of Strindberg, and the idea swept all over Europe. It became a way to experiment, away from mainstream art or its commercialized version – a way to bring down walls again. The development of theatre for young audiences and puppetry in the 1960s showed that theatre was definitely a socially relevant art.

Taking the optimistic broader perspective, it does seem that walls have been coming down between countries, classes and genres, from opera to dance; styles of productions, from the elaborate performances of both commercial and publicly funded theatre to the rich minimalism of Brecht and experimental forms; between acting practices, performers and audiences. The spectacular development of theatre training has brought amateur and professional actors closer and improved the social status of the acting profession.

Finally, looking at a century of theatre-making, a repertoire has evolved which can tell us much about theatre in western Europe at the end of the twentieth century. What we find on these stages are, first of all, the classics of world (generally meaning European) drama. Greek tragedy has long been a good test of changes in outlook and taste for both creators and audiences. We also find Shakespeare and the Elizabethan drama more so than Spanish drama of the golden age). There are Goldoni, Büchner and Kleist and what can be called the European national classics (Molière for one but very little Corneille, Racine or Hugo). We find Goethe; the late-nineteenth and early-twentieth-century classics – Chekhov, Ibsen, Strindberg, Hauptmann, Gorki, Synge, Shaw, Wilde and O'Casey; contemporary classics such as Claudel, Giraudoux, Sartre, Anouilh, Ghelderode, Genet, García Lorca, Valle-Inclán, Alberti and of course Pirandello, Brecht, Beckett and Ionesco.

Strangely enough, dramatists from eastern Europe like Molnar, and, to a lesser extent, Kohout, Mrożek, Havel, Babel and Bulgakov have been performed because they were socio-political critics of their own countries; Gombrowicz and Witkiewicz are also there. Only recently have important contemporary dramatists from the USSR like Erdman, Vampilov, Svarts and Slavkine been performed.

The contemporary dramatists that one can find performed in almost every western European country today include Frisch, Dürrenmatt, Zuckmayer, Schnitzler, Strauss, Bernhard, Kroetz, Dorst, Grass, Brasch, Fassbinder, Handke, Heiner Müller, Harald Mueller, M. Walser, Hein, Pinter, Bond, Arden, Enquist, Noren, Arrabal, Koltés and Obaldia. Quite obviously, German language dramatists (Swiss, Austrian and German) are in a very strong position.

Of course repertoire does not mean dramatists alone but companies and directors like the Théâtre du Soleil, the Grand Magic Circus, the Pip Simmons Group, Carmelo Bene, Luca Ronconi, Giorgio Strehler, Stein, Langhoff and Karge, and Catalan groups like Els Comediants, Els Joglars and la Fura dels Baus.

The creation of the Théâtre de l'Europe in Paris in 1983 has helped to showcase more directors from other European countries than before, although festivals like Edinburgh and Avignon have been better artistic encounters for much longer. Of course international tours are part of the various repertoires too all over Europe and dance is often incorporated into theatre seasons.

In a state of permanent reappraisal and fighting against the commercial power of television, the boulevard theatres all across Europe, mainly with imports from the United States and musicals such as Cats and Les Misérables, are also trying to survive.

With cautious optimism then, it can be said that European theatre in the 1990s is helping to build bridges between divided communities, opening new vistas and creating new networks (like the Informal European Theatre Meeting). It is at long last bridging the gap between the Council of Europe view of European culture and a strictly EC view of culture. It is, in fact, interweaving all of Europe's various hierarchies. Theatre may yet prove to be Europe's most fascinating frontier.

Philippe Rouyer
Bordeaux

MUSIC THEATRE

There are many forms of music theatre to be seen in Europe today. They range from plays with music to music dramas, musical comedies, chamber operas, comic operas, chancel operas, operas bagatelle and even children's musicals. Since the early 1980s, large-scale pop and rock concerts and related genres have also become increasingly theatrical. Given such variety, one would imagine that precise definitions would abound. The fact is, in European and North American theatre – and in other cultures influenced by those theatres – the terms 'music theatre' and 'musical theatre' (including their German, French, Italian and Spanish equivalents) have a wide variety of meanings and usages. No precise terminology defining the genre has, in fact, emerged. We can note, though, that in central Europe since the middle of the twentieth century, the term 'music theatre' has grown in use and generally refers to works growing out of the European tradition of opera and operetta in which music is used to interpret and emphasize the dramatic action.

Given this tradition – and while acknowledging these multifaceted musical forms – it should not be viewed as an exaggerated emphasis if we move opera here to the foreground of 'music theatre'. Traditional opera is itself both a musical and a theatrical genre as well as being exemplary for aesthetic and historical questions. It is also one of the greatest and most specialized achievements of European culture, invented in Europe and conveyed to the world from there.

This point of view is supported by the development of music theatre that we encounter in Europe since the end of World War II. The existence and survival of the 'musical' certainly connects to the basic form and inner structure of opera. The fact is, the *form* has been open to the influence and penetration of new developments since the sixteenth century; however, it also frequently resisted, indeed actively opposed, new developments at various points in its history.

Opera *practice*, on the other hand, recognized different opinions. It interpreted, explained and ultimately understood new works in their relation to earlier works. The opera displayed an especially impressive synthesis of various types of art. As well, it combined plot with both musical and spiritual abstraction, a combination which went beyond linguistic and national boundaries. It also contained within its form many individual forms of very diverse types. These might be just a few of the reasons why Baroque opera had such an enormous success (beginning primarily in Italy and Spain). One speaks here theoretically, but it was certainly far ahead of its time in historical terms.

In any event, it is possible to see from this that in whatever way a new musical stage-work presents itself, it is (be it in contrast or conformity) a part of the 'heritage' accumulated over four centuries which forms an inventory of works that can still be performed today. All are, of course, subject to varying traditions, rooted in fundamental musical and stage principles which in turn play a role in the specific development of the art. For example, the space in which the work is performed moved early on from the festive halls of the aristocracy to architecturally independent buildings, buildings which remain virtually unchanged today. A curtain still often separates the stage and auditorium and, between them, the orchestra. The proportions of the ground plan of both spaces correspond to those of the space above them. Together with the proscenium they are the main elements in the acoustics of the space.

Or take another example that even more

clearly establishes the relationship between the artistic and the organizational – the location of the conductor. It was an expression of the vocal soloist's superiority in opera that the conductor stood directly in front of the stage. In this way the singers saw the conductor most clearly, while the orchestra had to make do with a spatial relationship that corresponded more to the conductor's place in Wagner.

At the same time, the number of instruments grew and individual instruments became more independent. Thus they could bring to the eighteenth century – which had a considerably different understanding of the relationship between speech, song and acting – their own dowry of instrumental and thematic independence. When this was done it became not so much a change in dominance as a new partnership of equals – orchestra, auditorium and stage. Again, at this moment, opera moved forward. One can view nineteenth-century attempts by the instrumental groups to attain their own clarity and precision as similar to that of libretto seeking to approach spoken drama more closely.

Turning to musical stage-works created between the 1930s and the early 1960s, we see the situation change again: now the 'opera', or whatever the new work may be called, draws the instrumentation to itself. And it does so through an approach linked much more to later developments in chamber and ensemble music. In this instance, the stage action does not make use of either symphonic-theatrical or symphonic-chamber elements as interpretational but rather as an instrumental collective forming its own thoughts, creating its own themes much more independently and setting them down almost contrapuntally. In this way, they escape the holds of plot and the traditional musical-theatrical foundation.

The development of such an 'instrumental theatre' has led to the renunciation of plot, character development and even motivation in many instances. In their place have come attempts (mostly short ones), offering not only a more anecdotal form but also texts that deal with everyday issues. Authors and audiences quickly developed their interest in such stage realism. To that point, opera enthusiasts had favoured abstraction and fantasy but from then on, its authors led them into new approaches and much more contemporary themes. The medium was frequently chamber opera which was, if nothing else, certainly less expensive than full-scale productions. Through such works, the repertoire was renewed.

Today we can find side by side in the same theatre classical works like Monteverdi's *Orfeo* and modern works by Richard Strauss and Carl Orff; the many forms of music theatre exist almost as foils to one another. Each has its own ever-changing compositional vocabulary. Here, knowledge of structure not only is useful with respect to the many music theatre forms but at the same time allows one to see more easily the 'classical' connection.

The social function of these various forms of opera – both in the past and the present – connects to this as well. Classical opera was invented as a courtly entertainment and is still used in this way today by states and in diplomacy. In Europe it took, and continues to take, a leading role in the promotion of culture generally. Under dictatorships such sponsorship was carried out especially intensively because it was seen as supportive of particular governments. Opera was seen as carrying forward spiritual leadership and strength. There exists in this respect, however, a great difference between the national operatic creations of a Smetana or a Dvořák on the one hand and those of a Verdi or a Puccini on the other. The former aimed for artistic and spiritual independence of both people and countries. Thematically they used legendary heroes as well as real historical occurrences.

As for the latter, Verdi came to the view that longer subjects were required to develop theatrical possibilities fully if they were truly to move hearts and confirm social and public ideas. He wanted to build bridges to contemporary listeners by allowing them to make social and human connections. This development (now accepted as traditional) also forms a practical aesthetic and continues to connect to the development of the European and North American musical stage even in the 1990s. In this sense, opera and its still growing side genres, not only is maintaining its moral task, but also is still committed to such traditional elements as libretto, music, staging and, last but not least, artistic organization.

Of course, it is no coincidence that in the construction of late-twentieth-century cultural centres, there remains a not-so-subtle political and propagandist message aimed at forming ideological bonds between those who attend both large- and small-scale musical events. Aside from an interest in the music, they also offer a chance for everyone to dress up and be seen, especially when admission prices were – as in the immediate post-war years – not so high.

The allegorical side – regularly utilized in earlier times – had as its task the imprinting on to a people of national symbols relating to happiness and freedom, victory and the essential goodness of humanity. It was no different from the tournaments and processions by which seventeenth- and eighteenth-century rulers sought to inculcate these same feelings and thoughts in their people.

Opera and its later developments also brought progress in the sphere of ideology which meant that plot and character had to link to the whole in the same way as did words and music. From the mid-nineteenth century, as connections to courts loosened, the form found new freedom. This change, in the German-speaking world especially, released imaginations to create a series of extraordinary works, from *The Magic Flute* to *Fidelio*. In Italy, the way was paved for the *opera buffa* and composers such as Rossini, Verdi and Puccini, the Italian stage composers who have – as can be seen in retrospect – remained at the very top of the bestseller list, not only in their time but also throughout the entire twentieth century. One need only mention the names of operas such as *The Barber of Seville*, *Rigoletto* or *La Bohème* to understand how familiar all of their major works are. These Italian stars were later complemented by Weber, Wagner and Strauss among many others all across Europe working in the form. The nineteenth century clearly developed both the national and the international opera repertoire.

From 1945 on, the form of musical theatre changed and continues to change. Chamber works grew in increasing numbers, partly because of budget constraints but also because of challenges by still newer forms. In the United States particularly, small opera groups became increasingly popular. In the 1950s, there were no fewer than 325 chamber opera premières in North America, mostly dealing with contemporary issues and ideas, and mostly done by student groups.

This may still be one of the qualitative differences between European and North American developments. In Europe, where there is no tradition of student or amateur work in this field (though there were attempts at creating amateur opera ensembles in the 1950s and 1960s in Bulgaria) such performances – with only piano or chamber accompaniment – would have produced head-shaking reactions.

Traditional European approaches to opera must be given their due. Certainly they have had their influence in many parts of the world – the Americas, Australia, South Africa and New Zealand to name just a few locales where opera was imported. But even then, opera was and still is presented only in a few of the major cities, cities perhaps in which art patrons, music lovers and the well-to-do with nostalgia for Europe managed to find enough money to build an opera house in the first place. And in some of these places, the form also changed. One could again speak of relationships to historic opera form, to features found in the traditional Italian *buffa* and the French *comique*. In this development, the United States again assumed a very dynamic, self-confident approach to both tradition and the development of newer forms including what has become known as the Broadway style of music theatre.

Suffice it to say here that these changes, supported by innumerable degree-granting university programmes in music, led to a situation in which young artists moved forward innovatively, without worry, yet with enough concentration so that the formalities of opera tradition became merely functional. In this sense, Europe fell behind. But in relation to the maintenance of tradition, European strengths can still be felt in the 1990s but perhaps with less conviction than they once possessed.

Horst Seeger
Dresden
Translated by Stephanie Gunther

DANCE THEATRE

The evolution of much of theatrical dance in Europe since the middle of the twentieth century can be characterized as a movement towards freedom. It was freedom conceived in various ways. One was as the liberty to say what one wanted to say, rather than what a cultural or political bureaucracy demanded be said. Quickly in some areas, more gradually in others, ethical and political restraints, which had narrowed the range of themes that dance could depict, were pushed away. Then there was liberty to move. Classical ballet technique had already been found inadequate to portray contemporary themes, but by mid-century even the then-accepted styles of modern dance were deemed insufficient. Further experiments were undertaken. In time, some choreographers found the exploration of newly discovered movements so absorbing in itself that they chose to reject subject matter altogether. They wanted only to devise movements that were interesting for their own sake.

The concept of the role of dance in the lives of people was changing also. For dance in eastern Europe, goals were dictated by the government, which meant that *Swan Lake* was acceptable because it was harmless, but new works had to exhibit proper, political content. In the west, a variety of aesthetic, ethical, social and political causes had been available, but entertainment took precedence. After World War II, artistic possibilities burgeoned. Though less welcome in the east, the well of the tide could not be stopped. By the beginning of the 1990s nearly all of Europe was seething with new dance ideas that were bringing larger, more diversified audiences into the theatres. And choreographers were ready to serve diversified tastes.

In most European countries, ballet groups had long held a secure but minor position in opera houses. Now ambitious choreographers wanted more. Restless with merely providing a few divertissements while the singers caught their breath, dancers started to form small companies of their own which could play in smaller houses to audiences eager to see something out of the ordinary. Many such groups were born and died, but a number lived on, not only in the major cities. Some, notably that of Pina Bausch in Germany, even acquired such status as to take over opera houses, without foregoing their experimental character.

The newly independent companies presented a wide variety of dance styles. In the early years of the century, new kinds of movement had begun to develop in Europe out of the innovations of Rudolf Laban and Mary Wigman, whose work was continued by teachers in Britain, Estonia, Germany and Yugoslavia. After World War II, American companies, exhibiting a variety of styles, began to tour Europe and their influence was soon felt. But European choreographers worked out their own versions of the American idea of 'moving from the inside out', of starting with feeling and then finding the most appropriate physical form to communicate it. What resulted was not merely imitative; it was creative.

The first and most powerful American influence was that of Martha Graham. While her success in Europe was not immediate, the establishment of the London School of Contemporary Dance in 1966 marked a turning point for the acceptance of her technique and the capacity of her ideas to inspire young choreographers. Also in the 1960s, European visits by the companies of Merce Cunningham and Alwin Nikolais stimulated fresh developments.

As early as 1975 Richard Alston broke from the London School of Contemporary Dance to form his own company, Strider. By the 1980s Carolyn Carlson and Viola Farber, from the Nikolais and Cunningham groups respectively, had trained dancers who went on to form their own branches in cities throughout France. Among those who followed, Jean-Claude Gallotta and Maguy Marin, most notably, evolved markedly individual styles.

From the beginning of the century, new techniques had developed in response to the need to depict new subjects. Contemporary life could not be well represented by the polite, restrained carriage of classical ballet. Rather, it demanded a taut, sometimes tormented, sometimes aggressive body that had to contend with a world pervaded by tensions. Graham had called it 'nervous, sharp, and zigzag', and the new techniques reflected those qualities. Even when the subject was not explicitly contemporary, dance movements became more incisive, more angular than rounded, more struggling with the pull of gravity than happily defying it.

The trend was not limited to companies oriented to the modern dance nor to works dealing with contemporary issues. The Soviet Union demanded productions that condemned cruel czars while they praised the revolution. In Russia, Yuri Grigorovich's *Ivan the Terrible* (1975) berated the monarch with strong, vigorous movements. In Belgium the works of Maurice Béjart, like his *Messe pour le temps présent* (1967) blended strong, dynamic movement, elaborate spectacle and mysticism. In Estonia, Mai Murdmaa's rendition of Dostoevsky's *Crime and Punishment* (1991) used innovative movement to stress the emotional tension of the protagonist's struggle.

News about interesting premières spread quickly, and a number of choreographers staged works for groups in other countries. While this had been happening for many years, the scale was now quite unprecedented. Especially notable were the works created by Juri Kilián and Hans van Manen in the Netherlands that entered the repertoires of US companies. Dominating the move from the United States to Europe were the works of George Balanchine for whom a special trust was established to ensure that the requesting company was capable of performing the ballet and that it would be staged by someone who knew and respected not only the steps but also the spirit of the choreography. Works from the repertoire of modern dance moved more slowly, but an important

step was taken in 1990 when the José Limón company staged his *There is a Time* for the Mussorgsky Theatre in Leningrad.

The number of companies featuring mixed repertoires grew throughout this period. Typical was Alterballetto, which was established in the Bologna region of Italy in 1977. With Amedeo Amodio as artistic director, the repertoire also featured works by foreigners including the Americans William Forsythe and Glen Tetley. In Romania, Fantasio was founded in Constanta in 1979. The company performed classics like *The Nutcracker* along with original works by its director Oleg Danovski, who provided ballets on national themes, like *Vox Maris* to the music of Georges Enesco, and modern works, like *Study* to the music of Pink Floyd. Also in 1979, Iván Markó took over the Györ Ballet in Hungary, often choreographing to music by Hungarian composers such as Béla Bartók's *The Miraculous Mandarin* (1981).

Other companies were formed specifically to feature modern works. One was the Polish Dance Theatre in Poznań, founded in 1973 by Conrad Drzewiecki as a showcase for new choreography, often staged to music by contemporary composers. Another was the Contemporary Dance Theatre of Rome, founded in 1977 by Elsa Piperno, who was familiar with the Graham technique. A number of such private groups in various countries also featured ballets based on national folk themes. Companies specifically devoted to folk dance also flourished, especially in eastern Europe.

Many traditional ballet companies continued to perform the classics, while also commissioning new works. Germany, in particular, was able to do this extensively, since its many municipal theatres kept permanent ballet ensembles. Both native and foreign choreographers profited from this arrangement which made possible some worthy productions of ballets by John Cranko and John Neumeier.

So the classics survived, though often with changes geared to the tastes of a modern audience. *The Sleeping Beauty* was shortened, as lengthy passages of pantomime were deleted. After all, the viewers already knew the story and would be bored by its reiteration. Other variations involved changing the era or the setting of the story, an approach already used by opera directors. More drastic was Mats Ek's Swedish *Giselle* (1982) where in the second act the heroine's spirit dances, not in a moonlit grove, but in an insane asylum.

In other cases, however, important ballets

from the past were carefully preserved – or attempts were made to preserve them, since prior to the work of Laban no efficient system of dance notation existed. Still, for many years, person-to-person transmission kept some ballets almost consistently on view. The outstanding centre of such activity was Copenhagen where the nineteenth-century works of August Bournonville remained the proud possession of the Royal Danish Ballet. While some changes took place, special efforts were made to retain a distinctive style characterized by lightness and small, fast footwork. Along with its Bournonville heritage, the Royal Danish Ballet continued to commission new works from both native and foreign choreographers.

Other companies chose diverse paths in relating to their individual traditions. In Britain, London's Royal Ballet steered a largely faithful course, honouring the classical tradition created by Frederick Ashton. But Ballet Rambert was transformed into a modern dance company. One country that had chosen a distinctive identity all along was Spain, which continued to build on its remarkable styles of *flamenco* and *bolero*. Only in 1978 was a national ballet company finally established in Madrid. After all, in this time any country was free to establish its own dance identity, whether by preserving its past, or refining it, or discarding it in favour of some fresh, untried – possibly dangerous, but exciting – new path.

One rather new path that a number of European countries chose to embark on was that of dance publication. In the past half century the publication of dance books has multiplied, and many dance journals have come into existence. Their variety is now considerable. There are how-to books for the would-be ballet dancer or choreographer, biographies and histories, as well as books of criticism and dance analysis. Magazines range from the popular to the esoteric. Quality is equally varied. Within this period, dance scholarship has emerged as a viable discipline, its existence finally acknowledged with the formation of the European Association of Dance Historians in 1989.

Selma Jeanne Cohen
New York

THEATRE FOR YOUNG AUDIENCES

Theatre for young audiences as a specific form emerged in Europe in the second half of the nineteenth century. Theatrical elements had been used for the education of young people centuries earlier, however, with school and Jesuit theatres attaining great significance in European theatre history during the sixteenth and seventeenth centuries. These were performances by the pupils themselves intending to teach through impersonation. When staged for the public, they aimed at an audience of all ages. For in the large extended families of the time there was no distinction made between the lives of children and adults. So children as a matter of course were also members of the audience or participants in these theatre performances.

It was only when industrialization created a more bourgeois family unit, that the roles and way of life between the generations started to change. For children and adolescents, learning became the dominant occupation and school became the central means of attaining the no longer immediately accessible world of adults. A new literature for children and young people began to develop and finally a professional theatre for young audiences.

The staging of special performances for children and their parents initially had a purely commercial motivation. Theatres were traditionally poorly attended in the weeks before Christmas; in the late nineteenth century some enterprising theatre managers discovered that they could fill them with productions for children. Because suitable plays for young audiences did not yet exist, theatre managers simply created performances out of selections from the existing adult repertoire.

In Britain, the Christmas pantomime developed out of pantomime generally along with elements of the music hall and the burlesque; in the German-speaking countries, children's shows grew from Christmas fairytales, folk tales, children's ballets, the Parisian *féerie* and Viennese magic tricks. While the moralistic messages of these plays provided edification for young people, elaborate scenery, music and dance – usually without a real connection to the action – provided simple entertainment. Such Christmas performances spread very rapidly and remained the primary form of professional theatre for young audiences until late into the twentieth century.

At the turn of the century, the form began to be sharply criticized, particularly by those advocating reforms in teaching. But real change did not occur until reforms were initiated by socialists after World War I leading to the first state theatre for children being established in Hungary in 1919. Among its creators were composers Béla Bartók and Zoltán Kodály and literary critics György Lukács and Béla Balázs. In Czechoslovakia, Miroslav Disman attempted to establish a similar institution in 1918. In Germany, attempts were associated with the names of Edwin Hoernle, Walter Benjamin and Bertolt Brecht, though in these cases it was for a theatre primarily *with* children.

Only in Russia did the theoretical concepts lead to widespread implementation. Already in 1918, the People's Commissar for Education, Anatoly Vaslievich Lunacharski, presented a comprehensive 'children's theatre programme' which, among other things, called for the founding of professional theatres specifically aimed at young audiences. In 1920, the first state theatre for children was established in Moscow under the artistic direction of Henriette Pascar. The following year, the very young Natalia Satz (1903–93) founded the Moscow Theatre for Children and in the Ukrainian city of Kharkov, a state Theatre for Young Audiences was founded. In 1922, Alexander A. Briantzov founded the Theatre for Young Audiences in Petrograd. Satz, like Briantzov, saw her own work as a reflection of the new principles of education and creativity being espoused, an opportunity to give new focus to the countless children who had been neglected by war and revolution. For the youngest, they performed fairytales; for the slightly older, the Moscow theatre included plays with more contemporary topics. The Petrograd theatre also included plays based on themes from world literature (*Tom Sawyer*, *Til Ulenspiegel*, *Don Quixote*), as well as adaptations of classical works.

The Soviet models had significant influence across Europe. Professional theatres for young audiences following the Moscow prototype were established in Prague in 1934 and in Istanbul in 1935. In Glasgow, the Scottish Children's Theatre of Bertha Waddell emerged in 1925 and continued to operate as a touring company for decades. In Belgrade, Rodino Poriste was founded in 1938 by the dramatist Branislav Nušić, while in Zagreb, Djecje Carstvo was founded by the famous actor and director Tito Strozzi. From 1928 on, many companies formed in the Netherlands, the most significant being the Nederlands Theatre, formed in 1936. In France it was Léon Chancerel who, with his Théâtre de l'Oncle Sebastien, performed for children in the style of *commedia dell'arte* from 1929 on. In Portugal, Italy, Iceland, Spain and Sweden – though specific theatres were not established in the pre-war years – regular performances nevertheless took place for young audiences as they did in Austria (Theater der Jugend), in Denmark (Dansk Skoloscenen) and other countries, with student theatregoers paying next to nothing to get in following the precedent set by British groups. In countries such as Poland, Greece and Turkey – with long traditions in puppetry – children's theatre grew around that form as well.

World War II interrupted this development; it was only after the war that most companies could again operate. But as European politics were split into two camps after the war, theatre for young audiences also began to develop along entirely different paths. In western, southern and northern Europe, theatre artists simply took up again the type of work that had been so violently interrupted in 1939. In Belgium it was the Koninklijk Jeugdtheater Antwerpen, the largest such western European theatre; in the Netherlands it was the Scapino-Ballet of Hans Snoek, while in Britain many new groups formed doing what began to be called theatre-in-education. The fact is, though the adult theatre in western Europe grew and changed, theatre for young audiences remained almost the same as before the war.

Those under Soviet influence developed quite differently. In eastern European capitals and large industrial cities, state professional theatres for children and young people were established, technically and financially endowed as adult theatres, again following the Soviet prototype: from 1944 in Bulgaria, 1945 in Poland and Czechoslovakia, 1946 in the German Democratic Republic, 1950 in Yugoslavia and 1951 in Romania. Other theatres also received a mandate to open to young audiences. Where national traditions existed, they tied into *them*; where such traditions were not followed, Soviet plays were used as examples to create their own plays. Besides adaptations of folktales for very young audiences, plays with contemporary and historical subjects as well as dramatizations of classics were created. In addition, classic plays from each nation's own literature were brought into the repertoire.

Because of the structural and ideological similarities of theatres in countries which had been declared socialist, contacts grew between the various states from the end of the 1950s (there were, of course, similar contacts among the western European groups). This was to prove especially important for the exchange of experiences and developing new repertoire. In spite of their work, however, these youth theatres had great difficulty being recognized artistically. Too many performances were simply illustrations of ideology or pedagogical messages which, even in the eyes of their producers, had only negligible artistic worth.

In the early 1960s, contact between east and west was re-established and the founding of a world children's theatre organization discussed for the first time. At international children's theatre festivals in London and Venice in 1964, groups met, a constitution was outlined and on 7 June 1965, in Paris, the founding convention of the Association internationale du théâtre pour l'enfance et la jeunesse (ASSITEJ) was created under the direction of Léon Chancerel. Representatives of twenty-five European and North American states became charter members. Among those present were, besides Chancerel, Rose-Marie Moudoues, the Czech Vladimir Adamek, Gerald Tyler from Britain and Sara Spencer from the USA. The goal was an organization dedicated to supporting 'a theatre for children and youth at the highest artistic levels'. Structures were established and a series of national centres was set up, centres which would guarantee cooperation without limitations. At the same time, the constitution closed membership to amateur groups or groups in which children or young people themselves performed. No one at that time suspected – or even had grounds to hope – that international cooperation and global diffusion of theatre for young audiences had begun.

Following the politicization of the west that began in the mid-1960s and which became known in Europe as the Student Movement after the May 1968 riots in Paris, the question of society's responsibility to its children came into sharper focus. State-school programmes could not be quickly altered but the theatre, going beyond institutional structures, could be more closely connected to its audience's realities. Young intellectuals – teachers, psychologists, sociologists and, of course, artists – embraced the notion of free groups and worked, mostly collectively, for audiences of young people. These plays were often set in classrooms, playgrounds or streets. Often they dramatized examples of daily repression by those in control of politics and society, as well as in the workings of school and family.

Unemployment and environmental pollution, hostility toward foreigners, sexual enlightenment and forced sexual stereotyping were other key themes. Both realistic and emancipatory, as some of its creators named it, this theatre sought to help children and young people to understand real-life situations and encouraged them to surmount problems and alter the world. The young people in these plays were always the victors and would make allies of those adults who supported them. The West Berlin Grips-Theater with its managing director and most important author, Volker Ludwig, would become perhaps the best known representative of the theatres attempting to stimulate the social visions of audiences with wit and nerve. Even today, Grips's plays are performed in many parts of the world.

Nearly all the theatres for young audiences

that began after 1968 in western Europe – literally hundreds – had similar themes and goals. Most, though, existed only for a short time and rarely had permanent companies or spaces. Those in France (like Maurice Yendt's Théâtre des Jeunes Années), Italy (Carlo Formigoni's Teatro del Sole), Portugal (João Brites's Teatro o Bando) and Sweden (Suzanne Osten's Unga Klara) also began to develop alternative performance methods. Interest also began to grow among authors. Fantastic and symbolic styles were employed and later clowns and nonsense plays inundated the stages.

The generation of 1968 had become professionals and with their collective visions of a social utopia fading, the family itself became a subject for examination. As Alice Miller wrote, 'the first and worst damage a child can suffer is in the family'. But through Bruno Bettelheim it was also learned that folktales contained both pictures and symbols that corresponded to the often unknown inner reality of the child and these could establish help and courage for them. Thus was the fairytale rediscovered from the annual Christmas shows in the adult theatres. When it returned to use by theatres for young audiences, it was in a new form whose aim was to release children from their anxieties. In Sweden and Italy, this new exploration of fairytales was even rooted in existential approaches to children's fears of weakness, authority, sexuality, loneliness and death, using scripts from ancient Greece to today.

The changes begun in 1968 in so many western European children's theatres remained for a long time without any noticeable influence on eastern Europe. It was, of course, seen in eastern Europe in festivals and ASSITEJ activities. What was also seen were the obvious differences between the large and stately dramatic theatres for young audiences of the east with their well-trained artists (in the Soviet Union alone there were well over fifty such stages including a music theatre for children since 1965) and the small, barely subsisting, struggling free groups of the west. Nevertheless, during this time, while a self-chosen educational mandate was still the central theme for the western European companies, the theatre in eastern Europe was finally beginning to free itself from its ideological and pedagogical fetters and was beginning to make artistic criteria the guiding principle of its work.

Because it was still not permitted to question authority, western plays could not be used as models. Other approaches would have to be found. Inspired by the example of the Soviet writer Yevgeny Svarts, a number of authors turned again to folk forms, making clear the modern analogies. Or they created their own fairytales and parables. Thus the theatre managed to keep alive the old traditions, revealing folktales as genuine classics for children's theatre, always being able to interpret them in new ways.

As well, music and dance works for children were created along with pantomime and mixed forms (often actors and marionettes). Especially brave experiments were done by small companies in Poland and Czechoslovakia in the 1960s, experiments which were carefully observed by cultural authorities. That their influence on other socialist countries was only minimal was clearly due to political reasons but it was also in part due to the theatre buildings themselves with their traditional picture frame stages which limited experimentation. But slowly, such influences were felt especially when rehearsal spaces were converted to performance spaces and new theatrical methods and even texts of western European origin could be staged. One could see this process throughout the 1980s.

What effect political changes since the beginning of the 1990s will have on theatre for young audiences is not yet known. There is little hope that one will see the bringing together of the best of the two systems. Rather, the economic recession facing Europe in the first half of the 1990s and militant nationalism have caused many to believe that the financially cheaper western model will dominate.

The fact is, young people have no strong lobby anywhere on this planet which as a report issued in 1991 by the Club of Rome says, 'we seem openly determined to destroy'. Since the early 1980s, European theatre for young audiences has had an artistic variety and strength never before seen.

In the end, theatre for young audiences has been and continues to be a theatre of feeling and fantasy, a theatre that speaks most of all to the senses. And it is a theatre that from the beginning reached young people from all social levels. In this sense it has also been a folk theatre. All these qualities have made it increasingly interesting for adult audiences, not simply those parents and teachers who accompany their children to the theatre. The creation of a folk theatre for all generations, a folk theatre which has never given up its specificity as a theatre for young people, that is the achievement of theatre for young audiences in Europe. This has been a very real achievement because both young people and adults live in a world that no longer allows any real separation between the generations.

Wolfgang Wöhlert
Berlin
Translated by Varya Rubin

PUPPET THEATRE

In its long history European puppetry has developed various forms, and their synchronic existence today has become one of puppetry's characteristic features. For centuries, puppetry also connected to different genres including Medieval Mystery plays, *commedia dell'arte*, opera, variety, circus and melodrama, and was inspired as well by narrative forms including the popular tales of chivalry. The majority of these were adapted by puppeteers into folk styles utilizing such comic figures as Pulcinella, Polichinelle, Punch, Petrushka, Hanswurst, Kasper, Kašparek, Guignol, Tchantchès, Woltje, Cassandrino, Gianduja, Gerolamo and many others. Generally created as string-puppets or hand-puppets, very occasionally they became rod-puppets (*Hänneschen*) or even shadow-puppets (*karagöz*).

At the beginning of the twentieth century, avant-garde artists took a new interest in puppetry which resulted in the foundation of several serious puppet theatres by such artists as Paul Brann in Germany, Geza Blattner in Hungary, Vittorio Podrecca in Italy, Josef Skupa in Czechoslovakia and Sergei Obraztsov in the USSR. Paul Brann conceived his as a theatre based on stylized movement, his puppets taken as artificial actors. Geza Blattner experimented with materials and forms influenced by modern trends in plastic art. Vittorio Podrecca established a style for the puppet variety show and musical revue which gained great popularity, with some referring to his puppets as *Übermarionetten* after Edward Gordon Craig's notion.

Josef Skupa was also a master of the variety show, but his fame was mainly due to his invention of two contemporary comic figures, Spejbl and Hurvinek, who in their many sketches helped make fun of the foibles of the middle classes. Sergei Obraztsov, as a soloist, satirized traditional songs and Gypsy romances, mainly using hand-puppets. He was the first to use his bare hands as puppets with small balls on the forefinger. As the director of the Central State Puppet Theatre in Moscow from 1931 he created a unique and original theatre with a repertoire of fairytales, contemporary plays and satirical programmes using mainly rod-puppets operated to imitate human beings.

Despite the experiments of Blattner, it was the homogenous, imitative style of Brann and Obraztsov which prevailed. Obraztsov's influence especially grew after World War II, when his theatre began to tour all over the world. It was particularly influential in eastern Europe where new communist regimes were applying to puppet theatre their overall policies relating to the promotion of culture generally as derived and imported from the Soviet Union.

In the past, puppet theatres had primarily been the business of individuals and only rarely did they become the concern of larger groups. Traditionally, puppet companies were privately run and financially independent. During the early part of the twentieth century, however, social associations or municipal authorities began to offer support to certain groups. In the Soviet Union, immediately after the October Revolution, the new government went so far as to adopt a special policy to protect and support activities in the field, founding a network of state puppet theatres in the process. The focus was on the Central State Puppet Theatre in Moscow which retained prime responsibility for finding a new, progressive repertoire and for developing new means of expression for the art.

The idea of having one leading theatre in each country was also applied in the satellite countries though, as the Polish experience proves, not always successfully. Massive state support nevertheless accelerated the development of puppetry in eastern Europe through the foundation of an extensive infrastructure (a system of schooling, puppet theatre criticism, publications, and so on).

In western Europe, another system of protection and support developed but more slowly and, in some cases, more surely: the granting of modest subsidies by state, municipal and regional authorities, in most cases through the funding of individual projects. This system has been increasing to the point where in the 1990s, in such countries as France, Italy, Spain and Germany, the majority of puppet players now enjoy its benefits.

As a direct result of the great differences between these two systems, enormous variations in concept and structure developed in the puppet theatres of eastern and western Europe. In the west, for example, companies are generally small (two to six people), have a base in a workshop or rehearsal room and perform on tour in schools, arts centres and only occasionally in theatres. Only a few have their own theatres. In eastern Europe, however, most puppet companies have their own buildings with auditoriums, workshops, administrators and, if needed, their own means of transport. The average eastern European puppet theatre numbers about sixty employees and the larger ones, such as the Central Puppet Theatre in Moscow, as many as 300.

These structural differences were most clearly seen when Obraztsov's theatre started to tour throughout Europe and during the first international puppet festivals which began to be held in the 1950s. It was there – in Bucharest and Braunschweig – that western puppetry was first confronted with that of the east. Western puppeteers would often present refined ideas – Yves Joly's *Paper Tragedy* from France and his variety show items with gloves and hands, for example. But the strongest impulses came from the east, especially in the creative works of Margareta Niculescu of Romania and Jan Wilkowski of Poland, who produced large-scale shows in 'regular' theatres.

The most modern productions showed a wide variety of different sorts of productions and styles. Nevertheless, the inclusion of traditional forms was significant: the English continued to perform the comedy of Punch and Judy; the Italians – Pulcinella; the Romanians – Vasilache; the Hungarians – Vitez Laszlo; the Belgians – Woltje and Tchantchès; and the French – Guignol and Lafleur. German hand-puppet and string-puppet companies were still using the figure of Kasper, although his function as a folk representative was replaced by his function as children's entertainer and adviser. In France and Belgium, the traditional theatre was still using rod-marionettes sized according to their positions in the social scale (the emperor being the tallest); similar – though heavier – rod-marionettes in Sicily continued to present the adventures of Charlemagne's paladins.

The existence of all these theatres, however, was threatened by a falling-off of audiences who were turning to cinema and television for their entertainment. But with the help of historians and folklorists, tourist associations and municipalities, many of the companies survived, including the two major European shadow forms – Turkish *karagöz* and Greek *Karagiozis*.

Stylistically, large numbers of companies saw puppetry in the years after World War II as a derivation of actors' theatre and tried to adhere to the principles of homogenous stage reality. Puppetry itself was marked by the form of the puppets used, starting from their construction and type (hand-puppets, string-puppets or rod-marionettes) and finishing with the style of sculpting which in some cases was strictly imitative – even when stylized – and in others based on caricature. Some puppet masters achieved extraordinary results: Max Jacob and Carl Schröder in Germany with their hand-puppets; John Wright with his figures for the Little Angel Marionette Theatre in England; and Germany's Harro Siegel in his performances with carefully carved marionettes. The old variety show style slowly transformed itself into solo marionette cabaret such as those of Albrecht Roser with his famous German clown, Gustaf, and Gustaf's 'Ensemble'. Roser's puppet skills were matched only by his unique sense of theatricality.

By the beginning of the 1950s, eastern European theatre was obliged by the state to follow socialist-realism as both an artistic and a propagandist style. As well, companies were told to use the Soviet repertoire. The death of Stalin in 1953, however, relaxed these strictures and opened a period of relative freedom. Thus, at the end of the 1950s, Niculescu, Wilkowski and other eastern European artists were able to abandon the obligatory style of dramatic imitation and to undertake a new poetic and 'theatrical' theatre. Niculescu and Wilkowski especially emphasized the theatricality of their productions by often stressing the actual process of creation, sometimes focusing on the metaphoric use of different means of expression.

Wilkowski also exploited folklore as a source of inspiration, leading him to his greatest achievement (*Zwyrtala the Musician*, 1958). This interest in folk themes was common to many eastern countries (for example, Hungary, Bulgaria, Romania), because it served as an instrument for the introduction of young audiences to national themes.

More and more, young artists joined the new trends. In Bulgaria, puppeteers found other modern ways to use folklore in such productions as *Krali Marko* (1967). In Hungary, the unique State Puppet Theatre in Budapest explored folk motifs and musical repertoires using compositions by Bartók, Kodály and Stravinsky. In Sweden, Michael Meschke founded a large-scale theatre and produced shows based on famous works of world literature using varying means of expression (notably in *Ubu Roi*, 1965).

In the 1960s, puppetry experienced another artistic boom, again led by eastern Europe. In Poland each of the various puppet theatres competed in terms of originality and inventiveness. In Czechoslovakia, puppets were used to overcome officially imposed styles, first through the technique of 'black light theatre' and later utilizing live actors as part of the puppet stage composition. Right across Europe, the old masters, those still working in the imitative tradition, were being quickly outstripped by creators from the new generation. Even in the Soviet Union, Obraztsov's artistic monopoly was being broken by the Leningrad Bolshoi Puppet Theatre and later by theatres from the Baltic and Caucasus Soviet republics.

Craigian and Brechtian theories of theatre also influenced puppetry and were themselves creative and theatrical in just the ways that Craig and Brecht wanted. In many productions, puppeteers even abandoned the traditional puppet booths or screens to show themselves in action and step by step transformed themselves into performers. The formerly homogenous unity of setting and puppets was replaced by a heterogeneous scenic world of humans, puppets, masks and props. The puppet – considered as stage subject in the old theatre – now became an object or an instrument in the hands of the new 'players'. From this it was only a short step to the total atomization of the puppet as stage character, which from then on was often presented by a puppet *and* its manipulator along with a speaker or narrator. Thus the model of the ancient Japanese *bunraku* began to appear in European puppetry and developed in still different ways.

The new tendencies could be observed most strongly in Poland and Czechoslovakia. The Polish Poznań Puppet Theatre experimented with unusual deployments of space and a variety of means including 'object theatre'. In Czechoslovakia in the 1970s a new company, Drak, from Hradec Kralove, became a leader in puppetry due to the internationally acclaimed productions of its director, Josef Krofta, who enriched the language of puppetry with poetic and metaphoric images. Generally, his actors were visible generators of stage action in which the puppets took their place among several means of expression. Krofta's productions also briefly touched the poetic in object theatre but soon abandoned it for puppets alone.

The eastern European theatres have always tended to work in repertory with each group producing three or four shows a year, many more than the average western European group, which usually produced a series of projects according to their creative ability and financial means. Each of the projects would often take two or three years to prepare. Among the exceptions were some of the British and German permanent theatres.

As for repertoire, the subjects were similar everywhere: fairytales, adaptations of modern poetry and children's novels. In some countries writers were commissioned to write specifically for puppet theatres and young audiences. In this way, dramaturgy of a special poetic value was born and developed in Bulgaria. For adults the puppet theatres performed plays from other sources: Sophocles, Molière, Shakespeare, Corneille, Goethe, Büchner, Maeterlinck, Jarry, Dürrenmatt, Mrożek, Witkiewicz, and many others. In general, though, much of the repertoire consisted of adaptations of popular world literature including Asian epic narratives such as the *Ramayana* and the *Mahabarata*.

Western European puppetry in the 1980s started to give priority to a more 'visual' theatre, limiting the inclusion of 'literary' drama and thus being keen to accept the novelty of 'object theatre'. The replacement of the puppet by everyday objects resulted from the apparently overwhelming need for novelty experienced by a majority of artists. Object theatre productions also tended to emphasize the creative action of the performer who, in full view of the audience, suggested the fictional life of the presented object which thus functioned as a stage character. This kind of theatre was practised in many countries but became a specialty of French and Italian players. However, the appearance of object theatre did not put a stop to the existence of other forms of puppetry. All over Europe, in fact, a multimedia theatre flourished while France became famous for storytelling forms of theatre, visual theatre and what was known as material theatre. This last form achieved particular note in the productions of the Philippe Genty Company.

Spain continued to draw on the dramatic repertoire in the 1980s and also produced a 'visual' theatre in productions by La Claca. France and Italy also revived shadow theatre with special achievements by the Gioco Vita company from Piacenza. Germany tended to focus on object and material theatre. Scandinavian countries in their turn, showed sensitivity towards the visual/fine art aspects of puppetry.

Due to new social and financial support, western European puppetry grew and enriched its artistic potential at this time. It competed successfully with eastern European theatres which in the 1970s and 1980s seemed to lose their innovative dynamism, though the professional level of the performances remained high. Exceptions could be seen in the Soviet Siberian theatres and in some of the East German theatres which in the 1970s had developed their own styles based on the synergistic relationship between players and puppets (an exemplary production being Strindberg's *Miss Julie* by the Neubrandenburg Theatre).

The collapse of the Soviet political bloc greatly changed the financial situation for eastern Europe. The impoverished states and societies created in its wake were clearly not able to continue the policy of the communist governments, and puppet theatres, like all theatres, were facing major changes in the 1990s. It may well be that these countries will very soon be forced to apply the same support system practised for so long in western Europe.

Looked at as a whole and despite the previous division of Europe into two political blocs, European puppetry is in the 1990s a fairly unified whole and puppet artists have together experienced all the changes of their art from homogenous scenic reality to the modern stylistic of a 'theatrical' theatre with the process of creation itself as focus.

In part, this unity has been possible through the cooperation and frequent meetings of European puppeteers. In the period after World War II, the first such meeting was the Puppetry Week in Braunschweig (1957) and later the World Festival of Puppet Theatres in Bucharest (1958). The Bucharest Festival in particular had a tremendous impact on the development of puppet theatre. Repeated in the 1960s, very soon other festival initiatives joined them: in London, in Bielsko Biala (Poland), in Varna (Bulgaria) and in Cervia (Italy) among other cities. By the 1990s, most European countries were seeing several puppet festivals a year, with the most famous being that of Charleville-Mézières in France, which every three years gathered together more than a hundred companies from all over the world.

International activities in the 1990s are coordinated by an international association of puppeteers (Union Internationale de la Marionnette, UNIMA), founded in Prague in 1929. Every four years, UNIMA holds a congress, usually in Europe. UNIMA has national centres in virtually every European country and promotes the global development of puppetry, supports its various traditions, and organizes courses, conferences and festivals.

The successful development of puppetry has also become possible due to its growing infrastructure – puppetry training schools and publications. In western Europe, puppet centres – institutions supported by state or local authorities – maintain libraries, collect documentation, deliver information and organize exhibitions, courses, conferences and festivals. Again the best known is that in Charleville-Mézières, with its extensive programme of information, schooling and research activities.

The first regular school for puppet players and directors of puppet theatre was founded in 1952 in Prague as a department in the Academy of Art. It offered a diploma course at the university level. Later on, similar schools were founded in Poland, Bulgaria, East Germany and the Soviet Union. Professional training in western European countries was previously obtained only by means of courses or apprenticeships but in the 1970s departments of puppetry were founded in the Theatre Institute in Barcelona, in the Theatre School in Stuttgart, and in 1987 Charleville-Mézières opened a National Higher School of Puppetry. An agreement signed in 1990 by a majority of schools encouraged their close cooperation.

The first puppet journals in Europe were founded at the beginning of the twentieth century and after 1945 many of them were continued. Among the oldest is *Československý Loutkař* (*Czechoslovak Puppeteer*). Very soon other magazines appeared, such as *Teatr Lalek* in Poland, *Marionnettes* in France, *Animations* in Britain. There are also important specialist magazines in Switzerland, Italy, Spain, Germany and the Netherlands. In many countries, criticism of puppetry is now given space in general theatre journals.

Puppet theatre has been systematically researched in Europe since the nineteenth century. Today there are numerous publications which include studies of traditional puppetry, particular genres of puppet theatre, the history of puppetry both in specific countries and in Europe as a whole. There are also theoretical studies of puppet theatre including both its phenomenology and its semiotics.

Henryk Jurkowski
Warsaw

THE NATIONS AND
THEIR THEATRES

ALBANIA

The smallest country on the Balkan Peninsula in southeastern Europe, Albania is 320 kilometres from north to south and about 100 kilometres east to west (28,750 square kilometres or 11,000 square miles). Bounded on the west by the Adriatic Sea and the Strait of Otranto, on the north and east by the republics of former Yugoslavia and by Greece on the south, Albania's population of 3.3 million is divided into two major groups which form 98 per cent of the country: the Gegs in the north and the Tosks in the south. Greeks, Vlachs, Serbs, Bulgars and Gypsies make up the remainder. Tirana, the capital and largest city, has a population of about 300,000.

Located on important east–west trade routes across the peninsula, the territory that is now Albania has been invaded over and over again going far back into ancient history. The Turks invaded the country in 1385 and held it, except for a short period in the fifteenth century, until early in the twentieth century. Albania declared its independence on 28 November 1912. In 1939, the Italian dictator Mussolini invaded and in 1943, the German army took over the country. At the end of World War II, a communist government headed by Enver Hoxha (1908–85) took control and maintained power until 1985. Until 1961, foreign aid came primarily from the Soviet Union; after that date, the country turned to China for support. Through the 1970s and 1980s, Albania isolated itself more and more in an effort to achieve a pure form of communism.

Albania's theatrical history actually dates back to the fourth century BC when the country was known as Illyria. Its theatrical roots can be found in such ancient cities as Apolonia, Hexal (Bylis in Illyrian times), Klos (Nikaia), Finiq (Foinik), Butrint (Buthrotum) and Dyrrachium

among others. It was during the fourth century that a rich folk tradition developed in both theatre and other arts, a tradition which can be seen even today in the country's many dramatic forms.

Albania's modern theatre traces its roots to the last quarter of the nineteenth century – a period known as the National Albanian Renaissance – when the first Albanian drama was written and produced, *Dasma e Lunxhërisë* (*The Wedding of Lunxheria*, 1874) by Koto Hoxhi (1824–95). Later, Leonardo de Martino's (1830–1923) *Christmas Eve* was produced (1879). This movement also saw Shakespeare's works produced for the first time in the country – *Othello* in 1889 in the city of Korça.

Politically, throughout this period, a national independence movement grew both inside and outside the country and a large number of nationalistic theatre clubs – all of them amateur – were established. Among the major Albanian plays produced at this time were *Besa* (*The Given Word*, 1875) by Sami Frashëri (1850–1904); *Emira* (1883–4) by Anton Santori (1850–94); and *Vdekja e Pirros* (*The Death of Pirro*, 1906) by Mihal Grameno (1871–1931).

When national independence was finally achieved in 1912, the country's theatres began an even more active period of artistic development, creating as well a number of national artistic theatrical associations including Atdheu (Homeland) and Bashkimi (Unity). The most influential of the companies at this time were the Association of Fine Arts in Korça and the Bogdani Theatre in Shkodra. Though the plays produced by these groups tended to be historical in nature, they also dealt critically with social and political problems of the period.

In the 1920s and 1930s, tragedies on mythological themes by Ethem Haxhiademi
(1902–67), plays on national motifs by Gjergj
Fishta (1871–1940) and short comedies on
social themes by Kristo Floqi (1876–1949)
enriched the tradition of Albanian dramaturgy
with new artistic ideas and structures.

Although lacking technical means, schooling
and financial support and disregarded by
government and the wealthy, the theatre itself
was distinguished at this time by its passion,
critical sense and true-to-life spirit. Its ideal was
social emancipation and national identity.

By the 1930s, however, social criticism had
almost entirely disappeared from Albania's
theatres due to the generally conservative nature
of the government. In place of these earlier plays
came a dramatic literature that, at its best, was
allegorical and, at its least interesting, was both
sentimental and melodramatic.

Under Italian occupation, a new National
Liberation Movement developed as well as a
Partisan Theatre Movement which was at its
height between 1941 and 1945. The partisan
theatres operated not only in the cities but also
in the mountains among units of the National
Liberation Army and even in prisons. Lacking
scripts which could deal with the issues at hand,
the partisan theatres turned to improvised
musical sketches which were usually satirical in
nature. As the war went on, more literary
dramas began to be included as well. Yet even
in the written plays, the movement remained
essentially a political theatre, agitational as well
as romantic.

By 1944, the fascists were losing control and
the Anti-Fascist National Liberation Committee
held a congress in the city of Përmeti. Among
other things, it decided to formally recognize the
Central Theatre in the capital city, Tirana, as
the country's first 'professional' theatre and as
Albania's National Theatre. On 25 May 1945,
the Central Theatre was formally renamed the
State Professional Theatre; in 1947, the name
was changed again to the Teatri Popullor
(People's Theatre). In 1989 the company formally became the Teatri Kombëtar (National
Theatre).

Other groups were given similar professional
recognition by the state after 1947 and over the
next decade ten more professional dramatic
theatres and another fifteen variety theatres
(*estrada*) were set up across the country. As professional companies, these groups began to
upgrade their performance skills. Though many
approaches were examined, the most important

were those of the Russian director and teacher,
Konstantin Stanislavski.

Dramaturgy too developed significantly
during the 1950s as did opera and ballet. For the
first time, major works from the European
repertoire were seen in Albania performed by
Albanian professionals. A number of important
dramas by Albanian dramatists also began to be
included in the repertoire, among them *Toka
jonë* (*Our Land*, 1954) and *Halili dhe Hajria*
(*Halili and Hajria*, 1952) by Kol Jakova (b.
1916), and *Familja e Peshkatarit* (*The
Fisherman's Family*, 1955) by Sulejman Pitarka
(b. 1923).

During the 1960s and 1970s, government theatrical policy made national dramatic literature
a priority and the production of foreign plays
was significantly reduced. What the Albanian
theatre may have lost at this point in external
ideas, it made up in enriching the national dramatic tradition, raising the level of dramatic
writing and consolidating what can be called the
Albanian theatrical style.

By the 1980s, policies changed again and
European and other works from the world
repertoire once more found a place on the
national stages and a more balanced ratio of
national and international works was seen.
During this decade, the national theatres began
taking risks once again, presenting a wide range
of works dealing with major issues of the time.
Productions focused particularly on the relationship between individuals and society at large,
depicting most often the lives of simple working
people and the struggles they faced each day.

Of interest here is the fact that the official
theatres very often reflected one view of society
– usually an optimistic one – while many
others, including the variety theatres, reflected a
very different view, a more cynical one. At times
this dichotomy could be seen almost as stemming from different aesthetic principles, dialectical in their varying approaches. Each was
influenced in turn by national economic, social
and political changes. Despite these
philosophical differences, however, Albanian
theatre artists as a whole tended to remain loyal
to realism through the 1980s and generally
rejected experiments in form as well as what
might be called the dramaturgy of paradox.

In the 1990s, Albanian theatre aimed once
more at linking with and mastering the many
developments in world theatre – in terms of both
styles and schools – of which it was deprived
under the long period of communist censorship
which had ended as the decade began.

Pandi Stillu's 1955 People's Theatre production of Sulejman Pitarka's *The Fisherman's Family*, designed by Hysen Devolli.
Photo: Teatri Popullor Archive.

Structure of the National Theatre Community

In Albania in 1992, twenty-eight different professional theatrical groups existed – ten dramatic companies, fifteen variety groups, an opera-ballet troupe, a circus, and a puppet company. There were also ten smaller puppet companies. The largest concentration was in Tirana. This city alone boasted the Teatri Kombëtar, the Teatri i Operas dhe Baletit (Opera and Ballet Theatre), two variety theatres (Estrada and Estrada Ushtarit) and the Teatri i Kukullave (Puppet Theatre).

Through the early 1990s, all professional theatres in the country were completely state supported and operated in similar ways.

The largest company is the Opera and Ballet Theatre with over 400 singers, instrumentalists, dancers and artistic and administrative staff. The largest dramatic theatre in the country is the National in Tirana with fifty-five actors, four directors, three stage designers and other personnel. The variety theatres in Tirana have some forty actors, instrumentalists and singers on their payroll while the other six theatres each have from twenty-five to thirty staff.

Variety theatres give an average of three or four premières a year while drama and comedy theatres each give two or three premières annually. The majority of premières take place at the theatres in the capital.

Administratively, each theatre has an artistic council which acts as a consulting body to the director. The council looks at all new scripts and expresses its opinion about the value of the play. If approved, the script is passed for judgement to the Repertoire Commission (part of the Executive Committee of the district) but final decisions are given only by the District Party Committee. In the early 1990s, this system was still in place but was gradually being modified.

Government policy itself continues to be

aimed at the spread of the theatre to all the major towns of the country – a policy that had often been used to turn theatre into an effective method of state propaganda.

In addition to its professional groups, Albania also boasts more than 4,000 amateur groups which work in local town and village cultural facilities and which are usually attached to factories and agricultural cooperatives.

A national festival of professional theatres is held every three years (beginning in 1962) with the Aleksandër Moisiu Prize awarded for the Best Play in the festival. Other prizes awarded at the festival are for Best Direction, Performance and Design. Variety theatres also compete at these festivals for the Çajupi Prize for Best Production.

Until the 1990s, state subsidies kept ticket prices extremely low, usually equal to between one and three hours' work at the national minimum wage.

All theatre professionals, including designers and technicians, are members of the Writers' and Artists' Union and are traditionally entitled to a wide range of social benefits. Many work as well in film, television and radio. In total, the country has more than 1,000 actors, designers, singers, variety performers, puppeteers and musicians, all members of the union.

Artistic Profile

Companies

The Teatri Kombëtar is without doubt the country's most important theatrical institution. Throughout its history, it has consistently served as a school for the qualitative growth of other theatres. Its stage in Tirana has also been the venue for the most significant plays by the country's most important authors and the themes of its repertoire have been closely linked with fundamental national interests. Through its history, the Kombëtar company – usually numbering some sixty actors, directors and designers – has been Albania's major producer of historical plays on national subjects, plays which have attempted to throw light on significant periods, events and figures. Artistically, the theatre has tended to favour spectacular productions, large-scale visual design and an epic tragic style.

The country's second most important theatre – the Migjeni – is located in the city of Shkodra. Its favoured style can be described as romantic and the company has produced many poetic dramas featuring nationalistic themes (but themes specifically relating to the regional life of the northern highlands). Many of its productions have also dealt with the nature of individual freedom in its various struggles against communal habits, norms and conceptions.

The Çajupi Theatre in the city of Korça has dealt most directly with social and political issues, even including in its repertoire plays focusing on the National Liberation War itself. This interest has been seen as well when the theatre has staged classics from world dramatic literature with directors being encouraged to find parallels to national issues.

In the variety area – an area of enormous popularity – theatres have tended toward the staging of mostly satirical works. With a broad thematic spectrum of social issues to deal with, these theatres have generally played in mixed genres including everything from dance and music to painting, projections and film. Of particular importance in this regard have been the major variety theatres of Tirana and Shkodra, Fieri and Durrësi, which have staged a wide range of productions from comedy to fantasy, from large-scale musicals to modest revues. Virtually all of these companies have a strong critical edge to their work as well as an extremely contemporary sensibility.

Dramaturgy

Though Albanian dramaturgy lacks a significant historical tradition, during the last half of the twentieth century it has been linked with the ideals of socialist-realism, trying to reflect daily life, political problems and contradictions, and trying to place the Albanian people at the centre of the dramatic canvas.

The main shortcoming of this type of dramaturgy was its specific political agenda, extreme idealization of life and schematism of conflicts and characters. Most plays followed strict principles and concepts, all relating to the ideal of the struggle for social emancipation and national identity.

Three writers are of particular importance within the country's theatre. Kol Jakova is probably the most significant of the post-war writers. He tends to deal with social and economic concerns and is interested in the struggles of his characters to gain greater freedom. Jakova's psychologically well-drawn characters bear testimony to the disintegration of the traditional national patriarchal structure. His cleverly devised fables, sharp dramatic conceptions, unique language and laconic dialogue are hallmarks of his style. His major plays include *Toka jonë* and *Lulet e Shegës* (*Pomegranate Flowers*, 1977).

Fadil Paçrami (b. 1921) is another of the more successful playwrights of the post-war period, mainly in the 1960s, with such plays as *Shtëpia në bulevard* (*The House on the Boulevard*, 1963) and *Ngjarje në fabrikë* (*It Happened in a Factory*, 1969). Distinguished by his own political viewpoint and his consistent protest against conservative forces, he constructs his plays on a dialectical basis with conflicting groups of characters face-to-face in debate on keen political or ethical problems. He reveals the spirit of his characters through inner psychological tension which gradually emerges. His characters often seem fated, their destinies fixed beforehand.

The most prolific Albanian dramatist during the 1970s and 1980s was Ruzhdi Pulaha (b. 1942), a comic writer whose works dealt with conflicts between various social groupings. A problematic, optimistic yet militant writer, his plays are characterized by their recognizable everyday language and their reduction of dramatic time and space in an almost journalistic way. His most important works include *Zonja nga qyteti* (*City Lady,* 1974), *Maro Mokra* (1978) and *Mësuesi i letërsisë* (*The Literature Teacher,* 1986).

Another dramatist of note is Fadil Kraja (b. 1931) whose work focuses on historic issues of national importance. A creator of epic and monumental heroes with an almost spiritual commitment to the ideals of the nation, he consistently takes his subject matter from Albanian myth and legend. A dramatist of passion and pathos, Kraja's plays balance lofty ideals with spiritual struggle, national interest with personal commitment, honour and shame, law and belief. His two most often produced plays are *Baca i Gjetajve* (*The Patriarch of Gjetaj*, 1979) and *Gjaku i Arbërit* (*The Blood of Arbri*, 1981).

There are, as well, a large number of satirical comedies which have proven popular with audiences. Among the most produced are *Prefekti* (*The Mayor*, 1948) by Besim Lëvonja (1922–68); *Karnavalet e Korçës* (*The Carnivals of Korça*, 1961) by Spiro Çomora (1918–73); and *Fytyra e dytë* (*The Second Face*, 1968) by Dritëro Agolli (b. 1931).

Probably the most popular author during this period working almost exclusively with the variety theatres has been Pëllumb Kulla (b. 1940), a writer whose productions have involved strongly satirical character sketches, situational comedy and simple verbal humour. His works exist within the tension between dramatic cause and comic consequence, between what is possible and what is real. It should be said here as well that the paradoxes in his work have grown not so much from fantasy as from the realities of everyday Albanian life.

Directors, Directing and Production Styles

Sokrat Mio (b. 1902) was Albania's first important director of the modern period. Coming to prominence in the 1950s, Mio professionalized Albania's stages and his approach to the theatre had enormous influence on all those who subsequently went into directing as a career.

Following Mio's example, a large number of newly professionalized directors emerged. Pandi Stillu (1914–70) was given the country's highest cultural honour when he was named a People's Artist for his consistently committed work during the late 1950s and 1960s. Creating vivid stage portraits of the lives of ordinary people (generally through detailed psychological work with his actors) Stillu's career was highlighted by his productions of *Toka jonë* in 1954 and of the comic classic *Karnavalet e Korçës* in 1964.

People's Artist Pirro Mani (b. 1932) achieved note in the late 1960s through his ability to handle large casts and massive scenes in such plays as *Cuca e Maleve* (*Mountain Lass*, 1967). His later work focused even more on the development of actors through the creation of recognizable individual characters. His work has consistently dealt in contrasts: the serious with the humorous, the spiritual with the battles of daily living, the tragic with the grotesque. This latter ability was particularly evident in his handling of Brecht's *The Resistible Rise of Arturo Ui* in 1971. His work also showed him to be a master in the creation of stage atmosphere, as in *Fytyra e Dytë*.

Kujtim Spahivogli (1932–93) was another

39

Pirro Mani's 1971 People's Theatre production of Brecht's *The Resistible Rise of Arturo Ui*, designed by Agim Zajmi.
Photo: Teatri Popullor Archive.

strong director. In his productions of *Ngjarje në fabrikë* by Paçrami and *Banya* (*The Bath House*, 1973) by Vladimir Mayakovsky, he created an organic symbiosis of the dramatic and comic, the real and grotesque. He successfully experimented in elements of setting and acting, paying attention especially to the nature of feeling within a limited unit of time. His stagings were always dramatically expressive and within his eclectic style there converged the conventional, the visual, the symbolic and the naturalistic. He was also a distinguished teacher of acting.

Mihal Laurasi (b. 1930) is distinguished by his rigorous depictions of life in its metaphoric details. In his productions of *Njollat e murrme* (*Dark Stains*, 1968) by Minush Jero (b. 1938) and *Orpheus Descending* (1972) by Tennessee Williams, Laurasi managed to develop a genuine sense of ensemble playing with his actors.

Serafin Fanku (b. 1939) is another People's Artist who has achieved note as a director by successfully interweaving elegant pictorial compositions with very realistic performances. His work has also shown a particular sensitivity to the poetic, the figurative and the metaphorical. Among his most important productions have been *Fisheku në pajë* (*The Bullet in the Dowry*, 1967), *Baca i Gjetajve* (1979) and *Gjaku i Arbërit* (1981).

Esat Oktrova (b. 1930) is a director known for his philosophical, almost meditative productions. *Këneta* (*The Swamp*, 1968), one of his most characteristic shows, was at once philosophical and realistic, creating both emotional and spiritual power.

In the variety field, the best known director has been Gjergj Vlashi (b. 1928). Working in various styles, his productions have consistently displayed a keen sense of political satire through a very accomplished sense of burlesque.

Among Albania's many outstanding actors are a number who have been recognized as People's Artists. Among those who should be noted here are Naim Frashëri (1923–75), Kadri Roshi (b. 1927), Mihal Popi (1903–79), Zef Jubani (1910–58), Loro Kovaçi (1903–66), Sandër Prosi (1920–85) and Robert Ndrenika (b. 1942).

Josif Papagjoni

Music Theatre
Dance Theatre

Music and dance are used regularly in the country's many variety theatres but, for the most part, when one speaks of music theatre and dance theatre in Albania one is speaking of traditional opera and ballet. Only one company exists in the field, Tirana's Teatri i Operas dhe Baletit (Opera and Ballet Theatre) founded in 1953 as an extension of the Philharmonic Orchestra which was created in 1950.

Early on, the company staged a number of classical international operas and ballets. Perhaps the most important result was a significant improvement in opera and ballet training which led by the end of the 1950s to the staging of operas and ballets by Albanian composers.

The first of these national operas was written in 1958 by composer Preng Jakova (1917–69). Entitled *Mrika*, the work was distinguished as much by its lyricism as its nationalism. In 1968

Jakova composed another opera of note, *Gjergj Kastrioti Skënderbeu*. Jakova's pioneering works led to the creation of even more sophisticated operas later on, including *Komisari* (*Commissar*, 1974) by Nikola Zoraqi (1928–92); *Zgjimi* (*The Awakening*, 1976) by Tonin Harapi (1927–92); and *Goca e Kaçanikut* (*The Girl from Kaçanik*, 1979) by Raul Dhomi (b. 1945).

In the 1980s, Albanian operas and operettas sought a more popular appeal by utilizing a traditional international style; these later operas nevertheless relied heavily on recognizable Albanian types and situations. At root in the music could be heard the intonations of popular and patriotic Albanian folk songs which have long remained a permanent source of inspiration for composers.

Ballet has developed along much the same

Panajot Kanaçi's 1963 Opera and Ballet Theatre production of Tish Daia's *Halili and Hajria*, designed by Stavri Rafaei.
Photo: Teatri i Operas dhe Baletit Archive.

path. First came works from the international repertoire; later came ballets dealing with national themes and issues. Among the ballets which have stood out are *Halili dhe Hajria* (1963), composed by Tish Daia (b. 1926), choreographed by Panajot Kanaçi (b. 1923); *Cuca e maleve* (1972), composed by Nikola Zoraqi, choreographed by Agron Alia (b. 1931); and *Plaga e dhjetë e Gjergj Elez Alisë* (*The Tenth Wound of Gjergj Elez Alia*, 1987), composed by Feim Ibrahimi (b. 1935), choreographed by Alia.

Pandi Bello

Theatre for Young Audiences
Puppet Theatre

There are no companies in Albania specifically producing plays for young audiences. Rather, most companies – including the variety theatres – try to schedule at least one production annually which will be of particular interest to young audiences.

Plays written for teenagers and children mainly serve didactic and educational purposes but do little to introduce their audiences to fantasy, dream, play or fun. Only productions by the variety theatres include song and dance and some actually include the participation of children and teenagers in the cast. The situation was beginning to change only in the early 1990s.

In the area of puppet theatre, Albania has one major company in Tirana and another ten in smaller towns which mostly tour. There is no Albanian school for puppet theatre. Those wishing to work in the field usually graduate from the Art Academy in Tirana and then take training courses at the Tirana Puppet Theatre.

Albania's great folkloric wealth, however, is perhaps best demonstrated in puppetry since many of the plays are based on legends and stories. The well-known national tale *Fatbardha* (1951) was among the first professional productions of the modern period and remains popular.

In the years 1951–6 the bulk of puppet and children's plays staged came from abroad and presented images of the world within a rigorously predetermined morality. The repertoire was mainly of an informative and descriptive character at the expense of entertainment and spectacular features. The world of miracles and fairytales on the puppet stage particularly was deprived of elements of paradox, of free imagination and suggestiveness. Elements of evil – all forms of demons, monsters, witches, fear, violence and anxiety – were virtually forbidden from the stage or were presented in a schematized way. Charms, magic and miracles were also dismissed. In their place were moralism and didacticism of the most extreme kind. This began to change in the 1980s with the appearance once more of fantastic and miraculous elements in dramatized fairytales and folk legends.

Up to the mid-1950s settings too were static. Later they became movable and by the 1970s sculptural elements came into use which emphasized a new vividness.

As for puppet technique, finger-puppets were replaced from 1955 by marionettes. Musical backgrounds using live accordion replaced earlier and long outdated recordings.

Design
Theatre Space and Architecture

As Albanian theatre has been professionalized, design elements too have become more and more important. During the 1950s, most design was simply illustrative, gaining sophistication only in terms of its illusionistic qualities. In the 1960s, realism began to give way to less concrete images, while in the 1970s colour, symbolism and light played increasingly important

Shaban Hysa's design for the 1984 People's Theatre production of *Prometheus*.
Photo: Teatri Popullor Archive.

roles. It was also in the 1970s that the notion of conventional theatrical space began to be questioned and exploration began to be conducted in this area. All these elements could be seen in Albanian theatre design during the 1980s and into the early 1990s.

In technical terms, Albanian theatres have also improved over these decades. As the 1990s began, there were a dozen well-equipped theatre buildings across the country, all with revolving stages, sophisticated though basic lighting equipment, mechanical scene-changing capabilities and communications equipment.

Most are of the proscenium type with stage widths ranging from 9 to 15 metres, depths from 6 to 16 metres and in visible height from 6 to 18 metres. The Opera and Ballet Theatre is the largest hall in the country with 1,200 seats while the largest dramatic theatres are the Kombëtar with 550 seats and the Çajupi with 580.

Training

In 1959, a Higher School of Dramatic Art was established to meet the growing needs of the professional Albanian theatre. Attached to the People's Theatre, the school was named in honour of the great Albanian actor Aleksandër Moisiu (1879–1935). Seven years later, the school merged with similar schools of music and visual arts to create the Higher Institute of the Arts.

Located in Tirana, the Higher Institute's theatre programme trains young people for professional careers in virtually every area of dramatic art including all aspects of stage work, variety theatre and cinematography. The largest group of its students graduates from programmes in acting and directing; smaller numbers train in design, singing, music and choreography. The school uses the country's leading artists as its teachers.

The Higher Institute also has a library of over 70,000 volumes and offers university-level equivalencies in theatre, music, film and the visual arts.

Criticism, Scholarship and Publishing

Probably the most important work yet published on theatre in the country is the three-volume *Historia e Teatrit Shqiptar* (*History of Albanian Theatre*) published in 1983, 1984 and 1985 in Tirana. Complementing these volumes on the early traditions are a number of more general books on theatre and theatre aesthetics along with monographs on such national figures as actors Aleksandër Moisiu and Zef Jubani.

Since 1961, a bimonthly journal has appeared called *Teatri* which has published a great deal of theoretical and practical material along with playscripts. A quarterly journal called *Skena dhe Ekrani* (*Stage and Screen*) also publishes essays on both theoretical and practical aspects of theatrical and cinematic art as well as opera and variety theatre.

Regular reviews and commentaries have long been carried in newspapers and more popular magazines although they have not always been written by people with real qualifications. The first attempts at raising the level of critical journalism came after the opening of Albania's first university (in Tirana) in 1957, when critics began to receive proper training for the first time. In the decades that followed, one began to see some breakthroughs in both analysis and aesthetic considerations.

In the 1990s, a new democratic Albania made it possible for theatre criticism to assume an even wider freedom of expression and a new social dimension. Criticism now can present deeper analytical views and is able to judge from various aesthetic and methodological viewpoints. In earlier years, criticism was permeated by ideological and political dogmatism.

Even in the early 1990s, Albanian theatrical criticism still had a tendency to be more polemical than theatrical. Among the modern critics whose work has been more theatrically oriented are Ismail Hoxha (1931–73), Kudret Velça (b. 1929), Josif Papagjoni (b. 1950) and Miho Gjimi (b. 1942).

Josif Papagjoni
Translated by Emtela Lubomja

Further Reading

Fjalori Enciklopedik Shqipter. [Albanian encyclopedic dictionary]. Tirana: Akademia e Shkencave e RPSSH, 1985.

Gjini, Miho. *Pas Shfaqjes.* [After the spectacle: critical essays]. Tirana: Shtëpia Botuese Naim Frashëri, 1974.

——. *Teatri dhe koha: studime dhe artikuj kritikë.* [Theatre and time]. Tirana: Shtëpia Botuese Naim Frashëri, 1975.

——. *Trokitje në dyert e teatrit.* [Knocking at theatre's door]. Tirana: Shtëpia Botuese Naim Frashëri, 1967.

Historia e Muzikës Shqiptare. [A history of Albanian music]. Tirana: Shtëpia Botuese e Librit Shkollor, 1985.

Historia e Teatrit Shqiptar. [History of the Albanian theatre], 3 vols. Tirana: Shtëpia Botuese e Librit Shkoller, 1983–5.

Hoxha, Ismail. *Nga jeta në teatër, nga teatri në jetë.* [From life to theatre, from theatre to life]. Tirana: Shtëpia Botuese Naim Frashëri, 1983.

Kosova, Bardhyl. *Aleksandër Moisiu.* Tirana: Shtëpia Botuese Naim Frashëri, 1969.

Mjeshtëria e aktorit. [The art of acting]. Tirana: Shtëpia Botuese e Librit Shkoller, 1985.

Moisiu, Vangjel. *Aleksandër Moisiu.* Tirana: Shtëpia Botuese i Nëntori, 1980.

Papagjoni, Josif. *Teatri dhe aktori.* [Theatre and actor]. Tirana: Shtëpia Botuese Naim Frashëri, 1980.

Selimi, Skënder. *Arti i Koreografisë.* [Choreography as art]. Tirana: Shtëpia Botuese e Librit Shkoller, 1987.

Shita, Vehap. *Kur ndizen Dritat.* [In the limelight: critical essays]. Prishtina: Rilindja, 1977.

Shkurtaj, Gjovalin. *Kultura e gjuhës në skenë e në ekran.* [The nature of speech on stage and on screen]. Tirana: Shtëpia Botuese e Librit Shkoller, 1983.

Shllaku, Leo. *Zef Jubani.* Tirana: Shtëpia Botuese Naim Frashëri, 1962.

Velça, Kudret. *Rruga e zhvillimit të dramës sonë të re.* [The progress of the new Albanian dramaturgy]. Tirana: Shtëpia Qëndrore e Krijimtarisë Popullore, 1972.

Vlashi, Gjergj. *Regjisura në estradë.* [Directing for variety]. Tirana: Shtëpia Qëndrore e Krijimtarisë Popullore, 1987.

ARMENIA

The Armenian Republic, from 1920 until 1991 part of the Soviet Union, is located between the Black and Caspian Seas, between Georgia and Azerbaijan on the north and east, and between Turkey and Iran on the south and east. Once a potent kingdom bridging the borders of Europe and Asia – in 1947 it celebrated its two thousandth anniversary – modern Armenia was reduced to its present 29,000 square kilometres (10,670 square miles) through a succession of invasions and historic circumstances. Accepting Christianity as its state religion as early as AD 301 – the first state to do so – the Armenians quickly found themselves in conflict with their non-Christian neighbours.

Armenia was conquered in the sixteenth century by the Ottoman Empire. In 1828, Russia acquired most of present-day Armenian territory. Between 1894 and 1915, a series of Turkish massacres of ethnic Armenians took place and many of those remaining left their ancient homeland. In 1993, the country had a population of approximately 4 million with an additional 4 million ethnic Armenians spread around the world. The largest expatriate Armenian communities – each with its own theatre groups – can be found today in Georgia, Azerbaijan, the United States, Canada, Bulgaria, Egypt, France, Iran and Lebanon. Even today, but certainly prior to 1915, Armenian culture, commerce and politics can be found in many parts of the region, including Istanbul, Tbilisi and Baku.

In 1918, a modern Armenian Republic was established with its capital in Yerevan; following the dissolution of the Soviet Union, a new Armenian Republic was established in 1991.

The earliest reference to Armenian theatre is found in Plutarch's *Comparative Biographies*. It is stated there that the Armenian King Artavazd, son of Tigran the Great (d. *c.*56 BC), built a Hellenic theatre in his capital city of Artashat and that in 53 BC Euripides' *The Bacchae* was staged. Documentation also exists related to theatre during the early and late Middle Ages in the area. A professional theatre emerged in the nineteenth century.

Translations of Shakespeare into Armenian began to be published in the 1850s and staged in the 1860s. Among the most important translators was Hovhannes Mahseyan (1864–1931), who published twelve translations of Shakespeare's major plays, beginning with an enthusiastically received *Hamlet* in 1894. Bedros Adamian, Armenia's first great Shakespearian actor, had begun to popularize Shakespeare on stage in the 1880s. In 1883 he and his Armenian theatre company performed *Hamlet* at the Pushkin Theatre in Moscow and Adamian subsequently toured Russia for five years. Another major Shakespearian actor, Hovhannes Abelian (1865–1936), starred in *Othello* for twenty-five years beginning in the 1890s.

Major early Armenian playwrights include Gabriel Soundoukian (1815–1912), Hakob Paronian (1842–91), Alexander Shirvanzadé (1858–1935), Levon Shant and Derenik Demirjan. Soundoukian's comedy *Pepo* (1871), about a fisherman's rebellion against a conniving merchant, marks the foundation of Armenian realist drama. Written in Tbilisi, Georgia, the play is still performed in Armenia today, has been staged in Georgia and Azerbaijan, and has also been translated into French, Russian (by Maxim Gorki) and Ukrainian.

Hakob Paronian was a satirist whose stories contained much dialogue that lent itself easily to stage dramatization. His tragi-comedy about marital infidelity and judicial injustice, *Bagh-dassar Aghpar* (*Brother Balthazar*, 1886), was produced on the Western Armenian Stage in Constantinople, the capital of Ottoman Turkey. Through its exposure of the corrupt moral life of the Armenian upper-middle class, it became one of the most popular Armenian plays and has also been performed in Ukrainian, Georgian, Azerbaijani and Russian.

Alexander Shirvanzadé's domestic plays, such as *Iskhanouhi* (*Princess*, 1891), *Yevkine* (1901), *Ouner Eeravoonk* (*Did She Have the Right?*, 1902) and *Armenouhi* (1909), show the influence of Ibsen, particularly *A Doll's House*. In his family drama *Patvi Hamar* (*For the Sake of Honour*, 1904), material greed overcomes conscience and parental love, resulting in tragedy. By 1911, the play had been performed 300 times.

Levon Shant's neo-romantic symbolic drama *Hin Astvatsner* (*Ancient Gods*) was written in 1909 and staged to great acclaim at the Artists' Theatre in Tbilisi in 1913. The play stresses the idea of the liberation of the human spirit from all constraints. Other important works by Shant include *Oshin Bayl, Caesar* and *The Princess of the Fallen Castle*.

Written in 1923, Derenik Demirjan's grotesque comedy with political overtones, *Kaj Nazar* (*Nazar the Brave*), dramatizes the popular folk tale by the national poet Hovhannes Toumanian about how a stupid and weak person, by sheer luck of circumstance, becomes a fear-inspiring tyrant.

With the establishment of an Armenian Soviet Republic in 1920, stage art – along with Armenian society in general – embarked on a new phase of its development. Armenian theatre, as all Soviet theatre, faced the requirement of reflecting and endorsing the principles of the socialist revolution while attempting to preserve and develop its own traditions.

Levon Hakhverdian

Structure of the National Theatre Community

Through most of the post-World War II period there were two basic types of organization of the theatre in Armenia: state companies (*pettatron*), completely subsidized by the government, and the people's theatres (*zhoghtatron*), semi-amateur companies mostly in the small provincial towns. Most of the colleges and high schools put up their own amateur productions every now and then. All employees (including actors) of state theatres were on the payroll, regardless of their participation in a production. There were special bonuses for successful productions. As a rule each state company has a separate theatre building. State theatres have a chief director in charge of all artistic issues and an administrator overseeing business matters.

An important tool of state control was the artistic council (*geghkoroord*), made up in each company of ideologically sound individuals. It previewed all productions, confirmed the selection of plays and the distribution of roles. The ultimate power in all theatre-related matters rested with the Ministry of Culture.

The theatre community in Armenia since World War II includes about two dozen state theatres (half of those in Yerevan) and the same number of people's theatres. The Union of Theatrical Workers (UTW), founded in 1940 and serving as a sort of trade union, possessed certain coordinating capabilities and, during the Soviet period, provided extra ideological leverage.

From 1945 to 1991 the universal Soviet classification of artistic merit applied also to Armenia: the government granted the titles of Honoured Artist and, higher still, People's Artist of the Armenian SSR. In the 1970s the government established the Hovhannes Abelian Prize for outstanding contribution to Armenian theatre. In the Soviet period the Armenian theatre companies toured extensively in the USSR and occasionally abroad, and almost every year two or more of the better Soviet companies played on Armenian stages. Although there was no regular theatre festival, several international events took place in the 1970s and 1980s – a Shakespearian Festival in 1983, and Festivals of Armenian and Russian Drama.

After 1985 numerous non-state professional theatre companies emerged. These do not always have a building of their own and are mostly not subsidized by the government. Some are sponsored by private business or prosperous state enterprises, others attract enough spectators to carry on and some survive on sheer enthusiasm. The *geghkoroords* have lost most of their prominence, although the Ministry of Culture still allocates funds for the state theatres.

Ticket prices vary greatly but are kept within reach of the majority of theatregoers. The rehearsal period of a play seems to have decreased slightly compared with that of the Soviet period and ranges between three and four months on average.

In 1992 playwright Raphael Hakobjanian established the Stanislavski and Vakhtangov Foundation to promote theatrical revival in Armenia. Among its other activities, the foundation provides scholarships for theatre students.

Artashes Emin

Artistic Profile

Companies

Dramaturgy

Directors, Directing and Production Styles

On 26 August 1946, the Communist Party of the USSR passed a new law relating to theatres and their repertoires, specifically requiring plays to reflect the ideals of socialist-realism. Socialist-realism was essentially a theory of drama without conflict, drama that reflected a harmonious social order. As a result of this law, ideologically sound plays became rather colourless, replacing conflict with bombast, and genuine reflection of reality with idealization.

Serious plays were of little interest in such an atmosphere and comedy, a form which allowed playwrights to infringe on at least some taboos, became the genre chosen by most writers. It was also the form favoured by many leading actors, among them Tatik Sarian. In classic plays by writers such as Hakob Paronian and Gabriel Soundoukian and modern plays by writers such as Nairi Zarian, Sarian did a series of star turns portraying brilliant characters, at once simple and kind. Most of his work was staged by director Vardan Ajemian (1905–78) in Yerevan at the Paronian Musical Comedy Theatre. Ajemian also staged important productions of Armenian plays at the Leninakan Drama Theatre (among them, Zarian's historical tragedy, *Ara the Beautiful*).

At the same time, psychological realism still flourished at the Soundoukian Theatre. Among the many important productions staged there by director Armen Goulakian (1899–1961) were Lermontov's *The Unknown* and Tolstoi's *The Living Corpse*, both starring the great classic actor Papazian.

A thaw began after Stalin's death in 1953 and state control of the arts loosened significantly. At this time classical plays were again staged widely along with more modern plays with a much sharper critical tone. As a director, Ajemian was the foremost figure in Armenian theatre at this time, equally at home with the fantastic realism of Vakhtangov and the lyrical realism of Chekhov. His major productions ranged from *The Cherry Orchard* to musical comedies such as *Karineh* (Choukhajian), from Shirvanzadé's play *Namous* to Paronian's *Baghdassar Aghpar*.

Among significant productions during this period at the Soundoukian Theatre, many of which toured to Moscow, were Cassona's *The Trees Die Standing*, Figereydo's *The Fox and the Grapes*, De Filippo's *Saturday, Sunday, Monday* and Saroyan's *My Heart's in the Highlands*.

Many of those who worked with Ajemian became key figures in the development of Armenian theatre in the 1960s and 1970s, among them Hrachia Ghaplanian, who first emerged as an important director at the Young Spectator's Theatre in Yerevan.

During those two decades, many playwrights came to prominence as well, including Gourgen Boryan (author of *Under the Same Roof* and *On the Bridge*), Grigor Ter Grigorian (*The Last Carnations* and *Ah Nerves, Nerves*), Alexander Araxmanian (*Roses and Blood* and *Sixty Years and Three Hours*), Gevorg Haroutyounian (*The Heart Fault* and *Intersection*), Aramashot Papayan (*The World Has Really Gone Berserk*), Perj Zeytountsian (*The Saddest Man* and *The Legend of the Destroyed City*), Zarzand Darian (*The President of the Republic*), Zabel Asadour (1863–1934), one of Armenia's few female writers (*The Bride*), and Vardges Petrossian (*The Hippocratic Oath Is Heavy*).

47

Nishan Parlakian's 1984 New York
Armenian Church production of Zabel
Asadour's *The Bride*.
Photo: H. Kantzabed.

Many of these plays were produced not only
in Yerevan but also in smaller cities –
Leninakan, Kirovakan, Artashat, Kamo and
Kapan. They addressed issues about both the
ancient and immediate past of the nation but
more immediately they addressed the imperfec-
tions of the regime.

In 1968, the Yerevan Drama Theatre opened
under the artistic direction of Ghaplanian. It
established its own style, larger than life, broad
in character. Focusing on clear, somewhat
simple solutions to complex issues, its productions were dynamic and socially suggestive.
Among its successes were *The Diary of Anne
Frank* and Makayonok's *The Persecuted
Apostle*.

Throughout the 1980s, Armenian plays examined and re-examined the theme of 'power to
the people' as social changes began to rock the
Soviet Union as a whole. Many world classics
were looked at in this light, among them
Shakespeare's *Coriolanus* and *King John* (both
done by the Soundoukian Theatre), *Hamlet*,
The War of the Roses, and Stratiev's *The Bus* at
the Yerevan Drama Theatre and *Richard II*,

Lermontov's *Masquerade,* Shirvanzadé's *Chaos*
and Chekhov's *Three Sisters* at Kirovakan's
Abelian Theatre. Another notable production
was *The Criminal's Family* by Giacometti at the
Leninakan Drama Theatre.

Nineteen professional companies were oper-
ating in Armenia by the early 1980s including
three new ones in Yerevan – the Film Actors'
Theatre directed by H. Malian; the satirical
Camera (Chamber) Theatre founded by its
director Ara Yernjakian in 1982; and the
Experimental Youth Theatre founded by its
director Hratchya Ghazarian also in 1982.
Among the important productions in the early
years of the Film Actors' Theatre were *The
Decameron* and a work based on Medieval
Armenian proverbs, *The Foxbook*, while the
Experimental Theatre found success with
Mayakovsky's *Mystère Bouffe*.

Two music theatres also operate in Yerevan –
the Paronian Musical Comedy Theatre headed
by Armen Elbakian and the Spendiarev Opera
and Ballet Theatre (where the operas of Alexander Spendiarian, Tigran Choukhajian and
Armen Tigranian are regularly played). There is
also a State Youth Theatre headed by Yervant
Ghazanchian and two puppet theatres. The
Theatre Institute, a four-year college training
young people for the stage, presents several student productions a year as the final requirement
for graduation.

Until shortly after the dissolution of the
Soviet Union, the state-subsidized theatre in
Armenia made possible an excellent repertory
system which provided most artists with ongoing work and enabled directors, playwrights
and designers to stage engaging work for their
audiences. The Soundoukian Theatre in the
early 1990s, for example, staged productions
such as Berj Zeitountiants's *Unfinished
Monologue* about corruption in the business
world; Ibsen's *Enemy of the People*, starring one
of Armenia's foremost actors and the artistic
director of the company, Khoren Abrahamian;
and Jirair Ananian's musical farce *Carousel*
and *My House Is Not Your House*, a political
farce about the current housing shortage.
Ananian began writing for the stage, radio
and television in 1956. Through his many
comedy-farces about contemporary Armenian
moral and social mores – *Taxi, Taxi* (1972),
The Man From the Flying Saucer (Paronian
Musical Comedy Theatre, 1992) – Ananian
has become the Neil Simon of Armenian
comedy.

In the early 1990s the Yerevan Drama

Theatre, directed by Armen Khandigian, staged works such as Berj Zeitountiants's *The Great Silence* about the great national poet Daniel Varoujan, one of 300 intellectuals murdered at the outset of the 1915 massacres; the drama *The Eternal Return*, about the poet-writer Paroyr Sevak, a spokesman for Armenian rights in the Soviet Union; *Brother Balthazar* by the satirist Hakob Paronian, in which both the actors' costumes and the stage were designed in stark contrasting black and white; and an impressionistic production of *Julius Caesar*.

In 1992 one could also see Hakob Paronian's sex comedy *The Eastern Dentist* at the Youth Theatre, Armen Elbakian's production of Molière's *Georges Dandin* at the Paronian Musical Comedy Theatre, and the Gavit Theatre political collective creation *For the Sake of Gigos*.

By the late 1980s companies in Armenia were beginning to face many serious problems yet struggled to continue operating. This despite an enormous earthquake in 1988, the collapse of the Soviet Union and the political turmoil that followed through the early 1990s, an economic blockade by Azerbaijan and the struggle by the breakaway province of Nagorno-Karabakh; this despite economic chaos, only two hours of water per day in the capital in 1993, one hour of electricity, a fuel shortage and the departure of many from the profession to seek new lives in other countries. Theatre nevertheless continued to be staged and new groups amazingly continued to emerge.

Among the groups starting up in the 1990s were Studio Nork, Theatre Guild Laboratory, Satire Theatre, Raffi Muradian and Artur Khachaturian's Theatre on Wheels, Sonnet 101, Triangle, Studio 13, Bem, Gavit Theatre and the Ajemian Studio. Not all lasted very long in the new economic atmosphere. Even the Soundoukian Theatre faced major economic crises and as a result three smaller companies emerged – one run by director Mher Mkrtchian and known simply as the Mkrtchian Company; another by Sos Sarkissian called the Hamazgayin Theatre; and a third run by N. Tsatourian called Metro.

In 1993, Armenian theatre was almost completely without government support. As a result, it was struggling to regain both its stature and its audiences.

Levon Hakhverdian

Music Theatre
Dance Theatre

Music theatre in post-war Armenia evolved mostly through and around the Sate Opera in Yerevan (founded in 1933). The repertoire of its company over the years has included mostly western classical works of which many productions were Soviet premières such as Stravinsky's *Oedipus Rex*, Menotti's *The Consul*, Bellini's *Norma*, Donizetti's *Poliuto* and Bernstein's *West Side Story*.

Virtually every Armenian piece ever written for opera has also played on the State Opera stage.

The Paronian Musical Comedy Theatre was founded in 1944 in Yerevan.

The State Ballet Company gave its first performance in 1939 with Khachaturian's *Happiness*. Until Vilen Galstian took over as artistic director in the late 1970s, most of the productions were put together by guest choreographers from Russia (Moisaev, Lavrovski, Zanga). Galstian's productions of *Gayane*, *Spartacus*, *Masquerade* and *David of Sassoun* represented the result of a national re-evaluation of

Armen Goulakian's 1935 production of Hovhannes Toumanian's opera *Anoush*.

traditional ballet. Its dancers mostly come from the Yerevan School of Dance, established in 1936 from the School of Rhythm and Plastics which had been founded in 1930 by Srbouhy Lisitsian in Yerevan.

Emmanuel Manoukian

Theatre for Young Audiences
Puppet Theatre

Information not available at time of publication.

Design
Theatre Space and Architecture

Most influential on Armenian design tradition were Georgi Yakoulov's sets for *The Merchant of Venice* and Shirvanzadé's *Related with a Morgan* (both 1926, Yerevan State Theatre). He combined a colourful palette with almost architectural laconicism and a versatility of plastic solutions.

Michael Aroutchian headed a school of more academic professional designers over the following decades. This was occasionally stirred with ventures into theatre by such great painters as Yervand Kochar and Martiros Sarian, who did the opulent sets of *Almast* by Spendiarov for the opening of the Yerevan Opera in 1933.

The prevailing designs in the years that followed were marked by a movement between simple graphic solutions, use of architectural volumes and the constructivist approach. The war years reduced the theatre repertoire to historical dramas with a patriotic charge, where the original talent of Melixet Svaghchian blossomed, most markedly in the sets for Nairi Zarian's *Ara the Beautiful*.

The post-war years proved to be most trying for theatre designers. The non-conflict drama was asking for near-photographic solutions, stripped of any inspiration. This changed in the mid-1950s almost overnight with the arrival on the scene of the first graduates of the Yerevan Arts and Theatre Institute. They broke the naturalistic non-conflict spell, but lacked innovation, mostly reviving, with some expertise, long-forgotten trends and techniques.

The 1960s punctured the stagnation with increased exposure to new visual material and ideas from abroad. Theatre directors were the first to respond, but it was not until 1965, when Sargis Aroutchian designed the sets for Arthur Miller's *The Crucible* (Soundoukian Theatre, directed by H. Ghaplanian), that Armenian stage design attempted anything that could be called modern. The sets promoted a philosophic perception of the play, accentuating its mood with then-unorthodox means. This paved the way for others to experiment.

The renowned post-war painter Minas Avetissian designed a number of sets for opera, among which one for Khachaturian's (1903–78) *Gayane* showed sparkling wit and colours. Through the 1970s and 1980s a new generation of Armenian stage designers emerged, including Rouben Ghevondian, Vahagn Tevanian, Karen Gevorgian and Karen Grigorian. Among them, Yevgeny Sofronov was clearly the most innovative, experimenting with modernistic techniques, though his designs were mostly void of colour. The mid-1970s also brought along a growing awareness of the importance of costume, and Anahit and Gayane Arouthian contributed greatly towards more diversity and flexibility in costume design. Their best works included *The Barber of Seville*, *Macbeth* and *La Bohème*.

Sargis Aroutchian

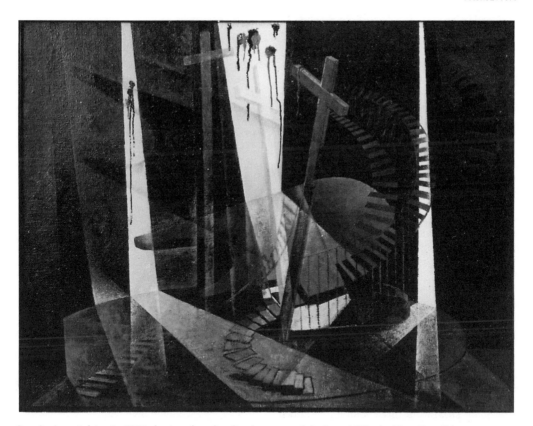

Sargis Aroutchian's 1965 design for the final scene of Arthur Miller's *The Crucible*, Soundoukian Theatre.

Training

Until 1944, when the Theatre Institute was founded in Yerevan, theatre professionals were trained in independent studios. The most prominent was the studio in Tbilisi (founded by O. Sevoumian) and the studio in Moscow (founded in 1918 by Ruben Simonov). Today, the institute in Yerevan offers five-year Master's degrees in acting, directing and theatre studies. Each year a different master teacher accepts a class of his or her own and carries it through to graduation.

University-level general humanities background courses (history, languages, and so on) are mandatory. Theatre training is also available at the Armenian Pedagogical Institute's theatre department (founded in 1972). The four-year master classes in acting and directing there are also led by leading actors and directors. At both schools tuition is free. Theatre technicians usually emerge through apprenticeship at the theatres themselves.

Designers often train at the Yerevan Fine Arts Academy or one of several other art schools. Costume designers sometimes come from fashion houses.

Some of the major companies, such as the Soundoukian and the Dramatic Theatre, now have their own studios.

Artashes Emin

Criticism, Scholarship and Publishing

Armenian theatre has been accompanied by theatrical criticism since the middle of the nineteenth century. Following 1945, routine reviews began to be augmented by more general articles commenting on theatrical developments. Some theoretical provisions were set forth, drawing from the experience of Russian and western theatre. A dispute about the future prospects of Armenian theatre arts evolved in the periodicals. Sargis Meliksetian, Rouben Zarian and Souren Haroutiounian, prominent scholars of the time, were succeeded by the graduates of the department of theatrology of the Yerevan Theatre Institute.

Their joint efforts contributed in the mid-1950s to the formation of an independent school of theatre scholarship. This promoted the publication of a number of studies on the history of the national theatre and its prominent personnel, resulting in a library of important works, among which are Georg Goyan's *2000 Years of Armenian Theatre*, Vahram Terzibashian's *The History of Armenian Playwriting* (in two volumes), Garnik Stepanian's *Outline of the History of Western Armenian Theatre* (in three volumes), Rouben Zarian's *Siranouysh* and *Petros Adamian* (in two volumes), Sabir Rizaev's *History of Armenian Directing*, Louise Samvelian's *Shakespeare and the Armenian Literary and Theatrical Culture*, Levon Hakhverdian's *History of Armenian Theatre (1901–1920)* and *Theatre Dictionary*, Henrik Hovanessian's *Medieval Armenian Theatre*, and the group project, *History of Soviet Armenian Theatre*.

The Art Institute of the Armenian Academy of Sciences is responsible for the bulk of these publications. In 1958 it incorporated a theatre department, with nearly a dozen scholars studying theatre and its history. The department is completing studies on nineteenth-century Armenian theatre, Armenian theatre communities in the United States and Egypt, and old Yerevan theatre companies. A complete history of the Armenian theatre in five volumes was in preparation in 1993.

This picture of Armenian theatre criticism would be incomplete without mentioning the memoirs of notables like Olga Goulazian, Vahram Papazian, Vagharsh Vagharshian and Gourgen Janibekian, which provide invaluable material, both critical and factual.

Armenian theatrical periodicals also have a history in Istanbul, Tbilisi and Baku since 1874. New productions in Armenia are regularly reviewed in the press both by columnists and freelance contributors, most of them professionals. The weekly *Taterakan Yerevan* (*Theatrical Yerevan*, founded in 1953) is published by the UTW and combines *Playbill*-type infomation with artistic profiles of companies and actors. The illustrated monthly *Arvest* (*Art*, founded in 1926) has a lengthy section on theatre and drama. Since 1990 an exclusively theatrical almanac has been published in Yerevan under the name *Bem* (*Stage*).

Levon Hakhverdian with Artashes Emin
Research assistance by Nishan Parlakian
Translated by Artashes Emin

(See also USSR. Because of war conditions in Armenia during 1992–4, it was not possible to obtain material for all sections of this article.)

Further Reading

Alexander, Edward. 'Shakespeare in Armenia'. *Shakespeare Quarterly* 9 (1958): 387–94.

Alexanian, Elena. '19th Century Armenian Realism and its International Relations'. *Review of National Literatures* 13: *Armenia* (1984): 45–63.

Allworth, Edward. 'Introduction to the Modern Drama of the Transcaucasus'. Introduction to *Evil Spirit (Char Voki)* by Alexander Shirvanzadé. Translated by Nishan Parlakian. New York: St Vartan Press, 1980. xi–xxvii.

Avagian, K., B. Haroutiounian, Sabir Rizaev, Levon Hakhverdian and L. Khalatian. *History of Soviet Armenian Theatre*. Yerevan, 1967.

Goyan, Georg. *2000 let armianskovo teatra*. [2000 years of Armenian theatre]. Moscow: Gosudarstvennoe Izdatel'stvo Iskusstvo, 1952.

Hakhverdian, Levon. 'Armenian Classical Drama and its International Context'. *Review of National Literatures* 13: *Armenia* (1984): 174–93.

Inglisian, Vahan. 'Die armenische Literatur'. In *Handbuch der Orientalistik*. Edited by B. Spuler. Köln: E.J. Brill, 1963. Vol. VII: 156–250.

Kagramanov, Nerses Voskanovich. *Dramaturgiia narodov SSSR na armianskoi stsene: 1876–1976*. [Armenian playwriting: 1876–1976].

Yerevan: Izdo-vo Akademiia nauk Armianskoi SSSR, 1980. 78 pp.

Parlakian, Nishan. 'Armenian Theater: An Update'. *Council on National Literatures World Report* 6 (1993): 14–40.

Rizaev, Sabir. *History of Armenian Directing.* Yerevan, 1963.

Tamrazian, Hrant Smbatovich. *Shirvanzadé, Gianka ev Kordza.* [Shirvanzadé, his life and work]. Yerevan: Haypethat Press, 1961.

Terzibashian, Vahram. *The History of Armenian Playwriting.* 2 vols. Yerevan, 1959–64.

Thorossian, H. *Histoire de la littérature arménienne des origines jusqu'à nos jours.* [The history of Armenian literature from its beginnings to the present]. Paris, 1951.

Tigranov, G. *The Armenian Musical Theatre.* 3 vols. Yerevan, 1956–75.

Two Thousand Years of the Armenian Theater. New York: Armenian National Council of America, 1954. 12 pp.

Verdone, Mario. 'Due agitka dell'armeno Egische Ciarenz'. [Two Agitkas by the Armenian Egische Ciarenz]. *Teatro Contemporaneo* 3, no. 5 (October 1983–January 1984): 209–25.

Zarian, Rouben. *Shakespeare and the Armenians.* Translated by Haig Voskerchian. Yerevan: Academy of Sciences, 1969.

——. *Theatrical Portraits.* Yerevan: 1956.

AUSTRIA

Austria is the country of Wolfgang Amadeus Mozart, Adolf Hitler and Arnold Schwarzenegger. Until the time when the Iron Curtain was dismantled, Austria was considered as the easternmost country in the west. Its geopolitical situation is thrown into relief by a list of Austria's neighbouring countries: Switzerland, Liechtenstein, Germany, the Czech and Slovak Republics, Hungary, Slovenia and Italy. Covering an area of 83,900 square kilometres (32,400 square miles), the country is divided into nine federal states or provinces. German is the mother tongue of most of its 7.8 million inhabitants (1.6 million of whom live in the capital, Vienna) though there are several linguistic minorities. Politically speaking, Austria is one of the western parliamentary democracies. As the successor state to the Austro-Hungarian Empire, which also had its political and cultural centre in Vienna, Austria feels entrusted with a centuries-old cultural legacy.

The inter-war period saw the emergence of a specific, historically evolved role for the country's theatre as the centre of the search for a national identity. On the one hand, Austria had the task of modernizing the grand tradition of the (imperial) theatres of the Austro-Hungarian Empire into what had become a small, deeply indebted republic. On the other hand, the many modern theatres established in the late nineteenth century had to fight desperately for survival, a remarkable task in view of the diminished population and the pauperization of the very classes that had supplied most of the regular theatregoers.

Six of the eight provincial capitals at that time also had well-established theatres with permanent ensembles and a high quality three-sector repertory (opera, operetta and theatre). Even many of the medium-sized and small towns were used to having permanent theatres whose seasons were highlighted by guest performances of touring stars or companies. The decline of the empire, with its dense network of German-language theatres, ushered in hard times for many of these establishments, since free movement was severely restricted by new borders, differing labour laws and economic barriers. Many of the smaller theatres found themselves hard put to engage quality artists. Economic hardship forced other leading performers and directors to emigrate, especially to Germany. Still, a number of magnificent new establishments attracted major talents to Austria: in 1920, the Salzburg Festival, founded by Max Reinhardt (1873–1943), Hugo von Hofmannsthal (1874–1929) and Richard Strauss (1864–1949), was inaugurated with the legendary open-air performance of *Jedermann* (*Everyman*), Hofmannsthal's adaptation of this morality play from the late Middle Ages. Due to its consistently high level of quality, the Salzburg Festival became – next to Bayreuth – one of the most important European festivals. Its unique combination of lovingly preserved local tradition and a sophisticated, international atmosphere soon attracted audiences from all over the world.

Works by such Austrian dramatists as Hofmannsthal, Arthur Schnitzler (1862–1931), Hermann Bahr (1863–1934), Ferdinand Bruckner (1891–1958), Franz Theodor Csokor (1885–1969) and Robert Musil (1880–1942), all great influences on German-language theatre, were, however, often staged in Austria only after they had been premièred abroad. In the 1930s, cabaret had a special standing in Austria, both aesthetically and politically. It was honed to perfection and gained an importance that went far beyond the scope of the small stages on which it was performed. Probably the most influential proponent of this politically agile but heterogeneous movement was Jura Soyfer (1912–39), whose main works (*Der Weltuntergang, Astoria, Vineta* and *Broadway Melodie 1492*) were revived in the 1980s and 1990s.

The invasion of Austria by German troops on 12 March 1938 and the annexation (*Anschluß*) of Austria by the Third Reich had a decisive impact on the nation's theatre life. Numerous Austrian artists had to leave the country because of their 'racial origins' or politics. It was also the time when many German artists who had found protection in Austria left the country. To name but a few, these included dramatists Carl Buck-mayer (1896–1977) and Ödön von Horvath (1901–38), composers Ralph Benatzky (1887–1957) and Ernst Krenek (1900–91), directors and theatre producers Max Reinhardt and Stella Kadmon (1902–89), writer and director Ernst Lothar (1890–1974), and actors Oscar Karlweis (1894–1956), Albert Basser-mann (1867–1952), Tilla Durieux (1880–1971) and Hans Jaray (1906–90).

Many of them had to live in hiding and found themselves banned from working. Some of them were mangled in the deathly machinery of the Nazi regime. Rudolf Beer (1889–1938), the administrator and director at the Volkstheater and the Raimundtheater, who was even briefly in charge of the Reinhardt stages in Berlin and finally artistic director of Theater in der Scala in Vienna, committed suicide after an interrog-ation by the Gestapo. Jura Soyfer, the young dramatist who wrote cabaret, died in a concen-tration camp, as did the cabaret artist Fritz Grünbaum (1880–1941), and the directors Carl Forest (d. 1944) and Friedrich Rosenthal (1885–1942). The introduction of auth-oritarian theatre laws in the Ostmark, as Austria was called, and strict supervision by Nazi Propaganda and Culture ministries ensured that theatres kept to Nazi-issued directives. In fact, Berlin used the structures of Austria's essentially elitist cultural establishments to put art and artists to the service of Third Reich propaganda. All theatres were 'Aryanized' and more often than not they were also nationalized.

Austrian Nazis, who had expected to make a career for themselves after the take-over, were only initially successful, such as the writer Mirko Jelusich (1886–1969), who spent some months in 1938 in the position of director of the Burgtheater. Joseph Goebbels, Hitler's propaganda minister, made appointments to the key positions: Lothan Müthel (1896–1965) at the Burgtheater (from 1939), Heinz Hilpert (1890–1967) at the Theater in der Josefstadt (from 1938), Walter Bruno Iltz at the Deutsches Volkstheater (from 1938), Heinrich Strohm (from 1939) and Karl Böhm (1894–1981; from 1943) at the Vienna State Opera.

The Ostmark was subjected to the same repertoire guidelines, bans, employment direc-tives (certificates of Aryan origin, certificates of political reliability) as Germany itself. The tra-ditional theatrical competition between Berlin and Vienna was consistently decided in favour of Berlin by the Nazis. Nevertheless, the Nazi leader appointed for Austria between 1941 and 1945, Baldur von Schirach, was permitted to make some regional concessions with a view to cultural independence.

With the ambitious and highly subsidized Reichstheaterfestwochen (German Theatre Fes-tivals) in 1938 and 1939, the Third Reich sought to advertise its cultural superiority to the world. Pompous events, such as the Raimund Week in 1940 and the Mozart Week and the Grillparzer Week in 1941, were designed to sub-jugate the works of these artists to Nazi ideology. There was steady resistance to the annexation of the mind: at the Burgtheater the Catholic resistance group of Karl Roman Scholz (1912–44) was active. When the group was denounced in 1942 by the actor Otto Hartmann, actor Fritz Lehmann along with musician Friedrich Wildgans and members of the technical staff were sent to prison.

With the onset of 'total war' Joseph Goebbels decreed a theatre ban on 1 September 1944. The staff was transferred to compulsory jobs in the arms industry; some theatre buildings, such as the State Opera and the Burgtheater, were severely damaged by bombs in the last year of the war.

In the Moscow Declaration of 1943, three Allied powers – the United States, the Soviet Union and Great Britain – declared that Austria had been the first victim of Hitler's policy of aggression and was to be freed from German oppression. This statement formed the basis of the Second Austrian Republic, which was founded on 27 April 1945. A further important statement of the declaration, which reminded Austria of its responsibility for participating in the war on the side of Hitler Germany, was soon forgotten.

From 1945 until 1955 Austria was divided into four occupation zones by the Allied powers.

Vienna was also divided into four sectors. The Soviets, who had liberated Vienna, decreed the immediate reopening of theatres. On 30 April 1945 the Burgtheater performed Franz Grillparzer's (1791–1872) *Sappho* at its interim home, the Ronacher Variety Theatre. In their occupation zone, the Americans supported the organization of the Salzburg Festival in 1945. Hofmannsthal's *Der Tor und der Tod* and *The Abduction from the Seraglio* by Mozart were performed. The provincial theatres in the French and British zones also opened their doors in the same year. The rapid restoration of artistic life led to revivals of productions from the Nazi period, pre-empting serious discussion on the role of art during the Nazi regime and preventing any new definition of Austrian art after 1945.

Only a few politicians in the Second Republic, such as the communists Viktor Matejka (1901–92), Vienna City Councillor for Culture, and Ernst Fischer (1899–1972), senior official in the Art Ministry and a great expert on world literature, tried to lure expatriate Austrians back to their home country. Some returned of their own volition, some came back as Allied cultural officials and participated in the redevelopment of cultural life in Austria.

Theatre played an important role when Austrians went searching for their identity after 1945. It was living proof of the collective psychological, emotional and intellectual state. By the plays performed and the style in which they were performed, theatres underlined the desire of Austrians to distance themselves from the Nazis. Being Austrian meant, first of all, *not* being German and, thus, not being involved in the terrors of the past. This attitude made it possible to regard the period of Austro-fascism (1933–8) and the Nazi regime as a mere interruption in a continuous period of democracy and republicanism. Sensitive spots appeared whenever the theatre touched on Austria-related taboos or religious convictions or spoke in favour of class warfare.

From 1948 onward, the Cold War also influenced Austrian theatre. Attempts at social criticism or criticism of Austria by the theatre were frequently labelled 'communist' and defamed. Thus an important Austrian theatre – the Neues Theater in der Scala – was ruined because it was said to propagate communism.

In order to heighten Austria's international reputation, policy-makers decided to subsidize expensive festivals. One audacious idea – to engage Bertolt Brecht in a senior position at the

Hans Moser in Axel von Ambessers's 1961 Theater in der Josefstadt production of Johann Nestroy's *Blue Funk*, designed by Hill Reihs-Gromes.
Photo: Barbara Pflaum.

Salzburg Festival – was not implemented. The Salzburg Festival has ever since, however, been characterized by famous actors and internationally renowned singers and musicians. On the other hand, the social element, festive mood and well-off, music-loving regulars seemed to become more important than innovative productions and the striving for new forms of art.

The Bregenz Festival, concentrating on classical operettas since 1946, has also developed into a big tourist attraction. The Vienna Festival was revived in 1955 so that Vienna could maintain its role as a metropolis of theatre and music.

For Austria, the year 1955 meant the State Treaty – and with it its sovereign status and 'ever-lasting' neutrality – and the reopening of the reconstructed State Opera and Burgtheater, again linked to the fate of the state in representational functions. The fact that cultural policy and funds focused on the establishment of 'high culture' only strengthened the scepticism towards Austria as a centre of modern and experimental art.

The largest part of the audience that has filled the major theatres in Vienna and in the provincial capitals (the owners of season tickets) in the decades since World War II has come from the educated upper-middle class. They are traditionally less interested in content or experiment than in the actors' performance. Austrian audiences therefore appreciate performance elements above all and have affectionate relationships with their favourite actors. While audiences at the numerous private comedy theatres and alpine folk-play theatres (amateur theatre) were moving away from the stage with the advent of television from the 1960s onward, audiences in the major cities survived every crisis. They continue to be interested in guest performances, festivals and open-air events in the summer, and are not deterred by high ticket prices. A tiny section of the public is open to experimental theatre and the avant-garde and usually fills the alternative theatres.

The progressive Austrian actors' law of 1922 was reintroduced in 1945. Actors with contracts enjoy a satisfactory social security status (pay, health and pension insurance). More often than not the management will give them leave for television, radio or film jobs. In the alternative theatres, the social situation of artists is significantly worse. For decades, they were paid only for performances and not for rehearsals, another reason why actors try to become integrated into the well-established theatres.

A general paradigm shift of politics and art became apparent in the period of single-party government of the conservative Austrian People's Party (1966–9), when the opposition in Austria's artistic and intellectual life began to pool their resources. With the social-democratic government under the leadership (1970–82) of Bruno Kreisky (1911–90), Austria took some major steps toward modernization – international contacts, new social relationships and new interests on the stage. One late effect of this cultural renewal was the occupation of the Arena St Marx (1976). This dilapidated slaughterhouse area, where the alternative events of the Vienna Festwochen had taken place, was occupied by artists, intellectuals and young people who wanted to prevent the proposed demolition of the slaughterhouse area and to establish an autonomous civic and cultural centre under a self-administration scheme. The summer of the Arena conflict, upgraded by solidarity from Canadian singer and poet Leonard Cohen (he called the Arena 'the best place to be in Vienna') was abruptly ended by the arrival of the municipal demolition machinery. Nevertheless, local and central policy-makers learned a lesson from this demonstration of independent youth culture and began to support the establishment of cultural centres and free theatre companies. Although this did not result in a redistribution of public funds in favour of free theatre companies, the economic situation at least allowed for an increase in the overall budget for culture. At the end of the 1970s, a general austerity policy meant a partial restriction on the freedom of production. In the 1980s many free companies, now recipients of state subsidies, sank into undistinguished production modes and socially irrelevant aesthetics.

Evelyn Deutsch-Schreiner

Structure of the National Theatre Community

The theatre plays an extremely important role in Austria's public life. This is indicated by the fact that not only is the Republic of Austria the owner of the world's largest theatre trust, the Bundestheaterverband (Association of Federal Theatres) whose 3,500 employees are responsible for 1,400 performances attracting 1.4 million spectators each season in Vienna, but also most of the country's many privately owned theatres receive public funds within the framework of a subsidizing system.

Subsidies to theatre make up a significant share of the public culture budget (national and provincial budgets) which in 1990 amounted to some 11 billion Austrian schillings (ASch),

approximately US$1.1 billion. Of this, museums and collections were allocated 9.2 per cent, music 3.7 per cent, and the performing arts (theatre and opera) 35.5 per cent. This represents almost four times what the state allocated to the promotion of sports. However, the entire public culture budget amounts to only 1.2 per cent of public expenditure or 0.7 per cent of the gross domestic product.

The lion's share of theatre subsidies traditionally goes to the national theatres, which are all part of the Association of Federal Theatres: the State Opera (2,280 seats), the Volksoper (1,577 seats), the Burgtheater (1,400 seats) and the Akademietheater (532 seats).

In 1990, the overall expenditure of the Federal Theatres amounted to ASch2.3 billion. Of this sum, ASch560 million was spent on pensions, while the revenue from ticket sales amounted to only ASch421 million; houses averaged about 80 per cent of capacity. In total, income covers about 28 per cent of expenditures with different cost-coverage ratios for individual theatres; the State Opera, for instance, has a cost-coverage ratio of 50 per cent. The deficit (about ASch1.6 billion in 1990) is entirely covered by public subsidies.

The fact that even permanently sold-out performances cannot pay for more than a fraction of production and operating costs is characteristic of this form of organization and is more or less accepted by the general public.

Public funds not only go to the four national theatres in Vienna, but also are allocated to the operation or support of various theatres and festivals all over Austria. Since the amount of funds from federal, provincial and municipal sources should theoretically reflect the social importance and the artistic quality of the respective activity, subsidies are frequently surrounded by controversy.

Vienna has for centuries been the theatrical capital of Austria. Apart from the national theatres, it is home to such important, long-standing stages as the Theater in der Josefstadt (since 1788), the Volkstheater, and the Theater an der Wien (1801), as well as a great number of smaller theatres and companies.

Although the number of theatregoers has clearly declined in recent decades, audience statistics are still impressive: in the 1989–90 season Vienna counted almost 4 million theatregoers (more than double the number of inhabitants and about the same as the number of cinemagoers). Of these, the two operas attracted 1 million visitors; the Burgtheater and the Akademietheater 400,000; the major private theatres 1.8 million in about 3,000 performances; and the more than fifty small stages and theatres without permanent location more than 600,000 visitors; expressed in terms of ticket sales this means about 12,000 tickets are sold

Claus Peymann's 1993 Vienna Festival/Burgtheater première of Peter Handke's *The Hour We Didn't Know Anything About Each Other*, designed by Karl-Ernst Herrmann.
Photo: Oliver Herrmann.

every day, the shares of music theatre and drama being roughly equal.

Ticket prices vary considerably: tickets to the opera cost between ASch15 (standing room) and ASch2,500; on average theatre tickets cost ASch200, about double the cost of a cinema ticket. There are, however, substantial discounts for unemployed people, students and military personnel.

The provincial capitals also have theatres of some size. In the 1989–90 season the province and town theatres attracted 1.3 million visitors in more than 3,000 performances. It is striking that all these theatres have long been prepared to accept substantial deficits in order to maintain cultural life in the provinces. While musicals by Andrew Lloyd Webber were attracting the biggest crowds in Vienna in the 1980s and early 1990s, the repertoire of provincial music theatres is to a certain extent dominated by operettas. There are also a great number of small theatres and other locations used regularly for performances, as well as a long amateur tradition.

Festivals are held annually in every Austrian province. The Salzburg Festival, with its 142 performances and 200,000 visitors in 1990, heads the list in terms of international prestige and economic size, followed by the Bregenz Festival (more than 100,000 visitors). For many smaller festivals (for example, Burgenländische Festspiele, Sommertheater Bad Ischl and Seefestspiel Gmunden) the economic impact for the region is significant. In spite of its intimate character, the Carinthischer Sommer (in the Carinthian towns of Ossiach and Villach) has gained an international reputation for its programme of contemporary music, church operas and children's operas. The Vienna Festival is another major festival also featuring guest performances by international companies. Two festivals with a considerable impact on the development of contemporary art are the Steirischer Herbst Festival in Graz, and the Ars Electronica in Linz.

Klemens Gruber, Rainer Maria Köppl

Artistic Profile

Companies

From 1945 to 1948, left-wing theatrical artists who had come back from exile tried to use the stage as a vehicle for both social criticism and general enlightenment. Günther Haenel (b. 1898), director of the Volkstheater during this period, used critical social drama to mark this new beginning. Other theatres too were willing to explore new territory. Under the directorship (1945–8) of Rauol Aslan (1890–1958) the Burgtheater increasingly presented Austrian dramatists who had been banned under the Third Reich: Arthur Schnitzler, Richard Beer-Hoffmann, Hugo von Hofmannsthal, Ferdinand Bruckner (*Krankheit der Jugend*), Franz Theodor Csokor (*Der 3. November 1918*), Fritz Hochwälder (1911–86) (with perfectly constructed and historically realistic plays such as *Das Heilige Experiment*), Franz Molnár (1878–1952) (*Liliom*) and František Langer (1888–1956) (*Peripherie*, a critical social study); much the same was true of the Theater in der Josefstadt, on whose studio stage Ödön von Horvath and Hans Weigel (1908–91) were performed. Leon Epp's (1905–68) theatre, Die

Insel (The Island), strove for a consistently literary programme.

The Neues Theater in der Scala (1948–56) was founded and managed jointly by the actors Wolfgang Heinz (1900–84), Karl Paryla (b. 1905) and Emil Stöhr (b. 1907), who had returned to Austria from their Swiss exile, and Günther Haenel. Their project was based on the idea of a workers' theatre which they had already developed in Zürich.

This theatre, often hailed as the 'working-class Burgtheater', pursued a programme of outspoken social drama. The company performed Johann Nestroy (1801–62) but also favoured Bertolt Brecht. The highly professional actors were unequivocally anti-fascist; many of them, in fact, had been persecuted by the Third Reich.

After the war, the Theater in der Josefstadt was directed by Rudolf Steinboeck (b. 1908), who had the daring to produce as its second show Brecht's *Der gute Mensch von Sezuan* (*The Good Person of Setzuan*), with Paula Wessely (b. 1907) in the title role.

The Salzburg Festival, however, remained rooted in tradition and continued to perform stately culture for the well-to-do and the elite after the war. From 1946, Max Reinhardt's famous production of *Jedermann* has been a sold-out highlight of the programme. Among the major actors portraying the title role have been Attial Hörbiger (1896–1981), Will Quadflieg (b. 1914), Walter Reyer (b. 1922), Curt Jürgens (1912–82), Maximilian Schell (b. 1930) and Klaus Maria Brandauer (b. 1944). Among the directors leaving their imprint on the festival in the immediate post-war period were Ernst Lothar, Leopold Lindtberg (1902–84) and Oscar Fritz Schuh (1904–84).

In this same period, the small theatre scene – the so-called 'cellar theatres' – was also lively: the Studio of the Hochschule (1945–50), the Kleines Theater im Konzerthaus (1949–58), the Theater am Parkring (1951–60), the Theater Kaleidoskop (1952–60), Die Tribüne (since 1953), Experiment am Lichtenwerd (since 1956), and in particular the Theater der Courage, founded in 1947 by Stella Kadmon to continue the pre-war cabaret *Der liebe Augustin*. These theatres were devoted to international contemporary plays, focusing particularly on Brecht, Günther Weisenborn, Jean-Paul Sartre, Jean Genet, Samuel Beckett and Eugène Ionesco. Many famous actors and directors started their careers there: the actors Kurt Sowinetz (1928–91) and Ernst Meister (1926–86); the director Erich Neuberg, who greatly influenced the style of theatre performances broadcast on television in the early stages of that medium; and the film and television directors Michael Kehlmann, Walter Davy (b. 1924) and Wolfgang Glück (b. 1929).

Cabaret in Vienna, famous in the 1930s, experienced a new heyday in the post-war period. Karl Farkas (1894–1971) and Ernst Waldbrunn continued to work in traditional cabaret forms and particularly shone in comic exchanges full of Jewish humour. Helmut Qualtinger (1928–91), Gerhard Bronner, Carl Merz (1906–79) and Georg Kreisler (b. 1922) developed a much more politically oriented cabaret style with black humour and 'dirty' language.

Qualtinger and Merz created a figure named 'Herr Karl' (Mister Karl) for an Austrian television play with the same title, broadcast in 1961 under the direction of Erich Neuberg. This stereotype of the malicious and sentimental Austrian lower-middle class was unequalled in its cutting representation of how Austrians analysed their past, and led immediately to a nation-wide scandal.

The period between 1955 and 1966 was characterized in government by a coalition

Helmut Qualtinger as 'Mister Karl'.
Photo: Barbara Pflaum.

between the two major political parties and was said to possess 'tomb-like calm' by socially aware artists. Resistance to this conservative cultural policy was a subcultural phenomenon. Its radicalism was mainly of an aesthetic nature, however. *Acht-Punkte-Proklamation des Poetischen Actes* (*Eight-Point-Proclamation of the Poetic Act*) by Hans Carl Artmann (b. 1921), for example, laid down rules of 'poetic action' by saying it was possible to be a poet without ever having written a poem. It also anticipated happenings and performance art independent of the well-known American avant-garde tendencies. The abandoning of strict borders among individual art forms awakened a new trend towards the 'integrated work of art' and revitalized the old avant-garde notion that 'art equals life'.

The avant-garde began to gather through a group of Viennese writers who, in spite of their differences, soon formed the Wiener Gruppe (Vienna Group). In close contact with painters and musicians, they established their base at the Art Club and Der Strohkoffer, a combination bistro and gallery, and at the leftist Catholic Galerie next to St Stephan run by Monsignore Otto Mauer. Not only did the representatives of the young *informal* painting style (Josef Mikl, Markus Prachensky and Arnulf Rainer) exhibit their works but also it was there and at the Theater in der Liliengasse that the members of the Wiener Gruppe read their works. The French Tachist painter Georges Mathieu at the same time performed his public paintings at the avant-garde theatre at the Fleischmarkt led by Herbert Wochinz and became one of the fathers of what has become known as Wiener Aktionismus (Viennese Actionism). Apart from marathon literary readings and happenings, there were processions and demonstrations (usually ending in huge parties) and, in 1958–9, a series of literary cabarets. In the summer they staged an 'open-air *commedia*' in a park, organized macabre parades and, for their last joint event, in 1964 staged the first performance of a multimedia children's opera.

The main protagonists were Friedrich Achleitner (b. 1930), Konrad Bayer (1932–69), Hans Carl Artmann, Gerhard Rühm (b. 1930) and Oswald Wiener (b. 1935). As in the literary cabaret, the dominating aspects were those anticipating happenings, a style of communication the Wiener Gruppe deliberately cultivated to distinguish themselves from the Austrian art and cultural establishment; and there was, of course, to compensate for the intellectual wasteland of the Nazi regime, innovative experimenting with expressionism, surrealism and dadaism – for example, the Austrian Raoul Hausmann (1886–1971) – on the content side, and innovative techniques in the handling of language.

An important contribution to avant-garde art came from the Wiener Aktionisten (Viennese Actionists), the performance-oriented anti-art movement that was a radical reaction to the prevailing conservative atmosphere. Hermann Nitsch (b. 1938), Otto Mühl ('paintings growing out of the canvas'), Rudolf Schwarzkogler (1940–64), Günther Brus (b. 1938), Valie Export (b. 1942) (Grapple and Touch Cinema), all from the visual arts, enjoyed a close relationship with the Wiener Gruppe. They elevated gesture into a movement-oriented, theatrical act. In various performances – *Pouring with Food and Blood*, *The Body as a Canvas*, *Self-Mutilations*, *Walling In and Walling Out* and *Trespassing of the Public Space* – they violated taboos of religion, sex and, often, good taste, aiming at a kind of therapeutic effect. Nitsch, in fact, developed a whole theatrical theory of what he called *Orgien-Mysterien-Theater* (Orgy Mystery Theatre).

The Burgtheater, in its renovated building (inaugurated in 1955) and directed by Ernst Haeusserman (1916–84) from 1959 to 1968, devoted itself to world literature. Leopold Lindtberg directed Shakespeare's historical dramas and a cycle of plays by dramatist Franz Grillparzer; Gustav Rudolf Sellner (1905–90) directed a cycle of ancient dramas in a space created by Fritz Wotruba (1907–75); and a Raimund cycle (Ferdinand Raimund, 1790–1836) was staged under the direction of Rudolf Steinboeck with stage design by Oskar Kokoschka (1886–1980), the famous expressionist painter.

The Theater in der Josefstadt, formerly the theatre of Max Reinhardt, was and still is a theatre centring on individual actors and a conversational tone. After Ernst Haeusserman, the theatre was directed (1959–69) by Franz Stoß (b. 1909). In a much-admired, unmistakably Viennese acting style, an experienced company played Anton Chekhov, Georges Courteline, Arthur Schnitzler, Hugo von Hofmannsthal, Franz Molnár, Luigi Pirandello and Ödön von Horvath, as well as polished light comedies.

From the standpoint of programming, the most interesting theatre in Vienna was probably the Volkstheater under the directorship of Leon Epp (1952–68). Epp presented Sartre, Camus, Genet, Ionesco and writers in the documentary style, such as Heinar Kipphardt, Peter Weiss and Rolf Hochhuth. With his production of *Mutter Courage* (*Mother Courage*) in 1963 Epp put a stop to the boycotting of Brecht in Vienna and from then on presented a Brecht production every year. Essentially, the theatre's seasons were devoted to Austria, with a special focus on Nestroy, a policy continued (1968–79) by Gustav Manker (1913–89), Epp's successor. Manker paved the way for the new generation of Austrian dramatists: Wolfgang Bauer (b. 1941), Peter Turrini (b. 1944) and Harald Sommer (b. 1935).

In the 1970s, the socialist one-party government under Bruno Kreisky led to a demand for a radical cultural policy. This awakened great expectations among Austria's cultural community: a spirit of departing for new territory left its lasting imprint on the cultural climate. The upheavals of 1968 had reached Austria with delay and in a very dissipated form. The new open-minded and multicultural atmosphere, however, did induce some changes in the institutionalized temples of art: under the directorship of Gerhard Klingenberg, the Burgtheater attracted some of the most important European directors: Jean-Louis Barrault, Peter Wood, Peter Hall, Otomar Krejca, Roberto Guiccardini, Luca Ronconi, whose classical productions (with Luciano Damiani) did not meet with general understanding but turned out to be epoch-making, and Giorgio Strehler, who, in Goldoni's *La Villegiatura*, was able to kindle a Mediterranean acting temperament in even the most serious-minded classical players. The theatrical landscape was given added colour by artists and companies such as the Komödianten am Börseplatz (Stock Market Comedians), 'practising Brechtians', and underground stages such as the Ateliertheater am Naschmarkt and the Kaffeetheater.

The commissioner of the Vienna Festival, Ulrich Baumgartner (1907–84), began in 1968 to lure the international world of theatre to Vienna under the motto 'European Comedians', from the Piccolo Teatro of Milan to the Vakhtangov Theatre from Moscow to avant-garde *café-théâtres* from Paris. In the following years Baumgartner succeeded in bringing companies, directors and productions to the Arena St Marx. These were to define European theatre in the 1970s and even in the 1980s – Peter Brook, Jérôme Savary (Magic Circus), Andrei Şerban, Ellen Stewart, and Joe Chaikin's Open Theatre.

Some years earlier, the Living Theatre from the USA caused a scandal in Vienna with its performance of *The Brig*.

A consequence of this open-mindedness was a sudden boom of independent theatrical producers, called 'independent companies'. Theatre in cafés, in the street and in pubs animated the world outside of establishment culture (on which they had hardly any influence). Some of these independent companies managed to create their own performing spaces and bridged the gap between underground theatre and the large civic companies. Artistically, the most important were the Ensembletheater (the former Kaffeetheater), the Gruppe 80 (Group 80) which developed out of the Komödianten im Künstlerhaus, and the Schauspielhaus, known as the Theater der Kreis (The Circle) in the late 1980s when it was under the direction of George Tabori. One should also mention here the mobile Fo-Theatre, which performed critical, socio-political drama in Vienna's municipal housing complexes.

Claus Peymann's 1974 Burgtheater production of Thomas Bernhard's *The Hunting Party*, designed by Karl-Ernst Herrmann.
Photo: Hausmann, Österreichischer Bundestheaterverband.

The theatrical institutions run by the state and the provinces, on the other hand, have stayed mostly with the traditional, for example, the slightly outdated bourgeois style of the Theater in der Josefstadt's seasons or the combination of popular classics and contemporary Austrian drama at the Volkstheater.

Under the directorship (1973–85) of Achim Benning (b. 1935) the Burgtheater devoted its seasons to actors' theatre in German dramas from the classical period and the *fin-de-siècle*. In addition, there were world premières of Václav Havel's plays, productions of Scandinavian, Irish and Russian dramatists and some works of Brecht. Brecht's plays, though, remained strangers to the Burgtheater, even under its new director, Claus Peymann (from 1986) and despite the efforts of Manfred Karge, the Brecht-trained director from Berlin.

Peymann did, though, make some remarkable attempts to change his audience and brought many young people to the Burgtheater and the Akademietheater. Peymann's seasons, with their focus on German-language contemporary drama – Thomas Bernhard (1931–89), Peter Handke (b. 1942), Peter Turrini, Elfriede Jelinek (b. 1946) – now represent formidable competition for even the smaller companies.

Dramaturgy

One of the most performed living Austrian playwrights in the 1970s and 1980s was Elias Canetti (b. 1905), the 1981 Nobel prize-winner for literature. The linguistic virtuosity of his dramatic parables *Die Hochzeit* (*The Marriage*, written 1931–2, published 1932), *Komödie der Eitelkeit* (*Comedy of Vanity*, written 1933–4, published 1950) and *Die Befristeten* (*The Numbered*, written 1952) was only belatedly recognized by theatre companies. *Die Hochzeit* was directed by Hans Hollmann at the Akademietheater in 1985 and by Axel Corti at the Salzburger Festspiele in 1988. *Komödie der Eitelkeit* was directed by Hermann Kutscher at the Schauspielhaus Graz in 1972 and by Hans Hollmann at the Burgtheater in 1979. Friedrich Kallina directed *Die Befristeten* at the Konzerthaustheater in Vienna in 1987.

Contemporary Austrian drama is focused around a revival of the critical social play depicting the working classes on the one hand and, on the other, a refined literary daring, represented by Peter Handke and Thomas Bernhard, the most internationally known Austrian

writers. From 1976 until his death in 1989, Bernhard was the Burgtheater's writer-in-residence and *Heldenplatz* was his last première. In his will, however, Bernhard, the 'democratic anarchist', prohibited further productions of his plays in Austria. Since 1989, Austrians wishing to see productions of Bernhard's plays can do so only abroad. Handke, author of *Kaspar* and *Offending the Audience*, has had many of his plays staged by Karl-Ernst Hermann, whose kindred visual spirit effectively reflects the writer's imagination on stage. In the early 1990s, Peter Turrini was the most frequently performed Austrian dramatist at the Burgtheater: *Minderleister* (directed by Alfred Kirchner), a piece on unemployment and the economic crisis, *Tod und Teufel* (*Death and the Devil*, directed by Peter Palitzsch), a drama about a sinning priest and arms deals, and *Alpenglühen* (directed by Claus Peymann), have been successes there.

The Akademietheater presented the world première of *Totenauberg*, a play about Martin Heidegger (1889–1976) and Hannah Arendt (1906–75) by Elfriede Jelinek, who had success at the Volkstheater with *Krankheit oder Moderne Frauen* (*Illness or Modern Women*).

Works by the two important writers of social drama, Felix Mitterer (b. 1948) and Heinz R. Unger (b. 1938), have been staged in many theatres across the country. The political drama *Republik des Vergessens* (*Republic of Forgetting*), Unger's contribution to the debate about Austria's relationship with fascism, had its première at the Schauspielhaus and at the Volkstheater. Felix Mitterer, author of *Kein Platz für Idioten* (*No Place for Idiots*) and *Die wilde Frau* (*The Wild Woman*), also had success with a modern version of *Jedermann* at the Theater in der Josefstadt.

Playwright Wolfgang Bauer, a radical chronicler of current history (*Magic Afternoon*, *Change*, *Shakespeare the Sadist* and *Die Kantine*), has also been performed at national theatres. The writer Ernst Jandl (b. 1925) is also a radical linguistic experimenter in his dramatic works *Die Humanisten* (*The Humanists*) and *Aus der Fremde* (*From Abroad*), voted play of the year by the journal *Theater heute* in 1980. The director George Tabori has also achieved success as a playwright in the last few years with *Mein Kampf* and *Goldberg-Variationen*. Among the writers emerging in the mid-1990s were Werner Schwab (b. 1958), a representative of verbally aggressive social drama (*Volksvernichtung oder Meine Leber ist sinnlos*/*Genocide* or *My Liver is Senseless*), and Robert Schneider (b. 1962).

Directors, Directing and Production Styles

While Austrian dramatists have left their imprint on theatre throughout the German-speaking world, and actors such as Romy Schneider (1938–82), Oskar Werner (1922–84), Helmut Berger (b. 1944) and Klaus Maria Brandauer became international stars, few internationally known directors emerged in Austria after World War II. Max Reinhardt died in exile in 1943. The Austrian-born film directors Billy Wilder (b. 1906), Fred Zinnemann (b. 1907), Otto Preminger (1906–86) and Fritz Lang (1890–1976) did not return to work in Austria.

Walter Felsenstein (1901–75) left Austria as a young man and worked in Germany as an actor, director and theatre director. Director of the Komische Oper Berlin (East Berlin) since 1947, he became one of Europe's leading directors of contemporary music theatre. Leopold Lindtberg, director at the Schauspielhaus Zürich while in exile, frequently returned to Austria after the war. His style greatly influenced the performance of the classics at the Burgtheater and in 1964 he directed the first performance of the stage version of Karl Kraus's (1874–1936) *Die letzten Tage der Menschheit (The Last Days of Humanity)* at the Theater an der Wien with Helmut Qualtinger, Karl Paryla and Otto Tausig.

In 1948 Berthold Viertel (1885–1953), a poet and director, returned to Austria. He returned from exile with more knowledge and his own translations of contemporary Anglo-American dramas. In the late 1940s and early 1950s he directed thirteen productions in Austria, for

George Tabori's 1993 Akademietheater production of his *Requiem for a Spy*, designed by Karl-Ernst Herrmann.
Photo: Ruth Walz.

example, Tennessee Williams's *The Glass Menagerie* at the Akademietheater.

Vienna-born Fritz Kortner, a well-known actor during the 1920s in Berlin, and a director in post-war Germany, offered some glimpses of radical realism in the 1960s (for example *Othello* in 1966 at the Burgtheater).

Hans Hollman (b. 1933) put his stamp on productions of classical plays in the FRG in the 1970s; most were adapted to address current issues. Otto Schenk (b. 1934), as director and actor, is the theatre's most popular performer at the Theater in der Josefstadt. His productions at the New York Metropolitan Opera were also widely acclaimed.

At the Schauspielhaus (Vienna) Hans Gratzer (b. 1941) produces exclusively contemporary drama. Many well-known German directors, such as Jürgen Flimm, Peter Zadek, Peter Stein, Hans Neuenfels, Achim Freyer and Andrea Breth, also work regularly in Austria. Stein has also been the artistic director of drama at the Salzburg Festival. George Tabori moved to Vienna in the late 1980s and began Der Kreis (The Circle), an experimental theatre and a school. His productions for Der Kreis and also at the Burgtheater and Akademietheater quickly made him one of the most influential personalities in Viennese theatre in the late 1980s and early 1990s.

The Slovene minorities in Carinthia and Styria, and the Hungarian and Croatian minorities in Burgenland, also pursue their own cultural activities in 'culture societies' or 'clubs', partly including amateur theatre. The same is true of foreign workers from Turkey and those from the former Yugoslavia. There is no professional theatre organized by or for these minorities.

Ulf Birbaumer

Music Theatre

Austria's reputation as a 'land of music' can be explained in more than one way: apart from the international repute of many works created there, along with the performers and music institutions of high artistic quality, the general public attributes enormous cultural importance to music. The media as well are interested in the form, especially works at the Vienna State Opera, a powerful symbol of the nation's cultural identity. They are also interested in its world-famous orchestra, the Vienna Philharmonic Orchestra, and festivals such as the one in Salzburg, which are strongholds of traditional culture. The enormous interest that the population showed in the reconstruction of the State Opera after World War II was telling proof of the special affinity Austrians have for music and music theatre.

Due to bomb damage to the building, the State Opera had to suffer ten years of 'exile'. Its first post-war performance, however, took place on 1 May 1945 – Mozart's *Hochzeit des Figaro* at the Volksoper, directed by Hermann Juch (b. 1908); from October 1945, it continued mostly at the Theater an der Wien (under the directorship (1945–54) of Franz Salmhofer (1900–75) until the reopening of the opera house on 5 November 1955. This decade, one of the most attractive in the opera's history, was shaped by its skill with the Mozart (and Richard Strauss) ensemble under the directorship (1943–5) of Karl Böhm. From 1945 onward, the ensemble gained an international reputation through singers such as Irmgrad Seefried (1919–88), Elisabeth Schwarzkopf (b. 1915), Hilde Güden (1917–88), Sena Jurinac (b. 1921), Wilma Lipp (b. 1925), Anton Dermota (1910–89) and Erich Kunz (b. 1909).

Herbert von Karajan (1908–89), who after Böhm's second period as director (1954–6) became artistic director of the opera (until 1964), introduced an era of internationalization which replaced the commitment to a permanent ensemble and a connected repertory. The focus was shifted to productions in the original language and attempts were made to lure attractive star singers to a kind of semi-*stagione* in Vienna. This system was followed by directors Egon Hilbert (1899–1968), director 1964–8, Heinrich Reif-Gintl (1900–74), director 1968–72, Rudolf Gamsjäger (1909–85), director 1972–6, Egon Seefehlner (b. 1912), director 1976–82 and 1984–6, Lorin Maazel (b. 1930), director 1982–4, and Claus Helmut Drese (b. 1922), director 1986–91. Drese complemented his overall strategy – superlative performers and directors, controversial repertoire – with some innovative activities motivated by his commitment to twentieth-century opera: productions with an experimental character staged at unusual locations (such as the Odeon and the Theater im Künstlerhaus) and designed to attract new audiences. Members of the opera-affiliated Opernstudio had an opportunity to test their skills in the performance of contemporary works (such as the first Austrian performance of Udo Zimmermann's *Weiße Rose* in 1987, or *Kehraus um St Stephan* by Ernst Krenek in 1990).

The two directors since 1991, the singer Eberhard Wächter (1929–92) and the former theatrical agent Ioan Holander, shifted the focus of their artistic strategy to the ensemble. This policy was less oriented towards brief stays by famous names but was geared more to longer-term contracts for young or not yet well-known singers.

Since 1991 the Vienna Volksoper, for fourteen years under the leadership of Karl Dönch (b. 1915), has had the same director as the Vienna State Opera. Its programme is traditionally characterized by a combination of works from the traditional operetta repertoire, a few mostly 'classical' musicals, rarely performed operas (such as *Lady Macbeth of Mtensk* by Shostakovich in 1991) and German-language productions of Italian operas (such as *La Bohème* by Puccini in 1984 or Mozart's *Da Ponte-Trias* in 1987–9), as well as works from the twentieth century.

As far as Austrian composers are concerned, in the State Opera contemporary opera has primarily been represented by Gottfried von Einem (b. 1918), *Dantons Tod* after Georg Büchner (1947 and 1967); *Der Prozeß* (*The Trial*) after Franz Kafka (1953 and 1970); *Der Besuch der alten Dame* (*The Visit*) after Friedrich Dürrenmatt (first performed in 1971, revived in 1989); *Kabale und Liebe* after Friedrich Schiller (first performed in 1976); and Friedrich Cerha (b. 1926), *Baal* after Bertolt Brecht (1981, revived in 1992) and *Der Rattenfänger* after Carl Zuckmayer (1987). The Wiener Schule (Vienna School), forced out of the country by the Nazis, conquered the opera stage after World War II, first through Alban Berg (1885–1935) – *Wozzeck* (first performed in 1930, then 1952 and 1955) and *Lulu* (1968) – then through Arnold Schoenberg (1874–1951) – *Moses und Aron* (1973). Ernst Krenek's first dodecaphonic opera, *Karl V*, was commissioned by the State Opera in 1933 but never reached the stage due to political reasons. The work was finally premièred in 1984. As far as the international contemporary repertoire is concerned, *Un re in ascolto* by Luciano Berio (1984), *Die Schwarze Maske* (1986) by Krzystof Penderecki and *Die*

Soldaten (1990) by Bernd Alois Zimmermann were successful with both the public and the media.

The Wiener Kammeroper (Vienna Chamber Opera), under the leadership of Hans Gabor (b. 1924) since its foundation in 1953, presents contemporary works on a smaller scale, complemented by open discussion sessions, for example Gerhard Schedl (b. 1957), *Der Kontrabaß* (1984); Herbert Lauermann (b. 1955), *Das Ehepaar* (first performance in 1987) and *Wundertheater* (first performed in 1988). The greater part of the approximately 120 annual performances of this medium-scale stage with only modest financial means is devoted to a deliberately broad repertoire. The Kammeroper is also very committed to the promotion of young talent (for example, through the International Belvedere Competition for opera and operetta, organized for the first time in 1982).

The Jugendstil-Theater is part of the psychiatric hospital at Baumgartner Höhe at Vienna's periphery. Designed by Otto Wagner (1841–1918) and reopened in 1980, since 1990 it has been the home of unconventional opera performances, presenting innovative interpretations, well-established contemporary works and experimental music.

In 1956 Marcel Prawy (b. 1911) introduced the Broadway-style musical to Austria with a Volksoper performance of Cole Porter's *Kiss Me Kate*. This type of popular music theatre gained special importance at the Theater an der Wien under the directorship (1965–83) of Rolf Kutschera and, especially, under the directorship (1983–93) of Peter Weck (b. 1930). Following Anglo-Saxon models, he produced hit musicals from the USA or London's West End, such as Andrew Lloyd Webber's *Cats*, which after seven years and 2,020 performances formed the basis of Vienna's reputation as a European musical metropolis. This was followed by attempts to use Austria-related themes to create an 'Austrian musical': *Freudiana* (Eric Woolfson, Brian Brolly and Lida Winiewicz, 1990) dealing with the intellectual world of Sigmund Freud, and *Elisabeth* (Sylvester Levay and Michael Kunze, 1992), devoted to the legendary Elizabeth of Bavaria (1837–98), wife of the Habsburg Emperor Franz Joseph (1830–1916).

The opera in Graz, Austria's second-largest home of music theatre, presents contemporary and rare works, as well as a traditional repertoire in new and even spectacular interpretations. Since 1990, its director, Gerhard Brunner (b. 1939), has been continuing this policy after eighteen years of the directorship of Carl Nemeth (b. 1926) came to a close with Wagner's *Ring* cycle (1988–9).

Other theatres in the provinces, offering both music theatre and drama, also mainly rely on a traditional repertoire. The Tirolean Landestheater and the Landestheater in Linz have gained additional recognition after 1945 due to their commitment to high-quality operas through first performances of contemporary works and an emphasis on modern composers.

Austrian festivals also combine a traditional programme with a commitment to contemporary or rare works. In the three decades until his death in 1989, Herbert von Karajan placed his unmistakable stamp on the Salzburg Festival. During that period the festival was predominantly dedicated to artistic perfection and opulence. During the Karajan era, Mozart's work was mainly presented by the directors Jean-Pierre Ponnelle (1932–88) – for example, *The Magic Flute* (1978) – and Michael Hampe (b. 1935) – *The Marriage of Figaro, Don*

Giovanni and *Così fan Tutte* (1982–91). This dedication to the *genius loci* continues to be one of the pillars in the policy of the present festival management under Gerard Mortier (b. 1944).

After World War II the commitment of the Salzburg Festival to contemporary music theatre began with the first performance of *Dantons Tod* by Gottfried von Einem in 1947. It became even more clearly visible in the 1980s, frequently in cooperation with the Vienna State Opera (Cerha, 1981; Berio, 1984; Henze after Monteverde: *Il ritorno d'Ulisse in patria*, first performed in 1985; Penderecki, 1986; Gerhard Wimberger (b. 1923): *Fürst von Salzburg*, 1987; Helmut Eder (b. 1916): *Mozart in New York*, 1991).

Since 1986, the Bregenz Festival has presented major operas staged with spectacular results on the Seebühne (for example, by Jérôme Savary), the lake-front stage which had mainly been used for operettas and musicals since 1946; and the Festival Hall (inaugurated in 1980) which shows works that are rarely seen elsewhere (for

Jérôme Savary's 1991 Bregenz Festival production of Bizet's *Carmen*, designed by Michel Lebois.
Photo: Monika Rittershaus.

example, Catalani's *La Wally*, first performed in 1990). The Seefestspiele Mörbisch has since its establishment in 1957 been devoted to operetta.

Since 1975, the Carinthischer Sommer has been presenting religious opera, especially through commissions to Austrian composers, and pieces for children, for example, Cesar Bresgen (1913–88), *Albolina* (1987). Founded in 1958, the Gesellschaft für Musiktheater (Society for Music Theatre) presents Baroque works in churches, mostly in the Vienna University church.

The diversity of contemporary Austrian music theatre also finds expression at the avant-garde Graz festival, Steirischer Herbst (Styrian Autumn). Within the framework of the festival, the opera in Graz presents important first performances such as *Aventures* and *Nouvelles Aventures* (first performed in 1970) by György Ligeti, *Orpheus und Eurydike* (first performed in 1973) by Ernst Krenek, Friedrich Cerha's three-act version of Alban Berg's *Lulu* (first performed in 1981), *Auszählreim* (first performed in 1986) by Otto M. Zykan (b. 1935), and *Amerika* (first performed in 1992) by Roman Haubenstock-Ramati (b. 1919).

When the Nazi era interrupted the development of modernity it led – especially in the domain of music – to a longer search for an indigenous point of view. The reception of the Vienna School and everything that came in its wake was delayed; post-war concert performances – as, for example, Berg's *Lulu* in 1949 by the Internationale Gesellschaft für Neue Musik (International Society for New Music, founded in 1922) – were rare. Gottfried von Einem had a special position. As early as 1947, the success of his *Dantons Tod* placed him in the limelight and he became the most frequently performed living composer. His work is marked by tonality.

Creators of more traditional opera include Helmut Eder, *Der Aufstand*, an appeal against violence and the abuse of power (1976); Cesar Bresgen, who uses an accessible musical

language in *Der Engel von Prag* after motifs by Leo Perutz (1978); Gerhard Wimberger, whose *Dame Kobold* is a musical comedy after Calderón de la Barca/Hugo von Hofmannsthal (1964). Ivan Eröd (b. 1936) revives earlier tradition in works such as *Orpheus ex machina*, a paraphrase of the Orpheus motif (1982).

The Vienna School was succeeded and further developed – apart from the work of emigrants such as Egon Wellesz (1885–1974) and Ernst Krenek – by composers such as Karlheinz Füssl (1924–92), Paul Kont (b. 1920) and Friedrich Cerha. György Ligeti wrote *Le Grand Macabre* (1978), a doomsday spectacle after Ghelderode, following the tradition of absurd drama. His work is now recognized in many parts of the world. A leader of avant-garde composers (and a leader in graphic notation) is Roman Haubenstock-Ramati, whose *Amerika* (1966, after Franz Kafka) is a panoply of simultaneously presented scenes. A total rejection of the 'Darmstadt School' (Stockhausen, Boulez and Nono), which had dominated the debate of ideas in the international avant-garde in the 1950s, became apparent in the vein of 'new tonality' seen in the work of Kurt Schwertsik (b. 1935). His *Fanferlieschen und Schönefüßchen* is a fairytale after Clemens Brentano and was presented in 1981.

Of younger composers, Herbert Lauermann and Gerhard Schedl have already left their artistic imprints. The multimedia emphasis is reflected by Otto M. Zykan's unconventional conception of the integral work of art (*Singers Nähmaschine ist die beste*, 1966/73). In the works of Dieter Kaufmann (b. 1941) sounds produced by the human voice, instruments and electronic devices are contrasted with one another.

The Hallucination Company, Drahdiwaberl, the Erste Allgemeine Verunsicherung and Wolfgang Ambros (with the 'Alpine musical' *Der Watzmann*) successfully represent Austrian rock theatre.

Isolde Schmid-Reiter

Dance Theatre

Austria's centres for classical and modern dance are Vienna, Graz and Salzburg. The Vienna State Opera Ballet is Austria's most important company. After World War II the ballet was led by Erika Hanka (1905–58) until 1958,

Dimitrije Parlic (b. 1919) from 1958 to 1962, Aurel von Milloss (1906–88) from 1963 to 1966 and 1971 to 1974, Wazlaw Orlikowsky, from 1966 to 1971, Richard Nowotny (b. 1926) from 1974 to 1976, Gerhard Brunner, from

1976 to 1990, Gerlinde Dill (b. 1933) from 1990 to 1991, and Elena Chernischova, from 1991 to 1993, when Anne Woolliams (b. 1936) took over direction of the company.

In her work, Erika Hanka strove for a modern style which integrated classical ballet. Her seasons featured the Diaghilev repertoire, works with contemporary music and ballets with a typically Austrian or Viennese flair, for example *Medusa* (1957). Aurel von Milloss was responsible for giving the programme a more international touch and created a number of works using contemporary composition, such as *Bolero* (1965) and *Estri* (1972). A lasting influence was exerted by Gerhard Brunner, who developed an excellent repertoire with very high standards of both choreography and music, and who also tried to create a specifically Viennese style.

The second classical troupe in Vienna is the ballet company at the Vienna Volksoper. Outside Vienna the companies in Graz and Salzburg are the only ones possessing supra-regional importance. Graz focuses on both the classical and contemporary repertoire while Salzburg deals with various forms and styles. Since 1992, Innsbruck has had a dance theatre, directed by Eva Maria Lerchenberg-Thöny (*Lamento* and *Rosa Winter*, both 1993), within the framework of the Tirolean Provincial Theatre.

At the beginning of the twentieth century, Grete Wiesenthal (1885–1970) and her sisters Elsa and Bertha began to experiment with modern dance. In the 1920s and 1930s the expressionist dancers Gertrud Bodenwieser (1890–1959) and Gertrud Kraus (1903–77) gained international recognition, as did Rosalia Chladek (b. 1905), an expressionist dancer and teacher. A lively modern dance scene did not come about, however, until the 1980s. An international dance boom, the Tanzbiennale in Vienna with its New-Dance Week, and numerous festivals with guest performances throughout the year significantly influenced the development of modern dance in Austria.

The Vienna Tanztheater Homunculus was

Hubert Lepka's *108 EB Chambermusic for Five Engines* at the 1991 WUK Dance Festival in Vienna.
Photo: Wolfgang Kirchner.

founded in 1981; in 1982 Liz King from Britain set up the Tanztheater Wien with its international company, a leader in this area for a number of years. The company closed in 1988. In 1982 the dance theatre Vorgänge was established in Salzburg.

By the early 1990s Austria had about forty companies with varying artistic standards. Homunculus continues to propagate modern expressionist dance with many of its dancers graduates of the Conservatory of the City of Vienna. Their training is based on Rosalia Chladek's system of movement. The greater part of the Homunculus repertoire is based on literature and literary sources. Its productions tend to deal with human relationships and issues relating to the individual versus society, for example, *Neue Räume I–III* (*New Rooms I–III*, 1990–2) and *Schlachthof für Engel* (*Slaughterhouse for Angels*, 1992).

Dancer-choreographer Sebastian Prantl (b. 1960) was trained in New York and for some time specialized in multimedia dance performances. In the early 1990s he returned to a more abstract dance language and extensively concerned himself with music, visual arts and architecture, for example in *Für die Vögel* (*For the Birds*, 1992) and *Klangsäule* (*Sounding Post*, 1993). Another dancer-choreographer is Willi Dorner. After training in the USA and France, his work was very much influenced by contact improvisation and the use of video techniques (*Fremdlingin/The Foreigner*, 1990). Other dancer-choreographers of note include Elio Gervasi, Bertl Gstettner, the performance artist Daniel Aschwanden, Dorothea Hübner, Aurelia Staub, Roderich Madl and Doris Ebner. Dancers Astrid Bayer, Sibylle Starkbaum and Rose Breuss concentrate mainly on solo performances. Social criticism appears in the choreography that Zdravko Haderlap devises for his Tanztheater Ikarus in Klagenfurt (Carinthia).

The Salzburg dance scene has been markedly shaped by the Vorgänge company, which was founded in 1982 by sports students searching for alternative forms of movement. The group quickly attracted international attention due to its fresh style and acrobatic elements. In the late 1980s it split into several groups: the companies of Editta Braun, Beda Percht (b. 1958) and his Cataracts (specializing in suspension and climbing events), Hubert Lepka and his Maschinen-Tanz-Theater, and the dance-comedy duo Ekke Hager and Wolf Jugner.

The Austrian choreographer best known internationally is Johann Kresnik (b. 1939), who received his training as a dancer in Graz. He moved to Germany in 1959 where, since the end of the 1960s, his dance theatre works count among the most radical and provocative examples of German dance theatre – *Paradies* (*Paradise*, 1968), *Familiendialog* (*Family Dialogue*, 1980), *Ulrike Meinhof* (1990) and *Frida Kahlo* (1992). His work is seen in Austria only through visiting dance companies.

Ursula Kneiss

Theatre for Young Audiences

Since the 1930s, Vienna has had, in its Theater der Jugend (Theatre for Children), an organization unique in tradition, size and structure. After 1918, Vienna was governed by the social democrats. Still known for its grandiose municipal housing complexes, the city established a Theatre for Children for two purposes. First, it was to promote popular education and provide young audiences from all sections of the population with aesthetic training through organized theatre visits in order to attack the educational monopoly of the upper classes. Second, the productions provided jobs for unemployed actors and filled gaps in Vienna's theatrical life.

After 1934 the organization, now officially known as Theater der Jugend, extended its activities, formerly restricted to children over the age of 10, to encompass primary school children. Subsidized from this point by the Ministry of Education, the theatre had to fulfil 'national' tasks and was soon taken over by Hitler's youth movement. After the war, the organization was slowly rebuilt, a theatre company re-established in the 1950s, and a permanent stage found for the company for the first time in its existence.

The structure of Theater der Jugend (TdJ) is still the same as in its founding years: an organization which arranges theatre visits for children and a theatrical production unit. Tickets are distributed through the schools: every school in Vienna appoints one of its teachers as a contact, who then informs the school about the group's activities and organizes ticket orders. The company, organized as a non-profit association, is financed by the Federal Ministry of Education and the Arts, the City of Vienna and the neighbouring provinces of Lower Austria and Burgenland.

The subscription scheme presents the company's own productions as well as outside productions, for example, from the Burgtheater, musicals and circus performances.

With the Renaissancetheater (550 seats), the Theater im Zentrum (230 seats), and the Zwischenraum (seventy seats), the TdJ has three permanent stages at its disposal and rents additional stages if the need arises.

Roughly 50,000 subscriptions were sold in the 1991–2 season; 558 performances of the TdJ's own productions were attended by 160,000 people. In addition, the TdJ's organization distributed just as many tickets for other theatres in Vienna. The TdJ has a staff of approximately 200, receives subsidies amounting to ASch60 million and has revenues of about ASch40 million.

The TdJ's collaboration with schools not only is the source of its high attendance rate but also restricts the artistic freedom of the theatre. Proposed productions have to be submitted to a pedagogic advisory board for approval. This board consists of teachers and representatives of various institutions (Catholic Family Association, Youth and Parents' Associations). The original task of the TdJ, to make 'education' available to broader sections of the population, was pursued after 1945 in such a way that the programme remained rather rigid: fairytales for children and modern classical plays for adolescents.

The years of 'proper' adaptations of popular tales, legends and mystic stories, carefully cleansed of any references to real life, was sold to schools on a subscription system by the TdJ – arguably the largest theatre organization for children in the western hemisphere until the early 1970s. It was then that socially critical productions by the Berlin Reichskabarett (later renamed Grips), with their many references to daily life, found their way to Vienna's cellar theatres. The first step came in 1971 with a performance of *Maximilian Pfeiferling*, by Carsten Krüger and Volker Ludwig (b. 1937), produced by Werner Prinz and Ingrid Greisenegger (b. 1940) at the cooperative theatre, Courage.

At the same time models of theatre for children from France and Italy provided incentives for the *Animazione* (Social Animation) movement, which, initiated in 1972 by the theatre experts Ingrid Greisenegger and Ilse Hanl (1943–90) at the Dramatisches Zentrum in Vienna, paved the way in Austria for a theatre *with* children. In contrast to the traditional theatre *for* children, addressing a quasi-imaginary child, *Animazione* aimed at helping children to express their own needs in group work, to discover creativity in role-playing, drawing, and discovering their environment. Animation concepts were used as basic materials, not only for school performances, but also in the professional theatres. In 1972 the Teatro del Sole staged its *Città degli animali* as part of the summer seminar of the Institute for Theatre Research in Eisenstadt.

In the 1990s, the Theater der Jugend focused on real situations experienced by children and adolescents, giving commissions to young writers and young directors, who put their own stamps on the productions.

In the provinces, theatre for children was traditionally reduced to Christmas pageants at provincial theatres and amateur theatres. In the 1980s, individual companies making theatre for children were established. Two of them succeeded in securing permanent stages for themselves – the Theater am Mirabellplatz (Toi-Haus) in Salzburg and the Theater des Kindes in Linz. Other companies perform at schools and in municipal meeting halls.

Today the Culture Department of the city of Vienna allocates ASch3.5 million to independent companies producing theatre for children. An advisory board decides on the distribution of this amount to the thirty to forty companies that apply for subsidies annually.

Momentum to the movement of theatre for children is now also provided by various international festivals. The year 1987 saw the first international children's theatre festival in Vienna, within the framework of the Vienna Festival. This event resulted in the foundation of an Austrian centre of the international ASSITEJ association. Since 1989, a group from Vorarlberg has been organizing the Luaga and Losna Festival, presenting international and Austrian companies and organizing conferences. In the province of Lower Austria a further international festival, Szene Bunte Wähne, presents performances in six different towns.

Marlene Schneider

Puppet Theatre

After the end of World War II Austrian puppet theatre was in a deplorable state. In order to survive, many puppet theatres had observed instructions issued by the Nazi-German Reichsinstitut for Puppet Theatre, which had an outlet in Vienna. They incorporated Nazi propaganda in their sometimes century-old texts. When the war was over, many of the theatres physically destroyed these old scripts, and sometimes even their equipment, for fear of reprisals. Thus, a treasure of traditional puppet material was lost forever. With only a few exceptions, the old puppet masters were unable to continue their work.

Post-war misery induced many young people to try their hands at puppet theatre. New companies evolved which did not understand the older traditions and, out of ignorance, took the propaganda style as their own. Even today puppet shows for children on television contain residual traces of this.

Two very well-known puppet theatres survived the war without damage. The Salzburger Marionetten (founded by Anton Aicher in 1913) continued their work and their tours abroad with immensely popular musical plays. At the Paris World Exhibition in 1937, the company was, in fact, awarded the gold medal. During World War II, its puppets were used as 'front-line-theatre'. After the war, it performed even major operas, such as Mozart's *The Magic Flute*, *The Abduction from the Seraglio* and *Don Giovanni*. The company can still be seen at the Salzburg Festival.

According to puppeteer Richard Teschner (1879–1948), puppet theatre was never supposed to be a miniature imitation of human theatre. Rather than giving human voices to his puppets, his creations acted in silence, accompanied by exotic music, in a mysterious, grotesque and unreal world. Teschner developed a specific technique based on Javanese models, for operating his puppets, a combination of rod and string techniques. In the beginning, Teschner performed for a small private circle – among the audience Gustav Klimt (1862–1918) and Alfred Roller (1864–1935). From 1925 onward, the performances were open to the public. From 1932 to 1948 he performed with his own Figurenspiegel. The name of the theatre stemmed from the circular concave mirror used to display the setting. Today, the remnants of Teschner's theatre can be seen in the Austrian Theatre Museum. The rare performances in this style still find enthusiastic audiences.

The economic recovery of the 1950s produced a pedagogical era of puppet theatre. Theatrical 'lessons' for children about traffic or brushing one's teeth resulted in a complete loss of traditional glove-puppet theatre. Most puppeteers viewed their work as merely a meagre source of income.

The only puppet theatre with a permanent stage today is the Wiener Uraniapuppentheater led by Hans Kraus. With his two puppet stars, Kasperl and Petzi, he has shaped the impression that Austrians have of glove-puppet theatre.

In its early days, Austrian television discovered glove-puppet theatre for children's programming. Wednesday afternoons have ever since been the time for puppet theatre on Austrian television.

In the course of time, puppet theatre has, more or less, lost its artistic dimension and is regarded only as nostalgic entertainment for children. In the 1960s some puppet theatres for adults were founded in Vienna, but had to close due to a lack of interest on the part of the public. The early 1970s saw a major upswing, and Ulrich Baumgartner, commissioner of the Vienna Festival, devoted the entire 1971 festival to puppet theatre and invited internationally renowned puppet theatres to Vienna.

Erwin Piplitz (b. 1939) was entrusted with the organization of the World Puppet Festival at the Museum of the Twentieth Century and he also founded the Pupodrom, the first contemporary Austrian puppet theatre. In 1984 the Vienna Festival was once more devoted to puppet theatre. A major exhibition at the Messpalast was a meeting-point for many young puppeteers and several companies presented their first public performances. Old techniques were rediscovered. This did not, however, represent the beginning of a new avant-garde tradition, as was the case for some eastern bloc companies, and most of the newly founded companies disappeared again.

In the 1990s, most of the puppet theatres perform for children. Some companies use contemporary forms and texts that also address an adult audience: the Lilarum Theatre (Vienna) presents fairytales for children and a separate programme for adults (Shakespeare's *The Tempest* in 1992); the one-man theatre by Christoph Bochdansky (Vienna); the Bavastel Company

(Kirchdorf, Upper Austria); and the shadow theatre of Klaus Behrendt (Vienna), which is especially focused on Asian shadow theatre, myths and legends. There are also some very good amateur and school puppet theatres. In 1989 the Theater der Jugend in Vienna closed its puppet theatre and thus put a stop to a tradition initiated by teachers in the 1930s.

In 1979 Austria joined the International Puppeteers Association (UNIMA); in the same year the first Mistelbacher Puppentage was held, the most important international puppet festival in Austria. A new series of festivals called Pupienale was established in Wels, which from 1994 was named Welser Puppentage. In Hohenems, the Homunculus Puppet Theatre Festival was created as a counterpoint to the Schubert Festival. This means that at present Austria has three international events devoted to puppet theatre.

Klaus Behrendt

Design

Stage and costume design in Austria are characterized by contrasting forces of great tradition on the one hand and avant-garde attempts to abandon that tradition on the other. During the Baroque era, sumptuous music-theatre pageants at the imperial court used all available means to represent the power and style of the emperor. Eventually, religious theatre and theatre for the common man began to make use of the stage painter. At the end of the twentieth century Viennese prop shops and costume workshops delivered their perfectly crafted scenery to theatres all over Europe.

In the early twentieth century Vienna became a centre of theatrical reform. The director of the opera – composer and conductor Gustav Mahler (1860–1911) – appointed Alfred Roller, a graphic artist, painter and professor at the progressive arts and crafts school, as the opera's head designer. In just over five years, the collaboration between the two men gave rise to a fundamentally new definition of opera as an integrated work of art. At the same time leading proponents of modernism, such as Kolo Moser (1868–1918), Remigius Geyling, Heinrich Lefler (1863–1919), Eduard Wimmer-Wisgrill, Oskar Kokoschka, and Oskar Strnad (1879–1935), to cite but a few, gathered experience at small theatres (*Fledermaus* cabaret) and at open-air stages. They presented their radical scenery projects in exhibitions and had them published. One example of the high quality of scenery and costume designs at the beginning of the twentieth century was the Wiener Werkstätte, which decisively influenced interior decoration at the time. It also designed and produced fashion and made Vienna a European fashion centre. After World War I these skills were utilized by productions – even on Broadway – for many years to come.

Tradition and attempts to break with it were also characteristic of the post-war period. The Burgtheater, the Vienna State Opera, and the Salzburg Festival succeeded in attracting the permanent services of domestic artists, such as Stefan Hlawa (b. 1896), painter and graphic artist of scintillating wit, and designers of international calibre, such as Lois Egg (b. 1913) at the Burgtheater and Günther Schneider-Siemssen (b. 1926) at the State Opera.

Another important factor for stage design developments after the war was the fact that leading personalities of the new theatrical trends of the inter-war period – Emil Pirchan (1884–1957) and Casper Neher (1897–1962), for example – continuously worked in Vienna. As well, numerous visual artists, such as the painter and poet Oskar Kokoschka and the sculptor Fritz Wotruba, cooperated in entire production cycles of the Burgtheater while painters such as Wolfgang Hutter, Ernst Fuchs, Arik Brauer, Karl Korab and many others were engaged for individual productions.

The fact that Austrian theatre has always been in a position to attract leading representatives of international stage design has made its mark. Wieland Wagner, Teo Otto, Jürgen Rose, Ita Maximowna, Josef Svoboda and, especially, Jean-Pierre Ponnelle have regularly worked at Austrian theatres. More recently, stage designers who want to implement their scenic visions as directors have found more than ample room for their ambitions, both in repertory and at festivals: among them, Karl-Ernst Herrmann, Wilfried Minks and Achim Freyer.

The training institutions for stage and

Achim Freyer's 1987 Burgtheater production of *Ovid's Metamorphoses*.
Photo: Matthias Horn.

costume design have contributed to the high standards, since only artists of international renown have been appointed as teachers. At present there are four training institutions, each of them headed by a professor active in international theatre. These include the Academy of Fine Arts in Vienna under Erich Wonder (b. 1944); the Academy of Applied Arts in Vienna under Axel Manthey; the Mozarteum University of Music and Performing Arts in Salzburg under Herbert Kapplmüller (b. 1941); and the University of Music and Performing Arts in Graz under Wolfram Skalicki. These artists are also active in day-to-day Austrian theatrical life.

Theatre Space and Architecture

Vienna has always been home to a great number of renowned theatre architects. The Opera House, designed by Eduard van der Null (1812–68) and August Siccard von Siccardsburg (1813–68), opened in 1868 and served as a model for major theatres in central Europe due to its rich ornamentation, its sober spatial arrangements and its excellent acoustics. The Hofburgtheater (later known as the Burgtheater) was a late work by Gottfried Semper (1803–79) and his partner Karl Hasenauer (1833–94), designed as a finale to the Baroque

tradition of theatres with tiers of boxes. The design was flawed by deficiencies with regard to acoustics and the range of vision, and at the inauguration (1888) it turned out to be already obsolete. Both buildings were so heavily damaged in the war that their reconstruction was actually a rebuilding, especially of their stages.

Austrian architects designed other theatrical buildings even outside Austria. The design team of Ferdinand Fellner (1847–1915) and Hermann Helmer (1849–1919) designed no fewer than forty-eight theatres and concert halls, especially in central and eastern Europe. Oskar Strnad's audacious designs anticipated the total theatre of Gropius and Piscator, Clemens Holzmeister designed the two festival stages in Salzburg while Wilhelm Holzbauer designed the new opera and town hall in Amsterdam.

The most urgent construction tasks connected with theatre in the post-war period were the reconstruction of the Vienna State Opera, heavily damaged by bombs and fire, and the Burgtheater, which had burned down only two days after the liberation of Vienna. In both cases the solution chosen was neither an exact reconstruction – which would have been possible – of the historically important buildings, nor entirely new buildings, but something between the two, a half-hearted and unsuccessful search for a combination of tradition and innovation. All undamaged building parts (especially the external walls, but also the grand staircases and the lobbies) were painstakingly preserved, but the auditoriums were clearly designed to tastes prevailing in the early 1950s. The stages were completely redesigned and brought up to the latest standards; at the Burgtheater, for example, there was a revolving stage by Sepp Nordegg (b. 1913).

The architects appointed for the politically important 'reconstruction' of the two national theatres (after a restricted competition) were Erich Boltenstern for the State Opera and Michel Engelhart and Otto Niedermoser (b. 1903) for the Burgtheater. They made it their task not so much to serve a new aestheticism or a new social objective, but rather to provide representative space for festive educational theatre.

Both competitions failed to pay any notice to Clemens Holzmeister, the designer of the first Salzburg Festival Hall (1926 and 1936–8) and creator of the sets for Max Reinhardt's legendary *Faust* production at the Salzburg Festival. Ignoring this man, recently returned from emigration, was absolutely typical of the period: change was fearsomely to be avoided. Holzmeister had designed the government quarter in Ankara during the years he spent in exile and had also worked on the idea of an 'ideal theatre' after studying ancient theatres. As a result, he designed various projects which were much discussed in expert circles. His projects for Salzburg, for instance, were a music stage on the Mönchsberg and a fascinating festival hall at Mirabellgarten. The designs were breathtaking in their audacity, entirely abandoning the concept of the proscenium arch stage. He searched

for new relationships between audience and players, integrating nature and the precincts of the town. The post-war period forbade an implementation of these ambitious schemes. By then, Holzmeister had already begun the battle for the completion of 'his' festival quarter in Salzburg and was offered the task of rebuilding the historical theatre in Linz and designing a new, smaller building for drama. This provided him with an opportunity to give a tangible example of what he planned to do for Salzburg. In both cases the theatre occupied a central point within the town; in both cases the new theatres were expected to meet the latest technological standards. In both towns the theatre projects were high-priority items on the cultural policy agenda and received a great deal of public attention.

In 1956 Holzmeister was commissioned to build a large festival hall in Salzburg to accommodate opera, concert and drama. He planned to build a theatre district, also including administrative offices and workshops, behind the protected walls of the former Imperial Stables in early Baroque style, next to his old festival hall, which had been badly scarred by an adaptation by the stage designer Benno von Arendt during the Nazi period. The new, large festival hall, ideally fitting into the historical centre of Salzburg, is today one of Austria's most beautiful modern theatres as well as a model of functional adequacy and technological perfection, displaying the possibilities a theatre architect may make use of in the late twentieth century. Holzmeister's festival district is more than just a group of important functional buildings. It is a symbol for a country seeking to unite a cosmopolitan spirit and indigenous values, tradition and innovation, aestheticism and technology.

The monumental lake-side stages in Bregenz and Mörbisch are of little inherent artistic value: platforms extended into the lakes to carry the sets of the respective festival productions. Similarly, many other open-air theatres harness natural or architectural beauty as an essential element of the atmosphere they create.

The new festival building in Bregenz, mainly designed to provide a roof for the open-air productions and for as many spectators as possible in case of bad weather, is an unadorned functional edifice.

No new public theatres have been established in the period under discussion. The only moves in this respect were the installation of technically well-equipped stages in multifunctional halls or civic centres, the establishment of rehearsal and experimental stages for the major theatres, and the creation of adequate stages for theatre schools, such as the Max Reinhardt-Seminar in Vienna designed by Peter Czernin.

Small and medium-size stages (for example the Theater im Künstlerhaus in Vienna) devised simple and convincing solutions for giving their theatres flexible spatial arrangements to be adapted for any kind of production.

A number of internationally renowned Austrian specialty companies regularly provide theatre technology. Among them are Waagner-Biro AG (Vienna Burgtheater, opera buildings in Geneva and Sydney); Wiener Brückenbau und Eisen Konstruktions AG (opera buildings in Vienna, Warsaw, Istanbul, theatres in Bratislava and Ostend); and PANI, active in stage construction and lighting technology.

Wolfgang Greisenegger

Training

Academies for music and the performing arts are located in Vienna, Graz and Salzburg. The Vienna Hochschule für Musik und Darstellende Kunst operates the solo voice and music drama department, the well-known acting and directing department (the Max Reinhardt-Seminar) and the film and television department. The Hochschule also runs a department of culture management, arts administration and public relations.

The Mozarteum, the famous Hochschule für Musik und Darstellende Kunst in Salzburg has, inter alia, departments for solo voice and music drama and for the performing arts (direction, acting and stage design).

The Vienna Akademie der Bildenden Künste (visual arts) and the Hochschule für Angewandte Kunst (applied arts) offer master classes in both stage and costume design.

Applications to these training institutes are

very high and include large numbers of German students. Only a few applicants are accepted every year from the several hundred that apply. On average, training lasts for four years and is completely paid for by the state.

Additional training options are offered at the Conservatory of the City of Vienna and various private actors' schools.

The theatre division of the Trade Union for Art, Media and Free Professions holds a 'stage admission exam' for graduates from private acting schools or private theatres. This exam is the legal prerequisite for the acting profession.

Actors' workshops in the 1970s led to the foundation of an acting class at the Dramatisches Zentrum in Vienna in 1979. For ten years it was a catalyst for theatrical activities outside the institutionalized theatres.

Rainer Maria Köppl, Klemens Gruber

Criticism, Scholarship and Publishing

In Austrian journalism, theatre reviews have a remarkably high priority. In supra-regional daily and weekly newspapers, theatre reviews – by far outstripping cinema or television reviews – are the most important columns where journalists deal with art and are given the biggest portion of the culture pages. Austria's best known art critics have always been theatre critics; O.M. Fontana (1889–1969) for the conservative daily newspaper *Die Presse* (*The Press*), Friedrich Torberg (1908–79) for the monthly *Forum*, Otto Basil (b. 1901) for *Neues Österreich* (*New Austria*) and as editor of the cultural magazine *Der Plan*, and Jacques Hanak for the socialist newspaper

Arbeiter-Zeitung in the 1950s and 1960s. Later important critics have included Hans Weigel and Hilde Spiel (1911–91) for the daily German newspaper *Frankfurter Allgemeine Zeitung* (*Frankfurt General Newspaper*) and Piero Rismondo for *Die Presse* until the 1980s; and in the early 1990s Sigrid Löffler for the weekly Austrian magazine *Profil* (*Profile*), Karin Kathrein (b. 1938) for *Die Presse* and the daily *Kurier* (*Courier*), Hilde Haider-Pregler (b. 1941) for the daily *Wiener Zeitung* (*Vienna Newspaper*) and Hans Haider (b. 1946) for *Die Presse*. The major foreign German-language newspapers also include regular features on Austrian theatre.

There are two specialized Austrian theatre magazines – *Die Bühne* (*The Stage*) and *Opernwelt* (*Opera World*). The weekly *Der Falter* gives information on cultural events of every type in Vienna. Austrian radio (Volkmar Parschalk, head of cultural programming) and Austrian television (Karl Löbl, head of cultural programming) cover premières at the larger theatres.

The Institut für Theaterwissenschaft (Institute for Theatre Studies) at the University of Vienna is the only advanced degree-granting theatre institution in Austria. Its faculty include guest professors from various parts of the globe and more than thirty local experts in areas such as theatre and media history, theory of the theatre, dramaturgy, theatre design and equipment, social and organizational history, music theatre and media theory. In addition, there are courses on directing and acting, dance, theatre and media law, as well as on non-European theatre. Various trainee programmes are offered (theatre and film direction, playwriting, and stage design) and students have the opportunity to attend rehearsals and work at theatres.

The institute also has a specialized library of approximately 50,000 volumes – among them a comprehensive collection of dramas from Count Ferdinand Palffy (1774–1840) from the eighteenth century and 160 magazines – as well as an audio-visual archive. Two offices house a collection of pictorial material and reviews (about 10,000 pictures, 27,000 theatre programmes and 800,000 theatre reviews). Since 1955, the institute has also been publishing the quarterly journal, *Maske und Kothurn: Internationale Beiträge zur Theaterwissenschaft* (*Mask and Cothurnus: International Contributions to Theatre Studies*). The Fachbibliothek für Theaterwissenschaft (Library for Theatre Studies) and the Wiener Gesellschaft für Theaterforschung (Vienna Society for Theatre Research) publish scientific studies such as complete yearly documentations on Austrian theatre productions.

The Austrian Theatre Museum is one of the most attractive theatre museums in the world. It regularly presents exhibitions and administers the former theatre collection of the Austrian National Library (more than 1 million objects, 100,000 of them stage and costume designs) and its department of theatre literature (70,000 volumes).

The works of many Austrian dramatists are regularly published in the Federal Republic of Germany. Agents in Austria expressly devoted

to drama are the Thomas A. Sessler Verlag, Vienna/Munich, the Hans Pero Bühnen- und Musikverlag and the Österreichische Bühnenverlag in Vienna. In addition, the publishers Residenz Verlag, Bundesverlag, Europa-Verlag, Jugend und Volk and Löcker Verlag publish drama and theatrical literature.

Two literary reviews, *Manuskripte* (Graz) and *Protokolle* (Vienna), also feature new scripts by Austrian dramatists.

The Vienna publishing house Universal-Edition, founded in 1901, is of tremendous importance for music theatre. Very early, it concluded copyright contracts with composers of the Vienna School – Schoenberg in 1908, Zemlinsky (1872–1942) in 1911, Berg in 1921 and Krenek in 1923 – and the firm's publishing programme has always been influenced by its concern for contemporary composers.

Klemens Gruber, Rainer Maria Köppl
Translated by Susanne Watzek

Further Reading

Abele, Hans. *Die Bundestheater in der österreichischen Wirtschaft.* [The federal theatres and their role in the Austrian economy]. Vienna: Österreich Bundestheaterverband, 1984.

Alexander, Gerda, and Hans Groll, eds. *Tänzerin, Choreographin, Pädagogin Rosalia Chladek.* [Rosalia Chladek: dancer, choreographer, teacher]. Vienna: Österreich Bundesverlag, 1980.

Behrendt, Klaus. *Puppentheater in Österreich.* [Puppet theatre in Austria]. Vienna: UNIMA Zentrum Österreich, 1987. 179 pp.

Breicha, Otto, and Gerhard Fritzsch, eds. *Aufforderung zum Mißtrauen: Literatur, bildende Kunst, Musik in Österreich seit 1945.* [Invitation to distrust: literature, visual arts, music in Austria since 1945]. Salzburg: Residenz, 1967.

Den Freunden zur Erhaltung des künstlerischen Nachlasses von Fritz Wotruba, eds. *Fritz Wotruba: der Bildhauer als Bühnenbildner.* [Fritz Wotruba: the sculptor as stage designer]. Bremen: Gerhard-Marcks-Stiftung, 1992.

Deutsches Bühnenjahrbuch: Theatergeschichtliches Jahr- und Adreßbuch. Theater, Film, Funk, Fernsehen. [German stage almanac: theatrical yearbook and address register. Theatre, film, radio, television]. Berlin/Hamburg: Genossenschaft Deutscher Bühnenangehöriger, 57. Jg. 1949–.

Drese, Claus Helmut. *Im Palast der Gefühle: Erfahrungen und Enthüllungen eines Wiener*

Operndirektors. [In the palace of emotions: experiences and revelations of a Viennese opera director]. Munich: Piper, 1993.

Engerth, Rüdiger. 'Der Wiener Aktionismus.' [The Vienna Actionism movement]. *Protokolle* (1970/71): 152–169.

Fuhrich, Edda, and Gisela Prossnitz, eds. *Die Salzburger Festspiele. Bd 1: 1929–1945. Ihre Geschichte in Daten, Zeitzeugnissen und Bildern.* [The Salzburg Festival. Vol. 1: 1929–45. Facts, memorabilia and images]. Salzburg: Residenz, 1990. 327 pp.

Goertz, Harald, ed. *Österreichisches Musikhandbuch. Österreichische Komponisten der Gegenwart.* [Austrian music almanac, contemporary Austrian composers]. Vienna: Doblinger, 1989. 248 pp.

Greisenegger, Ingrid, and Ilse Hanl. *Animazione: Texte zur Theaterarbeit.* [Animation: texts on theatrical work]. Vienna: Dramatisches Zentrum, 1975. 55 pp.

Greisenegger, Wolfgang. *Österreich Bühnenbildner der Gegenwart: Ausstellung im Tiroler Kunstpavillon in Innsbruck.* [Contemporary Austrian stage designers: exhibition at the Tiroler Kunstpavillon in Innsbruck.] Exhibition catalogue. Innsbruck: 1968.

——. 'Theater'. In *Clemens Holzmeister. Architekt in der Zeitwende. Sakralbau, Profanbau, Theater.* [Clemens Holzmeister. Architect at a time of change. Religious and profane buildings, theatre]. Salzburg/Stuttgart/Zürich: Verlag Das Bergand-Buch, 1978.

Hadamovsky, Franz. *Bücherkunde deutschsprachiger Theaterliteratur, Teil 2: 1945–79.* [Bibliography of German-language theatre literature, part 2: 1945–79]. Vienna/Köln: Böhlau, 1982. 407 pp.

Haider-Pregler, Hilde. *Theater und Schauspielkunst in Österreich.* Vienna: Bundespressedienst o.J., 1970. 228 pp. Published in English as *The Theatre in Austria.* Vienna: Federal Press Service n.d., 1970. 202 pp.

Jacobs, Montague. *Deutsche Schauspielkunst: Zeugnisse Zur Bühnengeschichte Klassischer Rollen.* [German acting: testimony to the history of classic roles]. Berlin: Henschelverlag, 1954. 539 pp.

Judtmann, Fritz. 'Die Baugeschichte des neuen Burgtheaters'. [The construction of the new Burgtheater] in *175 Jahre Burgtheater.* Vienna: 1955.

Kraus, Gottfried, ed. *Musik in Österreich: eine Chronik in Daten, Dokumenten, Essays und Bildern.* [Music in Austria: a chronicle of data, documents, essays and pictures]. Vienna: Brandstätter, 1989. 518 pp.

Landa, Jutta. *Bürgerliches Schocktheater: Entwicklungen im österreichischen Drama der sechziger und siebziger Jahre.* [Shocking the bourgeois: developments in Austrian drama in the 1960s and 1970s]. Frankfurt/Main: Athenäum, 1988. 198 pp.

Österreichischer Bundestheaterverband Bericht 1992/1993. [1992/93 report by the Austrian Federal Theatre Association]. Vienna: Austrian Federal Theatre Association, 1993.

Österreichisches Theaterjahrbuch. [Austrian theatre almanac]. Vienna/Berlin: 1964–71.

Prawy, Marcel. *Die Wiener Oper.* [The Vienna Opera]. Munich: Goldman, 1980.

Priessnitz, Reinhard. 'Die verbesserung von mitteleuropa – Mitglieder der Wiener Gruppe'. [The improvement of central Europe – Members of the Wiener Gruppe]. In *Das Größere Österreich.* [The greater Austria]. Edited by Kristian Sotriffer. Vienna: Edition Tusch, 1982. pp. 448–52.

Reinking, Wilhelm. *Spiel und Form: Werkstattberichte. Bühnenbildner zum Gestaltwandel d. Szene in d. zwanziger u. dreissiger Jahren.* [Play and form: designers and the transformation of stage design in the 1920s and 1930s]. Hamburg: Christians, 1979. 326 pp.

Reiterer, Albert F. 'Kulturelle Aktivitäten 1990: Ein statistischer Überblick'. [Cultural activities in 1990: a statistical summary]. *Kulturstatistik 1990.* Vienna: Österreichisches Statistisches Zentralamt, 1992. pp. 17–36.

Schreiner, Evelyn, ed. *100 Jahre Volkstheater. Theater-Zeit-Geschichte.* [100 years of the Volkstheater. Theatre-period-history]. Vienna: Jugend & Volk, 1989.

Seebom, Andrea. *Die Wiener Oper: 350 Jahre Glanz und Tradition.* [The Vienna Opera: 350 years of splendour and tradition]. Vienna: Ueberreuter, 1986. Published in English: New York: Rizzoli, 1987.

Sotriffer, Kristian, ed. *Das größere Österreich: Geistiges und soziales Leben von 1880 bis zur Gegenwart. Hundert Kapitel mit einem Essay von Ernst Krenek: von der Aufgabe, ein Österreicher zu sein.* [The greater Austria: intellectual and social life from 1880 to the present. One hundred chapters with an essay by Ernst Krenek: On the task of being an Austrian]. Vienna: Edition Tusch, 1982.

'Statistik der österreichischen Theater 1989/90'. [Statistics concerning Austrian theatres in 1989/90]. *Theaterstatistik 1989/90.* Köln: Deutscher Bühnenverein, 1991.

Tanz: 20. Jahrhundert in Wien. [Dance: twentieth century in Vienna]. Exhibition catalogue. Vienna: Österreich Theatermuseum, 1979.

Theater in Österreich. Verzeichnis der Inszenierungen. [Theatre in Austria. Catalogue of productions]. Vienna: Wiener Gesellschaft für Theaterforschung/Institut für Theaterwissenschaft/Universität Wien, 1980–.

Tschulik, Norbert. *Musiktheater in Österreich: Die Oper im 20. Jahrhundert.* [Music theatre in Austria: opera in the twentieth century]. Vienna: Österreich Bundesverlag, 1984.

Urbach, Reinhard, and Achim Benning, eds. *Burgtheater Wien 1776–1986. Ebenbild und Widerspruch, Zweihundert und zehn Jahre.* [Vienna Burgtheater 1776–86. Likeness and contradiction. 210 years]. Vienna: Österreich Bundesverlag u. Schroll, 1986. 263 pp.

Waechter-Böhm, Lisbeth, ed. *Wien 1945 davor/danach.* [Vienna 1945 before/after]. Exhibition catalogue. Vienna: Brandstätter, 1985.

Wiener Theaterjahrbuch. [Vienna theatre almanac]. Vienna: Forts, 1965–.

AZERBAIJAN

Situated in the eastern part of the Transcaucasian region, Azerbaijan shares borders with Russia, Turkey, Iran, Armenia and Georgia. It has a land area of 88,600 square kilometres (34,200 square miles), the Caucasus Mountains surround it on the northeast and southwest; to the east is the Caspian Sea. Its 1992 population was approximately 7.3 million, 1.7 million of whom live in Baku, its capital. Just over 88 per cent of the population are native Azeris. The other 12 per cent are composed of various ethnic groups including Russians, Lezgins, Talyshins and Jews.

The land has been the subject of foreign invasions for more than a thousand years. Between the seventh and tenth centuries the country was overrun by the Arab Khalifat; in the eleventh century, it was the Turks/Seljuks; in the thirteenth century, the Mongols. Azerbaijani culture began to prosper between the sixteenth and eighteenth centuries when the country, officially part of the Sevefid State, was ruled by Turkish dynasties. During this time, the arts of poetry, miniature painting and calligraphy achieved their heights.

The war treaties of 1813 and 1828 divided the Azerbaijan territories between Russia and Iran. With the development of the oil industry in the nineteenth century, Baku became the world's largest oil-producing centre and the country began to undergo an industrial boom. Capitalism began to develop at this time and European influence began to be clearly felt in all spheres of life.

In 1918, however, as a direct result of the Russian Revolution, Azerbaijan moved towards socialism and became the Azerbaijani Democratic Republic, a parliamentary democracy that lasted only two years. In April 1920, the Red Army overthrew the government and northern Azerbaijan became part of the new Soviet Union. It remained part of that Union until the USSR collapsed; in October 1991 it once again became an independent Azerbaijani Republic.

Azerbaijan today is a democratic secular state with a president and a parliament. Azeri is the majority language but Russian is widely spoken. The majority religion is Islam but there are significant numbers of Christians, Jews and Krishnas.

Historically, the country's culture has been defined by three specific influences – the culture of Islam, Turkish culture and European culture. During the Soviet period, socialism was more imposed than accepted and disturbed in many ways the country's natural historical development. Consequently the post-Soviet period has been marked by a complex search in all cultural processes for the synthesis of the national and the universal.

In terms of theatrical history, it is also possible to identify three specific periods: from the beginning to 1920 (the development of an indigenous culture); from 1920 to 1990 (the development of a Soviet culture); and from 1990 on (a new beginning and an attempt to synthesize the various influences).

Early Azerbaijani theatre was heavily involved in the art of the storyteller. Known as *ashyks*, they were singer-musicians and followed in the tradition of the tellers of epic legends. Other indigenous forms include *koskosa*, a kind of theatrical folk game; *garavelli*, rooted in the spring festivals much like the Dionysian festivals of Greece; folk puppet shows; and the religious spectacles of T'azieh ritually performed in specially built tents with a small raised stage area, actors working mimetically with the spectators separated from the performers.

Theatre in the European sense is a nineteenth-century phenomenon. The founder of Azerbaijani professional theatre is Mirza Fatali Akhundov (1812–78), an educator and a worshipper of European culture. He wrote six comedies in the western style, among the first in Islamic culture. Before the end of the nineteenth century, all had been translated into English, German and Dutch. Molièresque in style but identifiably indigenous in feeling, these comedies were successful on stage and have become a touch-point for Azerbaijani directors when renewal has been sought in the repertoire.

Akhundov's comedy *Sarguzashti-veziri-khani Lankarani* (*The Envoy of the Khan of Lenkoran*) was staged in 1873 in Baku by a group of teachers who had studied in European and Russian cities. This and other of Akhundov's plays were subsequently staged in other Azerbaijani cities including Giandja, Shusha, Sheki, Kuba and Nakhichevan, along with plays by Nadjafbek Vezirov (1854–1926). Also staged at this time was Gogol's *Revizor* (*The Government Inspector*) translated into Azeri. The deeper goal of all these productions, however, was essentially didactic.

After 1900, a number of other writers began to emerge. Most important among them were Abdurakhimbek Akhverdiev (1870–1933), Nariman Narimanov (1870–1925), Djalil Mamedkulizade (1866–1931) and composer and dramatist Uzeir Gadjibekov (1885–1948). Groups of actors were also beginning to appear – known as *tovarishestva* (friendship groups) – as early as 1906. Through various educational societies these troupes began to become more and more professional.

Some of the groups were allowed to play one day a week at the Tagiev and the Mailov Theatres in Baku (on a rental basis), stages put up by capitalist philanthropists at the beginning of the century and generally utilized by foreign touring groups. Between 1900 and 1920, these increasingly professional, western-style Muslim acting companies staged many national plays as well as plays by Shakespeare, Schiller, Geine, Dukandj, Gogol and Tolstoi.

The national plays that were most frequently staged were *Gadji Gara* by Akhundov, *Aga Mohammed Shakh Gadjar* by Akhverdiev, *Othello* by Shakespeare, *The Robbers* by Schiller, *Life of an Actor* by Dukandj and *Revizor* by Gogol. The first national opera, *Leili ve Medjnun* (*Leili and Medjnun*) written by Uzier Gadjibekov, was also staged at this time. There were also performances of classical

Azerbaijani *mugams*, national song recitals with many centuries of tradition.

Even as late as 1918, indigenous productions were staged with the support of private benefactors and theatre enthusiasts with educational interests. State and local authorities supported only foreign troupes and solo performers such as the Russian Fyodor Chaliapin. In 1919, the state decided to nationalize the Mailov Theatre but given the unstable political situation, no further steps were taken in the development of a national theatre.

Many theatre professionals of the time wanted to see more state activity in the field, hoping to make theatre a more public art which proclaimed social and moral concepts. Others wanted the state to support folk forms and non-western forms. To pious Muslims, who found European culture merely amusing, the development of a state-supported, western-style theatre was not a direction to be supported.

The result of this struggle was a rather sober form of western theatre filled with moral lecturing and philosophical and poetic stereotypes. Elements of this can still be seen today.

By 1920, all the theatres and their property were nationalized and the state began a monopoly on the legal staging of theatrical performances. State ideology became compulsory in the theatre with deviations, direct or implied, resulting in immediate bans of both the production and those participating in it. By the end of the 1930s, this control became a trigger for official repression.

The first new State Theatre was organized in Baku in 1920, joining the already existing Azerbaijani and Russian drama troupes and an opera troupe. The new State Theatre was created on the model of the popular Moscow touring company, Satir-Agit (Satire-Agitation). A year later, a small Azerbaijani troupe opened in Baku calling itself Tanqid-Tabliq (Critique-Propaganda). The popular success of this latter group was based on its comic sketches utilizing local character types, its political satire and witty dialogues. This theatre later changed its name to the Baku Workers' Theatre and moved to Azerbaijan's second biggest industrial city, Kirovabad (now called Giandja).

In Baku in 1922, the State Drama Theatre was officially opened, becoming in 1924 the Azerbaijan Academic Drama Theatre – known throughout the country as GAT – under the direction of the Russian director and actor, A.A. Tuganov (1871–1952). Tuganov tried to create an Azerbaijani version of the Moscow Art

Theatre and introduced the Stanislavski method into Azeri acting. The experiment was not a success since local audiences expected direct contact with their actors and rejected the fourth-wall aesthetics of the new style.

GAT's repertoire at that time was dominated by romantic, poetic and moralistic plays by Djafar Djabarly (1899–1934), philosophic morality plays and verse parables by Husein Djavid (1882–1944) and adaptations of Shakespeare (*Hamlet*) and Schiller. The public also went to see their favourite actors almost regardless of what play they were in.

The Baki Fakhla-Kandli Teatry (Baku Workers' and Peasants' Theatre) opened in 1925. In 1927, it was renamed the Baki Turk Ischi Teatry (Baku Turk Workers' Theatre) and from 1927 it began to work in the style of the Russian director Vsevelod Meyerhold. Its work was heavily agitprop and its visual approach constructivist. Biomechanics was used in the approach to performance. This was another short-lived experiment, however, and Meyerhold's ideas were not seen again until the 1960s.

Led by GAT, which followed the decreed cultural and theatrical aesthetics, theatre in the 1920s and 1930s played a significant and deter-mining role in the country's social life, particularly in the capital. At the same time, the social status of actors increased enormously. No longer considered as social exiles, they became respected and honoured artists.

Audiences of the time came from all social groups, indicative of the state's determination to create a classless society. Critical discussions dealt only with approved styles. Critics had to be for realism and against 'bourgeois formalism', for national tradition and against national 'short-sightedness', for an ideal-filled repertoire and against 'excessive entertainment'.

Ideological pressure increased significantly in the 1930s when the wave of repressions then sweeping the Soviet Union also touched Azerbaijani theatre. Fabricated political cases incriminated Djavid, Miza Sharifzade (1893–1937), Ulvi Radjab (1903–37) and other famous theatre practitioners. All were arrested.

In 1938, Adil Iskenderov (1912–78) was appointed principal director at GAT, a position he held until 1960. By the end of the 1940s, despite strict codification of theatre forms, new experiments began at GAT and one could see for the first time in Azerbaijani productions elements that could be described as baroque.

Adil Iskenderov's 1938 Azerbaijan Academic Drama Theatre production of Samed Vurgun's *Vagif*.

Iskenderov strove to combine aphoristic attacks with essentially motionless performances constructing productions in many new ways. Audiences easily understood the ideological codes and could identify with the ideas being expressed. Among his major productions were the verse drama *Vagif* (1938) by the poet Samed Vurgun (1906–56) and *Othello*.

A young director, Mekhti Mamedov (1918–85), joined GAT in 1945 and in 1960 became the principal director. His first directorial assignment for the company was *Twelfth Night* (1946), a high-spirited comic spectacle. This energy and spirit was characteristic of much of his future work – *Dancing Master* (1949) by Lope de Vega, and *Aligulu evlanir* (*Alikui Gets Married*, 1949) by Sabit Rakhman (1910–70). Despite his energy, Mamedov was not really able to break through the older traditions.

Tofik Kazymov (1921–80) became the director of GAT in 1963 and tried to usher in a new era. But ideological orientation of theatrical art was deeply rooted by this time and Kazymov, who had begun his career in Iskenderov's company, was unable to make real changes.

Kazymov's first production for GAT was *Antony and Cleopatra* and featured a much more spare design than had been seen at the theatre to that time. His next production was *Romeo and Juliet*, handled as a human love story in a hostile world. He later turned to Azeri plays – *San hamisha manimlasan* (*You Are Always With Me*, 1964) and *Mahv olmush gundalikar* (*Destroyed Diaries*, 1967), both by Ilyas Efendiev (b. 1914). Both these works tried to move away from established ideology and to throw light on everyday reality. He even dealt with the taboo subject of bribery in *Shaharin jaj qunlari* (*Summer in the City*, 1978), a play by the writer Anar (b. 1938).

One of Kazymov's most interesting experiments was *Olular* (*The Dead*, 1966), a tragicomedy by Mamedkulizade, in which he tried to synthesize contemporary trends with traditional Azeri theatre forms. A year later he staged the melodramatic parable *Sansiz* (*Without You*) by Shikhali Kurbanov (1925–67) and *Fyrtyna* (*The Tempest*) by Shakespeare, a fairytale interpretation in which one could see subtle notes of scepticism and disappointment with contemporary life.

At the end of the 1960s, Mamedov returned to GAT and staged a number of productions of classical works. Among them were Lev Tolstoi's *Qanly meyit* (*The Living Corpse*, 1968), Djavid's *Hajjam* (1970) and *Iblis* (*The Devil*, 1978) and, his most outstanding production, Mamedkulizade's tragi-comedy *Deli jeqingagy* (*Concourse of the Insane*, 1976).

This same period saw the Azerbaijani theatre grow into crisis as audiences simply stopped going to the theatre. Stereotypes abounded in all areas of culture and people seemed to simply lose interest in the arts. It became, therefore, a period of artistic renewal with directors seeking ways to connect the contemporary theatre with national forms. The process took place mainly outside GAT.

It was in 1975 that the Sheki Dovlet Dram Teatry (Sheki State Drama Theatre) opened in the city of Sheki. More precisely, the company reopened, having been in existence in the period 1931–49. The theatre's director was Guseinaga Atakishiev (b. 1949), who managed to find an effective blend of European plasticity, Brechtian epic forms, Russian realism and Azeri folk theatre. Even the Eastern European Grotesque found its way into his work.

Atakishiev also staged the work of modern foreign playwrights including Bulgaria's Racho Stoyanov, Hungary's S. Petöfi, Brecht (*Arturo Ui*) and Switzerland's Friedrich Dürrenmatt. In 1985, he moved to Baku where as director of GAT he staged Gorki's *Lower Depths*, Dürrenmatt's *Romulus the Great* (1986) and invited a guest director from the Berliner Ensemble to stage *Dreigroschenoper* (*Threepenny Opera*, 1987). Despite these efforts, Atakishiev could not establish an effective working relationship with the company and left the theatre soon after.

From 1977, the Russian section of the Young People's Theatre in Baku (called TUZ) began working with a young director named Azerpasha Neimatov (b. 1947). His productions, mostly musicals, were marked by a strict and reserved sense of style and extraordinary taste, quite different in feel from the ideologically based productions of GAT.

His productions, for both the Russian and Azerbaijani sections of the company, were quite strong and successful with audiences. Russian productions of note included *Noch posle vypuska* (*Night After Graduation*, 1975) by Vladimir Tedriakov, and *Bumbarash* (1976) by A. Gaidar. For the Azeri section, he staged *Danabash kendinin mektebi* (*The School of Danabash Village*, 1989) by Mamedkulizade, *Sabah chohdan bashlanyb* (*Tomorrow Began a Long Time Ago*, 1986) by Rakhman Ali-Zade

(b. 1947) and *Juchulama* (*The Dreams*, 1987) by Kamal Aslanov (b. 1946).

In 1979 the director Vagif Ibragimogly (b. 1949) became head of the Tadris Teatry (Theatre School) at the Azerbaijan Dovlet Indjasanat Institutu (Azerbaijani State Arts College). A cornerstone of his approach was his interest in principles of Asian theatre – suggestiveness, body movement more than text, the use of music and dance. He sought to find an Azerbaijani version of all these elements and tried to move theatre into a mytho-poetic direction, towards archetypes.

In 1990, Ibragimogly became head of the Theatre Juk (the name comes from an ancient Turkish cry for the dead, particularly for dead heroes). In this role, his ideas for a new theatrical form for the Azerbaijani public began to crystallize.

Another theatre which tried to break from the GAT mould – in 1991 GAT was renamed the Azerbaijan Dovlet Milli Dram Teatry (Azerbaijani National State Drama Theatre) – was the Kirovabad (Giandja) Dram Teatry (Kirovabad Drama Theatre). The company was first formed in 1932–3 on the base of the Baku Turk Workers' Theatre. Following the GAT model until the 1960s, it began to include at that time a number of new plays – *Buraja qajin* (*Come Here*, 1965) by the Turkish writer Aziz Nesin, *Hajatda qapan it var* (*Beware of the Dog*, 1964) by the Georgian writer G. Buachidze, and

even Brecht's *Threepenny Opera*. All these productions were directed by Nasir Sadykh-Zade (b. 1939). Sadykh-Zade later moved to Baku and, unfortunately, the theatre returned to a much more conservative style.

Another theatre that tried to find a new approach to repertoire was the Sumqait Dovlet Dram Teatry (Sumqait State Drama Theatre) under the directorship of Marakhim Farzalibekov (b. 1949). Farzalibekov staged several Soviet works – Bokarev's *The Steel Makers* (1976) and Lermontov's *Masquerade* (1971) – along with some Azerbaijani plays including Djabarly's *Vafaly Sarijja* (*The Betrayed Saria*, 1979). When he too moved on to GAT, the Sumqait lost its distinct focus.

A note here about the production of Russian plays in Azerbaijan. Since 1945, Russian plays have been regularly produced in the country but have not dominated the repertoire. Indeed, though it was mandatory early on to include Russian plays in the repertoire, it was also mandatory to include Azerbaijani works. Since 1991, many styles have begun to be seen in the country and many new voices heard. The old idea of one voice and unification of culture for ideological reasons is no longer tenable. On the other hand, across-the-board decreases in state support have meant that all Azerbaijani theatres in the early 1990s are searching for new ways to continue their explorations.

Structure of the National Theatre Community

Control by the state was a feature of Azerbaijani theatre for most of the twentieth century. Control was the essential responsibility of the Medeniyyet Nazirliyiyenin Teatr Idarasy (Directorate of Theatres of the Ministry of Culture). The directorate (or TI as it is known in Azerbaijan) was in charge of virtually everything – administration, financial policy, ideology and artistic policy.

In the mid-1980s, this began to change. Until that moment, the TI also acted as a censor and was given a private showing of every production in advance. From the mid-1980s, the censorship still officially existed but a much more liberal attitude began to make itself felt. It was rare, in fact, for productions to be stopped. After the breakup of the USSR and with the beginning of democratic reforms, much more creative and

economic independence was given to each theatre. The TI in the 1990s had virtually no control of theatrical activity.

There are twenty-four theatres currently functioning in Azerbaijan. Fifteen of them are in Baku, most in the downtown core. Ten of those are state owned – the Azerbaijan Dovlet Milli Dram Teatry, the Azerbaijan Dovlet Opera ve Ballet Teatry (State Opera and Ballet Theatre), the Azerbaijan Dovlet Misigili Komedija Teatry (State Musical Comedy Theatre), the Gosudarstvenny Russki Dramaticheski Teatry (State Russian Drama Theatre), the Azerbaijan Dovlet Qang Tamashachylar Teatry (State Young People's Theatre), the Qanglar Teatry (Youth Theatre), the puppet and marionette theatre Buta, the Azerbaijan Dovlet Juk Teatry (Theatre Juk), the Mugam Teatry (Mugam

The State Musical Comedy Theatre production of M. Shamkhalov and Z. Baghirov's *Mother-in-Law*.

Giandja, Saliany and Kakh, there are also puppet theatres. In Nakhichevan and Giandja, there are poetry theatres as well, named after Djavid and Zarrabi, respectively.

Numbers of actors in troupes vary from ten to a hundred people. For instance, in the Opera and Ballet Theatre, ninety-six; in GAT, ninety-six; in the Youth Theatre, thirty-nine; in the puppet and marionette, only ten. In the past, state funding was allocated annually in a lump sum. By 1992, rising inflation was sharply increasing production costs, even within several months. An average rehearsal period is three months with about sixty rehearsals scheduled.

The Azerbaijan Teatr Khadimleri Ittifagy (Union of Theatre Workers of Azerbaijan) is the only artistic and social benefit organization which represents theatre workers. It was registered in 1944 as the Theatre Society. In the past the Theatre Society, as well as other artistic organizations of Azerbaijan, was under state control and appeared to be a conduit of state ideology. Today it is an independent self-financing organization which genuinely represents the interests of theatre people. It has recently begun to organize tours for theatre people to festivals and conferences. In 1991, it established the Golden Dervish Prize for best director, actor and theatre critic of the year.

The major traditional theatre festival (Novruz) includes groups from Azerbaijan, middle Asia and Kazakhstan.

Theatre attendance in the 1990s dropped significantly due to the general political instability, the economic crisis and inflation. Since the end of the 1980s ticket prices have risen substantially, reaching 15–30 rubles, with movie prices only 10–20 per cent lower.

There is a theatre museum in Azerbaijan, although in 1992 and 1993 its materials were not displayed due to economic and organizational problems.

Theatre) and the Mahny Teatry (Song Theatre). The last two opened in 1990.

Three municipal theatres also exist – Tanqid-Tabliq (Propaganda and Agitation), Kamera Teatry (Chamber Theatre) and Theatre Mejdan (Square). The last two opened in 1992. The city's only studio theatre is the Opera Studio at the Azerbaijan State Conservatory.

State drama theatres also function in other cities of Azerbaijan – Giandja, Mingechaur, Sheki, Nakhichevan, Gazakh, Agdash, Shusha, Fizuli, Lenkoran and Kusary. In Nakhichevan,

Artistic Profile

Companies

The most important actors and directors in Azerbaijan have traditionally worked at GAT in Baku. The company, the most officially connected of all the troupes in the country, has traditionally been defined by the principles of educational aesthetics and its work has been based on romantic theatre traditions and principles of socialist art.

Under Iskenderov, a strong hierarchy developed inside the theatre and the productions themselves reflected prevailing cultural policies. Elements of this system remained as time went by though strict adherence to the system broke down.

It was at the end of the 1980s that the old aesthetic was galvanized for the last time in the social pamphlets which were put on stage. It still defined to a great extent successful performances of *Qyzyl tesht* (*Golden Jar*, 1987) by Seiran Sekhavet (b. 1950), directed by Bakhram Osmanov (b. 1962). The time itself seemed to demand accusatory, politically engaged productions, which in many ways went along quite well with familiar educational reasoning. Still, this last gasp only underscored the irreversibility of the evolution, the final breakdown of a didactic approach to theatre.

A specifically national quality is a distinctive trademark of the TMK troupe. Using a form close to singing, the troupe is divided into vocalists and dramatic actors. Vocalists are usually the actors with the highest professional training and who studied voice at a conservatory. Dramatic actors also learn rhythmical recitation and domestic-style singing. Essentially they play buffoon-type characters colourfully satirizing real-life situations. In this theatre, it is difficult to speak about a specific show, or about the integrity of movement or text. Nevertheless, the best performers from this troupe still manage a stable psychological and social contact with their audiences.

Also national in its way is the troupe of the Theatre Juk, which consists of fifteen actors and a director. In Juk's shows, words, song, music and movement are present in one undivided synthesis, somewhat similar to Indian *Katkhakali*. The actor's body remains the main and primary material of expression. Rehearsal periods at this theatre are lengthy and it is rare for them to stage more than one or two shows per year. The actors are constantly striving to materialize inner and intimate, sacred qualities of the human being through movement, searching for an image to express the nature of the spirit. This is more conceptual theatre than traditional, although it does appeal to national traditions and to eastern theatre forms with its meditative orientation.

Dramaturgy

By classic Azerbaijani dramaturgy is meant first of all plays by M.F. Akhundov, D. Mamedkulizade and A. Akhverdiev. Their best plays contain recognizable images of the national universe and actors readily incarnate these worlds on stage. More often than not, their respective visions appear fragmented and split and this tends to be emphasized in production of the plays.

In the 1960s, the most significant plays were by Sabit Rakhman and I. Efendiev, which still maintain a romantic perception of the world and offer clear and simple solutions. Rakhman, author of *Hoshbahtlar* (*Lucky People*), *Jalan* (*The Lie*), *Nishanly qyz* (*Engaged*) and others, created more comic characters, juicy epigrams and witty repartee. Efendiev, on the other hand, author of *San hamisha manimlasan* (*You Are Always with Me*), *Mahny daqlarda qaldy* (*The Song Stayed in the Mountains*) and *Mahv olmush qundaliklar* (*Destroyed Diaries*) created a more lyrical drama about everyday life though the domestic environment was still often romanticized and poeticized.

From the mid-1970s, other authors emerged such as Anar, Rustam Ibragimbekov (b. 1939) and Vagif Samedogly (b. 1939) who rejected romantic pathos and concentrated on the existential aspects of their characters.

Ibragimbekov, who wrote in Russian, is the author of *Zabytyi avgust* (*Forgotten August*), *Pokhozhyi na lva* (*The Lion-Like*), *Zhenschina pered zakrytoi dveriu* (*Woman at the Closed Door*), and many other plays. All are neo-realistic stories with a Baku backyard atmosphere, presented in a Chekhovian psychological style and constructed as complex parables. They offer their insights through the banal and ordinary.

Anar, another important author, wrote *Zangir* (*The Chain*), *Adamyn adamy* (*Insider to Insider*) and *Shaharin jaj qunlari* (*Summer in the City*) among others. In his works, he melds melodramatic collisions with social pamphleteering in which the 'between the lines' meaning prompts 'between the lines' theatrical decisions. In his comedies, he follows the aesthetics of the folk *garavelli*, whose characters are traditional trickster-jester types.

V. Samedogly, author of *Ugja dag bashynda* (*On the Top of a High Mountain*), *Baht uzuju* (*Wedding Band*) and *Jajda top-top ojunu* (*Playing Snowball in the Summer*), likes sharp grotesque situations. Though witty, his plays are ironic rather than accusative.

Two writers who emerged in the 1980s were Kamal Aslanov and Rakhman Ali-Zade. Aslanov, writing in Russian, is the author of *Da zdravstvuiet solntze* (*Long Live the Sun*), *Pravaia ruka Mirali* (*Mirali's Right Hand*) and *Rai v shalashe* (*Paradise in a Hut*). He writes well-made plays with unexpected turns of events. Quite often they present surreal situations or even completely absurd ones.

Ali-Zade, author of *Bizim kendin narlary* (*Pomegranates of our Village*), *Qohumlar* (*Relatives*) and *Dadashbala amalijjaty* (*Operation 'Dadashbala'*), prefers comedies of manners with juicy, sharp and even risqué dialogue. His plays are rooted in folk farce, but behind them one can always see the twentieth century.

Directors, Directing and Production Styles

A new direction in Azerbaijani theatre emerged in 1991 with the production of *Ogul* (*The Son*) directed by V. Ibragimogly, based on the epos *Kitabi Dede Korkut*. This new style moved away from illusionist aesthetics as well as from the traditional Italian box stage. This particular show was performed in a large room where the audience sat on the perimeter. The genre is identified as *iukhlama* (lamenting) and is not based on a particular literary text. Ibragimogly aimed to liberate the hidden motivations of human existence through expressive body movement and the magic of sound and rhythm. Actors were required to hear the music and the melody of the pronounced word. Depending on their own movement abilities and inner tuning, they materialized their reactions to what they were hearing. A key to this style is silence itself – its capacity to reach the innermost mind by bypassing words. To fulfil his ideas, Ibragimogly uses principles of eastern theatre, Brecht's epic theatre folk forms and elements of western European avant-garde theatre.

Music Theatre

The history of the State Opera and Ballet Theatre and the State Musical Comedy Theatre are both related to the name of composer and writer Uzier Gadjibekov. Gadjibekov, creator of the opera *Leili and Medjnun*, premièred his work in Baku in 1908. Based on a poem by Fizuli – an Azerbaijani poet of the sixteenth century – the opera starred the actor-singer Guseinkuli Sarabskii (1879–1945).

Leili and Medjnun is an eastern variant of *Romeo and Juliet* in which love of woman is transformed into love of God. *Mugam*-style singing laid a national musical basis for the composition, a perfect complement to the symbolic content of Fizuli's poetry. Unfortunately, numerous productions of the opera have turned it into more of a concert performance. A genuine *mugam* opera spectacle could show how unique a *mugam*-based theatre could be.

The State Opera and Ballet opened in 1920 and has kept up a repertoire of classical and contemporary opera, including works by other Azerbaijani composers. A milestone was its production of the opera *Kerogly* (1937), based on the national epic, starring Shovket Mamedova (1897–1981) and Biulbiul (1897–1963), who trained in voice in Italy. Both *Leili and Medjnun* and *Kerogly* have become calling cards for Azerbaijani opera.

Fatma Mukhtarova (1893–1972) was the first Azerbaijani opera singer to perform in such parts as Carmen, Delilah, Polina (*The Queen of Spades* by Tchaikovsky) and Marina (*Boris Godunov* by Mussorgski). The first director of national operas was Ismail Idayat-Zade (1901–51) and the company's best known conductors were Niyazi (1912–84) and Rauf Abdullaev (b. 1937).

The first musical comedy, *Ar ve arvad* (*Husband and Wife*) by Gadjibekov, was performed in Azerbaijan in 1909. In 1939 the Musical Comedy Theatre was created, a troupe with both Russian and Azerbaijani sections. The Russian section had a preference for classical operetta as well as contemporary musicals. The Azerbaijani section tended towards national musical comedies. In that genre there were productions which have become classics – *O omasyn bu olsun* (*If Not This One, Then That One*, 1910) and *Arshin mal alan* (1913).

Mekhdi Mammedov's 1976 State National Opera and Ballet Theatre production of Uzier Gadjibekov's *Leili and Medjnun*, designed by Elchin Aslanov.

Dance Theatre

Azerbaijan has preserved many rich dance traditions from ancient times. These are now being studied and developed thanks to various dance ensembles, predominantly state owned. Other than this classical choreography in which dance has a self-imposed meaning, there is not really a contemporary dance theatre in Azerbaijan. There are rather only choreographic elements used in contemporary productions.

Classical ballet is most often seen in works by foreign and Azerbaijani composers at the Opera and Ballet Theatre. The first national Azerbaijani ballet was staged in 1940 – *Qyz qalasy* (*Maiden's Tower*) to music by Afrasiyab Badalbeili (1907–76). It was choreographed and danced by Gamer Almaszade (b. 1915).

The best known Azerbaijani ballets are by composer Kara Karaev (1918–82) – *Jeddi gozal* (*Seven Beauties*, 1952) and *Ildyrymly jollar* (*By the Path of Thunder*, 1958), premièred in St Petersburg – and by composer Arif Melikov – *Mahabban haqynda dastan* (*The Legend of Love*, 1984), premièred in St Petersburg, *Min bir qegja* (*The Thousand and One Nights*, 1981) by Fikret Amirov (1922–84), choreographed by Nailya Nazirova, (b. 1936). These works were most frequently danced by Tamilla Shiralieva (b. 1946) and Vladimir Pletnev (1946–88), two of the country's most outstanding dancers.

Theatre for Young Audiences

Azerbaijan's State Children's Theatre, known as TUZ, opened in 1928 (with first a Russian and then, in 1931, an Azerbaijani section). The key figures early on were director Zafar Neimatov (1915–71), for many years the principal director of the theatre, and actors Agadadash

Gurbanov (1911–65) and Guseinaga Sadygov (1914–83).

Theatre for children and young adults in Azerbaijan was for a long time regulated by Soviet directives. The main goal of these theatres was to provide the ideological education of the new generation in the spirit of Soviet ideas. Any recommendations had to be approved by central Komsomol (Young Communist League) organizations. Pedagogically, they also had to be approved by the Academy of Pedagogical Sciences. Recommendations were very carefully and pedantically regulated: optimum ages for certain plays (pre-school, junior, intermediate, senior, adolescent); lengths of scripts; and specifics of aesthetic perceptions. Repertoire was obviously under strict control. Group attendance and collective discussions were encouraged. At the same time, ticket prices for youth theatres (as well as puppet theatres, which were in the same category) were kept very low with trade union organizations (also state owned) obliged to sponsor theatres. Such a system was in place practically until the beginning of the 1960s.

Changes in the socio-political and cultural situation of the USSR at the beginning of the 1960s had an immediate impact on the status of youth theatres. Ideological dictatorship weakened. Theatre institutions in Azerbaijan decided not to train actors for youth and puppet theatres, with conventional theatre training considered sufficient.

Directors found themselves allowed, on occasion, to stage shows outside the guidelines. However, the social prestige of youth theatres was declining, partly because of cuts in financial support and partly because of lower rates of pay for actors. Many working in the field were coming to youth theatres simply to get experience and would quickly move on to an 'adult theatre'.

Thanks to a relatively free creative atmosphere, Azerbaijani TUZ was able to use directors who were not so ideologically, aesthetically, or socio-pedagogically engaged. Among these were A. Neimatov, Namik Agaev (b. 1962) and Djannet Selimova (b. 1940). All showed their artistic opposition to the dominating aesthetics of GAT, and this was evident in their best productions – *Zabyty avgust* (*Forgotten August*, 1974) by Ibragimbekov (directed by Selimova) and *Kechan ilin son qegasi* (*The Last Night of the Passing Year*, 1978) by Anar (directed by Neimatov).

Theatre for teens in the USSR began as a repercussion of the youth movement of the 1960s. The Studio Theatre of G. Atakishiev followed in the same line when the entire acting class of the Arts Institute started its own theatre after completing training. This immediately became a genuine youth theatre, a theatre by the young, and not necessarily for particular age groups. The company set itself up as an official opposition to the repertoire and theatre aesthetics of GAT. This was later expanded by the creation of the Theatre Juk (headed by Ibragimogly), the Youth Theatre in Baku (headed by G. Atakishiev) and the studio Ahtarysh (Search) at the Sheki Theatre (headed by Farman Abdullaev (b. 1952)).

The most significant productions of the Ahtarysh were *Tanha padshakhyn naqyly* (*The Tale of the Lonely Padisheik*, 1988) after a comic parable by Anar, and *Ajri aqag* (*The Crooked Tree*, 1988) by F. Abdullaev.

Such youth theatres in the 1990s were working quite actively, including in their repertoire plays that were not staged at other theatres. Among their productions have been *Qatl qunu* (*The Day of the Execution*, 1989) after the novel by Azerbaijani author Yusif Samedogly (b. 1935), and *Leili ve Medjnun* (1991).

Puppet Theatre

Since the Middle Ages in Azerbaijan, puppet shows such as *Godu-godu*, *Shakh Selim* and *Kilimarasy* were widely staged. Puppets made out of rags or wood, or finger-puppets, were used and some of these shows are still presented at folk events today.

In 1931, through the initiative of actor Molla Aga Bebirli (1905–70), the Gosudarstvenny Kukolny Teatr dlia Detei (State Puppet Theatre for Children) was founded in Baku. In its early repertoire were fairytales such as *Ali-baba and the Forty Thieves* and *Aladdin's Magic Lamp* as well as *Gadji Gara* by M.F. Akhundov and *The Dead* by Mamedkulizade. From 1941 to 1945, the troupe began touring as an agitprop type theatre for young people. From the mid-1960s, when a permanent theatre was opened, adaptations and original plays from national Azerbaijani folklore were produced.

Namik Agaev, the theatre's principal director since 1987, quite often uses an actor-puppet double on stage. Agaev staged *Bulbul* (*The Nightingale*, 1989) based on Hans Christian Andersen, *Qyrmyzy renqin naqyly* (*The Tale of the Black Colour*, 1991) after a poem by the Azerbaijani classic writer Nizami (twelfth century) and *Pari Gjadu* (*The Witch*, 1988) by A. Akhverdiev.

In 1990, the Buta Puppet Theatre premièred in Paris *Arshin mal alan* after an operetta by Gadjibekov. The theatre, headed by Tarlan Gorchiev (b. 1953), used a combination of hyper-naturalistic aesthetics in the miniature space of a marionette theatre. The result was a lyrical musical comedy which created an unexpected effect of ironic distance and nostalgia.

There is no special institution for training puppeteers in Azerbaijan, nor is there an established system for training technical staff for puppet theatre. The majority of directors and actors, as a result, adapt their conventional theatre training. The deep-rooted folk background in this field is still being explored and is predetermining further development of the form.

Design

The stylistic search of theatre designers in Azerbaijan for years followed the directions of the Soviet Union. Until the 1960s, the visual designs did not go beyond decorative painted back curtains, lifelike costumes and a naive stage illusion recreating specific locations. These were the boundaries of the aesthetics within which the first professional Azerbaijani theatre designer Rustam Mustafaev (1910–40) worked. Such aesthetics were dominant in practically all theatres in Azerbaijan in the post-World War II period. They reached their conclusions and exhaustion in the theatre works of Nusret Fatullaev (1925–88), who worked with Iskenderov at GAT.

On the stage, Fatullaev called for precisely built architectural recreations, pieces designed for a single observation point and the illusion of perspective. His work was meticulous in both sets and costumes. At the same time, he created a stage space filled with ornament. With the director's predetermined frontal compositions and one-dimensional blocking (often played on the apron) anything mimetic was transformed into pathos and truth became stylized 'truthfulness'. This need to create illusion on stage was caused by the dominating ideology, in which realism was a panacea for fighting bourgeois formalism. Iskenderov and Fatullaev, at the same time, were actually trying to destroy the 'fourth wall' illusion, appealing to the audience's perception, which identified itself not so much with the general atmosphere of the stage but with the nicely ornamented words of pathos.

In the 1960s, when Tofik Kiazymov came to GAT, the theatre's designers were challenged with scenographic tasks rather than mimetic-decorative ones. The artist-decorator became the artist-scenographer and these tendencies began to spread to other Azerbaijani theatres.

The scenography of Elchin Aslanov in *The Dead* was the first to destroy the frame of illusionism. The stage itself showed its bareness, first, through the elimination of the painted backdrop, and second, by baring the theatrical machinery itself. The stage set became meaningful rather than illustrative. A tombstone became part of a house wall; two places of action became one, underlining the inseparability of life and death. The design became flexible thanks to the clever use of lighting; it 'acted' together with the actors. Frightening empty spaces emerged on this bare stage, all creating an atmosphere of uneasiness, alertness and fear.

Director Kiazymov and designer Aslanov blasted away the customary and the established from within. It was probably for those reasons that *The Dead* turned out to be a strange spectacle, both to audiences and to the more orthodox and dogmatic theatre critics. The first thaw was, however, irreversible and was an important part of the process of freeing stage design from its ideologically loaded mimetic function.

Azerbaijani scenography developed further in the work of Elchin Mamedov (b. 1946). Mamedov arranges the space for his shows metaphorically. Using most often softly faded

Elchin Aslanov's design for Tofik Kiazymov's 1967 Azerbaijan Academic Drama Theatre production of Djalil Mamedkulizade's *The Dead*.

colours, variations of light, textured costumes, and collages of objects, he focuses all of it on the metaphor. In *The Concourse of the Insane*, he created a two-level construction made of white painted beams, all wrapped in a cobweb, out of which characters struggle to free themselves. In *Danabash kendin mektebi* (*The School of Maktabash Village* by Mamedkulizade, directed by Neimatov), a miniaturized model of a village is built on the stage, creating an overall strangeness. In *Juhulama* (*Before You Go to Sleep* by Aslanov, directed by Neimatov) the stage set is surreal: a combination of a doctor's office and a shed for cattle. While creating these designs,

Mamedov is also often being ironic towards his objects.

The style of Diaghilev's *Russian Seasons* was incorporated by painter Torgul Narimanbekov (b. 1930) into his designs for the ballet *Thousand and One Nights*. The stage was framed by a brightly decorative and colourfully sophisticated back curtain, inside which was the magic world of Scheherezade's tales. The dancers' costumes were also designed by the artist in the same style as painted stage decorations. Overall, it created a visual environment which, in a sense, predetermined the musical and choreographic solutions.

Theatre Space and Architecture

All theatres in Azerbaijan are Italian-style proscenium arch buildings. GAT's stage measures 12 by 22 metres, the Musical Comedy Theatre 13 by 20 metres and the Opera and Ballet 12 by 18 metres. On occasion these theatres are also used for social events, meetings, conferences or even congresses.

Technically, most theatres are very poor:

there are no elevators beneath stages, no electronic equipment and limited lighting and sound capabilities. Many theatres – including GAT – are currently undergoing reconstruction.

This lack of difference in theatre buildings is, in fact, slowing down the development of theatre aesthetics today. Nevertheless, attempts are made. The Theatre Juk, for instance, has practically destroyed the boundaries of the Italian stage box in its productions, and its designer-scenographer (Rashid Sherif, b. 1953)

artificially recreates a 'theatre-under-the-tent' atmosphere.

Training

The only institution that provides theatre training in Azerbaijan is the Azerbaijani State University for the Arts, which from 1923 to 1945 functioned as the Baku Theatre Technical School, and from 1945 to 1990 as the Azerbaijani State Institute for the Arts. Acting students are trained in the Stanislavski system. Upon graduation, students receive diplomas and are assigned to one of the state-owned theatres.

In the past, directors' training included a two-year apprenticeship in Moscow or St Petersburg. The country's independence may broaden the choice of countries in which theatre students can train. There are no alternative theatre schools in Azerbaijan.

Criticism, Scholarship and Publishing

There are three major centres for theatre research in Azerbaijan: the department of theatre and cinematography at the Institute for Architecture and Arts of the Academy of Sciences of Azerbaijan, the Faculty of the History of Theatre at the Institute for the Arts of the University of the Arts, and the Theatre Museum.

There are no special theatre periodicals in Azerbaijan. There is an arts magazine, *Gobustan*, which regularly publishes materials on theatre. Also publishing occasional articles are newspapers *Madanijjat* (*Culture*) and *Adabijjat gazeti* (*Literary Gazette*). Other periodicals publish theatre reviews.

When surveying this situation, one must take into account the fact that the educational tendencies in Azerbaijani theatre have long been state controlled, while all aspects of social life have been extremely ideologized. Both have had tremendous impact on theatre research and theatre critics. As a result, practically all theatre research is done using the same methodology which supposes that theatre processes do not have their own rules but are always engaged by ideology. It is important to bear this in mind when appraising the works of the major authority in theatre research until the 1970s – Djafar Djafarov (1914–73). Also significant are the works of theatre scholars Gulam Mamedli (b. 1897), Makhmud Allakhverdiev (b. 1931) and Ingilab Kerimov (b. 1931), although most are more descriptive than anything else. In recent years, critics are much more often taking aesthetic viewpoints into account in their work.

The current necessity is to write a new history of Azerbaijani theatre, one that pays more attention to theatre discourse and inner theatre processes (synchrony and diachrony), discovering the hidden and open methods of resisting ideological pressure, analysing the psychology and sociology of audience perception and taking into account the differences in audiences.

There are, however, several useful works on theatre aesthetics and semiotics in Azerbaijan by directors Mekhti Mamedov, Rakhman Badalov (b. 1937) and Niyazi Mekhti (b. 1951).

There is no regular system for theatre criticism in the mass media, although some criticism does exist. Among the critics of note are Ilkham Ragimli (b. 1949), Mariam Ali-zade (b. 1950), Giulrikh Alibekova (b. 1928), Novruz Takhmazov (1947–91) and Aidyn Talybov (b. 1958).

Rakhman Badalov
Translated by Roman Koudriavtsev

Further Reading

Allakhverdiev, Makhmud. *Alaskar Alakbarov: Hajat ve jaradygylygy.* [Alaskar Alakbarov: life and creative journey]. Baku: Azerneshr, 1972. 234 pp.

——. *Azerbaijan halq teatry.* [Azerbaijani folk theatre]. Baku: Maarif, 1978. 233 pp.

Badalov, Rakhman. 'Bashlanqyg'. [The beginning]. *Gobustan* 3 (1980).

Djafarov, Djafar. *Azerbaijan dram teatry, 1873–1941.* [Azerbaijani Drama Theatre, 1873–1941]. Baku: Azerbaijani State Publishers, 1959. 417 pp.

——. *Redjisser sanati: M. Mammadovun jaradygylygy.* [The art of the director: the creative journey of M. Mamedov]. Baku: Azerneshr, 1968. 380 pp.

Ilkham, Ragimli. *Dramaturgija ve teatr.* [Dramaturgy and theatre]. Baku: Ishyg, 1989. 146 pp.

Ingilab, Kerimov. *Stanovleniye i razvitiie Azerbaijanskogo teatra (konietz XIX–nachalo XX veka).* [The genesis and development of Azerbaijani theatre from the nineteenth to the beginning of the twentieth century]. Baku: Elm, 1991. 293 pp.

Mamedov, Mekhti. *Azeri dramaturqijasynyn estetik problemleri.* [Aesthetic problems of Azerbaijani dramaturgy]. Baku: Azerneshr, 1969. 380 pp.

Mekhti, Niyazi. 'Bashlanmamish qundelikelerden parchalar'. [Excerpts from a never-started diary]. *Gobustan* 3 (1990).

——. 'Teatryn semiotikasy'. [The semiotics of theatre]. *Gobustan* 2 (1987).

Memedli, Gulam, ed. *Azerbajgan teatryn salmanesi, 1850–1930.* [Chronicles of Azerbaijani theatre, 1850–1930]. 2 vols. Baku: Azerneshr, 1975 and 1983.

Talybov, Aidyn. 'Nostalgia po rayu'. [Nostalgia for paradise]. *Teatr* 2 (1980).

——. 'Shafiqa Mammadova – Pyrpyz Sona'. [Shafiga Mamedova – dishevelled Sona]. *Gobustan* 3. (1987).

Yusifbeili, Tamilla. *Shekspir na Azerbaijanskoi stzene.* [Shakespeare on the Azerbaijani stage]. Baku: Azerneshr, 1974. 273 pp.

BELARUS

Also known as Belorussia (Byelorussia), Belarus has inherited the state traditions of the Great Lithuanian Principality (from the thirteenth to the sixteenth centuries), the Byelorussian People's Republic (1918) and the Byelorussian Soviet Socialist Republic (1919–91). In 1991, with the dissolution of the USSR, Belarus became an independent parliamentary republic, bordered by Poland, Lithuania, Latvia, Russia and Ukraine.

Situated at the meeting point of the Nieman, West Dvina and Dnieper rivers, Belarus has a territory of some 207,000 square kilometres (79,900 square miles) and a population of just under 10 million. With its capital in Minsk, a city of 1.6 million, the republic contains several different nationalities and ethnic groups. Linguistically, Belarussian and Russian are the major languages, with a minority speaking Polish.

Theatrical traditions in Belarus date back to pre-Christian times with elements still found even today. Prior to Christmas, Easter and other major holidays, for example, bears, cranes and goats are led from village to village as part of ritual celebrations, rounds are danced, specific songs are sung and incantations chanted.

A specific form of folk play – the *batleika* – involved puppet figures and took place before circled altars with the action placed within the two circles. The *batleika* directors (creators and owners of the puppets) showed these plays at fairs, on public squares and even in the homes of princes. Most of the scripts were adaptations of biblical tales such as *Czar Irod* and *Czar Maximilian*. Between the sixteenth and seventeenth centuries, literary dramas and comedies began to appear in church schools along with Mystery plays and interludes. Included among them were various peasant versions of what has come down to us as the Faust story.

By the nineteenth century, Belarussian theatre began to be connected to the national liberation movement and the production of works of art in the Belarussian language. One of the century's outstanding theatrical figures was Vincent Dunin-Martsinkevich (1808–84), a dramatist and director. He created a company from his own serfs and took them to the capital, Minsk, and other cities to perform such works as the comedy *Pinskaia Shliahta* (*The Noblemen from Pinsk*) and the pastoral-opera *Sialianka* (*Peasant Woman*). Both of these scripts are still played in Belarussian theatres.

At the beginning of the twentieth century, Belarussian intellectuals formed a series of amateur dramatic circles and began to produce their own plays such as *Pawlinka* by Yanka Kupala (1882–1942). In 1910, the company of Ignat Buinitsky (1861–1917), a leader of the national liberation movement, became the country's first professional theatre. The company toured both within the region and abroad (playing as far away as St Petersburg and Warsaw) and continued functioning through 1913. In 1917, Buinitsky, along with Flarian Zhdanovich (1884–1942), organized the First Belarussian Drama and Comedy Company. This group formed the base of the Belarussian State Theatre, now officially called the Kupala Belarussian State Academic Theatre and located in Minsk.

Until 1931, the State Theatre was headed by Evstigney Mirovich (1878–1952), an outstanding director, playwright and teacher as well as a proponent of the Russian realist school. He broke from amateurism in his work and filled his productions with popular folk elements and pastoral ethnographic approaches. Combined with psychological realism and impressive scenic design, his productions were immensely popular and he developed a number of important actors.

In the city of Vitebsk, a second professional group was formed in 1926. Called simply the Belarussian State Theatre No. 2 and now known officially as the Kolas Belarussian State Academic Theatre, the company was made up of recent graduates from a special training programme that had been established in Moscow for Belarussian students. The company's early work focused on the romantic style with impressive scenic images, symbols and sculptural design.

Shortly thereafter, still another troupe began which toured widely during the summer. This group was first known as the Belarussian State Theatre No. 3 and eventually based itself in Gomel. Running the new company was Vladislav Galubok (1882–1942), an impressive director, dramatist, actor and artist. It was during the company's first year of operation (1926) that communist authorities banned a performance of Kupala's tragi-comedy, *Tuteishia* (*The Local Folk*), the first time in the Soviet period that socialist dogma interfered with artistic creation. The incident had ramifications and Moscow's attempt to spread Russian culture and traditions within Belarus was perceptibly slowed.

During this period, authorities from Moscow were also attacking what they called 'formalism' in art along with 'bourgeois ideology' and 'cosmopolitanism'. Dramatists were being pressured to write plays with communist heroes who could clearly defeat class enemies. Directors were also pressured to stage them. Through the late 1920s and 1930s, those who did not conform were deported to work camps in Siberia or other areas of northern Russia. By 1937, many of these people had been murdered without trial or judicial inquiry.

Still in the 1920s, a number of revolutionary satire theatres (the so-called *terevsat*) began to appear in Minsk and Vitebsk. In 1931, a professional youth theatre – the Young Spectators' Theatre – was founded and in 1932, a Russian State Dramatic Theatre was started in Bobruysk (the company later moved to Mogilyov, then Grodno; today it is situated in Minsk).

Throughout this period, many smaller cities began to support companies. Municipal troupes were started in Mosyr, Pinsk and Gomel. There was also a Polish State Touring Theatre operating at the time. Between 1926 and 1947 (excluding the years of World War II), there was also a Jewish State Theatre operating in Minsk.

One failed experiment during the 1930s was an attempt to form a series of culturally correct, ideologically based groups in many of the smaller cities, the so-called *kolkhoz-sovkhoz* (theatres on collective farms). But the theatres did not attract many professionals and their low level of performance led to their rapid collapse.

During the war itself, almost all theatres in Belarus were closed. Many companies, in fact, transported their activities to Moscow and other Russian cities which seemed safer. Others were organized into collectives which gave regular shows for the troops. For an extended period during the war, Belarus was occupied by the Nazis and only the National Dramatic Theatre in Minsk was allowed to function. In 1943 in the city of Tomsk, Lev Litvinav (1883–1968) staged Kupala's *Pawlinka* with actors from the First Belarussian State Theatre, one of the theatrical highlights of the difficult war period. Other artists simply perished during this time, including the great Jewish actor-director Mikhail Zoraw (1903–42), who was murdered in the Minsk ghetto.

World War II wreaked unprecedented destruction on Belarus with nearly a quarter of the population lost. Those evacuated from the eastern front and those returning home at the war's conclusion shared one basic interest: a hope for a new and peaceful life free from lawlessness on the one hand and the secret police on the other. Unfortunately, such hopes proved naive. In cultural fields, prohibitions became even more severe. Authorities wanted to see class-conscious heroes on stage at the end of the war. One Belarussian play, Kandrat Krapiva's (1896–1991) *Mili Chalavek* (*The Sweet Man*) was banned because its hero – a rogue seeking a soft life during the war – did not meet official heroic guidelines.

However, many plays were staged which simply reflected the war experience, the struggles against the occupiers with specific acts of heroism. Some were effective dramatically; others were weak. But none of the produced plays was truly able to reflect the horrors of the war and its immediate aftermath. Those that came closest were interpretations of world classics, particularly Shakespeare. In 1946, Litvinav staged a powerful *Romeo and Juliet* which, in the hands of actress Irina Zhdanovich (b. 1906), focused on the power of a young woman in the face of death and destruction. The first Belarussian *Hamlet* was also staged at this time in Vitebsk by the Kolas Theatre's director Valery Bebutav. The script had been translated by Yuri Gawruk (1905–75) who, unfortunately, was serving time in a Russian *gulag*. As a result, his name was included neither in the programme nor on the season schedule.

In 1946, the Central Committee of the All-Union Communist Party was in almost total control of the country and it adopted several lamentable resolutions about art and literature. Among them was the Resolution on Improving the Repertoire for Dramatic Theatres, which had a severe impact right across the USSR. Following this resolution, each state-supported theatre had to produce two or three new plays each year which would further Soviet socio-political goals.

The result was numerous performances about industrial and agricultural workers attempting to meet or exceed quotas. Even in Krapiva's light comedy, *Hto smiajetsa aposhri* (*Whoever Laughs Last*), the situations had to be taken seriously – self-seekers and pseudo-scientists taking control of a science research institute only to be replaced themselves by party functionaries. Neither subject attracted audiences.

By 1953, a production of *King Lear* staged by Vasili Fyodorov (1892–1971) for the Russian State Theatre broke through this style and focused on the nature of hypocrisy and betrayal. This version of the play was punishing those in charge rather than those who followed. It was a clear sign of the times.

Throughout the decade, one could see various ideological approaches influencing theatre production and repertoire. Numerous plays were dealing with the life of Vladimir Lenin and, given the great number of such scripts, became known generally as Leniniana. Most of them distorted or concealed historical truth.

The Jewish State Theatre also suffered during this time as anti-semitism again reared its head in the post-war period. In 1948 in Minsk, a prominent Jewish actor and public figure, Solomon Mikhoels (b. 1890), was murdered. A year later, the State Jewish Theatre was closed down entirely, depriving the country of both its outstanding actors and its unique repertoire of plays – adaptations of Shakespeare such as *The Merchant of Venice* and dramatic versions of stories by such Yiddish writers as Mendel Moikher-Sphorim and Sholom Aleichem.

After the Communist Party Congresses of 1956 and 1959, there were several conscious attempts made to destroy the personality cult of Stalin but, despite some reductions, strong state censorship controlled all results. Socialist-realism released its choke hold on directorial

Boris Platonov as Aesop in Boris Erin's 1957 Kupala Theatre production of G. Figueiredo's *The Fox and the Grapes*.

style but attempts to move toward a more imagistic type of production were still discouraged.

Nevertheless, attempts at change could be detected in such productions as *The Fox and the Grapes*, a script by the Brazilian writer G. Figueiredo staged by Boris Erin (b. 1921). In this play we meet a kind of Aesop figure boldly speaking about spiritual and intellectual freedom. Played by the well-known actor Boris Platonov (1903–67), the character's willingness to die rather than to live the life of a slave immediately attracted audiences. In 1958, Erin staged a Turkish play, Nazim Ahkmet's *He Who Has Been Forgotten*, a realistic examination of moral problems and one of the first plays produced after the war which avoided distorted images and undue exaggeration. A production of Shakespeare's *Antony and Cleopatra* at the Russian State Theatre in 1964 staged by Russian director Vera Redlich took a uniquely personal view of human relations.

By the late 1960s, plays of symbol and paradox, farce and the grotesque began to be seen more and more in productions by younger directors such as Valery Rayevsky (b. 1939) and Boris Lutsenka (b. 1937). Rayevsky later found himself in trouble over a production deemed to be anti-Soviet – Vladimir Voinovich's *Hachu bits sumlennim* (*I Want to be Honest*, 1969). The production was eventually banned. His next production, later that same year, was Brecht's *Mann ist Mann* (*Man is Man*), a Belarussian première. In this production, a clear statement was made about the need to be human and the fact that human destruction simply cannot be justified. Two years later, Rayevsky staged Andrei Makayenak's (1920–82) popular comedy *Tribunal* with Genady Avsyanikaw in the lead role. At the same theatre, Lutsenka staged Makayenak's drama, *Zatsukani Apostal* (*The Hackneyed Apostle*). Both productions, attacking lies and deception, had great success and further established this director's reputation.

The 1970s also saw the production of a number of historical plays on Belarussian themes, some of which had been previously suppressed. Among these were plays by Konstantin Gubarevich (1907–87) – *Brestskaia Krepast* (*The Fortress of Brest*) and *Glavnaia Stavka* (*Central Headquarters*), about World War II and World War I respectively. In 1974, Lutsenka was named director of the State Russian Dramatic Theatre and for his first production staged Shakespeare's *Macbeth* as a study of personal degradation in a violent and evil world. Lutsenka later produced a powerful version of Brecht's *Die Dreigroschenoper* (*The Threepenny Opera*, 1976) and a dramatization of a novel by Alex Adamovich (b. 1927) called *Viartanne ý Khatin* (*Return to Khatin*, 1977), perhaps the first human portrait of the German occupying forces during the war. A similar theme – human struggle in the face of evil – was central to Lutsenka's production of the rarely seen Hungarian classic, Imre Madách's *Tragedy of Man* (1979).

Throughout the 1970s and into the early 1980s, many of these performances were criticized as being ideologically incorrect and contrary to the ideals of socialist art. But, though some of these productions were permitted to tour abroad, Lutsenka himself was not allowed to go with them and in 1980 he was removed from his post as head of the Russian State Theatre.

But Lutsenka had set a personal standard which was followed by many others in the 1970s and 1980s. Rayevsky staged at the Kupala Theatre in Minsk in 1974 a dramatization of Vasil Bykov's (b. 1924) novel *Aposhni Shants* (*The Last Chance*), a presentational piece with the dramatic intensity of a detective story. The same theatre saw a production of poet and dramatist Eugen Shaban's (1936–83)

play *Shrami* (*The Scars*) in 1977. As staged by Andrei Androsic (b. 1941), the play looked at the forbidden topic of black-market dealings. Rayevsky also staged in 1977 *Sviataia Sviatih* (*Holy of Holies*), a play by Ion Drutse (b. 1928) which had previously been banned in Moscow, Kiev and Chişinau.

Another important historical play emerged from the city of Vitebsk, Vladimir Karatkevich's (1930–84) *Vitsebskiya zvani* (*The Bells of Vitebsk*, 1974) about a people's revolt in the seventeenth century against religious as well as political repression. The 1976 success, *Simon-musica* (*Simon the Musician*), after a poem by Jakub Kolas (1882–1956), saw still another move toward non-realistic staging by Mazynsky. The difficult life of the play's young violinist hero became a national symbol of the historic fate of all Belarus.

Another play in the growing non-realistic style was *Solle* (*Salt*) which was to have been produced in 1980 at the Grodno Municipal Dramatic Theatre. The play, warning about the possibilities of ecological catastrophes such as would occur at the Chernobyl nuclear plant, was banned by municipal authorities, apparently because the subject was too controversial.

The plays of Alexei Dudarev (b. 1950) came to national note in the 1980s. Two of his scripts were staged at the Kupala Theatre and the Kolas Theatre in 1983, *Parog* (*The Threshold*) and *Vechar* (*Evening*), plays about the hopeless and uncompromising lives of people living under communism. Rayevsky staged Dudarev's 1984 play, *Radavia* (*The Soldiers*), about military behaviour in World War II.

As the 1980s went on, there were even franker discussions of problems. The destruction of the nation's agriculture by the collectivization of the 1930s was spoken of openly for the first time in Valery Maslyuk's (b. 1953) production of Bykov's *Znak Biadi* (*The Sign of Disaster*) produced in 1985 at the State Russian Dramatic Theatre.

Also in 1985, real social and political change began to be felt in Belarus. Each year thereafter until independence in 1991 showed elements of the changes and new perspectives as playwrights and directors suddenly felt able to speak about any subject from the stage. In 1987, director Mikola Piniguin (b. 1957) warned about the dangers inherent in revolutions in Gorki's *Dzetsi Sontsa* (*Children of the Sun*) at the Kupala Theatre. In Helena Popova's play *Zjitsio Karitsina* (*The Life of Karitsin*, 1986), Piniguin dealt with the moral and spiritual crises

The 1983 Kupala Theatre production of Alexei Dudarev's *Evening*, directed by Boris Erin.

being faced by generations brought up on a Soviet past but who were now contemplating breaking away. Also in tune with the times was Rayevsky's production of *Mudramer* (*Measuring Foolishness*, 1987) by Mikola Matukovsky (b. 1929) which satirized officials who were unwilling to think for themselves.

By the late 1980s and the collapse of the Soviet Union, a new national liberation movement was emerging. The production that most reflected this change in thinking was Piniguin's Kupala Theatre offering of Yevgeny Svarts's parable, *Drakon* (*The Dragon*, 1989) with lyrics by Leonid Dranko-Maysyuk (b. 1958). This witty, bright and sarcastic play called on audiences to do away with the dragon in themselves, to kill off the slave in their nature. In 1990, Piniguin staged Kupala's long-prohibited 1922 play *The Local Folk*. The production utilized the Belarussian *batleika* to tell its tale of an ordinary man caught up in an absurd and changing world. Another play reflecting the rapidly changing social life of the period was *Strastsi pa Audzeiu* (*Audzey's Passions*, 1989) a tale of a peasant trying to come to grips with his life under a collapsing political system. The play was written by Vladimir Butrameyev (b. 1953) and was staged by Rayevsky.

By 1991, Lutsenka re-emerged as artistic director of the State Russian Theatre and quickly began changing it from what it had been into a new cultural centre called Soglasie (Consent). One of its first productions was *Khristos e Antikhrist* (*Christ and Anti-Christ*) after the novel of Dimitri Merezkovski dealing with the nature of evil and the spilling of blood from generation to generation.

Following the declaration of independence by the new Belarussian Republic, one could see a clear desire on the part of theatre artists to experiment with new forms and styles. The New State Theatre Laboratory of Belarussian Drama, an independent stage under the direction of Mazynsky, began its life in 1991 with a series of absurdist plays by completely new writers. Similar experiments were beginning to be seen from other professional groups and even from some newly formed, independent semi-professional companies.

Mikola Piniguin's 1990 Kupala Theatre production of Yanka Kupala's *The Local Folk*, designed by Boris Gerlavan.

Structure of the National Theatre Community

Until the late 1980s, all professional companies in Belarus were considered to be state theatres and were subject to the general directions of the Belarussian Ministry of Culture (Directorate of Theatre and Music). Many of the older companies were being subsidized even before the war and the nationalization of theatres. Among these were the Kupala, the Russian State Theatre, the Belarussian Young Spectators' Theatre, the Young People's Theatre and the State Puppet Theatre, all in Minsk; and the Kolas Theatre in Vitebsk.

Added to this group later on were the State Academic Opera and Ballet Theatre, the State Theatre of Musical Comedy, and the Cinema Actors Theatre Studio. In 1990, two formerly amateur companies were also given state status in the cities of Mosyr and Slonim and in 1992 the People's Theatre of Molodechno became yet another state theatre.

A number of municipalities were also involved in subsidizing their own local companies as well as, in some cases, puppet groups in cities such as Mogilyov, Gomel, Grodno, Brest, Vitebsk, Molodechno and Bobruisk. But even Minsk municipal authorities were involved in supporting theatre groups such as the Minsk Dramatic Theatre which in 1992 added a young people's theatre studio called Where Am I?

Traditionally, artists were offered permanent contracts with wages set by the state which tied them to specific theatres. During the 1990s, this began to change with actors, directors and designers able to move between theatres much more easily and theatres themselves having more independence in setting wages. It was rare for any of the dramatic theatres to have composers or choreographers on their staffs. Instead, these people were hired on a per-production basis.

Most theatres offer from three to eight premières each season with productions usually kept in the repertoire for at least one or two seasons. New plays are seen between twice and four times each month with anywhere from ten to twenty productions usually kept in each theatre's active repertoire.

Tickets have traditionally been sold in blocks through unions, factories and educational institutions with tickets for the state theatres usually being the most expensive – the equivalent of three loaves of bread. Other prices are usually no more than one or two times the price of a film.

The Union of Belarussian Theatre Artists brings together state, studio and amateur groups to deal with issues of mutual interest. In 1992 it was chaired by the playwright Alexei Dudarev. In association with the State Ministry of Culture, the union has hosted a Belarussian National Theatre Festival every three years. In 1991, the union, in association with the Kupala Theatre, hosted an International Festival of Slavic Theatre.

State prizes for theatre are awarded by the Council of Ministers every two years. This same council, in association with the union, gives specific awards every three years to the leading director and designer (the Mirovich Prize); for musical theatre (the Alexandrovskaya Prize); for children's theatre (the Mazalevskaya Prize); for acting (the Buinitsky Prize); and for criticism and scholarship (the Krapiva Prize).

Artistic Profile

Companies

The largest and therefore the best known companies in Belarus are the Kupala, the Russian State Theatre and the State Academic Opera and Ballet Theatre in Minsk, and the Kolas Theatre in Vitebsk. The Minsk Dramatic Theatre is one of the major municipally supported theatres in the country.

Since 1990, a number of independent companies have also come into being, some traditional and some alternative in nature. Most are on a constant search for financial sponsorship. Many evolved from local amateur companies (the best of which were traditionally given the title of People's Theatres) and were often connected to trade unions or businesses.

The best known of the amateur groups are the Pinsk People's Theatre, the Grodno People's Theatre (connected to the Textile Workers' Union), the Krasnopolsky People's Theatre, the Borisov People's Theatre and the Minsk People's Theatre (connected to the Tractor Workers' Union).

From 1985 on, a number of theatre studios began to appear across the country, semi-professional groups which were funded by various commercial enterprises and which offered both productions and training. Many of the studios only had a short lifetime but others have survived and continue to remain popular. Among these are Act, Jest, the Historical Drama Studio and Abzats (all in Minsk) and the Experimental Theatre in Mozyr.

An Association of Studio Theatres emerged in the late 1980s and has been sponsoring an international festival each Christmas.

Dramaturgy

Modern Belarussian dramatic literature has generally followed European and Euro-American models. From the nineteenth century – starting with Vincent Dunin-Martsinkevich – most playwrights worked in a realistic mode focusing on language, character and the development of recognizable national heroes.

Few national works have stood the test of time; those that have were discussed in the opening section of this article. Among the significant writers discussed in that section are Yanka Kupala, Kandrat Krapiva, Konstantin Gubarevich, Andrei Makayenak, Eugen Shaban, Vladimir Karatkevich and Alexei Dudarev.

In an effort to further develop the dramatic form in Belarus, a playwrights' studio called Volnaya Scena (Free Stage) was begun in 1991. Working with young dramatists, the studio has produced first plays by a number of young authors. Most of these early plays, it might be noted, have been written in an absurdist style.

One playwright showing special promise is Ivan Chigrinav (b. 1934), author of the 1992 success *Zvon ne Malitva* (*Bells, Not Prayers*) produced at the Kupala Theatre.

Directors, Directing and Production Styles

For a discussion of directing, see previous material in **Artistic Profile** and the opening, historical section.

Music Theatre

The roots of Belarussian musical theatre can be found in pre-Christian rituals and other seasonal dramatic celebrations. Most included musical accompaniment. Folk plays (batleika) also included music.

More formal productions, operas in fact, date back to the seventeenth century when large musical plays (often Italian in origin) were done in castles and in amateur peasant productions. A more national repertoire began to be developed by Stanislav Manyushka (1819–72) whose best known opera is The Idyll, with a libretto by Dunin-Martsinkevich. The opera was produced in Minsk on three different occasions in the 1850s.

During the first decades of the twentieth century, many amateur groups staged musicals of various sorts. Full Belarussian operas began to be produced in the 1920s, among them Taras on Parnassus (1927) by composer Mikalaj Aladav (1890–1972). But a lack of suitable playhouses kept the form from developing significantly. This was corrected to some extent in 1930 with the opening of a Belarussian Studio of Opera and Ballet. The first productions staged were Rimsky-Korsakov's Zolotoi petushok (The Golden Cockerel) and Bizet's Carmen.

In 1933, the State Theatre of Opera and Ballet opened in Minsk with a repertoire of Italian, French and Russian works. Over the years, national operas were added into the repertoire including Mikhas Padgorny (1939) by Eugene Tsikotsky (1893–1970), U pushchah Palesia (In the Forests of Palesia, 1939) by Anatoli Bagatyrvov (b. 1913), and Kvetka shchastia (The Flower of Happiness, 1940) by Alexei Turankov (1886–1958). In these works, the musical and visual sources were clearly to be found in Belarussian folk music and visual art forms.

But even operas in the 1940s and 1950s had to deal with the rigours and limitations of being socialist in nature and had to follow Soviet prescriptions. This led to a significant reduction in their style and number.

In 1941, the war intervened to close down the State Theatre of Opera and Ballet. Reopened in December 1944 with an opera about a female partisan called Alesia, the State Theatre went on to produce a number of original works known mainly for their literary qualities and romantic style. Among the best of these from the mid-1940s to 1970 were Castus Kalinovsky (1947)

by Dimitri Lukas (1911–79); Nadezhda Durova (1956) by Anatoli Bogatyrov; Koluchaia Ruza (The Thorny Rose, 1960) by Yuri Semenyaka (b. 1925); Kali apadaelistva (When the Leaves Fall, 1968) by Semenyaka; Andrei Kastsenya (1970) by Aladov; and Zorka Venera (The Star Venera, 1970), again by Semenyaka.

The most consistent director of traditional operas over this period was the Russian, Boris Pokrovski.

Musically, Belarussian opera has been maturing over the years, intensifying the internal polyphonic structure and adding symphonic and even jazz elements. Composers and librettists were also turning to more dramatic subject matter, much of it with allegorical and often political meanings. These have included such works as Giordano Bruno (1977) by Sergei Kortes (b. 1935), Sivaia Legenda (The Grey Legend, 1978) by Dimitri Smolski (b. 1937) and Stsezkai zitsia (By the Path of Life, 1980) by Henryk Wagner (b. 1922).

Even directors were beginning to change their thinking about stage space. Semyon Shtein (b. 1928) staged a version of Prokofiev's War and Peace utilizing not only the stage but also the entire auditorium and had the chorus and soloists singing from various off-stage locations. In 1990, Shtein premièred Prokofiev's opera Magdalene as part of an international festival devoted to Prokofiev's works.

In 1991, the composer Sergei Kortes became the company's artistic director and a new emphasis began to be placed on further developing a national operatic repertoire. Produced were new works by Victor Soltan (b. 1953) and Andrei Bandarenka (b. 1955); a Children's Opera Studio was also formed.

Outside Minsk, the Musical and Drama Theatre of Bobruisk has been regularly staging musical comedies and operettas since its founding in 1958. In 1965, the company was reorganized and became the Mogilyov Municipal Musical Comedy Theatre with a repertoire of classical operettas and some not very successful musical comedies by Belarussian composers. In 1970, the company moved to Minsk where it became known as the Belarussian State Musical Comedy Theatre. Among the successful national operettas it produced have been works by Semenyaka, Rygor Surus (b. 1942), Vladimir Kondrusevich (b. 1949) and Andrei Mdivani (b. 1937).

Dance Theatre

Dance is another of Belarus's ancient arts with roots dating back to pre-history and connections linking dance forms to rituals and the dances of wandering performers. The first ballet companies were made up of feudal peasants and were formed in the seventeenth and eighteenth centuries at the palaces of princes and other feudal estates. The most famous were in the towns of Shklov, Slonim and Grodno.

With the most important dance companies based in St Petersburg and Warsaw, it was an artistic coup to have in the city of Vitebsk in the mid-nineteenth century a ballet company headed by the Polish ballet master Michal Pion. Over the next decades, dance became a significant part of the plays of Belarussian writers such as Dunin-Martsinkevich and Buinitsky.

The opening of the Belarussian State Opera and Ballet Theatre in 1920 included the creation of a ballet troupe under the leadership of ballet master and teacher Konstantin Alexyutovich (1884–1943). The new troupe set professional standards for the art for the first time in the republic and offered a repertoire primarily of classical ballets.

The first Belarussian ballet – *Salavei* (*The Nightingale*) – was created in 1939 by Alexyutovich to the music of Mikhail Kroshner (1900–42). Its subject matter was the peasant revolts that took place between 1860 and 1863.

In 1949, Muller staged *Kniaz-Vozera* (*The Lake Prince*) to music by Vasili Zalataryov (1872–1964). The work was notable for Muller's attempt to combine the principles of classical ballet with the choreography of folk dance forms. Over the next decade, there would be various attempts at reconciling the two forms and producing ballets on contemporary subjects. One could see this even in 1992 in Andrei Mdivani's ballet *Ragnega*, a work dealing with national history over a thousand-year period.

Two of the most popular composers for ballet during this time were Henryk Wagner (*Padstaunaia Niavesta*/*The False Fiancée*, 1958; *Sviatlo e tseni*/*Light and Shade*, 1963; *Paslia balu*/*After the Ball*, 1973) and Eugen Glebov (b. 1929), composer of *Mara* (*The Dream*, 1961), *Alpiiskaia Balada* (*Alpine Ballad*, 1967) and *Vibranitsa* (*The Chosen Woman*, 1969).

For the most part, the production of ballets during the 1950s and 1960s was done in strict conformity with Soviet guidelines on art and following the traditions of the Russian dance school.

It was Valentin Yelizarov who first broke with these traditions introducing modern dance and even avant-garde techniques in performances. In Yelizarev's most important works – *Carmen Suite* (1974), *Creation of the World* (1976) and *Til Eulenspiegel* (1978) – stage design and lighting became active elements in the works and there was an extraordinary unity with the music. He 'unshoed' the dancers, giving them both external and internal freedom to express the imaginative essences of their characters and to help them connect with audiences through what can be described as a unique ballet plasticity.

In addition to the State Ballet company, there are many smaller professional dance troupes and even amateur dance companies now working across the country. Most of them offer dance concerts on an occasional basis. The most important of these groups are the state ensemble Khoroshky, the Gomel Popular Ensemble of Song and Dance, the Brest ensemble Radoste (Joy) and the Grodno ensemble, Ranica (Morning).

There is also one pantomime theatre of note – Ruh (Movement) – which leans toward the avant-garde in its movement work and which has most often performed on the stage of the Belarussian State Philharmonic Concert Hall.

Theatre for Young Audiences

The first attempts to create a Belarussian theatre for young audiences took place in the early 1920s when the Young Spectator Company began operation in Minsk. Lasting from 1924 to 1926, the company focused on dramatizations of school classics.

In 1931, a new group in Minsk calling itself the Belarussian Young Spectators' Theatre came into being and operated for the next decade. Closing down in 1941, it reopened in 1956 as the Belarussian Republic's Young Spectators' Theatre with most of its actors and directors being recent graduates of the Theatre Institute. The company's post-war director was Lyubov Masalevskaya (1903–64); in her desire to rid the company of plays that simplified conflict and talked down to audiences she sought more recognizable Belarussian characters and situations where folk forms could be used. Her most important productions in this style were plays by dramatist Ivan Kozel (1928–70) such as *Paparats-kvetka* (*The Fern*, 1956) and *Nad hvaliami Serebrank* (*Over the Waves of Serebranka*, 1961).

Despite such exceptions, the company struggled for many years to find its own style using many different directors in the process. Throughout this exploration it was hampered by the need to meet Soviet aesthetic demands for such things as the obligatory triumph of positive heroes and other elements of socialist-realism. Among its successes in this exploration was Nikolai Sheyko's (b. 1936) production of the Russian play by Alexander Volodin, *S Lubimimi ne Rastavaitece* (*Do not Part with Loved Ones*), in 1972. In this production, Sheyko/Volodin

enlisted the audience's help in reflecting on the meaning of life, society and moral criteria.

In 1991, director Modest Abramov (b. 1942) took charge of the company seeking to transform the group into a cultural centre for young people, a place where the performance was just one aspect of its overall work. To this end, courses have been offered and productions have been staged dealing with the skills of those involved in the theatrical process from actors and directors to playwrights and backstage personnel. Shows in this style have been written by Svetlana Alexievich (b. 1948), Vladimir Mashkov (b. 1938) and Arthur Volsky (b. 1924). An improvised performance called *Super Sha* (*Super School Jokes*, 1992) was a popular series of grotesque miniatures, while *The Three Little Pigs* was produced only in English and done for classes studying that language.

From the 1950s to the 1990s, every company receiving state support was asked to stage at least one children's production each season. Unfortunately, these productions are often done without sufficient rehearsal, with young directors and with very small budgets. Nevertheless, two or three such shows are done annually by most of the companies and manage to find audiences.

Puppet Theatre

Belarus's national theatrical folk form – the *batleika* – was in its earliest manifestation essentially a puppet play. Despite this long and popular tradition, however, professional puppet troupes did not come into being until 1938 when the Belarussian State Puppet Theatre was opened in Gomel. During World War II, the company moved to the city of Dushanbe in Tadjikistan, but returned to Gomel to continue its productions as well as its training programmes.

In 1950, the State Puppet Theatre moved to Minsk but, without a permanent home of its own, it established several small troupes which toured regularly throughout Belarus doing productions in both the Belarussian and Russian languages. Run by director Arkadi Arkadiev (1897–1969), the company essentially produced dramatized fairytales such as *Dzed e zorau* (*The Old Man and the Crane*, 1952) by Vitaly Volski (1901–88). The company also began to stage occasional productions for adults.

In the 1960s, director Anatoli Lelavski (b. 1923) began to move in new directions, arguing that the puppet should not merely be a miniature actor. He argued for the artistic recognition of puppets as having their own logic rather than human logic. The result was a series of new performances with the puppets capable of being either realistic or not, psychologically true or grotesque in style. Among his major successes were *Srebranaia Tabakerka* (*The Silver Snuffbox*, 1961) by Zmitrok Byadulya (1896–1941), *Skazi svaio imia soldat* (*What's Your Name, Soldier?*, 1975) by Anatoli Viartinski (b. 1931), and two shows for adults – *Bozestvennaia comedia* (*The Divine Comedy*, 1971) by Isidore Shtock and *Levsha* (*Lefty*, 1978), after a story by Nikolai Leskov.

The Puppet Theatre finally obtained its own theatre in 1966 and this allowed it to develop its scenographic explorations. As well, the company began to include live actors in its productions. One of its successes in this area was a

1980 adaptation of Hans Christian Andersen's *The Nightingale* staged by Alexei Lelyavski (b. 1958). Lelyavski subsequently staged actor-puppet productions of *The Good Soldier Shweyk* in 1981 and Bulgakov's *Master and Margarita* in 1988. A number of Belarussian plays and stories have also been staged in this popular style.

One of the unique experiments of Lelyavski and the company has been the staging of full puppet operas, including Jules-Émile-Frédéric Massenet's *Cinderella* in 1992.

Since the 1960s, other state puppet companies have come into being in Brest, Mogilyov and Grodno. In 1986, a company called Lyalka (Doll) began operating in Vitebsk performing only Belarussian plays in the Belarussian language. In 1991, a municipal theatre was opened in Molodechno called simply Batleika.

The First Biennial Festival of Belarussian Puppet Theatre was held in Minsk in 1981; after 1983 it became an international festival.

There are, as well, some 600 amateur puppet companies in Belarus and a number of amateur puppetry festivals.

Design

Until World War II, design in Belarus meant scenic painting, and scenic painting (along with costume design) was basically realistic and illustrative in nature. Designers were considered technicians rather than creators and rarely had the opportunity to do anything other than what the director wished them to do.

In the decades since World War II, this has changed in great measure with designers now recognized as creative artists on their own, equal to playwrights and directors. Perhaps the first national designer to assert his independence was Armen Grigorianz (1918–76) at the Russian Dramatic Theatre and at the Kupala Theatre. In his best work, he refused to recognize realistic proportions and sizes, choosing instead to arrange his materials symbolically and imaginatively, often giving them a monumental, sculptural quality. His productions in this style have ranged from *King Lear* to Örkény's *Cat's Cradle* to Nazim Ahkmet's *Zabiti usimi* (*Completely Forgotten*).

Another important scenographer is Boris Gerlavan (b. 1937) whose work is distinguished by his always original use of scenic space. His designs for the Kupala Theatre have been consistently imaginative in their thinking – a swaying earth in Shakespeare's *The Tempest* (1986); a walled amphitheatre made from government desks in Matukovsky's *Mudramer*; and a church formed from candelabras for Chekhov's *Three Sisters*. Gerlavan works mostly with light, often changing it radically within each performance.

Alexander Salavyov (b. 1926) works at the Kolas Theatre and tends to combine picturesque and graphic principles in his scenic work. Often resembling paintings – light and shadow, subtle combinations of colours – his work can be described as scenographic impressionism. His work has been particularly effective in historical dramas and romantic plays such as a 1965 production of Raynis's *Vei Veterok* (*Blow, Breeze*) and plays by Karatkevich.

Theatre Space and Architecture

The only genuinely old theatre buildings still standing in Belarus are the theatre in Grodno (built in 1780), the Kupala Theatre in Minsk (1890) and the Mogilyov Theatre (1888). All are beautiful, cosy proscenium houses of about 500 seats with one or two balconies.

Of the remaining theatre buildings, most have been built since 1945. The State Russian Dramatic Theatre is actually older having been reconstructed from a former synagogue.

Most of these are also proscenium houses with one or more balconies and stages 12 to 15 metres wide, 18 metres deep and up to 10 metres high. In the Soviet period, most of these theatres also had to do service as congress and conference halls and were relatively large –

between 700 and 1,000 seats. It can also be said that most of them were built with more than a tinge of pomposity. Technically, few have more than a basic turntable stage, basic elevator devices and generally outdated lighting.

The largest of Belarus's theatres is the State Opera and Ballet Theatre with 1,200 seats. The smallest theatres are the studios which rarely have fewer than 200 seats.

Training

Formal theatre training existed in Belarus during the seventeenth and eighteenth centuries but by the nineteenth century had disappeared almost entirely. The tradition was re-established in the 1920s when both the Kupala and Kolas theatres set up training programmes for their actors. Both were based on training programmes already in existence in Moscow and St Petersburg.

In 1938, the Minsk Theatre School was established with two programmes – acting and dance. The war closed the school in 1941 but in 1945, dance programmes were re-established at the Ballet and Opera Theatre and at the Minsk Dance School.

The Belarussian State Theatrical Institute began soon after. In the early 1990s, under the name Theatrical Arts Institute, it was training actors, directors, stage and film designers, theatre critics and, since 1975, puppeteers.

The Minsk Institute of Culture also trains directors for amateur groups.

Virtually all performance training is based on the principles of Stanislavski although elements of the work of Meyerhold, Vakhtangov and Tairov have also been added.

Criticism, Scholarship and Publishing

Theatrical research and criticism evolved in the late nineteenth and early twentieth centuries in Belarus and was generally connected to the national liberation movement. Among the first to write theatrical criticism and publish in the field were well-known figures from the movement such as Yanka Kupala, Zmitrok Byadulya, Maxim Garetsky (1883–1939) and Alexander Vaznesenski (1888–1966).

By 1932, a weekly newspaper *Litaratura e Mastatstva* (*Literature and Art*) began to appear, carrying regular criticism of theatrical events as well as discussions on culture generally and news of cultural events.

In 1957, the Belarussian Academy of Science created a department of theatre and cinema (from 1977, simply the department of theatre) as part of the academy's Institute for Art Criticism, Ethnography and Folklore. Since that time, this department has been the centre for the most advanced studies of theatre history and theory. The department also contains a valuable archive of the history of Belarussian theatre and regularly publishes theatrical studies and monographs.

For many years, the director of theatre research at the Academy of Science's theatre department was Vladimir Niafiod (b. 1916) and much of the material published in the 1950s and 1960s was defined by party ideology rather than independent scholarship. A three-volume *History of Belorussian Theatre*, for example, was sharply criticized for its clear bias.

During the 1970s and 1980s, more independent studies were published. Among them were an examination of Belarussian theatre between the sixteenth and nineteenth centuries by Yuri Barishev (b. 1930) and studies of Belarussian dramaturgy by Stefan Lavshuk (b. 1944).

Almost all newspapers in the country today regularly publish reviews and reports about theatrical premières and since 1983 the magazine *Mastatstva Belarusi* (*Belarussian Art*) has offered more in-depth reports. In 1992, the magazine changed its name to *Mastatstva*.

One of several new publications to appear in the 1990s was *Teatralnaia Belarus* (*Theatrical Belarus*) which regularly publishes plays, opinions, reviews, debates, reminiscences and historical research along with brief information on premiéres across the country.

Two publishing houses regularly publish theatrical books and studies – Navuka e Tehnika (Science and Technology), connected to the Academy of Science, and Mastatskaia Litaratura (Art and Literature).

Vankarem Nikiforovich

(See also USSR)

Further Reading

Aliahnovich, Frantsishak. *Belaruski Teatr.* [Belarussian theatre]. Vilnia, 1924. 114 pp.

Barishev, Yuri. *Musikalni Teatr Belorusii.* [Belarussian music theatre]. Minsk: Navuka e Tehnika, 1990. 382 pp.

——, *Teatralnaia cultura Belorusii XVIII Stoletia.* [The theatrical culture of Belarus in the eighteenth century]. Minsk: Navuka e Tehnika, 1992. 296 pp.

——, and Oleg Sannikov. *Belaruski Narodni Teatr 'Batleika' e Iago Uzaiemasuviazi z Ruskim 'Viartepam' e Polskim 'Shopkai'.* [The Belarussian 'batleika' folk theatre and its intercommunication with Russian 'viartep' and Polish 'shopka']. Minsk: V-va Akademii Nauk BSSR, 1963. 42 pp.

Churko, Ulia. *Belaruski Balenti Teatr.* [Belarussian dance theatre]. Minsk: Navuka e Tehnika, 1983. 286 pp.

Gistoria Belaruskaga Teatra. [History of Belarussian theatre]. 3 vols. Minsk: Navuka e Tehnika, 1983–7.

Hrestamatia pa Gistorii Belaruskaga Teatra e Dramaturgii. [A reader on the history of Belarussian theatre and drama]. 2 vols. Minsk: Visheishaia Shkola, 1975.

Kaladzinski, Mikhail. *Teatr Lialek Savetskai Belarusi.* [The puppet theatre of Soviet Belarus]. Minsk: Navuka e Tehnika, 1976. 144 pp.

Narodni Teatr. [Folk theatre]. Minsk: Navuka e Tehnika, 1983. 512 pp.

Nekrashevich, A. *Belaruski Pershi Dziarzauni Teatr.* [The first Belarussian State Theatre]. Minsk: Beldziarzvidavetstva, 1930. 28 pp.

Niafiod, Vladimir. *Belaruski Teatr: Naris Gistori.* [The Belarussian theatre: a historical essay]. Minsk: Vidavetstva AN BSSR, 1959. 900 pp.

——. *Gistoria Belaruskaga Teatra.* [History of the Belarussian theatre]. Minsk: Visheishaia Shkola, 1982. 543 pp.

Pashkin, Yuri. *Russkii Dramaticheskii Teatr v Belorussii XIX veka.* [Russian drama theatre in Belarus in the nineteenth century]. Minsk: Navuka e Tehnika, 1980. 216 pp.

Sabaleuski, Anatol. *Belaruskaia Savetskaia Drama.* [Belarussian Soviet drama]. 2 vols. Minsk: Belarus, 1969. 143 pp., and Minsk: Mastatskaia Literatura, 1979. 220 pp.

Seduro, Vladimir. *Belorussian Theatre and Drama.* New York: Research Program on the USSR, 1955. 517 pp.

Stelmah, V. *Shliahi Beloruskogo Teatru.* [The ways of Belarussian theatre]. Kiev: Mistetsvo, 1964. 172 pp.

Vazniasenski, A. *Drugi Belaruski Dziarzauni Teatr.* [The second Belarussian State Theatre]. Minsk: Beldziarzvidavetstva, 1929. 25 pp.

BELGIUM

A small federalized country with a constitutional monarchy in northwestern Europe, Belgium has a land area of 30,500 square kilometres (11,700 square miles). Belgium is comprised of a Dutch-speaking region (Flanders, with a population of some 6 million); a French-speaking region (Wallonia, with a population of 3.5 million) and a small German-speaking minority in the east; and the officially bilingual capital of Brussels (with a population of about 1 million). Apart from the national government, each region (Flanders, Wallonia and Brussels) has its own government with regional authority.

Since the early 1960s, each region has managed its own cultural life as part of the federalization process. Each community has a totally separate minister and budget for culture and the theatre activities taking place in the different regions of the country are essentially independent of one another. There is one exception – the National Opera in Brussels, known as le Théâtre de la Monnaie in French and as De Munt (The Mint) in Flemish. It is one of the very few artistic institutions in Belgium to remain national.

Historically, Belgium was part of the Austrian Empire from 1713 after having been under Spanish rule for more than a hundred years. In 1797 France annexed the country. After Napoleon's defeat in 1815, Belgium and the Netherlands were set up as a united kingdom. Some Belgians were unhappy about this union and on 4 October 1830 they declared their independence.

In May 1940, shortly after the beginning of World War II, Belgium found itself unable to resist a German invasion and the country came under German occupation for four years.

Prosperity and high employment marked the post-war years, a period in which the two major linguistic groups grew more autonomous.

The French-Speaking Theatre

It was only after World War II that Belgium's French-speaking theatre gained the foundations for its institutional structure and a truly independent organization. Until 1940 the greater part of professional theatrical life in Brussels and the main cities of Wallonia consisted of tours by French companies or of French actors who were engaged to occupy the leading parts. In contrast, Belgian playwrights went to Paris in search of success. However, this was also the period in which Belgium knew its greatest playwrights – Maurice Maeterlinck (1862–1949), Fernand Crommelynck (1886–1970) and Michel de Ghelderode (1898–1962).

There were certainly striking attempts to create high-quality theatre in Brussels before this period. Among these were Jules Delacre's (1883–1954) Théâtre du Marais (1922–6). Delacre was a disciple of Jacques Copeau and a friend of Louis Jouvet. There was also the Théâtre du Rataillon (1930–5) of Albert Lepage (1895–1986), who was linked aesthetically to the Autant-Lara Laboratoire d'Art et Action in Paris. For certain periods the Théâtre du Parc came to the fore, for example at the end of the 1930s when a Belgian company developed under the control of Adrien Mayer (1899–1980). Opera also knew its periods of glory – for example, the Théâtre de la Monnaie played certain operas by Wagner before they appeared in Paris, and a few years later *Wozzeck* and *Salome*. Pre-war Brussels also enjoyed a blooming of vaudeville and music hall theatre in many locations, the last witness of which was the Théâtre de la Gaîté which closed in the 1970s.

The war years, with their prohibition of tours by French companies, encouraged the development of local theatre. After Fernand Piette (1907–78) and his Théâtre de l'Équipe, which was touring the country well before the war, Jacques Huisman (b. 1910) created the travelling company of the Comédiens routiers, modelling himself on the Frenchman Léon Chancerel. In 1943 Claude Étienne (1917–92) founded the Rideau de Bruxelles, which he managed until his death.

In 1948 the state organized the activity of the main companies in a system involving subsidies and certain conditions which have changed since. It created the Théâtre National and appointed Jacques Huisman as manager, a position he held until 1985. For a long time this institution benefited from half of all subsidies allocated to the theatre and was given the vast task of popularizing the theatre, both in Brussels and the provinces. The Théâtre National was a central element in the country's theatrical infrastructure and produced a repertoire consisting essentially of the classics, of a number of great modern authors, or of plays dealing with major ethical questions or sociological problems. National playwrights were rarely produced in this important theatre. Instead, they could mainly be found in the Rideau de Bruxelles. The Rideau's manager, Claude Étienne, produced several playwrights from the immediate post-war generation by applying a commissioning policy, and in addition performed foreign plays, showing a marked taste for contemporary English-language drama.

The other major professional companies of the 1950s in Brussels were the Théâtre du Parc, with an essentially traditional approach; the Théâtre des Galeries, more centred on light comedy, and with a contemporary repertoire; and the Théâtre de Poche, created in 1953 by Roger Domani (b. 1926). In Liège, the major groups were the Théâtre du Gymnase and the Théâtre de l'Étuve, which both tended to follow contemporary developments.

This period in general can be characterized by the priority of giving domestic employment to actors and other theatre people. This was accompanied by an aesthetic approach

Jacques Delcuvellerie's 1983 Groupov collective creation of *Il ne voulait pa dire qu'il voulait le savoir malgré tout.*

emphasizing readability, in line with the task of permanent education that the state encouraged, and in line with the frequently semi-professional origins of the companies. These policies led to a widening of the public to include the middle classes. Other common features of the theatre during these years were the low level of subsidization and the dominance of neo-classical aesthetics. This approach gradually created a gap between French-speaking Belgium and theatrical developments taking place during the same period in both France and Germany.

New wave theatre, or *le jeune théâtre* as it was called in French, emerged in Brussels during the 1960s. In 1963 Albert-André L'Heureux (b. 1946) founded the Théâtre de l'Esprit frappeur, which encouraged a repertoire marked by the Theatre of the Absurd, staged in a manner that was simultaneously irreverent and extremely artistic. Henri Chanal (1936–69) played a major if brief role in the renewal of theatrical forms, partly by his choice of repertoire (contemporary Belgian playwrights).

The gradual arrival of the new wave in the 1970s not only generated native playwrights very slowly but also changed the institutional situation. Works based on the absurd and the explosion of literary forms gave birth from 1970 onwards to the texts of Frédéric Baal (b. 1941) and his experimental Laboratoire Vicinal. Also in 1970, Marc Liebens's (b. 1937) Théâtre du Parvis opened the way towards a *théâtre critique*, influenced by the heritage of Brecht, eager to renew the repertoire and reflect on the use of playwrights.

The proponents of these new approaches were forced to create their own networks for production and distribution and were not absorbed into the major theatrical infrastructures. At the same time, the large theatres maintained a traditional approach.

Through the years, however, the oldest and most important of these new companies have progressively gained official recognition and financial stability.

Marc Quaghebeur

The Flemish Theatre

It is impossible to explain contemporary theatre in Flanders without first taking into account those socio-economic factors which determined the country's cultural and artistic rise both in the Middle Ages and in the twentieth century. As well, a susceptibility to pictorial language, to rituals and processions (largely inspired by the prevalent Catholicism) were also factors which contributed to a high standard of theatre in periods of economic boom. This is known not so much from the names of playwrights as from the number of texts originating in certain periods and from the revolutionizing of theatre and acting styles in others.

Neither should one forget that the Flemings have always had a close cultural relationship with the Netherlands. Joost van den Vondel (1587–1679), for instance, though born of Flemish parents, became the most important exponent of Holland's 'golden age' and playwright Hugo Claus (b. 1929) was first discovered by the Dutch before his work was widely performed in Flanders and abroad.

Around the turn of the century, the most famous French-speaking Flemish writers – Maurice Maeterlinck, Charles Van Lerberghe (1861–1907), Emile Verhaeren (1855–1916) and Charles De Coster (1827–79, the writer of *La Légende d'Ulenspiegel*, 1867) – came from and worked in cities such as Ghent, Brussels and Antwerp. As well, Michel de Ghelderode and Fernand Crommelynck not only were inspired by Flanders but also often referred to themselves as Flemings.

Historically, four serious secular plays are connected with the late Medieval chivalric culture – the so-called *abele spelen* (plays from the nobility) – *Esmoreit, Gloriant, Lanseloet* and *Van den Winter ende vanden Somer* (*Of the Winter and of the Summer*). These plays date back to the thirteenth century although the manuscripts were presumably copied in about the year 1400, and they provide a late testimony to the courtly tradition. As far as we know, they are originals and it has often been pointed out that there are also resemblances to Japanese Noh plays.

This series had been preceded by an extensive number of rather stereotypical Miracle and Mystery plays as well as dramatized hagiographies. The Christian emblematic drama is best represented by the *Seven Bliscappen van Maria* (*Seven Joys of Mary*), a life of Mary probably dramatized in the late fourteenth century or the early fifteenth century and from which only the first and last parts have survived. These plays and the performances of them are the first witnesses to a flowering Christian urban culture.

This bustling activity acquired bourgeois overtones when, from the fifteenth century on, the Rhetoricians formed 'chambers' and an organized theatre culture spread throughout the country. All sorts of plays with symbolic themes and allegorical characters emerged, the most famous and also the best of them being *Elkerlyc* (*Everyman* in English; translated as *Jedermann* in 1911 by the Austrian writer Hugo von Hofmannsthal). This play, about the relative value of earthly possessions when one is confronted with death, probably dates from the late fifteenth century and may well be the high point of Flemish and European Medieval drama.

The output of plays by the Rhetoricians was extensive, their continuous activities during the following centuries under Spanish, Austrian and French rule not only preserved the vernacular but also constantly motivated the amateur theatre, eventually laying the foundations for the establishment of the professional stage in the nineteenth century (in Antwerp in 1853, in Ghent in 1871, and in Brussels, the capital, in 1875).

In this same period, the Rhetoricians became important exponents of the Vlaamse Beweging (Flemish Movement), the struggle for cultural emancipation which, from 1840 onward, was devoted to achieving the use of the Dutch language in civil services.

It was the so-called 'historical triangle' of the Flemish professional stage (Antwerp, Ghent, Brussels) which laid down the main lines of twentieth-century Flemish theatre policy. The municipal theatres of these three cities have always contained the most important companies within their walls. However, their alliance with a predominantly bourgeois audience led to questions being asked about the true 'popularity' of these theatres.

This debate, among other causes, led to the founding of the Vlaamse Volkstoneel (Flemish People's Theatre) in 1919, a company that sought to go beyond the traditional municipal theatre limits in its attempts to appeal to a broader and more specifically Flemish audience. Calling itself militantly pro-Flemish, it pursued widely divergent theatre policies under various managements. Its most remarkable years, however, were spent under the direction of Johan de Meester, Jr (1898–1986), a Dutchman who set an international standard for the company. De Meester, following in the footsteps of Soviet experimenters such as Meyerhold, Tairov and Vakhtangov, achieved enormous note with his own expressionistic productions. After 1929, the artistic notoriety of the Vlaamse Volkstoneel was eclipsed by a new commitment to Flemish nationalism and Catholicism, a commitment that ultimately foundered. Yet even in this period, the theatre

managed to inspire such notable writers as de Ghelderode, Anton Van de Velde (1895–1986) and Paul de Mont (1895–1950).

It should be noted here that de Meester's experiments in expressionism were not the first in the Flemish theatre. That honour goes to Herman Teirlinck (1879–1967), who worked with the Royal Flemish Theatre in Brussels on such expressionistic works as *De Vertraagde Film* (*The Slow Motion Film*, 1922), *Ik Dien* (*I Serve*, 1923) and *De Man zonder Lijf* (*The Man Without a Body*, 1925). In these plays, the influence of Alexander Blok, Fernand Crommelynck and Luigi Pirandello is clearly discernible, as is that of Meyerhold and expressionist film.

After 1926, Teirlinck was also the first to adopt the so-called 'theatre of style', which was intended to integrate the new technical ideas introduced by the Bauhaus, the Van de Velde School run by Ter Kameren in Elsene, and Edward Gordon Craig.

During World War II, the three major Dutch-speaking companies in Antwerp, Ghent and Brussels remained active. But immediately afterwards, the Ghent company was dissolved for political and financial reasons and the Brussels company was allowed to decline until it had almost no significance. In the national search for a Flemish equivalent to the French-language Théâtre National there was almost no alternative but to confer the title on the Antwerp company, the only professional Flemish company of any standing that remained.

From this point on, the KNS (Koninklijke Nederlandse Schouwburg/Royal Dutch Theatre) of Antwerp was the official Flemish equivalent of the National Theatre and was directed to give 'artistic performances of a high order to be propagated on the widest scale and ... to promote the social standing and the vocational training of actors'. To this latter end, a Studio was created which could serve as both a training institution and an experimental theatre.

For the 1945–6 season, the company offered a full repertoire of works for Antwerp as well as a simultaneous touring programme for other Flemish cities, especially Ghent. In its turn, the Brussels company, now called the KVS (Koninklijke Vlaamse Schouwburg/Royal Flemish Theatre) was designated to produce 'new' theatre, a task for which it was neither prepared nor fit. In 1948, its commission was withdrawn and the company was designated simply an Associate of the KNS in Antwerp. The group at this point began working independently, and again began to develop its own profile.

Clearly, this multi-company National Theatre concept was not greeted with enthusiasm everywhere, most particularly not in Ghent where the Antwerp 'coup' was greatly resented, the quality of the National Theatre productions severely questioned, the nature of the repertoire and its domination by imported drama roundly denounced (Anglo-Saxon plays represented some 37 per cent of the work produced; French plays 20 per cent; Dutch and Flemish plays only 14 per cent).

The National Theatre was itself the dream of Herman Teirlinck and had been inspired by England's Old Vic and France's Comédie-Française. Intended to incorporate 'national dreams and aspirations', the choice of plays was left to the directors. But the demands of trying to stage a new production every week (a demand continued through 1960) and a new production fortnightly after that; the appointment of artistic directors with little vision; and bureaucratic and political interference, left Teirlinck's dream little chance of success.

In Ghent, the pressure to re-establish a professional company was increasing: in 1965, the national government, the province of East Flanders and the city of Ghent finally provided the financial means for the NTG (Nederlands Toneel Gent/Dutch Theatre Ghent) to emerge.

In Brussels, Victor de Ruyter's (1903–76) ambitious management had raised the KVS by 1960 to a position as the best and most important company in the capital. This contributed to the abolition of the National Theatre dream and the re-establishment of equivalent professional companies in Antwerp, Ghent and Brussels. In 1967, the National Theatre in Flanders was administratively abolished and replaced by a formula under which the three companies were able to present their productions on each of the three stages. The RVT (Reizend Volkstheater/Touring People's Theatre) and its Studio are more or less a continuation of the Vlaamse Volkstoneel and travel through Flanders performing in villages and smaller towns. With this structure still in place, there is little room for the idea of a National Theatre for Flanders.

A special word here about the three key chamber theatres which emerged in Flanders in

Dirk Tanghe's 1991 Dutch Theatre Ghent production of Cyriel Buysse's *The Family van Paemel*.

the 1950s: the Toneelstudio 50 (Theatre Studio 50) founded in 1951 in Ghent; the Theater op Zolder – Nederlands Kamertoneel (Theatre in the Attic – Dutch Chamber Theatre) founded in 1953 in Antwerp; and Het Kamertoneel (The Chamber Theatre) founded in 1953 in Brussels.

In all three instances, it was recent graduates of the Higher Institute for Dramatic Arts who were instrumental in creating the companies out of concerns about fossilization of the larger companies. The young directors created their own small playing areas, focused rehearsals on in-depth analysis of texts and offered performances of great intimacy and detail.

Early chamber performances involved the latest trends in dramatic writing: Beckett, Ionesco, Osborne and Adamov among others. But in spite of absurdist and existential influences, the acting style of the chamber theatres did not differ fundamentally from the more traditionally based acting style of the larger theatres. Other chamber theatres soon came into existence in cities where there had previously been no theatre at all (such as Kortrijk, Brugge and Mechelen) although the repertoire in these cities was much less avant-garde than in the major cities.

Through the 1950s and 1960s theatre in Flanders was essentially a mix of the traditional and the new, large companies and small. The sweeping social upheavals of May 1968, however, which questioned so many middle-class values, also had their impact on the Flemish theatre. By 1970, the social relevance of the theatre was once again a central issue. Artistic routine in the larger theatres and especially their hierarchical structure were denounced by both younger artists and critics.

As a result, a number of new companies appeared with names that echoed their revolutionary roots: Trojaanse Paard (Trojan Horse) in 1970; Vuile Mong en Zijn Vieze Gasten (Dirty Mong and His Filthy Friends) in 1971; and De Internationale Nieuwe Scene (The International New Stage) in 1972. The work of these groups was largely improvised and sprang directly from the day's political situation. Probably the most important production from these groups and this period was the Nieuwe Scene's *Mistero Buffo* (1972) by the Italian Dario Fo. Fo's work, in fact, would long remain the company's main source of inspiration.

As these companies moved into the 1970s, links with the more traditional theatre were re-established. By 1975, the companies were integrated into the subsidy system that had been redefined by the Theatre Decree of 1975 (see **Structure of the National Theatre Community**) and the political theatre movement in Belgium was given a solid base for further expansion.

There was not really a common denominator for the new theatre of the 1980s. The world at this time was no longer perceived as one open to change but rather as a chaos upon which every artist forced his or her own order. In this new approach, all theatrical means contributed: a wayward interpretation of a classical text and the rejection of the verbal in favour of the physical especially. Borderlines between the various disciplines dwindled. Dance and theatre came even closer together; sculptors became stage directors and multimedia-ism and spacial-ism became increasingly important. Representative of this trend is Jan Fabre (b. 1958), a director and designer who has worked with his own company – Helena Troubleyn in Antwerp – as well as with the Opera Company of Flanders. His productions have been regularly seen at various international festivals.

Finally, a word about dramatic productions on Flemish radio and television. The post-war development of the radio play in Flanders has been remarkable though it seemed likely at first that the culture of the 'image' would bring about the disappearance of the genre altogether, notwithstanding that important Flemish authors such as Johan Daisne (1912–78), Hubert Lampo (b. 1920) and Gerard Walschap (1898–1991) were writing plays for radio in the 1950s.

The turning point came in the 1980s with the inspiring influence of Dries Poppe (1921–92) who headed the radio department at the BRT (Belgian Radio and Television) from 1960 to 1986. Under his regime, radio technique and the possibilities of reception underwent a radical evolution. More importantly, young writers were attracted to the medium of radio through the influence of the Vereniging van Vlaamse Toneelauteurs (Society of Flemish Playwrights).

The result was the Werkwinkel Drama Radio (Radio Drama Workshop) started in 1982. Within a few years, a whole series of talented young drama writers had become active in radio, devoting themselves in fact almost exclusively to the form. Also, a faithful audience had been formed. Of the forty-eight new productions mounted by BRT's radio drama department in 1987, twenty-seven were written in Dutch and twenty-one in French.

Among the major Flemish radio dramatists, one must note Fernand Handtpoorter (b. 1933),

Guy Bernaert (b. 1940), Luc Van den Briele (b. 1930), Jaak Dreesen (b. 1934) and Marc Minnerose (b. 1923). Major directors include Michel de Sutter (b. 1946), Flor Stein (b. 1942) and Gui Laenen (b. 1944), who is also a writer.

On television, the first Flemish plays and series tended to be based on the work of authors who took their inspiration from country life, folklore or the illustration of a glorious past. Although credible and well-groomed productions were done, most suffered from a lack of dramatic power, wooden dialogue and, above all, weak writing. Even the use of well-known Flemish writers failed to change the situation.

In the mid-1970s, however, a genuine Flemish television dramaturgy began to develop as writers were given an opportunity to actually learn something of their craft. Probably the major television dramatist in the early 1990s was Roger van Ransbeek (b. 1936) whose plays, *Er was eens in december* (*Once Upon a Time in December*, 1978), *Place Ste-Cathérine* (1979) and *Wacht tot hij opbelt* (*Wait Until He Calls*, 1981), achieved national and even international fame.

Jaak van Schoor, Alfons van Impe,
Toon Brouwers, Marc Hermans,
Marianne van Kerkhoven

Structure of the National Theatre Community

French Community

In 1991, subsidies for theatre amounted to more than BFr775 million (US$26 million). The Théâtre National received about BFr150 million of this total. In addition another thirty-five theatres and companies are subsidized each year. The funds granted in this way (BFr370 million) are divided in widely differing amounts among traditional institutions and the oldest of the so-called 'independent companies', which share BFr275 million. The remainder is distributed to about twenty smaller troupes. In addition, some BFr41 million is reserved for aid to young artists or companies which receive little or no subsidies during the year. These subsidies are allocated on the basis of individual projects. The remainder is divided among the theatre for children and youth (BFr75 million), political participative theatre known as *théâtre-action* (BFr29 million), theatre performed in dialect, amateur theatre and support to festivals and associations which promote the theatre.

Thus the influence of the Théâtre National is no longer what it used to be at the time when it received half of the budget allocated to the theatre and had a virtually complete monopoly on decentralization policies.

Things also changed greatly during the 1980s in terms of decentralization and the theatre in Wallonia. A number of local and provincial theatre centres were created with their activities made up of local productions, co-productions with other Belgian theatres and guest appearances by visiting Belgian and foreign productions. This was true of the Atelier Théâtral de Louvain-la-Neuve that Armand Delcampe (b. 1939) began in 1969 on a university site where major international directors such as Otomar Krejca or Benno Besson were invited, and where it was possible to see the productions of Peter Brook and Ariane Mnouchkine; the same applies to the Théâtre de la Place in Liège, which succeeded the Théâtre du Gymnase, and to the Centre Théâtral in Namur. And as winning a public in Wallonia is often affected by the fact that the population is spread out across small towns with Medieval origins, there was even the creation in 1984 of a regional cultural centre – the Centre Dramatique Hennuyer.

The recent tendency to replace touring with local institutions which organize their own productions has been confirmed with the implantation of a permanent dance company (L'Ensemble) in the Maison de la Culture in Tournai and the transformation in Charleroi of the Théâtre de l'Ancre, into a regional creative centre. The only major travelling companies that remain are the Théâtre de l'Équipe, which continued its activities after the death of Fernand Piette in 1978, and the Théâtre de la Communauté de Seraing (Theatre of the Community of Seraing), which continues to perform in the genre of *théâtre-action* while taking its performances to working-class districts, and Les Baladins du Miroir, led by Nèle Paxinou (b. 1942), which continues the principle of fairground theatre. One might note here that companies such as those from Liège – the Théâtre Arlequin or the Théâtre d'Art – are tending to settle down.

Theatre in various dialects of Walloon also

remains very much alive and well through one professional company in particular, the Théâtre du Trianon.

There are as well a large number of theatre festivals. Among them is the Festival de Spa, begun by the Théâtre National but which became independent in 1990. Taking place each August, it brings together a dozen or so of the year's top Belgian productions. Another important festival is the Rencontres Internationales de Théâtre Contemporain (International Contemporary Theatre Encounters) in Liège which offers, during the months of September and October, a wide range of performances with special interest in groups from France and Quebec.

The Festival du Théâtre Jeune Public (held during Christmas and Easter) takes place in various spaces both in Brussels and across Wallonia and brings together twenty or so groups staging productions for children and adolescents, while the Festival Vacances-Théâtre de Stavelot (Stavelot Holiday Theatre Festival) and the Festival Bellione-Brigittines are both held each August in Brussels.

It is extremely difficult to be precise about the number of artists working at any given moment in Belgium's French Community: there have never been studies done in this area. It is simply possible to say that there are three unions which speak for actors and those in the performing arts, and that they have been important in gaining social recognition for their members. It should be noted here that one of these groups – the Union des Artistes – is not formally a union but rather a philanthropic association. It provides its members – younger and older members in particular – with financial support which comes from collections made each year within the theatre community generally and from audiences in particular.

As a whole, Belgium's French Community in 1991 included thirty-six companies which were receiving some form of subsidy along with many smaller groups working in the realms of *théâtre-action* and theatre for young audiences. Another fifteen or so groups received support for individual projects during the year.

The major prizes awarded each year include the Eve Awards given by the Performing Arts Journalists' Association for best direction, best actor, best actress and best choreography. A similar award is also given annually to the author of the year's best play by the writers' association, the Société des Auteurs et des Compositeurs Dramatiques.

As with the numbers of actual theatre workers, it is difficult to speak of a specific level of theatre ticket prices. These are extremely variable with the high end found at the opera – the Théâtre Royal de la Monnaie (BFr3,000–4,000) – while the lower end can be found at various smaller groups (about BFr200). Most companies also offer special student rates.

Marc Quaghebeur

Flemish Community

The Regent's Decree of 19 September 1945 institutionalizing the Nationaal Toneel (National Theatre) in Belgium was further elaborated in the Royal Decrees of 12 May 1952 and 14 September 1954. On each occasion the role of the National Theatre for Flanders was assigned to the Koninklijke Nederlandse Schouwburg (KNS) in Antwerp. The Royal Decree of 18 February 1964, however, was the first to provide a specific regulation for the professional theatre in Flanders. Limited subsidies were given to a number of other repertory companies and to a number of small companies (chamber companies). The idea of a National Theatre had not been altogether abandoned but proved impractical. From 1967–8 onwards the repertory companies of Antwerp (KNS), Brussels (Koninklijke Vlaamse Schouwburg – KVS) and Ghent (Nederlands Toneel Gent – NTG) received similar statutes and the 'national role' was spread over all three.

The Theatre Decree of 13 June 1975 divided theatre companies into four categories: repertory theatres, touring theatres, chamber theatres and experimental or educational theatres. Thanks to this Theatre Decree, subsidies in Flanders increased spectacularly over the next years: from BFr80.8 million in 1974 to BFr425.7 million in 1981. Starting in 1983–4, however, the Ministry of Cultural Affairs began calling a drastic halt to the increases. In 1990 the budget for subsidizing twenty-eight theatre companies was BFr529.1 million, and the budget for subsidizing fourteen fringe projects was BFr17 million. In relation to the GNP this was one of the lowest theatre subsidy budgets in western Europe.

In 1991 a new law was approved by the Flemish Executive: for the first time, dance, puppetry (*figurentheater*) and arts centres were seen as subsidizable according to standard norms. The new law took effect in 1993 and almost immediately, about fifty theatre

Franz Marijnen's 1990 KVS production of Eugene O'Neill's *Long Day's Journey Into Night*, designed by Santiago del Coral.
Photo: Leo van Velzen.

companies, five dance companies, eight arts centres and about seventy cultural centres began to be subsidized, some BFr1.5 billion in total. There are of course also financial interventions from the provinces and municipalities.

The first international Flemish theatre festival took place in Antwerp in 1958; from 1959 to 1975, it was known as the Festival of Flanders and played host to many international theatre troupes.

In 1977, the Kaaitheater (Quay Theatre) Festival was organized as a centennial present to the Royal Flemish Theatre (KVS). Mainly oriented towards the experimental and avant-garde, the festival was held in a tent on the Arduinkaai (Ashlar Quay), a street behind the KVS. From that time on, the Kaaitheater became a biennial event with performances held in various Brussels theatres. In 1985, the last Kaaitheater Festival was held and in 1987 it merged with Schaamte (Shame), a Brussels group producing avant-garde theatre and dance.

Since 1983, the city of Louvain has organized Klapstuc, a biennial international festival of modern dance. And since 1973, a biennial international puppet festival has been held in the cultural centre at Neerpelt.

Most international contacts of the Flemish theatre are with Holland and since 1946 they have been conducted through the agency of the Belgisch–Nederlands Cultureel Akkoord (Belgian–Dutch Cultural Agreement). Since 1987, an annual Flemish–Dutch Theatre Festival has been held bringing together companies from both countries and since 1990 alternating between Belgian and Dutch locations.

There is a specific Flemish Centre of the International Theatre Institute and a Vlaams Theater Instituut (Flemish Theatre Institute) which act as international contact points and which also publish their own magazines (*ITI News*, *Facts and Info*, and *Articles*). Each institute organizes various symposia, meetings and exhibitions. In 1992 the Vlaams Theater Instituut joined with the Dutch Nederlands Theater Instituut as EESV (Nederlands–Vlaams Instituut voor de Podiumkunsten).

Jaak van Schoor

Artistic Profile

Companies

French Community

It has been argued that the French-speaking community of Belgium is the second most active French-speaking area in the world.

Brussels is the most active centre with a large number of permanent companies and a significant number which appear for a show or two and then disappear, often started by young actors as a showcase for their talents. The permanent groups are more focused in their programming and generally work for a more specifically determined audience.

At the Théâtre National, run since 1990 by Philippe van Kessel (b. 1946), programming covers a broad range of repertoire – classic and modern – as well as the occasional new work.

The programme of the Compagnie des Galeries, directed by Jean-Pierre Rey (b. 1927), is predominantly commercial, concentrating on boulevard theatre. Alongside other established

companies with a more serious repertoire, the Théâtre du Parc offers a rich although conformist selection in a superb theatre more than two centuries old. Claude Étienne's Rideau de Bruxelles, under the wing of the Palais des Beaux-Arts, has developed a simultaneously classical and stylized approach since the 1940s.

New plays are also a regular part of the Brussels theatre scene. Roger Domani's Théâtre de Poche was for a long time the place for new foreign plays and theatrical scandals, but in the 1900s has mainly been staging plays concerned with contemporary mores.

In addition to these repertory theatres, two suburban theatres are based around specific actors, the Compagnie Claude Volter and the Compagnie Yvan Baudouin-Lesly Bunton.

There is also Henri Ronse (b. 1946) who created (in 1980) the Nouveau Théâtre de Belgique, where he works on a demanding, modern repertoire. He was the first, for example, to stage the works of German dramatist Thomas Bernhard in the French language.

Henri Ronse's 1991 Nouveau Théâtre de Belgique production of Paul Willems's *La Vita Breve*, designed by Nuno Côrte-Real.
Photo: Claude Lê-Anh.

Another new tendency connected with *théâtre critique* also appeared first in the capital – works filled with Brechtian alienation, cold images and a serious dramaturgical approach. This is seen in the Théâtre Varia where three directors – Philippe Sireuil (b. 1952), also a noted opera director, Michel Dezoteux (b. 1949) and Marcel Delval (b. 1949) – alternately staged plays in this style, usually contemporary pieces marked by profound dramaturgical investigation.

In the same way, the Atelier Sainte-Anne productions were mainly oriented towards contemporary German authors. Marc Liebens, the first of the directors to turn in this direction, founded the Ensemble Théâtral Mobile. Liebens renounced the idea of a fixed place in order to try and tour each of his productions, generally to the French-speaking cities of Brussels, Geneva and Paris.

This international perspective has also been a constant factor behind companies which practise an extremely physical style of theatre, *théâtre du corps*. Although Frédéric Baal's Théâtre Laboratoire Vicinal ceased activities in 1977, Frédéric Flamand's (b. 1946) Plan K and Baba Mebirouk's (b. 1948) Théâtre de Banlieue maintain this tradition and are well integrated in the international networks which continue the work of the avant-garde of the 1960s. The former Brussels sugar refinery occupied by Plan K was, till 1991, a meeting point for various companies pursuing *théâtre du corps*. Belgian and foreign productions of this kind also appear in Brussels in the Halles de Schaerbeek. But if one theatre should be mentioned for putting on international productions, it is the Théâtre 140 of Jo Dekmine (b. 1931). Since 1963, representatives of the most remarkable forms of 'alternative' theatre have come from around the world to this venue, linking experimentation with imaginative extravagance.

At the end of the 1970s, the new wave theatre could be easily divided among 'literary theatre', *théâtre critique* and *théâtre du corps*. But in the 1980s and 1990s the tendencies are far less clear cut and intellectualized, and even freer in form. However, there are exceptions: the more classical work of Bernard Damien (b. 1951) in the Théâtre du Grand Midi; the productions of Alain Populaire (b. 1947) and his Théâtre Impopulaire, increasingly founded on a sort of silent ritual; and the experimentation, based to a large extent on the plastic arts, of the Ymagier Singulier and its leading figure, Thierry Salmon

(b. 1957), who later pursued his career in Italy. Two experimental directors from Liège are Jacques Delcuvellerie (b. 1946) with his Groupov company and Isabelle Pousseur (b. 1961). Although they have their own specific characteristics, both tend to work in the style of the *théâtre critique*.

For the rest, many independent theatre projects from both Brussels and Wallonia are played in the Botanique, the new Brussels–Wallonia cultural centre based in the capital. Martine Wijckaert's (b. 1952) Théâtre de la Balsamine has also put on other groups, although with a greater orientation towards collective experimentation, based in particular on the expression of physical sensitivity.

Marc Quaghebeur

Flemish Community

In a city dominated by French culture, the Royal Flemish Theatre in Brussels has always been a symbol for the Flemish minority. This repertory theatre has consistently aimed at finding large audiences both in Brussels and the surrounding Flemish area. Artistically, the programming has represented a basic mix of serious and comic plays. From 1946 when Victor de Ruyter was appointed its artistic director and demanded increased rehearsal time, the company fought to be as good as the best French-speaking theatres in the city. Within a decade, de Ruyter achieved his goal and audiences increased significantly.

It was de Ruyter who produced the majority of Hugo Claus's work in Flanders and established a close relationship between director Jo Dua (1925–93) and leading actor Senne Rouffaer (b. 1925), a collaboration which resulted in a number of remarkable productions ranging from *Hamlet* to *Marat/Sade*. It was also de Ruyter who introduced Edward Albee's plays to Belgium, beginning with *Who's Afraid of Virginia Woolf?* in 1965.

When de Ruyter left, a more commercial approach was taken by his principal successor Nand Buyl (b. 1923). Commercialism notwithstanding, Buyl brought forward another Flemish playwright of note, the classicist Johan Boonen (b. 1939).

In 1959, Rudi van Vlaenderen (b. 1930) founded Toneel Vandaag (Theatre Today) in Brussels, a chamber theatre which introduced, among those of other writers, the works of Fernando Arrabal. He also organized Middagen van het toneel (Lunchtime Theatre). One of this company's most striking productions was Claus's adaptation of Seneca's play *Thyestes* directed by the author in an Artaudian style. The theatre closed in 1968.

The Brussels Kamertoneel (Brussels Chamber Theatre) opened in 1964 offering on a modest scale traditional, literary-oriented theatre. During the 1976–7 season, van Vlaenderen took charge of the company, temporarily renamed it the Brabants Kollektief voor Theaterprojecten (BKT – Brabant Collective for Theatre Projects) and moved the company towards a traditional international repertoire.

In 1972, Arturo Corso's (b. 1937) production of Dario Fo's *Mistero Buffo* opened at the Opera House of Brussels, the Muntschouwburg. This production of Fo's secular passion play was one of the highpoints of the season and was later seen at many European theatre festivals.

For some ten years between 1973 and 1985, the Jeugd en Theaterwerkgroep (Youth and Theatre Workgroup) produced creditable theatre for young people, often with plays written by their internationally known resident playwright Alice Toen (b. 1932). The company also endeavoured to introduce many German plays for young people (by Thomas Brasch and Lukas B. Suter, for example) but, despite being artistically successful, drew too little interest to be commercially viable.

In 1964, the deserted Beursschouwburg (Stock Exchange Theatre) was adopted as still another centre for Flemish theatre in Brussels. Serving first as a venue in the capital for smaller Flemish theatre productions, the Exchange gradually evolved its own company. A conflict concerning organization and ideology, however, brought about its demise in 1969, a loss since the company counted a number of interesting actors among its members.

The Beursschouwburg became a rallying point for a new generation of Flemish theatre and animated the city centre at various times with both individual performances and festivals such as the Mallemuntfestival, the Kaaitheaterfestival, Brusselement and the Vlaamse theatre circuit. All originated at the Exchange. In 1990, the Kaaitheater and the BKT merged resulting in still another concentration of Flemish theatrical activities.

Since its founding in 1853, the KNS (Koninklijke Nederlandse Schouwburg/Royal Dutch Theatre) has dominated theatrical life in the city of Antwerp. In 1945, as already discussed, the company was appointed the National Theatre and had to perform as well in Ghent, Brussels and dozens of other Flemish towns on a show-a-week basis. Under Walter Tillemans (b. 1932), however, house director between 1961 and 1984, the company's style and structure changed significantly.

Tillemans was strongly influenced by the ideas of Brecht and the working methods of the Berliner Ensemble. With a strong interest in the social relevance of theatre and its potential for affecting large audiences, he very successfully staged not only plays by Brecht, but also works by Shakespeare, the Czech dramatist Pavel Kohout and popular plays by the Flemish author Jan Christiaens (b. 1929).

The manager of the theatre during the first part of Tillemans's work there was Bert Van Kerkhoven (1906–84) and it was he who made a number of important administrative reforms and created opportunities for young actors and directors at the theatre. Van Kerkhoven, for example, introduced the 'three weeks system', allowing every production a continuous three-week run. It was also under his management that the concept of a single National Theatre was abolished and the exchange of productions between the Flemish companies of Brussels, Ghent and Antwerp introduced.

It was between 1972 and 1986, the years that the KNS was managed by Domien de Gruyter (b. 1921), that Tillemans realized some of his most successful productions. At the same time (1980), the company moved into the new Municipal Theatre, a huge complex with two houses. The building had actually been designed in 1959, a time of large-scale vision. By its completion eleven years later, most theatres had already returned to smaller scales as the favoured mode of operation. Trying to play in this over-large house cost the company enormous sums of money. By 1982, subsidies were decreasing across the board and in 1984, Tillemans left the company for a smaller group, the Raamtheater (Window Theatre). Shortly thereafter, de Gruyter too left the KNS.

Ivonne Lex (b. 1926), a popular actress, became the theatre's first female artistic director in 1986. She wanted the KNS to produce a repertoire in which classical productions would alternate with less traditional shows and which would appeal to a wide audience. But Lex was unable to fight the economics of the decade and when she stepped down as the company's director in 1991, the crisis in Flanders's oldest repertory company was greater than ever.

That same year, Tillemans was hired to

oversee a merger between KNS and the Nieuw Ensemble Raamtheater into a single company which would operate with three theatres at its disposal. It would take many years for the results of the merger to be seen.

Another Antwerp theatre of note is the RVT (Reizend Volkstheater/Touring People's Theatre) which was founded in 1945 by Rik Jacobs (1913–85). Brought under the aegis of the National Theatre in 1947 as its touring wing, the company came under the control of the municipality of Antwerp in 1967. Its quality during most of this time, unfortunately, was essentially amateur. In 1985, however, the RVT became an independent company with Peter Benoy (b. 1944) as its artistic director. The level of work began to be raised as Benoy took a much more contemporary approach to both the repertoire and the company. In 1991 the RVT changed its name to Zuidpool (South Pole).

Perhaps the most important chamber theatre of the 1950s in Antwerp was the Theater op Zolder (Theatre in the Loft), later called the Nederlands Kamertoneel (Dutch Chamber Theatre). Founded in 1953 by Tone Brulin (b. 1926), the company had a particular interest in new Flemish authors early on but later evolved into a fairly traditional bourgeois group. In 1967, the company moved to Maastricht in the Netherlands where it changed its name to the Groot Limburgs Theater. It closed some ten years later.

The Fakkeltheater (Torch Theatre), established in 1956 by a group of left-wing school teachers to bring politically rooted cabaret theatre to Antwerp, evolved through the 1960s into a fully professional company under the direction of Walter Groener (b. 1933). Since 1975, the company has played in two halls. In the 1980s, despite stressing the social relevance of its repertoire, the company seemed to lay greater emphasis on lighter-weight productions.

The TIL (Toneelgezelschap Ivonne Lex/ Ivonne Lex Theatre Company) began operations in Brussels in 1970 and moved to Antwerp in 1973 where it plays in two small theatres: Het Appeltje (The Little Apple) and since 1981 in Het Klokhuis (The Apple Core). The company also tours extensively in both Flanders and the Netherlands with a repertoire that is non-experimental but also non-commercial. Mostly, it thrives on the energy and talents of its director, Ivonne Lex.

In 1972, actor-director Will Beckers (b. 1947) and KNS dramaturge Toon Brouwers (b. 1943) founded the Nieuw Vlaams Theater (New Flemish Theatre) which produced a repertoire of exclusively Dutch-language plays, most created for this studio theatre. The first plays of such writers as Paul Koeck (b. 1940), René Verheezen (1946–87) and Roger van Ransbeek saw their original productions here. In 1984, however, the Flemish government withdrew its subsidy and the theatre was forced to close.

The Tie-3 Theatre, founded in 1977 by author-director Tone Brulin, attempted to connect Belgians to the Third World through theatre. In 1986, Eugène Bervoets (b. 1956) assumed the company's management and has maintained the same policy. In 1991 the company closed for lack of finances.

Of the numerous Antwerp companies engaged in producing 'new theatre' during the 1980s, the most prominent were De Witte Kraai (White Crow) which, under the direction of Sam Bogaerts (b. 1948) and actor-director Lucas Vandervost (b. 1957), consciously operated on the boundaries, and Akt, which amalgamated with Theater Vertikaal (originally founded in 1959) to form the Akt-Vertikaal in 1985. In 1987, White Crow and Akt-Vertikaal merged to form a new group called De Tijd (The Tide). De Tijd's director Ivo van Hove (b. 1958) and scenographer Jan Versweyveld (b. 1958) staged outstanding productions of Shakespeare's *Macbeth* and Wedekind's *Lulu* before moving to the Netherlands in 1990. De Tijd now works with Lucas Vandervost as artistic director and focuses on modern authors (for example, Botho Strauss) and specific aspects of dramatic writing.

Perhaps the most successful small Flemish theatre company in the early 1990s was the Blauwe Maandag Compagnie (Blue Monday Company) founded in 1984 by Luc Perceval (b. 1957) and Guy Joosten (b. 1963). The pair did a series of outstanding productions of both classical and contemporary plays including Lars Noren's *Nightwatch*, Chekhov's *The Seagull*, O'Neill's *Strange Interlude* and Strindberg's *The Father*. The company operated through most of this period without a theatre of its own and with only modest subsidy.

Turning to the Flemish city of Ghent, one must again go back to the decision to create a National Theatre in 1945–6 which effectively closed down the Ghent's own repertory company in favour of a visiting company. Strong resistance came from many quarters but especially from the then still existing Toneel School (Ghent Theatre School, 1911–59), which

Luc Perceval's 1991 Blue Monday Company production of Nestor de Tière's *Wilde Lea*.
Photo: Johan Jacobs.

wanted a professional outlet for its own activities.

In 1950, a group of students, led by their teacher Dré Poppe (b. 1922) decided to found Theatre Studio 50, although it was not until 1955 that a permanent home was found in the basement theatre, Arca. From that point on, it began to create a clear image for itself as an avant-garde company staging performances of plays by Ionesco and John Osborne in 1957 and Beckett (*Waiting for Godot*, 1959).

In 1965–6, a new major repertory company was formed in Ghent (Nederlands Toneel Gent/Dutch Theatre Ghent), with Dré Poppe as its first artistic director. Poppe's avant-garde interests were not pursued in the larger house; the repertoire consisted of classics and more commercial plays. Albert Hanssens (1916–81) replaced Poppe in 1967 adding exploration of the Flemish repertoire.

In 1973 Walter Eysselinck (b. 1931) succeeded Hanssens. Evincing a clear preference for the Anglo-Saxon repertoire, he mounted the first Flemish production of Peter Shaffer's *Equus*. Continuing an already existing though rather limited musical tradition, he also produced *Cabaret*. From 1976 to 1977 – under the direction of Jaak van Schoor (b. 1939) – there was a shift in emphasis towards the German repertoire.

It was under the direction of Jef Demedts (b. 1935) that an artistic committee was introduced, responsible for all artistic decisions. The company quickly became one of the most interesting in Flanders, staging productions ranging from *Lysistrata* to Ionesco's *Le Roi se meurt* (*Exit the King*). Since 1986, the company has reverted to the more traditional approach in policy-making. In 1991, Hugo van den Berghe (b. 1943) took over artistic control of the company and began what appeared to be a move toward a more accessible and popular repertoire.

Arena, another group, was essentially a private venture started in Ghent in 1969 with a keen interest in Genet and other avant-garde writers. Later on, it developed into a music theatre company and in 1985 became part of the Ballet van Vlaanderen (Flanders Ballet).

Jan Decorte (b. 1950) was undoubtedly a pacesetter in the 1980s with important productions of Hebbel's *Maria Magdalena*, Heiner Müller's *HamletMaschine*, Shakespeare's *King Lear* as well as of his own comedies. Jan Fabre also achieved international fame with his theatre of plastic overtones and repetitive movement.

Out of the merging of De Witte Kraai and Akt-Vertikaal sprang an important new company, De Tijd (The Tide), where the subtle acting of Lucas Vandervost and the spectacular imagery of Ivo van Hove were combined. Sam Bogaerts developed into a versatile and provocative director. Herman Gilis (b. 1951), who has his beginnings in the political theatre movement, regularly offers arresting displays of acting and directing. For all these directors – except Jan Fabre – the international repertoire remains an important source of inspiration.

In the Blauwe Maandag Compagnie, the directorial duo of Luc Perceval and Guy Joosten experiments with extreme adaptations of contemporary texts. Eugène Bervoets in Tiedrie, Gui Cassiers (b. 1960) in Stekelbees and Willy Thomas (b. 1959) in Dito'Dito also work with new plays, often of their own writing. Jan Lauwers (b. 1957) of the Need Company integrates classical texts with a strongly physical style.

Toon Brouwers, Alfons van Impe,
Jaak van Schoor

Dramaturgy

French Community

Without doubt, the country's best known playwrights are the symbolist Maurice Maeterlinck and Michel de Ghelderode; de Ghelderode is the author of some sixty works written in French, though a number were first performed in Flemish translation. The world created in these plays recalls the grotesque cavalcade of the Flemish fair and Pieter Brueghel's (*c.*1520–69) paintings. Well known too is Fernand Crommelynck whose play *Le Cocu magnifique* (*The Magnificent Cuckold*) has been performed in Russia, under the direction of Meyerhold, in a constructivist *mise-en-scène*.

This said, there have been many other playwrights of note whose works have been staged in Belgium both during and since World War II. Among them are Herman Closson (1901–82), author of *Le Jeu des quatre fils d'Aymon* (*The Four Sons of Aymon*); Georges Sion (b. 1913), author of *La Matrone d'Éphèse* (*The Matron of Ephesus*); Suzanne Lilar (b. 1901), author of *Le Burlador*; Charles Bertin (b. 1919), author of *Christophe Colomb*; and Jean Mogin (1921–86), author of *À chacun selon sa faim* (*To Each According to His Needs*). All took their inspiration from the ideas of writers such as Montherlant or Giraudoux. They use historical or mythical material in order to draw from it the moral dramas which exalt, in a timeless way, the highest sentiments or conflicts of traditional humanism.

Of other post-war writers, one should also note Paul Willems (b. 1912), author of *Il pleut dans ma maison* (*It's Raining in My House*), and Jean Sigrid (b. 1920), author of *Mort d'une souris* (*Death of a Mouse*). The former has his roots in German romanticism and allied himself to 'magic realism', which enjoyed great success in Belgian literature during the immediate post-war period. The latter, while not neglecting history, deals much more with contemporary issues. The work of these two playwrights came to real note only after 1965 with the birth of new approaches in the theatre and profound changes in Belgian society.

Of the later generations, one should mention Liliane Wouters (b. 1930), author of *La Salle des profs* (*Prof's Room*); Jean Louvet (b. 1934), author of *L'Homme qui avait le soleil dans sa poche* (*The Man Who Had the Sun in His Pocket*) which in the 1970s entered the repertoire in its Brechtian phase. Louvet is a Walloon who writes in French and was profoundly influenced by the 1960 strikes in the steel industry.

Brecht's influence is shown in the plays of René Kalisky (1936–81), who nevertheless sought to free his work from the principle of alienation and pushed on to the stage all the totalitarian regimes of twentieth-century European history, often taking this approach to nightmarish proportions. He was refused by the Théâtre National, which at the time was the only institution with the resources to produce his plays, and his major works were initially performed in Paris by director Antoine Vitez.

The authors who followed the generation of Louvet, Wouters and Kalisky have been performed by very different companies, depending on their affinities and types of writing. In Brussels the fantasies and linguistic verve of Pascal Vrebos (b. 1952) in a play like *Cyclochoc* or the bitter-sweet comedies about contemporary mores of Jacques De Decker (b. 1945) in *Petit-Matin* (*Early Morning*) are based on a more traditional approach. Piet Sterckx's (1925–87) *Voyage à Delft* (*Journey to Delft*) is based on wild imaginings and the universe of paintings and cartoon strips created by the author himself and his Théâtre de la Balançoire.

In the *théâtre critique*, one should mention the work of the writer of the Ensemble Théâtral Mobile, Michèle Fabien (b. 1945); the dramaturge of the Théâtre Varia, Jean-Marie Piemme (b. 1944); and Paul Emond (b. 1944) as well as Yves Hunstadt's (b. 1956) one-man shows, performed at the Atelier Sainte-Anne.

In Wallonia, Richard Hourez (b. 1946), author of *Le Terrain vaque* (*The Waste Land*) deals with the same issues as Jean Louvet, while Michel Voiturier (b. 1940), author of *Chronique locale* (*Local Story*), considers various social problems. Émile Hesbois (b. 1937) works in a more poetic register. His *La Corne du bois Gozette* (*A Corner of Apple Pie Wood*) is a free adaptation of Dylan Thomas's *Under Milk Wood*. Guy Denis (b. 1942), author of *Capiche prend le maquis* (*Capiche Goes Underground*), uses characters from his native Ardennes province where he successfully tours with his Capiche Arden Théâtre, while actress Francine Landrain writes texts for Groupov adapted to this company's specific experiments.

Marc Quaghebeur

Flemish Community

There is little doubt that Herman Teirlinck was Flanders's leading dramatist in the period from about 1922 to 1960 when his place was taken by Hugo Claus; of the two, Claus's reputation has outstripped that of Teirlinck. Not only was he awarded the National Drama Prize on four occasions – in 1965 for *Een Bruid in de Morgen* (*A Bride in the Morning*), in 1972 for *Vrijdag* (*Friday*) and in 1979 for two plays, *Orestes* and *Jessica* – but he proved himself immensely skilful in combining his dramatic skills with an outstanding sense of language.

In the period of the National Theatre, important writers in Flemish who were produced included Jozef Van Hoeck (b. 1922) whose play *Voorlopig Vonnis* (*Provisional Verdict*, 1957) was immensely popular, and Luc Vilsen (b. 1921) whose plays *De genaamde Greco* (*The Man Named Greco*, 1960) and *Joanna of de triomf van de democratie* (*Joanna or the Triumph of Democracy*, 1977) were also successful with audiences.

Performed even more often than Van Hoeck or Vilsen in the large theatres of Flanders was the work of Herwig Hensen (1917–89), especially *Het Woord Vrijheid* (*The Word Freedom*, 1963), *Morgen kan het te laat zijn* (*Tomorrow May Be Too Late*, 1963) and *De Rattenvanger van Hamelen* (*The Rat-Catcher of Hamelin*,

1970). All of these writers portray individuals in confrontation with a changing world.

The absurdist theatre was specifically adapted for Flemish audiences in the plays of Piet Sterckx, Pieter de Prins (b. 1926), Jan Christiaens and Georges van Vrekhem (b. 1925). International issues could be found in the work of Tone Brulin, who integrated political events into the theatrical concepts of Artaud, Grotowski and Brook. He was also the first to stage his own productions with various ethnic groups and the first to introduce the theatre of other cultures to Flemish audiences (for example Malaysia, Suriname, Egypt and Iraq). He also translated many plays from other cultures.

In 1982, Walter van den Broeck (b. 1941) received the National Award for Drama. By then he was already a much-performed author who caused the audience to identify itself with the trenchant language and slice-of-life plays such as *Groenten uit Balen* (*Greenings from Balen*, 1972), *Greenwich* (1974) and *De Tuinman van de Koning* (*The King's Gardener*, 1985).

Paul Koeck has been one of Flanders' most prolific playwrights since the late 1980s. His experience in journalism and the media has determined in part his social commitment – a trait which he shares with van den Broeck – and his crisp, direct style can be seen in such plays as *De Huurlingen* (*The Mercenaries*, 1973), *De Bewustmaker* (*The Consciousness Raiser*, 1983), *De Aardemakers* (*The Earthmakers*, 1986) and *Het Vincent-effect* (*The Vincent Effect*, 1986).

Johan Boonen (b. 1939) not only adapted Greek plays for the modern stage but also created a series of new plays which testify to his particular sense of theatrical metaphor, for example, *De Bokken* (*The Goats*, 1974), *Jozef Vek* (1975) and *De Blauwe Maarschalk* (*The Blue Marshal*, 1982). He wrote regularly for the Royal Flemish Theatre (KVS) in Brussels and also worked in film and television.

This familiarity with the media is typical of the generation that also includes Roger van Ransbeek and René Verheezen. Van Ransbeek wrote such plays as *The Beatles Forever* (1983) and *De Schuldvraag* (*A Question of Guilt*, 1986). Verheezen, who worked as actor-author-director, created a number of searingly realistic portraits with a taboo-shattering effect: *Onder Ons* (*Amongst Ourselves*, 1978), *De Caraïbische Zee* (*The Caribbean Sea*, 1980) and *Moeder* (*Mother*, 1985).

Despite the numbers of playwrights, none are able to survive on their writing for the theatre and therefore they – and with them the Vereniging van Vlaamse Toneelschrijvers (Association of Flemish Playwrights) – often try to reach audiences abroad, especially in the Netherlands. Despite appearances to the contrary, it is not easy for Flemish authors in Belgium to have their work performed in the Netherlands, even though many Flemish actors work there. In this respect, mutual recognition and cultural integration are still lacking.

Since the late 1980s, the Flemish Ministry of Cultural Affairs has made support for Flemish playwrights one of its priorities, providing support and financial grants for those whose new plays are premièred by Flemish theatre companies. This policy has helped but too many writers still remain marginal. This is true especially of writers such as Jan Decorte and Arne Sierens (b. 1959) whose work, though interesting, had not yet been seen in the large theatres as late as 1993.

Toon Brouwers, Alfons van Impe,
Jaak van Schoor

Directors, Directing and Production Styles

French Community

During the inter-war period (1918–39), numerous Belgian actors and actresses continued to go to Paris in order to further their career, as this was impossible in Belgium: this was the case, to name but a few, for Fernand Ledoux (b. 1897), Fernand Gravey (1905–70), Raymond Rouleau (1904–81), Victor Francen (1888–1977), Berthe Bovy (1887–1977) and Tania Balachova (1902–73), who was to become an outstanding theatre teacher. This tendency diminished after the liberation (1944) due to the creation of permanent companies in Belgium, although some actors, such as Raymond Gérôme (b. 1920) or Françoise Giret (b. 1929), continued to emigrate. In Belgium it was possible to see a number of distinguished actors. Even French or Swiss actors chose to exercise their profession in Belgium, where they found a job stability that France could not offer. The improvements in theatrical education resulted in new generations of actors being trained in the conservatories or colleges and going on to feed both the major theatrical institutions and the independent companies. The lack of a cinema industry in Belgium has meant that for some time now actors once again have been going abroad, drawn particularly by the greater possibilities that France offers on this level.

Marc Quaghebeur

Flemish Community

In Flanders, self-trained actors dominated the stages prior to 1948. In Antwerp, such actors constituted the core of the KNS until graduates of the Studio van het Nationaal Toneel (Studio of the National Theatre, from 1967 the Studio Herman Teirlinck) began to enter the profession. Therefore, actors of the older generation with little or no professional training, determined the National Theatre's acting style for many years.

The first significant director to work with the post-war KNS was Fred Engelen (1912–67). Not only were his productions prepared with a thoroughness unknown to that point but also he succeeded in introducing a new repertoire to the company (Brecht, Ionesco and adaptations of Hašek and Kafka). Walter Tillemans, his erstwhile pupil at the Studio, directed in much the same spirit but pursued a greater political commitment. Another director of note who made his career primarily with the Koninklijk Jeugdtheater (Royal Youth Theatre) in Antwerp is Jan Verbist (b. 1943).

In the 1960s, Jo Dua, one of Flanders' most talented directors, was responsible for a great many outstanding productions at the KVS, the Royal Flemish Theatre in Brussels, including Peter Weiss's *Marat/Sade*. In the 1970s, Senne Rouffaer (b. 1925), for many years one of the company's principal actors, also became one of its most celebrated directors.

In Ghent, a new repertory company was created in 1965 – the NTG (Nederlands Toneel Gent/Dutch Theatre Ghent) – with Frans Roggen (1911–78) directing many of its early

Franz Marijnen's 1968 Mechels Miniatuurteater production of Fernando Arrabal's *Fando et Lis*.
Photo: Institut Belge d'Information et de Documentation.

productions. One of its leading actors, Jef Demedts, was its artistic director from 1978 to 1991.

In youth theatre, Eva Bal (b. 1938) founded the Speeltheater (Play Theatre) in Ghent in 1979 and significantly changed the nature of performance style for her young actors, working with improvisations. She later worked in other European countries and became particularly well known in Germany.

The generation of actors and directors to emerge in the 1980s and 1990s has been even more mobile than its predecessors. Theatre and film actor Jan Decleir (b. 1946) built a successful solo career, especially with the plays of Dario Fo. Karel Vingerhoets (b. 1953) appears regularly at Antwerp's Raamtheater and has worked as well in the Netherlands, Germany and Austria. Franz Marijnen (b. 1943) has staged productions not only in Flanders but also in the United States and several European countries; in 1993 he became artistic director of KVS. Still another important director is Jan Fabre, who has staged both dramatic and operatic productions in various European and American cities. His work is noted for its highly visual, post-modern style.

Toon Brouwers

Music Theatre

French Community

The period after World War II saw the end of the long reign of Corneil de Thoran (1881–1953) in the Théâtre de la Monnaie. De Thoran, a stylish and authoritarian man, was the manager who brought figures such as Alban Berg, Lauritz Melchior and Kirsten Flagstad to Brussels. He paid constant attention to new developments in choreography and opera. De Thoran produced, apart from Belgian musical works such as those of Jean Absil (1893–1974), Marcel Poot (1901–88) and François Rasse (1873–1955), operas by Britten and Menotti, Stravinsky's *Rake's Progress* and even the German works such as *Dantons Tod* (*Danton's Death*), by von Einem. The war did not completely destroy the Brussels public's appreciation of German pieces, and in particular those of Wagner, which were introduced to Brussels by Maurice Kufferath (1852–1919) during the first twenty years of the century.

De Thoran was succeeded by Joseph Rogatchewsky (1891–1985), the leading tenor in the company, who continued his predecessor's approach and showed little inventiveness but maintained the idea of repertory programming with a permanent company. This decline corresponded exactly with the similar loss of public interest observed in other countries. The few attempts at innovation passed almost unnoticed, swamped by the concessions made to a public that was eager for new operettas and the easy successes of comic opera.

A new wind blew in 1959 with the arrival of Maurice Huisman (b. 1912). He had the foresight to bring to Brussels the French choreographer Maurice Béjart (b. 1927), who gave a new dimension to ballet, conceiving it as a total spectacle taking inspiration from all cultures. He immediately enjoyed great success with a version of *The Rite of Spring* (1959) that caused astonishment at first, but later went on to become one of the dance classics of the century. From then on Béjart became the spearhead of the house (which became the National Opera in 1963) and during the next twenty-five years choreographed dozens of new performances – *Symphonie pour un homme seul* (*Symphony for a Man Alone*, 1955), *9e symphonie* (*Ninth Symphony*, 1964), *Boléro* (1960), *Les Noces* (1965), *Baudelaire* (1968), *Bakhti* (1968), and so on.

Although they may seem less spectacular, the changes introduced to the opera house were no less radical. The idea of having a permanent company with a different opera every evening was abandoned. The variety in the performances (increased by regular visits from foreign companies) and a policy of renewal bore fruit, even if there was a certain amount of wear and tear during the 1970s. Huisman also created an Opera Studio and was instrumental in the creation of the Mudra, an important dance school run by Maurice Béjart.

In 1981 the arrival and work of Gérard Mortier (b. 1943) at the head of the Brussels Opera immediately made the house a major force on the international scene and progressively made it a focal point that was envied by other opera houses. Trained in Germany and

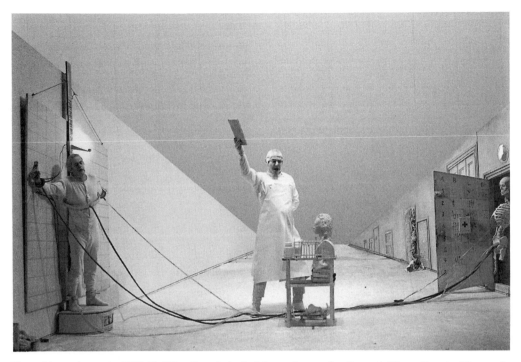

Hans Neugebauer's 1989 Théâtre Royal de la Monnaie production of Alban Berg's *Wozzeck*, designed by Achim Freyer.
Photo: Hermann J. Baus.

Paris, simultaneously public relations man and manager, Mortier made the Monnaie the most visible cultural institution in the country and successfully completed an audacious renovation of the building in record time (the flies of the stage were raised and new machinery installed). The building reopened in November 1986; with the help of two musical directors, John Pritchard and Sylvain Cambreling, Mortier revitalized the orchestra and choirs, and introduced several cycles of concerts and recitals. Producing five new shows per year, he imposed a style that encouraged a more theatrical approach to opera with permanent groups of singers who rehearsed performances long in advance under 'permanent' directors and well-known guests.

The departure of Maurice Béjart and the Ballet du XXe siècle for Lausanne in 1987 occurred when serious financial difficulties led ministers to impose budgetary cutbacks which threatened to restrict the prestigious, quality programme favoured by Mortier. In 1991 Mortier was selected to manage the Salzburg Festival and was succeeded by Bernard Foccroulle (b. 1953).

Undamaged by the war, the Théâtre Royal in Liège continued a fairly routine programme in the twenty years after the war (the ordeal suffered by many institutions placed under the supervision of an unenlightened municipal authority), apart from a few happier moments due to the enthusiasm of tenor André d'Arkor (1901–71), who managed the company between 1945 and 1966. The bulk of the house's performances at that time were made up of French opera (Liège has always been very open to French tastes) and the few classics from the repertoire that are sung in French. The opera, however, proved unable to revitalize itself and often reduced its activity to six-month seasons.

The transformation of the company dates from 1967, with the creation by the cities of Liège, Mons, Verviers and Charleroi of the Opéra de Wallonie (also called the Centre lyrique de Wallonie, and following the latest redivision of cultural responsibilities in Belgium, the Centre lyrique de la Communauté française). Since 1967 this non-profit association has been run by Raymond Rossius (b. 1926). Although the performances are prepared in Liège, they are also played in the associated cities (who thus saw their local productions disappear to the profit of Liège) and also regularly in other places as well.

The implementation of the new organization resulted in a marked improvement in quality. The new unit abandoned repertory and successfully renewed its public. Thanks to improvements in the theatre's technical facilities and increased audience comfort, a strengthened orchestra and choir, the creation of a modest ballet troupe, the opening of a small opera-studio given over to chamber productions and contemporary musical theatre and more ambitious programming, the company staged such productions as *Boris Godunov*, *Pelléas et Mélisande* and *Mathis der Maler*, along with new pieces such as *Cyrano de Bergerac* by Paul Danblon and *Liège-Liberté* by René Defossez (1905–88). In 1974 an Opérette de Wallonie was formed under the wing of the Liège-based house, and was based in the Grand Théâtre de Verviers. From 1981, an inclination towards spectacular productions moved the Opéra de Wallonie to present pieces such as *Carmen*, *Aïda*, *Samson et Dalila* and *Nabucco* in the Palais des Sports in Liège.

Fernand Leclercq

Flemish Community

The repertoire of the Antwerp Opera has always had a distinctly Flemish character. Mezzo-soprano Mina Bolotine (1904–73), baritone Renaat Verbruggen (1909–81) and tenor Sylvain Deruwe (b. 1927) succeeded one another as artistic directors, staging not only the international repertoire but also original Flemish works with a Flemish cast and an ensemble system following the German model. No star system operated, and the work of the director and designer was clearly more important in Antwerp than in Ghent.

Jan Blockx (1851–1912) was the first successful Flemish opera composer. His *Herbergprinses* (*Princess of the Inn*, 1896) and *De bruid der zee* (*The Bride of the Sea*, 1901) have been performed more than 200 times over the years. Paul Gilson (1865–1942) with *Prinses Zonneschijn* (*Princess Sunshine*, 1903) and August de Boeck (1865–1937) with *Winternachtsdroom* (*A Winternight's Dream*, 1902) shared this success. However, the work of younger generation composers – *Egmont* (1944) by Arthur Meulemans (1884–1966), *Jonker Lichthart*

(*Squire Lightheart*, 1928) by Jef van Hoof (1886–1959), *De mannen van Smeerop* (*The Man from Smeerop*, 1952) by Willem Pelemans (1901–91) and *Stroppe-la-corde* (1964) by Peter Welffens (b. 1924) – did not enjoy the same success.

Although traditionally French-oriented, the Ghent Opera became wholly Flemish during World War II, achieving comparatively high artistic levels under Hendrik Caspeele (1889–1980). After the war and a period of disorganization, Vina Bovy (1900–83), a singer of international renown, became one of Ghent Opera's most celebrated artistic directors (1947–55). She instituted a tradition of singing the Flemish, German and English repertoire in Dutch, and the French and Italian in French. This was continued from 1955 to 1961 by Constant Meillander (1897–1977).

Under the management of Karel Locufier (1904–72), however, priority was given to a varied repertoire including both operettas and the 'iron repertoire', now sung in the original language. During Locufier's tenure, the nineteenth-century concession system, in which the director took total financial responsibility, was abolished. From 1973, the company was administered by a non-profit association. Bart Lotigiers (b. 1914) continued these policies and introduced contemporary works. From 1978 on, Luigi Martelli (b. 1920) achieved great popularity with his emphasis on the Italian *bel-canto*. His grand gala productions, featuring world-famous stars, were enormous successes.

In 1981, the operas of Ghent and Antwerp amalgamated. Now called Vlaamse Opera (Flemish Opera), its first director was Alfons van Impe (b. 1921). Under van Impe's management, 'production' became an important artistic concept, with more preparation time, fewer performances and a different repertoire. Alban Berg's *Lulu*, Hindemith's *Mathis der Maler*, Janáček's *From the House of the Dead* were played, and Willem Kersters's (b. 1929) *Gansendonk* was performed for the first time. Public attendance fell, however, especially in Ghent. In 1986–7, interim directors Silveer van den Broeck (b. 1943) and Erik de Meester (b. 1947) tried to steer a more traditional course but staff strikes and a necessary renovation of the opera house in Ghent cut their period of management short.

In 1987, Gérard Mortier, the director of the Muntschouwburg in Brussels, was appointed manager of the newly reorganized company with Jef de Roeck (b. 1930) as its artistic director. Their artistic and financial policy plans, however, did not receive any support from the board of management; in December 1989 Marc Clémeur (b. 1953) was appointed the new manager. Clémeur's artistic plans stressed three main issues: attention to baroque music, contemporary music and an innovative Puccini cycle. His opera house – though with a smaller budget than the Muntschouwburg – intended to compete with opera houses and companies both in Belgium and abroad.

Micheline Heyse

Dance Theatre

Flemish and French Communities

In 1945, dance in Belgium could be divided into two categories: the classically oriented *corps de ballet* attached to the opera houses of Brussels, Antwerp, Ghent, Mons, Charleroi and Liège, whose main role was to provide the *divertimenti* in the opera productions, and the private modern dance companies, which aimed to renew the dance and win for it a place as an independent art.

Although their very existence was threatened by their lack of autonomy, independent budget and sound professional training, the ballets of the Brussels Opera House and the Antwerp Koninklijke Vlaamse Opera (Royal Flemish Opera) in particular were continually building and expanding a varied repertoire. The opera ballets used classical techniques grafted on to the French style of ballet, which had been introduced to Belgium by visiting companies and ballet masters, and the programmes were determined largely by the traditional opera repertoire. The performance of an autonomous programme by the opera's *corps de ballet* was very much an exception.

As a reaction against this state of affairs a small number of private groups began, led by advocates of free and expressive dance and the 'space and expression' theories of Rudolf von Laban. Chief among these groups were those of Lea Daan (Lea Gombert, b. 1906) and Jeanne Brabants (b. 1920) in Antwerp and Elsa Darciel (b. 1906) in Brussels. Thanks to them steps were taken towards the organization of dance training and the raising of professional standards in Belgium.

Immediately after World War II, initiatives taken in 1937 bore fruit and Les Amis de la Danse/De Vrienden van de Dans (Friends of Dance) was created. They organized seven National Dance Festivals between 1947 and 1953, featuring in particular solo dancers and private companies. When these festivals came to an end the opera once again provided the framework wherein the process of development could continue. The people, the financial means, the creative impulse in dance here moved from the private sector to the official institutions.

Without doubt the international breakthrough for Belgian ballet came in 1959 with the creation in Brussels of le Ballet du XXe Siècle (Ballet of the Twentieth Century) under the artistic direction of Maurice Béjart.

It was then, and has remained, an internationally inspired company, revolutionary in casting aside traditional hierarchy and equalizing the number and function of male and female dancers. The stylistic evolution of the Ballet of the Twentieth Century can be described as a passage from the content/idea-based ballet – *Le Sacre du Printemps* (*The Rite of Spring*) and *Boléro* to giant spectaculars such as *Nijinsky, Clown de Dieu*, *I trionfi de Petrarca*, *Notre Faust* and *Le Concours*. Béjart's productions are based on classical techniques but are enriched by a much more individual input by the choreographer. And central to all his work is the problem of contemporary humanity in conflict with society or with itself. Working in close connection with Béjart's company was Mudra, the Centre for Advanced Training and Research for Theatre Interpreters, created in 1969.

Following the departure of Maurice Béjart, the Ballet of the National Opera entered a period of transition with the arrival of the young, modern-style American choreographer Mark Morris, whose contract ended in 1991. In 1992, Bernard Foccroulle, the director of the opera, decided to host Anne-Teresa De Keersmaeker (b. 1960) and her company, Rosas.

The success of the Ballet of the Twentieth Century roused public interest outside Brussels and awakened a sudden political interest in dance among the powers that be. The establishment of the company in Brussels sharply outlined the lack of any such boast among the Flemish or Walloon communities. And so, within the framework of cultural autonomy which dominated the official political character of the time, two supplementary groups were projected, one for Flanders, one for Wallonia.

The creation of the Ballet (since 1976 Ballet Royal) de Wallonie took place in 1966. And yet this company could already look back upon a long history. The Ballet of Wallonia was, in fact, a merging of the three opera ballet groups of Charleroi, Mons and Liège. Hanna Voos (1910–90) was the artistic director of the group until 1977. Over the years the Ballet of Wallonia developed into a company with a classical repertoire (*Giselle*, *Swan Lake*, *Romeo and Juliet*, *Coppelia*) and for a long time was Belgium's only representative of the classical romantic ballet.

But her successor Jorge Lefèbre (1936–90), who was appointed in 1980, followed the path of Maurice Béjart and tried to forge a company in the neo-classical, modernist style, serving the imagination of a single choreographer. His most notable productions included *David Come Home*, *The Prodigal Son's on the Road Again*, *Carmina Burana* and *Carmen*. His later works led him in a narrative and popular direction, giving ballet a cohesion in terms of style and technique that was previously unknown. After his death in 1990 the articles of association of this dance institution were rewritten to form the Centre Chorégraphique de la Communauté française. Its functions were widened to include, in addition to its own productions, hosting and co-producing other artists, ensembles and companies. From that point on its artistic director, currently Frédéric Flamand, was to be appointed for a limited period and the director's mandate extended to ensure a high-quality artistic programme.

The Ballet van Vlaanderen (since 1976 the Royal Ballet of Flanders) was created in 1969, and between then and 1984 danced an extremely varied repertoire. Artistic director Jeanne Brabants aimed to offer as complete a selection as possible of dance techniques and styles to the Flemish public. This programming policy relied on the work of well-known international choreographers, but not to the exclusion of talented Belgians: Jeanne Brabants herself, André Lecleir (b. 1930), Aimé de Lignière (b. 1944) and even Béjart.

In 1984, however, Valery Panov was appointed artistic director/choreographer, and he radically changed this policy, staging only his own choreography. His repertoire consisted of evening-long classical ballets. Roughly speaking, his work may be described as technically virtuoso and dramatically strong. For his subjects, he consistently turned to world literature such as *The Three Sisters,* adaptations of Shakespeare, *War and Peace* (Tolstoi), *The Idiot* (Dostoevsky) and *Til Ulenspiegel* (De Coster). In all his work the emphasis is on spectacular stage effects and his hallmark is the virtuoso *pas de deux*.

With the appointment of Panov, the repertoire of the Ballet Royal de Wallonie and the Koninklijk Ballet van Vlaanderen was effectively exchanged.

In January 1987, Robert Denvers (b. 1942) became artistic director of the Royal Ballet of Flanders. It is now the perfect working sphere for graduates of the Stedelijk Instituut voor Ballet van Antwerpen (Antwerp Municipal Institute of Ballet). This professional school, unique in Belgium, combines a complete general education with ballet training, teaches the Russian Vaganova system for classical dance, and has produced a number of top male dancers of excellent merit and ability.

At the Vlaams Instituut voor Danspedagogie (Flemish Institute for Dance Pedagogics) in Antwerp, a two-year course trains teachers of classical and modern dance. The programme at this higher-education-level school is equally divided into practical, pedagogical and cultural-historical subjects.

Apart from the three large ballet companies there are a number of smaller modern groups. Rosas, based at the National Opera, came into being in 1983: directed by Anne-Teresa De Keersmaeker, this group has been prominently featured at various international festivals. Her works, *Rosas danst Rosas*, *Fase*, *Elena's Aria* and *Bartok/Aantekeningen*, all between 1983 and 1990, belong to post-modernist/minimalist dance, incorporating penetrating mathematical and repetitive movements. Micha Van Hoecke (b. 1944) also deserves attention. This ex-dancer from the Ballet of the Twentieth Century directs his own company, L'Ensemble, which divides its time between its base in the Belgian town of Tournai and Italy, where its work is co-produced (mixed forms of theatre and dance).

Numerous experimental dancers and choreographers (some of them emerging from the Mudra School) attract more and more attention from the media and convey a sense of new and bustling activity in the Belgian dance scene. In the French-speaking community, one should mention Pierre Droulers (b. 1951), Diane Broman (b. 1953), Nicole Mossoux (b. 1956),

Félicette Chazerand (b. 1955) and Michèle Noiret (b. 1960).

The 1980s saw the formation of more organized groups, such as the companies of Michèle Anne De Mey (b. 1959) and José Besprosvany (b. 1959). As well, a series of multimedia theatre companies also began to use dancers, including Plan K and the Théâtre Impopulaire, blurring the lines between these two art forms. This new open attitude toward dance has also allowed subsidized theatres to host and offer periods in residence to dance companies. These institutions, such as Théâtre Varia and the Atelier Sainte-Anne, have thereby offered stability to contemporary choreographers without the direct support of ballet institutions.

On the Flemish side also, numerous experimental choreographers should be noted. Among them are Roxane Huilmand (b. 1964), Marc Vanrunxt (b. 1960), Alain Platel (b. 1956), Ria De Corte (b. 1954), Rosette De Herdt (b. 1951) and especially Wim Vandekeybus (b. 1963), while Jetty Roels (b. 1947) has her own Centre for Multicultural Dance (Indian, Japanese) in Ghent.

Since 1990 many dance festivals have been organized in Belgium, most of them private initiatives. Their intention is to bring new thoughts and trends in dance to the attention of the public. There are, for instance, Klapstuc (Louvain), dance programmes of the Kaaitheater and the Singel, De Beweging (Antwerp), La Balsamine (Brussels) and the Festival Gestes in Brussels, among others.

From 1984 onwards a number of dance associations began to develop parallel activities with the aim of encouraging contemporary creative efforts, favouring new forms of dance at both the technical and choreographic levels. The non-profit association, Danse Plus, focuses on supporting young companies. It regularly organizes festivals or dance-exchanges aimed at showcasing young choreographers. Contredanse, still another association, is developing an Information and Documentation Centre for Dance in the Cultural Centre La Bellone and also publishes a *Guide de la Danse de la*

Frédéric Flamand's 1989 Plan K production of his *The Fall of Icarus*, designed by Fabrizio Plessi.
Photo: Pierre Daled.

Communauté française de Belgique (Guide to Dance in Belgium's French-speaking Community) and a magazine covering the contemporary dance scene.

Finally, a few words about mime. From 1952 onward, the Ghent-born M.A.J. Hoste (1912–77) did a lot of pioneer work in this field. In his native city, he founded both the Hoste-Sabattinitheater and the Academy of Mime (1955). Hoste drew his inspiration largely from Marcel Marceau. Both he and his most important pupil, Maria Van Heirbeeck (b. 1940) – Belgium's first female mime – were advocates and representatives of the *mime pur*.

All of Hoste's pupils, including Frederik Van Melle (1936–85), were to follow him in this respect.

In Antwerp, Herman Verbeeck (b. 1938), who followed in the footsteps of Étienne Decroux, also took revolutionary strides. He was in his turn followed by Jan Ruts (b. 1956) who achieved an international reputation with his company Pyramide op de punt (Pyramid on the Point) in the late 1970s. In Mechelen, another mime, Edwin Peten (b. 1942), created the Mechelse Mimestudio.

Rina Barbier, Patricia Kuypers

Theatre for Young Audiences

Flemish Community

The first youth theatre in Flanders was created in 1940 by puppeteer Jan Brugmans (1902–81) who called the new company De Zonnebloem (The Sunflower). In 1942 he met with financial problems and Joris Diels (1903–92) took over the initiative, giving the running of De Zonnebloem to Fred Engelen. After the war the city of Antwerp approved the Jeugdtheater (Youth Theatre) as an independent company with a separate subsidy and its own theatre. Actress Corry Lievens (1903–68) directed a company of some fourteen actors and the repertoire consisted largely of fairytales and stories adapted for the theatre, although classical plays – those of Shakespeare and Maeterlinck, for instance, and tone poems (Prokofiev) – were also featured. It was one of western Europe's first officially approved youth theatres. Gradually, the repertoire was modernized under the management of Joost Noydens (1968–87) and his successor from 1987 on, Walter Merhottein (b. 1934). In 1974, Toneelgroep Tentakel (Theatre Group Tentacle) came into being. Socially committed, the group offered a repertoire consisting mainly of collective creations. In 1985, struck from the subsidy list, the company closed down.

In Ghent the Nationaal Jeugdtheater (National Youth Theatre) operated from 1969 to 1979 under the direction of Hugo Vandercruyssen (b. 1936). They played in schools and in their own theatre, and their repertoire comprised mainly the work of contemporary playwrights like Tone Brulin, Hugo Meert (b. 1942), Freek Neirynck (b. 1949) and others. In

1978 the puppet theatre Stekelbees, begun in 1974, developed into a children's theatre with a critical contemporary repertoire.

As early as 1959, Jeugd en Theater (Youth and Theatre) had been founded in Brussels by Alice Toen (b. 1924) and Dries Wieme (1924–92). They set out to build a theatre that could connect with the world of children, a trend continued more strongly still from 1968 onwards, under the influence of Volker Ludwig and the Berlin Grips Theater. The plays written by Alice Toen herself were widely acclaimed both at home and abroad. Later on the company operated under the name Brialmonttheater, and its work was aimed at adult audiences. It closed in 1985.

In 1974 the political theatre-in-education group Vuile Mong en Zijn Vieze Gasten (Dirty Mong and His Filthy Friends) began to mount yearly productions, in circus style at first, and from 1980 using a narrative structure.

After working as a director and teacher of dramatic expression with other young theatres, Eva Bal created in 1979 the Speeltheater (Play Theatre) in Ghent. She used children as well as adults in her productions, which were generally based on improvisations relating to social situations. A children's drama school has since been added to this theatre. In 1979 Teater Poëzien (Theatre PoeSee) was created. They produced dramatized versions of poetry and poetic works.

At the end of the 1970s Flanders saw the emergence of a new form of youth theatre, in which actors and puppets performed together. Its founders were Luk de Bruyker (b. 1953) and Freek Neirynck of Teater Taptoe (Tattoo

Theatre) in Ghent, followed by the Mechels Stadspoppentheater (Mechelen Municipal Puppet Theatre) and Poppenteater Froe Froe and Black Out in Antwerp among others.

Since the 1970s a number of companies which normally play for adult audiences have occasionally put on productions for a younger age group. This has especially been the case with the Fakkelteater (Torch Theatre) and the Toneelgezelschap Ivonne Lex (Ivonne Lex Theatre Company) in Antwerp, the Mechels Miniatuur Teater (Mechelen Miniature Theatre) and the Nederlands Toneel Gent (Dutch Theatre Ghent). Since the beginning of the 1980s occasional youth theatre productions have also been made in a number of provincial towns. New style in youth theatre is clearly an initiative that comes from Ghent: the traditional way of working with children is an Antwerp characteristic. But everywhere there are signs of change. The Dutch examples in this area are being noted.

Toon Brouwers

French Community

Theatre for young audiences in French-speaking Belgium underwent a spectacular boom during the 1970s with the number of companies going from three to thirty-five. This was primarily due to new support from both public authorities and the Ligue des familles (Family League). In 1969 the league had created an Association for the Promotion and Distribution of the Theatre for Children and Adolescents while a governmental decree granted official recognition to companies 'for children' in 1973. With no past (or very little) and no places to perform, the new children's groups had the difficult tasks of getting into schools, and creating everything from scenography to scripts. As a result, most productions began to be written collectively, a form still widely used.

This style of theatre gives enormous importance to images, gestures and visual aspects. It has also invented new forms of playwriting – scenarios, image sequencing and children's gestures. Some plays are 'unpublishable' because the text is so slight or even non-existent, being made up of sounds, rumbles, languages that do not exist, or even musical language.

One of its major characteristics is that right from the start it challenged the simplistic division of the world into good and bad and opposed the clichéd use of garish colours, felt flowers and naive animals. Determined not to treat children as idiots, the Théâtre de la Vie in Brussels caused a stir in 1973 with *Arthur au pays des hommes*, which demonstrated a clear post-May 1968 anti-conformism.

The Théâtre Isocèle of Brussels, on the other hand, aimed right from the start to reach the sensitivities of children, rather than their intelligence; it encouraged intuition and emphasized the ambiguity of human relationships. It created the first 'real' productions for nursery schools: *La Maison timide* (*The Timid House*, 1977).

The Théâtre de la Guimbarde, also in Brussels, drew a good number of professionals into the theatre for children, working on well-known texts (Ionesco, Prévert, Svarts, Andersen, Gougaud) while distinguishing itself by its remarkable group activity.

Brussels's Théâtre de Galafronie, a champion of collective work, created a number of outstanding productions including *La Chasse au dragon* (*The Dragon Hunt*, 1980), *L'Arche de Noé* (*Noah's Arc*, 1982) and *La Soupe au crapaud* (*Toad Soup*, 1983).

Liège's Ateliers de la Colline create plays through workshops with children or adolescents in a region suffering from chronic unemployment.

In addition, many small companies are emerging, albeit without resources and without official recognition. Most show a tendency toward musical theatre, work with voice and ballet.

Companies working for a young public have also felt the need to create an instrument in order to represent and promote themselves to the public authorities – press, schools and general public. Based in Brussels, the Chambre des Théâtres pour l'Enfance et la Jeunesse (CTEJ: Chamber of Theatres for Children and Youth), founded in 1976, includes most theatre companies, as well as companies working with puppets for children, singers and even dance companies working in this field. The CTEJ also functions as a forum for ideas, comparisons and questions.

Catherine Simon

Marianne Hansé's 1983 Théâtre de Galafronie production of Didier de Neck and Bernard Chemin's *Toad Soup*, designed by Bernard Chemin and Jean-Claude De Bemels. Photo: Jean-Dominique Burton.

Puppet Theatre

Flemish Community

After World War II, three main types of puppet theatres were active in Flanders. First, the traditional rod-puppet theatres in Antwerp, Ostend and Brussels which had great popularity for mainly adult audiences. Second, a more epic puppet theatre as practised in Ghent by the plastic artists Albert Vermeiren (1915–89) in his Marionettentheater Nele, and by M.A.J. Hoste with Poppenspel't Masker. And third, the primitive glove-puppet theatre of Jan Brugmans (1902–81), Karel Weyler (b. 1913) and Louis Contryn (b. 1929). The latter took their inspiration not so much from the Dutch 'Jan Klaassen' tradition (comparable to Punch and Judy) but developed a personal yet still conventional style not so very different from existing puppet traditions.

All three groups shared naturalistic playing styles, but the latter two also had a pedagogical purpose while performing for children. The rod-puppet theatres used dialect while standard language seemed more appropriate for the two other groups.

In 1946 the first standard work on puppet theatre in Flanders was published: *Het poppenspel in de Nederlanden* (*Puppet Theatre in the Low Countries*, 1946) by Joris Vandenbroucke (1896–1980), the founder of the Ghent Spelleke van de Muide, which started a revival of puppet theatre in Ghent. By the 1970s, some twenty puppet theatres were active there.

Before and after the war, Jef Contrijn (1902–91) from Mechelen occupied an important place in the field. He was the first in Flanders to try to renew both repertoire and style. By 1975–6 his Mechels Stadspoppentheater Opsinjoorke (Mechelen Municipal Puppet Theatre Opsinjoorke) had become the most modern puppet theatre then performing in the country.

The real revival of the Flemish puppet theatre came in the 1970s when puppeteers began to perform in less conventional ways. Among the most important were Rik Hannon (b. 1928) of the Postiljontheater (Brussels), Danny Verbiest (b. 1945) of Malpertuus (Wemmel), Krikkemik (Alsemberg), Teater Taptoe (Ghent), Pompelfloerke (Brussels), Paljas (Roeselare), Joris Jozef (b. 1946) and Maaike (Hasselt).

The Mechelen Municipal Puppet Theatre also played its part in this revival, performing contemporary stories of their own written with completely new puppet characters. Their theatre no longer consisted of a cut-out rectangle separated from the audience by a curtain. Naturalistic and abstract characters alternated and the plays received more dramaturgical attention.

The most striking development in this revival was when combinations of puppets (or abstract figures and objects) and actors performed together. This was first seen at Teater Taptoe. Writer Freek Neirynck and designer Luk de Bruyker both specialized in this 'mixed' form and their company often toured abroad. One of the first performances in their style was Neirynck's *Thomas zit te dromen in de klas* (*Thomas Sits Dreaming in the Class*, 1981).

This mixed form of puppets and actors was also seen in the work of Froe-Froe and the Mechels Stadspoppentheater. The most important solo puppeteers of the 1970s were Joris Jozef, Jejem Piron (b. 1946) and Sonja Vandermaelen (b. 1947).

Freek Neirynck

French Community

Puppets appeared sporadically in Belgium during the seventeenth and eighteenth centuries and were widely present during the nineteenth century, whether rod-puppets, probably of Sicilian origin, or glove-puppets, of French or Italian origin. Until the beginning of the twentieth century puppets enjoyed great popularity. However, the two world wars, the arrival of the cinema, and industrial and social progress reduced the extent of these activities.

Traditional puppet theatres continue in urban centres. This is the case for the Théâtre Toone and its character 'Woltje' in Brussels, and the Théâtre Royal Ancien Impérial and the Théâtre des Marionnettes Liègoises and their 'Tchantchès' in Liège.

New developments occurred during the 1950s, mainly in Brussels: there was theatre in schools (Guignol, Triboulet), activities for television (Suzon (b. 1921) and Jean (b. 1906) Gerardy), a puppet academy (Le Perruchet), puppets used for the music hall and advertising (Les Farfadets, Les Pupazzi, Colibri and his masks), a travelling company (Les Marionnettes Saint-Gilloises) and many amateur theatres.

From 1970, young professional groups emerged, oriented toward both adults and children. There is the Théâtre Al Botroûle in Liège, which works in a traditional way; the Gare Centrale in Brussels, which deals with the relationship between the actor and puppet; and the Créa-Théâtre in Tournai, which investigates the process of creation itself, using actors, puppets and masks. In Namur there is Zygomars; in Brussels the Théâtre des Quatre Mains, which uses glove-puppets; the Théâtre du Tilleul in Brussels uses shadow silhouettes; Jeanpico in Brussels, performs 'object theatre' and finally the Tof Théâtre in Brussels concentrates on an analysis of the everyday.

Also worth noting is the opening in Tournai in 1987 of the Centre de la marionnette of the French-speaking community of Belgium, the objective of which is to develop this art by training, new performances, publishing and promotion.

Most of these professional theatres, experimenting with content and form, tend to operate as theatres for children and youth.

Francis Houtteman

Design
Theatre Space and Architecture

Flemish Community

In Flanders, as elsewhere in Belgium, external factors (including economics) have had great influence on scenic design in recent years. There are now, for instance, unequipped spaces outside traditional playhouses; there are resources in many new cultural centres; and there is

the impact of avant-garde movements in the visual arts. Continually dwindling budgets are a major factor severely limiting what may be spent on a given production. This usually means skimping on the use of space as well as on the elegance of the sets. And since few working in the theatre enjoy any real job security in Flanders, it is hardly surprising that there are only a few designers choosing to make a career in this area.

Since the 1970s, the more significant and interesting scenic designs have excelled in spatial and visual terms, though sometimes failing to capture the full dramatic potential. This is partly a result of the tendency to make theatrical design more autonomous, or at least of certain designers wanting to present their own way of seeing things. This attitude is not so different from that of certain directors who choose the unadorned architecture of existing buildings as their only set.

Indeed, it is possibly the inherent diversity of such contrasting points of view that led to the creation of a professional association for scenic designers in Flanders as well as to the relatively large number of books on scenic design now being published. There are also various institutions introducing courses on scenic design for the very first time.

Turning to the designers themselves, during the period of the National Theatre (1945–65) stage design in Flanders was limited to the pictorial tradition. From 1965, however, new scenographic concepts in design, often in unusual spaces, began to be introduced. Since the 1970s, Andreï Ivaneanu (1936–89) has worked extensively for the NTG (Dutch Theatre Ghent), while John Bogaerts (b. 1940), resident designer at the KNS (Royal Dutch Theatre), has become well known for his work on Brecht. Werner de Bondt (b. 1943) produced many strongly architectural designs for the Studio Herman Teirlinck. Other notable names in Flemish scenography include Jacques Berwouts (b. 1945) especially at the Arena in Ghent, Jerôme Maeckelbergh (b. 1945), who has designed productions for several theatres in Antwerp, and Marc Cnops (b. 1949), who has worked for most of the larger companies in Flanders and Holland. Roos Werckx (b. 1945) and Luc Dhooghe (b. 1939) have designed for the more experimental companies, as has the distinguished young scenographer Jan Versweyveld (b. 1958) who has been connected with De Tijd and Zuidelijk Toneel Eindhoven in the Netherlands. Another interesting and original scenographer is Niek Kortekaas (b. 1958).

Werner De Bondt

French Community

In the 1920s, it was the French who were most concerned with the notion of modernity and this concern spread to Belgian designers of the time. The major influences here were Jules Delacre of the Théâtre du Marais, Albert Lepage of the Théâtre du Rataillon and Belgians such as Marcel Baugniet (b. 1896), René Moulaert (1901–65), who made his career both in Flanders and Paris, Denis Martin (1909–83) and Ange Rawoe (1912–69). Another influence came from the area of graphic design. The French style remained dominant right into the 1950s and even today certain directors prefer French originality to Belgian creativity in the field.

Also of note here is the influence of Raymond Gérôme, whose spectacles at the Palais des Beaux-Arts had impact. Gérôme, in fact, regularly hired painters to do his designs and this element too can be seen in Belgian theatres.

By the end of the 1950s, it was television which gave a great deal of work to designers and which in turn influenced stage design. Innumerable television designers had learned their craft doing plays, ballets and even variety shows for television.

As was probably the case in most countries, the era of set designers soon gave way to an era of scenographers. Serge Creuz (b. 1924), a professor of stage design in the École de la Cambre in Brussels, fought for the official recognition of scenographers in his activities in the Association Belge des Scénographes, Techniciens et Architectes de Théâtre (Belgian Association of Scenographers, Architects and Theatre Technicians), drawing up a Scenographer's Charter and finally establishing in Brussels the Cultural Centre La Bellone.

La Bellone is the principal centre in the country devoted to the performing arts. Set in a beautiful eighteenth-century building, it regularly organizes exhibitions and houses a documentation centre. It is also the centre for various groups connected to the design field.

Alternative views on stage space first developed during the 1970s. During this period isolated experiments started to appear in productions: there was the scenography of the French Claude Lemaire for *Measure for Measure*, produced for the Théâtre du Parvis in 1972, followed by *I*, a play by Frédéric Baal for the Théâtre Laboratoire Vicinal – bizarre shells, created by the sculptor Olivier Strebelle (b. 1927), were used as costumes.

The birth of the Théâtre de l'Esprit Frappeur in the cellar of a private home in 1963 and the installation of the Atelier Sainte-Anne in the attic of another home in 1972 were also

Jean-Claude De Bemels's design for Philippe Sireuil's 1983 Théâtre Royal de la Monnaie production of Leoš Janáček's *Katia Kabanova*.
Photo: Paul Versele.

influential. These extraordinary spaces forced revaluation of the whole notion of theatrical space and its relationship with the public. Such challenges gave birth to some superb stage designs: the turning stage of the *Wunschkonzert* and the hen coop for *Ella* in 1980, a double acting area by Jean-Marie Fievez (b. 1948) for the Atelier Sainte-Anne; the voyeuristic designs of *Avec Ramsès* (*With Ramses*) and *Prothèse* (*Artificial Limb*) created by Jean-Claude De Bemels (b. 1945) in the same theatre in 1984. Each time the audience was designed along with the 'décor'.

In addition to the Atelier Sainte-Anne, other independent companies began in Brussels and needed to find places to perform. There was the Studio Levie, the Chapelle des Brigittines and the Ciné Rio. Then came a movement towards the many deserted barracks, following the example of the Théâtre de la Balsamine. Others discovered an abandoned theatre from the beginning of the century – the Théâtre Varia.

At the Dailly barracks, Martine Wijckaert and De Bemels reinvented *Nadobnisie i koczkodanie czyli zyelona pigulka* (*Dainty Shapes and Hairy Apes or the Green Pill*) by Witkiewicz, using the barracks as raw material, moving the audience from one room to another and finally deceiving it in a superbly 'theatrical' manner with partitions and false walls.

As for actual theatre architecture, companies found themselves working in a wide range of spaces, some never originally conceived of as theatres. Among traditional spaces it is important to note the beautiful Théâtre du Parc and the Théâtre Royal of Namur. But there are companies also working in the ancient market at Schaerbeek (the Halles de Schaerbeek) and in a former barracks (Théâtre de la Balsamine).

Other unusual sites have included the Grotto at Han which in 1948 was used for the première of Herman Closson's play, *Le Jeu de Han* (*The Play of Han*) staged by the Rideau de Bruxelles. Beersel Castle was long the site of a summer festival, while today the cellars of the Stavelot Monastery are the festival's host. The Monastery of Villiers-la-Ville is the locale each summer for large productions such as *Barabas* and *Cyrano de Bergerac*.

During the 1970s, cultural centres began to go up everywhere and provincial theatres found homes thanks to the efforts of Frank Lucas (b. 1922, Deputy Minister of the French Community). Medium-sized and even small Walloon towns (Marche-en-Famenne, Tournai, Libramont and Ottignies) have subsequently put up multi-use halls which have been regularly utilized by touring groups. As suggested by the scenographer Arik Joukovsky (1923–88), these spaces have been built of concrete with a simple scenic frame and an auditorium equipped with a variable rake. Lights can also be hung and the brick walls are designed in an undulating fashion to ensure good acoustics.

In the 1990s, the Théâtre Varia in Brussels was entirely renovated to make its scenic space flexible, more functional and more comfortable. During the same period, eight Brussels theatres had their technical facilities vastly upgraded thanks to financial support from the French Community.

By law, the Théâtre National has an obligation to support other groups as much as possible but since 1985 the company itself has suffered under financial pressure and staff shortages. Nevertheless, it has continued to allow its construction shops to be used by other local groups.

Catherine Simon

Training

Flemish Community

In the 1860s, the (still existing) Royal Conservatories of Ghent, Brussels and Antwerp started courses in diction and declamation following French traditions. They were taught by members of the literary and theatrical professions. Then, as now, conservatories practised a system of education following the best nineteenth-century training, as offered by the Conservatoire de Paris for instance. All followed the lines of musical training: a traditional master–pupil relationship was established involving only a small number of students. The students would be expected to surrender their intuitions and emotions to their master whose skills, experience and famous repertoire of parts had been acquired in a specific discipline. The apprentices would follow the master's example with the intention of equalling or surpassing his achievements.

In 1946, director Herman Teirlinck – a former teacher at the Brussels Conservatory – ensured that the new statutes creating the National Theatre included a section requiring the company to provide a training studio where young actors and technicians could learn advanced professional skills. The guiding principles of this newer-style training were related to four 'cultures': general culture, body culture, voice culture and acting culture. The advanced students formed a company in which their technical skills could be applied and tested before an audience. This approach was completely new in Belgium. The great freedom of these teaching methods, the talent of the first graduates and the inspiring presence of Teirlinck himself brought instant fame to the Studio. In 1948, Fred Engelen was appointed head of the Studio. Both his teaching and his work as a director continued along the lines laid down by Jan-Oscar de Gruyter (1885–1929) and Joris Diels.

In 1956, a new class of Studio graduates inspired Teirlinck to publish his book *Wijding voor een derde geboorte* (*Consecration for a Third Birth*) which later developed into the *Dramatisch Peripatetikon* (*Peripatetic Lessons About Theatre*, 1959), a profession of faith in the future of the theatre and the craft of the actor. At the best of times, the theatre training in the conservatories was but a preliminary training for the Studio.

In Brussels, Teirlinck was succeeded by his pupil Gust Maes (1893–1979), with whom Nand Buyl (b. 1923) later collaborated. One striking feature of the training offered was the creation of a course in kinetics in 1948 taught by Lea Daan both in Antwerp and in Ghent, and a course in eurhythmy taught by Elsa Darciel (b. 1915) in Brussels.

In Ghent, Frans Roggen came to teach drama in 1956. The appointments of Jet Naessens (b. 1915) in 1959 and Luc Philips (b. 1915) in 1962 to the staff of the Antwerp Royal Conservatory saw a change for the better: both curriculum and teaching improved.

The present curriculum, which has often been remodelled on that of the Studio, includes classes in acting, speech, diction, physical training, improvisation and psycho-pedagogics as well as a number of parallel courses (for example history of literature and theatre, art and culture, eurhythmy, methodology of the spoken word, and so on). The training programme is spread over three years. Within this framework each conservatory offers its own variations depending upon the special skills of the teachers.

In the field of design the School of Terkameren in Brussels deserves mention.

Also located in Brussels is the Rijkshoger Instituut voor Toneel en Cultuurspreiding (National Higher Institute for Theatre and Culture Propagation, now called the Hoger Instituut voor Toneel en Cultuurspreiding van het Gemeenschapsonderwijs). Created for the Dutch-speaking community in Belgium, it is the Flemish counterpart of the French community's Institut National Supérieur des Arts du Spectacle, with the difference that there is no actor training at the Hoger Instituut. This training takes place at the former Studio of the National Theatre in Antwerp. This institution became the Hoger Instituut voor Dramatische Kunst (Higher Institute of Dramatic Art) in 1966, and was renamed the Studio Herman Teirlinck in 1967. The curriculum was based on the joint essay *Over de opleiding van de tonelist* (*On the Actor's Training*, 1966) by Teirlinck and Alfons Goris (b. 1930), the director of the school since 1961. From then on, the institute received official status, a sound financial basis and finally, several years later, suitable accommodation.

In 1969, the Ministry of Culture decided to enlarge the Studio with the addition of a Kleinkunstafdeling (entertainment department). In 1991, Toon Brouwers took over the general management of the Studio while Jan Decleir became its artistic director.

A few words here about the Mudra School, founded in Brussels by Maurice Béjart. An international centre of research and advanced study for theatre performers, it was based on more or less the same pattern as the Studio, supported by the Belgian government but run as a private school until 1987. Its aim was to educate artists and theatre technicians in the broadest sense of the terms. Mudra also aimed to stimulate choreographic research and to offer multidisciplinary training.

Alfons Goris

French Community

In the French-speaking community, three Royal Conservatories were created in Brussels, Liège

and Mons at the start of the nineteenth century. They eventually added to their music department a performing arts department, now called *Arts de la Parole*, made up of a section for speech and a section for acting.

The speech sections number on average between ten and fifteen teachers and instructors and about fifty students who are selected by competition. Here students work, for instance, on the fables of the Middle Ages, La Fontaine, Bossuet and Voltaire, as well as Baudelaire, Rimbaud and contemporary poets. The principal course is completed with work such as voice training, phonetics, the history of literature and methodology.

The acting sections number on average some thirty teachers and instructors and slightly fewer than a hundred students, selected by competition. The disciplines taught (acting, voice training, body training, history of the theatre) are similar to programmes at major German and British schools.

At the start of the 1960s two high schools for the performing arts opened in Brussels, the INSAS (Institut National Supérieur des Arts du Spectacle et Techniques de Diffusion) and the IAD (Institut des Arts de Diffusion). These schools give an in-depth preparation for all the professions of the cinema, radio and television, but also have developed theatre sections. Thus, among the leading teachers currently at the INSAS are theatre directors from the new generation – themselves former graduates from the INSAS – such as Michel Dezoteux (b. 1949), Isabelle Pousseur (b. 1957) and Philippe Sireuil (b. 1952). They train actors (in a three-year study cycle) and stage technicians and directors (in a four-year study cycle). The school was founded by Raymond Ravar (b. 1927) and inspired by the French Michel Saint-Denis (the creator of the École de Strasbourg) who participated in person in the start-up of the INSAS, and by the French Pierre Aimé Touchard, who taught there for a number of years.

The IAD, whose programme does not differ greatly from that of INSAS, has been based for a number of years in Louvain-la-Neuve and is currently directed by Jules-Henri Marchant (b. 1940). One of the original features of the IAD is that it carries out activities in collaboration with the Centre d'Études Théâtrales of the Catholic University of Louvain-la-Neuve. The actors are trained for four years under the direction of famous theatre practitioners such as Armand Delcampe (b. 1939) and Pierre Laroche (b. 1931). The training given there, which is both theoretical and practical, is influenced by Jean Vilar's ideas on theatre.

The appearance of the INSAS and IAD drove the three French-speaking conservatories to depart from their more traditional academic approaches. New courses were created and contemporary playwrights (from Heiner Müller to Koltès) found a place beside Shakespeare, Molière and Claudel.

The Royal Conservatory of Brussels benefits from the existence in the capital of a large number of professional, subsidized theatres. The majority of its teachers are attached to these theatres as actors or directors: such is the case for Claude Étienne, Pierre Laroche and André Debaar (b. 1929). Its graduates therefore quickly move into these theatres.

Being denied this advantage, the Royal Conservatories of Liège and Mons have tended to concentrate more on pedagogy. On the one hand they train future speech and theatre teachers, while on the other they experiment in new teaching methods. Such activities were particularly developed in the Royal Conservatory of

Liège where René Hainaux (b. 1918) played a leading role for many years. Since 1970 some twenty foreign grandmasters of the theatre have been invited to Liège, including Kristin Linklater, Uta Birnbaum, Galina Morossova and Miroslav Dedic. It was also at Liège that a section of 'actor-animators' was created, supported notably by the European Social Fund. Also based in Liège is the Centre de Recherches et de Formation Théâtrales de Wallonie (Bureau de Liaison Internationale des Écoles de Théâtre: BLIET), a contact organization which grew from the International Theatre Institute, and the International Centre for Stage Movement Education.

Excellent actors have been trained at INSAS and IAD. But no doubt the greatest merit of these two institutions will prove to be their creation of a number of young and bold directors, who are now at the origin of some thirty new professional companies and several hundred productions annually.

Jean-Henri Drèze

Criticism, Scholarship and Publishing

Flemish Community

In Flanders, research in theatre was for many years the almost exclusive province of philologists and/or critics. This presupposes an approach to the subject through either texts or generalized history. Credible work of this last sort was done by Lode Monteyne (1886–1959), whose *Drama en toneel door de tijden heen* (*Drama and Theatre Through the Ages*, 1949) was long considered a standard.

Alfons van Impe continued along similar lines with his book *Over Toneel* (*About Theatre*, 1978). This book also talks about theatre policy. Jaak van Schoor combines historical and scientific viewpoints on the theatre in his *Een Huis voor Vlaanderen: Honderd Jaar Nederlands Beroepstoneel te Gent* (*A House for Flanders: A Hundred Years of Dutch-spoken Professional Theatre in Ghent*, 1971). He also produced a book on Flemish playwrights, *De Vlaamse Dramaturgie* (*Flemish Dramaturgy*, 1979).

Carlos Tindemans (b. 1931) first introduced sociology to theatrical history in his doctoral thesis, *Mens, gemeenschap en maatschappij in*

de toneelletterkunde van Zuid-Nederland (*Man, Community and Society in the Theatrical Literature of the Southern Netherlands*, Ghent, 1973). Tindemans's later handbook, *Drama en Theater* (Louvain, 1984) is still widely read.

It was in 1972 that dramatic theory was introduced as part of the curriculum in the department of Germanic philology at the Antwerp University Institutions (UIA), although it was initially only an optional course. In 1978, it was extended to a fuller programme with Tindemans as its director.

At the Catholic University of Louvain (KUL), a limited theatre curriculum began in 1979 and was extended to a full programme in 1987–8. The Louvain programme is also concerned with theatre practice and stages many student theatre productions. In 1991 the programme was integrated into the department of cultural studies, directed by Luc Lamberechts (b. 1945).

At both these universities, the theatre sections have strong ties with the respective departments of Germanic philology.

At the State University of Ghent, courses on the history and the development of theatre began in 1969; a full-time drama and theatre programme started in 1987–8 in the Drama and Theatre Centre under the direction of Jaak van Schoor. In 1992, theatre studies became an independent institute with full curriculum for licentiate students within the Faculty of Arts.

At the Free University of Brussels, seminars on educational theatre have been given since 1976. This has resulted in a series of publications, for example, *Het politieke theater heeft je hart nodig* (*Political Theatre Needs Your Heart*, 1982), *Het theater zoekt... Zoekt heet theater* (*The Theatre in Search of... In Search of the Theatre*, 1985 and 1986, 2 vols). In 1989, a chair was created for theatre studies. Nevertheless, there is still no independent theatrical institution in Brussels.

The theatre sections of the different universities each have their own emphasis: Antwerp is modern, methodologically oriented and rather theoretical while Louvain is more practical. Ghent tends towards the historical (Shakespeare, Belgian expressionism) and the Anglo-Saxon and Dutch-oriented theories. Brussels has had a keen interest in the newest Flemish international (also American) drama. But all facets of theatre (and film, especially in Ghent) are taken into account.

Important theatre collections are kept in the Archief en Museum voor Vlaamse Cultuur (Archive and Museum of Flemish Culture) in Antwerp. Ghent has had a Documentatiecentrum voor Dramatische Kunst (Documentation Centre for Dramatic Arts) since 1972. This is a private institution tied to and housed within the Ghent State University. It publishes a quarterly journal of its work, *Documenta*. The foremost critical quarterly review is called *Etcetera*. Information about the Flemish theatre can be obtained from the monthly periodical *De Scene*. The *Vlaams Theater Jaarboek* takes a retrospective view of the year's productions.

In terms of ballet and opera, Rina Barbier (b. 1945) has written several books: *Van opera-ballet naar Ballet van Vlaanderen* (*From Opera Ballet to the Ballet of Flanders*, 1973), *ABC van het ballet* (1978, 1980) and *Het Koninklijk Ballet van Vlaanderen* (*The Royal Ballet of Flanders*, 1983). A standard work in the field of opera is Karel Wauters's (b. 1943) *Wagner in Vlaanderen* (*Wagner in Flanders*, 1983).

Jaak van Schoor

French Community

Apart from the regular reviews in the daily and weekly press, French-speaking Belgium is not rich in critical material on the theatre. There is no specialist journal which closely follows and analyses the full range of productions throughout the seasons, allowing an historical overview.

As for journals which publish studies, analysis and theoretical articles, mention should be made of *Alternatives théâtrales* produced in Brussels and edited by Bernard Debroux (b. 1946). *Alternatives théâtrales* concentrates in particular on new wave theatre productions, especially those giving considerable attention to dramaturgy and criticism. *Cahiers Théâtre Louvain* is edited by Armand Delcampe and published as part of the activities of the Atelier Théâtre and the Centre d'Études Théâtrales at Louvain-la-Neuve. There is also a semiotic journal called *Degrés*, published in Brussels and edited by André Helbo (b. 1947), which features studies on the theatre. As for stage design, in 1977 Arik Joukovsky published the leading journal *Actualités de la Scénographie* in Brussels, although it moved to Paris in 1983. In the past, there were two major periodicals: *Théâtre de Belgique*, which appeared during the 1950s, and *Théâtre dans le monde*, published by the International Theatre Institute office in French-speaking Belgium until 1965.

Several publishers issue plays: the Éditions des Éperonniers, Le Cri and Les Éditions Labor (in the Espace Nord collection, which republishes great works from the past). The Didascalies collection of the Ensemble Théâtre Mobile has published some contemporary plays, occasionally accompanied by a critical dossier. The Rideau de Bruxelles has a collection featuring a number of Belgian plays that it has produced. There have also been some significant publications and distribution activities carried out by Éditions Promotion Théâtre/Émile Lansman.

Many documents on the history of the theatre and contemporary theatrical activity are gathered in the theatre section of the Archives et Musée de la Littérature in Brussels. The Maison du Spectacle has a collection of material dealing essentially with scenography, and it also functions as an exhibition space and meeting place for theatrical associations. The Archives et Musée de la Littérature produces various studies on the history of the theatre in French-speaking Belgium, regularly publishes specialist articles and exhibitions on this subject, and since 1983 has been publishing the *Annuaire du Spectacle de la Communauté française de Belgique* (*Theatre Yearbook of the French-Speaking Community of Belgium*).

Among the range of research activities, mention should be made of the social and economic studies of the theatre of Michel Jaumain (b. 1951) and his co-workers, presently based in the Centre d'Information et de Recherches sur l'Économie de la Culture et de la Communication (Information and Research Centre on the Economic Aspects of Culture and Communication) in Brussels. The group headed by Roger Deldime (b. 1939) at the University of Brussels deals with the sociological aspects of the theatre, especially in research on audience and reception. Studies on the theatre are published by Éditions De Boeck-Université (theatre series) and in the Archives du Futur collection, published by Labor.

Paul Emond
Flemish sections translated by
Jos van Gorp
French sections translated by
Philip Murgatroyd

Editor's note: The order of the placement of material on the French and Flemish communities in this article represents an agreement between the two communities and reflects their national desires in this regard.

Further Reading

Flemish Community

Alphenaar, Carel, et al. *De goden van het theater. 22 Nederlandse en Vlaamse toneelschrijvers aan het woord.* [The Gods of theatre: twenty-two Dutch and Flemish playwrights talking about their craft]. Harlekijkn: Westbroek, 1983.

Faits et Info. [Facts and info]. Brussels: Flemish Belgian Centre of the ITI, 1987.

Hellemans, Dina, et al. *Op de voet gevolgd. 20 jaar Vlaams Theater in internationaal perspectief.* [Sticking close to: twenty years of Flemish theatre from an international perspective]. Brussels: Free University of Brussels, 1990.

Hermans, Mark, and Jaak van Schoor, eds. *Dramaturgie in Vlaanderen/L'Art dramatique en Flandre/Playwriting in Flanders.* Antwerp: Flemish Belgian Centre of the ITI, 1974.

Olaerts, Ann, et al. 'Flemish Playwrights'. *Articles*, no. 7, Special issue (Summer 1991).

Theaterjaarboeken voor Vlaanderen. [Flanders theatre yearbook]. Antwerp: Flemish Belgian Centre of the ITI, 1966–.

van Schoor, Jaak. 'The Contemporary Flemish Scene'. In *An Anthology of Contemporary Belgian Plays, 1970–1982*, ed. David Willinger, 6–10. New York: Whitston, 1984.

——. 'Il teatro fiammingo prima del 1945'. ['Flemish theatre since 1945']. In *Storia del XX Secolo*. [A history of the twentieth century], ed. Tullio Gregory. Rome: Instituto della Enciclopedia Italiana, 1993.

French Community

Centre de Sociologie du Théâtre. *Théâtres et jeunes publics, 1970–1980*. [Theatre and young audiences, 1970–1980]. Brussels: Direction générale de la Jeunesse et des Loisirs, 1981. 335 pp.

Deldime, Roger, ed. *Le Théâtre belge de langue française.* [French-language theatre in Belgium]. Brussels: Éditions de l'Université de Bruxelles, 1983. 282 pp.

Emond, Paul. 'Un siècle de théâtre'. ['A century of theatre']. In *Cheminements dans la littérature francophone de Belgique au XXème siècle.* [Paths of French-language literature in Belgium in the twentieth century], 91–125. Quaderni di Francofonia, 4. Florence: Leo S. Olschki Editore, 1986.

En scène pour demain: Ou soixante ans de théâtre belge. [Stagings for tomorrow: sixty years of Belgian theatre]. Brussels: Libres Images aux Presses de la Bellone, 1988. 204 pp.

Jaumain, Michel. 'Le Théâtre dramatique francophone: cadre institutionnel et statut juridique depuis 1945'. ['French-language theatre: institutional framework and legal status after 1945']. *Courrier hebdomadaire du CRISP* (Centre de Recherche et d'Information Socio-Politiques), nos. 911–12 (1981). 65 pp.

Lilar, Suzanne. *Soixante ans de théâtre belge.* [Sixty years of theatre in Belgium]. Brussels: Renaissance du livre, 1952. 107 pp. Also available in English and Dutch.

Morckhoven, Paul Van. *The Contemporary Theatre in Belgium.* Brussels: Information and Documentation Institute, 1970. 125 pp.

Quaghebeur, Marc. 'The Current Situation of the French-language Theatre of Belgium'. In *An Anthology of Contemporary Belgian Plays, 1970–1982*, ed. David Willinger, 291–5. New York: Whitston, 1984.

——. 'Introduction to Belgian Theatre'. *Gambit* 11, nos. 42–3 (1986): 9–24.

——. 'Le Devenir du Jeune Théâtre en Belgique francophone'. ['The evolution of French-language theatre in Belgium']. *Les Dossiers du Cacef* 61 (1978): 23 pp.

——. 'Situation du théâtre en Belgique francophone'. ['Current situation of French theatre in Belgium']. In *Aspects du théâtre d'expression française*. [Aspects of theatre in the French language], 63–82. Gand: Frans Roggenstichting, 1982.

——. 'Une institution théâtrale à la croisée des chemins'. ['A theatrical institution at the crossroads']. *Jeu: Cahiers de Théâtre* 35 (1985): 111–25.

Renieu, Lionel. *Histoire des théâtres de Bruxelles, depuis leur origine jusqu'à ce jour*. [A history of the theatres in Brussels: from the beginnings to the present]. Brussels: Culture et civilisation, 1974. 1,200 pp.

BELORUSSIA

(see **BELARUS**)

BOSNIA-HERZEGOVINA

As part of the former Yugoslavia, the Republic of Bosnia and Herzegovina covered some 51,100 square kilometres (19,700 square miles). In April 1992 it proclaimed itself an independent country and in May of the same year became a member of the United Nations. At the same time, civil war began among the three ethnic groups which comprised the population of Bosnia and Herzegovina: Muslims, Serbs and Croats.

Located in southeastern Europe, this territory borders Pannonia (one of the most fertile plains in Europe) in the north and the Adriatic Sea in the south. This land is, in fact, the border between eastern and western Europe, between the Roman Catholic and Eastern Orthodox religions. Because of this location, its history is complicated both socially and historically over the more than ten centuries since the name Bosnia was first mentioned as an autonomous and independent country.

Numerous wars devastated the territory from the Middle Ages and the Crusades right up until the two world wars of the twentieth century. World War I, in fact, started in Bosnia and Herzegovina, when the Austro-Hungarian monarchy attacked Serbia after the assassination of the Austrian crown prince Franz Ferdinand in Sarajevo.

The more recent civil war, which started after the declaration of independence in April 1992, showed the complexity of the ethnic composition of the republic, which was one of six distinct federal units of the Socialist Federal Republic of Yugoslavia (1945–91). In November 1943, only three days before the meeting of the Anti-Fascist Committee of the National Liberation of Yugoslavia under the leadership of Josip Broz Tito and the Communist Party, it was decided that a separate federal republic of Bosnia and Herzegovina should be formed as a united community of Muslims, Serbs and Croats. To be an heir to the one which existed since December 1918, this newly founded Socialist Republic of Bosnia and Herzegovina was to be a continuation of the

Medieval Bosnia. In the new Yugoslav federation, it was to be the balance point between nationalist appetites of both Serbs and Croats, the largest constituents of the Yugoslav community.

With the disintegration of Yugoslavia in 1991, the balance among the ethnic groups of Bosnia and Herzegovina was tilted leading to armed conflict starting in April 1992. Within a year, more than two hundred thousand people had died and almost 2 million inhabitants had fled the country, which in 1991 had a population of some 4.4 million. Much of the fighting was in and around Sarajevo, the capital, which in 1991 had a population of 415,600. Other large regional centres were also part of the war zone – Banja Luka, Tuzla, Mostar, Zenica and Bihać.

The fate of Bosnia and Herzegovina was uncertain in 1994 and its political, demographic and cultural picture was changing day by day. It is unlikely, therefore, that a review of the history of the modern theatre in Bosnia and Herzegovina can show what future audiences can expect to see. Nevertheless, such a review can explain the circumstances which made Bosnia and Herzegovina the stage for one for the bloodiest tragedies of the twentieth century.

In the Medieval Bosnian state, theatre life corresponded to European standards. Jesters, jugglers and players from the Bosnian court were exchanged with artists from the Serbian and Dubrovnik courts. The name of one of the jesters, Pribinj, from the court of the Bosnian ruler Sandalj Hranić in 1410, even, comes down to us, an indication of his high regard. At the start of Turkish rule in 1463 theatre life began to distance itself from Europe's main trends. Theatrical life returned to folk forms including the Turkish shadow theatre, here called *karadjoz*. Echoing the Medieval comic theatre, it was played in the vernacular and developed typical local characters.

The first theatre in Bosnia and Herzegovina was built in Sarajevo within the living quarters of the English consul in the second half of nineteenth century. A similar stage was built shortly after by the German consul. Both had a mainly personal character and limited influence. Community theatres in Sarajevo and Tešanj, however, had a more public character but were pushed aside by touring theatre groups which performed plays with nationalist themes. At the same time, national theatres were being founded in other Yugoslav regions such as the Hrvatsko narodno kazalište (Croatian National Theatre) in Zagreb (1860), Srpsko narodno pozorište (Serbian National Theatre) in Novi Sad (1861) and Slovensko narodno gledališče (Slovenian National Theatre) in Ljubljana (1867).

After the occupation of Bosnia and Herzegovina by the Austro-Hungarian monarchy in 1879, a more modern theatre began to develop. Over the next forty years, theatre life in Sarajevo developed from modest community shows and the national romances of the touring groups into a much more bourgeois theatre, this according to the most important historian of the theatre of Bosnia and Herzegovina, Josip Lesić (1929–93). Unlike other Yugoslav republics, though, there were no permanent stages around which the theatre life could concentrate and around which a specific profile of theatre could be formed. This absence remains essentially true right into the 1990s due to the complexity of the ethnic composition and the absence of a specifically Bosnian national theatre which could form a unique and specific profile.

During the Austro-Hungarian period, touring groups from Serbia and Vojvodina were not allowed to perform nationalist plays. Despite the prohibition, groups did perform, the first one in 1879.

On the other hand, a Deutsches Theater (German Theatre) was founded in Sarajevo in 1881, and it was active, with little influence on the local populace, until 1894 when its building burned down. A few years later, Prvo bosansko-hercegovačko narodno pozorište (First National Theatre of Bosnia and Herzegovina) was founded in Tuzla, but its name was soon changed to Prvo srpsko bosansko-hercegovačko pozorište (First Serbian Theatre of Bosnia and Herzegovina). It survived less than a year. In 1912 the work of the Srpsko diletantsko pozorište (Serbian Amateur Theatre) was prohibited, and the work of the Zemaljsko narodno pozorište (National Theatre), founded in 1913, dissipated because of the beginning of World War I.

During the Austro-Hungarian period, Bosnia and Herzegovina had similar borders as it did in the Yugoslav federation. After World War I, Bosnia and Herzegovina became part of the new Kingdom of Serbs, Croats and Slovenes (the name of the first mutual state of southern Slavs in 1918) and the statehood of Bosnia and Herzegovina as an independent unit was questioned. Nevertheless, a permanent theatre was founded in Sarajevo. The Narodno pozorište (National Theatre) was established in 1920, but because of poor working conditions (the building itself was under renovation) was sent to visit the mainland and Dubrovnik, where the actors performed their first season. In October 1921, after a three-day celebration, the theatre was opened to the public.

In 1929, King Alexander Karageorgevich's dictatorship started and the new Kingdom of Yugoslavia was proclaimed. The territory of Bosnia and Herzegovina, as in the other parts of Yugoslavia, was divided into provinces. In 1931, in Banja Luka, the capital of Vrbaska province, another permanent theatre was founded. By World War II, there were two permanent theatres, in Sarajevo and Banja Luka. Both their programmes had totally Yugoslav repertoires including Bosnian and Herzegovinian drama. Each ethnic group had its own spiritual nourishment from the stage.

The organization of these theatres was directly connected with the state; administrators were appointed like those in other sectors of state administration. Theatres were also financially dependent on the state, and remained so throughout the Yugoslav federation period.

After the collapse of the Kingdom of Yugoslavia in 1941, the independent state of Croatia was formed; it annexed Bosnia and Herzegovina. During this period Narodno pozorište in Sarajevo changed its name and repertoire. For the first time the name showed the national character of the theatre: Hrvatsko državno kazalište (Croatian State Theatre). During its four seasons, no Serbian plays were performed. On the other hand, the repertoire was rich with pieces from 'Bosnian life', among which the most numerous were those by Ahmed Muradbegović, the artistic director.

The goal of the national liberation movement (partisans under the leadership of Tito and the Communist Party of Yugoslavia) was not only the liberation of the southern Slavs and their unification into a single state, but also a change of social system, a socialist revolution. Once this was realized, the new government took over control of all social and cultural activities and demanded the clear ideological orientation of culture. The *idea* was more important on stage than the execution of it and the number of people in the audience was more important than the quality of the audience. Theatre became a place for mass gatherings where performances were to articulate ideas which reflected the political moment. The pedagogical role of theatre was at the forefront, and theatre ensembles were forced occasionally to leave their buildings and play their work in various factory halls and cultural centres.

The government, clearly interested in developing a theatre network, opened many new theatres. Almost all the professional theatres in Bosnia and Herzegovina, in fact, were founded in the first decade after World War II. These included Narodno pozorište Tuzla (National Theatre of Tuzla, 1949), Narodno pozorište Mostar (National Theatre of Mostar, 1949), Narodno pozorište Zenica (National Theatre of Zenica, 1950), Pozorište za mlade (Youth Theatre, 1950) and the Kamerni teatar 55 (Studio Theatre 55, 1955). Their work continued until the civil war in 1992. Renovated and newly founded theatres took over the staff and the repertoire from those which had operated before World War II.

The period from 1945 to 1953 was characterized by a strong ideological control reflected in both production and dramatic literature. The repertoire consisted of mainly Russian classics (Chekhov, Turgenev, Gogol, Gorki and Ostrovsky) along with Shakespeare and Molière, of contemporary Soviet playwrights (Skvarkin, Kataev and Petrov), of plays by Yugoslav authors (Držić, Sterija, Stanković, Cankar and Krleža) and occasionally plays by contemporary playwrights (Humo, Kulenović and Ćopić). Contemporary playwrights were required to respect the theory of reflection; that is, to show reality on stage through a strictly ideological prism. The stage becomes, as Lesić says, 'utilitarian imitation of life' under the strict eye of the party.

Whenever it seemed that the stage showed the uglier face of reality, repression and punishment came into effect. The director of the Narodno pozorište Sarajevo, Skender Kulenović, was removed from office and his comedy *Djelidba* (*The Division*) which had its opening night at the beginning of 1948 was removed from the repertoire. *The Division* touched a nerve in looking at the relationship of the different ethnic groups. The communist government had earlier proclaimed that problem as having been positively solved. This was a taboo topic, out of the reach of anyone's critical questioning. These circumstances did not essentially change during the entire period of communist cultural influence. The equal representation of all nationalities also had priority in the selection of repertoire and theatre management which served as clear proof of the correct solution to the national question in both socialist Yugoslavia as well as in Bosnia and Herzegovina.

The period from 1953 to 1960 was characterized by a gradual loosening of political control in the theatre. One could also see the difference in the socialist system of the Soviet and Yugoslav models. The Communist Party changed its name to the League of Communists in 1952, and in the same year, during the Congress of the Writers of Yugoslavia, a plea was published which asked for an end to the practice of socialist-realism.

In the theatre, the sudden development of a network along with a lack of artists specifically from Bosnia and Herzegovina resulted in the need for guest actors and directors. Bosnian theatres turned into Yugoslav stages. In the newly founded theatres, especially in Tuzla, important actors and educated directors from Belgrade and Zagreb began to appear. The Malo pozorište (Little Theatre) was founded in Sarajevo at this time which, in its form (studio theatre) and its repertoire (plays with a critical orientation, dealing with existential questions) differed from all the other theatres in the republic.

Studio theatres became a trend in most of the larger centres in Yugoslavia, as well as in provincial centres of Bosnia and Herzegovina. Studio 64 was founded in Mostar in 1959. On the other hand, theatre as an educational tool was all but forsaken. Stylization in acting and abstraction in set design showed new approaches to theatre art.

Younger critics began demanding from directors creative risk, imaginative ideas and a real interpretation of literature. In such a climate the Malo pozorište was founded under the artistic directorship of Jurislav Korenić.

Liberal influences in politics became stronger between 1960 and 1970. At the same time, circumstances leading to the decentralization of Yugoslav society were becoming stronger as well. In the theatre, new trends were emerging. A festival of small stages was founded at the Malo pozorište. The concept of 'large stage' was not limited to physical dimensions but also applied to the importance which national theatres gave to the educational function of the theatre. Their programming policy had too often had to satisfy values affirmed by official policy. The small stages attempted to find new paths for the theatre. The Festival malih i eksperimentalnih scena (Festival of Small and Experimental Stages) welcomed very different creative attempts, artistic achievements and styles.

The first teaching institution in the field of set design was also founded at this festival –

Dramski studio 1967 (Drama Studio 1967). As well, the festival gave an opportunity to local audiences to see important contemporary theatres from abroad. One of the most important was the Living Theatre with their production of *The Brig*.

In the 1960s, numerous playwrights from Bosnia and Herzegovina emerged whose social and critical orientation was reflected more in their contemporary and historic themes (with implications for the present) than in their forms, which were mostly traditional.

The 1970s were characterized by a consolidation of these ideas, by further institutional development and by steps toward a definition of culture in Bosnia and Herzegovina. In this decade, local values gained even greater importance in Yugoslavia. More significance, for example, was given to the republics than to the overall federation. Collective decision-making, as a basic theory of self-management in socialism, had an especially negative influence on theatre art. This was reflected in the loss of the creative spirit of many capable individuals whose authority was undisputed in the 1950s and 1960s. The complex procedure involved in selection of repertoire (in which non-artistic personnel shared) was part of the creative crisis in the Bosnian and Herzegovinian theatre. The same happened in other parts of Yugoslavia.

As a reaction to the theatre crisis, new forms of non-institutional theatre emerged, like Pozorište u pokretu (Theatre on the Move) which performed in the mainland. The family theatre, Maska i pokret (Mask and Movement) with its specific organizational and aesthetic orientation was founded by Iva and Petar Mandić. Both were searching for a way to use puppets and movement as a medium for theatrical expression. This theatre continued its activity into the 1980s on the stages of Spain and the Netherlands. One-person scripts by Josip Pejaković, the leading actor of the Narodno pozorište Sarajevo (*Oj, živote – What a Life*) and by Zijah Sokolović, the leading actor of Kamerni teatar 55 (*Glumac je glumac je glumac – An Actor is an Actor is an Actor*) gained great popularity. These plays also gained an international reputation and were later translated into Polish, German, English and other languages.

There were as well important changes in the organization of the theatre. The Association of Professional Theatres of Bosnia and Herzegovina became a coordinator of events such as the Festival of Small and Experimental Stages, the

Festival of Professional Theatres of Bosnia and Herzegovina in Jajce, the Puppet Theatre Biennial in Bugojno, and the Parade of Professional Theatres in Brčko. Bosnia and Herzegovina's openness towards all Yugoslav authors was also defined through this association. A department of dramatic arts was opened at the Philosophy Faculty of Sarajevo. Directors, actors, playwrights and critics were all educated there. Nevertheless, there still remained a constant need for skilled artists from Belgrade and Zagreb.

Tito died in 1980, which marked the beginning of the end of the Yugoslavia in which Bosnia and Herzegovina had the opportunity to develop as an equal member of the federation. The basic principles in the country's politics and culture did not change: Bosnia and Herzegovina still provided a balance in the Yugoslav federation. But the Festival of Small and Experimental Stages did change its concept. From this point it included the best performances from all over Yugoslavia, a decision which showed that Bosnia and Herzegovina still functioned as a neutral territory on which all Yugoslavs could freely compete. This new concept, introduced by artistic director Miro Lasić, was opposed by both Sterijino pozorje (Sterija's Theatre), which had the reputation of being the most important theatre festival of Yugoslav plays in the country, and critics who complained about its lack of clearly defined aesthetic principles.

At the end of 1980s, the festival changed its name to the Festival jugoslovenskog teatra (Festival of Yugoslav Theatre) and in 1991, its last year, the name was changed again to Festival jugoslovenskih teatara (Festival of Yugoslav Theatres), a small but significant change which emphasized the unique character of each of the Yugoslav republics. In fact, the festival became a review of the biggest and the best performances from the Yugoslav repertoire.

The Academy of Dramatic Arts was founded in Sarajevo in 1980, finally ensuring the education of strong artistic personnel. At the beginning, the academy had only an acting department, but in 1989 a department for theatre directing was opened as well.

Ironically, the weakening of the authority of the political structure after Tito's death led to an enrichment of artistic life in the country. Bosnia and Herzegovina quickly gained a reputation for developing artists rather than political hacks. It also became a haven for artists who opposed the growing nationalism of Slovenia, Croatia and Serbia. In this atmosphere, a new theatre was founded, Otvorena scena Obala (Open Stage Shore), whose work started a trend called 'new primitivism'. Basically, it tried to recognize local culture, often in a naturalistic way.

The international success of the play *Tetovirano pozorište* (*The Tattoo Theatre*) by Mladen Materić (a prize at the international theatre festival in Edinburgh, a tour in the USA, Canada, France and Portugal) showed that the artistic originality of this work, originating in a spirit of 'new primitivism', held attractiveness for audiences.

National trouble in Yugoslavia became more intense at the end of the 1980s and the beginning of the 1990s. Bosnia and Herzegovina still welcomed authors and plays from other parts of the country. It was noteworthy that a Bosnian production by Narodno pozorište from Zenica appeared at Sterijino pozorje in 1990 with the first performance of *Sveti Sava* (*St Sava*), a drama by Siniša Kovačević, a Serbian author, which, because of its heretical views, was not performed in his home town. While in Belgrade, a performance was interrupted by a group of nationalist extremists who stormed the theatre.

Besides classics, the repertoire policy of most theatres in Bosnia and Herzegovina in the year before the war clearly placed an emphasis on the recognition of the Yugoslav dramatic heritage. Among the plays which found their place in the repertoire were *Lejla – Na božjem putu* (*Laela – in Search of God*) by Ahmed Muradbegović, *Požar strasti* (*The Flames of Passion*) by Josip Kosor, and *Pustolov pred vratima* (*A Vagabond at the Door*) by Milan Begović. Yugoslav television broadcast the first performance of the play *Djelidba* (*The Division*) by Skender Kulenović from Kamerni teatar 55. The presence of national political leaders at the opening night indicated the importance that this play was given by the then-current political authorities. Those same parties came to power in November 1990 and started the 'division' of Bosnia and Herzegovina, a division that would turn into an armed conflict in 1992. The last new play at the Narodno pozorište in Sarajevo before the war opened in March 1992 was Dževad Karahasan's drama *Čudo u Latinluku* (*A Miracle in Latinluk*), an adaptation of the first Bosnian play, *Nauk Krstijanski* (*Christian Learning*), written in 1616 by a Franciscan monk, Matija Divković. With it, the circle closed again and the horrors of destruction, known here from the Middle Ages, were renewed. Nevertheless, theatre production did not disappear completely in the demolished Sarajevo. The Kamerni teatar played the pacifist protest musical *Hair* and amateur plays were regularly staged in basements. The drama *U skloništu* (*In the Shelter*), by the contemporary playwright Safet Plakalo, was even recorded for television.

Structure of the National Theatre Community

The network of professional theatres in Bosnia and Herzegovina was one-third the size of that of Serbia and half that of Croatia. More specifically, there were six professional theatres located in five regional centres. None had been closed down, as had been the case in other Yugoslav republics, in the period after World War II. In fact, these theatres were centres of cultural life and very often went beyond the exclusively theatrical domain and had influence on their regions.

Because the first professional company was not founded until 1920, community theatre was an important way of organizing theatrical life. In 1945, amateur actors joined professionals and artistic leaders in the founding of new theatres. Community theatres, though, remained well developed alongside the professional ones. In smaller cities they were, in fact, a substitute for professional theatres and had similar repertoires. Subsidized by the state, these theatres functioned as professional theatres, but because of the lower budgets, they had shorter seasons. The highest artistic quality was reached in community theatres in Travnik, Visoko, Bugojno, Trebinje and Sarajevo. The most important festival of community theatres in Yugoslavia took place in Trebinje.

The theatres in Sarajevo, Banja Luka, Tuzla, Mostar and Zenica were connected to the state in terms of both budget and politics. Between 80 and 90 per cent of the funds originated from state budgets, mostly from the municipalities and the republic. Theatres were financed in direct relation to their proposed repertoire, a repertoire set by the theatre's artistic committee. A bonus system rewarded performances which won prizes at festivals or which were recognized by the federal ministry. The remainder of funds originated from ticket sales or from sponsorships. This marketing method became especially popular in the 1980s. Ticket prices were kept low, with discounting systems and subscriptions available to schools, military institutions and workers. In this way, theatres easily acquired full houses and audiences had access to inexpensive tickets.

In 1946, the Opera was founded in the biggest theatre in the republic, Narodno pozorište in Sarajevo, and in 1950 a ballet ensemble was founded. Other theatres nurtured an exclusively dramatic repertoire. Theatres generally planned eight new productions each season, but very often fewer productions were mounted, either because funds were reallocated or because high inflation shrunk budgets by the end of each season. The large number of employees in technical and administrative departments were ultimately an organizational burden for each theatre, but through increased self-management each theatre acquired the right to decide its own artistic direction. Nevertheless, the lack of imagination and lack of creative risk in many theatres was the direct result of employees' concern for their personal incomes. As members of artistic councils, government representatives and politicians also had great influence on theatre work, often taking on a censorship role.

Commercial theatre in Bosnia and Herzegovina did not, for the most part, exist. One-person scripts were almost always financially successful, though, being very easy to tour. They were also very much liked by audiences and seen in many parts of both Bosnia-Herzegovina and Yugoslavia. Many were also recorded.

The Association of Professional Theatres of Bosnia and Herzegovina, with its headquarters in Sarajevo, organized and coordinated national theatre activity, ran festivals and published dramatic literature and works of theatre theory.

The Festival of Small and Experimental Stages, founded in 1960, was long one of the most important Yugoslav theatre events. Lasting ten days, in its last years it showed eighteen productions selected by a federal jury and a jury from each republic who chose productions from their regions. A Golden Wreath was awarded to the best performance.

A Festival of Puppet Theatres of Bosnia and

Herzegovina took place every second year from 1970 alternating with a Federal Puppet Festival which gathered the best puppet productions from all over Yugoslavia. A Theatre Festival of Bosnia and Herzegovina, taking place every year in Jajce, did not select plays but allowed each theatre to decide which production to send.

From 1974 until the war, a festival of Bosnian authors took place in Brčko. This event did not have a major influence on theatre life, but was an opportunity for regional audiences to see performances from all the large centres.

Artistic Profile

Companies

It is difficult to divide the theatres of Bosnia and Herzegovina according to aesthetic criteria. All the theatres, founded or revived after World War II, had basically the same social role assigned to them by the new socialist society. That role was first of all educational, aimed at the spreading of literacy. Each theatre's programme was directed to an audience which was supposed to gain knowledge and education.

The largest company was the Narodno pozorište Sarajevo (National Theatre of Sarajevo), formed from parts of the partisan theatre group and from parts of an older ensemble. Its first performance after the war, *Sumnjivo lice* (*A Face You Cannot Trust*) by Branislav Nušić, took place on 26 May 1945. Its repertoire over the next decade included classical plays by both domestic and foreign authors, committed Soviet plays and propaganda pieces by contemporary playwrights. It followed a clear ideological orientation, turning the stage into a battleground for the transformation of society. Its style was essentially realistic and offered a still-life of the past without interacting with the reality surrounding it.

In the 1950s, young directors educated after the war (Jablan, Grigorović and Drašković) brought some changes (the Stanislavski method of acting and stylization in set design). This resulted in a more liberal attitude towards scripts. The acting ensemble became stronger and the theatre improved steadily until the mid-1960s when, due to the ageing of the ensemble, a crisis set in. After many of the older generation retired, there were simply not enough young, educated actors to take their places. Theatre seasons included mostly plays by contemporary playwrights from Bosnia and Herzegovina (Pašalić, Žalica, Fetahagić, Kapor and Miroslav Jančić, b. 1935) and adaptations of the literary heritage from Bosnia and Herzegovina. The ensemble regularly made tours abroad, mostly to Bulgaria, Czechoslovakia and Poland, and frequently visited other parts of Yugoslavia.

The theatre celebrated fifty years of existence – dating back to the 1920s – with a season that included *Kuća oplakana* (*The House Mourned*) by Rodoljub Čolaković (a revolutionary topic), *Kamen spavač* (*The Sleeping Stone*), an adaptation of Mak Dizdar's poetry (a historic topic), and *Dundo Maroje* (*Uncle Maroje*) by Marin Držić (a local classic). In the first half of the 1970s, its most notable performances were *Golgota* (*Golgotha*) by Miroslav Krleža and *Omar Paša Lataš* (*Omar Pasha Latas*) by Duško Andjić, which the theatre brought to Sterijino pozorje. Despite the arrival of some strong directors, among whom Sulejman Kupusović was the most important, an ongoing need for directors was clear. In 1977, a renovation of the building began and lasted for four years. The theatre continued its work during this period in the inadequate space of the police hall. The restored building, however, ultimately provided the ensemble with better conditions for work and a stage 40 per cent larger.

In the 1980s, the most important plays mounted included *Sprovod u Terezijenburgu* (*The Funeral in Theresienburg*) by Miroslav Krleža, *Hrvatski Faust* (*The Croatian Faust*) by Slobodan Šnajder and *Vojcek* (*Woyzeck*) by Georg Büchner. The first performance of the play *Gamlet* (a play on words on *Hamlet*) in 1986 resulted in a controversy around the Croatian writer Slobodan Šnajder.

The last season before the war was characterized by an absence of contemporary drama. The theatre remounted older performances (*Omar Paša Lataš*, 1977; *Hasanaginica*, 1986) and, challenged by the social changes, revived plays by authors whose works were almost forgotten after the war – *Požar strasti*, by Kosor, and *Na božjem putu*, by Muradbegović. The repertoire also included several classics including Bulgakov's adaptation of Gogol's *Dead Souls*, directed by Dejan Mijač, which won prizes at the Festival jugoslavenskih teatara, participated in the BITEF festival and visited the Soviet Union.

The Narodno pozorište Banja Luka (National Theatre of Banja Luka) is the second largest professional theatre in Bosnia and Herzegovina. After World War II it aimed its activity toward the whole region, and its mobility became one of its important characteristics. From the mid-1950s, after the appointment of Predrag Lazarević (b. 1929) as artistic director, it developed a repertoire accessible to everyone. The company moved from Shakespearian tragedy and comedy, Molière, Nušić's comedies and works by Jovan Sterija Popović, to the works of contemporary authors from Bosnia and Herzegovina including Miodrag Žalica (1926–93), Uroš Kovačević and Drago Mažar. In the late 1960s, the theatre's building was destroyed in a severe earthquake and for the next four seasons it worked in various inadequate spaces, even under a circus tent.

The company formed its own Theatre Commune in the 1970s and staged Brecht's *The Days of the Commune* in a factory. It also did work on method acting such as *Michelangelo Buonaroti* by Miroslav Krleža, *Mystère-Bouffe* and *The Bathhouse* by Mayakovsky, and *Vode se povlace* (*The Waters are Receding*) by Drago Mažar. All these performances were politically committed and formed a key part of the overall season. Such political commitment vanished in the 1990s and the theatre's repertoire once again, like other theatres in Bosnia and Herzegovina, returned to classics and plays by contemporary authors representing all Yugoslav republics.

The Narodno pozorište Tuzla (National Theatre of Tuzla) started its work with Nušić's comedy *Običan covek* (*An Ordinary Man*) on 30 March 1949. At the beginning it had only three professional actors and the rest of the ensemble was taken from the community theatre. Within the next ten years the ensemble became stronger and brought in professional directors and a number of actors from Belgrade and Zagreb. Among the most important was Dejan Mijač, who added contemporary foreign plays and Yugoslav and foreign classics (Shakespeare, Molière, Ibsen, Gogol, Cankar and Krleža) to the repertoire of folk plays and comedies. After performing Ahmed Murad-begović's *Rasemin sevdah* (*Rasema's Love Song*), the theatre tried to promote contemporary literature from Bosnia and Herzegovina.

Miodrag Mitrović and Derviš Sušić soon established themselves as playwrights at the Tuzla theatre. To celebrate the opening of its new building in 1953, the theatre started its own magazine, *Pozorište* (*The Theatre*), still the most important theatre periodical in Bosnia and Herzegovina.

Another theatre which began in 1949 was the Narodno pozorište Mostar (National Theatre of Mostar). Safet Pašalić, an experienced actor, was the first artistic director of the theatre. The ensemble was formed from actors in the partisan theatre, members of the local community theatre and occasional guests from Sarajevo. From the beginning, the repertoire leaned towards domestic drama, especially writers from the Mostar area – Aleksa Šantić, Svetozar Ćorović and Osman Djikić. After the first few seasons, the theatre grew steadily under the leadership of director Safet Ćišić and the dramaturge Skender Kulenović. In the 1960s, the theatre was helped by experienced guest directors and teachers while also allowing young directors and actors from Yugoslav theatre schools to work independently and establish themselves.

The Narodno pozorište Zenica (National Theatre of Zenica) began in 1950. During its first few years of existence, the theatre did not have a style and it resembled the community theatre from which it originated. By the mid-1950s, with the arrival of younger, educated directors, the theatre tried to establish an analytical approach to plays and also a new repertoire (including Brecht, Galsworthy, Dostoevsky and Kleist). In the 1960s, director Zdravko Martinović, dramaturge Zoran Ristović, designer Radovan Marušić and costume designer B. Marković completely transformed the theatre. Using guest directors who searched for new methods of expression, the company's Stanislavski approach to acting gained legitimacy on the stage. The director Jovan Putnik was inspired by the expressionistic and surrealistic theatre while still giving the same importance to acting and text. It soon became one of the most open theatres in Bosnia and Herzegovina, often working with guest directors who based their work on the modern trends ranging from surrealism and expressionism to the ritualistic and violent. Basing its repertoire on contemporary Yugoslav drama and the dramatization of Yugoslav prose, the Zenica theatre was among the most frequent participants at Yugoslav festivals and won numerous awards. In 1978 the theatre started operation in a modern building designed by architects Zlatko Ugljen and Jahiel Finci.

Studio Theatre 55 opened its doors in 1955. Founded by a group of professional actors and directors in the hope of offering an alternative to the national theatres, it has had a permanent ensemble since 1957. While other theatres traditionally formed their repertoires around national plays, this theatre selected pieces from international literature (Herman Wouk's *The Caine Mutiny*, Georg Büchner's *Danton's Death*, *The Diary of Anne Frank*, Brecht's *The Threepenny Opera* and *The Exception and the Rule*) which had a relevance to the political reality in Yugoslavia. The theatre's small stage influenced the style of acting. In the 1970s, it became the most popular theatre in Bosnia and Herzegovina with a season based on contemporary European avant-garde dramaturgy. Among its many successes have been *The Idiot* (after Dostoevsky), *Victor or Children in Power* by Roger Vitrac, *The Birthday Party* by Pinter, *Hamlet u selu Mrduša Donja* (*Hamlet in the Village of Mrduša Donja*) by Ivo Brešan, *The Effect of Gamma Rays on Man-in-the-Moon Marigolds* by Paul Zindel, *Endgame* by Samuel Beckett, and in latter years, *The Marriage* by the Polish writer Witold Gombrowicz, *Bijeli brak* (*The White Marriage*) by Tadeusz Różewicz, *Death of a Salesman* by Arthur Miller, and domestic texts from Bosnia and Herzegovina like *Nije čovjek ko ne umre* (*A Man's Got to Die*) by Velimir Stojanović (1940–88) and *To* (*It*) by Alija Isaković. After a fire in 1988, its building was renovated and improved. In the 1990s, it tried to form seasons exclusively based on domestic literature, thus somewhat losing its theatrical uniqueness.

The Pozorište za mlade (Youth Theatre) was formed in 1950 and its ensemble then consisted only of children. In 1964 it started working with its own professional ensemble but continued to perform until 1977 without its own stage. In 1977, it joined the puppet theatre. Its repertoire has generally been composed of domestic plays but, in recent years, it has tried to realize more ambitious performances based on plays by Aristophanes, Jarry and Edward Bond.

Dramaturgy

In the years since the first Bosnian play – according to Josip Lesić it was in 1885 when the drama *Majčin amanet* (*My Mother's Vow*) by Ivan Lepušić was written – Bosnian dramaturgy

has not produced a single classic such as Nušić, Sterija, Cankar or Krleža. Petar Kočić, with his satirical comedy *Jazavac pred sudom* (*The Badger on Trial*) is, however, one of the most important playwrights, but, like most playwrights, regularly changed his style and themes.

Skender Kulenović's comedies *Djelidba* (*The Division*) and *Večera* (*The Dinner*) were in form similar to Nušić's comedies, but their themes were new and their value was in their author's ability to invent original characters who bore characteristics of the time. His satire touched society's conscience burdened as it was with religious hatred and hostility. Kulenović also wrote, along with other authors from the early post-war years (1945–53), a specific form of drama taken from the Soviet Union, *agitovka*, a form of agitprop. Essentially propaganda, the characters were types, divided into 'black' and 'white'. Later on, playwrights tried to hide their social and political commitment by turning the types into real characters, adding elements from their social environment and motivation to explain their behaviour. Many such dramas criticizing society were written in the 1960s. It was at this time that Kulenović wrote his drama, *Svjetlo na drugom spratu* (*A Light on the Second Floor*), which describes the ambition, selfishness, envy and jealousy of characters who belong to the new socialist society and did not come from the 'reactionary' pre-war period. This important drama did not have a long life and could not be played in major centres, since it depicted the ambitions of the Communist Party as a source of human evil and social degradation.

Very few new plays were written in the 1950s. Three exceptions of note were Safet Pasalić and Miodrag Žalica's innovative *Rt prema mjesečini* (*Cape Moonlight*, 1958), *Glumci i rode* (*The Actors and the Storks*, 1959) and *Sviće ugašeni dan* (*The Dawning of a Dark Day*, 1962), all of which broke from realism.

The first drama that Miodrag Žalica wrote on his own was *Evropska trava* (*The European Grass*, 1963). Performed in the Kamerni teatar 55, *Evropska trava* was a parody of all avant-garde drama and it criticized playwrights who uncritically accepted such work as a model. Controversial, it was widely criticized and resulted in Žalica's long silence. In his drama *Pas koji pjeva* (*The Singing Dog*, 1968) Žalica turned to symbolism. His *Rimski dan* (*One Day in Rome*, 1976) secured him a unique place among authors writing on national history.

He approached contemporary society through a dialogue between the Roman poets Tibula, Propercio and Ovid in the court of Octavian Caesar.

An earlier historical drama was written by Miroslav Jančić, *Bosanski kralj* (*The King of Bosnia*, 1967). Through a hypothetical situation set in the court of the Bosnian king Tvrtko in the fourteenth century, the author analysed relationships among the various ethnic groups and religions in contemporary Bosnia and Herzegovina. Although allegorical, his analysis was based on the premise that domination by any one of the three nations would ruin the very foundation of Bosnia. In 1966 he had also written a drama, *Bosanska kuga* (*The Bosnian Plague*), a contemporary story which analysed, through the eyes of a character without a clear national identity (his father was a Serb killed by the Ustashas, and his mother was a Croat raped by the Chetniks), the history of Bosnia. The political commitment in these dramas, at the time of their production, was perhaps too obvious, which lessened their artistic value, but these dramas clearly warned about events which did come to pass.

Derviš Sušić's works are satirical treatments of the war and the development of socialism. In 1964, his novel *Ja, Danilo* (*I, Danilo*) was adapted for the stage. Sušić later wrote a series of dramas with themes from contemporary life – *Ne čekajuci Mijata* (*Not Waiting for Mijat*, 1966), *Jesenji cvat* (*The Autumn Blossom*, 1966), *Bujrum* (*At Your Service*, 1967) and *Baja i prijatelji* (*Baja and Friends*, 1971), which were mostly played in Tuzla. All end with the triumph of youth (justice) over a morally frustrated and degenerate society. Optimism and joy always bring healing in his works. With his historical chronicle *Veliki vezir* (*The Grand Vizier*, 1969) about the last days of Mehmed Pasha Sokolović, the grand vizier of the Turkish empire who governed during the peak of Turkish power and was responsible for many buildings in Bosnia, Sušić started his series of historical dramas. Among them are *Teferić* (*The Party*) and *Posljednja ljubav Hasana*

Kaimije (*The Last Love of Hasan Kaimija*). Sušić's best drama, *Veliki vezir*, is important because its universality touches the existential fears of every spectator.

The plays of Velimir Stojanović differ from the plays of most other writers in Bosnia and Herzegovina. He wrote only two dramas, *Nije čovjek ko ne umre* (*A Man's Got to Die*, 1978) and *Voćni dan* (*The Fruit Day*, 1981), but even they were enough to give him a special place in the country's dramaturgy. Unlike those authors who search for existentialist truth in national history, Stojanović is inspired by existential philosophy and by the avant-garde theatre of the 1960s. He is interested in the present moment, not in historic and existential meaning. In his plays the audience becomes an equal participant in the theatre event. His heroes are diabetics (*Nije čovjek ko ne umre*) or drunkards on a day they abstain from alcohol (*Voćni dan*). Their situation is always absurd, they have no future. But they are close to the spectators, speak their language, emphasize their mentality. Stojanović brings to the stage heroes who suffer and do not really live their lives.

Among other playwrights of note are Alija Isaković, author of *To* (*It*, 1979), *Generalijum* (1979) and *Hasanaginica* (1981), Nedzad Ibrisimović, author of *Ugursuz* (*The Rouge*, 1970) and *Karabeg* (*Kara-bey*, 1983), and Dževad Karahasan, author of *Kralju ipak ne svidja se gluma* (*The King Does Not Like the Actors, After All*, 1983) and *Čudo u Latinluku* (*A Miracle in Latinluk*, 1992). Authors whose work was interrupted by the war include Sena Mustajbašić – *Biće, biće* (*Will Be, Will Be*, 1987) and *Mrakuša* (1991) – and Darko Lukić – *Baseskija san o Sarajevu* (*A Dream of Sarajevo*, 1991).

Directors, Directing and Production Styles

For a discussion of directing, see previous material in **Artistic Profile** and the opening, historical section.

Music Theatre
Dance Theatre

Information not available at time of publication.

Theatre for Young Audiences
Puppet Theatre

Information not available at time of publication.

Design
Theatre Space and Architecture

Information not available at time of publication.

Training
Criticism, Scholarship and Publishing

Information not available at time of publication.

Despite the civil war, theatre life in Sarajevo continues. Several theatre groups have challenged the unreal situation of the besieged city with their work. Kamerni teatar 55 and Pozorište za mlade have mounted productions such as *Hair* (adapted by Marko Vesović and choreographed by Slavko Pervan), *Grad* (directed and designed by Haris Pasović) and *Waiting for Godot* (directed by Susan Sontag); plays by Euripides and Sophocles were also produced in 1993. The Sarajevo International Theatre and Film Festival held in October/November 1993 featured some of these productions.

Mair Musafija
Translated by Aranka Lengyel-Bosiljevac
and Irene Pauzer

(See also YUGOSLAVIA. Because of war conditions in Bosnia and Herzegovina during 1994, it was not possible to obtain material for all the sections. This article was based heavily on the research of the late Josip Lesić, a distinguished theatre historian who, in more ideal circumstances, would have written it.)

Further Reading

Borovčanin, Svetko. *Godišnjak jugoslovenskih pozorišta 1991–2*. [The yearbook of Yugoslav theatre 1991–2]. Novi Sad: Sterijino pozorje, 1992.

Cečić, Ivo, ed. *The Encyclopedia of Yugoslavia*. Vol. II: *Jugoslavenski leksikografski zavod 'Miroslav Krleža'*. Zagreb, 1982.

Dvadeset godina Narodnog pozorišta u Mostaru. [Two decades of the National Theatre in Mostar]. Mostar, 1967.

Lazarević, Predrag, Josip Lesić, and Mladen Sukalo. *Narodno pozorište Bosanske krajine Banja Luka 1930–80*. [The National Theatre of Banja Luka, 1930–80]. Banja Luka, 1980.

Lesić, Josip, *Drama i njene sjenke*. [The drama and its shadows]. 1991.

——. *Grad opsjednut pozorištem.* [A city obsessed with theatre]. Sarajevo, 1969.

——. *Istorija jugoslovenske moderne režije.* [The history of modern Yugoslav directing]. 1986.

——. *Jedan vijek bosansko-hercegovačke drame.* [A century of drama in Bosnia and Herzegovina]. Sarajevo, 1976.

——. *Narodno pozorište Sarajevo.* [The National Theatre of Sarajevo]. Sarajevo, 1971.

——. *Narodno pozorište Zenica.* [The National Theatre of Zenica]. Zagreb, 1978.

——. *Pozorišni život Sarajeva za vrijeme austro-ugarske uprave.* [The theatre in Sarajevo under the Austro-Hungarian monarchy]. Sarajevo, 1973.

——. *Sarejevsko pozorište izmedju dva rata.* [The Sarajevo theatre between the two world wars]. 1976.

——, ed. *Savremena drama i pozorište u Bosni i Hercegovini.* [The contemporary drama and theatre in Bosnia and Herzegovina]. Novi Sad: Sterijino pozorje, 1984.

Lesić, Zdenko. *Teorija drama.* [The theory of drama]. 3 vols. 1977–91.

Pavlović, Luka. *Pozorišne hronike.* [Theatre chronicles]. 3 vols. Sarajevo, 1969–78.

Stojanović, Velimir. *Šminka i znoj.* [Make-up and sweat]. Sarajevo, 1974 (theatre criticism).

BULGARIA

Located in southeastern Europe, north of Turkey and Greece and south of Romania, in 1988 Bulgaria's estimated population was 8.97 million people. Its land area is 110,900 square kilometres (42,800 square miles). Bulgaria, one of the oldest states in Europe, has a history which dates back to AD 681 when the central Asian Bulgars conquered part of the Balkan Peninsula and founded the First Bulgarian Kingdom. The Bulgars adopted the language and many of the customs of the conquered Slavs. Medieval Bulgaria was one of Europe's major military and cultural powers and Bulgaria flourished as a centre of Slavic culture and learning.

In 1396, along with the other Balkan states, Bulgaria was conquered by and became part of the Ottoman Empire, a situation that remained for nearly 500 years. In the Russian-Turkish War of 1877–8, Russia helped Bulgaria to win political independence but only the northern part of the country achieved its goal; the southern part, Eastern Rumelia, remained under Turkish control. In 1885, Eastern Rumelia was reunited with Bulgaria.

During World War I, Bulgaria fought on the side of Germany and Austria-Hungary and, when the war ended, lost some of its territory. During World War II, Bulgaria was again under German influence but its army stayed out of the war itself. In 1944, the Soviet Union declared war on Bulgaria and occupied the country. It was at this time that a government friendly to the USSR was set up and the country became officially known as the People's Republic of Bulgaria.

For most of the period that Bulgaria was under Ottoman rule, its arts looked towards Asia for models. In the 1840s, however, a Bulgarian independence movement – the so-called

National Revival – turned back towards Europe.

In the 1840s, European-style theatre began to appear again as part of this movement, an attempt to adopt European cultural values as quickly as possible after the hoped-for liberation of the country from the Ottomans. The earliest manifestations could be found in schools where recitations and readings of classical dialogues could be heard. By 1856, full stagings of dramatic pieces could be seen marking the beginning of the end for much earlier folk spectacles linked to forces of nature and magic.

Between 1864 and 1876, several theatre groups were formally established by Dobry Voinikov (1833–78) in Romanian cities including Braila, Gjurgevo and Bucharest. Under Voinikov, a leader in the National Revival movement, these groups included actresses for the first time and Bulgarian plays in the repertoire, including some by Voinikov himself and others by Vasil Droumev (1841–1901) and even the poet Hristo Botev (1847–76). These early plays were generally nationalistic in nature, historical in form and usually reflected the ideas of the revival movement. Even leaders in the movement – Ljuben Karavelov (1834–79), Atanas Ouzounov (1851–1907) and Bacho Kiro (1835–76) – found the dramatic form valuable as they attempted to communicate their ideas in script form.

Following the overthrow of the Ottomans in 1878, plans began for the establishment of Bulgaria's first state-subsidized theatre company in the city of Plovdiv. The company was formally established between 1881 and 1883 with the support of writers Konstantin Velichkov (1855–1907) and Ivan Vazov (1850–1921). In a number of articles, they argued that theatrical art is an important step in the spiritual development of a Bulgarian nation. When the company was finally established under the direction of Stephen Popov (1854–1920), it attracted leading amateurs who to that time had been able to play only in productions by the Plovdiv Printers' Society.

By 1888, the group brought a production to Sofia of the French play by Alexandre Dumas père, *Le Tour de Nesle* (*The Tower of Nesle*). So successful was the Plovdiv performance that the company decided to remain in the capital. A wooden theatre building, the Osnova, was constructed for them, on the same site where the current Bulgarian National Theatre stands. Opened on 4 December 1888, the group eventually called itself Salza i Smyah (Tears and Laughter) in 1892 and retained this name until 1904. Over the coming years, many of its leading actors and directors went to Moscow or St Petersburg for training while others went to Prague, Berlin, Vienna and even Paris. In 1904, the group was officially renamed the Bulgarian National Theatre and on 3 January 1904, a new building was opened for them.

Over the next eight years, the new National Theatre staged many of the world's classics – from Shakespeare and Molière to Schiller – along with plays particularly fashionable at the time – works by Ibsen, Hauptmann and Tolstoi. This repertoire gave the company's actors a chance to explore a wide range of styles and Bulgarian playwrights the possibility of developing new themes, widening Bulgarian theatre's philosophical range and bringing it closer to the European mainstream. It was at this same time that a number of well-known poets and novelists turned to the stage for the first time.

Theatre, in fact, moved to the centre of the country's cultural life at this point, touching on both aesthetic and ideological issues. Vazov underscored the democratic aspects of the revival and its public commitment to deal with human problems. Dimiter Blagoev (1836–1924) and many Marxist artists strove to include theatre in the social debate while other artists declared theatre to be the supreme cultural institution.

In the theatres themselves, performances were generally staged by actors rather than directors but as the National Theatre began to grow the role of the director grew as well. In the early years of its development, most of the National's directors came from abroad, often from cities such as Zagreb and Prague.

The National was the only state-subsidized company in the country at this point but other groups survived by touring their productions widely. Among the most important of these were the Savremenen Theatre and the Rosa Popova Company. Staging mostly modern plays by such authors as Gorki and Ibsen, these companies inspired the creation of new amateur groups. Among these were the many workers' clubs which wanted to use the art to propagate socialist ideas. Many actors who would later have important careers on the professional stage began their professional lives in this way.

The October Revolution of 1917 and its spread across the new Soviet Union provided further inspiration for politically and socially focused theatre artists. Directors became even more crucial in the interpretation of text and theatrical art was looked to as one of the chief analysts of the cataclysmic events of the time. Under the influence of the German expressionist movement and German directors such as Max Reinhardt, the Bulgarian director Geo Milev (1895–1925) moved from illusionistic realism on stage to what he called 'the supreme reality of art', focusing his work on poetic and metaphorical stage imagery. In 1923, Milev staged Ernst Toller's expressionistic masterpiece *Man and the Masses* with the active support of politically committed, party-based theatre and music groups.

In 1924, Hrissan Tsankov (1890–1971) became a director of the National, a position he held until 1944. In his productions, he sought, like Wagner, to synthesize all the arts including music, dance, poetry and even pantomime.

The major figure at the National from 1925 to 1977 was the great Russian actor-director Nikolai Ossipovich Massalitinov, formerly of the Moscow Art Theatre. During this period, he worked closely with Bulgarian actors and introduced and deepened the understanding of the theatrical reforms of Stanislavski and Nemirovich-Danchenko. Massalitinov sought to deepen the depiction of the complex bond between the individual and society. His work with actors led to new levels of performance, particularly in his own stagings of Bulgarian, Russian and western dramas treating everything from religion to politics in dramatic as well as satiric ways.

A more revolutionary political art was, however, slowly becoming dominant in the late 1920s and early 1930s. This movement was signalled by the creation in Sofia in 1930 of the politically committed company Sinite Blouzi (Blue Shirts). Over the years the company changed its name many times for political reasons – among its many names were Tribuna (Tribune), Narodna Szena (New Stage) and Realistichen Teatar (Realistic Theatre) – but throughout it managed to retain the purity of its political commitment. Its artistic leader during much of this time was Boyan Danovsky (1899–1976), who rooted his work in the ideas of Piscator, Brecht and Soviet revolutionary theatre.

In 1919, the first Bulgarian artists' union was founded through the initiative of Gyorgy Dimitrov (1882–1949), then secretary of the Workers' Trade Union. Called the Union of Actors, Musicians and Theatrical Employees, the new union advocated democratic principles, social sensitivity and the humanization of relationships between the state and the individual.

Two experimental theatres were formed at this time as well – the Teatar Studia (Theatre Studio) of Isaac Daniel (1894–1942) and the Opiten Teatar (Experimental Theatre) of Stephen Sarchadjiev (1912–65). Leading directors such as Massalitinov and Danovsky also set up special acting studios in this period and Todor Pavlov defined some basic principles of Bulgarian Marxist aesthetics, the theoretical foundations for Bulgaria's socialist theatre.

By the late 1930s, four state theatres were in operation but this number would change significantly after the revolution of 1944 and the formal change-over of Bulgaria into a socialist state. Almost immediately after the revolution, the number of state theatres jumped to twenty-six, some with specific audiences in mind. Among these were, the National Youth Theatre (founded in 1945) and the State Satire Theatre (1957). By state policy, theatres would no longer cater to the wealthy or the social elite but would attempt to make theatrical experience a part of everyone's life.

To fill the needs of the growing profession, the Bulgarian State Theatre Academy was founded in 1946 to train actors, directors, critics and puppeteers. In 1948 as well, a new magazine, *Teatar* (*Theatre*), was founded and in 1957 a weekly cultural newspaper began publication, *Narodna Kultura* (*Peoples Culture*). The aim of all these ventures was to create a socially connected theatre for the country, to examine historical process in dramatic terms and to analyse class struggles.

The earliest performances of Bulgaria's new socialist theatre generally depicted the revolution itself utilizing both national plays and plays from the Soviet repertoire. Western plays were seen less and less except where they could fit into the new scheme by analogy. Some of the plays produced were openly propagandist but others were emotionally effective. Massalitinov's stagings of Gorki's *Enemies* and Zidarov's *King's Mercy* depicted individuals in specific social situations and their psychological reactions. Danovsky's stagings of Gorki's *Egor Boulichov and the Others* and Ivanov's *Armoured Train* were more intellectual responses to the new society dealing with social and moral ideals.

In the late 1950s, following Stalin's death, dogmatic interpretations – socialist-realism for the most part – were relaxed in favour of a new kind of rationalization of the relationship between individuals and society as a whole. During the 1960s, it was the State Theatre of Satire which stood at the centre of this changing aesthetic. Suddenly the intellect was put at centre stage and one could see its free play in such productions as Mayakovsky's *The Bedbug*, staged by Danovsky; Gogol's *The Government Inspector* and Sukhovo-Kobylin's *Tarelkin's Death*, staged by Metody Andonov (1932–74); and productions of Dürrenmatt's *Frank V* and Petrov's *When the Roses Dance* by Grisha Ostrovsky. In these productions, official aesthetics began to crumble and a franker, more democratic dialogue began with the audience.

A new interest in the theatrical ideas of Meyerhold, Vakhtangov and Brecht also began to emerge in the 1960s, resulting in a range of productions that were both poetic and journalistic. Looking for more sophisticated means of performance, productions at this time ranged from spectacles to analyses of social laws, from vehicles for spectacular acting to flights of fantasy. Genres were no longer strictly observed; the lyrical and the ironic were mixed as were the tragic and the grotesque. Even improvisation found its way on to stages.

Theatrical space too began to be challenged, with more and more directors opting for small spaces rather than large, for flexible spaces rather than fixed, for non-traditional venues rather than the traditional proscenium houses. The work of both set and lighting designers also came to the fore at this time. The first of these new intimate theatres was Teatar 199 with a 199-seat auditorium. Here the theatre of sombre realism became merged between emotion and metaphor.

One of the most interesting developments of the 1970s was the appearance of a number of pantomime groups in cities such as Sofia, Sliven,

Roussé, Gabrovo and Silistra. Some dealt in classical mime while others connected the form to puppetry, clowning or folk material. One of the major companies is the Studio Pantomime of Velyo Goranov and Vasil Indjev; a decade later, Goranov started still another group, Movement.

Well into the 1980s, historical subject matter was used to deal with a range of contemporary issues that could still not be dealt with directly. This could be seen clearly in Kamen Zidarov's historical dramas *Ivan Shisham*, *Kaloyan* and *Cain and the Magician*; Nikola Rousev's *The Old Man and the Arrow*, dealing with the issue of power and the people; in Stephen Tsanev's *The Trial of the Bogomils*, a play about the relationship between freedom and violence, and *Saturday 23*, a drama about the anti-fascist uprising in 1923.

Throughout the 1970s particularly, many Bulgarian artists explored the spiritual and social memory of the people as well as questions of national morality. Still others began to explore the country's folk roots and used folkloric spectacle – carnival in nature – on the stage. One could see this clearly in many productions by director Ville Tsankov, such as *Masters*, written by Racho Stoyanov (1883–1951), and two plays by Petko Todorov (1879–1916), *The First Ones* and *Masons*.

By the end of the 1980s, the Bulgarian theatre again went through a period of restructuring and change caused by the collapse of the Soviet Union. These changes ranged from organizational structures to artistic policies and approaches. Several new experimental companies emerged in the wake of these changes not only in Sofia but also in smaller cities such as Plovdiv and Pazardjik.

Structure of the National Theatre Community

In 1992, Bulgaria had forty-six dramatic theatre companies in operation, in addition to twelve puppet theatres, nine state opera and ballet theatres, two operetta groups, the Workers' Opera Company in Sliven, the Youth Opera Company in Blagoevgrad, one national theatre for young audiences, and innumerable amateur and semi-professional theatre groups.

Seasons generally last about ten months, that is about 280 performances annually for each theatre operating in Sofia. In the provinces, the numbers of performances by each group are somewhat lower because many stages are shared by dramatic and musical or dance groups. Most companies operate on a repertory system with prices traditionally kept low through state subsidy. In the 1990s, the level of subsidy was being reduced.

Most musical theatres have at their disposal their own regular orchestras, choruses and ballet companies as well as their own scene-building facilities.

According to a 1980 survey, some 6 million people were attending theatrical performances each year.

For nearly fifty years, there existed in every major town and city elective councils of culture which were in charge of all cultural activities. The councils included representatives of cultural unions, writers, artists, film-makers, architects, musicians, actors, and so on. Working with representatives of different strata of society and different age groups, these councils set directions for each city, attempting to link national policies to local needs.

Artistic Profile

Companies

For discussion of companies, see the material on **Dramaturgy** and in the opening, historical section.

Dramaturgy

At the beginning of the twentieth century, one of the country's most popular playwrights was Ivan Vazov, whose plays *Toward an Abyss* and

Ivaylo made frank comparisons between past and present as they tried to find in tragedy the meaning of history. Romantic in tone, his plays reflected bourgeois reality following liberation from the Ottoman Empire. One of his most profound works in this style was *Outcasts*, a play depicting Bulgarian revolutionary émigrés living in Romania. In one of his comedies, *Job Hunters*, Vazov turned to the subject of social relations and the struggles involved in fighting for jobs and offices.

A second playwright of importance at this time was Anton Strashimirov (1872–1937) who fought against dogma, violence and cruelty in plays such as *Vampire* and *Mother-in-law*. At the same time, Petko Todorov was dealing in his plays with philosophical rebellion, with worldly pettiness and with the sombre race for bread and money.

National dramaturgy reached its peak in this period in the works of Peyo Javorov (1878–1914). Javorov's major plays, *At the Foot of Vitosha Mountain* and *When Thunder Strikes*, are both lyrical analyses of human relationships mixed with social injustice and political battles. In his works, love is a protest against violence and cruelty.

During the inter-war period, Bulgaria's stages became home to the satirist Stephen Kostov (1879–1939). Inspired by the comedic works of Vazov, his plays attack societal evils with genuine fervour. In such works as *The Golden Pit*, *Grasshoppers*, *The New Port* and *Healer*, he ridicules both ignorance and parsimony, the hunger for money, corruption and even the degradations of job-hunting. In *Golemanov*, he depicts a political demagogue striving after power through hypocrisy, bribery and humiliation.

During this same period, the plays of Yordan Jovkov (1880–1937) depict the martyr-like resistance of people to the ugliness of social injustice. His plays, *Albena* and *Boryana*, are poetic reinterpretations of the world, examining the nature of moral purity. Even spiritual life is examined in *Masters* by Racho Stoyanov, a writer looking for philosophical meanings at a time of moral tribulations. Specific political visions were offered by Nikola Vaptzarov (1909–42) in *The Ninth Wave* and Ljudmil Stoynov (1888–1973) in *Wolves and Sheep*.

Valery Petrov and Ivan Radoev moved Bulgarian drama in a more lyrical direction. Petrov's *When the Roses Dance*, a poetic comedy, showed the author's psychological insights into human emotions such as love. In such plays as *Theatre, My Love*, *The Moonlit Room*, *White Tale* and *Dream Button* he shows a unique ability to touch both adults and children, to deal ambiguously with important human issues, blending wise insight and artistic imagination, reality and fantasy. A master of aphoristic dialogue, Petrov plays with the double masks of tragedy and comedy, setting a basic optimism and idealism in his works.

Radoev also deals with the unconventional and some of his plays can be seen as poetic confessions. In such works as *Romeo and Juliet*, *Petrol*, *Criminal Song*, *The Cannibal*, *Globe Lightning* and *Dream* he touches on the mechanization and demeaning of human life. Focusing on spiritual emptiness and the problems of living in an atmosphere of demagoguery and shifting moral values, Radoev looks at the deformation of social relations and the dichotomy between morality and reality.

Dimitar Dimov is still another playwright of note who analyses human action and emotion and attempts to put his insights into a philosophical perspective. An imagistic, aphoristic writer, his plays *Holiday in Arko Iris* and *Women With a Past* are insightful socio-political statements about contemporary humanity.

Dragomir Assenov focuses on everyday compromises and civic responsibilities in such plays as *Birthday Party*, *Roses for Dr Shopov* and *Gold Reserve*.

Among the most important Bulgarian dramatists in the 1970s and 1980s were Stanislav Stratiev and Yordan Radichkov. Radichkov's most significant plays – *January*, *Bustle*, *Lazarus Up a Tree*, *An Attempt at Flying* and *Baskets* – are strange, visually powerful portraits of cataclysms usually caused by collisions between past and present. His characters are reflections of national memory, full of rich associations with folk traditions, freely mixing reality and imagination, modernity and history. His heroes are able to live in differing layers of time, to connect the living and the dead. Through comic insight, he manages to mingle the clear, down-to-earth life of today's people with the eternal qualities of nature creating a kind of carnival joke, a joke that is as sad as the balance-sheet of one's life.

Stanislav Stratiev, for his part, examines, in such plays as *The Roman Bath*, *The Bus*, *Buckskin Jacket* and *The Maximalist*, ugly and socially dangerous individuals who prefer to make life dogmatic and senseless. His plays are full of paradoxes as he attempts to understand social and psychological deformation especially as it applies to bureaucrats, demagogues and consumers. For Stratiev, the counterpoint is found in the moral stability of creative life, uncompromising and implacable.

In the early 1990s, authors were looking seriously once again at absurdist techniques, elements of the grotesque and other paradoxical approaches to reflect the changes taking place across the country. Among the most

successful of these new writers was Hristo Boychev.

Nevyana Injeva

Directors, Directing and Production Styles

For a discussion of directing, see the material on **Dramaturgy** and in the opening, historical section.

Music Theatre

Bulgarian music theatre, like spoken theatre in the country, has links that go far back in time to early religious cults and ritual performances. Evolving over the country's long history, the form slowly acquired its national characteristics, traits acutely different from traditional European approaches in terms of both repertoire and interpretation.

Opera and dramatic theatre usually took place in the same building with the same audiences attending on different evenings. As a result, audiences entered the theatre with criteria established along dramatic rather than musical lines. Their prime interest therefore was often more on plot than musical form.

Because of insufficient studies of early ritual-based music, it is necessary to begin an examination of the theatrical form somewhere in the middle of the nineteenth century. It was at that time that Bulgarian music was first beginning to influence the repertoire of orchestras of the Turkish garrisons as well as the new 'urban songs', as they were called. Simultaneously with this intonational penetration, the National Revival press began to express interest in the use of musical theatre.

After the liberation of the country in 1878, recognizably Bulgarian music became part of the repertoires of all the military brass bands, individual artists, amateur ensembles, and even music in schools. It was not long after that performances of operatic excerpts and later whole operas began to be performed by the newly created opera section of the Drama and Opera Company in Sofia, often with Czech singers taking part for lack of trained Bulgarians.

These performances, usually with a choir and an orchestra, immediately attracted attention and significant audiences. Such musical evenings

were historically followed by visits by foreign stars and eventually companies, most often from Italy. In this way, musical theatre generally and opera in particular made its way into the life of Sofia and other major cities across the country.

In 1908, the Bulgarian State Opera Society laid the foundations for a permanent opera theatre in Sofia (today known as the National Academic Theatre for Opera and Ballet). The first outlines of a future Bulgarian opera can still be seen in the work of conductor Gyorgy Atanassov – *Gergana* and *Tsveta*, whose effects on the public's conception of opera were themselves formed on models of western European and Slav classics.

In 1922, the Opera Society was financially taken over by the state. At that time, an impressive group of Russian singers and directors, some of whom remained with the company for several decades, gave new impetus to the form and raised professional standards. By the early 1930s, the presence of talented and well-trained soloists made it possible for the first time to include a considerable number of classics in the repertoire, many from the nineteenth century, along with many original works such as *Yana's Nine Brothers* by Lyubomir Pipkov, *Czar Kaloyan* by Pancho Vladiguerov, and *Salambo* by Vesselin Stoyanov.

The socialization of culture after 1944 also meant the introduction of Soviet opera to Bulgaria, including an influx of performers, directors and even teachers. By the 1950s, five State Opera and Ballet Theatres were founded and new opportunities for Bulgarian composers emerged.

Among the major modern composers are Parashkev Hadjiev, who wrote sixteen works for the musical theatre, some of which were toured to the former states of Czechoslovakia, the USSR and the German Democratic Republic; Marin Goleminov, creator of *Ivailo* and *The Zograph Zahariy*; and Simeon Pironkov, creator of a Brecht adaptation, *The Good Person of Setzuan*.

The repertoires of most of the country's opera theatres today generally include a wide range of European classics (Mozart, Rossini, Verdi, Gounod, Bizet, Smetana, Bartók), Russian classics (Tchaikovsky, Mussorgsky, Glazunov, Shostakovich, Prokofiev) and original Bulgarian works.

Probably the foremost director of opera in the country is Boris Pokrovsky.

A series of International Competitions for Young Opera Singers has long attracted significant attention abroad for Bulgarian musical performances and performers.

Alongside opera, operetta too has had great popularity within the country. Amateur groups were staging operettas as early as 1898 in Sliven, and in 1906 in Shoumen and Plovdiv. The first professional operetta company was founded by A. Sladarov in 1917. The company's first performance was in early 1918, *The Marquis Bonelli*, staged at the Odeon Cinema and Theatre.

The same year, P. Stoychev reorganized the Svoboden (Free) Theatre and staged a series of operetta and dramatic performances. In 1921, Bulgarian operetta performers proclaimed one of the world's first strikes of theatre artists, demanding better working conditions. The strike was supported by the General Trade Union. In December 1922, the Cooperative Operetta Theatre was founded to meet these goals and to formally establish operetta as a recognized art.

In 1942, the Artistic Operetta Company was founded under the direction of Mimi Balkanska and its repertoire included classic and new Viennese operettas, Russian operettas and Bulgarian works. In 1947, the company was taken over by the state and became known as the National Operetta. Its first director was Assen Rouskov. In 1948, the company was reorganized and renamed the Stefan Makedonski State Music Theatre.

Every season, classics such as Hervé, Offenbach, Strauss, Kalman and Lehar are supplemented by the works of more modern composers such as Cole Porter, Leonard Bernstein and Rudolf Friml among others. There are as well a large number of Bulgarian-written operettas which continue to attract significant audiences. Operetta companies also stage musical comedies, comic operas, musicals, farces and vaudevilles. Some have even tried to find links with popular music.

All music theatres regularly tour in their own regions. Audiences attend their performances on subscription and most performances are accompanied by lectures.

For many years, the annual Sofia Weeks of Music Festival were held and attracted performances from across the country and abroad.

Rosalia Bix

Dance Theatre

The roots of ballet in Bulgaria are comparatively young. In 1908, the Bulgarian Opera Society was founded, an organization which was the nucleus not only of opera but also of ballet. The creators of the society, without any national ballet models before them, turned to the choreographers of folkloric dance and in this way a unique form of Bulgarian ballet was created. The country's first choreographers, therefore – A. Dimitrov, R. Koleva and P. Radoyev – took part in the many stages of the development of a genuine national professional ballet.

For example, in 1914, Radoyev, created the first children's ballet school. Linked to the Bulgarian Opera Society after it was turned over to the state, the school quickly met the demand for new dancers.

Foreign models emerged on the Bulgarian stage in the early 1920s with regular visits by Russian dancers. As a result, a relatively large number of Bulgarian dancers decided to go abroad for their training, most to Russia, some to Berlin.

In the 1920s, free expressive dance as developed in Germany began to be seen in Bulgaria through guest performances. Among the companies of note were the Wiesental and Bodenwieser companies which included social themes in their works. It was chiefly Petrov who moved Bulgarian dance in a similar direction, both creatively and thematically. This bias and its non-contradiction between the classical school of dance and the German plastic school was an important formative influence in the country.

Anastas Petrov produced *Coppelia* in 1928 at the Sofia National Opera, a production which, while true to the original, nevertheless allowed some freedom of interpretation. His school performances ultimately became the most interesting performances of each theatre season. Petrov created not only professional dancers but also emotionally full-blooded artists who, in their systematic work with him, realized new choreographic work to the fullest.

Petrov advocated the development of a classical ballet repertoire and had a marked preference for romantic works, until then missing from the repertoire of Bulgarian groups. He later added *Giselle*, *Swan Lake*, *Esmerelda*, Glazunov's *Raimonda* and Frohman's *Sleeping Beauty*, after Petipa's original.

In 1937, Petrov created the first original Bulgarian ballet, *Yana and the Dragon*, to music by Hristo Manolov. Based on Bulgarian legends and folk traditions, the ballet spoke of freedom within an unjust society. The work became an immediate success and has remained part of the national repertoire.

Another innovator of national importance was Maria Dimova. A student of the German plastic school, she redirected the form toward Bulgarian folk dance which became her building material in an emotional rather than an ethnographic sense. She was also among the first to reveal a conscious social sense in the phenomena depicted, phenomena connected to the breakup of classes within society. Compositions such as *All Soul's Day*, *A Mother's Lament* and *Elegy* all figure largely in her popular solo performances and all summon up images of victims of advancing fascism.

Dimova's work, though not great in volume, marked the beginning of realistic quests in the Bulgarian ballet theatre whose early zenith was reached in Goleminov's dance drama *Nestinarka* (*The Fire Dancer*) produced in 1942. These two trends – the romantic and the realistic – existed simultaneously within Bulgarian dance.

After 1944 and the socialization of the arts, a new professional maturity could be seen in the national dance. One could also see certain trends. The most popular performances in the 1940s and well into the 1950s were those which, in one way or another, responded to the heroic ardour of the times. Among these was *Prometheus*, created by Petrov in 1945 to music by Beethoven; *The Red Poppy*, created by the Soviet choreographer N. Holfin in 1951 to music by Glière; and *Laurencia*, created by Nina Kiradjieva in 1953 to music by Crane. The dancers were mostly pupils of Petrov who quickly grasped and solved the problems of a socialist theatre. It is in their work that one could most clearly see the synthesis of the realistic and the romantic, the revelation of feeling and the soaring flight of ideas.

By the 1960s, new artists were beginning to appear. Leading the way among them was Petrov's student, Emanuil Manolov, at the Roussé National Opera; B. Kovachev in the city of Plovdiv; and G. and Stanislaw Yordanov in the city of Varna. The companies outside the capital began to become known for their dance experiments at this time, experiments that broke with the realistic work that had dominated since the 1940s and which moved the focus from literary to musical dramaturgy. Among the new composers being used were Ravel, Bartók and Stravinsky. In many cases, these were purely symphonic canvases standing out against a background of philosophic fables, comic grotesques and lyrical dramatic poems.

Violetta Konsoulova

Theatre for Young Audiences

Bulgaria has only one theatre devoted exclusively to performances for young audiences, the National Youth Theatre. The company, founded in 1945, has separate sections devoted to work for children and teenagers. Other companies also stage occasional performances for young people.

Since the middle of the nineteenth and throughout the twentieth century, schools included plays as part of their curriculum, usually in an effort to teach history and to instil a sense of national pride. The idea of staging performances on a professional level specifically for children was first discussed between the two world wars. By the end of World War II, professional performances had begun to be staged in Sofia, Plovdiv, Roussé, Varna, Bourgas and Sliven. Still incidental to the regular seasons, these special Sunday matinées – generally consisting of dramatizations of fairytales – were popular with families.

The establishment of a national children's theatre in Sofia was intended to speed up the development of the form and to function as an ideological/methodological centre for the development of theatre for young audiences. The new National Youth Theatre (NYT) began staging full seasons of plays for children and teenagers. Between 1960 and 1980 alone, more than 350 new plays for young audiences were staged across the country by the NYT and other groups. Included were works by most of the country's major playwrights including Valery Petrov, Nedyalko Yordanov, Pancho Panchev and Ivan Radoev. Many of the National's productions even in the 1990s were unusual blendings of reality and fantasy.

Interestingly, in addition to its primary work,

the National Youth Theatre also stages occasional plays for adults. From 1968, the company has also been the organizer of a biennial International Festival of Theatre for Children, Teenagers and Youth.

An experimental children's drama studio was started in the 1970s by the Varna Theatre. This studio, run by the brothers Danail and Raiko Raikov, brings together children between the ages of 6 and 15 who are interested in performing.

Since 1966, a triennial national series of workshops and discussions relating to theatre for young people has also been held. Including a national festival of performances for young people, these National Reviews of Theatres for Children and Adolescents have become a stocktaking on work being done and an opportunity to look at what might be done in the future.

Still another children's theatre festival has regularly taken place in the city of Turgovishte.

Puppet Theatre

The historical roots of Bulgarian puppet theatre – like Bulgarian theatre itself – can be traced far back in time to early dramatic rituals connected to seasonal celebrations. Many are connected to aspects of ritual magic. While they eventually took on Christian appearances, this did not essentially change their nature.

By the Medieval period, religious Mystery plays using puppets – among them, *Mara Lishanka* and *The Bride Going Out to Bring the Ox for the Wedding* – were being seen at charity events, family gatherings and children's celebrations. By this time, the ritual and magical elements were beginning to disappear and the productions were becoming much more independent.

These roots can also be seen in the actual construction of contemporary puppets from such things as corn cobs, brooms, gourds, napkins, spoons, wood or simply pieces of cloth. These improvised puppets represent a whole range of creatures from people to birds and other animals and their operation was done by hand, rod, wooden sticks or mechanical means. In addition they were operated by more traditional marionettes or even shadow-puppets.

Public theatrical performances date back to the eighteenth century. One of the earliest books

on the subject – Felix Kanitz's *Danubian Bulgaria* (1871) – describes a travelling company and has pictures of a puppet show on a box, a style that could still be seen in the 1990s at bazaars and fairs. Its characters are most often known as Kara Kolyo, Pena, Racho and Deshka and their adventures are anecdotal and generally concern everyday activities.

Still another type of performance seen regularly at fairs uses glove-puppets and is closer to the Punch and Judy/Petrushka tradition. The repertoire consists of short satirical sketches, pantomime and a great deal of fighting. Unlike the Kara Kolyo tradition, this style of performance produced no recognizable national type.

Both types of fairground puppets are characterized by musical accompaniment, usually drum or rebec but often simply songs.

It is generally agreed that the country's first professional puppet performance took place in Plovdiv in 1892 during the First Bulgarian Exhibition when Thomas Holden and his company gave a series of performances utilizing strongly mechanized marionettes.

In 1904, an organization of Czech *émigrés* called the Czech Society founded a marionette theatre in Sofia, a company which survived off and on until 1966. Its performances were in both Czech and Bulgarian and were usually intended for children. The company's repertoire included modern Czech plays and world theatrical classics. Its two leading characters were usually called Kapshtarek and Pepichek.

The country's first professional marionette theatre grew out of the work of a Bulgarian amateur group working at the Slavonic Interchange Society. Formed in 1923 by a Czech-trained architect, A. Donkov, the group was led from 1924 until her death in 1940 by the Russian actress V. Bazilevich. Under Bazilevich, the company attracted actors from several professional dramatic companies in Sofia. Its repertoire was dominated by dramatizations of classics and folk stories. In its productions, one of the most popular characters, the Puppet Fairy, was played by an actress. The company also published its own small newspaper, *Puppet Theatre*. Following Bazilevich's death, the company was dissolved.

A professional touring puppet theatre began operating from the city of Plovdiv in 1928 under the direction of S. Penchev and L. Georgiev, using actors from the Municipal Dramatic Theatre. The company's style was influenced two years later by a visit to Sofia of Podreca's Teatro dei Piccoli from Italy. In 1931, Penchev created his own Bulgarian Theatre dei Piccoli which toured the country that year with a satirical political play for adults.

During the war, K. Batembergsky began a private professional puppet troupe in Sofia which operated for eight years, closing its doors in 1950.

It was following the establishment of a people's socialist government in Bulgaria in 1944 that conditions materially changed for artists of all types, including those working in puppet theatre. As in other cultural fields, a network of theatres was established with the state taking on most of the financing. In 1946, an official state puppet theatre began to emerge under the direction of Mara Penkova. Two years later it was receiving state grants and had begun to call itself the National Puppet Theatre of Bulgaria.

Through the 1940s and 1950s, virtually all puppetry in the country was under the influence of European styles, particularly German and Czech. For the most part, puppet performances endeavoured to be simply dramatic performances in miniature. Both the directors and the actors were trained as dramatic actors and most of the performances used marionettes.

It was the emergence of the new National Puppet Theatre, however, which marked a significant turning point in this development. Penkova, a dramatic actress of long standing, was trained in puppetry in Germany but it was her meeting with the great Soviet puppet master Sergei Obraztsov during his tour of Bulgaria in 1945, which decisively changed the direction of her work.

Between 1946 and 1958, she staged some forty children's productions in which the intention to recreate miniature dramatic performances was, if not overcome entirely, at least significantly limited. The marionette was replaced by the glove-puppet. Petrushka and Javanese techniques were introduced. (About this same time, 1948, a circus performer, G. Saranov, founded a marionette company in Plovdiv which, among other things, staged whole operas.)

Among Penkova's first productions was a Bulgarian script, *The Boy and the Wind* by N. Trendafilova in which the protagonist is the wind. Using a large piece of free-flowing material for this character, Penkova's approach was a clear break from the realistic tradition which had dominated the form to that time. She pointed Bulgarian puppetry in a new direction and, though the artistic level of her own productions was not always high, she deserves enormous credit for her national contribution to the field.

Originally consisting of amateur actors, the company gradually became an exclusively professional group. In 1958, the company was taken over by directors Atanas Ilkov, Nikolona Georgieva and designer Ivan Tsonev and in 1964 changed its name to the Central Puppet Theatre.

From this point on professional dramatists began to show interest in the puppet form. In 1962, a puppet section was, in fact, founded at the Sarafov Higher Institute of Theatrical Art. By 1987, Bulgaria boasted twenty professional puppet companies across the country.

Elena Vladova, Vassil Stefanov

Lydia Alexandrova's State Puppet Theatre of Sliven production of Yordan Radichkov's *We Sparrows*.

Design
Theatre Space and Architecture

Although not particularly professional, set design in the period of the National Revival was quite original and highly idiosyncratic. Showing clear traces of five centuries of isolation, its enthusiasm and inspirational qualities visibly connected it to traditional religious and applied art, especially wood-carving and church painting. But even with such influences, there was a clear tendency towards western European realism. This is particularly true in the visual work of teacher and director Krastjo Pishurka, playwright and educator Dobri Voinikov, and in the work of the first academically educated Bulgarian painter, Nikolai Pavlovich. Their efforts laid the groundwork for a generation of professional designers after the liberation from Turkish occupation. Many of them came from abroad and their professional presence made Bulgarian stages gradually look like those of Vienna and Prague.

Among the key designers were Adolf Kapp, Otto Horeishi, Adolf Zello and Maestro Kvinto. Their work, together with sets produced in the Vienna studio of Frank and Hans Kautzki, established the academically realistic manner of design. During the first decades of the twentieth century, the designs of Aleksander Milenkov, a student of Hans Fraam and a typical representative of German decorative naturalism, became especially well known. Followers of a similar aesthetic were Vladimir Katzarov – a student of Frank and Hans Kautzki – and Ivan Enchev-Vidjo, who had trained in Munich.

As audiences grew, the primitive set design typical of the National Revival period was gradually replaced by the new Vienna-Prague style. By the 1920s, design was further influenced by the realistic ideas of the Moscow Art Theatre and expressionistic tendencies in modern German painting. A special role in establishing the latter tendency was played by the poet and director Geo Milev, the director of the National Theatre Bojan Danovski, and the painter, translator and critic Sirak Skitnik.

The 1920s and 1930s saw a brilliant generation of Bulgarian set designers begin to work. Many were young painters coordinating national tradition and new artistic approaches. Well educated and artistically aware, they were at the core of the vitalizing processes that drove the entire Bulgarian culture at the time. Most prominent among them were Pencho Georgiev, Ivan Penkov, Ivan Milev and Asen Popov.

In the late 1920s several young Russian painters settled in Bulgaria including Yevgeny Vashtenko, who had worked at Meyerhold's theatre, and Vladimir Misin. Both contributed to the growth of ideological differences in the field.

The sets of Penkov, Milev and Georgi Karakashev tended to be one-dimensional and decorative and reflected the influence of the Russian artistic circle known as Mir Izkustv (Art World) and the spirit of *art nouveau*. This work was explicitly opposed by other innovative designers who believed in the essentialness of the three-dimensional nature of the actor and a stage space with corresponding dimensions.

In the 1930s, constructivism replaced symbolism and the revolutionary theatres of the time moved in this direction. Tempted by these experiments, famous painters and graphic artists tried their hands at the theatre. Among them were Aleksandar Jendov, Georgi Popov-Jhon and Boris Angelushev.

Despite the formal prevalence of constructivism in Bulgarian set design, the approach remained relatively diverse until the end of the 1940s. During the socialist period, crises in the theatre were inevitably and naturally followed by crises in set design. Socialist-realism especially caused damage but did not manage to uproot entirely a spirit of experiment, thanks in great measure to the risks of professors in the Academy for Fine Arts. Among them were Dechko Usunov, Ljubomir Delchev and Ivan Penkov.

In the 1960s and 1970s, many of Penkov's students created dazzling sets on Sofia stages and in other cities throughout the country. In this regard, mention should be made of the sets of Stephan Savov for *Romeo and Juliet: The Gas Station* (1974), by Ivan Radoev, at the State Satire Theatre, and the sets by Mariana Popova for *Man of La Mancha* (1973) at the State Music Theatre. During this period, some of the famous artists of the Plovdiv School also turned to set design – Hristo Stefanov, Dimitar Kirov, Ioan Liviev, Ivan Kirkov and Svetlin Russev, as well as the architects Angel Ahrjanov and Georgi Trendafilov.

Several artists of the 1980s stand out for their impressive intellectual presence and outstanding plastic skills – Nevena Kavaldjieva, Krasimir Valchinov, Vjacheslav Parapanov, Stephan Popov, Elena Ivanova, L. Barabov and Ani Pulieva. During the mid-1980s, however, Bulgarian set design went into crisis despite the growth of prizes and, since 1986, annual exhibitions of the work of young designers. Many designers turned to mechanical and plastic models. Especially strong has been the influence of modern Polish design in this regard and that of populist German troupes. These show up as either minimalism or overt abundance, both superficially motivated by the aesthetics of post-modernism.

Petar Smiicharov

Training

The first professional theatre school in Bulgaria was founded in 1925 by Nikolai Ossipovich Massalitinov, a Russian *émigré* and a major actor at the Moscow Art Theatre. He had worked for almost three decades as a director at the National Theatre in Sofia. The theatre school was affiliated with the National Theatre and in the early days its students included some outstanding established Bulgarian actors who wanted to study there. Massalitinov had outstanding pedagogical skills and remarkable success in converting both his actors and his students to the Stanislavski system. That original theatre studio changed its name and status many times over the years and gradually evolved into the current National Academy for Theatre and Film Arts in Sofia.

The first State Theatre School was founded in Sofia in 1942. Also affiliated with the National Theatre, it was transformed in 1948 into a State School for Higher Theatre Education and became independent. In 1954 it became the Sarafov Higher Institute for Theatre Arts and in the 1990s was transformed into the National Academy for Theatre and Film Arts.

There are three main departments in the National Academy for Theatre and Film Arts. The oldest is the acting and directing department. In 1962 the department for puppet theatre was founded, and in 1973 the film department was established.

The academy also offers Master's degrees in acting, directing (since 1947), theatre criticism and research (since 1959), pantomime (1991), public speech (1991), acting for puppet theatre (1962), directing for puppet theatre (1977), theatre criticism and research for puppet theatre (1991), design for puppet theatre (1992), film and television directing (1973), film and television photography (1973), film criticism and script writing (1973) and animation (1979). There are also degree programmes in film montage (since 1990) and photography (1992).

The courses are either four or five years in length. A doctorate requires an addional three years and is offered in most subjects.

From their first year, students are organized in classes of not more than fifteen, with each class having an artistic adviser throughout its course of education. Most artistic advisers come from the ranks of the best Bulgarian theatre and film practitioners.

In the 1990s, several small, private drama schools were founded. The Private Theatre School for Higher Education is considered to be the most prestigious among them and was founded in 1991. It offers degrees in two specialties – acting and directing. A three-year course provides students with a diploma qualifying them as a professional actor or director; a four-year course provides students with a Bachelor's degree in these areas.

Criticism, Scholarship and Publishing

Bulgarian theatre criticism is considered to be a part of theatre rather than a part of journalism. Its prose tends therefore to be more analytical than entertaining. Those who work as critics also do so more as a sideline than as a sole profession.

Developed as an indelible part of the theatre in the middle of the nineteenth century, until the beginning of the twentieth century it bore characteristics of the theatre itself – amateurish, didactic and moralistic. Aimed at bolstering the spirit of the people, the tasks of the Bulgarian critic, artist, playwright and spectator merged eventually into one – that of the Bulgarian patriot writing, performing and applauding in the name of national liberty and the enlightenment.

At this same time, criticism started exerting aesthetic functions as well. Through the early part of the century, the proper balance between social and aesthetic criteria has frequently been debated, especially after the communist revolution when the consequences were very immediate and real.

From the beginning, therefore, Bulgarian theatre criticism grew to be an active partner in the theatre and drama. This perhaps explains why for a long time it was primarily supportive rather than critical. Those who worked as critics helped to establish the first professional companies and the National Theatre, promoted directors to the status of central figures in the theatre, and supported new tendencies in acting brought to the Bulgarian stages from graduates of foreign theatre schools.

It is rare in Bulgarian periodicals to find theatre critics as staff members. Criticism has always tended to be written either by journalists covering mainstream cultural and artistic events or by writers, playwrights, directors and literary critics. Many major writers have tried their hands at writing reviews. Among them have been Vasil Drumev, Ljuben Karavelov, Ivan Shishmanov, Ivan Vasov, Pencho Slaveikov, Sirak Skitnik, Pejo Javorov, Petko Todorov and Geo Milev. Among those who have specialized in writing criticism are Ivan Andreichin, Nikola Atanasov, D.B. Mitov and Gocho Gochev. One of them – Ljubomir Tenev (d. 1993), whose creative life spanned more than sixty years – was considered to be the doyen of Bulgarian theatre criticism for his highly imaginative and profoundly analytical writings.

Since the establishment of a degree in theatre criticism and research in dramatic arts at the National Academy for Theatre and Film Arts in 1959, Bulgarian theatre criticism has been written primarily by graduates of the programme. Yet even those who have been and are employed by periodicals are usually hired as editors rather than as theatre critics.

Before the communist revolution, overnight reviewing was the norm after an opening. During the communist period, reviews were usually published no sooner than a week after the opening. From the 1990s, theatre coverage depends totally on the publication, the importance of the theatre having the première, and the prominence of the artists involved in the production. Two weekly newspapers – *Kultura* (*Culture*) and *Literaturen Forum* (*Literary Forum*) – publish such reviews and longer articles on a regular basis. A monthly specialized magazine, *Theatre*, has, since its founding in 1946, been covering Bulgarian theatre throughout the country publishing reviews, articles, interviews and scripts – sometimes foreign – in each issue.

Since 1966 Narodna Kultura has been publishing plays (Bulgarian and foreign) in a series entitled *Theatre*. Since 1984 Nauka I Izkustvo has been publishing books on theatre history, theory and criticism in a series entitled *Theatre: The 20th Century*.

A complete study of the Bulgarian theatre (*History of Bulgarian Theatre*) was written by Pencho Penev in 1975. By 1993, it needed significant updating.

Kalina Stefanova-Peteva
Translated by Sylvia Golemanova, Boris Nymoushin
and Kalina Stefanova-Peteva

Further Reading

Bardijewska, Liliana. 'Literatura bulgarska: Dyskurs o narodzie'. [Bulgarian literature: discourse on the nation]. *Dialog* 7 (1986): 118–29.

Bulgarian Centre of the ITI. *The Bulgarian Dramatic Art*. Sofia: National Centre of Propaganda and Information, 1979. 68 pp.

Dinova-Russeva, Vera. *Bulgarian Set Design*. Bulgarian Artistic Publishing House, 1975.

Gradev, Dimiter, ed. *Bulgarian Puppet Theatre*. Sofia: Information Centre, 1979. 144 pp.

Guiorova, Sevelina. *Le Théâtre dramatique Bulgare*. [Bulgarian dramatic theatre]. Sofia: Septemvri, 1979. 120 pp.

Karakostov, Stefan L. *Bŭlgarskiiat teatŭr: osnovi na socialisticheskiia realizŭm, 1881, 1891, 1945*. [Bulgarian theatre: fundamentals of socialist-realism, 1881, 1891, 1945]. Sofia: Nauka i Izkustvo, 1982. 570 pp.

Klementiev, Boris, and Dimitar Grozdanov. 'The Artist and the Theatre: The First Exhibition of Young Set Designers'. *Izkustvo* 10 (1986).

Natev, Atanas. *Teatralma ideografiia: iavleniia, problemy, nasoki v dneshniia chuzhdestranen teatur*. [Theatre ideology: phenomena, problems and questions on the artistic nature of theatre]. Sofia: Partizdat, 1983. 338 pp.

——. *The Bulgarian Music, Theatre, Art*. Sofia: National Centre of Propaganda and Information, 1979. 135 pp.

Shoulov, Iosif. *The Bulgarian Theatre*. Translated by Elena Mladenova. Sofia: Foreign Language Press, 1964.

Sŭstav, Dimitŭr K. *Sŭvremenna teatralna teoriia i kritika: sbornik statii*. [Contempory theatrical theory and criticism: a symposium]. Sofia: Nauka i Izkustvo, 1980. 355 pp.

Zmiicharov, Petar. 'Personal Opinion in 40 Lines'. *Standart* 42 (1992).

BYELORUSSIA

(see **BELARUS**)

COMMONWEALTH OF INDEPENDENT STATES

(see **USSR**)

CROATIA

Located in southeastern Europe and one-fifth of the former Socialist Federal Republic of Yugoslavia, Croatia had a 1991 population of 4.8 million and a land area of 56,500 square kilometres (21,800 square miles). With its capital in Zagreb (703,800 inhabitants), 77.9 per cent of the population are Croats, 12.2 per cent Serbs, 2.2 per cent Yugoslavs, 1 per cent Muslims, 0.5 per cent Hungarians, 0.5 per cent Slovenes and 5.7 per cent others.

In the seventh century Croats settled the area of the former Roman provinces Panonia and Dalmatia. The first written Croatian document dates from the period of Duke Trpimir (852). In 925, Pope John X proclaimed the Croatian ruler Tomislav king. In 1102, Kálmán (from the Hungarian dynasty Arpad) became king, and Croatia formed a union with Hungary. In 1301, the French Anjou dynasty was brought to the Croatian throne. In 1572, Croatian nobility elected Ferdinand Habsburg and his dynasty as kings. In 1868, Croatia became a Hungarian dependant in the dual Austro-Hungarian monarchy.

The Croatian parliament broke off relations with Austria-Hungary on 29 October 1918. Along with other southern Slavs, they united in the State of the Slovenes, Croats and Serbs. This state joined the Kingdom of Serbia to form the Kingdom of the Serbs, Croats and Slovenes on 1 December 1918. In 1929 King Alexander Karageorgevich renamed the country as the Kingdom of Yugoslavia.

Following a short-lived and futile resistance, the Kingdom of Yugoslavia capitulated before the Axis powers, and under the patronage of these powers the Independent State of Croatia was declared on 10 April 1941. At the same time, many areas of Croatia started the anti-fascist struggle.

The Federal Republic of Yugoslavia, established in May 1945, was held under a one-party communist regime by the leadership of the Croat, Josip Broz Tito (1892–1980). In 1963, the state was renamed the Socialist Federal Republic of Yugoslavia; Croatia became the Socialist Republic of Croatia. Between 1989 and 1991, economic, political and national crises in the state intensified rapidly. The first opposition parties since 1941 were founded in 1989, and the first post-war democratic elections were held in 1990. A new constitution announced the determination to establish an independent Republic of Croatia, and on 25 June 1991 the Republic of Croatia was proclaimed as a sovereign and independent state. The Republic of Croatia was internationally recognized in January 1992. It is now a member of the United Nations.

Theatrical life in Croatia developed similarly to that in other western European countries. Liturgical plays in Latin from the eleventh century mark the beginning of recorded theatrical events in the territory. In the thirteenth century, under the influence of popular festivities which were flourishing in the southern parts of Croatia (Dalmatia) under Italian influence, numerous Medieval sacral theatrical forms were developing. In Dubrovnik, secular, religious and humanistic theatres developed from the fourteenth century.

The comedy writer Marin Držić (c.1508–67), whose comedy *Dundo Maroje* (*Uncle Maroje*, 1551) was widely performed, won recognition during the Renaissance. In the city of Hvar, a community theatre was built in 1612. In Dubrovnik, the Baroque theatre was represented by Ivan Gundulić (1589–1638) and Junije Palmotić (1607–57).

Until 1607, theatrical life was also developing

within ecclesiastical schools and religious orders (particularly the Jesuits, Paulists and Franciscans). By the close of the eighteenth century, numerous German and Italian travelling companies could be found performing in public places throughout Croatia. It was at the beginning of the nineteenth century that Zagreb established itself as the political and cultural centre of the nation. In 1840, the first Croatian professional theatre was founded in Zagreb within the framework of the programme of national renaissance. Its organizational structure has changed little over the years; in 1846 the first Croatian opera – Vatroslav Lisinski's (1819–54) *Ljubav i zloba* (*Love and Malice*) – was performed there.

Playhouses in other Croatian towns opened in the second half of the nineteenth century featuring mostly German and Italian theatre and opera companies. Theatre manager Stjepan Miletić (1868–1908) from Zagreb modernized Croatian theatrical life significantly. By the end of 1945, all theatres in Croatia were staging professional performances in the Croatian language. The situation was the same even in cities like Rijeka and Zadar, which had been under Italian occupation and which had seen only amateur companies perform in Croatian.

Like many other periods in the history of Croatian theatre, the period that followed World War II and the formation of the new Yugoslavia was marked by significant political activity. Theatrical life in Croatia was characterized by new political orientations generally and the growing power of the Yugoslav Communist Party in particular. Parts of Croatian national territory previously under Italian control (the northern coast and some islands) were united at this time with Croatia. Croatia entered this new period extremely aware of its rich theatrical tradition and its five centuries of stage continuity.

Even during World War II, cultural life was active in Croatia. In partisan units, many artists formed theatre companies continuing pre-war, left-oriented, theatrical traditions. The repertoire of the partisan theatres included national classics of patriotic-heroic tendencies (mostly nineteenth-century romantic plays), foreign satires (often Gogol), contemporary political plays and various collage-type programmes. In all larger towns and cities, a rich theatrical heritage continued to flourish throughout the period. Since a large majority of theatres were spared destruction during the war, in the period right after, with the communists taking power in 1945, theatrical life continued and grew without major pauses or significant changes.

In the late 1940s and early 1950s, the national theatres of the former Yugoslavia began to change their names, but their internal structure remained mostly, if not entirely, the same. The post-war years put the theatres in a special and privileged position. Generous and bountiful government grants elevated cultural life to a stately level. The new cultural policy, characterized by educational intentions in the broadest sense of the words, led to the foundation of a series of permanent professional theatres even in small cities which lacked any theatrical tradition; many of these, however, were later closed down when they proved to be financially infeasible.

Compared to 1940, the number of professional theatres in Croatia quadrupled. The great demand for artists and other theatre workers laid the foundation for advanced education in all aspects of stage art. This turned into a surprising impetus for theatrical life. Quickly all the dramatic arts – including opera and dance – took centre stage. Theatres could not satisfy the demand for tickets. And because ticket sales followed the Soviet model and were sold mostly through unions and factories, tickets could not be bought easily. In fact, until the mid-1950s Croatian theatre closely imitated that of the Soviet Union.

The repertoire of the period was also remarkably narrow in focus and Soviet influenced. Theatres staged national classics: Marin Držić and Miroslav Krleža (1893–1981); contemporary patriotic Croatian writers; Russian and Soviet playwrights from Griboedov, Ostrovsky and Gogol to Leonov, Škvarkin and Simonov; and they did not stage Mayakovsky, Bulgakov or Erdman. Carefully chosen international classics were staged with a stress in production on socialist and leftist tendencies (Shakespeare, Molière, Goldoni and Balzac), as were a few contemporary western playwrights who criticized the political and social characteristics of their societies (Arthur Miller's *All My Sons*). Opera and ballet were not so completely determined by this repertoire policy but even there Russian and Soviet composers prevailed. Works that might have given rise to ideological doubt were studiously avoided (for example, Wagner was not done until 1952).

A strict ideological orientation, where the least vagueness was punished by condemnation in the press and removal of the play from the repertoire, resulted in simplified acting and directing patterns of a neo-romantic character. Features, clothes and behaviour clearly distinguished positive characters from negative ones. From the beginning of each play the viewer was forced at this time to accept such one-sided interpretations. Questions were not allowed on either side of the footlights. It was mandatory that a play, the joint venture of an entire company, express a clear ideology or be a history lesson or a picturesque explanation of simplified psychological categories. The director's overall task in this structure was simply to achieve the correct stage and spatial relations of actors within the strictly realistic setting. Training of actors was reduced to an interpretation of two Stanislavski principles – 'living the role' and 'living through'. Thus the 1940s and 1950s were characterized by simplicity and schematic qualities.

As Yugoslavia moved away from the socialist bloc and its national and political development took a new turn, the strict canons of socialist-realism in the cultural field were also gradually abandoned. This new direction was 'formally' sanctioned in a paper by Miroslav Krleža, a leading Croatian man of letters and also a dramatist. Read at the Congress of the Writers' Union in Ljubljana in 1952, this call for freedom and pluralism of artistic attitudes started changing the image of theatrical life almost overnight.

This proclaimed pluralism was soon established in practice and changes were seen in the repertoire. Socialist-realist plays by Soviet writers – burdened as they were by schematic displays of socialist ideology – were the first to go, along with similar attempts by Croatian authors. They were replaced by Giraudoux, Anouilh, a series of American contemporaries such as Williams and Miller, and representatives of the avant-garde of the 1950s such as Ionesco

and Beckett. Soon, all barriers to new theatrical expression were removed and stages were opened to all modern literary tendencies. French existentialist playwrights, contemporary British authors, various followers of the avant-garde, a series of boulevard successes from the European capitals and Broadway, satirical and critical dramatic visions by Polish and Czech writers, explorations of Brecht's corpus, experiments with Artaud's theoretical principles and echoes of the Living Theatre all became part of Croatian theatre from the mid-1950s onward. Ethical questions were now considered in a mythological context and there was experimentation with language. New genres, like the fairy-tale and the grotesque, were introduced.

Theatrical life underwent significant structural changes, however. National institutions ceased to be the only places of artistic importance. Theatre artists searched for more unconventional organizational forms and as a result, new theatres were opened and new festivals established. This had both positive and negative consequences which were still being felt in the 1990s.

Among the foreign companies which have had particular influence following visits to Croatia in the period between the 1950s and the 1980s, one should mention the Théâtre National Populaire from France with Jean Vilar and Gerard Philippe (1955), the Piccolo Teatro from Milan with Giorgio Strehler's *Arlecchino, servitore di due padroni* (*Servant of Two Masters*, 1955), Laurence Olivier and Vivien Leigh in *Titus Andronicus* directed by Peter Brook (1957), performances of the Comédie-Française, the Vienna Burgtheater, leading Russian theatres, Polish and Czech companies, and a vast array of various representatives of avant-garde movements who appeared regularly at numerous festivals.

Structure of the National Theatre Community

The organizational structure of Croatian theatre is the result of historical development and specifics of the internal administrative and financial systems of the country. Present-day Croatian theatres inherited many of their organizational aspects of theatres from former states which had influence in the region (the Austro-Hungarian Empire, the Kingdom of

Yugoslavia and the Socialist Federal Republic of Yugoslavia).

The method of management which, with minor transformations, existed until 1991 and the announcement of a new Theatre Act, was also determined in the post-World War II period. It was then that the workers' self-management system was introduced as the principal administrative model, not only in business, but also in educational and art institutions. Such an internal administrative structure, created primarily for business firms, significantly limited the creative freedom of theatre. As an example, following public announcement of a vacancy, candidates applied as for any other job. If appointed they could hold, say, the position of manager for four years with the possibility of reappointment for another four.

In the case of national houses with three companies, each would have its own manager but the manager would not have authority to decide on a single important issue regarding the functioning of the theatre (choice of repertoire, engagement of company members, or financial policy). The manager was obliged by law to execute the decisions of artistic councils (consisting of artists employed by the theatre and of the council which, aside from the theatre representatives, comprised members delegated from other social and political entities).

This system was borrowed from politics and was never really suitable for theatre since it did not place any kind of executive power in an artistic authority. It was also practically impossible to terminate an artist's engagement. Consequently, an actor's first engagement could well remain a permanent one until retirement. Administrative and artistic managers, therefore, could only partly formulate a theatre's style.

Ad-hoc companies, some of which staged whole seasons and remained active over many years, or those gathering around a single project and then disbanding, managed to avoid such complicated organizational schemes. Theatres without companies, but with strong artistic and dramaturgical leadership, have also been appearing since the mid-1960s. They employ directors, designers and actors from various institutions exclusively for performances of a single play. These theatres are also mobile. They tend to function in non-traditional venues while successfully retaining a high quality level and a provocative repertoire. Not burdened by an administrative apparatus, in their best seasons they represent some of the strongest fermenting agents of modern Croatian theatre.

After World War II, theatre in Croatia was financed from state funds. Until the mid-1950s, theatres were financed directly according to fixed rules of budget distribution. Subsequently, theatres received their grants through a national Fund for Culture. This fund was created by taking roughly 0.3 per cent of the wages of all employed people. The fund supported professional theatres on national, regional and municipal levels. All theatres would submit repertoire proposals to fund committees. Funds were granted therefore on the basis of a particular season's attractiveness rather than for the name or tradition of an institution. Since 1991 theatres have also been financed by various sponsoring agencies.

Dramatic theatres normally perform four or five plays per season; opera houses up to three operas; and ballet theatres two ballets during a season lasting from September to the end of June. Independent companies, artists coming together around a single project, or individuals presenting monodramas, pantomimes, recitals or the like also compete for funding from the same sources. Grants usually cover up to 70 per cent of estimated costs with the rest being covered by box-office income and, more recently, sponsors' support and advertisements.

Theatre tickets in Croatia have traditionally been inexpensive (average price for an opera is US$3–4, while seats for dramas cost no more than US$2.50). Festival tickets tend to be three times the price of normal tickets. All large theatres offer tickets to students and groups at reduced prices. A wide spectrum of various season tickets are also offered, especially by the national theatres.

In total, there were twenty-three professional theatres operating in 1993 – four national theatres, six dramatic theatres, two independent theatres, one Italian-language dramatic theatre (in Rijeka) and one theatre doing musical, operatic and dramatic plays. There were five puppet groups and four theatres for young audiences.

Croatia hosts about ten regular festivals annually. The Dubrovačke ljetne igre (Dubrovnik Summer Games, since 1950) is one of the most important. The aesthetics of theatre in natural, open spaces (squares, streets, churches, fortresses and palaces) are explored in this ancient city on Croatia's southern coast. Many classic Croatian plays by Hanibal Lucić (*c*.1485–1553), Držić, Gundulić, Ivo Vojnović (1857–1929) and Krleža, as well as world classics by Sophocles, Shakespeare, Calderón, Molière, Goldoni and Brecht, have been done at this festival. Its musical segments – concerts, operas and ballets – are also international in character.

The Splitsko ljeto (Split Summer, since 1954) is also an international drama and opera festival while the Osiječki operni bienale (Osijek Opera Biennial, since 1970) is dedicated mainly to modern opera. Other festivals of note include the Gavelline večeri (Gavella Evenings, Zagreb, since 1973), Dani satire (Days of Satire, Zagreb, since 1976) and the Marulovi dani (Marulo Days, Split, since 1990).

Since 1987, Zagreb has also been host to Eurokaz, a festival of international avant-garde and experimental theatre. An international festival of children's theatre, Festival djeteta (since 1958) takes place yearly in Šibenik.

Puppet theatres can be seen at several festivals, of which the Medunarodni festival kazališta lutaka/Pupteatra internacia festivalo (International Puppet Festival, Zagreb, since 1968) is held mainly in Esperanto.

Artistic Profile

Companies

The oldest Croatian professional theatre, the Croatian National Theatre in Zagreb (founded in 1840), developed out of the national need for a cultural and political identity during a time of struggle against foreign political and cultural domination. In the organizational and structural sense, this theatre was a combination of the Vienna Burgtheater and the Prague Narodni Divadlo (National Theatre). For over a century and a half it was the centre of numerous nationally significant events. Its initial goal was to popularize the national language and literature, a task of significant educational importance. Organized originally as simply a dramatic theatre, the National added opera and ballet troupes. This led to a number of problems regarding management and space but the model of a central multi-genre playhouse has remained.

Besides the Croatian National Theatre in Zagreb, there is a Croatian National Theatre in Osijek (since 1907), a Croatian National Theatre in Split (since 1920) and the Ivan Zajc Theatre in Rijeka (since 1945) with the same multi-company structure.

In addition to these national theatres, Croatia has a number of dramatic theatres and other theatres specializing in comedy and operetta. Among the most noteworthy are the Dramsko kazalište Gavella (Drama Theatre Gavella) in Zagreb founded in 1954, the Zagrebačko gradsko kazalište Komedija (Zagreb Municipal Comedy Theatre, since 1950), the Satiričko kazalište Jazavac (Badger Satire Theatre) in Zagreb, since 1964, Theatre Etc. (Zagreb, since 1966), Hrvatsko narodno kazalište Varaždin (Croatian National Theatre of Varaždin, since 1945), and the Kazalište Marina Držića (Marin Držić Theatre, Dubrovnik, since 1944).

Among youth and children's theatres, the most important are the Zagrebačko kazalište mladih (Zagreb Youth Theatre, since 1948), the Zagrebačko kazalište lutaka (Zagreb Puppet Theatre, since 1945) and the Kazalište lutaka Zadar (Puppet Theatre of Zadar, since 1952). The most important independent companies are Teatar u gostima (Guest Theatre, Zagreb, since 1974) and Glumačka družina Histrion Zagreb (Histrion Acting Company, Zagreb, since 1975).

The years after 1953 were marked by a pronounced liberalization in policy and the organizational structure changed. Numerous young actors and directors abandoned the huge, often bulky national theatre institutions to form smaller dramatic theatres. They quickly showed how ossified the traditions of the larger established institutions had become. Newly formed theatres like the Zagrebačko dramsko kazalište (Zagreb Drama Theatre, 1954, now called the Dramsko kazalište Gavella/Drama Theatre Gavella) and Theatre Etc. (founded in 1966) soon became centres of innovation in repertoire, interpretation and organization. With these somewhat larger theatres now operating, several companies in smaller centres began to disappear (Zadar, Šibenik, Karlovac and Pula).

Dramaturgy

The first post-war years of strict ideological orientation resulted in a strong interest in past events and a glorification of recent history by playwrights. Soviet plays were regarded as the ideal. In the mid-1950s, after political and ideological liberalization, Croatian dramatists turned to western European and American models. Their works reveal the influence of Jean Giraudoux and Jean Anouilh, particularly in the motifs of ancient myths. The influence of Arthur Miller and Tennessee Williams is evident in the rendering of scenes from an urban environment.

Since the 1960s, Croatian dramatic literature

and the repertoire of numerous theatres have been completely open to virtually all modern international dramaturgical developments. This has resulted in a heterogeneousness of genre and topics in contemporary Croatian dramatic literature.

The influence of Miroslav Krleža was both significant and extensive in the national drama. His dramatic work between the two wars developed in several cycles. Early on came his symbolic-expressionist work, best represented by *Kraljevo* (*Kermes*, 1915), an expressionist drama whose importance was confirmed only after its 1970 presentation in the Gavella Drama Theatre in Zagreb. He later turned to Scandinavian variations of the form. In 1958, he added a third act to his best known drama, *U agoniji* (*In Agony*, 1928), and wrote a fantasy drama *Aretej ili Legenda o svetoi Ancili* (*Areteus or The Legend of the Holy Ancila*, 1959) in which he analysed the position of an intellectual threatened by political murder in a totalitarian regime. Dramaturgically, the play is reminiscent of the author's early experimental phase.

In the early 1950s, plays about the recent war were replaced by dramas based on detailed psychological studies. Marijan Matković's (1915–85) cycle *Igra oko smrti* (*Playing Around Death*) is the best example of this strain in dramatic literature. This cycle of ten plays belonging to different dramaturgical models deals with the lives and destinies of people from the mid-1930s to the end of World War II.

Mirko Božić (b. 1919) wrote *Pravednik* (*The Just*, 1961) after several plays about the war. *The Just* deals with personal resistance and morality during the war.

Traditional social drama did not disappear from the stage. It was present in the later works of Josip Kulundžić (1899–1970) such as *Klara Dombrovska* (1955). In the 1920s, the same author experimented with expressionism and in 1953 ruffled ideological censors with his play *Čovjek je dobar* (*Man is Good*) by posing the problem of good and evil in warring political parties.

Comedy writers of the time included Dragutin Gervais (1904–57), author of *Karolina Riječka* (1952), and Joža Horvat (b. 1915), author of *Prst pred nosom* (*Before One's Nose*, 1947). Pero Budak (b. 1917), another writer of note, dealt with rural life in *Mećava* (*Blizzard*, 1952).

The thematic elements of existentialism, dilemmas of choice, freedom and action, and relation to authority entered Croatian drama in the mid-1950s under the influence of contemporary French and American writers. The most important play of this movement was Ranko Marinković's (b. 1913) *Glorija* (1955), on the whole one of the most successful Croatian plays. *Glorija* is a Miracle play, structurally resembling Pirandello's work. It explores humanity's ideological confinement by dogma and our desire for freedom of action. Matković's *Heraklo* (1958), the second part of the trilogy *I bogovi pate* (*Gods Suffer Too*) is about the problems of an individual who struggles against the cult of personality. The play is a modern projection of the myth of Heracles.

The relation of the individual to the state, the theme strongly present in Croatian theatre at the time, has been dramatized by Ivan Supek (b. 1915) in *Heretik* (*Heretic*, 1968) and by Nedjeljko Fabrio (b. 1937) in *Reformatori* (*Reformers*, 1967).

The central figure of the new generation of writers who formed themselves around the literary journal *Krugovi* (1952–8) was Antun Šoljan (1932–93), an author who excelled in all genres, even anonymously pursuing his independent ideas in the harshest times of communist autocracy. His work had decisive bearing on latter-day Croatian literature. The plays *Galilejevo uzašašće* (*The Ascension of Galileo*, 1967), *Brdo* (*The Hill*, 1967) and particularly *Dioklecijanova palača* (*Diocletian's Palace*, 1969), *Romanca o tri ljubavi* (*A Romance of Three Loves*, 1967) and *Bard* (*The Bard*, 1987) dramatize all the dilemmas of the contemporary intellectual troubled with doubt over the possibility of survival in a totalitarian society.

Šoljan's plays, technically unconventional and abounding in puns, were a great innovation in modern Croatian drama. In the genre of radio drama he achieved national and even international success (*Čovjek koji je spasio Nizozemsku/The Man Who Saved the Netherlands*, 1983). The same generation also brought forth Čedo Prica (b. 1931), who earned recognition with his play *Ostavka* (*Resignation*, 1986), and Ivan Kušan (b. 1933), whose politically provocative play *Svrha od slobode* (*The Purpose of Freedom*, 1971) met with strong communist opposition.

Another interesting figure is Radovan Ivšić (b. 1921). Since 1945 he has lived and worked in Paris. His most important work, *Kralj Gordogan* (*King Gordogan*, written in 1943, performed and first published in France in 1968, then in Croatia in 1975) was written under the influence of Alfred Jarry and French surrealism.

Poetic plays of note were written by Nikola

Šop (1904–82), Jure Kaštelan (1919–90) and Vesna Parun (b. 1922). Fadil Hadžić (b. 1922) wrote some thirty comedies. Ivan Raos (1921–87) started experimenting early with dramatic form and expression. The strong spirit of the avant-garde is also felt in the works of Zvonimir Bajsić (1925–87) and Ivica Ivanac (1936–88), whose *Odmor za umorne jahače ili Don Juanov osmijeh* (*A Break for Tired Riders or Don Juan's Smile*, 1961) synthesizes echoes of Beckett and poetic-intellectual structures present in the best European drama of the time.

Ivo Brešan (b. 1936) represents these tendencies in later Croatian drama. His grotesque tragedy *Predstava Hamleta u selu Mrduša Donja* (*A Performance of Hamlet in the Village of Mrduša Donja*, 1971) uses Shakespeare cheerlessly to depict dictatorship by a single political party; his *Predstava Hamleta u selu Mrduša Donja* is probably the most internationally successful Croatian contemporary play. In his other plays Brešan, working with total precision, employed the same intertextual technique to analyse totalitarian society.

Tomislav Bakarić (b. 1941) is a writer who explores the historical destiny of Croatia, whereas Ivan Bakmaz (b. 1941) boldly experiments with form and language under the influence of the European Theatre of the Absurd. Slobodan Šnajder (b. 1948) distinguished himself as a dramatist and by founding the theatrical journal *Prolog*. His best plays are *Kamov: smrtopis* (*Kamov: Deathscript*, 1978) and the internationally performed *Hrvatski Faust* (*Croatian Faust*, 1982). Both dramatize biographies of Croatian literary and historical figures in an attempt to present views of contemporary political reality.

The playful authorial trio of Tahir Mujičić (b. 1947), Boris Senker (b. 1947) and Nino Škrabe (b. 1947) works jointly within the spirit of postmodernism. Their plays, collected as *Porod od tmine* (*Descendants of Darkness*, 1979), respond to historical questions of the time with witty linguistic pastiches. Miro Gavran (b. 1961) is a particularly skilful writer of dialogue, and many of his plays have been performed abroad, especially his *Čehov je Tolstoju rekao zbogom* (*Chekhov Said Goodbye to Tolstoi*, 1989).

Directors, Directing and Production Styles

Among Croatian directors, the work of Branko Gavella (1885–1962), particularly in the period after World War II, deserves special mention. From 1914 he directed over 250 dramas and operas within the former Yugoslavia. From 1930 to 1947 he worked abroad (Czechoslovakia, Bulgaria and at La Scala in Italy) and returned to Croatia after 1949. A founder of higher education for actors and directors, a theoretician of the theatre and a theatre scholar, he distinguished himself particularly as a director of national plays (Držić, Vojnović and Krleža) and those of Shakespeare.

Others who also played an important role in contemporary Croatian theatre include Tito Strozzi (1892–1970) and Tomislav Tanhofer (1898–1971). Marko Fotez (1913–76) became popular as the director of Marin Držić's comedies. Vlado Habunek (b. 1906) earned recognition in the United Kingdom, Germany and the United States, while Kosta Spaić (b. 1923) worked in Finland, Switzerland, Germany, the UK and the USA. Other prominent Croatian directors include Mladen Škiljan (b. 1921), Bogdan Jerković (b. 1925), Dino Radojević (1927–86), Tomislav Durbešić (b. 1928), Vladimir Gerić (b. 1928), Božidar Violić (b. 1931), Georgij Paro (b. 1934), Joško Juvančić (b. 1936), Petar Selem (b. 1936), Tomislav Radić (b. 1940), Miro Metimorec (b. 1942), Petar Veček (b. 1942), Želimir Mesarić (b. 1944), Ivica Kunčević (b. 1945) and Marin Carić (b. 1947).

Music Theatre

Music theatre started playing an important role in Croatia as early as 1846 when the first Croatian opera was performed in Zagreb – Vatroslav Lisinski's *Ljubav i zloba* (*Love and Malice*). After national operatic life began to flourish, Croatian artists started performing on world stages: Matilda Mallinger (1847–1920) sang Eve on the opening night of Wagner's *Die Meistersinger von Nürnberg* in Munich in 1868. Baritone Josip Kašman (1847–1924) performed in the first season of the Metropolitan Opera in 1883, while Milka Trnina (1863–1941) was one of the great world Wagnerian sopranos at the turn of the century. A longstanding tradition of national opera and operetta developed through the twentieth century.

Croatia has four opera companies and one company specializing in operetta and musicals. Seasons last, on average, for nine to ten months.

Operatic companies in Croatia are independent artistic organizational segments of particular National Theatres and are located in Zagreb, Osijek, Split and Rijeka.

The Croatian operatic repertoire is connected to the beginning of national opera in the middle of the nineteenth century. It developed between two tendencies: the European tradition of the Italian belcanto and the search for indigenous elements of folk music. All schools of musical style in the following years, from neo-romanticism to expressionism and even modern variations verify the constancy of this polarization.

Jakov Gotovac (1895–1982) became famous with his comic opera *Ero s onoga svijeta* (*Hero from the Other World*, 1935). His post-war works were also based on folk music – *Mila Gojsalića* (1952), *Stanac* (1950) and *Dalmaro* (1964). The later works of Ivo Tijardović (1895–1976), author of the most popular national operetta, *Mala Floramye* (1925), were more in the vein of traditional opera spectacles with late romantic characteristics (*Marko Polo*, 1960, and *Dioklecijan*, unperformed).

The exceptionally productive and diverse composer Boris Papandopulo (1906–91), a representative of the neo-classical style and a brilliant instrumentalist and expert on orchestras, distinguished himself by his operas *Rona* (1965) and *Kentervilski duh* (*The Spirit of Canterville*, 1979). The works of Ivan Brkanović (1906–87) are characterized by their great dramatic force – *Ekvinocij* (*Equinox*, 1950, based on the play by I. Vojnović) and the opera-oratorio *Zlato Zadra* (*The Gold of Zadar*, 1955).

Ivo Lhotka-Kalinski (1913–86) composed the monumental musical drama *Matija Gubec* (1947) and a series of small operas for radio and television, mostly based on the texts of Serbian dramatist Branislav Nušić – *Analfabeta* (*Ignoramus*, 1954), *Putovanje* (*Journey*, 1956), *Dugme* (*Button*, 1957) and *Vlast* (*The Power*, 1958).

Natko Devčić (b. 1914) is famous for his opera *Labinska vještica* (*The Witch of Labin*, 1957), Tihomil Vidošić (1902–73) for the comic opera *Stari mladić* (*The Old Youth*,

1960) and the productive composer Bruno Bjelinski (1909–92) for the children's opera *Pčelica Maja* (*Little Bee Maja*, 1963) and a series of one-act chamber operas.

The works of Silvije Bombardelli (b. 1916) belong to the vein of humanistic realism. His most popular opera is *Adam i Eva* (1967). The works of Stjepan Šulek (1914–86) include librettos inspired by Shakespeare's plays and hold a special place in contemporary Croatian opera. The musical dramas *Coriolanus* (1959) and *The Tempest* (1969) express his understanding of music, pervaded by the perfection of neo-classical form.

Milko Kelemen (b. 1924) introduced revolutionary orientations and theses into Croatian music. His experimental operas were inspired by existentialist philosophy and the Theatre of the Absurd. He created a new synthesis of music, words, dynamic action and modern expressive possibilities for scenes in *Novi stanar* (*The New Tenant*, 1964, based on Ionesco), *Ubu Roi* (1965, based on Jarry), *Siege* (1970, based on Camus) and *Apocalyptica* (1979).

Ivo Malec (b. 1925) employed new, mechanically synthesized sound in his dance drama *Prije doručka* (*Before Breakfast*, 1958) and in what he called a 'stage poster', *Victor Hugo: jedan protiv svih* (*Victor Hugo: One Against All*, 1971) for the Avignon Festival.

Miro Belamarić's (b. 1935) operas *Love of the Lord Perlimplin* (1975, based on García Lorca) and *Geschichten aus dem Wienerwald* (*Stories from the Vienna Woods*, 1993, based on Horvath) also received acclaim. Ruben Radica (b. 1931) with his opera *Prazor* (*The Dawn*, 1991), Igor Kuljerić (b. 1938) with *Moć vrline* (*The Power of Virtue*, 1977) and *Richard III* (1987, based on Shakespeare), and the avant-garde composer Silvio Foretić (b. 1940) with *Semi-Mono-Opera* (1979) for a single performer, voice, piano and percussion, also made a significant impact in modern Croatian opera.

Radio operas and operas composed for television constitute a particular operatic sub-genre. Ivo Lhotka-Kalinski and Stanko Horvat (b. 1930) worked effectively in this branch of music theatre.

Musical theatre generally started developing in the late 1950s. Among the composers particularly successful in the genre have been Ivo Tijardović – *Katarina Velika* (*Catherine the Great*, 1959), Stjepan Mihaljinec (b. 1935), composer of *Ja i moje drugo ja* (*Me and My Other Self*, 1963), Milivoj Krbler (1939–71), composer of *Plava limuzina* (*Blue Limousine*,

1963), and Alfi Kabiljo (b. 1935), composer of *Jalta, Jalta* (1972).

Ivica Krajač (b. 1938), Karlo Metikoš (1940–91) and Milijenko Prohaska (b. 1925) are authors of works belonging to the genre of rock opera – *Gubec beg* (1975) and *Grička vještica* (*The Witch of Grič*, 1979). Vlado Štefančić (b. 1930), director, and Sanda Langerholz (b. 1932), actress, particularly distinguished themselves in this demanding genre.

Among the major Croatian directors of opera are Vlado Habunek, Kosta Spaić and Petar Selem.

Among the numerous Croatian singers who have distinguished themselves on an international level are Zinka Kunc-Milanov (1906–89), who belonged to the repertory company of the Metropolitan Opera from 1937 to 1962, Srebrenka (Sena) Jurinac (b. 1921), a member of the Vienna National Opera from 1944 till the end of her career, Dragica (Carla) Martinis (b. 1922), a leading singer of the Vienna National Opera, Božena Ruk-Fočić (b. 1937), who gained popularity in Europe with her dramatic and powerful interpretations of Verdi and Wagner heroines, Ljiljana Molnar-Talajić (b. 1938), Gjurgja (Georgine) Milinković (1913–86), Marjana Radev (1913–71), who appeared at La Scala and Covent Garden, Biserka Cvejić (b. 1923), a famous alto and a member of the Metropolitan Opera and the Vienna Opera, and Nada Putar-Gold (b. 1923), a member of the Berlin and Frankfurt Operas.

Other singers of note include Ruža Pospiš-Baldani (b. 1942), Dunja Vejzović (b. 1943), another famed Wagner interpreter who also distinguished herself in the works of several modern composers (Berg, Bartók and Schoenberg), the famous tenor Josip Gostič (1919–63), a permanent guest of the Vienna National Opera, Krunoslav Cigoj (b. 1949), Vladimir Ruždak (1922–87), a renowned baritone who sang the contemporary repertoire of Hanze and Dallapiccola along with other composers at the Hamburg Opera and the Metropolitan, Ferdinand Radovan (b. 1938), and the most famous bass-baritone of Croatian origin, Tomislav Neralić (b. 1917), a longtime member of the German Opera in Berlin, who excelled in the Wagnerian repertoire. Other famous bass singers were Franjo Petrušanec (b. 1938), Giorgio Surian (b. 1954), who performed mostly at La Scala, and Neven Belamarić (b. 1949).

Opera conductors of international acclaim include Milan Sachs (1884–1968) of Czech origin and Lovro Matačić (1899–1985). Sachs was a famous conductor of Smetana, Janáček, Wagner, Strauss and Stravinsky. In both the pre- and post-war periods, Matačić was particularly famous for his conducting of Wagner's *Lohengrin* (Bayreuth, 1959), Bizet's *Carmen* (La Scala), Giordano's *Andrea Chenier* (Vienna National Opera) and Wagner's *Ring der Nibelungen* at the Roman Opera.

Mladen Bašić (b. 1917) is a famous conductor of the modern repertoire (Ravel, Britten and Prokofiev) and was director of the Salzburg Opera. From 1976 he was director of the Mainz Opera. Berislav Klobučar (b. 1924) has conducted the Vienna National Opera since 1953 and has conducted at La Scala, Bayreuth and the Metropolitan Opera. Miro Belamarić (b. 1935) frequently makes guest appearances on European and American stages, while Nikša Bareza (b. 1936) has conducted in Zürich since the 1970s, and later became director of the Graz Opera and conductor of the Vienna National Opera. Already world renowned, Vjekoslav Šutej (b. 1951) belongs to the youngest generation of Croatian conductors.

Dance Theatre

There are four professional ballet companies in Croatia, all part of national theatres. Within the theatres they act both as independent artistic bodies and as part of opera performances. Besides these companies, which perform the traditional, classical and contemporary repertoire and are the main collaborators of national music and ballet production, Croatia has several independent dance troupes. These troupes are more oriented toward avant-garde programmes, and are experimental in both musical and choreographic terms.

Despite the diversity of the national tradition, contemporary Croatian ballet is marked by two major streams: choreography and dance which follow the tradition of the great 'white' ballets and which contain elements of the Russian school from the 1920s, and new tendencies in dance art, which originate from the principles of Laban. Russian classical ballet and choreography was brought to Croatia/Yugoslavia in the mid-1920s by the members of the Froman family, headed by Margareta Petrovna Froman (1886–1970), a choreographer and director. Through her own activities, she founded the classical style of Croatian ballet.

For their part, Ana Roje (1909–91) and Oskar Harmoš (1891–1992), both students of Legat, incorporated elements of the Russian school with specific elements of national folk dance. They were members of numerous international troupes (including the Ballets Russes), leaders of their own dance schools in Croatia and abroad, and dancers and teachers in Zagreb. Mia Čorak Slavenska (b. 1916) started her career as a ballet dancer in Zagreb, but from 1937 danced abroad, spending a great deal of time as prima ballerina of the Ballets Russes de Monte Carlo. From 1944 she performed in the United States with the Metropolitan Opera (1954–5) and was director of her own troupe.

In the styles of European dance which have been developing since the 1960s, Croatia is well represented by Milko Šparenblek (b. 1928), a dancer and choreographer. Beginning his career in Zagreb, he moved to Paris in 1953 and began performing with Charrat, Béjart and Tcherina. In 1957 he embarked on a career as a choreographer (Sanders's L'Echelle). His speciality is contemporary dance and the transposition of non-ballet musical works into dance performances (Monteverdi, Beethoven, Berlioz, Mahler and Mozart). For several years, Šparenblek led the ballet of the Metropolitan Opera, the Gulbenkian Ballet of Lisbon, and the Ballet de Lyon. He returned to Zagreb in the 1980s.

Composers of note since 1945 include Krešimir Baranović (1894–1975), who wrote Licitarsko srce (The Gingerbread Heart, 1924) and The Chinese Story (1955), Bruno Bjelinski (1909–93), who explores new possibilities of sound in his ballet stories for children – Pinocchio (1959), Peter Pan (1966) and Puss in Boots (1977), Silvije Bombardelli, Ivan Brkanović (Heloti, 1966), and Boris Papandopulo – Žetva (Harvest, 1950), Grand Hotel (1967) and Tri kavalira frajle Melanije (Three Suitors of Lady Melanie, 1976).

Radical innovations in Croatian music and dance were introduced by Branimir Sakač (1918–79), composer of Simfonija o mrtvom vojniku (Symphony for a Dead Soldier, 1959), Milko Kelemen, Čovjek pred zrcalom (Man in Front of a Mirror, 1963) and Napuštene (The Abandoned, 1964), Ivo Malec, Mákete (1961), Prije doručka (Before Breakfast, 1958), Apprendre à marcher (1961) and La Voix du silence (1972), a synthesis of several stage genres, and Frano Parač (b. 1948), Carmina Krležiana (1986).

Theatre for Young Audiences

Croatia has a long tradition of professional theatres and acting troupes which perform programmes for children and young people. The first professional theatres of this type were founded after 1945 and by 1993 Croatia had four such theatres. In regions which do not have them, stage activities for children and youth are organized as part of existing theatre institutions.

The development of Croatian theatre for children and young people can be followed through several stages. In the first period after 1945, these theatres had only a didactic and propagandist function, with a marked ideological orientation. The repertoire followed the official aesthetic-political orientation of the country and was patterned after the Soviet model of theatre pedagogy. Besides its educational purpose (that is, to educate future audiences), these theatres discreetly but strongly directed young people towards aesthetic uniformity. This could be best seen from their repertoires which included mostly Soviet playwrights.

Later, during the period of liberalization of the country's cultural policy, these theatres slowly changed into workshops whose artistic structure, as well as repertoire, has a twofold purpose. The first is education; through numerous acting and dance studios led by professional directors and teachers, these theatres prepare amateur performances. The second activity, which is emphasized especially in the work of the most famous youth theatre in the country, the Zagrebačko kazalište mladih (Zagreb Youth Theatre, founded in 1948), is marked by a repertoire suited to more mature adolescents and even adults. This repertoire, which is often radical and experimental, is performed by professional actors and avant-garde directors.

In the 1990s, the repertoire of these theatres became pointedly pluralistic, presenting a wide range of themes. Dramatized fairytales and stories are performed for the youngest audiences while collective creations often grow out of special workshops which aim to stimulate the creativity of young people themselves. Older audiences can regularly see not only national and world classics (Držić and Shakespeare), but also works by contemporary national playwrights whose works were not initially intended for such audiences. At times, the repertoire of youth theatres actually offers contemporary plays on a par with the most daring achievements of national and local theatres.

Puppet Theatre

The first puppet theatre in Zagreb was founded in 1920, but until 1945 this type of art did not have any professional continuity though many renowned painters, sculptors, actors and composers were involved with it. In the 1990s, Croatia has five professional puppet theatres, several puppet sections which work as parts of youth and children's theatres, as well as several independent puppet companies. These puppet theatres tend to be very mobile, and they perform throughout the country.

The education of puppet-makers and puppeteers is not systematically organized but there are courses and seminars at the Academy of Dramatic Art and at the Teachers College. Numerous Croatian puppeteers were educated abroad (mostly in Czechoslovakia and Poland). Both international and national puppet festivals are organized every year.

Among puppet techniques, the most popular are guignols and the modified Javanese technique of stick-puppets; marionettes are not so common. Puppeteers who use the technique of the shadow theatre or varied forms of black light theatre are few. Following modern tendencies in contemporary puppet art, techniques include stage appearances by live actors who connect to particular puppets through costumes. The traditional square or semicircular screen as well as the old marionette box are disappearing, so the visual obstacle between performers and audience is broken.

According to the development patterns and artistic tendencies of this genre, the repertoire of the puppet theatres follows two basic lines: an educational repertoire for all ages of children and adolescents for whom the puppet theatre often presents their first contact with the stage (fairytales for children, stories from national and world literature for adolescents), and a repertoire which tries to create new forms of expression and a new experience for demanding theatregoers.

Shortly after World War II, the Družina mladih (Company of the Young) was established by Vlado Habunek and Radovan Ivšić from Zagreb. Its unconventional repertoire (Chekhov, Merimée) achieved a decisive change and made puppet theatre an eminent theatrical form. The most popular Zagreb directors and designers include Vojmil Rabadan (1909–88), Borislav Mrkšić (b. 1925), Berislav Brajković (b. 1925), Berislav Deželić (1920–82), Velimir Chytil (b. 1925) and Davor Mladinov (b. 1927). Branko Stojaković (1937–92) and Mojmir Mihatov (b. 1952) work in Zadar.

Poet and translator Luko Paljetak (b. 1943) is also one of the most important puppet directors in the country. Another leading director is Zlatko Bourek (b. 1929), a brave and unconventional experimentalist, who brings together drama and elements of puppet animation. He is also a skilful designer of masks and costumes, a painter, graphic artist and maker of animated films. He became widely known for his adaptation of Tom Stoppard's *Dogg's Hamlet* (Theatre Etc., Zagreb, 1982) with actors and puppets.

Croatia hosts both a Children's Festival in Šibenik and an Esperanto Puppet Festival in Zagreb.

Design
Theatre Space and Architecture

Most of the theatre buildings in Croatia were built in the late nineteenth and the first half of the twentieth centuries and were architecturally influenced by the Austro-Hungarian and Italian style. As a separate but important historical fact, it should be noted that a theatre on the island of Hvar was started in 1612 in the local arsenal. This theatre was given its present neo-classical shape in 1803. Most of these buildings are, in fact in a classical, neo-classical or neo-Baroque style and still function as national, regional and city theatres. All major Croatian theatres, however, date from the nineteenth century.

In the 1970s and 1980s, many of these historically and architecturally interesting buildings were modernized. Special attention was given to modern stage equipment, lighting and comfort, while keeping in mind the need to preserve the authentic architecture of the original structure.

Among Croatia's many famous historical buildings, the following should be mentioned: Dubrovnik, opened in 1864, in the neo-classical style, architects Miho Klaić (1829–96) and Emilio Vecchietti (1830–1901), the first Croatian theatre architect, and restored in 1987; Osijek, built in 1866, completely restored in 1986, the building was heavily damaged in 1991 as a result of the Serbian war; Šibenik, 1879; Varaždin, 1873, neo-classical, the first theatre by the famous Viennese architect Herman Helmer; Rijeka, 1885, designed by Helmer and Fellner; Split, 1893, architects Vecchietti and Ante Bezić (1849–1906), reconstructed after a fire in 1979 by Božidar Rašica (1912–93); and Zagreb, 1895, neo-Baroque, by Helmer and Fellner.

After 1945, specialists and architects were busy with adaptations, restorations and reconstructions. Many multi-use halls were built after the war.

One of the major theatre designers of the century was Ljubo Babić (1890–1974). Others of the early part of the century include Marijan Trepše (1897–1964), Krsto Hegedušić (1901–75) and the Russian-born Vladimir Ivanovich Žedrinski (1899–1974). After the war, among the first designers to emerge were Zvonko Agbaba (b. 1919) and Aleksandar Augustinčić (b. 1921) who were using abstract elements and unconventional materials (glass, metal and plastics). Sophisticated realism was represented by the work of Miše Račić (1921–87), and poetic realism by Kamilo Tompa (1903–89) and Edo Kovačević (1906–93). The avant-garde painter Edo Murtić (b. 1921) brought further abstraction to set design.

Zagreb designers Boško Rašica (1912–93) and Vjenceslav Richter (b. 1917) approached the stage as a given volume and worked out their designs scenographically as a meeting point of several multidimensional surfaces. They also experimented with new materials, recalled traditional scenographic solutions and worked on the functionality of the space, always keeping in mind important pictorial details.

Painter and graphic artist Zlatko Bourek (b. 1929) is a singular personality on the contemporary Croatian scene for costume design, and other visual forms of production (animated film clips, masks, and so on). His solutions often contain elements of grotesque humour and the macabre.

It is interesting to note that well-known Croatian 'naïve' artists have also tried their hands at scene design. In their pictorially and colouristically recognizable way, Ivan Generalić (1914–92), Ivan Rabuzin (b. 1919) and Ivan Lacković Croata (b. 1932) are just a few who have worked in recent Croatian theatre.

Among designers emerging in the 1970s and 1980s, the most notable are Drago Turina (b. 1934), a daring and constructive artist, who often receives awards at international festivals, Zlatko Kauzlarić-Atač (b. 1945), an exquisite designer and painter, and Dinka Jeričević (b. 1947), whose designs are at once imaginative and functional.

Costume design as an independent profession developed only after 1945. Among major designers have been Vanda Pavelić-Weinert (1911–79), Inga Kostinčer (1925–73), Iva Škomrlj (b. 1932) and Diana Kosec-Bourek (b. 1937).

Training

Similarly to the entire national school system, artistic education in Croatia is organized as a part of the state educational system. Besides individual courses, workshops and seminars for dance disciplines (not intended for professional stage artists), there is no alternative private system of education in the arts. Schooling of future artists is organized at the primary, secondary and university levels, but primary and secondary education can be obtained only in music and ballet.

The art college with the longest tradition is the Music Academy of Zagreb (founded in 1921), which offers courses in several other cities. To receive a degree, musical artists (singers, conductors and players) need at least four years of study and professional training.

Before 1945, there were no schools or academies for actors. Some secondary schools connected to the National Theatre in Zagreb, however, were organizing professional training in theatre arts which lasted two to three years. Although there were several (the oldest was founded in 1896), these schools had no professional continuity. Schools for directors and other theatre workers simply did not exist at all.

Organized study for all professions in theatre arts started after World War II. A State School for Actors was organized in 1945, and the Academy of Dramatic Art, with departments for acting and directing, in 1950. The length of study for acting is four years. The first academy for directing and broadcasting/radio was organized as a graduate school; one could enter only after finishing two years of higher education in liberal arts. Later, following the needs of modern media technology, the academy opened new departments for film and television as well as dramaturgy.

Scene and costume design still do not exist as organized studies so most Croatian artists receive this kind of training through practice in theatres after getting a degree in one of the fine art disciplines (painting, sculpture, graphic art or architecture).

Today in all departments of the Zagreb Academy of Dramatic Art (acting, theatre and broadcast directing, film and television directing, photography, editing, and dramaturgy), there are about 145 students. Every year, about 120 candidates apply to the acting department, but the average number of those accepted is about one in ten. Both acting and directing are four-year undergraduate programmes; students also receive a complete education in liberal arts. The major courses of the curriculum are acting, stage speech, stage movement, theory of music, history of music, history of national and world theatre, history of literature, theory of drama, psychology, mask, costume, and so on. Teachers are prominent Croatian artists, historians, drama and theatre theoreticians, writers, and dramatists.

Education is free but many theatres give scholarships anyway to individuals to ensure the renewal of their troupes. After completing courses, students get a Bachelor's degree. Most start performing while still at the academy.

There are no legislative regulations which would direct graduates towards particular theatres or particular parts of the country. Relations and contracts among young actors, directors and theatre institutions are based on personal agreements and contracts. Lack of engagements, however, does not imply social insecurity; after two years of even temporary appearance on the stage, actors have the right to join a trade union, and get social security (medical insurance and pension).

The academy fosters the constancy of the national stylistic tradition, being at the same time active in the implementation of experimental scenic and literary movements. It was the academy which introduced avant-garde playwrights such as Ionesco and which turned the theories of Brecht, Artaud, the Living Theatre, Barba and others into practice.

Students of the Academy of Dramatic Art in Zagreb (since 1981 a part of the University of Zagreb) have participated in numerous international festivals, competitions and encounters of student theatres.

Criticism, Scholarship and Publishing

The tradition of theatrical criticism dates back to the mid-nineteenth century. Critiques first appeared in daily and weekly newspapers then in literary journals and professional periodicals. Since the inception of radio and television (the 1930s and 1950s respectively), these media have been dedicating some of their cultural programmes to theatre as well.

The pluralism of present stage life has resulted in the pluralism of critical methods and methodologies. All dailies and weeklies in the country (about ten of them) engage permanent critics for columns on culture. Some critics keep the same position for several years, trying to influence theatrical life and audience judgements. There are also about ten literary periodicals in the country, and most of them have special sections on theatre. However, since all these are monthly or bimonthly publications, there are rarely reviews of current theatrical events in them. These publications are reserved for scholarly analysis. All Croatian radio stations give consideration to and comment on theatrical events; performances are noted, commented upon, critically evaluated, and broadcast (in full or in parts) by national television.

Methods of theatre criticism have tended to reflect the dominant ideology of the country. Till the beginning of the 1950s, the prevailing style was socialist-realism. Aesthetic pluralism, originating in the literary and philosophy areas, developed later.

Regardless of the amount and diversity of critical opinion, critics have little influence on the practices of particular theatres. Job security (theatrical engagement) for actors, and even directors, was guaranteed by law until 1991. Some critics also engaged in practical work and worked themselves as theatre managers or heads of certain theatre areas.

Theatre theory is taught today both at the department of comparative literature (University of Zagreb) and at the departments of directing and dramaturgy at the Academy of Dramatic Art. There is no major in theatre, but a multidisciplinary approach, through various departments where it has been studied, has caused a sudden expansion of this discipline. Today Croatia has numerous scholars who carry out research into various aspects of modern theatre studies.

The most important recent Croatian theatre scholars include Slavko Batušić (1902–79), Ivo Hergešić (1904–77), Marko Fotez (1915–76), Marijan Matković (1915–85), Borislav Mrkšić (b. 1925), Frano Čale (1927–93), Vladan Švacov (b. 1930), Branko Hećimović (b. 1943), Petar Selem, Nikola Batušić (b. 1938), Zvonimir Mrkonijć (b. 1938), Maja Hribar-Ožegović (b. 1938), Darko Gašparović (b. 1944), Igor Mrduljaš (b. 1945), Boris Senker (b. 1947) and Slobodan Prosperov Novak (b. 1951). The Institute for Literature and Theatre Studies of the Croatian Academy of Arts and Science in Zagreb brings together scholars engaged in theatre studies.

Since 1945, several theatre journals and periodicals, mostly monthlies and bimonthlies, have been published in Croatia – *Scena* (Zagreb, 1950), *Teatr* (Zagreb, 1955–8), *Kazalište* (Osijek, 1955–73) and *Prolog*, later *Novi Prolog* (Zagreb, since 1968). Articles and essays on the history of theatre, documentation and theatre archives are also published in the *Chronicle* of the Institute for Literature and Theatre Studies (Zagreb, since 1975).

Valuable documentation is published in commemorative anthologies and almanacs issued by almost all Croatian theatres on their anniversaries. Croatian theatre scholars used to publish their papers in the journals and periodicals of the former Yugoslavia (*Pozorište*, Tuzla; *Scena*, Novi Sad; and *Dokumenti slovenskega gledališkega in filmskega muzeja*, Ljubljana).

Croatia does not have a house specializing in the publishing of plays or theatre studies but most of the leading publishing houses do publish dramatic texts and books on theatre and drama. National theatres and the Critics' Association appear as publishers as well. The major publishers on theatre are Zora (Zagreb), Matica Hrvatska (Zagreb), Školska knjiga (Zagreb), Centar za kulturnu djelatnost (Zagreb), Izdavački centar (Rijeka), Književni krug (Split) and Hrvatsko društvo kazališnih kritičara i teatrologa (Zagreb).

Nikola Batušić
Translated by Martina Mencer Salluzzo

(See also YUGOSLAVIA)

Further Reading

Batušić, Nikola. *Hrvatsko narodno kazalište u Zagrebu 1840–1860–1992*. [Croatian National

Theatre 1840–1860–1992]. Zagreb: Školska knjiga, 1992. 212 pp.

——. *Povijest hrvatskog kazališta*. [The history of Croatian theatre]. Zagreb: Školska knjiga, 1978. 542 pp.

——, Branko Hećimović, and Ranko Marinković, eds. 'Il teatro croato del dopuguerra'. *La Battana* 91–2 (1989): 175 pp.

——, Georgij Paro, Jozo Puljizević, and Petar Selem, eds. 'Posljeratna hrvatska drama i kazalište'. [Croatian drama and theatre after the war]. *Scena* 2–3 (1974): 151 pp.

Batušić, Slavko. 'Das kroatische Theater'. [The Croatian theatre]. In *Theatergeschichte Europas* [History of European theatre], vol. 10, pp. 242–62. Edited by Heinz Kindermann. Salzburg: Otto Müller, 1974.

Cindrić, Pavao, and Slavko Batušić, eds. *Hrvatsko narodno kazalište 1894–1969: enciklopedijsko izdanje (Enciklopedija s poviješnim pregledom razvitka HNK)*. [Croatian National Theatre 1894–1969: encyclopedic edition (Encyclopedia and historical survey of the development of the Croatian National Theatre)]. Zagreb: Naprijed, 1969. 721 pp.

Dani hvarskog kazališta – eseji i grada o hrvatskoj drami i kazalištu. [Essays on Croatian theatre and drama]. Vol. 10: *Hrvatska dramska književnost i kazalište od predratnih revolucionarnih previranja do 1955*. [Croatian dramatic literature and theatre from pre-war revolutionary turmoil to 1955]. Split: Književni krug, 1983. 412 pp.

Dani hvarskog kazališta – eseji i grada o hrvatskoj drami i kazalištu. [Essays on Croatian theatre and drama]. Vol. 11: *Suvremena hrvatska drama i kazalište*. [Contemporary Croatian drama and theatre]. Split: Književni krug, 1984. 374 pp.

Foretić, Dalibor. *Nova drama – svjedočenje o jugoslavenskim dramatikama i njihovim scenskim refleksima*. [New drama – Yugoslav dramatics and their stage reflection]. Rijeka: Izdavački centar/Novi Sad: Sterijino pozorje, 1988. 423 pp.

Gašparović, Darko. *Pismo i scena – dramaturški analekti*. [Writings and stage – dramatic analogues]. Rijeka: Izdavački centar, 1982. 144 pp.

——, ed. 'Contemporary Croatian Drama'. *The Bridge* 55 (1978): 120 pp.

Hećimović, Branko. *Antologija hrvatske drame*. [Anthology of Croatian drama]. 3 vols. Zagreb: Znanje, 1988. 1,385 pp.

——. *Repertoar hrvatskih kazališta 1840–1860–1990*. [Repertoire of Croatian theatres 1840–1860–1990]. 2 vols. Zagreb: Globus i Jugoslavenska akademija znanosti i umjetnosti, 1990. 1,423 pp.

——, ed. 'Das kroatische Drama des 20. Jahrhunderts'. [Croatian drama in the twentieth century]. *Die Brücke* 51–3 (1977): 343 pp.

——. *Dramaturški triptihon*. [Dramatic triptych]. Zagreb: Hrvatsko društvo kazališnih kritičara i teatrologa, 1979. 188 pp.

——. *Suvremena drama i kazalište u Hrvatskoj*. [Contemporary drama and theatre in Croatia]. Rijeka: Izdavački centar/Novi Sad: Sterijino pozorje, 1987. 509 pp.

Kroflin, Lidija. *Zagrebačka zemlja Lutkanija*. [Zagreb Puppetland]. Zagreb: Medunarodni centar za usluge u kulturi, 1992. 163 pp.

Marjanović, Petar, ed. 'Anthology of Works by 20th Century Yugoslav Playwrights'. *Scena* 7–8 (1985): 511 pp.

Novak, Slobodan Prosperov, ed. *Dubrovačke ljetne igre 1950–1989*. [Dubrovnik Summer Festival 1950–89]. Dubrovnik: Festival Dubrovnik, 1989. 219 pp.

Perković, Zdeslav. *Arhitektura dalmatinskih kazališta*. [Dalmatian theatre architecture]. Split: Logos, 1989. 74 pp.

Selem, Petar. *Otvoreno kazalište*. [Open theatre]. Zagreb: Hrvatsko društvo književnih kritičara i teatrologa, 1979. 216 pp.

——. *Različito kazalište*. [A different theatre]. Rijeka: Izdavački centar, 1985. 170 pp.

Senker, Boris. *Pogled u kazalište*. [A look into theatre]. Zagreb: Hrvatsko društvo kazališnih kritičara i teatrologa, 1990. 272 pp.

CYPRUS

The island nation of Cyprus is located in the northeastern corner of the Mediterranean Sea about 65 kilometres (40 miles) south of Asia Minor, present-day Turkey. According to history and legend, the 9,250 square kilometre (3,570 square mile) island was first colonized by Greeks in about the twelfth century BC; today about 80 per cent of the Cypriot population speaks Greek and follows the Greek Orthodox Church. In the sixteenth century AD, predominantly Muslim Turkish settlers began arriving on Cyprus and today represent most of the other 20 per cent of the population of 665,000 people.

The island's crucial geographical position – it commanded the trade routes to both the Middle and Far East – made it an important outpost from earliest times. After the Trojan War, the Achaeans began colonizing the island and by the fifth century BC the Hellenes were the dominant group. As such, Cyprus became involved in the cultural revolution of the Greek world which culminated in the Golden Age of Athens. Among Cypriots who contributed to Athenian culture at the time were Zenon of Kitium (334–262 BC) and the poet Stasinos.

As with most major Hellenic centres of the period, theatres played a key part in the cultural, religious and political life of Cyprus: three ancient theatres have been excavated to date on the island at Soli, Salamis and Curium. As theatre faded in importance in the Graeco-Roman world, so too did it fade in Cyprus.

Over the course of its more than 3,000-year history, the island has been a microcosm of the power struggles in this part of the world. Not only has it been under Greek control but also it has been part of many other empires, including the Assyrian, Egyptian, Persian, Roman and Byzantine, with the Greek-speaking Byzantines ruling the island for some 800 years. Between the late twelfth and the fifteenth centuries, it was a Frankish kingdom. In 1489, it came under the control of the Venetians.

The Turks conquered Cyprus in 1570 and ruled Cyprus until 1878, when it was ceded to Britain, which formally annexed it in 1914. Most Greek Cypriots, however, desired political union with Greece and the movement for union, called *enosis*, intensified after World War II into a guerrilla campaign against the British. Turkish Cypriots, for their part, sought partition of the island into Greek and Turkish sections.

In 1960, Cyprus became an independent state, a republic, under terms which forbade either *enosis* or partition. The constitution called for a Greek Cypriot president and a Turkish Cypriot vice-president, with 70 per cent of the seats in the legislature allocated to Greeks and 30 per cent to Turks. The divisive elements of the Zürich Agreement, by which the Republic of Cyprus came into existence, resulted in an unworkable constitution. This led to strife; finally in 1974, Turkey invaded the island, taking advantage of a coup initiated by the Greek military *junta*.

History records only four plays by Cypriot authors prior to 1878. Under English rule, however, theatrical activity was encouraged and many productions are recorded of plays by Cypriot, Greek and western European authors during the early part of the twentieth century.

Schools tended to produce classical Greek tragedies and played an important role in maintaining the historical links with Greece. Professional artists also played in political and satirical theatrical revues imported from the Greek mainland. There were as well many visits by professional theatre groups from Greece.

With the start of World War II, visits by

Greek companies all but ceased and it became difficult even to bring in foreign films. By 1942, the necessity of providing locally produced entertainment had become obvious, not only in Nicosia but also in the smaller towns and villages. It was in this year that four theatre groups sprang up in the capital – United Artists, the Lyric Theatre, the New Lyric and the Orpheus.

The repertoire of all these theatres consisted mainly of operettas (Austrian and Greek), musical and satirical revues, and locally written plays, generally comedies, involving representations of local customs. Until the 1940s, theatrical entertainments in the villages were performed only by men. Some young girls of 15 and 16, however, ignored social convention during the war and took to the stages. Clearly a base was being established at this time for the development of a truly indigenous Cypriot professional theatre.

Those working in other art forms also contributed to the new professionalism. Among them were the poets Costas Montis (b. 1914), Lefteris Yiannides (1914–86), Tassos Stephanides (b. 1917) and Costas Markides (1896–1968); composers such as Achilleas Lymbourides (b. 1917), Yiangos Michaelides (1897–1972) and Yiangos Bonis (1913–62); and even painters such as Telemachos Kanthos (b. 1910) and Costas Stathis (1916–89). All these major artists worked with theatre companies.

In 1945, another fully professional dramatic theatre called Prometheus was established with the support of not only the country's trade unions but also AKEL, a left-wing political party. Run by Tefkros Anthias (1903–68) and Adamantios Lemos (b. 1908), who had fled from occupied Greece, the company was instrumental in developing a strong group of professional actors, among them George Pastel (1926–68), who would later star in *The King and I* in London's West End. Another Greek director, Costis Michaelides (1913–83), also came to Cyprus at this time to work with Lirikon, as well as some of the other developing theatres outside the capital.

With the end of the war, professional Greek companies again resumed their tours to Cyprus and cinemas once again began offering inexpensive entertainment. But indigenous professional theatre on Cyprus had established a foothold and would not be wiped out.

Despite a lack of assistance for this movement by the British colonial government, the Kypriako Theatro (Cyprus Theatre Company) was formed in 1950 by Achilleas Lymbourides and Andreas Lantsias (b. 1926), embracing many of the best older actors and attracting many new ones, with Nicos Pantelides (1906–84) as a leading actor. Like United Artists, the company specialized in light comedies, almost exclusively Greek, although they occasionally did dramas and musicals.

The period between 1955 and 1959 was a period of armed struggle against the British. The British, for their part, had an army of some 30,000 to keep the island under control. When the British imposed evening curfews in the major centres, it became virtually impossible to keep the theatres operating.

In 1960, with the island's newly won independence, the New Theatre was formed in Nicosia. Plays by such writers as Arthur Miller, George Bernard Shaw and Alejandro Casona were seen here for the first time along with original plays by developing Cypriot writers. The spaces were those that were found to be available – often cinemas and old restaurants.

At this same time, the Music Academy of Cyprus established the country's first professional drama school with most of its teachers imported from Athens. From this school sprang still another theatre, the Arts Theatre, modelled on the Karolos Koun Arts Theatre in Athens.

In an attempt to encourage state assistance to the arts, the various theatre troupes formed themselves into a single major company called OTHAK (Cyprus Organization for Theatrical Development). Early on, OTHAK received modest support from both the Cypriot and Greek governments. Its first production was Büchner's play, *Danton's Death*. The company's first artistic director was Costis Michaelides.

OTHAK functioned for only a few seasons but it did manage to produce a number of important plays by such authors as Aristophanes, Shakespeare, Miller and even Peter Ustinov. It also served as an important theatrical home for many younger Cypriot artists who had studied abroad in Great Britain, the United States, Greece and the Soviet Union.

Because of financial problems, the high-minded aims of OTHAK soon faded and the company, renamed Ethos, had to revert to light comedies and satirical revues to attract audiences and to meet rising costs. In 1966 the company began to face direct competition from still another group, the Papademetris Company – founded by Demetris Papademetris (b. 1936) – which was doing more or less the same kind of work.

In December 1963, the new Cypriot government faced its first serious political challenge, one that culminated in inter-communal clashes across the island. Theatre people were caught in the middle of this struggle and had great problems. Despite this, two young directors, both connected to OTHAK, chose to establish new theatres at this time – Vladimiros Kafkarides (1932–83) and Nicos Shiafkalis (b. 1934).

Kafkarides's New Theatre company, founded in 1967, staged a variety of plays, ranging from classics to musicals: Carlo Goldoni's *La Locantiera* and an adaptation of Nikos Kazantzakis's *Kapetan Michalis*, both in 1967, Savvas Savvides's (b. 1918) *Military Coup*, and Aristophanes' *Peace* in 1968. The Shiafkalis Group focused on American and European plays including works by Albee (*Who's Afraid of Virginia Woolf?*, 1968) and Behan (*The Hostage*, 1968). Surprisingly, given the difficult political situation, the government – through its Ministry of Education (Cultural Service) – found funds to subsidize both.

Shortly thereafter, a press campaign began –

actively supported by performers, directors and literary magazines – aimed at pressuring the government to formally establish a state theatre. The government turned to UNESCO for advice. UNESCO, in its turn, recommended a feasibility study be done. In the 1960s, the noted Greek director, Takis Mouzenidis, head of the National Theatre of Greece, was sent to Cyprus to conduct the study. Mouzenidis eventually recommended the creation of a state theatre and in 1971 the Theatre Organization of Cyprus (THOK) was formed with the Athenian actor and director Nicos Hadjiskos as its artistic director.

In November 1971, the new company gave its first performances – Aeschylus' *Agamemnon* at the Municipal Theatre in Nicosia (from that time on the company's permanent home) and a modern Greek play, Gregoris Xenopoulos's *Man of the People* in the city of Limassol. The company's associate artistic director was the noted Greek director and teacher Socrates Karandinos, the driving force behind the establishment of the State Theatre of Northern Greece. Karandinos, with the support of

Nicos Shiafkalis's 1974 THOK production of Arnold Wesker's *Roots*, designed by Nicos Couroushis.

Cypriot directors such as Kafkarides and Shiafkalis, helped to solidify the company's administrative structure and added many Greek and foreign plays to the repertoire.

Equally important at this time was the emergence of the Cyprus Broadcasting Corporation (CBC) which since independence had played a leading role in promoting theatrical art through radio and television. CBC produced many plays through the 1960s: among them were representative works by Shakespeare, Molière, Ibsen, Strindberg, Chekhov, Shaw, Pirandello, Brecht, Ionesco, Miller, Williams, O'Casey, and García Lorca.

One of CBC's most unusual events was a full television production of the ancient Greek comedy *Samia* (1974) by Menander. In 1969, CBC went so far as to set up its own theatre company which produced plays for live audiences and then restaged them for television broadcast. The company, run by CBC general director Andreas Christophides (b. 1937) and director Evis Gabrielides (b. 1927), operated for two years offering a wide variety of plays, both European and Greek, in an attempt to focus attention not only on the historical development of the theatre but on modern trends as well. One example of the latter was the company's 1971 production of Beckett's *Waiting for Godot*.

Another group of note at this time was the Experimental Stage in Nicosia. Founded in 1972, the company experimented both with new plays and new styles of production operating in a seventy-seat theatre in an old house in a suburb of the city.

In 1974, the island was invaded by Turkey, a shattering blow to many fields of activities. Overnight, the republic was deprived of 35 per cent of its lands and 45 per cent of its resources. One-third of the island's 600,000 population was turned into refugees who suddenly had to be fed and housed. Everything from the Experimental Stage to THOK was on the edge of extinction.

It was THOK, however, which rose to the theatrical challenge, undertaking a tour to Greece with two plays, both written by Cypriots. The first, Loukis Akritas's *The Hostage*, clearly expressed the spirit of resistance (in this case the resistance of the Greeks against German occupation many years earlier); the second, Michalis Pashiardis's *The Water of the Dragon*, dealt with the rich traditions of the Cypriot countryside.

In spite of the fact that the Municipal Theatre in Nicosia was only a few metres from the Turkish army's outpost, THOK also continued performing three times each week in Nicosia to nearly full houses. As well, the company toured widely to the rest of the non-occupied island.

Important to understand in the development of THOK is its role not only as a theatrical producing organization but also as a catalyst for theatrical development across the whole island. The THOK mandate quickly evolved to include the encouragement of Cypriot playwrights through an annual drama competition for both adult and children's plays (this is also done by the CBC); the granting of financial assistance for the upgrading of stage facilities in towns and villages; and the granting of financial and technical assistance to professional theatre groups willing to tour the island.

During its first ten years, THOK did much to improve the general level of theatrical work across Cyprus in the field of theatre for young audiences and generally to raise the professional standard of theatre.

But the 1980s were a turbulent decade for theatre in Cyprus and after ten years of production, THOK began to be criticized for neglecting development work and monopolizing state subsidy for its own productions. In response, a number of non-profit, 'free' groups came into being and THOK was given responsibility for developing guidelines for state financial and technical assistance for them. These included the registration of all free groups as legal non-profit entities, their control by artists themselves, and their willingness to tour the island. The groups were also required to use Actors' Union members. Since 1988, a THOK official has been directly responsible for the free groups has to oversee the groups financially and to keep the THOK council informed about their activities.

The government of Cyprus and the House of Representatives (the budget of THOK has to be approved by both as well as by the Council of Ministers) have favourably responded to the demand for theatre decentralization. THOK promoted this demand by granting subsidies to the two existing theatre groups in Nicosia – Satiriko and Theatro Ena – and supporting the setting up of a third one, ETHAL, in Limassol, the second biggest city in Cyprus. The company was later renamed Praxis (Action). At the same time, THOK responded favourably to the demands of local authorities to acquire their own theatres in multi-use halls. So the municipalities of Limassol and Paphos were assisted financially to turn two old cinemas, the Palace and Zena, into modern theatres.

A number of local authorities, such as those of Agros, Pedhulas and Palaehori, were also assisted to acquire small halls. Paralimni and Larnaca (the third largest city) also now have their own open-air theatres.

This development policy of THOK is also reflected in the growth and disposal of its budget. State assistance to THOK (which was US$180,000 in 1971) reached US$3 million in 1991, of which US$800,000 was to be used for development projects.

Some words must also be said here about the Turkish theatre on Cyprus which, until 1960, was essentially non-professional in nature. During the late nineteenth century and the first half of the twentieth century, traditional Turkish plays bearing the characteristic influence of Anatolian drama were presented in Turkish areas of the island.

The forms of Turkish theatre included the *gölge oyunu* (shadow play), the shadow theatre *Karagiozis*, the storytelling theatre called *meddah* and religiously inspired morality plays. Social problems were dealt with mostly in short satirical works.

In the period immediately following World War II, a number of non-professional theatre clubs came into being in Turkish areas. The most important of these was the Brothers Club, a group that staged mostly modern plays.

Despite this interest in European drama, it was clear that the Brothers Club was taking its cues from the nationalistic and reformist ideas of the Turkish president, Kemal Ataturk. This could be clearly seen in dramas such as *Vatan Yahut Silistre* (*Homeland*, 1908) and *Gulnihal* (1909) by the Turkish writer Namik Kemal.

Other important non-professional Turkish theatre groups through this period have been the Turk Teavün Cemiyeti, the Tiyatro Ve Ses Akademisi (Academy of Drama and Sound), the Turk Academi Tiyatrosu (Turkish Theatre Academy) and Halk Kulubu (People's Club). Even sports clubs were staging plays from time to time and, in almost all cases, the role of theatre was aimed at counterbalancing the Greek Cypriot demand for *enosis*.

Following Cypriot independence, the various theatre clubs maintained their activities and were even joined by other amateur groups such as the Guzel Sanatlar Dernegi (Fine Arts Association), which specialized in light comedies. It was not until February 1963, however, that the first Turkish Cypriot professional theatre came

into being, a company called Ilk Sahne (First Stage). Founded in Nicosia by Uner Ulutug (1939–78), a graduate of the State Theatre Conservatory in Ankara, the company's first production was *Kôr* (*The Blind*, 1963) by Turkish playwright Vedad Nedim Tor. The company closed down in December 1963 because of serious political problems in the community.

A new theatre group called the Kibris Turk Tiyatrosu Ilk Sahne (Cyprus-Turk Theatre First Stage) was born in 1965; Ulutug and Kemal Tunc (b. 1938) were the founders. The company performed in a school hall and did both Turkish and local popular plays. In 1970, the Ilk Sahne company came under the sponsorship of the State Department of Youth, Sports and Culture.

Following the Turkish invasion of the island in 1974, Ilk Sahne changed its name to the Cyprus-Turkish State Theatre, gained additional financial support and increased both the size of its company and the number of productions it staged. At the same time, its politically rooted productions all but ceased and were replaced almost exclusively by light comedies and thrillers.

In 1980, four actors from the Ilk Sahne/State Theatre were dismissed by management for staging a play that was considered to be too socialistically oriented. Later that same year, the four – Yasar Ersoy (b. 1951), Erol Refikoglu (b. 1946), Osman Aklas (b. 1954) and Irsin Refikoglu (b. 1950) – were hired by the Municipal Council representing the Turkish quarter of Nicosia to set up a new professional theatre, the Nicosia Turkish Municipal Theatre.

This company, still active in the 1990s, focuses on community issues, Turkish-Cypriot concerns and even more general issues. Using both traditional Turkish theatrical forms and

The founders of the Turkish Municipal Theatre in their 1991 production of *War in the Gulf*.

modern plays, the company seeks to represent the concerns of the Turkish Cypriot community.

During the 1980s, a number of amateur groups also began to appear across the island.

Structure of the National Theatre Community

As the 1990s began, Cyprus could boast of five professional theatres in operation – four in Nicosia and one in Limassol. Each of these companies was receiving subsidy from the government representing about 70 per cent of the group's overall costs. The companies, on average, were producing between three and six shows each year. In general, about one in seven of these plays were by Cypriot authors, one in five by Greek authors and the rest by mostly European or American authors. Most of the companies also tour the island with the THOK company a regularly invited guest to the annual Epidaurus Festival of ancient drama in Greece.

In addition to these dramatic companies, three other groups regularly stage satirical revues, musicals and comedies.

All professional actors are members of the Cyprus Actors Union, founded in 1962. As of 1991, the union had eighty-two members, all of whom were graduates of recognized theatre schools. Only union members are allowed to perform on professional stages and only theatre school graduates can become members of the union.

The union has done much to improve working conditions among theatre professionals as well as raising salaries. The union has also been involved in promoting bilateral exchanges, cultural relations and finding scholarship funds for young actors to study abroad. As well, it is involved in the organization of various seminars in cooperation with national and foreign cultural agencies. Most active in this regard have been Cultural Centres in Cyprus run by the UK, the USA, the former USSR, France, Germany, Bulgaria and Greece.

A Playwrights Union has also existed since 1969; in 1991 it had fifty-six members.

Other international activities are organized by the Cyprus Centre of the International Theatre Institute (established in 1977) which regularly publishes materials about Cypriot theatre and which organizes regular pan-Cyprian theatrical congresses, mostly focusing on the role of theatre in protecting and enriching national identity.

One particularly interesting aspect of theatrical life in Cyprus is the relatively large number of festivals which take place each year. The oldest is the open-air festival in the city of Limassol, which is held every July. Begun in 1966, the Limassol Festival includes not only spoken theatre but both dance and music as well, with companies coming from as far away as India and the United States. Limassol also hosts a theatre festival each September during its annual Wine Festival. This latter festival shows clear links to the ancient Athenian theatre festivals during which comedies were shown amidst much eating, drinking and celebrating.

The Nicosia Festival is also held each September and includes, in addition to local companies, at least one major theatre company from Greece. Special efforts are made, however, to produce Cypriot plays. To this end, the Playwrights Union for many years co-sponsored a competition for one-act plays by Cypriot authors. Special funds have also been made available to allow a major director to stage either a Greek or Cypriot play during the festival.

Another special theatre festival is arranged annually during the month of September by the Cyprus Tourism Organization in cooperation with THOK. Utilizing the Roman theatres at Curium and the Odeon in Paphos (a small open-air theatre) as well as a small square outside a Medieval monastery in the centre of the cosmopolitan resort Ayia Napa in the Famagusta District, the festival focuses on ancient Greek tragedies and comedies and is extremely popular with tourists to the island.

Artistic Profile

Companies

Between 1971 and 1981, subsidy to the official state theatre, THOK, almost tripled. During this period, it maintained a company of some twenty-five actors and two resident directors.

Most of THOK's actors are graduates of Greek theatre schools; some have studied in other parts of Europe or in the United States. The company stages seven or eight productions each year with a number of them later touring.

The first resident directors of the company were Vladimiros Kafkarides, who had studied in the USSR, and Nicos Shiafkalis, a graduate of the Guildhall School of Drama in London. In 1975, Evis Gabrielides became the company's resident artistic director. In 1977 Nikos Charalambous (b. 1941) was added to the list of resident directors. Guest directors work regularly with the company. Most come from Greece; others have come from the USSR, Germany and the United States.

In general, THOK limits its works to spoken drama; revues and musical comedies are left to other groups to perform. The company has staged plays from the ancient Greeks to modern European and American classics. The company has also toured abroad with some regularity appearing most often in Greece but with increasing frequency in other parts of Europe.

In addition to its regular company, THOK also has a children's theatre company.

With THOK at the centre of Cypriot theatrical life, a number of other companies have developed over the years providing more specialized types of programming. In 1983, the New Theatre was formed by Vladimiros Kafkarides, determined to bring theatre to the widest possible public and taking as one of its mandates tours to the smallest communities on the island. Kafkarides, who died shortly after the company's founding, wanted the new company to pay special attention to Greek plays and socially oriented European writers such as Dario Fo.

In 1986, the New Theatre company split in two. One group of its actors withdrew from the main company and established its own troupe called Satiriko. Satiriko declared that it would continue Kafkarides's policies and established its reputation in the production of both Greek plays and innovative European dramatists, focusing on a realistic production style.

In 1987, director Andreas Christodoulides (b. 1951), trained in England, established another small company in an old warehouse near Nicosia's Famagusta Gate. This group, called Theatro Ena, has tended to produce mostly European and American writers, including Samuel Beckett and Tennessee Williams.

There are two other theatres of note, both of them amateur but operating on a permanent basis. The People's Theatre is based in a suburb of Nicosia – Aglandjia – and was founded in 1959. The company produces mostly Greek comedies which it later tours to villages and refugee camps on the island. The second company is called ACT Theatre (Anglo-Cypriot Theatre) and performs mainly in English. The company was founded in 1981 and did about forty productions during the 1980s. Its repertoire ranges from classical drama to contemporary slapstick comedy.

Dramaturgy

With the exception of a single Medieval Mystery play, the earliest examples of Cypriot playwriting date to the conclusion of the long Turkish occupation period at the end of the nineteenth century. This occupation left the pages of Cypriot dramatic history almost blank; almost, but not entirely. There were a few Cypriot-written plays but most were created by Cypriots living abroad, mainly in Greece. These writers were clearly influenced by Greek playwrights who, in their turn, were influenced

Nikos Charalambous's 1990 THOK production of Euripides' *The Phoenician Women*, designed by Angelos Angeli.

by French, German and Italian drama, mostly in the fields of musical revues and farce comedies.

Near the end of the nineteenth century there were some generally unsuccessful attempts at writing historical drama and melodrama. More successful were attempts at the musical revue form by writers such as Costas Markides (1896–1968), a doctor who, after studying in Athens, successfully introduced the form in Cyprus. Markides's revues were both political and social in nature.

Another dramatic form which gained national popularity in the years just after World War II was the musical character play, the so-called 'ethographia' (recording of customs). These plays were written in the Cypriot dialect and their themes were generally taken from village life.

In modern Cypriot drama – those plays that have emerged since 1960 – two very clear themes have regularly appeared: the need for self-determination and the equally strong need for improved living conditions. Both are seen in plays even from the late 1940s and early 1950s, a period that saw a number of major strikes involving miners and those in the building trades.

Two plays of note from this period in the republic's history are *The Unworthy One* (1962) by Rina Katselli (b. 1938) and *In the Depths of the Earth* (1984) by Michalis Pitsilides (b. 1920). Both reflected the struggle for independence as well as strikes by the workers.

Other major events in Cyprus' recent history have also been reflected by modern writers. The military coup of July 1974 against the then elected president Archbishop Makarios (1913–77) and the Turkish invasion of that same year are found in three 1984 plays: *Old Comrades* by Christos Zanos (b. 1946), *An*

Unexpected Meeting by Pambis Anayiotos (b. 1954) and *Dry Martini* by Panos Ioannides (b. 1935).

The problems of uprooting in the wake of the Turkish invasion was dealt with in *This War Was Also Fought* (1986) by Kyriacos Efthymiou (b. 1954); Katselli's *Inner Searching* (1979); and *Cruel Angel* (1986) by Maria Avraamides (b. 1939). One of the few plays written entirely in the Cypriot dialect deals with an attempt to preserve the island's traditions – Michaelis Pasiardis's (b. 1941) play, *Gatani*.

Other plays represent an attempt to use Cypriot history to underline contemporary problems. These include *Monks* (1972) by Christakis Georgiou (b. 1929); *Onisilos* (1981) by Panos Ioannides (b. 1935); *Ioannikios* (1983) and *The Lionheart in Cyprus* (1985) by Andros Pavlides (b. 1946); and *In the Kingdom of Cyprus* (1986) by George Neophytou (b. 1946).

The final four plays to be mentioned in this stocktaking are *The Empire* (1983) by Antonakis Evgeniou (b. 1920), which deals with the fall of empires generally after World War II; *The Stripping* (1987) by Ianthi Theocarides (b. 1938), which deals with the threat of nuclear atomic catastrophe; *The Anatomy of a Revolution* (1986) by Costas Kirris (b. 1928) and *The Bosses* (1982) by Andreas Fantides (b. 1932), both of which deal with revolutionary movements.

Directors, Directing and Production Styles

For a discussion of directing, see previous material in **Artistic Profile** and the opening, historical section.

Music Theatre

Music theatre in Cyprus as such does not exist. There are no opera or operetta companies functioning on a permanent basis.

This said, a number of small professional theatre groups during and after World War II did regularly stage revues, musicals, comedies, even Viennese operettas, responding to a demand across the island for light entertainment.

In the 1960s, two companies – one run by Demetris Papademitris (b. 1936) and the other by Dora Kakouratou (b. 1945) – were established primarily to stage American-style musicals. Both were still functioning in the early 1990s.

The satirical revue, a style especially popular in Greece, has been regularly imitated in Cyprus with great success.

Dance Theatre

Cyprus has a long folk-dance tradition and visitors to the island regularly see folk-dance groups performing at festivals and other more local celebrations. Among the best known groups are Susta, Sikali, Vasilitzia and Shiakallis.

The development of dance theatre itself is more related to the history of dance schools. Many exist on the island but are traditionally attended by young girls and then primarily for social rather than theatrical reasons. With so many schools in existence, however, a number of small groups have emerged to stage a range of productions from *The Nutcracker* (1991) and *Coppelia* (1992) to several modern pieces.

The most active of these dance groups include Chorotheatro under the direction of Ariana Economou (b. 1951); Diastasi, twenty dancers under the leadership of choreographer-teacher Maria Mesi-Angelides (b. 1960), Christia Gabrielidou (b. 1961) and Nadina Mouyiasi (b. 1955); and Synthesi, which has created several programmes of original work.

Theatre for Young Audiences
Puppet Theatre

The first professional children's theatre in Cyprus was founded in 1967 by the National Youth Council under the leadership of actor Neophytos Neophytou (b. 1939). The company, unfortunately, survived for only two seasons.

In 1976, THOK established its own Children's Stage; it has been operating ever since. The company, first under the artistic directorship of Evis Gabrielides, has two or three productions per season and attracts large audiences.

In 1983, the New Theatre set up a children's stage under the direction of Vladimiros Kafkarides. The company focused on children in the 5–12 age range.

The most popular form of puppet theatre on Cyprus is the shadow theatre known as *Karagiozis*. With clear Greek and Turkish links, the shadow theatre was immensely popular in the late nineteenth century and in the years before the advent of cinema. It was revived during World War II and had a significant following in the immediate post-war period. When cinema and television became common, however, the form began to decline in popularity yet it continues to exist even today.

In its Cypriot form, the shadow theatre is essentially a one-person show. The *karagiozopehtis* (shadow puppet manipulator) is hidden behind an opaque screen and moves the brightly coloured puppets (generally caricatured figures cut from hard paper) according to the needs of a sketchy scenario.

There are about ten stock types. The most popular and important figure is Karagiozi himself, a typical representative of folk wisdom, cleverness and cunning. The scenario allows for significant amounts of improvisation, and audience reaction plays a major role in the development of the plot. For decades, this was the only form of entertainment in the rural parts of Cyprus.

Design

Until the 1960s, set design in Cyprus was traditionally a painter's art and painted backdrops were heavily relied on by such pioneers as Telemachos Kanthos (b. 1910), George Mavrogenis (b. 1923) and Yiannis Rousakis (b. 1930). During World War II, many of their designs were done on paper cement sacks that were stitched together.

Just before 1960, the late Nicos Zografos, a painter/stage designer from Greece, came to Cyprus, designed several productions and began to show local artists new directions in this field.

Under his guidance, Lonias Efthivoulou (b. 1922) made his appearance, first working with amateur and then with professional theatres. After Cyprus gained its independence, several artists began to study design abroad in such countries as Greece, England, France, Italy, the USA, Russia, Czechoslovakia and Bulgaria.

In the decades that followed, several important designers emerged, including Nicos Couroushis (b. 1937), Klara Zacharaki Georgiou (b. 1938), Andy Bargilly (b. 1940), Costas Kafkarides (b. 1942), Andreas Ladommatos (b. 1940), Stefanos Athienitis (b. 1948), Angelos Angeli (b. 1952), Andreas Charalambous (b. 1947) and Stavros Antonopoullos (b. 1955). Yet even in 1993, none was able to make a living from stage design alone. Most were also teaching art at various public or private schools.

Design styles vary from the most conventional to the most contemporary, from naturalistic to highly symbolic. THOK productions tend to be the most designed. In the rest of the companies, design is much more modest because of finances.

Theatre Space and Architecture

The first professional groups to spring up after the war found themselves totally without playing spaces to house productions. As a result, old warehouses or music halls were turned into theatres, as were cinemas on dark nights. Professional productions were, therefore, limited to larger towns where such buildings were available.

In Nicosia, one of the most beautiful cinemas was the Papadopoulos; it was a favourite with both actors and audiences. Built at the beginning of the century, it was a copy of an eighteenth-century Viennese theatre complete with stalls, balconies and galleries. Later renamed the Melpo, it was demolished in the 1970s to make way for a shopping arcade. Another former cinema that was also destroyed by the shopping centre boom of the 1970s was the Magic Palace, a huge hall with a façade that imitated classical style.

In Limassol, the favoured houses in the 1950s and 1960s were the Yiorthambli and the Rialto. In Famagusta, the Hatzihambis Theatre, and in Larnaca, the Rex. Stage facilities in all these cities were primitive and actors often had to work under truly difficult conditions.

In the late 1950s, the municipality of Nicosia began to build a magnificent new multipurpose theatre with a seating capacity of 1,200. Completed in 1967, it is used as the main stage for THOK. On some nights it is also used for concerts, ballet, and so on. In Limassol and Paphos, the municipalities – also with the financial assistance of the republic through THOK – have turned two former cinemas into modern theatres with very good stage facilities.

It should also be noted here that because of weather conditions, it is almost impossible to perform indoors in Cyprus from May to October. During this period, theatre groups generally perform outdoors.

Virtually every town in the unoccupied area of the country now has its own open-air theatre. The most impressive are the ancient Theatre of Curium and the Odeon of Paphos, which are both used extensively by theatre companies. In Nicosia, there is also a replica of an ancient amphitheatre, the Makarios Amphitheatre, seating about 2,000 people. This too is used often in the summer months.

In the late 1980s, smaller municipalities began to demand their own halls, and some have already succeeded with the financial help of the government through THOK. Today, villages such as Pedoulas, Agros, Paralimni and Palaehori all have their own small theatres.

Training

There are no theatre training schools in Cyprus. For professional training most Cypriot artists go to Greece; a number go even further abroad.

Criticism, Scholarship and Publishing

Theatre criticism appears regularly in daily and weekly newspapers as well as in quarterly literary magazines or limited circulation publications. Most of the criticism in the popular press is written by journalists with only modest theatrical background.

The literary magazines *Cypriot Letters* and *Paphos* in the 1940s and 1950s were among the first to publish theatre criticism. In the 1950s, *Eleftheria* and *Democratis* were pioneers in theatre criticism among newspapers. More recently, the literary magazines *Intellectual Cyprus* and *New Epoch*, which started publication in the late 1950s, began devoting several pages to theatre. *The Cyprus Chronicles*, a literary magazine published in the 1960s and early 1970s, was noted for its radical approach to theatre criticism. The earliest attempt at publishing a theatre journal in Cyprus was during World War II when Costas Montis began publishing the short-lived *Theatre*.

Until 1980, theatre books were published by authors at their own expense and were circulated among friends. Since 1980, the Cyprus Playwrights Association has published regular collections of one-act plays written by its members.

Christakis Georgiou, Nicos Shiafkalis

Further Reading

Chrysanthěs, Kypros. *Theatrikes apodeltióseis kai dyo monoprakta*. [A theatrical scrapbook and two one-act plays]. Nicosia: Theatriké Syllogé Kai Vivliothéke, 1978. 57 pp.

Ersoy, Yiassar. *The Turkish Cypriot Theatrical Movement*. Nicosia: privately printed, 1975.

Mousteris, Michalis. *Istoria tou Kupriakou Theatrou*. [History of the Cypriot theatre]. Limassol: Fili Press, 1983.

——. *Chronologikh Istoria tou Kupriakou Theatrou*. [Chronological history of Cyprus theatre]. Limassol: Fili Press, 1988. 300 pp.

The Theatrical Organization of Cyprus. *Ta Sekachrona tou THOK*. [Ten years of THOK]. Nicosia: Proodos Press, 1982.

CZECH REPUBLIC

The origins of Czech theatre can be found in dramatic elements of the rites and customs of the various Slavonic tribes native to the region. Theatrical history itself dates back to the Middle Ages with texts of both religious and secular works being found in various cities. During the Renaissance, Czech humanist-inspired didactic theatre existed. Baroque folk theatre also played a significant role, with some of its traditions surviving into the twentieth century. Court theatre too was performed, mostly in foreign languages, at country castles and palaces of the nobility.

In 1724 the first public theatre, the Count Špork Opera Stage, opened in Prague. In 1739 Prague's Divadlo v Kotcích (Kotce Street Theatre) became the home for various international groups interested in staging opera and dramatic performances. This theatre also introduced burlesque theatre with Harlequin and Hanswurst figures, pantomime ballet, and the first attempts at Czech-language professional theatre. Theatrical activity changed slowly from Italian to German dominance on the stage.

In Prague during the second half of the eighteenth century, a small group of Czech patriots tried to revive the dying Czech-language theatre. The new company used the Nostitz Theatre, built by Count Nostitz-Rieneck in 1783, and renamed it the Stavovské divadlo (Theatre of the Estates) in 1798. One of central Europe's best equipped theatres during this time, it became the site of many important theatrical events, including the 1787 première of *Don Giovanni*, conducted by Mozart. Still another group – Vlastenské divadlo (Patriotic Theatre) – emerged in 1786 under the leadership of playwright Václav Thám (1765–*c*.1816).

In the first half of the nineteenth century, Czech theatrical activity again was focused on the Theatre of the Estates. Under the direction of dramatist and director Jan Nepomuk Štepánek (1783–1844), a Czech-language theatre group began performing alongside a German troupe on Sunday afternoons. Here, works by writer Václav Kliment Klicpera (1792–1859), the romantic actor and playwright Josef Kajetán Tyl (1805–56), and composer František Škroup (1801–62) were brought to life. During the nineteenth-century movement known as the National Revival, the theatre became a platform for emancipation efforts of the nation.

The first provisional 'national' theatre – Prozatimní divadlo (Provisional Theatre) – opened in 1862. A new romantic composer, Bedřich Smetana (1824–84), created a series of operatic works using the Czech language, works which led to the creation of a Czech national opera. The country's artistic longing for recognition as a culturally independent entity culminated in the opening of the Národní divadlo (National Theatre) where opera, drama and ballet performances could be staged. Its building was constructed between 1868 and 1883 through a series of public donations. The creation of this National Theatre became a model for all other professional groups in the country. A vast theatre network soon developed around cities such as Plzeň and Brno.

At the beginning of the twentieth century, two important people assumed leading roles with the National Theatre: director Jaroslav Kvapil (1868–1950), who introduced symbolism and impressionism to a predominantly realistic stage; and composer Karel Kovařovic (1862–1920), who improved both the dramaturgy and the professional quality of the opera stage. At this time, new operatic works by Antonín Dvořák (1841–1904) and Leoš

Janáček (1854–1928) began to be performed in Prague and Brno. The leading choreographers, Augustin Berger (1861–1945) and Achille Viscusi (1865–1945), laid the groundwork for the development of Czech ballet. The Theatre of the Estates and the Neues Deutsches Theater (New German Theatre) in Prague remained especially prominent in this development along with the numerous German theatres performing in towns such as Ústí nad Labem, Liberec and Brno, cities still inhabited by German minorities.

At the forefront of theatrical activity in independent Czechoslovakia after 1918 was director Karol Hugo Hilar (1885–1935), an artist with a keen interest in expressionism. His appointment as drama director of the National Theatre in 1921 opened up a rather traditional stage to world and domestic artists. Otakar Ostrčil (1879–1935) led the great growth in opera.

In the field of dramaturgy, significant contributors included Karel Čapek (1890–1938), his brother Josef (1887–1945), and František Langer (1888–1965).

During the same period, a number of younger avant-garde artists emerged in Prague. In 1926 directors Jiří Frejka (1904–52) and Jindřich Honzl (1893–1953) founded Osvobozené divadlo (Liberated Theatre) as a section of the artistic club Devětsil. Their vision of the modern stage was closely linked to contemporary European avant-garde tendencies, especially those in Russia and France. These directors joined forces with the composer and director Emil František Burian (1904–59) to form a still newer image of poetic theatre.

In 1930, Frejka, who promoted constructivism in his productions and *commedia dell'arte* acting, moved to the National Theatre, and synthesized his experience with the literary orientation of the larger stage. Burian realized his programme of synthetic and poetic theatre on the stage of Divadlo 34 (D34).

The focal point of Honzl's work at this time also shifted and he became linked with the surrealist movement and cooperation with the actors and authors Jiří Voskovec (1905–81) and Jan Werich (1905–80). The Liberated Theatre became the centre of their dark-edged satirical work and remained influential for several generations.

From 1939 to 1945, during the period of German wartime occupation, theatre in the so-called Protectorate of Bohemia and Moravia was largely censored and controlled by Nazi officials. For the most part, Czech drama was suppressed and foreign drama severely limited. As the German occupation progressed, Jewish artists were finally forced to abandon careers in the theatre. Certain avant-garde groups were forcibly shut down (including Divadlo 34) and in 1944 large numbers of theatres were closed.

During this dark period in Czech theatre, many major artists emigrated; some were sent to concentration camps, such as the writer Josef Čapek; many others were executed: the dramatist Vladislav Vančura (b. 1891), actress Anna Letenská (b. 1904) and director Josef Skřivan (b. 1902) among others were all sentenced to death in 1942.

Numerous artists imprisoned in the Terezín ghetto added a unique chapter at this time to Czech theatre history. While waiting to be transported to the concentration camps, they performed for children and adults. Composers Hans Krasa (1899–1944) and Viktor Ullmann (1898–1943) even created new opera works there.

Following the end of the war, a period of relative political freedom occurred lasting until 1948. Most of the previously persecuted artists returned from abroad and from concentration camps. Theatres that had been controlled by the Germans were turned over to the state for use by Czech groups. At this time, Prague and other smaller cities experienced the spontaneous emergence of newly formed ensembles such as Velká opera (Great Opera) and Vesnické divadlo (Village Theatre). Perhaps the most popular ensemble of the period was Divadlo satiry (Satire Theatre) in Prague.

In February 1948, the communists took control of the country. Though their cultural policies secured social stability for theatres, free artistic development was stopped; through the mid-1950s, dogmatic theories of socialist-realism dominated the stage. Virtually all contemporary western plays disappeared from the repertoires at this time, replaced by approved Soviet plays and dramatic works from other socialist countries. The domestic authors were forced to write in the newly approved agitprop style. The official powers allowed only certain classical plays to be performed, while suppressing the best works of the pre-war playwrights. Even the acting styles had to conform to an ideologically distorted interpretation of Stanislavski.

Once again, many theatres were forbidden to perform, including the Satire Theatre and the Great Opera; many major artists were no longer permitted access to the stage. All theatre that

Alfréd Radok's 1966 National Theatre production of Gorki's *The Last Ones*, designed by Josef Svoboda.
Photo: Jaromír Svoboda.

was neither realistic nor Russian – even in modern dance and pantomime – was suppressed. Policies were established not only by artistic directors, but also by the Communist Party's hierarchical social system. Members of the party attended political congresses and conferences which set themes, styles of expression and working methods for the theatres.

In charge of the Municipal Theatre at Vinohrady since 1945, Frejka was finally forced to leave the company at the beginning of the 1950s. Burian distanced himself from his creative work after some unsuccessful attempts at employing the government's desired style. Other artists, such as Voskovec, chose once again to leave the country. Among those under attack at this time were Saša Machov (1904–51) and Ivo Váňapsota (1906–52), who laid the foundations for the modern Czech ballet. Both died as victims of hatred in the poisoned political atmosphere.

In the mid-1950s, after the death of Stalin, a so-called 'thaw' emerged in which the political pressure slowly relaxed. At this time, Jan Werich and Miroslav Horníček (b. 1915) revived the clowning tradition of the Liberated Theatre on the stage of Divadlo satiry ABC (ABC Satire Theatre) which existed from 1955 to 1962.

During the 1960s Czech theatre experienced another brief period of relative political freedom, again returning to European contexts while retaining the financial advantages of working in a highly subsidized cultural environment. This was especially true at the National Theatre in Prague and at the Statni divadlo (State Theatre) in Brno. At these theatres, the country's leading directors had outstanding actors and the best resources at their disposal.

From 1956 to 1961, director Otomar Krejča (b. 1921) led the drama ensemble of the National Theatre. He synthesized a poetic vision of modern drama with the tradition of psychological, realistic acting. His achievements – as well as the unique style of another extraordinary director, Alfréd Radok (1914–76) – contributed to this theatre's most important period. Artists such as director Václav Kašlík (1917–89) and conductor Jaroslav Krombholc (1918–83) also helped create a movement towards a new form of opera theatre. Radok even began a series of experiments involving the simultaneous use of both film and stage. These experiments ultimately led to the creation of the Laterna Magika (Magic Lantern) in 1958, a project that Radok collaborated on with his brother Emil (b. 1918) and the renowned stage designer Josef Svoboda (b. 1920).

In 1965, Krejča left the National Theatre and started his own group in Prague – the Divadlo za branou (Theatre Behind the Gates). This small company quickly created a theatre workshop based on a Chekhovian dramatic style.

At the same time many small theatres were begun whose repertoires were similar to those of other European 'cellar' theatres.

Founded in 1958 by Jiří Suchý (b. 1931), Ivan Vyskočil (b. 1929) and Ladislav Fialka (1931–91), Divadlo na zábradlí (Theatre on the Balustrade) became a significant centre for many of these new groups. The company achieved international fame in the mid-1960s with Jan Grossman's (1925–93) productions of Beckett, Kafka, Jarry and Václav Havel (b. 1936), the company's resident playwright at that time.

During this period, one could find numerous theatrical approaches in the Czech theatre ranging from Brecht to Theatre of the Absurd, from poetic theatre to clearly nationalistic plays. It was during the mid- to late-1960s as well that many experiments in form and style abounded in pantomime and black light theatre. Cabarets flourished as did other forms of satirical theatre. Analogous processes were occurring in ballet and opera. And in set design, Svoboda's work was becoming known world-wide. Clearly, it was during the 1960s that Czech theatre found a recognized place within the European mainstream.

In August 1968, however, the doors were closed once again when Warsaw Pact troops invaded the country. The so-called Prague Spring was followed by almost a year of continuing opposition within the cultural community among others. As a result, the government, with the help of a massive network of secret police, decided finally to wipe out artistic opposition by force.

Many major artists once more left the country at this time in fear of their lives. These included Alfréd Radok, who left days after the invasion, actor Jan Triska (b. 1936), actor and dramatist Pavel Landovsky (b. 1936), dramatists and writers such as Milan Kundera (b. 1929), Pavel Kohout (b. 1929) and Ludwik Aškenazy (1921–86). Theatres such as the Divadlo za branou were closed down (1972) as were studio theatres connected to the large state companies.

Those who remained in the country found themselves forced to leave the major cities. This group included such important personalities as

Grossman, Jan Kačer (b. 1936) and Miloš Hyns (b. 1921). This was also the fate of a number of dissident dramatists such as Havel and Josef Topol. The same fate was true for eminent critics, theoreticians and historians who were not permitted to work in their own fields and were in effect blacklisted. These names, in fact, could not even appear in the media as the government attempted to wipe them from the memories of the nation once and for all. Even magazines devoted to theatre were closed down. Undesirable performances – including certain Soviet plays – were simply banned and international contacts severely limited.

Through the 1970s, the political struggles continued with younger artists adopting many of the 'opposition' approaches of their banned predecessors. As a result, many plays produced at this time included imaginative and coded political messages. As political pressure mounted against these theatres in the largest cities, much of the creative activity simply shifted to the provinces, where a great number of small studio ensembles sprang up. At the same time, many of the provincial ensembles began playing in the larger cities, especially in the suburbs of Prague, where they attracted large audiences of young people. Their success created an even wider spectrum of amateur and semi-professional 'cellar' theatres in Prague.

It was at this time as well that handwritten copies of banned works began to be circulated and in this way the texts of these plays were kept alive. Another response was the development of a form of theatre known as *bytové divadlo* (apartment theatre), in which important actors and actresses such as Vlasta Chramostova (b. 1926) performed in private flats for selected audiences.

Given this situation and adding to it the constant scrutiny of an active state censorship (especially strong in Bohemia), the general level of public performance began dropping across the country.

By 1987, the communist leadership of the country, in a state of political turmoil because of the policy of *perestroika* (restructuring) in the Soviet Union, began to loosen its grip on cultural activities. A number of artists returned to Prague from the provinces.

In November 1989, the communist leadership was removed and shortly thereafter, Havel, a man who had served many years in jail for his political views and the clear leader of the dissident movement, was named president of Czechoslovakia and in 1993 of the new Czech Republic.

While it was still part of the Czech and Slovak Federal Republic, there were in total forty-one Czech-language theatres operating seventy-nine different ensembles across the country. These companies were playing in seventy-six theatre buildings.

For purposes of comparison, in 1960, there were eighty-two Czech theatre groups (seventeen working in Prague); in 1970, seventy-nine (fourteen in Prague); 1980, seventy-seven (twenty-two in Prague); in 1990, seventy-nine groups (twenty-one in Prague).

Jindřich Černý, Ladislava Petišková

Structure of the National Theatre Community

See CZECHOSLOVAKIA for structure 1945–92.

Artistic Profile

Companies

Prague, the national capital, is the country's largest city with a population in 1990 of 1.2 million. It also boasts the highest concentration of theatre companies in the country. The largest theatre institution in Prague and therefore the largest in the country is the Národní divadlo (National Theatre).

The National Theatre has three ensembles – a drama company, a ballet company and an opera company. The different companies alternate use in the National's various theatres.

As the country's official state theatre since

Miroslav Macháček's 1968 National Theatre production of Dürrenmatt's *The Anabaptists*, designed by Josef Svoboda.
Photo: Jaromír Svoboda.

1929, the National has always faced the strongest political pressures. In the immediate post-World War II period and especially in the post-1956 period, the National reached its artistic heights because of the strong directors, designers and actors working there. The 1970s and 1980s saw it decline in all areas – its drama company as well as in its opera and ballet productions. Its repertoire became increasingly conservative and the theatre's working methods became outdated.

One exception during this period was the work of director and actor Miroslav Macháček (1922–91), who helped the drama company maintain some semblance of quality in productions such as Stroupežnický's *Naši furianti* (*Our Pigheads*, 1980) and an outstanding *Hamlet* in 1982.

Since 1989, the National has been attempting to restore and rejuvenate its ensembles under a series of new artistic directors. The drama company, directed by Ivan Rajmont (b. 1945), has oriented itself toward a contemporary European repertoire, while the opera company, working under Eva Herrmannová (b. 1929), and the ballet company, under Vlastimil Harapes (b. 1946), are both struggling to bring these troupes to world level once again.

The next largest theatre in Prague is the Divadlo na Vinohradech (Vinohrady Theatre) founded in 1907 as the Vinohrady Municipal Theatre. Competing with the National throughout its history for artistic leadership, the company has long maintained a tradition of being a true actors' ensemble. Early on, the company worked exclusively in the areas of psychological realism; from 1945, Jiří Frejka synthesized realistic and avant-garde approaches applying this new style to both classics and contemporary works in plays such as Neveux's *Le Voyage de Thésée* and Griboedev's *Woe from Wit* (both 1947).

During the 1960s, the theatre was run by František Pavlíček (b. 1923) and the company became known for productions by directors Luboš Pistorius (b. 1924) and Jaroslav Dudek (b. 1932) and new plays by Kohout, Aškenazy and Ivan Klíma (b. 1931). Many of these works – such as the 1963 Čapek–Kohout *War Against Salamanders* – were anti-illusionistic and spectacular. In the 1970s and 1980s, many television and film stars worked at the theatre and the repertoire was adjusted to accommodate them.

In 1989, actress Jiřina Jirásková (b. 1931) took over direction of the Vinohrady and succeeded in making it Prague's best attended theatre with a repertoire of popular plays and well-known actors. Its most successful play in the early 1990s was Kohout's *Ubohý vrah* (*Poor Murderer*).

The Prague Municipal Theatre was an amalgamation of several small stages in the city. Originally created in 1950 by artists from the Vinohrady under the direction of Ota Ornest (b. 1913), the theatre tried to promote a more intimate style of acting, often staging contemporary western plays during its first twenty years of existence.

Its most important director was Alfréd Radok who, after leaving the National, staged major performances of such plays as Gogol's *The Marriage* (1963) and a Poor Theatre version of Romain Rolland's *Play of Love and Death* (1964). The company's resident playwright during this period was Vratislav Blažek (1925–73).

Since 1989, the company has operated three theatres under the direction of the dramaturge Jan Vedral (b. 1955). The 'K' Theatre focuses on a contemporary repertoire; the ABC on comedies and musicals; the Theatre Rokoko works with new actors and directors in the Spolek Kašpar (Club Kaspar).

The Realistické divadlo (Realistic Theatre) operates in a space which has a tradition of folk theatre extending back into the 1870s. In the 1950s, under the direction of Karel Palouš (b. 1913), it became a workshop producing plays in a dogmatically interpreted Stanislavski style but it also began to present new plays and was involved in early productions of literary reformers such as Pavlíček and Kohout. During the 1970s, productions by Pistorius kept the public going to see its work. In the late 1980s, it had become a Prague base for directors who had made a name for themselves in the provinces in the previous decade. Among these were Karel Kříž (b. 1941), the director of the theatre since 1991, Miroslav Krobot (b. 1951) and Jiří Fréhar (b. 1938).

In 1991, the company changed its name to Labyrint (Labyrinth) and set itself up as a cultural centre for Prague's 'left bank'. Its new repertoire tends toward the intellectually challenging, often in connection with experiments in the field of stage design.

Many of Prague's fringe theatres or cellar theatres can trace their origins back to the literary cabaret, Reduta, founded in 1957. Created in opposition to the official 'big' theatres, the first of these unofficial companies was Divadlo na zábradlí founded in 1958. This company worked in a variety of genres and styles including drama, pantomime, song and cabaret. The leaders of the theatre's drama section were theorist/director Jan Grossman and playwright Václav Havel. Under their leadership, the company created a unique Czech version of Theatre of the Absurd in the 1960s. Both were forced to leave the theatre in 1969 for political reasons, however; despite the popularity of Havel's work, many of his later plays were known only from underground editions and foreign performances.

In addition to Havel's plays, the company also staged plays such as Jarry's *Ubu Roi* (1964), Kafka's *The Trial* (1966) and absurdist versions of plays such as *Hamlet* (1978) and *Macbeth* (1981). During the 1970s and 1980s, the company operated on an underground basis and was under regular attack by the authorities. Run by film director Evald Schorm (1931–88) during this period, Divadlo na zábradlí was the most important theatre in Prague at the time. In 1988, after Schorm's death, Grossman returned to the theatre and in 1991, in association with playwright Karel Steigerwald (b. 1945), became its artistic director. His major successes, not surprisingly, were with plays by Havel – *Largo Desolato* in 1990 and *Pokoušení* (*The Temptation*) in 1991.

Činoherní klub (Drama Club), founded in 1965 as a loose association of stage directors and actors, is another actor-oriented company which through the years has had a number of exceptional directors working with it – among them, founders Jan Kačer, Jaroslav Vostrý (b. 1931) and playwright-director Ladislav Smoček (b. 1932). Working in extremely small spaces, the company also developed its own writer's workshop under Smoček's direction developing not only Smoček's own absurdist satires such as *Podivné odpoledne Dr Zvonka Burkeho* (*The Strange Afternoon of Dr Zvonek Burke*, 1966) but also the work of Alena Vostrá (1938–92) in such plays as *Na ostří nože* (*On Knife-Edge*, 1968) and Pavel Landovsky in such plays as *Hodinový hoteliér* (*The Hour Hotel Keeper*, 1969). Even 'new wave' film directors such as Jiří Menzel (b. 1938) and Evald Schorm worked there. But through the 1970s and 1980s, many of its leading figures were forced to leave the company. Despite this, the ensemble remained vital under the direction of critic, actor and later translator Leoš Suchařípa (b. 1932) and retained its faithful audience. In 1990, Vostrý once again took charge.

Divadlo za branou was founded by Otomar Krejča after his departure from the National Theatre in 1965. Krejča's productions for the group took an existential approach to modern classics (including several Chekhov works) and were staged with extraordinarily powerful performances by his actors. The theatre was closed in 1972 for political reasons, and Krejča left the country in 1976, but re-established his theatre in 1990 as Divadlo za branou II (Theatre Behind the Gates II).

One other small stage of note in Prague during the period was the Semaphor Theatre, a cabaret created in 1959 by composer Jiří Šlitr (1924–69) and actor-singer-playwright Jiří Suchý. The group's most popular show was the 1962 production of *Jonáš a tingl tangl* (*Jonah and the Tingle Tangle*). During the 1960s, the theatre nurtured a number of very talented singers.

Ne-divadlo (Non-Theatre) was started in 1964 by Ivan Vyskočil, an author, actor and professional psychologist. Vyskočil, one of the founders of Theatre on the Balustrade, staged a number of his own plays. During the 1970s and 1980s, he staged these and other works in non-theatrical venues around Prague and even outside the city. Often improvisatory in nature, his works attacked a nihilistic system which sought to manipulate society.

The Jára Cimrman Theatre, founded in 1967, was noted for its burlesque attempts to demystify national myths. Its two founders have also been its two artistic centres – Zdeněk Svěrák (b. 1936) and Ladislav Smoljak (b. 1931). Many of its programmes deal with the life of its non-existent namesake, Jára Cimrman.

The city of Brno, with a population of 400,000, is the country's second largest theatre centre. From the end of the 1950s, a drama ensemble from the State Theatre offered a special programme of popular political folk theatre including Brecht under the direction of playwright Ludwík Kundera (b. 1920), dramaturge Bořivoj Srba (b. 1931), director Evžen Sokolovský (b. 1925) and artistic director Miloš Hynš.

In 1959, the National Theatre company was joined by a political satire troupe called Večerní Brno (Evening Brno). In the 1960s, a number of small groups also came into being. The most important of them include Husa na provázku (Goose on a String, later known as Theatre on a String). Created by Peter Scherhaufer (b. 1942), Eva Tálská (b. 1944) and Zdeněk Pospíšil (b. 1944), the company's work showed the Czech penchant for translating verbal metaphors into visual ones. Throughout its existence, the company was an oasis of dramaturgical imagination full of spontaneous expression and non-ideological poetry. It was from this group that the internationally acclaimed mime, Boleslav Polívka (b. 1949), emerged.

Ha-divadlo was founded in the town of Prostějov by Svatopluk Vála (b. 1946). Later run by Arnošt Goldflam (b. 1946), the company's production method is based on equality among the dramatic word, physical actions and graphic scenic images. Utilizing both montage and free association, the company has been operating in Brno since 1980.

Studio Y was founded in 1963 in the city of Liberec by director-actor-playwright and designer Jan Schmid (b. 1936). In 1978, the company, noted for its comic rearrangement of reality, moved to Prague where it continues to operate into the 1990s.

The director Ivan Rajmont, head of the drama ensemble of the National Theatre since 1989, was the founder of the Činoherní studio (Drama Studio) in the town of Ústí nad Labem in 1972, a company which became known for its absurdist productions and for the opportunities that it afforded both young playwrights and directors who could no longer work in Prague for political reasons.

In addition to these companies, the country also boasts a wide range of semi-professional and even amateur alternative theatres which have been operating not only in Prague but also in most cities since the late 1980s. All are characterized by their lack of interest in traditional forms and styles and their opposition to traditional social reality. One of the most important of these groups was the Divadlo na okraji (Theatre on the Edge) which operated in Prague between 1970 and 1986 under the direction of Zdeněk Potužil (b. 1947).

Jindřich Černý

Arnošt Goldflam's 1991 Ha-divadlo production of Ladislav Klíma's *The Human Tragicomedy*, designed by David Cajthaml.
Photo: Jaroslav Prokop.

Dramaturgy

The death of Karel Čapek in December 1938 effectively marked the end of pre-war Czech dramaturgy. In the years just after World War II, prose writers and poets such as Jan Drda (1915–70) and Josef Kainar (1917–71) turned to the stage with contemporary domestic plays and satires.

Ideological pressure from the Communist Party after 1948, however, soon forced dramaturgical development away even from this direction and towards socialist-realism. Those who did not follow the new line found their plays banned. Even the plays of Čapek and Langer disappeared. It was only after the thawing of Stalinist politics in the late 1950s that dramatists were at long last able to move away from the stiff conventions of dictated aesthetics. Among the first to do so was František Hrubín (1910–71), who in 1958 saw his Chekhovian-styled play, *Srpnová neděle* (*August Sunday*), staged at the National Theatre in Prague. His next play, *Křišťálová noc* (*Crystal Night*), followed in 1961.

Other writers did not fare so well. Important plays by Jiří Kolář (b. 1914), for example,

simply never reached the stage; among these were *Chléb náš vezdejší* (*Our Daily Bread*, 1949) and *Mor v Athénách* (*Plague in Athens*, 1961).

Among the many important Czech dramatists who were working during these years, several stand out. Among them are Josef Topol and Václav Havel, perhaps the two poles of Czech dramatic art, Milan Uhde (b. 1936), Ivan Klíma, Milan Kundera, Pavel Kohout and Pavel Landovsky.

Topol was the resident author in the National Theatre workshops of Otomar Krejča. A sensitive analyst of human relations, in his works – at once simple and imaginative – he examines the impact of social evils on human intimacy. Among his major works are *Jejich den* (*Their Day*, 1960), *Konec masopustu* (*End of the Carnival*, 1963), *Kočka na kolejích* (*Cat on the Rails*, 1965), *Hodina lásky* (*Hour of Love*, 1968) and *Sbohem, Sokrate* (*Goodbye, Socrates*, 1976).

Havel, already mentioned as resident author of the avant-garde Theatre on the Balustrade, deals in an absurdist way with the mechanisms of totalitarianism in relation to individual human beings. Among his most important

Jan Grossman's 1990 Theatre on the Balustrade production of Havel's *Largo Desolato*, designed by Ivo Žídek.

works are *Zahradní slavnost* (*The Garden Party*, 1963), *Vyrozumění* (*The Memorandum*, 1965), *Vernisáž* (*The Opening*, 1975), *Largo Desolato* (1984) and *Pokoušení* (*The Temptation*, 1985). At his best, he creates moving parables about the fate of contemporary humanity.

Of the others previously mentioned, Uhde in his *Král Vavra* (*King Vavra*, 1964), Klíma in his *Zámek* (*The Castle*, 1965), and Kundera, another product of Krejča's workshop, in much of his work as both playwright and novelist, have all leaned toward the absurd. Among Kundera's important plays are *Majitelé klíčů* (*Owners of the Keys*, 1962) and *Ptákovina* (*Stuff and Nonsense*, 1968), a burlesque parable on the theme of human might, and an adaptation of a Diderot novel, *Jakub a jeho pán* (*Jacques and his Master*, 1970). This latter play, with Kundera *persona non grata* at the time, remained in the theatre's repertoire at Ústí nad Labem for fifteen years with the director, Evald Schorm, officially credited as its author. Kahout has been more varied in his works, including in his *August, August, August* (1967) and his play *Ubohý vrah* (1971).

In addition to the dramatists from the Činoherní klub such as Ladislav Smoček, Alena Vostrá and Landovsky referred to previously, three other dramatists of note include the Brecht-inspired Ludwík Kundera, author of *Totální kuropeni* (*Total Cock's Crow*, 1964) and *Labyrint světa a lusthaus srdce* (*Labyrinth of the World and Paradise of the Heart*, 1983); satirist Vratislav Blažek, author of *Třetí přání* (*The Third Wish*, 1960); and František Pavlíček, author of several problem dramas such as *Zápas s andělem* (*Fight with the Angel*, 1959) and *Nanebevstoupení Sašky Krista* (*The Assumption of Saska Kristus*, 1967).

Oldřich Daněk (b. 1926) was one of the more interesting writers in the post-1969 period adapting historical themes in plays such as *Vévodkyně valdštejnských vojsk* (*The Duchess of Wallenstein's Troops*, 1981). Among the writers who emerged in the late 1970s and 1980s, the most promising have been Daniela

Fischerová (b. 1948) with her *Princezna Turandot* (*Princess Turandot*, 1986), and Karel Steigerwald, the author of several analytical dramas on Czech history such as *Tatarská pouť* (*The Tartar Fair*, 1979) and *Dobové tance* (*Period Dances*, 1980).

The works of Bohumil Hrabal (b. 1914) have also become extremely popular thanks to frequent dramatizations of his stories. Among his most popular works have been *Bambini di Praga*, (*Children of Prague*, 1978) and *Hlučná samota* (*Too Loud a Solitude*, 1984), a work which combines a torrent of tavern talk with poetic realism. Extremely popular on the small stages have also been the plays of Josef Kainar, author of such works as *Ubu se vrací* (*Ubu Returns*, 1988), Jiří Suchý, author of *Jonah and the Tingle Tangle* (1962), and Ivan Vyskočil, author of *Haprdáns or Hamlet, Prince of Denmark* (1981).

One writer whose works have begun to enjoy popularity in the post-1989 period is Karol Sidon (b. 1942). Two of his plays achieved note in the early 1990s – *Shapira* (written in 1972) and *Labyrint aneb Cirkus podle Komenského* (*The Labyrinth or The Circus According to Comenius*), a play also written in 1972 but produced only in 1991.

Finally, it should be noted that during the 1970s and 1980s, when so many significant dramatists were simply not allowed to have their plays performed, many of them worked collectively with particular theatres and created theatrical events that were less literary than theatrical. As such, many of these works cannot be easily defined in print and so remain uniquely tied to productions at specific theatres.

Helena Albertová, Jana Patočková

Directors, Directing and Production Styles

For a discussion of directing, see previous material in **Artistic Profile** and the opening, historical section.

Music Theatre

The oldest opera houses in the country are those of the Theatre of the Estates (1783) and the National Theatre in Prague but other Czech

cities such as Brno, Ostrava, Olomouc, Plzeň, Ústí nad Labem, Liberec and Opava also have long traditions. In the years following World

War II, new opera houses were constructed in the latter three cities as well as in Brno.

Just after World War II, Prague became the only city in the country to be able to boast two opera houses – the National and the Velká opera 5 května (Grand Opera of 5 May) – the Velká playing in what was formerly the Neues Deutsches Theater (later called the Smetana Theatre) between 1945 and 1948. Under the direction of composer Alois Hába (1893–1973), whose quarter-tone opera *Matka* (*The Mother*) was premièred in Munich in 1931, the Velká developed into an ambitious avant-garde ensemble and became home to some of the country's most important musical talents of the time – conductor Karel Ančerl (1908–73), conductor and director Václav Kašlík, designer Josef Svoboda and director Alfréd Radok. The ensemble's emphasis on only the most contemporary of operatic works clearly distinguished it from virtually all the other companies in the country. In 1948, this young and progressive ensemble merged with the National Theatre's opera company.

Through the late 1940s and well into the next decades, most other Czech opera houses tried to develop a balance between national and international works including a number of Russian operas, especially by Prokofiev.

The base of the Czech repertoire has consistently been found in the works of Bedřich Smetana and Antonín Dvořák. The leading conductor in the immediate post-war period was, without doubt, Václav Talich (1883–1961).

It was in Brno that the operatic works of the great Czech composer Leoš Janáček first came to national attention. Janáček took realistic dramatic works and set them to music, among them, Preissova's *Jenůfa*, Ostrovsky's *Kátá Kabanová* (*The Storm*) and Čapek's *Věc Makropulos* (*The Makropoulos Affair*). These works, which incorporated the composer's realistic style with ethnic motifs, became favourites with conductors as well as with such designers as Svoboda and František Tröster.

A number of Czech directors also made important reputations during this time by focusing on works by Janáček and other national composers. Among the major directors were Ferdinand Pujman (1889–1962), Václav Kašlík and Luděk Mandaus (1898–1971).

During the 1950s and 1960s, still another Czech composer of note came to national attention, Bohuslav Martinu (1890–1959), and his major works were produced widely. Among these are *Mirandolina*, premièred at the National Theatre in Prague in 1959, *Julietta*, premièred at the National Theatre in 1938, and *Řecké pašije* (*Greek Passions*) which was produced successfully both in Prague and Brno in the 1960s.

Because productions of new works from the west were discouraged in the 1960s and 1970s by government policy, external influences became less and less significant. On the positive side, this forced Czech artists to become more and more imaginative in developing their own work but it also left the country without any real sense of the latest contemporary trends in the field. It was only when Czech opera groups were invited to travel abroad on official tours that foreign work could be seen and that Czech work could begin to penetrate beyond eastern Europe. It was an appearance by Prague's National Theatre Opera Company at the Edinburgh Festival in 1964 that marked the discovery by the west of the works of Janáček.

The work of certain other artists attracted special attention to a number of the smaller Czech opera companies. Of particular note was the work in the city of Ostrava of conductor Jaroslav Vogel (1894–1970), an outstanding interpreter of both Wagner and Janáček as well as the author of a fine monograph on Janáček; in the city of Olomouc of composer Iša Krejčí (1904–68), author of several fine operas including a 1946 adaptation of Shakespeare's *Comedy of Errors* called *Pozdvižení u Efesu* (*Uprising in Ephesus*); and in the city of Plzeň of conductor Bohumír Liška (1914–90) whose work on such composers as Britten and Prokofiev gave his company a special place in the national repertoire.

Director Bohumil Hrdlička (b. 1921) started his career in Ostrava but quickly began working all across the country. Many still consider his 1957 production of Mozart's *The Magic Flute* as definitive. Set in a recognizable post-war milieu, giving the priests contemporary costumes, all overseen by concentration camp watchtowers, its avant-garde qualities set it clearly against the official aesthetic doctrines of the period. Hrdlička eventually left Czechoslovakia for a career in German-speaking Europe where he was instrumental in introducing Janáček's work.

Two other Czech operatic artists of note who also made major reputations outside the country were conductor Zdeněk Chalabala (1899–1962), who worked extensively with Moscow's Bolshoi Opera Theatre, and Václav Neumann

Bohumil Hrdlička's 1957 National Theatre production of Mozart's *The Magic Flute*, designed by Josef Svoboda.
Photo: Jaromír Svoboda.

(b. 1920), who worked mostly with Berlin's famous Komische Oper.

Other notable Czech composers in the decades since the end of World War II have been Jan Hanu (b. 1915), creator of the 1965 opera *Pochodeň Prometheova* (*The Torch of Prometheus*), and Josef Berg (1927–71), creator of the 1967 opera *Eufrides před branami Tymenu* (*Euphrides Before the Gates of Tymen*).

In the early 1990s there were nine opera houses/ensembles in Czech territory, mostly based around Prague.

Ivan Vojtěch

Dance Theatre

The development of dance theatre, particularly ballet, in the Czech Republic after 1945 can be divided into several clearly defined stages. The first, in the immediate post-war years, is characterized by the growth of the genre generally within the purview of opera performance and its attempts at this time to break away from the domination of opera.

The major figures in this development were the choreographers Saša Machov in Prague and Ivo Váňapsota in Brno. At the National Theatre, Machov attempted to create a specifically Czech national ballet with Zbyněk Vostrák's (b. 1920) *Viktorka* in 1950, while in Brno, Váňapsota developed an outstanding ensemble working from the Diaghilev repertoire.

A second phase began in the 1950s when national policy demanded that art conform to the realistic ballet-drama favoured by the Soviets. In works of this type, form was all but ignored and movement was the guiding force. Perhaps the single choreographer from this period whose work was of real note was Jiří Němeček (b. 1924), a seasoned director who helped create the idea of full-length dramatic ballets. In his work, stage design played a significant role as it did in his 1959 production of Jan Hanuš's *Othello*, which was designed by Josef Svoboda.

A third phase can be said to have begun in the early 1960s with the development of a more poetic ballet based on specific dance expression, economy of movement, exaggeration and metaphor. At the cost of almost losing classical dance entirely, choreography of this period stepped out of the narrowly defined, canonized territory of the classical *pas*. The period ushered in a new era of modernization and individual choreographic expression. The number of shorter ballets in the repertoire increased significantly.

Among the important choreographers emerging at this time were Luboš Ogoun (b. 1924) and Pavel Šmok (b. 1927), who jointly founded the independent Prague Ballet which operated between 1964 and 1970. Not connected to a specific theatre, the company often toured abroad and became an experimental laboratory for all Czech ballet. Typical of this work early in the decade was Ogoun's 1963 production of *Hiroshima* in Brno to the concrete music of William Bukový. Later on, the period was characterized by Šmok's choreography to Janáček's *Listy důvěrné* (*Intimate Letters*, 1968). Still another choreographer of note here was Jiří Blažek (b. 1923).

The political turmoil of 1968 and the Prague Spring brought about a return to the spiritual and political climate of the 1950s. Connections abroad were closed down and Czechoslovak dance lost all contact with the rest of the world. During this time, many important artists emigrated – among them, Jiří Kyliân (b. 1948), who in 1975 became artistic director of the Nederland Dans Theater – and artistic standards at home dropped significantly.

One exception to this trend was the work during this time of the Prague Chamber Ballet under the direction of Pavel Šmok. His *American Concert* (1977) to the music of Dvořák and his 1986 work, *Clear Night* to the music of Schoenberg, were highlights of Czech dance during this decade.

A number of younger artists began to develop during the late 1980s when dance troupes began to be founded outside the official structures and in some cases in direct opposition to them. Among the most important were Miroslav Kura (b. 1924), a brilliant dancer-actor, Marta Drottnerova (b. 1941), the first Czech ballerina of world standard, and Vlastimil Harapes.

As the 1990s began, a dozen ballet ensembles were operating in Prague, Brno, Plzeň, Ostrava and several smaller cities. As well, there were several travelling professional dance ensembles (such as the Czechoslovak State Song and Dance Ensemble founded in 1948) which were attempting to maintain the country's folk tradition. Travelling ballet troupes such as the Ballet Prague (1964–70) and its successor, the Prague Chamber Ballet (founded in 1970), were also of importance to the growth of the art across the country.

Of the permanent ensembles, the oldest, the strongest artistically and the largest is the ballet troupe of the National Theatre in Prague with more than 120 members. Other theatres with large ballet troupes connected to them are the Brno State Theatre (sixty members) and the Ostrava State Theatre (fifty members). The Laterna Magika in Prague also has a large dance ensemble at its disposal.

The country's dance community has a major publication in the field, *Taneční listy* (*Dance Journal*).

Vladimír Vašut

Pantomime

Pantomime has always been of special interest in Czechoslovakia but during World War II it moved into the realm of the avant-garde and almost disappeared in the experiments of directors and choreographers. By 1948, it fell victim to ideological bans which tried to eliminate from the Czech theatre everything that was not socialist-realism in style. Pantomime at that point became simply a branch of dance training.

It was the French artists Jean-Louis Barrault and Marcel Marceau, whose films were shown in Czechoslovakia, who inspired a new generation to take the form seriously and to re-create it as an independent genre. By the end of the 1950s, a number of small mime companies were started, the most important one by Ladislav Fialka, the co-founder, artistic director and leading figure of the pantomime troupe of the Theatre on the Balustrade.

The uniquely stylish and poetic profile of his pantomime was, on the one hand, based on ballet technique and, on the other, on a strong feeling for plasticity. Involving as well a strong sense of the romantic tradition, such full-length works as *Cesta* (*Path*, 1962), *Blázni* (*Fools*, 1965) and *Knoflík* (*The Button*, 1968) were remarkable for their unique blend of the fantastic and the picturesque along with a genuine political point of view.

In contrast to Fialka's work was that of Ctibor Turba (b. 1944) and Boris Hybner (b. 1941), who at their Alfred Jarry Pantomime Ensemble (which operated from 1968 to 1972) worked in an absurdist style. They rejected traditional mime masks as well as white face, and their intentional ugliness, shocking aggressiveness and black humour took their theatrics to daring extremes. Perhaps their most impressive piece in this style was the 1968 work *Hara-kiri*.

Another mime of particular importance both inside and outside the country during the 1970s and 1980s was Boleslav Polívka. An actor with Brno's Theatre on a String, Polívka went on to create a series of mime performances in which he achieved a genuine synthesis of poetry and intellectual-political clowning. He was at his most inventive in such works as *Pépé* (1974), and *Šašek a královna* (*The Jester and the Queen*, 1983).

Through the late 1970s and 1980s, pantomime became extremely popular because it could, without words, speak to an audience about officially banned subjects. The development of the genre brought into existence ten different mime ensembles of various styles including Křesadlo (Flint) which from 1973 was led jointly by Václav Martinic (b. 1937) and Nina Vangeli (b. 1946). In 1981, the Braník Pantomime Theatre was founded in Prague as a home in which these and other guest ensembles from abroad could perform.

A mime department has existed since the 1980s at the Musical Academy of Performing Arts in Prague and since 1989, a number of private mime companies and schools have come into existence.

Ladislava Petišková

Theatre for Young Audiences

The tradition of staging plays for young audiences in the Czech Republic is a clear continuation of a form that had its modern beginnings in Russia. Czech performances, however, vary greatly from naturalistic retellings of classic children's fairytales and often include original poetic works which may or may not have didactic purposes.

The first Czech professional theatre for young people was founded in Prague in 1935 by Míla Mellanová (1899–1964). After the war, three new companies began: in Prague, the Jiří Wolker Theatre (1953); in Brno, the Julius Fučík Theatre (1955–65); and in Ostrava, the Petr Bezruč Theatre (1951). All staged productions exclusively for schools.

In the 1960s, however, director Jan Kačer began staging performances for adults as well at the Bezruč Theatre, extending the notion of theatre for the young in the process. Kačer had particular success with František Pavlíček's topical adaptation of Hans Christian Andersen's *Slavík* (*The Nightingale*) and the plays of Jan Jílek (b. 1933).

Beyond these companies specializing in the field, a number of other companies also included occasional performances for young people. One of the most consistent in this regard was Prague's Pocket Theatre, headed by mime Zdenka Kratochvílová (b. 1936).

Young people were also enormously attracted to the workshop productions directed by Eva Tálská at Brno's Theatre on a String and by Jan Schmidt at Prague's Studio Y.

For the record, Czechoslovakia was one of the founding members of ASSITEJ (International Association of Theatre for Children and Young People). The organization's first international congress was held in Prague in 1965.

Drahomíra Čeporanová

Puppet Theatre

Puppet theatre had an enormous popularity in the Bohemian countryside at the end of the eighteenth and the first half of the nineteenth centuries. Dozens of wandering puppet troupes helped to preserve the Czech language as well as the sense of nationhood in the predominantly German environment. It is in this historical context that modern puppetry in the country must be understood.

The earliest of the modern ensembles in Czech territories was that founded in Plzeň in 1930 by Josef Skupa (1892–1957). In 1945, this company changed its name to Divadlo Spejbla a Hurvínka (Spejbl and Hurvínek Theatre) and moved to Prague. The company was one of three professional troupes in operation before World War II. In 1948, when puppetry was included in the nationalization of the country's theatres, this art was given the same professional status as other theatrical forms.

By 1949, a network of professional puppet troupes was in evidence across the country, but their members were most often being recruited from amateur groups. One man who contributed to the overall process of professionalization at this time was Jan Malík (1904–80) who as far back as 1930 had a reputation as a reformer in the field.

In 1949, Malík founded the Ústřední loutkové divadlo (Central Puppet Theatre) in Prague, a company which operated for many years in the pictorial tradition perfected by the Soviet puppet master Sergei Obraztsov. Utilized were traditional stick-puppets and this signifi-

cantly influenced the choice of repertoire. From 1950 on, this company set the standard for all other groups in the country. Its 1952 production of the fairytale *Zlatovláska* (*The Golden-Haired Princess*) by poet Josef Kainar is still one of the mainstays of Czech puppet dramaturgy.

By the second half of the 1950s, however, Malík's style was felt to be too dependent on words, relegating the puppet to be simply an illustrative object. The base of opposition was found in the experimental group Salamandr in the Spejbl and Hurvínek Theatre as well as among puppetry students at the Academy of Performing Arts, founded by Skupa in 1952 as the world's first university-level school of puppetry.

The development of the genre in the ensuing years can be characterized as an oscillation between two poles: on the one hand, productions which represented the world realistically, and on the other, productions which strove to achieve a non-realistic communication with the viewer. It is this latter direction which has led the form into further evolution in the development of a poetics of theatrical objects and the exploration of stage metaphor.

Occurring at the same time as a general resurgence of interest in the marionette tradition, this exploration can be seen in the innovative work of the company Drak (Dragon), based in the city of Hradec Králové. Founded in the mid-1960s by Vladimír Matoušek (1900–77) and under the later direction of Jan Dvořák (b. 1925), the company has played a significant role in the development of the form through the audacious dramaturgy and directorial inventiveness of Dvořák, Josef Krofta (b. 1943), the design and technological virtuosity of Petr Matásek (b. 1944) and the woodworking arts of František Vítek (b. 1929).

Drak productions tend to be combinations of puppets, live actors, and stage props, with the props capable of interpretation in many ways. The company has performed in many theatres for both children and adults. Among their major successes are *Šípková Růženka* (*Sleeping Beauty*, 1976), *Sněhurka* (*Snow White*, 1979), *Popelka* (*Cinderella*, 1982) and the philosophical allegory *Píseň života* (*Song of Life*, 1985).

Another puppet company of note is the Naivní divadlo (Naive Theatre) in Liberec. Founded in 1949 as the Loutkové divadlo v Liberci (Liberec Puppet Theatre), the group changed its name in 1968. The company is especially known for its *mateřinky* productions, plays intended for the youngest of children which take playfulness and fantasy as artistic guides. The company's key figure is stage designer-puppeteer Pavel Kalfus (b. 1942).

The Spejbl and Hurvínek Theatre has continued to retain its own position in the field thanks to the leadership of Skupa's successor, Miloš Kirschner (b. 1927). The company also continues as one of the country's most popular groups, thanks to its high standards and its productions for both children and adults. Of special note here are the appearances in many of the productions of the company's namesake characters, the mythical and very popular Spejbl and Hurvínek, who first appeared in the 1920s.

These positive developments in the art, however, have led to an enormous dependence on directors and a certain underestimation of the puppet itself as a means of expression. Nevertheless, the form's popularity remains high.

Early in 1993, there were in total ten professional Czech puppet groups, all state subsidized. In addition there were dozens of amateur groups and several black light companies. The most significant of these groups was the independent Černé Divadlo (Black Theatre) founded by Jiří Srnec (b. 1931) in 1964. Their productions – such as *Létající velociped* (*The Flying Bicycle*, 1975) and *Alenka v říši divů* (*Aspects of Alice*, 1989) – exist on the border between pantomime and puppet theatre with objects moving in a kind of fantastic free-play.

Another group, Vedené divadlo (Guided Theatre), had a short existence in Prague between 1969 and 1972 under the direction of Karel Makonj (b. 1947). This company, in its 1969 production of Camus's *Le Malentendu* (*The Misunderstanding*), introduced giant mannequin-like puppets to the stage which have been used subsequently by others.

Perhaps the most marked contemporary trend in Czech puppetry is the simultaneous use of both puppets and live actors, a style particularly used by both Drak and the Naive Theatre.

Finally, it should be noted here that one of the oldest puppet magazines in the world, *Český loutkář* (*Czech Puppeteer*), was founded in 1912. In 1929, UNIMA (the International Puppeteers' Union), was founded in Prague.

Miroslav Česal, Nina Malíková

Design

Czech stage design in the second half of the twentieth century has been closely tied to movements in the field of art from the pre-World War II period. Cubist architecture – a movement centred around the work of Pavel Janák (1882–1956) – entered Czech theatre around 1920 under the banner of expressionism and cubo-futurism.

Introduced by such artists as Vlastislav Hofman (1884–1964), Bedřich Feuerstein (1892–1936) and Jiří Kroha (1893–1974), the approach was developed further by František Tröster. Tröster's discovery of dramatic space in

the 1930s anticipated the principle of sculptural architecture of the 1960s.

Soviet constructivism provided the lead for Czech avant-garde movements of the 1920s and helped to create a new individual style – 'poetism' which claimed as its inspiration such artists as Mayakovsky, Apollinaire, Picasso and the dada movement. This movement was translated on to the stage by director Jindřich Honzl and the architect Antonín Heythum (1901–54). The centre of its activities was the Osvobozené divadlo in Prague in 1925.

This is also where Emil František Burian

began his career. Burian and Miroslav Kouřil (1911–84) employed slide and film projection in their work at the D34 Theatre, dramatically linking into the overall visual composition. Their 'theatregraph', patented in 1938 and directly connected to film technology of the 1936–8 period, involved the use of a transparent projection area across the front of the stage.

The onset of World War II and the nationalization of all the professional theatres in 1948 disrupted the natural evolution of design in the country. The need to follow prescribed forms and the 1968 occupation by Soviet forces further prevented free development in the field. Despite this, there were short spurts of significant creative activity in the years just prior to 1948 and in the twelve years from 1956 to 1968.

In Prague, it was the Grand Opera of 5 May which began to develop entire programmes around the work of the country's most imaginative designers – notably Josef Svoboda – in the immediate post-war period (1945–8). Svoboda's work showed not only imagination but also simplicity and his career quickly brought him to the stage of the National Theatre and later abroad.

After a short period in which he experimented with socialist-realism, he developed, in collaboration with Krejča and Radok, the idea of psycho-plastic space capable of expressing a wide range of changes in dramatic settings. Svoboda's 1957 design for Bohumil Hrdlička's production of Mozart's opera The Magic Flute indicated new ways to exploit the visual aspects of the stage through both technique and technology especially in the use of lighting.

At the world exposition held in Brussels in 1958, Svoboda presented a programme with director Emil Radok and the Laterna Magika company utilizing the polyekram, still another innovation on this new road. In 1959, these new approaches won Czechoslovakia First Prize at an international design competition in Brazil (the São Paulo Biennial) and Tröster was awarded a Gold Medal as the Best Foreign Stage Designer. These were the first of many such awards picked up by Czech designers at this event in the coming years including Svoboda himself, Jiří Trnka (1912–69), Vladimír Nývlt (b. 1927) and Oldřich Šimáček (b. 1919).

It was international design successes such as these which inspired the creation in 1967 of a similar Czechoslovak event, the Prague Quadrennial, the largest international exhibition of stage design and theatre architecture in the world.

In the mid-1960s national trends led to designers such as Zbyněk Kolář (b. 1926) and Vladimír Šrámek (b. 1927) stylizing dramatic reality into strongly aesthetic abstract or symbolic signs, while solitary and purely visual art productions were created by Zdeněk Seydl (1916–78).

Toward the end of the 1960s, stage stylization began to be separated into specific elements either accentuated or taken out of normal contexts. By 1975, a new 'action' stage design began to be seen which consisted of a constant confrontation of empirical and dramatic realities with the on-stage actor as their living arranger. Costume too became a new focus of artistic dramatic expression. This was seen as early as 1964 in the designs of Libor Fára (1925–88) for the Grossman production of Jarry's Ubu Roi at the Theatre on the Balustrade.

Through the 1980s, characteristic design has been determined most often by graduates of various stage design schools. Neither painters nor architects, the designers of this later period such as Jaroslav Malina (b. 1937), Jan Dušek (b. 1942), Miroslav Melena (b. 1937), Jan Konečný (b. 1951), Ivo Žídek (b. 1948) and Marta Roszkopfová (b. 1947) are specialists whose work represents even more contemporary examples of action stage design. The earliest movements in this direction came from Otakar Schindler (b. 1923) and seem to connect to the Poor Theatre movement of the 1960s in which there is an absolute minimum of design expression. This has also been a significant part of the style of the small theatres of the mid-1980s with action stage design being left behind by these newer approaches.

Perhaps the single dissenting design voice during this period was Jan Vančura (b. 1940), who allowed himself to be inspired by the romantic designs of the nineteenth century.

Early in the 1990s, collage and assemblage seemed to be favoured approaches on the Czech stage and there was a developing trend toward decoration and even kitsch in the work of Daniel Dvořák (b. 1954) and Karel Glogr (b. 1958). This was first seen in costume design, which acted as a bridge of sorts between the older and newer styles. Among those who are working in this way, the key figures are Jindřiška Hirschová (b. 1922), Helena Anýžová (b. 1936), Irena Greifová (b. 1939) and Josef Jelínek (b. 1949).

Věra Ptáčková

Theatre Space and Architecture

Most theatre buildings in the Czech Republic have been built in the traditional Italian style. The oldest ones have all been declared historical monuments. Of architectural as well as theatrical significance are Prague's Stavovské divadlo (Theatre of the Estates, 1783), a building in the classical style designed by Anton Haffenecker, which housed the world première of *Don Giovanni* in 1787, and the National Theatre, built in 1883 from donations by Czech citizens during the major period of national revival.

In Brno, the most significant building is the Mahen Theatre, completed in 1882. Unique also is the Baroque-style Castle Theatre built in 1767 in Český Krumlov which has been preserved in its entirety including original stage decorations and props.

At the time of the creation of the Czechoslovak state in 1918 there were, in total, twenty-three independent theatre buildings of which twenty-two are still used for productions. After 1918, the network was further enlarged with the addition of buildings and halls in smaller towns.

Among the significant theatres since 1945 are the 620-seat open-air theatre built in 1958 in Český Krumlov, with a revolving stage by Joan Brehms (b. 1907), and the Janáček Opera in Brno which has two side-stages and one rear-stage, and was built in 1965 by the team of Jan Vísek (1890–1966), Vilém Zavřel (b. 1910) and Libuše Žáčková (b. 1921). This theatre boasts 1,383 seats, a 20 by 22 metre stage and an orchestra pit that can hold ninety musicians.

The 796-seat Workers Theatre in Zlín was built in 1967 by Miroslav Řepa (b. 1924) and František Rozhoň (b. 1926) and has a 19 by 23.5 metre stage. The ground plan of the auditorium is based on the Gropius oval of a conventional theatre. A segment of the proscenium can be used as a forty-musician orchestra pit.

The Workers Theatre in Most, built in 1987 and designed by Ivo Klimeš (b. 1932), has a trapezoid stage which narrows from 31 metres to 16 metres with a depth of 13.6 metres. The proscenium arch is 7.5 metres high and has a width ranging from 12 to 21.5 metres. The auditorium seats 500 spectators.

The National Theatre's New Scene in Prague is an open space designed by Karel Prager (b. 1923) in 1983. The auditorium seats 510 and has space for twenty-four musicians.

Vladimír Adamczyk

Training

State conservatories exist at the secondary school level (13 to 18 years of age) for the training of actors, musicians and dancers in three cities: Prague (though the conservatory was founded in 1808, the drama department was founded only in 1919); in Brno (founded in 1919); and in Ostrava (1959).

Advanced training is provided by the Akademie múzických umění (Academy of Performing Arts) in Prague (founded in 1946) and the Janáček Academy of Musical Arts in Brno (1947). Both institutions train students as professionals for theatre, music and film and as teachers in these fields. Since 1952, the Academy of Performing Arts has also had a special chair in puppet theatre, one of the first in the world. In terms of facilities, both academies have their own theatres and opera studios.

A number of so-called People's Art Schools offer theatre training across the country during evening hours for amateurs.

Helena Albertová

Criticism, Scholarship and Publishing

The foundations for modern Czech theatre analysis were laid by Otakar Zich (1879–1934) in his seminal book, *The Aesthetics of Dramatic Art* published in 1931. In this work, Zich argued for theatre as a dynamic concert of a wide range of elements while at the same time laying the broad foundations for taking a semiotic approach to art.

The later Prague structuralists too found their work directly growing out of Zich's essential ideas. Among them were Roman Jakobson (1896–1982), Petr Bogatyrev (1893–1971), Ján Mukařovský (1891–1975) and still later, Jiří Veltruský (b. 1919), who left the country in 1948.

The development of Czech structuralism was interrupted in the late 1940s and early 1950s by official government positions which attempted to deny that this movement had validity for socialist art. As a result, there was virtually no collaboration at this time between theatrical science, aesthetics and more general theories on art. Theories were, in fact, developed almost by accident as a by-product of the activities of dramatists, directors (particularly Jan Grossman) and critics. Most appeared as essays rather than books. Interestingly, when Mukařovský's *Studies of Aesthetics* was published in 1966, semiological research – particularly as it related to music theatre and the work of Ivo Osolsobě (b. 1928) – was clearly tied to structuralist concepts.

In the post-war years, Czech theatre science developed a wider institutional base with Chairs of Theatre Science established at Charles University in Prague and at the University of Brno. The Prague Chair was held early on by František Götz (1894–1974), former dramaturge of the National Theatre; later it was held by historians Jan Kopecký (b. 1919) and František Černý (b. 1926).

In history, the Czech Academy of Science created an important four-volume *Dějiny českého divadla* (*History of the Czech Theatre*), published by the Academia Prague between 1969 and 1983, covering Czech theatre from the Middle Ages to 1945.

Since 1959, national theatre documentation has been done by the Divadelní ústav (Theatre Institute) in Prague. The documents themselves are housed in the National Museum in Prague and the History Museum in Brno.

Of special theories, mention should be made of the work by Růžena Vacková (1901–82), *Výtvarný projev v dramatickém umění* (*The Role of Stage Design in Dramatic Art*) published in 1948; and *Česká scénografie 20. století* (*Czech Stage Design in the Twentieth Century*) by Věra Ptáčková (b. 1933) published in 1982.

In the immediate post-war years, the key journals for theory and criticism were *Divadelní zápisník* (*Theatre Notebook*), and *Otázky divadla a filmu* (*Problems of Stage and Film*). From the end of the 1950s, a new generation of critics and theorists collected around the periodicals *Divadlo* (*Theatre*) and *Divadelní noviny* (*Theatre News*), both of which ceased publication in 1970.

In the late 1970s, the most important place for theatre criticism was *Scena* (*Stage*) which in the 1980s became a centre for critical attacks on official cultural policies. In 1986, *O divadle* (*About Theatre*), a *samizdat* review, became a voice for theatrical dissidents. Since 1989, a number of new publications have also begun to appear, among them, *Divadelní revue* (*Theatre Review*) which began publication in 1989; *Svět a divadlo* (*World Theatre*) which began in 1990; and *Divadelní noviny* (*Theatre News*) which began in 1992.

Petr Pavlovský
Translated by Jan Krčmář and Caroline Vocadlo

(See also CZECHOSLOVAKIA)

Further Reading

Bezděk, Zdeněk. *Československá loutková divadla, 1949–1969*. [Czechoslovak puppet theatres, 1949–69]. Prague: Divadelní ústav, 1973. 160 pp.

Černý, František. *Měnivá tvář divadla aneb Dvě století s pražskými herci*. [Changeable face of theatre, or two centuries with actors from Prague]. Prague: Mladá fronta, 1978. 319 pp.

——, ed. *Dějiny českého divadla*. [History of the Czech theatre], 4 vols. Prague: Academia, 1969–83.

——, ed. *Divadlo v Kotcích. Nejstarší pražské městské divadlo 1739–1783*. [Theatre in Kotce. The oldest Prague Municipal Theatre 1739–83]. Prague: Panorama, 1992

Císař, Jan. *Divadla, která našla svou dobu*. [Theatres that resonated with their time]. Prague: Orbis, 1966. 126 pp.

Fencl, Otakar. *The Czechoslovak Theatre Today*. Prague: Artia, 1963. 84 pp.

Goetz-Stankiewicz, Markéta. *The Silenced Theatre: Czech Playwrights Without a Stage*. Toronto: University of Toronto Press, 1979.

Hájek, Jiří, Olga Janáčková, and Vladimír Just. *Divadlo nové doby 1945–1948*. [Theatre of a new age 1945–8]. Prague: Panorama, 1990.

Herrmannová, E., E. Illingová, and M. Kuna. 'České hudební divadlo v letech 1945–1960' [Czech musical theatre 1945–60]. In *Příspěvky k dějinám české hudby II*, [Contributors to the history of Czech music II] ed. Milan Kun, 155–232. Prague: Academia, 1972.

Just, Vladimír. *Proměny malých scén*. [Changes in the small theatres]. Prague: Mladá fronta, 1984. 344 pp.

Konečná, Hana, ed. *Čtení o Národním divadle. Útržky dějin a osudů*. [The National Theatre: on its history and its fate]. Prague: Odeon, 1983. 412 pp.

Kopáčova, Ludmila, and Jana Paterová, eds. *České divadlo*. [Czech theatre]. Vol. 2, *Divadla studiového typu*. [Studio theatre], by Milan Obst, Jan Kolář, Jan Dvořák, Miroslav Křovák, Vlasta Gallerová and Vladimír Just. Prague: Divadelní ústav, 1980. 87 pp.

Kopáčova, Ludmila, Jana Paterová, Otakar Roubínek, and Jonatan Tomeš, eds. *České divadlo*. [Czech theatre]. Vols. 6 and 8, *O současné české režii*. [About contemporary Czech directing], by Jan Císar, Jan Czech, Michal Lázňovský, et al. Prague: Divadelní ústav, 1982–3.

Nadvornikova, Marie. *Postavy ceskeho divadla: vyberova bibliografie kniznich publikaci a clanku z divadelniho tisku 1945–1980*. [Productions of the Czech theatre: selected bibliography of books on theatrical activities, 1945–80]. Publikace Statni vedecke knihovny v Olomouci, 4. Olomouc: Statni vedecke knihovny v Olomouci, 1983. 85 pp.

Osolsobě, Ivo. *Divadlo, které mluví, zpívá a tančí*. [A theatre which speaks, sings and dances]. Prague: Supraphon, 1974. 242 pp.

Procházka, Vladimír, ed. *Národní divadlo a jeho předchůdci*. [The National Theatre and its predecessors]. Prague: Academia, 1988. 623 pp.

Ptáčková, Věra. *Česká scénografie 20. století*. [Czech theatre design in the twentieth century]. Prague: Odeon, 1982. 365 pp.

Šormová, Eva. *Divadlo v Terezíně 1941–1945*. [Theatre in Theresienstadt, 1941–5]. Theresienstadt: Severočeské nakladatelství, 1973.

Trensky, Paul I. *Czech Drama Since World War II*. White Plains: Sharpe, 1978.

CZECHOSLOVAKIA

(Historical Overview)

A pre-1918 map of Europe would not have contained the country's name in any modern form or even have shown the location of this small central European entity, which was bounded by Germany, Austria, Hungary, Ukraine and Poland. Known for much of the twentieth century as Czechoslovakia or, more precisely, the Czechoslovak Republic, the name corresponded to the country's two largest ethnic groups, the West Slavonic Czechs and Slovaks. On 1 January 1993, the country formally split into two independent entities to be known from that point as the Czech Republic and the Slovak Republic.

Prior to the separation, the Czech and Slovak Federal Republic had an area of 127,900 square kilometres (49,400 square miles) and a population of some 16 million, with about two-thirds living in the Czech territories of Bohemia and Moravia; the remaining third lived in Slovakia. Along with the Czechs and Slovaks, the country included several other smaller national groupings – Hungarians, Poles, Germans and Ukrainians (Ruthenians).

Historically, it was the defeat of Germany and its Austro-Hungarian allies in World War I which directly led to the emergence of many new independent states in central Europe including, on 28 October 1918, the independent Czechoslovak Republic. For the next twenty years it was arguably the most economically successful country in Europe. From a cultural point of view, the period was also one of its most fertile.

In 1938, however, Hitler demanded the surrender of the Sudetenland in which German minorities were living. At that same time, a move toward Slovak autonomy within the Czechoslovak union intensified. In 1939,

despite the annexation of the Sudetenland, German troops invaded Czech territories and occupied them under the name of the Protectorate of Bohemia and Moravia. Slovakia became an independent state subordinate to Hitler's Germany. Southern and eastern territories were in turn occupied by Hungarian forces.

In 1945, the country (without its eastern territories) returned to its pre-war name of the Czechoslovak Republic. In 1948, the communists took power and the country became part of the Soviet bloc. In 1960, the name was changed once more, this time to the Czechoslovak Socialist Republic. In the early 1960s there began a reform process that culminated in the 1968 Prague Spring, but this was ended in August of that year by the entry of Warsaw Pact armies and Soviet occupation of the country. Communist rule was restored as was strong political dependence on the Soviet Union.

In 1977, as cultural and economic losses mounted, a group of dissidents issued a call for new freedoms under the name Charter 77. It was this movement that was responsible for the so-called Velvet Revolution of November 1989, which saw one of the signatories of Charter 77, playwright Václav Havel (b. 1936), become the country's new president.

In 1990, at the request of the Slovaks, the country's name was changed once again to the Czech and Slovak Federal Republic. But the name change proved to be insufficient recognition of the cultural and historical differences between the two peoples and, after extended political wrangling, both Czechs and Slovaks agreed to split the country into independent entities.

Structure of the National Theatre Community

Prior to 1945, theatre activity in Czechoslovakia was sponsored by a wide variety of sources including the state, municipalities, cooperatives and private producers. In June 1945, however, an official state decree formally abolished the concept of private theatrical production, nationalized all theatre buildings and moved professional theatres under the exclusive management of state and cooperative bodies.

In 1948, parliament passed another theatre law (replacing one that dated back to 1850) which legalized the new directions in this field. For most theatre artists, the initial changes appeared to be for the good. Among other things, social standards improved significantly and, in just a few years, a wide-ranging network of professional theatres was created. In the largest cities – Prague and Bratislava – highly subsidized, multi-ensemble theatres came into being; in smaller cities, single-ensemble but still highly subsidized companies began operating with the responsibility of touring within their regions. Even small villages were visited by the state-sponsored Vesnické divadlo (Village Theatre) which operated between 1945 and 1960 and which between 1954 and 1960 also had a German ensemble. In 1951, the state also supported the founding of a Polish-language theatre in Český Těšín.

Under this system, the state took responsibility for up to 80 per cent of a theatre's costs. In return, a theatre was required to produce a certain number of performances per season. In addition, the state provided capital for long-term development, the refurbishing of theatre buildings and even for the construction of new ones.

Through the federal Ministry of Culture (till 1968; during 1969–92, the Czech Ministry of Culture and the Slovak Ministry of Culture), grants were given to local authorities which controlled both theatrical budgets and their artistic profiles. The local authorities also had to approve all personnel appointments at the theatres, whether of artistic directors or actors. Once approved, the artists were usually put on long-term contracts which severely limited movement between theatres. The contracts themselves corresponded closely to work codes in force generally across the country. Salaries were based on an artist's education, professional training and experience but were significantly influenced by their political conformity. Traditionally ticket prices were kept very low (about one hour's wage) to allow the greatest access to the theatre for the greatest number of people.

Right across the system, the state (with the help of shadow operations) maintained strong censorship until the political changes of 1989. Leading positions were almost invariably filled by members of the Communist Party, often with access to secret information. During the 1970s and 1980s, this turned into a directive system with ingenious bureaucratic precautions. Theatres were told to produce within a very narrow range of plays; specific plays were impossible to stage; and every employee of a theatre was studied for 'political integrity'.

The overall system – despite minor changes in 1957 and 1978 – essentially remained unchanged until 1989 when all forms of censorship were abolished. In the early 1990s, however, the country's many theatres were still trying to find a new system of state support which would work effectively and without state control. With these many changes, only a few companies remained under the direct sponsorship of the state; most others were turned over to municipal sponsorship. Still others were operating on a private sponsorship or commercial basis.

The same situation was true for the country's substantial Hungarian ethnic minority which had permanent professional companies in Komárno and Košice with Ukrainians also having a subsidized company at Prešov.

Alongside the professional theatre, amateur theatre also boasted a long tradition in both Czech and Slovak territories.

This said, the transformation of the economy in the early 1990s, the accompanying rise in the cost of living, and the political problems between Czechs and Slovaks, were producing serious declines in theatre attendance all across the country making long-term planning for everyone working in theatre extremely difficult.

Field researchers and staff

(See also CZECH REPUBLIC and SLOVAK REPUBLIC)

DENMARK

The first plays written in the Danish language date to the end of the fifteenth century and use Medieval Morality and scholastic plays as their model. During that same period, however, most of Europe was already moving away from ecclesiastical traditions and beginning to develop newer dramatic forms. From this single example, it becomes clear that there has long been a delay in mainstream European culture reaching this small Scandinavian country in the northwest corner of Europe, with the peninsula Jylland (Jutland) the only fixed link to the continent. Composed of more than 500 islands, of which Fyn and Sjaelland (Zealand) are the largest, Denmark (and its theatre) – though continental traditions have always been obvious – has at the same time developed original features which have made it more than just a miniature version of larger and more dominant cultures.

Historically, the relationship with the European mainland goes far back in time. Between the ninth and twelfth centuries – the so-called Viking period – Danish warriors regularly attacked the European coast. By the twelfth century, however, the Danes had themselves been converted to Christianity and their dreams of European domination had been replaced by peaceful trading voyages. The history of Denmark as a sovereign state dates back to about the tenth century.

Today, Denmark (not including Greenland) with its land area of 43,000 square kilometres (16,600 square miles) is the smallest of the five Scandinavian countries, with Norway nearly eight times larger and Sweden some ten times larger in size. But Denmark's population is greater than that of Norway and about half that of Sweden. Copenhagen, the capital, remains the largest city in all of Scandinavia.

With its population of 5.1 million (1990), Denmark has long been one of the tiniest linguistic regions of Europe. Though Danish is the official language, most Danes also speak English and/or German. Because learning a foreign language has been so important in Denmark's history, foreign cultural influences have been brought into the country.

Just as the Latin drama of the Catholic church was the main model for Danish drama until the Lutheran reformation of 1536, the Danish theatre in the centuries that followed took its main inspiration from German, English, Dutch and French models. Touring groups from these countries regularly visited Danish royal castles during this time.

The first Danish public theatre was built in Copenhagen in 1663 by a Dutchman who had received special permission from King Frederik I (1609–70) to build a permanent stage for these many touring companies. Unfortunately, the economic base for his *Schouwburg* turned out to be rather weak. The theatre quickly went bankrupt and in 1666 the building was destroyed.

In 1722, a second theatre was opened, this one created through the efforts of a French actor, René Magnon de Montaigu. Montaigu came to the court of Christian V (1646–99) in 1686 as head of a French theatre company but the company was dismissed when a new king, Frederik IV (1671–1730), came to the throne. Frederik preferred opera singers to actors and brought in an opera troupe from Germany. As compensation for his company's dismissal, however, Montaigu was given permission to open a new theatre where Danish plays as well as foreign plays could be performed. At the same time, Montaigu initiated the first training for Danish actors.

Montaigu's new theatre opened on 23 September 1722 in Lille Grønnegade (Little Green

Street) in Copenhagen with a performance of Molière's *L'Avare* (*The Miser*) in a Danish translation. Only three days later, a totally new Danish comedy was premièred, *Den politiske Kandestøber* (*The Political Tinker*). This was the first of a series of comedies written by the great Norwegian-born writer Ludvik Holberg (1684–1754).

Holberg, a professor at the University of Copenhagen, used a combination of French and Italian comic forms. Unlike the plays of Molière, however, which were highly polished, Holberg's plays were plain, full of common sense and with a matter-of-fact tone. They spoke less to regal audiences in the new theatre than to the common people. Immensely popular then and even today, the plays have not only formed the backbone of Danish theatre but also set the Danish linguistic style while preaching a philosophy of moderation.

Montaigu's theatre, unfortunately, was forced to close in 1728 because of a fire that destroyed most of the Danish capital. Before the theatre could reopen, the pietist king, Christian VI (1699–1746) had succeeded his father and the building was entirely demolished. No new theatre was built again until the accession of the next king, Frederik V (1723–66).

Frederik V's theatre opened on 18 December 1748 and, after a short period of private ownership, was taken under direct royal patronage with the king assuming full responsibility for it. Known from that time as the Kongelige Teater (Royal Theatre), the same building was used until 1874, when a new theatre was opened only a few metres from the old one.

Outside Copenhagen, the city of Odense saw its first theatre built in 1795. In the decades that followed, many other major cities saw theatres go up as well.

It can be fairly said that until 1849 – the year when the country's absolute monarchy was replaced by a constitutional one – the history of the Danish theatre was essentially the history of the Royal Theatre. In 1849, the Royal Theatre's various privileges were subsumed into a federal and municipal grant system which, in principle, opened the possibility of operating a theatre to anyone.

Perhaps the most important change in connection with the Royal Theatre's transition into a 'national' theatre had to do with the notion of subsidy and its cost to the state. The majority of the parliamentarians of the time came from outside the capital and were not considered to be part of the cultural elite. Most therefore argued

that the bulk of theatrical financing should come from the municipality and suggested that the state should turn the operation over to a private corporation, a point of view still occasionally heard today.

Another argument had to do with the repertoire. Should the theatre continue doing mixed programmes involving spoken drama, ballet and opera or should these forms be offered on different evenings, perhaps in different theatres? Mixed programmes, in fact – often on the same evening – continued until the 1960s.

Many new theatres did open after the changeover of the Royal Theatre's status, most staging comedies, operettas and revues. The first to open was the Casino in 1848, followed by the Folkteateret (People's Theatre) in 1857, the Dagmar Theatre in 1883, the Nørrebro Theatre in 1886 and the Ny Teater (New Theatre) in 1908.

Outside the capital, most large cities were also building or establishing theatres for local amateurs as well as for the touring companies whose numbers were steadily growing during the nineteenth century. Two of the oldest are the Helsingør Theatre built in 1817 (since moved and rebuilt in the museum town of Århus) and the Rønne Theatre built in 1823 on the island of Bornholm and still used for summer performances.

In 1878, Ålborg, the largest city in the northern part of Jutland, became home to one of the largest stages outside the capital. This made it possible for some of the major touring groups to play extended seasons (as long as six months) outside Copenhagen. Århus, located in the eastern part of Jutland and the country's second-largest city, opened its first theatre in 1900 and was calling upon an active group of local players right from the beginning.

The city of Odense started building another new theatre in 1914 for its regional company. The company was later challenged by groups working in even larger, more comfortable and privately owned buildings in the city.

Throughout the twentieth century, the basic framework of Danish theatre did not change significantly from that of the nineteenth century, although the Casino was torn down in 1939 after movie theatres had made its repertoire of folksy melodramas and operettas obsolete. Also disappearing at this time was the Dagmar Theatre whose repertoire of contemporary foreign dramas made it a significant competitor for the Royal.

A popular revue theatre, the Apollo, opened

in 1931 in Copenhagen but was destroyed in January 1945 by Danish Nazis in revenge for bombings by the resistance. By war's end, the Danish theatre scene had pretty much been returned to what it was prior to the war.

By 1955, the government found itself subsidizing up to 50 per cent of the operating budgets of the various regional theatres with municipalities covering the other half. This practice became law in 1963 when Denmark passed its first official Theatre Act. As well, provisions were included at the time covering grants to touring theatre companies, a move resulting in the amalgamation of three different touring groups – each from a different political and education grouping – into a single national touring company called the Danske Teater (Danish Theatre).

Though the law covered only regional theatres, other theatres in the capital found themselves under financial pressure in the mid-1950s, and five different companies closed between 1954 and 1962. In 1970, a revision to the Act made it possible for smaller companies also to receive government funding if they sold tickets as part of a seasonal, multi-theatre package.

The new Act rescued many of these groups including many significant companies which started in the 1960s such as the Fiolteatret in Copenhagen (founded in 1962), the Svalegangen (Gallery) in Aarhus (1963), Jomfru Ane (Virgin Ane) in Aalborg (1967) and Banden (The Gang) in Odense in 1969.

The new legal situation also aided the country's largest private theatre, the Ny Teater (1,007 seats) which also had found itself in 1971 on the brink of closing because of a major operating deficit. By becoming part of the new group and selling season tickets, the theatre immediately became eligible for government funding and was quickly able to re-establish its operations.

In 1973, still another revision to the Act extended financial support on this basis to all theatres in the country.

At the end of the 1970s, these statutory provisions were being used to allow, for instance, Copenhagen's theatres to form themselves into a single large group called simply the Greater Metropolitan Regional Stage. As well, the Danske Teater and the Jyske Opera (Jutland Opera) became members of a group of touring companies known as the Rejsende Landsteater (Touring Country Theatre).

Only the Royal Theatre remained independent, with its budgets having to be approved on an annual basis by the national parliament. This situation remained in effect until 1990.

Structure of the National Theatre Community

Because Danish theatres are all part of municipal, regional or national groupings, most Danish companies operate within strictly defined administrative structures. Seasons – generally September to June – have to be planned far in advance and are usually limited to three or four productions per year per company. Rehearsals are usually between eight and twelve weeks.

Most actors work on per-show or per-season contracts. Actors working on longer-term contracts tend to be found only at the Royal Theatre and at the major regional stages.

Since the introduction of these administratively large theatre groupings, new approaches in ticket arrangements have also come into play. The administrative centre for group sales is a cultural organization called Arte which offers theatregoers tickets to all the groups, in this case in the capital, and can tailor season ticket packages to allow theatregoers to see many different companies on one subscription. Outside Copenhagen, ninety-three different local theatre societies have come together to make similar ticket purchasing arrangements. Known as Danmarks Teaterforening (Danish Theatre Organization), it arranges season packages involving various touring groups.

The theory behind such structures, of course, is an attempt to widen the net of those interested in theatre. Recent studies, however, have shown that audience composition has not changed significantly over the years. The largest part of the theatregoing public is still composed of the well educated, the affluent, the middle aged and the middle class. The new ticket purchase arrangements have simply allowed the same people to attend more frequently.

County theatres – those which are neither national, regional nor private – are exceptions to this ticket arrangement and their funding is divided evenly between the various counties and the state. Feeling the economic pinch during the 1980s, the counties began rethinking their level of financial support as the 1990s began.

The most highly funded theatre in the country has traditionally been the Royal Theatre with annual public funding in 1991–2 of 230 million kroner (about US$46 million). In the same year, Copenhagen's Greater Metropolitan Regional Theatre (made up of the ABC Theatre, the Avenue, the Betty Nansen, the People's Theatre, the New Theatre, the Riddersalen and the Rialto) had combined public funding of about a quarter of that amount, 60 million kroner. With the closing in 1991 of the Ny Teater, the overall sum was to be reduced further.

From 1992, the government decided to replace this type of funding with specific grants which must cover the overall operations at each theatre. This is good in many ways since it means that each theatre's board of directors finally has the freedom to set its own artistic priorities, something not easily done under the previous system.

Funding for the regional theatres as a whole equals some 90 million kroner while the Touring Theatre receives another 30 million. County theatres received 40 million in 1991–2 while the Touring Children's Theatre alone received some 12 million kroner.

Aside from these sums, the Ministry of Culture spends approximately another 15 million kroner on independent projects.

Entering the 1990s, public subsidy was averaging about 40 per cent of ticket prices which ranged from US$8 to US$38 at the Royal Theatre and from US$10 to US$30 at the various regional theatres. As such, the lowest individual ticket prices were about the same as those being charged for films.

Looked at historically, it is interesting to note that when the Royal Theatre opened in its present building in 1874, the cheapest seats were equivalent to the daily wage of a skilled labourer. Today, the same seats are barely half an hour's wage. The figure, of course, is somewhat deceptive since behind today's ticket price is an enormous amount of public subsidy.

Danish actors are members of the Dansk Skuespiller Forbund (Danish Actors' Association) while writers generally join the playwrights' federation, Danske Dramatikeres Forbund. Designers are members of Sammenslutningen af Danske Scenografer (Association of Danish Scenographers) with backstage personnel connected to the Teatertekniker Forbundet (Union of Theatrical Technicians). In 1992, there were approximately 1,400 members in the actors' union.

There are two national/regional festivals held in the country each year with the biggest one held each September in Århus.

Artistic Profile

Companies

In the mid-1960s most inspiration came from the United States, with its hippie and beat cultures, and groups like the Living Theatre, Open Theatre, Firehouse Theatre, Bread and Puppet Theatre and La Mama became models for other theatres. In 1966 a Copenhagen group was established on this foundation. They chose the name Christianshavnsgruppen; it became the first Danish theatre laboratory.

However, it was not the first theatre laboratory in Denmark. In 1966 a student of Jerzy Grotowski's, the Italian director Eugenio Barba (b. 1936), moved his own theatre group from dubious conditions in Oslo, Norway, to a permanent place in Holstebro, Denmark, and even obtained grants. This unique situation was due neither to Barba nor to his Odin Theatre, but to the simple fact that Holstebro, in fierce competition with the neighbouring town of Herning, needed an artistic trump card (Herning seemed to have a monopoly on modern painting and sculpture). The Odin was suggested as that card and in just a few years, the town became known as what has since been called a 'cultural model'. The town had clearly obtained an artistic attraction in the Odin that made it shine both nationally and internationally.

Given this background, Barba might have seized the opportunity to create behind closed doors in an art-for-art's-sake environment. However, he did not. He built his theatre laboratory in a strictly Grotowskian spirit – experimental work based on physical and psychological training – while at the same time arranging Danish, Scandinavian and international theatre seminars and guest performances. Simultaneously he published works by some of the most influential theorists and experimenters of theatre in the twentieth century – Piscator, Meyerhold, Eisenstein and Grotowski. Between 1965 and 1974, he published the journal *Theory and Technique of Theatre*. While the Odin Theatre's performances, with their fascinating, sensual and sometimes anxiety-provoking set designs and body language, appealed only to a limited audience, the journal, the publishing business and especially the seminars were directed to a large and mixed crowd of actors, directors, dramatists, students, teachers and theatre aficionados. A three-day Dario Fo seminar in 1980, for example, managed to attract more than 1,000 people to Holstebro from all over Scandinavia.

The Odin Theatre has toured widely, particularly in southern Europe and South America, where the group has shown great ability in crossing cultural and human borders. Though only a few Danish theatre groups have been directly inspired by Barba and the work of his group, many are greatly indebted to the company's social and artistic commitment which constantly radiates from the activities in Holstebro.

Another well-known theatre group has been the curious company called Solvognen (Sun Wagon). Identified with the Copenhagen free city of Christiania (the abolished Bådsmandstræde Barracks, occupied by squatters in 1971), Solvognen was anything but a typical theatre group. Though it participated in theatre discussions and seminars and even staged some 'traditional' performances, the mark of the group was that of an extended collective, individual anonymity and a large but loosely defined membership. Its plays were created by a core group living in Christiania, and its mammoth productions were staged in the Grey Hall, one of the huge shops of the abolished barracks. Working without municipal or governmental grants, everything was done by volunteers or unemployed people.

In its first years of existence – the early 1970s – the group performed something best described as street and action theatre. Solvognen saw everything – political events, oppression, wars or demonstrations – as an opportunity for a play, an action or a happening. The city, the street or an institution was always used as stage and set. Its spectators were huge audiences of passers-by, merchants or participants in the event.

The dramaturgy of Solvognen was as simple as it was classical: the prerequisite for each play, happening or action was a large audience. The group went looking for it wherever it might be, in the street, in the square or through radio. And it usually succeeded in finding it.

Another theatre of note outside the establishment has been Kirsten Delholm (b. 1945) and Per Flink Basse's (b. 1949) Billedstofteater (Pictorial Theatre). Since 1977, the group has created unusual events in streets and squares with silent formations and parades. A good deal of surrealist ambiguity is hidden in its work as well as some elements of the absurd. But the Billedstofteater is not alone. British-born Trevor Davis (b. 1949), a long-time resident of Denmark, presented in 1980 a Festival of Fools, an impressive international meeting of corporeal mime and dance theatre. The festival was repeated annually thereafter with dancers, clowns and one year a *fakir*, who hung himself with hooks above Købmagergade (a busy street in Copenhagen). For some years after that, Davis also directed an Århus Festival Week, which offered an even wider selection of theatre, dance, music and performances. In 1990 he returned to the capital as director of the new theatre Kanonhallen, established in part of the abolished Østerbro Barracks. It is a flexible playhouse used by various groups for specific projects.

By the 1980s, Denmark's avant-garde had become quite well known and charter air flights from 1987 enabled everyone with artistic ambitions who wanted to be seen in New York to travel easily. Many groups started to tour and international experiences in dance and theatre washed over these many 'aspiring artists' as they were called in government cultural-economic reports. This international 'wash' has continued into the 1990s.

Dramaturgy

Naturalism dominated Danish playwriting in the immediate post-war period and the style was given new life by the influence of British kitchen-sink naturalism in the late 1950s. In general, Danish playwriting was imitative rather than innovative during this time.

Changes began to be felt in the early 1960s when the usually conservative Danish Radio began to commission new plays and radio theatre started to function as a workshop for the development of new writers. Another influence at this time was the Student Theatre which quickly picked up the plays of the French absurdists. Even summer revues (played in various Danish resorts) began to take on a hard satirical edge and eventually made their way to television where they found large audiences.

Perhaps the most prominent dramatist of the 1960s, 1970s and 1980s was Ernst Bruun Olsen (b. 1923) who, after a number of successful radio plays, had an enormous success at the Royal Theatre in 1962 with a musical revue called, in both Danish and English, *Teenagerlove*. The script focused on the creation of a pop singing idol.

Olsen was an actor before he began writing and later became a prominent director especially of his own works. Though he has called his plays folk-melodramas, there are deeper themes at work and one can see in them an updating of the ideas of the playwright Kjeld Abell (1910–61).

Memories of ideals deserted in the pursuit of economic security, small worlds versus bigger ones – often built around the music of earlier periods – are repeated themes in plays such as *Bal i Den Borgerlige* (*Dance at the Pub*, 1966) and *Da Jazzen kom til Byen* (*When Jazz Came to Town*, 1982). Olsen deals with the nature of art, and plays with theatrical reality in his comedy about Holberg and his theatre, *Den poetiske Raptus* (*The Poetic Craze*, 1976); with van Gogh in *Postbudet fra Arles* (*The Mailman from Arles*, 1980); and with theatre director Betty Nansen (1873–1943) in *Betty Nansen på Betty Nansen* (*Betty Nansen on Betty Nansen*, 1990).

During the 1970s, the favoured theatrical style featured political debate with Leif Petersen (b. 1934) its major exemplar. After several radio plays and the production of a number of one-act stage plays at the Student Theatre, Petersen had a breakthrough at the Gallery in Århus with *Alting og et Posthus* (*Everything and a Post Office*, 1969), a grotesque realistic comedy about the middle-class dreams of people at the bottom of the social ladder.

Ernst Bruun Olsen's 1962 Royal Theatre production of his *Teenagerlove*, designed by Helge Refn.
Photo: Tórgen Mydtskov.

Throughout the 1970s, Petersen's politically rooted scripts were played regularly by the touring theatres, and even the Royal Theatre staged his work successfully. In 1972, they did *Pengene* (*Straight Talk*) as a 250th anniversary celebration of the opening of Holberg's first theatre. The play, with each succeeding production, has proved its staying power as a witty and theatrically imaginative exposure of the brutal, class-dominated society, to which Holberg, despite his satirical attacks, ultimately submitted.

Petersen has also long been a spokesperson for the training of dramatists, first as Chair of the Dramatic Studio (started in 1976 by the playwrights' federation, Danske Dramatikeres Forbund) and later as Chair of the Ministry of Culture's Theatre Council. Even so, it is still rare for dramatists in Denmark to have genuine on-the-job experience. The closest one gets to this is the playwright-in-residence programme started by the Århus Theatre in 1977.

The major innovator in Danish drama during the 1980s was Sten Kaalø (b. 1945) who was the first of the dramatists to be in-residence at Århus. He wrote associative, psychologically investigative poetic dramas, his major plays include *Komedie i Grænselandet* (*Comedy at the Border*, 1977) about a meeting between two well-known Danish poets; *Alfa and Omega* (1980) about the painter Edvard Munch; *The Giraffe of New Orleans* (1981), an anarchic comedy; and *Berninis Børn* (*Bernini's Children*, 1986) a black comedy of war.

Kaalø's successor as dramatist-in-residence at Århus, Svend Åge Madsen (b. 1939), is a novelist who has managed to transfer to the theatre the fascinating philosophical arguments of his novels. His works, both figuratively and directly, connect with the plays of Luigi Pirandello, particularly in *Nøgne Masker* (*Naked Masks*, 1987) where Madsen has Pirandello meeting Freud. Two other Madsen plays are also intellectual experiments – *Det Sidste Suk* (*The Last Breath*, 1986) and *Svar Udbedes* (*Answer Requested*, 1987).

Heino Byrgesen

Directors, Directing and Production Styles

While Ernst Bruun Olsen has been his own congenial director and while several younger writers have also tried their hands at directing their own plays, most Danish directors since World War II have rarely been the midwives of new plays. One exception has been Klaus Hoffmeyer (b. 1938) who began his career in 1961 by staging plays by the Danish absurdist, Jess Ørnsbo (b. 1932). As a director, Hoffmeyer has been a provocateur of sorts, especially for Ørnsbo, and together they have created a number of productions of plays which often unconventionally challenge the more popular theatre. Working mostly at the Århus Theatre in the 1970s and 1980s, he later had great success with *Fra regnormenes Liv* (*From the Lives of Worms*) by the Swedish Per Olov Enquist at the Royal Theatre (1981) and with his staging of Wagner's *Der Ring des Nibelungen* at the Jutland Opera between 1984 and 1987. Another success was his production of Rainer Werner Fassbinder's *Der Müll, die Stadt und der Tod* (*Garbage, City and Death*) at the Mammoth Theatre in Copenhagen in 1987.

Sam Besekow (b. 1911) in the 1930s belonged to the experimental avant-garde. By the 1990s, he was seen as the Danish director who was doing most to protect traditional approaches mostly by using stars. This was clear even in his 1991 production of Dürrenmatt's *Der Besuch der alten Dame* (*The Visit*) at the Aveny Theatre.

Kaspar Rostrup (b. 1940) is still another important Danish director who has made a theatrical virtue out of not accepting the limitations of the spaces he works in (especially proscenium houses). He has done this both by finding justifications in the text in plays such as *Peer Gynt*, which he staged at the Ålborg Theatre in 1970, and in what might be called spatially free, total theatre productions that he staged while artistic director of the Gladsaxe Theatre between 1984 and 1991 starting with Holberg's *Niels Klim*.

Peter Langdal (b. 1957) is a director with a sense of the unusual who first came to note in 1973 with a production called *Plys og Plastik* (*Plush and Plastic*) utilizing the flexible theatrical space of the Gladsaxe Theatre. His staging of Holberg's *Erasmus Montanus* at the Betty Nansen Theatre the following year solidified his growing reputation for the new and daring.

Langdal's productions often deal with the conflict between mere knowledge and common sense and tend to have a circus bent to them. This shows through in both new works and productions of the classics such as *A Midsummer Night's Dream* (1986) and *Peer Gynt* (1989). In 1986, Langdal staged Holberg's

225

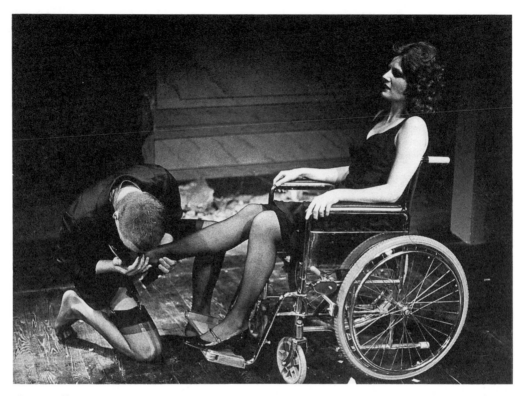

Klaus Hoffmeyer's 1987 Mammoth Theatre production of Rainer Werner Fassbinder's
Garbage, City and Death, designed by Bjarne von Solberg.
Photo: Freddy Tornberg Film/Video.

Jeppe på Bierget (*Jeppe of the Hill*) at the Dramaten in Stockholm and, in 1990, Shakespeare's *A Winter's Tale* at the Central-teatret in Oslo. His love of slapstick comedy and apparently improvised gags hides a very firm analysis of text, especially in classical dramas.

Birthe Johansen

Music Theatre

Between 1940 and 1990, more than eighty productions of new Danish operas were seen on national stages, television and radio with more than forty of them staged between 1970 and 1990. From the 1940s to about 1970, most of these were large in scale; since 1970, the chamber form has been the most favoured.

The major producer in the period from 1940 to 1957 was the Royal Theatre in Copenhagen which staged fourteen new operas. In the seven-year period between 1957 and 1964, however, it staged none. During the same seven-year period, in fact, the only new operas staged in the country were done at the Student's Opera in Copenhagen – *Kniven* (*The Knife*) by Vagn Holmboe (b. 1909) – and at the Music Academy of Jutland – *Mette* by Bent Lorentzen (b. 1935), the most active music theatre composer of the time.

Between 1965 and 1970, new Danish operas were again staged at the Royal. Among them are *Historien om en moder* (*History of a Mother*) by Thomas Koppel (b. 1944), *Belisa* by Poul Rovsing Olsen (b. 1922), *The Labyrinth* by Per Nørgaard (b. 1932), *Udstilling* (*Exhibition*) by Ole Schmidt (b. 1928), *Macbeth* by Herman

Koppel (b. 1908) and *Faust 3* by Niels Viggo Bentzon (b. 1919) in a visiting production from the Kieler Opera.

Between 1970 and 1990, most new operas were again staged outside the Royal with the Jutland Opera leading the way with fifteen productions.

There are many possible reasons for the Royal's decision to move away from new opera but one of them was certainly the nature of Nørgaard's work, *The Labyrinth*. Audiences did not seem to understand the advanced tonal language while more avant-garde musicians saw it as a genuflection to conventional opera.

In the years since 1970, Danish music drama also moved into many new areas: happenings, instrumental theatre, dance theatre, film music, television music and opera for national tours. One such experiment was *Sonata for Four Opera Singers* by Mogens Winkel Holm (b. 1936), produced by the Society for Young Music Artists in Copenhagen.

In Århus, the Opera Group staged several new works including *Nice Day Today, n'est-ce pas, Ibsen* by Henning Christiansen (b. 1932), *Bulen* (*The Bump*) by Svend Nielsen (b. 1937) and *Skyggen af en drøm* (*Shadow of a Dream*) by Erik Jørgensen (b. 1912). Some of these works were later shown on television and heard on radio. In total, seventeen operas by contemporary Danish composers have been shown on television since 1960.

Disappointingly, very few of the new Danish operas have been given second productions. Even those that have been staged only once have had generally limited runs: only fifteen have been performed more than ten times; only five more than twenty times. Few have been toured to other theatres.

Given this situation, it is little wonder that audiences, especially in the capital, have the impression that the production of contemporary Danish opera is a marginal matter. However, it appeared that both the Royal and the Jutland Opera were willing to undertake new productions on a regular basis again in the 1990s should additional funds become available.

Mogens Andersen

Dance Theatre

For more than 200 years, Copenhagen's Royal Ballet has had a virtual monopoly on dance theatre in Denmark and the name most closely associated with the company has been that of August Bournonville (1805–79). Bournonville's romantic ballets are still staged regularly and remain a popular part of the repertoire.

Modernization of the Royal Ballet began in 1932 with the hiring of Harald Lander (1905–71). Lander introduced the newer Russian school of ballet training and, for the first time since Bournonville, the company engaged its own resident choreographer. Lander put his own clear mark on the Royal's repertoire in the 1930s and 1940s and even recreated a number of Bournonville's ballets, the most important being *Étude* with music by Knudaage Riisager (1897–1974) inspired by Czerny. This ballet, a choreographic fantasy about ballet training, was premièred in 1948 and has subsequently been staged in many parts of the world.

Lander left the company in 1951 due to policy disagreements with the company and was soon hired as the ballet master of the Paris Opera. Before leaving the company, however, he initiated a ballet festival (1950) where international audiences became aware of the well-preserved Danish dance tradition. This festival also helped make the Royal Ballet's international reputation.

As well, Lander hired the Russian-born teacher, Vera Volkova, in his last year with the company and she became responsible for training a whole new generation of Danish soloists. The leading ballet masters through the 1950s and early 1960s seemed to have no real ambition to put their own choreographic marks on the repertoire, though both Niels Bjørn Larsen (b. 1913) and Frank Schaufuss (b. 1921) did create several ballets. Foreign choreographers also began to work with the company at this time.

In 1955, the Russian-born George Balanchine staged *Concerto Barocco* and *The Sleepwalker* with the company; that same year, the English choreographer Frederick Ashton premièred his *Romeo and Juliet* to music by Prokofiev. The following year, Balanchine began work with the company on *Serenade* and *Apollon Musagetes*.

The year 1957 saw the creation of one of the landmarks of Danish ballet when the Swedish choreographer Birgit Cullberg staged

Månerenen (*Reindeer on the Moon*) to music by Knudaage Riisager. Over the next few years, Cullberg became the company's unofficial choreographer-in-residence and produced enormous successes with ballet versions of *Miss Julie* and *Medea*. As late as 1985, she staged an enormously popular *Pulcinella* with the troupe. In 1960, French choreographer Roland Petit staged *Carmen* and the English choreographer Kenneth MacMillan put together a popular evening of three short pieces – *Dances Concertantes, Under the Earth* and *Solitaire*.

In 1963, dancer Flemming Flindt (b. 1936) made his choreographic début with a television version of *Enetime*, a work based on Eugène Ionesco's one-act play, *The Lesson*. The following year he was invited to produce the ballet at the Royal Theatre. In 1966, he was named ballet master of the Royal and quickly began including a number of his own works in the repertoire. Flindt's modern dance theatre had a significant influence in bringing a new and younger audience to its productions. Especially

important in this regard was *Dødens Triumf* (*The Triumph of Death*), a work from 1972 with music by Savage Rose. Flindt also created new productions of *Swan Lake* and *The Nutcracker*. He ended his time at the Royal in 1978 with a personal reinterpretation of a nearly forgotten Bournonville ballet, *The Toreador*.

The Flindt period is remembered as well for the inclusion of works by a number of important foreign choreographers such as the American Paul Taylor (*Aureole*, 1968), which showed the company in bare feet for the first time, the Mexican-born José Limón (*Morens Pavane/The Moor's Pavane*, 1971), the American Glen Tetley (*Pierre Lunaire*, 1968, *Le Sacre du Printemps*, 1978, and *Firebird*, 1981) and the English Antony Tudor (*Lilac Garden*, 1970).

John Neumeier from the Hamburg Ballet staged a *Romeo and Juliet* with the company in 1974 and he returned to stage another full-length ballet, *A Midsummer Night's Dream*, in 1980. Neumeier also premièred the full-length ballet, *Amleth*, in 1985.

Flemming Flindt's 1964 Royal Theatre production of his *Enetime*, designed by Bernard Daydé.

In 1978, Flindt was replaced by Henning Kronstam (b. 1934), who returned to Bournonville for inspiration, especially in 1979, the centennial of Bournonville's death. Kronstam wanted to strengthen the company's ability to handle the classical repertoire as well and in that same year, Erik Bruhn (1928–86) staged a new production of *Giselle*.

During the 1980s, a number of younger dancers and choreographers – some from Denmark, some from abroad – found their way to the Royal Ballet but none really managed to put their mark on the repertoire during the decade.

Heino Byrgesen

Theatre for Young Audiences
Puppet Theatre

Until the 1950s, children's theatre in Denmark was used either for educational purposes or for simple entertainment. The educational theatre took place mostly in schools where groups such as Danish Schoolstage saw to it that the next generation of audiences became familiar with the classics of Danish drama: Holberg, Henrik Hertz (1798–1870) and Johan Ludvig Heiberg (1791–1860), to name just a few. These were solid performances but the repertoire was very narrow, neither up-to-date nor in touch with the lives of young people.

The entertainment-style children's theatre mostly took place during school holidays, especially at Christmas time, when 'real' theatres – which never normally gave children a second thought – put on stage everything that adults like to think of as appropriate for children, most especially talking animals and flowers.

By the 1960s, these two types of theatre for children – despite some attempts by Danish Schoolstage to introduce new Danish dramas to their young audiences – had deteriorated almost completely and the best one could hope for were well-done dramatizations of classic children's books such as *Treasure Island*.

It was Finnish-born Tove Jansson with her Mumi-goblins and Swedish-born Astrid Lindgren with her Pippi Longstocking who made the first breakthroughs in Danish children's literature. The work of both these writers was based on a new type of children's literary creation, one which was free of any superior point of view and one which created its own artistic models.

In Danish theatre, the Jansson–Lindgren model was taken up in the 1960s by Jytte Abildstrøm (b. 1934) and Vibeke Gaardmand (1940–81), who separately created two unique companies for young audiences. Their work was not intended to be especially revolutionary but

rather just an alternative of sorts to the old-fashioned styles. The work had several basic premises: to let children themselves focus on the world either seriously or with a sense of fun; to create a series of performances about children's lives involving their own conflicts, dreams and hopes; to create a style that used the child's sense of wonder and the child's own reactions without talking down to them; and to connect fantasy to both reality and the child's own psychology.

In creating such a theatre, improvisation became a useful tool and much improvised theatre for young people was seen in Denmark in the 1970s. The resulting shows were characterized by a recognizable social realism and a willingness to debate issues. Productions tended to focus on the rigidity of the school system and on children's conflicts in the home and school.

During the 1980s, such social engagements continued but the style and content evolved into a more mythic framework using fantasy and non-realistic settings. In such work, the child's inner and outer worlds were able to come together.

As of 1993, there were some one hundred Danish theatres for young audiences spread across the country. Among the most important were Theatre Artibus (founded in 1969), the Theatremill (1974), the Umbrella Theatre (1968) run by Ray Nusselein according to his ideas of playing for children and his experiments using fine art as a model for his shows, Månegoegl (Funny Moon, 1981), the Jytte Abildstrøm Theatre (1970), Group 38 (1972), Theatre Terra Nova (1985) and Theatre-in-Balance (1987). Each of these companies was creating theatre with wit, depth and dramatic quality.

At the same time, the older style of children's theatre still appears regularly. Most of these

The 1992 Jytte Abildstrøm Theatre production of her *Mother's Day*, designed by Nils Goetzche Frederiksen.

traditional groups now call themselves 'family theatre' and actually make money, which is more than many of the more contemporary groups manage to do.

But it is clearly the contemporary groups which are connecting with audiences and which children themselves most want to see. Their themes remain strong and modern, each following its own ideas and each developing in its own unique way.

The Marionette Theatre is located in the King's Garden, Copenhagen. It is a small outdoor theatre combining children's and puppet theatre. Every year, when Copenhagen Commune's summer entertainment programme commences, the Marionette Theatre also has its première. And every year it becomes a small theatrical event in itself. To its credit, the Mari-

onette Theatre represents both a balance between tradition and renewal and the special relationship existing between children and adults that has characterized the best of Danish children's theatre in recent years.

The Marionette Theatre creates two productions during its summer season. Normally the first production is a teasing commentary on the established adult theatre's own theatrical events. The second production is often a specially conceived interpretation of a traditional work – Hans Christian Andersen, for example. In both productions it is the child's perspective on the world that is paramount in setting objectives for the direction and interpretation of these works.

Beth Juncker

Design

A new era on Danish stages began with the set designs of Svend Johansen (1890–1970). His visual language was unique and he joined a group of artists who signalled the breakthrough of modernism in Denmark. Johansen's interest in set design was sparked by a lengthy visit to Paris where his eye was caught by the Diaghilev-Ballet, with set design by Derain, Matisse and Picasso. Fuelled by these impressions, he gradually developed his own very personal style where shapes and colours formed an original musicality. His *commedia dell'arte* characters were unsurpassed in their rhythmic plasticity. These figures were later transferred to Holberg's gallery of comic characters where his most unique example could be seen in *Mascarade* at the Royal Theatre, 1954. Among the many sets Johansen did for the Royal Theatre were Ravel's *Bolero* (1942), Mozart's *Abduction from the Seraglio* (1936), Verdi's *Aïda* (1949) and Shakespeare's *As You Like It* (1951).

Among the modernists who followed him were the sophisticated Helge Refn (1908–85) and the brutally abstract Erik Nordgreen (1921–87). Refn, too, went to Paris and became a student of Fernand Léger; in the period 1929–31 he was at the Théâtre Pigalle with Louis Jouvet. In 1937 Refn won the Diplôme d'Honneur at the World Exhibition in Paris for a brilliant model of an experimental stage. Refn's means of expression were crystal clear: a picturesque structural language with a simple sophisticated and brilliant colour scheme. Behind the gracious, sometimes surrealistic style would often be a powerful severity. Among his memorable productions are Shaw's *Caesar and Cleopatra* (1945), Schiller's *Don Carlos* (1946), Albee's *Little Alice* (1966), Massenet's *Manon* (1969), Strindberg's *To Damascus* (1971) and Shaffer's *Amadeus* (1982).

With the death of Refn, the Gallic inspiration in Danish set design came to a temporary end.

Lars Juhl's 1988 Den Jyske Opera design for Richard Wagner's *Das Rheingold*, directed by Klaus Hoffmeyer.

The next generation found their main inspir-ation in Germany. Lars Juhl (b. 1943) was one of the first who went to Germany for his educa-tion; for three years he was a student at the Teo Otto School in Düsseldorf. The designs of Juhl are characterized by a tight stage composition with a classical perspective letting floor and depth appear as spacious as possible. Within a fixed frame the often exuberant imagination of Juhl then unfolds. Juhl created the set designs for the Royal Theatre's productions of Gershwin's *Porgy and Bess* (1970), Strindberg's *Erik XIV* (1974) and the Jutland Opera's *Der Ring des Nibelungen* (1983–7).

In the 1980s and 1990s Steffen Aarfing (b. 1955), educated at the Architectural School of the Art Academy, became one of the country's foremost designers. His background as an architect and his unerring sense of aes-thetics (influenced by the German expressionism of the 1980s) led to a renewal of Danish set design. His most remarkable productions have been Strauss's *Kalldeway Farce* (1983), Christopher Hampton's *Dangerous Liaisons* (1986), Fassbinder's *The Bitter Tears of Petra von Kant* (1989) and García Lorca's *Blood Wed-ding* (1992).

The National Theatre School has produced of late a group of very talented set designers. Among them are Nina Flagstad (b. 1957), Bente Lykke Møller (b. 1956) and Kim Witzel (b. 1956). All have shown an expressive figurative language in their work.

Bente Scavenius

Theatre Space and Architecture

Most Danish theatre buildings from the nineteenth century – proscenium houses all – are still in use although many of them have undergone transformations of one sort or another. In 1931, for instance, the Royal Theatre was given an annexe stage. The Royal's New Stage or, as it is more popularly known, the Birdhouse, opened that year in what became a combined radio and theatre building near the Royal's main theatre (though in 1945, Danish Radio left the building). Between 1983 and 1985, the entire theatre complex was renovated leaving the larger main stage for opera and ballet and the 1,000-seat New Stage almost exclusively for plays.

Other older theatres in the capital have also undergone renovations in recent years, mainly to reduce the number of seats and/or to expand the stage. The Avenue Theatre, opened in 1919 as the 800-seat Phoenix Theatre, reduced its seating to 400 in 1982. The Nørrebro Theatre in 1986–7 decreased its seating capacity from 920 to 600 while the People's Theatre in 1989–91 also decreased seating in its main stage to 615 while increasing its two secondary stages, the Hippodrome and the Snoreloftet (Loft) to 220 and 110 seats respectively.

The regional theatres too moved to the crea-tion of a series of annexe stages. Århus opened its 279-seat Scala Theatre in a former cinema in 1955 and soon after added a 110-seat basement Studio. The 480-seat Odense Theatre added an eighty-seat second stage called the Vaerkstedet (Workshop) in 1963. In 1986 the company added another 450-seat theatre, the Sukker-kogeriet (Sugar Factory) in an industrial area of the city. The 469-seat Ålborg Theatre added a fifty-seat basement stage in 1970 and in 1983 also built a 150-seat Little Stage.

Perhaps the most significant document to appear in Denmark in recent years related to theatre building was the 1969 Ministry of Culture Report no. 517. This report contains a whole series of recommendations for the crea-tion of new theatre spaces in the country. Its main premise is that the old fixed theatre spaces with defining proscenium arches are outdated. Calling for the separation between audiences and performers to be softened and new spatial relationships developed, the report urges stylistic flexibility as the foundation for the crea-tion of both new spaces and any renovations that might be undertaken.

One question not dealt with in the report was the ideal size of new theatre spaces. In a prac-tical way, however, Danish architects had been answering that question for a number of years simply by renovating the older spaces or creating new theatres out of former cinemas.

Nils Koppel (b. 1914), designer of the Gladsaxe Theatre in 1964, argued during the 1970s that there was a logical connection between a theatre's size and its technical stan-dards. The larger the theatre, said Koppel, the less intimacy there was, and less intimacy must be made up for by greater and more expensive technology.

During the 1970s and 1980s, smaller, more flexible and more intimate theatres were preferred to large ones. Even those that had earlier created 'fixed' smaller theatres began to renovate them in an effort to break down the rigid separation between stage and spectator.

As for the Royal, in 1978 the Ministry of Culture held an open competition for a new playhouse. Its thinking at the time was that what was needed was a large flexible stage of 750 to 900 seats and a second stage of at least 175 seats. However, such a stage was never built.

Between 1983 and 1986, the main stage of the Royal was renovated in an effort to make the theatre somewhat more flexible and to allow improvements in the theatre's technology.

Since the 1980s, a number of new spaces for touring theatres have gone up outside the capital. Most are multi-use facilities such as the Vordingborg Education Centre (built in 1980), the Morsø Highschool-College Theatre (1984) and the Kolding Theatre-Congress Cultural Building (1991). In all these new facilities, both stage and seating are movable.

Elin Rask

Training

Until the twentieth century, the training of Danish theatre professionals was exclusively practical. That is, there were no schools *per se* and training, such as it was, took place within the various companies. In 1959, Århus University began offering courses in dramatic literature and theatre history. Seven years later, Italian director Eugenio Barba began offering classes and seminars in Holstebro as part of his newly created Odin Theatre. That same year, the Christianshavn Group was formed and began offering workshops inspired by various American experimental models (the Living Theatre, the Open Theatre, Bread and Puppet, and La Mama).

During this same period, the Ministry of Culture began looking into the whole question of theatre training and in 1967 delivered a report calling for the creation of a national theatre academy in Copenhagen. Towards the end of 1968, the Statens Teaterskole (National Theatre School) was started by the ministry although most of the recommendations included in its report of the previous year were ignored.

As a result, when the National Theatre School opened – essentially to train actors, directors and designers – there were strong arguments about its direction and its relationship to the existing theatres in the country. At the root of this debate was the question of whether it was a training centre for the traditional theatre or whether it should act as a laboratory for new theatre forms and ideas, especially those coming from the United States and Poland.

In its early years under its first principal, actress Berthe Qvistgaard (b. 1910), an attempt was made to satisfy both viewpoints. Very quickly, many teachers and students left the school in protest. In 1979, Arne Skovhus (1932–83) became principal and the school achieved some stability by committing itself to traditional approaches. After Skovhus's death, actress Lone Hertz (b. 1939) became principal of the school and the National moved even further towards traditional approaches. This led to more in-fighting at the school and to confrontations with the Ministry of Culture. Hertz resigned in 1990 and, in 1991, the university scholar Olav Harsløf (b. 1945) became principal.

As of 1992, the National also added the training of theatre technicians while newer schools in Århus and Odense had begun to train actors.

Jytte Wiingaard

Criticism, Scholarship and Publishing

Danish theatre research is mainly done at the Institute of Theatre Scholarship at the University of Copenhagen and at the Institute of Dramaturgy at the University of Århus.

Torben Krogh (1895–1970) was the University of Copenhagen's first professor of theatre scholarship and was influenced by the German positivist traditions. Krogh tended to work from archaeological positions in reconstructing theatres of previous periods and wrote several important books about early Danish theatre, forming a strong base for ongoing research in the field. Krogh's research has been continued by Klaus Neiiendam (b. 1938) who has also written widely on Danish theatre history as well as on the theatre history of other European countries.

Since 1970, contemporary theatre itself has become a subject for researchers. Kela Kvam (b. 1931) has not only written about contemporary theatre generally in both Denmark and abroad but also organized festivals for politically committed group theatres. Another scholar working in this area is Bent Holm (b. 1946) who has written about the theatre of Dario Fo. Holm was also one of the people who introduced semiology into Danish theatre scholarship and effectively analysed *commedia dell'arte* from a semiological viewpoint in his 1991 study *Solkonge og Månekejser* (*King of the Sun and Emperor of the Moon*).

Inspired by American semiotic models, additional research is now going on in Copenhagen focusing on communicative aspects of theatre, radio and television as well as on audience reception.

Dramaturgical studies have been the main focus at Århus although research into educational drama has lately become another subject of interest. Århus has worked particularly closely with the nearby Odin Theatre in such areas as acting and performance analysis and the evolution of new dramatic forms. Research has also been done on cultural politics, audience composition and theatre for young audiences. In 1992, a two-volume *History of Danish Theatre* was published by a group of scholars from Århus and Copenhagen.

As for theatre reviewing in newspapers, the tradition goes back to 1748 with the opening of the Royal Theatre. Over the years, a tradition of relatively long written reviews developed and by the mid-twentieth century newspapers were regularly giving space to what could be called in-depth reviews in such papers as *Berlingske Tidende*.

Probably the most influential theatre reviewer after World War II was Svend Kragh-Jacobsen (1909–84), an aficionado of naturalism who was able to place the productions he saw into an historical perspective. He also combined theatre reviewing with research and criticism on ballet. Following Kragh-Jacobsen in the dance position at the newspaper was Erik Aschengreen (b. 1935) who also began teaching the first courses in theoretical dance education in the country at the University of Copenhagen. On the dramatic side, Kragh-Jacobsen was replaced by Jens Kistrup (b. 1925) whose criticism tended to be director-oriented and focused on the relationship between the theatrical event and society.

One critic particularly interested in the political group theatres was Henrik Lundgren (1948–90) who covered the field from the 1960s until his death.

Two no longer operating theatre magazines of note were *Harlekin* and the Odin Theatre's *Teatrets teori og Teknik* (*Theory and Technique of Theatre*), both published in the mid-1960s. No other journals have emerged to take their place.

Jytte Wiingaard
Translated by Hanne Lerdorf

Further Reading

Ascani, Karen, ed. *Teatro danese nel Novecento*. [Danish theatre in the twentieth century]. Biblioteca teatrale 41. Rome: Bulzoni, 1983. 125 pp.

Blum, Jacques. *Teaterliv i København*. [Theatre life in Copenhagen]. Copenhagen: Tiderne skifter, 1989.

Brostrøm, Torben, and Jens Kistrup. *Dansk Litteraturhistorie*. [History of Danish literature]. Vol. 6. Copenhagen: Politiken, 1977.

——, and Mette Winge. *Danske digtere i det 20 århundrede*. [Danish writers in the twentieth century]. Copenhagen: Gad, 1982.

International Theatre Institute. *Teater i Danmark*. [Theatre in Denmark]. Yearbook. Copenhagen: Danish Centre of the International Theatre Institute, 1965–92.

Jensen, Stig Jarl, Kela Kvam, and Ulla Stroemberg. *Dansk teater i 60'erne og 70'erne*. [Danish theatre in the 1960s and 1970s]. Copenhagen: Borgen, 1983.

Kragh-Jacobsen, Svend. *Teatermosaik*. [Theatre mosaic]. Copenhagen: Lademann, 1979.

Kvam, Kela, Janne Risum, and Jytte Wiingaard, eds. *Dansk teaterhistorie*. [History of Danish theatre]. 2 vols. Copenhagen: Gyldendal, 1992.

Rask, Elin. *Trolden med de tre hoveder: Det Kongelige Teater siden 1870, bygningshistorisk og kulturpolitisk*. [The troll with three heads: the

Royal Theatres since 1870]. Copenhagen: Akademisk forlag, 1980.

——, and Leif Tuxen. *Ej blot til lyst – også en arbejdsplads. Det Kongelige Teater foer og efter ombygningen.* [Not only for pleasure – also a working place. The Royal Theatre before and after the rebuilding]. Lyngby: Dansk historisk håndbogsforlag, 1987.

——. *Teatersemiologi.* [Semiology of theatre]. Copenhagen: Berlingske leksikon Bibliotek, 1976.

——. *Teaterforestillingen.* [Theatre performance]. Gråsten: Forlaget Drama, 1980.

Wiingaard, Jytte. *Teater og kommunikation.* [Theatre and communication]. Copenhagen: Borgen, 1983.

ENGLAND

(see **UNITED KINGDOM**)

ESTONIA

A small country of some 47,000 square kilometres (18,000 square miles) and 1.5 million inhabitants on the east coast of the Baltic Sea between Latvia and Russia, Estonia is populated by people of Finno-Ugric origin who have lived on this land for nearly 5,000 years. In the thirteenth century they were subjugated by German crusaders and later the country came under Polish, Swedish and (since 1710) Russian rule. For almost 700 years, a small German minority remained the dominant class and was the source of occasional amateur theatricals.

In 1809, a resident professional theatre in Tallinn was established and performed mostly in German. Native Estonian theatre was created as part of a national awakening in 1870 when the nationalist poet Lydia Koidula (1843–86) wrote and staged her plays. Initially alien to many people, theatre activity spread with amazing rapidity and innumerable villages quickly formed amateur groups to produce translations, adaptations and original plays, mostly comedies, including some by Shakespeare and Molière.

In 1906, the first professional Estonian repertory company, the Vanemuine, began operation in the university town of Tartu. Later that year, the Estonia company followed in Tallinn while in 1911, the Endla company opened in Pärnu. In each case, the buildings were financed by nation-wide, public campaigns reflecting the close connections between the country's arts and its people. In their artistic aims, these theatres, especially the Vanemuine under the leadership of Karl Menning (1874–1941), followed the major artistic trends of their time, early on focusing on realism, psychological insight and ensemble acting. Ibsen, Bjørnson, Hauptmann, Sudermann and Gorki quickly became staples of the repertoire. The first decade of these companies also saw the emergence of the greatest Estonian playwright, August Kitzberg (1855–1927) and the novelist Eduard Vilde (1865–1933), who also wrote for the theatre.

The period between 1918 and 1940 saw

Estonia, a society without sharp class differences, once again politically independent and this brought about an upsurge in cultural interest. Free at last from the restrictions of czarist censorship and national oppression, the theatres – until then financially supported by special societies which had a say in forming both their companies and repertoire – now began to be directly supported at both state and municipal levels. By 1940, Estonia had seven fully professional theatres (three of them in the capital Tallinn) and four semi-professional theatres (with small professional cores) in less urban provincial centres. The country's first opera and ballet troupes were also opened in that period.

Country-wide, the overall number of productions rose from seventy-seven in 1920–1 to 114 in 1937–8; the number of theatregoers also grew from 300,000 to 700,000. Artistic standards as well were rising and plays were receiving both longer rehearsal periods and extended runs. The technical side was also improving; by the 1930s all theatres had cycloramas and some had revolving stages. Lighting became more important. Stage designs were no longer simple illustrations but an active part of the production. The role of the stage director was also being steadily enhanced; artistic directors like Ants Lauter (1894–1973) of the Estonia and Priit Põldroos (1902–68) of the Tallinn Töölisteater (Workers' Theatre) were decisive in forming the overall image of their companies. But most Estonian directors were also actors and all these troupes were in a sense actors' companies. Stage personalities like the versatile Paul Pinna (1884–1949) and the tragedienne Liina Reiman (1891–1961) were veritable cult figures during their long careers.

In its artistic directions, the Estonian theatre of the 1920s was catching up with symbolism and was also venturing into expressionism with translations of Maeterlinck, Strindberg, Kaiser and Toller among others. Experimentalism also tinged the discovery of older European classics, especially Shakespeare. The 1930s were marked by a return to realism, and native drama again became important. By the end of the decade, in fact, it made up roughly one-half of the repertoire though only two or three comedies by Hugo Raudsepp (1883–1952) and the two plays of the great Estonian novelist A.H. Tammsaare (1878–1940) can be called masterpieces. The main achievements of this period were the spreading of theatre to all areas of the country and to all levels of the population as well as the establishment of solid professional criteria.

In the history of the Estonian people, the crucial year was 1940, when Estonia, along with the other Baltic states (Lithuania and Latvia), was annexed by the Soviet Union. Hitherto, cultural development had been largely self-regulating and organic; suddenly everything was subjected to both a rigid censorship and bureaucratic administration. All theatres were quickly nationalized; the societies that had created and run them were dissolved. In the years following, the repertoire was filled with Soviet plays.

From 1941 there followed three years of devastating war and Nazi occupation with its own harsh rules. When the Soviet army returned in 1944, about 70,000 Estonians, remembering the atrocities of the first Soviet occupation, fled the country with a high percentage of artists and intellectuals among them. From this point, Estonian culture developed in two distinct branches – the culture at home and the culture in exile. In some fields, like poetry and fiction, the small and dispersed exile community held pre-eminence right up until the mid-1960s. Theatre, however, more dependent on material conditions, needs physical and financial support and these were difficult to find abroad. Attempts to form professional Estonian companies in Germany and Sweden in the late 1940s quickly failed. From that time on, the exile theatre was continued but strictly on an amateur basis functioning more to unite refugees than anything else. Nevertheless, important exile groups have continued to exist in Stockholm and Toronto with smaller groups operating in the United States, Britain and Australia. In their repertoire, all have largely stayed with pre-1940 plays. Of the several hundred plays written by Estonians in exile, only a few – some comedies by Arvo Mägi (b. 1913), several satires by Ilmar Külvet (b. 1920) and the symbolist dramas of Bernard Kangro (b. 1910) – may have lasting value.

In Estonia itself in the 1940s, most theatre houses lay in ruins. Only the Estonia Theatre was rebuilt after the war (1947). The Vanemuine and the Endla companies received new houses only in 1967. Early in the post-war period, there was real enthusiasm for building the country up again as a national entity but this desire soon faded as Stalin's terror-based policies prevailed. In 1949–50 there were, in fact, mass deportations, forced collectivization of the countryside, and ideological witch-hunts. The goal was to exclude western influences. Leading stage directors of the previous period were removed from their posts. Several provincial theatres were closed in 1950–1.

In 1949, the Estonia, which had been a music-and-drama theatre since its inception, was turned into exclusively a music theatre. From that point, there remained only one Estonian-language drama troupe in Tallinn (this despite the creation in 1948 of a Russian-language drama theatre in the Estonian capital). Soviet occupation also encouraged a constant influx of Russians and the proportion of non-Estonians rose in the country from less than 10 per cent in 1940 to some 40 per cent in 1990. Most immigrants, however, had no theatregoing interest and the Russian theatre in Tallinn has had chronic audience problems. In fact, the repertoire of the theatres consisted of mostly lifeless Soviet plays while the box office depended on a handful of acceptable classics. The only Estonian playwright who was acceptable to Stalinist taste was August Jakobson (1904–63) but his plays about relentless class struggle quickly disappeared after Stalin's death. Even the creation of a professional puppet theatre in 1952 had little effect.

The general production style at this time (called ironically Stanislavskian) was a mixture of drab realism and clichés. It was usually safer for the director to model his production on an officially approved example from Moscow or Leningrad; it remained for the actor to find some enlivening touches. So it was the actors – people like Kaarel Karm (1906–79), Ants Eskola (1908–89) and Aino Talvi (1909–92) – whom audiences came to see, if they came at all. The main thing about the bleak post-war decade was that theatre simply survived.

After the death of Stalin in 1953 conditions began to change slowly for the better, though each step towards greater freedom was accompanied by fierce critical battles. Gradually the repertoire widened, admitting more classics and contemporary western writers. For Soviet authors new problems and areas of life were opened up; their characters again started to look like living people. In native drama, plays by Juhan Smuul (1922–71), Egon Rannet (1911–83) and Ardi Liives (1929–92) brought fresh realism and poetic insights. In staging, individual stylistic differences reappeared as directors reasserted themselves. There was a tendency to move away from restrictive pseudo-realism towards more imaginative solutions. A notable foreign influence at this time was

Brecht, while the most prominent Estonian figures of the 1955–70 period were Voldemar Panso (1920–77), founder of the Noorsooteater (Youth Theatre, 1965) in Tallinn, and Kaarel Ird (1909–86), who led the Vanemuine. Theatre attendances soon reached pre-war levels and continued to rise.

In the 1960s, a new, freer and more sophisticated generation made its way in virtually every artistic field. Young directors and actors were more conscious of developments elsewhere reading avidly about Artaud, Grotowski, Peter Brook, and the American avant-garde, though opportunities to see such work were practically nil. They relied less on the text of a play than on visual symbols, metaphors and physical action. In general, their productions were aggressive, defiant, even hysterical – as a reaction to tightening ideological pressure after 1968. Later, they turned toward quasi-religious and spiritual sources. Proponents of the trend were the directors Jaan Tooming (b. 1946), Evald Hermaküla (b. 1941) and partly also Kaarin Raid (b. 1942). Its effect was felt in absurdist-influenced plays by Paul-Eerik Rummo (b. 1942), whose *Tuhkatriinumäng* (*The Cinderella Game*, 1969) is the best example of a play built on an imaginary situation, Mati Unt (b. 1944), Enn Vetemaa (b. 1936) and Vaino Vahing (b. 1940).

By the end of the 1970s, the metaphoric-physical trend had largely spent its force. Also, a general stagnation of the Soviet system became more and more pervasive. A time of weariness, loss of direction and stylistic eclecticism set in. In certain ways realistic and psychological modes returned, but avant-garde attempts did not disappear entirely. A turning towards history, 'the roots', was noticeable, for example in the plays of Jaan Kruusvall (b. 1940) and Rein Saluri (b. 1939), staged by Mikk Mikiver (b. 1937).

The coming of the Gorbachev *perestroika* (restructuring) in 1985 and an open resurgence of national aspirations in 1987 brought about great changes. Censorship was suddenly abolished; subjects, authors and plays previously banned were now able to reach the stage; guest performances by foreign troupes in Estonia and visits by Estonian theatre people abroad became more common; there was a flurry of small experimental groups. Theatre actively participated in the national struggle, which finally led to the re-establishment of Estonia's political independence in 1991.

Approaching the mid-1990s, the arts were

again at a crossroads. For years they were a channel for expressing, however allusively, opposition to Soviet rule. Now free, they were having to rethink their function. At the same time, the overall economic decline was making their financial position even more precarious, resulting in a wave of lightweight commercial productions. Freedom had come, but so had poverty. Theatre, like the whole Estonian nation, was undergoing a period of transition when high hopes often mixed with despair.

Structure of the National Theatre Community

There have never been private or commercial theatres in Estonia; all theatres have been permanent repertory companies with a number of plays in constant rotation aiming to appeal to a wide range of tastes. Only the amateur Hommikteater (Morning Theatre, 1921–4) with its expressionistic focus and the still semi-professional Workers' Theatre of the 1920s with its left-wing sympathies had a more specialized image. The avant-garde of the 1970s had to work within the rigid Soviet system, with small groups of like-minded experimentalists trying to function somehow inside the larger companies. Only since about 1990 have semi-professional experimental groups been able to work on their own.

Under the Soviet system, all theatres were centrally funded by the Ministry of Culture, which also appointed their managers and artistic directors. The state paid about 85 per cent of all costs; the remaining 15 per cent came from the box office. The same system has continued to work in independent Estonia, though each theatre's leadership is no longer appointed by the state. In future, municipal and private sponsorship as well as box-office returns will obviously have to take a larger share.

In 1992, there were ten professional theatres in Estonia. Six were working in Tallinn: the opera-and-ballet theatre Estonia, Eesti Draamateater (Estonian Drama Theatre), Noorsooteater (Youth Theatre), Vanalinna-stuudio (Old-Town Studio), a comedy theatre founded in 1980 by the popular actor Eino Baskin (b. 1929), the Russian Drama Theatre, and Nukuteater (Puppet Theatre). Operating outside Tallinn were the Vanemuine in Tartu, the Endla in Pärnu, the Ugala in Viljandi, and the Rakvere Teater in Rakvere.

Each of these theatres used to travel widely (especially in summer), giving performances not only in towns but also in villages. In the early 1990s, however, such travels were curtailed for lack of finances. In 1987 (the last year for which accurate figures are available), there were altogether seventy new productions in the country with 4,500 performances and 1.7 million spectators. Most drama troupes had twenty-five to thirty members with the average rehearsal period being two months. As of 1992, with widespread poverty and rocketing ticket prices everywhere, audiences were diminishing, troupes were being reduced, actors were being hired annually instead of on five-year contracts (the former practice), productions were having shorter runs and rehearsal periods were having to be cut.

Professional interests have traditionally been represented by the Estonian Theatre Workers' Union, a blanket organization for all theatre people, with specialized subsections. Together with the Ministry of Culture, it also gives annual awards for each season's best productions, performers, designers, and so on.

As well, there are about 1,000 amateur groups in Estonia, the more regular among them having formed a league of their own. These groups successfully organized two international alternative theatre festivals under the name Baltoscandal at the summer resort town of Pärnu in 1990 and 1992. During the 1970s and 1980s, a number of biennial Estonian theatre festivals were held but by 1992 all had been discontinued. The only remaining effort in this area was the Baltic Theatre Festival, which, in addition to the three Baltic states, has also included Belarus and some guest performances from outside the region; it changes its host (Baltic) country each year.

Artistic Profile

Companies

All Estonian theatres work on much the same principles and have a common audience orientation, so differences are relatively minor, depending on the acting tradition of the company and the artistic preferences of its director. Among the drama companies, three are of particular significance – the Estonian Drama Theatre, the Youth Theatre and the Vanemuine. The Estonian Drama Theatre, founded in 1916, has had a varied history. From 1949 to 1965 it was the only Estonian-language drama theatre in Tallinn. Its troupe, the largest (about fifty people) and best in Estonia, was formed from three previously existing Tallinn companies (and, as a result, has always been less unified than those of other theatres). The skills of its actors have come out most strongly in large-scale classical productions. It worked most effectively under the artistic direction of Voldemar Panso from 1970 to 1977 and Mikk Mikiver (1977–85); later it worked under a collective leadership and eventually had to cut its

troupe to thirty-five. It is the nearest approach to a classical theatre in Estonia in terms of acting, style and repertoire. But through the 1980s and into the 1990s it became more open to experimentation, and four or five of the best Estonian directors regularly work there.

The Youth Theatre, whose name is somewhat misleading, was founded in 1965 by Voldemar Panso primarily to provide Tallinn with a second Estonian-language drama theatre. Panso led it from 1965 to 1970, and his ethos continued there under the direction of Mikk Mikiver from 1970 to 1974. At the time, the company formed a more unified ensemble than that of the Estonian Drama Theatre, and its productions were livelier. Panso's ideas were a mixture of Stanislavski and Brecht, but he also relied on his own unique intuition and imagination. Thus he became the prime agent in overcoming the narrowly conceived 'realism' of the 1950s. Among his more than fifty productions (both for the Estonian Drama and for the Youth Theatre) the most successful were those of world classics (Shakespeare, Ibsen and Shaw)

Evald Hermaküla's 1986 Estonian Drama Theatre production of Shakespeare's *The Tempest*, designed by Vadim Fomichev.
Photo: Peeter Laurits.

and of Estonian authors (Tammsaare and Smuul); he largely managed to avoid the usual Soviet fare. From 1974 to 1986, under the leadership of Kalju Komissarov (b. 1946), the Youth Theatre took a more political turn, but that was counterbalanced by the work of other directors, like Mati Unt. In the early 1990s, with a new and younger leadership, the Youth Theatre underwent drastic changes. It had to abandon the large auditorium that it rented in a Soviet-style 'culture palace' and began playing mostly in a 100-seat hall. The acting ensemble was accordingly cut from thirty to eighteen.

The oldest Estonian theatre, Vanemuine, is at present the only theatre that houses three separate companies for opera, ballet and drama. In certain productions, especially operettas and musicals, they are often combined. The whole post-war period in the Vanemuine was strongly influenced by the personality of Kaarel Ird, who led it from 1944 to 1950 and again from 1955 to 1986. Basically a drama director, he staged a number of outstanding musical theatre productions as well, and was able to keep the three companies in balance. With his old-style, left-wing approach, he was most successful with plays that had a clear social message and with folk comedies; he also systematically staged new Estonian dramas. The Vanemuine was the place where, thanks to Ird's protection, the leaders of the avant-garde of the 1970s, Jaan

Tooming and Evald Hermaküla, could experiment freely.

Dramaturgy

Drama has never been a leading literary genre in Estonia; only a few important writers, like August Kitzberg or Hugo Raudsepp from the pre-war period, have had careers primarily as playwrights. Stylistically, Estonian drama reached maturity when Ibsenian realism was dominant, and in many ways this has remained the norm. Also, since Estonia has no verse play or native expressionistic traditions, neither of these forms has had any real repercussions in its drama. The established genres by 1940 were folk drama/comedy, drawing-room drama/comedy, and realistic problem plays; their modifications continued to function within the Soviet framework.

Of the writers who resuscitated drama in the mid-1950s the most important was probably Juhan Smuul. A controversial figure who had glorified Stalin in poetry, he now defended a more humane and tolerant attitude and showed a real gift for humour. Never a conscious innovator, he still broke norms and forms, thus preparing the ground for younger authors. Of his five plays, only the folk drama *Kihnu Jõnn* (1964) and the *bravura* comic monologue

Kaarel Ird's 1974 Vanemuine production of Oskar Luts's *In the Backyard*, designed by Georg Sander.
Photo: Gunnar Vaidla.

Polkovniku lesk (*A Colonel's Widow*, 1965) will probably remain; the others belong to their period.

In the wave of non-realistic drama from the late 1960s and early 1970s, some of the best plays were written by authors who had only a passing interest in the theatre. The most popular playwright of the 1970s was Enn Vetemaa. Though his early plays were somewhat innovative, he later turned to a more realistic format, though even here there are often surrealist elements. Vetemaa loves the well-made play with its plot turns and character revelations. He also has a satirist's eye for the vices of egoism, hypocrisy and vanity. His best plays, like *Jälle häda mõistuse pärast* (*Woe from Wit Again*, 1975), somewhat resemble Dürrenmatt; his weaker pieces tend towards easy commercialism where the poor in brains and pure in heart inherit the earth.

Vahing, Unt, Saluri and Kruusvall were still dominating the dramatic scene in the 1980s but there was no clearly commanding figure. The difference between the early realistic and the later non-realistic modes was being blurred; elements of both were often mixing.

Perhaps in retrospect, the late 1980s and early 1990s will be seen as the time of Madis Kõiv (b. 1929). A physicist by profession, his plays (like *Faehlmann*, 1982, with Vaino Vahing, about a leader of the national awakening; and *Kokkusaamine* (*A Meeting*, 1991) are highly intellectual and strongly visionary.

Directors, Directing and Production Styles

The work of the two outstanding directors of the 1950s and 1960s, Voldemar Panso and Kaarel Ird, has been discussed in connection with the Youth Theatre and the Vanemuine. In the avant-garde of the late 1960s, the leading figure was Jaan Tooming. In his series of large-scale productions, mostly based on the works of the Estonian classics Kitzberg, Tammsaare and Vilde, that trend reached its peak in the 1970s. They were characterized by a liberal use of symbols, metaphors and the grotesque in depicting hypocrisy, greed and ambition, and a final pointing towards spiritual values. The latter tendency was even more pronounced in Tooming's later productions, but his approach had become more subdued and his touch less sure. The work of the other leading experimentalist, Evald Hermaküla, has been both more intellectual (continuing the Brecht line) and more anarchic.

The avant-garde also showed a strong interest in indigenous Estonian (and wider, Finno-Ugric) folklore as well as Oriental sources, both used for greater ritualization of performance. There were only a few attempts at breaking the barrier between stage and audience, however, and even less of an attempt at collective creation.

As in drama, the distinction between realistic and non-realistic production modes was generally lost in the 1980s; and again, there was no dominating personality. Instead, there was a group of about ten directors whose development, with all the normal ups and downs, was of general interest. In this period of 'postmodernist' eclecticism, it is perhaps fitting to end with the name of Mati Unt. Extremely versatile – a novelist, playwright, dramaturge, director and critic – he has been a presence on the literary and theatrical scene since the middle of the 1960s, always alert to the new and the vital. His best productions show a sophisticated mind, conscious of complicated cultural backgrounds and the often ironic dilemmas of the world dramatists he usually stages.

Jaak Rähesoo

Music Theatre

Plays with music as well as operas were first staged by the German theatre in Tallinn at the end of the eighteenth century. The nascent Estonian amateur theatre often interspersed action and speech with singing and dancing; the first operettas were put on in the 1880s; in 1899 the Vanemuine showed its first opera, Étienne Méhul's *Joseph*. Achieving professional status at the beginning of this century, the Estonia and the Vanemuine continued as combined music-and-drama theatres where actors and singers mixed in various genres.

The aims of Hanno Kompus (1890–1974), who started systematic opera productions at the Estonia in the 1920s, were to have a balanced repertoire where different national schools

(Italian, German, Slavonic, and so on) were equally represented, and to match each with a suitable production style. He also staged the first native opera, *Vikerlased* (*The Estonian Vikings*, 1928) by Evald Aav (1900–39), which established the line of national romanticism in the genre.

A general turn towards realism in the 1930s affected the opera as well, for example in the psychological ensemble work of Eino Uuli (1906–76), influenced by Stanislavski's music theatre productions. It was to his advantage that many Estonian singers were also good actors. A special feature of the Estonia of the 1930s were the witty and elegant operetta productions of Agu Lüüdik (1897–1949). The opera company of the Vanemuine, always less brilliant vocally than that of the Estonia, received a boost in 1933 when Eduard Tubin (1905–82) became its conductor. Operettas were also staged in the smaller theatres.

During World War II, almost half of the music company of the Estonia fled to the west. Despite that, it was turned into an exclusively music theatre in 1949, cutting the vital link with developments in drama. But the greatest soloists of the post-war period, Tiit Kuusik (1911–90) and Georg Ots (1920–75), continued the actor-singer tradition and passed it on to present-day stars, like Anu Kaal (b. 1940), Hendrik Krumm (1934–89) and Teo Maiste (b. 1932).

Soviet occupation tilted the repertoire heavily towards Russian opera. Stalinist taste mummified nineteenth-century forms and abhorred modernity; in the opera it fostered a bizarre combination of petty realism and pomposity.

In contrast to drama and ballet, opera production style was not revolutionized in the 1960s. Here growing freedom primarily meant a wider range of modern composers; many contemporary classics were introduced into the Soviet Union by the Estonia or the Vanemuine, especially in the productions of Udo Väljaots (1916–79), helped by the conductor Neeme Järvi (b. 1937). Among Väljaots's major suc-

cesses was Tubin's remarkable psychological opera, *Barbara von Tisenhusen* (1969).

At the same time, the laconic and forceful Verdi productions and the exuberant and ironic Rossini productions of the director Paul Mägi (1917–73) turned the Estonia decisively towards classical Italian opera, and that trend has been continued by Arne Mikk (b. 1932), whose work, influenced by the production ideas of German opera director Walter Felsenstein, has again emphasized theatrical imagery and psychological motivation.

Another source of growing theatricality has been musical comedy, present since the early 1960s; Voldemar Panso, though primarily a drama director, was among its pioneers.

At the Vanemuine, which continued as the sole music-and-drama theatre in Estonia, the social interests and realistic taste of Kaarel Ird also marked his opera productions; even more important were his 'folk-musicals' using popular Estonian songs – another manifestation of the country's search for its artistic roots.

Among more recent opera directors, Ago-Endrik Kerge (b. 1939) and Neeme Kuningas (b. 1955) have a liking for heightened theatricality (sometimes employing the theatre-within-theatre device) and the grotesque. The old unity of song and dance has often inspired the choreographers Mai Murdmaa b. 1938) and Ülo Vilimaa (b. 1941) (see **Dance Theatre**).

Musical comedy is occasionally staged by other theatres as well, though the number is not comparable to that of the operetta in the pre-war repertoire. Modern recording facilities have enhanced the role of music in drama productions, however. Among the innovations of the avant-garde of the 1970s was its turning to all sorts of hitherto unlikely sources, from pre-Renaissance and Oriental music to contemporary rock, as an effective comment on the events of a play; often the main 'actor' in climactic scenes was the music. That development has continued to reach even more remarkable levels of sophistication.

Kristel Pappel

Dance Theatre

Estonian dance theatre, born in the 1920s, was influenced by both the Russian ballet and various modern dance movements including Isadora Duncan and the German *Ausdruckstanz*

of Rudolf von Laban. A synthesis of all these forms was aimed at by Rahel Olbrei (1898–1984) who formed a permanent dance troupe at the Estonia in 1926. Her main concern in both classical and modern ballets was the dramatic integrity and psychological motivation of the performance. Another important group, connected with the Estonian Drama Theatre, was that of Gerd Neggo (1891–1974), started in 1924. From there came the founder in 1935 and director till 1973 of the Vanemuine dance company, Ida Urbel (1900–83). Her pantomimic, epic, rustic and forceful style was especially fitting in ballets dealing with native mythology, like *Kratt* (*The Goblin Thief*, 1943) by Eduard Tubin.

The Soviet occupation in 1940 closed private dance schools, but in 1946 a state-run school was opened in Tallinn. Its nine-year course followed the methodology of the famous Russian ballerina, Agrippina Vaganova. In this way, the language of classical ballet was canonized, all expressions of modern dance suppressed. The uniformity of style left a deadly stamp on post-war ballet productions, though *Swan Lake*, staged at the Estonia in 1954 by the Moscow choreographer Vladimir Bourmeister, became something of a landmark of classical maturity.

Great changes occurred in the 1960s when a new generation of Estonian choreographers appeared. Though trained in classical ballet (usually in Moscow or Leningrad), they were open to modern dance and experimental influences. Their search for a more abstract 'symphonic' language, for ritual, for heightened visual images and metaphors echoed that of the young drama directors. They preferred the laconic expressionism of shorter ballets, often using the music of modern composers, like Bartók, Stravinsky, Barber, Prokofiev and Berio.

The most outstanding among them has been Mai Murdmaa, who has worked at the Estonia since 1963 and led its ballet since 1973. She has moved away from following a strict storyline to a more direct expression of emotions. As in drama theatre, the growing ideological pressure of the 1970s subsequently brought her to a deeper consideration of national roots, and to an examination of the opposition of spirituality and repression, in full-length ballets based on the music of various Estonian composers – Eino Tamberg (b. 1930, *Joanna tentata*, 1971), Veljo Tormis (b. 1930, *Eesti ballaadid/Estonian Ballads*, 1980), Kuldar Sink (b. 1942) and Arvo Pärt (b. 1935).

At the Vanemuine in Tartu, whose dance company is not as rooted in classical ballet as

Mai Murdmaa's 1992 Estonia production of *The Don Juan Play*.
Photo: Harri Rospu.

that of the Estonia, a similar role has been played by Ülo Vilimaa. He began as a brilliant dancer in 1962, then became a choreographer, and has since 1973 led the troupe. Following the line of Ida Urbel, he has laid greater stress on 'free plastique' and historical or ethnographic stylization, using elements of Estonian folk dance.

The social upheaval and re-establishment of national independence in recent years have also opened dance theatre to contemporary trends such as jazz dance, multimedia, and so on, and,

in 1990 and 1991, festivals of modern dance were held in Tallinn. Modern dance is also the basis of a new professional group, Nordstar, founded in 1991. Growing international contacts – for example, the production of *Fröken Julie* (*Miss Julie*) by the Swedish choreographer Birgit Cullberg at the Estonia in 1991 – have further revitalized Estonian ballet. The role of amateur groups, like the Leigarid, in rediscovering authentic folk dance must also be noted here.

Lea Tormis

Theatre for Young Audiences

Most Estonian theatres usually stage one or two plays for children annually, mostly during the New Year season. A more systematic approach was taken in the inter-war period by the Draamastuudio Teater, one of the constituents of the present Estonian Drama Theatre. Its repertoire consisted of traditional fairytales and dramatizations of popular children's books.

During the Soviet period, plays were added to reinforce ideological indoctrination, most orthodox in the Stalinist years, less dogmatic later. The Youth Theatre, though primarily a regular drama theatre, has still tried to justify its name by staging a greater number of plays for children.

The interest of the avant-garde in the late

1960s in ritual, authentic folklore and 'uncorrupted' audiences often made them turn to children: Evald Hermaküla frequently staged children's productions in the 1970s, and in 1989 a semi-professional children's theatre, grown out of the Jaan Tooming acting studio, was founded in Tartu.

Most productions for children address preteens; teenagers tend to be taken to adult performances.

Amateur theatricals by children and young people at schools or in special 'circles' have always been lively; many such circles have worked for decades, renewing themselves constantly, and they regularly come together for public festivals.

Puppet Theatre

Estonia had no native puppet theatre tradition, though puppets could occasionally be seen in circus programmes. In 1937 the Estonian Drama Theatre started marionette shows as part of its children's theatre activities, and they continued after the war. A separate puppet theatre was founded in Tallinn in 1952; the company also tours widely across the country. Its director from 1952 to 1981 was Ferdinand Veike (b. 1924); since 1981 it has been Rein Agur (b. 1935).

Until the 1970s, its repertoire consisted of plays for smaller children with the actors using glove-puppets or rod-puppets from behind a screen. In later years, the theatre has tried to

widen its audience and appeal to adults with productions such as Shakespeare's *A Midsummer Night's Dream* and *Romeo and Juliet*. In these productions, the actors often manipulate puppets of various sizes and constructions openly on the stage, alternating puppet scenes with scenes involving live actors.

The Estonian Puppet Theatre, a member of UNIMA (the International Puppeteers Union), has toured in many parts of the former Soviet Union, in Scandinavia and Germany. Puppet performances are also staged by several amateur groups.

Jaak Rähesoo

Rein Agur's 1984 Puppet Theatre production of Shakespeare's *Romeo and Juliet*, designed by Rein Lauks.
Photo: Ann Tenno.

Design

Professional Estonian theatre design came into being when post-Ibsenian realism began paying greater attention to authentic detail on the one hand, while *art nouveau*, on the other, aimed at a highly stylized symbolism. The outstanding painterly qualities of the latter trend were best represented by Roman Nyman (1881–1951). Expressionism, cubism and constructivism with their restless play of surfaces and angles found an echo in the settings of Aleksander Tuurand (1888–1936), who also explored the new possibilities of lighting. Most designers were influenced either by the French orientation of the Pallas Arts School in Tartu or by the more eclectic approach of the School of Applied Arts in Tallinn.

Post-war theatre artists were hampered by the poor physical conditions of temporary acting spaces and the dull, pedantic and cluttered 'realism' of official Stalinist taste. But the best traditions of earlier periods were carried on by

Voldemar Haas (1898–1982) and the costume artist Natalie Mei (1900–75). They also created a romantic visual image for plays on early Estonian history. Both later taught at the Tallinn Art Institute, from where most Estonian theatre designers of the post-war period have come.

As with other aspects of the theatre, stage design was revolutionized again in the 1960s. A total visual impression, combined with symbol and metaphor, again became dominant with designers preferring a spare, laconic, abstract solution. From this point, both stage and costumes were usually designed by the same artist, guaranteeing a more unified style. In the 1970s, the notion of creating a total environment invaded the scene; a richness of detail reappeared with every object directly or symbolically involved in the action. A director and a designer often formed a more or less permanent partnership, like Voldemar Panso and Mari-Liis Küla (b. 1924), or Mikk Mikiver and Aime Unt

(b. 1941) in drama theatre. In music theatre, where the painterly qualities of the scenery are more important, the leading artists have been Eldor Renter (b. 1925), who often collaborated with the director Paul Mägi, Lembit Roosa (b. 1920) and Kustav-Agu Püüman (b. 1937). All have been immensely helped by the outstanding scene-painters Frits Matt (1909–92) and Uno Kärbis (b. 1926).

Kustav-Agu Püüman, Jaak Rähesoo

Theatre Space and Architecture

The first Estonian theatres, erected between 1906 and 1913 by nation-wide donations, were imposing buildings in the *art nouveau* style and objects of intense national pride; all were destroyed in World War II. Only the Estonia was restored, more or less, to its former shape. The new buildings of the Vanemuine and the Endla from 1967 represented austere functionalism. The new Ugala, opened in 1982 in the small southern town of Viljandi, is at present the best theatre building in Estonia.

All these theatres have large proscenium stages with revolves and auditoriums seating between 600 and 800 people. Most also have secondary stages for audiences of about 100, used for more experimental or intimate productions.

Technical facilities have been gradually improving at all Estonian theatres, but they still lack much in modern technology.

Guest performances outside the major cities are usually given in community centres or village clubs, which number around 400. The short and often rainy summer makes outdoor performances a constant risk, but some still take place, usually presenting modified versions of indoor productions.

Jaak Rähesoo

Training

Initially professional actors were recruited from the ranks of the local amateurs. The first important acting school was the Draamastuudio (1920–33) in Tallinn, led by Paul Sepp (1885–1943) and Hilda Gleser (1893–1932). It functioned with the financial help of a special supporting society. The training was theoretically Stanislavskian but in actuality it was quite eclectic.

Of its five graduating classes, the most important was the first one, which in 1924 founded the Draamastuudio Teater, one of the sources of the present Estonian Drama Theatre, and included the future theatre leaders, Priit Põldroos and Leo Kalmet (1900–75).

A state-financed acting school at the Tallinn Conservatoire functioned between 1938 and 1941; one class finished. After the war its work was continued by a theatre institute, which had three graduating classes, but in 1950 it was closed. During the following Stalinist hiatus, a class of Estonian actors was taught at the Lunacharsky Theatre Institute (GITIS) in Moscow.

All post-war training was strictly Stanislavskian.

In 1957 an acting school was again opened at the Tallinn Conservatoire. With a four-year programme of theoretical and practical courses, the Conservatoire has graduated the bulk of present-day professional actors in Estonia. The founder and director of the school till his death in 1977 was Voldemar Panso, who had studied stage directing in Moscow under Stanislavski's pupils Maria Knebel and Alexei Popov. Panso's teaching always remained basically true to the principles of psychological realism though he was not dogmatic. The school also absorbed influences from a wide variety of sources both national and international, from Brecht to Grotowski.

From time to time, various theatres have also established their own studios, usually two-year acting programmes.

Most Estonian stage directors began their careers as actors, though the Tallinn acting school graduated a small group of directors in 1976. Others received their educations in Moscow or Leningrad.

Theatre scholars have generally studied either at special institutes in Moscow or Leningrad or in departments of history or philology at Tartu University. Most technical professionals receive practical on-the-job training at the theatres.

Reet Neimar

Criticism, Scholarship and Publishing

In the inter-war period, most daily newspapers had regular theatre critics, many well-known writers among them, but only Artur Adson (1889–1977) published a book-length selection of his articles (1938). In 1934, the monthly *Teater* appeared, providing additional outlets for critical writing. The magazine ceased operation in 1940.

From being a watchdog of Soviet orthodoxy in the 1940s and early 1950s, criticism again became an expression of personal views after 1956. The leading critical publications of the whole post-war period have been the cultural weekly *Sirp ja Vasar* (founded in 1940; in 1989–90 called *Reede*; since 1991, called *Sirp*); the monthly *Teater, Muusika, Kino* (*Theatre, Music, Film*, founded in 1982); and the annual *Teatrimärkmik* (*Theatre Notebook*, 1961–81), which changed its title to *Teatrielu* (*Theatre Life*) in 1982.

As in many countries, theatre people have been active memoir-writers. Most theatre books have been published by or with the help of the Estonian Theatre Workers' Union. They include historical surveys, studies of individual theatres, actors and directors and collections of documents. Selections of essays have appeared from well-known theatre directors such as Voldemar Panso and Kaarel Ird, and from several critics.

Important translations into Estonian include works by Stanislavski, Meyerhold, Brecht, Artaud and Peter Brook. There is no single play publishing house; several publishers issue scripts.

The main repository of theatre history is Teatri- ja Muusikamuuseum (Museum for Theatre and Music) in Tallinn, founded in 1931. Research groups also work at the Estonian Theatre Workers' Union and at the Institute of History in Tallinn.

Jaak Rähesoo
Translated by Jaak Rähesoo

(See also USSR)

Further Reading

(Editor's note: *Many of the following titles, though available only in Estonian, do have major summaries in one or more other languages.*)

Adson, Artur. *Das estnische Theater*. [Estonian theatre]. Tartu: Akadeemiline Kooperatiiv, 1933. 64 pp.

——. *Teatriraamat*. [Theatre book]. Stockholm: Vaba Eesti, 1958. 230 pp.

Järv, Ants. *Väliseestlaste teater ja draama*. [Estonian theatre and drama in exile]. Tartu: Tartu Ülikool, 1991. 198 pp.

Kask, Karin. *Eesti nõukogude teater 1940–65*. [Soviet Estonian theatre 1940–65]. Tallinn: Eesti Raamat, 1987. 592 pp.

——. *Shakespeare eesti teatris*. [Shakespeare in the Estonian theatre]. Tallinn: Eesti Riiklik Kirjastus, 1964. 274 pp.

——. *Teatritegijad, alustajad: Eesti teatrilugu kuni 1917*. [Theatre-makers, initiators: history of Estonian theatre till 1917]. Tallinn: Eesti Raamat, 1970. 264 pp.

Matt, Frits. *Eesti teatri lavapilt*. [Stage design in the Estonian theatre]. Tallinn: Kunst, 1969. 180 pp.

Paalma, Vilma, Merike Vaitmaa, and Uno Heinapuu, eds. *'Estonia' lauluteatri rajajaid*. [Founders of the 'Estonia' Music Theatre]. Tallinn: ENSV Teatriühing & Eesti Raamat, 1981. 308 pp.

Tormis, Lea. *Eesti balletist*. [On the Estonian ballet]. Tallinn: Eesti Raamat, 1967. 228 pp.

——. *Eesti teater 1920–1940*. [Estonian theatre 1920–40]. Tallinn: Eesti Raamat, 1978. 504 pp.

Valgemäe, Mardi. *Ikka teatrist mõteldes*. [Thinking always about theatre]. Stockholm: Välis-Eesti & EMP, 1990. 188 pp.

Viiding, Riina, and Rein Heinsalu, eds. *Estonian Theatre*. Tallinn: Estonian Theatre Union, 1989. 160 pp.

FEDERAL REPUBLIC OF GERMANY

(see **GERMANY**)

FEDERAL REPUBLIC OF YUGOSLAVIA

(see **SERBIA-MONTENEGRO** and **YUGOSLAVIA**)

FINLAND

Bounded by Sweden, Norway and Russia, Finland, a Scandinavian country, has one of the largest land areas in Europe – 360,300 square kilometres (139,000 square miles). Of this, one-third is north of the Arctic Circle.

From 1154 to 1809 Finland was ruled by the Kingdom of Sweden. Before declaring itself independent in 1917, Finland was a Grand Duchy within the Russian Empire.

With a 1992 population of 5 million, the majority speak Finnish, a language belonging to the Finno-Ugric family. The second official language is Swedish, spoken by 6 per cent of the population.

Since the latter half of the nineteenth century the forest industry has been one of the mainstays of Finland's free market economy. Products of the metal and engineering industries comprise some 40 per cent of total exports.

The Finnish theatre has its roots in the rites of the Finno-Ugric peoples: the village games and rituals, marriage and burial ceremonies, as well as bear-hunting rituals. Formal theatrical performances date from the sixteenth century. Long isolated from European influence due to its remote location, Finnish schools began performing didactic plays in Latin praising hard work and diligence. Plays were also performed in Swedish at the Academy of Turku. Contacts with European theatre began at the end of the eighteenth century, when touring groups started arriving in coastal towns, mainly from Sweden, Germany and Russia.

The motivation to create an indigenous professional theatre was launched by nationalistic movements in the nineteenth century. The first professional theatre ventures were in the Swedish language, with the first permanent group founded in 1867; the company relied on Swedish actors until 1916. Swedish as spoken in Finland, however, was not considered refined enough to serve on the stage. The same prejudice was felt towards the Finnish language. Nevertheless, a Finnish-language professional theatre – Suomalainen teatteri (Finnish Theatre, later the National Theatre) – was founded in 1872. Dramatic literature had been written in Finnish since the 1820s, offering the theatre a good basis to start its activities. In 1847 students from the town of Kuopio had performed *Silmänkääntäjät* (*The Magician*), written by Pietari Hannikainen (1813–99); the first Finnish opera, *Kaarle kuninkaan metsästys* (*King Charles's Hunt*), composed by Frederik Pacius (1809–91), libretto by Zachris Topelius (1818–98), had been performed in 1852 by amateurs. When the Finnish Theatre was founded in 1872 it already had at its disposal eighty-nine plays written in Finnish.

It was playwright and producer Kaarlo Bergbom (1843–1906), assisted by his sister Emilie Bergbom (1834–1905), who became the first director of the Finnish Theatre. A former journalist, Bergbom's views on drama were influenced mostly by the German romantic theatre and especially by the style of the Meiningen Company, creating crowd scenes with a large cast and using historically precise and abundant settings. The Finnish Theatre was from the beginning divided into drama and opera departments. Oskari Vilho (1840–83) became director of the drama department; he had received his actor's training in Sweden. In the beginning the theatre functioned mostly as a touring company. The Finnish-speaking population of Helsinki was at the time very small, only about 7,000, so the theatre had to reach its spectators by touring to the provinces.

The initial plan for the Finnish Theatre was to further develop a Finnish dramatic literature and to bring to the Finnish public classical world drama. From its first years, the repertoire included Shakespeare, Molière, Goethe, Schiller, Gogol, Tolstoi and Calderón. Contacts with theatre in the other Nordic countries were also lively. Ibsen's *Doll's House*, for example, was presented in Finland less than a year after the world première. The tragedy *Daniel Hjort* by J.J. Wecksell (1838–1907) is considered the most notable masterpiece of drama in the Swedish language before Strindberg.

The early success and vitality of the Finnish Theatre was also due to the charisma of talented star actors such as Ida Aalberg (1853–1915), who joined the company in 1874 and grew into an internationally famous tragedienne remembered for her roles as Juliet, Hedda Gabler, Mary Stuart and Nora. Another notable star was actor Adolf Lindfors (1857–1929), a hearty and intelligent interpreter of Molière and also director of the theatre from 1907 to 1914.

From the beginning, theatre was considered an important means to propagate the Finnish language, Finnish culture and the growing nationalism. A strong amateur theatre tradition also helped make the art form familiar across all social classes.

Alongside the Finnish Theatre at the turn of the century, new theatres emerged in several parts of the country. Two parallel movements in the 1880s – the urban labour movement and the rural youth club movement – created amateur companies, many of which later became professional. The labour movement adopted theatre as one of its main cultural interests and used it as an instrument in its fight for cultural and socio-economic change. Often, two theatres would be founded in the same locality – a workers' theatre and a so-called middle-class theatre. The division reflected the prevailing social atmosphere and became especially marked after the civil war of 1917. The repertoires of the theatres did not differ greatly, but certainly their publics did. Only one workers' theatre still exists today – the Tampere Workers' Theatre.

Other important theatre centres were established in Turku, Kuopio and Vyborg, the latter town annexed by the Russians in 1945. These towns had already built theatres in the 1880s. As their artistic positions became established, the companies began performing in repertory with permanent staffs. Touring companies functioned mainly in the summer with the actors often setting up tours to cover debts accumulated from costume purchases.

The Swedish-language theatre – using the Swedish dialect spoken in Finland – gained an established position by 1916; until that year the new theatre building in Helsinki had been operated by groups from Sweden. Thereafter the Svenska teater i Helsingfors (Helsinki Swedish Theatre) became the leading stage for the country's Swedish-language drama. In 1919 Swedish-language professional groups were also founded in Turku and Vaasa.

When naturalism reached Finland at the turn of the century, Bergbom's grandiose style came under severe criticism. After he retired, the Finnish National Theatre went through a period lacking coherence in style until Eino Kalima (1882–1972) became director of the theatre in 1917, a post which he occupied until 1950, and established for the country's leading stage a style of expression based on Stanislavski's psychological method.

The workers' theatres also adopted new styles. German expressionism influenced directors Kosti Elo (1873–1940, head of the Tampere Workers' Theatre from 1919 to 1940), Mia Backman (1877–1958, director of the People's Theatre in Helsinki from 1914 to 1934) and Eino Salmelainen (1893–1975, director of the Tampere Theatre from 1925 to 1934, director of the Helsinki Workers' Theatre from 1934 to 1940, and director of the Tampere Workers' Theatre from 1943 to 1960). Many performances were simply copies from German stages. The most original forms were to be found in the plays of the Finnish expressionist playwrights Lauri Haarla (1890–1944), Hagar Olsson (1893–1978) and Arvi Kivimaa (1904–84). Expressionism had a long-lasting effect on the style of acting: the stylized, strong outbursts of emotion typical of expressionism were long popular on stage. To scenography, expressionism brought a new importance emphasizing the scenic qualities of setting. The notion of stock sets was quickly abandoned. A neutral frame became one of the elements required to mould the space and emphasize the required atmosphere.

As well as expressionistic plays, most theatres offered a diversified repertoire. Operettas enjoyed great popularity both in the workers' theatres and in the middle-class theatres. The same operetta might, in fact, be successfully performed in three different theatres in Helsinki simultaneously. Towards the end of the 1920s a wave of light comedies and farces by domestic playwrights conquered the theatres. The economic depression obliged the theatres to attract spectators with an ever lighter repertoire.

Economically, theatres at this time were subsisting on very limited resources. The state and some municipalities were giving modest subsidies, but theatrical activity was mainly financed through ticket revenues and other things such as lotteries. Private entrepreneurs also sponsored dramatic arts. Between 1918 and 1927, a heavy amusement tax caused theatres enormous difficulties to the point where they simply could not survive without subsidies. The situation eventually became absurd: what the state gave with one hand as aid, it took back with the other hand in the form of the amusement tax. In 1926, however, the National Theatre and the National Opera gained a more secure economic basis when they were granted a licence share of 19 per cent of state lottery revenues. This also marked the beginning of the present-day system for financing the arts, sciences and sports from the pool and lotto revenues of the national lottery.

During both world wars, theatre activity was significantly reduced. Numerous theatre groups toured the front offering entertainment to soldiers in an effort to boost the general morale. Propaganda and entertainment theatres also presented productions including works from the classical repertoires.

By 1945, twenty-four professional theatres were receiving state aid, three of which were Swedish-language theatres. Furthermore, numerous amateur stages aimed at becoming professional. Yet only a few of the actors in professional theatres had received professional training. Only one Finnish-language theatre school existed in the country, and the leading Swedish-language stage maintained its own school for actors. Most actors sought their way into the profession following the long route from amateur companies to apprenticing with professional theatres and, if they were sufficiently talented, progressively obtaining more important roles.

In the 1950s the questioning of the theatre's role as an institution of art and its social significance began. The need to settle accounts in the aftermath of the world war, the threats of the Cold War, the scarcity of all goods in the post-war period, and the social instability left by a general strike formed a contrast with the idea of theatres as hermetic temples of the arts. The ground was favourable for changes both in the form and content of theatre.

After the war most cities still had a workers' theatre and a middle-class theatre. Both theatres required municipal subsidy. As resources were scant, pressure was brought to bear to unite the theatres. Turku was the first city to create on such terms a municipal theatre in 1943, the Turku City Theatre; the same course of development continued in nearly all the cities during the 1950s. An alternative to the city theatre was a stock company governed by the municipality. The unification of middle-class and workers' theatres had the drawback that the public of the formers workers' theatres did not, at least temporarily, recognize the new city theatres as their own. A few attempts were made at creating workers' theatres on a purely ideological basis but they were short-lived.

Theatres became the focus of each city's cultural life. Audiences grew steadily, with the exception of 1962 when an extraordinary number of television sets were sold and audience statistics fell.

Active exchanges with foreign countries, however, again raised the status of theatre. Among the notable foreign companies that visited the country were the Berliner Ensemble, the Piccolo Teatro di Milano and the Royal Shakespeare Company. The organizing of a world congress for the International Theatre Institute (ITI) in Helsinki in 1959 represented another opening for international contacts. Finnish theatre groups also started making tours abroad. The National Theatre dared to take a Molière performance to Paris while the Tampere Workers' Theatre took a play by Camus. The exchange of visiting groups became especially active between Nordic countries.

Even though a widespread base of amateur theatre had made drama a form of folk art in Finland, the theatre public still belonged to the higher social classes and educational levels. Due to distances, theatres reached rural populations only on their occasional summer tours. Subject matter also tended to adhere to the conventional tastes of middle-class people.

During the 1960s many theatre people started to feel a need to influence society through art. In the background was Brecht's idea that art can change the world. Prominent innovators arose such as Ralf Långbacka (b. 1932) and Eugen Terttula (1926–88) who reformed the theatre both artistically and socially. An unprecedented break from the conventional was a production by Kalle Holmberg (b. 1942) for the Helsinki Student Theatre of *Lapualaisooppera* (*The Opera of Lapua*, 1966) by Arvo Salo (b. 1932) and Kaj Chydenius (b. 1939), a satire of the fascist movement in Finland in the 1930s.

As theatre people became more socially oriented in their productions, greater concern was also felt about offering theatre to all social groups in the population. This was to affect both the content of drama and the administration of the theatres.

Such was the objective of the group movement of the late 1960s. This generation, which had only recently left training schools, founded a number of 'free' groups that toured the country offering performances to formerly neglected groups – children, young people, workers and those living outside urban centres. The first of these free groups were the Swedish-language Skolteatern (the School Theatre, formed in 1960), and the Finnish-language groups Kom-teatteri (the Kom Theatre, 1969), Ryhmäteatteri (the Group Theatre, 1967), Ahaa-teatteri (the Ahaa Theatre, 1970) and Penniteatteri (the Penny Theatre, 1970–87).

Established theatres too became concerned about reaching a wider public strata. Eight regional theatres were founded at this time receiving more state subsidy than other theatres; in return they were required to serve the local population of a vast area either by touring in the region or by organizing transport for the public to their theatre. Their repertory policy was meant to take into account the usual regional features and they were also to develop contacts with local writers and amateur groups.

While the mainstream of the established theatre repertoire remained conventional, the general picture was not that of stagnation. The most interesting directors continued working in the larger theatres and in the best cases succeeded in breaking routines and bringing in new ways of expression. Perhaps the best examples of this were the Långbacka–Holmberg era at the Turku Municipal Theatre (1971–7) and Jouko Turkka's (b. 1942) at the Helsinki City Theatre (1975–82).

Up to 1990, Finnish theatres continued to enjoy a period of active growth. Over a rather long time the numbers employed by theatres had grown faster than the theatre schools were able to train them and there was practically no unemployment in the field. The situation changed in 1991 due to a deep economic recession; theatres began to reduce their activities and unemployment has grown.

Helsinki, Tampere and Turku have remained the main theatre centres. However, theatres of other cities, such as the municipal theatres of Kajaani, Kuopio, Lappeenranta, Oulu and Vaasa, have periodically attained a high artistic level and attracted attention nation-wide.

Anneli Suur-Kujala

Structure of the National Theatre Community

Finland has a dense network of theatres with no fewer than twenty-eight cities boasting professional companies subsidized by public funds. Virtually every city over 25,000 inhabitants, in fact, has a theatre.

In 1993, there were sixty-two professional companies in total of which thirty-seven were operating on a permanent, established basis, including the National Opera and the National Ballet in Helsinki. Of the remaining twenty-five, seventeen were operating as free groups with eight other companies working exclusively in the dance field.

Three of the theatre groups also are deemed to be national companies: the Finnish National Theatre and the Swedish National Theatre (both based in Helsinki) and the Tampere Workers' Theatre, the only workers' company in the country still in operation. These national companies receive subsidy from both state and local authorities, with the state subsidy significantly higher.

There are eight designated regional theatres operating across the country which, since 1978, are also required to tour in their regions.

Finland's Swedish-speaking minority has eight Swedish-language groups operating, four well-established and four smaller groups. All other theatres in the country work exclusively in Finnish.

Of the sixty-two theatres, five specialize in productions for children. There are also several small puppet groups working exclusively for young audiences. In fact, most Finnish theatres (which all tend to work in repertory) stage at least one production each season for children.

The larger theatres – such as the Finnish National Theatre and the Helsinki City Theatre – have permanent companies of about fifty actors; medium-sized theatres tend to have companies of about thirty. About 500 actors work annually on a show-by-show basis. Administrative and technical staffs are about twice as large as the artistic staffs.

The Espoo Theatre close to Helsinki uses its stage primarily for visiting productions from across the country and abroad as well as for a small number of its own productions done by jobbed-in actors.

Salary scales across the country are about average for the Nordic countries and correspond to the general wage level for people with academic training such as teachers. Trade unions are strong and virtually 100 per cent of the theatre community belongs to one union or another – actors, directors, designers, technicians, and so on. The permanent theatres belong to the Finnish Theatre Union while the free groups belong to the Theatre Centre. Theatres follow agreed scales for wages and are not allowed to hire untrained personnel at lower wages.

Actors generally work on two-year contracts which, at the actor's choice, can be renewed. In practice, theatres cannot give notice to an actor with a permanent contract. Directors generally work on fixed-term contracts and move between theatres quite freely. Freelance actors grew in number in the 1990s as did the number of groups which emerge for a production or two and then disappear. The system utilized in the larger groups has been the subject of much recent criticism, especially by the small groups who have long argued for greater flexibility.

With business sponsorship in culture almost non-existent, public subsidy in Finland, a small economic market, is the indispensable impelling force that keeps cultural activity moving forward. Even box-office revenues are insignificant in comparison to public subsidy, but such a high level of subsidy is more or less the norm in most Nordic countries. In 1993, state subsidy was 193.5 million Finnish marks (US$35 million), with another 240 million marks (US$43 million)

coming to theatres from local authorities. The National Opera received direct subsidy, not included in the above figures, of an additional 122.5 million marks (US$22 million).

Theatregoing grew after the war to about 1.1 million people in 1960 and to 2.6 million in 1972. Since that time the number has varied between 2.4 million and 2.6 million spectators annually. The number is impressive given that it represents around 50 per cent of the country's 5 million inhabitants. In the most densely populated areas of southern Finland and the provinces of Häme and Uusimaa, the number of tickets sold is virtually equal to the number of inhabitants.

The reason for the theatre's continuing popularity in the country can probably be attributed to the number of new theatres constructed in the 1960s and 1970s – fourteen – and the consequent growth in the number of seats available. The period corresponds to a general urbanization of Finnish society.

Most of the new Finnish theatre construction was financed by local authorities who wanted to improve each city's cultural image while also making a positive impact on their local economies through spin-off commercial activity and increased tourism.

During the warm summer months, theatrical activities often take place outdoors. Staged not only by professionals but also by hundreds of amateur theatre groups, these outdoor productions can be seen in parks and include both comedies and classics as well as children's theatre. The best known outdoor theatre in the country is the Pyynikki Theatre in Tampere.

There are as well innumerable summer festivals, the biggest one organized each August in Tampere. Each June, a dance festival is organized in Kuopio and each July an opera festival is held in a Medieval castle in Savonlinna. Other festivals for children's groups and amateur companies take place during both winter and summer.

Riitta Seppälä

Artistic Profile

Companies

The Finnish National Theatre was founded in 1872. Under the direction of Kaarlo Bergbom,

it started as an authentic folk theatre performing also on extensive tours around sparsely populated rural areas. Eino Kalima (director of the theatre between 1917 and 1950) brought the

Stanislavski method to Finland and led to a new professional standard in the theatre. Arvi Kivimaa, who succeeded Kalima as director and remained there until 1974, opened wider contacts with European theatres; the same policy was followed by Kai Savola (b. 1931, managing director of the theatre from 1974 to 1992), who promoted foreign visits and invited renowned guest directors such as Yuri Lyubimov, Lev Dodin and Otomar Krejca. In 1992 Maria-Liisa Nevala (b. 1943) was appointed managing director of the theatre. Since 1902, the National has functioned in the same three-stage building; there is a fourth stage in a neighbouring building.

As in other leading theatres, the most prominent actors of the National have remained loyal to the company for decades, though some have also become popular movie stars such as Aku Korhonen (1892–1960), Ella Eronen (1900–87), Tauno Palo (1908–82), Joel Rinne (1897–1981), Jussi Jurkka (1930–82), Pentti Siimes (b. 1929), Eeva-Kaarina Volanen (b. 1921) and Tarmo Manni (b. 1921).

The theatre's repertoire tends to be varied, including national and foreign drama, classical and modern plays. There are ten to fifteen premières each year with about twenty plays kept in the repertory. Music theatre is very rarely presented at the National.

The leading Swedish-language company in Finland is the Swedish Theatre in Helsinki. Its activities as a national stage began in 1916 when two groups – one from Sweden and a Swedish-speaking group from Finland – were united; it continues performing in a building from 1866. Director Nicken Rönngren (1919–54) contributed notably to the development of the theatre; he trained a group of skilled actors and raised the theatre's artistic level to an international standard. Among the theatre's most notable actors have been Gerda Wrede (b. 1896), who also directed the actors' school functioning in the theatre, Axel Slangus (1890–1965), Erik Lindström (1906–74) and May Pihlgren (b. 1904). The company has fostered Swedish-language drama by Finnish playwrights and also has a solid music theatre tradition. The theatre has a total of eighty employees; thirty are artistic staff.

The Tampere Workers' Theatre, the only remaining workers' theatre in the country, was taken under special protection by the state in the 1980s. Founded in 1901 as an amateur theatre, it became a professional theatre during the period when Kosti Elo was its director

Eino Salmelainen's 1958 Tampere Workers' Theatre production of Camus's *Les Justes*.

(1919–49). Eino Salmelainen, director of the theatre from 1943 to 1964, influenced theatre nation-wide through his original productions at the Workers' Theatre. He freed Finnish acting from theatrical clichés and put new emphasis on psychological accuracy. During the period that Salmelainen was director of the theatre, he created a strong sense of ensemble and an exceptionally close contact with audiences. This has been passed on to later generations by the company's core of long-time actors. The Workers' Theatre not only functions in a modern building inaugurated in 1986 but also performs on two stages at its former building. Since the 1970s, the Workers' Theatre has not had any political alignment and the company's repertoire has been oriented to as wide an audience as possible without compromising its artistic ambitions.

The Tampere Theatre, founded in 1967, is another major theatre in the city. Though it is a private shareholders' company, it also receives subsidy from state and local authorities. The theatre has three stages and a staff of about ninety; its repertoire tends toward new foreign plays and large-scale music theatre productions.

They presented, for example, the first performances in Finland of *West Side Story* and *Phantom of the Opera*.

Municipal theatres in Finland came into being as the result of a compromise on cultural policy. In the 1940s, when most towns had both a workers' theatre and a so-called bourgeois theatre, financial resources were no longer sufficient to maintain both and they were united to form a municipal theatre. Today they receive quite substantial aid from local authorities.

The Helsinki City Theatre was founded in 1965, and gained a new building with three stages in 1967. Following on the work of two earlier theatres, it inherited a repertory of folk drama, old and new, and light music theatre. In the 1970s the theatre became noted for productions by directors such as Jouko Turkka. Ralf Långbacka, director of the theatre from 1983 to 1988, strove to break from the norms of large established theatres by adding in small productions committed to current issues. Attempts were also made to break down institutionalization by dividing the theatre into three artistically independent units. During Raija-Sinikka Rantala's (b. 1946) time as director, the theatre has added an independently functioning group, the Yhdestoista hetki (Eleventh Hour), directed by Kalle and Ritva (b. 1944) Holmberg.

The Turku City Theatre, founded in 1946, is the country's oldest municipal theatre entirely maintained by local authorities. The theatre's new building was inaugurated in 1962 and presently it has three stages with a staff of 120; it produces eight to ten premières per year. The artistic level of the Turku City Theatre has kept it among the country's front-line stages with the years 1971–7 as the theatre's most prosperous period. Under the direction of Ralf Långbacka and Kalle Holmberg it became the country's most artistically important theatre. Even after the Långbacka–Holmberg period, though, the theatre continued to produce works of national interest and has been particularly successful experimenting with productions outside the theatre's premises.

The municipal theatre in Oulu, founded in 1965, is the largest in northern Finland. It functions in a building constructed in 1972 with three stages, and has a staff of about a hundred employees. The theatre has influence over a vast area covering Lapland and northern Sweden; half its spectators come from outside Oulu itself. In addition to folk drama the theatre has also produced some experiments. Among these was 'theatre in the service of life', produced in the 1980s, which consisted of a series of twenty-four plays on current issues. Each had a

Kalle Holmberg's 1972 Turku City Theatre production of Aleksis Kivi's *Seven Brothers*, designed by Kaj Puumalainen.

rehearsal period of one day. Interest in national playwrights has also marked its repertoire.

The municipal theatres of Lahti, Kuopio and Jyväskylä have also developed into major professional theatres with high standards.

At the end of the 1960s a group theatre movement arose in Finland as a protest against most of the established theatres. The group theatres' objective was to democratize theatre art and to reach those groups of the population for whom theatre had been unattainable because of economic, social or geographical reasons.

The first to be founded was the Ryhmäteatteri (Group Theatre) in 1967. It became a leader of the experimental theatre movement after Arto af Hällström (b. 1952) and Raila Leppäkoski (b. 1950) became its directors in 1981. Its repertory generally consists of new plays written specifically for the group and adaptations of classical drama. Appealing especially to students, the group performs on its own stage in Helsinki in the winter and during the summer in a historical fortress on the island of Suomenlinna just off the coast of Helsinki.

The Kom-teatteri (Kom Theatre) began its activities in 1969 as a Swedish-language company directed by Kaisa Korhonen (b. 1941), but it evolved into a Finnish-language group within a year. Initially left-leaning, the group stages mostly new Finnish plays. Many young writers, in fact, have worked with the group on a staff basis. Music takes a central role in the productions of the Kom Theatre. Composer Kaj Chydenius and producer Pekka Milonoff (b. 1947) deserve mention among the artistic directors of the theatre.

A number of theatre groups started up towards the end of the 1980s. Among the most interesting are the two Swedish-language groups, Viirus and Mars, and the Finnish-language theatre groups, Q-teatteri (Q Theatre) and Eurooppa 4 (Europe 4).

Of the eight regional theatres in the country, the municipal theatre of the city of Kajaani, founded in 1906, has consistently offered the most original repertoire. It has also functioned as the regional theatre for the province of Oulu since 1978. Kari Selinheimo (b. 1944) became director of the theatre in 1973 and since that time the company has attracted attention nationally for its ability to combine contemporary drama with folk themes. It has been the most dedicated of the regional theatres in its search for plays with regional connections while also dedicating a portion of its artistic resources to productions for young audiences. Even there,

it has regularly searched for new forms of expression.

Finland's two Swedish-language regional theatres – the Vasa and the Åbo Svenska (in Turku) – work together to take tours to the Swedish-speaking area of the Gulf of Bothnia and the large archipelago along Finland's west coast.

At the same time, the Lilla Teatern (Little Theatre) in Helsinki has also regularly staged more alternative theatre productions in Swedish. Founded in 1940, the Lilla Teatern began its life as a variety theatre. After 1955, director Vivica Bandler (b. 1917) turned it into one of the country's more significant avant-garde companies. In 1967, actors Lasse Pöysti (b. 1927) and Birgitta Ulfsson (b. 1928) became directors of the theatre and began to establish a new repertoire by commissioning plays on contemporary issues by Swedish-language writers living in Finland. Many of the writers worked closely and collectively with the company. The group's many cabaret performances also reacted to political issues of the day. Its most recent director, Asko Sarkola (b. 1945), has added other plays to the repertoire ranging from classics to light comedies. Most of its Swedish-language productions today are later restaged with the same actors in Finnish.

Dramaturgy

The great national writer Aleksis Kivi (1834–72) laid the base for Finnish dramatic literature. Most directly influenced by Schiller, Holberg and Shakespeare, Kivi's plays combine multifaceted realistic characters with a solid dramatic structure and a rich poetic language. His masterpiece was *Nummisuutarit* (*Cobblers of the Heath*), written in 1864 and first staged in 1875 at the Finnish Theatre. Considered the first major work of Finnish national drama, this tragi-comic tale of a cobbler's unfortunate marriage proposal continues to inspire new interpretations on the country's stages.

A contemporary of Kivi's, Minna Canth (1844–97) was the first social-realist in Finnish drama. Influenced by Ibsen, she fought for improved social status for women and for the social rights of the less fortunate. She was interested in those trapped on the edges of society and her play *Anna-Liisa* (1895) tells the story of a young woman from a puritanical village who kills her new-born baby. *Työmiehen vaimo* (*The Worker's Wife*, 1885) deals with the tragic fate of an alcoholic. The comedy *Papin perhe* (*The Vicar's Family*, 1891) is a bourgeois drama with the family's internal relations a microcosm of the power structures of Finnish society of the time. Canth's plays are still studied and in the 1970s especially they inspired several new, politically oriented productions.

Maria Jotuni (1880–1943) is another early master of Finnish dramaturgy. With pitiless satire and multifaceted characters, she describes the selfishness, mediocrity, cruelty and self-complacence of the society around her. The most popular of her plays has been *Tohvelisankarin rouva* (*Wife of the Henpecked Husband*, 1924) and *Miehen kylkiluu* (*Man's Rib*, 1914).

These various Finnish classics all engendered a mainstream of essentially realistic dramas and those later writers who diverged from realism rarely received positive responses from audiences.

The 1930s and 1940s saw the appearance of a number of journalist-playwrights who wrote a large number of interesting plays dealing with everyday life. Among the important playwrights of this period were Mika Waltari (1906–79) and Estonian-born Hella Wuolijoki (1886–1954), a colleague of Brecht's, whose play *Sahanpuruprinsessa* (*Sawdust Princess*) inspired Brecht's *Herr Puntila und sein Knecht Matti* (*Herr Puntila and his Man Matti*). Wuolijoki wrote regularly about Finnish peasant culture in such works as *Niskavuori* and excelled in portraits of strong female characters.

During the 1950s, there was a trend towards smaller and more intimate stages and this had its effect on playwriting of the period. *Eros ja Psykhe* (*Eros and Psyche*) and *Poltettu oranssi* (*Burnt Orange*), written in verse by poet Eeva-Liisa Manner (b. 1921), were influenced by modern psychology and psychoanalysis as were the plays of Walentin Chorell (1912–83), who wrote in Swedish. Veijo Meri (b. 1928), a well-known prose writer, wrote several absurdist comedies such as *Sotamies Jokisen Vikiloma* (*Private Jokinen's Wedding Leave*).

Paavo Haavikko (b. 1931) broke away most boldly from the traditions of realism. He often used history as a base for his portraits of bureaucracy, power and power struggles. Combining epic myth with anachronistic elements, his early plays received strongly negative criticism. He finally had success with *Agricola ja kettu* (*Agricola and the Fox*) which takes place in Finland during the Reformation; the main character, Mikael Agricola, was a disciple of Martin Luther. The play's theme – a small nation caught between superpowers – was later taken up in other plays including the libretto for an opera, *Ratsumies* (*The Horseman*).

Social change was reflected clearly in 1960s dramaturgy in such plays as *Lapualaisooppera* (*The Opera of Lapua*, 1966) written by Arvo Salo. The decade saw many reinterpretations of historical events from anti-bourgeois points of view as well as many plays, often on local history, written collectively.

Probably the foremost name among Finland's socially committed writers is Jussi Kylätasku (b. 1943). Working initially with director Jouko Turkka, he wrote the drama *Runar and Kyllikki* which was written in 1971 but was not staged for another three years because most theatres' boards were nervous about staging a play about a sexual murder and the mental violence undergone by a weak individual in a small rural community. In his later plays, Kylätasku regularly turned to historical events to comment on current political happenings. His play *Gracchuskan pojat* (*Gracchuskan's Sons*, 1982) is set in ancient Rome, *Maaria Blomma* (1980) and *Haapoja* (1990) deal with religious fanaticism.

A number of trained dramaturges have emerged in recent years from the Theatre Academy and many have themselves turned to playwriting, often outside the realistic mode. Among the most interesting are Jussi Parviainen (b. 1955), author of *Jumalan rakastaja* (*God's Lover*, 1984), and Juha Siltanen (b. 1959), author of *Foxtrot* (1991).

Directors, Directing and Production Styles

For most of Finland's theatre history, directors have played a central role. Alongside their creative work on various productions, they have often served as artistic directors of theatres responsible for a company's overall artistic profile.

In the period just after World War II, three directors of note stand out. For Eino Kalima, long-time director of the Finnish National Theatre, the post-war period was his most creative and the culmination of his artistic career. At the beginning of the century, he had studied in Moscow and had been greatly influenced by the work and ideas of Stanislavski. In his own productions, he strove to eliminate the superficial from the actor's work in order to achieve a new kind of psychological realism. He did not believe in simply imitating reality on a stage but sought rather an intuitive, internal reality. Kalima's masterpieces were his Chekhov productions; their delicate Slavic atmosphere and the profound personality of his characters left a lasting mark on all subsequent Chekhov interpretations in Finland.

A second prominent director was Wilho Ilmari (1888–1983), head of the Turku City Theatre for some thirty years. Ilmari was also a follower of the Stanislavski method; his most lasting contributions, however, were his many innovations in actor training.

Eino Salmelainen, director of the Tampere Workers' Theatre from 1943 to 1964 was first a follower of expressionism, later of the Stanislavski style and in the 1950s of the French absurdists. Near the end of his career, he again turned to psychological realism. Always opposed to emotionally expressionless acting – a clear misreading of Stanislavski's ideas – he consciously strove for expressive force in his work though always with the utmost simplicity.

His apparent radicalism, his coordination of text and movement, his aversion to the conventional and his deeply penetrating readings of text engendered many new interpretations. Among his numerous innovative productions were Camus's *Les Justes* (*The Just*), Aleksis Kivi's *Cobblers of the Heath* and Hella Wuolijoki's *Niskavuori* series.

During the 1950s and 1960s – with Arvi Kivimaa running the National Theatre – director Jack Witikka (b. 1916) staged a great number of productions which again sought to break away from realism. His approach was extremely visual to the point of being almost cinematic. He also let the actor explore more than usual. Among his important productions were the Finnish premières of several plays by Beckett, including *Endgame* and *Waiting for Godot*, as well as plays by Albee, Pinter, Miller and Osborne.

Brecht's influence on Finnish theatre was most evident in the 1960s. Younger directors attacked earlier generations of directors for their

Ralf Långbacka's 1977 Turku City Theatre production of Büchner's *Danton's Death*.
Photo: Kari Hakli.

Jouko Turkka's 1979 Helsinki City Theatre production of Maiju Lassila's *Wise Virgin*.

lack of social and political commitment. Ralf Långbacka, one of these new voices, combined precise intellectual analysis with a socially oriented approach in his own productions. He challenged the large repertory theatres to become more vital and fought to create an ensemble of thinking, creative artists. During his time as director of the Turku City Theatre (1971–7), the company became the most vital in the country. His productions were not limited to Brecht but his *Galileo* was a highlight of the period. Among other authors he staged with great success were Shakespeare, Chekhov and Büchner. He later also staged a number of outstanding productions of operas. In the 1990s, his influence on theatre in Finland extended into the area of teaching and even into theory as he became a noted analyst of theatre and dramatic art.

Långbacka's co-director at the Turku City Theatre was Kalle Holmberg. Holmberg first achieved fame in 1966 with his production of Arvo Salo's *The Opera of Lapua* for the Helsinki Student Theatre. Both the form and the content of the production were protests against the notion of opera and theatre as merely beautiful and entertaining. The production inspired many of the developing, politically oriented, theatre groups which were emerging by the early 1970s.

Holmberg has reflected his times with sensitive intuition and he has come a long way since his early, Brecht-inspired folk opera style. During the time he worked in Turku, he won admiration of both critics and a wide segment of the public for his dynamic production of Aleksis Kivi's *Seven Brothers* in which he stressed movement and portrayed the Finnish people with both humour and criticism. In his later work, he turned to dramatizations of Dostoevsky novels and mythical interpretations from the epic *Kalevala*.

This artistically important period at the Turku City Theatre was followed in the second half of the 1970s by a flourishing period at the Helsinki City Theatre under Jouko Turkka. At the beginning of the 1970s, Turkka had first come to attention as a provocative director. He often created interpretations of Finnish classics which shattered romantic clichés with coarse neo-realistic descriptions of the common people. In this, he worked closely with young playwrights who themselves were concerned about social problems, growing urbanization and crime. Among his important works at the Helsinki City Theatre was Hannu Salama's (b. 1936) *Siinä näkijä missä tekijä* (*Where There's*

a Deed There's a Witness) in which he used simultaneity to create an overview of the Finnish civil war and its historical consequences. Another of his outstanding productions was Maiju Lassila's (1868–1918) folk comedy *Viisas neitsyt* (*A Wise Virgin*). When in the 1980s Turkka began teaching, he again caused controversy with his emphasis on a physical form of naturalism and emotional expression. In the 1990s, he worked most often on television.

During the 1970s, many of the smaller groups that came into existence preferred to move away from the notion of an all-powerful director and chose instead to work collectively. Unfortunately, the results were not impressive and by the 1980s strong directors again came to the fore.

Many of the strongest have been women. Kaisa Korhonen, another Brecht-influenced director, started her career with the Kom Theatre and came to public attention with productions of plays by Brecht and Gorki. Her productions portrayed the family and the middle classes with both severity and disillusion. Throughout her career, she has tended to work with small, closely knit groups in which the actors' personalities are allowed to emerge and influence the productions. Her later works, especially with the Musta Rakkaus group in Tampere, have tended to be more imagistic requiring audiences to make mental connections. Intuition, emotion and a continuous search for new methods have marked her work.

Another director of note working with the Kom Theatre has been Laura Jäntti (b. 1950). A consistently experimental director, she has given special weight to visual and musical aspects in her productions. Concerned especially with the psychology of relationships between men and women, her productions of two Shakespearian plays, *The Tempest* and *Richard III*, were played with women in the leading roles. Probably her best work was Märta Tikkanen's (b. 1935) *Punahilkka* (*Little Red Riding Hood*) done for the Turku City Theatre in 1987. The play deals with a marriage inferno, female subordination, repressed sexuality and the passage of problems from one generation to another.

Since 1981, the Ryhmäteatteri has followed a markedly experimental line, regularly digressing from prevalent currents. Its two directors – Arto af Hällström and Raila Leppäkoski – were among the first to move away from the sociopolitical viewpoints of the 1970s. Avoiding easy answers, they preferred to simply raise questions and to offer new ways of seeing the key issues. As well, they dealt with space in innovative ways seeking more direct contact with their audiences and turning each production into a new adventure. In doing this, the company even turned to world classics; Hällström's own

productions of Molière were consistent highlights.

In the 1990s, no specific trends are yet clear though experiments in the dance field have had influence in the theatre.

Anneli Suur-Kujala

Music Theatre

When the Suomalainen teatteri was founded in 1872, it had both spoken theatre and opera sections. The Finnish National Opera, which derived from the opera section of the Suomalainen teatteri, is the only institution in Finland specializing in music theatre. Yet almost all professional theatres in Finland have included music theatre in their repertory. From the early twentieth century, Hungarian and Viennese operettas as well as folk plays accompanied by music became major box-office attractions that permitted the financing of productions of more serious drama. In the 1950s American musicals began competing for success with the operettas. Right into the 1990s, stage musicals retained their leading position in spectator statistics. Perhaps the country's all-time favourite has been the often-revived folk-based musical play *Tukkijoella* (*Loggers' River*) by Teuvo Pakkala (1862–1925) (originally presented in 1899).

The 1970s were a boom period for Finnish music theatre. Politically oriented, its leading figure was composer Kaj Chydenius. His *Opera of Lapua* marked the way for critical and satirical musical drama with the Kom Theatre the most consistent representative of the trend.

Music also gained importance in spoken drama and many prominent musicians specialized in theatrical music, as in the case of Jukka Linkola (b. 1955) and Atso Almila (b. 1953), who both composed music for stage musicals and opera.

The year 1975 marked the rise of new Finnish opera with presentations of *Ratsumies* (*The Horseman*) composed by Aulis Sallinen (b. 1935) and *Viimeiset kiusaukset* (*The Last Temptations*) by Joonas Kokkonen (b. 1921). The works were critically well received and also enjoyed great success with the public. In both cases, the operas were tonal and the scenic composition founded on recognizable Finnish dramatic realism. *The Horseman*, particularly,

offers several interwoven levels of text (the libretto is by the renowned lyric writer Paavo Haavikko) while the hero in both operas is the hard-working Finnish male raised to a mythical scale.

The Last Temptations remains the only opera composed by Joonas Kokkonen but quickly achieved the status of a national classic. It competes for that title with the opera *Pohjalaiset* (*The Ostrobothnians*, 1923) composed by Leevi Madetoja (1887–1947); the theme of the latter is the struggle for independence of the Finnish people during czarist rule in the nineteenth century. The opera reveals much about the self-esteem of the newly independent country and about its strong nationalism. The musical structure of *The Ostrobothnians* has its roots in Finnish folk melodies.

Aulis Sallinen has continued composing music for opera with exceptional success. After *The Horseman* he composed the opera *Punainen viiva* (*The Red Line*, 1978), based on a famous novel. The red line symbolized the right to vote obtained by Finns during Russian rule, as well as the bloody fight for survival in the backwoods of eastern Finland.

In 1983, *The Last Temptations* and *The Red Line* were presented as part of a tour to the Metropolitan Opera House in New York. The Finnish National Opera has also presented them in London, Moscow, Zürich and several cities in Germany.

Another internationally famous opera by Aulis Sallinen, *Kuningas lähtee Ranskaan* (*The King Goes Forth to France*) was composed as a joint commission from the Savonlinna Opera Festival and the Royal Opera, Covent Garden, in 1983. The world première of the work was in 1984 in Savonlinna, and the London première in 1987.

Of Sallinen's operas, *The King Goes Forth to France* is most distinctly a musical drama. Its post-modern approach was especially emphasized musically and directorially in the Covent Garden production. Sallinen's fourth opera was based on the hero Kullervo in the Finnish national epic *Kalevala*. Kullervo crystallizes the bitterness and vindictiveness which result from a lack of love in the world. In this version, Kullervo becomes a criminal destroying all that crosses his path. First presented in Los Angeles in 1992, the opera was the inaugural presentation of the new National Opera House in Helsinki in 1993.

The opera *Veitsi* (*The Knife*) by Paavo Heininen (b. 1938), with a libretto by Veijo Meri, is a multi-focus musical work. Postmodern in style, *Veitsi* is Finland's first urban opera: most national operas deal only with characters in an agrarian society or with historical figures. Prior to *Veitsi*, Heininen had composed *Silkkirumpu* (*The Damask Drum*) based on Japanese *Noh* drama.

Also of note are the operas *Vincent* (premièred at the Finnish National Opera in 1990) composed by Einojuhani Rautavaara (b. 1928), and the 1975 *Hyönteiselämää* (*Insect Life*) by Kalevi Aho (b. 1949). Aho had earlier composed the operatic monologue *Avain* (*The Key*) for a baritone and thirteen musicians. It was first presented in Helsinki and later by the Hamburg State Opera.

Several explanations have been sought to justify the vitality of opera as an art form in Finland. The Savonlinna Opera Festival was revived in 1967 and its existence obviously inspired opera composers. The presentation in 1970 in Savonlinna of the opera *Juha*, composed by the 1920s modernist composer Aarre Merikanto (1893–1958), contributed to launching a boom in opera composition; both the work and the impressive presentation (directed by Kalle Holmberg, who later directed all the premières of the operas by Aulis Sallinen) undeniably demonstrated music theatre's vast theatrical possibilities.

Even so, it is difficult to explain why so much more music theatre is composed in Finland than anywhere else in Europe. One reason might simply be that almost without exception, all new works find enthusiastic producers. Even before its opening, the new opera building had a list of new music theatre productions lining up to be presented there. Among these were *Det sjungande trädet* (*The Singing Tree*), a first opera by the academician Erik Bergman (b. 1906), as well as a first opera by composer Jouni Kaipainen (b. 1956).

Dance Theatre

Until the 1960s, professional dance in Finland consisted almost solely of classical ballet. The ballet of the Finnish National Opera started its activities in 1922 and it was possible even then to fill the group with students trained in Helsinki by dance teachers from St Petersburg or by Finnish teachers who themselves had been trained there.

Prior to the foundation of the company, dance performances were presented in Helsinki mostly by foreign guest dancers, the most distinguished being the ballet troupe of the Maryanski Theatre from St Petersburg. Also a performance by Anna Pavlova inspired Finnish dance amateurs to undertake the serious study of dance.

A performance by Isadora Duncan in 1905 at the Finnish National Theatre encouraged amateur dancers to study the new free dance; Maggie Gripenberg (1881–1976) was the most noteworthy among them. She started her studies in Dresden and continued at the Jacques Dalcroze school in Geneva. The first modern Finnish choreographer to obtain international recognition, she won first prize in a choreography competition in Brussels in 1939.

Her contribution as choreographer and teacher was crucial to the birth of the Finnish dance theatre. She created abstract choreographies based on rhythm for her own company's performances as well as works with marked German expressionist influence. Gripenberg also choreographed for the ballet of the Finnish Opera, including a production based on the music *The Tempest* by Jean Sibelius (1865–1957); she also did choreography for the Finnish National Theatre among dramatic companies.

One of Gripenberg's most prominent students, Irja Hagfors (1905–88), performed in the 1930s with the Harald Kreutzberg dance group among others in Germany; she later worked as a choreographer in Finland.

The 1960s was a period of transition for the

art of dance in the country. Riitta Vainio (b. 1936), who studied modern dance technique in the United States under Nadia Chilkofsky, started teaching modern dance regularly and, with her students, founded a dance group that bore her name. Classical ballerina Tamara Rasmussen (1927–92) studied jazz technique with foreign teachers, founded a dance school and soon mounted performances with a group of her students. Some of Maggie Gripenberg's students founded the group Praesens, which offered regular dance theatre activities and was active through the 1970s.

The achievements of Riitta Vainio as pedagogue and choreographer laid the foundations for professional modern dance in Finland. Her productions were influenced by American postmodernism. In Finland in the 1960s, a period dominated by classical ballet, her works were so new and revolutionary that she had only a small following even in artistic circles. Riitta Vainio's work as a teacher was better understood and valued; her students became the founders of the first dance theatre groups of the 1970s and 1980s.

The first of these groups was the still-active Dance Theatre Raatikko founded in 1972; choreographer Marjo Kuusela (b. 1946) was one of its most active members. Kuusela was trained in literature as well as dance and her artistic work was linked to Finnish realism and theatre. Her first works were based on national plays from the end of the nineteenth century which dealt with the conditions of Finnish labourers, especially working-class women. The themes of her productions were in line with leftist cultural interests in the 1970s which tried to integrate intellectual values with the labour movement. The problems of Finnish society and its people remained a central theme in Kuusela's productions into the 1990s though the style of her works has moved from realism. Her later works were freer in form than the dance dramas from the beginning of her career. The eclectic nature of her movement has developed from her former search for simplicity to a greater sensitivity and subtlety of nuance. In addition to the Raatikko Dance Theatre, Marjo Kuusela has created dance theatre productions for the Finnish National Ballet and for the dance group of the Helsinki City Theatre, among others. At the Raatikko her work is carried on by choreographer Marja Korhola (b. 1954) whose works are marked by an agile fantasy and satire.

Operettas and musicals have always been popular in Finnish theatre but the dance groups performing in these works were usually amateurs. During the boom of operettas and musicals at the Helsinki City Theatre in the 1960s and 1970s (when the theatre often had three musical productions in its repertoire), performances were mounted with the best professional freelance dancers in the capital, dancers with classical and modern schooling. This was not as difficult as it seemed since regularly functioning dance groups – other than the Finnish National Ballet – did not yet exist. Gradually these freelancers formed a highly professional elite, and the question of forming a permanent group in connection with one of the biggest theatres in the country became inevitable.

In 1973 the Helsinki City Theatre engaged a group of six dancers on a permanent basis along with Liisa Priha (b. 1941) as ballet master and choreographer. The dancers not only performed in the theatre's musical productions but also created their own productions each year. The group gradually grew and gained status for Finnish dance, especially during the period that it was led by Jorma Uotinen (b. 1950) who had performed with Carolyn Carlson's group at the Paris Grand Opera. Uotinen led the group of twelve dancers between 1982 and 1991 when he was named director of the Finnish National Ballet. During his leadership the image of the group changed. Uotinen represents a dance theatre that in style and technique reminds one of Carolyn Carlson's aesthetics. His works are composed of strong and aesthetically mastered scenic visions, where dancers, lighting, costumes and objects combine in seamless cohesion to create a mythical world. His works have always strongly reflected the spirit of the times, receiving a sympathetic response especially from younger audiences. In 1991, Carolyn Carlson was director of the Helsinki City Theatre's dance group.

In the beginning of the 1990s several small dance groups were also functioning on a regular basis in Finland, of which two groups in Turku – the Aurinkobaletti and Dance Theatre Eri – started off as theatre dance groups. Eri, formed by a group of five dancers, boasts a high technical level. The group has also startled audiences with its unusual choice of themes including the status and feelings of sexual minorities.

Auli Räsänen

Theatre for Young Audiences

As in other Nordic countries, before the rise of small independent theatres in Finland, performances for children were generally limited to a single annual fairytale staged at Christmas. On the other hand, Finland was self-sufficient as far as these plays went since it had its own storyteller, Zachris Topelius, a journalist and critic, who wrote some thirty children's plays based on Finnish and international folk tales in the 1850s and 1860s. It is worth noting that Topelius was also the first to call for an indigenous Finnish drama in 1842.

For generations, children were limited to the magic circle of Topelius's plays, which were didactic and full of black-and-white morality. As well, in the course of a hundred years, their treatment also became stereotyped and flat.

Topelius thus became a symbol for the left-leaning generation that created independent theatres in the late 1960s and the early 1970s and took up children's theatre with great enthusiasm. They considered that fairytale elements blurred the child's conception of reality and they discarded Topelius and along with him the entire fairytale tradition.

The interaction and exchange of ideas at inter-Nordic seminars arranged in the early 1970s provided an important influence for the new children's theatres. 'To the children' and 'with the children' were the watchwords with which the new touring companies set out to activate the public.

To compensate for the lack of instructive, socially critical children's plays, texts were made according to the individual needs of each group. They had an epic structure and made use of ingenious dramaturgical cuts. They dealt with motorization, pollution, the dangers of drugs and smoking, developing countries and social problems. Regardless of the scope of the issue, the pattern was to present one problem and its solution. Information and instruction were served up through fantasy elements, imaginary creatures and magic tricks. Style was sought in the 'aesthetics of scarcity' of the Medieval market theatre, since on tour performances had to be staged in a variety of spaces. The reality of the situations depended on actors' skills; characters were deliciously caricatured types.

The greatest impact of these instructive plays was that they opened the doors of schools and day care centres to the independent groups.

The Finnish children's theatre reconquered

the fairytale in the mid-1970s. The group theatre movement had passed from simplistic social preaching to a deeper view of the world and humanity, from agitprop to socialist-realism. In the children's theatre, fairytales were thought to express people's deepest wishes and social morality.

The renaissance of fairytales and the return to their human wisdom and philosophy did not follow the same pattern in Finland as in other Nordic countries. In Finland it was the result of an increasingly lively cultural exchange with the east European countries and the encounter with the vitality of their interpretation of folk tales and classics. Translations of children's books and pedagogical works from those countries revitalized the consciousness of the country's own folk heritage, and led to a realization of the potential offered to children's theatres by fairytales, stories and nonsense rhymes. The message aimed at the mind was succeeded by a breakthrough of emotion and experience; the warmth and colour of folk tales provided the tone for many years. The approach differed from the western trend in which theoretical writings shifted emphasis to an analysis of the significance of fairytales in terms of depth psychology.

Folklore was also adopted in Finland as a means of viewing the world, a weapon against multinational 'trash culture'. The colourfulness of the folk tradition was used for aesthetic purposes: by emphasizing visual elements, children's understanding of theatre could be developed along with their comprehension of the significance of various elements of expression in the arousing of emotions and associations.

The independent companies were the pioneers of Finnish children's theatre, though its development has also been retarded by the financial and intellectual underestimation these companies have suffered. The continuity of children's theatre has depended on touring companies. Though the institutional theatres' former reluctant and merely dutiful approach has changed and artists have started to take more interest, the activity of the institutional theatres is still seasonal and children's productions still have not achieved an established position within them.

In the early 1990s, some 3,500 performances were being given annually for children. Touring companies accounted for 40 per cent of these performances.

In 1993, there were about thirty independent theatre and dance companies regularly doing special performances for young audiences. Specific groups staging such productions included the Swedish-language Skolteatern (founded in 1960); the puppet theatres Vihreä Omena, Peukaloppotti, Sampo, Hevosenkenkä and Mukamas. Ahaa-teatteri and Teatteri forty-one were specializing in school performances, while the modern dance companies Raatikko, Hurjaruuth and Mobita were also staging regular productions for children.

During the second half of the 1980s the children's theatre in Finland rose in social esteem, which led the state to grant special assistance for the foundation of such theatres. Thus the theatres Teatteri Pieni Suomi in Helsinki and Teatteri 2000 in Tampere were founded through special state assistance.

Although the Finnish theatre has always been highly aware of its national and educational vocation, it has not been so conscious of the continuity of its role and how to safeguard it. Finland has lagged behind other Nordic countries regarding the systematic development of children's theatre and the 'preparation' of new generations of spectators.

Raija Ojala

Puppet Theatre

Finland, as other Nordic countries, lacks an indigenous puppet theatre tradition. Some forms of folklore could be considered reminiscent of puppet and mask theatre, such as the masks and figures used in feasts celebrating the killing of a bear, or the disguises of the *nuuttipukit*, door-to-door strollers celebrating the end of Christmas festivities. Finland joined the centuries-old and highly developed European tradition of puppet theatre only in the nineteenth century. Travelling troupes touring to Stockholm and St Petersburg occasionally also visited Finland, and performed, among their repertoire, scenes from various classic works.

Paper and shadow figures as well as glove-puppets were brought to Finland as toy gifts from trips to Europe. Around the same period, some artistically minded adults became enthusiastic amateur puppeteers, giving performances to small audiences, among them the painter Albert Edelfeldt (1854–1905).

In 1909, Kalle Nyström (1865–1933) founded the Marionetteatern in Helsinki and ran it continuously for twenty years. The performances were aimed at an adult audience and told of current happenings in artistic spheres and of celebrities such as Sibelius. Children had their own performances. In 1915 Bärbi Luther (1898–1979) began performing exclusively for children in kindergartens using shadow figures. In the 1930s the puppet theatre Marionettiteatteri Fennia flourished, presented by artist Arvo Avenius (1901–72) among his other amusement park activities.

After World War II, puppet theatres sought and found a new language and new styles. Two noteworthy visits from abroad were made to Finland: in 1949 French puppeteer Jacques Chesnais performed and in 1950 the Russian Sergei Obraztsov. They inspired enthusiasm for puppetry and Finnish puppeteers began presenting public performances showing their influence. The names of Harriet (b. 1891) and Nikolai (1871–1956) Schmakoff as well as the puppet theatre Laipn Nukketeatteri presented by Annikki Setälä (1900–70) should be mentioned. Mona Leo (1903–86), the grande dame of Finnish puppet theatre, started her own puppetry activities in 1952, and her modern approach marked the epoch. Other pioneers worthy of mention were the Kasper Theatre of Irja (b. 1930) and Matti (b. 1926) Ranin, as well as Eine Helke-Viljanen (b. 1922) from Helsinki. This pioneering period was followed by a lull until the beginning of the 1970s, when interest in theatre for children brought a boom and much new enthusiasm for puppetry.

Four professional puppet theatres were founded in Finland of which the oldest, Nukketeatteri Vihreä Omena (Green Apple Puppet Theatre), began in 1971. The founder and artistic director of the theatre was Sirppa Sivori-Asp (b. 1928).

Teatteri Hevosenkenkä (Horseshoe Theatre) was founded in 1975 in Espoo; it performs also in the Finnish National Theatre. Kirsi Aropaltio (b. 1945) was its founder and first artistic director.

Nukketeatteri Sampo (Sampo Puppet Theatre) was founded by Maija (b. 1950) and Bojan (b. 1955) Baric in 1977 in Helsinki and specializes in marionette performances.

The Finnish-Swedish bilingual puppet theatre Teatteri Peukaloppotti-Teatern Tummetott was founded in 1976 in Vaasa. Artistic director Kristiina Hurmerinta (b. 1950) has also served as artistic director of the annual International Puppetry Festival. Peukaloppotti-Tummetott theatre, working under the title of Pandora's Stage, has presented profound, visual performances mostly for adult audiences. Nukketeatteri Sytkyt of Kuopio also started its activities in the 1970s.

During the 1980s puppetry activities in Finland continued to grow with Teatteri Mukamas founded in Tampere. Semi-professional puppetry companies were also created around the country. Among others, the City Theatres of Turku and Hämeenlinna included puppetry performances in their regular repertoires presented by their own cast of actors as well as guest artists. Many solo puppeteers started performing in other parts of the country, for example Teatteri Olga. Nukketeatteri Suomen Turku has mounted performances together with amateurs and children including the historic play *Daniel Hjort* in the Turku Castle and *The Passion Play* at Easter in the Cathedral of Turku.

In addition to the performing companies, there are two puppetry centres in Finland where workshops, training, public performances and other happenings are organized all year round: Musta and Valkea Ratsu (Black and White Horse) in Sysmä, and Nukketalo (Doll's House) in Pieksämäki.

Between 1981 and 1990 the International Puppetry Festival in Vaasa gathered both Finnish and foreign puppeteers, historians and critics. In addition to the guest performances, the festival offered training and workshops, exhibitions and street happenings. After 1990, the event became something of an arena for visual artists.

Two museums offer collections of Finnish puppetry: the Theatre Museum in Helsinki has a permanent collection of theatre puppets created between 1951 and 1968 by the Finnish puppetry pioneer Mona Leo; the museum also mounts exhibitions of puppetry. The Haihara Doll Museum in Tampere has a collection of theatre puppets from the beginning of the century including some rare pieces. As well, the Finnish Broadcasting Company, YLE, has a permanent exhibition of animation puppets.

Puppetry is not yet included as a separate course in the curriculum of the Theatre Academy, but a short training course for puppetry professionals is offered annually.

A range of puppetry training at different levels is also organized in adult education institutes, by the church, and in many other institutions, mostly on an amateur level. Most Finnish puppeteers are self-taught and have sought professional training abroad.

From the beginning, Finnish puppetry has had a narrow and difficult path since the art form was not very highly valued. State assistance and municipal subsidies to qualified puppet theatres were, as a result, quite modest. Nevertheless, during the 1990s a breakthrough and a new fruitful period for the form was beginning as qualified puppeteers were raising the artistic level of productions. Many were also seeking new contacts abroad, exchanging artistic and training experts with, among other countries, Czechoslovakia, the United States, France and Russia.

UNIMA-Finland, the Finnish Centre of the International Puppeteers Union was founded in 1984; it now has 300 members, proof of the new interest in Finnish puppetry art. Members include puppeteers from both professional and amateur companies, instructors, researchers, students and authorities from cultural organizations.

Maiju Tawast

Design

Scenography as a form of art is considered to have begun in Finland in the years just after World War I. At the turn of the century and still during the 1910s most theatres used stock sets chosen from what was available and best suited to the play. Standard sets included, for example, a pine and a birch forest, an exotic forest, the interior of a country cottage and a rococo parlour. On the other hand, the most important performances since the turn of the century had set designs specially commissioned from painters. So, for example, the set for the play *Pohjolan häät* (*The Wedding in Pohjola*), presented at the inauguration of the new Finnish

National Theatre in 1902, was done from sketches by the renowned painter Pekka Halonen (1865–1933).

The traditional realistic style of set designs also awakened growing criticism in the early 1920s as a trend against the limitations of realism gained support. The most noteworthy representatives of the new current were painters Eero Snellman (1890–1951), Henry Ericsson (1898–1933) and Yrjö Ollila (1887–1932). Whereas Snellman was influenced by the pictorial and decorative art of the Ballets Russes in Paris, set designs by Ericsson for Helsinki stages represent one of the earliest Finnish applications of the ideas of Adolphe Appia and Edward Gordon Craig.

Expressionism arrived late and was only a brief phenomenon on Finnish stages (1922–6). Director Kosti Elo in cooperation with set designer Jussi Kari (1887–1953) produced several strongly conventionalized performances for the Tampere Workers' Theatre accentuating subjectivity and the shattering of the ego in the horrors of war. These elements were often reflected through strong and dark colours, and effective lighting. The style was most clearly applied in Tampere to interpret new expressionist plays. Among Kari's most successful sets were those for Toller's *The Machine Wreckers* and Georg Kaiser's *Gas*.

Expressionism also had a fruitful influence on scenography. The importance of visual planning for a performance became self-evident. Eventually the distinctive external features of expressionism faded but, in the best cases, the power of expression and suggestiveness remained.

Another remarkable pioneer of set design was Matti Warén (1891–1955), who worked mainly for the Finnish National Theatre (he was on contract to the theatre from 1927 to 1951). The versatile Warén did not represent any specific trend but adapted various expressive means to suit the needs of the play: on the one hand, imaginative, lush and fairy-book set designs with skilful use of colour, and on the other, a bare simplicity and highly developed sense of form in his interpretations of tragedies. Belonging to this latter style, the set he designed for *Kullervo* by Aleksis Kivi in 1934 is perhaps the most remarkable example of set design from the early period of Finnish scenography. Like Jussi Kari, the basis of most of Warén's set designs link him with pictorial scenography.

The most notable representatives of architectural set design, which gained importance in the late 1920s under the influence of the modernists, were sculptor Wäinö Aaltonen (1894–1966) architect Alvar Aalto (1898–1976) and painter Yrjö Ollila. They designed the set for Hagar Olsson's expressionistic, socially critical play *S.O.S.* Their sets represented undoubtedly the most daring trend in Finnish set design at the time; constructivism never really gained support in Finland, nor did dadaism or other non-realistic trends.

Certainly the most innovative set designer of these three was Alvar Aalto; his sets for the Turku Theatre in 1930 emphasized with simple means the social and anti-war themes of *S.O.S.* His were also the first designs in Finland using projections and one can see a connection with Erwin Piscator's and Laszlo Moholy-Nagy's work.

Set designers in the 1940s turned back to realism. But the lack of materials during the war put restrictions on many plans. Among the most noteworthy of the new generation was Leo Lehto (1912–74), who experimented with new materials and developed a revolving auditorium for the Pyynikki Summer Theatre.

Stage lighting became an important element in the 1950s. Once again, an interesting phase began in the theatre: modernism with its bare forms left its mark on scenic expression also. An example from this period was the set by Rolf Stegars (b. 1914) for *The Dream Play* at the Finnish National Theatre (1959) in which set changes were done mainly through lighting. The existential sense of the play gained strength against the bare scenes and this approach worked even for interpretations of absurdist plays. One of the most notable examples of this trend was the static and foreboding design by Pekka Heiskanen (b. 1929) for Samuel Beckett's *Endgame* at the Finnish National Theatre in 1957.

A reaction against aestheticism in the 1960s was most evident in the designs of Kari Lilla (1943–82) for plays directed by Kalle Holmberg. Reality forced its way into the theatre in the form of rough planks, used in 1966 both for *Ubu Roi* and for *The Opera of Lapua*. Rusty iron plates were also a favoured material at the time.

In the 1970s, designs became plainer, partly due to new performing conditions, as touring companies and regional theatres began working in factories and gymnasiums. Against a minimal set, costumes often became a dominant element of design. Actor and costume designer Liisi Tandefelt (b. 1936) was influential at this time, having done pioneering work both as a designer

Kalle Holmberg's 1966 Helsinki Student Theatre production of Arvo Salo's *The Opera of Lapua*, designed by Kari Lilla.

and an educator; her costume designs had a personal flare often strongly marked by the artisan's needlework. The *art nouveau*-style wardrobe Tandefelt designed for *My Fair Lady* in 1986, in fact, won the Gold Medal at the Prague Quadrennial in 1987.

One of the phenomena marking the Finnish theatre in the 1980s was the transfer of the performing space from theatre buildings to industrial premises. Tiina Makkonen (b. 1952) created original and visionary solutions of space arrangement for such premises. Using natural materials and handicraft along with lighting that could mould the space, she created a strong and coherent atmosphere closely connected to each production. Her scenography often appealed to memories and associations on a very personal level, giving each production an intimate character.

Ensio Suominen (b. 1934) has created impressive solutions for the problems of large stages; in his interpretations of classical works he combines in an exceptional way the monumental and the needs of the production. With apparently modest means, he creates a dimensional tension that crystallizes the essential contradiction of each play. Lighting is also incorporated with a unity that emphasizes the cinematic quality of his set solutions.

The diversity of general theatre aesthetics of the 1980s and 1990s also prevails in scenography. It is therefore difficult to indicate a single or obvious tendency. As well, the unprecedented solutions that new techniques have made possible and a return to the ideals of the Poor Theatre make it difficult to generalize. A great change has, however, taken place with a new accent on the visual. As such, the links between scenography and drama have become even closer.

Heta Reitala

Theatre Space and Architecture

Theatre design in Finland after World War II is concentrated in the period 1951–87, when ten large theatres were built. Finnish architects have always emphasized the public character of theatre buildings. It was only in the 1980s that alternative planning surged alongside monumental theatre architecture as smaller flexible studio theatres were preferred and theatre was linked to other cultural activities in multipurpose buildings providing facilities for various leisure activities. Thus architects have also had a considerable influence on the identity of Finnish drama activities.

The fundamental conception in Finnish theatre projects has been the ideology of theatre as an establishment-like institution, according to which large-capacity auditoriums and flexibility for stage modifications create a basis for the activity. Theatre planning has also been marked by the objective of providing variety in repertoire, requiring the installation of several stages in the same building. This rationalization of the use of space for performances and storage has also helped cut costs. The decisions on the arrangement of the space and the choice of materials for the foyers and the auditoriums have emphasized the ceremonial character of the theatre.

The strong urbanization that took place in the 1960s in Finland and the resulting growth of the urban population brought with it a need for new theatre buildings. In addition, an increase in leisure time caused particular social problems. Theatre was seen as a solution which could help adapt citizens to modern lifestyles. Cities started seeking independent culture policies to fulfil their new needs, and they founded theatre institutions, which required large theatre buildings.

The state supported the construction of theatres between the 1960s and the 1980s while stressing the democratic rights of all citizens to enjoy cultural services irrespective of where they lived. Thus theatre can now be seen in modern theatre buildings throughout the country. Theatre buildings now also exemplify the essence of modern Finnish architecture and have become landmarks of cultural history.

The Small Stage of the Finnish National Theatre was built in 1952–4, designed by Kaija Siren (b. 1920) and Heikki Siren (b. 1918). This solution brought forth new tendencies in the dramatic arts and accentuated everyone's right to participate in cultural activities in post-war society. Thus the National also gained a studio stage permitting a greater variety in repertory. This building was the first modern theatre house in Finland.

The Helsinki City Theatre by Timo Penttilä (b. 1931) with a large auditorium seating 920 and a small auditorium seating 300 was opened in 1967. Penttilä's main idea was to break with conventional stage planning and discreetly accommodate a volume of 100,000 cubic metres into green park surroundings.

In 1983 the Lahti City Theatre took over a new theatre house designed by Pekka Salminen (b. 1937). The theatre has three different stages which can be modified to permit everything from large opera productions to small-scale performances. The building can hold 1,200 spectators and is one of the most prominent examples of concrete construction in Finnish architecture. Salminen also sought architectural solutions that would especially encourage young people to participate in cultural activities.

For Alvar Aalto the Greek theatre has always been a central source of inspiration in his architectural plans for libraries, art museums and universities. Between 1975 and 1987 the city theatres of Rovaniemi, Jyväskylä and Seinäjoki were built according to designs by Aalto. The buildings follow the same principles as his opera house in Essen, Germany, although they are considerably smaller. All these buildings are part of an administrative and cultural centre in the heart of the city. His concept was the creation of a meeting-place for citizens, a civic square symbolizing democracy surrounded by the city hall, a theatre and a library.

Marjatta (b. 1927) and Martti (b. 1928) Jaatinen planned the Tampere Workers' Theatre, completed in 1985. The theatre building of 85,000 cubic metres can seat between 750 and 920 spectators. This architect couple sought a modern identity for the old workers' theatre and its red brick walls maintain the traditional aspect of the industrial environment of the city of Tampere.

Timo Koho

Training

Through the early history of the Finnish theatre, professional training was usually obtained through practical apprenticeships – working in the theatres. An actual school for actors functioned in the Finnish National Theatre between 1906 and 1920, and at the Swedish Theatre between 1910 and 1973. The formal training of Finnish-speaking actors began in 1920 at the Finnish School of Drama and continued till the beginning of World War II in 1939. In 1943, the Theatre School of Finland was founded. Ten years later it also started training directors and scenic designers; in 1962 the training of designers was transferred to the Academy of Industrial Arts.

Director and actor Wilho Ilmari was the first rector of the Theatre School of Finland, from 1943 to 1963, and built the actors' training programme on a solid Stanislavski base.

A single theatre academy was unable to satisfy the growing demand for professionally trained actors. The provincial theatres particularly had to use actors whose only training was acquired through amateur companies. To meet the demand, a course for actors was started at the University of Tampere in 1966. Since 1964 the university has also been training directors and dramaturges.

In 1973 a Training Centre was founded at the Theatre School of Finland offering a diversity of courses lasting from a few days up to ten weeks for actors, directors, dramaturges and technical staff. Finnish as well as foreign teachers have been invited to teach there. Professionally stimulating, these courses have been especially important for actors lacking solid basic training.

During the 1970s, training became more consciously oriented towards a common curriculum for actors, directors and dramaturges. Theatre history, dramatic literature and language are now common to all courses. Besides performance skills, acting students are also taught subjects such as music, speech, physical education and acrobatics. The programme for students, whose mother tongue is Swedish, takes into consideration the traditional features peculiar to the Swedish-language theatres of Finland. The dramaturge's courses concentrate on the translation of plays and creative writing. Directing students are also taught repertoire planning in addition to the subjects directly related to their field.

The whole curriculum has as its objective preparation of productions. Practical experience therefore is obtained through work in their own student theatre. The students can, however, acquire experience with the methods of work in professional theatres through joint productions mounted in cooperation with theatres around the country.

In 1979 the Theatre School of Finland became the Theatre Academy, assuming both Finnish- and Swedish-language theatre training. It is one of three university-level state schools in the arts. The four-year programme includes courses in acting, direction, dramaturgy, dance pedagogy, lighting and sound. As at other universities, higher degrees can be taken, including a doctorate in theatre arts. It has been considered important that the instructors at the Theatre Academy be the best actors and directors in the country and that they maintain a live relationship with theatre work.

Criticism, Scholarship and Publishing

Traditionally all Finnish newspapers publish theatre criticism. The leading newspapers employ salary-based theatre critics, the smaller ones contract freelance writers. Besides writing critical articles, they also interview, prepare news items and present opinions. Until the early 1990s newspapers gave extensive coverage to theatre; rarely was a première at a professional theatre left uncovered. Till the 1960s the more noteworthy performances usually received two articles in the same newspaper: a quick evaluation and first impressions on the morning following the première, and a few days later a more thorough analysis. By the 1990s, that custom was no longer possible and cultural news was generally being given less column space.

Newspaper critics rarely have a theatrical background and therefore most criticism concentrates on literary evaluation. Thus the most outstanding critics are those who have also developed their skills in analysing performances.

Among the most important theatre critics in the post-war period have been Sole Uexküll (1920–78) and Jukka Kajava (b. 1943); also Maija Savutie (1910–87) who wrote for the leftist newspaper *Kansan Uutiset*, and editor Olavi Veistäjä (1908–88) from the newspaper *Aamulehti* in Tampere. Two books of critical articles by Uexküll and Savutie have been published: *Sole Uexküll: Kriitikko Teatterissa* (*Sole Uexküll: A Critic in the Theatre*), and *Maija Savutie: Kohti elävää teatteria* (*Maija Savutie: Towards Living Theatre*).

The first theatre magazines were published in Finland around World War I. The magazines were well edited but short-lived due to financial difficulties. In 1945 several theatre organizations founded the publishing firm Kustannus Oy Teatteri, which began immediately publishing the magazine *Teatteri*. To the present day, it has remained the only professional theatre magazine in the country. In the beginning the magazine appeared twice a month but gradually the numbers were reduced to ten per year. The style of the magazine has also changed from a news magazine to deeper and more critical themes. The articles are most often written by theatre professionals, directors, actors and educators.

Kustannus Oy Teatteri is the only publishing firm in the country dedicated solely to theatre; lack of funds has permitted the firm to publish only a few plays in addition to the magazine. Commercial publishing houses, as well as the theatre academies and theatre organizations, have also published some theatre literature.

The study of dramatic literature and theatre history has been included in the curriculum of the Helsinki, Turku and Tampere universities since the 1960s. Research is mainly concentrated on the history of the Finnish theatre. Among the most renowned researchers have been Timo Tiusanen (1936–85), who did work on Eugene O'Neill (Helsinki University) and Irmeli Niemi (b. 1931), who has done research into theatre history and on audiences.

In the beginning of the 1980s, the Theatre Academy added research to its curricular programme. As an experiment, research on the actor's work during the rehearsal process was carried out with both the director and the actors themselves participating (an example of this kind of research was done in 1983 with Kalle Holmberg directing a Dostoevsky production with five actors). Since 1988 it has been possible to do doctoral dissertations at the Theatre Academy on subjects such as the work of directors, actors and dramaturges, including analytical reports.

Anneli Suur-Kujala
Translated by Eva Jarne-Kautto

Further Reading

Finnish Theatre Today. Helsinki: Finnish Centre of the International Theatre Institute, 1971. 71 pp.

Heikkilä, Ritva. *Sata vuotta suomalaista teatteria*. [A hundred years of Finnish theatre]. Helsinki: Central Organization of Finnish Theatre Associations, 1972.

Koski, Pirkko. *Kansan teatteri*. [Peoples theatre]. 2 vols. Porvoo: Helsingin Teatterisäätiö, 1987.

Koskimies, Rafael. *Suomen kansallisteatteri 1902–50*. [The Finnish National Theatre 1902–50]. 2 vols. Helsinki: Otava, 1953, 1972.

Niemi, Irmeli. *Teatteri – Suomen kulttuurihistoria II*. [Theatre – Finnish cultural history II]. Porvoo/Helsinki/Juva: WSOY, 1980.

——. *Teatteri ja tanssitaide – Suomen kulttuurihistoria III*. [Theatre and dance – Finnish cultural history III]. Porvoo/Helsinki/Juva: WSOY, 1982.

Orsmaa, Taisto-Bertil. *Teatterimme kääne. Ekspressionismi suomalaisessa teatterissa*. [The turning point of Finnish theatre. Expressionism in the Finnish theatre]. Helsinki: Gaudeamus, 1976.

Paavolainen, Pentti. *Teatteri ja suuri muutto*. [Theatre and the great migration]. Helsinki: Kustannus Oy Teatteri, 1992.

Savutie, Maija. *Finnish Theatre: A Northern Part of World Theatre*. Translated by Philip Binham. Helsinki: Finnish Centre of the International Theatre Institute, 1980.

——. *Kohti elävää teatteria*. [Towards living theatre]. Helsinki: Teatterikorkeakoulu – Valtion painatuskeskus, 1986.

Tiusanen, Timo. *Teatterimme hahmottuu*. [Our theatre takes shape]. Helsinki: Kirjayhtymä, 1969.

FRANCE

France has coastlines on the Atlantic Ocean, the English Channel (La Manche) and the Mediterranean Sea; its land area is 550,000 square kilometres (212,200 square miles). There were 40 million inhabitants in France in 1945 and 56 million in 1990 (including 25 million in the workforce). In 1945, 30 per cent of the population was under the age of 19. In 1990, more than 12 per cent of the population was over 65 and 10 per cent were living alone. Between 1950 and 1970, the purchasing power of the average French salary doubled; between 1970 and 1980, workers' salaries increased by 50 per cent. In 1959, the cultural consumption of a household was 5 per cent of the average budget. In 1990, it was 8 per cent.

In order to make up for an acute crisis in housing after the war, an unprecedented effort was made in the 1950s, and more than 25 million houses were built. As a result, suburbs developed very quickly, transforming the rural France of the 1940s into the urban France of the 1990s. An increase in the number of cars (less than 20 per cent of households had a car in 1953, more than 80 per cent had one in 1990), the rebuilding of the rail and road networks, and the introduction of aircraft for domestic travel changed ideas of mobility and relationships between French social classes. This explosion of productivity, development of spare time and increase in expenditures for leisure – combined with a state policy showing more concern for culture, for example, the creation of a Ministry for Cultural Affairs in 1959, directed by André Malraux (1901–76) – should have led to an explosion of theatre during this time, an explosion linked to the general improvement in educational level. Unfortunately, it did not.

Undoubtedly, television (from 1954 in France), combined with the new mobility, helps to explain this state of affairs. All the efforts in cultural and theatrical development must be put into this context despite the fact that cultural spending by the state and local communities (FFr16 billion in 1990, approximately US$2.66 billion) have also increased significantly.

The fact is, from 1945 on, theatre became a national matter both geographically and socially, with decentralization the absolute keynote of state action in the field. Gradually local communities became involved, first cities, then the départements (counties) and eventually the régions (provinces).

When the war ended in France, not many theatres were actually operating and a serious rethinking of the role of the arts took place, a rethinking influenced by the wartime collaboration with the Germans in Paris between 1940 and 1944. From this came the Entertainment Order of 1945 which required licences for producers of shows. Theatre people, however, were suspicious of the state whose officials at the time were almost all either leftist or Gaullist, interventionists both. Theatre professionals also complained about overwhelming taxes on performances and what they felt were excessive trade union rules.

Despite state support for 'serious' art, audiences with money still preferred the *théâtres de boulevard* and their diet of light comedies. However, the *new* post-war audience – those discovering theatre for the first time – seemed to prefer seeing the classics and was generally suspicious of novelties. The result was a split in focus between state-subsidized theatres, which aimed at the new audiences, and the private boulevard theatres, which kept supplying well-to-do patrons with what Brecht called culinary plays by writers such as Jean de Lettraz

(1897–1967), Roger-Ferdinand (1898–1967) and Sacha Guitry (1885–1957).

At the same time, a number of small, independent theatres emerged on the Left Bank of Paris. Those involved with them were often more teachers than creators, concerned with directions for both theatre and society. The results set *théâtre de boulevard* directly in opposition to the more socially engaged theatre; official (and conservative) companies such as the Comédie-Française found themselves challenged by the Théâtre National Populaire (TNP) of Jean Vilar (1912–71); theatres outside Paris competed with theatres in Paris; and private theatres found themselves confronted by the independent avant-garde theatres which would ultimately launch the careers of writers such as Samuel Beckett (1906–89) and Eugène Ionesco (1912–94), authors who questioned the very nature of the theatre. As new techniques appeared in acting which went far beyond rhetorical postures, the traditional French repertoire simply disintegrated through the appropriation and rejection of classics, through the discovery of foreign authors, and through the adoption of techniques and recipes of what became known over the next decade as Theatre of the Absurd.

Between 1945 and 1990 then, theatre in France changed in every way: aesthetically, geographically, institutionally, economically, socially, and even politically. During this period, there emerged as well a progressive split between the state and society as a whole. By the late 1980s, however, the effects of privatization and the concept of art as merchandise began to transform theatrical art in France. Clearly, throughout this period, theatre had to think and rethink itself time and again.

The period since 1945 cannot be explained without some reference to what happened before. The birth of the modern French theatre goes back to André Antoine (1858–1943) and his *Manifeste pour le Théâtre Libre* (*Manifesto for a Free Theatre*, 1890), to the Théâtre d'Art of Paul Fort (1872–1960), also in 1890, and to the foundation of the Théâtre de l'Oeuvre of Aurélien Lugné-Poe (1869–1940) in 1893. The development of the art of directing, whether naturalist or symbolist, of theatre as a singular art with a specific language, led Romain Rolland (1866–1944) to try and create '*un nouvel art pour un monde nouveau*' ('a new art for a new world'). A movement to make theatre a popular art, a people's art, started with Maurice Pottecher (1867–1960) in Bussang in 1895,

followed by Firmin Gémier (1869–1933), first to play the role of Père Ubu in 1896.

The first official Théâtre National Populaire opened in 1920 in Paris at the Palais du Trocadéro (razed to make room for the Palais de Chaillot in 1935). Another attempt was made at the Vieux Colombier, which was operated from 1913 to 1924 by Jacques Copeau (1879–1949). Copeau then moved his work to Burgundy, far from Paris, where he remained until 1929. As early as 1913, Copeau had published his *Essai de rénovation dramatique* (*Essay on Dramatic Renewal*). Similar initiatives came later from the Compagnie des Quinze of Michel Saint-Denis (1897–1971) and the Compagnie des quatre saisons founded by Jean Dasté (b. 1904), André Barsacq (b. 1909) and Maurice Jacquemont (b. 1910) in 1937 (which became La Saison nouvelle in 1941).

The birth of the directors' group known as the Cartel, which from 1927 to 1939 produced 300 plays (seventy classical pieces, 162 French contemporary pieces and sixty-two foreign contemporary plays), framed the new ideology: theatre was a school for society, a moral and spiritual adventure. In making such an approach, the Cartel was at the service of both classical and modern texts – Chekhov, Pirandello, Jean Giraudoux (1882–1944). A professional association, the Cartel also aimed at taking theatre back from the commercial market. The state was urged to support their initiatives and help French theatre free itself from *théâtre de boulevard* which had experienced its own golden age in the 1930s with a cult of stars and a belief in theatre as pure entertainment. The Cartel argued for technical, physical and artistic training for the actor and directorial and design stylization: bare stages were favoured by Copeau and Louis Jouvet (1887–1951). The Cartel was against expressionism, however, rejecting Appia, Craig and Antonin Artaud (1896–1948).

Led by Charles Dullin (1885–1949), Jouvet, Gaston Baty (1885–1952) and Georges Pitoëff (1884–1939), the Cartel advocated a new kind of ensemble acting, a repertoire of important plays and a search for new audiences. At a time when the state was supporting only the Comédie-Française, the Opéra, and the Opéra-comique, the Cartel connected to both the militant left and Catholic action groups such as the Fédération du Théâtre ouvrier de France (Federation of Working-Class Theatre in France) in 1931, the Groupe Octobre from 1927 to 1936, and the touring Comédiens Routiers (1929–39) of Léon Chancerel (1886–1965) which were all trying to develop a kind of popular theatre.

Along with the Popular Front in 1936, the Cartel took part in the establishment of a national cultural policy for theatre which, post–1945, was realized in the state's movement toward decentralization. Dullin, who was at the Théâtre de l'Atelier in the 1920s, was arguing for decentralization as early as 1937. With a passion for *commedia dell'arte* and Elizabethan theatre, he saw directing as an art which could transpose reality. In his work, he developed techniques of flexible theatrical space allowing more direct contact between author and audience. His influence was important on a whole generation of actors including Jean Vilar.

Louis Jouvet, another leader of the Cartel, died on the very day he was appointed a councillor for theatrical decentralization. He had worked at the Comédie des Champs Elysées from 1925 to 1934 and then at the Athénée from 1934 to 1940. From 1945 to 1951 (he was in Latin America during the war) he staged works by Giraudoux, Molière (1622–73) and Jean Genet (1910–86). In his productions – including *Les Bonnes* (*The Maids*, 1947) – he was able to mix truth and pretence, a lack of ornamentation and aestheticism. He was also an impressive theorist, leaving a considerable number of essays on theatrical method.

Gaston Baty, for his part, ran La Chimère in Saint-Germain des Prés, the studio of the Champs Elysées (1924–8) and the Théâtre Montparnasse (1930–47). The first person to introduce Brecht into France (*The Threepenny Opera*, 1930), Baty's intelligence and intuition were hallmarks, as was his great knowledge of lighting and strongly individualistic interpretations. He eventually devoted himself to the art of the puppet. In *Le Masque et l'encensoir* (*The Mask and the Censer*, 1920) and *Rideau baissé* (*Curtain Down*, 1949), he wrote effectively about his experiences.

Georges Pitoëff, another in the Cartel, was the first director in France of *Six Characters in Search of an Author* by Pirandello (1923). At the Théâtre des Mathurins (1934–9), this exquisite actor and his wife, Ludmilla Pitoëff (1895–1951), a director and scenographer, was an experimenter who created an enormously rich repertoire (212 plays by 115 authors of twenty nationalities). Criticized for being too eclectic and for turning too much to a foreign repertoire, he was not asked by the Comédie-Française in 1936 – as were Copeau and other members of the Cartel – to advise on the future

of the company, the oldest in France.

At liberation in 1945, theatre was still clearly Parisian. The favoured authors of the *théâtre de boulevard* were maintaining their popularity while the authors favoured by the Cartel, especially Giraudoux, were also selling strongly. Jouvet, for instance, produced Giraudoux's *La Folle de Chaillot* (*The Madwoman of Chaillot*) at the Athénée in 1945.

But there was other activity as well. The distinguished actor and director Jean-Louis Barrault (1910–94) directed *Le Soulier de satin* (*The Satin Slipper*, 1943) by Paul Claudel (1868–1955) at the Comédie-Française and soon took over the Théâtre Marigny where, with his wife, actress Madeleine Renaud (b. 1900), he had a series of successes from 1946 to 1959: *Les Fausses Confidences* (*False Confessions*) by Pierre Marivaux (1688–1763), *Hamlet*, *Phèdre* (*Phaedra*), *Les Nuits de la colère* (*Nights of Anger*) by Armand Salacrou (1899–1989), *Partage de midi* (*The Break of Noon*, 1948) by Claudel and *The Oresteia* (1955).

Actor and theorist Antonin Artaud and producer-director Jean Vilar also achieved new fame in the immediate post-war period. Artaud's works became known and he even spoke publicly at the Vieux Colombier in January 1947, while Vilar began to produce a series of extraordinary productions in Paris, including Strindberg's *Dance of Death* and Eliot's *Murder in the Cathedral* (1945); Henri Pichette's (b. 1924) *Les Epiphanies* and Jacques Audiberti's (1899–1965) *Le Mal court* (*Evil on the Run*) in 1947 (both were directed by Georges Vitaly (b. 1917) at the Noctambules and the Théâtre de Poche).

In 1944, Jean-Paul Sartre (1905–80) saw his *Huis clos* (*No Exit*) played for the first time at Vieux Colombier. He followed this with *Morts sans sépulture* (*No Tomb for the Dead*) and *La Putain respectueuse* (*The Respectful Prostitute*) at the Théâtre Antoine in 1947. The post-war playwriting boom continued with several plays by Albert Camus (1913–60) – *Le Malentendu* (*The Misunderstanding*), *Caligula*, starring Gérard Philipe (1922–59) and *Les Justes* (*The Just*) in 1949.

André Obey (1892–1975), Director of Performing Arts in the Secretary of State's office, was administrator of the Comédie-Française from 1945 to 1947 and made links between the new dramas of the post-war period and the tradition of the well-made play.

Jean Anouilh (1910–87), a steady and prolific author, would also put his mark on theatre of the period, beginning with his adaptation of *Antigone* (1944) and later his *Colombe* (1951) at the Théâtre de l'Atelier directed by André Barsacq.

At the same time, André Roussin (1911–87) established himself as the best comic author of the *théâtre de boulevard* with *La Petite Hutte* (*The Little Hut*, 1947), *Les Oeufs de l'autruche* (*The Ostrich's Eggs*), *Nina* (1948–9) and *Lorsque l'enfant paraît* (*When the Child is Born*) in 1951. The writing team of Pierre Barillet (b. 1923) and Jean-Pierre Grédy (b. 1920) had a series of successes at this time in the *théâtre de boulevard* with *Le Don d'Adèle* (*Adele's Knack*) in 1951.

In this context, it might be more appropriate to consider the year 1951 as the real starting point of the contemporary period. The Festival d'Avignon had begun in 1947 under Vilar. In 1951, he was named director of the Théâtre National Populaire. The Avignon/TNP adventure would quickly put its mark on the years 1951 to 1969. Under Vilar, actors would become part of a genuine ensemble, scenery would be reduced to the most essential elements with new attention being paid to costume, lighting and music. There would also be a new repertoire of French and foreign plays (though very few by contemporary authors). In approaching theatre in this way, the TNP was to become a leader, both a moral force and a stylistic innovator.

From 1952, the small theatres on the Paris Left Bank (especially the Théâtre de Babylone) would become springboards for both writers and new groups, as the Concours des Jeunes Compagnies (Competition for Young Companies) had been when it began in 1946. Decentralization during this time also saw the gradual growth of theatres from the centre to various Parisian neighbourhoods and even to neighbourhoods just outside Paris. Among the first was the Centre Dramatique de l'Est. Later companies would appear in other parts of the country, including Saint-Étienne (1947), Toulouse (1949), Rennes (1949) and Aix (1952).

Gérard Philipe, Jean Vilar and Jean Negroni in Vilar's 1953 Théâtre National Populaire de Chaillot production of Heinrich von Kleist's *The Prince of Homburg*.
Photo: Agence de Presse Bernand.

Through the 1950s, the poetic theatre of writers such as Georges Schéhadé (1910–89), author of *Monsieur Bob'le* (1951), and the Theatre of the Absurd cut deeply into both the certainties of literary tradition and the foundations of theatre itself. Added in were elements ranging from the distant and exotic to concepts of negritude and the politics of the French-speaking Third World in plays by writers such as Édouard Glissant (b. 1928), Aimé Césaire (b. 1913) and Kateb Yacine (1929–89). All mingled and clashed with the still newer writings of Eugène Ionesco – such as *La Cantatrice chauve* (*The Bald Soprano*, 1950), *Victimes du devoir* (*Victims of Duty*, 1953), *Jacques ou la soumission* (*Jacques or the Submission*, 1955) and *Rhinocéros* (1960) – and plays by Beckett – such as *En attendant Godot* (*Waiting for Godot*, 1953), *Fin de partie* (*Endgame*, 1957), *La Dernière Bande* (*Krapp's Last Tape*, 1960) and *Oh! les beaux jours* (*Happy Days*, 1963, at the Odéon-Théâtre de France starring Madeleine Renaud and Jean-Louis Barrault), all directed by Roger Blin (1907–84). During the 1960s and 1970s, many others in France began to write in similar ways, including Robert Pinget (b. 1920), Jeannine Worms (b. 1928), François Billetdoux (1927–91) and Roland Dubillard (b. 1923).

Arthur Adamov (1908–70) tried to connect the social and political to the contemporary world through his version of absurdist theatre but it seemed to require more traditional means of exposition and language. It was a dilemma that a new generation represented by André Benedetto (b. 1934) and the political theatre generated by the 1968 student movement tried to confront. Jacques Audiberti, Jean Vauthier (1910–92) and Jean Genet, who mainly appeared as a perfect anti-Claudel, tried to renew the language of dramatic text and the notion of theatre space. Genet became the master of theological inversion through his blind belief in blasphemy. Thanks to his language and bold dramatic devices, his theatre defined a magic ceremonial whose trinity rested on evil, death and the absolute. *Les Nègres* (*The Blacks*, Théâtre de Lutèce, 1959, directed by Roger Blin) expressed the metaphor of the quest for identity without ever mixing up the stage and the world. Marguerite Duras (b. 1914) and Nathalie Sarraute (b. 1900) are two other writers of note also related to this trend.

The new theatre of the 1950s and 1960s offered a dramaturgy of refusal, turning its back on both theatre and language while the Theatre of Reality (even the existential works of Camus and Sartre) seemed conventional by comparison, a dated form by the 1960s which had interest only for its political and social messages. The new theatre sought metaphysical dimensions, constantly re-evaluating the relationship between language and death, continuously inventing new forms in which character magnified a quest for new identity – aesthetic, political and social. Artaud became influential. In his seminal essays, *Le Théâtre et son double* (*The Theatre and its Double*), mostly written in the 1930s, he wrote that 'breaking through language to find life is to make or remake the theatre'. It became part of the new challenge.

It was this new theatre too which developed and even sped up decentralization in France, thus continuing to encourage the ideal of creating a people's theatre. This was also the goal of the Théâtre National Populaire with its own roots in the work of the Cartel. All roads seemed to lead to the discovery of new writers, directors and companies, to research into theatrical form and the rejection ultimately of text. Its influence was clear even in modernizing the Comédie-Française.

The discovery of Bertolt Brecht in 1949 by directors such as Jean-Marie Serreau (1915–73), Vilar and Dasté and the subsequent visit in 1954 of the Berliner Ensemble with *Mutter Courage und ihre Kinder* (*Mother Courage and Her Children*) and in 1955 with *Der Kaukasische Kreidekreis* (*The Caucasian Chalk Circle*) added a new element to the dramaturgy of French decentralization. Ending up as a kind of directors' theatre, the great texts of the past were reinterpreted and recreated in an effort to reach a new audience of spectator-citizens. This was done as well with the magic of Giraudoux, the surrealism of Jean Cocteau (1889–1963) and even with the message plays of Camus and Sartre. By the 1960s, it all ended up in a rather bourgeois passive consumption. The more radical, however, continued to urge a Theatre of Refusal, one which separated those who enjoyed the traditional literary qualities of a play from those who pressed directors to abandon text altogether.

As the Theatre of Refusal slowly freed itself from the psychological and the philosophical, the theatre based on plot and dialogue – long the staple of the French stage – went into crisis. The new theatre challenged speech and its processes almost entirely. It broke conventions and abolished logical development. Clear in Ionesco as well as in Beckett, it allowed analogical thought to replace discursive thought. Now form controlled theatrical content and, in fact, made the theatre more theatrical. No longer seeking to portray life mimetically, theatre itself became a language of possibility and pretence.

The stage became literally that, a place where character disappeared and the overwhelming presence of the actor took over. There was no action in this anti-theatre, no characters, no language with which to communicate. Yet language was the medium of that same incommunicability. Verbal images became theatrical and their incommunicability was theatrically communicated. Everything became a sign though not necessarily a meaning. Laughter had revenge as an absolute weapon of derision, both tragic and comic.

Very quickly, though, this Theatre of the Absurd became conventional, recognizable and comfortable for audiences. Not only was Ionesco's *Rhinocéros* a popular success at home and abroad but in Paris it was a personal triumph for Barrault in the part of Bérenger.

In the late 1960s, Brechtian aesthetics tended to replace the aesthetics of the absurd and there was movement toward mythical and lyrical documentary theatre, often based on collective creation and improvisation. Done with actors from marginal social groups, the first experiments were by director Armand Gatti (b. 1924). Added into the mix once more was Artaud's Theatre of Cruelty. One could see a continuity from Genet's work in the late 1940s and 1950s to the work of directors such as Jorge Lavelli (b. 1932), Jérôme Savary (b. 1942) and Victor García (1934–82), who put their marks on the development of theatre in France beginning in 1965. In their approaches, theatre was a group activity where text, directing and acting had to be rediscovered each time. Turning away from literary tradition, these communes of actors slowly discovered a militancy which continued the attack on text; between 1975 and 1980, even the director became suspect.

In this respect, the development of Ariane Mnouchkine's (b. 1939) Théâtre du Soleil in

Armand Gatti's 1976 production of his *The Passion of General Franco by the Emigrants Themselves* at the Ney-Calberson warehouses, Paris.
Photo: Agence de Presse Bernand.

Paris became a microcosm of the national transformation of theatre between the 1960s and the 1990s: from text-based theatre to improvisational work, from collectively created plays to the creation of 'méta-pièces' ('metaplays').

As new buildings went up all over the country as part of decentralization, traditionally trained theatre people turned more and more to nontraditional venues. By 1970, the Cartoucherie (Armoury) at the Château de Vincennes in east-end Paris had become home to the Théâtre du Soleil's experiments. This very non-traditional space had enormous impact on the group's approach to production. Each play sprang from an almost total reorganization of the spatial elements and new relationships were created each time with the audience. It was important to the group that spectators took part in these dramatic 'mysteries'. Actors even changed and made up before the audience.

This rethinking of space seems to have come to France from New York's Off-Broadway and led to the birth of a generation of 'crisis directors' who would and could work in any location, under any circumstances, often helped not by set 'designers' but by stage 'scenographers'.

Probably the most important director – aside from Jean Vilar – of the late 1950s and early 1960s was Roger Planchon (b. 1931), both a new Jouvet and the most consciously Brechtian of the new French directors. Planchon went from the Théâtre de la Comédie (Lyon) in 1950 to the Théâtre de la Cité (in neighbouring Villeurbanne) in 1957, which became the new TNP in 1972. He also showed his productions in Paris and toured abroad extensively. He influenced many other directors including Ariane Mnouchkine, Bernard Sobel (b. 1936), Armand Gatti, Jacques Lassalle (b. 1936), Jean-Pierre Vincent (b. 1942) and Patrice Chéreau (b. 1944). Through him, the director's importance grew.

But Planchon was not the only influence. Many foreign companies were also attracting attention (especially the Living Theatre which appeared in Paris in 1961). A backlash of sorts could be seen in the work of directors such as Roger Blin who wanted to revive the idea of an unobtrusive director at the service of dramatic text. Blin did this for Beckett, while Serreau did it for Césaire, Yacine, Brecht, Adamov, Ionesco and Michel Vinaver (b. 1927).

The authors born of decentralization such as Guy Foissy (b. 1932) were innovating outside of Paris at a time when text and author were being called into question in Paris. René de Obaldia

(b. 1919), on the other hand, turned the absurd into a celebration of words and language and, along with Jean Tardieu (b. 1903), became popular in the decentralized theatres. But audiences generally were not prepared to accept actors or the theatre as the advance guard of society or even the actor as a saint who, through art, would be condemned to be burned at the stake or who was undertaking on behalf of society an act of self-sacrifice as Grotowski urged in his book *Towards a Poor Theatre* (published in France in 1969).

Audiences preferred more traditional productions by groups such as the Théâtre National Populaire, which continued to give them access to the classical, national and international established repertoire. Appreciation of novelty was grudging, except occasionally in the case of the Théâtre du Soleil or the Grand Magic Circus (*Zartan* in 1970), a kind of anti-Théâtre du Soleil. At the same time, the *théâtre de boulevard*, also in crisis, was struggling to regain its audiences.

By the 1970s, the Théâtre du Soleil had become a synthesis of all the aesthetic and social experiences of the 1960s. In existence since 1964, it was almost from the beginning made up of actors who wanted to research and work collectively. Each of its productions, especially after 1970, was a feast, but one with critical distance. Audiences almost always had to move around within the space and Mnouchkine's actors always seemed to present a series of powerful stage images, sometimes historical in nature. In 1970, their production of *1789* looked back to the French Revolution. They spoke of the illusion of history in *L'Age d'or* (*The Golden Age*) in 1975. In 1979 it was *Méphisto*, after which they began a series of Shakespearian pieces – *Richard II* in 1981, *Twelfth Night* in 1982, and *Henry IV (Part I)* in 1984. In 1985, they discovered a contemporary tragedy in *L'Histoire terrible mais inachevée du roi Norodom Sihanouk, Roi du Cambodge* (*The Fearful and Yet Unfinished History of Norodom Sihanouk, King of Cambodia*), and in 1988 *L'Indiade ou L'Inde de leurs rêves* (*The Indian Saga or the India of their Dreams*), two texts which sprang from collective creation and were ultimately written by Hélène Cixous (b. 1938), a feminist writer who had previously written *Portrait de Dora* (*Portrait of Dora*, 1976). From its birth, the story of the Théâtre du Soleil was, to a very great extent, the rediscovery of relationships between theatre and history.

Perhaps influenced by Théâtre du Soleil's

success, a number of theatres in the 1970s – including the Comédie-Française – had begun to commit themselves to full seasons of new plays. In 1970–1, for example, the Comédie-Française staged plays by Romain Weingarten (b. 1926), Dubillard, Billetdoux, Jean-Claude Grumberg (b. 1939), Obaldia, Foissy and Robert Pinget. Lucien Attoun (b. 1935) launched his Théâtre Ouvert in 1971, a place where scripts by new writers such as Enzo Cormann (b. 1954) and Michel Deutsch (b. 1948) were read and presented as works-in-progress.

A survey about plays performed in decentralization venues published in 1972 provided a good overview of the period since 1945. During that time, 412 different authors were produced. The most popular were Molière (136 productions), Shakespeare (eighty-four), Brecht (forty-eight), Alfred de Musset (1810–57: thirty-six), Marivaux (thirty-four), Ionesco (thirty), Eugène Labiche (1815–88: thirty), Chekhov (twenty-eight), Racine (1639–99: twenty-six), Pierre Corneille (1606–84: twenty-four), Claudel (twenty-four) and Pirandello (twenty-three). Rounding out this group were Obaldia (twenty productions), Giraudoux (eighteen), Anouilh (eighteen), Beckett (seventeen), Audiberti (eleven), Foissy (eleven), Gatti (nine), Fernando Arrabal (eight), Planchon (seven) and Adamov (six).

It was in the period after 1968 that France genuinely opened its theatres to Europe and beyond. It was the Nancy Festival (1963–83) which took the lead and showed the work of a whole new generation of directors and an approach to theatre that was close to ritual – Jerzy Grotowski, Robert Wilson, and the American Bread and Puppet Theatre.

At home, classics continued to attract interesting directors: *Richard II* directed by Patrice Chéreau in Marseille in 1970; *Hamlet* directed by Daniel Mesguich (b. 1952) at Nanterre in 1977; *Antony and Cleopatra* and *Troilus and Cressida* directed by Planchon for the TNP in 1978; *The Winter's Tale* directed by Lavelli at Avignon in 1979; and *The Cherry Orchard* (1981) directed by Peter Brook, a major figure of the period who settled at the Bouffes du Nord theatre in Paris in 1974 with an epoch-making production of *Timon of Athens*.

Most of these productions, not surprisingly, were marked by film aesthetics. Dramatic writing continued to be challenged. Obviously, a return to dramatic text did not mean that the text had to be used in a traditional way. Following the complex social climate of the 1970s, the rebuilding of theatre in the 1980s would have to be based on elements other than text. Served by directors such as Brook, Antoine Vitez (1930–90), Patrice Chéreau, Daniel Mesguich, Jacques Lassalle, Bernard Sobel, Roger Planchon, Georges Lavaudant (b. 1947) and a host of young directors, the theatre in the late 1970s and into the mid-1980s became a place to question history and to critique society, a place to question text and explore. The fact that directors such as Vincent, Vitez and Lassalle – nurtured on critical postures – all ultimately became heads of the Comédie-Française in a way validated the importance of their work in the 1970s.

There was as well in the 1970s an explosion of *café théâtres* (cafés providing theatre performances under very modest circumstances) mainly in Paris. The socially conscious plays produced were another reaction to a society becoming more and more technical and consumer-oriented, a reaction by those concerned with issues such as the environment.

These heirs of the Théâtre du Soleil all had their own ideas about writing and theatre space. Chéreau deconstructed scenes to provide new meaning while Brook used the empty shell of the Bouffes du Nord to make the most of actors from various nationalities all speaking French with their own accents. All moved away from the notion of mimesis. The influences of a range of international theatrical minds could be detected: Klaus Michael Grüber, Robert Wilson, Giorgio Strehler and Peter Stein among others.

During this period, theatre literally moved outside the walls, outside of the centre of Paris and outside many of the traditional dramatic structures. Yet it was still the director who had the last word even if he was also an actor such as Vitez or Planchon.

The arrival of a socialist government in 1981 meant major increases in government support to the arts as a whole (grants doubled between 1982 and 1986) and seemed to augur a new golden age for the French theatre. But that age was at best a silver one. Audiences in the 1980s favoured a passive consumption of easy shows and were not prone to anything but spectacular novelty. This said, there were exceptions: the wonderful work of Brook, whose creations were one success after another – *Carmen* by Bizet (1838–75) in 1981, *The Mahabharata* in 1985 and *The Tempest* in 1990 – and the Théâtre du Soleil, who returned to basics with the aforementioned *Norodom Sihanouk*, *L'Indiade* and its Greek series, *Les Atrides*, begun in 1990.

Alain Françon (b. 1945), one of the most promising directors of the new generation, and his Théâtre Éclaté was more typical, however, offering Eugene O'Neill's *Long Day's Journey into Night* in 1982, *L'Ordinaire* by Vinaver in 1983, *Chambres* by Philippe Minyana (b. 1946) in 1986, and a superb production of *Hedda Gabler* in 1986.

Even with reinforced budgets, the theatres outside Paris did not do much for new authors though some of their productions were extraordinary – Marcel Maréchal (b. 1937) at the Théâtre de la Criée in Marseille; Michel Dubois (b. 1937) in Caen; Jacques Rosner (b. 1936) in Toulouse; Jacques Nichet (b. 1942) in Montpellier; Daniel Mesguisch at the Théâtre de la Métaphore in Lille. These theatres of the decentralization offered more and more touring coproductions of established plays becoming, in the process, huge standardizing machines. When directors decided to co-produce, artistic choices were clearly reduced significantly.

Government-supported theatres seemed to give up on new work, preferring re-readings of classical texts. During the 1988–9 season alone, there were nine productions of *Don Juan* by Molière, and at the beginning of 1990 there were seven productions of *Le Misanthrope*. It was in a sense a return to the influence of the Cartel and their goal of deriving artistic, civic and moral consciousness from great texts, particularly French texts. Even touring groups began to disappear as local Cultural Centres started to grow in number across the country. In the private theatres too, with production costs increasing, the tendency moved even more towards spectacle in order to compete with television.

The creation of the Molière Awards in 1987 gave the theatre world a chance to show its unity and vitality. Staged for television, however, the Molières, in seeking to find national recognition and publicity, risked losing the theatre's soul. The fact was that few plays were broadcast on television, and theatre people, with the exception of those known from the *théâtre de boulevard* and the television programme *Au théâtre ce soir* (*Theatre Tonight*), were not sufficiently known to make the Molières a hit on the medium. Even outside Paris, those who were running the Maisons de la Culture weren't sure of the value of televised national awards since such a production might even dissuade audiences from seeing a production that evening.

Theatre in the 1980s and early 1990s also had to struggle against the cinema. When directors began to cast film stars, the actors' presence became more important than the script, even if the director was well known: Jacques Lassalle directed *Tartuffe* at the Théâtre National de Strasbourg in 1983 and cast film star Gérard Depardieu (b. 1948) in the title role; Roger Planchon had Michel Serrault (b. 1928) play *L'Avare* (*The Miser*) in 1985–6, and he later directed *George Dandin* with Claude Brasseur (1905–72). Eventually, something authentic seemed to disappear.

As well, major directors (Chéreau, Lavelli and Savary) began to direct operas and it seemed to become difficult eventually to do theatre on anything less than an epic scale. By the end of the 1980s, a new move began aimed at again rethinking what had been accomplished through decentralization. But by this time, the state had statutory obligations outside Paris. If all the institutions were redefined, it would have significant artistic and financial ramifications. Outside Paris, major sums were now being used more for the survival of companies and buildings than for creation itself. Spiralling costs and high deficits had become the norm. Ultimately, though, help was given to a number of independent, young and imaginative companies for script development as well as for publication and full production.

The long suffering of the private theatres, however, seemed to come to an end thanks to special help from the state and the city of Paris as private theatres became centres of discovery once again. Ironically, they had also been invaded by the production and administration methods of the state theatres, while the state theatres in turn had been won over by notions of popular success and profitability. Everywhere, a kind of neo-boulevard mentality was established in the 1990s favouring entertainment over more serious reflection. Though it had a new shape, the debate between cultural democratization and art was still intact.

The most serious, though, continued to struggle on. At Chaillot, then at the Comédie-Française, Antoine Vitez tried courageously to do 'an elitist theatre for everybody'. Jean-Pierre Vincent in Nanterre (as Patrice Chéreau had before him) along with Lassalle at Strasbourg and then at the Comédie-Française, tried to alternate between new works by young authors and the reinterpretation of classical texts. The Théâtre National de la Colline (which opened in 1988) was entirely committed to new French and foreign plays under its director, Jorge Lavelli.

The setting up, with some difficulties, of a pan-European company at the Odéon in Paris – the Théâtre de L'Europe in 1983, directed by the Italian Giorgio Strehler until 1990, then by Lluís Pasqual (b. 1951), one of his disciples – gave Paris the possibility of seeing a wide range of new productions: *L'Illusion* by Corneille in 1984, directed by Giorgio Strehler; Pirandello's *Six Characters* directed by Vincent in 1987; *King Lear* in Swedish, directed by Ingmar Bergman, in 1984; *The Possessed*, after Dostoevsky, in English, directed by Yuri Lyubimov in 1984–5; and the Katona Jozsef Theatre from Budapest with *The Three Sisters* in Hungarian, directed by Támas Ascher in 1988. Dreamed of since 1955, the Théâtre de l'Europe gave concrete expression to the opening of French theatres to the entire European community.

The 1990s seemed to be showing, as critic Bernard Dort (1929–94) said, that theatre performance in France was at long last coming of age.

Structure of the National Theatre Community

Jean Vilar spoke of a communion between theatre and audience, between the traditional and the new. Art, according to post-war government policy, however, should be for everyone. This latter concept was the aim of those who created decentralization: from the great originators such as Dasté, Vilar, Maurice Sarrazin (b. 1925), Hubert Gignoux (b. 1915) and Baty, to the later cultural barons such as Marcel Maréchal, Roger Planchon, Jacques Rosner, Antoine Vitez and Jacques Nichet. Attempting to get nearer to the French as a whole, rather than just to Parisians, decentralization was to give birth to an accessible theatre, theatre which could be done by people one might meet on the street (for they would belong to a permanent, resident company). Theatre in this sense was to be a national test laboratory for social and cultural relationships.

After Jacques Copeau moved to Burgundy, many other travelling and regional groups began to emerge. Between 1946 and 1952, five Centres Dramatiques (Dramatic Centres; from the 1960s they were called National Dramatic Centres or CDNs) were founded: the Comédie de Saint-Etienne (1947) under Jean Dasté; in Rennes – the Comédie de l'Ouest (1949) under Gignoux; in Toulouse – the Grenier de Toulouse (1949) under Maurice Sarrazin; and in Aix-en-Provence – the Centre Dramatique du Sud-Est (1952) under Baty. The last member of the Cartel, Baty died before he could work in Marseille where the company was moved in 1969 and renamed the Théâtre National de Marseille in 1975. Directors of these theatres were appointed by the state and a structure was established by which directors could rise up to more and more important companies. It was in this way that directors such as Jacques Fornier (b. 1926; 1971–2), André-Louis Perinetti (b. 1933; 1972–5), Jean-Pierre Vincent (1975–83), Jacques Lassalle (1983–90), Jean-Marie Villegier (b. 1937; 1990–3) and Jean-Louis Martinelli (b. 1955; 1993–) were all appointed directors of the Théâtre National de Strasbourg.

The end of this first period of theatrical decentralization coincided with the arrival of Charles de Gaulle (1890–1970) in power in 1958 and the creation of the Ministry of Cultural Affairs in 1959. This ministry added to the Centres Dramatiques a series of what were called Troupes Permanentes (Permanent Companies) in various cities across the country. In many cases, however, they were troupes without stages which wound up using less than ideal community union halls.

A second era in the history of decentralization had in fact begun with the promotion of Roger Planchon's Théâtre de la Cité to the status of a Troupe Permanente in 1957 and the foundation of the Centre Dramatique du Nord by André Reybaz (1932–89) in 1960.

The first Minister of Cultural Affairs, André Malraux, backed by de Gaulle, launched still another movement – establishment of a series of what were called Maisons de la Culture (Houses of Culture) across France, another level of the continuing decentralization. These superimposed themselves on the Centres Dramatiques or, as they were built, actually took the Centres Dramatiques in.

Those troupes and centres established just outside Paris (from the 1960s on) were known as 'le théâtre hors les murs' ('theatre outside the walls'), in other words, suburban theatres. These included the Théâtre de l'Est Parisien founded by Guy Rétoré (b. 1924) as La Guilde in 1951. Its extraordinary work bore the deep mark of Vilar and the influence of the Berliner Ensemble and Roger Planchon; it was enormously popular (more than 18,000 subscribers, for example, in 1964).

In 1987, the Théâtre National de la Colline was founded. Directed by Jorge Lavelli, it was dedicated almost exclusively to new work. The Théâtre de la Commune d'Aubervilliers became a Troupe Permanente in 1961 and the Théâtre des Amandiers in Nanterre moved into the Maison de la Culture in Nanterre in 1968. It was directed by Pierre Debauche (b. 1930) and Pierre Laville (b. 1942) from 1968 to 1975. Patrice Chéreau settled at the theatre in 1982 and focused on contemporary writing – in particular the works of Bernard-Marie Koltès (1948–89) – and the development of a structure involving theatre, cinema and training. Jean-Pierre Vincent replaced him in 1990.

The foundation in 1965 of the Association Technique pour l'Action Culturelle (ATAC, as it was called, an association for cultural action) brought all the directors of cultural organizations together to further focus artistic consciousness and management.

From 1972, directors of the National Theatres were being nominated for three-year terms by the Ministry of Culture on the advice of local communities. This often led to conflicts which were more political than aesthetic, although the two were usually linked. The fact that these companies were funded by both the state and local municipalities complicated the issue and increased the costs of running these huge machines to the point where subsidies were not enough to cover even the artistic costs.

The French theatrical map by the mid-1970s became even more difficult to read. First there were the National Theatres, of which the government was reluctant to create new ones. Then there were the Dramatic Centres, the Permanent Companies, the Houses of Culture, the Centres d'Action Culturelle (Centres for Cultural Activites) and the Centres de Développment Culturel (Centres for Cultural Development). There were also suburban theatres and private theatres. There were as well the many independent companies (the youngest

Patrice Chéreau's 1983 Théâtre des Amandiers Nanterre production of Bernard-Marie Koltès's *The Battle of the Black Man and the Dogs*.
Photo: Agence de Presse Bernand.

and most militant encouraged by the success of the Théâtre du Soleil) which in 1972 created the Association pour le Jeune Théâtre (Association for New Theatre).

Suddenly there were theatres and theatre organizations everywhere. The problem was that in becoming social and political, most seemed to forget their artistic duties, and that theatre was first and foremost an art of communication and perhaps collective communion.

Administratively, the French theatre became a kind of pyramid. At the top was the Direction des Théâtres et Spectacles (Directorate of Performing Arts), which remains dependent on the Ministry of Culture for funding and policy. It has authority for all theatre institutions in France including the Maisons de la Culture. The work of the Directorate of Performing Arts is connected to twenty-two regional offices. In setting policy, it attempts to find a balance between those independent companies which have no established space and the well-established institutional structures.

The Directorate is also responsible for the five National Theatres – the Comédie-Française (founded in 1680), the Théâtre National de l'Odéon-Europe, the Théâtre National de Chaillot, the Théâtre National de La Colline and the Théâtre National de Strasbourg.

The Directorate is also involved in the management of the country's twenty-seven National Dramatic Centres. Their goals are defined by a three-year schedule of conditions, the last being the precise artistic programme of the director. This schedule – originally drafted in 1972, modified in 1982 and strengthened in 1991 – lays down the number of productions per season that must be done (two productions or co-productions per year of which at least two in any three-year period must be new works by living authors). In 1993, the state was funding these theatres at a level of about 50 per cent, the remaining 50 per cent being given by local communities or being found by the companies through box-office receipts of not less than 20 per cent. Artists' salaries were required to be at least one-third of the budget with administrative and technical costs not over 50 per cent.

Added to the theatrical map and taking into account the growing role of local and regional communities in cultural planning, a series of Centres Dramatiques Régionaux (CDRs – Regional Dramatic Centres) were set up beginning in 1982. Funded equally by state and local authorities, these now include the Théâtre

Régional des Pays de Loire in Angers; the Atelier du Rhin in Colmar (tending towards musical theatre); the Théâtre de la Soif Nouvelle – the CDR of Martinique; Quai Ouest-Théâtre Quotidien de Lorient in Lorient; Les Fédérés, Centre National de Création d'Auvergne in Montluçon; the Centre Dramatique Régional of Poitou-Charentes; the Théâtre des Deux Rives Centre de Création in Haute-Normandie in Rouen; the Théâtre Populaire de Lorraine in Thionville; and the Compagnie Gilles Bouillon in Tours (which offers opportunities to recognized artists who may have been previously working in less than optimum conditions).

The various Houses of Culture, which Malraux saw as the cathedrals of the twentieth century, have been an element both of progress and complication on the cultural and theatrical map. Between 1961 and 1971 more than a dozen were built: in Le Havre (1961), Bourges (1962), Caen (1963), the Théâtre de l'Est Parisien (TEP) in Paris (1963), Amiens (1965), Thonon-les-Bains (1966), Firminy (1966), Saint-Étienne (1968), Grenoble (1968), Rennes (1969), Reims (1969), Nevers (1971) and Châlon-sur-Saône (1971). Many more were planned. The original plans, in fact, called for twenty Maisons de la Culture to be built across the country.

Often set up in places where there was already a Permanent Company, these Houses of Culture had a multi-artistic vocation, in many cases aimed at reaching a wider public. Jointly funded by the state and the towns they were resident in, they were headed by a director (an administrator, a scholar-critic or even a stage director) who became head of a not-for-profit voluntary organization with a board of directors. The setting-up of these Houses of Culture should have led to the creation of varied-use buildings. It was quickly realized, however, that neither the state nor the towns would be able to realize such ambitious programming (in 1966, in fact, people talked about a House of Culture in each of the ninety-five French départements as well as in the overseas territories).

Because of the enormous costs connected with the Houses of Culture, more modest structures began to be created. These included twenty-four Centres d'Action Culturelle by 1990 and another twenty-six Centres de Développement Culturel (CDCs). This movement, which started in 1970, saw the establishment of organizations which were concentrated on the immediate and wide diffusion of art ('churches around the cathedrals').

The complexity of this overall mission, the

weight of the structures, and the administrative, political, artistic and cultural arguments created, led in 1990 to the creation of a new structure – the Scènes Nationales (National Stages) – which brought together all the former structures except the CDNs, of which there were sixty-seven by 1993. The directors of the Scènes Nationales were in charge of organizing and supporting the touring of CDNs and major companies, welcoming into residence any theatre and dance creator who wished to use their space to create a production.

Ironically, decentralization actually meant more theatres for Paris and the area immediately around it (an area of some 13 million people). This led to strong political opposition. In 1993, Paris had – in addition to everything it had in the 1940s and 1950s – the Théâtre de la Ville (rebuilt in 1968), the Théâtre de la Cité Universitaire (three theatres), six neighbourhood theatres (for example, Carré Silvia Monfort and Théâtre de la Plaine) and rental spaces such as the Athénée-Louis Jouvet, the Théâtre de la Tempête and the Théâtre de la Bastille. An economic balance has long been sought between the subsidized theatres (both in the provinces and in and around Paris) and the private theatres, which felt the former were competing unfairly for audiences.

The Directorate of Performing Arts as a result found itself also responsible for the 1,200 or so professional independent companies in the country. These groups, founded by actors or directors with particular artistic visions, are generally inexpensive to operate and often extremely interesting. In many ways, they made up for the disappearance of many large repertory companies through the years while they provided an artistic outlet for younger directors unable to get into more established groups because of the nature of the work they wished to pursue.

Events such as the Concours des Jeunes Compagnies and the traditional help given to tours and teaching from 1946 to 1967 were replaced first by a Commission d'aide aux Animateurs (Commission for the Support of Cultural Animation) in 1964, then by the Commission d'aide aux Compagnies Dramatiques (Commission for the Support of Drama Companies) from 1974 to 1982. In fact, after 1968, all these institutions were called into question and the debate on popular theatre was revived.

The development of and fight between state-supported, locally supported or non-supported companies was the French equivalent of the alternative theatre movement which significantly altered theatrical structures in many other countries. It did as well in France at the time going far beyond debates about subsidies and recognition of specific companies. The founding of the Action pour le Jeune Théâtre in 1971 reflected this new direction and followed by several years the publication of an official report on the General State of Theatre (1965) and a national meeting in Villeurbanne (1968), both of which were also connected to these profound changes.

By 1973, there were even demonstrations in Paris against the Minister of Culture who reproached theatre people for begging with an alms bowl in one hand and a Molotov cocktail in the other. Nevertheless, the demonstrations went on, led by the Théâtre du Soleil and director Jean-Pierre Vincent along with many others. But also involved were those responsible for decentralization who were trying to operate on smaller and smaller budgets.

Eventually, this movement was neutralized by the state, though it was modestly supported by local communities which were politically hostile to any show of centralized power. After 1982, regional committees made up of teams of experts took the major responsibility. Composed of theatre specialists and journalists close to the field, they have in fact allowed quicker recognition of new companies. Despite significant funds since 1982, however, regional budgets have not been sufficient to ensure the operation of both the established and the new groups.

By 1993, the situation had become less confused: some of the more promising companies were being funded at the regional level while other top-ranking companies were being supported through the Directorate of Performing Arts. On the plus side, all the subsidized companies were being encouraged to sign three-year agreements with their home cities.

From forty subsidized companies in the 1960s, the national total had grown to seventy-five in 1972, 146 in 1981, 304 in 1984, and 398 in 1990. These numbers, of course, reflect only the companies whose grant applications were approved. Many more were unable to be supported.

In total, the National Theatres received in 1990 some FFr276 million (US$46 million) in support while the Dramatic Centres received FFr220 million (US$37 million); the National Youth Theatres received an additional FFr15 million (US$2.5 million). More than half of the subsidies, it should be noted, were given to companies or people working in and around Paris.

As for the private theatres, they still exist almost exclusively in Paris. There were forty-seven operating in 1990. In 1964, a Fund to Support Private Theatre was established through a surtax on tickets, state support, help from the city of Paris, and a voluntary contribution from members of the Association du Théâtre Privé. This fund has, in fact, generated FFr50 million (US$8 million) every year since 1989.

One must here acknowledge that the private theatres played an important role in the development of new plays in the 1950s and for a long time have developed audiences, authors and independent directors. The Directorate of Performing Arts is even helping certain projects in this area. These include scripts submitted by directors, new plays whose productions are proposed by authors, and first revivals by private theatres. Support can also be requested by an institution, a festival, a subsidized drama company or a private theatre group.

As for festivals, since the 1950s they have expanded all across the country. Also supported by the Directorate of the Performing Arts and local communities, the success of festivals in France owes much to the example of Avignon.

In 1947, an Avignon Art Week was held, organized by Jean Vilar with the help of Jeanne Laurent (1902–89). It welcomed 4,000 spectators for seven productions. A second festival was held in Avignon in 1948. By 1990, the Festival d'Avignon had a budget of more than 30 million francs (FFr4 million given by the state; FFr6 million by the city of Avignon; FFr3.5 million by the département; FFr1.3 million by the région, FFr5 million from private patronage, and FFr9 million from box-office receipts). More than 120,000 people attended some 250 shows (not including Avignon's fringe).

As early as 1951, such festivals began to find new audiences – those on holiday. Because a play seemed not too expensive for a city to

Antoine Vitez and Ludmila Mikael in Vitez's 1987 Festival d'Avignon production of Paul Claudel's *The Satin Slipper*, designed by Yannis Kokkos.
Photo: Agence de Presse Bernand.

support, the idea spread. It wasn't even necessary to be in a historical place, but the examples of Arras, Angers, Sarlat, Nîmes and Dijon prove that, with the help of the state, a festival in an historic area can be the crowning achievement for local cultural efforts with the possibility of giving works (usually classical) important recognition and large audiences.

The Festival International Universitaire (International University Festival) in Nancy from 1963 to 1968, which became the Festival Mondial du Théâtre (World Theatre Festival) from 1968 to 1983, was a laboratory for new work and a meeting place for young and innovative companies. This has also been the focus of the Festival Sigma in Bordeaux (since 1965). While the Théâtre des Nations – an initiative of the International Theatre Institute – focused (most often in Paris) on important international companies.

A number of festivals developed in the area around Paris: the Festival d'Aubervilliers (from 1961 to 1965); the Festival de Nanterre (from 1965 to 1967); the Festival du Marais, which started in 1962 as a means to save the area and give it back its beauty; and the Paris Quartiers d'Été (since 1989). The largest Paris festival in the 1990s was the Festival d'Automne (since 1971); it now begins the official Paris theatre season and is an echo of the festival in Avignon. Devoted to new theatrical and choreographic creation, it is an important showcase for innovative artists.

In 1980, the Directorate of Performing Arts supported ten festivals with subsidy of some FFr5 million; by 1990, the numbers had grown to fifty-four and FFr15 million.

Among other French festivals of note are the Festival de la Marionnette in Charleville-Mézières (every two years since 1972); the Semaine de la Marionnette in Paris; the Festival International des Francophones in Limoges (since 1984 a gathering of companies and productions from the French-speaking world); the Festival de Théâtre de Rue in Aurillac, called Éclats since 1986 (devoted to the street arts, as is a festival in Châlon since 1986, the two gather more and more French and foreign companies); the Printemps des Comédiens in Montpellier (since 1987); Turbulences in Strasbourg (since 1991); Mimos, the international festival of mime in Périgueux (since 1982); the International Theatre Festival and Les Inattendus in Maubeuge (since 1987); the Festival Nouvelles Tendances in Rennes (since 1991); the Rencontres Charles Dullin in

Villejuif, a testing ground for young companies (since 1979); and Théâtre en mai in Dijon (since 1990).

The need for a structure to coordinate the various institutions operating in France led to the setting-up in 1975 of the Office National de Diffusion Artistique (ONDA). By 1993, ONDA was perhaps the best informed agency in the country on the activities of theatre companies in France, whether subsidized or not. It was also advising local communities and festival organizers and was even helping finance such activities (the budget of ONDA was FFr18 million in 1990). A touring office helped to ensure that programmes were harmonized, thus avoiding two companies in the same town at the same time. ONDA was also working closely with a network of companies and organizations at the European level to ensure coordination internationally.

There are, finally, more than 4,000 amateur groups operating across the country under the umbrella of the Fédération National du Théâtre d'Animation (National Federation of Theatrical Activities).

Concerning cultural funding, it is of interest to note the growth of state support from 1945 to 1993 in terms of both real funds and what they represent in terms of a percentage of the national budget. In 1991, the budget for culture in France was FFr11 million in 1945 and FFr15 million in 1955 (0.17 per cent of the national budget). It was up to FFr1.5 billion in 1960 (0.38 per cent of the budget); FFr2.7 billion in 1970 (0.37 per cent); FFr4.8 billion in 1981 (0.41 per cent); FFr8.5 billion in 1982 (0.76 per cent); and FFr10.5 billion in 1990 (0.91 per cent of the national budget of the state). The symbolic figure of 1 per cent, talked about since 1936, was formally reached in the 1993 budget.

As for theatre's share of that funding, the subsidies for five companies in 1940 (again in constant 1991 figures, as are all other figures which follow) totalled FFr160,000. This grew to FFr3 million for twenty-six companies in 1944. In 1945, the figure rose to FFr3.6 million. In 1949, the Paris theatres alone received FFr2.3 million while those outside Paris got FFr3.2 million.

In 1957, a total of FFr78 million was shared among the Comédie-Française (FFr57 million), the Centres Dramatiques (FFr8.8 million), organizations (FFr4.2 million), Paris theatres (FFr2.7 million) and festivals (FFr5.3 million).

In 1970, theatre received FFr229 million,

including FFr64 million for the Comédie-Française, FFr60 million for the National Theatres, FFr63 million for other theatres outside Paris, FFr8 million for companies, and FFr27 million for the Houses of Culture. By 1975, the total subsidy given to theatre was FFr385 million; in 1980, FFr344 million; in 1982, FFr688 million; in 1985, FFr800 million; and in 1990 over FFr1 billion.

During the 1978–91 period, the spending by cities of more than 150,000 inhabitants grew from FFr120 million to FFr400 million; départements, FFr148 million in 1990, four times what was spent in 1975; and régions about 2.5 francs per inhabitant in 1990.

As for the social nature of the theatre audience in France, the great goal of decentralization was to give back to the regions a taste for theatre, and to the area around Paris a taste for popular theatre, the theatre which, according to Roland Barthes (1915–80), 'is a theatre which has confidence in man'. Just after the war, the interest was in *théâtre de boulevard* in Paris, but the decentralized Paris companies (such as the TNP and suburban groups from the 1960s on and the artistic success of the experimental Left Bank theatres beginning in the 1950s) saw audiences growing and gaining new interest in the art generally. Nevertheless, the goal of developing the 'non-audience' (in the suburbs and among the working classes) on the whole did not happen even in the illusory 1968 period which supposedly gave power to the workers. What the audience did become was institutionalized and the debate between cultural structures and art

only complicated the situation even more.

According to several surveys, professionals and top executives today make up 30 per cent of French audiences, with mid-level executives making up another 25 per cent. Hourly employees make up less than 10 per cent and students about 25 per cent. A 1990 survey showed that Paris's private theatres attracted some 3.5 million spectators; the National Theatres about 700,000; the CDNs about 1.6 million; and the 1,200 or so independent companies in the country, about 5 million people.

The idea of decentralization also led to the creation of audience associations. These have survived even if their functions have changed. Their aim was to eliminate the barriers which prevented people from going to the theatre, to select productions for support, and to offer subscription programmes. This is where an important chapter in the history of the theatre audiences was written by the Amis du Théâtre Populaire (ATP). Officially founded in 1954, the ATP was a national federation of audience associations and aimed at promoting popular theatre in France. The ATP had 15,000 members in 1954 and 55,000 by 1959. There are still about forty ATPs today, with several hundred members each.

There are as well a large number of unions in the country representing virtually every area of professional theatrical endeavour. Not a union, the Société des Auteurs et Compositeurs dramatique (Society of Playwrights), founded in 1777, has come to play a very active role in the defense of France's dramatists and performing arts in general.

Artistic Profile

Companies

Whether they were focused on naturalism like Antoine, symbolism like Lugné-Poe or focusing on a stylized theatricality in the service of the people like the Cartel, companies in France prior to World War II tended to be groups of actors who centred around important and innovative personalities. It was Copeau more than anyone else who initiated the modern concept of the troupe in France and his ideas in this regard became rallying cries for everyone involved in

the renewal of the theatre from the late 1930s onward.

In 1924 Copeau, whose influence continues to remain strong, left Paris and his Vieux Colombier (which he founded in 1913) to set up a troupe in Burgundy. With a deep belief in the role of the dramatic author in the theatrical experience, he wanted his productions to be based on ensemble playing and he pioneered in the modern use of a bare, neo-Elizabethan stage and *commedia dell'arte* stylization.

Until Copeau's experiments, the only true

company in France was the Comédie-Française, founded in 1680 and a development in its way of Molière's early touring Illustre Théâtre. From its creation, the company – with the exception of the ten-year period 1789–99 – retained a monopoly on the production of French drama.

Since 1850, the general administrator of the Comédie-Française has been appointed by the government. Operating as both a private company and as a society of shareholders (with sociétaires appointed for life) it still sees itself in the 1990s as the official guardian of French tradition although after 1960 it began to present contemporary classics like Ionesco and began as well to invite foreign directors.

In 1936, its new general administrator, Édouard Bourdet (1887–1945), asked Jouvet, Dullin and Baty to help him reorganize the company and its two theatres – the Comédie

Richelieu and the Odéon – and the idea of true ensemble playing grew. The ideas of the Cartel and the Front populaire – in which the notion of a permanent company became essential – led to the establishment of such troupes across the country as a foundation of decentralization.

In fact, each of the five regional centres created between 1946 and 1952 had a company of fifteen actors built around a leading figure. The idea had been articulated by Copeau in his manifesto, *Le Théâtre populaire*, written in 1941 but not widely read until many years later.

It was the appointment of Roland Pietri (1910–86) as head of the new permanent company in Colmar in 1946 which began the movement. This was followed by the appointment of Copeau's son-in-law, Jean Dasté, in Saint-Étienne in 1947; Maurice Sarrazin in Toulouse in 1949; Hubert Gignoux in Rennes in 1949;

Guy Trejan and Roger Planchon in Planchon's 1974 TNP Villeurbanne production of Molière's *Tartuffe*, designed by Hubert Monloup.
Photo: Agence de Presse Bernand.

289

and Gaston Baty in Aix in 1952 (Baty, unfortunately, died before taking up his position).

A number of other permanent troupes began to emerge in the 1950s, many of them later becoming incorporated into the new Centres Dramatiques Nationaux (CDNs) in the 1960s. Among the most important of these were the Théâtre populaire des Flandres (1954) which later worked alongside the Centre Dramatique du Nord under André Reybaz (the discoverer of the dramatist Vauthier and the French-speaking Belgian, Michel de Ghelderode); the Théâtre de Bourgogne, which in 1960 became the Centre dramatique de Bourgogne; Planchon's troupe in Lyon became a permanent troupe in 1957 when it moved to Villeurbanne, a working-class town outside Lyon.

It was the development of these permanent companies which led in 1963 to the second phase of decentralization – the establishment of the Maisons de la Culture (Houses of Culture) which most often housed one of the CDNs and its troupe.

During this same period, a number of artists formed their own independent companies. Among them Jean-Louis Barrault and his wife, Madeleine Renaud, who resigned from the Comédie-Française and established the Compagnie Renaud-Barrault at the Théâtre Marigny in Paris. As well, the Théâtre National Populaire was founded during this time (directed by Jean Vilar from 1951 to 1963 and then by Georges Wilson (b. 1921) until 1970), operating at the Théâtre de Chaillot in Paris and serving as a constant challenge to the Comédie-Française.

Planchon's discovery of the plays of Adamov, with whom his company regularly worked, and his encounter with Brecht in Paris in 1955, were, for this man of neo-Elizabethan sensibilities, branding experiences. They would bend his company's style naturally towards an epic theatre. Impassioned by history, his group was the first in France to focus on the undercurrents of economic and social conditions in the interpretation of classical works. Molière's *Georges Dandin* was interpreted in 1958 as a realistic scene of provincial life in the seventeenth century. His interpretation of *Tartuffe* (1962) was equally controversial because, in the relationship between Orgon and Tartuffe, he revealed homosexual undertones.

Throughout his career Planchon also staged many contemporary texts with his group. Vinaver's *Aujourd'hui ou Les Coréens* (*Today or The Koreans*) in 1956 and Adamov's *Paolo*

Paoli in 1957 were among the most successful of his premières. From 1961, along with his work as director of the troupe and actor, he also turned to playwriting. His first play was *La Remise* (*The Stable*, performed in 1962).

Marcel Maréchal, also a native of Lyon, created the Compagnie du Cothurne with a group of student friends in the style of Planchon. He was soon put in charge of the small Théâtre des Marronniers in 1960, then the larger Théâtre du Huitième in 1968. In 1975, he became director of the Théâtre National de la Criée in Marseilles. Influenced by classics as well as by the discoveries of plays by his contemporaries, his company's work was marked by a close collaboration with three writers: Audiberti, Louis Guilloux (1899–1980) and Vauthier. He premièred Audiberti's *Cavalier seul* in 1963 and Guilloux's *Cripure* in 1967. Jean Vauthier wrote most of his later works for Maréchal. *Le Sang* (*The Blood*) in 1970 was a major work, as was *Ton nom dans le feu des nuées, Elisabeth* (*Your Name in Tongues of Fire, Elisabeth*). In his stagings, at times exuberant and sober, Maréchal excelled in the mixture of grotesque and pathetic elements.

Guy Rétoré founded a troupe, La Guilde, in 1950 to play in the Paris suburbs. Thanks to his obstinacy, this theatre became the Théâtre de l'Est Parisien in 1962.

Jean Vilar had created the Avignon Festival in 1947 and later established himself at the 3,000-seat Théâtre de Chaillot in Paris. Inspired by his experiences at the Palais des Papes in Avignon, the immensity of the space led him to a rapid shifting of actors and a new style of acting based on the rhythm of the language, changes of level and inclined planes. The staging of *Le Cid* with Gérard Philipe in the title role completely broke old notions of static acting.

The goal of Vilar at the TNP was to put theatre within everyone's reach, to make it a 'public service, like gas, water, electricity'. He also organized in the working-class suburbs the 'TNP Weekend' where, for one price, audiences were given two plays, a dance, a concert and food. It was a great success. But as these were costly, he eventually decided to bring workers to the theatre rather than vice versa. Searching for popular models of theatre in the histories of Athens and Elizabethan England, he performed Greek tragedies and Shakespearian dramas offering historical plays in which theatre's social role was emphasized. The journal *Théâtre Populaire* claimed that Vilar's influence on the later provincial dramatic centres and on French festivals was immense. Vilar resigned from the TNP in 1963 and returned again to the Avignon Festival. Georges Wilson succeeded him and took essentially the same political approach.

After 1968, those who wanted a political theatre questioned Vilar's goal of 'a theatre which unites'. The argument was that true political theatre should divide the public, and should represent the ongoing struggle of the classes.

The protest movement of May 1968, libertarian in its views, wanted to create a new world where relations between individuals would be established. Certain people tried to realize these ideals through collective creation. In effect, the desire to escape the classic repertoire was born through the freedom of creating new works, the fruit of the collective voice. The notion of the written text itself was put into question. Operating most often from improvisations, sometimes from adaptations of stories, it was from this dream that Le Théâtre du Soleil was born, under the direction of Ariane Mnouchkine. Its approach became the model for many other popular and alternative theatres. The company

was formed in 1964 with a group of theatre students, following the model of Brecht's cooperative Berliner Ensemble in which all important decisions are made jointly, each member of the group assumes all the domestic tasks of the community. Their first success was with Arnold Wesker's *La Cuisine* (*The Kitchen*) in 1967 (the first Wesker play to be performed in France), then *A Midsummer Night's Dream*, a play which had great influence on the overall style of the company. Importance was accorded to movement and acrobatics. Two of the principal roles, Titania and Oberon, were taken by dancers from the Maurice Béjart Company.

Beginning in 1969 with *Les Clowns*, Mnouchkine also began to create her own dramatic texts. Each of the actors participated in their working out as well as in the staging. Because of Mnouchkine's interest in *commedia dell'arte*, she also began to use masks. In this way, she forced actors to perform more with their bodies. The plays *1789* (created in 1970), *1793* (1972) and *L'Age d'or* (1975) represent triumphs of such collective creation. Using the large

Ariane Mnouchkine's 1981 Théâtre du Soleil production of Shakespeare's *Richard II*, designed by Claude François.
Photo: Agence de Presse Bernand.

Armoury of Vincennes in east-end Paris where the troupe set up headquarters, the plays took place in various locations, the spectators finding themselves always at the heart of the action and in this way also participating in the creation of the show.

During rehearsals for *L'Age d'or*, members of the company even toured factories and performed in front of workers, asking them what they thought. In 1979 with *Méphisto*, Mnouchkine adapted a Klaus Mann novel not yet published in the west. In the 1980s, Mnouchkine recruited new actors and sought her model in the Oriental theatre, mounting at this time a cycle of Shakespearian tragedies. In the 1990s, she created the *Atrides*.

Two other important troupes were born directly from the experience of Théâtre du Soleil. Jean-Claude Penchenat (b. 1937), after having been part of Mnouchkine's company, founded his own troupe, the Théâtre du Campagnol. He mounted novel adaptations (Dickens's *David Copperfield* in 1977) and showed the French public several Goldoni plays which had not been previously translated, notably *The Player* in 1992. The Théâtre de l'Aquarium was founded by Jacques Nichet in 1967 from a university troupe very close to Théâtre du Soleil. Their shows were born from the transposition of narrative texts refocused through the eyes of current politics (*Les Guerres Picrocholines*, in 1967, was an adaptation of *Gargantua*). All were the fruit of collective creation by the actors as orchestrated by Nichet. Thus in 1976, *La Vieille Lune tient la jeune lune toute une nuit dans ses bras* (*The Full Moon Holding the New Moon In Its Arms All Night*) was a play about the occupation of factories.

A number of other troupes also work on the model of Théâtre du Soleil. Jacques Kraemer (b. 1937), director of Théâtre de Lorraine, wrote in 1970 *Splendeur et misère de Minette la bonne Lorraine* (on the problem of exhaustion of the iron mines of Lorraine) also based on the improvisational work of the troupe. Jérôme Savary, director of the Grand Magic Circus, also worked in the same style. His production *De Moïse à Mao* (*From Moses to Mao*, 1973) was also a collective creation.

The idea of the company changed again in the 1980s and a whole new generation of directors and actors came to life through the establishment of a company even if it was just for a few productions. The reasons were clear: by this time, it had actually become necessary to form a company to receive grants. Some of these new groups toured in the Centres Dramatiques or the Scènes Nationales created from 1990. This temporary company approach has become the norm at many of the Centres Dramatiques.

In this sense, it may still be said that only the Comédie-Française and the Théâtre du Soleil continue on as true permanent companies even in the 1990s. Nevertheless theatre life continues to revolve around individuals and groups such as Bruno Boëglin (b. 1951) and his Novothéâtre (founded in 1977); Gilles Chavassieux (b. 1934) and his Ateliers lyonnais (founded in 1975); Jean-Louis Martinelli and his Compagnie du Réfectoire (1971); Jean-Pierre Vincent, who first came to national attention with his Théâtre de l'Espérance in 1972; and Philippe Adrien (b. 1939) and Jean-Claude Fall (b. 1944), who established their Atelier de recherche et de réalisation théâtrale (Workshop for Research and Theatrical Production) in 1974.

Other groups of note include Théâtre de l'Unité founded in 1968 by Jacques Livchine (b. 1943); Robert Gironés (b. 1942) and his Théâtre de la Reprise (founded 1971); Ballatum (1972); Théâtre de la Chamaille (1972); Quatre Litres 12 founded (1972) by Michel Massé (b. 1947); La Rumeur founded in 1977; Royal de Luxe founded (1977) by Jean-Luc Courcoult (b. 1955); les Fédérés (1981); the Emballage-Théâtre/Compagnie Pépie-Klamm, founded by Eric Da Silva (b. 1957); le Cirque Aligre, founded in 1979 and which disbanded in 1985; Archaos founded in 1985; and Zingaro founded in 1987.

One of the more striking changes in the 1990s was the increasing presence of female directors across the country. Among them are Brigitte Jaques (b. 1946); Anne Delbée (b. 1950); Claudia Staviski (b. 1956) and her L'Ange rebelle/Compagnie Je-Ils (founded 1976); Jeanne Champagne (b. 1948) and her Théâtre Écoute (1981); Chantal Morel (b. 1958) and her Groupe Alarmes; and Sophia Louchachesvsky (b. 1955) and her Les Amis de (1987).

Among younger directors who have established their own troupes are Stéphane Braunschweig (b. 1965) and his Théâtre Machine, Robert Cantarella (b. 1957) and his Compagnie des Ours (founded in 1984), and Stanislas Nordey (b. 1966), creator of ensemble productions such as *Bêtes de style* (*Animals With Style*, 1991) and *Calderón* (1993).

Dramaturgy

French playwriting changed more in the twentieth century than it had from the Renaissance to the end of the nineteenth century. Dramatic authors gradually abandoned both unity of action and the need to create illusion. The notion of genre (tragedy, comedy, drama) also no longer held, with writers creating scenes from their imaginations without concern for fixed forms. The more generic term 'play' became used from 1880 on and gradually superseded other specific designations.

French theatre in the first half of the twentieth century gradually gave up its isolation and opened to foreign influences including Oriental models and the expressionism of northern Europe (Germany and Scandinavia). The visionary and iconoclastic work of Alfred Jarry (1873–1907), Guillaume Apollinaire (1880–1918), Roger Vitrac (1899–1952), Antonin Artaud and Paul Claudel – starting with Lugné-Poe's production of Claudel's *L'Annonce faite à Marie (The Announcement Made to Mary)* in 1912 – helped French theatre move even further from tradition.

Yet the years of the war and the immediate post-war period seemed rather conservative, with the existentialist and committed theatre (*théâtre engagé*) of Sartre, Camus and Armand Salacrou, the psychologically rooted literary theatre of Giraudoux, the very well-made ironic plays of Anouilh, the neo-classical plays of Henri de Montherlant (1896–1972), and even the poetic theatre of Cocteau and later Audiberti turning towards the modern. It was during the 1950s and 1960s, particularly fertile in terms of theatre, that the avant-garde actually revolutionized playwriting, thanks to Beckett, Ionesco, Adamov, Genet and Vauthier. These writers were soon followed in their audacity by a number of other playwrights such as Pinget, Weingarten, Schéhadé, Boris Vian (1920–59), Obaldia, Dubillard and Billetdoux.

The student protest of May 1968 revived interest in a more overtly political theatre and moved theatre away from the more obviously avant-garde. There was a return to political theatre – notably in Gatti – in the 1970s while the plays of Vinaver at the same time developed a kind of everyday, neo-Brechtian realism. Since the 1980s, on the other hand, the earlier avant-garde writers have become the modern classics.

Jarry's *Ubu Roi* (1896) was the first important play of the new avant-garde. Heir of Lautréamont (1848–70) and Rimbaud (1854–91), Jarry did not concern himself with pleasing the public in this play which, inspired by *Macbeth*, was a parody of historical drama but one which subverted everything. Based on the aesthetics of farce, *Ubu Roi* was absolutely indifferent to depth of character or logicality of scenery. Realism was banished from the stage and the influence of Freud helped abolish the line between dream and reality, releasing the imagination.

The *Manifeste du Surréalisme (Manifesto of Surrealism)* by André Breton (1896–1966), whose first version dates from 1924, eulogized imagination, madness and Freudianism. Surrealist theatre was to be rooted in the unusual. Its dramatic authors were to create a new form of illusion. Instead of representing truth as it was, they acknowledged that their play was simply a hoax. No longer concerned with the support of the public, the surrealists were appreciated only by a small number of the initiated. The reaction of most was general incomprehension.

It was not until the 1950s that these experiments found popular support. *Les Mamelles de Tirésias (The Breasts of Tiresias)*, by Apollinaire, dates from 1917. Apollinaire offers, in an absurd style, the phenomenon of transsexualism, the metamorphosis of Thérèse into a man. In *Victor ou les enfants au pouvoir (Victor or the Children in Power)*, a parody of the *drame bourgeois*, Roger Vitrac, in 1928, put on the stage a child with the height of a grown-up; that is, a deliberately false character. Both plays have been continuing favourites with alternative companies.

The work of Paul Claudel seems classical on the surface, but with the first performance of *L'Annonce faite à Marie* in 1912 and of *Tête d'or (Head of Gold* in 1924 (written in 1889), a new era for the 'position of the new man' opened up. With *Le Soulier de satin (The Satin Slipper)*, written in Japan between 1921 and 1924 and premièred in its shorter version by Barrault in 1943 with music by Arthur Honneger (1892–1955), Claudel pioneered new ways for French theatre; time and place were played with, action was presented simultaneously, acts were repaced by days. Most theatrical conventions were blown up, and space and acting were used to express the physicality of poetic language. Such writers prepared the way for the dramatic revolution of the 1950s.

The 1940s are characterized, in terms of theatre, by their dramaturgical classicism. As existentialists, Sartre and Camus produced their principal plays at the end of World War II and just after. They made the stage a place of debate and judgement. Their theatre, linked to the chaos of the war, responded to the aspirations of audiences of the time. As such, they enjoyed great success. In *Les Mouches* (*The Flies*), a play produced by Dullin during the war, Sartre utilized ancient mythology to denounce the occupation. *Huis clos* (*No Exit*), played at the Vieux Colombier in 1944, presented the world as hell and put forward the notion of action as the foundation of freedom. He spoke of torture in *Morts sans sépulture* (*No Tomb for the Dead*, 1946), of racism in *La Putain respectueuse* (*The Respectful Prostitute*, 1946), of political relationships in *Les Mains sales* (*Dirty Hands*, 1948), of individual liberty in *Le Diable et le Bon Dieu* (*The Devil and the Good Lord*, 1951), *Les Séquestrés d'Altona* (*The Condemned of Altona*, 1959) and *Les Troyennes* (*Trojan Women*, 1965). He looked at the relation between artists and power in *Kean* (1952). Sartre dealt with theory in *Un théâtre de situations* (*A Theatre of Situations*, 1973).

Camus, with long practical experience in the theatre, created *Le Malentendu* (*The Misunderstanding*, 1944) after the liberation. This play was a theatrical version of his philosophical thesis, *Le Mythe de Sisyphe* (*The Myth of Sisyphus*). In 1945, in *Caligula*, an exuberant neo-romantic drama, he gave the image of freedom pushed to its limits, its theme closely linked to imprisonment, a subject to which the public was then particularly sensitive. In 1947, in *L'État de siège* (*The State of Siege*) he brought to the stage his novel *La Peste* (*The Plague*) which had already had great success. The play, however, did not achieve equal success. He subsequently had a triumph with *Les Justes* (*The Just*) in 1949 with Maria Casarès (b.1922). From that moment, Camus devoted himself more and more to theatre, involving himself in the staging of his own plays or adapting foreign scripts.

Salacrou, who in the 1930s had staged foreign plays and historical dramas, after the war turned towards a social form of quasi-existential theatre, which put violence in an historical context – *Les Nuits de la colère* (*Nights of Anger*, 1946), *Dieu le savait* (*God Knew It*, 1950). He also created a number of satirical comedies denouncing bourgeois morality, such as *Une femme trop honnête* (*A Woman Too Honest*, 1956). His works were a constant meditation on the tragedy of the human condition, a cry of revolt against evil, a witness to the helplessness of a generation which had seen two world wars.

The existentialist theatre was the expression of a philosophy, then new, born of a sense of the absurdity of the world. But Sartre and Camus felt that all existence was absurd – certainly the old rhetoric was absurd – conserving as it did a rational order which was lost in the absurdity of language.

Boris Vian, a poet, novelist and playwright, was both an existentialist and an absurdist with a zany touch of surrealism. Extremely popular after his death with the post-1968 generation, he began his dramatic career in 1948 with a burlesque and cruel work, *L'Équarrissage pour tous* (*Squaring Off for All*), that made him a charismatic figure for the Parisian existentialists. A posthumous production of his play, *Les Bâtisseurs d'empire* (*The Empire Builders*) in 1959 assured his later reputation. To a very great extent, his personality bridges the gap between Sartre and Camus on the one hand and writers like Ionesco, Adamov and Beckett on the other.

Jean Giraudoux, whose works had been remarkably served by Louis Jouvet, had been prolific between the two wars. *Sodome et Gomorrhe* (*Sodom and Gomorrah*) was his only new work during the occupation. The preciosity of his style, which was situated in the line of Marivaux, characterized the works of this playwright, who was originally a novelist. He oscillated, in his choice of themes, between wonder and subjects which, even though apparently borrowed from ancient mythology, treated the most current of contemporary events. Thus *La Guerre de Troie n'aura pas lieu* (produced in English as *Tiger at the Gates*, 1935), though apparently dealing with the past, was actually dealing with the threat of the impending armed conflict with Germany. One of his best plays, *La Folle de Chaillot* (*Madwoman of Chaillot*) was directed by Jouvet in 1945.

Henri de Montherlant, poet, novelist and dramatic author, created his first play, *La Reine morte* (*The Dead Queen*), in 1942. He excelled with essentially historical and Christian themes such as his 1948 *Le Maître de Santiago* (*The Master of Santiago*) and his 1954 *Port-Royal*. His works, perhaps too perfect and too long, moved between the sobriety of the classic tragedy and the pure lyricism of romantic drama.

Jean Anouilh made his début in theatre in 1932 with *L'Hermine* (*The Ermine*) and continued to write for the theatre until the 1970s.

He divided his approximately forty plays into the categories 'pink, black, brilliant, grating and costumed'. In all his plays he denounced the mediocrity of life. One can also find there the recurring character of a pure, young girl trying to survive in a corrupt world, as in his *Antigone* (1944). Anouilh's playwriting was also characterized by a neo-Baroque style which manifested itself by often creating a play within a play – *La Répétition ou l'amour puni* (*The Rehearsal or Love Punished*, 1950). His writing style was characterized by a grating humour which mixed bitterness with fantasy. This literary theatre, like the existentialist theatre, which existed parallel to it, has also aged somewhat poorly, but it is still widely performed.

From the 1950s onwards, boulevard theatre in the Guitry-Aymé-Achard tradition remained active even though it went through various crises. Writers such as Félicien Marceau (b. 1913) with *L'Oeuf* (*The Egg*, 1956), Françoise Sagan (b. 1935) with *Un Château en Suède* (*A Castle in Sweden*, 1960), Maria Pacome (b. 1923) with *Apprends moi Céline* (*Teach Me Celine*, 1978), Loleh Bellon (b. 1925) with *Le Coeur sur la main* (*Heart on Your Sleeve*, 1980), and especially Jean Poiret (1926–92), author of the immensely popular *La Cage aux folles* (1973), and Françoise Dou̇n (b. 1928), author of the successful *Hit Parade* (1975), maintained a long line of entertaining, witty and occasionally thoughtful plays.

As for the poetic theatre represented by Jean Cocteau, it also fluctuated between classicism and modernism. A poet, novelist and film-maker, Cocteau made his début in 1917 with *Parade*, a ballet created in collaboration with Pablo Picasso and Erik Satie (1866–1925). His major theatrical production was between the two wars. During this time, he adapted a number of myths – *Orphée* (1926) and *La Machine infernale* (*The Infernal Machine*, 1933). After the war, he wrote only two plays: *L'Aigle à deux têtes* (*The Two-Headed Eagle*, 1945), where a queen is confronted by an anarchist, then *Bacchus* (1952), a play whose success was overshadowed by its blasphemous aspects. In 1962, he created in Tokyo *L'Impromptu du Palais-Royal*. Cocteau was involved directly in the staging of his plays and was

Pierre Mondy's 1973 Théâtre du Palais Royal production of Jean Poiret's *La Cage aux folles*, designed by André Levasseur.
Photo: Agence de Presse Bernand.

particularly interested in masks, costumes and designs for which he had an exuberant imagination.

Also emerging in the post-war period was Jacques Audiberti, a devoted reader of Victor Hugo (1802–85), the Parnassian poets and Lautréamont. His first important work was *Quoat-quoat* in 1946 followed the next year by *Le Mal court (Evil on the Run)* which enjoyed great success. From that point on, Audiberti gradually moved toward the *théâtre de boulevard*, especially from his *L'Effet Glapion (The Glapion Effect)* in 1959, which has become a minor classic. Altogether he wrote about fifteen neo-romantic plays with a very traditional structure, in which Manichean characters abound and where *coups de théâtre* and dramatic peripaties give intrigue the primary place. His brilliant plays, using a jubilant language, appeared as a celebration of words. His overflowing lyricism and his enormous Baroque exuberance and fantasy were his dominant characteristics.

To some extent Henri Pichette and Georges Schéhadé belong to the poetic theatre. Both were poets before turning to the stage. Pichette made his début with *Les Epiphanies (The Epiphanies)* in 1947, a drama played at the Noctambules, in which the action revolved about the life and death of a poet. He wrote *Nucléa* in 1952, a play about the dangers of nuclear war, returning to a classical style of poetry, and giving life once again to the Alexandrine. But the play was a failure and Pichette turned away from theatre.

Schéhadé, a Lebanese poet writing in French, produced most of his dramatic works from 1951 to 1965: *Monsieur Bob'le (Mister Bob'le*, 1951), *La Soirée des proverbes (Evening of Proverbs*, 1954), *Histoire de Vasco (History of Vasco*, 1956), *Le Voyage (The Voyage*, 1961), *Les Violettes (The Violets*, 1961) and *L'Émigré de Brisbane (The Immigrant from Brisbane*, 1965). Two recurring themes appear in his work, that of the voyage and that of waiting, both linked to a thirst for purity. The surrealistic dreamlike poetry which fertilized these scripts fascinated Jean-Louis Barrault, who premièred three of his plays.

The two great lyricists of the period were undoubtedly Jean Genet and Jean Vauthier. Genet's dramatic works were written in two periods. After his five novels (written in prison), he turned to playwriting. *Haute surveillance (High Surveillance*, written in 1945 and produced in 1949) and *Les Bonnes (The Maids*, produced in 1947), two contemporary trage-dies, offered the spectacle of a ceremony where the quest was to find the self, a quest that drove the protagonists to murder. Genet took his characters from two oppressed groups: prisoners and servants. In the later plays, the quest expanded to society at large. The second half of his dramatic work was written between 1955 and 1957. In *Le Balcon (The Balcony*, produced in 1960), he brought to the stage society as a whole and the number of characters housed also increased. Also he abandoned the enclosed theatre to create a brilliant theatrical structure, inspired by Gordon Craig's screens. *Les Nègres (The Blacks*, 1959) and *Les Paravents (The Screens*, 1966) were a diptych on the subject of colonization, posing the problem of image on a political level. Genet was spatializing his quest with an aesthetics of discontinuity. After *Les Paravents*, a grandiose work that subsumed all his former writings, Genet ceased writing for the theatre, turning to the Black Panthers and the Palestinian cause.

Jean Vauthier wrote *Capitaine Bada*, his first play, in 1949; it was premièred in 1952 by André Reybaz. In 1956, he wrote *Le Personnage combattant (The Fighting Man)*, in 1961, *Le Rêveur (The Dreamer)* and in 1966, *Badadesques*. In all these plays, the recurring character is the artist. With *Les Prodiges (Prodigies*, written in 1957 and first performed in 1970) he created a domestic tragedy of modern life; also in 1970 he adapted *The Revenger's Tragedy* by Cyril Tourneur as *Le Sang (Blood)*. *Ton nom dans le feu des nuées, Elisabeth (Your Name in Tongues of Fire, Elisabeth)* was a neo-Elizabethan rewriting of *Arden of Faversham* and was magnificently staged by Marcel Maréchal, who had become Vauthier's most faithful interpreter.

In Fernando Arrabal, the same type of blood cruelty could be found though his works can also be linked to the poetic tradition and to the surrealistic theatre of personal fantasies and psychoanalysis. His Théâtre Panique (Pan's Theatre) is a theatre of sadistic and physical attack on the bodies of partners: whippings, chained women (*La Grand Ceremonial/ The Great Ceremonial*, 1961), torture victims, scenes of necrophilia (*Le Lai de Barrabas/The Lay of Barrabas*, 1969), and cannibalism (*L'Architecte et l'empereur d'Assyrie/The Architect and the Emperor of Assyria*, 1967).

Soon after World War II the playwrights who were going to revolutionize the European stage began to appear: Ionesco, Beckett and Adamov. All three were foreign-born but lived in France and wrote in French: Beckett was Irish, Ionesco Romanian and Adamov Russian-Armenian.

In 1950, Ionesco's *La Cantatrice chauve* (*The Bald Soprano*) was performed at Noctambules staged by Nicolas Bataille (b. 1926). Because of the play's apparent incoherence, it was considered a hoax and did not attract a large public. Some months later, Jean-Marie Serreau introduced Adamov, also at Noctambules. This script was *La Grande et la Petite Manoeuvre* (*The Big and the Small Manoeuvre*).

In 1953, Roger Blin directed Beckett's *En Attendant Godot* (*Waiting for Godot*). This former secretary to James Joyce was totally unknown, although he had already written most of his novels. The production was a quasi-

success and Beckett began attracting attention. So too did some of the other writers of the French avant-garde. In 1969, twenty years after the creation of these first plays, Beckett received the Nobel Prize. The following year, Ionesco was invited to join the Académie Française.

One might ask why this movement took so long to be recognized. Unlike the avant-garde novel, which began to be seen in 1963 in manifestos such as *Pour un nouveau roman* (*Towards the New Novel*) by Alain Robbe-Grillet (b. 1922), the new theatre did not have a leader or a theoretician behind it. Beckett and Vauthier entrenched themselves behind a wall of almost total silence. Only Ionesco offered insight into the new style of playwriting in his

Lucien Raimbourg, Jean Martin, Pierre Latour and Roger Blin in Blin's 1953 Théâtre de Babylone production of Samuel Beckett's *Waiting for Godot*, designed by Sergio Gerstein. Photo: Agence de Presse Bernand.

Notes et contre-notes (*Notes and Counter-Notes*), a work published in 1966. In it, he gathered together a series of interviews, articles and papers written since 1950. Adamov, in *L'Homme et l'enfant* (*Man and Child*), an autobiographical book completed in 1967, also supplied some indications on the genesis of his plays. He also wrote a preface in 1955 which, despite its briefness, also offered information on the new orientation of these dramatists. Genet wrote one for the third edition of *Les Bonnes* in 1963.

All these authors, then, gave birth in the 1950s to a theatre whose roots stretched back to Jarry, a theatre which no longer tried to please the public but which put existence in question and which generated anguish. Determined to bring to the stage humanity in its most profound form of alienation, these writers criticized the *théâtre de boulevard* for its superficiality. On the other hand, they refused to give in to didacticism. Their conception was also very different from Brechtian theories and those of the American theatre, where social issues predominated. They equally condemned realism as an imitation of the false because to them imagination was of greater interest. Attentive to their own minds, they considered the dream, this 'other scene' as Freud called it, to be a world very close to the theatrical universe because of its unlimited sense of space and fantasy. This triple refusal – not to please, to teach or to imitate – led them to reduce stage action to apparently simple renderings and to create characters without equivalents in reality, more symbolic than anything else. All traditional aspects of character were removed. Their protagonists, often without names, pasts or histories, rarely acted. Space also became imaginary and no longer had to function as a reflection of reality or time.

In this new avant-garde, many followed the example of Ionesco, Adamov and Beckett and broke through language. For some of these writers, language was simply a source of illogicality and contradiction. Rather than generating sense, it generated nonsense. It was a source of irritation and misunderstanding. This concept of language echoed concerns heard since the 1920s. Freud, whose work was familiar to Beckett, Ionesco and Adamov, first suggested the essential falseness of language, seeing it as a vicious circle where humanity was most abused. The whole system broke down if individual memory and social consensus could not work together. In creating characters without memory, these dramatists presented beings who had also lost language.

For bilingual writers like Beckett, Ionesco and Adamov, these ideas were reinforced and further divided any hope of meaning. Beckett's case, in particular, was without precedent in the history of literature. Though he had written his first novels in his mother tongue, English, it was in French that he finally chose to write. His plays especially were written in French. From the 1960s, he moved back and forth between French and English, writing in both languages and often giving a second version of the same play in the other language. His was an *oeuvre* with genuine echoes.

It was because the very function of communication was put into question that a new language had to be created, a language characterized by an alternation between long monologues (which isolated protagonists in their solitude) and dialogues (which no longer functioned as question and answer).

Ionesco's *La Cantatrice chauve* stands out in this respect. It was the first time that language in theatre became pure derision. In order to show language as non-communication, Ionesco, a great reader of the surrealists, held up to ridicule the entire Aristotelian notion of logic. After this play, in *La Leçon* (*The Lesson*, 1951) and *Jacques ou la soumission* (*Jacques or the Submission*, 1950), Ionesco pursued this question of language. From *Les Chaises* (*The Chairs*, 1952), to *Amédée* (1953) to *Le Nouveau locataire* (*The New Tenant*, 1954), he meditated on the loneliness of being imprisoned by things, and things which seemed to proliferate in an endless way. The entry on stage of Bérenger in 1957 marked a turning point in his dramaturgy. Even though he continued to dismantle language, he did reintroduce a certain lyricism, linked to the growing expression of his metaphysical themes.

The problem of evil in the world from that moment became central to Ionesco. The four plays in which Bérenger appears – *Rhinocéros* (1958), *Tueur sans gages* (*Killer Without Security*, 1959), *Le Roi se meurt* (*Exit the King*, 1962) and *Le Piéton de l'air* (*Pedestrian of the Air*, 1962) – constituted a sort of tetralogy. Ionesco gave his protagonists a primary place, returning to a certain classicism. *La Soif et la faim* (*Hunger and Thirst*, 1964) connected to this cycle. From this point, the works became more and more metaphysically dense and began to take on an autobiographical resonance. In *Ce formidable bordel* (*This Fabulous Bordello*,

Jean-Marie Serreau's 1961 Théâtre de France Odéon production of Eugène Ionesco's
Amédée, designed by Peter Knapp.
Photo: Agence de Presse Bernand.

1973), based on the only novel that he wrote, he expressed his quest for the sacred and for the 'Manifestation', in the orthodox use of the term. In his two last plays, *L'Homme aux valises* (*A Man and his Suitcases*, 1975) and *Voyages chez les morts* (*Voyages to the House of the Dead*, 1980), Ionesco returned to his past. Theatre had supplied him with characters and dramatic locales, but it was the material of his personal journals which he now used. Rather than abandoning his concern with language, he chose to close his last play with a long monologue, a monologue where language is again dealt with as it was in *La Cantatrice chauve*.

In Ionesco's wake, a number of playwrights treated language in a burlesque or dreamlike style. Romain Weingarten, poet and dramatic author and also influenced by the surrealists, created work in the discordance of dialogue which consistently provoked uneasiness. His first play, *Akara* (1948), was followed by *Les*

Nourrices (*The Wet Nurses*, 1961) and *L'Été* (*Summer*, 1966) which brought on stage two adolescents and two cats (of which one was played by Weingarten himself). The play was an enormous success. In 1970, he wrote *Alice dans les jardins du Luxembourg* (*Alice in the Luxembourg Gardens*), in which he showed a little girl who, after having killed her mother, meets a giant egg inhabited by a certain Dodu; the dialogue functions here like an absurd and cruel game.

Robert Pinget, a novelist and, as a playwright, very close to Beckett, also put on stage, in his type of chamber theatre, people who do not communicate. Thus in *La Manivelle* (*The Crank*) two old men reassess their memories without really making contact. The theme of incommunicability is also at the centre of the work of Roland Dubillard, both an actor and dramatic author. His key works date from between 1960 and 1970. From his first play,

Naïves hirondelles (*Innocent Swallows*, 1961), he created characters who are simply unable to communicate and who exchange platitudes and clichés. His *La Maison d'os* (*The House of Bones*, 1962) was a drama of 'me' isolated in silence.

The paradox of René de Obaldia, a poet and playwright, lies in his power to play with language in virtuoso ways as he showed in 1960 with *Génousie*, his first play and later in *Du vent dans les branches de Sassafras* (*Wind in the Sassafras Tree*). In *Monsieur Klebs et Rosalie* (*Mr Klebs and Rosalie,* 1975) the heroine is a robot who talks in clichés, even in absurdities.

François Billetdoux, like Ionesco, uses language in an absurd way. An actor and novelist, his first play was done in 1955, *À la nuit la nuit* (*To the Night at Night*), and in 1959 *Tchin-Tchin* (*Cheers*). Written in a narrative, everyday style that he would continue to use in the future, where his protagonists gradually liberate themselves from conventions. His *Silence, l'arbre remue encore* (*Silence, the Tree Stirs Still,* 1967) and his *Réveille-toi Philadelphie* (*Wake-up, Philadelphia,* 1981) are allegories with a fantasy atmosphere where a character ages as the audience watches.

If one finds in Beckett and Adamov the same suspicion towards language as in Ionesco, their works are also characterized by physical exaggerations of the body. The body, for them, is also dramatic. The body, in earlier theatre, was only a mediator, a transmitter of a voice, support for a costume. But in their work, the body is exposed in its sufferings. Hideous and repulsive, it becomes vile. In their determination to humiliate the body, these writers are also heirs of the Theatre of Cruelty. For Beckett it was metaphysical cruelty. He puts on stage a world of old people, blind, lame, paralysed or even legless, lost in terms of the roles they played in their lives. The body has failed them and is now the instrument of a permanent moral torture, of physical and metaphysical cruelty. These sado-masochistic beings, thrown together with their disabilities for eternity, pass time to make themselves suffer better. The aged body, worn out and sick, is the centre of their alienation. They carry ostentatiously the stigmata of their dependence. A merciless tyrant, the body tortures their souls.

There are two key periods in the works of Samuel Beckett. The first, beginning with *Waiting for Godot* in 1953 to *Oh! les beaux jours* (*Happy Days*) in 1960, was centred on the miseries of the body. The mute body was sometimes even shown without words which might make clear the message. This was the case in the two mimo-dramas, *Acte sans paroles I* (*Act Without Words I,* 1957) and *Acte sans paroles II* (1960). *Oh! les beaux jours* marked a turning point for Beckett which became quite clear after *Comédie* (*Play,* 1964). From this point, Beckett's dramatic writing transformed itself under the influence of the experience of writing novels. In the series of 'dramaticules' which he began to create, it was voice rather than body which became primary. He often put on the stage a character who alone tells a story. The monologue begins to dominate. Beckett systematically exploits parts of the body. Sometimes he puts on stage one or more characters who speak about themselves in the first person – *La Dernière Bande* (*Krapp's Last Tape,* written in 1958, produced in 1960) and *Comédie;* sometimes in the third person about an absent character or a character who is present but remains mute – *Solo* (1980), *Impromptu d'Ohio* (1982) and *Fragment de théâtre II* (1960); sometimes in a voice off stage addressing itself or speaking to someone else, such as *Dis Joe* (*Eh Joe,* 1965), a play written for television; *Cette fois* (*That Time*), *Berceuse* (*Rockaby,* 1981) and *Pas moi* (*Not I,* 1975). In all these instances, the play becomes a form of autobiography.

It was the 'cruelty of blood', however, which bathed the works of Arthur Adamov and his followers. The body, for him, was doubly victimized, individually and socially, always a disaster for the protagonists. All the plays of Adamov had as their themes incommunicability and the suffering of the body. The threat of death, the kicks which might come from the other at any moment, all this made terror strong in his works. It is found in *La Grande et la Petite Manoeuvre* (*The Big and the Small Manoeuvre,* 1950), *L'Invasion* (*The Invasion,* 1950), *La Parodie* (*The Parody,* 1951), *Le Sens de la marche* (*Looking Forward, 1953*) and *Tous contre tous* (*All Against All,* 1953).

Le Ping-Pong (written in 1954 and first performed in 1955) and *Paolo Paoli* (completed in 1955 and staged in 1957) represented a turning point in Adamov's works. In discovering Brecht, he separated himself from Ionesco and from Beckett, putting back into question the whole conception of his writing. These new works showed a political engagement both partisan and didactic. In *Le Printemps 71* (*Spring 71*) Adamov was clearly influenced by Brecht's *Days of the Commune.* In *La Politique des restes* (*The Politics of Remains,* 1959), the influence of

Brecht could also be felt since Adamov offered a theme similar to that of Brecht's *The Exception and the Rule* – class justice.

After this period of political engagement, Adamov, undermined more and more by his own neuroses, turned toward the mysterious world of the psyche. He wanted to reconcile the two styles of his earlier writing. *M. le modéré* (*Mr Moderate*), written in 1967, appeared to be a return to the playwriting of the first period, though reflecting his politico-social preoccupations. *Off Limits* (1969) appeared as a series of happenings in which characters expressed their fantasies, and as a condemnation of American drug users. Finally, with *Si l'été revenait* (*If Summer Had Returned*) in 1970, Adamov returned to the dreamlike universe found in his early works. Returning at the end of his life to his first preoccupations, he finally found an equilibrium between dream and political engagement.

The political protest of May 1968 and the years which followed threw momentary discredit on the avant-garde as the politically committed theatre found realism a better form within which to work. But the movement away from realism continued.

The theatre of Armand Gatti reflected his hard experience in the wartime concentration camps (*L'Enfant rat/The Rat-Child*, 1959). This son of an Italian immigrant worked strongly against fascism (*La Passion du Général Franco/The Passion of General Franco*, 1969), the atomic bomb (*La Cigogne/The Stork*, 1968) and the Vietnam war (*V. comme Vietnam/V. as in Vietnam*, 1967). His theatre avoided didacticism through a style of writing where the real and the imaginary merged, but the abundance of his lyricism sometimes led to confusion.

Aimé Césaire, a poet from Martinique, became the voice of negritude. This political

Jean-Marie Serreau's 1965 Théâtre de France Odéon production of Aimé Césaire's *The Tragedy of King Christophe*.
Photo: Agence de Presse Bernand.

militant attacked colonialism from his first play, *Et les Chiens se taisaient* (*And the Dogs Were Silenced*, 1956), through *La Tragédie du roi Christophe* (*The Tragedy of King Christophe*, 1964) and *Une saison au Congo* (*A Season in the Congo*, 1967), this last play about the assassination of Patrice Lumumba, president of Zaïre.

Kateb Yacine wrote in French a hymn to Algeria and to the Algerian revolution in plays such as *Le Cadavre encerclé* (*The Corpse Surrounded*, written in 1955, clandestinely performed in 1958) and *Les Ancêtres redoublent de férocité* (*The Ancestors Increase Their Ferocity*, 1967). In 1972, he returned to Algeria where he dedicated himself to theatre in Arabic.

It was Planchon who discovered Michel Vinaver in 1956 through his *Aujourd'hui ou les Coréens* (*Today or The Koreans*). The play was about a meeting between an injured young French soldier working for the United Nations and a young Korean in his homeland, now devastated by war. The great success of Vinaver would come in 1977 with his *Iphigénie-Hotel* (*Hotel Iphigenia*, written in 1959), with *Les Travaux et les jours* (*Works and Days*, 1980) and *Les Voisins* (*Neighbours*, 1986), the last two directed by Alain Françon.

Jean-Claude Grumberg, a Jewish Parisian, places his widely performed *L'Atelier* (*The Workshop*, 1979) in his own milieu. Premièred at the Odéon, it dealt with the life of a small clothing workshop between 1944 and 1952. In this resolutely naturalistic play, the actresses playing the dressmakers really sewed the clothes that the audience watched them make.

Mention should also be made here of the works of Jean Paul Wenzel (b. 1947) whose most successful play has been *Loin d'Hagondange* (*Far From Hagondange*, 1977) directed by Patrice Chéreau; Michel Deutsch whose most successful play has been *Féroe, la nuit* (*The Faeroe Islands at Night*, 1989); and Pierre Laville, author of *Les Ressources naturelles* (*Natural Resources*, 1974), *Le Fleuve rouge* (*Red River*, 1981) and *Retours* (*Returning*, 1988).

From 1977, Bernard-Marie Koltès allied hyper-realism to lyricism in a rather unbridled way. Patrice Chéreau staged his work, most notably *La Nuit juste avant les forêts* (*Darkness Before the Woods*), *Combat de nègre et de chiens* (*The Battle of the Black Man and the Dogs*, 1983), *Quai Ouest* (*Quay West*, 1985) and *Dans la solitude des champs de coton* (*Solitude in the Cotton Fields*, 1985). His posthu-

mously produced *Roberto Zucco* (done in Berlin in 1990 and directed by Peter Stein) caused some scandal in France when staged in 1992 by Bruno Boëglin.

Two female novelists who turned to the stage should also be mentioned: Nathalie Sarraute and Marguerite Duras. Sarraute is best known for her *C'est beau* (*Simply Beautiful*, 1975) and *Pour un oui, pour un non* (*Yes or No*, 1986). Duras's best stage works include *L'Amante anglaise* (*The English Mistress*, 1968), *Suzanna Andler* (1976) and *Savannah Bay* (1983). Both evolved a theatre built on everyday language and cliché inspired by Beckett. Their success has inspired many other women to approach the theatre as well including Marie Redonnet (b. 1949), author of *Mobie Dicq* (1989).

What characterized the late 1980s and early 1990s was the forceful return, inaugurated by Beckett, of the monologue, and even longer fully scripted plays. Among the writers of note working in this way were Philippe Minyana, author of *Inventaires* (*Inventory*, 1987); Enzo Cormann, author of *Credo* (1982) and *Sade – Concerts d'enfer* (*Sade – Hell Music*, 1989); and Jérome Deschamps (b. 1947), a pupil of Vitez and trainee actor with the Comédie-Française, who founded the Compagnie Potron Minet with Macha Makeïeff and Michèle Guigon in 1978; the grimly comic plays he staged, all popular hits, include *Les Petits Pas* (*Small Steps*, 1986), *Les Frères Zénith* (*The Zenith Brothers*, 1990) and *Les Pieds dans l'eau* (*Wet Feet*, 1992).

Directors, Directing and Production Styles

Directing in France from the 1930s to the 1980s saw the development of two radically opposed approaches. From Copeau, the Cartel and Jean Vilar – and Jean-Louis Barrault in a more decorative and flamboyant way – came a group of directors who argued for absolute fidelity to the script. The actor was seen as an interpreter whose function was to reveal the text, usually on an empty stage. The performance was a mediation between text and audience intended, as Vilar once put it, to improve the moral and civic quality of society.

From the 1960s, however, came the era of directors – creators themselves and not just interpreters – for whom the script was an occasion to offer up an elaborate physical system of signs with actors in the service of a director's vision more than of a playwright's. From the sobriety of the earlier empty stage came designs which were more and more sophisticated. Among this latter group of directors were Antoine Bourseiller (b. 1930), Lavelli, Mesguich and, more overtly political, Chéreau, Vincent and Lavaudant.

Barrault, a student of Dullin, believed deeply in the director's responsibility to text. An actor by training, Barrault, in the 1930s, came into contact with Étienne Decroux (1898–1991), the great teacher of mime, and Decroux became another major influence on Barrault's conception of acting. Before the war, he produced three productions in Paris which all suggested that a play's emotional centre could be related to the expressive power of the body, the actor's physical presence. In *Autour d'une mère* (*Around a Mother*), a show done in 1935 at the Atelier (an adaptation of Faulkner's novel *As I Lay Dying*), he revealed his enormous talents as a mime. He reintroduced into French acting the long-lost language of the body. He also brought into the Renaud-Barrault Company the young Marcel Marceau (b. 1923) in the role of Harlequin in Jacques Prévert's (1900–77) mime drama, *Baptiste*. Marceau, who had also studied with Decroux and who was very influenced by Chaplin, was well on his way to becoming the world's most famous mime. His early work had a tragic hint to it though he later turned more toward the comic.

A second, crucial contact for Barrault was with the writer Paul Claudel, whose work he staged regularly. Their long association was particularly fertile. It was his *Numance* (after Cervantes) in 1937 that started his friendship with Claudel. Clearly influenced by Artaud, his first major success as a director was *Le Soulier de satin* in 1943. He often referred to himself as the midwife of Claudel's plays, notably of *Partage de midi* (1948), of *L'Echange* (*The Exchange*, 1951), and of *Tête d'or* (*Head of Gold*, 1959).

Barrault was also one of the first of his time to adapt for the stage non-dramatic works. He staged his version of *Le Procès* (*The Trial*) by Kafka in 1947. In 1967, he staged an adaptation of Flaubert's (1821–80) *La Tentation de Saint Antoine* (*The Temptation of Saint Antoine*), in collaboration with Maurice Béjart (b. 1928) and his dance company. This type of work would continue to be done by Barrault through the 1980s and was extremely influential.

While continuing to stage Claudel in the 1950s and 1960s, Barrault turned more and more to the avant-garde, premièring plays by Vauthier (*Le Personnage combattant* in 1956) and Ionesco (*Rhinocéros* in 1960).

Roger Blin, who had worked in Barrault's early productions, was also a student of Dullin's and a friend of Artaud's. He staged Adamov's *La Parodie* in 1952, and premièred Beckett's *Waiting for Godot* in 1953 at the Théâtre de Babylone, a production whose opening became part of the history of the French stage. He went on to do *Endgame* (1957), *Krapp's Last Tape* (1960) and *Happy Days* (1963). Blin devoted himself equally to the work of Genet. He staged *The Blacks* in 1959, and directed *The Screens* in 1966 with the Renaud–Barrault Company. From this association with Genet came the valuable *Lettres á Roger Blin* (*Letters to Roger Blin*), a precious volume which reveals the aesthetic theories of Genet.

When Blin died in 1984, Pierre Chabert (b. 1938) succeeded him as the primary director of Beckett, although Beckett himself staged *Krapp's Last Tape* in 1975. Chabert, however, created with him most of the 'dramaticules' (as Beckett called them) which he created from then to the end of his life. In 1983, he staged *Berceuse*, *Impromptu d'Ohio* and *Catastrophe*. He also adapted one of the first novels of Beckett, *Mercier et Camier* in 1987, in collaboration with Beckett himself and also staged *Compagnie* (*Company*) in 1984, one of Beckett's last narrative works.

With the same concern about style and detail that characterized Barrault and Blin, a number of directors became connected with the new avant-garde writers. Among them were Nicolas Bataille, Marcel Cuvelier (b. 1924) and especially Jean-Marie Serreau, also trained by Dullin and among the first to bring Brecht's works to France. It was Serreau who in 1949 staged Brecht's *The Exception and the Rule*. In 1950, he staged Adamov's *La Grande et la Petite Manoeuvre*, then premièred in 1954 Ionesco's *Amédée* and later *La Soif et la faim* at the Comédie-Française.

Jacques Mauclair (b. 1919) was a student of Jouvet. A friend of Ionesco's, he staged *Victimes du devoir* (*Victims of Duty*), then *Le Roi se meurt* (*Exit the King*) in 1963, and restaged *Les Chaises* in 1967. He was also linked to Adamov, for whom he staged *Le Ping-Pong* in 1955.

Claude Régy (b. 1923), a strongly independent director wary of proscenium stage conventions, committed much of his career to the staging of contemporary dramatists, both French and foreign. Among those whose works he staged were Marguerite Duras, Nathalie Sarraute, Botho Strauss, Harold Pinter and Peter Handke.

By the 1960s, the production of new plays was slowing down. Innovations began to situate themselves in directing. An era of directors and scenographers was beginning. Some of them simply preferred to hear their own voices, refusing entirely the text of authors, a declaration of theatrical emancipation. It was here that adaptations reached their apogee. This was also the era when everyone wanted to 'dust off' the classics, to offer new versions of the great plays of the past, to find a new language and idiom. One could speak then of the *Electra* of Vitez (and not necessarily of the *Electra* of Sophocles). He staged versions of the work in 1966, 1975 and 1987. Directors turned as well to opera, even more fixed in tradition.

The influence of the American Living Theatre was large in France in the 1960s. Julian Beck and Judith Malina, its creators, worked from a series of strong archetypal images. In 1971, *Le Regard du sourd* (*Deafman's Glance*), the first play of Robert Wilson to be presented in France, was done at the Nancy Festival and was a revelation for the French public. The production unfolded as a series of dreamlike images with few words. The same year, France also discovered the productions of the Polish director Tadeusz Kantor, who staged Witkacy's *La Poule d'eau* (*The Water Hen*) at the Nancy Festival. A painter allied to dadaism and growing out of constructivism, Kantor assigned a still newer role to the theatrical director who now became part of both the decor and the production.

Since the 1960s, a number of great directors have also emerged. One cannot ignore the importance of Mnouchkine, Planchon or Maréchal, of whom much has already been said. A few additional words must be said here about Antoine Vitez, a director with a strong background as a translator of plays (especially Greek and Russian) and as an actor. He began his directorial career in 1966 with his first version of Sophocles' *Electra* at the Maison de la Culture in Caen. He staged as many contemporary authors as classics and quickly distinguished himself by his treatment of the latter which were for him like 'trapped battleships' seen only through curtains of a distant era, porters of strangeness for contemporary audiences. But rather than simply updating them, Vitez emphasized in his productions their very strangeness. With his love of language, he returned to the Alexandrine, insisting on its musicality while refusing to use the commonplace under the pretext of being natural. If the theatre had become the art of cutting and montage with the text as living material for directors to form in their own ways, Vitez returned to text in all its splendour. He was the first, for example, since the nineteenth century to stage the complete *Hernani* (1985), whose text was always trimmed. In 1987 at Avignon, he staged the complete version (never before performed) of Claudel's *Le Soulier de satin*, which lasted an entire night.

For Vitez, theatre performed a social function inseparable from its aesthetic function. Establishing himself in 1972 at the Théâtre des Quartiers d'Ivry – a left-wing suburb of Paris – he sought to reconnect theatre to society. He remained there until 1981, when he was named director of the Chaillot. In 1988, he became head of the Comédie-Française. Always a believer in an 'elitist theatre for all' Vitez's influence had been and remained immense in the French theatre of the 1990s.

Antoine Bourseiller, one of the more promising young directors of the 1960s, became head of the Nancy Opera in 1985. He earlier staged important productions of Billetdoux's *Va donc chez Torpe* (*So Go to Torpe's*, 1961); Leroi Jones's (Amiri Baraka) *Metro fantôme* and *Dutchman* (both in 1965); and *Onirocri*, an original musical he wrote for the Avignon Festival in 1973.

Patrice Chéreau, though fifteen years younger than Vitez and Bourseiller, emerged nevertheless as a director at the same time as they did. Interested early on in Marivaux, he staged several of his plays in a strong, Planchonesque style. As staged by Chéreau, one found in them a cruel universe in the sense of de Sade, a universe very distant from traditional Marivaux. This was clear in his 1973 production *La Dispute* (*The Dispute*). Turning on the picture-frame stage, he revealed its walls and exposed its machinery, as did many directors in the 1960s and 1970s who tried to challenge its limits. In demystifying it, however, Chéreau was also celebrating the inherent magic which this stage was capable of generating.

From 1975, he turned to the staging of opera, distinguishing himself for his enormous visions, such as his 1976 production of Wagner's *Ring* cycle. The director of the Théâtre des Amandiers in Nanterre from 1982, he premièred the plays of Bernard-Marie Koltès from 1983 and subsequently became Koltès's regular director.

Paris never played such an international role,

culturally speaking, as it did in the twentieth century. Painters such as Picasso and Dali, sculptors such as Brancusi, and writers such as Joyce, Beckett, Ionesco, Cioran, Adamov and Arrabal settled in the city for all sorts of reasons, some political, some of the writers simply attracted by its vivacity. This was also true for three great directors – Jorge Lavelli, Giorgio Strehler and Peter Brook.

Lavelli was an Argentine of Italian ancestry who settled in Paris in 1960. His career was marked by two passions – the discovery of new writers and the staging of operas. It was Lavelli who premièred in France the works of the Polish dramatist Witold Gombrowicz. In 1963, he staged Gombrowicz's *Le Mariage* (*The Marriage*), and in 1976 a play by the Argentine writer Copi (*L'Homosexuel*). His taste for modern authors blossomed still further when he became director of the Théâtre de la Colline in 1988, where he played contemporary scripts exclusively. Lavelli's career in opera began in 1974 in Angers, with *Idoménée*. It marked the first in a series of major stagings in large theatres where he showed a Baroque imagination.

Giorgio Strehler began working regularly in France in 1983 when he was given the direction of the Théâtre de l'Europe because of his vast experience with the European repertoire.

Peter Brook moved to Paris from England in the 1970s. He had made his début at Stratford in 1946 where he staged both Shakespeare and opera. He started his Centre International de Recherche Théâtrale (International Centre of Theatrical Research) in 1971 and staged *Orghast*, an exploration of language, in Persepolis. Influenced by Artaud and fascinated by African and Indian civilizations, he went to Africa in 1974. From this point on, his company became truly international, mixing people from all backgrounds. In 1974, Brook's company opened at Les Bouffes du Nord, an old proscenium house in north Paris, with a production of *Timon of Athens*. In this old theatre, he tried to revive Elizabethan theatre for a modern audience. Eager to exploit the potentialities of the human voice, he also staged operas there: in 1981 he produced an intensely dramatic version of *Carmen* called *La Tragédie de Carmen* and in 1992 *Improvisations autour de Pelléas*

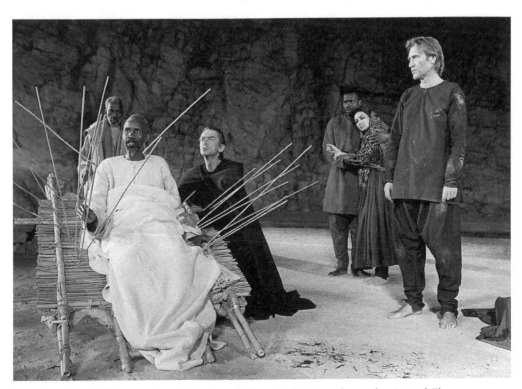

Peter Brook's 1985 International Centre of Theatrical Research production of *The Mahabharata*, designed by Chloë Obolensky.
Photo: Agence de Presse Bernand.

(*Improvisation on Pelleas*), after Maeterlinck. His work is the symbol of all that is modern in the theatre: combinations not yet exploited, signs borrowed from very different universes. *The Mahabharata*, premièred at Avignon in 1985, was Brook at his best. In the same way he mixed the Elizabethan and Italian stage, integrating actors of different cultures and genres such as theatre and opera. Brook, in his widely translated theoretical volume *The Empty Space* (1968), also showed himself to be an intellectually provocative master with the fertile style of Artaud.

Two other directors of note should also be mentioned: Jean-Pierre Vincent, who evolved a neo-Brechtian style of directing which he brought with him to the Comédie-Française when he ran that company from 1983 to 1986; and Georges Lavaudant, a master of theatrical collage and stage image, for instance with Pirandello's *The Mountain Giants* (1981).

Music Theatre

Opera in France is considered today as the preserve of the triumphant nineteenth-century bourgeoisie. This is particularly true of the Opera House in Paris built by Charles Garnier in 1875. It is essentially a conservative art which distances audiences from issues of the day, although in its popular form, operetta, contemporary subject matter is often addressed.

The range of French opera is quite large with the traditional repertoire played regularly but with more and more incursions being made by experiments in form, experiments that move us from the realm of traditional opera to what is often simply theatre with music. Today one can find in France everything from Wagner to Alban Berg, from Stravinsky to John Cage and Bertolt Brecht.

The most modern attempts seem to be trying to bring down completely the barriers between the various forms and sub-genres in an attempt to integrate them. Opera has also attracted major directors for decades. Jean Vilar, between 1964 and 1969, staged a number of operas after he left the Théâtre National Populaire. Among them were *Jerusalem* in Venice and *Don Carlos* in Verona, both by Verdi and both rather conventional.

Jorge Lavelli has staged a whole series of operas ranging from *Medea* in 1967 (an adaptation of Seneca's play by Jean Vauthier with music by Greek composer Iannis Xenakis) to *La Celestina* (with music by Maurice Ohana for the Paris Opera in 1988), from Mozart's *Idomenea* to Gounod's (1818–93) *Faust,* from Campra's *The Carnival of Venice* in 1975 to Debussy's (1862–1918) *Pelléas and Mélisande* in 1977 (the first modern French opera) to Strauss's *Salomé* in 1986. Most of his productions have been designed by Max Bignens.

Patrice Chéreau, working closely with his scenographer Richard Peduzzi (b. 1943), directed an epoch-making *Ring* cycle in Bayreuth between 1976 and 1980 conducted by Pierre Boulez (b. 1925). Chéreau has been quite successful in bringing to opera his personal politics and aesthetics. Earlier he staged Offenbach's *Tales of Hoffmann* at the Paris Opera (1974), Berg's *Lulu* (1979) and Mozart's *Lucio Silla* (1980) at Nanterre-Amandiers and (in 1992) Berg's *Wozzeck* at the Châtelet in Paris. Chéreau has said on several occasions that his major regret in the field is not being able to find singers who can really act or actors who can really sing.

Many directors seemed to have tried their hands at opera to see how far they could go in changing the form. Among them, Yannis Kokkos (b. 1944) who staged Berlioz's (1803–69) *La Damnation de Faust* (*The Damnation of Faust*), a popular French classic, partly as an attempt to liberate theatrical design from its illustrative function; Daniel Mesguich, who staged *The Ring* in Nice and in Paris in 1988 with singers and stagehands talking together near the end; Antoine Vitez (Monteverdi's *Orfeo* in 1981) and Peter Brook (Bizet's *Carmen*), who both explored the music of theatre and the theatricality of music through histrionic challenges to their singer-actors. Others have tried to integrate in the Greek style, the visual, the musical and the spoken word.

From 1969, a new form – known in France as *théâtre musical* – emerged, trying to rediscover the kind of total theatre that all practitioners had been dreaming of for more than a century.

Opera became a place for experiments in sound with the help of contemporary composers, as well as in voice and visual aspects. Unfortunately, it did not attract the public, who still preferred traditional opera and operetta.

In the 1970s, rock music began experimenting with ways to make itself more theatrical and these 'operatic' experiments drew large audiences of young people. Experiments, however, remained either avant-garde or highbrow.

It should be noted here that French operetta never evolved into musical-comedy nor did it ever derive a more modern form or content. One exception was noteworthy but short-lived. Jean Vilar in 1961 staged a production called *Loin de Rueil* (*Far from Rueil*, music by Maurice Jarre, b. 1924) at the TNP's second house which involved music and thus can be called the only real French musical-comedy. The numerous productions of opera and operetta by director Jérôme Savary do not alter the picture: in his productions the dichotomy between opera/theatre and audience remains both social and aesthetic.

Credit must be given to the Paris Autumn Festival for renewal and development in both music theatre and contemporary music; Avignon has also hosted many experiments ranging from works by Claude Prey (b. 1925) to works based on pieces by Samuel Beckett.

Prey in all his work has tried to emphasize the music of theatrical gesture and the theatrical qualities of musical gesture. In *Young Libertad* (done for the Opera Studio at Lyon in 1976), a group of young Americans in the 1930s musically recount their experiences as a social group and build the show on the revolt that made them into a group. Prey uses collages of various musical types. In his *Grisélidis* (1977), director Antoine Vitez plays with the complexity of verse forms organizing the space into three distinct areas – one for the actors (horizontal), one for the singers (vertical), and one for the musicians (front and back). This music theatre is clearly Brechtian in its distancing of the various theatrical elements.

Among others of note who have worked in the field, one should mention Pierre Barrat (b. 1931), who founded the Atelier d'Angers and later the Atelier du Rhin (now part of the Opéra du Rhin); Georges Aperghis (b. 1945), who created the Atelier théâtre et musique in Bagnolet in 1975 and has done some important experiments there; and Michael Lonsdale (b. 1931), a leading actor with a concern for the texture of voice and who plays with music, movement, instruments and voice in a polyphonic way.

Music has also stopped being a mere extra in theatre. It has been used effectively by director Serreau in plays by Kateb Yacine, Max Frisch and Bernard Dadié (b. 1916). From 1982, the Théâtre du Soleil has used music in its Shakespeare cycle as well as in its *Norodom Sihanouk* (1985), building a scenography and a performing space that makes the extraordinary instruments and sounds of Jean-Jacques Lemêtre (b. 1952) full participants in the structure of each production.

Jean Prodromides (b. 1927), who composed marvellous music for a production of Aeschylus' *The Persians* for French television in 1961 and who has since written music for productions at Nantes, for the Opéra du Rhin, and the Nancy Festival, is quite right when he says that the major importance of opera since 1955 is that it has rediscovered more lesser-known older works than it has given new opera works to the contemporary world.

The fact is that alongside the opera in Paris and the Opéra Comique (in the Salle Garnier and the Salle Favart) in the 1930s there were some seventy municipal opera groups and thirty-five casinos staging summer seasons. The linking of the Salles Garnier and Favart was an attempt by the state to create a cultural policy which would widen the audience for opera.

In 1947, a network was established by the state between all the municipal operas but the thirteen cities involved in the experiment felt that the actual subsidy being offered was far too modest. From that point, the state offered grants only to specific companies and the notion of decentralization was badly stalled in the music theatre field.

By 1955, however, a network of provincial opera groups was set up and the state made a significant financial commitment to encourage the production of new works, revivals, and exchanges between the fifteen opera houses whose seasons would henceforth be devoted entirely to opera and ballet. In 1964, the network again tried to focus on municipal operas; after a series of further refinements, this network became in 1985 the Réunion des théâtres lyriques de France (RTLF). Sixteen structures made up the network in 1993.

In 1968, a report by Vilar, Béjart, Boulez and Camille Demangeat (1905–85) had proposed a reorganization of opera in France. Presented to André Malraux, Minister of Culture, it

André Engel's 1992 Opéra Bastille production of Dimitri Shostakovich's *Lady Macbeth of Mtenšk*, designed by Nicky Rieti.
Photo: Moatti/Kleinefenn.

advocated a decentralized network very similar to the current RTLF.

The Opéra Bastille, designed by Carlos Ott (b. 1946), opened its doors on Bastille Day 1989 and began its first season in March 1990. The building, enormously expensive, was the cause of vicious political and artistic controversy in its first seasons. Though it will not necessarily ensure the interest of large audiences in opera, seats are not overly expensive by opera standards. Its repertoire used to lean to the experimental including versions of Mozart's *Magic Flute*, and *Madame Butterfly*, both directed by Robert Wilson.

Dance Theatre

In France, dance has always been linked to opera and theatrical performances generally since the time of Louis XIV (1638–1715) and Molière. The Ballets Russes de Serge Diaghilev (1909–29) was one of the key elements in changing perceptions of dance theatre in the country; another was the ideas of Antonin Artaud, who argued the importance of the body in the theatrical experience.

Ballet, in fact, remained close to opera until 1958, when Serge Lifar (1905–86) was replaced as director of the French National Opera Ballet, a position he had held since 1931. Terming himself a choreo-author, Lifar saw dance as a totally autonomous field.

Maurice Béjart began experimenting in the field in 1955 and his subsequent works opened up new vistas for dance: Stravinsky's *Rite of Spring* in 1959 and Ravel's (1875–1937) *Bolero* were just two of many early Béjart works that changed people's perception about the form. In 1967, Béjart and his composer-colleague Pierre Henry (b. 1927), who worked with concrete and electronic music, premièred the *Messe pour le temps présent* (*Mass for Today*) at Avignon, and later staged with Jean-Louis Barrault *La Tentation de Saint Antoine*, an adaptation of a Flaubert work as an experiment in total theatre.

Every summer from 1966 to 1969, Béjart choreographed another work in Avignon's

Palais des Papes, the showcase location of the Avignon Festival. It was Béjart who, more than anyone else in France, began the concept of dance theatre. Arguing that the twentieth century is the century of dance and that gesture has become more important than the word, Béjart creates ballets in which it is the audience rather than the artist who has the possibility to verbalize.

Influenced by the films of Jean-Luc Godard (b. 1930), Béjart also argues that there is nothing to understand in dance; rather it is simply something to see and hear. His later works resort to a collage of texts actually spoken by actors: *Malraux ou la métamorphose des dieux* (*Malraux or The Metamorphosis of the Gods*, 1986), *Ring um den Ring*, a comment on Wagner for the Paris Opera (1990), *Mort subite* (*Sudden Death*, 1991) for Berlin and *Pyramide* (*The Pyramid*, 1992).

Artaud's theories on the body along with the ideas of Gordon Craig on the *Übermarionette* came together in a network of collaborating fields and piqued Jean-Louis Barrault's interest in mime, a prelude in a sense to much contemporary dance.

It is Étienne Decroux, however, who is really considered as the father of modern mime in France: it was Decroux who taught Barrault and Marcel Marceau. Decroux invented a language of gesture in stage space. Close to Craig's ideas, he provided a technical basis for those concerned with total theatre, for those who want to speak and think with the whole body and not just the voice.

Robert Wilson's *Deafman's Glance*, presented in Europe in 1971, coincides with the beginnings of dance theatre in France. Wilson's use of mime, the frozen gesture effect as well as his use of actors as both puppets and dancers, was a breakthrough for both choreographers and directors.

Marceau is another exploring in this area. A pupil of Charles Dullin and Barrault, Marceau created a stage everyman in his Bip, a creation which at once harkened back to the imitative tradition and went beyond it.

Jacques Lecoq (b. 1921) began his stage-work in mime and later discovered masks. He founded a school of mime in Milan in 1952 (working with Giorgio Strehler's Piccolo Teatro) and made significant contributions to the study of *commedia dell'arte*. He later returned to Paris and established another school. One should also mention here the work of Yves Klein (1928–62, French discoverer of the ideas of John Cage and

Merce Cunningham) and Karine Saporta (b. 1950), who brought the ideas of Jerzy Grotowski into the realm of French dance. Saporta, in charge of the Caen Centre chorégraphique from 1981, was given *carte blanche* by the Avignon Festival in 1988 to investigate the moving frontiers between theatre and dance. She had earlier used texts yelled through a megaphone in *Pleurs en porcelaine* (*Porcelain Tears*) in Avignon in 1984. Her adaptation of Shakespeare's *The Tempest* (*La Princesse de Milan*, 1991) split the characters of Ferdinand and Miranda into several dancers who moved with a kind of pre-Raphaelite style. Perhaps the most important influence in the field since the late 1970s in France has been the German, Pina Bausch.

Among the French choreographers working in these general areas one must also mention Odile Duboc (b. 1941) who relies on a deep knowledge and practice of classical ballet and literature to create pure choreography; Angelin Preljocaj (b. 1947) who explores realms of surrealism; Maguy Marin (b. 1951), Jean-François Duroure (b. 1964), Caroline Marcadé (b. 1952) and Jacques Patarozzi (b. 1947), who work in what can only be called dance theatre; and the organic dance creations of Brigitte Lefèvre (b. 1944), Catherine Diverrès (b. 1959), Bernardo Montet (b. 1957), François Verret (b. 1955) and Daniel Larrieu (b. 1947), who have worked with water, and slowness, and have been influenced in various ways by Japanese *Buto*.

For all of these choreographers, the arts are closely related and labels do not matter. For them, word and intellect are no longer seen as the sole vehicles for meaning. There are also strong links for them between scenography and choreography. Like Peter Brook they are fascinated by the effects achieved by the body in empty space and the tales communicated by dancers. They are also not afraid to use spoken text.

Maguy Marin, a former student of Béjart, is the most consciously theatrical of this group. *May B* (1984) is a homage to Beckett which uses the text as a basis for movement and image. In *Cendrillon* (*Cinderella*, 1987, for the Lyon Opera Ballet) grotesque masked dolls remind us of a fair and puppetry. In *Cortex* (1991) objects from supermarkets are arranged in carts while shop assistants walk to the apron and yell bits of sentences. In 1993 she revisited classical ballet, staging *Coppelia* for the reopening of the Lyon Opera. Her work, like that of Jean-Claude Gallotta (b. 1950), can be seen as cinema-ballet as much as theatre-ballet.

Dominique Bagouet (1953–92), in charge of the Montpellier Choreographic Centre from 1980 until his death from AIDS, created more than thirty-five pieces of dance theatre relying heavily on visual artists and musicians in his fascinating grammar of slanting gesture.

One must also mention here Joelle Bouvier (b. 1959) and Régis Obadia (b. 1958), who start from the actor's awareness of body and lead us to the depths of instinctive and raw emotion; Claude Brumachon (b. 1959) who refuses story, costumes and other traditional theatrical means focusing almost exclusively on gesture; and Régine Chopinot (b. 1952), the *enfant terrible* of French dance theatre, whose 1988 work, *KOK*, was about the theatricality of boxing. Chopinot's work almost totally escapes labelling. In *Noir-Salle* (*House Out*, 1988), Charles Cre-Ange (b. 1954) has Alcestis dancing and speaking lines from Molière's *Le Misanthrope* while three Célimènes dance around him.

Jean-François Duroure was a pupil of Pina Bausch. His *La Maison des plumes vertes* (*House of Green Feathers*, 1988) is a moving solo piece for a Baroque clown while Jean-Claude Gallotta is concerned with the animalism and obscenity of humanity. His *Romeo and Juliet* (1991) is 'dance to cover the noise of useless words'.

François Verret loves to use text repeated via a looped tape, and literary excerpts as counterpoint to simultaneous and repetitive actions. Interested as well in hyper-realism, he has been criticized for his *Où commencer* (*Where to Start*, 1992) for creating a piece which mixed actors and dancers.

Dance in its various forms has steadily increased in audience size since the 1970s. In 1988, there were 4 million spectators for dance performances. Between 1980 and 1992 the number of state-supported companies has increased from ten to thirty. There were almost eighty dance groups operating in the country in 1993.

The creation of the Théâtre Contemporain de la Danse (Contemporary Dance Theatre) in 1984 has allowed dance companies from across the country to find a space for reception and residence, training, information, legal assistance and even public performance while in Paris. All these measures came as part of the decision by the state to establish, along the lines of decentralization, national and regional choreographic centres. In 1993, there were eighteen such centres (most established between 1981 and 1985).

The roots of this movement began with the creations of national ballet companies distinct from the ballet troupes of the ten opera-ballets. The national ballet companies included the Ballet National de Marseille (director Roland Petit (b. 1924), founded in 1972), Ballet du Rhin (1973), Théâtre du Silence, la Rochelle (1973), Ballet de Nancy (1978), and the Théâtre chorégraphique de Rennes (1978). Those centres were in addition to the Paris Opera Ballet (now autonomous) and the ten troupes belonging to the Network of French National Operas – the RTLF (see **Music Theatre**).

The choreographic centres are directed by the most promising French choreographers with a national system of promotions operating. In 1985, a Choreographic Production Centre was opened in Orléans.

In 1990, an important report called *Profession Danseur* (*Profession Dancer*) was released which redefined to a very great extent the status of dancers in France. Since that time, the Society of Playwrights has opened a special section for dance.

Dance has been part of the Avignon Festival since 1966 and now accounts for one-third of its programming. The Paris Autumn Festival also offers support for modern and post-modern dance. Many other festivals now have dance as a regular part of their programming. Since 1987, Châteauvallon has hosted a regular Théâtre National de la danse et l'Image Festival. Since 1970, the Bagnolet Meetings have become a centre for debates and a showcase for new work; since 1988, they have become international in nature. In 1982, a Dance Cinema Archive through French television was created to store and lend films and videos about dance.

Theatre for Young Audiences

Historically, theatre for young audiences was linked to the religious and educational system until the birth of quasi-state school movements (like the Education League of Jean Macé in 1866) and to the development of state schools from the 1880s. From this point relationships were established between schools and theatre for children.

Though the Cartel had a policy on theatre for children and youth, it was Léon Chancerel who started the Théâtre de l'Oncle Sébastien (1935), the first French theatre for children. His early seasons included Gignoux's *Le Pavillon chinois* (*The Chinese Pavilion*, 1935) and *Les Aventures de Ludulu* (*Ludulu's Adventures*, 1937). He produced *Treasure Island* at the Théâtre de la Porte Saint-Martin in 1952, the mecca of boulevard theatre in Paris.

After World War II, Miguel Demuynck (b. 1921) launched Théâtre de la Clairière (1949); other companies like Théâtre Scaramouche, Compagnie des Enfants, Théâtre Bonjour and Compagnie de l'oiseau sur la branche (Bird on a Branch Company) were started. This led to the creation of the Association for Theatre for Children and Youth, presided over first by Chancerel, later by Rose-Marie Moudouès (b. 1922).

The decentralization movement was deeply interested in theatre for children but suffered from a problem of definition (similar to amateur and university theatre). For most, it was a professional theatre made by adults for children from ages 4 to 16 rather than creative drama or role-playing by children for children (more or less supervised by parents or teachers). Awareness came late to France that theatre and education are fields where ideology and the training and integration of children in society can be developed.

From the 1960s onward, with the development of child psychology and psychoanalysis and the rise of new teaching methods, the imagination of children, their world outlook and language became the materials on which the imagination of artists began to work. Maurice Yendt's (b. 1937) Théâtre des Jeunes Années from 1968 on sought not to escape reality in their productions but to understand it. With the rise of television and media culture, theatre for children became a way to fight against subliminal indoctrination by images. The challenge became how to turn theatre for children into a space for freedom against the coercive adult world and into a tool for the discovery of theatre *per se* by children.

One can understand why the Ministry of Education decided to interfere. The libertarian post-1968 wave deepened the gap between an entertainment-oriented theatre for children and an educative and political one which does not forget the child's or teenager's imagination. The French system did not take theatre much into account so the Ministry of Education established very strict rules for the acceptance of plays to be performed in schools.

The 1972 guidelines set up a regional selection committee; the order was amended in 1977 and the choice of plays was transferred to the headmasters in each school. An *Inquiry into the Cultural Practices of the French* (1973) discovered that 67 per cent of the under-16 age group never went to the theatre and that only 16 per cent went more than once in the previous year.

Those in charge of cultural policy in the decentralization structures and the Maisons de la Culture after 1960 realized that theatre could not develop audiences if it had not been part of one's childhood. The Maisons de la Culture therefore (mainly in leftist and communist cities) set up children's units; the Avignon Festival from 1969 to 1975 (except for 1973) also put on plays for children.

There were about ninety children's and youth companies in the Paris area and seventy in the provinces by 1973; only twenty received grants.

In 1973, a National Theatre for Children (TNE) was established under the direction of Antoine Vitez, for whom theatre and puppetry were counterweights to literary texts. It had a free ticket policy but it began to charge when other theatres complained.

The setting up of six National Dramatic Centres for Children and Youth from 1978 on was a further response. These included a company in Nancy which, under the name Théâtre Jeune Public, published a magazine, *Strapontin* (*Flip-up Seat*, circulation 26,000) and focused on teenagers in their programmes.

Another was the Théâtre la Fontaine in Lille which today is called the Grand Bleu. Others include the Théâtre du Gros Caillou (Big Pebble Theatre) in Caen; the Théâtre du Préau (*préau* is a covered outdoor playing area at French schools); and the Théâtre de la Pomme Verte (Green Apple Theatre) founded in 1970 by Catherine Dasté (b. 1939) in Sartrouville. Dasté wrote and directed plays such as *Les Musiques magiques* (*Magic Music*, 1960) with Graeme Allwright, a well-known singer of country, bluegrass and folk songs. She turned Pomme Verte into a model children's theatre company for the 1970s. Françoise Pillet (b. 1944), who took over from Dasté in 1980, has rediscovered the relationship of children with theatrical illusion and knows how to make opera, painting, photography, scripts and books share the stage.

The Compagnie Daniel Bazilier (marionettes)

The 1985 Compagnie Daru–Compagnie Jean Pierre Lescot production of Dante's *Divine Comedy*.
Photo: Brigitte Pougeoise.

became a national company in 1978, settled in Saint-Denis to 1987 and tried to introduce children and teenagers to contemporary theatre. Scripts based on well-known literary texts were often used. Much is made of the aesthetic function of light and scenography, for instance in *L'Exception et la règle* (*The Exception and the Rule*, 1985, adapted from Brecht) and *Barbe Bleu* (*Blue Beard*, 1989). The company is now in Montreuil.

The Théâtre des Jeunes Années, founded by Maurice Yendt, an amateur group from 1960 to 1968, became permanent and professional in 1968 in Lyon. In 1980 it opened its own theatre. Yendt writes and directs only for young audiences and published most of his plays in *Cahiers du soleil debout* (*Standing Sun Notebooks*). Their repertoire shows what a true theatre for young audiences can do: *La Machine à théâtre* (*The Theatre Machine*, 1970), *Le Roi-clown* (*The Clown King*, 1971), *Le Rossignol et l'oiseau mécanique* (*The Nightingale and the Clockwork Bird*, 1972) and *Mathias et la tempête* (*Mathias and the Tempest*, 1973) all caused a stir in Lyon and broke new ground in how to adapt the moral of a tale to the present. *Histoire aux cheveux rouges* (*The Story of Red*

Hair, 1973) dealt with everyday racial prejudice; *Kikerikiste* (1975) dealt with our technological society; *La Poupée de chiffon* (*The Rag Doll*, 1977) was a very Brechtian play on property and social justice. Yendt founded the biennial International Meetings for Theatre for Children and Young People in 1977. It remains the only real children's theatre festival in France today.

The setting up of the six National Dramatic Centres for Children has enabled theatre for young audiences to make giant strides in terms of increased state support, numbers of performances and box-office income. In 1982, for example, there were 1,250 performances and 219,000 tickets sold.

As well, non-specialized companies also do theatre for the young. In 1979, 62 per cent of companies had given 15,000 performances for children, 41 per cent of which were in schools. These included the Patrice Bigel/La Rumeur company (founded in 1977) and the Théâtre Écarlate. The Théâtre en Miettes (Breadcrumb Theatre) staged *Chanson de Roland* (*Song of Roland*) in 1980; by 1987 the play had been performed more than 500 times. Both it and the Théâtre des Chimères are based in the Aquitaine region and both managed to survive thanks mainly to theatre for young audiences.

In 1987, there were 150 such companies in the Paris area and 160 more in the provinces. Such groups also perform in the fringe festival at Avignon. Some specialize in clowning (Clown Compagnie, Compagnie Embarquez and Compagnie de l'Araignée) and circus performance while others are involved in music theatre (la Carrerarie, Lyon).

The latest trend is storytelling, not in the manner of the Théâtre des enfants of Roland Pilain (b. 1907), who exploited children's literature, but as a multicultural exercise, often very critical of society even when it is an adaptation of well-known fairytales, such as the Grimms' *Hansel and Gretel*. The idea that there are clearly identified age groups from 4 to 16 years is on the wane just as the notion that theatre for adults and for young audiences are two different genres.

The Théâtre de la Clairière (Theatre in the Clearing, founded by Miguel Demuynck in 1949), remains the model for a theatre for children which starts from creative drama and role-playing; Demuynck writes plays that bring out social machinery for children to use and for their own imaginations to understand. The feeling is that theatre should mainly be used as a critical tool to understand reality – *Le Pêcheur d'images* (*Fisherman of Images*, 1969), *Chez moi, dans mon quartier* (*At Home in My Neighbourhood*, 1970) and *Les Impossibles* (*The Impossibles*, 1981).

Jean (b. 1927) and Colette (b. 1931) Roche have been working since 1971 in the Champagne-Ardennes region and mix the poetry of childhood and the living presence of theatre. There is the Naïf Théâtre of Richard Demarcy (b. 1942), whose *Grotte d'Ali* (*Ali's Cave*, 1973) revealed a vivid theatrical imagination.

One should also mention the inventive Théâtre du Galion in Nantes; the Compagnie de l'Olifant; the Compagnie du Trèfle in Annecy; the Compagnie du Pélican; the Compagnie Lucien Morisse (b. 1932); which presents a theatre of the imagination; the Compagnie de l'Echelle à Pau, now defunct, which used vegetable puppets; and Théâtre de Cuisine, a kind of micro-theatre verging on the Italian style of object theatre. More recently, companies of note have been the Théâtre des Opérations in Evreux, which has managed to help youngsters enter the closed world of theatrical tragedy; Le Point du Jour (Peep of the Day), which has presented highly painterly and theatrical shows; the Lichen Compagnie; and the Théâtre de Cavale, which since 1982 has been mixing the arts of theatre and photography so that the performance of the actors and the images meet and counteract.

Though themes in theatre for young audiences vary, it must be said that in France the educational aspect of the work still prevails over the artistic. The shows, though hoping to make children and young people discover the magic of theatre, still feel that they must prepare them for various aspects of daily living.

Puppet Theatre

Considered in France for generations as an art for children, puppetry today is shedding its child-oriented image. It is, in fact, becoming an avant-garde art linked to major advances in contemporary theatre.

Guignol – its most popular form – was invented by Laurent Mourguet (1769–1844) in Lyon. Guignol commented on political life in a very satirical way. From 1849 it was gagged by censorship. Starting about 1860, M. Onofrio collated and codified Guignol scripts turning this famous puppet into a parlour pastime for well-educated children.

Everybody knows Guignol but it has not much to do any more with the grotesque and satirical puppet tradition of the funfair booths. Paul Claudel in *L'Ours et la lune* (*The Bear and the Moon*, 1917) showed interest in puppetry while Alfred Jarry and his Théâtre des pantins burlesqued puppets in creating *Ubu Roi*. Later, the surrealists, such as Pierre-Albert Birot (1876–1967), and the Laboratoire Art-Action (Art and Action Lab, 1919–33) of Louise Lara (1876–1952) and Édouard Autant (1903–75) tried to turn puppetry into an art of fantasy.

The same movement that made children's theatre a technique in the service of pedagogy also restricted puppets to a school skill in which the lifelike imitation of real beings was paramount. Of course the theories of Craig on the

Übermarionette, the ideas of Artaud, the work of Barrault on mime, the theatrical practices of Tadeusz Kantor, the writings and the practice of Gaston Baty (he created Théâtre Billembois/ Wooden Ball in 1932 with its hero, J.F. Billembois), and reflections on theatrical space as an empty space on which one could build another kind of artistic reality, have all led the art of puppetry today to become a poetic art form which can both manipulate and subvert reality and meaning.

In the 1950s, the pioneering work of Yves Joly (b. 1908) and Georges Lafaye (1915–88) set the modern perspectives for French puppetry, which were adopted by other artists in the 1970s.

With the creation of the National Marionette Centre (CNM) in Paris in 1970 funded by the Ministry of Culture, puppet and marionette artists have been able to meet. In 1992, the CNM had a membership of more than seventy.

Many festivals, such as the international one organized by Jacques Felix (b, 1923) with his Petites Comédiens de Chiffon (Little Rag Actors) since 1961 (with an audience of 120,000 in 1989) and the Cergy Biennial (1977, 1979), Marionette Week in Paris (since 1981), the Val de Marne Biennial (founded in 1987; sixteen companies and nineteen shows in 1991), are helping the rise of the art; so has the creation in 1980 of the International Institute for Marionettes by Jacques Felix in Charleville-Mézières. From 1985 the institute has been run by Margareta Niculescu, the well known theatre director from Romania. In 1987, she opened the Higher National School of Puppetry. The school accepts fifteen pupils between the ages of 18 and 26 each year. Studies are freee and last three years, In 1988, Niculescu began publication of a magazine, *Puck*, which aims at reflecting on, being a meeting point for, and a place of confrontation between, puppetry and other arts in order to understand contemporary theatre in new ways.

There are about 250 marionette companies (many of them single person companies), 40 per cent in the Paris area, but there is no permanent puppet house in France. In 1989, thirteen companies received direct grants from the Directorate of Theatre and the Performing Arts.

Alain Recoing (b. 1924) and his Théâtre aux Mains Nues (Theatre of Naked Hands) worked with Gaston Baty; since 1958, he has devised mixed shows with all types of puppets, and has managed to build bridges between all the arts. His productions – *La Ballade de Mr Punch* (*Mr Punch's Ballad*, 1976) with Antoine Vitez for Théâtre de Chaillot, *Polichinelle* (*Punch*, 1985), *Gilgamesh* (1988), *Le Nain* (*The Dwarf*, 1990, for the Théâtre National de Strasbourg), and *La Poudre d'intelligence* (*The Powder of Intelligence*) by Yacine (on tour, 1992) – show an artist aiming at both adult and young audiences.

One should also mention here the work (from 1956) of Lucien Morisse, who puts texts into images telling stories – *Le Petit Prince* (*The Little Prince*, 1969), *Les Quatre saisons* (*The Four Seasons*, 1980) with music by Vivaldi, and *Bulle ou la voix de l'océan* (*Bubble or the Ocean's Voice*, 1988). Claude (b. 1929) and Colette (b. 1930) Monestier (Théâtre des Tournemains, 1958, then Théâtre sur le Fil, 1970) have been inventing forms from gestures, and insist on the relationship between the manipulator, the puppet and the public. The 'making' process is their theme – *Légendé pour un trou* (*Legend for a Hole*, 1971), *La Grosse Tête* (*The Large Head*, 1990). The Marionnettes Géantes de Metz of Raymond Poirson (b. 1929) since 1954 and his son Jean (b. 1959) since 1989 have given unforgettable shows including *Don Quichotte* (*Don Quixote*, 1974), *Le Maléfice de la Phalène* (*The Spell of the Moth*, 1975) adapted from García Lorca, *Oratorio pour une vie* (*Oratorio for a Life*, 1982) and *Passion* (1988).

Massimo Schuster (b. 1950), who came from the Bread and Puppet Theatre, created l'Arc en Terre in 1981. He settled in Marseille and uses extraordinary shapes in his work – *Ubu Roi* (1984), *Le Cid* (1986), *Le Bleu, blanc, rouge, et le noir* (*The Blue, White, Red and Black*, 1989), the last an opera for puppets with a libretto by Anthony Burgess.

The Compagnie Bazilier from Montreuil (founded in 1988) works both in children's and puppet theatre while the Compagnie Daru (1973) carries out contemporary analyses of myths and legends mixing forms and modes of expression including shadow theatre, miniature paintings from the Middle Ages and puppets.

The Jean Pierre Lescot company (formerly the Phosphènes, founded in 1968) plays upon popular tradition and everyday imagery using puppets of all kinds as well as shadow theatre. Georges Sorel and the Château de Fables started in 1980. They play with objects, particularly books.

Amoros et Augustin have been a shadow theatre since 1976 and did beautiful work with W.W. Liking, a Cameroonian woman who

Massimo Schuster's 1984 l'Arc en Terre production of *Ubu Roi*.
Photo: Brigitte Pougeoise.

settled in the Ivory Coast. They had success with *Sunjata, l'épopée mandingue* (*Sunjata, the Mandingo Epic*). The Théâtre de l'Ombrelle has been, since 1977, mixing shadow puppets and actors on a micro or macro scale in which sound, particularly the disembodied voices of nursery rhymes, are very important.

The Compagnie Dougnac (from 1953) has always insisted, first for adults and more and more for younger audiences, on the presence of the manipulator to underline the theatrical illusion. It also uses mime, dance and music. Since 1964, the Compagnie Houdart-Heuclin has been working with voice and music using important literary texts – *Phaedra* (1987, adapted from Racine), *Le Tourment de Dieu* (*God's Torment*, 1990) a poem by Alain Bosquet (b. 1919), and *Descartes, veille-je ou si je dors* (*Descartes, Am I Awake or Asleep?*, 1990). Hubert Japelle (b. 1938) and Théâtre de l'usine (Factory Theatre) since 1978 in Cergy have been using a verbal and visual idiom which cannot be reduced to speech. The puppets become instruments of direct collective communication which is both socially legitimate and artistically necessary – *Macbeth* (1975), *La*

Cité invisible (*The Phantom City*, 1985, adapted from Kafka), and *Les Nuits blanches* (*White Nights*, adapted from Dostoevsky).

Jeanne Vitez's Chemin creux since 1986 has been using masked actors whose gloves are marionettes: the hand is the life of the character and the actors are at the disposal of their hands. After each show the children take over the set and space. Emphasis is laid on the making of the puppets, which can be as modest as two pieces of cloth knotted together.

Finally, one must mention Philippe Genty (b. 1938), who has imposed puppetry as a major, multidisciplinary art on the general public. A graphic designer by trade, Genty is fascinated by the relationship between matter and life. He has used all the images of the unconscious. Going beyond fashion, his work can be surrealist, hyper-realist or post-modern. His are creations of inner landscapes which might shock were it not for the incomparable and often comic mastery of the manipulation, the use of music, the choice of materials and his stunning organization of space. Often mixing actors and puppets, his major productions have included *Rond comme un cube* (*Round Like a Cube*,

1982), *Sigmund's Follies* (1983), *Désirs Parades* (*The Parade of Desires*, which has had more than 400 performances since 1986) and *Dérives* (*Drifts*, 1989).

Design

The function and art of stage design in France has changed significantly since World War II. From an art of painting and decoration, design has become the much more all-inclusive art of scenography with its implications for stage space.

Prior to the war, designers, like Christian Bérard (1902–49), who often worked for Louis Jouvet, saw the set as a tool for the interpretation of text, an element which would elegantly clothe the dramatist's world. Almost always conceived in the Italian style, the proscenium stage (even when bare, as Copeau urged) was part of an overall picture and painters were almost always involved. Georges Douking (1902–87) worked with Gaston Baty from 1928 to 1937, later designed in Aix but made his career designing for the private theatres and for the opera in Paris.

André Boll (1896–1983), another painterly designer of note, had been influenced by the designs of Léon Bakst for the Ballets Russes and had also worked for Baty, Dullin and Jouvet. Suzanne Lalique (1899–1988), head of the scenery workshops, best exemplifies the Comédie-Française style, while Félix Labisse designed Barrault's production of *Partage de midi* (1948) and Léonor Fini (1907–84) designed stylish and sumptuous classical productions such as *Bérénice* in 1955.

Georges Wakhévitch (1907–84) did more than 200 designs for operas, 300 for plays and another 160 for films, a master without equal in France and a painter who stood for poetic realism and the beauty of flamboyant neo-romanticism. He designed for the Comédie-Française and for Barrault as well as for the private theatre.

One of the last great figures working in this style was Yves Bonnat (b. 1912) with more than 250 productions to his credit in theatre, opera and film. Influenced by the Ballets Russes and dance, Bonnat tended to design on a large scale. He also had mastery over outdoor work and used lighting effectively to make the set part of the overall spectacle. A man of the classics, Bonnat became a moderator in the evolution of design through his later work as a counsellor for the Ministry of Culture.

The work of Léon Gischia (1903–91) in the 1950s marked a turning point in design. Working with Vilar, Gischia saw the set not as decoration but as an aid to meaning for the production. This became clear in his productions of *Murder in the Cathedral* (1945) and Goldoni's *Les Rustres* for the Théâtre National Populaire in 1961. A painter, Mario Prassinos, also worked with Vilar seeking to find the universal ideas in each text in spaces that had been stripped down to bare boards and black curtains. The set, in productions such as *Macbeth* (TNP, 1961), was for him the creation of a mental landscape.

Among those designers working with the new small theatres in Paris, Jacques Noël (b. 1924) stands out for his work on such productions as Ionesco's *Les Chaises* (1952), on Brecht (*The Exception and the Rule*, 1950) and Adamov's *Le Ping-Pong* (1955). Noël designed Roger Blin's production of Beckett's *Fin de partie* (*Endgame*) in 1957. In each of these instances, he was able to totally transform the stage and help the director discover new elements in the work.

Jean-Denis Malclès (b. 1912) worked regularly with Jean Anouilh and was equally at home in the private theatres and at the Comédie-Française. Always respecting the given space, he created a series of stylized settings using costumes as an extension of the set itself.

One designer who worked both in and outside Paris was André Acquart (b. 1922). In Paris his severe, free-standing abstract structures, close to sculpture, could be seen in Genet's *Les Nègres* (1959) and *Les Paravents* (1966), Planchon's production of *Troilus and Cressida* (1964) and Max Frisch's *Tryptich* (1983).

The designer who most consistently joined painting and scenography was Gilles Aillaud (b. 1928), who worked regularly after 1972 with Klaus Grüber. For him, the set became part of the universal theatrical space where even props could enlighten deeper meanings (*Hamlet-Machine*, 1979).

After studying the problems of both theatrical architecture and settings, René Allio (b. 1924), cognizant of Brecht's design ideas, looked once again at painting as an element of narrative discourse. He worked with Roger Planchon for more than a decade from 1955 and argued that the depth of a theatre (more than its height or length) could be most effectively used to create dramatic designs. Between 1960 and 1972 he designed more than thirty productions for theatres outside Paris; in the 1970s he began designing for film.

A designer influenced by the sophistication of stage lighting is Alain Batifoulier (b. 1943). His commitment to freedom of movement on the stage was clear in his light designs for Molière's *Le Malade imaginaire* (*Imaginary Invalid*, 1978) in Marseille for Maréchal and his *Les Trois Mousquetaires* (*Three Musketeers*, 1983) which eventually was taken on world tour. Its setting – varying levels and panels – was both simple and effective. He later worked with director Daniel Mesguich.

Allio and Aillaud contributed significantly to the change-over from design to scenography but they were not alone. Among others who were moving in this same direction were Guy-Claude François (b. 1940), Richard Peduzzi and Yannis Kokkos. François worked regularly with Ariane Mnouchkine at the Théâtre du Soleil (*L'Age d'or*, 1975; *Les Atrides*, 1986) while Peduzzi has worked most closely with Patrice Chéreau. Peduzzi demands an architecture which is either exaggeratedly large or small and which is always left incomplete. It is enigmatic. His set for *Hamlet* in 1988 was a slanting parquet, at once a setting sun and a Renaissance façade on which actors walked, never really making exits or entrances. Kokkos worked with various directors and emerged as part of Antoine Vitez's creative team first in Ivry, a Paris suburb, and then at the Théâtre de Chaillot in Paris. His was an enchanted realism in which lighting augmented the space between the actor and his shadow. More concerned with the sensual effects of costume than historical accuracy, he was fascinated by film and loved to have actors isolated in light.

Richard Peduzzi's design for Patrice Chéreau's 1981 TNP Villeurbanne production of Ibsen's *Peer Gynt*.
Photo: Agence de Presse Bernand.

Jean-Pierre Vergier (b. 1944) owes much to the art of photography in his work which is at once romantic and expressionistic. Working very closely with Georges Lavaudant, he is probably France's best representative of what has come to be called Image Theatre.

Within the new scenography, lighting has come to play a more important role. Now used as an abstract and pictorial medium, light is used by many French designers to create images that are neither illusionary nor decorative. Among the key designers in this area, one should mention Pierre Saveron (1908–75), who worked with Vilar in Avignon, and André Diot (b. 1935), who moved from television to theatre and worked with Chéreau on productions featuring 'incomplete light' and light *contre-jour*.

Alain Poisson did all the lighting for Jérôme Savary's Grand Magic Circus, while Patrice Trottier (b. 1947), working at the same time as Diot, turned away from aesthetic lighting to the Brechtian style of full non-expressive light. He also worked regularly with Mesguich and Vitez.

Jacques Polieri (b. 1928) has proposed replacing the setting with a series of constructed images made by strobe lights and infography. He has called for a ring-shaped theatre which would revolve during performances and which could also be used for video transmissions. In 1971, he published a visionary book on these ideas, *Scénographie/semiographie* (*Scenography/Semiography*).

Theatre Space and Architecture

In 1903, Romain Rolland proposed a new type of theatre which Firmin Gémier realized in his Théâtre National Ambulant in 1920. It reminds one of Artaud's proposal for portable sheds in the late 1920s.

Despite these ideas, the Italian stage with its proscenium arch still dominated French theatrical thinking even after World War II. Most of the sixty Paris theatres were proscenium arch stages of which the Palais de Chaillot (built in 1937) was the most recent. In fact, no new theatres would be built in all of France until 1957 when the 700-seat Comédie de Strasbourg (by Pierre Sonrel, 1903–84) was completed.

With the Ministry of Cultural Affairs' decision to establish a series of Maisons de la Culture across the country, new thinking began on the nature of theatrical space and theatrical architecture.

Jean Dasté gathered a group of experts together in Saint-Étienne in 1957 to work out plans for a series of theatres which could seat 1,200. The result was a semicircular theatrical design with virtually no visual obstructions for the audience. The stage was, in Greek amphitheatre style, lower than the house.

Most of the Maisons de la Culture which were subsequently built followed this model but contained only between 800 and 900 seats and, where funds permitted, a second hall which was transformable. The buildings were also ideally to contain space for exhibitions and even cinemas. Twenty such Maisons de la Culture

were planned between 1964 and 1970. Twelve would ultimately be built between 1965 and 1987. Most used enormous amounts of concrete, were merely functional and quite severe.

Though their brutal architecture has been softened in the 1980s, these amphitheatre-type stages marked the end, more or less, of the proscenium stage as an assumed theatrical space in France. Architects such as Pierre Sonrel, René Allio and Bernard Guillaumot (b. 1926) have evolved other styles in their theatre designs. Guillaumot worked on the Théâtre des Amandiers at Nanterre, the Théâtre de Villeurbanne, the Entrepôt Lainé at Bordeaux and the Théâtre National de Marseille-la-Criée. He also restored the Théâtre Roger Salengro (an old municipal theatre) at Lille in 1989.

The first theatre to be actually constructed within Paris since 1937 was the Théâtre de la Ville (formerly Théâtre Sarah Bernhardt) in 1968. The space, designed by Jean Perrotet (b. 1925), an associate of V. Febre (b. 1927), is a rectangular auditorium sloping towards a low stage.

From the 1970s, many non-traditional spaces have been renovated and turned into active theatre spaces. Among them, the Cartoucherie (Armoury) of Vincennes on the east side of Paris (used by the Théâtre du Soleil) and the Théâtre des Bouffes du Nord in the north end of Paris used by Peter Brook since 1974.

In 1982, an ambitious plan for the renovation

The Montpellier Opera house.

and construction of new playhouses was put into place by the Ministry of Culture in close collaboration with various municipalities, départements and régions. New buildings went up in Montpellier (a 2,000-seat opera house), Sarlat, Bergerac, Melun-Sénart, Nice, Saint-Denis and Marne-la-Vallée. The last is a 900-seat theatre (with a 200-seat studio) by Jean Nouvel (b. 1945) located close to EuroDisney. An old fishmarket in La Rochelle and an old sugar warehouse in Bordeaux were also converted into theatres.

Other important renovations have taken place in Pau, Suresnes (the Théâtre Jean Vilar), at the Arsenal in Metz, at the Opera in Compiègne, the Grand Théâtre in Bordeaux, the Opera in Lyon (done by the architect Jean Nouvel), and at the Vieux Colombier in Paris, the original house of Jacques Copeau, which became the second stage for the Comédie-Française in 1993.

Training

The Conservatoire National d'Art Dramatique dates back to 1786 when it was called the École Royale de Déclamation. It became the Conservatoire d'Art Dramatique in 1808 and in 1812, a special class was added reserved only for actors of the Comédie-Française.

In 1946, the Conservatoire was reorganized under the direction of Pierre Abram (who remained as director until 1955). The Conservatoire was again reorganized in 1974, when Jacques Rosner took over its direction. From 1983, Jean-Pierre Miquel (b. 1937) has been its director.

The 1974 restructuring ended graduation examinations and mandatory courses, and opened the school to less traditional training methods. A variety of approaches are now studied and graduating productions are regularly seen at the Avignon Festival.

Entrance to the Conservatoire is extremely difficult with more than 1,200 candidates for thirty places. As well, those seeking entrance must have studied for a year in a regional or municipal conservatory or in a private theatre school. Students are accepted between the ages of 18 and 24. There are no fees. The other major national school is the École du Théâtre National de Strasbourg. The École de la rue Blanche is a high school, its students study for two years either in technical theatre or acting. Each year fifty actors and 110 technical people are accepted.

Since 1976, twenty-one regional conservatories have also existed with two- to three-year theatre training programmes. Such schools have existed since 1976 in Lille, and since 1981 in Bordeaux. There are also seventeen municipal conservatories and about sixty municipal theatre schools offering training for a fee.

Some schools of architecture also offer programmes in theatre architecture.

In the late 1970s, many of the National Dramatic Centres began their own schools. Among them are the École de Chaillot created by Antoine Vitez in 1982 and later taken over by Jérôme Savary; and the École de Nanterre, created in 1982 by Patrice Chéreau and training actors for stage and film in a two-year programme.

There are also many private schools, some well known such as the Cours Simon (founded in 1925), the École d'art dramatique Périmony (founded 1961), the École Charles Dullin (founded 1921), Le Cours Florent (founded 1967), the Atelier Voutsinas (1960), the École Balachova (1967) and the École Lecoq (founded by Jacques Lecoq in 1956). There are well over a hundred such schools in the Paris area and another sixty in the provinces.

Professional theatre training is generally not provided on the university level though there have been some attempts to change that. There are, however, some excellent university programmes in the study of theatre theory, history and criticism.

Criticism, Scholarship and Publishing

The many upheavals in French theatre since 1945 have much to do with the evolution of theatre criticism during this period. Until the late 1940s, criticism was predominantly literary and textual. The development in France of Russian formalism, semiotics and structuralism (Propp's *Morphology of the Tale*, 1929, translated into French in 1965), the structuralist approaches of Claude Lévi-Strauss (b. 1908; *Structural Anthropology*, 1958) and the development of philosophical existentialism (Sartre's *Being and Nothingness*, 1943) are at the roots of more modern French dramatic and theatrical criticism.

With the rise of the Cartel in the 1930s, the theories of Henri Gouhier (1898–1988) on *The Essence of Theatre* (1943) and on *L'Oeuvre théâtrale (The Theatrical Work*, 1958) and Jacques Scherer (b. 1912) and Étienne Souriau (1892–1979) helped to redefine dramatic and theatrical activity, particularly in terms of how theatrical meaning is communicated. Scherer, who created the Theatrical Studies Institute at the Sorbonne in 1950, published *La Dramaturgie classique en France* that same year, a work that examined the problems of internal

and external dramatic structure (ranging from character and action to conditions of performance). His work established a necessary link between them.

The study of external structures led to the creation by Denis Bablet (1930–92) of a Performing Arts Unit at the National centre for Scientific Research (CNRS). From 1970, the centre published a series called the *Voies de la création théâtrale (Ways of Theatrical Creation)* which gave stage design and performance a structural, ideological and aesthetic importance they had never previously enjoyed.

The work of Bablet on the history of stage design as a source of meaning is itself the offspring of seminal works, such as Pierre Sonrel's *Traité de scénographie (Treatise on Scenography*, 1943) and Léon Moussinac's (1890–1964) *Traité de la mise en scène (Treatise on Staging*, 1948). Odette Aslan and Georges Banu (b. 1943) took over from Bablet at his death.

Starting from a structuralist-aesthetic approach, Étienne Souriau's *Les Deux cent mille situations dramatiques (The Two Hundred Thousand Dramatic Situations*, 1950) studied the dynamics of theatrical function and the way they interacted in a text to produce the dramatic situations that space and design helped to externalize.

It was probably Roland Barthes, one of the original editors of the journal *Théâtre Populaire* (published from 1953 to 1964) who did more than anyone else to identify theatre as an ideological activity which produced meanings and who criticized mere reproductions of reality on the stage. Representation was not to be defined as imitation. Theatre was to be seen as a complex system of signs and meanings intended for an audience.

Influenced by Brecht, Barthes wrote extensively about the theatre in his journal; although he did not write a book on theatre as such, he did write in 1975 in *Barthes By Barthes* that 'performance is a universal genre through which the world is seen; theatre does not signify, it signals'. His *Sur Racine (On Racine*, 1963) started a new battle between the ancients and the moderns, adding a socio-psychoanalytic dimension to a predominantly structural and semiotic approach.

Later on, Anne Ubersfeld (b. 1925) on the socio-semiotic side in *Lire le théâtre (Reading Theatre*, 1977) and in *L'École du spectateur (School for Theatregoers*, 1981) develops Barthes's method further as well as the methods of Bernard Dort. Dort, the best structural and ideological critic in France of Brecht's plays and theories, reconciles the literary and theatrical approaches in his study, *La Représentation émancipée (The Performance Freed*, 1988).

Another important semiotician of theatre is Patrice Pavis (b. 1947), who managed on the theoretical side to bring together all the contemporary definitions of the major active, critical and semiotic concepts used in drama and theatre in his *Dictionnaire du théâtre* (1980).

The sociological approach to theatre has been examined by Jean Duvignaud (b. 1923), who tried to bring together the relationships between dramatic structure and acting practice on the one hand and social structures and behaviour on the other. His *Sociologie du théâtre: essai sur les ombres collectives (Sociology of the Theatre: An Essay on Collective Shadows*, 1964) examines 500 years of mainly European drama.

Anne-Marie Gourdon (b. 1938) has examined the sociology of the audience in her 1982 study, *Théâtre, public, perception*. This rich modern critical environment has also produced several valuable studies on the history of French theatre (particularly by Jacqueline de Jomaron, b. 1921) and even on the avant-garde (by Michel Corvin, b. 1930). It should be noted as well that a number of important dramatists, directors and actors have published sometimes fundamental books on their art, among them Ionesco, Vinaver, Barrault, Brook, Vitez and Mesguich.

Although this strong critical activity has not necessarily resulted in a better kind of theatrical reviewing in the newspapers, the old figure of the drama critic who could make or break any play he chose to is fast dying. Critics like Jean-Jacques Gautier (1908–86) in *Le Figaro* and Pierre Marcabru in *France-Soir* are no longer so feared by the theatre world; critics Colette Godard (b. 1926) and Michel Cournot (b. 1922) both in *Le Monde* and Guy Dumur (1922–91; *Le Nouvel Observateur*) and Jean-Pierre Thibaudat (b. 1946; *Libération*) continue to influence audiences, often using semiotic critical vocabulary without pedantry.

Radio (as compared to the 1950s) and television seem to play a lesser role in audience awareness even though Pierre Laville's weekly broadcast from 1984 to 1988 on the public television channel A2 helped viewers to discover most of the major theatrical figures.

Book publishing in the field has not been as significant as it could have been since the late 1970s but efforts have been made by the Ministry of Culture since about 1985 to improve the situation and publishers have begun to publish plays for sale in connection with major openings.

Much material has been preserved by various libraries. The performing arts department of the Bibliothèque Nationale (at the Bibliothèque de l'Arsenal in Paris and the Maison Jean Vilar in Avignon) and the libraries of the Comédie-Française and the Opéra Garnier in Paris, are major theatre resources. Until the creation in 1994 of a Centre National du Théâtre in Avignon, the only national theatre museum was the International Museum of the Marionette in Lyon, mainly focusing on guignol.

The oldest theatre journal in France is the *Revue d'Histoire du Théâtre* founded in 1949 by Auguste Rondel (1858–1934) and sponsored by the Société d'Histoire du Théâtre (itself founded in 1932). Every fourth issue of this quarterly journal includes a world theatre bibliography prepared by the Society.

In 1953, Roland Barthes, Guy Dumur, Robert Voisin, Bernard Dort and Jean Duvignaud founded *Théâtre Populaire*. There were fifty-four issues published until 1964. The journal sought to bring what they considered to be a mass-medium back to the people who had lost it to a rather conservative bourgeoisie. Each issue of the journal contained a new play and most defended the decentralization movement. The journal was accused of being Marxist, dogmatic, anti-Comédie-Française and pro-Brecht. Its issues nevertheless remain a tool of inestimable worth for researchers.

La Revue Théâtrale was started by Paul Arnold in 1945 and existed until 1959. It tried the same line as *Théâtre Populaire* but had a much more aesthetic outlook.

In 1970, *Travail Théâtral* began publication (thirty-three issues from 1970 to 1979). Published in Switzerland by French critics and scholars Denis Bablet (1930–92), Émile Copfermann (b. 1934), Françoise Kourilsky (b. 1933) and Bernard Dort, it tried to take up the torch of *Théâtre Populaire*. Also Marxist and Brechtian, it offered a panorama of the trends that animated the contradictory ways of theatre both before and after 1968.

Théâtre/Public, a venture of Bernard Sobel's Ensemble Théâtral of Gennevilliers, has been mainly funded by that Dramatic Centre; since 1974 (115 isssues as of 1994) it has carried interviews, thematic material and essays about the relationship between theatre companies and their audiences, education and culture.

In 1966, the first issue of *ATAC-Informations* appeared (the publication ceased operation in 1980). Published by the Association Technique pour l'Action Culturelle, which brought together all the organizations of decentralization, it included the programmes of most cultural organizations while accentuating new productions and tours. It also contained good material on theatres for young audiences and theatrical structure generally.

Acteurs published a hundred issues between 1982 and 1992, and is an accurate reflection of theatrical activity both in Paris and across the country during that period. Intended for audiences, its editor, Pierre Laville, wrote extensively on theatre life in all its forms. The magazine also published a play in each issue with an accompanying file on the author and the company staging it.

Other publications of note during this period included *L'Art du Théâtre* (connected to the Théâtre National de Chaillot, it published ten issues from 1985 to 1988 under the editorship of Georges Banu); *Les Cahiers de la Comédie-Française*, begun in 1991, is a quarterly under the editorial direction of Jean-Loup Rivière (b. 1946); *Théâtre en Europe* appeared from 1984 to 1988 (nineteen issues) and was connected to the Théâtre de l'Europe of Giorgio Strehler. The intention of the last-named was to engage European theatre people in a dialogue about theatre art.

From 1951 to 1968, the International Theatre Institute published *Théâtre dans le Monde/World Theatre*. A French/English bilingual publication, its issues served as a link between theatres and troupes, reinforcing as well the work of the ITI's Theatre of Nations Festival.

One current French journal is basically devoted to the publication of plays – *L'Avant Scène: Théâtre*, which has appeared twice monthly since 1949. In 1993 it was up to issue number 934. It is the distant descendant of *La Petite Illustration* and *France Illustration*, well known to French theatre lovers since the early 1900s.

Most of the national theatres, the CDNs, the Scènes Nationales and other important companies publish their own magazines and occasionally scripts of plays that they are performing. In this, they are following another tradition started by Jean Vilar, whose Théâtre National Populaire regularly published production scripts and photographic material.

Philippe Rouyer
with contributions in Artistic Profile
and Criticism by Marie-Claude Hubert
Translated by Isabelle Barth with
Varya Rubin, Sandra Widmer and Roseana Young

Further Reading

Abirached, Robert. *La Crise du personnage dans le théâtre moderne*. [The crisis of character in modern drama]. Paris: Grasset, 1978. 400 pp.

Adamov, Arthur. *Ici et maintenant*. [Here and now]. Paris: Gallimard, 1964. 250 pp.

Aslan, Odette. 'Patrice Chéreau'. *Les Voies de la création théâtrale* vol. XII. Paris: CNRS, 1986.

Auteurs dramatiques français d'aujourd'hui. [Contemporary French dramatists]. Amiens: Trois Cailloux/MC Amiens, 1983. 237 pp.

Bablet, D., and M.L. Bablet. *Le Théâtre du Soleil ou la quête du bonheur*. [The Théâtre du Soleil or the quest for happiness]. Paris: CNRS, 1979.

——, and J. Jacquot, eds. 'Théâtre du Soleil, Shakespeare, Arden, Beckett'. *Les Voies de la création théâtrale* vol. V. Paris: CNRS, 1977. 456 pp.

Banu, Georges. *Peter Brook*. Paris: Flammarion, 1991. 264 pp.

——. *Le Théâtre: sortie de secours*. [Theatre: emergency exit]. Paris: Aubier, 1984.

——. *Le Théâtre ou l'instant habité*. [Theatre or the peopled minute]. Paris: L'Herne, 1992.

Barthes, Roland. *Sur Racine*. [On Racine]. Paris: Seuil, 1963.

Benhamou, Anne Françoise, et al. *Vitez: toutes ses mises en scène*. [All the plays directed by Vitez]. Paris: Jean Cyrille Godefroy, 1981. 282 pp.

Blin, Roger. *Souvenirs et propos*. [Remembrances and proposals]. Paris: Gallimard, 1986.

Boissard, C. *Danse: dix ans de développement de l'art chorégraphique*. [Dance: ten years of development of choreographic art]. Paris: Réunion des Musées Nationaux, 1993. 197 pp.

Brown, Frederick. *Theater and Revolution: The Culture of the French Stage*. New York: Viking Press, 1980. 490 pp.

Busson, Alain. *Le Théâtre en France: contexte socio-économique et choix esthétiques*. [Theatre in France: socio-economic context and aesthetic choices]. Paris: Documentation française, 1986. 140 pp.

Cadona, J., and C. Lacroix. *Les Chiffres clé de 1991: annuaire statistique de la culture*. [Key figures for 1991: statistics for culture]. Paris: Documentation française, 1991. 127 pp.

CENAM. *La Danse en France/Dance in France*. Paris: CENAM, 1988.

Centre National des Marionnettes. *Compte rendu des deuxièmes assises nationales de la Marionnette, Charleville-Mézières, 22–24 sept. 1982*. [Report of the second conference of the National Puppet Centre, Charleville-Mézières, 22–24 Sept. 1982]. Paris: Centre National des Marionnettes, 1982.

Chabert, P., ed. 'Samuel Beckett'. Special issue of *Revue d'esthétique*. (1986). 475 pp.

Chéreau (les années): Nanterre-Amandiers, 1982–1990. [The Chéreau years: Nanterre-Amandiers, 1982–90]. Paris: Imp. nat., 1990. 347 pp.

Copfermann, Émile. *Vers un théâtre différent*. [Towards a different theatre]. Paris: Maspéro, 1976. 191 pp.

Corvin, Michel. *Le Théâtre nouveau en France*. [New French theatre]. 4th ed. Series Que sais-je?: Le point des connaissances actuelles, no. 1,072. Paris: Presses universitaires de France, 1974. 127 pp.

——. *Molière et ses metteurs en scène d'aujourd'hui*. [Molière and his directors today]. Lyon: University of Lyon Press, 1985.

Deutsch, Michel. *Inventaire après liquidation*. [Stock-taking after bankruptcy]. Paris: L'Arche, 1990.

'Dix ans de théâtre: 1981–1991'. [Ten years of theatre: 1981–91]. *Acteurs* 92–3 (July–August 1991).

Dort, Bernard. 'Entre la nostalgie et l'utopie: esquisse pour une histoire du théâtre français au XXème siècle'. [Between nostalgia and utopia: a sketch of a history of French theatre in the twentieth century]. *Cahiers Théâtre de Louvaine* 43 (1980): 7–35.

——. *Le représentation émancipée*. [Performance comes of age]. Arles: Actes-Sud, 1988. 184 pp.

——. *Théâtre public*. [Public theatre]. Paris: Seuil, 1967.

——, et al. *Avignon: quarante ans de festival*. [Avignon: forty years of a festival]. Paris: Hachette/Avignon Festival, 1987. 235 pp.

Dullin, Charles. *Ce sont des dieux qu'il nous faut*. [Gods are what we need]. Paris: Gallimard, 1969. 240 pp.

Durand, J.O. *Tous spectateurs: la belle aventure des amis du Théâtre Populaire*. [Spectators all: the fine adventure of the Friends of Popular Theatre]. La Tour d'Aigues, Ed. de l'Aube, 1992. 203 pp.

Duvignaud, Jean. *Sociologie du théâtre: essai sur les ombres collectives*. [Sociology of the theatre: an essay on collective shadows]. Paris: Presses universitaires de France, 1965. 585 pp.

Fournel, Paul. *L'Histoire véritable de Guignol*. [The true history of Guignol]. Lyon: Federop, 1975. 298 pp.

Gourdon, Anne-Marie. 'La Formation du comédien'. [The actor's training]. *Les Voies de la création théâtrales* vol. IX. Paris: CNRS. 280 pp.

——. *Théâtre, public, perception*. [Theatre and its perception by the public]. Paris: CNRS, 1982. 253 pp.

Green, Anne Marie. *Un festival de théâtre et ses compagnies: le Off d'Avignon*. [A festival and its companies: Off-Avignon]. Paris: L'Harmattan, 1992. 223 pp.

Guy, J.M. *Les Publics de la danse*. [The dancegoing public]. Paris: Documentation Française, 1991. 479 pp.

——, and L. Mironer. *Les Publics du théâtre*. [The theatregoing public]. Paris: Documentation française, 1988. 238 pp.

Hopkins, Patricia, and Wendell M. Aycock. *Myths and Realities of Contemporary French Theatre: Comparative Views*. Lubbock, TX: Texas Technical Publications, 1985. 195 pp.

Hubert, Marie-Claude. *Ionesco*. Paris: Seuil, 1992.

——. *Le Théâtre*. Paris: A. Colin, 1989.

Ionesco, Eugène. *Notes et contrenotes*. [Notes and counternotes]. Paris: Gallimard, 1962. Published in English: New York: Grove Press, 1964. 271 pp.

de Jomaron, Jacqueline, ed. *Le Théâtre en France: de la Révolution à nos jours*. [Theatre in France: from the Revolution to the present day], vol. 2. Paris: A. Colin, 1989. 614 pp.

Jourdheuil, Jean *Le Théâtre, l'artiste et l'État*. [Theatre, the artist and the state]. Paris: Hachette, 1979.

Jouvet, Louis. *Témoignages sur le théâtre*. [An eye-witness's report on theatre]. Paris: Flammarion, 1952.

Kokkos, Yannis. *Le Scénographe et le héron*. [The scenographer and the heron]. Arles: Actes-Sud, 1989. 215 pp.

Lang, Jack. *Le Théâtre et l'État*. [The theatre and the state]. Bibliothèque de droit public 78. Paris: Librairie générale de droit et de jurisprudence, 1968. 380 pp.

Latour, G. *Petites Scènes, Grand Théâtres: le théâtre de création, 1944–1960*. [Small stages, great theatres: the creative theatre, 1944–60]. Paris: 1986. 303 pp.

Lavelli, Jorge, and A. Satgé. *Lavelli, opéra et mise à mort*. [Lavelli, opera and its death]. Paris: Fayard, 1979. 269 pp.

Laville, Pierre, ed. *Théâtre: 1991–1992*. Paris: Hachette, 1992. 431 pp.

Madral, Philippe. *Le Théâtre hors les murs*. [Theatre in the Paris suburbs]. Paris: Seuil, 1969. 254 pp.

Maréchal, Marcel. *La Mise en théâtre*. [Staging the theatre]. Paris: UGE, 1974. 232 pp.

Mignon, Paul Louis. *Le Théâtre au XXème siècle*. [Theatre in the twentieth century]. Paris: Gallimard, 1978. 371 pp.

Rio, M.N., and M. Rostain. 'Aujourd'hui, l'opéra'. [Opera today]. *Recherches* 42 (1980). 287 pp.

Robinson, Jacqueline. *L'Aventure de la danse moderne en France, 1920–1970*. [The adventure of modern dance in France, 1920–70]. Bougé, 1990. 380 pp.

de Saint-Pulgent, M. *Le Syndrome de l'opéra*. [The opera syndrome]. Paris: Laffont, 1991.

Sandier, Gilles. *Théâtre en crise: des années 70 à 82*. [Theatre in crisis: from 1970 to 1982]. Paris: La pensée sauvage, 1982. 487 pp.

——. *Théâtre et combat*. [Theatre and battle]. Paris: Stock, 1970. 368 pp.

Schumacher, Claude. *Forty Years of Mise en Scène*. Dundee: Lochee, 1986.

Simon, Alfred. *Dictionnaire du théâtre français contemporain*. [A dictionary of contemporary French theatre]. Paris: Librairie Larousse, 1973. 255 pp.

Souriau, Étienne. *Les Deux cent mille situations dramatiques*. [Two hundred thousand dramatic situations]. Paris: Flammarion, 1950. 250 pp.

Stewart, E.R. *The Decentralisation of French Theatre 1940–1952: The Association Jeune France and the Centres Dramatiques*. Warwick: University of Warwick, 1985.

Sueur, Monique. *Deux siècles au Conservatoire d'art dramatique*. [Two centuries at the National Acting School]. Paris: CNSAD, 1986. 235 pp.

Temkine, Raymonde. *Le Théâtre au présent*. [Present-day theatre]. Lectoure: Bouffonneries, 1987. 328 pp.

——. *Le Théâtre en l'État*. [The state and/of theatre]. Paris: Éditions Théâtrales, 1992. 253 pp.

Ubersfeld, Anne. *L'École du spectateur*. [School for theatregoers]. Paris: Éditions sociales, 1981. 352 pp.

——. *Lire le théâtre*. [Reading theatre]. Paris: Éditions sociales, 1977. 280 pp.

Vessillier, Michèle. *La Crise du théâtre privé*. [The crisis in the private theatre]. Paris: Presses universitaires de France, 1973. 227 pp.

Vilar, Jean. *Jean Vilar par lui-même*. [Jean Vilar by himself]. Avignon: Maison J. Vilar, 1991. 340 pp.

——. *Théâtre, service public et autres textes*. [Theatre is a public utility and other writings]. 2nd ed. Paris: Gallimard, 1986. 556 pp.

Vinaver, Michel. *Le Compte rendu d'Avignon*. [The Avignon report]. Arles: Actes-Sud, 1987.

——. *Écrits sur le théâtre*. [Writings on the theatre]. Lausanne: L'Aire théâtrale, 1982. 330 pp.

'25 ans de décentralisation: les auteurs'. [Twenty-five years of decentralization: the dramatists]. Special issue of *ATAC-Informations*. (September 1972). 52 pp.

Vitez, Antoine, and Émile Copfermann. *De Chaillot à Chaillot*. [From Chaillot to Chaillot]. Paris: Hachette, 1981.

Whitton, David. *Stage Directors in Modern France*. Manchester: Manchester University Press, 1987. 307 pp.

Yendt, Maurice. *Les Ravisseurs d'enfants: du théâtre et des jeunes spectateurs*. [Wonder for children: theatre and young audiences]. Arles: Actes-Sud, 1989. 179 pp.

GEORGIA

A Georgian kingdom has existed since at least the third century BC but, like its neighbouring Caucasus republics (Azerbaijan and Armenia), it has long been a battleground for powers in the region. Georgia's last king abdicated in 1801 and the region became, first, part of Russia and, from 1917, part of the Soviet Union. In the early years of the USSR, the three republics were united into what was called the Transcaucasian Soviet Federal Socialist Republic. In 1936, each of the three became a separate constituent republic. In 1990, following the dissolution of the USSR, Georgia became an independent nation once again.

Located along the southern edge of the Black Sea, Georgia is bordered by Turkey to the west, Armenia and Azerbaijan to the south and Russia to the north and west. The republic has an area of 69,700 square kilometres (26,900 square miles) and had a 1989 population of 5.3 million. Its capital is Tbilisi (formerly known as Tiflis). Approximately two-thirds of the population are native Georgians who speak a south Caucasian language. Russian and Armenian are also spoken widely.

Georgia has a long literary history. Its major national epic is the thirteenth-century poem *The Knight in Tiger Skin* by Shota Rustaveli. Its earliest theatre space dates back to the third century BC and can be found in the mountain town of Uplistsikhe. Though no texts survive – no doubt due to the innumerable wars that have taken place in the area – it is clear that performances did occur at least 1,800 years ago.

Archaeologists have found connections between the ancient theatres and modern acting styles, styles that show their roots in folk forms, squares filled with the sounds of music and drums, comedy, improvisation, pageant and masquerade. The festive nature of Georgian theatrical art also seems to be directly connected with traditional Georgian taste for singing and dancing and a tendency towards celebratory re-enactments of the heroic. The nation's continuing protests against foreign domination and the recognition of one's duty to give up everything if necessary to protect national freedom have long been reflected in both Georgian plays and larger-than-life performing styles. Hallmarks include bold speech, extremes of feeling and violent passion.

In the Medieval period, the folk theatre added masks (*berikaoba*) and performances often became open protests against conquerors. Satirical performing styles and public accusations seem to have been common in the period. The theatre apparently was a favoured place for defending the national interest.

From the nineteenth century, Georgia's relations with its powerful Russian neighbours improved and in the second half of the century, Russian styles – particularly realism – became dominant in all the arts. The first Georgian dramatist of note to work in the realistic style was the nineteenth-century writer Gyorgi Eristavi. In 1850, Eristavi founded his own theatre and produced several new realistic plays. Unfortunately, he was unable to find financial support from the government – often the subject of attack in the plays – and audiences were not large enough to keep the company operating.

In 1879, a second company, which would ultimately become known as the Rustaveli, began operating in Tiflis. It was created by Ilya Chavchavadze (1837–1907) and Akaki Tsereteli (1848–1915), two important Georgian writers. They attempted to make their theatre a centre for the most advanced ideas on liberty and social humanism and wanted their plays to be part of the new realism as well. The theatre quickly gained a large following and both Georgian and Russian works as well as world classics could be seen on its stage. Stylistically, the company managed to blend the concept of national liberation with a deeply rooted folk style. Productions ranged from vaudevilles to Georgian comedies, from plays by Schiller to tragedies such as Monti's *Caio Gracco*.

After 1917, Georgia became a democratic republic. Arguing for theatre's social responsibility at this time, director Kote Mardzhanishvili (1872–1933), said the theatre must be regarded 'as a temple. It needs now to become a rostrum ... [which] must keep up with the tempo of contemporary life. ... [It] must bring joy to the people and cheer their spirit.'

Mardzhanishvili's ideas were deeply influential during this time as he sought to combine the realistic principles of the Russian theatre with the heroic and romantic traits of the Georgian style. Among the authors regularly produced by him were the Russian realists Chekhov and Gorki, the latter a personal friend. Mardzhanishvili was also close to both Stanislavski and Nemirovich-Danchenko, with whose Moscow Art Theatre he worked for three years.

Mardzhanishvili's importance in the development of the modern Georgian theatre cannot be overstated. He not only raised the general level of the stage but also created a new way of working for both the actor and other directors. He developed the notion of 'company' in Georgia and also created an 'ideologically correct' repertoire. There had been Georgian directors of note before him – Valerian Shalikashvili (1874–1919), Alexander Tsutsunava (1881–1955), Mikhail Koreli (1876–1949), Kote Andronikashvili (1887–1954) and Akaki Pagava (1887–1962), all of whom worked in the realistic tradition – but it was Mardzhanishvili who more than anyone else brought Georgian theatre into the modern period. In his productions, realism was never merely photographic but rather boisterous and passionate; never restricted, generalized or faceless but rather monumental, epic and exaggerated. It was this unique brand of realism that most characterized the Georgian stage and set it apart from the Russian style of realism.

Working mostly at the Rustaveli Theatre through his long career, Mardzhanishvili in 1928 started a new company in Kutaisi, a small city with a very long cultural tradition. Working with him were the dramatists Shalva Dadiani (1894–1959) and Polikarp Kakabadze (1895–1972) along with a large number of well-

known novelists, poets and even theatre critics. It was this literary base that became the core of the new theatre.

Mardzhanishvili's main focus in his new theatre was obviously contemporary drama. Among the successful works created there were satirical comedies such as Kakabadze's *Kvarkvare Tutaberi* (1929) and Dadiani's *Deep Into the Heart* (1928) and serious dramas such as Karlo Kaladze's (1907–89) *The Way It Was*, Demna Shengelaya's (1896–1980) *The White* (1928) and Dia Chianeli's (1891–1937) *Bail* (1929).

In addition, there were plays from the international repertoire such as Ernst Toller's *Hoppla, wir leben!* (1928) and from the European repertoire such as Karl Gutzkow's *Uriel Acosta*. All these works proclaimed ideas of noncompromise and human courage, sense and spirit. Mardzhanishvili went deep into the nature of human conflict and to the core of heroism.

After two years of operation in Kutaisi, the company moved to the capital where it became known simply as the Second Drama Theatre of Georgia. When Mardzhanishvili died in

Shota Agsabadze's 1937 Rustaveli Theatre production of Shakespeare's *Othello*.

1933, its name was officially changed to the Mardzhanishvili Theatre.

During the 1930s and beyond, Georgian plays presented a series of Soviet-style heroes – workers, peasants and representatives of the new Soviet intelligentsia. Among the better plays in this style was Kakabadze's brilliant comedy, *The Collective Farmer's Wedding* (1934), which depicts life on a collective farm through a series of colourful and memorable characters. The Georgian theatre continued to grow in both size and quality during this period.

Though the major theatres were unable to perform regularly during World War II, theatrical traditions were maintained through special performances by 'front groups' which brought together leading writers, directors and actors and played for army units on the front lines. And because so many performers were on the front lines, innumerable sketches and theatrical miniatures were created within hours after major events occurred, creating pieces filled with both joy and a firm belief in victory.

Following the war, the two major Tbilisi theatres began mounting larger-scale productions once again, productions aimed at reflecting the scale and the horrors of the war experiences.

History plays dealing with Georgia's past continued to be produced regularly both during the war and in the immediate post-war period. At least three writers – Sandro Shanshiashvili (1888–1979), Iona Vakeli (1898–1953) and Ushangi Chkheidze (1898–1953) – wrote separate plays during this time about the great Georgian military leader of the twelfth century, Gyorgi Saakadze.

In the 1940s and 1950s, Shakespeare and Schiller, long favourites of the Georgian theatre, were regularly taken up by the companies who found both writers close to the romantic Georgian spirit. One of the major productions of the period at the Rustaveli was *Othello* (1937) staged by Shota Agsabadze (1896–1966). Othello's revenge in this production was not only for his honour but also for the abuse he felt of the ideal, of universal harmony, of faith and justice. The roles of Othello and Iago were played by two of the great stars of the Georgian theatre at the time – Akaki Khorava (1895–1972) and Akaki Vasadze (1899–1978).

Other productions staged with equal originality and success included *Antony and Cleopatra*, directed by Vakhtang Tabliashvili (b. 1914), and *Richard III* and *Mary Stuart* staged by Vaso Kushitashvili (1894–1962), all at the Mardzhanishvili Theatre.

Also staged during this time were major productions of plays by Lope de Vega, Goldoni, Beaumarchais and Shaw, among others. In Dimitri Alexidze's (1910–84) production of Sophocles' *Oedipus Rex* (1956, Rustaveli), Oedipus and Jocasta were each played by four actors of significantly different ages – Akaki Khorava, Akaki Vasadze, Sergo Zakariadze (1909–71) and Erosi Manigaladze (1925–82). Through the 1950s and beyond, Russian classics were also frequently seen in Tbilisi, plays by Pushkin, Lermontov, Gogol, Ostrovsky and Sukhovo-Kobylin.

During the 1960s, many of the younger directors began turning away from realism and began experimenting with other forms. These experiments soon became clashes of age, with older actors and directors determined to stay with realistic styles and younger ones trying to find new methods of expression.

The plays of Nodar Dumbadze (1928–84), for example, focused on inner reality while Mardzhanishvili Theatre director Grigori (Giga) Lordkipanidze (b. 1928) experimented in productions of non-realistic plays such as *I, My Granny, Iliko and Illarion* (1960) and *I See the Sun* (1963). Lordkipanidze and other Georgian directors of note – including Robert Sturua (b. 1938) – returned to Dumbadze's plays later in equally important productions of *Don't Worry Mama* (1964), *Sunny Night*

Alexander Takaishvili's 1951 Mardzanishvili Theatre production of Gogol's *The Government Inspector*.

(1967) and in an adaptation of his novel, *The White Flags* (1974). The latter was staged at the Rustaveli by Lordkipanidze with the central role played by another outstanding actor, Otar Megvinetukhutsesi (b. 1938).

In the 1960s actors and directors of varying ages began to move in these new directions, denouncing heroic and romantic styles as anachronistic and attempting to find new meanings even within realism. But a lack of audience interest as well as official orthodoxy worked against the new approaches and prevented these experiments from reaching any kind of fruition. By the early 1970s, realism was once again the dominant form, albeit a Georgian realism.

This could be seen in Robert Sturua's stunning production of Arthur Miller's *The Crucible* (1965) at the Rustaveli Theatre. Sturua's actors created a profound and elaborate protest against the trampling of justice and barbaric violation of human laws. One could note change as well in Mikhail Tumanishvili's (b. 1921) production of Anouilh's *Antigone* (1968) at the Rustaveli, intellectual debate at its highest while at the same time reaching deep into the Georgian soul.

During the late 1960s and 1970s, Georgian literature itself was the focus on stage, a movement led by the critic Beso Zhgenti (1903–76), who urged theatres to focus on their own world and their own issues. Audiences responded well to these stagings which brought to their view powerful and recognizable characters, genuine debate and a new kind of stage language.

Brecht's aesthetics most clearly emerged on Georgian stages during the 1960s as well. In 1964, when the debate between the traditional and the new was at its height, Dimitri Alexidze staged Brecht's *Der Dreigroschenoper* (*The Threepenny Opera*) at the Rustaveli. In the production, Alexidze showed just how wide Brecht's new imagery could be for directors, and many young directors quickly took up the challenge. In the late 1960s, Sturua followed this direction producing brilliant productions of both *Der gute Mensch von Sezuan* (*The Good Person of Setzuan*, 1969) and *Der kaukasische Kreidekreis* (*The Caucasian Chalk Circle*, 1975). Sturua's approach to the latter play focused on Brecht's humanism. In 1974, Sturua, arguably Georgia's most important director, staged in the Brechtian style Kakabadze's

Giga Lordkipanidze's 1960 Mardzhanishvili Theatre production of Nodar Dumbadze's *I, My Granny, Iliko and Illarion*.

Kvarkvare using direct address to the audiences, songs, signs, and so on. Even his Shakespearian productions, *Richard III* and *King Lear*, showed clear Brechtian influences.

During the 1970s and 1980s, Georgian theatre continued to develop within the framework of a tightly prescribed Soviet multinationalism maintaining close contact with both new developments in Russian theatre and developments among the theatres of the other Soviet republics. The plays of Russian dramatists Mikhail Shatrov and Alexander Gelman were regularly seen. During this same period, companies from other republics played in Tbilisi and the two major Georgian companies toured to other parts of the USSR. The Rustaveli company in particular enjoyed enormous success abroad with its productions of plays by both Brecht and Shakespeare.

After the disintegration of the Soviet Union in 1990, Georgia once again became an independent nation. On the positive side, censorship in all the arts was eliminated and experimentation

began to flourish, But as political euphoria turned into civil war, theatre workers and the intelligentsia generally found themselves caught between decreasing state support on the one hand and attacks in the press on the other. This was not a siuation supported by the leader of the republic since 1992, Edward Shevardnadze (b. 1928), but it was a reality and represented a real danger to all Georgian theatre artists. By 1993, Georgian theatre, like the country itself, was suffering significantly.

Nevertheless, theatres were still active and several new productions were staged in 1993. Among them were Calderón's *La Vida es Sueña* (*Life is a Dream*) directed by Sturua at the Rustaveli, *A Midsummer Night's Dream*) directed by Tumanishvili at the Film Actors' Theatre, *Antony and Cleopatra* directed by England's Hilary Wood, and *Bakhtrioni* (text by Vaja Pshavela) directed by Temur Chkeize at the Mardzhanishvili. And audiences were still attending.

Structure of the National Theatre Community

By 1989, a network of thirty-four professional theatres had been established across the country, fifteen in Tbilisi alone. Others operated in regional centres such as Telavi, Chiatura, Gori, Rustavi, Kutaisi, Sukhumi, Batumi, Tskhinvali, Poti, Makharadze, Zugdidi and Akhaltsikhe.

Each of the theatres has traditionally followed the lead of those in the capital which, in turn, long followed directives established in Moscow. After 1990, enormous changes began which were still not clear by 1993.

For many years, one of the exemplary provincial theatres was the Meskhishvili in Kutaisi, a town whose traditions in theatre go back many centuries and have become an important part of its cultural profile. The company regularly invited in directors from other Georgian provincial companies and has had particular success with productions staged by Giorgi Kavtaradze (b. 1946) from the Georgian Theatre in Sukhumi. Returning the visits was the Meskhishvili's director, Yuri Kakulia (b. 1921), who staged Fadaev's *The Young Guard* and *Banya* (*The Bathhouse*) by Mayakovsky in Sukhumi. Such direct interchanges set a precedent among Georgian groups.

Georgian theatre unions trace their roots back to the Drama Society founded by the Georgian writer and statesman Ilya Chavchavadze in 1881. In 1945, it became the Georgian Theatre Society with Akaki Khorava its first chair. In 1987, the society became the Union of Theatre Workers with Giga Lordkipanidze as its chair. The union is representative of all areas of theatrical creativity and deals with both immediate and long-term social and material concerns. It has responsibilities as well in training and professional development and also has its own publications from time to time.

As a rule, Georgian theatres employ only graduates of recognized theatre schools. But there have been cases in which talented artists without degrees have been hired. All actors are contracted to particular theatres but may, with agreement, appear as guest artists on occasion at other theatres.

Honorary state titles recognize long-term contributions. In 1993 there were 444 Honoured Artists, 182 People's Artists and fifty-nine Honoured Art Workers.

Festivals of various sorts have been a regular part of Georgian theatre life. In 1979, 1982 and 1985, Soviet Youth Festivals were held in

Tbilisi, while in 1984 a Transcaucasian Puppet Festival was held.

Among major Georgian troupes which have toured abroad have been the Metekhi and Rustavi Drama Theatres, the Chavchavadze Theatre from Batumi and the Georgian State Opera and Ballet Theatre from Tbilisi.

(*See* USSR *for additional background on Georgian theatre structures, 1945–90*)

Artistic Profile

Companies

The two most important dramatic theatres in Georgia are the Rustaveli and the Mardzhanishvili Theatres in Tbilisi. Both have long histories and have been associated with a series of outstanding directors. Through the 1970s and 1980s, the work of the Rustaveli's artistic director, Robert Sturua – especially on the plays of Shakespeare and Brecht – has brought the company national and international acclaim and invitations to festivals world-wide.

Sturua quickly became a master of the epic form and used it to good advantage not only in Brecht but also in the works of Shakespeare including *Richard II* and *King Lear*. Concerned with the nature of spiritual destruction of the individual, Sturua synthesized the epic form with, on the one hand, tragic grotesque and outrageous buffoonery and, on the other, concrete realities and political events.

Another theatre of note is the Studio Theatre of Film Actors founded in 1977 in Tbilisi. Composed of recent graduates from the Theatre Institute, the company began its life by remounting productions done by the actors while still in school but quickly moved on to establish a repertoire ranging from García Lorca to Russian classics by Fadaev and Svarts, from modern Georgian dramatists to established international classics by such writers as Thornton Wilder and Molière.

Several smaller cities boast two different theatres, each with their own specific theatrical approaches: in Sukhumi they are the Abkhazian and the Sukhumi Georgian Theatres; in Tskhinvali one company operates in Georgian and another in the Ossetic language. Notable productions have been staged by theatres in the Abkhazian, Adzharian and South Ossetic Autonomous Republics within Georgia.

Still another important theatre is the Rustavi in the city of Rustavi. Formed in 1967 by Giga Lordkipanidze as an offshoot of the Mardzhanishvili, the newly independent theatre has effectively blended experiment with tradition. Among its important productions have been *Cyrano de Bergerac* and Korostilev's *A Hundred Years Later* (both 1968), Gorki's *Lower Depths* (1969) and in the 1970s, Anzor Kutateladze's version of *The Seagull*.

In Kutaisi, the Meskhishvili Theatre has kept up an outstanding acting tradition, while the Dadiani Theatre of Batumi is quickly becoming one of Georgia's best.

Until the vast changes in the Soviet Union occurred, the Griboedov Russian Drama Theatre in Tbilisi played a significant role in the theatrical life of the capital. Founded in 1845, the theatre's mandate was to promote cooperation between Russian and Georgian culture. Appealing primarily to the large number of Russian speakers in Tbilisi, the company presented a wide range of Russian and foreign classics as well as plays by leading Georgian dramatists. A number of major Russian directors did regular guest productions at the Griboedov, among them Giorgi Tovstonogov, long-time director of the Bolshoi Dramatic Theatre of Leningrad.

One of the oldest theatres in the country is the Armenian Drama Theatre, founded in 1863 in Tbilisi. With a repertoire of Armenian, Georgian and foreign contemporary plays, the theatre was headed in 1993 by Mikhail Grigorian (b. 1940), a student of Mikhail Tumanishvili. With roots going back as far as the 1820s, this Armenian company has had successes with a wide variety of authors ranging from Soundoukian to Gogol, and from Shakespeare to Shanshiashvili.

It should be noted as well that for many years, a national festival was held in Tbilisi showcasing outstanding productions from the regions. Held intermittently, the festival ceased entirely after 1990.

Dramaturgy

There are a number of important Georgian

writers creating for the stage. Throughout its history, the Mardzhanishvili Theatre has worked closely with writers and has regularly produced the work of such notable playwrights as G. Abashidze, Nodar Dumbadze, T. Chiladze, A. Chkhaidze and many others.

Of these, the most important plays are perhaps Chkhaidze's *The Bridge*, and Chiladze's drama, *Pages from the Family Album*. During the 1980s, Chiladze produced two plays of particular note, *Role for a Young Actress* and *Variations on a Contemporary Theme*, the latter directed by Robert Sturua at the Rustaveli.

Other writers of note during the 1980s have included A. Ckhaidze, author of *From Three To Six*; Shadiman Shamanadze, author of *Open Verandah*, premièred at the Rustaveli; and Lali Roseba, author of *Première* and *Provincial Story*.

Directors, Directing and Production Styles

Georgia has produced a large number of outstanding directors. Without doubt, the dominating force in the first half of the twentieth century in Georgia was Kote Mardzhanishvili. Even in his first professional production, Lope de Vega's tragedy *Fuenteovejuna*, staged at the Rustaveli Theatre in 1922, he clearly demonstrated his immense theatrical imagination and his special ability drawing larger-than-life performances from his actors. In his hands, the play became a testimony to heroism combining both pathos and brilliant festivity. His glorification of the heroic spirit was clearly in line with the attitudes of the epoch.

Mardzhanishvili was quite clearly attracted to the size and grandeur of classical plays. 'The cornerstone of art of the future', he once said, 'is seen in the masterpieces of the past. Those who do rather than those who talk will be the real creators of the new culture.'

Following his famous *Fuenteovejuna*, he turned to *Hamlet* and through this production he reflected on humanity's future and the future of the age. In his production, actions literally exploded on the stage forcing his characters into acts of courage. As played by Ushangi Chkheidze, *Hamlet* synthesized the dreams of all artists.

Mardzhanishvili attempted a wide range of styles including plays by German expressionists such as Toller, Kaiser and Werfel and he even tried to stage Mayakovsky's *Mystère Bouffe* outdoors (a plan he was eventually forced to give up on). He also regularly staged Georgian authors such as Shanshiashvili, Kakabadze and Dadiani. He believed deeply that a nation's theatre had to be rooted in its plays and argued for the Rustaveli to find authors who could create large dramas with heroic-romantic characters.

Following in Mardzhanishvili's footsteps was Sandro Akhmeteli, another outstanding director who strove to create a heroic and monumental form of theatre. Sensing the potential value of theatre to its society, Akhmeteli possessed an acute sense of the age and a profound understanding of the problems confronting his time. Rather than having his actors working toward an everyday image, he worked towards what he called a 'national rhythm'. His productions were therefore rooted in a distinct rhythmical structure and were supported by razor sharp characterizations. His creations showed people as heroic, dynamic and larger than life.

Two of his 1928 productions particularly stood out in this regard – *Break-up* by B. Lavrenyov and *Anzor* by Shanshiashvili (an adaptation of a Moscow Art Theatre play popular at that time called *Armoured Train 1469*). Both plays showed people struggling for

Robert Sturua's 1980 Rustaveli Theatre production of Shakespeare's *Richard III*.

justice and how their battles transformed society. In the first play, the people were sailors; in the second one, partisans. Both these productions were immensely popular but probably none was more popular than his version of Schiller's *The Robbers*, which he called *In Tyranny* (1930). Akhmeteli was executed in 1937.

Another major figure in Georgian directing was Mikhail Tumanishvili. One hears, in fact, of the Theatre of Tumanishvili and the School of Tumanishvili. Often using an acting style rooted in the exaggerated and the grotesque, his work with actors was almost always based on improvisation.

Perhaps the best known of Georgia's contemporary directors is Robert Sturua. Heading the Rustaveli company, Sturua continued Mardzhanishvili's interest in reinterpreting classics. A student of Tumanishvili, however, Sturua learned from his teacher not only how to work closely with actors but also how to use scenic space effectively. Though his methods were often in contradiction ot Tumanishvili's, Sturua's debt to his mentor is clear.

Sturua's work is also highly metaphoric, an element that has put him into conflict with actors on several occasions. Yet his ability to work both actively and analytically with them has enabled his productions to challenge every tradition. All these elements can be seen in his best work, especially daring productions of *Caucasian Chalk Circle*, *Kvarkvare*, *Richard III* and *King Lear*.

Still another director of note is Temur Chkheidze, who, in most of his work at the Mardzhanishvili Theatre, has tried to find contemporary parallels in the scripts he stages. His productions – especially Shakespearian productions such as *Othello* starring Otar Megvinetukhutsesi – often show individuals fighting against the larger evil of society. Alienation in its many forms usually plays a key role in his interpretations.

Music Theatre

Musical performance has a tradition in Georgia dating back to the ninth century when professional singers first began making appearances in various cities. The movement, however, was discouraged by church authorities and the process of development slowed considerably. A professional music theatre began to emerge in the second half of the nineteenth century under the influence of the Italian opera company in St Petersburg. The first steps saw the construction of a small opera house in 1851 and the presentation of scenes from various Italian-style operas such as Glinka's *Ivan Susanin* (1856) and Verstovsky's *Askold's Grave* (1857). The first full-length opera performed was *Lucia di Lammermoor*.

Between 1883 and 1893, the Russian composer Mikhail Ipolitov-Ivanov (1859–1935) became conductor of the Tbilisi Opera House and regularly staged established works, again mostly from the Russian repertoire. These included works by Tchaikovsky, Rimsky-Korsakov and Dorgomyzhski. He also staged his own opera, *Treachery*, based on the play of that name by Sumbatashvili-Juzhin (1857–1927), a Georgian who became known in Russia as Sumbatov. This development was aided considerably by visits to Georgia by Tchaikovsky and Anton Rubinstein, who conducted Georgian orchestras. Another regular visitor was the famous Russian star, Fyodor Chaliapin.

Between 1886 and 1890, Tchaikovsky himself visited Tbilisi five times, staging his own operas *Eugene Onegin, Mazepa* and *Fairy*.

First through translations of Italian and Russian classics into Georgian – mostly by Ilya Kargareteli (1867–1959), also known for his collected *Georgian Folk Songs* – a number of Georgian composers eventually turned to writing operas themselves. Among them was Zakaria Paliashvili (1871–1933), now considered the founder of Georgian opera and creator of *Absalom and Eteri* (1919), *Daisi* (1923) and *Latavia* (1928). These are lyrical, romantic operas which show both psychological and social motivation.

Another outstanding early composer was Meliton Balanchivadze (1863–1937). Balanchivadze, the father of the choreographer George Balanchine, is the composer of the opera *Treacherous Darijan* (1926). Dimitri Arakishvili (1873–1953) is the creator of an opera about Georgia's national poet, *The Legend of Shota Rustaveli* (1914) while Victor Dolidze (1890–1933) authored a fine comic opera, *Keto and Kote* (1919) and the opera *Lela* (1922).

It was the building of the Tbilisi Opera and Ballet Theatre in 1896 (now called the Paliashvili Opera and Ballet Theatre) which spurred the development of the form and which led to the golden age of Georgian opera in the period between 1918 and 1921.

Among the major Georgian opera composers of the immediate post-war period one should mention Shalva Meshvelidze (1904–84), whose *Legend of Tariel* was staged in 1946; Archil Kereselidze (1912–84), whose *Bashi Achuki* was staged the same year; and Shalva Azmaiparashvili (1903–57), composer of *Khevisberi Gocha*, staged in 1952.

In the 1960s, 1970s and 1980s several notable operas were written by Otar Taktakishvili (1924–89) – *Mindia* (1961) and *Abduction of the Moon* (1978); David Toradze (1922–83) – *Northern Bride* (1957); Revaz Lagidze (1921–81) – *Lela* (1975); Alexander Bukia (b. 1906) – *Uninvited Guest*, a comic opera (1950); and Archil Chimakadze (1919–91) – *Maia of Tskneti*, also a comic work (1980).

In the late 1980s and early 1990s, several new operas by the composer Bidzina Kvernadze (b. 1928) were staged in Tbilisi. These included *The Martyrdom of St Shushanik* and *Medea*.

In 1993, the conductor and artistic director of the Tbilisi opera was Jano Kakhidze (b. 1936).

A few words are needed here about operetta, another popular form in Georgia. Professionally produced operettas have been seen on Georgian stages since 1934 when the Vaso Abashidze Musical Comedy Theatre was founded in Tbilisi. Since its founding, works from the world repertoire as well as new operettas by Georgian composers have been successfully staged.

Dance Theatre

As with music theatre, the first steps in the development of a professional dance theatre took place in Georgia in the second half of the nineteenth century. In 1851, dancers from St Petersburg performed a series of classical ballets including *Giselle*. Such performances continued to draw appreciative audiences and in 1886, a ballet theatre was constructed and a Georgian ballet group formed led by Maria Perini (1873–1939). In 1916, Perini formed a Ballet Studio and its graduates formed the core of the Tbilisi Ballet Company.

In 1920, the dancer and choreographer Mikhail Mordkin (1880–1944) took over as director of the group and continued focusing on the classical Russian repertoire staging such works as *Swan Lake*. It was not until Vakhtang Chabukiani (1910–92) came along, however, in the 1930s that classical ballet became truly Georgian in character. A graduate of the Petersburg Ballet School (1929), in 1941 he became the Tbilisi company's leading dancer and began his work as a reformer in the field.

Heroism and romanticism were characteristics of Chabukiani's style both as a dancer and choreographer. This said, he also regularly challenged the refined delicacy of ballet and gave male dancers an active leading role in the work. Ultimately, he combined classical Russian ballet with Georgian folk-dance traditions to create a form of dance that is uniquely Georgian. Among his major productions are *Heart of the Mountains* (1941), *Sinatle* (1947), *Laurencia* (1948), *Gorda* (1950), *For Peace* (1953), *Othello* (1957), *Demon* (1961), *Bolero* (1971) *Hamlet* (1971) and *Apasionata* (1980).

From 1950 to 1973, he was the artistic director of the Tbilisi Choreographic School. When he left, he was replaced by Gyorgy Alexidze (b. 1941).

Ballet companies have also been formed in connection with the opera theatres in Batumi and Kutaisi.

The Georgian State Dance Company was founded in 1954 by Nina Ramishvili and Iliko Sukhishvili. It has toured world-wide, with great success.

As for the art of mime, despite some experiments in this area by Kote Mardzhanishvili at the end of the 1920s, the genre was essentially disregarded until the late 1970s. It was in 1978 that the Rustaveli Theatre Institute decided to add a mime section to its programme though students were to be accepted only every four years. In 1982, this programme became the State Pantomime Theatre under the direction of Amiran Shalikashvili (b. 1939) and Kira Mebuke (b. 1952). Shalikashvili later became first president of the International Association of Pantomime which was formed in Tbilisi in 1993.

Theatre for Young Audiences
Puppet Theatre

Stanislavski argued that professional actors should regularly play for children as well as for adults. This was the model for many years in Georgian theatres with productions for young audiences being mixed into the repertoires using the same actors as adult performances.

The first theatre specifically set up to perform for young audiences was the Rustavi Youth Theatre in the city of Rustavi. Initially connected to the Mardzhanishvili Theatre, the Youth Theatre formally separated in 1967 setting up its own company (made up mostly of recent graduates of the Theatre Institute) under the direction of Giga Lordkipanidze. Its first production was Rostand's *Cyrano de Bergerac*. Other productions have included Georgian and Russian classics such as Gorki's *The Lower Depths* and Dumbadze's *The Verdict* and adaptations of well-known children's fairytales such as Hans Christian Andersen's *The Emperor's New Clothes*.

In the early 1970s a Youth Drama Theatre was established in the city of Akhaltsikhe. Its first actors were also recent graduates of the Theatre Institute under the directorship of Nana Demetrashvili (b. 1936). The company's repertoire early on was based on productions done while the actors were still at the institute: *The Collective Farmer's Wedding* by Kakabadze, *Romeo, Juliet and the Darkness* after a story by Y. Otchenashek and *The Wisdom of Death* by Chkhaidze.

Still another company, this one in Tbilisi, was established in the early 1970s. Known as the Metekhi Youth Studio Theatre, it was originally housed in a church and its premises determined to a very great extent its production style.

Among its important productions early on were *People, Look at the Vine*, based on a story by Sandro Mrevlishvili (b. 1937), *42–74*, based on two pieces by Mayakovsky, an adaptation of Ostrovsky's *How the Steel Was Tempered*, and Shakespeare's *Hamlet*.

Other theatres across the country soon began to add into their own repertories productions specifically for young people. In many cases, they simply brought in graduating productions from the Theatre Institute introducing in this way a new generation of actors and directors. Thus, for example, in 1986 the graduating class of Professor Gizo Zhordania established the Theatre Studio on the Rustaveli Theatre's Small Stage. The first season consisted of the group's graduation productions – *The Diary of Anne Frank*, *The Samanishvili Stepmother* by David Kldiashvili (1862–1931), and *It Might be Windy Tonight* by Boris Vasiliov.

Two other groups of note are the Russian-Georgian Youth Theatre and the Russian Youth Theatre. Both are marked by a vividness of stage images and their careful choice of repertoire.

Georgia also boasts two puppet theatres which regularly present adaptations of Georgian, Russian and foreign classics. Perhaps the best known of the two is the Marionette Theatre of Rezo Gabriadze. Its productions of *Marshal de Fantiere's Diamonds*, *Alfred and Violetta* and *The Autumn of My Spring* are among the many outstanding works staged by the group, each full of the deep wisdom that can help young people resolve the problems of growing up.

Puppet companies exist as well in Sukhumi, Batumi and Kutaisi.

Design

The close working relationship between scenographers and stage directors has been of significance in the Georgian theatre as far back as the middle of the nineteenth century when such collaborative work was first seen at the Eristavi Theatre. By the turn of the twentieth century, such an approach was taken as a given

in the creative process and by the 1930s such visual collaboration was at its peak.

Among the major designers during this period were Josef Charlemagne (1880–1957), Irakli Gamrekeli (1884–1943), Valdimir Sidamon-Eristavi (1889–1943), David Kakabadze (1889–1954), Kiril Zdanevich (1892–1967),

Elene Akhvlediani (1901–75), Tamar Abakelia (1905–53), Peter Otskhali (1907–37) and Soliko Virsaladze (1909–88).

Totally free in their choice of artistic means, styles and trends, these scenographers thought in terms of stage space and architectural constructions rather than pictorial realism. They were visually unconfined in their romantic perceptions of nature and the universe. Most worked in both dramatic and musical theatres.

Of this first great generation, Gamrekeli was perhaps the most brilliant. Discovered by director Kote Mardzhanishvili at an artist's exhibition where he saw Gamrekeli's illustrations for Wilde's *Salome*, the two men went on to create many productions together including one of *Salome*. Later in his career he worked closely with Sandro Akhmeteli as well and was instrumental in determining a monumental and heroic style which would become a hallmark of the Rustaveli Theatre. In total, Gemrekeli created more than forty stage designs in his long career.

Gamrekeli always attempted to utilize stage space in new ways. His most consistent characteristic was the creation of a single visual element which would express the thematic essence of a work, frame the directorial concept and give the production a visual rhythm and dynamism. Sometimes it was done with a monumental arch creating a vista against which the action was set (*In Tyranny*); other times it was with a fortress set against a picturesque landscape, a throne room containg columns and arches, or with a series of crowning mountain caps.

Kakabadze was another scenographer who felt that the effectiveness of a design lay not so much in its literal interpretation of dramatic theme as in its overall plasticity, expression and quality of form. Kakabadze, however, found his work coming into conflict with strictures calling for more literal interpretations which followed the norms of socialist-realism. As a result he was severely persecuted during the later years of his life and often found himself unable to work.

He regarded space as the essence of form (including human form) and his work tended towards an abstract, fixed, unchangeable framing of the stage. In some instances this was represented by a painted backdrop or an architectual construction. Rarely was there need for any embellishments beyond these elements. In his 1928 design for Toller's *Hoppla, wir leben!* at the Mardzhanishvili Theatre, for instance, he created a pleated structure which was alternately lit from two sides. The play of light on fabric created unique playing areas which could easily be moved from one part of the stage to another.

Other important designs by Kakabadze were seen in David Kldiashvili's *The Samanishvili Stepmother* (1937), Dadiani's *Yesterday's People*, and in Herzel Baazov's (1904–38) *Itska Rizhinashvili* (1937) among others.

Another master was Peter Otskheli, who spent nine years at the Mardzhanishvili Theatre before dying at the hands of the Soviet police at the age of 30. Also giving preference to massive forms, his designs were nevertheless extraordinarily fine and precise in detail – tall curved staircases, unusually shaped armchairs, solitary trees with drooping branches or yellow flowers against backgrounds of grey and white.

Among his major designs were Dadiani's *Right in the Heart* (1928), Shelly's *The Cenci* (1930) and Dadiani's *The Unbridgeable Gap* (1935), all at the Mardzhanishvili. In Moscow, he designed Ibsen's *Master Builder* (1931) as well as works by Schiller and Victor Gusev for the Korsh Theatre and the Maly. In 1937 he was awarded a first prize by Stanislavski for his designs for *Rigoletto* and in 1939, he was aweared a posthumous gold medal at the International Exhibition of Stage Design in London.

Through the 1940s and early 1950s, socialist-realism closed down many of the visual experiments by Georgian designers. Artists suffered severe penalties if they veered from accepted norms. Professional humiliations, insults and even persecutions were common under the Stalinist dictatorship. Beyond those already mentioned in this regard, Lado Gudiashvili was another who suffered both professional and personal attacks.

The second generation of designers emerging at this difficult time had the task of trying to preserve the rich traditions of their predecessors while dealing with continuing demands from above. The result was the production of many faceless artistic works on the stage, plays of dull quality presented in dull ways. A few artists finally emerged, however – among them Josef Sumbatashvili (b. 1919) – who helped reopen the gates to visual as well as directorial experiment in Georgia from the 1960s onwards.

Theatre Space and Architecture

Theatre architecture can be traced back to at least the third century BC in Georgia. The remains of an ancient theatre from this period can still be seen in the town of Uplistsikhe (near Tbilisi).

From the modern period, the earliest theatre building put up dates from 1847–51, a 700-seat theatre built in the style of the late Renaissance inside a Caravansaray (a kind of merchant's inn) in central Tbilisi. Designed by architect John Skudri, the theatre and its foyer were designed by Grigori Gagarin (1818–93) in an oriental style. Unfortunately, in 1874 the building was destroyed by fire.

The architect Vladimir Shretter completed the construction of the Tbilisi Opera and Ballet Theatre (today the Paliashvili Opera and Ballet Theatre) in 1886. Although it combined European and Russian theatre construction with boxes and three balconies, the façade was designed in a Moorish style. In 1973, this 1,200-seat theatre caught fire but it was rebuilt retaining all the original architectural details.

The major dramatic theatre in Tbilisi was completed in 1861. In 1921 it was officially named the Shota Rustaveli Theatre. The façade of the theatre is monumental, while inside the hall is spacious with four semicircular balconies and a series of balconies surrounding the proscenium stage. The building was reconstructed in 1949 in a slightly modernized form.

The Public Theatre, built in 1909, has been the home of the Mardzhanishvili State Drama Theatre since 1930. With 800 seats, this basic proscenium house is more functional than architecturally beautiful.

Other traditional theatres exist in the cities of Gori (500 seats, 1939), Zougdidi (600 seats, 1944), Sukhumi (600 seats, 1952), Batumi (a 700-seat oval, 1953), and Kutaisi (a 1,200-seat oval, 1955).

A more modern 1,000-seat theatre with an enormous foyer, a pool and a winter garden exists in Telavi. In 1977, a Russian Theatre (the Griboedov Theatre) was built in Tbilisi. With 1,200 seats, it has a two-storey marble foyer with a balcony and side boxes.

Training

The Rustaveli Theatrical Institute, the republic's only training institution, was founded in Tbilisi in 1923. In its earliest days, it built on the Theatre Studio of Akaki Pagava and Pagava served as its first head. Among those subsequently running the school have been the great director Mardzhanishvili and Sandro Akhmeteli. Among its many outstanding teachers, five have been elected to the Georgian Academy of Science.

Starting out simply as an actor training institution, it later added in programmes for directors, theatre historians and theatre critics as well. In the mid-1960s, a musical-comedy programme was started and during the late 1960s puppetry and mime programmes were also introduced. Also in the late 1960s, the directing programme was expanded to include not only stage directing but also television and film directing, directing for puppet theatre and even directing for dance. Today, playwrights, camera operators and film critics also are trained at the institute. Most of the programmes run four years with a few as long as five.

For many years, classes were held under the auspices of Tbilisi's two major theatre troupes, the Rustaveli and the Mardzhanishvili. In 1939, however, all classes were centred at the institute and recognized at the secondary level. Taking over as rector at that time was the acclaimed People's Actor Akaki Khorava.

One unusual type of training at the institute is the special courses offered to cultural animators, people who will find careers in cultural organizations, cultural centres and amateur groups.

Because minority language theatre companies also exist within Georgia, training is offered as well in both Russian and Armenian. Until 1989, the institute also offered training for artists from other republics in the USSR such as Turkmenistan.

The school has managed to build over the years a style of performance and directorial study that is recognizably Georgian but which is clearly based on the ideas of many Russian

Mikhail Tumanishvili's 1975 Georgian Theatrical Institute production of Fadaev's *On Behalf of the Young Army.*

masters, including, Stanislavski, Nemirovich-Danchenko, Meyerhold and Vakhtangov. Students also study closely the Georgian models created by Mardzhanishvili and Akhmeteli. From time to time, the institute has also experimented with combining actors' and directors' programmes and though this has generally worked well it is still not a regular part of the programme.

In 1992, programmes in stage design and playwriting were added.

In 1993, the school was renamed the Georgian State Institute of Theatre and Cinema.

Criticism, Scholarship and Publishing

Georgia has a long tradition of theatrical criticism and particularly the collection of theatrical information and memorabilia. The first to begin collecting such material was King Archil II (1647–1713). Others, including the writer Sulkan Saba Orbeliani and King Teimuraz II, maintained the tradition. The state continues to have large holdings of theatrical materials because of this early interest.

The earliest criticism dates from the mid-eighteenth century when a number of established writers turned to theatre as a subject for critical analysis. Mikhail Tumanishvili (1818–85) was the first of many professional theatre critics in Georgia. Included in this list are many public figures who wrote on theatre over the years.

Since the 1920s, criticism, history and theory have been one of the major professional departments at the Georgian State Institute of Theatre and Cinema. In addition to training, the institute also publishes its own books and historical studies on both theatre and film.

One of the major critics of the century in Georgia was Dimitri Djanelidze (b. 1904) who established norms in the field, did research and wrote about contemporary productions. He also wrote several seminal studies on Georgian theatre including *The Folk Origins of the Georgian Theatre* (1948) and *The History of the Georgian Theatre* (1965).

Other critics of note included Sergei Amaglobeli (1899–1937), Beso Zhgenti, Grigor Bukhnikashvili (1897–1971) and Shalva Abbehaili (1894–1968).

Among the major critics writing since World War II are Nadezhda Shaloutashvili (b. 1918), Natela Urushadze (b. 1923), Eteri Gougoushvili (b. 1925), Vasil Kiknadze (b. 1929), Nodar Gurabanidze (b. 1929), Nino Svangiradze (b. 1918) and Aleko Shaloutashvili (b. 1929).

In general, critics are a part of the theatrical process. That is, they traditionally attend a preopening performance (a dress rehearsal or a preview). Discussions take place, often with some of those involved in the production, and usually within a week or so of the opening reviews begin to appear in the local newspapers. Magazine and journal reviews appear weeks or even months later. In recent years, television and radio reviews have also been done.

Specialized publications go back to the nineteenth century when a daily newspaper began to appear called *Theatre*. It was published in Tbilisi from 1885 to 1891. In the period just prior to and just after World War I, *Theatre and Life* appeared daily in the capital while *Theatre and Cinema* has been appearing daily since 1992.

Among the key theatre magazines and journals are *Khelovnebis Drosha* (*The Arts*), a monthly founded in 1924, and *Khelovneba* (*Art*), founded in 1927 as *Soviet Art* and renamed in 1989.

Khelovneba is also the name of one of the country's leading theatre book publishers; another of importance is Teatraluri sazogadoebis gamomtzemloba (Theatre Society Publishers).

Eteri Gougoushvili

(See also USSR)

Further Reading

Aleksidze, Dimitri. *Msakhiobis aghsrdis sakitkhisatvis.* [Training an actor]. Tbilisi: Literatura da Khelovneba, 1956. 204 pp.

——. *Rejisoris mushaoba spektakles.* [The director's work on performance]. Tbilisi: Literatura da Khelovneba, 1961. 261 pp.

Djanelidze, Dimitri. *Kartuli teatris istoria udzvelesi droidan XVIII saukunemde.* [History of Georgian Theatre]. Tbilisi: Literatura da Khelovneba, 1965. 603 pp.

——. *Rustaveli da sakhioba.* [Rustaveli and theatre essays]. Tbilisi: Literatura da Khelovneba, 1958. 302 pp.

——. *Sakhioba.* [Theatre essays]. Tbilisi: Literatura da Khelovneba, 1968. 227 pp.

Gogolašvili, Margarita. *Meskhetis teatris.* [The Meshketi Theatre]. Tbilisi: Sakartvelos teatraluri sazogadoeba, 1976. 91 pp.

Gougoushvili, Eteri. *Budni i prazkniki teatra.* [Working days and holidays of the theatre]. Tbilisi: Literatura da Khelovneba, 1971. 254 pp.

——. *Kote Mardzhanishvili.* Tbilisi: Sakartvelos teatraluri sazogadoeba, 1972. 545 pp.

——. *Simartlis gsit.* [On the road of truth]. Tbilisi: Sakartvelos teatraluri sazogadoeba, 1985. 292 pp.

Gurabanidze, Nobar. *Gamarjvebis gzit.* [On the road to victory]. Tbilisi: Literatura da Khelovneba, 1984. 303 pp.

——. *Mravalsakheoba teatrisa.* [The diversity of the theatre]. Tbilisi: Literatura da Khelovneba, 1972. 407 pp.

——. *Rejisori, msakhiobi, scena.* [The director, the actor, the stage]. Tbilisi: Literatura da Khelovneba, 1968. 363 pp.

Ioseliani, Djaba. *The Comic and Georgian Mask Comedy.* Tbilisi: Ganatleba, 1982. 206 pp.

Kalandarishvili, Mikhail. *Problemi rejisuri Sandro Akhmeteli.* [Sandro Akhmeteli: staging problems]. Tbilisi: Literatura da Khelovneba, 1986. 126 pp.

Kiknadze, Vasil. *David Kidiashvili's teatri.* [David Kidiashvili's theatre]. Tbilisi: Literatura da Khelovneba, 1973. 205 pp.

——. *Kartuli rejisoris istorii narkvevebi.* [Essays on the history of Georgian stage direction]. Tbilisi: Sakartvelos teatraluri sazogadoeba, 1982. 477 pp.

——. *Sandro Akhmeteli.* Tbilisi: Literatura da Khelovneba, 1977. 431 pp.

Mrevlishvili, Maliko. *Kartuli sastseno metkvelebis phonetikuri gapudzvlebi.* [Basic phonetic principles of Georgian stage speech]. Tbilisi: Ganatleba, 1966. 153 pp.

Nikolaishvili, Barbale. *Kartuli sastseno metkveleba.* [Georgian artistic speech]. Tbilisi: Ganatleba, 1979. 378 pp.

——. *Mkhatvruli kithvis khelovneba.* [The basic principles of artistic speech]. Tbilisi: Literatura da Khelovneba, 1971. 194 pp.

Shaloutashvili, Nadezhda. *Grusinsko–ukrainskie teatralnie sviazi.* [Georgian–Ukrainian theatrical relationships]. Tbilisi: Literatura da Khelovneba, 1984. 281 pp.

——. *Mogobrobis gzebit*. [On the road of friendship]. Tbilisi: Sakartvelos teatraluri sazogadoeba, 1978. 379 pp.

——. *Ostrovsky kartul szenaze*. [Ostrovsky's plays on the Georgian stage]. Tbilisi: 1958. 208 pp.

Shvangiradze, Nino. *Tamar Chavchavadze*. Tbilisi: Literatura da Khelovneba, 1973. 470 pp.

——. *Teatraluri etiudebi*. [Theatrical essays]. Tbilisi: Literatura da Khelovneba, 1964. 197 pp.

Tumanishvili, Mikhail. *Osndm repetitsia daitzskeba*. [Until the rehearsal has begun]. Tbilisi: Sakartvelos teatraluri sazogadoeba, 1977. 283 pp.

——. *Rejisori midis teatridan*. [The director braves the theatre]. Tbilisi: Sakartvelos teatraluri sazogadoeba, 1980. 263 pp.

Urushadze, Natela. *Msakhiobis Khelovneba*. [The actor's art]. Tbilisi: Literatura da Khelovneba, 1957. 248 pp.

GERMAN DEMOCRATIC REPUBLIC

(see **GERMANY**)

GERMANY

German theatre has always been, and still is, grounded in and guided by theory and cultural political objectives. For over two hundred years the guiding idea has been one of a national theatre. In Germany a national theatre means not only an institution, but also an intellectual concept, originally in opposition to the political and cultural fragmentation of the small feudal principalities. Out of these efforts on behalf of a national theatre there evolved many of the factors that continue to influence German theatre and its concepts even today.

In the last third of the eighteenth century, the German bourgeoisie began to see theatre as a medium for the expression of its self-assurance and political emancipation, a public forum for the articulation of its thoughts, feelings and advocacy of the ideals of the Enlightenment. Theatre was supposed to help prepare an intellectual ground for national unity beyond the frontiers of the many sovereign principalities. 'National' in this sense was not conceived of as 'nationalistic'; the dramatic repertoire included classics of world drama from every age, although plays that fit in with bourgeois German customs and beliefs were preferred and this did not stand in the way of a European universalism. At the same time, though, popular and more critical forms of theatre – including those developing from the traditions of the English–German strolling players and *commedia dell'arte* – were relegated to the background and even prohibited. The only surviving traces of these forms were kept alive in Viennese folk theatre and in puppet theatre.

The national theatre of the German bourgeoisie was to be a state-supported institution with a social mission and was to be funded

340

accordingly. But as it could not come into being without the aid of the minor princes, the most important of the newly established theatres (in Mannheim, Vienna and Weimar) were also court theatres. The Prussian constitution of 1808 had already designated theatres as 'national educational institutions' classed alongside museums and universities, though they were not put under the auspices of a minister of culture but rather remained 'commercial' enterprises entrusted to a minister of trade or even a chief of police.

The revolution of 1848–9 further reactivated the ideas of a cultural nation-state and established political advocacy for a national theatre but also without result. Hopes became pinned more and more on individual cities that had, by the turn of the century, attained a high degree of cultural self-confidence backed by both economic and political power. It was only with the change from empire to republic in 1918–19, however, that the conversion of court theatres into state or (in some cases) municipal theatres took place.

This trend was seen at the time as a movement from a 'commercial' to an 'arts' theatre and was accompanied by theatres and audiences taking matters into their own hands. The Deutsches Theater (German Theatre) in Berlin, as one example, was founded by actors in 1883 as an artist-run theatre and was the first in which the idea of a national theatre came close to being realized. Seven years later the Verein der Freien Volksbühne (Popular Stage Society) was formed in Berlin and, growing out of the tradition of workers' educational societies, was the first major cultural institution for workers and the lower-middle class. The Freie Volksbühne rapidly developed into a powerful supra-regional movement and is still the largest audience organization in western Germany today.

The German national theatre movement, however, was not content with a single representative theatre centre. Its goal had always been a comprehensive network of publicly subsidized theatres with a national cultural mission. It is a sad irony that the long-hoped-for and much discussed Reichstheatergesetz (State Law on Theatres), which was to have consolidated the German public theatres, was in the end enacted by the Nazis in 1934. State subsidy after this time was *dirigisme* in the extreme and the Reichstheaterkammer (State Theatre Centre) simply a means of political surveillance. A lack of familiarity with the idealistic republican roots of the national theatre concept led western

occupation forces at the end of World War II to try and introduce an entirely different system.

The German theatre itself had already succumbed to the pressures of war in September 1944. By 1945, Hitler's Greater German Reich lay in ruins, several regions of the old 1937 borders were severed off, and the rest of Germany was partitioned into American, British and French occupation zones in the west, and a Soviet occupation zone in the east. Dependent on the two power blocs, East and West Germany rapidly grew apart politically, to the point where two separate German states were established in 1949. The Federal Republic of Germany (FRG) was created in a 248,000 square kilometre (95,700 square mile) area of the western occupation zones, the German Democratic Republic (GDR) in a 108,000 square kilometre (41,700 square mile) area of the Soviet zone. Although Germany was reunited in October 1990, and the 61 million inhabitants of the former FRG and the 17 million inhabitants of the former GDR are once again living under a single social and political system, theatrical conditions were so different between east and west during this long period that the two traditions need to be discussed separately here.

Theatre in the West Zone/FRG

Most German theatres were destroyed or damaged in the war and acting companies dispersed. For the public, however, few things seemed more urgent than being able to go to the theatre again. Theatres and makeshift stages reopened almost immediately and enjoyed tremendous popularity despite primitive conditions and the considerable distances that had to be travelled on foot.

At first the cultural policies of the occupation powers favoured the establishment of commercial theatres in order to prevent the reappearance of a centralized publicly funded system, as in the days of the Nazis. Otherwise, theatre was regarded as an important tool for 're-education', and used as such through control of the repertoire among other things. 'Suitable' dramatic material was established through a list of approved plays and a programme of translation. Yet the re-educative zeal of the Theatre Section of the US Information Control Division was perhaps debatable, since half of all the American plays the US military government made available to the Germans were light comedies, farces and thrillers. This light entertainment was not going to do much to reinstil the virtues of democracy. Concentration on an anti-communist policy in any case replaced anti-fascist re-education programmes by the end of 1947.

Allied control commissions issued licences to reopen theatres after checking each applicant's political past; nevertheless official appointments of new artistic directors were already being made by German civic and state authorities from 1946 on. In this way, the subsidized public theatre model prevailed again, reinforced by federalist pressures and exacerbated by the partition of the country into zones. Early on, these theatres functioned without the financial security of group sales. Nevertheless, acting companies rapidly sprang up, and three important directors returned to leading positions. Karl Heinz Martin (1888–1948), one-time artistic director (1929–32) of the Berliner Volksbühne, took over the Hebbel Theater, by then the leading theatre in West Berlin; Heinz Hilpert (1890–1967), one-time artistic director of the former Reinhardt-Bühnen in Berlin (Deutsches

Jürgen Fehling's 1949 Bayrisches Staatsschauspiel München production of Friedrich Hebbel's *Maria Magdalene*, designed by Wolfgang Znamenacek. Photo: Rudolf Betz.

Theater), was for a short time artistic director in Frankfurt am Main before going on to found a Deutsches Theater in Constanz and later in Göttingen; and Gustaf Gründgens (1899–1963), artistic director of the Berliner Staatstheater (Berlin State Theatre) since 1934, became the artistic director of the Städtische Bühnen Düsseldorf (Düsseldorf Civic Playhouse) from 1947 to 1951. The last two actually preferred to work in the 'provinces' instead of Berlin, even though they had themselves helped make Berlin into a national theatre capital. Artistic continuity was also assured with the return to the theatre of such well-known directors as Jürgen Fehling (1885–1968; last production, 1952) and Hans Schweikart (1895–1975). Among the younger generation who had just begun to make a name for themselves, Karlheinz Stroux (1908–85), Hans Schalla (1904–83), Gustav Rudolf Sellner (1905–90), Harry Buckwitz (1904–87), Boleslav Barlog (b. 1906) and Günther Rennert (1911–78) now got their chance as directors and soon as artistic directors.

The repertoire of Berlin's Hebbel Theater reflected efforts to examine the recent past. Even during its first post-war season, it featured several anti-fascist plays written in exile, the most successful of which, both in the east and the west, was *Professor Mamlock* by Friedrich Wolf (1888–1953). Performed along with it were works dealing with the fight against the Nazis by Georg Kaiser (1878–1945), Franz Werfel (1890–1945) and Bertolt Brecht (1898–1956). Through these authors, artistic director Martin also established a link with the political theatre tradition of the Weimar Republic. The Hebbel Theater's dramaturge, Günther Weisenborn (1902–69), drew on his own experience to portray the resistance movement in his 1945 *Die Illegalen* (*Outside the Law*), written during his Nazi imprisonment.

The most effective model for the development of a contemporary repertoire turned out to be the Zürcher Schauspielhaus (Zürich Playhouse). Since 1933 it had been the most important German-speaking theatre outside the Nazi sphere of power. It had been a haven for many exiled actors, directors and writers, and it was where most of the new plays, which were to dominate the West German stage till well into the 1950s, were first performed: plays of the French, British and American avant-garde (Giraudoux, Sartre, Eliot, Wilder and O'Neill), the German exile drama (Brecht, Zuckmayer and Kaiser), and modern Swiss authors, Max Frisch and Friedrich Dürrenmatt.

Successes in western Germany of plays that had been banned as ideologically unacceptable in the Soviet zone signalled the political polarization between east and west. Typical examples included Thornton Wilder's *The Skin of Our Teeth*, which was seen by almost half a million people in the western zone between 1946 and 1948, not least thanks to its catchy German title, *Wir sind noch einmal davon gekommen* (*Made it Again!*); Jean-Paul Sartre's prototypical existentialist play, *Les Mouches* (*The Flies*, 1943), whose January 1948 Berlin première became a controversial political issue following a public debate with the author; and *Des Teufels General* (*The Devil's General*) by Carl Zuckmayer (1896–1977), the most frequently produced play of the post-war theatre in the western zones. All three had received their German-language premières at the Zürcher Schauspielhaus. Conversely, Konstantin Simonov's *Die russische Frage* (*The Russian Question*), which took a critical look at the United States, was banned in the western zones after its première in May 1947 at the Deutsches Theater in East Berlin. The Cold War had broken out on stage.

The 20 June 1948 currency reform in the western zones even more formally ushered in the division of Germany into two separate states. In many places, it was a decisive moment for the theatre as well. Because West German citizens suddenly found themselves with no more than 40 marks in new currency (not even a week's wages), many people could no longer attend the theatre and attendance dropped by an average of 60 per cent. This spelled the end for most commercial theatres.

The 1950s was a time of reconstruction for the theatre. A building boom began in 1951 which lasted until 1966. In addition to the forty-five surviving theatres that required only partial restoration, twenty were entirely rebuilt. As well, fifty-four new theatres were built along with as many new touring houses in cities without resident companies. Audience demand was, however, overestimated. While attendance had grown to 20 million per season in 1956, the theatres now built were simply too big.

Extremely long artistic directorship appointments brought stability to the operations in Bochum, Stuttgart, West Berlin, Düsseldorf, Frankfurt am Main, Munich (Kammerspiele – Studio Theatre) and Göttingen. A number of theatre festivals were also founded.

Recklinghausen's Ruhr Festival, in the middle of the coal-mining district, seemed to be living proof of a developing relationship between workers and culture. It began in 1947. In 1951 it was decided to build a colossal festival theatre which, however, opened only in 1965. In 1951 the Richard Wagner Festspiele (the Bayreuth Festival) reopened with radically new ideas, and the same year saw the foundation of the Bad Hersfeld Summer Festival in Hessen near the GDR border and the Berliner Festwochen (Berlin Festival), both cultural-political 'showcases' aimed at the east.

The West German theatre of the 1950s can in retrospect be characterized as conservative, conditioned by the conventions of a society in the process of re-establishing itself, a society making necessary daily compromises. The artists and their essentially bourgeois public were in agreement for the most part. The only peripheral disturbances and innovations came from the three great returned exiles, Bertolt Brecht, Fritz Kortner (1892–1970) and Erwin Piscator (1893–1966), already prominent as pioneers of a politically committed and artistically revolutionary theatre prior to 1933. Their return to the German theatre, repeatedly put off and greeted with hostility, was not to show a lasting effect until quite late. Brecht's productions at the Berliner Ensemble influenced theatre methods in the west, although it was only after his death that performances of his plays increased in the FRG. With only a few early exceptions, West German boycotts of his plays in 1953 (due to suppression of the East German workers' uprising), in 1956 (over the invasion of Hungary) and in 1961 (over the building of the Berlin Wall) did little to hinder the growing Brecht-boom.

For his part, Kortner, long famous as an actor in the expressionist theatre, spent two futile years trying to act again before beginning a new career in 1949 as a director in Munich and Berlin. His December 1950 production of Schiller's *Don Carlos* at the Hebbel Theater created the first major scandal of the post-war West German theatre, and his career continued to be dogged by controversy thereafter. All the same, and almost unnoticed, he became the teacher and model for the next generation of theatre professionals. Piscator, who did not return from exile until 1951, was for a decade limited to relatively insignificant work, primarily in the provinces, before he was appointed artistic director of the Berliner Freie Volksbühne in 1962, where he managed a spectacular revival of his political documentary theatre, ushering in a new theatrical epoch in West Germany.

Until that time, the West German theatre of the 1950s demonstrated little social and political engagement. Still, there was a general sense of something missing: where was the new German drama? There were no plays dealing with the new realities of the FRG. The depiction of German society in the few new plays was unfocused and abstract. Symbolic dramas and imported Theatre of the Absurd dominated the repertoire.

At most, the university theatres constituted a sort of *Sezession*. Deliberately distancing themselves from the publicly owned professional theatres, the university theatres were primarily intended as homes for new writing. Another kind of *Sezession* was the 'experimental' theatre which developed as an offshoot of the state and municipal theatres themselves and was a form of alternative theatre in new studio and workshop venues that had been opening in rapid succession since 1957.

About 1962 – even before the general politicization of culture by the student protest movement – change occurred in practically all aspects of West German theatre. This could be detected in the emergence of at least four new phenomena. The first was the emergence of a pronounced *Regie-Theater* (directors' theatre), especially by Peter Zadek (b. 1926) in his production of Brendan Behan's *The Hostage* in Ulm as early as 1961. During the artistic directorship of Kurt Hübner (b. 1916), Zadek left his mark on the work of the Bremen Schauspiel (Bremen Playhouse), which gained national prominence for what became known as the *Bremer Stil* (Bremen style, 1962–73). In 1964 the Berliner Theatertreffen (Berlin Theatre Encounter) came into being primarily as a directors' festival to which major productions were invited annually. A new generation of German directors soon became noticeable including, from the mid-1960s, those who were reworking the classics and others who were rediscovering bourgeois realism.

Second, and even more noticeable, was the unexpected emergence of German authors with message-plays that fulfilled the hopes for a contemporary German drama which could attract attention abroad. The 1961–2 success of two Swiss dramatists – Max Frisch with *Andorra* and Friedrich Dürrenmatt with *Die Physiker* (*The Physicists*) – already heralded the trend, although they still used traditional forms, the parable and the grotesque. Further analysis of contemporary issues was brought to life in timely plays by Martin Walser (b. 1927), docudramas by Rolf Hochhuth (b. 1931), Heinar Kipphardt (1922–82) and Peter Weiss (1916–82), and in more experimental forms such as Weiss's *Marat/Sade* (1964). This new political theatre was triggered – as it had been previously in the Weimar Republic – by Erwin Piscator and was developed and continued by Peter Palitzsch (b. 1918), who left the Berliner Ensemble in 1961 to come to the west where he spread the principles of Brechtian political theatre, and by Hansgünther Heyme (b. 1935), a pupil of Piscator's.

In 1966 a third new phenomenon became apparent, the idea of a Volkstheater, a theatre for the people. The rediscovery and enthusiastic reception of the works of dramatists of the interwar years such as Ödön von Horváth (1901–38) and Marieluise Fleisser (1901–74) prepared the way for it, and authors such as Martin Sperr (b. 1944), Rainer Werner Fassbinder (1946–82) and Franz Xaver Kroetz (b. 1946) put it into practice.

Fourth, and lastly, it became clear that the values of the 'old' theatre were now to be questioned: this occurred in the First Frankfurt 'Experimenta' in 1966, an avant-garde theatre festival where Peter Handke's (b. 1942) *Publikumsbeschimpfung* (*Offending the Audience*) received its première. Handke's *Sprechstücke* (speaking plays) and Fassbinder's anti-theatre were the extreme forms of expression for a new media-consciousness that was having its heyday in happenings at the time. It was retroactively supplied with a theoretical background in 1969 with the German publication of the theatrical writings of Antonin Artaud, Peter Brook and Jerzy Grotowski.

The theatre was deeply affected by the student movement of 1968. This was a time of extraparliamentary opposition and was analogous to the May Revolution in Paris. The new cultural revolution was no longer aimed simply at the theatre's traditional aesthetic and function, but also against the very institution itself, its fossilization and its 'authoritarian' spirit, leading to demands for a radical structural reform and worker-participation in all areas and on all levels. 'Democratization', meaning the participation of actors, dramaturges and other theatre professionals in the decision-making process, became the model for several theatres from 1969–70 on.

The student movement brought few lasting changes to the theatre, but it did promote the idea of theatre 'collectives' and created a new awareness of theatre's potential for social effect. The populist ideal was not only a genre but also a general production principle. For a short time it even led to the revival of agitprop and street theatre and its non-political counterpart, the active participation of the audience. Two productions by Peter Stein (b. 1937) served as examples of the ambivalent relationship between politics and art at the end of the 1960s: his 1968 production of Weiss's *Vietnam-Diskurs* (*Vietnam Discourse*) in Munich and his 1969 production of Goethe's *Tasso* in Bremen. In the first they were mutually incompatible and failed on both fronts; in the second they were shown to be capable of a synthesis that established the early fame of the director and his young company.

The circle of actors around Stein from 1970 on formed the nucleus of the Berlin Schaubühne am Halleschen Ufer (Playhouse on the Halleschen Ufer) founded in 1962 and renamed when it moved to the Lehniner Platz in 1981. The most important theatre in West Germany in the 1970s and early 1980s, it combined the artistic excellence of a highly subsidized private theatre with many of the structural features of a politically motivated independent company – a paradoxical model of how productively the spirit of 1968 could be united with tradition.

But the protest movement also spawned a theatre counter-culture that created new forms out of these new methods, explored other performance venues, made use of topical material, and above all appealed to a specific public: political groups, labour unions, citizens' groups, apprentices, school children, university students, suburban residents and immigrants. This new target-group theatre derived substantial inspiration from research into the theatre of the Weimar Republic and the Russian Revolution, while the actual impetus came from guest tours of the Living Theatre, the Bread and Puppet Theatre and various other New York Off-Off-Broadway companies at the end of the 1960s. In the FRG, independent theatre companies, mostly started by university students and graduates of theatre schools, focused on local issues. They did not form a coherent organization, although they were united in their rejection of the traditional division of labour and in their adaptation of techniques borrowed from the circus, revue theatre, *commedia dell'arte* and cabaret. Most were also attempting to create a more physical theatre with an emphasis on corporal mime. At the end of the 1970s they were more or less lost in the wake of international clown power and the so-called 'fool' movements.

This wide spectrum of styles was typical of the *Freie Szene* (alternate theatre scene) at the time and of the semi-professional fringe. Today its centres are primarily in Berlin, Hamburg (Kampnagel-Fabrik/Kampnagel Factory venues), Frankfurt and Munich, but it has also established itself in the provinces. One of its last major political manifestations was involvement in the peace movement during 1983–4, in conjunction with many public theatres. Its most lasting achievement was probably its interest in creating a modern children's and youth theatre relevant to the times.

One consequence of the dominance of public theatres in Germany is that alternative theatre movements are almost always immediately coopted by them. State and municipal theatres also produced an alternative theatre of their own, as, for example, in companies formed around directors with distinctive techniques, such as George Tabori (b. 1914), Peter Löscher (b. 1938) and Roberto Ciulli (b. 1934), which frequently became the basis for newer independent theatres. More importantly, *Sezessionen* of this type in the 1970s looked for alternate performance spaces as a reaction against the conventional fourth-wall prosceniums of the newly built theatres with their monumental anonymity and sterility. Backstage areas (rehearsal stages and scene shops, for example) were often themselves turned into alternative stages, or there was a temporary move – in a virtual wave of trendy protest – out of concrete fortresses into barns, closed-down film studios, exhibition halls, factories and even slaughterhouses. The Berliner Schaubühne, which changed its performance area with each production, was a model in this regard.

The position of the public theatre was qualified further by a drop in attendance beginning in the mid-1960s which it was unable to recoup. The audience for music theatre decreased by about 1 million and for plays by about 2 million. From 1971 on theatres suffered repeated financial crises that threatened their very being, especially with austerity measures beginning in 1982. Turning to new forms of audience development and increased public relations, theatres became more open about their operations, took new interest in young audiences, sponsored public discussions and theatre 'events', went out into the streets and justified their existence by emphasizing local connections. Internally, they responded to their organizational problems and identity crises with increased dramaturgical staff. The idea of a locally based theatre was somehow vitiated, however, by frequent changes in artistic directorships. In 1972, 1979 and 1985 it grew into a veritable merry-go-round for artistic directors which in turn meant a total change not only of management but of practically all the acting companies as well.

West German drama itself began to bloom in the 1970s. A host of new playwrights took their places alongside already well-known ones, though the theatres did not always exhaust the rich fund of topical plays. At the high point of this development came the founding of the highly regarded Mülheimer Theatertage (Mülheim Play Festival) in 1976 and its well-endowed annual playwright's award.

Artistically, from 1975 on, West German theatre was further stimulated through the increased reception of East German plays – Heiner Müller (b. 1929), Volker Braun (b. 1939), Stefan Schütz (1944), Christoph Hein (1944) – and an influx of writers, directors and finally actors from the GDR. Their ideas of style injected new life into a tired directors' theatre.

New changes began again in the late 1970s when the FRG was shaken by terrorism (1977) and plunged into hysteria. From then on, West German theatre began to show definite signs of a de-politicization which – coinciding with a simultaneous revival of interest in history but also a turning away from the ideals of the Enlightenment – resulted in a rediscovery of the psyche and the irrational, and a narrowing focus on national, even regional, nostalgia which found its expression in, among other things, a revival of annual regional festivals.

Theatre in the Soviet Zone/GDR

Directly after the war a large number of theatre companies got together in the Soviet occupied zone which included an as yet undivided Berlin. They had the support of the Soviet military administration; eight days after the capitulation (8 May 1945) it was already under orders to issue permits. Many of the Soviet officers put in charge of the arts had come out of a tradition of respect for German culture and saw it as an effective means of anti-fascist re-education. Although all productions had to have the approval of the occupation authorities, there were, in the beginning, no restrictions on the

repertoire or on the choice of actors or artistic directors. Prominent actors received extra rations and other privileges. The first post-war performance in Berlin took place on 27 May 1945, significantly, a classic German farce, *Der Raub der Sabinierinnen* (*The Rape of the Sabines*).

The first impetus for an intellectual and artistic revival came from the few anti-fascist artists who had survived the Hitler years in Germany, such as actor Ernst Busch (1900–80), playwright Günther Weisenborn and director Fritz Wisten (1890–1962), who had been senior director of the Theater des Jüdischen Kulturbundes (Jewish Cultural Association Play Society) in Berlin from 1936 to 1941. It also came from returning communist exiles, among them playwright Friedrich Wolf, actor and director Gustav von Wangenheim (1895–1975) and journalist Fritz Erpenbeck (1897–1975).

The first production of the initial post-war season with a message behind it was Lessing's *Nathan der Weise* (*Nathan the Wise*), directed by Fritz Wisten at the Deutsches Theater (artistic director: Gustav von Wangenheim), followed shortly by the Hebbel Theater's German première of Friedrich Wolf's anti-fascist *Professor Mamlock*, written in 1934. Both were repeatedly performed, heralding the beginning of an anti-fascist, democratically oriented theatre.

Simultaneously, theatre began to respond to the need for an intellectual renewal and a re-establishment of links with the outside world that had been cut off by the Nazis. Thus international classics and twentieth-century works, French, American and above all Russian (Chekhov, Gorki and Svarts), also found their way into the repertoire. From 1947 on, however, modern western European and American drama began to be replaced by contemporary Soviet plays. Even contemporary West German drama became subject to ideological approval. Thus attempts by Erich Ponto (1884–1957), the first post-war artistic director of the Dresdner Staatsschauspiel (Dresden State Playhouse), to mount a production of Zuckmayer's *Des Teufels General* ended with his dismissal, and Wolfgang Borchert's (1921–47) anti-war play, *Draußen vor der Tür* (*Waiting on our Doorstep*), which had thirty-six productions in West Germany by 1949, had to wait many years before making its way on to an East German stage. Plays by Friedrich Wolf and Günther Weisenborn, together with Soviet propaganda plays and plays about the Russian

Helene Weigel and Bertolt Brecht rehearsing his and Erich Engel's 1951 Berliner Ensemble production of Brecht's *Mother Courage*, designed by Teo Otto and Heinrich Kilger. Photo: Heiner Hill.

Revolution, were, however, officially sponsored, and soon formed the core of the contemporary repertoire.

In contrast to the regional nature of theatre in the western zones, a centralized theatre, dominated by Berlin, was soon established in the east zone. Prominent exiles and their comrades-in-arms from the pre-1933 period began to fill key positions: Wolfgang Langhoff (1901–66) took over the Deutsches Theater in 1946, hiring as his chief dramaturge one of the most renowned drama critics of the Weimar Republic, Herbert Jhering (1888–1977); in 1949, Bertolt Brecht and Helene Weigel (1900–71), together with director Erich Engel (1891–1966), founded the Berliner Ensemble. In 1954, Fritz Wisten, director of the Theater am Schiffbauerdamm (Schiffbauerdamm Theatre) since 1946, moved his company to the newly rebuilt Volksbühne on Luxemburgplatz. They were all united in the fundamental conception that it was the theatre's job to make a contribution to world peace, democratic renewal and social justice, regardless of what theatrical tradition its members came from or what artistic theories they held. In this sense they identified themselves with the fundamental aims of the GDR when it was founded in 1949, and were prepared to contribute their talents to building its intellectual and cultural foundations.

Conditions – at least at the beginning – were favourable. Theatre, like culture in general, was regarded and valued as an integral part of society, helping to construct a new social system. To achieve this end, most accepted significant restrictions on personal freedom, restrictions which ultimately limited the theatre's field of action to the demands, concepts and norms of a particular political ideology. On the other hand, this position forced artists to take theatrical concepts and turn them into social concepts; that is, to develop forms of art which could have a genuine effect on society.

Out of this there evolved a notion of theatre, on the part of both the audience and the theatre community itself, which could include all genres, and in which the 'realistic music theatre' of Walter Felsenstein (1901–75) had as respected a place as children's and youth theatre, or puppet plays. Derived from German Enlightenment ideas of a national theatre, this notion led to the creation of complex infrastructures – the development of ensembles and a state-organized system of theatre training.

At the same time, the theatre as a whole lost much. The tendency towards centralized and GDR-specific theatre prevented the adoption of alternative forms of theatre developed in western Europe and the United States after the war. The few innovative attempts to parallel developments on the international scene were either broken off or reduced to a kind of parochialism, and artists who resisted found themselves unable to work.

Thus, in the first half of the 1950s theatre in the GDR had already begun a confrontation between representatives of Stalinist cultural policies with their aesthetic of socialist-realism, and artists who wanted to link the beginning of a new socio-political structure to an openness to modern European artistic developments. The quarrels between the bourgeois-humanist theatre tradition, revived after 1945 and reinforced by the ideals of the Stanislavski system, and the revolutionary avant-garde tradition of theatre, primarily represented by Brecht's theory and practice, did enormous damage to the development of East German theatre with its counter-productive confrontations and ideologizing of the two most important approaches to theatre developed in Europe in the twentieth century. For decades, its repercussions hampered East German theatre from making use of the wider German tradition of modern art (the Bauhaus, for example) or even contemporary developments in European art.

Despite the accompanying loss of creative talents who were either prevented from working, stopped working or left the country – such as the head dramaturge of the Deutsches Theater, Heinar Kipphardt, and Brecht pupil Egon Monk (b. 1927) – people in the theatre managed to overcome this unproductive and politically orchestrated quarrel through practical, creative work, thereby strengthening their own self-image. A not-insignificant contributing factor was the effect of Brecht's work in Europe after his death, as well as the achievements of the Berliner Ensemble as seen, for example, in its productions of Brecht plays such as *Leben des Galilei* (*Galileo*) under the direction of Erich Engel, and *Der aufhaltsame Aufstieg des Arturo Ui* (*The Resistible Rise of Arturo Ui*) under the direction of Manfred Wekwerth (b. 1929) and Peter Palitzsch (b. 1918). Within the GDR, the Brechtian concept of theatre became the generally obligatory form of theatre, though again with a doctrinaire narrowness that disregarded its international dimension. Outside the GDR, East German theatre was, in fact, Brechtian theatre, and inside the country itself the adoption of Brechtian concepts remained within the confines of an ideological parochialism.

At the beginning of the 1960s some theatres in the GDR had developed a specific profile. The Deutsches Theater in Berlin gained international recognition by productions of both German classics and Russian realism. Benno Besson (b. 1922), drawing on his experience of working with Brecht and in French theatre, made a substantial contribution to the Stanislavski-oriented German realist acting tradition, shaped primarily by Wolfgang Langhoff. His production of Peter Hacks's (b. 1928) adaptation of Aristophanes' *Peace* (*Der Frieden*) was one of the most successful and influential productions during this period.

The Maxim Gorki Theater, founded in 1952, made an important contribution to the acceptance of both east and west European contemporary drama as well as indigenous drama under the artistic directorship of Maxim Vallentin (1904–87), already well known as the head of communist agitprop theatre groups before 1933.

Elsewhere in the country, a few theatres also made notable attempts to find an identity of their own. The Staatsschauspiel Dresden developed its own *Dresdner Stil* (Dresden style) under the artistic directorship of Hannes Fischer (1925–89), while at the Volkstheater Rostock (Rostock People's Theatre) during the 1960s, artistic director and manager Hanns Anselm Perten (1917–85) mounted important experimental productions of the works of Peter Weiss, Rolf Hochhuth and several Latin American playwrights. In the small mining town of Senftenberg, led by director Horst Schönemann (b. 1927) and dramaturge Armin Stolper (b. 1934), the company tried out new possibilities of making theatre relevant to local workers. Director Fritz Bennewitz's (b. 1926) attempts at Brecht, Shakespeare and modern interpretations of German classics at the Meininger Theater and, from the 1960s on, at the Deutsches Nationaltheater Weimar (German National Theatre of Weimar), were equally noteworthy.

Theatre right across the GDR gained wide public acceptance during these years with an annual audience attendance of nearly 16 million (out of a population of 17 million). After the dissolution of the Volksbühnenverein (National Stage Society) which organized audiences, such developmental work was taken over by the Federation of Labour. These activities brought many people into contact with theatre for the first time. In subsequent years, however, this type of organized theatre attendance lost its significance as a means of developing a productive relationship between the theatre and its audience.

After the building of the Berlin Wall around the western sector of Berlin in 1961 and the accompanying exodus of theatre people to West Berlin, East German theatre began to focus more on social contradictions within the GDR itself. A new generation of playwrights, among them Heiner Müller and Peter Hacks, challenged theatre to take a critical look at the existing social conditions in the country. This came up against solid resistance from the political leadership, and more than one production was banned and reprisals taken against the artists involved. Among other things, Wolfgang Langhoff was forced to step down as artistic director of the Deutsches Theater for his production of Hacks's *Die Sorgen und die Macht* (*Anxieties and Power*). In spite of that, theatres stepped up efforts to engage society in a critical dialogue. Allied to this was the growing power of the *Regietheater* with its enthusiasm for experimentation, especially with classical drama, and attempts to overcome the Stanislavski–Brecht dualism, above all on the part of the younger generation of directors. Thus the 1968 production of Goethe's *Faust*, co-directed by Adolf Dresen (b. 1935) and Wolfgang Heinz (1900–84), became a watershed for future productions of this major German classic, with its unconventional staging and interpretation, questioning Faust's role as an exemplary figure. But it also led to another clash with the authorities, and as a consequence Heinz stepped down as artistic director of the Deutsches Theater.

At the Berliner Ensemble, Manfred Wekwerth was able to tie into the successes of the 1950s with his production of Brecht's version of *Coriolanus*, while the productions of younger directors like Matthias Langhoff (b. 1941), Manfred Karge (b. 1938) and choreographer Ruth Berghaus (b. 1927) established their own claims to an independent and non-doctrinaire application of Brechtian techniques.

Political developments in eastern and western Europe at the end of the 1960s also encouraged forces for social and cultural reform in the GDR. In opposition to official dogma a number of attempts were made to connect theatres to their communities. Among the theatres attempting this was the Landestheater Halle (Halle Provincial Theatre) under the directorship of

Gerhard Wolfram (1922–91) and Horst Schönemann from 1966 to 1972. Despite important artistic achievements and a successful programme of involving the audience from the city's huge industries and academic institutions, however, they were unable to break through official structures. Only in the late 1980s did Peter Sodann (b. 1936) at the Neues Theater Halle (Halle New Theatre) succeed in these efforts.

A similar idea – theatre as urban cultural centre and meeting-place – was attempted by Benno Besson when he took over the artistic directorship of the Volksbühne in Berlin in 1969. After several successful years, however, he was also defeated by the well-fortified state system.

The expatriation of singer-songwriter Wolf Biermann (b. 1936) in 1976 and the protests of a host of well-known artists against such arbitrary measures, was a clear signal of the worsening political conflicts. As a consequence, a number of important developments were broken off. In 1978 Besson left the Volksbühne and from then on directed only abroad. Along with him, Langhoff, Karge and a number of famous actors also left the theatre and the GDR. Berghaus's tenure as artistic director of the Berliner Ensemble had already ended the year before. Together with directors Bernd K. Tragelehn (b. 1936) and Einar Schleef (b. 1944) and playwright Karl Mickel (b. 1935) she had tried to revive this internationally famous company, now threatened by a stylistic hardening of the arteries. Similar attempts, made by Jürgen Gosch (b. 1943) with his production of Büchner's *Leonce and Lena* at the Volksbühne, and by younger directors like Herbert König (b. 1944) and Frank Castorf (b. 1951) at the smaller provincial theatres at the beginning of the 1980s, all ran up against severe criticism from local authorities. It was not until Heiner Müller's productions of *Der Auftrag* (*The Task*) and *Macbeth* (adapted from Shakespeare) at the Volksbühne, that this style of free association and metaphoric theatre won wider public acceptance.

The crisis of theatre structures and the whole theatre system sharpened through the 1970s. Specifically, binding contracts, which were touted as a social achievement, but which, in effect, could not be terminated, prevented the free movement of theatre practitioners as well as economic competition between them. Many directors and choreographers freed themselves from these unproductive conditions by

mounting guest productions both inside and outside the GDR.

Among others, the Verband der Theaterschaffenden (Association of Theatre Artists), founded in 1966 as an independent professional body of artists, made repeated attempts to reform the system right up to the last days of the GDR, but kept running up against fierce resistance from the state. Attempts on the part of both professionals and amateurs to form independent theatre companies also had little success. Only some rock musicians and singer-songwriters such as 'Karls Enkel' (Karl's [Marx] Grandchildren) and groups like 'Pankow' and 'Schicht' (Shift), succeeded in creating a new form of musical theatre.

Of particular significance for the independents was the Zinnober (Vermilion) Company, operating since 1980 and consisting mainly of professional puppeteers. A closed community, it managed to create a space for itself to live out and present alternative lifestyles while making contacts with the traditional working-class and Bohemian district of Berlin. It was no accident that this first independent East German company disbanded after reunification.

The 1980s were marked by a unique personal style of creativity among younger and middle-generation directors that was nevertheless strongly tied to the traditions of German theatre. In Berlin, besides Alexander Lang (b. 1941), who began as an actor with the Deutsches Theater and went on to become one of the country's leading directors, there was the work of Thomas Langhoff (b. 1938), above all in productions of realistic plays (Chekhov, Ibsen and Hauptmann), and Rolf Winkelgrund (b. 1936), whose productions of plays by the South African playwright Athol Fugard and the Polish playwright Tadeusz Różewicz combined the seldom-used techniques of the grotesque with the realist tradition.

In 1974 in Schwerin, a mid-sized city in the middle of a farming region, director Christoph Schroth (b. 1937) and his ensemble embarked on a programme of populist theatre aimed at direct involvement in the issues of the day. With a number of important productions, a few spectacular ones among them, they managed to maintain this focus for fifteen years.

Similar attempts to revive stagnating city theatres with politically committed and artistically innovative productions were made in Senftenberg and later in Weimar by directors Peter Schroth (b. 1940) and Peter Kleinert (b. 1947), and in Schwedt by director Freya Klier (b.

1950). Frank Castorf started to do the same in the small northern city of Anklam, but was able to develop his style further only as guest director in such places as Karl-Marx-Stadt (Chemnitz), Halle, Gera and Berlin. His approach questioned all accepted and prescribed values, philosophical as well as artistic, and was an extreme expression of a tendency that was becoming more and more common in the intellectual life of the GDR.

As a consequence of *glasnost* and *perestroika* in the Soviet Union, social commentary played an increasingly important role in the theatre in the last years before the fall of the Wall and the end of the GDR. With productions of new plays by Heiner Müller, Christoph Hein, Volker Braun and other GDR playwrights, as well as contemporary Soviet works – predominantly social-commentary plays – and in politically updated productions of the classics, many in the theatre community expressed their dissatisfaction with existing social conditions and raised a protest against a fossilized political system. The theatre became one of the few places where the social crisis could, at least to some extent, be aired in public. Many theatre artists were among the leaders of anti-government expression and demonstrations during the upheavals in 1989.

With the reunification of Germany on 3 October 1990, the five East German regions (formerly fourteen administrative districts) joined the FRG as states. From this point on, East German theatre had to accommodate itself to the social and economic conditions of the FRG. Despite financial support from West Germany in the early days of this change-over, the process of integration nevertheless involved considerable upheaval showing itself in, among other things, a rapid drop in audience attendance tantamount to an increase in dealing with market conditions. By 1992 the possibility of making long overdue changes to the theatre system was only hesitantly appearing. Most obviously, the East German theatre had lost its importance as a social conscience and as a forum for public discussion of repressed or prohibited subjects. As a result, the theatre community was suffering an identity crisis as well as a crisis of creativity, and many theatres were searching for new themes and vocabularies to respond to the change. Most were also still struggling to establish a new relationship with their audience.

Structure of the National Theatre Community

As of 1992, West Germany (including West Berlin) had eighty-seven public theatres with about two hundred regularly used performance spaces, about eighty additional continually active private theatres, between thirty and forty touring agencies which regularly sent productions to towns without theatre companies of their own, twenty-eight summer festivals, and innumerable independent, professional, 'alternative' theatre companies. In addition, there were countless puppet theatres, cabarets, intimate theatres, *Dialektbühnen* (companies performing plays in regional dialects), and amateur theatre groups, as well as several outdoor stages with their own (occasional) productions.

In East Germany (including East Berlin) in the mid-1980s, there were sixty-five public theatres operating on 188 permanent stages. Among them were nine puppet theatres, three children's and youth theatres, and one revue theatre. In addition, nine independent cabaret companies enjoyed a status similar to the public theatres. There was also a theatre which produced shows only in Low German (attached to the Staatstheater Schwerin in Mecklenburg). The German-Sorbian Volkstheater Bautzen (Bautzen National Theatre) for its part alternated performances between German and Sorbian, thus reflecting the cultural interests of the Sorbian community, a local Slavic minority.

Private theatres and alternative groups were not allowed in East Germany, apart from a few private puppet and fairytale theatres. Independent companies were possible only from the mid-1980s on. East Germany also had a host of open-air stages.

When the country was finally unified, there was clearly an enormous number of performances. In the 1990–1 season, the number was about 35,000 in the West German public theatres alone, about 28,000 in the private theatres, 7,700 in commercial tours and 1,300 in festivals. Official statistics list a total of 72,000. Audience attendance stood at about 28 million: 17 million for the public theatres, 7 million for the private theatres, 1.6 million for the various festivals and an estimated 2.5 million for touring shows. On a per capita basis, this meant an average of forty-six visits to the theatre per every hundred inhabitants of West Germany and West Berlin per year. In East Germany, the average was even higher. As in West Germany, the public theatres usually work in repertory. Every year, some 650 to 700 new productions were added to the repertoire, giving a total of about 1,800 per year.

Financially speaking, theatres in Germany are the legal and financial responsibility of individual states, regions and local municipalities. The federal government itself has no cultural powers; its responsibilities are limited to such things as underwriting guest tours abroad, subsidizing theatres in the border regions, financing specific festivals and paying for theatre in the capital.

Within these groupings, theatre received the largest proportion of cultural subsidy (about 36 per cent of municipal cultural budgets, for example, compared to 15 per cent for music, 14 per cent for museums and 13 per cent for libraries).

Subsidies for public theatre in West Germany amounted to 2.4 billion Deutschmarks (DM) in 1990. Put another way, the public purse contributed an average of DM 128 to every ticket (equivalent to the daily wage of a mid-level employee). Only 15 per cent of the total costs were covered by box-office income. Of the rest, municipalities contributed some 57 per cent and state governments up to 43 per cent. The designations 'state' or 'municipal' theatre, therefore, indicated who bore the brunt of the funding. As a rule, however, state governments also shared in subsidizing municipal theatres just as larger cities in turn help finance state theatres.

Besides state theatres and municipal theatres there are also smaller theatres that receive multiple funding from combined sources, mostly town councils. Fourteen of these today constitute a Landesbühne (regional theatre), a kind of 'municipal theatre on wheels', a non-commercial touring company which continuously plays in the particular region whose name it bears.

During the period of the GDR, public theatres there received state subsidies that accounted for some 85 per cent of their total budgets. The size of the subsidy, the size of the company, as well as target-figures for audience attendance were all set by the central government based on such things as population and artistic importance. This system ensured regular financing for all theatres.

In keeping with the East German political system, there were three different levels of legal responsibility and support: municipalities, district soviets, and the state theatres; the state theatres (all in Berlin) were directly under the control of the Ministry of Culture.

Though states and municipalities carry financial responsibility for the public theatres, they do not run them. Instead they appoint artistic directors (on five-year contracts as a rule) and hand all rights over to them including hiring the company and deciding on programmes. The artistic director is required only to remain within the budget and follow its necessities.

In East Germany too artistic directors were appointed this way but at the same time were more accountable to the responsible political bodies and were required to take direct instructions from them. The artistic director, for example, only proposed annual budgets and season choices for approval. All theatres were also under the political supervision of the respective party organs.

The problem of high costs long ago raised the question of just what makes German theatre so expensive. It is not possible to give a sweeping answer. One thing is sure, however: compared to the size of creative personnel, there is an inordinately large technical, administrative and house staff in virtually every German theatre, in part because practically every theatre has its own workshops for sets, costumes and props. In the last decades in East Germany, the number of non-creative personnel increased so sharply that there were two technical or administrative employees for every artist during the 1980s. In general, actors, directors and other dramatic theatre creative personnel are more clearly in the minority whereas in musical theatre, with its large orchestras, choruses and ballet corps, the numbers are more even.

Opera and ballet are therefore cost-intensive by their very nature, and in drama the highest cost-factor is precisely that which its quality depends upon, namely the fact that it is a repertory theatre which needs an ensemble that gives actors the opportunity to develop their versatility.

Costly too are the high expectations of originality and quality that come with each and every production. This leads to long periods of rehearsal, intensive planning and conceptual preparation, and lavish supporting materials (voluminous programmes and documentation, public discussions, and allied events). Dramaturges – a specialty and a significant 'frill' of the German theatre – are mainly responsible for this.

Multipurpose theatre complexes dominate the German theatre scene. Only theatres in large metropolitan centres and in the Rhine-Ruhr region can afford to specialize in a single type of performance; in the smaller towns they have to restrict themselves to dramatic theatre only.

German theatre, despite collective production methods, still has a strict hierarchical management and a sharply defined division of labour in its technical and workshop operations. This high degree of specialization has allowed the survival of a number of uncommon tradespeople such as armourers, dyers, milliners and moulders.

Legally and socially, actors are no different from other employees. They are offered long-term contracts with job-security provisions tied to seniority, and are entitled to pensions, medical coverage, unemployment insurance, and holidays. They also have a right to 'comparable employment', a peculiarity that translates into being given showcase parts if their contracts are not going to be renewed.

In East Germany, too, the social status of actors was comparable to other workers, with rights to old-age pensions, medical care, paid vacations and rest periods regulated by pay agreements between the artists' union – to which almost all theatre workers belonged – and the Ministry of Culture. The average wage was marginally higher than the average income of the rest of the population, but was below the income of other professions or trades with comparably long training periods. Almost all East German theatre workers were graduates of colleges or technical institutes.

In accordance with universally binding GDR labour laws, all contracts with artists were of indefinite duration, so that, in effect, it was possible for an artist to quit a company only at the individual artist's own request. This regulation often led to the fossilization of acting companies.

The Bühnengenossenschaft is the union representing the interests of all stage-workers while the Deutscher Bühnenverein (German Theatre Association) is the national association of theatre managers, producers and authorities. Disputes are arbitrated and settled by arbitration courts and wage commissions. Production is often made more difficult by the great variety of working agreements which are inconsistent with the specific conditions of work in theatre.

In East Germany, a similar union included all artistic activity (not only theatre, but also orchestras, museums, cinemas and film). As well, there was the Verband der Theater-schaffenden (Association of Theatre Workers) with some 3,000 members, including other theatre-related occupations: directors, dramaturges, set designers, theatre academics and critics. The association's activities were directed to professional development, organizing study trips within the GDR and abroad (predominantly eastern Europe), and documentation of productions. In addition, the association sponsored colloquiums around important productions, as well as festival-like Werkstatt-Tage (Workshop Days) for all types of theatre activities. From 1985, it sponsored a special Werkstatt des jungen Theaters (Youth Theatre Workshop).

To develop audience attendance, public theatres – also commercial theatres and local cultural offices in towns without theatre companies – offer subscription series for eight to ten shows at a reduced rate. Over a quarter of all theatre visits are by subscription, and they account for more than one-third of box-office income. The subscription system, however, imposes certain restrictions on theatre operations. It demands the early planning of a fixed number of premières, places management in a strait-jacket of deadlines, and denies the flexibility of quickly dropping failed productions and taking advantage of successes. Nevertheless, there is not a theatre that would do without this guaranteed income, and experience shows that some new works, particularly in the music theatre, would never have had more than one performance without it.

Theatre clubs in West Germany often choose a selection of shows from more than one branch of a theatre's operations and from more than one theatre. Frequently they buy up an entire house. The two big theatre clubs have a long history. The Volksbühne (National Stage Society), founded in Berlin in 1890, was given its own theatre in 1914 and became the model for similar clubs elsewhere. Since 1920, many of these groups have been amalgamated into national organizations. The Theatergemeinde (Theatre Community), founded in 1919, organized theatre attendance primarily outside the major cities, maintaining its own *Wander-bühne* (touring stage) and supporting amateur theatre. The Nazis closed its operations during the war but both organizations re-established themselves, the former in 1948, the latter in 1951. Primarily ticket distributors, they still, however, follow some of their old cultural-political programmes in their own magazines, newsletters, conferences and playwrights' awards. The Volksbühne, for example, seeks to be for working people, while the Theatergemeinde sets great store by Christian and western values. Attendance figures for both have dropped from 5.5 million to 3.5 million per year since the 1960s. By the early 1990s, they represented only 17 per cent of the public theatre's income primarily because their block buying has given them greater reductions than in the case of subscriptions. Members of these theatre clubs generally belong to less affluent, politically weaker segments of society: clerks, government employees, housewives, pensioners, and, with a membership of 12–13 per cent, high school and university students.

In East Germany, all ticket prices were kept inordinately low; on average, less than the hourly wage of workers. Regular attendance there was assured through a broadly based system of subscriptions which included factories and other institutions. Frequently, however, tickets were bought but not used, so that sold-out houses might be only half-filled. Because of this, many theatres tried to design a more variable subscription system with greater individual choice.

Although Germany is dominated by public theatres, other types of theatres have also developed and lasted. They too are supported by public funds, although to a much lesser extent. Private theatres receive barely 4 per cent of all theatre subsidies. Berlin's Schaubühne nevertheless receives sufficient funding that it can compete with any state or municipal theatre. A few smaller private theatres that regard themselves as 'art theatres' base their budgets almost entirely on public subsidy. In Stuttgart and Berlin public funding even includes so-called boulevard theatres and, in Hamburg, a theatre for shows in dialect. New and unique for the German theatre are three houses doing large-scale musicals, opened in Hamburg and Bochum. They were regularly playing works by Andrew Lloyd Webber and together accounted for an audience of 1.3 million in 1990 alone.

Commercial touring companies are also relatively new. Until well into the 1960s, rural districts were served only by the travelling stages of the Landesbühnen and a few municipal theatres. But there grew a demand for theatre that could not be met by what was available. This resulted in the 1970s in the construction of large arts centres with proper theatres. Tour producers (about thirty-five of them in 1992) filled the gap

in the market and have, since 1980, formed a syndicate offering some 130 productions a year. They serve more than 300 rural communities. Many of their productions are simply vehicles for television stars or partially recast and recycled productions from the public theatres (generally tried and therefore usually true standard theatre fare) for which local authorities pay more than they can recoup in ticket sales. Since the funds come out of public budgets, this is also a form of indirect subsidy.

Among the West German independent groups that achieved great prominence through the 1970s are a few that have long since attained the status of major cultural institutions. Many, however, have simply disbanded, but new independent groups are always springing up, especially in eastern Germany.

In East Germany, amateur theatre had a special place and there were about 900 groups existing alongside the professional theatres, supported by factories, schools, universities, churches and local arts centres. In the case of a great many of these groups, artistic matters were in the hands of a theatre professional. During the 1950s and 1960s especially, a few of these groups showed exceptional ability, particularly the Berliner Arbeitertheater (BAT), the Berlin Business College students' theatre (premières of many of Heiner Müller's plays, directed by Bernd K. Tragelehn), and the Arbeitertheater Schwedt (Schwedt Workers' Theatre) in collaboration with Benno Besson. Beyond that there were about 1,500 groups putting on children's plays in schools, churches and Youth Pioneer clubhouses.

Finally, a word about festivals. In East Germany, the Berliner Festtage hosted foreign companies from 1957, as well as orchestras, soloists and guest performances from the various regions of the GDR. The Dresdner Musikfestspiele (Dresden Music Festival) opened in 1978 primarily for opera and ballet from both inside and outside the GDR. The Shakespeare-Tage (Shakespeare Festival) in Weimar and the Händel-Festspiele (Handel Festival) in Halle also belonged to the annual festival schedule, while the Musik-Biennale in Berlin, devoted to contemporary music, included modern opera, music theatre and ballet. There were only two festivals devoted exclusively to theatre, in 1987 and 1989.

In West Germany it was the Berliner Theatertreffen, the Mülheimer Theatertage, the Ruhrfestspiele and the Wagner Festspiele in Bayreuth that set the tone, and they are still the most important events in reunified Germany today. Also of prime importance is the Theater der Welt (Theatre of the World), held every two years since 1981 under the sponsorship of the (West) German Centre of the International Theatre Institute. A Biennale der europäischen Gegenwartsdramatik (Biennial of Contemporary European Plays) was first held in Bonn in 1992.

There are as well two other kinds of festivals, one primarily local – Opernfestspiele München (Munich Festival of the Opera), Maifestspiele Wiesbaden (Wiesbaden Spring Festival) – the other, summer festivals in tourist areas, such as the ruins of the monastery in Bad Hersfeld

(Hessen), the Luisenburg-Naturbühne (Luisenburg Natural Stage) near Wunsiedel (Franken), the Bergtheater Thale (Thale Theatre-on-the-Mountain in Sachsen-Anhalt), the Felsenbühne Rathen (Rathen Cliff Stage in Sachsen), the steps of the Schwäbisch Hall Cathedral, the rococo theatres in the palaces of Schwetzingen and Ludwigsburg (Baden-Württemberg), the Goethe-Theater in Bad Lauchstädt (Sachsen-Anhalt), and some sixty more of the same.

The Oberammergau Passion Play is especially popular with foreign tourists and is held every ten years in the upper Bavarian town of Oberammergau.

Artistic Profile

Companies

FRG

With Berlin as capital of the newly reunited Germany, the city, now numbering 3.4 million, has the opportunity of once again becoming the most important theatre centre in the country. The capital became the dominant cultural centre only with the founding of the empire in 1871, and the centre of German theatre only with the rise of director Max Reinhardt (1873–1943). Not till the Weimar Republic, however, was it the undisputed theatre capital, a position once again lost – for West Berlin – after 1945, especially with the isolation that came with the building of the Wall in 1961. With a population of 2.1 million West Berlin was large enough, however, not to let one theatre alone monopolize its cultural life.

Elsewhere in the FRG between 1945 and 1990 cultural significance had little to do with either the size of the city or the size of the theatre. Thus cities with a population between 300,000 and 400,000 such as Mannheim, Wuppertal and Bochum had theatres that made a bigger name for themselves than those in cities with populations of half a million like Essen, Dortmund, Hannover or Nürnberg, and even mid-sized cities of 120,000 to 140,000 like Göttingen, Heidelberg and Darmstadt could match them.

The major influences, of course, were the artistic directors who not only were impresarios but also gave the theatres their identity. Soon after the war, artistic directors Erich Engel,

Hans Schweikart and Gustaf Gründgens had already laid the groundwork for a high level of ensemble acting at the Münchner Kammerspiele and the Düsseldorfer Schauspielhaus, still hallmarks of these companies. From 1951 to 1961 the Staatstheater Darmstadt stood out under Gustav Rudolf Sellner's artistic directorship for the high literary quality of its plays and its avant-garde style. The Deutsches Schauspielhaus in Hamburg became a magnetic ensemble theatre under Gründgens from 1955 on, and again achieved a national importance under Ivan Nagel (b. 1931) from 1972 to 1979, while the Kurt Hübner period at the Bremer Schauspiel (1962–73) is almost legendary. People liked to speak of a Bremer Stil then but neither a style nor a method was the important thing; instead it was the fact that many creative directors and designers were able to work with a youthful acting company and stimulated one another's creativity. Director Peter Zadek worked there regularly as did Wilfried Minks (b. 1931), who had a lasting influence on scenography. As well, directors Klaus Michael Grüber (b. 1941), Peter Stein, Rainer Werner Fassbinder, Hans Neuenfels (b. 1941), Peter Palitzsch and Hans Hollmann (b. 1933), and designers Karl-Ernst Herrmann (b. 1936), Erich Wonder (b. 1944) and Jürgen Rose (b. 1937), together with the leading lights of the new generation of actors – Bruno Ganz (b. 1941), Edith Clever (b. 1940), Jutta Lampe (b. 1943) and Margit Carstensen (b. 1940) – also worked in Bremen. The group became the epitome of a lively, versatile director's theatre, one extremely receptive to European modernism. This was continued in Stuttgart from 1966 till the late 1980s, where many of the above-mentioned names cropped up again regularly. Palitzsch, for example, was artistic director of the Schauspiel till 1972, and Claus Peymann (b. 1937) built up an equally effective ensemble from 1974 to 1979.

In the 1970s, West Berlin became a trend-setter through the work of the Schaubühne. Joining Peter Stein and his company core from Bremen were actors Otto Sander (b. 1941), Libgart Schwarz (b. 1941) and later Udo Samel (b. 1953), and directors such as Grüber, Frank-Patrick Steckel (b. 1943) and later Luc Bondy (b. 1948). The American Robert Wilson also directed there. The intensive conceptual background research (including seminars and rehearsal notes) by the dramaturge Dieter Sturm (b. 1936) was indispensable for their stagings, as was Botho Strauss (b. 1944) as an adapter of plays. The company staged only four or five productions each year but they set new standards for Germany which spread widely through television and film. The Schaubühne combined radicalism, artistic perfection and social commitment. Between 1980 and 1984, the group also worked with Turkish artists, performing regularly for immigrant workers.

The Schauspielhaus Bochum is another good example of the importance a theatre can achieve – and also maintain – in a not very big city, even with changes in artistic directors, goals and styles. When artistic director Hans Schalla stepped down after twenty-three years in 1972 (his predecessor had been at the helm for thirty years), a completely new era began under Zadek. A rigidly formal literary style gave way to a lively populism, and neo-expressionist acting was displaced by entertaining realism. Another sharp change followed under Peymann in 1979 and Steckel in 1986. Yet it always remained a vital director's theatre, putting the

Peter Stein's 1974 Schaubühne production of Maxim Gorki's *Summer Folk*, designed by Karl-Ernst Herrmann.
Photo: Helga Kneidl.

spotlight on the actor without sacrificing anything in conceptual integrity.

More troubled and controversial, but often distinguished by extraordinary triumphs, were the artistic directorships in Köln and Frankfurt am Main. In Köln it was Hansgünther Heyme between 1968 and 1979 and Jürgen Flimm (b. 1941) from 1979 to 1985. In Frankfurt am Main these were the very interesting Palitzsch/Neuenfels years, 1979–85. In Bonn from 1981 to 1991, Peter Eschberg (b. 1936) and subsequently Manfred Beilharz (b. 1938) were resourceful in finding new scripts, particularly from contemporary authors.

GDR

All theatres in the GDR were encouraged to evolve distinct profiles regardless of the size or location of the city they were situated in. As in the FRG, this was directly influenced by the quality of the directors of the theatre. But the high quality of the various state acting schools (all teaching fundamentally similar principles) ensured quality ensembles even in smaller cities. However, movements that seemed even slightly radical were quickly closed down by narrow-minded local politicians (Frank Castorf's work in Anklam was one example).

The pull of Berlin was very strong for both actors and directors. The fact is, outside Berlin, only a few ensembles managed to maintain high standards over longer periods of time, two being the Schwerin Schauspiel from 1974 to 1989 and the Dresdner Staatsschauspiel in the 1950s and again from the late 1970s.

Thus, in almost all GDR theatres – and the Berlin theatres were no exception – periods of significant achievement alternated with periods of stagnation. Add to this the not insignificant factor that many important GDR directors left the country for political reasons – Benno Besson, Matthias Langhoff, Manfred Karge, Adolf Dresen, Jürgen Gosch, Bernd K. Tragelehn, Einar Schleef, Piet Drescher (b. 1940), Herbert König, Freya Klier and Alexander Lang among others – and it is easy to understand some of the difficulties encountered by companies at every level.

Most artistic directors were removed after the political change-over in 1990 and ensembles in search of new images were forced to undergo painstaking reorganization. In this difficult process, only a few theatres – among them, the Deutsches Theater and the Maxim Gorki Theater in Berlin, the Dresdner Staatsschauspiel, the Neue Theater Halle and the Freien Kammerspiele Magdeburg (Magdeburg Free Chamber Players) – have been able to preserve their image or to shape it anew. Others – including the Berliner Ensemble – were evolving in very different ways (see **GDR Directors, Directing and Production Styles**).

Dramaturgy

FRG

It should not be taken for granted that contemporary German playwrights play a dominant role in the German theatre, nor is it even a general rule. The theatres see themselves mainly as *musées imaginaires*, keeping world drama alive. Even so, their general literary orientation does not mean that they produce museum-pieces; instead most use new interpretations and formal experiments to the point of recasting each play in totally modern idioms.

In all, German-language plays take up less than half the repertoire. In planning their seasons West German theatres largely follow a convention that has evolved over the last few decades. In this relatively balanced scheme, eight types of play keep turning up regularly. Originality lies in the individual choices within each class and the contrasts between them. From a literary-historical point of view, the types of play are, first, classics of world drama, with an emphasis on ancient Greek, Shakespeare (Germany's most-produced playwright) and Molière; second, German classics: Lessing, Goethe, Schiller, Kleist and Büchner; third, European drama from the turn of the century, very broadly defined as from Ibsen, Strindberg and Wedekind to Chekhov and Schnitzler; fourth, modern classics such as Brecht (statistically, Germany's second most-produced playwright), Horváth, Pirandello and O'Casey; fifth, more recent European repertoire such as Sartre and Beckett; sixth, more recent German repertoire such as Frisch or Weiss; seventh, contemporary foreign plays by writers such as Sobol, Koltès and Ayckbourn; and eighth, contemporary German-language plays, regardless of whether the playwright is West or East German, Austrian or Swiss.

Each of these types will often be included in a single season. But beyond the more important plays of antiquity there are some gaps in the classical repertoire. Missing to a large extent are plays of the Spanish golden age, French classics (Corneille and Racine) and the English Restoration.

The fourth class of plays – modern classics – varies the most. Here, as occasionally with the third, many new plays and even playwrights are rediscovered, revived and reassessed, and were especially during the 1960s and 1970s. Among them, in roughly chronological order, were Carl Sternheim, Sean O'Casey, Ödön von Horváth, Marieluise Fleisser, Georges Feydeau, the young Brecht (especially his *Lehrstücke*), Isaak Babel, Maxim Gorki, Nikolai Erdmann, the Living Newspaper of the Weimar Republic (Peter Martin Lampel, Ferdinand Bruckner and Friedrich Wolf), Ramón de Valle-Inclán, Italo Svevo, Ernst Barlach and Hans Henny Jahnn. All experienced a renaissance after their rediscovery, especially Horváth. A list like this also shows how much elbow-room a theatre with a good dramaturge has, even within a rigidly defined historical canon.

The weight of tradition, however, is such that an ambitious director's theatre feels itself more challenged by the canon than by contemporary plays, which are left with only limited room in the repertoire. For all that, there is no dearth of contemporary German playwrights today and many of them are, or were, at the same time actors, directors, dramaturges, or otherwise closely connected to the theatre.

Looking back, it can be fairly said that West German drama generally was in bad shape until the 1960s. The cupboard of playwrights who had stayed in Germany turned out to be empty in 1945, and only Brecht and Zuckmayer among the exiles got more than a temporary place in the repertoire. Beyond the classics, it was mainly comprised of plays from France, the United States, and, from 1957 on, above all from England.

The Swiss Max Frisch and Friedrich Dürrenmatt represented all German-speaking drama. Wolfgang Borchert's *Draußen vor der Tür* was promising, but the author died the day before its 1947 première. In 1961, works by Tankred Dorst (b. 1925), Günter Grass (b. 1927) and Martin Walser were the first contemporary German plays since the war to be taken seriously and raised hopes that a genuine West German drama – everywhere prayed for, deeply felt and almost already talked into existence – would finally appear with a new generation of writers, even if it was still in the familiar guise of the parable play, the grotesque society comedy, or the Theatre of the Absurd.

The big change came, and quickly, from quite another quarter altogether, namely with politically specific, realistic and often documentary dramas, such as Heinar Kipphardt's *Der Hund des Generals* (*The General's Dog*, 1962) and *In der Sache J. Robert Oppenheimer* (*The Case of J. Robert Oppenheimer*, 1964), Rolf Hochhuth's *Der Stellvertreter* (*The Deputy*, 1963) and Peter Weiss's *Marat/Sade* (1964) and *Die Ermittlung* (*The Investigation*, 1965). The West German theatre had finally begun to examine issues repressed for over a decade such as Nazism, German war crimes, the war, and world affairs in general with a toughness appropriate to the subject. German guilt was also the subject of *Eiche und Angora* (*The Rabbit Race*, 1962) and *Der schwarze Schwan* (*The Black Swan*, 1964) by Walser, *Helm* (1965) by Hans Günther Michelsen (b. 1920) and Kipphardt's *Joel Brand* (1965).

It remained a trenchant theme even during the student movement of the late 1960s as writers turned primarily to international events: Weiss's *Gesang vom Lusitanischen Popanz* (*The Song of the Lusitanian Bogey*) and *Vietnam-Diskurs*, Hochhuth's *Soldaten* (*Soldiers*) and *Guerillas*, and *Das Verhör von Habana* (*The Havana Interrogation*) by Hans Magnus Enzensberger (b. 1929). Documentary drama experienced a comeback beginning in 1978; many of the aforementioned documentary-style plays were revived, and Kipphardt's *Bruder Eichmann* (*Brother Eichmann*, 1983) was added as a variation.

The 'revolutionary' years for German playwriting were also revolutionary for the theatre. But reality was a better show. Student protests and demonstrations outdid the drama on the stage and took its place. Following a period of long overdue reflection, theatres and writers emerged with even better techniques than before but also lost some of their positive relationships. Thus the achievements of the directors' theatre since 1968 corresponded less and less to playwriting trends, while playwriting was now, after its pioneer stage, about to enter an 'expansionist phase'. After débuts by Sperr, Fassbinder, Handke and Gerlind Reinshagen (b. 1926) and the beginning of Heiner Müller's recognition in the west, Tankred Dorst finally made the breakthrough with *Toller* in Stuttgart in 1968. George Tabori arrived in West Berlin with *Cannibals* in 1969 and promptly became a 'German' author, and the first play by Harald Mueller (b. 1934) made it to the Munich stage the same year. Thomas Bernhard (1931–89)

Peter Palitzsch's 1965 Württembergische Staatstheater Stuttgart production of Peter Weiss's *The Investigation*, designed by Gerd Richter.
Photo: Werner Schloske.

first emerged as a playwright in Hamburg in 1970, Kroetz got his start with a scandal in Munich in 1971, and Germany first got to know critic and dramaturge Botho Strauss as a playwright in Hamburg in 1972.

These newly emerging writers – many more could be named – belonged to no literary group or movement, nor even to the same generation, but their individual themes, styles and concepts taken as a whole amounted to a watershed in German drama.

A number of trends emerged. Two prominent political playwrights rediscovered private life: Walser with *Die Zimmerschlacht* (*Home Front*, 1967) and Frisch with *Biografie* (*Biography*, 1968). In 1966 Martin Sperr's *Jagdszenen aus Niederbayern* (*Hunting Scenes from Lower Bavaria*) provided the first example of a realistic folk play, depicting the helplessness of socially marginalized groups and their need for expression. Austrians Wolfgang Bauer, Harald Sommer and Peter Turrini made typical contributions to the genre, while in Bavaria thay came from Fassbinder, primarily with *Katzelmacher* (*Wop*, 1968), Kroetz with much of his work from *Hartnäckig* (*Stiff-Necked*, 1971) to *Bauern sterben* (*Farmers Die*, 1985), and Herbert Achternbusch (b. 1938), primarily with his monodramas *Ella* (1978) and *Gust* (1984).

Sketches of lower-middle-class life by Wolfgang Deichsel (b. 1939) showed that the Hessian dialect was once more dramatically viable for the stage, while Thomas Strittmatter (b. 1961) did the same for the Baden dialect with his first play, *Viehjud Levi* (*Levi the Cattle-Jew*, 1982). Writing in the Fränkisch dialect were Fitzgerald Kusz (b. 1944), Tankred Dorst – especially in his village tragedy *Korbes* (1988) – and, since 1990, Kerstin Specht (b. 1961). Another whole genre was devoted to exposés on the world of workers, minor clerks and asocial outsiders. Here too, Kroetz must be mentioned, followed by Heinrich Henkel (b. 1937), Gerlind Reinshagen (*Eisenherz/Ironheart*, 1982), Karl Otto Mühl (b. 1923) and Peter Greiner (b. 1939).

The genre of dramatized biography simultaneously experienced an important revival in plays about artists, in which writers reflected on their own relationship to society through historic figures. The very present and pressing theme of politics and the writer was preeminent. Grass started it in 1966 with his critique of Brecht in *Die Plebejer proben den Aufstand* (*The Plebeians Rehearse the Uprising*); Dorst showed Toller's failure during the Munich Soviet Republic and, in *Eiszeit* (*Ice Age*, 1973), Hamsun showed himself weighed down by his Nazi-collaborator past. Weiss's *Hölderlin*

(1971) depicted the eighteenth-century poet as a closet revolutionary, and Gaston Salvatore (b. 1941) announced the end of all revolutionary hopes in *Büchners Tod* (*Büchner's Death*, 1972).

The most conspicuous trend, and one that lasted into the 1990s, has aimed at a new critical approach to the German past and present. Many of the later national retrospectives might be called *Deutsche Stücke* (German plays), as Dorst called his play-cycle begun in 1975. Brechtian models – *Arturo Ui, Schweyk, Furcht und Elend des Dritten Reiches* (*Fear and Misery in the Third Reich*) – remained a staple in the West German repertoire, but from 1975 on they were complemented by Heiner Müller's scenic-montages which questioned the official GDR version of history while touching on unresolved questions of the past. These new plays, for the most part, tried to get at symptomatic features of daily life under fascism and of the post-1945 reconstruction, and combined historical records with biography. Gerlind Reinshagen's *Sonntags-kinder* (*Sunday's Children*, 1976) and *Rotter* (1977) by Thomas Brasch (b. 1945) were models of this type of historical play which found its most important and successful exponent in Klaus Pohl (b. 1952) and plays such as *Das Alte Land* (*The Old Ground*, 1984) and *Karate-Billi kehrt zurück* (*Karate Bill Comes Back*, 1991). Even George Tabori's comic excursions into German history such as *Mein Kampf* (1987) were unsettling, and war and apocalyptic doom made a strong comeback in plays such as Dorst's *Merlin* (1981), Harald Mueller's *Totenfloß* (*Raft of Death*, 1986), Rainald Goetz's (b. 1954) *Krieg* (*War*, 1987), and Brasch's *Frauen, Krieg, Lustspiel* (*Women, War, Comedy*, 1988).

But at the same time, with a swing of the pendulum in the opposite direction, drama began to concern itself with the *neue Sensibilität* (new sensitivity) of West German intellectuals and seemed happiest to be about nothing but itself – theatre about theatre. There was a boom in monologues, revues and party chitchat. Early in the 1990s, nothing was considered more antiquated than a 'well-made play' so there was a lot of experimentation with free forms (collage and over-painting) and the aesthetic of fragmentism was exercising an apparently irresistible fascination. Exemplary models of such themes and production styles could be found in the works of Botho Strauss and Tankred Dorst, who – at least in this respect – were, for all their differences in style, the proto-

typical western German playwrights of the 1990s.

GDR

The traditional literary orientation of the German theatre was reinforced in the GDR by the didactic function officially assigned to the theatre. It was supposed to educate people to the goals of the state. Historical and intellectual traditions played an important role. Paramount, therefore, were those philosophical, political and artistic trends that marked human progress. In the minds of its political leaders, socialism was called upon to realize the ideals of a 'progressive' humanity, and this official cultural policy worked against any questioning of the idea of progress. Historical and contemporary works along with intellectual positions which did so (such as the German romantics, Nietzsche, the Frankfurt School or even the Theatre of the Absurd) were officially denounced as decadent and went unpublished. Not until the 1970s was there any softening of this position, albeit without any fundamental change.

The classical repertoire was tailored accordingly. Shakespeare, Lessing, Goethe and Schiller were the uncontested champions of this inheritance. Büchner too was part of it with the Greek classics being added in the 1960s and Kleist joining them relatively late in the 1970s. The Spaniards, above all Calderón and Lope de Vega, were still relatively well represented in the 1940s and 1950s, but later Molière and Goldoni took on increasing importance. Russian plays were actually a significant part of the repertoire right from the beginning, but whereas Gorki was able to maintain his place the whole time, productions of Ostrovsky, Gogol, and Soviet revolutionary plays grew rarer, while Chekhov became the most important Russian playwright from the 1970s. A similar shift occurred with English-language playwrights: in the mid-1960s Shaw was supplanted by O'Casey.

Contemporary foreign drama was dominated by east European writers, mostly didactic plays and comedies early on. From the beginning of the 1960s, more and more works of social commentary found their way into the repertoire, primarily from Czechoslovakia, Hungary and the Soviet Union. Clearly, criticism of social ills in other socialist countries was easier to get past the censor than the home product. The high point of this development came in the 1980s with the plays of Russian playwrights Mikhail Shatrov and Alexander Gelman.

The inclusion of contemporary west European drama (which, from the GDR's point of view, included West German drama) was highly selective for both ideological and economic reasons. Theatres had only very limited funds of hard currency at their disposal to pay western royalties. Still, works by Günther Weisenborn and Wolfgang Borchert, by Rolf Hochhuth, Martin Sperr, Martin Walser and Heinar Kipphardt (especially *Bruder Eichmann*) were the most often performed West German plays. The works of Friedrich Dürrenmatt, Max Frisch and Peter Weiss were also performed with relative frequency.

Modern English drama was represented by Arnold Wesker, Ewen McColl, Brendan Behan and Peter Shaffer; American by Arthur Miller and Lillian Hellman; French by Sartre and Vercors. Absent altogether from the repertoire until 1987 were the absurdists (Beckett and Ionesco), although there was a remarkable receptivity to modern Polish drama. The elements of the grotesque and the absurd portrayed by playwrights, Slawomir Mrożek, Tadeusz Różewicz and Ireneusz Iredynski were interpreted in a manner considered suitable for the GDR stage.

From its beginnings, GDR drama was heavily under the influence of Bertolt Brecht and Friedrich Wolf. Both had helped shape the avant-garde political theatre of the Weimar Republic, and both were exiles returning to East Berlin to mould the new German drama. Close as they were to each other, both intellectually and politically, they also had totally different concepts of drama and theatre. Whereas Wolf wrote plays according to Aristotelian theory and was thus continuing in the tradition of German bourgeois drama, Brecht's theories and techniques of epic theatre had already broken with this tradition in the 1920s.

The first post-war plays dealing with the immediate past and present adopted conventional forms, however, not least because Brechtian theories were largely unknown. Among them were Fred Denger's (b. 1920) *Wir heißen euch hoffen* (*Invitation to Hope*), Hansjörg Schmitthenner's (b. 1908) *Ein jeder von uns* (*Any One of Us*), and Wolf's *Wie die Tiere des Waldes* (*Like Animals in the Wild*).

It was immediately after the founding of the GDR in 1949 that the political leadership began calling for the creation of a 'new drama' which reflected what was best in the new social life.

Playwrights' responses differed widely. While some – like Wolf with *Bürgermeister Anna* (*Mayor Anna*), Gustav von Wangenheim with *Du bist der Richtige* (*Some Mothers do Have Them*), and Karl Grünberg (1891–1972) with *Golden fließt der Stahl* (*Golden Flows the Steel*) – more or less came up with *apologias* for the 'new life', writers like Peter Hacks, Heiner Müller and Erwin Strittmatter (b. 1912) in the early 1950s (under the influence of Brecht) began, in their own ways, to use the German past and contemporary GDR society to depict the contradictions of historical process. This reappraisal of the past – above all the Prussian and Nazi past – was combined with laying bare the contradictions and mistakes of GDR society, considered as consequences of this past.

Significant in this respect was Müller whose first published play, *Der Lohndrücker* (*Wage Squeeze*), already portrayed the Nazi past's serious and continuing influence on the present. It was also the constant theme of his other works written in the 1950s but produced only later, plays such as *Die Schlacht* (*The Battle*), *Die Umsiedlerin* (*The Displaced Person*), and *Germania Tod in Berlin* (*Germania Death in Berlin*). With his second play, *Die Holländerbraut* (*The Dutch Bride*), Strittmatter also brought the Nazi past together with the problems of post-war reconstruction. His first dramatic offspring, *Katzgraben*, the story of a village after 1945, was originally produced by Brecht, who used it to come to methodological grips with the problem of depicting the contradictions of the new society.

Hacks, who had emigrated to the GDR from the Federal Republic, chose the servility and automatic obedience of the Prussian tradition as primary targets for his historical comedies, *Die Schlacht bei Lobositz* (*The Battle of Lobositz*) and *Der Müller von Sanssouci* (*The Miller of Sans Souci*).

Besides this developing East German theatrical mainstream there were also other important attempts in the 1950s which were not, however, taken as far. Among them, Heinar Kipphardt's satire on GDR cultural officialdom, *Shakespeare dringend gesucht* (*Desperately Seeking Shakespeare*); Hedda Zinner's (b. 1907) *Der Teufelskreis* (*Vicious Circle*), in which her handling of the Reichstag fire trial anticipated the techniques of docu-drama; and composer Hans Eisler's (1898–1962) attempt to deprive the Faust character of Goethe's heroic dimensions, using a folk-play style. Eisler's play, actually written as a libretto for an opera, came up against hefty criticism from party intellectuals, with the result that the text made it on to a GDR stage only some thirty years later. Brecht, who was working on a similar theme at the time, put aside his *Turandot oder Der Kongreß der Weißwäscher* (*Turandot, or The Congress of White-washers*) as a result of this situation.

At the beginning of the 1960s Müller and Hacks opened a new dimension in the portrayal of GDR reality. Müller's *Die Umsiedlerin* and *Der Bau* (*Construction*) and Hacks's *Die Sorgen und die Macht* and *Moritz Tassow* set new standards for dealing with the inherent contradictions of socialist society. All these plays fell foul of official policy and were banned; that is, they were removed from the repertoire after their premières. Such repressive attitudes towards unvarnished depictions of reality also affected younger playwrights such as Hartmut Lange (b. 1937) whose peasant comedy, *Marski*, was also forbidden, and Volker Braun, who had to wait several years before his first major play, *Kipper Paul Bauch* (subsequently *Die Kipper/The Tippers*) saw the stage.

The hit of the day was *Frau Flinz*, a modern adaptation of *Mother Courage*, written for Helene Weigel by Helmut Baierl (b. 1926), which differed from the original in that it conjured up a harmony between 'ordinary people' and the state.

Similar tendencies cropped up in plays by Helmut Sakowski (b. 1924) (primarily village comedies), Rolf Schneider (b. 1932) (*Einzug ins Schloß/Our Home's a Palace*), Rainer Kerndl (b. 1928), Claus Hammel (1932–90) and Rudi Strahl (b. 1931) in his *In Sachen Adam und Eva* (*In the Matter of Adam and Eve*). Many of these works had long runs. Nevertheless, only in adaptations of novels were writers able to go beyond the narrowest of official approaches.

Alfred Matusche (1909–73) was a special case. His sensitive and poetic plays tended to deal with the tragic or tragi-comic situations that people got into and they tried to bring a new and original flavour to GDR drama. He was particularly known for his play *Die Dorfstraße* (*The Village Street*), written in 1954 and dedicated to German–Polish reconciliation, and for his biographical drama, *Van Gogh*.

A new phase of GDR drama began about the same time as the theatre's didactic function changed and theatre became more open in the late 1970s. Analysis of the past and the present was introduced into plays about great world-historical processes. If Heiner Müller in *Zement* had already tried to confront the question of the

Russian Revolution with events taken from classical antiquity, from this point on many playwrights began taking their material directly from history. Among their favourite topics were revolutionary events from outside Europe. In 1975 Volker Braun wrote *Guevara oder Der Sonnenstaat* (*Guevara, or The Sun State*); a year later he took a piece of early Chinese history for his *Großer Frieden* (*The Great Peace*), and followed it up in 1979 with *Dmitri*, an adaptation of Schiller's play about the false czar Dmitrius.

Christoph Hein drew on English history for *Cromwell*, and the bourgeois revolution in China for *Die wahre Geschichte des Ah Q* (*The True History of Ah Q*), based on a short story by Lu Hsün, while Stefan Schütz examined relevant works of world literature with moral rigour and grotesque satire, analysing the nature of power in socialist society – *Odysseus' Heimkehr* (*The Return of Ulysses*), *Heloise und Abelard* and *Der Hahn* (*The Rooster*). Jochen Berg (b. 1948) cleverly encoded mirror-images of contemporary conditions into his adaptations of Greek classics. And after *Leben Gundlings Friedrich von Preußen Lessings Schlaf Traum Schrei* (*Gundling's Life of Frederick of Prussia Lessing's Sleep Dream Scream*), *Hamletmaschine* (*Hamlet-Machine*) and *Der Auftrag* (*The Task*), it was clear that Heiner Müller had discovered new ways to bring the present face to face with world history.

Side by side with these 'world-historical' themes, drama was also developing in another direction, namely plays that took a critical look at daily life in the GDR. Among the most significant were Ulrich Plenzdorf's (b. 1934) *Die neuen Leiden des jungen W.* (*The New Sufferings of Young W. [erther]*), Claus Hammel's *Die Preußen kommen* (*The Prussians Are Coming*), Adolf Wendt's (b. 1948) *Die Dachdecker* (*The Roofers*), Jürgen Gross's (b. 1946) *Match*, Volker Braun's *Tinka* and *Schmitten*, and comedies by Rudi Strahl, which were all major popular successes.

Drama in the GDR went through still another boom in the 1980s. In addition to the already established writers, a whole new generation of playwrights came to the fore, not only wanting to play their part in changing political conditions, but also making it difficult for theatres to mount their plays partly because of their unconventional form. These playwrights found a forum for their unpublished work in the Werkstatt-Tagen des DDR-Schauspiels (GDR Playwrights' Workshop), held every two years in Leipzig by the Verband der Theaterschaffenden, where they were able to put on their works and discuss them with theatre professionals. Forty playwrights took part in the last workshop in 1988.

The most talented of the newcomers were Lothar Trolle (b. 1944) and Georg Seidel (1945–91). Trolle, who had already made his début in the 1970s with clown plays and his (unproduced) comedy, *Greikemeier*, mainly depicted the life of ordinary people using a coldly distanced tone to throw his acute psychological observations into relief – *24 Sätze über eine Frau* (*24 Propositions About a Woman*), *Weltuntergang I und II* (*The End of the World I and II*) and *Hermes in der Stadt* (*Hermes in the City*). Seidel proved to be an especially acute analyst of the stagnancy of the GDR in his plays, *Carmen Kittel* and *Villa Jugend* (*Villa of Youth*). Uwe Saeger (b. 1948) had similar aims in mind with his *Flugversuch* (*Test Flight*) and *Außerhalb von Schuld* (*Beyond Guilt*), as did Irina Liebmann (b. 1943) with *Berliner Kindl*.

Müller, Braun and Hein, who had all in the mean time acquired international reputations, also subjected GDR society to strong criticism in their later plays. In his five-part opus, *Wolokolamsker Chaussee* (*Wolokolamsker Avenue*), Müller made apparent the crises of socialism; similarly, Braun's *Die Übergangsgesellschaft* (*Society in Transition*) and Hein's *Ritter der Tafelrunde* (*Knights of the Round Table*), both written in the hope of a possible renewal, turned out to be the writing on the wall for East German society. Transition was also the theme, though less hopefully, in plays by both these authors set during World War II: Hein's *Passage* and Braun's *Transit Europa*.

Directors, Directing and Production Styles

FRG

The West German theatre is and was above all a theatre for directors. As such, its primary focus has been on the classics. During the Nazi era, 'faithfulness to the original' was supposed to preserve the classics from serving any political purpose, but after the war the idea was mere ideological baggage which made relationships to the present more difficult. During the 1940s and 1950s a conservative reverence for the 'undying', eternal classics was typical at most theatres.

One of the first post-war West German directors to challenge this was Jürgen Fehling, who over twenty-five years had established himself in Berlin as a major contemporary interpreter of Shakespeare and as a passionate, ecstatic and hauntingly visionary interpreter of Kleist, Hebbel, Grabbe, Hauptmann and Barlach. For many he was the most inspired director of a very 'Germanic' type of metaphysical theatre that was somewhere between a dance of death and a will o' the wisp humour. Obsessed, however, with the absolute nature of his work, and incapable of a moderate response to existing conditions, he was unable to settle in the post-war theatre. Four productions in Berlin and four in Munich were examples to be marvelled at, but they did not genuinely influence theatre styles.

It was different for Gustaf Gründgens who, as artistic director of the Berliner Staatstheater, had protected Fehling from the Nazis and had acted in some of his productions (*Don Juan* and *Richard II*). As actor, director and theatre manager, Gründgens re-established himself after the war as a virtuoso in all fields, sovereign and exact. Stylistically, he prolonged the classicism of his earlier productions, taking the plays out of their historical context, paring issues down to existential questions, emphasizing formal principles, and raising productions to the level of 'high art'. With that notion of 'faithfulness to the original' he became an eloquent opponent of 'irresponsible experimentation', but in Düsseldorf and Hamburg he was also a proponent of modern drama with productions of Eliot, Sartre's *Les Mouches*, Osborne's *The Entertainer*, and several premières of such writers as Thomas Wolfe, Carl Zuckmayer, Hans Henny Jahnn and Brecht's *Heilige Johanna der Schlachthöfe* (*St Joan of the Stockyards*). Devoted to Goethe's *Faust*, he played Mephisto in his own Hamburg production of both parts of the tragedy (1957–8). This was arguably the theatre event of the decade and starred Will Quadflieg (b. 1914) in the title role.

In the 1950s, a tendency towards abstraction developed and it found its most significant expression in Wieland Wagner's (1917–66) neo-archaic productions of Wagner in Bayreuth and Sellner's productions of the Greek classics in Darmstadt, both starting in 1951. Sellner's stylization, meant to emphasize the essence of the play, not only simplified the set to basic geometric forms that were catching on everywhere, but often gave it a modish streamlined look. The acting was ritualized; the actors became instruments of choreographic strategies.

The realism of Kortner's productions in Munich and Berlin was distinct from these typical phenomena of the directors' theatre of the time. For Kortner, the actor was central, and he demanded the highest standard of realistic acting. Kortner's detailed analysis tried to find concrete elements in each text, which were then illustrated in production, primarily through eloquent gesture. He replaced pathos with impassioned reason and broke through rhetoric with slow pacing and silence. His characters had to negotiate their emotions through an obstacle course of props on a crammed set full of nooks and crannies, and their reactions were freed from social convention, often to the point of vulgarity, in order to emphasize their humanity. This subversion of traditional polish and pace aroused opposition, but it did turn old plays into fresh experiences, whether Schiller's *Die Räuber* (*The Robbers*, 1953 and 1959); Shakespeare's *Twelfth Night* (1957, 1962), *Othello* (1962) and *Richard III* (1963); Goethe's *Clavigo* (1969) or Lessing's *Emilia Galotti* (1970). The stage as an examiner of human nature was Kortner's credo and his achievement.

Theatre as a political forum was Erwin Piscator's goal. He first achieved this during the Weimar Republic and then brought it back to life in the West Germany of the early 1960s. His textual readings and concepts combined political consciousness, topicality and historical analysis into productions requiring techniques that only Piscator himself seemed able to practise and preach. But Brecht's theoretical writings were also having their effect and were responsible for new insights into such an approach. Directing became understood as more than simply an adequate realization of a drama on the stage. The director was now seen as an original artist as well as an adapter and, if need be, an artist with the right to totally rework a play. This idea was not restricted to the political left but could also come from more conservative quarters such as Rudolf Noelte (b. 1921), a pupil of Fehling's who, like him, went his own way. He followed Kortner's principles of characterization but showed his characters helpless and isolated in a stagnant society. The melancholy fatalism of his approach to realism was especially characteristic of his productions of turn-of-the-century works by Sternheim, Chekhov (*Three Sisters*, Stuttgart, 1965), Strindberg and Gerhart Hauptmann (*Die Ratten/The Rats*, Berlin, 1977), but also in Molière's *Le Misanthrope* (Salzburg, 1973; Hamburg, 1975).

The change of attitude towards the classics appeared none the less abrupt and radical, despite the continuity which Kortner's and Noelte's work provided. In 1965 Heyme scandalized his Wiesbaden audience with a version of *Wilhelm Tell* that gave the Swiss uprising and fight for freedom all the traits of an outbreak of fascist mass hysteria. The production was a continuation of what was just beginning in the realm of docu-drama, namely catching up with the Nazi past. Four months later, Peter Zadek presented Schiller's *Die Räuber* as a piece of trashy theatre, using the idioms of pop, comics, western and horror movies. These were deliberate provocations and 'anti-authoritarian' protests against the ubiquitous clichés surrounding the classics. Both Schiller and Shakespeare were reclaimed as our contemporaries, which signalled their vitality in advance. Relevancy soon became the general trend. Finally, the discovery of Brechtian techniques of historicizing was a dialectical solution to make the classics relevant. Thus, when Peter Stein advertised his 1971 production of Ibsen's *Peer Gynt* as 'a nineteenth-century play', he was able to bring out its relevance to the present precisely because of this historical distancing.

West German directors no longer make their mark through the imposition of individual styles. Their importance and their quality is determined less by their uniqueness than by a heightening of what they have in common with others. Judged by the number of invitations to the Berliner Theatertreffen, Zadek, Stein and Peymann are the most important directors by far, but each in a different way. Zadek's idea of theatre has been influenced by his years in England, and he sets great store on entertainment, vitality, spectacle and even sensationalism. In search of theatrical adventure, he does not shy from using tastelessness as a shock tactic. Stein was Kortner's assistant and his experiences in the student movement of the 1960s had a decisive influence on him. His idea of theatre includes meaningful effect, intellectual rigour and social awareness. Peymann comes out of student theatre and has preserved much of its spontaneity and charm.

This trio also works in different contexts. Although he twice held the post of artistic director and for years preferred to work with such leading actors as Rosel Zech (b. 1942) and Ulrich Wildgruber (b. 1937), Zadek has remained a nomadic director, occasionally taking time out to work in television or film. Stein's major work consists of some thirty

Claus Peymann's 1977 Württembergische Staatstheater Stuttgart production of Goethe's *Faust II*, co-directed and designed by Achim Freyer.
Photo: Werner Schloske.

productions with essentially the same team that he formed at the Berliner Schaubühne; only in recent years has he begun to work abroad. Peymann, originally a guest director at numerous theatres, took his Stuttgart ensemble – including actor Gert Voss (b. 1941), dramaturge Hermann Beil (b. 1941) and director-designers Karl-Ernst Herrmann and Achim Freyer (b. 1934) – to Vienna via Bochum practically unscathed, and steadily grew in the process. Peymann has become as important a catalyst as he is a director, uniting a great number of creative talents into a highly effective whole. Under him, Niels-Peter Rudolph (b. 1939) directed Botho Strauss, Achternbusch directed his own work, Manfred Karge and Matthias Langhoff produced several premières of plays by Thomas Brasch and Heiner Müller, and George Tabori evolved his own style.

Finally, there is also a difference in their dramaturgy. Zadek has built up a distinctive repertoire using extremely varied approaches ranging from anarchy to acceptance. High points were his sixteen Shakespeare productions – breaking new ground with *Measure for Measure* (1967), *King Lear* (1974) and *Othello* (1976)); his grasp of Ibsen, Chekhov and Wedekind – outstanding were *The Master Builder* (1983), *Ivanov* (1990) and *Lulu* (1988); his introduction of modern Irish and English playwrights into the German repertoire; and also his love for musicals and revue-like productions. Apart from Tankred Dorst, he was, however, out of touch with contemporary German playwrights. Stein, however, turned to a different author for practically every production, and to the Greek classics and Shakespeare only after extensive prior scenic experimentation. An attempt at a thematic and historical series began to emerge with Brecht's *Die Mutter* (*The Mother*, 1970), Vsevolod Vishnevski's *Optimistic Tragedy* (1972) and Gorki's *Summerfolk* (1974). Generally not specializing in any author, he staged only the three major plays by his former dramaturge, Botho Strauss: *Trilogie des Wiedersehens* (*Three Acts of Recognition*, 1978), *Groß und Klein* (*Big and Little*, 1978) and *Der Park* (*The Park*, 1984). Peymann focused on the tension existing between the two polarities of his work, the

German classics and his contemporaries Peter Handke, Thomas Bernhard and Gerlind Reinshagen. Classics were to be staged as modern plays; modern plays as classics. Thus he not only directed surprisingly contemporary explorations of Kleist (*Das Käthchen von Heilbronn*, 1975; *Die Hermannschlacht/The Battle of the Teutoburger Forest*, 1982) and interpretations of Goethe (*Faust I* and *II*, and *Iphigenie auf Tauris/Iphigenia on Tauris*, all 1977), but also imposed a rigorously pointed and highly visual form on Bernhard's hypertrophy. Peymann directed twelve of Bernhard's premières, from the author's début to his death. With this commitment to Bernhard and with his efforts on behalf of many other contemporary German writers, he stands alone among West German directors.

To give an idea of the range of styles besides those of Zadek, Stein and Peymann, it is necessary to mention a few other names, representative of many. On the one hand there is the group of those who, like Peymann, gathered top-flight ensembles around themselves as artistic directors, and developed them further without dominating them. Palitzsch, the old master, who began as part of Brecht's team and returned later to the Berliner Ensemble, was particularly selfless in allowing even artistic opposites to work with him and his leading actors. Dieter Dorn (b. 1935), artistic director (since 1983) at the Munich Kammerspiele, has also succeeded in integrating an outstanding ensemble, already largely brought together by August Everding (b. 1929) into an effective working unit, as has Jürgen Flimm at Hamburg's Thalia Theater since 1985. And on the other hand there are the extremes, the restless loners in the system who, like Zadek, keep testing the limits of the stage. Grüber's productions – including some operas – have this sense of the unusual. With no concession to audience expectations, often hermetic and with an almost incommunicative stillness, he shows people as wanderers, caught in the past, playing end-games. *Winterreise* (*Winter's Journey*) with the Schaubühne ensemble in the Berlin Olympic Stadium (1977) was a spectacular example. Heyme, with his extreme productions of Schiller and the Greek classics, and Neuenfels as unpredictable provocateur, also belong in this class. But perhaps the subtlest triumph of the director's theatre was that the 'return of the actor' could be proclaimed in 1976 when Bernhard Minetti (b. 1905) played Minetti in Bernhard's play *Minetti*.

GDR

In East Berlin, the capital of the GDR from 1949, theatres developed distinct identities over the decades. The most important in the new post-war state was the Berliner Ensemble, founded in 1949. Here Bertolt Brecht and his wife Helene Weigel were able to put into practice his concept of a theatre for the scientific age, as argued in his *Kleines Organon für das Theater* (*The Little Organon for the Theatre*). The Ensemble used a broad repertoire which included, besides Brecht's own plays – particularly his late plays and adaptations – works by Molière, Goethe, Kleist, Gorki, Johannes R. Becher (1891–1958) and Erwin Strittmatter.

Working alongside Brecht was a host of other directors such as Erich Engel, Bertold Viertel (1885–1953), Egon Monk, Benno Besson, Peter Palitzsch and Manfred Wekwerth, as well as designers such as Teo Otto (1904–68), Karl von Appen (1900–81), Caspar Neher (1897–1962) and Heiner Hill (b. 1913). In choosing his actors, Brecht was careful to maintain a productive balance of experienced players – Helene Weigel, Therese Giehse (1898–1975), Ernst Busch, Leonard Steckel (1901–71), Curt Bois (1901–91), Gerhard Bienert (1898–1986), Erwin Geschonnek (b. 1906) – and younger actors such as Angelika Hurwicz (b. 1922), Regine Lutz (b. 1928), Käthe Reichel (b. 1926), Ekkehard Schall (b. 1930), Fred Düren (b. 1928) and Heinz Schubert (b. 1925).

After Brecht's death, his protégés – Wekwerth, Palitzsch and Besson – along with Erich Engel, defined the new look of the Ensemble with their own productions of Brecht. *Der aufhaltsame Aufstieg des Arturo Ui* (*The Resistible Rise of Arturo Ui*), directed by Wekwerth and Palitzsch in 1959, and the 1964 production of *Coriolan* (after Shakespeare), directed by Wekwerth and Joachim Tenschert (1928–92), contributed substantially to the Berliner Ensemble's international reputation.

From the mid-1960s on, younger directors like Ruth Berghaus, Wolfgang Pintzka (b. 1928), Manfred Karge, Matthias Langhoff, Uta Birnbaum (b. 1933), Hans Georg Simmgen (b. 1933), Bernd K. Tragelehn, Einar Schleef and Peter Kupke (b. 1932) experimented with both form and content in an attempt to save the Berliner Ensemble from turning into a Brecht museum. Despite a series of successes, external political pressure and internal strife prevented a genuine revitalization. In 1992 the Berliner Ensemble was privatized and turned into a

limited company under directors Matthias Langhoff, Fritz Marquardt (b. 1928), Peter
Palitzsch and Peter Zadek, with playwright
Heiner Müller involved as a silent partner. To
what extent this restructuring will lead to new
developments remains uncertain.

Even during the Nazi era the Deutsches
Theater, which Max Reinhardt had made into
Germany's première showcase, remained true to
Reinhardt's humanistic and artistic principles
under director Heinz Hilpert – at least to the
extent that this was possible under a dictatorship that pervaded all areas of life. Thus its first
post-war artistic director and former Reinhardt
actor, Gustav von Wangenheim, and his successor, Wolfgang Langhoff, who took over in
1946, were able to rebuild an ensemble very
quickly by drawing directly on the Reinhardt
era. With its productions of German classics and
Russian realists it set the standard for realistic
acting in the following years. Besides Langhoff,
former Zürichers Wolfgang Heinz, Karl Paryla
(b. 1905) and Emil Stöhr (b. 1907), who had

joined the Deutsches Theater with part of the
ensemble of the Vienna Neues Theater in der
Scala (New Theatre in the Scala) when it was
shut down in 1956, also contributed substantially to its success.

Besson, like many actors from the Berliner
Ensemble, had also gone over to the Deutsches
Theater, opened it to the creative stimulus of a
gesture-oriented tradition whose goal was
'deliberate theatricality'. His productions of *Der
Frieden* (Peter Hacks, after Aristophanes),
Molière's *Tartuffe*, Sophocles' *Oedipus
Tyrannus* and his production of Yevgeny
Svarts's political fairytale, *The Dragon*, famous
for Horst Sagert's (b. 1934) imaginative set, also
helped the Deutsches Theater achieve international recognition. Under artistic director Wolfgang Heinz (from 1964), who perpetuated the
German and Russian tradition of realistic acting
(above all with his productions of Chekhov)
directors Friedo Solter (b. 1933) and Adolf
Dresen also stood out, the former especially
with an interpretation of Lessing's *Nathan der*

Friedo Solter's 1966 Deutsches Theater production of Gotthold Ephraim Lessing's *Nathan
the Wise*, designed by Heinrich Kilger.
Photo: Pepita Engel.

Weise (*Nathan the Wise*) that gave full scope to his actors' comic talents, the latter primarily with productions of O'Casey, Shakespeare and Kleist.

In the 1980s Alexander Lang, a protégé of Gerhard Wolfram (who had been running the theatre since 1973), became the Deutsches Theater's leading director. Drawing on his experience as an actor and exploring acting styles that had been long ignored in Germany, he sparked his actors' vitality and imagination in vividly realized scenes that turned the philosophical and literary content of the plays into adventures that kept audiences constantly and actively involved. His greatest successes at the time were Shakespeare's *A Midsummer Night's Dream* and Büchner's *Dantons Tod*. Lang later evolved a concept of Theater der Zusammenhänge (Theatre of Correlation), which was supposed to lead the spectator to historical insights through existential questions raised by a disparate array of dramatic works grouped together in special projects designed to show their relationship to one another.

When Dieter Mann (b. 1941), who had started as a young actor with the Deutsches Theater twenty years before, became artistic director in 1984, the productive relationship between tradition and experimentation remained the guiding principle. Heiner Müller's productions of his own plays, *Lohndrücker* (1987), *Hamletmaschine* (1990) and *Mauser* (1991), and Frank Castorf's productions of Bulgakov's *Paris, Paris* and Ibsen's *John Gabriel Borkman*, brought a new artistic dimension to the company. Thomas Langhoff, artistic director since 1991, has, in his turn, drawn once again on the realistic tradition of his father, Wolfgang Langhoff.

Berlin's Volksbühne under Fritz Wisten was also noted for its wide-ranging repertoire, from contemporary plays like Sartre's *Nekrassov* to classical tragedies. The great comedies of world theatre, however, formed the core, and gave the Volksbühne its distinctive image. Its greatest success was with Goldoni's *Servant of Two Masters* with Rolf Ludwig (b. 1925) as Truffaldino and directed by Otto Tausig (b. 1922), another actor and director from the Vienna Scala. With Wisten's departure in 1961, the theatre lost its importance until Besson took over as artistic director in 1969.

In close collaboration with Heiner Müller and directors Matthias Langhoff, Manfred Karge and Fritz Marquardt, Besson made the Volksbühne a real home for artistic experiment and public festivities. Taking the theatre 'collective' as his point of departure, Besson saw theatre as a model for society, 'a laboratory of social imagination'. A precondition for such a theatre was, for him, freeing the actor's creativity through the traditions of European folk theatre, *commedia dell'arte* above all, and also developing the audience's capacity for pure aesthetic enjoyment. Besson's concept was most evident in what he called 'spectacles', events in which he used various spaces throughout the theatre building to mount pieces of differing themes and styles, letting the audience choose from among a variety of opportunities. Besson also believed in a close involvement with the audience, especially workers, which ranged from taking plays from workers' theatres and then redoing them professionally (often in adaptations by Müller such as *Horizonte/Horizons*) to holding creative seminars for weeks at a time in factories in Italy and Berlin. After the Besson era came to an end in 1978 there were still some outstanding individual successes – such as Jürgen Gosch's production of Büchner's *Leonce und Lena*, Fritz Marquardt's productions of several Müller plays (*Der Bau, Die Umsiedlerin*), Müller's own productions of *Der Auftrag* and *Macbeth* and, in recent years, Frank Castorf's productions of Paul Zech's *Das trunkene Schiff* (*The Drunken Boat*) and Schiller's *Die Räuber* – but in general the image of the Volksbühne declined, as did its audience. Frank Castorf took over as its artistic director in the 1992–3 season.

Still another East Berlin theatre of importance was the Maxim Gorki Theater, founded in 1952, which grew out of an ensemble of young actors whose goal was to develop the Stanislavski method. Under artistic director Maxim Vallentin the Gorki specialized in contemporary drama, especially plays from the GDR, other east European countries and the Soviet Union, with a particular emphasis on the works of Gorki. Through close connections to major Berlin industries, the Gorki developed a loyal and steady audience whose interests and needs determined the theatre's identity. Under Vallentin's successor, Albert Hetterle (b. 1918), an actor with the ensemble since 1954, the theatre remained true to its artistic tradition – political commitment and entertainment. During the 1980s it was primarily through the work of Thomas Langhoff (Chekhov's *Three Sisters* and Shakespeare's *A Midsummer Night's Dream* among others) and Rolf Winkelgrund, that the Gorki again reached a very high standard of artistic achievement and played a real part in the social debate both before and during the great transition which led to reunification.

Only a few theatres in other cities of the GDR had lasting reputations. It may be said of the Leipzig and Rostock theatres, but in the end they too had all the signs of stagnation. The Volkstheater Rostock (Rostock People's Theatre), run with only a brief interruption by Hanns Anselm Perten from the beginning of the 1950s into the 1980s, was distinguished by its repertoire. Open to plays from all over the world, the theatre featured South American drama alongside works by Peter Weiss and Rolf Hochhuth. Leipzig was a similar case, where Karl Kayser (b. 1914), artistic director from 1958 to 1989, devoted much of the repertoire primarily to Soviet drama, and in more recent years, to important plays from the GDR.

Most of the other theatres changed their artistic image according to the artistic director of the day. Thus it was not uncommon for theatres in smaller centres to find themselves rudely awakened from years of insignificance, as a talented director and his group of co-workers moved in. That happened in the 1950s in Senftenberg, sparked by Horst Schönemann, in Meiningen in the 1960s under Fritz Bennewitz, in Rudolstadt in the 1970s under Klaus Fiedler (b. 1938) and in Anklam in the 1980s under Frank Castorf. With few exceptions, therefore, it is not possible to speak of the artistic profiles of GDR theatre with reference to the theatres themselves, but rather to the creative personalities pursuing their careers through various cities, not infrequently with Berlin as their goal.

This pattern is perhaps seen most clearly in the team of Gerhard Wolfram and Schönemann, whose peregrinations took them practically through the whole of the GDR. After he started as a director in Senftenberg, Schönemann teamed up with dramaturge Wolfram at the Gorki in Berlin in 1959 where, together with director Hans Dieter Mäde (b. 1930), they built up the theatre's reputation with a national and international contemporary repertoire, which satisfied the audience's demand for airing the problems of daily life as well as providing high-quality entertainment.

In Halle, under the difficult conditions of a culturally neglected and environmentally damaged industrial region, Wolfram as intendant and Schönemann as artistic director managed to champion the idea of a theatre working closely with its audience, calling itself the 'people's soapbox', and quickly made the Landestheater Halle into one of the leading theatres in the country. Plays and revue-like sketches about the social and psychological problems of the region were developed in close contact with people from major chemical plants and laboratories. These *Anregungen* (initiatives), as they were called, afforded spectators ample opportunity to take an active role in what was being presented. Coupled with it was an attempt to put into practice new ways of working together through collaborative creation on the plays and also participation in the decision-making process.

It wasn't long, however, before Schönemann and Wolfram came up against the limitation of a community theatre, and together left for Berlin in 1972 where they took over the Deutsches Theater. In 1979 Schönemann went to Dresden to become artistic director of the Staatsschauspiel, and in 1982 political intrigue persuaded Wolfram to follow his friend and take over the management there. Even in this artistically more traditionally oriented city, they managed to realize their ideals of a politically committed and artistically innovative theatre. They managed to turn the Staatsschauspiel, which had been stagnating for years, into one of the top theatres in the country. Wolfgang Engel's (b. 1943) productions of, for example, Hebbel's *Die Nibelungen*, Kleist's *Penthesilea* with Cornelia Schmaus (b. 1946) in the title role, and Goethe's *Faust*, were especially famous for their alarming and topical analogies to the present and their vivid use of a whole range of theatrical vocabulary. On a more personal level, Wolfram both promoted Engel's career and shielded him from political attacks.

At the Mecklenburger Staatstheater in Schwerin, Christoph Schroth together with dramaturge Bärbel Jaksch (b. 1945) began, in 1974, to put together a populist political theatre strongly influenced by Piscator's ideas. Particularly successful were the Schwerin *Entdeckungen* (explorations), theatre events which followed in the footsteps of the Halle 'initiatives' and also Besson's 'spectacles', in which several productions, exhibitions of artists' works, readings and other activities were all part of a single thematic evening designed to get the public actively involved. Best known was his production of both parts of Goethe's *Faust* in one evening, seen by over 100,000 people from all over the GDR, and also a 'Greek spectacular' comprised of three plays on the Trojan War (*Iphigenie in Aulis*, *Agamemnon* and *The Trojans*) and Aristophanes' *The Acharnians*, all

Wolfgang Engel's 1984 Staatsschauspiel Dresden production of Friedrich Hebbel's
Nibelungen, designed by Jochen Finke.
Photo: Hans-Ludwig Böme.

devoted to the theme of war and peace. In 1989, Schroth left for the Berliner Ensemble, where he had previously been very successful as a guest director, specifically with his production of Shatrov's *Blaue Pferde auf rotem Gras* (*Blue Horses in a Red Field*).

The Städtische Theater Karl-Marx-Stadt (Karl Marx Stadt (now Chemnitz) Municipal Theatre) also played an important role in the 1970s and 1980s under artistic director Gerhard Meyer (b. 1915). Together with directors Hartwig Albiro (b. 1931) and Piet Drescher, he created a theatre of clarity, realistic detail and poetic beauty which responded to the interests and needs of this small Saxon industrial centre's audiences, and at the same time developed a nation-wide reputation for discovering and nurturing new talent. Many actors like Jutta Wachowiak (b. 1940), Cornelia Schmaus, Christian Grashof (b. 1943) and Ulrich Mühe (b. 1951) started here on their way to top

theatres in Berlin. Gerhard Meyer also gave Frank Castorf the chance to continue his unconventional approach in productions of Müller's *Der Bau* and Ibsen's *An Enemy of the People*, after Castorf was fired from Anklam.

Between 1983 and 1987 as a polemic against the Deutsches Nationaltheater Weimar tradition (bearing the stamp above all of Fritz Bennewitz's important productions of Shakespeare, Goethe and Brecht in the 1960s and 1970s) directors Peter Schroth and Peter Kleinert, who both came out of Wolfram's Halle Theater, evolved an approach to the classics and contemporary plays that reflected the contradictions of the times with imagery derived from modern associative techniques. Their productions of Shakespeare's *Measure for Measure* and *Twelfth Night*, and Volker Braun's *Siegfried Frauenprotokolle Deutscher Furor* (*Siegfried: A Women's Brief on the German Madness*) were significant examples of this style.

Music Theatre

In 1900, opera, operetta and ballet frequently composed more than 50 per cent of the monthly repertoire of both court theatres and the larger

municipal theatres. In connection with the larger call on funding associated with musical productions, the consequence was a certain competitive mentality within the theatre which was quite productive. The popularity and success of musical theatre works prompted theatre managers to establish separate theatres for opera and operetta, in the tradition of the large *Residenz* cities, like Berlin, Dresden and Munich, which had court opera facilities that lived on as separate opera houses. This trend has continued in the larger municipal theatre complexes of cities such as Stuttgart and Leipzig run under a general management, where each of the branches has managed to assert an unofficial administrative and subsequently artistic independence.

Court theatres had actually been opened to the middle classes and the bureaucratic elite as early as the end of the eighteenth century. Opera, operetta and ballet thereafter experienced a quantitative audience increase that reached its high point just before World War I. This evolution had a significant influence on the perception that the opera house was nothing but a showplace for 'society', from which certain social classes were excluded on principle. A coterie of highly specialized 'connoisseurs' was built up and the majority of the propertied classes saw such people as drawing-room ornaments. Accordingly, artists aimed for superficial effects, theatricality and individual star performances. Anything that could disturb was eliminated from the repertoire and the purely musical or decorative were emphasized.

During the 1920s, a noticeably new creative energy emerged, which was to have a decisive effect. Along with new styles of performance, the hallmark of this new development was a breaking of all previous taboos, with social commentary, satire, and topics of intellectual immediacy now included. Not infrequently the standard of performance was extraordinary, for example at the Kroll-Oper (Kroll Opera) in Berlin at the end of the 1920s. This trend came to an abrupt conclusion with the emergence of the Nazis, and many top-ranking musicians and composers were soon driven into exile. The Nazis were unable to replace what was lost.

Opera and ballet, however, remained permanent parts of the thinking as well as of the structure of the overall German theatre system. Still primarily perceived of as theatre, they are also increasingly judged by the standards of director's theatre.

FRG

In 1990, there were fifty-four permanent opera companies in West Germany, although they did not all put on regular daily performances. The seven largest – Munich, Berlin, Hamburg, Düsseldorf (together with Duisburg), Frankfurt, Stuttgart and Köln – are of international relevance. During the 1970s, the Nürnberg Opera along with the Bremen, Kassel and Darmstadt Operas rose to a position of national importance with the high quality of their production standards and a repertoire that was exemplary in its inclusion of contemporary works; in the 1980s, the Gelsenkirchener Musiktheater im Revier (Music Theatre in the Coal District) and the opera company of the Städtische Bühnen Bielefeld (Bielefeld Municipal Theatre) also distinguished themselves. Seven of the larger opera companies also have affiliations with experimental studio theatres. There are no commercial opera houses.

In West Germany, opera, operetta and musicals have about the same attendance as drama (including children's and youth theatre) – about 6.5 million admissions per year. Costs are higher, however: opera, in fact, accounts for over two-thirds of the national theatre budget and is thus the most cost-intensive sector, three times as expensive as drama. Perhaps this has contributed to the opera's elitist reputation. Public surveys, however, suggest the opposite. Opera is widely accepted and popular even with young people and plays to full houses more often despite higher prices, which are considerably more than double the price of a theatre ticket. Because opera's capacity is thus stretched to the limit and the demand frequently outstrips supply, subscriptions have had to be limited.

Like dance, music theatre has an international character: one-third of the country's nearly 8,000 artists are from abroad. The bigger houses are also part of the international star circuit, and therefore often overshadow the ensemble idea and repertory system. The modern trend of doing opera in its original language for artistic reasons thus also becomes a matter of practical necessity.

Opera, with over half the performances, dominates Germany's music theatre repertoire. The Broadway-style musical is gradually supplanting the operetta, which in 1975 still enjoyed twice as many performances as this imported genre but in 1988 was surrounded by it. The repertoire of operas is much more 'museum' than that of dramas, and scarcely rejuvenates itself. Mozart and Verdi are still the staples, followed by Puccini and Wagner. Lortzing's *Spielopern*, once the staple of the smaller houses, dropped off markedly during the 1980s, Offenbach taking their place. Richard Strauss and Rossini are also frequently performed. Characteristic trends since the mid-1970s have included a renaissance in the works of Monteverdi and a revival of Baroque opera, particularly Händel (1685–1795); Mozart's *Idomeneo* and *Titus* joined the stock of the repertoire; and Slavic opera, especially Janáček, aroused great interest. Notable, too, was the rediscovery of works on the threshold of modernity by the Austrians Alexander von Zemlinsky, Franz Schreker and Erich Wolfgang Korngold.

Quantitatively speaking, modern opera hardly counts. Nevertheless, Alban Berg's *Wozzeck* and *Lulu* have become standards, and Arnold Schoenberg's *Moses und Aron* (*Moses and Aaron*) is performed continually. But works by living composers make up only 3–4 per cent of total productions. Yet a commitment to the modern has always been an important ferment for opera as theatre, and also for injections of new creativity into older works. The avant-garde, since 1945 completely under the influence of Schoenberg's twelve-tone *Serialismus*, for its part disdained 'impure' opera, and whoever meddled with the theatre at all – such as Werner Egk (1901–83), Boris Blacher (1903–75), Wolfgang Fortner (1907–87) and Hans Werner Henze (b. 1926) – preferred to write for the ballet, where the audience's rhythm-bound identification with the dancer allowed modern music to slip in practically incognito. The sparer nature of modern music was also more readily accepted where it served to support or heighten a scene, as in Carl Orff's (1895–1982) musical settings of antique dramas and Medieval and Baroque Christian plays. It was not till the late 1950s that pre-war composers for music theatre returned to the West German stage with 'literary opera' – Egk, Ernst Krenek (1900–91), Fortner (*Bluthochzeit*/*Blood Wedding*, 1957), Rolf Liebermann (1910–92) and, as of 1960, Blacher.

In the mean time a new generation, along with Henze and Giselher Klebe (b. 1925), had already turned its attention to the stage. Henze has remained the most versatile and successful contemporary opera composer. His musical vocabulary accommodates both a flexible use of the twelve-tone technique and quotations from the traditional repertoire, and raw drama as well as lyricism. He has explored all imaginable forms, from the fantastic opera, such as *König Hirsch* (*The Stag King*, 1956), through musical settings of literary classics, from the psychological realism of his chamber operas to an updated version of *opera buffa*, from the Mystery play (*Die Bassariden*/*The Bassarides*, 1966) and vaudeville to political parables (*We Come to the River*, 1976), children's operas and musical dramas. Since 1971 he has also been directing his own works more often, and in 1988 founded the Biennial for Contemporary Music Theatre in Munich.

What Henze tried to achieve through variety, Bernd Alois Zimmermann (1918–70) strove to find through simultaneous use of a multiplicity of idioms. His pluralistic opera, *Die Soldaten* (*The Soldiers*), is total theatre in the most sophisticated sense, which, since its 1965 première in Köln, has become the benchmark for West German opera and a fixture in the repertoire.

Mauricio Kagel (b. 1931 in Buenos Aires, living in Köln since 1957) went a third way. For him, music theatre was meaningful only as a reflection of its materials and limits. He reinterpreted opera's traditional elements and techniques of performance by interchanging their relationships and combining them with non-musical elements, which enabled him to write opera by either avoiding or transcending it. Thus his 1971 Hamburg première of *Staatstheater* (*State Theatre*), which he directed himself, is a 'scenic composition' and a staging of music, where events on stage illustrate the musical process: analysis turned into parody. Beyond these paradoxes, contemporary music theatre composers are, then as now, still having success with literary operas: Aribert Reimann (b. 1936) with *Lear* (1978) and *Troades* (1986), Wolfgang Rihm (b. 1952) with *Jakob Lenz* (1979) and *Oedipus* (1987) among others.

That opera can be both gripping and relevant was already shown as early as 1927 by the Kroll Opera in Berlin under the direction of Otto Klemperer (1885–1973) with productions by Fehling and Gründgens. As director of the Hamburgische Staatsoper (Hamburg State Opera) from 1946 to 1956, Günther Rennert took up the thread again when he tried to make his singers into actors and to articulate the dramatic action of operas by Rossini, Mozart, Verdi and Strauss for the stage, turning them into psychologically sophisticated music theatre. His recognition of the moderns (Stravinsky and Britten) acted as a catalyst, and half of his productions were consistently devoted to them. Rennert also carried on in this spirit elsewhere, especially in Stuttgart, but also at the Salzburger Festspiele (Salzburg Festival) and in Munich, where he again took up the post of director of opera from 1967 to 1976, and was mainly assisted by set and costume designer Rudolf Heinrich (1926–75), who came out of Felsenstein's school of 'realistic music theatre'.

Wieland Wagner (1917–66), grandson of Richard Wagner, had the most lasting effect on operatic set design. In Bayreuth in the 1950s, he took risks with a radically new approach to his grandfather's work, an approach which he later revised, improved and consolidated in a second phase (1961–5). He 'uncluttered' both stage and costumes by eliminating illustrative décor, and – like Appia, Craig and the expressionists before him – replaced naturalistic illusion with an abstract set composed of disc-like ramps, cubes and steps, using a strict lighting and colour scheme to reveal deeper levels of archetypal symbolism. He did the same in Stuttgart, his 'winter Bayreuth', where he gave Rennert some friendly competition with sixteen productions between 1954 and 1966; and also

in all the great German opera houses as well as several dozen outside the country, where he allowed realistic tendencies to come back into play, mainly in the non-Wagnerian repertoire from Gluck to Berg.

Rolf Liebermann was the third great creator of West German music theatre. From 1959 to 1973 he was director of the Hamburg Opera and again from 1985 to 1989 (in between he was at the Paris Opera, 1973–80). As the composer of three often-performed operas in the 1950s, the future of his *métier* was particularly close to his heart. He passed twenty-one commissions for new work on to colleagues, thus establishing the now universal practice of promoting fellow artists. Liebermann strengthened the ensemble, gave substantial support to the ballet, and opened his opera house to the world through guest tours and reciprocal invitations, thereby giving it a star aura. At the same time, Sellner was taking the Opera in West Berlin into an era of world-class status,

Patrice Chéreau's 1976 Bayreuth production of Wagner's *Rheingold*, designed by Richard Peduzzi.
Photo: Siegfried Lauterwasser.

accentuated especially by premières of Henze, Klebe, Blacher and Reimann, and the visual power of sets by designers Filippo Sanjust (1925–92) and Michel Raffaelli (b. 1929).

In the 1970s, music theatre underwent a change due to a powerful new Europe-wide momentum coming from directors. It was most evident in Wagner productions, particularly the *Ring des Nibelungen* (*The Ring Cycle*), where the abstract and archaic gave way to historically concrete and socially relevant interpretations, as in Leipzig (1973–6), and in the 1976 Bayreuth production by French director Patrice Chéreau and the scenographer Richard Peduzzi. The latter is more popularly known as the 'Ring of the Century' – and not only because it marked the centennial of the Bayreuth Festival. While Bayreuth owed this production to two Frenchmen, it owed two others to East Germans.

In 1972 Götz Friedrich (b. 1930), until then head director of East Berlin's Komische Oper, staged a realistic and pointedly political *Tannhäuser*, and in 1978 Harry Kupfer (b. 1935) made his début in Bayreuth (after more than twenty productions in the west) with *Der Fliegende Holländer* (*The Flying Dutchman*), which was a realistic phantasmagoria. Both directors have since become important, not only for Bayreuth, but also for all German music theatre: Kupfer for productions in Dresden, Berlin, Frankfurt, Köln, Stuttgart and Hamburg; Friedrich for his work in Stuttgart, Hamburg (where he was head director, 1973–83), and at the Deutsche Oper (German Opera) in West Berlin, where he became administrative director in 1981.

The fascination of opera as musical drama is due as well to renowned designers who also tried their hand at directing, like Jean-Pierre Ponnelle (1932–88), Rudolf Heinrich and Sanjust as early as the 1960s, and Herbert Wernicke (b. 1946) and Achim Freyer at the end of the 1970s. The latter's Stuttgart productions of Philip Glass and *Der Freischütz* (1980) caused a particular sensation, as did his *Zauberflöte* (*The Magic Flute*, 1982) in Hamburg. Liebermann had already drawn on the talents of a lot of theatre directors; in the 1970s a host of innovative directors brought a whole new creative concept to the opera – Grüber, Neuenfels, Bondy, Heyme, Günter Krämer (b. 1940), and many more.

Between 1977 and 1987 the Frankfurt Opera under Michael Gielen (b. 1927) became a funnel for all these trends. Gielen's directorship stands as a shining example of West German music theatre, mainly because of the work of Neuenfels (*Aïda*, 1981) and Ruth Berghaus, but also because productions were part of an overall concept of consistently high standards.

GDR

Although far smaller than West Germany, East Germany had about the same number of theatres staging operas, operettas and ballet. Among them were some of international calibre, such as the Deutsche Staatsoper and the Komische Oper in East Berlin, the Leipzig Opera, and the Semper Opera in Dresden.

Of the GDR's sixty-four theatres, forty-three were also, or even exclusively, engaged in the presentation of musical works. Of these, there were thirty-five multipurpose theatre complexes and eight purely musical houses. The Komische Oper Berlin and the Staats-Operette Dresden (Dresden State Operetta) were the only new post-war additions among them. Out of roughly 28,000 performances in all genres of theatre – with an attendance of 10.1 million (1985) – more than a quarter were musical: opera (9.6 per cent), operetta/musicals (13.6 per cent) and ballet (5 per cent), accounting for 41.3 per cent of total audience attendance. Out of 1,000 works to be seen from a total of 1,768 productions in 1985, there were ninety-one operas, a hundred operettas and musicals, and forty-five ballets, almost 40 per cent of them by GDR composers and choreographers.

The first seasons after the war were devoted to the classical repertoire and to authors suppressed by the Nazis. The works of Schreker, Hindemith, Berg and Weill reflected the younger generation's need to catch up with what they had missed under the Nazis, but there was no broad audience for these works. During the 1950s, meanwhile, influential ideologues, misinterpreting certain tenets of Marxism, dismissed early twentieth-century opera, which had already joined the ranks of the classics, as either 'formalist' or 'alienated from the people'.

After the foundation of the GDR, and in accordance with state cultural policies, writers and composers were given contracts that gave them a fairly secure income during the creation of their works. In the 1960s, a slightly higher proportion of new works entered the repertoire, encouraged by various forms of financial assistance, bonuses and an emphasis placed on them for propagandist purposes. The Verband der Theaterschaffenden and the Komponisten Verband, that is the composers, directors and librettists themselves, supported this with initiatives of their own, in part with lavishly expensive music and theatre festivals which were primarily dedicated to modern works, and where new works were showcased. Interestingly, musical life in the GDR was not absolutely subordinated to the state; criticism was mostly aimed at details of text, music or production. From the 1950s on, there was mounting evidence of cosmetic text-changes and variable versions. One glaring example is Paul Dessau's (1894–1979) *Verhör des Lukullus* (*The Interrogation of Lucullus*, 1951), whose title was changed to *Verurteilung des L.* (*The Conviction of L.*) for no apparent reason.

From the end of the 1950s, it became a matter of pride for the smaller theatres, too, regularly to put on original productions of new operas or German premières of operas from abroad. This was largely a matter of opera in the grand

style, filling out a whole evening, while chamber operas and other lesser genres trailed behind due to lack of demand.

The most important and influential opera composers of the older generation were Ottmar Gerster (1897–1969), Paul Dessau, Rudolf Wagner-Régeny (1903–69), Jean Kurt Forest (1909–75), Wilhelm Neef (b. 1916), Karl-Rudi Griesbach (b. 1916) and Robert Hanell (b. 1925); of the younger, Gerhard Rosenfeld (b. 1931), Siegfried Matthus (b. 1934), Rainer Kunad (b. 1936) and Udo Zimmermann (b. 1943), later the artistic director of the Leipzig Opera. Practically all these composers tried to use either parable or history as allegories for the political problems of the day and the problems of everyday life, and to evolve traditional European opera further in the direction of a stronger reliance on acting and text, as well as integrating new compositional techniques.

From the end of the 1970s on, there was a revival of interest in chamber opera, especially

Walter Felsenstein's 1968 Komische Oper production of Sergei Prokofiev's *The Love of Three Oranges*, designed by Valeri Lewental.
Photo: Arwid Langenpusch.

as a result of the competitions sponsored by the Dresdner Musikfestspiele (Dresden Music Festival), and theatres turned to alternative playing areas – foyers, rehearsal stages, former cinemas – to accommodate them. These works were often highly individualistic in both content and form, increasingly abandoning the structure of classical opera for a tendency towards what has been called instrumental theatre.

Children's opera, mostly performed – after the English model – by adults (examples of performances by children for children are rare), has always been in plentiful supply in the individual regions, written by conductors. For a long time these works imitated traditional opera, but in a fairytale setting. Smaller-scale, pedagogically oriented small-cast productions caught on only in the 1970s, with a growing interest in the instrumentation of the modern orchestra and the use of the elements of song, as well as the integration of theatre and opera in general.

Classical opera, of course, always took absolute precedence, which is a phenomenon that clearly distinguishes opera from the theatre. From time to time, leading opera houses in the GDR would produce one original production a year, but at the same time much emphasis was placed on contemporary interpretations of the classics, underlining the relevance of opera as an art form.

Operetta, as the traditional form of light entertainment, continued in its time-honoured fashion from 1945 on with works by Millöcker, J. Strauss, Zeller, Lincke and Lehár that had come to be regarded as classics.

The question of the renewal of the operatic form as a genre of theatre was taken up again in the GDR from about 1950 on, mainly with Felsenstein's work at the Komische Oper. His concept of 'realistic music theatre' and the production techniques he developed gained international influence in the 1960s, and were spread by directors of the Felsenstein School, above all by Götz Friedrich, Joachim Herz (b. 1924) and Harry Kupfer, who later went their own way. In the 1970s and 1980s, Ruth Berghaus, coming from the dance theatre, took part in this work, as did Christian Pöppel-Reiter (b. 1941), Christine Mielitz (b. 1949) and Peter Konwitschny (b. 1945). In search of greater publicity, producers of dramatic theatre such as Adolf Dresen, Alexander Lang, Wolfgang Langhoff and the playwright Heiner Müller started staging operas.

Dance Theatre

There are dance companies attached to virtually all the opera companies in Germany. However, it is not in all cases possible to speak of these as a distinct branch of dance for in the smaller theatres, with only a dozen dancers, the ballet is largely absorbed into the opera where it exists mainly to perform interludes in older operas and operettas and to form chorus lines for musicals. Nevertheless, even these dance companies put on their own performances, although only in the case of twenty or so theatres do they manage between forty and ninety shows a year.

Hamburg and Stuttgart are still among the most important homes of dance in western Germany, that is they have long had autonomous, internationally respected ballet companies and large receptive audiences. There are extensive dance activities as well in Munich, Berlin and Düsseldorf/Duisburg, which also have relatively autonomous ballet companies of sixty to seventy-five members. In addition, Köln, Frankfurt, Wuppertal and Bremen became particularly important for modern dance in the 1980s even though these cities have much smaller companies and audiences.

Although Germany did not have a pronounced tradition of ballet before World War II, audiences increased steadily from the 1950s to the end of the 1980s. In 1990 ballet attendance in western German public theatres was some 1.3 million; from 1970 to 1986 the number of performances rose from 761 to 1,832. It is thus quite possible to speak of an emancipation of dance but the decisive part played by artists from abroad must be taken into account.

FRG

After 1945, ballet did not take up the *Ausdruckstanz* (German expressive dance) of the expressionist generation – the strongest German contribution to the history of dance – but instead caught up with other developments in ballet that it had missed. Exponents of modern dance like Mary Wigman (1886–1973), Harald Kreutzberg (1902–68), Dore Hoyer (1911–67) and Kurt Jooss (1901–79) could not gain a foothold after World War II and were reduced to doing one-person touring shows and giving classes. French, British and American touring companies, however, set new standards for the FRG and pointed the trend toward a new classical-romantic style. Choreographers and ballet masters from these countries soon followed.

A genuine German impetus for a West German ballet renaissance, however, came from composers. Egk's 1948 *Abraxas* in Munich was the first and – due to the scandal caused by the fact that it was banned – by far the most influential. Blacher, Henze, Fortner and Klebe also composed for traditional ballet. The dance company of the West Berlin Municipal Opera, since 1954 under the direction of Tatyana Gsovsky (b. 1901, Moscow), showed this to advantage. As at the East Berlin Staatsoper (State Opera) earlier, Gsovsky became the most important force in the revival of the ballet-drama. At the same time in Wuppertal, Erich Walter (1927–83), the first of the new German choreographers, based his ballets on the *danse d'école*, a foundation on which he built for the next two decades in Düsseldorf.

The 1960s were the crowning years of the classical renaissance. Rolf Liebermann persuaded George Balanchine to turn the Hamburg Staatsoper into the first European outpost of his New York City Ballet. *Apollon musagète*, *Orpheus* and *Agon* entered the German repertoire along with many other Balanchine company classics until 1971.

In Stuttgart, artistic director Schäfer appointed South African John Cranko from London's Royal Ballet as director of ballet in 1961, which totally changed the German ballet scene. With great determination, Cranko built up a new company with soloists Marcia Haydée from Brazil, Richard Cragun from the United States, Egon Madsen from Denmark and Birgit Keil (b. 1944). Joining them as well was an English team of directors that speedily brought the technical quality of the company to perfection. The new Stuttgart style – full of vitality, explosive and colourful – used the classical vocabulary in a very individual, relaxed and frankly natural way, often even with humour.

As a choreographer, Cranko believed in ballet with a plot that filled a whole evening. His breakthrough with the public came in 1962 with Prokofiev's *Romeo and Juliet* followed in 1965

by Tchaikovsky's *Eugene Onegin* and in 1969 by *The Taming of the Shrew*. The Petipa classics were also reworked in new dramaturgical terms, and in concerto ballets Cranko claimed new ground in every direction.

He consolidated his work by reorganizing the ballet school. The catchwords *Stuttgarter Balletwunder* (Stuttgart ballet miracle) were already making the rounds in 1963, and local enthusiasm was confirmed by guest tours all over the world. Nor did it wane after Cranko's early death in 1973. Marcia Haydée, who took over as director in 1976, managed to maintain the character of the company through a process of constant renewal and also with the help of choreographers like Kenneth MacMillan, Glen Tetley, Maurice Béjart and Hans van Manen as well as others from the company itself.

One of them was American John Neumeier (b. 1942), another choreographer who thinks in dramaturgical terms, and a committed teacher, guiding his audience along new paths, first as director of ballet in Frankfurt (1969–73) and then in Hamburg. In building up his repertoire he pursued a long-term programme of full-length narrative ballets from which there emerged entire cycles, among them a recreation of the Diaghilev/Nijinsky ballets, a Tchaikovsky trilogy, and five Mahler adaptations. Increasingly, he turned to the great works of music and world literature.

Critical opinion is split over the monumental and reverential nature of these works. While Neumeier goes from triumph to triumph in Hamburg as well as abroad, some critics reproach him for what they see as regressive tendencies. This divergence of opinion is symptomatic of the situation as a whole, for Germany has in the mean time seen the evolution of a 'dance theatre' that is in many ways the antithesis of ballet.

The name dance theatre emphasizes the theatrical aspect of a much broader form of dance that is not subject to formal limitations. Its affinity to theatre is in fact greater than to opera. This is seen quite literally in the fact that dance theatre has been included in the Berliner Theatertreffen since 1980, that Pina Bausch (b. 1940), the leader of this new trend, calls her choreography 'plays', and that the Bochum Playhouse has had a 'dance theatre' since 1986.

A distancing from all balletic techniques and canons of style was not the only thing that was veiled under this apparently neutral concept; there was also a total revolution in content. Topicality, everyday life, social pressures and violence were the new themes, while techniques derived from American modern dance companies and the Nederlands Dans Theatre, which had been touring Germany since the 1960s, and from German expressive dance, whose importance was now being recognized, albeit belatedly. Practically all the innovators came out of Jooss's department of dance at the Folkwang School in Essen or the Wigman Studio in Berlin.

Early focal points were the Westberliner Akademie der Künste (West Berlin Academy of the Arts) and the Internationale Sommerakademie des Tanzes (International Summer School of Dance) in Köln. In Köln the future leading lights of the new movement were awarded their first prizes in the young choreographers' competition: Pina Bausch, Susanne Linke (b. 1944), Gerhard Bohner (1936–92), a devotee of Bauhaus dance theories, but also of Artaud, and Hans Kresnik (b. 1939), the dance platform's political demonstrator and narrator of nightmarish tales of terror and brutality. The way into the big theatres lay open.

In Bremen, Kresnik was the first to take over a ballet in a public theatre in 1968; the opera-ballet in Köln was transformed into a collectively run forum for dance in 1971; it was Bohner who first used the name 'dance theatre' for his group experiments at the Landestheater in Darmstadt (1972–5). Pina Bausch followed his example in Wuppertal in 1973. In 1978 Bohner and Reinhild Hoffmann (b. 1943) took over in Bremen from Kresnik, who went to Heidelberg only to return eight years later.

The dance theatre was unable to make further headway in the public theatres, but it became the most important German contribution to the international dance scene anyway, thanks to the outstanding artistry of Pina Bausch. If she began her choreographic work with music by Gluck, Mahler, Stravinsky, Weill and Bartok, by 1978 she had left all such connections behind in favour of a more associative technique with loosely connected scenes, repeated leitmotifs, collage, improvisation and cinematic transitions. Demonstration, variety-show formats, and alienation served to expose the clichés of social rituals and behavioural roles, while confusing sets (ponds and fields of carnations) and inventive business (such as an invasion of crocodiles and hippopotamuses) counteracted the

Pina Bausch's 1978 Tanztheater Wuppertal production of *Kontakthof*, designed by Rolf Borzik.
Photo: Ulli Weiss.

banality of everyday life centred on the battle of the sexes, lack of communication, and the pleasures and pains of human intimacy.

If 'dance theatre' was conceived as an alternative to ballet, American-born choreographer William Forsythe (b. 1949), since 1984 director of the Frankfurt ballet, represents the most radical confrontation of ballet with itself. His work has elements in common with Pina Bausch's – breaking formal barriers, using dialogue and film, highlighting the importance of the set, calling the works 'plays', and treating them as works-in-progress. Yet it has different roots. Forsythe always presents dialectical turn-abouts of old 'Balanchine' forms into new functional relationships. His choreography is the art of the dance reflecting upon itself, an exploration and a historical critique of his own work, and evinces a strong interest in theory and mathematical structure, yet is never dry but consistently exciting and engaging. After his début with the Stuttgart Ballet in 1976, Forsythe was entrusted with the original première of Henze's *Orpheus* (1979), while a new direction and fundamentally new conception of dance began to show itself most clearly in *Gänge* (*Gaits*, 1983) and *Limb's Theorem* (1990).

The upswing in West German dance also included a lively professional fringe, behind which, in turn, was a large amateur movement. More and more independent companies were formed from 1975 on, mostly influenced by Bausch, using dance as a commentary on the realities of daily life. Almost exclusively comprised of women, ten to fifteen companies were already performing regularly in the 1970s, and by the 1980s the number was well over fifty. The centres today are Berlin and Munich, and lately also Köln.

The first national dance forum was held at Frankfurt's Theater am Turm (Theatre at the Tower) in 1983; and a nation-wide touring festival entitled BRDance (Federal Republic Dance) was established in 1990.

GDR

Gret Palucca (b. 1902), whose school in Dresden had been shut down by the Nazis, reopened it on 1 June 1945, perhaps the earliest post-war dance activity in Germany. Soon after, Henn Haas (1907–89) founded the Theater des Tanzes (Theatre of Dance) in Weimar, and a little later Mary Wigman opened her dance studio in Leipzig, Dore Hoyer took over as

director of the former Wigman School in Dresden, Marianne Vogelsang (1912–79) founded a dance department at Rostock College, and Grita Krätke (1907–89) a dance studio in Schwerin. Jean Weidt (1904–88), returning from French exile, began work in Berlin with the group Junger Tänzer (Young Dancers) in 1948.

Almost all these dance instructors came out of expressive German dance but, nevertheless, there was now a more marked orientation towards theatre and what was called *Bühnentanz* (stage dance).

The big opera houses in Berlin, Dresden and Leipzig had large ballet companies of great power. Beyond that there were forty-two dance and ballet collectives, in part independent ensembles with their own repertoires or with their own approach to existing repertoires but also as integrated parts of opera or operetta companies. A few specialized in the variety show and revue format – Friedrichstadtpalast (Friedrichstadt Palace), Kleine Revue (Little Revue); others in choreographed adaptations of folklore – Tanzensemble der DDR (GDR Dance Ensemble), Staatliches Folkloreensemble (State Folklore Ensemble) and the Ensemble for sorbische Volkskultur (Sorbian Folk Ensemble).

GDR television also had its own ballet company, mainly for variety shows and revues. An equally capable ballet troupe was part of the army's Erich-Weinert-Ensemble. There were, however, no independent dance companies.

The Deutsche Staatsoper Berlin was the model in the ballet field. Here, between 1945 and 1952, Tatyana Gsovsky built up not only a powerful company, but also an exciting repertoire including Gluck, Ravel, Stravinsky, Prokofiev, Tchaikovsky, and the first original ballet of the post-war era, Leo Spies's *Don Quixote*. Her trademark was an artistry that lived up to the traditions of classical ballet. Her successors, Lilo Gruber (b. 1915) and Egon Bischof (b. 1934) continued her work and were able to build on it with modern works (including Henze, Balanchine and Cranko).

The 1950s brought an increasing vitality to dance in the GDR, at which time however the ongoing and unproductive quarrel between classical and modern resulted in a decision that hampered future development. With respect to the grand narrative ballet, the state theatre conference of May 1953 determined that henceforth classical ballet and folk dance were to be the acceptable forms. The German expressive dance, from Laban to Jooss and Wigman, was officially disregarded and, to a certain extent, even discredited.

Ballet companies devoted most of their activities to, and were mainly interested in, dramatic ballets and dances, with a definite preference for the grand style; but in addition, a variety of efforts were made – especially from the 1960s – to develop a ballet concertante (that is, symphonic dance) and to revive the chamber ballet tradition. This was also reflected in new libretti and compositions, often created in close collaboration with dance ensembles. One of the remarkable characteristics of GDR ballet was that leading composers created works whose contemporary musical vocabulary itself had a stimulating effect on the choreography. During the 1950s and 1960s, a considerable number of new ballets were especially influential. *Neue Odyssee* (*New Odyssey*), with libretto by Albert Burkat (1906–75) and music by Victor Bruns (b. 1904), was performed eighteen times throughout the GDR and also abroad; *Das Recht des Herrn* (*The Master's Prerogative*), by the same team, was performed twenty-five times, and the fairytale ballets of Karl-Rudi Griesbach and Wolfgang Hohensee (b. 1927) were no less successful. Since then a whole galaxy of prominent composers has written for the ballet, among them, Hans-Jürgen Wenzel (b. 1939), Georg Katzer (b. 1935), Rainer Kunad and Fidelio F. Finke (1891–1969). Bernd Köllinger (b. 1944), dance-dramaturge and later director of ballet at the Komische Oper Berlin, also made a substantial contribution to this trend with his libretti. Since the 1970s the ballet has won a wider audience and taken its rightful place alongside the other theatre arts.

Besides Berlin and Dresden, Leipzig also became another important ballet centre in the 1950s. Emmy Köhler-Richter (b. 1918) built up the repertoire by including most of the standard works plus original productions of new ballets. Her successor, Dietmar Seyffert (b. 1943), staged Stravinsky's *Sacre* (1981), one of the few genuinely successful productions of this important work. In Halle, Henn Haas put on at least one original ballet a year from 1957 to 1970. He was a particularly communicative choreographer and used his skills to convince composers of the validity of his ideas and commissioned many new compositions for his choreographic ideas.

Although professional collaboration with Soviet guest artists intensified from 1961 on, German ballet masters, choreographers and dancers still determined the life of the dance.

East European dancers enhanced the capability of the smaller ensembles, and guest soloists made occasional appearances with leading companies, but dance in the GDR never acquired a truly international character.

Since he began as a choreographer with the Komische Oper in the early 1960s, Tom Schilling (b. 1928) has made a substantial contribution to the uniqueness of GDR ballet and to the development of a new style. Starting with the prevailing dramatic style characteristic of Lilo Gruber's and Emmy Köhler-Richter's theatrically inspired creations, he adapted Felsenstein's 'realistic opera' to the different conditions and potential of ballet. His rare choreographic and musical imagination overcame the formal strictures of orthodox choreography with freer, more informal handling, and with his method of artistic synthesis he succeeded in creating modern and moving ballets which integrated techniques of German dance with the formal vocabulary and techniques of classical ballet.

The *Neuer künstlerischer Tanz* (new creative dance) of Gret Palucca, and her decades of teaching, also had a major influence on this trend. She developed a system out of German dance by combining it with other techniques. Practically all GDR ballet-artists, choreographers especially, were directly or indirectly influenced by her work, and in this sense were all students of Palucca.

The term *realistisches Tanztheater* (realistic dance theatre), not to be confused with west European *Tanztheater* (dance theatre), has meanwhile also caught on. The concept owes something to Felsenstein's terminology, and denotes a form of theatre which uses dance as its means of expression, integrates national traditions, and strives for both exact and convincing portrayals of emotions and social conditions.

Tom Schilling's work at the Komische Oper was also important and subsequently spread from there throughout the GDR. It was noticeable in the individualized work of Joachim Ahne in Rostock and Schwerin, and also in the work of Harald Wandtke (b. 1939) in Dresden and Udo Wandtke (b. 1944) in Weimar. A unique variation and form all her own was evolved by Irina Pauls (b. 1961) in Altenburg, and later at the Leipziger Schauspielhaus (Leipzig Playhouse), in a series of original ballets based on topical themes. In the 1980s, Arila Siegert (b. 1953) founded the Tanztheater am Schauspielhaus (Playhouse Dance Theatre) in Dresden. With her various chamber ballets, her choreographic collaborations with the theatre company (for example, for Shakespeare's *Sonnets*), and in her full-length guest productions – for example, *Othello und Desdemona* at the Komische Oper or *Medealandschaften* (*Medea Landscapes*) at the Leipzig Opera House – she was clearly following the tradition of German expressive dance and trying to revive it.

Hermann Rudolph's (b. 1935) works were stamped by a completely different individual style. It was especially at Karl-Marx-Stadt/Chemnitz that he created his own unique versions of standard works.

The history of dance theatre in the GDR is recorded in its dance archives in Leipzig, built up by Kurt Peterman (1930–84). The archives have records of 234 registered choreographic works created between 1961 and 1983, mostly chamber ballets to contemporary music, and more than a thousand ballets which have been premièred since 1949.

There have been more than 500 amateur groups in the GDR. Some of them approached professional standards and went on to attract attention, especially at the annual festival at Rudolstadt. Their repertoires typically included a number of premières.

Theatre for Young Audiences

FRG

In West Germany, no one seemed to care about children's and youth theatre until the end of the 1960s. Children were normally taken to so-called *Weihnachtsmärchen* (Christmas plays), mostly simple dramatizations and productions of Grimm's fairytales, or to Gerdt von Bassewitz's *Peterchens Mondfahrt* (*Little Peter's Trip to the Moon*), and at the opera, to Humperdinck's (1854–1921) *Hänsel und Gretel*. The only theatres which had a separate repertoire for children were the municipal theatres in Nürnberg and Dortmund, from 1948 and 1953 respectively. Few private theatres did children's shows; among the exceptions was the Münchener Märchenbühne (Munich Fairytale Stage), founded in 1953 and mounting shows in its own Theater der Jugend (Young People's Theatre) since 1957.

The student movement of the 1960s, however, looked on children as a disenfranchised minority. Author and journalist Melchior Schedler (b. 1936), basing his ideas on the theories of Brecht and Benjamin and a study of Asja Lacis's techniques, came up with provocative ideas for young people's theatre. At the same time, educational theorists developed models for teaching children through role-playing, and tried them out. The Deutscher Bühnenverein took a survey to determine what was needed, and called for more activity in children's theatre.

Some independent groups had already put all these recommendations into practice. One of them was the Reichskabarett (Reich's Cabaret) in Berlin, out of which, in 1971, came the Grips-Theater, the first and still the most important young people's theatre in Germany. Its founder and director, Volker Ludwig (b. 1937), built an operation whose goals, organization and methods became a model. From 1969, he began writing, with a variety of co-authors and his ensemble, a series of plays urgently needed by such a new emancipated children's theatre.

Relying on fairytale elements in the beginning, but on the trail of real-life problems (*Stokkerlok und Millipilli*), his plays dealt with the experiences of young spectators, took their side and represented their points of view in order to give them courage and to strengthen their self-confidence and awareness. Authoritarian parents, caretakers or police officers, schoolyard crises and imposed gender-roles were the major subjects. All these problems seemed solvable through cleverness (*Grips*) and solidarity. But topical social problems were also touched on: prejudice against foreign workers (*Ein Fest für Papadakis*/*Papadakis's Party*, 1973), youth unemployment (*Das hältste ja im Kopf nicht aus*/*That Really Takes the Cake*, 1975, the first German play for teenagers), pollution of the environment, exploitation of the Third World, and threats to peace.

Finally, Grips also made attempts to deal with German historical guilt in *Voll auf der Rolle* (*Totally in Character*, 1984) by Leonie Ossowski, and Ludwig's *Ab heute heißt du Sara* (*As of Today Your Name is Sara*, 1990). With his play about Berlin, *Linie 1* (*Line 1*, 1986), a powerful plea for living together in tolerance, Ludwig also conquered the adult theatre and won the Mülheimer Playwright's Prize. Grips also set the standard for productions. Comic effects, wit, songs and the intensity and directness of theatre-in-the-round fulfilled the often dreamed of notion of a truly populist theatre. The programmes helped digest the educational purposes of the plays.

If the Grips-Theater kept its leading role, it was not without competition. In 1973, the Rote Grütze (Red Berry) staked out its own distinctive territory as the most important company with regular participation by its children's audience. The group was able to teach children about sex in a playful, humorous way – *Darüber spricht man nicht!!!* (*We Don't Talk About Such Things!!!*) – the problems of puberty, drugs and brutality in relationships between the sexes were other themes which were based on long periods of research in the community. In Munich, the Theater der Jugend, with its own acting company since 1973, made a name for itself with social-commentary plays for young people by Helmut Walbert (b. 1937) and Werner Geifrig (b. 1939) (for example, *Bravo Girl*, 1975). Similar tendencies flourished at the Frankfurt Theater am Turm from 1976 until it was shut down by political pressure in 1979.

Other writers made a stronger appeal to the imagination and built their plays around circus acts and clown-comedy without, however, sacrificing their realistic bases; among them, Paul Maar (b. 1937) with his hit *Kikerikikiste* (*Cock-A-Doodle-Doo Box*, 1973), and Friedrich Karl Waechter (b. 1937) with his equally popular *Schule mit Clowns* (*Clowns in our School*, 1975) and *Kiebich und Dutz* (1977).

Independent groups have diminished in number since the wave of new companies that sprang up in the mid-1970s. However, children's and youth theatres were able to establish themselves as a separate department in a dozen public theatres and as the special domain of the regional theatres. The children's repertoire of the 'average' municipal theatre, mostly consigned to studio-productions, is – besides Grips plays – comprised of the popular fairytales of east European writers (Yevgeny Svarts among others) and the cheeky entertainments of Ken Campbell (*Fazz und Zwoo*, which was premièred in Germany in 1970), as well as success stories adapted from other media, such as Astrid Lindgren's *Pippi Longstocking* and the three parts of Otfried Preußler's *Räuber Hotzenplotz* (*Hotzenplotz the Robber*). The Grimm Brothers' and Andersen's fairytales, earlier expelled from the repertoire, also started a slow comeback in the 1980s.

During these years, changes, differentiations and new concepts in the theatre for young audiences were mostly influenced by Swedish and Dutch models. Besides this, youth theatre clubs have multiplied since the mid-1980s. These are initiatives launched by public theatres and directed toward schools, not only bringing young people into the theatre but also letting teenagers perform there. For the rest, the FRG's Kinder- und Jugendtheaterzentrum (Centre for Children's and Youth Theatre), founded in 1989, represents the overall theatrical interests of young people.

GDR

Within a year of the end of World War II, Leipzig's Theater der Jungen Welt (Theatre of the Young World) opened as the first professional children's and youth theatre. The date was 7 November 1946 and the first production was Erich Kästner's (1899–1974) children's story, *Emil und die Detektive* (*Emil and the Detectives*). In 1949, another theatre opened in Dresden (Theater der Jungen Generation/ Theatre of the Young Generation), and in 1950 in Berlin the Theater der Freundschaft (Theatre of Friendship). Others followed: in 1952 in Halle, the Theater Junger Garde (Theatre of the Young Guards, now called the Thalia Theater); in 1969 in Magdeburg, the Theater für Junge Zuschauer (Theatre for Young Audiences) which as of 1990 was called the Freie Kammerspiele (Independent Chamber Players).

Most were subsidized municipal operations with ensembles of between forty (Leipzig) and 180 (Berlin) and their own stages holding audiences of between 350 and 500. Very modest ticket prices made it possible for every child to attend regular school-organized theatre outings. In Dresden, Berlin and Halle, the companies were established as independent legal entities; in Leipzig and Magdeburg they were part of the municipal theatres until 1989.

The goal was to have their activities expand through the network of municipal theatres. As well, a state ordinance of 1963 committed every theatre to put on at least two special productions for children each season. A few theatres – Schwerin, Brandenburg and later Erfurt – built up extensive repertoires for children, but most restricted themselves to the traditional fairytales at Christmas. As adult audiences declined during the 1970s, however, even these theatres discovered the audience potential of children's theatre. Because of this, the children's audiences eventually grew to make up some 40–50 per cent of total attendance, and more than 300 children's productions in all genres began to be staged annually. Probably the most popular author of fairytales at the time was Peter Ensikat (b. 1941). Beyond this there were hundreds more amateur groups, among them thirty-five Pioniertheater (Youth Pioneer Theatres) that sprang up in the years after 1960 as part of the state youth organization. During the 1980s there was also an increasing number of independent groups performing at cultural centres, resorts, municipal festivals and factory celebrations.

National children's theatre conferences were held in 1953, 1955 and 1958 and an Arbeitsgemeinschaft der Kinder- und Jugendtheater (Union of Children's and Youth Theatre Workers) was founded in 1959. These all provided the opportunity to share experiences. As well, the GDR Centre of ASSITEJ (International Association of Theatre for Children and Young People) was founded in 1967, and a Büro für internationale Fragen des Kinder- und Jugendtheaters (International Office of Children's and Youth Theatre) was established in 1974 to encourage cooperation in all areas of children's and youth theatre production. Since 1976, it has sponsored annual international seminars for directors, and since 1977, seven-week workshops in Halle as well as new play competitions.

Until 1990 Ilse Rodenberg (b. 1906) was director of the International Office and she regularly encouraged foreign tours by GDR groups to promote children's theatre in other countries. Initially this took GDR performances to the FRG and other west European countries; later, it took them to Asian, Arab and African countries. This office was also the first to document and build up a collection of records of children's theatre from all over the world. In 1966, the first International Festival of Children's and Youth Theatre took place in East Berlin with twenty-five countries participating.

Children's and youth theatres did not evolve theories of their own until years later. In the beginning theatres had an educational role, and productions were seen simply as lessons. Performances consisted of fairytales with social commentary, a few classical works and plays from the Soviet youth theatre, available for the first time in translation.

Hans Rodenberg (1895–1978), who was given the task of starting the Berlin Theater der Freundschaft in 1950, was the first to evolve a concept of political theatre for children, based on his experience with the revolutionary workers' theatre before 1933, his knowledge of Soviet children's theatre from his years of exile, and Edwin Hoernle's (1883–1952) theories of a proletarian children's theatre. His intention was to inculcate the generation of children who went through the war and upon whom the Nazis had left their stamp, with humanist, anti-fascist and anti-capitalist values. Rodenberg built up a repertoire for three different age-levels, established the first educational section in a theatre, and succeeded in getting writers to collaborate. His programme was followed by other theatres that therefore evolved in much the same way.

The repertoire was dominated by contemporary German and Soviet plays about young people confronted with political decisions and the relationship of the individual to the collective. Among them, *Du bist der Richtige* (1951) by Gustav von Wangenheim; *Schneeball* (*Snowball*, 1950) by V.A. Lyubimova; and *Das rote Halstuch* (*The Red Neckerchief*, 1951) by S. Mikhalkov. Then came the fairytales, primarily by Soviet authors (Yevgeny Svarts and Samuel Marshak), and occasional comedies by Molière, Goldoni and Shakespeare, as well as plays that were directly related to the school curriculum – Schiller's *Kabale und Liebe* (*Love and Cabal*), Friedrich Wolf's *Die Matrosen von Cattaro* (*The Sailors of Cattaro*) and Brecht's *Die Gewehre der Frau Carrar* (*Señora Carrar's Rifles*).

If writers managed to come up with gripping historical subjects expressing children's points of view and encouraging their self-awareness – *Tom Sawyers großes Abenteuer* (*Tom Sawyer's Big Adventure*, 1953) by Hanus Berger and Stefan Heym; *Die Jagd nach dem Stiefel* (*The Great Boot-Hunt*, 1961) by Albert Pederzani; *La Farola* (1964) by Hanus Burger – these qualities were nevertheless still lacking in plays dealing with children's own experiences. State directives on education, and politically imposed 'non-conflict situations', prevented not only portrayals of generational conflicts, but also the development of truly meaningful contemporary children's plays.

The children's theatre in Dresden, under artistic director Rolf Büttner (1915–76) from 1956 on, made up for this lack by borrowing plays from the contemporary adult repertoire – *Und das am Heiligabend* (*And on Christmas Eve Too*) by Vratislav Blazek and *Die Aula* by Hermann Kant. Hans-Dieter Schmidt (1926–78), artistic director at Leipzig from 1959 to 1978, did the same with dramatizations of successful fiction – *Tinko*, after Erwin Stritt-matter; *Die Wolken ein Stück näher* (*A Little Closer to the Clouds*) after Günter Görlich.

The Berlin Theatre of Friendship, under artistic director Ilse Rodenberg from 1959 to 1973, got young poets interested in children's theatre and with them developed a new dramatic form for fairytales in particular. Instead of the prevailing politically predetermined characters and plots, these writers had faith in the poetic truth of the originals in plays like *Der gestiefelte Kater* (*Puss in Boots*) by Heinz Kahlau (b. 1931), *König Drosselbart* by Heinz Czechowski (b. 1935), and *Das bucklige Pferdchen* (*The Little Hump-Backed Horse*) by Elke Erb (b. 1938) and Adolf Endler (b. 1930).

In the process, an inspired use of epic theatre techniques also turned out to work well for children's theatre. Young director Horst Hawemann (b. 1940) in particular came up with productions whose most important quality was the demands they made on the actors to be in complete control of their characters in order to be open to the reactions of the children. It was

argued that this would allow children to participate with their own imaginations in such plays as *Tschintschraka* by G. Nakhutzshvili (1970), *Das bucklige Pferdchen* (1973) and *Die Herren des Strandes* (*Masters of the Shore*, 1971) by Friedrich Gerlach and Georg Katzer, after Jorge Amado. With productions such as these, children's theatre freed itself from its pedagogical strait-jacket and won artistic acclaim, even from theatre critics.

While Horst Hawemann and Mira Erceg (b. 1945) left their stamp on the Berlin Theatre of Friendship, their guest productions also became the standard for the new Magdeburg Theatre when it was opened in 1979, where Karl-Friedrich Zimmermann (1937–85) continued their work from 1979. Right from the beginning, Magdeburg made works of international drama accessible to its young public – *The Playboy of the Western World* by Synge, *Mann ist Mann* (*A Man's a Man*) by Brecht. Although Dresden had no outstanding directors, under artistic director Gunhild Lattmann (b. 1936) it nevertheless managed to build a consistently

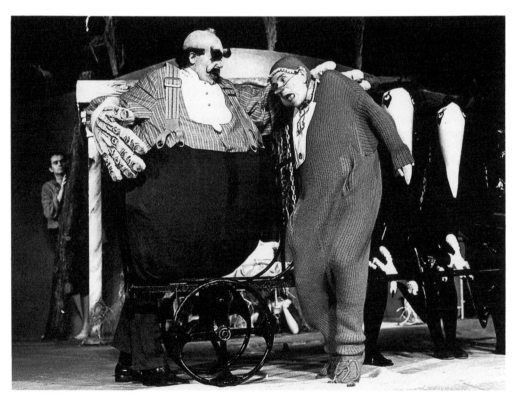

Karl Friedrich Zimmermann's 1985 Theater für Junge Zuschauer Magdeburg production of Peter Hacks's *The Children*, designed by Günter Altmann.

adventurous ensemble of younger actors around a core of experienced artists. Here they made the first, and most effective, breakthrough regarding the isolation of children from the world of adults, and also made the theatre into a meeting-ground for all generations through thematically linked performances, for example, Shakespeare's *Hamlet* and Letser's *Der kleine Prinz von Dänemark* (*The Little Prince of Denmark*). As well, they did parallel productions for adults and children and, through a variety of dramatic offerings and informative evenings, offered special events for both young and old.

Since the end of the 1980s, other theatres have been trying to expand in the same direction and are now known as *Familientheater* (family theatres). Plays from western Germany, Sweden, Holland, as well as new plays by former GDR authors, led the way in this trend. The fantasy plays of Horst Hawemann (*Kokori*, 1979; *Die Katze/The Cat*, 1986), Albert Wendt

(*Sauwetterwind/Foul Wind Brings Bad Weather*, 1981; *Vogelkopp/Birdbrain*, 1985), Peter Hacks (*Die Kinder/The Children*, 1984) and Manuel Schöbel (b. 1960) (*Prinz Tausendfuss*, 1987), all insisted on the individual's right to self-determination, and had the courage to assert their own ideas about life against a stagnant society.

After the 1990 reunification, the five East German children's theatres continued as municipal operations, with new, smaller theatres being opened in Cottbus and Güstrow. In order to hold on to and use their relatively rich resources of personnel and space more efficiently, however, and at least to some extent make up for all the facilities that were closed after 1990, these theatres also began to broaden their artistic and social activities to become more like municipal cultural centres for young people.

Puppet Theatre

There is a long tradition of puppet theatre in Germany although its audience is limited and many people still look on it as merely entertainment for children. Yet there has been an upswing since the 1970s which has given puppet theatre a chance to be taken seriously as an adult art form.

FRG

After 1979, the number of regularly performing puppet theatres with their own performance spaces and repertoires rose from seventeen to about forty. Adding in amateurs, some 350 puppet theatres were operating at any one time. Many were small – one to three person operations. The two largest, with companies of fifteen, being subsidized municipal institutions. The Hänneschen Theater in Köln, founded in 1802, was a family concern until 1926; the Augsburger Puppenkiste (Puppet Chest), founded by Walter Oehmichen (1901–77) in 1948, is still led by his family, although attached to the municipal theatre.

The Köln rod-puppet theatre is a well-loved and time-honoured local institution which, with its fixed Rhineland puppet characters, belongs to the realm of folklore. The Augsburg

marionette theatre is more ambitious from a literary standpoint (*Der kleine Prinz/The Little Prince* by Saint-Exupéry and *Faust*), and also has more of a universal appeal with fairy-tales, adventures and traditional stories. Since 1959 it has also put on about 800 television shows.

Two prominent puppet theatres came out of the inter-war years: Max Jacob's (1889–1967) Hohensteiner Handpuppenspieler (Hohenstein Hand-Puppet Players), which made the popular fairground children's hero, Kasper (a Punch-like figure), culturally acceptable; and the ingenious puppet-builder Harro Siegel's (1900–85) marionette theatre in Braunschweig. Siegel started his own puppet festival in 1957.

Other important initiatives in the field were launched by Ludwig Krafft (1901–77) with the founding of the Munich Puppentheatermuseum (Puppet Theatre Museum, 1940), and by puppet theatre historians Hans R. Purschke (1911–86) and Fritz Wortelmann (1902–76), who inaugurated the Deutsches Institut für Puppenspiel (DIP: German Institute for Puppet Theatre, disbanded in 1991) in Bochum in 1950 and the annual Figurentheater der Nationen (World Puppet) festival (FIDENA) in 1957. Wortelmann took on the task of building greater public awareness with his journal, *Der*

Puppenspieler (*The Puppeteer*), which from 1963 to 1990 appeared under the title *Figurentheater*.

Figurentheater was intended not only to be a more comprehensive term but also to serve notice of the puppet theatre's claims to being a genuine art form. The model was marionettist Albrecht Roser (b. 1922) with his clown, Gustaf. An active champion of puppet theatre craft, he was co-founder of the Verbandes Deutsche Puppentheater (Association of German Puppet Theatres) in 1968, an association which represents the interests of the profession. In Stuttgart he launched a number of initiatives by creating a puppet theatre society and managed to start a municipal *Figurentheater* as a stage for guest tours, finally even succeeding in getting a four-year diploma curriculum in puppetry accepted in the Academy of Music and Performing Arts in 1983. Since 1988 his colleague, Werner Knoedgen (b. 1947), has been the head of this department, the only

The Grandma marionette in Albrecht Roser's 'Gustaf and His Ensemble' puppet theatre, founded in Stuttgart in 1951.
Photo: Albrecht Roser.

academic puppeteer training school in the FRG. He also has published a phenomenology of the *Figurentheater* in 1990 (*Das unmögliche Theater/The Impossible Theatre*).

Puppet theatre has its own publisher since 1976, Frankfurt's Puppen & Masken (Puppets & Masks), which published the first comprehensive yearbook and directory in 1990, fulfilling the very necessary function of acquainting the *Figurentheater* world with itself.

Most West German puppet theatres perform for both adults and children with hand-puppets, marionettes and rod-puppets being the usual forms. Open stages, putting puppeteers in full view, are starting to catch on. Improvisation is more often talked about than practised. Mobility, of course, plays a significant role with guest tours and the many puppet festivals helping to ensure survival. Some puppet theatres hold regular workshops. With his literary *Figurentheater, die bühne* (the stage) in Berlin, Peter K. Steinmann (b. 1935) manages to be a model of versatility going from chamber style to street theatre to television.

There is also a great variety of genres. There is scarcely a *Figurentheater* that would do without fairytales, but a literary repertoire can also be found almost everywhere, even if seldom very wide-ranging or particularly original. Many include cabaret and parody; animal stories and adaptations from other media are especially popular. They also do opera (as Harro Siegel had already done) and even musicals. Occasionally they also experiment with abstract figures and unusual subjects or colours.

Reunification has given a further boost through cooperation between the two former Germanies; in 1991, the Deutsches Forum für Figurentheater und Puppenspielkunst (German Figurentheater and Puppet Players' Forum) was set up in Erfurt.

GDR

The historical roots of puppet theatre in East Germany can be found primarily in the traditional marionette theatre in the region of Saxony; in the innovations of the 'Hohensteiners', Max Jacob, Karl Iwowski (1904–70) and Theo Eggink (1901–75); and in the puppet plays put on by the revolutionary movement before 1933, such as those of Otto Griebel (1895–1972) and Herbert Oestreich.

The key ingredient for the many-sided development of the puppet theatre in the GDR after 1949 was the generous state support of amateur groups, the establishment of a series of state puppet theatres, and the formation of a support system of institutions and organizations. Immediately after 1945, over a hundred private puppet theatres were in operation; the number was later reduced by dogmatic cultural policies. Nevertheless, high-profile artists such as Carl Schröder (b. 1904), Felix Lorenz (1907–87), Hans Frannek (b. 1908) and Herbert Oestreich were able to exercise a formative influence. An important impetus came from the first guest tour of the Moscow State Puppet Theatre under Sergei Obraztsov in 1951. Besides the important Soviet repertoire, puppeteers also took up the stick-puppet, practically unknown in the GDR till then, which soon reigned supreme in all state theatres. In short order, some eighteen new puppet theatres were opened.

With the transition from individual artists to ensembles in regular theatres, a division of labour ensued which resulted in separate workshop and production operations with performing, directing and technical departments, out of which there developed a professional class of puppet-builders, scene painters, and puppet theatre dramaturges and directors.

Corresponding to the various levels of its audiences (pre-school, primary school, young adults and, increasingly, adults) the repertoire was made up of fairytales, traditional Punch and Judy shows (*Kasperspiele*), adaptations of children's plays and contemporary children's literature, as well as topical plays and puppet musicals. The repertoire expanded after the Ministry of Culture and the Verband der Theaterschaffenden introduced competitions.

Puppet plays came in both free and conventional forms and also made use of interaction between the puppet and the visible puppeteer; hand-puppets, stick-puppets and marionettes were commonly employed, but experimental puppets were not ignored.

Because puppet theatre came from an amateur tradition, for the most part, the puppeteers' qualifications have, since the 1950s, been raised through courses and seminars leading to professional diplomas. The establishment of a puppet theatre department in the Ernst Busch Theatre Academy in Berlin was a particularly important advance.

Puppet theatre enjoyed another noticeable upswing from the 1970s on, and took its proper place as a recognized performing art. Professional publications and professionally trained critics, in the journal *Theater der Zeit* (*Theatre of Our Time*), also contributed, as did the State Puppet Theatre Collection in Radebeul.

Festivals and competitions had an effect on raising artistic standards. These were an indicator of achievement in terms of aesthetic theories, artistic reputations and repertoires, and served as a forum for discussions on standards and practices. Prizes for both puppet theatre and freelance puppeteers were regularly awarded by state institutions and community organizations.

In the late 1970s, adaptations of fairytales seemed to dominate the form, although attempts were being made to gain recognition for the Kasper figure – that is the clown character – as a genuine folk-figure. Schröder's productions got a lot of attention in this respect, as did solo puppeteers Frieder Simon (b. 1930) and Peter Waschinsky (b. 1950). The latter's *Kasparett* was a breakthrough in bringing the Kasper figure up to date and, in his Neubrandenburg production of Barry Hines's *Der Teilhaber* (*Partner*), he showed just how important and artistically successful adaptations of contemporary theatre can be for the puppet stage.

The early 1980s saw the tradition of puppet plays for adults taken up again along with an increase in professionalism. Simultaneously, there was a noticeable political commitment on the part of puppet players in productions like Brecht's *Furcht und Elend des Dritten Reiches* (*Fear and Misery in the Third Reich*) and Arrabal's *Guernica*. Contemporary works such as Hacks's *Der arme Ritter* (*The Poor Knight*) and scenes from *Adam und Eva* shared the repertoire with poetic children's productions. With their production of *Der Jäger des verlorenen Verstandes* (*The Huntsman of the Lost Mind*), Berlin's Zinnober Group turned the Kasper tradition into a high level of artistic and topically relevant social commentary.

In 1984 at the UNIMA (International Puppeteers Union) World Congress in Dresden, students of the Ernst Busch Theatre Academy brought new dimensions to the political puppet theatre with their treatment of the theme of war and peace in a production of *Simplizissimus: Szenen aus dem Dreißigjährigen Krieg* (*Simplizissimus: Scenes From the Thirty Years War*).

By the 1987 festival, the puppet stage saw very different forms, traditions and works of world drama such as *Miss Julie*, staged by Knut Hirche (b. 1951) in Neubrandenburg; *Striptease* (Karl-Marx-Stadt/Chemnitz), *Cyrano de Bergerac* (Erfurt) and *Die Jüdin von Toledo* (*The Jewess of Toledo*; Dresden). Children's shows

Marlies and Knut Hirche's 1987 Puppentheater Neubrandenburg production of August Strindberg's *Miss Julie*.
Photo: Bernd Lasdin.

also began to take on ethically relevant themes, such as tolerance.

Attempts to depict the role of the individual in society and history were evident in 1990. Striking references to the present appeared in *Macbeth*, adapted by Ronald Mernitz (b.

1958), staged by Lois Frank (b. 1960), and topical subjects such as *Handgemenge* (*Street Fight*; Freie Gruppe Lavendel/Lavendel Independent Players, Berlin) were devoted to questions of this type. The trend was also evident in the best solo performances.

Design

Wherever there was a directors' theatre, there was also a great emphasis on set design. At the outset of his career Max Reinhardt was already attaching visual artists to his work, and the early-twentieth-century reforms in theatre were, in Germany, primarily reforms in set design – *Stilbühne* (styled stage), *Reliefbühne* (sculptured stage) and *Bauhausbühne* (Bauhaus stage). Both expressionism and constructivism found their most popular forms of activity in the theatre. The demands made on the set as co-creator of the production were always high and there was a concomitantly acute awareness of the problems involved, an eagerness to experiment

and a mastery of the craft on the part of set designers.

After 1945 it was possible to fall back on this high standard of the pre-Nazi era, but the means were lacking at first. Thus necessity became the mother of art and scenery that was symbolic or impressionistic, appealing to the spectator's imagination to make up for what was missing, became the prevailing style. It performed no illusionistic function, and can be considered to be modern to the extent that it supported and enhanced the expression of the play and its meaning rather than illustrating scenes and actions. Unified sets, on which all the scenes could be played without change, were common. What was important was not the set's illustrative capacity but the functional use of the designer's art.

Caspar Neher was the most prominent of the set designers who had made a name for themselves during the Weimar Republic. Brecht, who worked with him again from his 1948 *Antigone* to his death, called him a 'set-builder'. Neher's designs were defined by a clearly articulated architectonic of stage floor, structure and separation of areas, and were enlivened by the gestures of his figures and the rhythm of his costume design colours.

Despite the anti-illusionist nature of his constructions, Neher had long ago given up epic theatre as a specialty. His work was extremely versatile in both opera and drama, often with as many as twenty productions a year, and he worked primarily with Oscar Fritz Schuh (1904–84).

The work of Teo Otto was even more all-embracing. He, too, had been working with leading directors before 1933; during his wartime exile he designed a new production every two weeks at the Zürich Schauspielhaus. Without doubt, he became the most sought-after German set designer of the post-war era. Otto's style was more painterly, uniting surrealistic influences with montage in poetically suggestive images and powerful colour. He preferred the open stage and a décor comprised of representational fragments. He used simultaneous playing areas, projections, and shimmering, fast-changing gels.

In East Germany, the two set designers who came into prominence after 1945 were Karl von Appen and Heinrich Kilger (1907–70). Primarily working with directors such as Brecht, Langhoff and Besson at the Berliner Ensemble and the Deutsches Theater, they discovered new design possibilities that became the model for theatres throughout the 1950s and 1960s. Kilger and von Appen were both essentially seeking expressive use of stage-space through the performer's relationship with set and props. The artistic nature of the space was emphasized first by the box set and later by an open set which defined itself through the action and changed along with it.

The generally accepted principle of set design in the 1950s was to have only a fragment of the actual environment shown. Interior and exterior could interpenetrate and combine. The goal was to stimulate the creative imagination of the spectator. Kilger and von Appen took pains to find

this visual vocabulary which avoided the illusionistic and the illustrative. Outstanding examples were von Appen's set for *Der kaukasische Kreidekreis* (*The Caucasian Chalk Circle*, Berliner Ensemble, 1954; directed by Brecht) and Kilger's highly versatile set for *Der Frieden* (*Peace*, Deutsches Theater Berlin, 1962; directed by Besson). Although both designers were models for the next generation, only Kilger was actually a teacher, on the staff of the Berlin-Weißensee Academy of Fine Arts from 1947 to 1970.

Horst Sagert, a pupil of Kilger's, opened new avenues of set design in his work with Besson during the 1960s. For *Der Drachen* (*The Dragon*, Deutsches Theater, Berlin, 1965) Sagert created an image of a fantasy world which was meant to sharpen the meaning of the play and emphasize its metaphorical nature. Later Sagert managed to enrich the impressionistic nature of his images, for example, *Dona Rosita bleibt ledig* (*Dona Rosita Stays Single*, Deutsches Theater, 1970), so that throughout the 1970s and 1980s his work remained very representative of GDR set design, if only through a very few productions.

Besides the individual styles of these ranking designers, a sort of prevailing style, characteristic of the era, developed in West Germany in the 1950s. Many productions were characterized by an abstract ordering of scenic elements, mostly called 'stylization' but meaning fundamentally a simplification of the set, which saw the stage as a psychic space in contrast to reality. Through the use of revolves, spotlights or profile lights it revived the more common forms of expressionism, and found its most durable foundation and most successful application in the work of Wieland Wagner, who came out of set design to direct opera.

Against this there was another form of simplifying the set, as conceived by Brecht and Neher, which became still another element in West German theatre in the 1960s. This involved the use of an empty playing area with a few symbolic but concrete movable pieces of scenery, plainly visible lighting instruments and often descriptive signs or projections. Wilfred Minks, the most influential set designer of this period, took up aspects of didactic theatre in his formalized sets which were not, however, meant to fill or symbolize anything but rather to assert the aesthetic of the set as its own justification. At first they were show-window-like box stages, geometrically aligned along vertical and horizontal axes, with quotes from pop and op art

Klaus Michael Grüber's 1970 Württembergische Staatstheater Stuttgart production of Heinrich von Kleist's *Penthesilea*, designed by Wilfried Minks.

and modern technology (wall-size photographs, neon lights, reflective surfaces, plexiglass and synthetic materials).

The emancipation of set from both play and director was announced for the first time in an unusual theatre event in Bremen in 1968, created by Wilfried Minks, with the ironic title *Gewidmet: Friedrich dem Großen* (*Dedicated to Frederick the Great*). Achim Freyer, Karl-Ernst Herrmann and Erich Wonder – all, like Minks, active as directors in the mean time – later also 'directed' similar plays of autonomous imagery which did not rest on the customary dramatic foundation. Minks's 'show-windows' increased in richness and texture (sand, lawns, water and natural wood) from 1969 on and then instantly became the trademark of West German set design in the 1970s.

Besides Herrmann, whose work concentrated on Stein and Peymann, and his pupil Wonder, who designed the most interesting sets for Luc Bondy, Jürgen Flimm and Hans Neuenfels, Axel Manthey (b. 1945) – with his sets for Alfred Kirchner (b. 1937), Jürgen Gosch, Ruth Berghaus and finally his own productions – and Rolf Glittenberg (b. 1945) – who had studied with Otto and Minks and mainly worked for Bondy and Flimm – emerged as representatives of a new 'theatre of images'. Their styles were very different – Wonder, 'the cameraman of spaces', introduced cinematic principles into the theatre along with an artistically powerful lighting design – yet their demand for an independent semantic was the same.

The play no longer determined the set designer's function; instead the designer, together with the director, situated the play within a certain space, or confronted the play with it. It was possible to have enigmatic sets that could no longer be deciphered with the help of the play, and had more to do with environments, installations and performance pieces than with symbols. At the same time, traditional forms of communication also began to change.

Ruth Berghaus and Erhard Fischer's 1960 Deutsche Staatsoper production of Paul Dessau's
Die Verurteilung des Lukullus, designed by Heiner Hill.
Photo: Marion Schöne.

The stage changed its relationship to the spectator, plays were put on in foyers, the public could wander around the various scenes, and with larger projects the company even moved out of its regular theatre, as was the case with Grüber, Stein and Zadek on repeated occasions beginning in 1974.

In East Germany, too, set designers began to look for open theatre-spaces, where a variety of playing configurations and audience accommodation could be set up. By abandoning the traditional fourth-wall opposition between audience and actor – supposedly to provoke new ways of perception – new playing spaces sprang up in such locations as foyers, rehearsal stages and basements. Occasionally the proscenium stage itself was turned into an auditorium and the auditorium into the stage.

Otherwise, even with the many similarities during the 1970s and 1980s, developments in East Germany took a different course from those in West Germany. Gaining in importance were styles of set design that gave up historical concreteness for the time–space shifts of parables with their changing time sequences, alternating levels of time and strong symbolic effects. This led to sets which could point beyond concrete historical situations to show past, present and future as a continuous process.

Set design for music theatre further sparked creative developments in the 1980s. Work of great intensity emerged, particularly under directors Ruth Berghaus and Harry Kupfer (for example, *Die Verurteilung des Lukullus*, Deutsche Staatsoper, Berlin, 1983; set design by Hans-Joachim Schlieker, costumes by

Marie-Luise Strandt). Set design was making more and more use of variable time-levels and time-shifts. Modern costumes were supposed to indicate contemporary topical references.

The set for Heiner Müller's production of *Macbeth* at the Berliner Volksbühne in 1982 (set design by Schlieker; costumes by J. Harnisch) – the shabby façade of a backyard in Berlin – made allusions to contemporary reality in order to depict the historical drama of lust for power in completely incongruous circumstances. An example of contracting the world 'within the girdle of these walls' occurred in Alexander Lang's production of *Dantons Tod* (Deutsches Theater, Berlin, 1981), where designer Volker Pfüller (b. 1939) turned the stage into a Punch and Judy show decked out with red cloth.

In the 1980s, attitudes changed with respect to what constituted a finished set. The 'open' set concept, which was defined exclusively by action and props, was once again supplanted by closed sets with detailed scenery. There was an evident preference for certain design-motifs with metaphorical significance. Thus, the world was shown as a ruin, a heap of rubble, a prison, a theatre-within-a-theatre, a circus ring, a glass house, a waiting room or a labyrinth.

Throughout the 1980s, set design became increasingly important to the realization of the intentions of the production, not only in illustrative effects but also in encoded scenic details. This trend showed up in an increasingly hermetic scenic vocabulary (for example, *Urfaust*, Berliner Ensemble, 1984; directed and designed by Sagert), whose images demanded to be deciphered but almost always left over something that remained obscure. An imagistic style, as in Freyer's and Wilson's productions

in West Germany, did not develop, however.

The 1980s also saw the emergence of a new generation of designers such as Frank Hänig (b. 1955), Hartmut Meyer (b. 1953), Bert Neumann (b. 1960) and Peter Schubert (b. 1959), all graduates of the Berlin-Weißensee Academy of Fine Arts. They partly revived the methods of the constructivists.

In West Germany, director Grüber was the most visible proponent of the primacy of the set, basing himself on artists like Eduardo Arroyo, Gilles Aillaud and Antonio Recalcati. Achim Freyer and American-born Robert Wilson combined their origins in the fine arts with the craft of the director. In the 1990s, both were working in an imagistic style, each along a different path. Freyer, born in East Berlin, began his West German career in 1973, designing for the Kölner Oper and the Staatliche Schauspielbühnen in West Berlin and Stuttgart. His designs were so predominant, however, that the step to taking total control as director seemed only logical and was, moreover, the way for him to gradually free his art from the demands of the play. Wilson's first production in Germany was in 1979 at the Berliner Schaubühne. His subsequent collaborations with Heiner Müller and Tankred Dorst have signalled an increasingly literary orientation for the imagistic style drawing on classical mythology and works of classical antiquity, Shakespeare, Wagner and Kafka. But also Grüber's and Stein's style has undergone a change with 'super-realistic', larger-than-life effects – Grüber's *Hamlet* (1982); Stein's *Three Sisters* (1984), *The Hairy Ape* (1986), and *Roberto Zucco* (1989) – which could lead back to the illustrative set, and even – as a third phase in a dialectical development – to the illusionistic.

Theatre Space and Architecture

Of the many theatre buildings in Germany today, some go back to the seventeenth and eighteenth centuries, with many others going back to before World War I. But in the overall total, the number of old theatres is not very large, and only a very few have preserved their original fabric unchanged. Some theatres – five in Munich and three in Stuttgart among others – were restored as historic monuments or as faithful reconstructions of their originals, but by

far the greatest number were new buildings built since 1945. Following the difficult post-war period of makeshift stages and studio theatres (mainly 1948–51), the 1950s saw the beginning of a wave of construction that created far more seating than was necessary to replace what was destroyed in the war or had become obsolete.

In East Germany, on the other hand, investment in theatre construction was almost exclusively directed to rebuilding, reconstruction, modernization and adaptation – despite heavy war-damage and obsolete buildings and technology. Decisive in this respect was a cultural policy which put primary emphasis on the classical German cultural tradition, claiming it in the name of political renewal, and maintaining a guarded attitude towards twentieth-century innovations. Only a few new theatres were built, among them the Leipzig opera house in the 1950s and a new Friedrichstadtpalast (built as a revue theatre) in Berlin in 1984. There was some temporary rebuilding immediately after the war, for example, the old Friedrichstadtpalast as early as 1945, followed by the Metropoltheater in Berlin (today the Komische Oper, repeatedly renovated), the Schauspielhaus in Leipzig, the Nationaltheater Weimar, the Landestheater in Halle and the Volksbühne am Luxemburgplatz in Berlin (repeatedly renovated from top to bottom).

Priority was, for the most part, given to historical reconstruction. The first reconstruction of von Knobelsdorff's Staatsoper (State Opera) in Berlin, destroyed during the war, was carried out between 1951 and 1955. A second, in 1986, restored its valuable historic architecture and interior. In a long-standing feud over the rebuilding of the Semper-Oper in Dresden, the plan to rebuild the theatre as part of a group of historic buildings on the banks of the Elbe won approval. In the 1970s and 1980s the Deutsches Theater and Kammerspiele Berlin as well as the art nouveau theatre in Cottbus, were still being refurbished in a similar fashion. These measures, aimed mainly at reconstruction and modernization, were not without consequences for East Germany, where practically all theatres continue to rely on the traditional spatial solution of stage-auditorium opposition.

Despite much higher spending and more efficient use of funds, new construction in West Germany was also more in line with the close of the nineteenth century than with the twentieth. State and municipal authorities only very rarely allowed theatre professionals to participate fully in the planning process and few architects were specialists in theatre design, exceptions being Gerhard Graubner (1899–1970) and Werner Ruhnau (b. 1922). The necessity of multipurpose stages determined the architectonic functions, which, in the case of opera, were unthinkable without a conventional orchestra pit between stage and auditorium. The necessity of bringing together two or three playing areas under one roof (main theatre, smaller theatre, and/or studio theatre), and of the inclusion of enlarged prop, set and technical shops, was often taken as a licence to overbuild. A theatre's place in a city's architectural scheme also appeared to be predetermined, virtually confined to rebuilding on former sites and incorporating architectural remnants wherever possible. Ideologically, theatre design was also defined by the image of the 'prestigious' cultural edifice in the heart of the city. Since incorporation of classical temple elements had been exhausted, no convincing general overall style emerged. In the beginning it sufficed to generalize functional structures into the exterior surface, and set the smaller cube of the fly gallery on top of the larger cube of the auditorium and working areas. Later, there was a preference for additional architectural refinements, such as asymmetrically stacked terraces up to the fly gallery, masking the tower, or covering the whole thing with a bowl as in Dortmund (1966) or with a curved shell as in Düsseldorf (1970).

Inside the houses, the relationship between audience and play was fixed by the proscenium arch. In the big theatres, there were no alternatives to the proscenium arch; the most that could be done was to optimize it. This was attempted by making the separation between auditorium and stage more fluid through variable openings, elevating orchestra pits, and vaulted apron stages, which none the less continued to follow the fourth-wall convention.

Because of poor sightlines from the sides and from above, attempts were made to get away from the traditional system of boxes and dress circles, which were also often suspect as a badge of social importance. Resolving the dress circles into terraced balconies (*Schlitten* – sleds), aligned towards the stage in sweeping curves – introduced by Gerhard Weber (b. 1909) at the Hamburg Staatsoper in 1955 – offered a way out. In theatres with fewer than 900 seats, this type of staggered auditorium was cheerfully dispensed with in favour of evenly raked seating in the form of an hexagon or arc, as in a lecture hall.

Stage technology, installed in many of the new theatres by Walther Unruh (1898–1973) and Adolf Zotzmann (1912–89), was almost always of the highest standard, with integrated hoist, rotation and wagon systems. Powered drive systems and precision pulleys extended the possibilities of the flies, revolving stages and incorporated lift stages. Even the backstage and wings were equipped with wagons.

Directors, however, hardly ever used this

technological surplus to the degree anticipated. Set changes are no longer fundamental to set design and only rarely is the set actually changed during a play, but advances in stage technology are still helpful for a quick strike and set-up.

By contrast, heavily utilized rapid advances in lighting technology developed simultaneously with production demands. Early on, the principle of concealing the technology had already been breached by hanging many of the lights in front of the stage. Mechanical dimmers were replaced by electric ones, then by electronic systems that allowed the whole lighting plot of a production to be programmed into a computer, which was an important step for the further development of the profession of lighting designer.

In East Germany, on the other hand, such technologies lagged behind. East German industries did little research and development, and the cost of new technology was too high. Thus computer-programmed stage technology and electronic lighting and acoustic equipment, for example, were mostly earmarked for the larger theatres, while smaller ones for a long time had to make do with older equipment. Besides, installation of ever more complex and costly technology into older theatres and traditional spaces remained controversial; that artists would make effective use of it was not a self-evident proposition.

Since the 1970s, the focal point for advanced technological theatre architecture in East Germany had been cultural centres (Palaces of Culture) which sprang up in many of the larger cities. Designed to be prestigious multipurpose complexes – theatres, conference centres and exhibition halls – as a rule they did not include their own regular production company, with the exception of the Theater im Palast (Theatre in the Palace) in Berlin. This group, although without a permanent ensemble, was able to mount a very extensive repertoire of produc-

Erich Mendelsohn's 1928 Universum cinema housing the new stages of the Schaubühne in Berlin, designed by Jürgen Sawade.
Photo: Ruth Walz.

tions using guest actors, touring shows, exhibitions and readings.

The Friedrichstadtpalast in Berlin was a special case. The latest advances in auditorium design were realized here, with the best possible sightlines and a generously laid-out stage, where the divide between audience and performer seems practically non-existent. Its modern technology allows quick scene changes, whether stage, artificial ice surface or swimming pool, so it is ideally equipped for revue theatre.

In East Germany, a host of performance spaces also evolved out of rehearsal stages, foyers or adapted basements and attics, with only the simplest technical and scenic equipment. These initiatives were an expression of a desire to put into practice methods already developed in west European alternative theatres. Important for the development of East German theatre, in the end such changes did not lead to new conceptual strategies of theatre architecture, technology or stage design.

That is consistent with the fact that even in West Germany nothing of the sort happened either, despite a richly varied theatre scene and a wider range of alternative theatre. Thus, for example, for all of Werner Ruhnau's advocacy of open stages, hardly any were built, and theatres-in-the-round exist only for alternative functions such as the Ulmer Podium (Ulm Podium Stage, 1969). Flexible stages, as in the Mannheim Nationaltheater's Little Theatre, were never fully used, due to the high labour costs involved in doing change-overs. Individual high-tech variable stages with complete technical ceilings or mobile lighting banks, and modular platforms – either in the house as a whole or at least in seating sections – did not emerge until the 1960s. In 1981 the Berlin Schaubühne reached an optimum flexibility in its new quarters, where the whole house (70 by 33 metres) can be completely closed off, by means of soundproof rolling doors, into three separate halls permitting almost any kind of arrangement or combination of arrangements to be made.

During the 1970s, the traditional role of the theatre architect changed. Only a few cities were still waiting for a new theatre. Karlsruhe got a theatre in 1975, Heilbronn and Esslingen in 1982, Bremen got its Schauspielhaus in 1984, the Hannover and Bruchsal Landesbühnen got permanent homes in 1987, Essen got its opera house in 1988 (after Aalto's award-winning design of 1959), and Pforzheim got its theatre in 1990. All other architectural activity was confined to renovation and expansion, updating technology, asbestos removal and historical reconstruction. Few theatres were built in the provinces; instead more multifunctional buildings were built.

Training

FRG

Despite countless private theatre schools and acting teachers, professional actors' training in West Germany is virtually monopolized by eight public theatre schools: academies in Berlin, Hamburg, Hannover, Frankfurt, Stuttgart, Saarbrücken, Essen, Munich and Bochum.

The last two are municipal, the others are state institutions. An average of thirty-five students attend each of these schools whose programmes run for four years. There are fifteen to twenty teachers per school, about half of them well-known actors, directors and specialists in various fields. Applications to these schools have risen enormously through the years. If there were an average of eighty candidates per school for the annual theatre school auditions in 1975, there were ten times as many ten years later for eight to ten places each.

The curriculum generally consists of four areas: first, breathing/voice/diction/singing; second, body/movement; third, improvisation/collective creation; and fourth, theory (both dramatic literature and theatre history). Though teaching methods differ, attempts at reform – culminating in a five-day theatre school congress in Berlin in 1973 – seem to reinforce similar trends in all the schools. Although Stanislavski and Brecht styles dominate, and Artaud and Grotowski provide additional stimuli, the whole does not amount to a systematic national method. Rather, German training is a mix of several international methods.

Singers are also trained in state and municipal institutions, namely in twenty music academies, and in studios attached to the Munich, Köln and Düsseldorf operas. A common complaint is that future singers do not get enough training in acting and musicals.

Dance training as a rule starts in childhood and is continued at the music academies or is concentrated in the renowned dance centres of Hamburg, Berlin, Stuttgart and Munich.

Set designers come out of the nine art academies.

There is no regular overall training for directors as such. This area of training is still in its infancy in West Germany; in Essen and Munich it is an adjunct to actors' training; in Hannover and Frankfurt, a post-graduate curriculum. More promising is the music theatre directors' programme, which was started in Hamburg in 1973 and in Munich in 1986 by opera general director August Everding as an integrated study, involving music academies, university drama departments and local theatres. Since 1988 there has been an analogous course for drama directing in Hamburg and, as of 1993, in Munich.

After learning a trade and working in the theatre for several years, theatre technicians can get their degrees by supplementing their practical qualifications at a technical school, by additional studies (Darmstadt), or at the Theatertechnisches Seminar (Theatre Technical Seminary) at Recklinghausen. In 1987 the Technische Fachhochschule Berlin (Berlin Technical College) started a course in technical training for theatre.

GDR

Theatre training in the GDR took place exclusively in state schools. In Berlin, acting, directing, choreography and puppet theatre training were specialties; in Rostock, acting; in Leipzig, acting, choreography and theatre studies; and in Potsdam-Babelsberg, acting.

Singers and musicians were trained in five music academies, in Berlin, Dresden, Leipzig, Weimar and Rostock; directors for music theatre at the Musikhochschule (Music Academy) in Berlin.

There were three professional dance schools, in Berlin, Leipzig and the Palucca Academy in Dresden.

Art colleges in Berlin and Dresden had set-design departments which, in the broadest

sense, included costume and scenic design.

Professional qualification as a theatre technician came after learning a trade in the theatre and taking courses at a special cultural technology institute in Berlin. A few specialized courses were also available, such as one in moulded properties offered as part of Eduard Fischer's (b. 1916) workshop attached to the Berliner Ensemble.

Theatre courses at Humboldt University in Berlin were best known for their interdisciplinary integration of theatre history with cultural history and social science, a programme now being used by Leipzig University. Theatre courses at the Leipzig Theatre School were, until the 1980s, more strongly based in practice, with a primary emphasis on drama/dramaturgy. These courses were to be continued at the Music and Theatre Academy there.

Theatre schools generally offered comprehensive in-service courses for academic and professional development. These courses also aimed at providing additional training for specific groups such as theatre managers and critics. Additional professional development was offered by the Verband der Theaterschaffenden.

Training and professional development were, for the most part, free. Occasional fees were low and studies were supported by grants and, in the case of professional development, by generous union regulations.

There was a rigid quota, based on national needs in each category, and all graduates were guaranteed a job, a regulation which worked against artistic competition in the long run. There was a constant lack of new generations of singers and musicians; however, the ratio between theatre school candidates and admissions was ten to one, but was diminishing during the 1980s.

A policy of *Praxisbeziehung* (cooperative education) dominated most training schools, that is a close interaction between formal study and practical work. In a variety of ways this policy contributed to a high degree of professionalism in many areas. The Leipzig Theatre School, for example, was internationally known for its model system, where acting students spent two years of basic training in the school itself and an additional two years being integrated into different theatres through special studios. Besides encouraging professionalism, the cooperative system also encouraged a company spirit and a consciousness of theatre's effect on society. But it was hard to develop alternative models and techniques in theatres; in theatre schools it was not possible at all.

A methodological theory of theatre school training was developed in the GDR, and achieved international importance during the 1960s and 1970s. It was chiefly worked out by Rudi Penka (b. 1923) as a synthesis of the Stanislavski tradition and Brecht's theories of acting, and was further elaborated in the classroom and through aspects of pedagogical technique such as role-playing and role-theory as well as being organically related to movement, voice, music, and so on. The resulting model was not regarded as a binding 'method', but as a methodological foundation for creative alternatives. The model became the common property of acting schools in the GDR, proving itself in many theatres.

After reunification, theatre schools in eastern Germany found themselves in the process of having to adapt to the FRG training system. Thus the Rostock branch of the Berlin Hochschule was to become an independent entity; the Theaterhochschule Leipzig was to be gradually incorporated into the Musikhochschule; and the Fachschule für Tanz Leipzig was to be taken over by the Leipzig Oper among others.

Criticism, Scholarship and Publishing

Despite their name (*Theaterverlag*), German drama publishers are not primarily concerned with publishing plays. Rather, they are literary agents publishing the plays they represent in acting versions that generally do not make it into bookshops. Because the four major ones are subdivisions of large publishing houses, however, they do nevertheless publish plays.

Of course all drama publishers in their capacity as literary agents are essential to ensuring that any plays reach the public at all, and there are about eighty of them in Germany, including music publishers. But only about twenty of them are of any importance for the repertoire of public theatres.

Most contemporary German playwrights belong to Frankfurt's Verlag der Autoren, which has about ninety members. Frankfurt's Suhrkamp Verlag – which has assembled the largest market share of successful authors – represents Brecht, Fleisser, Weiss, Bernhard, Frisch and such contemporary playwrights as Dorst and Handke as well as the later Beckett, Bond, García Lorca, O'Casey and Shaw.

Frankfurt's S. Fischer Verlag focuses on modern German classics (Hofmannsthal, Schnitzler and Zuckmayer) and Americans from O'Neill, Williams and Miller to Shepard, Simon and Woody Allen, as well as early Beckett and Fugard.

Hochhuth is the only prominent German playwright represented by Hamburg's Rowohlt Verlag, which specializes in English playwrights from Pinter to Ayckbourn and Hare, as well as French writers such as Sartre and Camus. Since 1978 it has been getting competition from the Bremen Litag, which represents other contemporary British playwrights.

East German playwrights tended to be represented by Berlin's Henschelverlag, although an independent Autorenverlag (an artist-run agency), comprised of younger East German playwrights, was formed in 1989.

Music theatre publishing is dominated by Mainz's Schott Verlag, which, besides Wagner and Richard Strauss, represents the majority of the moderns (Hindemith, Orff, Henze, Zimmermann and Reimann among others). Leipzig's Breitkopf und Haertel is also an important music publisher.

Plays and playwrights are published only if they have proven themselves on stage or fit into the paperback play series put out by Suhrkamp, S. Fischer and Rowohlt. Verlag der Autoren publishes a selection of plays in its *Theaterbibliothek* (*Library of Plays*) series. The most important repositories of new plays are Suhrkamp's *Spectaculum* series (fifty-four volumes with six or seven plays each, 1956–92), and a number of substantial collections containing works of individuals or different authors (for example, *Dialog*), put out by Berlin's Henschelverlag, partly in conjunction with the Aufbau Verlag and Verlag Volk und Welt (both Berlin).

Professional journals such as *Theater heute* (*Theatre Today*) and *Theater der Zeit* (East German, until 1992), have also included plays in each monthly edition since 1960 and 1966 respectively, half of them new German plays. The larger theatres like to publish texts of original or première performances in their programmes, and these often turn into books.

Documentation is supplied by the theatres themselves and by the Deutscher Bühnenverein, and until 1990 also by the Verband der Theaterschaffenden. Handbooks, monographs on directors and actors and, more rarely, historical treatments are available in bookshops, but books on film are more popular. A half-dozen publishing houses in Berlin and Köln are making efforts to produce high-profile books on theatre.

Purely academic writing on theatre is for the most part confined to unpublished dissertations. Theatre arts courses are now a fixture in ten German universities as well as in the Hochschule für Music und Theater in Leipzig; theatre studies has its own department in two universities in Berlin (the Freie Universität and the Humboldt-Universität) and also in Munich and Köln. High enrolment has given teaching priority over research, although the Forschungsinstitut für Musiktheater (Music Theatre Research Institute) at the University of Bayreuth in Thurnau is still able to devote itself to producing something as complex as a multi-volume encyclopedia.

The largest theatre collections and archives are housed in the University of Köln's Theatermuseum in Castle Wahn, and in the Deutsches Theatermuseum in Munich. A Gesellschaft für Theaterwissenschaft (Society for Theatre Research) was founded in 1991 to encourage greater activity in the academic field.

Theatre criticism finds its most important outlets in five or six national newspapers; in the weekly *Die Zeit*; and monthly journals such as *Theater heute*, *Die Deutsche Bühne* (*The German Stage*) and *Opernwelt* (*Opera World*). Criticism is specialized into genres and is the domain of about two dozen travelling 'star' critics and a few regional correspondents. Their influence is not as great as their victims claim because audience attendance is to a large extent organized in advance; but its effects are more long-lasting than might be expected because critics recycle their verdicts in jury decisions (theatre conferences, competitions, surveys and retrospectives, and filter them down into colourful images that stick.

A specialty in the GDR was extensive production archives compiled by the Verband der Theaterschaffenden. These are being continued today by the *Zentrum für Theaterdokumentation und -information* (Centre for Theatre Archives and Documentation), Berlin.

Günther Erken (FRG), Rolf Röhmer (GDR) with Werner Gommlich, Gunter Kaiser, Joachim Näther, Horst Seeger, Käthe Seelig,

Peter Ullrich, Wolfgang Wöhlert
Translated by Hans Werner

Further Reading

FRG

Arnold, Heinz Ludwig, and Theo Buck, eds. *Positionen des Dramas. Analysen und Theorien zur deutschen Gegenwartsliteratur.* [Views of the drama: analyses and theories of contemporary German literature]. Munich: C.H. Beck, 1977. 287 pp.

Büscher, Barbara. *Wirklichkeitstheater, Straßentheater, Freies Theater. Entstehung und Entwicklung freier Gruppen in der Bundesrepublik Deutschland 1968–1976.* [Political theatre, street theatre, free theatre: the creation and development of independent companies in the Federal Republic of Germany 1968–76]. Frankfurt/New York: Peter Lang, 1987. 506 pp.

Daiber, Hans. *Deutsches Theater seit 1945.* [German theatre since 1945]. Stuttgart: Reclam, 1976. 428 pp.

Davies, Cecil William. *Theatre for the People: The Story of the Volksbühne.* Manchester: Manchester University Press, 1977. 181 pp.

Deutscher Bühnenverein, ed. *Theaterstatistik.* [Theatre statistics]. Köln: DBV, annually.

——. *Was spielten die Theater? Bilanz der Spielpläne in der Bundesrepublik Deutschland 1947–1975.* [What did the theatres produce? A listing of the repertoire in the Federal Republic of Germany, 1947–75]. Köln: DBV, 1978. 112 pp.

——. *Was spielten die Theater? Werkstatistik.* [What did theatres produce? Repertoire statistics]. Köln: DBV, 1992.

——. *Wer spielte was? Werkstatistik.* [Who played what? Repertoire statistics]. Köln: DBV, 1992.

Deutsches Bühnenjahrbuch. Das große Adreßbuch für Bühne, Film, Funk und Fernsehen. [German stage yearbook: directory for stage, film, radio and television]. Hamburg: Genossenschaft Deutscher Bühnen-Angehörigen im Verlag der Bühnenschriften-Vertriebs-GmbH, annually.

Ely, Norbert, and Stefan Jaeger, eds. *Regie heute. Musiktheater in unserer Zeit.* [Directing today: contemporary music theatre]. Berlin: Quadriga, 1984. 248 pp.

Hayman, Ronald, ed. *The German Theatre. A Symposium.* London: Oswald Wolff, 1975. 287 pp.

Herzfeld-Sander, Margaret, ed. *Essays on German Theatre.* New York: Continuum, 1985. 356 pp.

Hofmann, Jürgen. *Kritisches Handbuch des westdeutschen Theaters*. [A critical guide to West German theatre]. Berlin: Guhl, 1981. 356 pp.

Innes, C.D. *Modern German Drama. A Study in Form*. Cambridge: Cambridge University Press, 1979. 297 pp.

Ismayr, Wolfgang. *Das politische Theater in Westdeutschland*. [Political theatre in West Germany]. Königstein/Taunus: Athenäum, 1985. 496 pp.

Jauslin, Christian, and Louis Naef, eds. *Ausgangspunkt Schweiz: Nachwirkungen des Exiltheaters*. [Starting point Switzerland: influences of exile theatre]. Willisau: Theaterkultur-Verlag, 1989. 300 pp.

Kässens, Wend, and Jörg W. Gronius. *Theatermacher. Gespräche mit Luc Bondy, Jürgen Flimm, Hansgünther Heyme, Hans Neuenfels, Peter Palitzsch, Frank-Patrick Steckel, George Tabori, Peter Zadek*. [Theatremakers. Conversations with ...]. Frankfurt: Athenäum, 1987. 211 pp.

Kayser, Ruth. *Von der Rebellion zum Märchen. Der Etablierungsprozeß des Kinder- und Jugendtheaters seit seinen Neuansätzen in der Studentenbewegung*. [From rebellion to fairytale: the establishment of theatre for young audiences since its renewal in the student movement]. Frankfurt/New York: Peter Lang, 1985. 228 pp.

Kreuzer, Helmut, ed. *Deutsche Dramaturgie der sechziger Jahre*. [German drama and theatre in the 1960s]. Tübingen: Niemeyer, 1974. 182 pp.

Lackner, Peter. *Schauspielerausbildung an den öffentlichen Theaterschulen der Bundesrepublik Deutschland*. [Actor training in public theatre schools in the Federal Republic of Germany]. Frankfurt/New York: Peter Lang, 1985. 256 pp.

Lange, Wigand. *Theater in Deutschland nach 1945. Zur Theaterpolitik der amerikanischen Besatzungsbehörden*. [Theatre in Germany after 1945: the theatre politics of the American occupation forces]. Frankfurt/Cirencester, UK: Peter Lang, 1980. 775 pp.

Linke, Manfred, ed. *Theater/Theatre 1967–1982*. Berlin: Zentrum Bundesrepublik Deutschland des ITI, 1983. 352 pp.

Patterson, Michael. *German Theatre Today: Postwar Theatre in West and East Germany, Austria and Northern Switzerland*. Theatre Today Series. London: Pitman, 1976. 129 pp.

Regitz, Hartmut, ed. *Tanz in Deutschland. Ballett seit 1945. Eine Situationsbeschreibung*. [Dance in Germany. Ballet since 1945: a descriptive account]. Berlin: Quadriga, 1984. 192 pp.

Rischbieter, Henning. 'Theater'. In *Die Geschichte der Bundesrepublik Deutschland*. [The history of the Federal Republic of Germany], vol. 4, ed.

Wolfgang Benz, 86–130. Frankfurt: Fischer Taschenbuch, 1989.

Rouse, John. *Brecht and the West German Theatre: The Practice and Politics of Interpretation*. Ann Arbor, MI: University Research Press, 1989. 223 pp.

Rühle, Günther. *Theater in unserer Zeit*. [Contemporary theatre]. 3 vols. Frankfurt: Suhrkamp, 1976–92.

Schlicher, Susanne. *TanzTheater. Traditionen und Freiheiten. Pina Bausch, Gerhard Bohner, Reinhild Hoffmann, Hans Kresnik, Susanne Linke*. [Dance theatre: traditions and freedoms ...]. Reinbek bei Hamburg: Rowohlt Taschenbuch, 1987. 286 pp.

Schmidt, Jochen. *Tanztheater in Deutschland*. [Dance theatre in Germany]. Frankfurt: Propyläen, 1992. 259 pp.

Schneider, Rolf. *Theater in einem besiegten Land. Dramaturgie der deutschen Nachkriegszeit 1945–1949*. [Theatre in a conquered land: German post-war dramaturgy 1945–1949]. Frankfurt/Berlin: Ullstein, 1989. 144 pp.

Schneider, Wolfgang. *Kindertheater nach 1968. Neorealistische Entwicklungen in der Bundesrepublik und West-Berlin*. [Children's theatre after 1968: neo-realistic developments in the Federal Republic of Germany and West Berlin]. Köln: Prometh-Verlag, 1984. 114 pp.

Schubert, Hannelore. *Moderner Theaterbau. Internationale Situation, Dokumentation, Projekte, Bühnentechnik*. [Modern theatre architecture: the international situation, documentation, projects, stage technology]. Stuttgart/Bern: Krämer, 1971. 222 pp.

Schulze-Reimpell, Werner. *Development and Structure of the Theatre in the Federal Republic of Germany*. Translated by Patricia Crampton. Köln: Deutscher Bühnenverein and Bonn-Bad Godesberg: Inter Nationes, 1979.

——, ed. *Stücke '76–'90. 15 Jahre Mülheimer Dramatikerpreis*. [Plays from 1976 to 1990: fifteen years of the Mülheimer Prize]. Köln: Prometh, 1991. 192 pp.

Sebald, W.G., ed. *A Radical Stage: Theatre in Germany in the 1970s and 1980s*. New York: St Martin's Press, 1988. 197 pp.

GDR

Belkius, Gert, and Ulrike Liedtke, eds. *Musik für die Oper? Mit Komponisten im Gespräch*. [Music for opera? Conversations with composers]. Berlin: Henschel-Verlag, 1990. 352 pp.

Dieckmann, Friedrich, ed. *Bühnenbildner der Deutschen Demokratischen Republik. Arbeiten aus den Jahren 1971 bis 1977.* [Stage designers of the German Democratic Republic: designs from 1971 to 1977]. Berlin: Sektion DDR der OISTAT, 1978. 120 pp.

——. *Ensembles der Deutschen Demokratischen Republik: Theater, Ensembles, Schulen, Institutionen.* [Ensembles of the German Democratic Republic: theatres, ensembles, schools, institutions]. Berlin: Henschel-Verlag, 1973–89.

Felsenstein, Walter, and Siegfried Melchinger. *Musiktheater.* [Music theatre]. Bremen: Schünemann, 1961. 106 pp.

Funke, Christoph, Daniel Hoffmann-Ostwald, and Hans-Gerald Otto, eds. *Theater-Bilanz 1945 bis 1969. Eine Bild-dokumentation über die Bühnen der Deutschen Demokratischen Republik.* [Theatre survey 1945 to 1969: a visual documentation of the stages of the German Democratic Republic]. Berlin: Henschelverlag Kunst und Gesellschaft, 1971. 392 pp.

Hoffmann, Christel. *Theater für junge Zuschauer. Sowjetische Erfahrungen – sozialistische deutsche Traditionen – Geschichte in der DDR.* [Theatre for young audiences: Soviet experiences – German socialist traditions – history in the GDR]. Berlin: Akademie-Verlag, 1976. 252 pp.

Klunker, Heinz. *Zeitstücke, Zeitgenossen. Gegenwartstheater in der DDR.* [Contemporary theatre, plays and artists in the GDR]. Hannover: Fackelträger-Verlag, 1972. 235 pp.

Kranz, Dieter. *Berliner Theater: 100 Aufführungen aus drei Jahrzehnten.* [Theatre in Berlin: 100 productions from three decades]. Berlin: Henschel-Verlag, 1990. 518 pp.

Material zum Theater. Beiträge zur Theorie und Praxis des sozialistischen Theaters. [Material for the theatre: contributions to the theory and practice of socialist theatre]. Berlin: Verband der Theaterschaffenden der DDR, 1972–89. 222 issues.

Mittenzwei, Werner, ed. *Theater in der Zeitenwende. Zur Geschichte des Dramas und des Schauspieltheaters in der Deutschen Demokratischen Republik 1945–68.* [Theatre in changing times: history of the drama and of performance in the German Democratic Republic 1945–68]. 2 vols. Berlin: Henschelverlag Kunst und Gesellschaft, 1972. 396 + 482 pp.

Neef, Hermann and Sigrid. *Deutsche Oper im 20. Jahrhundert: DDR 1949–89.* [German opera in the twentieth century: GDR 1949–89]. Berlin: P. Lang-Verlag, 1992. 595 pp.

Nössig, Manfred, ed. *Die Schauspieltheater in der DDR und des Erbe (1970–74).* [Stage performances in the GDR and their legacy (1970–74)]. Berlin: Akademie-Verlag, 1976. 264 pp.

Pietzsch, Ingeborg, Gunter Kaiser, and Detlef Schneider, eds. *Bild und Szene. Bühnenbildner der DDR 1978 bis 1986.* [Stage design in the GDR from 1978 to 1986]. Berlin: Henschelverlag Kunst und Gesellschaft, 1988. 119 pp.

Profitlich, Ulrich, ed. *Dramatik der DDR.* [The drama of the GDR]. Frankfurt: Suhrkamp Verlag, 1978. 472 pp.

Puppentheater gestern und heute. [Puppet theatre yesterday and today]. Dresden: Staatlich Kunstsammlungen, 1977. 191 pp.

Puppentheater der DDR: eine Bestandsaufnahme. [The puppet theatre of the GDR: a stocktaking]. Leipzig: UNIMA-Zentrum der DDR, 1984. 60 pp.

Schneider, Wolfgang, ed. *Kinder- und Jugendtheater in der DDR.* [Theatre for children and young audiences in the GDR]. Frankfurt: Dipa, 1990. 110 pp.

Seeger, Horst, ed. *Jahrbuch der Komischen Oper.* [Yearbook of the Komische Oper]. 12 vols. Berlin: Henschel-Verlag, 1961–73.

——. *Jahrbuch Musikbühne.* [Yearbook of the music stage]. 4 vols. Berlin: Henschel-Verlag, 1974–7.

——. *Jahrbuch Oper heute.* [Yearbook of opera today]. 12 vols. Berlin: Henschel-Verlag, 1978–89.

Swortzell, Lowell. *Theaterarbeit in der DDR.* [Documentation of GDR theatre performances]. 19 vols. Berlin: Verband der Theaterschaffenden der DDR, 1976–90.

Theater in der DDR. [Theatre in the GDR]. Issues 1–14. Berlin: Zentrum DDR des Internationalen Theaterinstituts, bi-annually.

Theaterwerkstatt in Halle. Die Werkstatt-Tage des Kinder- und Jugendtheaters von 1977 bis 1990. [Theatre workshop in Halle: workshops for theatre for children and young audiences from 1977 to 1990]. Berlin: Ostdeutsche Sektion der ASSITEJ, 1991. 110 pp.

Wer spielte was? Bühnenrepertoire der DDR. [Who played what? The stage repertoire of the GDR]. Berlin: Direktion für das Bühnenrepertoire, 1977–87 annually.

GREAT BRITAIN

(see **UNITED KINGDOM**)

GREECE

The Aegean Sea houses most of the Greek islands and separates mainland Greece from Asia. The largest Greek island, Crete, is located in the eastern part of the Mediterranean basin while the Ionian Islands to the west (Odysseus' Ithaca among them) bear witness to the fusion of myth and fact of both the ancient Hellenic and Roman civilizations which flourished in this ancient waterway. The Balkan countries of Albania, Bulgaria, Turkey and the former Yugoslavia border Greece to the north.

Clearly, Greece's geographical position – a crossroads between Europe and Asia – accounts for part of its uniqueness. It has also been at times a curse, making Greece a natural stopping or starting point for the ambitions of other nations. More often, however, it has been a blessing which the nation exploited in many positive ways, assimilating knowledge and culture from both near and distant civilizations, transforming them, recreating them and ultimately developing its own matrix, clearly the prototype of western civilization.

Greek's modern period dates to 1821 when the Greek people achieved independence after 400 years of Ottoman rule, a period that failed to impose Islamic values on the recalcitrant nation. Some of the country's present 132,000 square kilometres (51,000 square miles) of territory were, in fact, not liberated until much later. In 1912, Thessaloniki was returned to Greek control while it was not until 1947 that the islands of the Dodecanese were returned by Italy. In the 1990s, over 10 million people speak modern Greek with the vast majority of the population practising the Greek Orthodox religion. There is a small Muslim minority in northeastern Thrace.

Modern Greece is a parliamentary republic with a more-or-less figurehead president elected every five years. Between 1981 and 1988, a socialist government was in power; it made cautious attempts to nationalize many industries but, by and large, the country has operated as a free market economy since World War II. More than 4 million people live in the capital, Athens, and the nearby seaport area of Piraeus; this area is the centre of not only government and business for the country but also its active cultural life.

Despite Athens' dominance in cultural matters, other cities are also very active. Thessaloniki, for example, though a lively northern port and business centre, is also a university town with a 2,300-year-old tradition of literary creation and intellectual debate. Major archaeological finds from Pella, ruins and beautiful sculpture from Zeus' ancient city of Dion, and above all, the treasure of the Macedonian royal tombs excavated in Vergina, all give a clear sense that this is a city where the arts have been nurtured. A State Theatre of Northern Greece was established there in 1960 and has since given impetus to theatre life not only in the city itself but in the surrounding areas as well.

Greece's third-largest city is Patras in the northwestern Peloponnesus, another thriving seaport which has a long cultural tradition, including a municipal theatre dating from 1871. The building – the Apollon (Apollo) – was built by the German architect Ernst Ziller, who was also responsible for both the municipal theatre and the Royal Theatre (now the National Theatre) in Athens and a theatre on the Ionian island of Zakynthos. The Apollo was renovated in 1970 and in 1988 it became the Municipal and Regional Theatre of Patras. Its director from 1988 to 1991 was Maya Lyberopoulu (b. 1940) who staged full seasons there involving classics, modern plays and even experimental work. Many of the company's productions have been staged within the context of the Patras International Festival.

Many other smaller cities also have theatres. The Ionian islands of Zante and Corfu, in particular, were cultural centres long before the mainland was liberated. The first theatre in modern Greece, in fact, was built on Corfu in the seventeenth century.

It is Crete, however, with its Minoan palaces, Medieval castles and fortresses and Venetian fountains which has retained a singular type of culture that embodies music, dance, singing, oral poetry, storytelling and theatre. Its summer festivals regularly attract large Greek and foreign audiences.

This portrait of modern Greece, however, is very different from the Greece that emerged from World War II. Nazi occupation from 1941 to 1944 was followed by a ruinous civil war which did not end until 1949. These two wars left Greece a ravaged country full of bitterly disillusioned people.

Amidst that desolation, a handful of young playwrights set out in search of the nation's and their own identity. Until that time, poetry and prose had been the dominant genres in modern Greece but after the war, drama seemed to be the most appropriate vehicle to express the quest for a new identity. Since 1950, in fact, the theatre – always a form of entertainment through which Greeks could learn – has continued to attack ignorance and complacency, faded ideals, alienation and dehumanization while exploring authority and, more recently, personal relationships of every kind.

Greek playwrights were encouraged and inspired by other intellectuals and theatre practitioners. In 1943, Karolos Koun (1909–87), founder and director of the Theatro Technis (Art Theatre) delivered a lecture/manifesto in which he stated his belief in

the crystallization of emotions, the removal of everything redundant in the artistic composition of a concept, after a profound analysis of the reality of the world outside us.... To offer an aesthetic experience today, we must advance towards new forms, new concepts, towards contemporary means of expression which emerge from the needs of our inner and outer realities.

The left-wing intelligentsia, some of whom had created Theatre in the Mountains (a form of agitprop theatre used during the resistance against the Nazis but even more during the civil war) also made concerted efforts to promote a modern Greek dramaturgy and new acting methods. This took both daring and time since the country was bitterly divided, there was no government cultural policy in place and both direct and indirect censorship occurred regularly.

The National Theatre was the country's most prestigious troupe but it too had been decimated by the war and the ensuing civil strife. Some directors – including Dimitris Rondiris (1899–1981) – refused to work there during Nazi occupation. Eleni Papadaki, an outstanding actress, was killed during the civil war, possibly as an act of provocation. Other people simply left for personal reasons.

But there was still Katina Paxinou (1900–78), the greatest tragedienne of her time, and her husband, the actor-director Alexis Minotis (1904–90), who eventually became director of the theatre. With them came a younger

Katina Paxinou in Alexis Minotis's 1955 National Theatre of Greece production of Euripides' *Hecuba*, designed by Kleovoulos Klonis.

generation of actors. Minotis's greatest contribution at this time was the revival of ancient Greek drama.

Those who could not or did not wish to be employed by the National Theatre for political reasons formed new companies and performed mainly in Athens. Some toured the provinces after Palm Sunday, traditionally the end of the winter theatre season in Greece. With only a few exceptions, the common denominator in these efforts was the presence of a single individual who established a company and brought together people who shared the same artistic vision.

One of the first companies created after the liberation from the Nazis was Enomeni Kallitechnes (United Artists). The company broke with existing practices in the theatre by challenging the traditional actor-manager approach which put all artistic power in one person's hands. Aspiring to high-quality performances of plays which anticipated or reflected social developments and political concerns, the company aimed its work at lower-class audiences who traditionally did not attend the theatre.

Other groups with similar aims followed. In 1949, the Realistiko Theatro (Realistic Theatre) began, and in 1959, the Dodecati Avlea (Twelfth Curtain). All of these companies offered opportunities to young artists, among them Vassilis Ziogas (b. 1937) and Costa Mourselas (b. 1931). In 1955, the To Elleniko Laiko Theatro (Greek Popular Theatre) was founded by Manos Katrakis (1908–84). Its aim was to 'implement the essential principles of popular theatre to increase lower-class audiences' without lowering standards.

Few of these companies managed to survive very long. There was no Ministry of Culture to support them until 1971 and culture was not on the agendas of local authorities. Indeed, it was not until the 1980s that local festivals, cycles of cultural events or even regular summer festivals began to appear with any regularity or sense of community. These proliferated under the encouragement of an imaginative and inspired Minister of Culture, the internationally known actress Melina Mercouri (1932–94).

The new ministry subsidized established companies to tour widely in an effort to decentralize cultural life and to bring theatres to even small towns in the mountains. Within the ministry, a Secretariat for Youth was founded in 1982 and for many years it was responsible for an extremely ambitious programme involving theatre and theatre education. It organized seminars and conferences for teachers; it provided students all over Greece with free theatre tickets; and it devised proposals for the Ministry of Education to introduce theatre into the school curriculum.

In the 1960s, however, there was no Ministry of Culture to try to develop theatre in this politically tumultuous period. The Conservative Party ruled Greece from 1952 to 1963 when the Centre Union Party headed by George Papandreou (b. 1919) came to power. After a period of political unrest, Papandreou was forced to resign and the country saw a series of caretaker governments, political bribery and manipulation. A *coup d'état* by a group of colonels took control of the government in 1967 and the new regime lasted seven dismal years.

During this *junta* period, many intellectuals, theatre people and artists were forced to flee the country. Those who could not or chose not to leave were initially stunned by the almost total overthrow of the country's democratic traditions. Eventually, though, they found means and methods to evade censorship and publish, lecture, hold discussions and even perform. The goal in virtually all cases was to raise the consciousness of the public.

Playwrights in particular felt an increasingly urgent need to probe and reveal the true character of those around them. Restrictions on freedom of speech acted both positively and negatively. Theatre – like most art forms – became very political. The little *boîtes* (pubs featuring singers) in the ancient Plaka section of Athens became the meeting-places for discussions of contemporary Greek theatre and new productions. One of them, the *boîte* Apologia (Defence), where discussions were held on Sunday mornings and performances throughout the week, was closed down by the *junta* on the pretence of lack of ventilation.

Another venue at this time for new, experimental, subversive writing and performance was the Piramatiki Skene (Experimental Stage) founded by Marietta Rialdi (b. 1943), an actress, director and playwright. Performances were usually followed by discussions with the audience in the small, underground (literally a basement) theatre, and speakers were invited to give talks on progressive, avant-garde developments in the arts.

Even supposedly commercial companies took the risk of producing plays which clearly 'instructed' audiences that each individual citizen was responsible for the current political situation and that each would have to initiate action if they wanted it changed.

In 1973, Jenny Karezi (1935–92) and Costas Kazakos (b. 1935), both very popular, politically committed theatre and film stars, staged *To megalo mas Tsirko* (*Our Grand Circus*), a play by the patriarch of modern Greek drama, Iakovos Kambanellis (b. 1922). Utilizing virtually every theatrical device known, their production reminded audiences how the Greeks had forced the Bavarian King Otto to grant them a constitution and how they had fought against various forms of oppression. All the recognizable codes were there: characters and designs from the popular shadow theatre, *Karagiozis*, songs from the period of German occupation, a narrator instructing a street urchin, and an exquisite Cretan singer, Nikos Xylouris (1936–80), whose singing and general demeanour kindled ancient memories of heroes, epics and bards.

The production could have been interpreted as a way to defuse political tensions but audiences understood the real meaning. They also realized that it would take courage to confront the colonels but that it could be done.

Together with politicians working underground and many who travelled abroad to organize resistance against the *junta*, theatre people joined with all those who eventually rose up against the regime and compelled them to admit defeat.

All along the National Theatre was carrying on the invaluable tradition of performing ancient Greek drama at the giant outdoor theatre at Epidaurus and the smaller outdoor Herod Atticus Theatre in Athens. The company also staged indoors other classics and modern plays including works by Shakespeare, Lope de Vega, Jonson, Calderón, Molière, Goldoni, Marivaux, Lessing, Kleist, Goethe, Chekhov, Ibsen, Strindberg, Pirandello, O'Neill, García Lorca, Beckett, Williams and even Caryl Churchill. Among the highlights of the National's productions through the decades have been performances of *King Lear* (1938) with Emilios Veakis (1884–1951), Pirandello's *Enrico IV* (1967) with Dimitris Horn (b. 1921), Dürrenmatt's *The Visit* (1961) with Katina Paxinou, Beckett's *Happy Days* (1980) with Vasso Manolidou (b. 1914) and Ionesco's *Exit the King* (1992) with George Michalacopoulos (b. 1938).

But for all its qualitative importance, rarely did the National take risks or venture into contemporary drama before it had proven itself elsewhere. As for modern Greek plays, its general rule until the late 1960s seemed to be that the repertoire include only farces or moralistic dramas by established writers such as Nikos Kazantzakis (1883–1957), Gregoris Xenopoulos (1867–1951), Angelos Terzakis (1907–77), Pandelis Prevelakis (1909–87) or George Theotokas (1905–66). Occasionally the theatre would stage plays from the late Cretan Renaissance, a neo-Greek renaissance in the seventeenth century of which eight plays are extant (two lyrical tragedies, one historical tragedy, three comedies, a pastoral drama and a religious Mystery).

There were, of course, a few exceptions such as Kambanellis's *I Evthomi Mera tis Demiourgias* (*The Seventh Day of Creation*, 1956), a play that concerned itself with modern Greek post-war reality. But it is fair to say that the National Theatre, contrary to its own charter, followed rather than introduced new trends in national and even international dramaturgy.

The company which led the way in producing new plays was Karolos Koun's Art Theatre, which is where serious Greek drama not only became respectable after the 1950s but became successful at the box office as well. It was this success that encouraged many other groups – the National among them – to produce new plays.

Commercial theatres focused on the staging of farces and comedies from both Greece and abroad (most often French) along with a uniquely Greek theatrical genre called *epitheorisi*, a kind of variety revue in the Spanish *zarzuela* tradition. In 1894, an Italian company presented such a variety show, *Gran Via*, and it proved immensely popular with its topicality and message of freedom from rules, both social and artistic. The form was copied and eventually adapted for Greek audiences. The *epitheorisi* is now filled with pungent political satire which relates it, albeit indirectly, to the Aristophanic tradition.

It was and still is a form that reflects the perpetual flow of things (indeed, numbers can be withdrawn or added to accommodate current events), uses mixed media, offers possibilities for experimentation and has an acute sense of stage rhythm. Its stock characters and use of the vernacular (an element not to be taken for granted on early Greek stages because of the so-called Language Problem) are two other significant aspects of this genre. It is, in fact, formal characteristics rather than thematic concerns which can be most clearly seen in many contemporary Greek plays. The characters in Mourselas's *Ekinos ke Ekinos* (*This One and That One*, 1972), for example – their appearance and clownish movements, the witty repartee – remind one of the *compère* and his innocent friend with a hundred questions found in every *epitheorisi*.

The fact is, the *junta* temporarily stopped an unprecedented flowering of the arts in modern Greece. During the seven years the nation was 'being cast', as the dictators called their rule, many things were written or created underground or became elliptic and esoteric, often gaining in interest, depth or universality because of this. When the *junta* was removed from power in 1974, many self-exiled artists returned home from France, Germany, Italy, Sweden and the United States. Greek artistic creation has been enriched by this experience abroad and many of the groups seem determined to retain the vital exchange.

At the same time, playwrights have picked up the earlier threads and are now creating work unhampered by censorship or unassimilated foreign influence. One is able to see clearly the literary kinship between the poetic work of the nineteenth-century dramatist Dionysios Solomos (1798–1857) and the works of Loula Anagnostaki's *Nike* (*Victory*, 1981) and *I Kasseta* (*The Cassette*, 1984). One can see the connections as well between Constantine Cavafis (1863–1933) and Kambanellis's *O Aoratos Thiasos* (*The Invisible Troupe*, 1988). In each case, the dramatists use the earlier material to illuminate modern concerns and perspectives.

On the other hand, a playwright such as Vassilis Ziogas clearly anticipates the ideas of Derrida and Foucault in his plays *Paschalina Pehnithia* (*Easter Revels*, 1966) and *I Gami* (*The Weddings*, 1987), written in 1964 and 1970 respectively. In both plays, Ziogas explores the structures of power and authority and asserts the right of individuals to be different. The uniqueness of the individual and the responsibility not to surrender one's freedom of choice are also focal points of Anagnostaki's work.

Several new companies were created just after the fall of the *junta*. The most significant was Amphi-Theatre, founded and directed by Spyros Evangelatos (b. 1940). Concentrating on rarely performed and virtually unknown Greek plays of the eighteenth and nineteenth centuries, the company has created memorable productions with plays from the Cretan Renaissance such as *Erotocritos* (staged in 1975) and from the Byzantine era such as *Digenis Acritis* (staged in 1989–90), a play based on the twelfth-century epic which marks the beginning of modern Greek literature.

Through the 1970s and 1980s and into the early 1990s, the Greek theatre witnessed a continuous round of creativity and productivity. Smaller groups – along with the Koun Art Theatre, the National and the Stoa (Arcade) Theatre, which has devoted itself almost exclusively to staging modern Greek plays – have again made Athens a real theatre capital. The same energy can also be seen outside Athens in the State Theatre of Northern Greece and at many of the regional theatres. These theatres have also become hospitable venues for a score of very good dramatists who clearly represent the diversity, social concern and philosophical and poetic flights of the modern Greek psyche.

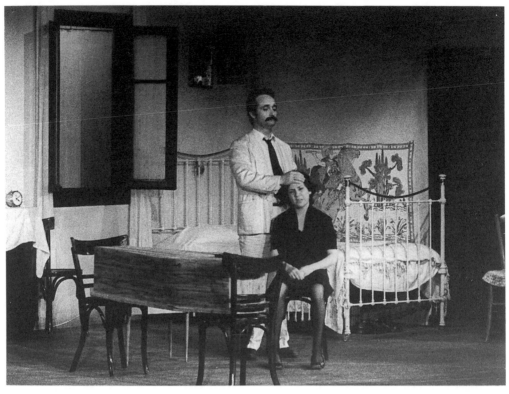

Thanassis Papageorgiou's 1975 Stoa Theatre production of George Dialegmenos's *Auntie Passed Away. Stop*, designed by Yorgos Ziakas.
Photo: Kostas Goudis.

Structure of the National Theatre Community

The Ministry of Culture subsidizes two theatres completely – the National Theatre and the State Theatre of Northern Greece. The National in 1992–3 received US$4.5 million while the State Theatre received US$3.8 million. In addition, the Karolos Koun Art Theatre receives a state subsidy of 80 per cent of its annual budget for the two theatres it runs.

In addition to these three major groups, the ministry contributes nearly 50 per cent of the budgets of the country's eleven regional theatres and spends a further US$1 million or so on another thirty non-profit companies. Decisions are made in this latter area by a special committee appointed by the minister. The committee is also involved in funding commissions of new plays and translations.

Until the first six regional theatres were established by the ministry in 1983, it was rare to find companies working on a regular basis outside the major cities. Among those few that did exist were the Theatriki Lesche (Theatre Club) in Volos, the Theatriko Ergastiri (Theatre Workshop) and Piramatiki Skene Technis (Experimental Stage) in Thessaloniki, the Thessaliko Theatro (Thessaly Theatre) in Larissa and the Eteria Theatro (Theatre Company) in Crete.

In Greece, the theatre season usually begins in October and ends one week before Easter. A few of the Athenian companies might visit Thessaloniki or other smaller cities after that and some theatres remain open until the end of May. After that many theatre people begin work at the country's two most prestigious theatre festivals – in Epidaurus and Athens. Others begin work on light entertainment productions (comedies and *epitheorisi*) to be offered in open-air theatres during the summer.

During the winter season, the number of theatres in Athens varies from ninety (1989–90) to sixty (1991–2) depending on the state of the economy and available subsidies.

The country had eleven regional theatres in 1993–4 located in Agrinio, Calamata, Crete, Ioannina, Komotini, Lamia, Larissa, Patras, Rhodes, Serres and Veria. In addition to the State Theatre in Thessaloniki, the Experimental Stage has also operated there since 1979.

On occasion, companies from Athens tour the provinces or television stars capitalize on their fame and form a touring company for a limited but remunerative number of performances in smaller towns.

Prior to the creation of regional theatres, there were only a handful of municipal theatres and privately run provincial companies. The agreement signed between the ministry and the local authorities was that each would contribute 50 per cent of the theatre's annual budget provided that the theatres employed at least ten actors, promoted modern Greek plays and toured their region.

Though it is still too soon to assess the achievement of these institutions as a whole, problems have emerged, mainly because of tight-fisted local authorities. But it is clearly a system that can only raise standards in these smaller centres even when that appears to go against the will of the local community. A tour of Beckett's *Oh, les beaux jours!* (*Happy Days*), for example, with a very good actress, Despo Diamardidou, in the leading role, played to packed theatres in many towns in northern Greece despite initial concern about the choice of play.

The regional theatre in Larissa was founded by the actress Anna Vagena (b. 1947) as the Thessaliko Theatro ten years before it became an official regional theatre. Its director from 1983, Costas Chianos (b. 1942), worked very hard to gain community support and achieved artistic note by exploring new approaches to the performance of ancient Greek drama. Working with the outstanding tragedienne Lydia Coniordou (b. 1953), Chianos has directed stunning performances of Euripides' *Electra* and *Iphigenia in Taurus* as well as Aeschylus' *Choephori* in which he incorporated traditional elements of music, costume and dance. The company was later invited to perform at Epidaurus and at festivals abroad.

The city of Volos inaugurated a building in 1990 with a series of performances by companies invited from Athens and elsewhere. Plans are now underway to establish its own company. Similar plans are also underway in Tripoli for restoration of the Malliaropoulio Theatre, built between 1906 and 1909. In its early years, the theatre housed opera companies and touring performances by well-known actors, Greek and foreign.

There has always been a strong amateur movement in Greece, with the longest continuously operating companies located in Mytilene (Lesbos), Corinth and Chios. The Dramatic Society in Corinth organizes an annual festival of amateur theatre as does the Homeric Cultural Centre, which hosts a biennial festival on various Aegean Islands. Another such festival was established on Ithaca in 1975 and many well-known professionals made their début at that festival.

The Epidaurus Festival begins each year at the end of June and goes through to the end of August. Exclusively devoted to performances of ancient Greek drama, this festival takes place in the well preserved ancient theatre, which has its superb acoustics. On occasion, other events occur at the theatre: Verdi's *Requiem* was presented by La Scala from Milan in 1981 while Peter Hall brought his *Oresteia* in 1982 and produced three Shakespearian plays there in 1988. Maria Callas (1923–77) also sang in Epidaurus in 1957.

Few of the other ancient theatres are used on a regular basis. The festival of ancient Greek drama at Philippi and Thasos is a northern Greek event that each summer welcomes performances from across the country. Performances have also been given at Dodona (twenty-two between 1960 and 1981) under the auspices of the Society of Epirotic Studies. Because performances are not allowed at the theatre at Delphi, companies wanting to work there use the ancient stadium. Most performances there are part of annual conferences held on ancient Greek drama sponsored by the European Cultural Centre. In 1988, for instance, the British dramatist Tony Harrison wrote his play *Trackers of Oxyrhynchus* for performance at the stadium. The play was later staged in a revised version in the United Kingdom.

The Athens Festival is a two-and-a-half-month summer festival which includes theatre, music and dance. Performances are now almost exclusively held at the outdoor Herod Atticus Odeon, a Roman theatre located at the foot of the Acropolis which seats about 5,000.

For a number of years in the 1980s, Theatriki Syntechnia (Theatre Guild), a company directed

Karolos Koun's 1965 Karolos Koun Art Theatre production of Aeschylus' *The Persians*, designed by Yannis Tsarouchis.

by Nikos Armaos (b. 1943), organized a small but interesting festival of alternative theatre at the old open-air cinema Averof in Athens. Groups such as Eugenio Barba's Odin Teatret from Denmark and the Centro Sperimentale di Roma from Italy have appeared there.

Between 1986 and 1990, a festival was held in the ancient theatre – another Roman Odeon – in Patras under the direction of the composer Andreas Mikroutsikos (b. 1947). The festival featured a number of experimental pieces including happenings and bus-ride readings.

On an irregular basis, a summer festival also takes place in the city of Heraklion on Crete with both Greek and foreign participants. A Renaissance Theatre Festival is held in the Medieval Cretan city of Rethymno.

The most important festival in northern Greece (usually in October–November) is Dimitria, organized and mainly sponsored by the city of Thessaloniki with support from both the Ministry of Culture and private sources.

Of the many theatre associations and unions, the most powerful are the Actors Union and the Playwrights Association. The Actors Union has some 3,000 members and negotiates contracts with all professional theatres. No contract is signed for less than three months even if a company is giving a single performance. Rehearsals are usually five hours per day and normally last two months; 80 per cent of each subsidized company must be made up of Actors Union members.

The Playwrights Association from its inception in 1908 has functioned very effectively as a royalty-collecting agency. It has also established programmes for the translation of plays and has conducted seminars for young playwrights. Its main mission is the promotion of modern Greek plays and the monitoring of subsidized theatres to ensure that they devote a good part of their repertoires to plays by Greek writers.

The Ministry of Culture is also interested in the promotion of modern Greek dramaturgy and subsidy is usually dependent on a commitment to produce such plays. It has also established a Playwright's Award with prizes for both established and new writers. The National

Theatre is obligated to present the plays which win the first prizes. The Karolos Koun Award is an annual prize for the best produced Greek play along with prizes for actors, directors and designers. The two top drama school graduates are awarded the annual Lambeti Prize named in honour of the actress Elli Lambeti (1926–83).

Athens also boasts more than thirty commercial theatres.

Until 1989, there were two state television channels. There are now numerous private ones as well. Directors interested in film are subsidized by the Hellenic Film Centre, a department within the Ministry of Culture.

Artistic Profile

Companies

The Charter of the National Theatre, published in the *Government Gazette* of 1930, states that it was established to foster 'the concept of beauty and to promote Greek dramaturgy and theatre... to perform plays from the ancient, Medieval and modern repertoire together with the best of foreign drama.' Founded in 1930, among its early directors were personalities of great culture, people who had spent years studying theatre both in Greece and abroad, and whose ambition it was to familiarize Greek audiences with the best of the modern repertoire. They viewed the National Theatre as a venue where the public would be 'educated' as European citizens, endowed with a supreme heritage.

It was because of this heritage that they considered it of paramount importance to revive the tradition of staging ancient drama. Fotos Politis (1890–1934), the first director of the company, already had experience at staging ancient Greek plays. His opening production for the National was Aeschylus' *Agamemnon* (1930). Dimitris Rondiris, director of the National from 1934, devoted his career almost exclusively to the staging of ancient drama and was influential in establishing the Epidaurus Festival in 1954 and the Herod Atticus performances of ancient Greek drama in 1955.

Alexis Minotis, one of the greatest Greek actors of the twentieth century, contributed to the revival of ancient Greek drama by adopting naturalistic and expressionistic elements in both his acting and directing. The earlier declamatory style and the techniques of lighter forms were rejected as being too superficial for these plays. For Minotis it was essential to rely on 'intuitive forces' in an effort to interpret the poet's intentions.

Other directors were engaged by the National to direct for the festivals. Among them were Alexis Solomos (b. 1925) who directed both tragedy and comedy and wrote extensively on ancient drama; Takis Mouzenidis (1911–81), a director who spent much time in his career promoting an appreciation of ancient drama at universities in various parts of the world; Minos Volanakis, a sensitive and imaginative director who also headed the State Theatre in Thessaloniki at different times; and Spyros Evangelatos, a daring and innovative director who later founded the Amphi-Theatre. Later directors of the National include Stavros Doufexis (b. 1933), George Michaelides (b. 1938) and Nikos Charalambous (b. 1941), who has taken a ritualistic, ceremonial approach to his work on the ancient plays. Only since the 1980s has the National allowed younger directors such as Yannis Houvardas to present what can be called less reverent interpretations to the public.

Prior to 1974, the National was not particularly committed to the production of contemporary Greek plays though the powerful Playwrights Association ensures that it does include some in its annual repertory. The fact that the National also tends to pay lower royalties than some other theatres has not helped improve this situation. Nevertheless, since the fall of the *junta* in 1974, the National has at least been more open to contemporary plays which have dealt with some of the painful issues of the recent past.

Perhaps the most interesting have been Pavlos Matessis's (b. 1934) *Exoria* (*Exile*, 1987), a play about the traumas and the destructiveness of the Greek civil war of the late 1940s; and Vassilis Ziogas's *The Weddings* in which the central character, a woman well past her prime, proceeds to reject all the forms of oppression she has experienced as daughter, wife and mother, transcending the absurdity of existence by creating her own personal myth.

For a number of years, the National toured

the country with its company, Arma Thespidos (Thespian Chariot) but this task is now handled by the regional theatres.

The State Theatre of Thessaloniki became the State Theatre of Northern Greece (STNG) in 1960 thanks to the efforts of the Macedonian Prime Minister (later president of Greece) Constantine Caramanlis. Even before it became the STNG, some very good actors played there including some who worked on productions in 1943–4 during the German occupation.

STNG has had a series of dedicated and inspired directors at its helm and as a result has been a point of reference for theatre life in all of northern Greece for many years. Its two touring units, created by Spyros Evangelatos during his period as the theatre's director (1977–89), were in fact the inspiration and base for the three regional theatres in northern Greece – Komotini, Veria and Serres. From 1966, the STNG participated regularly in both the Epidaurus and Athens Festivals and in the festivals at the ancient theatres at Philippi and Thasos.

STNG was also the first theatre to allow a woman, Koula Antoniadou (b. 1948), to direct an Aristophanic comedy at Epidaurus and has achieved a reputation for inviting daring and irreverent directors such as Andreas Voutsinas to direct there.

The theatre also has its own drama school and regularly uses students in its productions in addition to well-known guest artists from Athens. The STNG has made it a conscious policy to employ local talent as far as possible and it has nurtured many fine actors as well as designers such as Apostolos Vettas (b. 1945), directors such as Peppi Economopoulou (b. 1945) and Pavlos Paganopoulos (b. 1948), and composers such as Herakles Paschalides (b. 1953).

The oldest and in many ways the most well-respected of the major Greek companies is the Karolos Koun Art Theatre. It too has a very successful theatre school attached to it which provides most of the actors for its two companies.

In July 1941, probably the worst year of the German occupation, Koun advertised 'for the discovery of new talent in the theatre'. About a year later – October 1942 – the performance of Ibsen's *Wild Duck* marked the birth of a company that literally changed the theatrical scene in Greece. In a very early lecture-manifesto (August 1943) Koun proclaimed: 'We do not do theatre for the sake of theatre. We do not do theatre for a living. We do theatre to enrich ourselves and the public that follows us, so that we can all help to create a far-reaching, spiritually rich, civilization of the highest integrity for our country'.

Koun has been true to his proclamation, certainly more so than anybody else in post-war Greece. In the Art Theatre Drama School Koun trained some of the most sensitive and competent stage workers. With his students, and occasionally with other actors, he presented scores of Greek plays and introduced numerous new playwrights, encouraging in this way both the National Theatre and other smaller experimental groups to do the same. However, as he admitted himself, he deliberately staged good foreign drama during the first fifteen years of his long career as director of the Art Theatre, hoping to provide the stimulus necessary for the pioneers of the new era in modern Greece.

Further, Koun has presented ancient Greek tragedies and comedies in revolutionary ways, sometimes causing artistic scandals such as his first production of Aristophanes' *The Birds*. In 1959, performances of the Aristophanes play for the Athens Festival at the Herod Atticus Theatre were cancelled, allegedly in the name of decency and respect for tradition and religion.

In 1977, in the same theatre, several members of the conservative government sat, albeit uncomfortably, through Koun's interpretation of Aristophanes' *Peace*, where a *Karagiozis*-type Trygaeus, with an enormous phallus, seduced Opora (Fruitful).

World acclaim had come earlier in the form of invitations for tours in the United States and Europe and participation in the World Theatre Season in England. In 1977, during the celebration of thirty-five years of his work, in Paris, the opening speech was made by Eugène Ionesco.

In Thessaloniki, the Experimental Stage started in 1979 as an offshoot of a cultural association called Techni (Art). Now one of the most successful and stable theatres in the area, its founder was Nikeforos Papandreou, the former director of the STNG drama school. The company has struck a happy balance between what one might call good entertainment and more demanding theatre. It has done plays from a wide variety of styles including outstanding productions of Beckett's *En attendant Godot* (*Waiting for Godot*), Ionesco's *Jeux de massacre* (*Massacre Games*), Shakespeare's *A Midsummer Night's Dream* as well as works by Mishima and modern Greek plays.

One of the more adventurous alternative

Karolos Koun's 1959 Karolos Koun Art Theatre production of Aristophanes' *The Birds*, Designed by Yannis Tsarouchis.

groups in Athens is Diplous Eros (Double Eros), founded by Michael Marmarinos (b. 1957) and Amalia Moutousi (b. 1960). Performing in the basement of a downtown commercial theatre, the company has chosen to explore various interpretations and approaches to particular texts. Typical was its 1992 cycle called *Medea*. It encompassed three different performances: the first was based on the classical text by Euripides; the second on Heiner Müller's *Material: Medea*; the third was a mime show. Three actresses played the different Medeas.

Some of the fringe theatres in Athens are included in the generously subsidized companies, because of the high-quality work they do, for example Skene and Stoa. Others depend mainly on a rather limited but loyal audience, for example Kathreftis (Mirror). The audiences of the latter type of fringe theatre are attracted by the special kind of drama performed there: poetic, dramatized prose or poetry, or spectacles related to comics, as is the case with the Omada Theama (Spectacle Group) of Yannis Kakleas, who has also experimented with forms of Theatre of Cruelty. Nikos Hatzipapas and Titina Halmatzi, founders of Mayiko Theatro (Magic Theatre), have emphasized the visual

aspects of performances and have transformed entire spaces to perform plays such as Marlowe's *Dr Faustus*.

Dramaturgy

When one talks about Greek theatre the assumption, in both east and west, is that one is actually talking about ancient Greek theatre, since the classical Greek heritage seems to have transcended every spatial and temporal boundary. Modern Greek theatre is admittedly a late offshoot on the international scene, but in its rather brief existence it has produced a considerable number of plays of excellent quality. Since about 1950, many new plays have become box-office successes through the consistent and concerted efforts of devoted and inspired theatre people. They have also been translated into many languages: German, Russian, Dutch, Romanian, Hungarian, Italian and Spanish; fewer have been translated into French, and still fewer into English.

Where does 'modern' begin and what do modern Greek playwrights concern themselves with? We need to clarify certain things since

411

every history of modern Greek literature begins with the Byzantine border ballads and the epic of Digenis Akritas, written in Greek in the tenth century AD. Also, most of them stop around 1950 and their references to drama are scanty and totally unbalanced with regard to other genres of literature. Arbitrarily then, we shall be talking about Greek dramatic production since 1950 since the general consensus is that modern Greek theatre came of age after World War II.

The special conditions which have influenced modern Greek theatre are directly related to socio-political factors and they have been the formative agents of contemporary drama. Events such as World War II, the underground resistance during the German occupation, and the civil war compelled playwrights to adopt a new stance towards human existence, a stance which precludes a pre-ordained, compartmentalized society. Within this broader context, playwrights have probed and examined a variety of issues in an incisive, imaginative and often humorous way, in plays of depth, sensitivity and, ultimately, of powerful poetry.

So Greek playwrights since 1950 have written to exorcise the ghosts of the past and to define their identity as it emerged through the wounds of their youth and young adulthood. In *The Ghost of Mr Ramon Navarro*, Pavlos Matessis employs a sympathetic but cutting tone, sometimes verging on sarcasm, to criticize the kind of pre-1950 existence where even one's love life was regulated by others as well as by decrees and dictums.

In the same play Matessis also deals with what most Greek playwrights consider a congenital human characteristic, namely the desire for freedom, and expresses it symbolically through the idea of the journey (or its ironic reversal, stagnation), a motif as old as the poetry of Homer and as recent as that of Cavafis, but also very appropriate for the Greek people, who have a history of years of journeys and voyages, of colonization and uprooted refugees, and desperate, confused immigrants. At a deeper level, another, equally important, theme of the play is dread.

Earlier than Matessis, Kambanellis in 1957 had written a genuinely compassionate account of a group of people, small families and individuals, which he called *The Court of Miracles*. The play marked a turning point in modern Greek dramaturgy and constituted the necessary requiem for an era that had irrevocably passed, while at the same time providing an introspective look into Greek

reality. In his court of miracles, we are offered a panoramic view of vices and virtues, of ugliness and beauty, of prosaic detail and flights of imagination, of a deeper sense of duty and honesty and wicked fraud, of irrepressible sexuality and platonic love, of mundane factuality and poetry; in short, of the world of modern Greece.

Each character has a problem and a dream, and all are persecuted by the uncertainty of their lives; they do not own the place they live in and cannot even be sure that their miserable existence will continue as it is for very long. A construction boom has already started and civil engineers visit ominously from time to time, measure width and length, and finally take over. They are going to build a new apartment block, while the people from the yard are exiled to yet another temporary residence, since to buy their own place can only be a dream. 'We were born refugees . . . haven't you learned to stomach that yet?', one of them says.

The sudden, the unexpected, the impersonal power outside ourselves that regulates our lives, is a fact of life that Greeks, according to Kambanellis, have come to accept with a stoicism gained through constant upheavals experienced in the short span of their individual existence. Where do the people of the yard (this threshing-floor of existential struggle, as Kazantzakis views Greece and the world in general) go from here? Kambanellis, in his later plays, and the younger generation of playwrights have tried to follow the development of events to discover what the picture of Greece might be at the new 'resting place'. They have tried, that is, to reveal the new Greek identity as it has developed in the second half of the twentieth century.

Margarita Lyberaki expresses a very ambivalent attitude in *The Saint Prince* (1972). Alexios, the prince (in some parts of Greece 'prince' means 'beggar'), returns to his home after many years of travel and ascetic life. Although he longs to be recognized by his family he remains disguised and finally leaves again, convinced that such ties will hamper his journey to self-knowledge.

In *The Bottle*, Vassilis Ziogas is sceptical about the sincerity of human relationships but considers them inevitable since the 'area' of human ambience is so limited. Pavlos Matessis, Stratis Karras and Loula Anagnostaki view the human bond as the only comfort in humanity's struggle to face the daily dread of its existence.

In an almost psychoanalytical way, playwrights drag the hidden facts of post-war Greek society up to the surface and coerce the audience into looking at whatever the mirror reflects. Lyberaki's *The Other Alexander* is a study of the disintegration of the old order of destructive hatred between opposing political systems, the disgusting nature of an informer society, disorienting eroticism, and the search for a new identity. It is a powerful picture of a divided society confused about the direction in which to go. The image of a world divided and in a state of demolition is sustained throughout *The Other Alexander* in various ways. At the end of the play, however, the household has collapsed, the father moans like a trapped animal and the mother distractedly repeats 'Where are my children? I want my children.'

However, the paradox of hope enfolded in destruction is found surrealistically floating in Ziogas's *Easter Revels* and *The Bourgeois Mythology*. And yet it is not so paradoxical in the light of the existential philosophy which post-modern playwrights have assimilated through Kazantzakis and others and which claims that possibilities exist for people when they have reached the nadir of despair. Ziogas describes the three acts of the play as Crucifixion, Epiphany and Resurrection. He claims that Resurrection offers hope for a better life, better than the one people are given at birth. However, people have to destroy the old world before they can inhabit a new one. They have to work toward destruction and risk before they have completed their 'preparations'.

In Lyberaki's *The Other Alexander* we observe the collapse of a system, find hints of dynamic new beginnings and suggestions of methods for a new start. In *Easter Revels* the plans are carried out and chaos ensues, leaving those who had been unwittingly excluded perplexed and unprepared.

Most of the playwrights who aimed at sensitizing their audiences to the political situation soon realized that to reach a wider public they had to use either easily recognizable 'props' from the folk heritage or obvious foreign symbolism. In *Oh, Dad, What a World!* Kostas Mourselas used features from *epitheorisi*. Kambanellis adapted Kafka's *The Penal Colony* for his 1970 play; while George Skourtis, perhaps the most openly didactic of these writers, went to the *Karagiozis* (shadow puppet) stock-room for his implements. The goal was to return to roots by research, study and presentation of the past, to find out and convey recognizable patterns through which the 'lesson' could be taught. For Skourtis and to some extent, Mourselas,

Demitris Kehaidis, Karras and other playwrights, the need to acquire self-knowledge within one's defined 'space' (that is, the social environment of contemporary Greece) demands first priority. In this respect their work is different from that of Anagnostaki, Matessis and Ziogas who consider the individual's commitment to freedom the impetus which will demolish authority in its social form.

Any audience will certainly be reminded of Beckett's tramps in *Waiting for Godot* as they watch Peter and Paul (two of the three characters in *The Nannies* by George Skourtis) in the opening of the play, sipping their *ouzo*, trying to solve the problem of Peter's loosely hanging last button, while at the same time desperately looking around for anyone who will give them a job – the means, if not the reason, to survive. Their names, however, which might have biblical overtones for a European or North American audience, would evoke the same kind of response from a Greek spectator that Tom, Dick and Harry might elicit from an Anglo-Saxon. They thus transcend the superficial, realistic part of themselves and become symbols; they become Everyman. They are ignorant types who have been enticed into a moribund environment, pressed by necessity.

The symbolic aspect of these characters is skilfully sustained by constant allusions to easily recognizable shadow theatre types. Like them the tramps do a burlesque skit to express their joy at the assurance of food, drink and shelter. They run and jump and turn somersaults; they even make actual references to two shadow theatre characters, Karagiozis and Hatziavatis, whom they used to impersonate in amateur performances when they were young.

Anagnostaki in *Social Occasion* (1969), Terzakis in *The Step-Son* (1969), Matessis in *The Ceremony* (1977) and Kambanellis in *The Four Legs of the Table* (1978), to mention only a few, portray this same dead or dying world, full of deception and corruption. With the self-knowledge that humanity can acquire by looking at its own image, these dramatists imply, people may become fearless and dare to live in spite of imminent death.

Minor or simply different issues have been the concerns of other playwrights. Manolis Korres, for example, castigates social complacency with regard to old age and illness. Marios Pondicas delves in the dark regions of individual or communal guilt while Constandina Vergou optimistically examines the possibilities after guilt is taken to extremes. George Maniotis examines oppression within the family and/or by social structures. George Christofilakis examines relationships between men and women, old and young, in the austere agrarian environment of mountainous Greece and scratches the painful wounds of the civil war, but his plays are more than that. *To Telos* (*The End*), in particular, is about human dignity, compassion and deep affection beneath rough treatment and behaviour.

Andonis Doriadis, among others, finds his material in the oppression of the *junta* regime. George Dialegmenos has given us a number of 'photographs' of great definition of the neighbourhood family, characters and situations of the small-time salesman, the small-time adulterous wife, the small-time torturer. His plays, however, also serve to point a finger at a tendency towards obsequiousness, sadism and maternal oppression. He fights to get rid of guilt for crimes past, underhandedness and self-complacency and tries to cut the often strangling umbilical cord between the individual and the family or tradition.

Demitris Kehaidis, another writer of note, sees his people 'travelling' to some place, carrying all their possessions, literally and figuratively, on their backs. Some of these possessions are the endowments of national upheavals, others are simply human.

To Panegyri (*The Festival*), in which a mother marries off her very young daughter to a much older man, is Kehaidis's most significant play so far. The title is, of course, ironic and the play makes it clear that the playwright does not view life as a panegyric. Behind the lights and the fun, that is, is the reality of wretchedness and misery. In the play this is visually conveyed by means of a rough blanket which hangs from a branch to 'cover' the makeshift household where self-deception, laziness and conniving thrive only a few yards away from bright lights and dressed-up people.

In his play *The Bottle* (1973), Ziogas shares Kehaidis's concept of life as a deceptive *panegyri*, supposedly a festive occasion. He also views life as an enticing whore who tempts man into living by the occasional 'sweet hour'. The two images, the *panegyri* and the whore, have something in common: they both offer ephemeral joy and distract man from the treadmill of bondage. Moreover, life or existence is both a threshing-floor and a cylinder from which there is no escape.

Nearly forty years after Kambanellis's *The Court of Miracles*, Greek playwrights appear to be seeking to forge a strong link with the Greek psyche of the past (through imagery, myth, tradition and even history) without any false respect for their ancestry, while creating a new frame of reference and powerfully exercising their prerogative to exist. At the same time they are articulating the poetry and the beauty, ultimately the healing effect, of human relationships.

This said, one must especially mention other specific plays and playwrights which make very special points. One such is a long monologue entitled *The Coat* (1984) by Marietta Rialdi; it is one of the most moving accounts of people ageing, being unwanted and feeling useles.

Loula Anagnostaki fights for the prerogative of the individual to commit a decisive act – even if negative – which will justify that person's existence. The recognition of the uniqueness of this act is a step towards self-knowledge, and this in turn leads to a state of freedom.

One of Anagnostaki's major plays, *Victory*, is about immigration and the experiences of ongoing misery. It is also about human existence and the wanderings of people who travel the road unsuccessfully. It is ultimately about the efforts of a group of people to complete the 'ceremony' of life, to perform the 'marriage' which will justify and guarantee the continuation of their existence. *Victory* demolishes prefabricated visions of victory and reveals truths to people of honesty, integrity and dignity.

Ultimate self-knowledge is the reference point of the journey in many modern Greek plays and it is equated with the pursuit of freedom.

Modern Greek playwrights have defined their 'space'. 'I live in chaos,' says one of Ziogas's characters in *The Bottle*, but it is a chaos containing everything. They have also acquired some degree of self-knowledge which enables them to see that they too are like other travellers in the world. They have striven to free themselves from the restrictive shackles of superimposed systems, institutions and authority in general. The braver ones have also accepted the fact that Ithaca did deceive them, gave them no 'beautiful journey' and that the Medes will finally pass. The only possible guide for them is the warm touch of another human being.

Although Elefthero Theatro (Free Theatre) was a group that started with Greek and foreign plays, it later concentrated on *epitheorisi*. Its work was unique in that it was one of the few examples of serious theatre written collectively. Also, its kind of *epitheorisi* was actually a

Karolos Koun's 1987 Karolos Koun Art Theatre production of Loula Anagnostaki's *The Sound of the Gun*, designed by Yorgos Patsas.
Photo: Dimis Argyropoulos.

commentary on the genre itself, of political, social and other issues, not least of which was the aesthetics of theatre itself as it had been experienced before the group's inception. The members of Elefthero Theatro (with the inevitable withdrawals and additions) worked as a group from 1970 to 1978.

Directors, Directing and Production Styles

For a discussion of directing, see previous material in **Artistic Profile** and the opening, historical section.

Music Theatre

The first Greek opera company in Athens performed *The Candidate*, a comic opera in three acts by the Corfu composer Spyridon Xyndas (1814–96), as its inaugural play in 1888. The play had been previously performed in Corfu in 1867, but there is no other information about that performance. Until 1888 then, the Greek public was familiar only with Italian opera, and Greek composers wrote their music to Italian librettos. That first company toured to Egypt, Turkey, France, Italy and Romania but because of a shortage of funds, it broke up in 1890.

In 1900 Dionysios Lavrangas (1864–1941), a composer-conductor, headed another attempt, this one at the Municipal Theatre of Athens. The company operated until 1943.

It soon became clear that few singers would be able to pursue careers in Greece. Most perfected their craft in Italy, Germany and Austria and usually remained abroad after that. This practice unfortunately remained the same in the 1990s for, although Greece had produced such artists as Maria Callas, Agnes Baltsa and Costas Paschalis, a lack of opportunity at home still compelled most of the very talented to seek careers elsewhere.

On the positive side, there is now an Opera House in Athens which occasionally tours to other cities such as Thessaloniki, Corfu, Volos and Patras. It regularly takes part in the Athens Festival, often inviting in star soloists, Greek and foreign. Both the Opera House and the Athens Concert Hall have encouraged Greek composers by staging new Greek operas or even commissioning them. Operas by Mikis Theodorakis, Thanos Mikroutsikos, Yorgos Kouroupos, Yorgos Sisilianos and Perikles Koukos have been included in the programmes of both institutions.

Operettas were an immensely popular genre before World War II, as were programmes of *epitheorisi*. New fads from Europe and North America became popular in Greece mainly through this style of theatre which attracts big crowds even today.

Theodorakis wrote his *Song of the Murdered Brother* in 1962 and in it he attempted to wed a variety of elements – tragic imagery and choral effects, folk songs and dance. In 1973 Kambanellis's *To Megalo mas Tsirko* (*Our Grand Circus*) depended heavily on music using recognizable codes, the songs referring to specific political situations.

Both Theodorakis and Manos Hatzidakis tried their hand at *epitheorisi* in 1962; the first created *Omorfi Poli* (*Beautiful City*) and the second *Odos Oniron* (*Street of Dreams*). Hatzidakis also created a script called *Pornography* in 1982. Another composer, Mimis Plessas, wrote *O Dromos* (*The Street*) which was closed by the *junta* which considered it subversive. Plessas has also composed a rock opera, *Orpheus and Eurydice* which was performed in Athens in 1980.

The commercial theatre has had greater success with foreign musicals. Aliki Vouyouklaki has staged *Cabaret*, *Evita*, *My Fair Lady* and *Annie* while Smaroula Yuli has produced *Chicago* and *Guys and Dolls*. Other companies have done *Jesus Christ Superstar* and *Oh, Calcutta*. In 1975 Yannis Chioles directed Tania Tsanaklidou in *Piaf*.

Hatzidakis also created music for his *Six Popular Paintings* (a ballet) in 1950. He claims that what he was trying to do was to render an audiovisual interpretation of six popular *rebetika* songs.

In the Athens Festival of 1993 Theodorakis presented *Medea* as 'a lyrical tragedy'.

Dance Theatre

The pioneer in this area was Rallou Manou (1915–88). A dancer, teacher of dance and a choreographer at the National Theatre between 1948 and 1952, for over thirty years she was responsible for the choreography in numerous ancient Greek plays at the Herod Atticus Theatre and Epidaurus. She also choreographed a version of *The Birds*, directed by Karolos Koun in 1959.

Manou founded the Hellenic Chorodrama in 1951 and worked with a large group of talented artists who were equally responsible for such memorable productions as *The Accursed Serpent* and *Six Popular Paintings*. Among them were composer Manos Hatzidakis, and the artist-designer Nikos Hatzikyriakos-Gikas. All contributed to this new form of theatre.

Virtually all the major theatrical choreographers were unafraid to enrich classical ballet movement, music or design with traditional folk elements. Zouzou Nikoloudi, another major choreographer, concentrated almost exclusively on the choruses of ancient Greek drama. She, too,

choreographed *The Birds* by Koun in 1962, but went beyond choreography to present dance theatre based on the myths found in ancient plays. Lia Meletopoulou was also inspired by ancient myths but her work was far more influenced by modern dance than by traditional elements.

Sophia Spyratou (b. 1949) founded the dance theatre Chororohes (Dance Flow) in 1989. By 1991 she had managed to rent an old school building which she transformed into a multipurpose centre with a small theatre upstairs, rooms for dance training, halls for music and other events. Since 1989 she has directed many shows and her company has participated in festivals in Greece and abroad. Spyratou uses diverse material for her performances – poetry, short stories, myths and legends, folk songs and parodies. One of her most interesting performances was *Scenes of Women's Madness* (1991) in which heroines of Euripides and Shakespeare – Cassandra, Ophelia, the Mad Mother and others – 'meet diachronically, at a common point, opening the window of madness. It is about the common fate of women, through drama and prose'.

Omada Edafous (Ground Group) was established in 1986 by the director Dimitris Papaioannou and the dancer Angeliki Stellatou. The work of the group defies characterization although dance and theatre are certainly involved. In their shows, the group's members have collaborated with sculptors, composers, artists and athletes. They have performed in an old soap factory, on an island, at the University of Patras and at festivals in Barcelona, Valencia, Seville and Antwerp. Both Chororohes and Omada Edafous are subsidized by the Ministry of Culture.

Theatre for Young Audiences

Karagiozis and Punch were the favourite entertainment for both children and adult audiences in early post-revolution Greece. However, the need for a more sophisticated theatre, exclusively for children, produced, among other things, a volume of plays as early as 1896 by Gregorios Xenopoulos, the playwright of the Astiko Theatro (Bourgeois Theatre). In 1903 Constantinos Chrestomanos (1867–1911) produced a pantomime especially for children.

There were no immediate follow-ups. Efrosyni Londou (1888–1973) and Antigone Metaxa (1905–71) formed their companies – *of children* – in the early 1930s. Both of them were teachers; Londou was distinguished by the League of Nations for her play *The Song of Peace*, while Metaxa, also an actress, became best known by children as the radio character Aunt Lena.

School theatre has always been part of the Greek educational system. In fact, one could probably say that the beginnings of modern Greek theatre can be traced to school productions in the Greek communities bordering the Danube. Influenced by the Enlightenment, the teachers chose plays from Greek antiquity and with their students created performances focused on both the art of theatre and the morale of the audiences.

Together with some of the best Greek schools, foreign educational institutions in Greece sponsored by the French, German, Italian and American governments carried on the tradition of school theatre into the twentieth century. Karolos Koun, in fact, started his career as a director at Athens College, where he worked as an English teacher.

During German occupation, the artist Spyros Vasiliou, the director Socrates Karandinos and the translator Vasilis Rotas (1889–1977) devoted much of their time to puppet theatre. At about the same time Barba-Mystousis, a special kind of puppet theatre named after its main character, was created by Eleni Theochari-Perraki. In the mountains, Rotas and Kotzioulas created puppet performances addressed to children along with resistance theatre for the adults.

In the 1950s a number of professional companies for adults presented occasional plays for children. Director Takis Mouzenidis was involved with these as was Katina Paxinou who produced *The Snow Fairy* with professional actors. In Thessaloniki, actress Mary Soidou offered children's productions for more than thirty years.

Today children's theatre is a thriving industry in Greece. Both the National Theatre and the State Theatre of Northern Greece have occasionally produced plays for children but theirs are not systematic, consistent efforts. Some of the subsidized companies in Athens and some of the regional theatres also produce plays for children but in the main this domain belongs to the private sector. The companies perform over the weekend and on holidays or they arrange special performances for schools. They use such diverse material as versions of Aristophanic comedy, Bertolt Brecht's *The Caucasian Chalk Circle*, children's plays by Greek or foreign playwrights or musicals including some with ecological or anti-consumerist messages.

One of the most ingenious forms of children's theatre was devised in the 1970s by Eugenia Fakinou. She used empty cans and called her theatre Tenekethoupoli (Can City); while the performance was going on she allowed and encouraged the children to participate and alter the course of events and decide what the ending would be.

Xenia Kalogeropoulou, a successful actress and president of ASSITEJ (International Association of Theatre for Children and Young People) in Greece, houses her children's theatre at Porta (Door), where she also performs plays for adults. She often directs and writes her own plays and her *Ulisindband* has been translated into English, French, Turkish, Hebrew, Romanian and other languages. Another good actor, Dimitris Potamitis, is the founder of a children's theatre, the repertoire of which includes foreign and Greek plays.

In both the last two companies, established in the 1970s, the actors are professionals and their performances are prepared as meticulously as any show for adults. They also inspired others who endeavoured to engage young audiences with both the spectacular and the thematic parameters of their performance. Theatro tou Eliou (Theatre of the Sun), Thiasos '81 (Troupe '81), Kafetheatro Amletinos (Café-Theatre Amletinos) and Aeroplio (Airship) are a few of the many groups now doing work exclusively for children.

Another theatre group, Parodos, introduced theatre games in 1976. Lakis Kouretzis, a leading figure in Parodos, has worked all over Greece, engaging young children in theatre games and training others to do the same. His book, *Theatre for Children in Greece*, is the standard guide for any teacher or actor working in the field.

Radio theatre for children is best known for a series of programmes called *Lillipoupoly* (*Lilliput City*) devised by a team of writers, composers and actors and supported by Manos Hatzidakis, the well-known composer, who was in charge of this area of the Greek Broadcasting Corporation.

Puppet Theatre

While writers and intellectuals were trying to establish *demotiki* (the spoken vernacular) as the means of expression for both poetry and prose, a new form of popular theatre was being cultivated unobtrusively in post-revolution Greece, the shadow theatre, or *Karagiozis*. Here it must be immediately clarified that the shadow theatre is not a puppet theatre in the usual sense of the term. It does not belong to the same tradition and did not develop from it. The basic implements of the shadow theatre are a piece of white cloth, figures with movable parts and some form of lighting. The figures are either black and white or coloured, cut out of cardboard, or drawn on specially prepared animal skins. Most important, of course, is the *Karagiozis* player who, behind the screen, manipulates the figures with strings or sticks, imitates the different characters, sings, creates sound effects and generally orchestrates the performance.

The form is named after its leading figure, an ugly hunchback. Many have wondered where he came from and how he managed to captivate audiences. Why did he appeal to such a vast and varied public? Why did his popularity last so long? How did he influence the Greek theatre?

Although there are some indications that *Karagiozis* existed before the Greeks won their independence from the Turks, the bulk of the evidence seems to suggest that this form of popular theatre came to Greece, oddly enough, with the fall of the Ottoman Empire and reached its climax in the first few decades of the twentieth century. The first people to write on Greek *Karagiozis* were the French Louis Roussel and the Italian Giulio Caimi. The shadow theatre was 'discovered' by scholars and theatre people around 1920, later became fashionable, and acted as a stimulus for creative experimentation. Fotos Politis, a former director of the National Theatre, Vasilis Rotas, the foremost translator of Shakespeare in Greece, Theodore Synodinos (1880–1941) and critic Andreas Karandonis (1910–88) have all written plays of varying degrees of success using the *Karagiozis* background as a basic element. In 1963 the editor of the periodical *Theatro* dedicated an entire issue to *Karagiozis*.

The best documented work so far is the article 'World Shadow Theatre and the Greek *Karagiozis*' by Dionysis Flabouras, published in *Zygos*, a periodical which deals with architecture, the plastic arts and decoration. Flabouras traces the origin of shadow theatre to eleventh-century China and challenges the notion that *Karagiozis* developed from the mysteries at Eleusis or Kaviros.

Almost the moment that Greece was liberated and Greeks who had previously lived in Constantinople and the thriving cities of Asia Minor came across the border, *Karagiozis* made its appearance. Whether it pre-existed in any other form, the *Karagiozis* that the immigrants brought to mainland Greece, Piraeus and Patras in particular, was the Turkish *karagöz*. This is significant because the Turkish figure was a foul-mouthed character, and the entertainment often relied on vulgarities to produce laughter. It was rejected by Athens and pitched its tents in ports or other places where a variety of people in transit gather. Soon, however, Karagiozis lost his phallic appendage which was transformed into a very long arm, always ready to dispatch blows to anybody weaker than himself. Some of the particularly obscene characters disappeared altogether and new characters, Greek characters, were introduced.

All were representatives of the variety of temperament and mentality of the population comprising the new Greek state. These included the pseudo-aristocratic (with obvious western influence), the redneck Barbayiorgos, the strong unadulterated highlander from central Greece, Corfu natives, Cephalonians, and, later on, Stavrakas from Psyri, a rough section of Athens.

Most importantly, new stories, mainly dealing with events and characters from the Greek revolution, replaced the Turkish tales, which meant that Greek folk elements, fairytales, superstitions, songs and dances, came to the aid of this new, popular entertainment.

One other hero from Greek history, Alexander the Great, accompanied by his most famous generals, Antiochus and Seleucus, appeared on the *berde* (screen) and soon became one of the more popular characters. However, he lost all his *hauteur*, acquired human warmth and was sometimes deliberately confused with St George. Feeling restrained about presenting a saint on the lit-up screen, the *Karagiozopaihtes* (manipulators) replaced him with an undisputed hero and the play *Alexander the Great and the Accursed Snake* became a favourite story. Ancient Greek tragedies, Greek mythology and the Bible also served as sources of inspiration, and so one can now see plays like *Oedipus Rex*, *The Riddles* (related to the Sphinx of Thebes), *The Seven Monsters* (a strange combination of Hercules' feat with the Lernaian Hydra and the Apocalypse), and *Theseus, the Minotaur and Karagiozis*.

Most of the important *Karagiozopaihtes* were illiterate, yet they seem to have been able to appreciate fully what would captivate the imagination of their audiences, possibly because their sense and judgement were unadulterated by any feigned aesthetics or foreign influences. After *Karagiozis* was 'purified' in both speech and movement, the audiences of the shadow theatre included men, women and children from all strata of society. Its success was such that sometimes other professional touring troupes would have to pack up and go as soon as the *Karagiozis* arrived.

By 1920, there were fifteen shadow theatres in Athens alone. One of them, Andonis Mollas's, had its theatre beside the ancient temple of Zeus until the Tourist Organization demolished the theatre in 1934. Many others roamed all over Greece, adding new figures and stories and technical innovation as they went along. The group of Epirus *Karagiozopaihtes* in particular was responsible for some of the most significant developments. The peak was shortly after 1920 and lasted roughly until the late 1940s.

Post-war *Karagiozis* tried to adjust to modern times, but all it could really change or develop were the stories, hence *Karagiozis the Astronaut*. The technical aspects had already been perfected to such an extent that they sometimes became an encumbrance or otherwise detracted from the spontaneity and simplicity of the spectacle. In any case, the cinema and then television proved too strong a rival for *Karagiozis*.

In the 1990s, there were still one or two shadow theatres in Athens and some of the old *Karagiozopaihtes* have taught their children the art. A professional union was established in 1925, and in October 1977 a *Karagiozis* school was started. Recently, interest in *Karagiozis* from abroad has come in the form of invitations to perform or to hold workshops in Europe and the United States. The seal of respectability for shadow theatre came from the University of Thessaloniki which in the 1980s began to offer a course on *Karagiozis*.

Without doubt, however, for about a hundred years (1830–1940), *Karagiozis* was the best established, most generally accepted form of entertainment in Greece. It emphasized patriotism in times of peace; acted as a history lesson for the masses; and it preserved many important facets of folk tradition. Folk songs, beliefs and sayings, fairytales and superstitions, customs and habits, codes of ethics and social institutions were incorporated, usually, but not always, in a comic form.

Another reason *Karagiozis* became so popular was that, through comedy, humour or light satire, it was a constant and active if indirect social protest. The typical setting for a *Karagiozis* performance consists of a beautiful *seraglio* on the right and a ramshackle hut on the left. The disparity is all too obvious; there is always social injustice and inequality. Those representing authority or a higher social class are always well dressed, Karagiozis and his family are always barefoot, in tatters and starving. The Turkish characters are usually those in positions of power and authority. They are oppressive or even violent, or have hired others to do their dirty work for them. The only way the establishment can avoid a predicament is either by using cunning or simply running; Karagiozis does both. It is made clear that Karagiozis steals because he is hungry, and he is hungry because society has not provided for him or equipped him to make an honest living. The rich and powerful do not steal food or money because they have so much of both. They can be wise and generous because they can afford it.

However, Karagiozis has his own moral code. He steals because he has to, not for sport, and he receives the blows as he says 'for an idea' not for money. Survival is the supreme motto. And yet he never appears as a traitor; in fact, traitors are some of the most hateful figures in *Karagiozis* stories.

Not even death escapes irony; it, too, is laughed at or becomes an occasion for a joke so that the audience will not leave the theatre grieved. Following the princess's death and Alexander the Great's suicide Karagiozis laments: 'Oh neighbours, go and get shrouds and graves for me to sell!'

Karagiozis was never a staunchly political theatre, polemically engaged in social criticism. Thanasis Fotiades is probably right in saying that *Karagiozis* was always careful not to overstep the boundary which would endanger its existence.

It is this that many Greek playwrights satirize in their plays, employing *Karagiozis* techniques in an ironic fashion, so that through familiar patterns their audiences come to recognize some of the harmful national traits which they as playwrights want to see eliminated from the new Greek self. What they insinuate, in plays like Skourtis's *The Musicians*, Metsos Efthymiades's *Fondas*, Kehaidis's *Backgammon*, Karras's *The Strongmen* and others, is that social and political awareness are the only means to combat pre-established authority and that expecting a clever racket to change one's life is simply self-deception. That is, while they acknowledge the fact that Karagiozis, with his anti-heroic attitude, manages to survive in an absurd world, they urge a more assertive existence for human dignity.

Design

At the beginning of the twentieth century the Royal Theatre ordered its settings from Germany. Freelance directors, like Constantinos Chrestomanos, ordered theirs from Italy. The style was very much in the Italian tradition of impeccable perspectives, outlined architectural details and folds.

The first important Greek designer was Panos Aravandinos (1886–1930), who contributed to the establishment of design as part of the creative work of theatre. His first setting was prepared in 1916 for the *epitheorisi Xifir Faler* at the new theatre in Neo Phalero.

When the National Theatre was established, its director, Fotos Politis, engaged Kleovoulos Klonnis (1907–88), trained in France, and also hired the costume designer Andonis Fokas (1889–1986). The latter worked at the National for about forty years creating over ten thousand costumes for plays by Shakespeare, Molière, Goldoni, Gogol, Shaw and O'Neill among others. He also created memorable costumes for ancient Greek tragedies, using colours from the natural ambience of the ancient sites and theatres together with those of modern folk tradition.

The first moves against design realism occurred at Koun's Art Theatre where Diamandis Diamandopoulos (b. 1914) and Yannis Tsarouchis (1910–89), two important Greek artists, started designing in the 1930s. Tsarouchis continued his collaboration with Koun for a long time, the zenith being his almost surrealistic work for *The Birds* in which the idea of the bird was rendered by a tassel of feathers that was stuck to each actor's bottom.

Tsarouchis's main thrust was for a fusion of ancient and modern traditions. He eventually designed *Trojan Women* and *Seven Against Thebes*, the first in an open-air parking lot in Athens, the second at the site of the mythological action.

Tsarouchis and Diamandopoulos, like Koun, were influenced by Kondoglou, all of them trying to incorporate elements from modern Greek reality into their work. At the same time Nikos Hatzikyriakos-Gikas made a dynamic entry into Greek theatre with cubism.

Yannis Stefanellis (b. 1915) is another designer who has worked with Koun, at the National Theatre and very often in the opera.

Fantastic, phantasmagoric sets, costumes and masks are typical of Dionysis Fotopoulos (b. 1943) who works with the same ease with commercial theatre companies and those doing experimental theatre (he worked with Peter Hall on the 1993 Lysistrata, with the National Theatre).

There are two Fine Arts Schools in Greece of university status – the older one in Athens, and a very recently established one in Thessaloniki. The private fine arts school Vakalo also has a very good reputation and some of the finest artists and designers are among its graduates.

A number of Greek designers work exclusively abroad. Yannis Kokkos (b. 1944) has worked with Antoine Vitez and Jacques Lasalle in Paris and has designed for operas in Vienna.

He now also directs and was awarded the Prague Quadrennial First Prize in 1988. Nicolas Georgiadis worked as a stage designer with the Theatre Royal in London, La Scala in Milan, the Berlin Opera, the Vienna State Opera, the Metropolitan Opera of New York and the Paris Opera. He also taught at the Slade School of Fine Art in London, where he had been a student.

Stefanos Lazaridis (b. 1944) also had a successful career in the United Kingdom. He worked with John Copey for many years and has designed the sets for many operas. Chloe Georgaki-Obolensky and Theoni Vachlioti-Aldredge (b. 1932) are two other designers who have pursued international careers. The first created the designs for Cacoyannis's *Trojan Women* in Spoleto in 1963 and has also worked with Peter Brook. Vachlioti-Aldredge works mainly in New York where she has received a number of Tony Awards. She was also awarded an Oscar for her costumes for the film *The Great Gatsby*.

Nikos Charalambous's 1993 State Theatre of Northern Greece production of T.S. Eliot's *Murder in the Cathedral*, designed by Stavros Andonopoulos.
Photo: Nondas Stylianidis.

Theatre Space and Architecture

The ancient theatres of Greece are most impressive for their variety. From the island theatre at Thasos, where the sea is visible through the tall pines, to the theatre at Dodona with its austere mountain scenery; from theatrical Delphi where Mount Parnassus towers over the auditorium and the silver-grey olive groves sweep down to the sea, to the serenity of the giant theatre at Epidaurus, set in the grounds of Aesclypius' sanctuary. All are impressive and historically important.

The poet George Seferis spoke of these auditoriums as 'empty shells of theatres' and it takes no more than a small act of the imagination to conjure up the life they once possessed, the tiers undulating in diffused light like the fluting of a shell: all this, of course, before time crept up on the stone of which these theatres were built and dulled the brightness, or covered them under mounds of protective soil.

Many of the ancient Greek theatres – some thirty-five of them – are empty today, sad spectres of the glorious past. The drama, however, that once educated – in the truest sense of the word – the audiences that came to these temples of Melpomene and Thalia is not dead. It is performed regularly in some of them and on special occasions there are performances even in the more remote and less well-preserved ones.

In a series of important articles, Professor Fanis Kakridis relates the concave line of the *koilon*, the hollow 'shell' of each theatre, to the circle of the orchestra. These he further connects to the line of the horizon in the background and to the all-encompassing effect of both structure and setting, as the dome of the sky ultimately lures the eye upward. Returning to the *koilon*, he reminds us of the social segregation it presupposed and describes the different groups occupying their allotted space: priests, lords, generals, ambassadors, chief magistrates, senators, other dignitaries, and then the older men, their sons (mature citizens who would potentially exchange positions with some of the occupants of the lower tiers), the young men, and finally the women (and the slaves assisting them) with the children.

Kakridis carefully reconstructs the invisible network that not only united these segregated groups but also guaranteed the continual communication between audience and actors, whether the latter were the chorus around the

thymele, the protagonists on the *logeion*, or the *deus ex machina* on the *theologeion*. He then proceeds to point out the relationship between the ancient Greek theatre and the Christian Orthodox church with its particular architectural details, the special arrangement of the icons on the altar, and especially the format of the Orthodox Mass. He concludes by drawing attention to the actual *agon* which was enacted in the theatre each time during each performance, and surmises that

> the cosmic order, as it is expressed by the ancient theatrical edifice, forms the framework for ancient drama in its most profound essence; consciousness of a relentless supreme power is essential if the drama is to reveal man's passion for his liberation. ('On Theatre' in *To Vema*, June/August 1976)

The architecture, acoustics, ambience, and naturally the texts still make audiences fill the empty shells, where social stratification is not quite as strict as when the names of arch-priests were carved on the marble thrones of the amphitheatres.

On the other hand, the climate allows for other open-air spaces to be used in the summer for different theatre events. The Roman odeons, Venetian fortresses and castles, mountain-sides, playgrounds and even ancient sites are used for performances and local festivals from May to September. In 1976, for example, composer Yannis Xenakis created *Polytropon*, an extravaganza of music and art, an exemplary piece of total theatre for the local people of Mycenae and the busloads of visitors attracted there. Homeric passages were read by actors, a French percussion band created a dramatic frenzy and there were slides of Agamemnon's gold mask blown up to gigantic size on the red hillside.

An amphitheatre was built on Lycabettus, the highest hill in Athens, in the 1960s and it has been used for all types of theatre since. The rocky peaks of the hill and the big open space near the theatre became part of Andrei Şerban's La Mama production of ancient Greek tragedy in the 1970s. The sentinels on the rocks, the setting sun at the beginning and the rising moon at the end of the performance created a magical atmosphere.

Old quarries in remote areas of Athens were also used for performances before 1985, when the city was the Cultural Capital of Europe; Minos Volanakis used the quarry in Vyronas (where a full-scale festival of theatre and music is now held) for performances of *Waiting for Godot* in 1983. With basic changes, some of these places became settings for Peter Brook's *Mahabharata*, Peter Stein's *Oresteia* and other performances during this time.

In the winter, the National Theatre performs on the two stages of its neo-classical building in central Athens. The larger one is a proscenium while the smaller Nea Scene (New Stage) has movable seating and a flexible performing space. In the past, an underground garage was also used for smaller productions. The National uses another large theatre in Athens from time to time, the Rex. They have even hired private theatres on occasion.

The State Theatre of Northern Greece uses the theatre in the Association of Macedonian Studies building as its main venue, a nineteenth-century-type space with an Italian stage. Also used is the Yperoo (Loft) in the same building. A third venue, the old Vasiliko Theatro (Royal Theatre) next to the White Tower, the landmark in Thessaloniki, has been restored and so the STNG uses it as well, especially when its main stage is occupied during the Dimitria Festival (October to November) each year.

Very few of the regional theatres work in buildings created specifically for the purpose. Most are located in former cinemas or even restructured power stations, as is the case in Calamata. Most of the older theatres in Greece have proscenium stages although there are notable exceptions. The Karolos Koun Art Theatre, with its two separate companies, works in what was the original basement (220 seats) of the Orpheus cinema. The original owner of the complex, the State Council Court, reclaimed it but the Ministry of Culture declared the Basement, as the theatre is popularly called, a scheduled space, and a triumphant performance of García Lorca's *Yerma*, directed by Mimis Kouyoumtzis, marked its new phase in 1993, after almost three years of being shut for restoration.

Koun's second theatre is located in the ancient Plaka on a street named after the tragic poet Phrynichos. The building was an old timber warehouse but was specially redesigned as a Renaissance-type theatre, with a thrust stage, by the theatre architect Mano Perakis, who won a Gold Medal for his work at the Prague Quadrennial in 1991. It seats 240 people and major productions have been directed there by Yorgos

Lazanis, the eldest of Koun's artistic inheritors. The two companies collaborate on the ancient Greek drama they present each year at Epidaurus and in Athens.

Plaka, at the foot of the Acropolis, is the oldest part of Athens and also the site of the Amphi-Theatre, another restructured building. About 150 years old, the space seats 200, and gives the impression of being an amphitheatre while actually being quite a flexible space.

Other companies work in a variety of venues. Among those working in restored, old, neo-classical houses are Skene, Theatro Exarchion and Masks, while several are working in old cinemas – Amore, Anichto Theatro and Stoa. Others work in non-theatrical spaces such as printshops – Embros; warehouses – Aplo Theatro; office spaces – Piramatiko Theatro tis Polis; or even old bakeries – Theatro tou Fournou.

There are quite a few new theatres, equipped with new technology, owned by cultural and educational institutions, local authorities or schools. One of the best theatres in Athens was built on the suburban grounds of Athens College in the 1970s. Civic or other cultural centres usually build multipurpose halls and either invite companies on special occasions or sponsor a resident theatre group for a length of time.

Invaluable information about older theatres in Greece, some of which are used or are being restored at present, is contained in Nikos Babounakis's book *Norma's Spectre*.

Alexandra Triandi, a *lieder* singer, conceived the idea of a multipurpose concert hall for Athens in about 1950. She did not, however, live to see it completed. It was, in fact, only opened in 1991. Performances during 1992 included Strauss's *Elektra*, Sophocles' *Electra* done by Moscow's Taganka Theatre (directed by Yuri Lyubimov), and various dirges from the tragedies where Electra is a main character. Perhaps the most interesting event was the commissioned chamber opera *Pylades* by George Kouroupos (libretto by Giorgos Heimonas, a leading prose writer and a sensitive translator of ancient Greek drama), directed and designed by Dionysis Fotopoulos.

The May–June 1993 cycle was called *Eleni* and it included Strauss's *Die ägyptische Helena* (*The Egyptian Helen*), Gluck's *Iphigenie en Tauride* (*Iphigenia in Taurus*), a commissioned opera by Thanos Mikroutsikos (b. 1947), *I Epistrofi tis Elenis* (*Helen's Return Home*) and Euripides' *Helen* by the Cyprus State Theatre, directed by Nikos Charalambous. The carefully planned Athens Concert Hall (with excellent acoustics) has already become a reference point for cultural life in the capital.

Training

Theatre education has undergone many changes since 1974, the year that the *junta* collapsed. Since that time, many young people have supplemented their drama school educations with related university degrees while others attended schools abroad or participated in seminars and workshops, or worked at international or local festivals.

Before World War II, however, young actors and directors apprenticed themselves to masters in Paris, Germany or Austria. Although Paris continues to remain an attraction, since the war London, Poland and to a lesser degree New York have exerted a growing influence. Theatre innovators like Jerzy Grotowski, Peter Brook and Eugenio Barba have become a source of inspiration for many young theatre artists.

Until recently, courses on Greek and foreign drama were only occasionally taught at the Universities of Thessaloniki and Crete as part of the School of Philosophy. A department of theatre studies, however, was established at Athens University in 1990 but its courses are purely theoretical. A department of theatre was inaugurated at Thessaloniki in 1992 and includes practical work so that its graduates will be able to pursue careers in the theatre as well as in the classroom. There is also a theatre studies programme at the University of Patras.

The National Theatre and the State Theatre of Northern Greece each have a drama school attached to them and the candidates who pass the entrance examinations (no more than twenty per year) receive free education. Since 1983 – according to the law on theatre training – private drama schools, owned by theatre companies (as in the case of the Art Theatre), associations, the Conservatory of Athens, or individuals, are required to comply with much more stringent rules with regard to infrastructure, qualifications of instructors and curricula.

Both before they enter and when they graduate, all drama school students have to pass exams conducted by committees comprised of actors specially appointed by the Ministry of Culture.

Specialized instruction is also now being offered at centres or workshops, usually in three-year programmes, financed partly by the Ministry of Culture and EC funds. The Centre for Research and Performance of Ancient Greek Drama, run by a highly qualified team of theatre practitioners and scholars, offers courses on choral movement, voice, acting, mask-making and theory.

All drama schools are considered higher institutions of education, and the curriculum, set by law in 1983, includes acting, improvisation, movement, dance, voice, music, singing, dramaturgy, theatre history, history of modern Greek literature, film history and practice, costume design and mask-making.

The National Theatre Drama School has had a long tradition of training students, especially in ancient Greek drama, while the Art Theatre School has won a reputation for atmospheric and physical improvisational acting.

The Hellenic Centre of the International Theatre Institute (ITI) has often invited teachers from Russia, England, Poland and elsewhere and sponsored workshops where young actors work on specific aspects of acting, movement or voice. In 1989, for example, the Russian Alexei Gnussev demonstrated his technique of plastic movement to actors. In 1985, directors, actors, composers and choreographers explained and presented their different approaches to work related to the ancient Greek chorus.

The French Institute, the British Council, the Goethe Institute and others have regularly provided opportunities for contact with what is new or experimental in the art of theatre in Europe and North America.

Criticism, Scholarship and Publishing

The most significant organization for theatre research in Greece is the Museum and Centre of Greek Theatre Studies, headed by the playwright Manolis Korres. Apart from its invaluable exhibition items and the books which its founder, the theatre historian Yannis Sideris (1898–1975), started collecting in about 1930, its staff offers excellent services to both researchers and theatre artists.

During the 1990s, the Hellenic Centre of the ITI was engaged in a wide range of research under the title 'Modern Greek Theatre at the Close of the Twentieth Century: Production Potential and Conditions of Reception'.

The Goulandri-Horn Foundation has theatre as the focus of its research, seminars and conferences. The National Research Foundation does specialized research in the area of theatre, and research related to theatre is also done in Greek universities. While in the past academics usually dealt with the philological aspects of ancient Greek drama, recent scholarship has examined practical considerations in the productions of these plays.

Nikos Hourmouziadis's books on *Production and Imagination in Euripides: Form and Function of the Scenic Space* (1965) and *Terms and Transformations in Ancient Greek Tragedy* (1984) are very good examples of this direction. In the four essays comprising the latter book, he examines space, time, image and silence and the relationship to them of each of the tragic poets at different periods in their careers.

Modern approaches, both to ancient and modern Greek drama, are adopted by critics as well, but perhaps the most important achievement is the fact that modern Greek theatre has become material for university courses and serious research. Traditional methods are still employed for research on the Cretan Renaissance Theatre and what is called the Aegean Sea Theatre, perhaps because new material is constantly being discovered and initial emendation and explication deserves priority. The Aegean Sea Theatre plays, written in the seventeenth century, bear fascinating resemblances to the English morality and Mystery plays. They were written by either Jesuit or Christian Orthodox priests and teachers, aiming to instruct and refine their students, resident at church schools in various Aegean islands.

Annual conferences on ancient Greek drama, held at Delphi, involve scholarship and criticism, presented in the form of papers or discussions, for a select international audience. The proceedings are usually published in a volume each year.

A considerable number of plays, Greek and foreign (in translation), are published by various firms in Greece, together with volumes of criticism. Houses such as Ermes, Estia, Kedros, Gnossi, Kastaniotis, Dodoni and others specialize in publishing plays, theories and editions on design and costume.

The cultural sections of the national and commercial banks have also sponsored the publication of plays and books on theory. The Cultural Association of the Moraitis School is an organization fostering scholarship on modern Greek civilization and general education. Under the editorship of the writer Nikos Kasdaglis and later Kostis Skalioras, and in collaboration with the National Bank, they published a series of nearly forty translations of plays that had already been produced. These ranged from Euripides and Aristophanes to Samuel Beckett; the aim is to keep excellent translations from disappearing. Plays are also sometimes published in theatre programmes along with other materials relevant to the production.

Aliki Bacopoulou-Halls

Further Reading

Bakounakis, Nicos. *Norma's Spectre*. Athens: Kastaniotis, 1991.

Chrysostomidis, Alekos. *Popular Theatre*. Athens: Smirniotakis, 1989.

Evangelatos, Spiros. *Again About Erotokritos: An Attempt to Identify the Poet*. Athens: Kastaniotis, 1989.

Fotopoulos, Dionysis. *Costume Design in the Greek Theatre*. Athens: Commercial Bank, 1986.

——. *Masks Theatre*. Athens: Kastaniotis, 1980.

——. *Stage Design in the Greek Theatre*. Athens: Commercial Bank, 1987.

——. *Tales Beyond the Façade*. Athens: Kastaniotis, 1990.

Grammatas, Theodore. *Modern Greek Theatre and Society*. Athens: S.D. Vassilopoulos, 1990.

'Greek Festivals'. *Thespis* 8 (December 1972): 18–23.

Greek Opera. Athens: Ministry of Culture, 1988.

Halls, Aliki Bacopoulou-. *Modern Greek Theatre: Roots and Blossoms*. Athens: Diogenis, 1982.

Hatzipandazis, Thodoros, and Lila Maraka, eds. *Athenian Epitheorisi*. 3 vols. Athens: Ekdotiki 'Hermes', 1977.

Kaftantzis, Yorgos. *Theatre on the Mountains of West Macedonia During the German Occupation*. Athens: Yati, 1990.

Kaimi, Julio. *Karagiozis or The Ancient Comedy in the Soul of the Shadow Theatre*. Translated by K. Mekkas and T. Milias. Athens: Gavriilidis, 1990.

Koun, Karolos. *Social Position and Aesthetic Policy of the Art Theatre*. Athens: Glaros, 1943.

——. *We Make Theatre for Our Soul*. Athens: Kastaniotis, 1987.

'Le Drame Antique en Grèce Moderne'. *Thespis* 1 (May 1964): 47–69.

Michaelides, George. *Modern Greek Playwrights*. Athens: Cactus, 1975.

Minotis, Alexis. *Empirical Theatre Education*. 2nd ed. Athens: I Ekdosis ton Filon, 1988.

Mouzenidis, Takis. 'The Revival of Ancient Greek Drama'. *Thespis* 8 (December 1972): 24–8.

Myrsiades, Linda S. *The Karagiozis Heroic Performance in Greek Shadow Theatre*. Translated by K. Myrsiades. Hannover: Hannover University Press, 1988.

Paxinou, Katina, and Alexis Minotis. *Long Journey to Ithaca*. Athens: Epikerotita, 1989.

Pontani, F.M. *Teatro Neoellenico*. Milan: 1962.

Puchner, Walter. *Greek Drama Theory – Twelve Studies*, vol. B. Athens: 1988.

Regional Theatre of Larissa. *15 Years of Theatre in Thessaly*. Larissa: Regional Theatre of Larissa, 1991.

Regional Theatre of Patras. *The First Three Years*. Patras: Regional Theatre of Patras, 1991.

Sakellariou, Haris. *The Theatre of the Resistance*. Athens: Thema, 1989.

Siatopoulos, Demetrios. *The Theatre of Romiosyni*. Athens: Philippotis, 1984.

Sideris, Yannis. *History of Modern Greek Theatre*. Athens: Kastaniotis, 1990.

——. 'The Playwrights of the Modern Greek Theatre'. *Thespis* 2–3 (May 1965): 9–43.

——, et al. *The Modern Greek Theatre: A Concise History*. Translated by L. Vassardaki. Athens: 1957.

Solomos, Alexis. *Theatre Directory – Persons and Things of the Theatre World*. Athens: Kedros, 1990.

Techni Experimental Stage. *1979–90: Eleven Years of Theatre in Thessaloniki*. Thessaloniki: 1990.

Terzakis, Angelos. 'Contemporary Theatre in Greece'. *Thespis* 8 (December 1972): 32–3.

'Théâtre et Compagnies'. *Thespis* 1 (May 1964): 26–43.

'The Greek Playwrights and Their Problems'. *Thespis* 8 (December 1972): 45–50.

Vakalo, Yorgos. *Short History of Scenography*. Athens: Kedros, 1979.

Vitti, Mario. *Function of Ideology in Greek Ethographia*. Athens: Keirmena, 1974.

Walton, J. Michael. *Living Greek Theatre: A Handbook of Classical Performance and Modern Production*. New York: Greenwood Press, 1987.

GREENLAND

(see **DENMARK**)

HUNGARY

The first Hungarians – seven different tribes – arrived in the Carpathian Basin in central eastern Europe at the end of the ninth century, the accepted date being AD 896. Duke Árpád, their chief leader, founded a dynasty at that time which ruled the country for 400 years. The first Magyars accepted Roman Christianity and, under the leadership of King István, organized in the tenth century a politically independent state.

From the fourteenth century onwards, members of other European dynasties (including the Anjous, the Jagellos and the Habsburgs) sat on the Hungarian throne. As a consequence, there were times when Buda, the reigning centre of the country, was actually capital of a huge political conglomerate reaching from Poland to Dubrovnik. Between 1458 and 1490, the country experienced an era of civic and intellectual prosperity under the reign of Matthias Corvinus (1458–90), an outstanding statesman, ambitious military commander and eager man of letters. His court became a centre of Renaissance culture, a Societas Litteraria Danubiana (Danube Literary Society) was established, and a fabulous library of valuable codices – the Bibliotheca Corviniana – was built up.

After the battle of Mohács in 1526 and the seizure of Buda by the Turks in 1541, the country quickly fell apart: the north and west were taken by the Habsburgs; Transylvania became an almost independent principality (though it remained under Turkish influence); and central Hungary came under direct Turkish rule for the next 150 years. At the end of the seventeenth century, the Habsburgs took control, changing one foreign rule for another. In 1703, Ferenc Rákóczi II (1676–1735) led an uprising; in 1848 came a War of Independence when young radicals Lajos Kossuth (1802–94), a famous orator and politician, and Sándor Petőfi (1823–49), an excellent lyric poet, among others, inspired the nation. Both these attempts at independence were, however, crushed, the latter with the help of the Russian army.

On the basis of the so-called 'compromise' of 1867 between the Habsburg Dynasty and the Hungarian nation, a new political framework, the Austro-Hungarian Empire, was brought to life. Economically successful, the empire was also a political organization of many nations, and of many nationalistic aspirations. At the end of World War I, however, the empire ceased to exist. New political entities were created and Hungary lost two-thirds of its earlier territory in the realignment. Some 3 million Hungarians also became minorities in the newly defined surrounding states: Austria, Czechoslovakia, the Soviet Union, Romania and Yugoslavia.

From 1919 to 1945, Hungary was a kingdom whose head of state was a resident governor. In 1946, it became a republic which between 1949 and 1989 was known as the People's Republic of Hungary. On 23 October 1989, the country's communist constitution was formally changed and the name of the country reverted to the Republic of Hungary.

As a consequence of these changes, Hungary today is a small country of 93,000 square kilometres (35,900 square miles) with 11 million inhabitants, almost all of them ethnic Hungarians. The capital city is Budapest, with a population of 2 million. There are six provincial centres with populations over 100,000 – Miskolc, Debrecen, Pécs, Szeged, Győr and Székesfehérvár.

The history of Hungary's theatrical culture also reaches back into much earlier times and parallel European developments. Folk plays and theatrical celebrations related to Christmas and Easter can be traced back to the eleventh century. Documentation can be found on *ioculatores* dating from the thirteenth century. During the Renaissance, chiefly under the reign of Matthias Corvinus, an interest in stage spectacles and humanistic dramas spread across the country.

In 1558, Péter Bornemisza (1535–85), a Protestant preacher, wrote a version of Sophocles' *Electra*, the first significant work of Hungarian dramatic literature. During the same period, Bálint Balassi (1554–94) wrote an Italian-inspired poetic pastoral drama. Soon, the religious controversies of the era began to appear in dramatic form in such plays as Mihály Sztárai's (d. 1575) *Az igaz papságnak tüköre* (*The Mirror of True Priesthood*).

During the nearly 150 years of Turkish occupation, which extended mainly over the central section of Hungary, cities on the western and northern fringes of the country went on with religious performances while the Jesuits, Piarists and Pauline orders began producing school dramas all across the country. As the years went on, such school performances increased; by the eighteenth century more than 4,000 were recorded.

From the middle of the eighteenth century, professional theatres began to be established. The company of László Kelemen (1762–1814) was a pioneer in this development, giving its first performance at the still-functioning Várszínház (Castle Theatre) in Buda on 25 October 1790. Two years later, another company began to give performances in Kolozsvár, in the Transylvanian part of the country.

After decades of strolling companies, in 1833, a Hungarian troupe, consisting of the best actors of the time, settled for four seasons in Buda, offering a rich repertoire of classical and contemporary plays, musical-comedies and operas. The same company took over a newly built proscenium theatre in Pest and opened it on 22 August 1837. In 1840, the theatre was licensed by the parliament as the Nemzeti Színház (National Theatre). From this point on, other permanent theatre buildings were erected in major cities.

In 1875, the Népszínház (People's Theatre) opened a new building with its own repertoire of musical plays and fashionable operettas. In 1884, the Magyar Királyi Operaház (Royal Hungarian Opera House) opened; from 1896 onwards, the Vígszínház (Comedy Theatre) began to stage well-known boulevard dramas of the period. It was from this theatre that the playwright Ferenc Molnár (1878–1952) and later the actress Lili Darvas (1902–74) would set out on world careers.

Between 1904 and 1907, the Thália Társaság (Thália Society) tried to introduce contemporary drama and new types of acting. Its founders included György Lukács (1885–1971), later to become famous as a philosopher and aesthetician; Sándor Hevesi (1873–1939), an innovative director; and Zoltán Kodály (1882–1967), a composer and musicologist.

Hungarian operetta also came into its own in this period in such new theatres as the Magyar Színház (Hungarian Theatre) and the Király Színház (King's Theatre), mostly through the work of such successful composers as Ferenc (Franz) Lehár (1870–1948), and Imre Kálmán (1882–1953).

Both enlivened the former waltz and polka

melodies of the Strauss era with rhythmic forms based on Hungarian folk music: the fast and syncopated *csárdás* and the slower *hallgató* (a kind of rubato song). These elements became basic characteristics of this new style and were met with enthusiasm throughout the country and even abroad. The form was rejuvenated and Hungary became one of its leading practitioners.

During 1919, the revolutionary Republic of Councils set itself the task of making theatrical culture available to the masses. After the defeat of the republic, however, a number of leaders of this representative progressive art movement had to emigrate. These included such major figures as László Moholy-Nagy (1895–1946) who, together with Farkas Molnár (1897–1945), designer of the so-called 'U-Theatre', had a leading role in the Bauhaus movement. János Mácza (1893–1974), another *émigré*, became a renowned figure in Soviet art theory, while Lajos Kassák (1887–1969), poet became editor of the multilingual periodical *MA* (*Today*), which carried information on the experiments of theatrical 'isms' in Europe.

At home, two great directors left their marks on the work of the Nemzeti Színház between the two world wars: Sándor Hevesi, who attracted attention not only with his analytical abilities but also with his ambitious cycles of Shakespeare's plays, and Antal Németh (1903–68), who, from 1935 on, tried to introduce new artistic directions in both repertoire and staging.

It was between the world wars, too, that Gusztáv Oláh (1901–56) developed into one of the country's foremost scenic designers and directors. Working with Oláh in the Opera House was Kálmán Nádasdy (1904–80), an outstanding director and pedagogue.

In the decades just prior to World War II, the Vígszínház (Comedy Theatre) and the Belvárosi Színház (Downtown Theatre) were among the most successful privately operated theatres in Budapest. At the Vígszínház, Dániel Jób (1880–1955) was in charge, and he had a penchant for refined naturalism. The director of the Belvárosi Színház was Artúr Bárdos (1882–1974), known primarily for his interest in new styles and new talents.

At the beginning of World War II, Hungary's political and military links with Germany grew closer. One of the consequences of this was the application of the so-called Nazi Nürnberg-statutes' – anti-Jewish laws – which justified the exclusion, persecution and in many cases annihilation of several hundred Jewish intellectuals, scientists and artists, a number of them notable for their struggles against growing fascist influences. The Független Színpad (Independent Stage) under the direction of Ferenc Hont (1907–79) and the Madách Színház (Madách Theatre), headed by Andor Pünkösti (1892–1944), became active centres of intellectual resistance. In 1944, the fascist government collapsed during the siege of Budapest. But many important artists were killed, including one of the most outstanding directors, Árpád Horváth (1900–44).

In September 1944, Soviet troops entered Hungary to drive out the Germans. Almost as soon as the front moved on, provincial theatre companies in Szeged, Miskolc, Pécs and Debrecen began bringing performances again to the war-ravaged country. Budapest at the time was still a battleground. Pest, on the eastern bank of the Danube, was freed on 18 January, and on the 28th of the same month a 'liberty matinée' was held in the miraculously intact building of the Magyar Színház.

Under the leadership of Tamás Major (1910–86), the Nemzeti Színház began work with performances in its 'Little House' in March 1945 since its main building was badly damaged (it would not open until October). In April 1945, Zoltán Várkonyi's (1912–76) Művész Színház (Art Theatre), and later the Fővárosi Operettszínház (Municipal Operetta Theatre) was opened. The Belvárosi Színház and the Szabad Színház (Free Theatre) started performing in May.

The homeless company of the Vígszínház resumed work at a former cinema with Gorki's *The Lower Depths*. In June, Ödön Palasovszky's (1899–1980) avant-garde theatre began to perform, but survived for only about six months.

The reorganized provincial theatres continued to operate following the earlier circuit-system. Classified into four categories depending on their quality and size, the companies regularly visited well-defined areas of the country.

Between 1945 and 1949 all theatres except the state-subsidized Nemzeti Színház and the Operaház functioned as private enterprises, but runaway inflation soon forced most of them into bankruptcy. In 1948, broad community support helped to establish a new puppet theatre called Mesebarlang (Cave of Fairy Tales), the antecedent of the present-day Állami Bábszínház (State Puppet Theatre).

It was at this point that theatres across the country were reorganized into a more formalized state system which, at first, did not change the companies significantly. But new demands on the repertoire revealed just how great a change this would ultimately be. A number of playwrights and dramatic works which had been banned for political reasons in previous years were suddenly allowed to be performed. Exiled playwright Gyula Háy (1900–75) returned from the Soviet Union and quickly achieved new renown with his *Tiszazug* (*The Midwife*, 1945) and *Isten, csátsz, paraszt* (*God, Emperor, Peasant*, 1946). Theatres also began to play the works of Lajos Bíró (1880–1948), a successful scriptwriter who had moved to Hollywood, and Béla Zsolt (1895–1949), a spokesman for bourgeois and liberal views. Audiences also got to see the works of Lajos Kassák and Tibor Déry (1894–1977), both significant representatives of the Hungarian avant-garde. Gyula Illyés (1902–83), a famous lyric poet, also had several plays performed at the Nemzeti Színház.

Beginning to appear at this time as well were a significant number of performances of Russian and Soviet plays. Gogol and Ostrovsky joined Maxim Gorki, whose works had been regularly produced. New productions of French, English and American plays allowed audiences to catch up on a repertoire they had missed during the long years of war. Budapest theatres, for example, began to perform Noël Coward, Garson Kanin, George S. Kaufman, Arthur Miller, J.B. Priestley, John Galsworthy, Armand Salacrou and John Steinbeck as well as Jean Anouilh and Jean Giraudoux.

New approaches in stage direction and acting also began to appear. At the Nemzeti Színház, along with the more naturalistic style of director Béla Both (b. 1910), Tamás Major struck a shriller, sometimes haranguing, tone of voice, whereas Endre Gellért (1914–60), representing a younger generation, successfully applied the psychological insights of the Stanislavski method.

At the Vígszínház, the young Endre Marton (1917–79) revived earlier traditions while the newly formed Művész Színház was introducing a more sentimental and dynamic style in the productions of Imre Apáthi (1909–60) and Zoltán Várkonyi. Traditional, somewhat naturalistic trends, however, remained the norm in stage design.

Many companies looked towards a new kind of realistic acting at this time based on what they had seen or heard of Soviet models, Stanislavski's writings not yet being available in Hungarian translation.

The development of a new repertoire was the first problem of the Állami Operaház (State Opera House). In August 1946, Aladiá Tóth (1898–1968) took charge and invited German-born Otto Klemperer to be its conductor. Klemperer remained there for four years, concentrating chiefly on the reinterpretation of Mozart's operas. Mussorgsky and Tchaikovsky also took their place in the programming while operas by Gluck and Smetana added colour; contemporary music was represented by works such as Benjamin Britten's *Peter Grimes*. And the time had come at last to stage *A csodálatos mandarin* (*The Miraculous Mandarin*) by Béla Bartók (1881–1945).

Between 1945 and 1949, the Nemzeti and the Madách began building audiences by paying new attention to the working classes. The short-lived Munkás Opera-barátok Társasága (Workers' League of Opera Supporters) had similar ambitions, providing exceptionally cheap seats and trying to raise audience levels. The playhouses were filled every night and things looked bright for the future. Unfortunately, economic troubles and the appearance in Hungary of an extremely dogmatic and schematic Soviet approach to art – socialist-realism – began casting shadows for the decade ahead.

The year 1948 marked the centenary of the outbreak of the War of Independence against Habsburg oppression and became notable in its own right as the 'Year of the Change'. It was during 1948, with the nationalization of the banks and large-scale industry, that important social and political transformations truly began to take place auguring significant changes in the cultural field as well. In 1949 all theatres were formally nationalized.

The task of reorganization in Budapest was, of course, different from that in the provinces. In the capital city, many old spaces took on new artistic functions. Among the early changes was the establishment of an Úttörő Színház (Young Pioneers' Theatre), which catered to young people in the 10–14 age bracket; at the same time, the Ifjúsági Színház (Youth Theatre) was building up a repertoire for those in the 14–18 age group. A Magyar Néphadsereg Színház (Theatre of the People's Army) began staging classics such as Schiller's *William Tell* as well as more contemporary plays, which tended to become lessons in both patriotism and socialism.

In the provinces, permanent companies were reorganized in Debrecen, Győr, Miskolc, Pécs

The Hungarian State Opera House in Budapest.

and Szeged; another company shared responsibility for the towns of Kecskemét and Szolnok. Suddenly freed from commercial pressures, these companies at their best were able to present plays of genuine literary value; at worst, they provided cultural information for quickly growing audiences. Shortly after, the Állami Faluszínház (State Rural Theatre) was launched. Later renamed the Déryné, it operated a series of touring companies which played in towns that, for reasons of distance or lack of technical facilities, were inaccessible to other troupes. All the provincial companies offered a varied repertoire including not only spoken drama but also operettas, plays for children and, in Szeged and Miskolc, opera.

By 1951, the changes started to become obvious. The Budapest theatres began shifting towards a 'universal' programming policy which, more than anything else, reflected the state's cultural intentions. During each season at each theatre, there would be at least one production of a world classic (most popular were Shakespeare, Molière and Lope de Vega); a Russian play (Gogol, Chekhov and Gorki were seen in virtually every Budapest theatre every season); a work by a classic Hungarian author to represent tradition; and finally, something contemporary, preferably socialist, ideally by a Hungarian writer. Every company's repertoire rested on these four cornerstones – not bad in and of themselves – but the uniformity of the seasons was less than inspiring. The situation became even more difficult as political interference became rigid and schematic.

By the mid-1950s an official 'thematic plan' was formulated and a state Dramaturgical Council set up to control its implementation. The subject matter of a play became more important than its artistic merit or even its suitability for a particular company. Two notable exceptions to these policies should be mentioned here – the premières of *Fáklyaláng* (*Torch-flame*, 1952) by Gyula Illyés, and *Galilei* (1956) by László Németh, both produced by the Nemzeti Színház. Both plays were later forbidden for ideological reasons.

The Twentieth Congress of the Communist Party of the Soviet Union in 1956 encouraged the use of satire, a genre which Hungarian writers had already begun to use in such scripts as Ernő Urbán's (1918–74) *Uborkafa* (*The Upstart*, 1953) and Tibor Déry's *Talpsimogató* (*The Bootlicker*, 1954). Ferenc Karinthy's (b. 1921) tragedy *Ezer év* (*A Thousand Years*, 1955) probed still deeper into the social problems of Hungarian life while Imre Sarkadi's (1921–61) drama *Szeptember* (*September*, 1955) focused on tragic conflicts in the life of the peasantry.

The changing social role of the artist was also recognized during this period. The Association of Hungarian Stage and Cinema Artists was organized in 1950 and through its library of theatre books, conferences and national festivals, played an important role in theoretical and practical work too. As a sign of respect for the arts and artists, the distinctive titles Merited Artist and Outstanding Artist were also instituted in 1950. For promising young actors, the Mari Jászai Prize – named after a famous Hungarian actress – was set up. Through the efforts of actress Hilda Gobbi (1913–88), two homes were established for retired actors.

But the work actually being seen on the stages across the country was becoming depressingly pedestrian with only foreign performances standing out against an increasing greyness. Among the foreign groups which had some genuine impact at this time were the Soviet puppeteer Sergei Obraztsov and his company, the innovative productions of the Komische Oper of East Berlin and the stimulating novelty of China's Beijing Opera.

But if the theatre being seen was less than brilliant, there was certainly a great deal of it. In the five years between 1950 and 1955, the number of performances almost doubled (from 6,113 in 1950 to 11,088 in 1955), while the number of tickets sold rose from 2.5 million in 1950 to 5.5 million in 1955, this in a country of only 10 million inhabitants.

The year 1956 marked a major national popular uprising which was, however, soon crushed by Soviet troops. In its aftermath, political and social tensions remained high. In December 1956, the newly formed Hungarian Socialist Workers' Party issued guidelines on cultural policy calling for innovative approaches in the theatre and encouraging artists to express themselves more forcefully.

The launching of the Irodalmi Színpad (Literary Stage, now renamed the Radnóti Theatre), and the start of summer performances at the Körszínház (Theatre-in-the-Round) in 1958, provided a framework for these new aspirations. In 1960 Imre Eck (b. 1930) organized the Pécsi Balett (Pécs Ballet), noted for its modern style, in the city of Pécs. That was also the year when the Petőfi Színház (Petőfi Theatre), the first Hungarian theatre devoted to musicals, was formed, with Miklós Szinetár (b. 1932) as its artistic director. The Vígszínház, which had been renamed the Theatre of the Hungarian People's Army in 1951, was given back its former name in 1960.

In 1958, under Dezső Szilágyi (b. 1922), the Állami Bábszínház began to stage performances utilizing several different ensembles throughout the country. Utilizing outstanding literary and musical works, the company regularly produced pieces by Bartók, Kodály and later György Ligeti (b. 1923); they also staged Stravinsky's *Petrushka*, and Benjamin Britten's *The Prince of the Pagodas*, for adult audiences.

The Thália Színház (Thália Theatre) was launched in 1963, under the direction of Emil Keres (b. 1925) and Károly Kazimir (b. 1928), and quickly became the home of a highly interesting line of plays noted for their concern with and sensitivity to social problems.

Hungarian theatre life suffered a loss in 1964 when the Nemzeti Színház closed down following demolition of its renowned but ageing building. In 1966, the company began playing in a renovated building of the former Magyar Színház.

As the 1960s approached, the schematic themes of repertoire planning began to loosen and Hungarian dramatic literature turned to a re-examination of the country's recent history. *Fekete bárány* (*Black Lamb*, 1957) by Endre Vészi (1916–87) was the first play in this new style and was quickly followed by Lajos Mesterházi's (1916–79) *Pesti emberek* (*People of Budapest*, 1958) and Imre Dobozy's (1917–82) *Szélvihar* (*Storm*, 1958). In 1959 *Kormos ég* (*Smoky Sky*) by József Darvas (1912–73) focused attention on the dilemmas confronting intellectuals. Similar problems were analysed in a dissimilar way by Endre Fejes (b. 1923) in his *Rozsdatemető* (*Rust Burial Ground*, 1963), about the lifestyle of the proletariat and about its missed historical responsibility. In *Életem Zsóka* (*My Darling, My Life*, 1963), Károly Szakonyi (b. 1931) explored the deep disillusionment of the artistic world. The same theme received impressive treatment in Imre Sarkadi's *Elveszett paradicsom* (*Paradise Lost*) in 1961, and in his *Oszlopos Simeon* (*Simeon the Stylite*, 1967). Political and psychological tensions were dealt with in Miklós Hubay's (b. 1918) *Csend az ajtó mögött* (*Silence Behind the Door*, 1963) and *Késdobálók* (*Knife Throwers*, 1964). István Csurka (b. 1934), with his *Ki lesz a bálanya* (*Fall Guy for Tonight*) put on at the Thália Studio in 1969, bitterly gave the last rites to a lost generation.

The aftermath of World War II called forth poetic remembrances like the musical *Egy szerelem három éjszakája* (*Three Nights of a Love*, 1961), by the trio of authors Hubay, István Vas (b. 1910) and György Ránki (b. 1907) and *Gellérthegyi álmok* (*Dreams on Gellért Hill*) by Ferenc Karinthy. Political problems of post-revolutionary periods were openly dealt with in works such as László Gyurkó's (b. 1930) *Szerelmem Elektra* (*Electra, My Love*, 1968). Toward the end of the 1960s,

a new theme, the ever-present conflict between people and politicians, made a strong bid for attention in Hungarian drama in such plays as Hubay's ruthless *Néró játszik* (*Nero Playing*, 1968) and Gábor Görgey's (b. 1929) often-revived *Komámasszony, hol a stukker?* (*A Gun for Five?*, 1968).

István Örkény (1912–79), the country's outstanding absurdist, marked this period indelibly with his *Tóték* (*The Tóth Family*, 1967), a gripping historical grotesque. His *Macskajáték* (*Catsplay*, 1971) was another popular success which was widely performed abroad as well. Later, he successfully built up a whole series of political-historical plays such as *Vérrokonok* (*Blood Relatives*, 1974), *Pisti a vérzivatarban* (*Pisti in the Holocaust*, 1979) and *Forgatókönyv* (*Screenplay*, 1982). Suddenly there were no obstacles to the performance of works which had been banned during the 1950s as 'formalistic' (Brecht's works included). As a result, there was a sudden influx of plays whose style and structure demanded a different approach as

Gábor Székely's 1971 Pesti Theatre production of István Örkény's *Catsplay*.

well. Experimentation flourished at this time and was almost uniformly 'form-breaking'. Over the next few years these experiments divided themselves into more familiar categories – epic, narrative, documentary, metaphoric, dramatic parables, and theatre of 'alienation', among others. As new forms emerged, so too did a new generation of directors and actors.

The national uprising of 1956 had brought to the surface many underlying difficulties. This led by 1964 to the development of theories aimed at achieving a 'new system of economic management'. Though these theories were never quite realized, cultural policy nevertheless was forced to fund various types of analytical surveys and studies, most of which emphasized the need for new directions in the arts. Still, many dramas – generally critical of the new directions – were suppressed and many authors and artists from both Hungary and abroad were labelled as decadent, pessimistic or counter-revolutionary. The works of Ionesco, Genet, Mrożek and Czech writer Bohumil Hrabal were, for example, considered undesirable. New works by major Hungarian writers were also delayed or refused production entirely. Among them, *A Kegyenc* (*The Favourite*) by Gyula Illyés, *Pisti a vérzivatarban* (*Pisti in the Holocaust*) by István Örkény, *Takarítás* (*Cleaning Up*) by Péter Nádas (b. 1942) and *Hallelujá* by Mihály Kornis (b. 1949). As a result, new performance styles were developed by young directors in an effort to mirror the growing political tensions; these efforts intensified after the 1968 military intervention by Warsaw Pact forces in Czechoslovakia.

These new styles were most effectively represented by the Twenty-fifth Theatre, founded by László Gyurkó. Existing from 1970 until 1977, it became a stimulating institution typical of the decade in its experiments. Others also left their imprints. Gábor Székely (b. 1944) in Szolnok, József Ruszt (b. 1937) in Kecskemét and Gábor Zsámbéki (b. 1943) in Kaposvár all flatly refused the obligatory optimism and began to work in a new 'objective' style, demanding an ensemble approach and an intense yet deeply passionate kind of acting. Following a run in Budapest in 1972 of the Royal Shakespeare Company's production of *A Midsummer Night's Dream* directed by Peter Brook, new debates started on such subjects as 'theatre versus literature' and the role of directors. These debates, to a very great extent, polarized the various generations.

As part of these changes, the artistic directorship of the Nemzeti Színház was given to Endre Marton in 1971. Until his untimely death in 1977, the company's productions of both classical and modern Hungarian plays gave a distinct role to this theatre. After his death, debate emerged on the very role of a 'national theatre'. One viewpoint, represented by the literary historian and critic Péter Nagy (b. 1920), the new managing director of the Nemzeti Theatre, underlined the responsibility of such an institution to give priority to indigenous dramatic literature. Directors such as Székely and Zsámbéki, on the other hand, argued that the leading theatre of a country should be concerned about artistic quality first and only then about developing a national repertoire.

In 1982, the Várszínház was taken over by the Nemzeti as its second stage; its earlier 'little theatre', the Katona József Theatre, was turned into an autonomous institution under the joint leadership of Székely and Zsámbéki. During the same year, Dezső Malonyay (b. 1921) became the managing director of the Nemzeti with László Vámos (b. 1928) as its artistic director. The new leadership began to develop a new repertoire on the twin principles of 'being true to both the national past and present-day Hungary without nationalistic flag-waving' and being 'internationalist, and receptive to what the world has to offer without indiscriminately adopting foreign fads'. It was in this spirit that classical plays such as *Magyar Elektra* (*Hungarian Electra*), by Péter Bornemisza, and the *Csíksomlyói passió* (*The Passion Plays from Csíksomlyó*) written during the eighteenth century, joined the national repertoire. More contemporary Hungarian literature was represented by such works as Illyés's *Tiszták* (*Albigenses*, 1970) and *Ádvent a Hargitán* (*Advent in the Hargita Mountains*, 1986) by András Sütő (b. 1927). The staging of an ambitious Hungarian historical rock-opera *István a király* (*István the King*, 1983) by Levente Szörényi (b. 1945) and János Bródy (b. 1946) in a production by Imre Kerényi (b. 1943) was a commercial and artistic success.

A cycle of Shakespearian chronicle plays was staged at the Várszínház in 1984, while Molière and Victor Hugo represented French classical drama. The approach remained essentially the same during the early 1990s.

Structure of the National Theatre Community

For historical and economic reasons, Budapest has a larger proportion of Hungary's theatres than its size alone would indicate, with about half of the country's forty permanent theatres based there. Individual provincial theatres, however, frequently have more than one company, with many boasting additional sections devoted to opera, ballet, children's theatre and puppetry.

From an economic point of view, there are five types of theatres in the country: the state theatres, owned and supported directly by the Ministry of Culture; the municipal theatres, owned and supported by city councils; the private theatres, mostly situated in Budapest; alternative theatres; and open-air theatres.

As the 1990s began, there were four state theatres, all based in Budapest – the Nemzeti, the Magyar Állami Operaház, the Népszínház and the Játékszín (Play Stage).

The Nemzeti has two houses – both proscenium spaces – one of 671 seats and the other of 258 seats; the Opera House has two proscenium spaces of 2,186 and 1,261 seats. The Népszínház and the Játékszín have only one stage each (the former with 333 seats, the latter with ninety-nine seats).

There are, in addition, twelve municipal theatres in Budapest (operating seventeen stages) and an additional thirteen municipal theatres in other cities operating twenty-one stages. The city of Pécs in the south has four stages, while the cities of Győr and Miskolc have three each. The largest of the provincial municipal theatres has 765 seats, the smallest seventy.

A number of private theatres also began operation from 1980, with some actually being subsidized. Among them, the Karinthy, Domino and the Független Színpad.

During the 1980s, many small alternative theatres established themselves, contributing to the development of new acting styles, using pantomime, modern dance-theatre, and elements from Grotowski's Poor Theatre methods. Some of them – the Arvisura Company, the R.S.9 Studio, the Térszínház (Space Theatre), Természetes Vészek (Natural Disasters) and the Andaxinház – have produced works of impressive quality.

There are also fifteen to twenty open-air theatres across the country, with Budapest, Szeged and Gyula having the longest traditions.

András Mikó and György Székely's 1952 Municipal Operetta Theatre production of Ferenc Lehár's *The Earl of Luxembourg.*

Operating only during the summer, they range in size from 339 seats to 8,139 in Szeged. In any given year, there are about 12,000 performances given in Hungary, with about 5.5 million spectators attending.

Most towns and villages too small to have their own theatres are regularly visited by the touring companies of the Népszínház and the Állami Bábszínház. Each year these two groups give some 3,500 performances.

Subsidy for the state and municipal theatres generally ranges from 30 to 50 per cent of total costs. Children's theatres generally receive even higher subsidies. On the box-office side, until about 1985, prices of tickets were centrally fixed. In the early 1990s, however, prices began to fluctuate with the cost of productions.

Overall, the country's theatres had a total of 6,200 employees in 1989, about one-third of them artists; the other two-thirds were technical and administrative staff.

All Hungarian theatre workers belong to the Színházi Dolgozók Szakszervezete (Theatre

Workers' Union), which negotiates salaries and benefits. A second organization, the Magyar Színházművészeti Szövetség (Association of Hungarian Theatre Artists), has separate sections for actors, stage directors, designers, dramaturges, reviewers, stage managers and those representing the musical sections of the theatres. This association attends exclusively to professional and artistic issues.

Artistic Profile

Companies

The Nemzeti Színház, Hungary's best known theatre, usually puts on between eight and ten new productions in its two buildings each season, while another ten to twelve works from earlier years are maintained in the repertoire. In 1987, in honour of the company's 150th anniversary, a complete history of the theatre was published.

The Vígszínház, the second oldest company in the country, has operated two stages since 1967 with the Pesti Színház serving as its second theatre. Specializing in sophisticated comedies – especially those of Molnár – it has developed a whole generation of playwrights working in this genre. Its name, however, does not restrict its policy to comedies only. One can also find serious plays on its stage, ranging from Chekhov to O'Neill, from Bulgakov to Mrożek, from Dostoevsky to Ionesco and Arthur Koestler as well. It also produces the works of contemporary Hungarian playwrights. István Örkény, for example, was its resident author between 1971 and 1979. László Márton (b. 1939), artistic director of the theatre from 1985, succeeded in staging new Hungarian musicals, like *Képzelt riport egy amerikai pop-fesztiválról* (*Imaginary Report on an American Rock Festival*, 1973) and *A padlás* (*The Attic*, 1988), both composed by Gábor Presser (b. 1948).

The Madách Színház, also with its own second stage, is the third major theatre in Budapest. Its repertoire includes a range of domestic and foreign classics mixed with contemporary works thus following the traditions of the Nemzeti. At the same time, the company has also managed to include a long run of the Andrew Lloyd Webber musical *Cats* in its repertoire. Since then, the theatre has specialized in presenting new Hungarian musicals, like *Doctor Herz* (1988) and *Mária evangéliuma* (*The Gospel of Mary*, 1991), with music in both cases by László Tolcsvay (b. 1950). Popular comedies tend to be put on at the Madách's

Kamaraszínház. The styles of the different productions at Madách are generally as varied as the choices of the repertoire and have run the gamut from the profound psychological insight of Gorki's *The Petit Bourgeois*, staged by the theatre's artistic director (1972–89) Ottó Ádám (b. 1928), through the intellectual tension of Camus's *Caligula*, staged by György Lengyel (b. 1936), to the subtly ironic interpretation of Dumas's romanticism as seen in Tamás Szirtes's (b. 1945) production of *Edmund Kean*. *Ghetto*, written by the Israeli Joshua Sobol, as well as García Lorca's *The House of Bernarda Alba*, have also been seen at the theatre.

The Thália Színház was created in 1961 and the company moved into its present playhouse in 1971. Throughout this period, until his retirement in 1991, Károly Kazimir (b. 1928) was both its general manager and artistic director. Through Kazimir, the Thália has also become closely linked with productions of Budapest's Körszínház (Theatre-in-the-Round). The Thália has regularly included in its seasons productions that were originally premièred at the latter. These are most often epic productions staged largely on the model of Piscator's *War and Peace* and include productions of *The Divine Comedy*, the Finnish epic *Kalevala*, the Asian epic *Ramayana*, Boccaccio's *Decameron* and even a new version of the *Casanova* story. The Thália's own Studio Theatre also offers a wide range of plays including works by Kafka, Beckett and Schnitzler. In 1991, the building became the permanent seat of the Rock Theatre and changed its name to the Arizona Theatre. The Körszínház, in its turn, became an independent institution under the name of the Globe Theatre, offering a varied repertoire in a variety of styles.

The Katona József Színház officially separated from the Nemzeti in 1981, determined to realize more experimental ideas. The scale of its repertoire has since been wider than at the Nemzeti. As well as innovative productions of classics such as *As You Like It*, *Coriolanus* and

The Three Sisters, the company has also staged Bulgakov, Pinter and contemporary Hungarian playwrights such as György Spiró (b. 1946). In 1988, the company became a founding member of the Italian Giorgio Strehler's Paris-based Union of European Theatres. Throughout the 1980s and into the 1990s the company toured widely in Europe and the Americas.

The Játékszín, operating since 1978 under the general management of Gábor Berényi (b. 1927), has chosen as its role the staging of largely ignored Hungarian dramas. The theatre has also done a lot for contemporary Hungarian writers, both launching and relaunching their plays. The Játékszín does not have its own company but borrows actors from other theatres. In most seasons, some fifty to sixty actors perform in its productions. Likewise, directors and designers are also recruited from other companies.

In the early 1990s, there were four provincial companies which had also established solid reputations. The Csiky Gergely Színház, in the town of Kaposvár, developed a company of such high standards that a book entitled *A Kaposvár jelenség* (*The Kaposvár Phenomenon*) was published in 1984 to explain its methods. In 1974, Gábor Zsámbéki became its artistic director and László Babarczy (b. 1941) its manager in 1978; together they were able to bring in a number of original young directors including Tamás Ascher (b. 1949), János Ács (b. 1949), Péter Gothár (b. 1947) and István Szőke (b. 1942). Often calling on actors to direct, the company has had major success with a wide range of playwrights including Peter Weiss (*Marat/Sade*, 1966), Brecht, Chekhov, Gombrowicz and even Sophocles.

In 1979, Imre Csiszár (b. 1950) became director of the Miskolci Nemzeti Színház (Miskolc National Theatre) in the northeastern part of the country. Ten years later he became director of the Nemzeti in Budapest. As is usual with most provincial theatres, Miskolc tries to offer a wide range of programming. Included in its repertoire have been Shakespeare (*As You Like It*, *Macbeth*), Goldoni (*Servant of Two Masters*), Ibsen (*Peer Gynt*), Maeterlinck (*The Blue Bird*) and Wedekind (*Lulu*). The theatre's presentation of the Hungarian classic *Az ember tragédiája* (*Tragedy of Man*) in 1984 was notable for its unique approach, 'as performed by the inhabitants of a Hungarian village'. In later years the company has had success with plays by John Arden (*Sergeant Musgrave's Dance*, 1985) and Sartre (*Les Mains sales/Dirty Hands*, 1989).

The Szigligeti Színház in Szolnok has also built up an outstanding repertoire of Hungarian premières of foreign plays under István Paál (b. 1942), from 1981 to 1986, and György Schwajda (b. 1943). The company had successes with Mrożek (*Tango*, 1978), Jarry (*Ubu Enchainé*, 1979), Beckett (*Endgame*, 1979), a rarely produced satire by Bulgakov (*The Purple Island*, 1981), Pinter (*The Birthday Party*, 1980, and *Betrayal*, 1984), Sternheim (*The Strongbox*, 1982), Wedekind (*King Nicholas*, 1983) as well as the first Hungarian staging of an early version of *Vassa Zheleznova* (1987) by Gorki, a stage adaptation of Pasternak's *Doctor Zhivago* (1988) and Yukio Mishima's Japanese drama *Sado Koskakufujin*, (1989). All these plays testify to the extensive orientation of this company in modern world literature.

The Hevesi Sándor Színház in the city of Zalaegerszeg in the southwestern corner of Hungary showed that it was possible to develop both a new ensemble and a new permanent theatre during this period. After a cautious beginning, the company began regular seasons in 1982–3. The first season included a pantomime-style performance of *The Miraculous Mandarin* by Bartók. The company's repertoire later included Jacobean drama (*The White Devil* by Webster), Brecht's *Baal*, a double bill of Brešan's *The Performance of 'Hamlet' from the Village Mrduša Donja, County Blatuša*, and an early tragedy by the romantic playwright József Katona (1791–1830), *Jeruzsálem pusztulása* (*The Destruction of Jerusalem*, 1985). The company has staged Witkiewicz's *Az őrült és az apáca* (*The Madman and the Nun*, 1986) and a modern *Švejk* (1989). The theatre has also done important developmental work with children (open rehearsals, playing and teaching world classics). Since 1985, the theatre has hosted an annual Open Forum where directors and actors work on new plays in the presence of the playwrights.

The Nemzeti Színház in Pécs and the Petőfi Színház in Veszprém should also be mentioned in this stocktaking for having brought to audiences the works of two great contemporary Hungarian playwrights in the 1960s and 1970s. Pécs produced ten plays by Gyula Illyés, while the Petőfi Theatre produced another six of his dramas. The Petőfi also regularly staged the works of László Németh.

Though psychological realism is still the dominant feature of Hungarian theatre in both acting and directing, it is certainly not the only style that one finds. There are, in fact, hardly any twentieth-century initiatives in world theatre which have not been seen or, at the very least, experimented with on the Hungarian stage.

Dramaturgy

Through most of the nineteenth century, romanticism dominated Hungarian drama. These plays – led by the great dramatic poem, *Az Ember Tragédiája* (*The Tragedy of Man*), written between 1859 and 1860 by Imre Madách (1823–64) – aimed at both the highest literary values and outstanding stage effects. The Madách play, a philosophical work in the epic tradition of Krasinski and Ibsen, was one of the few works of the period to achieve both these aims. It remains Hungary's 'national' drama and is still regularly produced.

By the turn of the new century, romanticism was being replaced by the more realistic well-made play. The first Hungarian dramatist to achieve international fame was a master of the new form, Ferenc Molnár, adapting this French form to Hungarian circumstances. Molnár's

Endre Gellért, Tamás Major and Endre Marton's 1955 National Theatre production of Imre Madách's *The Tragedy of Man*.

plays were perfect vehicles for conveying both the feelings and the thoughts of the modern age. His dramaturgy also inspired many other playwrights, popular in their time but almost totally forgotten in the decades since. Most of these works, unlike Molnár's, had the form but lacked any real substance.

Worth noting here are the works of Molnár's master, Sándor Bródy (1863–1924), and some of Bródy's contemporaries, particularly Milán Füst (1888–1967), whose works are considered today to be precursors of the absurd.

When World War II ended, there was a burst of new dramatic energy in the country and numerous plays found their way into production. Few had any lasting value. When playwriting began to be dominated by socialist-realism in the 1950s, the level of drama deteriorated still further. Only the plays of Gyula Háy stood out – *Haben* (*Have*) and *Az élet hidja* (*The Bridge of Life*) – excelling in their ability to deal with genuine issues while still following the official guidelines.

The rigidity of the prevailing ideology relaxed in the period 1953–6 and a few new and interesting figures began to appear, among them Endre Vészi and Erno Urbán whose topical *Zeitstücke* were considered extremely daring at the time.

After the revolution of 1956 and the national shock caused by its armed repression, Hungarian dramatists turned to more introspective themes. Imre Sarkadi (1921–61) perhaps best exemplified this tendency by combining an absurdist attitude towards life with a realistic presentation on stage. He gave almost tragic utterances to the loss of ideals at the time in such plays as *Oszlopos Simeon* (*Simeon the Stylite*) and *Elveszett paradicsom* (*Paradise Lost*).

Moral rather than political issues tended to dominate the plays of the late 1950s and 1960s, with the works of Gyula Illyés and László Németh standing out, authors whose major plays have been mentioned in earlier sections of this article. During the 1970s, it was István Örkény who expressed most effectively the moral dilemmas of the period in a series of absurdist tragedies which included *Tóték* (*The Toth Family*) and *Macskajáték* (*Catsplay*), plays which achieved international fame.

From the middle of the 1970s, a new generation of playwrights began to emerge with a range of problem plays that again ran into difficulties with authorities who directly interfered with approval for their production. Géza Beremény (b. 1946) was one such writer. He seemed to be speaking for a whole generation in *Cubic Space* (1976) as his hero struggled in vain simply to get a decent place to live. His *Halmi* (1979) spoke about the grievances of a drop-out son, a young man who loses his father, is unable to accept anyone else and finally commits suicide.

Another of these writers was György Spiró, who dealt with historical conspiracy in his *Nyulak Margitja* (*Margaret of the Rabbits*). He followed this with a sarcastic picture of theatre and art under pressure in an occupied country in *The Imposter* (1983). His *Csirkefej* (*Chickenhead*, 1986) presented a powerful story of contemporary moral decay; later, he did the libretto for a musical called *Ahogy tesszúk* (*As We Do It*), a disillusioned yet entertaining portrayal of average people trying to survive in a crumbling world.

Péter Nádas also achieved a reputation in the late 1980s with a trilogy – *Takarítás* (*Cleaning Up*), *Találkozás* (*The Meeting*) and *Temetés* (*The Burial*). All three plays were actually written between 1977 and 1980 but had to wait a decade before they could be staged. Concentrated, reduced almost to the purity of chamber music, these plays deal with everyday situations, using memory as a kind of uncertainty principle as they reach into the world of modern ritual.

Passion and obsession characterize the plays of Mihály Kornis. *Hallelujah* (1981) is a bitter and boisterous comedy with exuberant theatricality. His *Kozma* (1986) is, in contrast, a tragedy that successfully mixes mythological and contemporary elements reflecting current ethical and political questions. His 1989 play, *Körmagyar* (*Hungarian Round*), is a clever Hungarian updating of Arthur Schnitzler's *Reigen* (*La Ronde*) to present-day circumstances.

The plays of György Schwajda speak ironically about the hopelessness of honesty. These include *A bohóc* (*The Clown*, 1966), *A Csoda* (*The Miracle*, 1978) and his *Ballada a 301-es parcella bolondjáról* (*Ballad of the Idiot in Cemetery Block 301*, 1989).

Zsigmond Báthory (1992), a realistic historical tragedy by László Márton, should also be noted here. This unusual work was written for the occasion of the two hundredth anniversary of Hungarian theatre in Transylvania.

Gábor Zsámbéki's 1986 Katona József Theatre production of György Spiró's *Chickenhead*.

Directors, Directing and Production Styles

Between 1945 and 1990, Hungarian directors worked in a range of styles from Stanislavski-oriented psychological realism to the absurd, from mixed forms to Brechtian. One of the few directors in the country to work in all of these styles was Tamás Major.

Major began his career in a realistic vein with plays such as Gorki's *Yegor Bulichev* (1947) but within a decade had moved to an uproarious plebeian manner in his production of Shakespeare's *Merry Wives of Windsor*. It was Major who introduced the epic theatre of Brecht to Hungary in his 1962 production of *Galileo*. Late in his career, he turned his hand to a surrealistic-absurdist rendering of Peter Weiss's drama, *Song of the Lusitanian Bogey* (1970).

Other directors have not been so eclectic in their approaches. Endre Marton has tended toward well-organized neo-classical productions in such plays as García Lorca's *The House of Bernarda Alba* (1955) and Imre Madách's *Moses* (produced in 1967), but he showed that he too could adjust to more theatrical styles in his stagings of Weiss's *Marat/Sade* (1966) and Dürrenmatt's *Play Strindberg* (1973).

The productions of Zoltán Várkonyi (1912–79) proved his intellectual wit, his sense of theatricality and his superior talent in leading his actors. He created a heart-rending *La Guerre de Troie n'aura pas lieu* (*Tiger at the Gates*) by Giraudoux (1976); he has also put on stage stylistically perfect performances of Molnár's comedies, such as *A testőr* (*The Guardsman*, 1966) and – as his last work – created a highly sophisticated political metaphor in István Örkény's *Pisti a vérzivatarban* (*Pisti in the Holocaust*, 1979).

István Horvai (b. 1922) has been at his best when using his profound psychological sensitivity, as in his Chekhov productions, returning several times to *The Three Sisters*, *Platonov*, *Uncle Vanya* and Gogol's *The Diary of a Madman* (1967). Ottó Ádám has developed an almost puritan realistic style, presenting for

example Miller's *A View from the Bridge* (1960), and revivals of Hungarian playwrights from the turn of the century, truly recreating the mood and atmosphere of those years. Of equally impressive interest were his modern stage adaptations of epic poems such as *Paradise Lost* (1970), the *Ramayana* (1971) and the *Kalevala* (1979) as well as *Til Ulenspiegel* (1980) and *Everyman* (1983). László Vámos is another director who has worked in a wide range of genres, keeping a very conscious balance between theatrical fantasy and a well-disciplined performance in such productions as *Hamlet* (1962) and Beckett's *Oh, les beaux jours!* (*Happy Days*, 1971), while regularly staging classical operettas such as *Orphée aux enfers* (*Orpheus in the Underworld*) by Offenbach (1979). Earlier, in 1972, he had staged the Hungarian première of Britten's opera *A Midsummer Night's Dream*.

Among the younger directors, György Lengyel began his career at the Madách Theatre as a faithful interpreter of contemporary Hungarian authors such as Endre Illés (1902–85) and Magda Szabó (b. 1917), and later showed his skills as a director with major classics such as Ibsen's *Peer Gynt* (1971), Gogol's *Dead Souls* (1976), and a philosophical and architectonic rendering of Madách's *The Tragedy of Man* (1981).

Early in his career, József Ruszt worked in the Budapest alternative theatre with Péter Halász (b. 1953), founder of a group which came to prominence in New York in the 1970s, SQUAT Theatre. Ruszt, however, turned towards literary masterworks, creating a kind of 'ritual theatre' in *Troilus and Cressida* (1973), Marlowe's *Doctor Faustus* (1978) and Wagner's *Tristan and Isolde* (1988). László Márton (b. 1943) has consistently shown an extraordinary sense of rhythm and tension in such plays as Molière's *L'École des femmes* (*The School for Wives*, 1973) and a brilliant poetic imagination in his rendering of Kleist's *The Prince of Hamburg* (1980). He was also the director of the first Hungarian popular musical, *Imaginary Report on an American Rock-Festival* in 1973.

Music Theatre

Music theatre – particularly opera – has been an integral part of the repertoire since the beginning of professional theatre in Hungary. The

opera division of the Nemzeti Színház, in fact, was staging major operatic works as far back as 1837.

In 1884, the 1,400-seat Magyar Királyi Operaház (Royal Hungarian Opera House) opened; between 1888 and 1891 it was run by Gustav Mahler, who would later achieve world fame as a composer. Under the management of Miklós Radnai (1892–1953) and László Márkus (1882–1948), and with the work of such outstanding stage directors as Gusztáv Oláh and Kálmán Nádasdy, the theatre maintained extraordinarily high standards. After World War II, the Operaház had to contend with the difficult conditions facing all theatrical organizations. In 1953, it added a 2,200-seat house and developed it into its second theatre under the name of Erkel Színház (Erkel Theatre).

The operas of Ferenc Erkel (1810–93) – director of the Opera Division of the Nemzeti from 1837 until his death – along with those of Bartók and Kodály have been the mainstays of the national repertoire; internationally, programming includes most of the major pieces of operatic literature from Mozart to Stravinsky, from Wagner to Alban Berg.

Newer Hungarian operas from the 1950s were mainly in the romantic style but from 1957 on, a more open approach to all the arts gave rise to several new styles. Mihály Hajdú's (b. 1909) *Kádár Kata* (1959), for example, was written in a folk-ballad style; Sándor Szokolay's (b. 1931) *Vérnász*, based on García Lorca's *Blood Wedding* (1964), took this style further and became a major success. András Mihály's (b. 1917) *Együtt és egyedül* (*Together and Alone*, 1966), was actually set during World War II and showed an even more modern dramaturgy as well as a nettled tone. In 1969, the company staged Emil Petrovics's (b. 1930) *Bűn és bűnhődés* (*Crime and Punishment*, based on Dostoevsky's novel); through the late 1970s and 1980s, even more new operas came into the repertoire. Part of the credit for this growth in the number of new works must go to Miklós Lukács (1905–86), managing director of the Opera House between 1966 and 1978. He had previously served as one of the company's conductors in the period between 1943 and 1966. In 1990, Endre Ütő (b. 1947) became artistic director of the company.

Opera also has a long tradition in the provinces with independent opera ensembles operating in Szeged and Debrecen; between 1954 and 1959, an opera company operated in

András Mikó's 1981 Erkel Theatre production of Béla Bartók's *Bluebeard's Castle*.

Miskolc; since 1959, a company has operated in Pécs and, since 1975, in Győr. It is, in fact, in these provincial towns, that some of the most unusual works have been staged: Carl Orff's *The Moon*, Hindemith's *Mathis der Maler* (*Mathis the Painter*), Werner Egk's *Peer Gynt*, Prokofiev's *War and Peace*, and Gottfried von Einem's *Danton's Death* have all had their Hungarian premières in Szeged. The operatic branch of the National Theatre in Pécs was the first Hungarian theatre to stage Hindemith's *The Long Christmas Dinner* and Shostakovich's *Lady Macbeth of Mtsenšk*. Debrecen's company has featured Benjamin Britten's adaptation of *A Midsummer Night's Dream*, Malcolm Williamson's *Our Man in Havana* and the Menotti opera *Amelia Goes to the Ball*. As well, most provincial companies also have their own music theatre divisions.

In Budapest, where just about every theatrical interest has its own building, there are additional companies for the performance of productions representing light musical theatre in all its manifestations; even the leading dramatic theatres occasionally stage Broadway-style musicals.

Operetta too has been an important part of Hungarian theatrical life since the 1860s and the Fővárosi Operettszínház in Budapest has produced works by such internationally recognized masters of the form as Ferenc Lehár, Imre Kálmán, Viktor Jacobi (1883–1921) and Albert Szirmai (1880–1967). More recently, the company has produced works by Pál Ábrahám (1892–1960) and Szabolcs Fényes (1912–86). Since 1985, the company has staged annual six-week seasons in Munich featuring major hits from its repertoire such as Johann Strauss's *Die Fledermaus*, Offenbach's *The Grand Duchess of Gerolstein*, Lehár's *The Land of Smiles*, *Der Graf von Luxembourg* and *The Merry Widow*, Suppé's *Boccaccio*, and Kálmán's *Gypsy Love*, *Csárdás Queen* and *Countess Maritza*. The company's well-known operatic revue, *Ball in the Savoy* by Ábrahám, and Jenő Huszka's (1875–1960) *Mária főhadnagy* (*Lieutenant Maria*), with its romantic associations of the 1848–9 Hungarian War of Independence, have also maintained a popular place in the repertoire.

Since the 1960s, the Operettszínház has begun to play Broadway-style musicals, including *Kiss Me Kate*, *My Fair Lady*, *Fiddler on the Roof*, *West Side Story* and *Chicago*. The company also has a second stage, the Zsebszínház (Pocket Theatre), in which small-scale musicals can be staged.

The Rock Színház is a relatively new company created and run by Tibor Miklós (b. 1947) and Mátyás Várkonyi (b. 1950) which opened in 1982 with Andrew Lloyd Webber and Tim Rice's *Evita*. The company followed this success with its own original musical, *Sztárcsinálók* (*Starmakers*). In 1986, the Ministry of Culture took over direct subsidy of the company. Throughout this period it has managed to produce ambitious regular seasons of original and foreign productions including *Farkasok* (*Wolves*), *Üvöltés* (*Scream*), *A krónikás* (*The Chronicler*) and *A bábjátékos* (*The Puppeteer*), as well as such internationally famous musicals as *West Side Story*, *Hair* and *Les Misérables*. In 1991 it went into partnership with the former Thália Theatre, renaming the new enterprise the Arizona Theatre.

Dance Theatre

Since the middle of the nineteenth century, outstanding solo dancers have been active in Hungary but the development of ensemble stage dance started in earnest with the opening of the Budapest Operaház in 1884. Formal ballet instruction was quickly organized under the auspices of the Operaház by Nicola Guerra (1865–1942), who was in charge of the ballet ensemble from 1885 until 1915. One of the highlights of these early years was a visit by Diaghilev's famous Ballets Russes, featuring Anna Pavlova, in the 1912–13 season.

From this time until 1930, Budapest saw the work of a succession of choreographers representing many different styles. But none proved to be of any real significance until Polish-born Jan Cieplinski (1900–72) took over guidance of the Operaház's ballet. Cieplinski was able to transplant the achievements of the Diaghilev company with genuine authenticity to the Hungarian stage during the 1930s as well as to experiment with Hungarian motifs. Later, the work of Gusztáv Oláh, both as stage director and ballet manager, contributed further to the rising standards of ballet at the Operaház.

Two of the most significant personalities of

Hungarian ballet, Ferenc Nádasi (1893–1966) and Gyula Harangozó (1908–74), also made their first appearances in the 1930s. Nádasi joined the Operaház in 1937 and produced significant results, especially in dance teaching. From 1950 until 1961, he served as ballet director of the ensemble. Harangozó was a talented and temperamental dancer and choreographer. His first choreography was the ballet *Csárdajelenet* (*Tavern Scene*), which had its première in 1936. In 1945, an 'oriental' version of Béla Bartók's *A csodálatos mandarin* (*The Miraculous Mandarin*) was staged by Harangozó; in 1956, using another approach, he set the ballet in a modern city.

In the post-war period, out of twenty ballets produced between 1945 and 1949, fifteen were based on music composed in the twentieth century. Among those composers were Bartók, Stravinsky, Debussy, Ravel, De Falla, Gershwin and Prokofiev as well as Hungarians Ferenc Farkas (b. 1905) and Sándor Jemnitz (1890–1963). The creation between 1949 and 1952 of such major professional folk dance ensembles as Néphadsereg Művészegyüttese (People's Army Dance Ensemble) the Duna Művészegyüttes (Danube Art Ensemble) and the Magyar Állami Népi Együttes (Hungarian State Folk Ensemble) also had a positive effect on dance in Hungary as did direct access to and acquaintance with Soviet ballet. The Állami Balettintézet (State Ballet Institute), which opened in 1950 to train professional dancers, was based, in fact, on a synthesis of the Soviet Vaganova system and the Hungarian Nádasi method of dance instruction.

Starting in 1959, Imre Eck, then a young choreographer, made his appearance on the national ballet scene. Eck first gained fame as founder of the Pécsi Balett/Ballet Soprianae (after the Latin name of Pécs) whose style and repertoire became significant through his efforts. From 1961 to 1966, the first five seasons of its existence, the Pécs ensemble created a striking and stimulating style of its own, which – though closely linked to classic ballet – drew freely from the stage idioms of modern dance, jazz, acrobatics and pantomime. The composers of the music upon which Eck based his choreography were virtually all contemporaries and almost all Hungarian.

In the 1970s, László Seregi (b. 1929), became

Iván Markó's 1979 Győr Ballet production of his *Lovers of the Sun*.

the leading choreographer at the Operaház. He combined elements of the Harangozó-type national ballet with Soviet ballet style. To this, he added ideas from Hungarian folk dance, his refined stage sense, ingenuity and multiplicity of vision. His successes have ranged from a classical approach in two Bartók pantomimes via a lyrical, almost surrealistic approach in *A cédrus* (*The Cedar Tree*, 1975) to a highly theatrical rendering of *Romeo and Juliet* in 1985.

The Győri Balett (Győr Ballet) was organized by Iván Markó (b. 1947) in 1980 in the western Hungarian town of Győr. Markó had worked for many years with the Maurice Béjart company in Brussels, and quickly proved himself well qualified to train young dancers and to create with their help a unique dance theatre combining imaginative choreography with beautiful dancing. Among his major works are *Az igazság pillanata* (*The Moment of Justice*, 1980), *Haydn getanzt* (*Haydn Danced*, 1982), *Boldog lelkek* (*Happy Souls*, 1983), *Izzó planéták* (*Glowing Planets*, 1984), *Ecce Homo* (1986) and *Prospero* (1987).

The ballet ensemble of the Operettszínház also regularly stages its own events, most often based on the one-act dance plays of Richárd Bogár (1924–86). Ballets based on fables and fairy stories are staged annually for children by Éva Géczy (b. 1921) also within the framework of the Operettszínház.

Since 1981, an annual Táncfórum (Dance Forum) has been held in Budapest where young choreographers have an important opportunity to present their latest chamber ballets.

Theatre for Young Audiences

Many adult theatres in Hungary today produce shows for young audiences regularly, usually one per season. In Budapest, the József Attila Színház, for instance, often does plays such as *The Little Prince*, while the Thália Színház almost always includes in its regular repertoire original plays directed at young people. The Játékszín also regularly stages new plays, as does the Radnóti Miklós Színpad. The Mikroszkóp Színpad, better known for its adult political cabarets, also offers itself as a venue for entertainment for children, often featuring Péter Levente's (b. 1943) unique happenings. These build extensively on the normal activities of children.

The Arany János Színház plays exclusively for children. Its repertoire ranges from the indispensable *Wizard of Oz* to *Az ördög három aranyhajszála* (*The Three Golden Hairs of the Devil*), the latter derived from an old folk tale. There are also productions for the 10–14 age group, such as Molière's *Les Fourberies de Scapin*, Shakespeare's *Two Gentlemen of Verona*, and even musicals such as Lionel Bart's *Oliver!*

One can add to these the creative dramatic approaches of Katalin Sólyem and Jutka Halász (the latter working most often with the experiments of József Ruszt). In Ruszt's work, children have the opportunity to attend rehearsals and can comment on the work as it is happening.

In the provinces, too, just about every theatre has regular performances for young people using the same actors, directors and designers who do adult productions.

According to one statistical survey done in 1984, Hungarian theatres produced some 300 plays for children over the thirty-five-year period ending in 1980. Some 65 per cent were by Hungarian writers; the rest were either classics or works of contemporary foreign authors.

Puppet Theatre

Puppetry has a long history in Hungary; its roots can be traced far back into folk customs. This includes the *Bábtáncoltató Betlehemezés* (*Bethlehem Play with Dancing Puppets*) performed by peasants. Using an enclosure designed as a church, the puppets (Herod, the Devil, shepherds) are moved from beneath the stage and use scripts that have been passed down orally. Similar forms can be found in both Poland and Ukraine.

By the eighteenth century, marionettes were being seen in Esterházy Castle in productions under the musical direction of no less a personage than Jószef Haydn. In the nineteenth century, puppet productions were being seen regularly on fairgrounds, a tradition still seen today. Family dynasties of these early puppeteers began to be established at this time (Korngut and Hinz are just two of the well-known names in the field) and here too their modern inheritors maintain the tradition (the Korngut-Kemény family in particular, who work in Pest).

Early on in the twentieth century, Lóránd Orbók (1884–1924) did a number of experiments aimed at developing literary puppet plays between 1910 and 1914. Géza Blattner (1893–1967), working just after World War I, was the first in Hungary to use the *wayang* technique of Indonesian origin with plays written by Béla Balázs (1884–1949). In 1925 he left for Paris and in 1929 opened a puppet theatre there, Arc-en-Ciel. His version of the Hungarian classic *The Tragedy of Man* by Madách won a Gold Medal at the 1937 World's Fair in Paris.

Béla Büky (1899–1978), another twentieth-century pioneer, was particularly interested in shadow theatre and in the folkloric world of peasants. His transparent coloured figures conveyed the simple humour of the tales and the sad tragedies of folk ballads. Between 1941 and 1945, István Rév (1898–1977) established a Nemzeti Bábszínház (National Puppet Theatre) in which he gave ten productions (epic works, light operas, comedies) for adults and another six for children. One of these latter performances, *Toldi*, based on a Hungarian epic poem, had been produced 750 times by the early 1990s and was still going strong. Rév's figures use a special internal control and small pedals.

The Állami Bábszínház, Hungary's largest puppet theatre, was founded in 1949. Basing its repertoire on a mixed series of shows – some for adults, some for children – it became an official state theatre in 1958 and started its own school in 1962. In 1976 it moved into its own building in Budapest, with an auditorium seating 380.

Today, the Állami Bábszínház has two buildings in Budapest plus eight subsidiary troupes which tour the provinces with differing repertoires. In total the company has 220 members, sixty of whom are puppeteers.

Generally, four new puppet plays for children and one for adults are staged annually with about thirty to thirty-five works kept in the repertoire. In each instance, the company aims not for a scaled-down imitation of adult theatre but rather for a unique genre which works on its own, mixing literature, art and music with reality and fairytale effects. In an average year, the company stages 1,400–1,500 performances and is seen by nearly half a million people, mostly children. In addition to puppet versions of such classic fairytales as *The Sleeping Beauty*, *Hansel and Gretel*, *Snow White and the Seven Dwarfs* and *Cinderella*, they also produce a number of modern fairytales for children based on both Hungarian and foreign literature.

Since 1964, the theatre has staged a series of puppet productions for adults as well, including puppet adaptations of *A Midsummer Night's Dream*, Bartók's *A fából faragott királyfi* (*The Wooden Prince*) and Stravinsky's *Petrushka*, in 1965. The theatre has had success with a series of full-scale 'puppet musicals', including Bartók's *A csodálatos mandarin* (*The Miraculous Mandarin*, 1969), Stravinsky's *L'Histoire du soldat* (*A Soldier's Story*, 1976) and pieces by Ravel, Britten and Mozart. Brecht, Dürrenmatt, Van Itallie and Mrożek dramas were also shown to be good choices for puppet interpretations.

In 1982, the company began doing puppet versions of great epics: *Odüsszeusz a tengerek vándora* (*Odysseus, Wanderer of the Seas*) opened the series, and was followed by a stimulating puppet version of the Finnish epic, *Kalevala* (1984) and the *Ramayana* (1989). The company's directors have included Dezső Szilágyi and Kató Szőnyi (1918–89). Iván Koós (b. 1927) was its longtime resident designer with Vera Bródy designing puppets.

Apart from the Állami Bábszínház, there are three other professional puppet companies in operation in Hungary. The Bóbita Bábszínház (Bóbit Puppet Theatre) of Pécs was founded in 1981 and is sponsored by the Nemzeti Színház of Pécs. The company holds children's performances regularly – both in its own building and in small towns and large villages in Baranya County. Eger, in northern Hungary, has its Harlekin Bábegyüttes (Harlequin Puppet Company) founded in 1985, which offers puppet shows for children, while Miskolc boasts a company called Csodamalom (Miracle Mill), which has been operating since 1990.

Design
Theatre Space and Architecture

On 23 August 1786, the Habsburg Emperor Joseph II decided to dissolve the Carmelite Order, to secularize their convent in Buda, and to transform their church into a theatre. He commissioned Farkas Kempelen (1734–1804), an engineer, to realize the project. On completion, the building was called the Castle Theatre and remains in use to the present day as the second stage of the Nemzeti Színház.

In 1812, a second theatre – with a capacity of 3,500 – opened its gates on the Pest side of the Danube. It was called the German Theatre and the overture for the official opening was composed by Beethoven. The theatre was classical in style and had four storeys. An arched portico and statuary decorated the front. It was used almost exclusively for operas and the theatre burnt down in 1947.

The next building to house a Hungarian theatre company was erected in the city of Kolozsvár (today Cluj, Romania) in 1821. This was followed in 1823 by a theatre in Miskolc and in 1831 by a small but very beautiful classical temple of art in Balatonfüred. This theatre was decorated with the inscription 'Patriots to the Nation!'

Perhaps the most important architectural step in the country's theatre history was the opening of a new building in Pest in 1987, also in the classical style, which in 1840 would become the National Theatre of Hungary, the Nemzeti Színház. Designed by the company's own technical director and modified by a local architect, this building operated through 1908 when it was demolished. At that point, the company moved into the building of the Népszínház (People's Theatre), a space that had opened in 1875. The company remained there until 1964, when that building was also torn down.

From 1860 onwards many theatres were built across the country, most of them (including the Vígszínház) by the famous Viennese planning office of Hellmer and Fellner. Perhaps the highest achievement in Hungarian theatre building during the last part of the nineteenth century was the Royal Opera House in

The Budapest Vígszínház (Comedy Theatre) in 1926.

Budapest, designed by Miklós Ybl (1814–91). Inaugurated in 1884, this was the first theatre in Europe to employ the so-called Asphaleia system, a hydraulic device for raising, sinking and tilting parts of the stage and working the flies. The system operated effectively for nearly a hundred years until it had to be dismantled for a general reconstruction.

The newest theatre in Hungary was erected in Győr in 1978, using modern technical equipment. A proscenium space, its architectural uniqueness lies in the shape of its roof which rises in a wide curve to a peak (containing the grid). The building includes a major mural by the Hungarian artist Victor Vasarely (b. 1908).

In the 1980s, many old theatres dating back to the turn of the century began to be modernized and restored to their original styles. Included in these architectural renovations were theatres in Veszprém, Pécs, Budapest and Debrecen.

By the end of the 1960s, there was a renaissance of open-air summer theatre in Hungary. This had begun with the reopening of the Open Air Theatre on Margaret Island in Budapest in 1951, followed by the Szegedi Szabadtéri Játékok (Szeged Open-Air Festival) in 1959. In 1960 the Budai Parkszínpad (Buda Park Theatre) began its outdoor productions; in 1964 the Gyulai Várszínház (Castle Theatre in Gyula) turned the courtyard of a sixteenth-century brick castle into an attractive site for theatrical productions. Since 1969 the beautiful Baroque main square of Szentendre, a scenic old town in the hills north of Buda, has served as an enchanting backdrop for still another group of masked and costumed comedies.

The earliest of these was built in 1930 in Szeged where, on a huge square in front of the Votive Church, a temporary wooden stage was erected. In 1959, a permanent auditorium and a huge 600 square metre stage was constructed in its place. An outdoor theatre was built in 1938 on Margaret Island. The theatre, which held over 3,000, was damaged during World War II but was reopened in 1951. Since then it has been used for operas as well as operettas, musical plays and open-air concerts.

Training

Professional training for actors started in Hungary in 1865 with the aim of preparing performers chiefly for the Nemzeti Színház. This limited goal was expanded in 1947–8 when the Színművészeti Akadémia was renamed the Színház és Filmművészeti Főiskola (College of Theatre and Film Art) and began offering training as well for stage directors, dramaturges, film directors, camera operators, film editors and producers. In the 1960s, courses also began to include training for television. In 1971, the government raised it to university level.

Each year some 500–600 young people apply for admission to the school's acting department. These numbers are reduced to about fifty by a three-stage written and oral examination system followed by extended performance auditions. At the end, two groups of twenty-four to thirty acting students each are admitted.

Practical subjects in the school – above all the craft and mastery of acting – are taught by leading professionals. During their first two years, students are not allowed to accept outside contracts but in their third and fourth years they are free to do so. Much time and effort is devoted to physical training such as gymnastics, acrobatics, fencing and dancing. Diction and singing (including voice training) also play an important role in the curriculum.

The college has its own stage and auditorium, the Ódry Színpad, which hosts from eight to ten student productions each year representing a wide variety of genres and styles. These are seen by both invited members of the profession and the public.

The training of puppeteers is handled exclusively by the Állami Bábszínház, which starts its classes at two- or three-year intervals. During the four semesters of the puppeteers' course, three days a week are devoted to theoretical subjects and three to the practice of puppeteering. The most talented graduates are usually offered contracts by the theatre.

Those interested in stage design are trained at the Magyar Képzőművészeti Főiskola Díszlet-Jelmeztervező Tanszék (Department of Scenery and Costume Design of the Hungarian College of Fine Arts). A two-year degree course has also recently been instituted at the Színház és Filmművészeti Főiskola for theatre technicians.

Criticism, Scholarship and Publishing

Theatre history became a discipline in its own right in Hungary during the mid-nineteenth century. The initiative had been taken by the Kisfaludy Társaság (Kisfaludy Society), a national organization whose history contest in 1882 was won by József Bayer (1851–1919) for his study *A nemzeti játékszín története* (*The History of the National Stage*). The trail blazed by Bayer was followed by Jolán Kádár Pukánszky (1892–1989) who produced valuable research based on his own studies of national theatre archives.

Since the 1930s, additional generations have become interested in theatre research, including such important scholars as Ferenc Hont, Géza Staud (1906–88), György Székely (b. 1918) and Ferenc Kerényi (b. 1944). Hont carried out extensive research on Hungarian Medieval theatre activities while Staud specialized in the castle theatres in feudal residences during the eighteenth and nineteenth centuries as well as on Jesuit school theatres during the seventeenth and eighteenth centuries.

Székely's work has focused on theatrical genres, while Kerényi worked mostly on the history of Hungarian theatre in the first half of the nineteenth century. All four of these scholars have also been active in the contemporary Hungarian theatre as dramaturges, editors and/or directors.

The Színház és Filmművészeti Főiskola (Hungarian College of Theatre and Film Art) actually had a department of theatre studies as early as 1946. It closed in 1953. It was followed by a number of other centres of research: the Országos Széchenyi Könyvtár Színháztörténeti Gyűjteménye (Theatre History Collection of the National Széchenyi Library) in 1949; the Országos Színháztörténeti Múzeum (National Museum of Theatre History), incorporating the Bajor Gizi Színészmúzeum (Bajor Gizi Actors' Museum), in 1952; and the Magyar Színházi Intézet (Hungarian Theatre Institute) in 1957.

Since the 1960s, these research organizations have produced a number of important works, including *Régi magyar drámai emlékek* (*Relics of Hungarian Drama*, 1960), *Magyar Színháztörténet* (*Hungarian Theatre History*, 1962) and *A színház világtörténete* (*A World History of the Theatre*, 1972). The Magyar Tudományos Akadémia Színháztudományi Bizottsága (Committee on Theatre Studies of the Hungarian Academy of Sciences), established in the early 1960s, catalogues and acts as a coordinating and supporting body for Hungarian research on theatre history and theory.

There are several publishing houses which regularly issue books on theatre. Gondolat deals mostly with theoretical and historical works; Múzsák works in the musical field. From time to time, Szépirodalmi and Magvető publish volumes dealing with the overall history of the Hungarian stage. The Magyar Színházi Intézet tends to do specialist publications, for example, *Adattári Füzetek* (*Files from the Archives*), *Színháztörténeti Füzetek* (*Notes on Theatre History*) and, since 1977, *Színháztudományi Szemle* (*Review of Theatre Research*). *Színháztechnikai Fórum* (*Forum on Theatre Engineering*) is a quarterly published by OISTAT (The International Organization of Scenographers, Theatre Architects and Technicians) and the Magyar Színházművészeti Szövetség Színháztechnikai Szakosztálya (Department of Theatre Technology of the Association of Hungarian Theatre Artists) publishes on the subject of stage technology. In recent years, the Akadémiai Kiadó (Akadémiai Publishing House) has also taken an interest in theatrical subjects. Its first publication on the subject was a *History of the Hungarian Theatre, 1790–1873* (1990).

There are also a number of theatre weeklies, periodicals and specialized journals. *Színházi Élet* (*Theatre Life*) attempts to cover the national scene and is issued weekly, while *Színház* (*Playhouse*) publishes monthly. *Hungarian Theatre – Hungarian Drama*, published in English, German and Russian since 1980, is a kind of yearbook, while *Hungarian Theatre News* (also available in the same three languages) appears three times annually. Both are published by the Hungarian Theatre Institute, the national branch of the International Theatre Institute. Comprehensive writings about theatre are regularly published in the English-language *New Hungarian Quarterly*, a periodical mainly in circulation abroad.

The national dailies all carry reviews of new theatre productions, especially those opening in Budapest. A number of leading reviewers have also published selections of their writings, usually arranged around specific topics.

György Székely, Péter Nagy

Further Reading

Alpár, Ágnes. *A fővárosi kabarék műsora 1945–1980*. [The programme of Budapest cabarets 1945–1980]. Budapest: MSZI, 1981.

Belitska-Scholtz, Hedvig. *Théâtre forain de marionnettes et de guignols en Hongrie*. [Itinerant puppet and marionette theatres in Hungary]. Charlesville-Mézières, France: IMPR Moderne, 1976.

Bőgel, József, and Lajos Jánosa, eds. *Scenographia Hungarica*. [Scene design in Hungary]. Budapest: Corvina, 1973.

——, eds. *Scenographia Hungarica, 1970–80*. [Stage and costume design in Hungary, 1970–80]. Budapest: Corvina, 1983.

Borsa, Miklós, and Pál Tolny. *Az ismeretlen Operaház*. [The unknown opera house]. Budapest: Műszaki, 1984.

Csillag, Ilona, ed. *A százéves színésziskola*. [The one-hundred-year-old acting school]. Budapest: Magvető, 1964.

Dénes, Tibor. *Le Décor de théâtre en Hongrie: passé-present*. [Hungarian stage design: past and present]. Munich: Danubia, 1973.

Dienes, Gedeon. *A színpadi tánc története Magyarországon*. [The art of theatrical dance in Hungary]. Budapest: Múzsák, 1989.

Gabnai, Katalin. *Gyermekszínház Magyarországon*. [Children's theatre in Hungary]. Budapest: Múzsák, 1984.

Gábor, Éva. *A Thália Társaság, 1904–08*. [The Thália Society, 1904–08]. With a summary in English. Budapest: Hungarian Theatre Institute, 1988.

Hont, Ferenc, ed. *Magyar Színháztörténet*. [Hungarian theatre history]. Budapest: Gondolat, 1962.

Kaposi, Edit, and Ernő Pesovár, eds. *Magyar Táncművészet*. [The art of dance in Hungary]. Budapest: Corvina, 1983. Published in English, 1985.

Kerényi, Ferenc, ed. *A Nemzeti Színház 150 éve*. [150 years of the National Theatre]. Budapest: Gondolat, 1987.

Keresztury, Dezső, Géza Staud, and Zoltán Fülöp. *A magyar opera és balettszcenika*. [Hungarian opera and ballet scenography]. Budapest: Magvető, 1976.

Kocsis, Rózsa. *Igen és nem*. [Yes and no]. Budapest: Magvető, 1973.

Kun, Éva. *Die Theaterarbeit von Sándor Hevesi: Ungarns Beitrag zur Reform des europäischen Theaters im 20. Jahrhundert*. [Sándor Hevesi's work in the theatre: the contribution of Hungary to the twentieth-century reform of European theatre]. Munich: Kitzinger, 1978.

Lengyel, György. *A magyar színház ma*. [The Hungarian theatre today]. Budapest: Népművészeti Propaganda Iroda, 1984.

Mályusz-Császár, Edit, and Judit Szántó. *A magyar színháztörténet rövid vázlata*. [A brief outline of Hungarian theatre history]. Budapest: Hungarian Theatre Institute, 1979.

Manherz, Károly, ed. *Hungarian State Ballet Institute*. Budapest: State Ballet Institute, 1981.

Nagy, Péter. Foreword to *Théâtre hongrois d'aujourd'hui – dix auteurs – dix pièces*. [Hungarian theatre today: ten authors, ten plays]. Budapest: Corvina Publications Orientalistes de France, 1979.

——. *Le Théâtre classique français en Hongrie*. [French classical theatre in Hungary]. Budapest: Akadémiai, 1969.

Selmeczi, Elek. *Világhóditó bábok*. [World-conquering puppets]. Budapest: Corvina, 1986. 212 pp.

Siklós, Olga. *A magyar drámairodalom útja 1945-től 1957-ig*. [Hungarian dramatic literature from 1945 to 1957]. Budapest: Magvető, 1970.

Staud, Géza. *Adelstheater in Ungarn*. [Theatres of the nobility in Hungary]. Vienna: Verlag der Österreichische Akademie der Wissenschaften, 1977. 393 pp.

——. 'La Formation du nouveau public des théâtres en Hongrie après la IIe guerre mondiale'. [The development of new theatre audiences in Hungary after World War II]. In *Das Theater und sein Publikum*, ed. Heinz Kindermann. Vienna: Verlag der Österreichische Akademie der Wissenschaften, 1977. 421 pp.

——. 'Le Théâtre théâtral en Hongrie'. [The theatrical theatre in Hungary]. *Maske und Kothurn* 1 (1969): 39–44.

——. *Magyar Színháztörténeti bibliográfia*. [Bibliography of Hungarian theatre history], 2 vols. Budapest: Magyar Színházi Intézet, 1976.

——, ed. *A Budapesti Operaház száz éve*. [One hundred years of the Budapest Opera House]. Budapest: Zeneműkiadó, 1984.

Székely, Csilla. 'American Dramas on the Hungarian Stage, 1918–1965'. *Hungarian Studies in English* 3 (1967).

Székely, György. *A Nemzeti Színház*. [The National Theatre]. Budapest: Gondolat, 1965.

——. *Magyar Színházak*. [Hungarian theatres]. Budapest: Magyar Színházi Intézet, 1973.

——. 'The Thália Society: 1904–1908'. *Theatre Research/Recherches Théâtrales* 10, no. 2 (1969): 110–15.

——, ed. 'A Theatrical Guide to Hungary'. *Theatre Research/Recherches Théâtrales* 9, no. 1 (1967): 5–14.

——, ed. *Magyar színháztörténet 1790–1883*. [A history of the Hungarian theatre: 1790–1883]. Budapest: Akadémiai Kiadó, 1990.

——, Mihály Conner, and István Szilágyi. *A magyar színészet nagy képeskönyve*. [The great picture-book of Hungarian acting]. Budapest: Corvina, 1984.

Szilágyi, Dezső, ed. *A mai magyar bábszínház*. [Contemporary Hungarian puppet theatre]. Budapest: Corvina, 1978.

Tezla, Albert. *Hungarian Authors: A Bibliographical Handbook*. Cambridge, MA: Harvard University Press, 1970.

Várszegi, Tibor, ed. *Fordulatok*. [Rotations]. 2 vols, with summaries in English. Budapest: Typovent, 1992.

ICELAND

Iceland is an island of 103,000 square kilometres (39,700 square miles) situated in the north Atlantic Ocean, between Norway and Greenland. The island is believed to have been uninhabited until the ninth century when Norse Viking outlaws began to settle there. They brought with them concubines and slaves captured in the British Isles, most of them in Ireland, who later intermingled with the Norse settlers. The island was considered 'fully settled' by the mid-tenth century.

In AD 930, the settlers established the Althing, one of the oldest parliaments in the world, which gathered annually at Thingvellir near Reykjavík, now the only city and present capital. Christianity was officially adopted in AD 1000, the result of fine diplomacy rather than genuine faith, though 'heathen' worship was still tolerated for years after that. Iceland was Roman Catholic until 1550, when the last Catholic bishop was executed at Skálholt in southern Iceland. The country is now officially Lutheran.

Iceland lost its independence to Norway in 1262, and the Norse in turn lost the country to Denmark. Consequently, Iceland went through centuries of degradation and extreme poverty. Independence was regained in gradual steps and was fully realized in 1944, when the last links with Denmark as a ruling country were severed and Iceland was declared a republic. The parliament is situated in Reykjavík and is still called the Althing. Politically, Iceland is a democracy, with a general election every four years. Nearly all governments since 1944 have been coalitions.

In 1992, Iceland had some 255,000 inhabitants, more than half of whom lived in Reykjavík and the surrounding towns. The language is Icelandic, a Germanic language, and this is often considered by the inhabitants to be a unifying factor and a living definition of their existence as a nation. Of importance here is the fact that Icelandic has changed so little through the ages that a modern Icelander can read both the Eddic poems and the ancient sagas, which makes Icelandic a classical language that is still alive.

Iceland has a great literary heritage in the Eddic and Skaldic poems, composed in the eighth, ninth and tenth centuries, and notably in the sagas, written in the twelfth and thirteenth centuries. Though there is a rich tradition of storytelling, there is scant evidence of early performances even as primitive ritual.

For centuries Iceland was exclusively a rural society. Theatre, in the modern sense of the word, was therefore late to put down roots in the country and instead of Medieval strolling players or court jesters, one found vagrants roaming from farm to farm, earning their living by telling tales and singing songs and ballads. There were no theatrical troupes as such but the dramatic element was present from the earliest times, as evidenced by the dramatic form of some of the Eddic poems. Whether these were ever performed as dramatic dialogues remains to be proven.

Historical sources are clearer in relation to the dramatic games of the students at the two cathedral schools, at Hólar and, especially, at Skálholt. Written accounts from the mid-eighteenth century describe a ceremony known as *Herrandótt* (Lord's Night), which closely resembles the Boy Bishop tradition and the French Feast of Fools, as well as a satirical speech resembling the *sermon joyeux*. This later led to dramatic performances in the strict sense and the birth of Icelandic drama with the satirical comedies of Sigurdur Pétursson (1759–1827), who with *Sladur og trúgirni*

The 1966 National Theatre of Iceland's production of Sigurdur Pétursson's *Gossip and Gullibility*.

(*Gossip and Gullibility*, 1796) and *Narfi* (1799), was Iceland's answer to Molière and Holberg.

Iceland experienced a slow growth in urbanization during the nineteenth century. Amateur theatre groups were formed in small towns and fishing villages and consisted of pupils from the schools and interested craftsmen and merchants. This growth of Icelandic theatre from the grassroots may partly explain the enormous popularity of modern Icelandic theatre, where year after year the total number of spectators exceeds that of the entire population. There is still today some give and take between the professional and amateur theatres, and the latter is, socially at least, very important.

Reykjavík, the nineteenth century budding capital, soon took the lead and saw the first performances of the only plays of that period to have lasting value. These were first plays by very young playwrights: *Skugga-Sveinn, The Outlaws* (1862), by Matthías Jochumsson (1835–1920), and *Nýársnóttin* (*New Year's Eve*, 1871), by Indridi Einarsson (1851–1939). Both playwrights were disciples of the artist-stage designer and theorist Sigurdur Gudmundsson (1833–74), the first Icelandic man of theatre to have a theoretical base for his work. Gudmundsson urged writers to make use of folkloric as well as historical motifs for their plays so that audiences could be enlightened and made aware of their national identity. This ideal was closely linked with the struggle to preserve the Icelandic language under foreign rule (amateur productions in Danish were predominant) and part of the nation's struggle for independence. The first plays of Jochumsson and Einarsson made effective use of folk motifs and both writers also penned historical epic dramas, Einarsson in the unperformed *Sverd og bagall* (*Sword and Crozier*, 1899) and Jochumsson in *Jón Arason* (*The Last Bishop*, 1900).

A major event came in 1897 when Leikfélag Reykjavíkur (Reykjavík Theatre Company – RTC) was established by the amalgamation of earlier amateur groups. Thus was born a permanent theatre company consisting of a handful of individuals of outstanding although amateur talent. It was and still is democratically run by the actors themselves, who from the outset aimed at professional goals. The basic ideas were to secure the growth of playwriting and raise the standards of production. The new company found a home in a small intimate theatre, the Idnó, and remained there until 1989, when it moved into the new Reykjavík City Theatre.

The history of this company up to the mid-1940s can be divided into several periods. The first ten years served to emphasize theatre as a meaningful form of art and not just amusement. The second period, often labelled the 'Icelandic period' or the 'golden age', lasted from 1907 to 1920 and was characterized by the fact that every season there were one or two premières of Icelandic plays. The Icelandic repertoire, then consisting only of plays by Jochumsson and Einarsson, was enriched by Einar H. Kvaran (1859–1938) with, for example, *Léhardur fógeti* (*Bailiff Leonard*, 1913), as well as by Jóhann Sigurjónsson (1880–1919) with plays such as *Fjalla-Eyvindur* (*Eyvind of the Mountains*, 1911) and *Galdra-Loftur* (*The Wish*, 1914), and Gudmundur Kamban (1888–1945) whose *Vér mordingjar* (*We Murderers*, 1920) marks the end of the era. Einarsson and Kvaran also served as stage directors during the formative years while the repertoire was in transition from Danish and French vaudevilles to Ibsen, German realism, and new Icelandic plays. The Norwegian playwrights Björnstjerne Björnson (1832–1910) and Ludvik Holberg (1684–1754) were often produced, as were Schiller, Shaw, Dumas and Zola.

The 1920s were a period of re-evaluation. A new generation of actors came to the fore, some of whom had been professionally trained abroad, and the isolation of Icelandic theatre was permanently broken as evidenced by the fact that Pirandello was staged in Reykjavík no later than in Paris or Berlin. This was also a period when the company felt that the time had come to attempt Shakespeare and Strindberg. Reinhardt-inspired actor Indridi Waage (1902–63) became the leading director and was joined toward the end of this period by Haraldur Björnsson (1891–1967), among the first Icelandic actors to receive formal training (at the Royal Theatre, Copenhagen). The third leading actor and director, Lárus Pálsson (1914–68), arrived on the scene in 1940, after years of training and acting in Copenhagen. The 1930s were marked by ups and downs, partly due to the Depression, and the most important new Icelandic works of that period were probably Waage's and Emil Thoroddsen's (1898–1944) dramatizations of Jón Thoroddsen's (1818–68) nineteenth-century novels, *Piltur og stúlka* (*Lad and Lass*, 1933) and *Madur og kona*

(*Man and Woman*, 1934); the ideology behind those productions was that of the 'popular theatre' movements in Germany and France earlier in the century.

By the 1940s the RTC consisted mostly of professional actors. Acting as a profession was gaining confidence and getting organized. In 1941 the Union of Icelandic Actors was established, with leading actor Thorsteinn Ó. Stephensen (1904–92) as its first chair. Stephensen, who became the first director of Icelandic Radio's drama department, was also to play a role in the politically complex preparations for the opening of the National Theatre. The early 1940s were the heyday of home-made, often topical revues, some of which were played in the Idnó Theatre alongside RTC productions, while the RTC itself was strong enough artistically to form the National Theatre's ensemble.

The idea of a National Theatre was quite old by this time, first put forward by Sigurdur Gudmundsson and his group of followers around 1860. Later Indridi Einarsson led the campaign that resulted in a Bill being passed by the Althing in 1922, and the exterior structure of the building was completed in the early 1930s. Funding was secured through a specially created entertainment tax, which was also intended to cover the eventual running costs of the theatre itself. Unfortunately, this money was channelled to different official enterprises during the Depression thus delaying the whole project. For more than a decade, the building stood without life and a group of young Icelandic actors went abroad, mainly to England, to pursue studies. At home, the first privately run drama schools were being established.

World War II and the following years were a period of enormous economic upheaval, which also made its mark on theatre as there was now money to finish the National Theatre building. New funds also went to the Reykjavík Theatre Company and to other groups of professionals that came into temporary existence, as well as to numerous amateur groups around the country of which the Akureyri Theatre Company was the most important, a group which often reached professional standards. The repertoire of the RTC was varied and rich, ranging from Ben Jonson (*Volpone*) and Shakespeare (*The Merchant of Venice, Hamlet*) to Gogol (*The Government Inspector*), Ibsen (*Peer Gynt, Hedda Gabler, A Doll's House*), Maxwell Anderson, Maugham, Coward, Kaj Munk, Priestley and O'Neill, among others. Of the new Icelandic plays the most notable were *Gullna* hlidid (*The Golden Gate*, 1941), by David Stefánsson (1891–1968), which was based on a folk tale, and which broke all attendance records; Sigurdur Nordal's (1888–1972) *Uppstigning* (*Ascent*, 1945), dealing in experimental form with the problems of identity; and Gudmundur Kamban's *Skálholt* (1945), which had seen first production in Copenhagen in 1933. All three plays have remained in the Icelandic repertoire and all were directed by Lárus Pálsson.

The opening of the National Theatre in 1950 meant more than just a new theatre building, a national institution and a symbol of independence. It meant that actors would, for the first time, be paid a monthly salary and be offered long-term contracts. Although professionally trained and with the artistic ambition of professionals, the actors and directors for the most part had to earn their livings elsewhere between stints on the stage. The existence of the National meant that finally a nucleus group would be able to devote its entire efforts to its art and consequently form a more homogenous company. Until that time theatre work had to be supplemented by work in radio drama, which began in 1930. But clearly, the opening of the National Theatre, under artistic director Gudlaugur Rósinkranz (1903–77), marked the advent of a modern theatre in Iceland. Although most of the actors from the Reykjavík Theatre Company were recruited by the National, a few idealists, including the popular leading actors Thorsteinn Ó. Stephensen and Brynjólfur Jóhannesson (1896–1975), decided to keep the RTC going in order to give the National competition. In 1964, the RTC also adopted the system of engaging a seasonal company and thus became fully professional, while still democratically run by the actors themselves.

The National Theatre gave a tremendous boost to the theatrical arts of Iceland and greatly enhanced popular interest in theatre. During the 1940s it was rare to have more than ten productions on during a season in Reykjavík, five or six by the RTC and one or two by other companies, with the addition of some light revues, cabarets or operettas. Suddenly the number was doubled and audiences were receptive. This number was later to increase still more. The repertoire of the National Theatre consisted, as it had done and continued to do with the RTC, of Icelandic plays old and new – although it did not make an immediate difference to playwriting – foreign classics, modern plays and plays for children. Opera, especially, and ballet also gained a

foothold at this time. From the outset, the National Theatre produced one or two operas each year, mostly chosen from the nineteenth-century Italian repertoire.

In general, during the period between 1945 and 1963 the theatre was based on a solid realistic approach, the keywords being truthfulness and naturalness. This applies to the meticulous and earnest work of the Stanislavski-inspired Gunnar Róbertsson Hansen (1901–64) a leading director with the RTC after the National Theatre opened, as well as the work of his successors, actors-directors Gísli Halldórsson (b. 1927) and Helgi Skúlason (b. 1933), and the discerning taste of lyrically gifted Lárus Pálsson in his 'humanistic mission' in the theatre. This also applies to Indridi Waage, although the intensity of his best work led him towards expressionism and mysticism. This realistic predominance, however, did not exclude certain stylization when dealing, for instance, with classical plays, especially by such playwrights as Holberg, Molière and Shakespeare.

The 1960s were characterized by a number of social changes and these were in turn reflected in significant changes in style and taste in theatre productions – a heightened sense of values together with a growing awareness among theatre artists of their social responsibilities. By this time, post-war wealth and affluence began to show even more predominant signs of a hollow materialism and it was becoming evident to many artists that the fast-increasing population of the Reykjavík area and the numerous towns around the coasts was gradually losing touch with its rural origins and even its history.

The RTC recruited its first artistic director, Sveinn Einarsson (b. 1934) in 1963, and had by then a small company of actors under long-term contracts (made possible by a subsidy from the Reykjavík City Council). It was ready and able to tackle the challenge of competing with the National Theatre on a more equal basis than previously. Iceland had seen the advent of absurdist plays in Baldvin Halldórsson's (b. 1926) acclaimed production of Beckett's *Waiting for Godot* at the RTC in 1960 and Helgi Skúlason's productions of Ionesco's *The Lesson* and *The Chairs*, with the National Theatre following suit over the next few years with several outstanding productions of plays by Ionesco (*Rhinocéros*, *The Bald Soprano*) and Pinter (*The Caretaker*), for the most part directed by Benedikt Árnason (b. 1931), establishing him as the leading director at the

National, a position he retained into the 1990s while directing more than fifty productions there.

Also in 1960, the independent fringe theatre group Gríma (Mask) was established, which was to prove partial to the new wave of absurdist writing. The National Theatre, in spite of its many popular successes with fine productions of foreign plays, had failed throughout its first decade to make a significant difference to playwriting and the condition of playwrights. This was to change dramatically during the 1960s and all the above-mentioned factors were crucial in affecting that change.

Gríma was to last until 1971 and was in essence a literary theatre, dedicated to new-wave drama from Europe and new Icelandic experimental playwrights. With nearly all its members simultaneously contracted to other theatres, notably the National, the group fostered many talents, such as actress Kristbjörg Kjeld (b. 1935), designer Magnús Pálsson (b. 1929), director Brynja Benediktsdóttir (b. 1938), the first in a line of many outstanding female stage directors who emerged in Icelandic theatre over the next ten years, and theatre director Vigdis Finnbogadóttir (b. 1930), who was artistic director for the RTC for six years (1973–9) and subsequently was elected the president of the Icelandic Republic in 1980.

Gríma produced first plays by playwrights such as Oddur Björnsson (b. 1932) and Svava Jakobsdóttir (b. 1930). Björnsson's early plays were absurdist satires and fantasies, unabashedly theatrical one-acters, such as *Köngulóin* (*The Spider*, 1963) and *Amalía* (1964), while Jakobsdóttir's début play and Gríma's last production, *Hvad er í blýhólknum?* (*What's Contained in the Cornerstone?*, 1971), was a clear-headed look at women's position in society, underlining women's right to a proper career and equal rights. Its staging was inspired by the realism of German documentary drama and was directed by newcomer Maria Kristjánsdóttir (b. 1944), who was to become one of the most meticulous stage directors. In addition to Icelandic playwrights, Gríma also presented work by Sartre, Genet, Arrabal, Ionesco and Beckett.

In 1969, another independent, experimental theatre group emerged, Leiksmidjan (Theatre Workshop) under the leadership of Moscow-trained director Eyvindur Erlendsson (b. 1937). The Theatre Workshop created only two productions before disbanding in 1971 – Sigurjónsson's *The Wish* (1969) and *Frísir kalla*

(1971). These productions broke new ground in stressing the importance of the actor's expression through body and voice rather than the writer's craft. Both showed a meaningful and probing return to myth and folk motifs, the traditional sources of Icelandic theatre. The Workshop thus signified a return to basics, a re-evaluation of theatrical means. The Workshop itself disbanded too soon for their innovations to have significant influence, but the nucleus of the group re-emerged in Akureyri in 1973 when the Akureyri Theatre Company was reorganized to become the only professional theatre outside Reykjavík under the artistic leadership of director/playwright Magnús Jónsson (1938–78). The Akureyri Theatre Company, like the RTC, was and still is democratically run by actors.

Individuals from the Workshop, including director Thórhildur Thorleifsdóttir (b. 1945) and leading actor Arnar Jónsson (b. 1943) who left the Akureyri Theatre Company, were instrumental in establishing Althýduleikhúsid (People's Theatre) in Akureyri in 1975, which began as a radical left-wing touring theatre aimed at a working-class audience. This group, in effect, continued from where the Workshop had left off and included playwright Bödvar Gudmundsson (b. 1939), whose epic political allegory *Skollaleikur* (*Blind Man's Buff*, 1977), played in a style reminiscent of *commedia dell'arte* complete with half-masks, was the company's major success. Here Thorleifsdóttir's background in dance began to emerge as a unique asset in her directing. Despite great energy and genuine dedication to its ideals, however, the People's Theatre was soon faced with severe financial difficulties and the group was forced to reorganize its activities. In 1978, the theatre was re-established in Reykjavík where it has remained ever since with easier access to audiences. The People's Theatre of the 1990s bore little resemblance to the idealistic group it set out to be in the late 1970s and its repertoire was predominantly that of an intellectual, avant-garde fringe theatre.

Contemporaneous with the endeavours of the Theatre Workshop, another significant and short-lived group, loosely connected to the RTC, emerged. This was Litla leikfélagid (Little Theatre Company), which stressed group efforts at creating drama, making use mostly of resources within the company, often by way of improvisation. Its outstanding productions were *Einu sinni á jólanótt* (*Once Upon a Christmas Eve*, 1969), directed by Gudrún Ásmundsdóttir

(b. 1935) which, like Theatre Workshop's *Frísir kalla* two years later, marked a significant return to folk motifs by way of improvisation, and *Poppleikurinn Óli (Óli, the Rock Musical,* 1971), an anarchic, critical look at modern society and its conditioning of the individual. This was co-directed by Pétur Einarsson (b. 1940) and Stefán Baldursson (b. 1944) who thereby made his entrance into Icelandic theatre and was later to become one of the most sought-after and active stage directors in the country. Baldursson became artistic director of the RTC in 1980 (a post he held until 1986) and artistic director of the National Theatre in 1991. Several actor-playwrights emerged from this group, most notably Kjartan Ragnarsson (b. 1945) and Thórunn Sigurdardóttir (b. 1944), who both prefer to direct first productions of their own plays and approach playwriting and the themes of their plays from the point of view of the director.

The 1970s produced further examples of theatre created by groups of actors, often aimed at special audiences and played in schools and factories. The most significant productions in this vein came, however, not from individual groups but from the National Theatre itself with

Ínúk (1974), directed by Brynja Benediktsdóttir, who throughout the 1970s and 1980s was among the most innovative directors working at the National, and *Grænjaxlar (Greenhorns,* 1977), directed by Stefán Baldursson. *Ínúk* was created from anthropological concerns with the fate of primitive societies of hunters, in this case Greenlanders, and was aimed at primary schools. The production, with its innovative yet simple mixture of primitive song, dance and ritual, together with a clear and almost naïve exemplary story, caught on with the general public and eventually became a favourite at international theatre festivals and was subsequently seen in nineteen countries.

The most significant development of the 1980s was a new awareness of scenography, which made such an impact that it may even be called a revolution. One has to go back to the years before 1980 in order to find traditional, three-dimensional scenery complete with painted flats. As part of this development, stage designers have become far more involved in all levels of a production than ever before. New materials have been brought in and anything is permissible in order to underline a feature, theme or the very nature of a work. Consequently, a typical professional production in

Brynja Benediktsdóttir's 1974 National Theatre production of *Ínúk.*
Photo: Kristinn Benediktsson.

Iceland in the 1990s was likely to present the viewer with a carefully thought-out total concept, incorporating visual aspects that were suggestive in their fantastical or lyrical abstractions rather than realistic. This helped to bring out and stress a variety of acting styles.

Structure of the National Theatre Community

Theatre today in Iceland remains the most popular form of live entertainment. In the late nineteenth century there was very little else in the way of amusement, but its popularity remains genuine. Although attendance dropped significantly with the advent of television in 1966, the number of spectators attending theatres per year frequently outnumbers the national population.

The National Theatre, the Reykjavík Theatre Company, the Akureyri Theatre Company and the People's Theatre all receive significant subsidy from official sources, either the state or town councils, although the existence of the People's Theatre is very much in question at the time of writing due to severe budget cuts. Other theatre groups have a more minimal subsidy.

Though subsidy on the whole is modest, it is still important. Even the National, with its twelve to fifteen productions annually, struggles to cover 50 per cent of its costs at the box office.

Artistic Profile

Companies

The 1980s saw a profusion of new Reykjavík-based theatre groups, most of which were short-lived due to lack of funding and a shortage of playing spaces, yet throughout the decade these groups presented well over a hundred productions in Reykjavík alone. Some of these groups, such as Gránufjelagid and Thíbilja, have sometimes based their work on improvisation, while others, such as the Pinter-inspired Pé-theatre and the Grínidjan (Comic Studio), remained closer to convention, the latter concentrating its efforts on comedy and farce.

The most active groups and among the most important ones are Frú Emilía, developed in 1986 around the creative partnership – the first of its kind – of dramaturge Haflidi Arngrímsson (b. 1954) and director Gudjón P. Pedersen (b. 1956), whose various sources of influence include dance theatre, street theatre, visual theatre and the new German drama of the 1970s and 1980s, and the Egg Theatre, which was a one-man theatre and was established in 1981 by actor Vidar Eggertsson (b. 1954) who was intent on exploring the nature of the relationship between actor and audience and created his own version of Beckett's *Not I* (1983) to that end. The Egg Theatre has since produced further solo shows as well as new Icelandic plays

experimenting with the nature of dramatic form, most significantly Árni Ibsen's (b. 1948) *Skjaldbakan kemst thangad líka* (*The Turtle Gets There Too*, 1984).

Throughout the 1970s and 1980s, the more established theatres (the National, the Reykjavík Theatre Company and the Akureyri Theatre) continued to master a variety of styles necessary for their homogenous repertoires. All continue to present audiences with a variety of theatrical experiences. The Akureyri Theatre is more limited than the two Reykjavík theatres, since the company is much smaller and it produces only about four productions each season. Both Reykjavík theatres have continually stressed the importance of new writing juxtaposed with modern work from other countries as well as classics such as Shakespeare, Molière, Goethe, Schiller, Ibsen, Strindberg, Chekhov, Gorki, the Greek tragedies and comedies, and modern classics such as Brecht, Beckett, O'Neill, Williams, Miller and others.

The National Theatre had major successes with new Icelandic plays throughout the 1970s and established Gudmundur Steinsson (b. 1925) at that time with fine productions of his biting allegorical satires of modern lifestyles, such as *Lúkas* (*Matthew*, 1975), *Sólarferd* (*Viva España*, 1976) and *Stundarfridur* (*A Brief Respite*, 1978), the last mentioned breaking

Stefán Baldursson's 1979 National Theatre production of Gudmundur Steinsson's *A Brief Respite*, designed by Thórunn S. Thorgrímsdóttir.
Photo: Jóhanna Ólafsdóttir.

box-office records. Meanwhile the RTC established Kjartan Ragnarsson as well as Birgir Sigurdsson (b. 1937), whose realistic dramas are essentially a critique of values and whose central characters are on a genuine, philosophical quest for an alternative to the corrupting influence of materialism. His outstanding play to date is *Dagur vonar* (*A Day of Hope*, 1987).

During the 1980s, the National had several popular successes with imported musicals but gradually seemed to lose the knack for effectively producing new work, with the exception of plays by Ólafur Haukur Símonarson (b. 1947). Símonarson's plays, staged by Thórhallur Sigurdsson (b. 1946), were done in an expressionistic style characterized by sharp lighting, disjointed sets and a heightened acting style. In the 1990s, the National Theatre seemed again ready to take the lead in developing new work.

At the RTC, the 1980s saw Ragnarsson come into prominence both as playwright and director, abandoning the closed form and realistic structure of his earlier plays in favour of

an open, epic form coinciding with a shift of attentions from modern themes to historical ones. In 1989, the company moved out of the old, and by this time run-down, Idnó Theatre and into a new, highly modern theatre called Borgarleikhúsid (City Theatre).

Dramaturgy

One of three opening productions at the National was Lárus Pálsson's adaptation of Halldór Laxness's (b. 1902) classic novel *Íslandsklukkan* (*The Bell of Iceland*), which achieved immediate popular success and has remained central to the NT repertoire. This success may have been instrumental in the great novelist's turning to playwriting: over the next few years he wrote four important plays, demanding works for the stage, strange mixtures of the absurd and the symbolic, at once satirical and lyrical. Not all of them achieved popularity, however. These plays are *Silfurtúnglid* (*The Silvery Moon*, 1954), with its theme of pure, unspoiled life contrasted with the world of show business where everything is for sale, and *Dúfnaveislan* (*The Pigeon Banquet*, 1966), a fine Taoist comedy of values. *Strompleikurinn* (*The Chimney Play*, 1961) and *Prjónastofan Sólin* (*The Sun Knitting Factory*, 1966), on the other hand, did not do so well with audiences. During the 1970s and 1980s, however, a number of Laxness's novels were adapted for the stage and met with tremendous success.

Another playwright to have left his mark on the period was Agnar Thórdarson (b. 1917) who, apart from his first play – an historical account of the fates of the last descendants of the Norse settlers in Greenland – mainly describes the bourgeoisie of Reykjavík in a humorous well-made play. His most popular work remains the comedy *Kjarnorka og kvenhylli* (*Atoms and Madams*, 1955). Jónas Árnason (b. 1923) also had his first work for the stage, the musical comedy *Delerium Bubonis* (1959), performed in the 1950s, but his major works belong to the period after 1960 and his most significant contribution was the fine comedy *Skjaldhamrar* (*Operation Shield Rock*, 1975), a meeting of pre-war and post-war values.

With other productions of new work during the 1950s it was often as if the theatres lacked faith and made the effort to put on new Icelandic plays out of a sense of duty rather than any genuinely felt dedication. The real breakthrough came with *Hartíbak* (*Hard-a-Port*, 1962) by Jökull Jakobsson (1933–78) directed by Gísli Halldórsson, which broke box-office records at the RTC, running for three successive seasons. Here was a writer with a fine ear for the local, everyday speech of common people, which he supplemented with impressionistic lyricism and a uniquely nostalgic brand of tragicomedy. During his short career Jakobsson wrote some twenty plays for stage, radio and television, making effective use of the influences of writers such as Chekhov and Pinter and towards the end of his life it had come to be generally expected that new Icelandic plays would draw the greatest number of spectators each season.

Although Jakobsson's example became an encouragement for aspiring playwrights, the development towards a serious tackling of Icelandic realities was effected by a number of intertwining developments. Thus most of the new playwrights during the 1960s, apart from Jakobsson, were inspired by the Theatre of the Absurd, a liberating force for Oddur Björnsson, Erlingur E. Halldórsson (b. 1930) and Birgir Engilberts (b. 1946).

The National Theatre soon accepted the challenge proposed by the RTC and by Gríma and also produced a number of first plays by new writers. These included Gudmundur Steinsson with *Forsetaefnid* (*The Presidential Candidate*, 1964), who, after writing two subsequent plays for Gríma, came to prominence as a leading playwright at the National Theatre during the 1970s; and Birgir Engilberts, a highly original absurdist who was fostered by the National itself, where he worked as a stage designer for many years. Engilberts's first and best known play was *Loftbólur* (*Bubbles*, 1968), a highly satirical allegory on the destructive power of materialism. The National Theatre also produced most of the subsequent plays of Oddur Björnsson, the excellent one-act absurd satires *Jódlíf* (*Yolk Life*, 1964) and *Tíu tilbrigdi* (*Ten Variations*, 1968), and the full-length plays *Dansleikur* (*Dance Play*, 1974) and *Meistarinn* (*The Master*, 1976), where the dramatic potential of Björnsson's theatricalism began to be fully realized.

The 1960s also saw the premières of most of Halldór Laxness's plays at the National Theatre and the RTC, while stage adaptations of some of his novels became a major attraction during the 1970s and 1980s and made a significant contribution to the development of Icelandic playwriting. Sveinn Einarsson's adaptations of *Kristnihald undir Jökli* (*Christianity at the Glacier*, 1970) was particularly popular. Bríet Hédinsdóttir's (b. 1937) adaptation of *Íslandsklukkan* (*The Bell of Iceland*, 1981) and Stefán Baldursson and Thorsteinn Gunnarsson's (b. 1940) adaptations of *Salka Valka* (1982) were also successes. Hédinsdóttir, an actress and director at the National Theatre, also did adaptations of work by other writers during the 1980s, most significantly of *Jómfrú Ragnheidur* (*Maiden Ragheidur*, 1981), from Gudmundur Kamban's *Skálholt*, and *Svartfugl* (*The Black Cliffs*, 1986).

Looking at Icelandic plays as a whole after World War II, one can clearly see that they are often in themselves idealistic warnings of the dangers inherent in the corruption of traditional values and their replacement by commercialism. Too often, however, the serious, moralizing impulse has a lumbering effect except when camouflaged with humour. These issues run throughout all of Laxness's plays, as well as the plays of Jökull Jakobsson and Gudmundur

Steinsson. They are a predominant feature of Agnar Thórdarson's plays as well, and the backbone in all of Jónas Árnason's plays.

We find similar concerns in Svava Jakobsdóttir's allegorical plays of the 1970s and 1980s; Nína Björk Árnadóttir (b. 1941) and her delicately woven texture juxtaposing realistic dramas of the roughness of everyday life with soft-spoken lyricism; Birgir Sigurdsson's rough-edged realism with its mythical undertones; and Birgir Engilberts's absurdist allegories (where they are inherent in the very structure of the plays); and, to a lesser degree, in the works of absurdist Oddur Björnsson.

Kjartan Ragnarsson is far more concerned with the individual fate of his characters as portrayed against the backdrop of an unjust and apathetic society, a note struck in his first play *Saumastrofan* (*The Atelier*, 1975), which gave an element of freshness, and in all of his later plays, whether they deal with modern or historical themes. Ólafur Haukur Símonarson's plays are realistic, almost claustrophobic portrayals of close-knit groups of people, normally working class, caught in personal combat with one another and their past. His major contribution to Icelandic playwriting includes the trilogy *Milli skinns og hörunds* (*Under the Skin*, 1984), comprising *Milli skinns og hörunds*, *Skakki turninn í Písa* (*The Leaning Tower of Pisa*) and *Brotlendíng* (*Wreckage*). Although Símonarson in his first full-length play, *Blómarósir* (*Lovely Lasses*, 1979), as well as in his book to the musical *Grettir* (1980), paid homage to the early tradition of grotesque satire and larger-than-life character portrayal, his subsequent plays show a preoccupation with realism, although the language he uses frequently remains expressionistic, fantastic and lyrical.

Árni Ibsen

Directors, Directing and Production Styles

For a discussion of directing, see previous material in **Artistic Profile** and the opening, historical section.

Thórhallur Sigurdsson's 1984 National Theatre production of Ólafur Haukur Símonarson's *Under the Skin*.
Photo: Jóhanna Ólafsdóttir.

Music Theatre

While in the 1930s and 1940s operettas were occasionally performed on the small stage of Idnó, either by the Reykjavík Theatre Company (for example, *Nitouche* by Hervé, 1941) or by others, including the Music Society, opera performances on a regular basis were in need of a stage until the National Theatre opened its doors in 1958.

Director Gudlaugur Rósinkranz made it his policy to pioneer in this field. A few weeks after the official opening of the theatre, the Royal Swedish Opera gave guest performances of *The Marriage of Figaro*, and within a year the National had staged its own first opera – *Rigoletto* under the musical direction of Victor Urbancic (1903–58) with Stefan Islandi (b. 1907) as the Duke of Mantua and Gudmundur Jónsson (b. 1920) in the title role. More productions were to follow, under the baton of either Urbancic or Robert Abraham Ottósson (b. 1912) – *Die Fledermaus*, *La Traviata*, *Cavalleria Rusticana*, *Pagliacci*, *Die Zauberflöte* and *Tosca* among others. In the 1960s the interest diminished somewhat, but important performances were *Il Barbiere di Sivillia*, conducted by Ottósson, and *Madame Butterfly*, directed by the Swede Leif Söderström and conducted by the Swede Niels Grevillius. These productions were interspersed in the repertoire with Viennese operettas and American musicals.

Until this time, Icelandic singers generally made their careers abroad but a new generation of singers decided to stay in Iceland at this time and were instrumental in the new growth of opera productions.

The repertoire generally was still conventional and the only experiments into modern music composition were *The Medium* by Menotti, performed by the RTC in Idnó in 1952, two short operas by Thorkell Sigurbjörnsson (b. 1938), *Apaspil* (*Monkey Playing*) and *Plastic Flowers*, performed at special festivals in 1960 and 1963, and his children's opera *Rabbi*, a joint venture of the Children's Music School and the RTC in 1967. Sigurbjörnsson's short opera was the first composed by an Icelander though in the 1940s Sigurdur Thórdarson (1895–1968) had written an operetta, *Í álögum* (*Spellbound*), which was performed in 1942.

The first full-length Icelandic opera was *Thrymskvida* (*The Lay of Thrym*), a comic opera based on the Eddic poems. This was at the National Theatre (NT) in 1974 and by then the interest in opera had increased with record-breaking productions of *Carmen* and *Die Fledermaus* (fifty performances during one season). *The Lay of Thrym* was followed in 1982 by Atli Heimir Sveinsson's (b. 1938) first opera, *Silkitromman* (*The Silken Drum*) in a production which was subsequently seen at the Simón Bolívar Festival in Caracas in 1983.

The outstanding opera success of the 1980s was at the NT – *Un Ballo in Maschera*, with popular tenor Kristján Jóhannsson (b. 1948) in the lead. However, opera has been produced less frequently at the NT of late. This is due in great part to the fact that in 1979 the Icelandic Opera was founded, and Icelandic opera history during the 1980s and early 1990s was mainly written there. It is a society (with the status of a free group), with no permanently engaged ensemble but a house of its own. It has put on two or three productions a year, thus increasing audience choice in the field. The repertoire, with the exception of two children's operas by Britten, has been on much the same line as at the National. The Icelandic Opera has, however, managed to produce *Aïda* and *Otello* on its small stage; outstanding productions have included *La Traviata*, *Il Trovatore*, *Die Zauberflöte* (1991) and a double bill of *Carmina Burana* and *I Pagliacci*. Its artistic director at the start was Gardar Cortes (b. 1940), followed in 1992 by Ólöf Kolbrún Hardardóttir (b. 1949), both popular singers. Other singers of that generation, singing at both houses, include the tenor Sigurdur Björnsson (b. 1932), the mezzo-soprano Sigrídur Ella Magnúsdóttir (b. 1944) and the baritone Kristinn Sigmundsson (b. 1951), to mention but a few. Among the younger opera favourites is the coloratura Sigrún Hjálmýsdóttir (b. 1955) and the baritone Bergthór Pálsson (b. 1957).

Productions have been directed by Thórhildur Thorleifsdóttir and Bríet Hédinsdóttir (Icelandic Opera), and Sveinn Einarsson (NT). Conductors have included Ragnar Björnsson (b. 1926), Jean-Pierre Jacquillat, Gilbert Levine, Maurizio Barbacini and Robin Stapleton.

Some of the younger singers have formed yet another opera group, Óperusmidjan, aiming at broadening still further the choice of repertoire.

Sveinn Einarsson

Dance Theatre

Dance theatre first gained a proper stage in Iceland with the opening of the National Theatre in 1950. In 1952 the theatre began its National Theatre Ballet School, which in the 1990s was still the country's only ballet school.

Ásta Nordmann (1904–86), a pioneer in Icelandic ballet, was the first Icelander to go abroad for training (Leipzig and Copenhagen) and for years was responsible for all choreography in theatre productions in Reykjavík. She also ran her own ballet school until the National Theatre came into existence. Most of her students later taught ballet themselves, organized school productions for the public, and in the late 1940s one of her students, Sigrídur Ármann (b. 1928) established her own private school which is still operating.

An Association of Icelandic Ballet Dancers was founded in 1947 and briefly ran its own ballet school with the long-term aim of setting up a ballet company. The association gave a production of Les Sylphides and other shorts in 1949.

Ármann choreographed the first Icelandic ballets, Eldurinn (The Fire, 1950) and Ólafur liljurós (1952), to Icelandic music. These were both seen at the National Theatre.

Some of the outstanding early talent from the National's school went abroad to develop careers; these included Helgi Tómasson (b. 1942) who for a long time was a soloist with the New York City Ballet and later became artistic director of the San Francisco Ballet.

It took twenty years of groundwork before the National Theatre felt that the time was ripe to establish its own ballet company. Íslenski Dansflokkurinn (Icelandic Dance Company) was founded in 1973. The company is independent although it operates under the general auspices of the National Theatre.

The Icelandic Dance Company does productions of both classical and modern ballets and its small corps of ten to twelve dancers has taken part in the theatre's own productions, especially the occasional musical theatre works and classical operas that are produced. The company has frequently been supplemented with foreign guest dancers and choreographers as well as with Icelandic dancers who otherwise work abroad.

The most significant productions of classics by the company include Alan Carter's Coppelia (1975), Yuri Chatal's The Nutcracker (1977), both featuring Helgi Tómasson as guest; Sir Anton Dolin's Pas de Quatre (1978) and Giselle (1982), with Ásdís Magnúsdóttir (b. 1954) in the title role as well as María Gísladóttir (b. 1953) as guest, and Tómasson in the role of Albrecht; and Birgit Cullberg's Miss Julie (1983), with Ásdís Magnúsdóttir in the title role and Niklas Ek as Jean. The modern repertoire includes Marjo Kuusela's Tófuskinnid (The Fox Skin, 1979), Jochen Ulrich's Blindisleikur (Blind Man's Buff, 1980), to an Icelandic libretto and music, and Ed Wubbe's Stödugir Ferdalangar (Constant Travellers, 1986).

Among the leading Icelandic choreographers are Nanna Ólafsdóttir (b. 1948) with Turangalila (1983) and Daphnis and Chloe (1985), the first full-length ballet by an Icelandic choreographer, Hlíf Svavarsdóttir (b. 1949) with Amalgam and Duende (1986), and Ingibjörg Björnsdóttir (b. 1948) with Requiem (1983).

Theatre for Young Audiences

The first experiments in Icelandic children's theatre were made in 1930 in the middle of the Depression by a group of young enthusiasts called Litla leikfélagid (Little Theatre Company), who produced a number of original pieces for children. During the 1930s and 1940s the Reykjavík Theatre Company sporadically produced children's plays, but it was not until the 1950s that children's theatre became a regular feature of Icelandic theatre.

The National Theatre has featured such productions on a regular basis since its inception, with one children's production a year, mostly foreign fairytales featuring songs.

The Reykjavík Theatre Company produced one children's play a year from 1965 to 1973, all original Icelandic pieces. The Akureyri Theatre Company has also produced one children's play a year, usually of foreign origin.

A special children's and youth theatre group,

which among other things paid visits to schools, worked within Althýduleikhúsid (People's Theatre) from 1980 to 1982. Apart from this no specialized children's theatre has operated in Iceland. About 15 per cent of the productions of amateur groups are, however, aimed at children or young people. A national centre of ASSITEJ (International Association of Theatre for Children and Young People) aimed at furthering the interests of children's and youth theatre was formed in Iceland in 1990.

Sigrún Valbergsdóttir

Puppet Theatre

Although it has no national tradition to build upon, puppet theatre plays an important role in Iceland's theatre life. There are four puppet theatre groups in the country with constant activity, and several others that come and go.

The first to be formed (in 1952) was Íslenska brúduleikhúsid (Icelandic Puppet Theatre), which is still performing, mainly with carved, wooden marionettes.

Leikbrúduland (Puppetland) was founded in 1969. It is at present Iceland's biggest puppet group and has a permanent theatre in Reykjavík. Works are built on the abundant sources of Icelandic folk tales, rather than on any specific tradition of puppetry. Since the 1980s the company has toured widely.

Brúdubíllinn (Puppet Bus), literally a theatre in a bus, drives between Reykjavík's playgrounds during the summer and tours all over the country.

Sögusvuntan (Saga Apron) is another small travelling repertory theatre. It plays in the capital as well as in other towns across the country, usually in kindergartens and schools.

In addition to these, Messíana Tómasdóttir (b. 1940) has, with her Strengjaleikhúsid (String Theatre), experimented with puppet theatre for adults in such productions as *Bláa stúlkan* (*The Blue Girl*, 1984).

UNIMA Iceland, the national centre of the International Puppeteers' Union, was founded in 1976 and has some forty members.

Hallveig Thorlacius

Design

With the advent of professional theatre and the emergence of the National Theatre, professionally trained scenographers entered an area hitherto dominated by naturalistic painters. Lárus Ingólfsson (1905–82) became head of design at the National after studies and a brief career in Copenhagen. Ingólfsson and his followers were primarily concerned with a realistic and even naturalistic recreation of reality, true to the tradition and standards set by Sigurdur Gudmundsson in the nineteenth century.

After 1960, the repertoire in Icelandic theatre became more homogenous, and a new generation of actors and directors with new attitudes began making their presence felt. Simultaneously, new scenographers began developing their individual styles. These included Magnús Pálsson, with his sculptural approaches; Messíana Tómasdóttir, with her carefully worked symbolism of colour schemes; Steinthór Sigurdsson (b. 1933), who has remained true to the realistic tradition; and Sigurjón Jóhannsson

(b. 1939), who for twenty years has developed a personal style based on a feeling for the quality of Icelandic nature, which on one level harks back to Gudmundsson. Jóhannsson brought new materials into his sets and, for example, made ingenious use of giant, floating cloths, which by the use of complicated fly systems were made to go through various metamorphoses when carefully supplemented by lighting.

During the 1980s Icelandic theatre saw a revolution in stage scenery, the most significant development of the period, and Jóhannsson played a significant part in this. The designer became involved at this time in the total vision of a production, often creating an impressive abstraction which both underlined and added dimension to the total meaning of the theatre work to be seen. Leading designers in this field have been Thórunn S. Thorgrímsdóttir (b. 1951), Gretar Reynisson (b. 1957) and Gudrún S. Haraldsdóttir (b. 1956).

Sigurdur Pálsson

Theatre Space and Architecture

The oldest Icelandic theatre is a small wooden building with corrugated iron cladding dating from 1897. Built in a neo-classical style, it stands in the centre of the Old Town by the lake in Reykjavík and served the Reykjavík Theatre Company until 1989.

The Akureyri Company has a theatre of a similar type built in 1906. It stands in a prominent position in the town and is richly decorated with wood-carvings. Both houses were built with various functions in mind and have a simple stage and rectangular auditorium with a single balcony. They have undergone extensive alterations, however, and have only been used as theatres again in recent decades.

The National Theatre (built between 1928 and 1950) in Reykjavík is the first building in Iceland intended solely as a theatre. It is built of concrete and has external decorations reminiscent of columnar basalt, with a finish of ground Icelandic rock. Its architectural style is a variation on neo-Gothic which the architect, Gudjón Samúelsson (1890–1950), termed 'cliff-style'. Inside the theatre there was a traditional auditorium seating 660, with two balconies and boxes on either side of the proscenium arch, a fly tower, an orchestra pit and a revolve in the stage floor. The theatre has recently undergone extensive interior renovation and alterations, and now has a sloping auditorium floor and a balcony; in its new form it seats 522.

The newest and best equipped theatre in Iceland is Borgarleikhúsid (City Theatre) in Reykjavík, built between 1976 and 1989. It is situated in the new city centre and is constructed of concrete with a large aluminum roof. Designed by Gudmundur K. Gudmundsson

The National Theatre in Reykjavík photographed in the early 1950s.
Photo: Photosport.

(b. 1937), Ólafur Sigurdsson (b. 1935) and Thorsteinn Gunnarsson, the building is a good example of modern Icelandic architecture. It houses two auditoriums: the larger is fan-shaped with a sloping floor and seating for 536, while the smaller is hexagonal with versatile seating arrangements for 270. The main stage has a large revolve, an orchestra pit, fly tower, backstage and two side-stages.

In addition, many buildings throughout the country can be and are used as temporary theatres; some of them have quite good stages and are substantially equipped.

Thorsteinn Gunnarsson

Training

Theatre training has not long been in existence in Iceland. It was begun during the 1930s and 1940s by actors who had received training abroad, mostly at the Royal Theatre in Copenhagen. These actors gave private lessons or even ran their own schools in Iceland for short periods of time.

Haraldur Björnsson gave lessons and so did Soffía Gudlaugsdóttir (1898–1948). The Drama School of Lárus Pálsson was started in

1940 and remained in operation for twenty years.

The National Theatre Drama School began in 1950 and the Reykjavík Theatre Company's Drama School in 1959; both featured regular actor's training based on European models. Both schools closed down between 1969 and 1972 in order to get a state-run drama school started. Over the next few years, two schools were launched: in 1972, young aspiring actors set up the SÁL-Drama School; in 1975, the state-run Leiklistarskóli Íslands (Drama Academy of Iceland) was started, featuring a four-year acting course.

Students at the Drama Academy run their own public theatre in their final year of studies, offering three productions, one of which is of a new Icelandic play. In their third year, the students also give a production for children, which is open to the general public.

Helga Hjörvar

Criticism, Scholarship and Publishing

Apart from incidental comments on theatre and theatre-related activities in journals and various other sources, the first theatre criticism *per se* was reviews in the Reykjavík newspapers of Sigurdur Gudmundsson's production of *Skugga-Sveinn* in 1862. These mainly consisted of an analysis of the play itself, but have also become important documents in theatre history, since they comment on the effect that Gudmundsson's sets had on the audience and give a description of them. Theatre reviews were reserved for productions of new Icelandic plays well into the twentieth century, but with the arrival of professional actors on the scene such reviews became regular features in the papers.

The average theatre reviews have been and to a great extent still are closely related to literary criticism, since most of the reviewers have had some academic training in literature and literary analysis. A typical Icelandic theatre review therefore gives a fairly thorough literary analysis of the play while discussion of the production itself is minimal, and understanding of the nature of the work of actors and directors, especially, is often missing.

Because of the inherent nature of Iceland's small society where everything happens at close range and the critic can expect to encounter theatre people every day, few reviewers last long enough to make their presence really felt. There have been important reviewers, however, who have enjoyed long careers, especially Ásgeir Hjartarsson (1910–74) who was active from 1948 until 1972, and Ólafur Jónsson (b. 1936) whose reviews appeared from 1968 until his untimely death in 1984. In their time these two were considered leading reviewers by the public and professionals alike. Both lacked theatrical background, and Hjartarsson never claimed to be anything but an interested amateur, although his sensitivity and good taste enabled him to assess productions and individual performers with relative accuracy. His obituaries on some of the best first-generation actors display insight and awareness of technique. Through long practice both these reviewers acquired insight into the complex workings of theatre and an ability to give evidence of various acting styles. Jónsson, especially, was a demanding reviewer, an outstanding literary analyst more than anything else, with a taste for genuine intellectualism, but sometimes quite merciless in his absolute honesty.

Two important critics, Jón Vidar Jónsson (b. 1955) and Páll Baldvin Baldvinsson (b. 1953), emerged during the 1980s. Both pursued theatre studies abroad and shared an understanding and insight into the working of a theatre, which gave them a fresh approach, but both were soon to become actively involved with professional theatre and did not pursue their critical careers for more than a few years. At the time of writing, Súsanna Svavarsdóttir (b. 1958), is the one critic who towers over the scene and whose strongly stated opinion is greatly respected by the public, as well as by many theatre people.

Research into theatre history is still in its infancy in Iceland. The first theatre historian was Lárus Sigurbjörnsson (1930–74), who for many years was associated with the RTC as literary adviser, but whose main job was that of curator for the Reykjavík City Archives. Sigurbjörnsson wrote a book about Sigurdur Gudmundsson's contribution to Reykjavík cultural life, as well as a bibliography of Icelandic plays and foreign plays in translation, including all the ones that were never produced. This was published in 1949. Steingrímur J. Torsteinsson (b. 1911) complemented Sigurbjörnsson's bibliography and wrote a thematic account of the earliest Icelandic playscripts up to 1870.

Sveinn Einarsson has written a history of Icelandic theatre, the first volume of which deals with roots and sources from earliest times to the late nineteenth century. This appeared in 1991. In this study, Einarsson goes back to the settlement to trace all possible evidence of performances of any kind, pointing out that

Iceland, like other countries, did have games, dance and rituals that incorporated dramatic elements. The second volume deals with theatre until 1920.

There have been several dissertations on Icelandic plays and individual playwrights which were written as part of a degree in either Icelandic studies or general literary studies at the University of Iceland, including Helga Kress's (b. 1939) thesis on Gudmundur Kamban and his early works, and Frída Á. Sigurdardóttir's (b. 1940) pioneering study of the plays of Jökull Jakobsson.

Actors' biographies normally do well on the best-seller lists, but lately books about actors' lives tend to be in the form of an extended interview rather than proper biographies founded on research. The earliest biographies of actors are Njördur P. Njardvík's (b. 1936) life of Haraldur Björnsson and critic Ólafur Jónsson's life of Brynjólfur Jóhannesson. Actors' autobiographies are rare.

New plays do get published, but only recently on a regular basis. Hence final editions of produced plays may be hard to find. This is especially true of plays produced after 1960; only three out of some twenty plays by Jakobsson were published during his lifetime, which will be problematic for the editors of the complete works, now being planned for publication.

The leading Icelandic publisher, Mál og menning, has published Helgi Hálfdanarson's (b. 1911) translations of Shakespeare's complete plays as well as his translations of the complete Greek tragedies. The Frú Emilía Theatre has in recent years been very active in publishing the texts of everything they perform, as well as devising a successful series of playreadings of the classics, which they have also published. These include plays by Molière, Chekhov, Gorki and Ibsen.

Oddly enough, play publications were more common during the first half of the century, when editions of performed and unperformed plays abounded. The rare appearance of a new play on the Reykjavík stage between 1920 and 1950 may partly explain this, since publication was often the only outlet for the playwright.

Árni Ibsen

Further Reading

Einarsson, Sveinn. *Íslensk leiklist I*. Reykjavík, 1991.

Friis, Erik J., ed. *Modern Nordic Plays – Iceland*. New York: Twayne, 1973.

Haugen, Einar, ed. *Fire and Ice: Three Icelandic Plays*. Reykjavík, 1967.

Janzon, Leif, ed. *Nordisk Teater*. [Nordic theatre]. Stockholm, 1988.

Magnússon, Sigurdur A. *Icelandic Crucible*. Reykjavík, 1985.

Sigurbjörnsson, Lárus. *A Bibliography of Icelandic and Foreign Plays in Translation*. Reykjavík, 1949.

IRELAND

An island in the north Atlantic Ocean, separated from the coasts of Scotland, England and Wales to the east by the Irish Sea, and separated from France to the south-east by St George's Channel, Ireland is one of the least densely populated countries in Europe, with a total area of 70,300 square kilometres (27,150 square miles), and a population of only 5,093,372, according to the 1991 census. The main urban centres, Dublin and Belfast, are located on the eastern seaboard, with smaller concentrations of population in the west and north, including Galway, Cork, Limerick and Derry. The island is made up of two distinct political units: the Republic of Ireland (whose official name is Eire), composed of the twenty-six counties of the south and northwest (population 3,523,401), and the province of Northern Ireland (often referred to as Ulster), made up of the six counties in the northeast of the island which are part of Great Britain (population 1,569,971). Dublin is the capital of Eire, in which a democratically elected parliament, the Dáil, meets. Although the people of Northern Ireland, like those of Scotland and Wales, elect representatives to the Westminster parliament in London, Belfast acts as the administrative centre of the province. English is spoken in all parts of the island, although Irish is the first official language of Eire. Both parts of the island are part of the European Community.

Irish history – and hence Irish theatre history – is unusual in a European context because of the island's continuing colonial and post-colonial relationship with Great Britain. When the first Anglo-Norman colonizers arrived in Ireland in AD 1169, they encountered an Irish-language (or Gaelic) culture with a complex literary tradition; they did not, however, encounter any form of theatrical performance.

While early Gaelic literary culture placed strong emphasis on recitative poetry and storytelling, it did not include aspects of personification and dramatic dialogue which could be recognized as theatrical. Consequently, there are important differences between the ways in which early Gaelic culture resonates in contemporary Irish theatre as compared to the other arts, particularly poetry and music. From the earliest Miracle plays of the twelfth century, theatre in Ireland was linked to the island's colonization by England, and was confined to secure centres of colonial administration. Hence, in spite of the existence of the thriving Smock Alley Theatre in the eighteenth century, many of the most talented members of the Irish theatre community, including playwrights such as George Farquhar (1678–1707) and Richard Brinsley Sheridan (1751–1816) focused their careers on the London stage. Similarly, although nineteenth-century Ireland had a popular and patriotic theatre, the most successful Irish theatre practitioners worked outside the country – a group which included writer and producer Dion Boucicault (c.1820–90), Oscar Wilde (1854–1900) and George Bernard Shaw (1856–1950).

As Wilde and Shaw were establishing themselves in the London theatre in the 1890s, events were taking place in Ireland which were to establish, for the first time, an Irish theatre of major importance which was more than a provincial or colonial derivative of the London theatre. The founders of what was to become the Abbey Theatre (founded 1899), Augusta Gregory (1852–1932), William Butler Yeats (1865–1939), Edward Martyn (1859–1923) and later John Millington Synge (1871–1909) were members of the privileged landowning classes whose forebears had patronized the

Smock Alley Theatre. Their writings indicate an awareness of the 'little theatre' movement in England and France, French symbolist theatre, the naturalism of Ibsen and Zola, and, in Yeats's case, Japanese Noh. However, they were also, to varying degrees, believers in the doctrines of cultural nationalism, looking for the expression of a national distinctiveness in the arts. Like other cultural nationalists in early-twentieth-century Europe, they saw peasant life, folklore and mythology as the repositories of an authentic national existence which, they believed, in Ireland's case had been suppressed by British colonialism.

The founding of the Abbey took place in a period in Irish history extending from 1891 to 1916 when Irish nationalist aspirations were expressed primarily in cultural terms, in which theatre, poetry, traditional Irish sports and the Irish language were key elements. When in 1916, an unsuccessful but historically important nationalist uprising was quelled, there were two playwrights among its executed leaders, Patrick Pearse (1879–1916) and Thomas Mac Donagh (1878–1916). In the years following 1916, militant nationalists gained increasing support, and in 1919 a war of independence began, culminating in the twenty-six counties of southern and northwestern Ireland being granted independence from Great Britain in 1921. This in turn was followed by a short but divisive civil war in 1922.

After 1922, Irish culture was in a period of consolidation, and the nationalist art forms that had been revolutionary for a previous generation became part of official state cultural policy. In 1924, the Abbey Theatre was given a state subsidy, and since that time the Abbey has been run by a board of directors, some of whom initially had little or no theatrical background. Accordingly, morally ambiguous works, such as the poetic symbolist theatre of Yeats, became increasingly marginalized, as did the works of Sean O'Casey (1880–1964). O'Casey began his career with realistic representations of Dublin's slums, such as *The Shadow of a Gunman* (1922) and *Juno and the Paycock* (1924). However, his critiques of prevailing religious and political pieties, which extended to formal experiments with satire and allegory in his later works, increasingly put him at odds with members of the Abbey's board of directors. When his third play, *The Plough and the Stars* (1926), which dealt critically with the 1916 Rising, met with organized demonstrations and official disapproval, O'Casey left Ireland for London. In his self-imposed exile, one can see an emblem of the malaise that was to enter Irish cultural life in the middle decades of a century that had begun with such promise.

Throughout the period between 1924 and the late 1950s, mainstream Irish theatre, and the Abbey in particular, was dominated by plays of peasant life by rural playwrights such as Lennox Robinson (1886–1958) from Cork and George Shiels (1881–1949) from Ulster. This conservative dramaturgy followed the conventions of realism, using a proscenium stage, the illusion of a 'fourth wall' between stage and audience, sequential narrative structure, consistent characterization and absence of overtly poetic language. However, it employed these conventions in the representation of an idealized rural life, which was fast disappearing (if it had ever existed), conforming to a puritanical moral code. Hence, an officially promulgated rural ideal was presented to increasingly urban audiences as reality.

The same institutionalization of a revolutionary cultural stance took place in the area of Irish-language theatre. One of the earliest productions by the Irish Literary Theatre in 1901 was the first professionally produced play in the Irish language, *Casadh an tSugain* by Douglas Hyde (1860–1949). In its time, the creation of an Irish-language theatre constituted a revolutionary gesture in the project of 'de-anglicizing Ireland'. However, the implementation of plans to transform post-independence Ireland into an Irish-speaking state increasingly became a dogmatic xenophobia which stifled artistic experimentation. In 1945, for instance, four of the seven plays produced by the Abbey were in the Irish language – a proportion that did not reflect the use of Irish in society at large, suggesting a gulf of unreality between the national theatre and the population it was supposed to represent. However, the predicament of the Dublin-based Abbey needs to be contrasted with the experience of an Irish-language theatre, Taibhdhearc na Gaillimhe, founded in 1928. Located in Galway near one of the major remaining pockets of indigenous Irish-speaking population, it continues to produce original Irish plays, and translations of English and European works.

In 1945, therefore, while most of Europe was in the process of reconstructing civil society from the ruins of World War II, Ireland, which had remained neutral during the conflict, was in a period of cultural isolation. The official post-independence ideology of reviving a rural,

Catholic, Gaelic-speaking society led to protectionist trade policies which slowed economic growth to a virtual standstill. In the cultural sphere, Irish isolationism was implemented by punitive literary censorship, which banned the works of almost every major Irish and world writer of the twentieth century.

Although the Abbey of 1945 reflected this cultural conservatism, its unchallenging dramatic fare found a wide popular audience, and a prestige from the days of Yeats and Synge remained. This, it has been argued, was partly responsible for an upsurge in amateur theatrical activity throughout the country in the mid-1940s. New theatre buildings appeared in the small towns of Tralee, Killarney and Birr; annual amateur festivals were launched in Sligo and Dundalk, and in 1953 the competitive All-Ireland Amateur Drama Festival began in the town of Athlone.

While the burgeoning amateur theatre provided the training ground for the next generation of the Irish theatre community, many remember the Gate Theatre productions of Hilton Edwards (1903–82) and the English-born Michael Mac Liammoir (1899–1978) as their first inspirational experience of the theatre. The Edwards–Mac Liammoir company, the Dublin Gate Theatre Studio (founded 1928), brought to Ireland theatrical performers of international stature, such as Dame Sybil Thorndike and Orson Welles. Similarly, like the amateur Dublin Drama League (1919–41), the company provided an opportunity for Irish audiences to see theatrical forms other than sentimental peasant realism. The Gate's 1944 season, for instance, included Eugene O'Neill's American colloquial tragedy, *Desire Under the Elms*; the 1945 season featured Thornton Wilder's expressionistic play, *The Skin of Our Teeth*. Furthermore, at a time when the peasant realist productions of the Abbey left little room for scenographic experiment, the Adolphe Appia-influenced designs of Hilton Edwards provided a visual excitement unavailable elsewhere in the country. The Edwards–Mac Liammoir company continued in this capacity until Mac Liammoir's death in 1978, and their commitment to world theatre, new Irish writing, and emphasis on design have been upheld by the current Gate Theatre.

Given the stringency of Irish censorship laws throughout the 1930s, 1940s and 1950s, however, the room for theatrical experiment and change was limited. Hence, while World War II forms a watershed in the cultural history of most European nations, it was of less importance in Ireland than the economic and social changes that occurred in the late 1950s. Beginning in 1958, the Irish government began to encourage, for the first time, industrialization and participation in world markets, in contrast to the post-independence emphasis on the protection of an idealized rural culture. In 1962, Ireland applied for membership of the European Economic Community, which it joined a decade later. In 1992, it ratified a treaty on European unity.

Ireland's entry into the world economy coincided with two major turning points in the development of contemporary Irish theatre. In 1957, the first Dublin International Theatre Festival was held, giving a new life to the stiflingly introverted Irish theatre. The second major event took place on the fringes of the festival, as the Pike Theatre Club successfully challenged the censorship of theatrical performances. The Pike had earlier achieved success by producing a play rejected by the Abbey, *The Quare Fellow* (1954) by a working-class Dublin writer, Brendan Behan (1923–64). Behan went on to win international acclaim for the English translation of his satiric second play, *An Giall* (1958; later expanded and translated as *The Hostage*). The boisterous, hard-drinking life of Behan and many of his fellow writers of the period has attained a legendary status, particularly among Irish expatriate communities; in retrospect, this self-destructiveness begins to look like a sad, but understandable, response to a collapsing, entropic cultural environment.

The changes that took place in Irish social, cultural and economic life after 1958 were described by one contemporary as 'a deep and far-reaching cultural revolution'. The introduction of television in 1962 and the modernization of the school curriculum shortly thereafter simultaneously increased the opportunities for rapid development and created the demand for more development. It was against this background of profound cultural transformation that two of the leading playwrights of contemporary Ireland first came to prominence. Brian Friel (b. 1929), from Omagh, County Tyrone, and Thomas Murphy (b. 1936), from Tuam, County Galway, found themselves the focus of both Irish and international acclaim after early successes, Friel with *Philadelphia, Here I Come!* (1964) and Murphy with *A Whistle in the Dark* (1961). In each case, the play adapts the Ibsenesque structures of the previous generation's rural dramas to create characters who are disoriented and dislocated, obsessively remembering a past they are forced to reject. It was also during this period that John B. Keane (b. 1928), a playwright from Kerry, in the southwest of Ireland, wrote the harsh, naturalistic plays of rural life on which his reputation rests – *Sive* (1959), *The Field* (1965) and *Big Maggie* (1968). Several of Keane's plays had their first productions with amateur groups – a point indicative of the continued vibrancy of the amateur movement.

The mood of optimism with which the 1960s began in Ireland was shattered, however, by the events of 1969 in Northern Ireland. The Anglo-Irish Treaty which ended the War of Independence in 1921 allowed the six counties of the northeast of the island to remain as a part of Great Britain. Unlike the population of the Irish Republic, more than 90 per cent of whom are members of the Roman Catholic faith, two-thirds of the population of Northern Ireland are members of Protestant churches, many of Scottish Presbyterian origin. Believing their cultural and religious identity more secure within the context of Great Britain, most of this Protestant community, known as Loyalists or Unionists, resist any attempt to unite Northern Ireland with the Irish Republic. Hence, Northern Irish political life since 1922 has been divided between unionism and republicanism, with the Unionists holding what amounts to a permanent majority. In 1969, attempts by northern Catholics to change this situation sparked a violent response from Unionist paramilitaries, which in turn led to rioting, the involvement of the British army, and the re-emergence of Republican paramilitary groups. In spite of numerous attempts to resolve the conflict, Northern Ireland remains trapped in a state of low-intensity three-way civil war, marked by sectarian assassinations, bombings, rioting and a high-profile army and police presence.

In the middle years of the twentieth century, politically deadlocked Northern Ireland shared the cultural stagnation of the Irish Republic, albeit for different reasons. Until 1951, the two principal theatres in Northern Ireland were the Belfast Arts Theatre (founded 1946) and the Ulster Group Theatre (1941–60), the latter producing unchallenging peasant realist plays for Belfast audiences similar to those being staged by the Abbey in Dublin. In 1951, however, the Lyric Theatre was established in Belfast to stage major works of world theatre, new Irish drama, and – most specifically – the verse plays of Yeats, a policy that it continues to implement today. In spite of its association with Yeats's plays (which have strong links to Irish cultural nationalism), the Lyric has maintained an active disengagement from the polarized politics of Northern Ireland, winning support from all sections of the community. Indeed, the accomplishment of the Lyric in this regard was highlighted in 1960, when the Ulster Group Theatre closed after a controversy surrounding *Over the Bridge*, a play by Sam Thompson (1916–65) which dealt with sectarianism in the Belfast shipyards.

Ireland thus entered the 1970s in a contradictory state in which economic expansion and atavistic violence existed side by side. With an increasingly large and affluent middle class, theatre audiences increased, so too did state subsidies. In the late 1960s, both the Abbey and the Lyric moved into new theatre buildings with substantial funding from the Arts Councils of Ireland and Northern Ireland, respectively. In 1971, the Gate Theatre received government funding for the first time, and since that time there has been a general increase in the variety of theatrical forms receiving state assistance; moreover, there has been a growing tendency for the Arts Councils of Northern Ireland and the Irish Republic to provide joint funding for projects relating to the island as a whole. The growth of third-level education in this period also contributed to the expansion and diversification of the theatre, providing both better-informed audiences and, through university drama societies, many key theatre personnel.

It has been claimed that the ongoing Northern Ireland conflict has acted as the 'conscience' of the increasingly consumerist Irish Republic. Indeed, much of the most challenging Irish theatre of recent years has been in explicit response to the 'Troubles' (as the Northern Ireland conflict is euphemistically known). For instance, Brian Friel's play, *The Freedom of the City* (1973), uses a Brechtian device of multiple narrators and non-sequential narrative structure to create both a response to an incident in which British soldiers killed thirteen civilians in 1972, and a commentary on the way in which contemporary Irish culture interprets such events. There is a similar semantics of structure at work in *Spokesong* (1976) by Belfast writer Stewart Parker (1941–88), which uses circus arts to transform the bicycle into a metaphor for balance in a violently unbalanced society. More recently, Frank McGuinness (b. 1953), a writer from Donegal in the Irish Republic, has made an impressive imaginative leap across the Irish cultural divide with *Observe the Sons of Ulster*

Marching Towards the Somme (1985), which deals with the individual and communal sense of identity of a group of Unionist men. However, the most far-reaching cultural venture to arise from an awareness of the dangerous rifts in Irish society has been the Field Day Theatre Company, founded in Derry, Northern Ireland, by a group of leading figures in the arts, including Brian Friel.

The violence in Northern Ireland has not, however, been the only challenge to the new economic and cultural confidence. While the standard of living for the middle classes in both urban and rural areas has improved significantly since 1959, there has also been an alarming growth in unemployment and emigration during the same period. Sprawling suburbs with young populations have grown up around the urban centres of Dublin, Limerick, Cork, Galway and Belfast where there are areas in which the

unemployment rate exceeds 50 per cent and social problems, including drug abuse and violent crime, are rife. Meanwhile, emigration by young people, particularly from rural areas, continues in patterns that date from the mid-nineteenth century. Between 1841 and 1851 the population fell from 8.2 million to 6.6 million through starvation, emigration and disease. In the Great Famine (1845–9) 1 million died; between 1847 and 1854 1.6 million emigrated to the United States. Indeed, Ireland's population today is half of what it was in 1840, even though the country did not suffer significant depopulation in either of the world wars. Moreover, Ireland is unusual in European terms in that it has not experienced the influx of immigrants from the developing world which has characterized demographic change in former European colonial powers.

The theatre has responded to these cultural

Garry Hynes's 1985 Druid Theatre Company production of Synge's *The Playboy of the Western World*, designed by Frank Conway.
Photo: Mark Kilroy.

shifts in a number of ways, which range from the works of Friel and Murphy to reinterpretations of older scripts dealing with rural Ireland undertaken by the Druid Theatre Company from Galway (founded 1975). Similarly, many of the most challenging new companies of recent years, including Rough Magic and Passion Machine from Dublin (both founded 1984), have developed performance styles which reflect the urban, electronic media culture that constitutes the reality of life for the majority of the Irish population today.

In spite of the challenges faced by contemporary Irish society, Irish theatre (and, indeed, the arts in general) continues to expand and develop, with a noticeable proliferation of new theatre companies and arts festivals since the early 1980s. This expansion has led to such dramaturgical diversity that there is no longer any one style of theatre which can be identified as 'Irish', as was the case in the mid-twentieth century. Indeed, there is perhaps no better yardstick against which to compare the Irish theatre of the 1990s with the theatre of the 1940s and 1950s than the Dublin Theatre Festival of 1991. Dublin was European City of Culture for 1991 – something which would have been unthinkable in 1945. The 1991 Festival (not unlike the festivals of previous years) featured a programme of more than forty plays, including the premières of six new Irish plays, the Schiller Theater of Berlin's *Macbeth*, a Kabuki version of *Hamlet* by the Tokyo Globe Company, and challenging visual work by the French company of Philippe Genty and Archaos. In spite of this scope and diversity, for many the highlight of the festival was provided by the Gate Theatre, when, for the first time ever, all of the works for theatre by Dublin-born writer Samuel Beckett (1906–90) were presented together by leading Beckett interpreters from around the world. This high-profile celebration of the Irish writer who has perhaps contributed most to twentieth-century theatre is in sharp contrast to the first Irish production of a Beckett play, when in 1955 the tiny Pike Theatre staged *Waiting for Godot* (1953) amid controversy surrounding 'crudities' of language in the text. Such concerns, largely the product of an insecure and insular cultural identity, seem quaintly historical in the Ireland of the 1990s, where the friction between a complex, distinctive national culture and a postmodern world culture has given the Irish theatre a dynamism that equals that of the most celebrated years of the Irish Renaissance of the early years of the twentieth century.

Structure of the National Theatre Community

The Irish theatre today is in a period of rapid expansion, with an increasingly well-organized network of companies, organizations and theatre spaces. The largest segment of the theatre community continues to be the extensive amateur movement, whose activities in both Eire and Northern Ireland are coordinated by the Amateur Drama League (ADL), representing 200 member companies and between 500 and 600 other companies ranging from the long-established (such as the Dublin Shakespeare Society, established in 1907) to the ephemeral. Unlike professional theatre, the amateur movement is not concentrated in urban centres of population; although there are a number of urban-based companies, most amateur productions originate in the hundreds of small communities scattered throughout rural Ireland.

There is a complex two-way interaction between the amateur and professional theatre communities. Until recent developments upgraded professional theatre training in Ireland, most professional theatre practitioners had served an apprenticeship with an amateur company. Moreover, as funding bodies place increasing emphasis on urban-based companies touring rural areas, many of the venues essential to a successful tour are maintained by amateur companies. This input is returned in festival adjudications, training workshops, and occasional directing engagements undertaken by professionals who choose to work with amateurs. Moreover, while developing playwrights often find amateur companies willing to perform new work, established writers such as Belfast-based Martin Lynch (b. 1950) have introduced a new element into the amateur/professional relationship with drama projects involving large amateur casts (sometimes numbering over a hundred people) created in collaboration with an entire community.

The distinction between amateur and professional status differs slightly between Northern Ireland and the Irish Republic. Actors, directors and other theatre professionals (with the exception of technicians, who are represented by one of the country's largest unions, SIPTU) are represented in the Republic by Irish Actors Equity, which recognizes two classes of union membership – full members and permit-holders. The latter category includes actors with an established record (often with amateur companies) who are permitted to work for a professional company. Permit-holders can apply for full membership after holding five permits. In Northern Ireland theatre professionals (again, with the exception of technicians) are represented by the Scottish office of British Actors' Equity, which has effectively abolished the distinction between full and provisional membership. Hence, after one professional production in Northern Ireland most theatre artists attain full union membership. A reciprocal agreement exists between the two unions which permits full members of each to work in the other's jurisdiction for a period of one year. The 1992 minimum rate of payment for Equity actors in Northern Ireland was higher than in the Republic, at IR£214 per week (US$375) as compared to IR£137 per week (US$240), although in both cases most performers earned salaries above the minimum (considerably so in the case of well-established actors).

In 1992 there were 285 Ulster members of Equity working in the theatre (the union also represents 130 variety artists), to which can be added 900 full Equity members and 375 permit-holders in the Irish Republic, for a total professional community of 1,560 actors, directors, designers and choreographers. These theatre artists come together to produce plays in a number of different ways. A limited number are members of permanent companies with their own theatre building, such as the Abbey in Dublin, the Lyric in Belfast, or the Druid Theatre Company in Galway. Others are members of permanent companies, such as Charabanc or Tinderbox in Northern Ireland, who are not attached to a single theatre space and so must rent a venue, tour, or find an alternative performance space; theatre-in-education companies fall into this category. Most members of the theatre community, however, are freelance workers, who are either hired for a single production by one of the permanent companies, or who are hired by producing theatres with an artistic director (but no resident company), such as the Gate in Dublin.

Of course, these distinctions are not absolute, and theatre artists move from company to company. Druid, for instance, not only has its own theatre space, but also has an established policy of touring nationally and internationally. Field Day is a touring company; however, it premières its work in Derry, and is strongly associated with the city's Guild Hall. On the whole, however, companies attached to a theatre building tend to produce more work; the Abbey, for instance, offers performances for fifty-two weeks of the year. A touring company such as Field Day, on the other hand, tours only in the autumn, and produces no more than two plays each year. Hence, even taking into account a rehearsal period averaging three to four weeks, some companies which are permanent (in so far as they maintain salaried administrative staff) employ performers only for relatively short periods of time.

The situation of playwrights is even less secure than that of performers. The Society of Irish Playwrights, which acts as a playwrights' union for all of Ireland, in 1993 had over 120 members, for whom it agrees royalty rates in conjunction with the Irish Writers' Union, and arranges workshops and rehearsed readings. Yet few of its members earn their living exclusively through writing for the theatre, and many, particularly in Northern Ireland, turn to writing for television. A small percentage receive Arts Council subsidies, either directly through bursaries and commissions, or indirectly as a writer-in-residence attached to a major theatre or a university. Several notable writers combine writing with a full-time career in education. There are a number of annual writing awards, including the O.Z. Whitehead Award, offered by the Society of Irish Playwrights; however, benefits are primarily in terms of public and peer recognition.

The pattern of partial state subsidy also extends to theatre companies and producing theatres. While several large producing theatres, such as the Gaiety in Dublin, are self-financing, twenty-five of the major companies with established production records receive some form of Arts Council subsidy. In the case of companies touring both the Republic and Northern Ireland, funds may be granted by both Arts Councils. In 1991 grants ranged from a high of almost IR£2 million (US$3.5 million) granted to the Abbey Theatre, down to IR£800 (US$1,400) given to the Actors and Playwrights Theatre in Dublin. Apart from the five companies who received the top grants of more than

IR£100,000 (US$175,000) in 1991 (the Abbey and Gate Theatres in Dublin, the Lyric in Belfast, the Druid in Galway and TEAM, a theatre-in-education company) the average grant was in the vicinity of IR£10,000 to IR£20,000 (US$17,500 to US$35,000), which is insufficient in itself for the operation of a company with full-time personnel. These grants are supplemented in some cases by additional subsidies for the maintenance of theatre buildings. However, this does not help companies without a permanent theatre building, among whose number are many new groups receiving no state funding through other channels.

Given the necessarily limited nature of state subsidy, therefore, the theatre's continued existence depends largely on financial success at the box office. It is a matter of some concern, however, that the most heavily subsidized organizations, the Abbey and the Gate, also have the highest ticket prices, with the best seats selling for IR£14 (US$25). Many of the smaller companies sell tickets in the vicinity of IR£7 (US$12), which is still twice the price of a cinema ticket (IR£3.50, or US$6). Hence, attending the professional theatre remains primarily a middle-class activity, in spite of the work of CAFE (Creative Activity For Everyone), an organization dedicated to developing the arts in marginalized sections of the community.

While the Irish theatre celebrates its achievements with an annual awards ceremony, the Harvey Theatre Awards, the real focus of the theatre year is the Dublin Theatre Festival, which takes place in late September and early October. Unlike other arts festivals in Belfast, Galway and Derry which bring major international companies to Ireland, the Dublin Theatre Festival is dedicated almost exclusively to theatre. However, even outside the festival periods, the theatre has a high profile in Ireland, due in part to public awareness of the disproportionately large number of Irish playwrights of international reputation. Writers such as Brian Friel, Tom Murphy and Frank McGuinness are seen as part of a writing tradition extending back through O'Casey, Yeats, Synge, and the writers of the eighteenth century. As such, major playwrights are widely recognized public figures, and an internationally successful production is often a cause for national pride. New plays by well-known writers are the subject of substantial media coverage, and there is an active interest in Irish theatre in the universities. Of more financial significance is the increased importance of this living cultural tradition for the tourist industry, which plays a key role in the Irish economy. This has resulted in some theatres making less adventurous dramaturgical decisions in the summer months, hoping to capture the potentially large tourist audience with the works of internationally recognized writers. However, it also suggests a motivation for increased government funding for a cultural activity whose success or failure has economic implications for the country as a whole.

Artistic Profile

Companies

In the 1990s Irish theatre companies covered a wide spectrum of organizational profiles, ranging from the subsidized theatres operating from their own buildings in the capitals of Dublin and Belfast, to the hundreds of amateur companies based throughout the country.

The transitional state between amateur and professional status in which many new companies exist is exemplified by the 1992 situation of Glasshouse Productions (founded 1990), a Dublin-based group committed to performing new plays by and about women. At a time when subsidies are not available for new companies and corporate sponsorship is difficult to find, all four members of Glasshouse hold full-time jobs outside the theatre, and have taken equal shares of any profits from the three plays they have produced thus far. A company such as Glasshouse could develop in one of two directions: if the company's financial problems continue, it could dissolve (as many similar companies do every year), with its members becoming either freelance professionals or amateurs associated with other groups; or, it could develop into a fully professional fringe company.

Three of the most important professional companies of recent years – Charabanc of Belfast, Passion Machine and Rough Magic from Dublin – have evolved in just this manner. Indeed, a company such as Glasshouse looks to

Charabanc as an example of what it is possible to achieve from outside the theatrical mainstream. Made up largely of women, Charabanc's first production, *Lay Up Your Ends* (1983), set the pattern for their future work. Dealing with a strike by female Belfast mill-workers in 1911, it was researched by the group and written in conjunction with playwright Martin Lynch for presentation to a Belfast audience. Lacking a theatre building of their own, Charabanc reach audiences through touring – a policy which has won them a growing international reputation and with it,

funding from the Northern Ireland Arts Council.

Passion Machine Theatre Company, by contrast, remains rooted in the community where it was founded in 1984 by two Dublin secondary school teachers, Roddy Doyle (b. 1958) and Paul Mercier (b. 1958), who still teach in the suburbs of North Dublin. Recognizing that few of their students – part of Dublin's large population of working-class and lower-middle-class youth – attended the theatre, they began writing plays about urban life using colloquial comedy and popular music, performed in venues such

Lynne Parker's 1990 Rough Magic production of Wilde's *Lady Windermere's Fan*, designed by Barbara Bradshaw.
Photo: Amelia Stein.

as Dublin's SFX Centre, best known as a rock music venue. Since 1984, Mercier's plays, such as *Wasters* (1984) and *Home* (1988), have reached a wide audience, totalling 79,000 in 1989 alone. However, in spite of their box-office success and Arts Council funding, they employ only one person (an administrator) on a full-time basis.

Rough Magic began as a group of actors and directors who met while university students at Trinity College, Dublin. It was formed to première new British and American works and initially each member of the company took a share of production profits. However, as individual company members earned wider reputations, they began to work with other groups on a freelance basis, and the company now contains only three full-time personnel – an administrator and two directors. Currently in receipt of Arts Council funding, the group has increasingly presented new Irish work and challenging reinterpretations of older Irish material, such as a 1990 production of Oscar Wilde's *Lady Windermere's Fan* (1892), which featured an all-male cast, each of whom played a variety of roles.

Key personnel in one of Ireland's most nationally and internationally acclaimed companies, the Druid Theatre Company of Galway, began their careers, like Rough Magic, in a university drama society, in this instance associated with University College, Galway. However, Druid's university influence was tempered by the involvement of amateur actors from An Taidhbhearc, an Irish-language theatre founded in 1928. Beginning in 1975 under the direction of Garry Hynes (b. 1953), Druid began a series of radical reinterpretations of classic Irish representations of rural life and this which evolved into a period of involvement with playwright Thomas Murphy in the mid-1980s. Although Hynes subsequently left the company to become artistic director of the Abbey Theatre, Druid has continued to thrive, performing for thirty-one weeks in 1990, maintaining its own theatre building and employing seven full-time non-performance personnel, partly on the basis of a substantial Arts Council grant.

Druid's status as a major company developed over a decade of consistent achievement; Field Day, by contrast, has been a major company since its inception in 1979. Founded in Derry by a group including Brian Friel, actor Stephen Rea (b. 1947) and poet Seamus Heaney (b. 1939), the high public profile of its members gave the company an immediate cultural importance. Indeed, Field Day has been the subject of considerable scholarly interest since the early 1980s, inspired in part by the idea that it forms a 'fifth province' that transcends Irish cultural differences (Ireland was historically divided into four provinces). Other critics, however, charge that Field Day constitutes yet another incarnation of an Irish nationalism which would marginalize Ulster Unionists. As well as touring new plays by Friel and other Irish dramatists, including Thomas Kilroy (b. 1934), Field Day has published an influential series of pamphlets and a controversial anthology of Irish writing, edited by Field Day founder and leading Irish literary critic, Seamus Deane (b. 1940). Like Charabanc, Field Day is a touring company with no theatre building of its own.

As Field Day was in the process of formation, the Gate Theatre in Dublin was facing a crisis precipitated by the deaths of its founders, Michael Mac Liammoir (d. 1978) and Hilton Edwards (d. 1982). However, since the mid-1980s, the Gate has successfully managed the transition from a theatre company headed since 1928 by two men who acted, directed, designed, wrote and produced, to a producing theatre run by an artistic director, in the early 1990s Michael Colgan (b. 1950), an arts administrator of considerable ability; indeed, the vitality of the Dublin Theatre Festival in the mid-1980s was due in part to his efforts. Although Colgan began his career as a director, his role as the Gate's artistic director became largely managerial, consisting of the hiring of freelance directors and performers to produce specific scripts. None the less, the Gate maintained certain distinctive qualities associated with its founders, most notably high design standards and frequent appearances by directors of international standing, including Michael Bogdanov and Steven Berkoff from England, and Walter Asmus of Germany. Moreover, although the Gate takes its name from its Dublin premises, it has an established international touring record, and a policy of staging occasional productions at the larger Gaiety Theatre, also in Dublin. In addition to its administrative staff, the Gate employs seven production personnel; it receives an Arts Council grant, which in 1991 amounted to IR£442,000 (US$773,500).

Finally, the two theatres that most clearly represent the 'theatre establishment' in Ireland – the Abbey in Dublin and the Lyric in Belfast – are both in a period of transition, and, some might say, crisis. Both theatres receive substantial Arts Council funding; in 1991, for instance, the Abbey received half as much funding again as all other theatre companies in the Irish Republic combined. However, with exceptions such as the Abbey's 1990 production of Brian Friel's *Dancing at Lughnasa*, the Irish productions winning national and international acclaim in recent years have been produced by companies such as the Druid and Charabanc. Druid, for instance, regularly sell 95 per cent of all available tickets for their productions; the Abbey averages houses of 68 per cent (albeit 68 per cent of a 628-seat auditorium). Hence, the fringe has, in a sense, become the mainstream – leaving the established mainstream theatres in an uncertain position. Both theatres have responded to this situation by bringing talented individuals from younger companies into their organizations. The Lyric, for instance, appointed Martin Lynch, best known for his work with Charabanc and community groups, as writer-in-residence in the late 1980s. In an attempt to end a period of uncertainty and a rapid succession of artistic directors, the Abbey appointed Garry Hynes of Druid to its top position in 1990. However, in early 1993 she announced that she would be leaving at the end of that year. The Lyric continues to struggle, declining audiences making adventurous dramaturgical choices difficult; the Abbey, on the other hand, shows signs that it will use its substantial human and fiscal resources to move toward a consistent level of achievement which would justify its claim to be Ireland's national theatre.

Dramaturgy

When in 1898 the poet and playwright Yeats founded the organization that was to become the Abbey Theatre, he initially called it the Irish Literary Theatre. This origin – and the word 'literary' in particular – signals a distinguishing characteristic of Irish dramaturgy, and the continued dominance of the playwright as the most important figure in contemporary Irish theatre.

As the history of Irish theatre indicates, the work of Brian Friel holds a central place in Irish writing for the theatre since 1945. Friel was born in Northern Ireland, and now lives in the Irish Republic; his work has been premièred by major theatres in both political states. From his early writing in the 1960s to his plays for Field Day in the 1980s and 1990s, Friel's work has acted as the barometer of a rapidly changing society. More importantly, in a country which – particularly since 1969 – has seen itself trapped by its history, Friel's plays have used the immediacy of theatrical performance to interrogate our understanding of past events.

Atypical of Friel's work in structural terms, *Faith Healer* (1979) is a concentrated exploration of the indeterminate nature of memory. The play is made up of four monologues, each delivered on an almost bare stage by one of three interrelated characters – Frank, a travelling faith healer, Teddy, his manager, and Grace. Although there are points at which their accounts of the events leading up to Frank's murder outside an Irish pub agree, there are significant contradictions. Grace claims she and Frank were married; Frank says they were not. Teddy claims the relations linking the three were purely professional; the other characters indicate otherwise. With no criteria to judge among the three versions of the same story presented to them, the audience is left with a relative truth created in the moment of telling, suggesting that there may be no access to absolute truths about the past.

This concern with the indeterminate nature of history is evident in all of Friel's recent work. *Translations* (1980), set in rural Donegal in 1839, employs a variation on the conventions of theatrical naturalism; although the play is performed entirely in English, some of the characters are understood to be speaking in Gaelic, and some in English. Hence, in a play which explores the degree to which language 'shapes the contours of reality', there are gulfs of incomprehension between characters. Similarly, *Making History* (1989) uses an epic structure to contrast the squalid defeat of a seventeenth-century Irish-Catholic chieftain, Hugh O'Neill, with the making of the historical myth of his heroic resistance.

More recently, *Dancing at Lughnasa* (1990), which won awards in New York and London, continues Friel's concern with memory. Suggesting Tennessee Williams's *Glass Menagerie* in its use of a narrator recalling a series of linked vignettes from his past, the play highlights another aspect of Friel's texts – the absence of a single dominant character. Dealing with five sisters, the young son of one of the sisters, and their brother, the focus shifts from character to character throughout the play in a style similar to the work of Chekhov. Indeed, the ensemble nature of earlier Friel plays, such as *Living Quarters* (1977) and *Aristocrats* (1979), forms a logical prelude to his adaptation of Chekhov's *The Three Sisters* (1981), which in some ways forms a model for *Dancing at Lughnasa*.

Friel has not been alone in adapting important works of European theatre for the Irish stage. Just as Friel's own play, *Translations*, had explored the impossibility of pure translation from one language to another, so too have Irish dramatists been concerned with translation as an act of cultural appropriation in the contemporary theatre. The 1980s and 1990s have seen Friel, Thomas Kilroy and, most notably, Frank McGuinness adapt plays by Ibsen, Chekhov, Brecht and García Lorca into an English idiom that is distinctively Irish. These established dramatists have been joined in their exploration of world theatre by a number of leading poets who have adapted works of classical Greek theatre for Irish audiences. In 1985, for instance, Tom Paulin (b. 1949) created a version of Sophocles' *Antigone* entitled *The Riot Act* for Field Day; in 1989, Brendan Kennelly (b. 1936) wrote a version of Euripides' *Medea*; and in 1990, Field Day founder Seamus Heaney adapted Sophocles' *Philoctetes* as *The Cure at Troy*. All of these translations and 'versions' both challenge insular definitions of Irish cultural identity and reaffirm the distinctiveness of the Irish use of English, seeking to establish a difficult balance between the local and the global.

The plural interpretations of reality implicit in the work of Friel and other Irish writers can be understood as functions of both Ireland's colonial past and the country's current engagement with wider cultural horizons. This concern with multiplicity is also important in the work of Thomas Kilroy, in particular *Talbot's Box* (1977) and *Double Cross* (1986). In *Talbot's Box*, an actor playing Matt Talbot, a Dublin dock-worker who led a secret religious life of fasting, prayer and self-mortification, is entrapped in a claustrophobic box set, where he is questioned and persecuted by a group of actors, each of whom takes on a variety of roles, challenging the singular integrity of his identity. *Double Cross* continues Kilroy's exploration of the actor–character relationship in the context of two Irish men, Brendan Bracken (1901–58) and William Joyce (1906–46), who were responsible for English and German propaganda, respectively, during World War II. Bracken and Joyce are played by the same actor (Field Day founder Stephen Rea in the original production) and interact with each other by means of pre-recorded voices and a large video screen suspended above the stage.

Although they have been successful outside Ireland, Friel, McGuinness and Kilroy have directed much of their work towards Irish audiences, an aesthetic once described by Friel as 'talking to ourselves'. Indeed, the responses of Irish audiences to their plays often differ significantly from those of English and North American audiences, indicating delicate nuances of meaning peculiar to the Irish use of English. In this regard, it could be argued that the international reputation of one of Ireland's most challenging playwrights, Thomas Murphy, has suffered because his powerful plays depend in part upon his subtle command of colloquial speech. Born in the rural west of Ireland, Murphy has been a professional playwright since the early 1960s, during which time he has written twenty plays, including several of the most acclaimed works of recent years.

Bailegangaire (1985), which means 'the town without laughter', was first produced by Galway's Druid Theatre with Siobhan McKenna (1923–86) in the leading role of Mommo. Set in the kitchen of a small cottage which, the stage directions state, 'should be stylized to avoid cliché', the play is structured around the senile Mommo's attempts to tell how the town of Bailegangaire came to be so named. Prompted by her daughters, Dolly and Mary, each of whom is tormented by her own past, Mommo's tale stops, restarts and repeats itself, until, in the play's final moments, it arrives at a conclusion that unites past and present, narration and dramatic ostentation. *Bailegangaire*'s revelatory ending echoes similar moments in other plays by Murphy, notably *The Sanctuary Lamp* (1975) and *The Gigli Concert* (1984). Murphy's stylized naturalism, with its contrasting moments of brutality and transcendence, makes his theatre comparable in some ways to magic realist fiction.

While the work of these leading playwrights continues to develop in challenging new directions, it would be an injustice to suggest that they are the only writers of importance in the contemporary Irish theatre. There are now a number of playwrights working in the Irish language who have shown themselves capable of exploring new ideas and forms. These Irish-language writers range from an emerging new generation to established writers such as Criostoir O Floinn (b. 1927), whose reputation dates from 1966, when he won acclaim for his play *Cota Ban Chriost*. Moreover, there are now several generations of English-language playwrights of international stature writing plays for the Irish stage on a regular basis. For

Garry Hynes's 1985 Druid Theatre Company production of Tom Murphy's *Bailegangaire*, starring Siobhan McKenna.
Photo: Amelia Stein.

instance, 1992 saw a new play from Tony Award-winner Hugh Leonard (b. 1926), whose first play was produced in 1956 and whose *Stephen D* (1962), an adaptation of a novel by James Joyce (1882–1941), was profoundly influential in its cinematic use of narrative and location. However, 1992 also brought plays from new writers such as Dermot Bolger (b. 1959), who began writing for the theatre in the late 1980s. Indeed, the 1992 Dublin Theatre Festival featured the première of six new Irish plays (two in the Irish language) and that number again were performed in the twelve months leading up to the festival. It would

therefore appear that, given the reservoir of writing talent that exists in Ireland, the dominance of the written word in the Irish theatre will continue into the foreseeable future.

Directors, Directing and Production Styles

Following the visit to the 1982 Dublin Theatre Festival of Polish director Kazimierz Braun and his Artaud-influenced Wrocław Contemporary Theatre Company, Irish director Patrick Mason (b. 1951), actor Tom Hickey (b. 1938) and

Tom Hickey in Patrick Mason's 1983 Abbey Theatre production of *The Great Hunger*, designed by Bronwen Casson.

writer Tom MacIntyre (b. 1933) began collaborative work on a series of performances that challenges both the primacy of language in the Irish theatre and the stability of the written script. Mason, whose extensive directing credits range between opera, premières of new Irish writing and memorable productions of classic plays by Shaw and Chekhov, is best known for his work in the Abbey's experimental studio, the Peacock, and in the Gate Theatre, where he has developed a directorial style that emphasizes emotively powerful visual images. When directing the first production of Frank McGuinness's *Observe the Sons of Ulster*, for instance, he draped the back of the stage with a gigantic Union Jack and this has since become associated with the text. Tom Hickey began his career with Dublin's Focus Theatre, which trains actors in techniques based on the work of Stanislavski, and worked in television before establishing himself as one of the foremost Irish stage actors of recent years. A tall, thin figure, Hickey has said that his early training was often at odds with his own propensity towards 'physical bizarreness' and a fascination with oddities of movement and expression, which he has lately developed through mime. In 1984, Hickey's playing of J.P.W. King in the première of Tom Murphy's *The Gigli Concert* created a physically eccentric character of tragic dimensions. The third member of the group, Tom MacIntyre, was primarily known for his fiction and poetry prior to working with Mason and Hickey.

In the spring of 1983, Mason, Hickey and MacIntyre began work on a performance deriving from *The Great Hunger*, a long poem by Patrick Kavanagh (1904–67) dealing with the emotional sterility of rural life in Ireland during the 1940s. Through a process of collaborative writing and improvisation, a performance was created in which objects (bellows, a wooden female icon, a mirror), movements (swinging on a gate) and fragments of language ('Christ will be the green leaves that will come') were given symbolic resonances. Moreover, when *The Great Hunger* toured Edinburgh, Moscow, New York and London, it changed in response to its surroundings; the text was transformed yet again in 1986 when it was re-mounted at the Peacock after post-performance dialogues with the audience. Mason, Hickey and MacIntyre created three more works in this imagistic style, *The Bearded Lady* (1984), *Rise Up, Lovely Sweeney* (1985) and *Dance for Your Daddy* (1987), all of which have had a major influence on subsequent Irish theatre practice.

In spite of such attempts to break with script-based performance, most Irish directors today work with an acute awareness of the weight of a major writing tradition. Hence, the usual challenge faced by the Irish director is twofold: the nurturing of new writing, and the continuous reinterpretation of earlier Irish writing. Of the numerous directors who have succeeded in both areas, Joe Dowling (b. 1948) and Garry Hynes have achieved particular prominence. Dowling has directed the premières of a number of important Irish plays, including Brian Friel's *Aristocrats* (1979). However, it was his direction of Sean O'Casey's *Juno and the Paycock* for the Gate Theatre in 1986 which suggested the ability of the Irish theatre to renew itself by reinterpreting its textual legacy. With the aid of the intense stage presence of actor Donal McCann (b. 1943), Dowling broke with the comic sentimentalism which had traditionally characterized productions of the play, instead emphasizing stylistic contrasts within the text, playing some scenes to bring out music hall influences, and others with a graphic realism which contradicted the myth of picturesque poverty that the play is often made to support. One of the most influential productions of the 1980s, it reached international audiences when it travelled to New York and Jerusalem.

Garry Hynes's reinterpretations of works from the early part of the twentieth century have had a similar impact. Although Hynes directed the first production of Murphy's *Bailegangaire* for Galway's Druid Theatre in 1985, her earliest success had been with a tense, unsentimental series of productions of J.M. Synge's *Playboy of the Western World* in the late 1970s. Hynes's work is characterized by a meticulous attention to the written word (particularly when working with texts by living writers) and what one actor has called 'rawness and attack'. With her appointment as artistic director of the Abbey Theatre in 1990, she continued her radical interrogation of early Abbey writers, including Sean O'Casey and Lennox Robinson, introducing into familiar realist texts elements of stylization which contradict audience expectations, thereby forcing an examination of those expectations. While similar experiments had been attempted by smaller theatre companies, Hynes has been able to maximize the symbolic resonances of the Abbey as Ireland's national theatre to point to a rethinking of Irish culture taking place at the core of the institutionalized mainstream.

The dialectic in Hynes's work between the

need to partake of a distinctively Irish tradition, and the need to break with elements of that tradition, has been a powerful creative force in contemporary Irish performance practice. For example, an older generation of actors still active in the theatre provide tangible links to a past tradition when they appear in new works or new interpretations of existing scripts. Perhaps the most outstanding instance of an actor whose presence established links between the past and the present in the Irish theatre was Cyril Cusack (1910–93), whose professional career began in 1917, and who was still performing until shortly before his death. Conversely, there are younger actors whose performances have given new life to established aspects of the Irish tradition, notably Barry Lynch (b. 1959), whose international reputation has grown considerably since the late 1980s. Among the most challenging performances of recent years, however, have been those of Barry McGovern (b. 1948) in texts by Samuel Beckett. In particular, McGovern's one-man show, *I'll Go On* (1985), based on the novels *Molloy* (1948), *Malone Dies* (1948) and *The Unnamable* (1950), uses the estrangement, irony and solitude implicit in the situation of an actor alone on a stage in ways which recall Beckett's own explorations of the semantics of theatrical form. For Dowling, Hynes, McGovern and other prominent members of the contemporary Irish theatre community, the need for reinvention of an established tradition has led to a constant search for innovation.

Christopher Morash

Music Theatre
Dance Theatre

The most traditional and, at the same time, original Irish theatre performance of which music and dance are an integral part is that of the Tralee-based National Folk Theatre, Siamsa Tíre. Founded by its artistic director, composer Pat Ahern (b. 1932) in 1974 to create and develop new stage material drawn from the wealth of Irish folklore, it now consists of a small performance company backed by more than sixty part-time performers. Each drama, based on Irish folk tales or history, recreates, through a mixture of mime, music, song, dance, and the Irish language, the life of an older rural Ireland with butter churning, rope twisting, corn-sheaf flailing or cobbler or thatcher at work. Both solo and choral arrangements of traditional airs are used, played on the *bodhrán* (a traditional handheld skin drum), flute and fiddle, while the dance style derives from the unique step-dancing of north Kerry, as taught by the nineteenth-century blacksmith's son, Jerry Molyneaux, and handed down directly by his pupils. Choreographers with backgrounds in ballet and contemporary dance have been added to develop a distinctive dance form from traditional origins. *Ding, Dong, Dedero – Forging the Dance* (1991) breaks new ground in this respect. Molyneaux tells his own story, the mainstage setting is his father's forge, with the kitchen and the musicians on facing side-stages. The company works from its own theatre as well as from three rural training centres where performances can be given; it has also performed in leading theatres throughout Ireland, north and south on British and Irish television and toured Britain, France, Germany, Italy, Canada and the United States.

Original musicals have been numerous, despite inadequate funding. Notable were a 1958 musical, *The Heart's a Wonder*, based on J.M. Synge's *The Playboy of the Western World*, while a musical by James McKenna, *The Scatterin'* (1960), about four Dublin teddy boys, had three subsequent productions, each with different music. The original Pike Theatre production used Irish ballads in rock rhythm with overture and ballet music; it was later rescored twice, in 1962 for a London production, and again in 1973 for an Abbey production. The 1991 revival, using popular songs of the 1950s, was by the Passion Machine company, whose productions often make effective use of popular musical idioms.

In recent years, music and dance have become integral to, if not the actual theme of, many Irish plays. A prime example is the Abbey Theatre's 1992 Tony Award-winning play by Brian Friel, *Dancing at Lughnasa*, which received a nomination for best choreography. Set in August 1936, when dances were still held in parts of Ireland to celebrate the feast of the pagan god Lugh, the play's action is triggered by the

Patrick Mason's 1990 Abbey Theatre production of Brian Friel's *Dancing at Lughnasa*, designed by Joe Vaneck.

music supposedly coming from a battered old radio. 'The Mason's Apron' causes the wild impromptu reel from its female characters, recreating the days before age and the need for respectability prevented them from attending the local dance. 'Dancing in the Dark' from Ambrose and his Orchestra draws one of them back into romantic ballroom dancing with the continually deserting father of her illegitimate son, and Cole Porter's 'Anything Goes' sends another into a long-forgotten demonstration of ballroom technique with the same feckless partner, while an African chant accompanies their brother's recollections of his days as a missionary priest, when he became the converted.

Just as dance is essential to Friel's eighteenth play, so is music – specifically opera – important in much of the work of Thomas Murphy. In *The Gigli Concert* (1983), the need of an Irish building contractor to sing like Italian operatic tenor Beniamino Gigli – a need that infects the English quack psychiatrist he consults – is the essence of the play, which uses recordings of no fewer than thirteen different Gigli arias, with the climax embodied in the solo rendering of 'Te Che a Dio Speigasti'. Director Patrick Mason, who also directed *Dancing at Lughnasa* and is noted for his direction of opera, considers Murphy's whole dramatic construction musical, likening the speeches of the three main characters in his 1975 play *The Sanctuary Lamp* to arias.

The Abbey Theatre has been linked to music and dance since its co-founder, W.B. Yeats, wrote his then-revolutionary *Plays for Dancers*, inspired by Japanese Noh plays. Since 1989 the Abbey has staged an annual Yeats Festival, using modern dance techniques within plays such as *At the Hawk's Well*, as well as using dance to unite three or more plays with related themes under the titles of *The Cuchulainn Cycle* (1989), *Masks of Transformation* (1990) and *Sacred Mysteries* (1991). Appropriately, the American director of these productions, James W. Flannery, is not only a scholar and critic, but also a singer. The specially commissioned music for these productions has fused new music and popular music idioms.

The Abbey has also commissioned incidental music for plays from Shaun Davey (b. 1948), composer of *The Brendan Voyage* and *The Relief of Derry Symphony*, and associated particularly with the plays of Stewart Parker and Frank McGuinness. Similarly, Field Day Theatre Company commissions original music from musicians like Donal Lunny, who scored

Seamus Heaney's *The Cure at Troy*, a producer and performer of best-selling albums both on his own and with a number of Irish groups. His music combines traditional and popular idioms, and he has worked extensively in film and television.

The Dublin company which comes closest to the complete mingling of speech, music and dance in its drama is the young and experimental Co-Motion Theatre Company. For the 1990 and 1991 Dublin Theatre Festivals, for instance, it produced *The Sinking of the Titanic* and *The Tain bo Cuailgne*, respectively, which used a mixture of dancers (required to act) and actors (required to dance). The first play centred around J. Bruce Ismay, owner of the White Star Line, which built the *Titanic*, while the second told the great Celtic epic taken from the twelfth-century Ulster Cycle of manuscripts, in which war breaks out between the forces of Connacht and Ulster in 300 BC over the possession of a magical white bull.

While productions such as these suggest an inclination on the part of Irish theatre practitioners to explore movement, the Irish theatre dance companies which would otherwise provide the resources and context for such developments are in a precarious state, in spite of the establishment in 1981 of a professional support body, the Dance Council of Ireland. In 1990, for instance, there were only sixty-six professional theatre dance performances in the entire country, and by 1991 there was only one permanent professional dance company in Ireland – Daghdha – employing four dancers. Since the early 1980s, there have never been more than twenty-seven professional dancers in full-time, permanent employment in Ireland at any one time.

Daghdha (the company's name is derived from that of an Irish mythological god) is based at the Thomond College of Education (part of the University of Limerick since 1991), whose physical education programme for secondary school teachers is the only such programme in the country to employ a dancer-in-residence. The successful link between Daghdha and the University of Limerick suggests that the absence of such training facilities elsewhere in the country contributes to the weakness of Irish dance culture. Moreover, while companies such as Daghdha and the Barefoot Dance Company (founded in 1979) spend much of their time conducting performances and workshops for secondary school children, any interest in dance which these school visits may elicit is thwarted by the absence of an advanced dance academy.

The Irish dance community has identified a further obstacle to future development in Arts Council funding policy for dance, which is oriented towards specific projects, rather than granted for the maintenance of permanent companies. Consequently, establishing prolonged artistic continuity and developing an audience are persistent problems, as the infrastructure of the dance community is constantly confronted by its own provisionality. And yet, in spite of these constraints there is innovative work being done in Ireland in the area of modern dance. For instance, the Dance Theatre of Ireland (founded in 1989) has worked with designer Robert Ballagh (b. 1943) to unite developments in the Irish visual arts with modern theatre dance. Even more challenging has been the work of composer Robert Doyle (b. 1949), who has created music for performances by Operating Theatre (founded in 1987) and Icontact Dance Theatre (founded in 1989), incorporating elements of new music, performance art and modern dance in works such as *The Tower of Babel* (1992), which was characterized by one reviewer as a 'cerebral, multi-layered, often obscurantist flow of images'.

In the area of classical ballet, the situation is even more unstable than is the case with modern dance. In 1947, Joan Denise Moriarty (c.1915–92) founded the amateur Cork Ballet Company, and, building on its success, went on to found the state-supported Irish National Ballet in 1974. In 1978 the company premièred her first full-length ballet, based on J.M. Synge's *The Playboy of the Western World*, with music by the Irish traditional music group, the Chieftains; this was followed in 1981 by *The Tain*, based on *Tain bo Cuailgne*. In spite of these accomplishments, the Arts Council terminated its structural funding for the Irish National Ballet in 1989, one year after ending financial support for the Dublin City Ballet (founded in 1979). Since that time, ballet activity in Ireland has been sporadic, with Arts Council grants restricted to individual projects, while in Northern Ireland Arts Council money is largely directed towards subsidizing English and Scottish touring companies.

While classical theatre dance struggles to exist in Ireland, opera on the Italian model appears to have established itself as an integral part of the Irish theatre after a period of relative neglect. Beginning in 1705 with a production of an early English opera, *The Island Princess*, an active operatic culture flourished in Dublin during the eighteenth and early nineteenth centuries,

nurturing at least one composer of note, Michael Balfe (1808–70). However, opera in Ireland was a victim of the colonial cultural power-struggles of the late nineteenth and early twentieth centuries, when it went into something of an eclipse. Hence, as many of the great state-funded opera companies were being formed in other European countries in the first half of the twentieth century, opera was low on the Irish cultural agenda, in spite of the widespread popularity of individual performers, notably Count John McCormack (1884–1945).

In the absence of significant state enthusiasm for opera, the maintenance of an operatic tradition in Ireland initially fell to volunteer organizations, most notably the Wexford Opera Festival. It was founded in 1951 by Dr Tom Walsh (1911–88) with a performance of Balfe's *Rose of Castile* (1857). The participation of professional performers, directors and designers increased yearly, establishing an international reputation for the festival. In particular, the Wexford Festival has established an important place for itself in the opera world with its revivals of rarely performed works. For example, a 1979 Wexford Festival production of Luigi and Federico Ricci's *Crispino e la Comare* led to an increase in critical interest in these seldom-heard composers of *opera buffa*. Other recent festival productions have included Jószef Haydn's *L'Isola Disabitata*, with Irish mezzo-contralto Bernadette Greevy (b. 1939) in 1982, and Giuseppe Gazzanigia's *Don Giovanni Tenorio, or The Stone Guest*, staged in 1988. The festival continues to present six performances of three operas over an eighteen-day festival in late October, in conjunction with associated events such as art exhibitions and choral recitals.

While the Wexford Festival attracts many of the world's leading operatic talents, in contrast to many other European opera events it receives only 28 per cent of its funding from the state, and continues to generate the remainder through the efforts of a volunteer committee. In contrast to the Wexford Festival, Belfast-based Opera Northern Ireland received a 1991 Northern Ireland Arts Council grant of ST£444,600 (US$778,050), which it used to present a more conventional repertoire, including productions of Puccini's *Tosca* and Mozart's *The Magic Flute*. Although these performances were co-produced with the Dublin Grand Opera Society (the recipient of IR£250,000, or US$437,500, from the Irish

Arts Council), thereby concentrating resources and funding from both Northern Ireland and Irish Republic sources, Ireland is still far from having an adequately funded national opera company.

Carolyn Swift, Christopher Morash

Theatre for Young Audiences

From the late nineteenth century until the present day, one of the most popular theatrical forms in Ireland has been the pantomime, which is directed at audiences under 12 years of age. The basic structures of the pantomime (or 'panto', as it is often called) have varied little over the years, using familiar narratives from traditional children's literature – such as *Cinderella, Jack and the Beanstalk*, or *Aladdin and His Magical Lamp* – interspersed with inoffensive topical jokes, slapstick, songs, direct addresses to the audience, spectacular special effects, and appearances by well-known comedians, of whom Jimmy O'Dea (1899–1965) is remembered with particular affection. Certain pieces of stage business are so well established that they evoke traditional participatory responses from the audience. Although the Abbey staged Irish-language pantomimes in the 1940s, today pantomimes are performed primarily during the Christmas season in Victorian theatre buildings, such as the Gaiety and the Olympia Theatres in Dublin or the Everyman Palace in Cork.

While this traditional form continues to thrive, since the mid-1970s youth theatre has taken new directions, which may be subdivided into theatre *for* the young and theatre *by* the young. In the latter category, most schools include the staging of a play as a primary (ages 5–11) or post-primary extracurricular activity, and there are a fluctuating number of amateur youth theatre groups throughout the country, whose work is coordinated by the National Association for Youth Drama. There is also an organization, the Irish Student Drama Association, which coordinates the work of university theatre groups.

Founded in 1974, the Dublin Youth Theatre is one of the longest established youth theatres in Ireland, staging plays by Brecht, Shakespeare and Brian Friel, as well as collectively written productions. Membership is limited to ninety, and is by audition only. While the company's production standards are high, its primary aim is to further the personal and social development of its members. In Belfast, the Ulster Youth Theatre (founded 1984) has similar aims, employing professional adult directors who work with youths from all sections of the divided community over a six-week residential period. The Ulster Youth Theatre began by staging popular Broadway musicals, but later started to create its own challenging, non-naturalistic scripts, such as its 1989 production, *Now That's What I Call Gore!*, dealing with political violence.

Equally exciting has been the emergence of adult-staffed theatre companies whose work is aimed at young audiences. Two such companies came into being in 1984, Graffiti (based in Cork) and Wet Paint (based in Dublin), both of which now receive Arts Council funding. Similarly, two Northern Ireland based companies – Big Telly (founded 1990) and Replay (founded 1989) – receive funding from the Northern Ireland Arts Council for their touring productions. Graffiti uses an epic, ensemble style of performance based on improvisations to present plays and drama workshops to children through the school system. Wet Paint works with youth clubs (through the Dublin Youth Services Council) in areas not usually associated with the theatre. Developing their performances through workshops, its members work in a style which they call 'provocative naturalism' to present works of topical interest.

The longest established Irish theatre-in-education company, however, is TEAM, which emerged in 1975 from the Young Abbey company founded by director Joe Dowling. Although based in Dublin, the company tours throughout much of the Republic, reaching an estimated 10,000 school children each year. TEAM develops its text with an established playwright over an extended consultative period, producing a play which is then performed with accompanying workshops. Host schools pay the company a daily fee, which supplements a substantial Arts Council grant and limited funding from the Department of Education. While TEAM's productions deal with issues such as alcoholism, sectarianism and human rights, the company has a policy of

The 1991 TEAM production of Maeve Ingoldsby's *Firestone*.
Photo: UCD Audio Visual.

non-didacticism, aiming instead to produce works which will be 'catalysts for further discussion'. TEAM employs four administrative staff, including an artistic director, and up to twelve other theatre professionals, including Equity actors.

All five major Irish companies which work with young audiences have toured their work outside Ireland through their membership in ASSITEJ (International Association of Theatre for Children and Young People). The three companies based in the Irish Republic have also presented plays at the Dublin Theatre Festival,

marking a desire to bring their work to wider audiences. However, TEAM's collaboration with leading Irish playwrights provides the best instance of the mainstream interacting with a type of theatre which remains on the margins of most theatre criticism. In particular, two works written by Frank McGuinness in conjunction with TEAM, *Borderlands* (1983) and *The Gatherers* (1984), have achieved acclaim from the critical community as plays worthy of praise regardless of the audiences to whom they are directed.

Christopher Morash

Puppet Theatre

Dublin in the eighteenth century had one of the most important puppet theatres in the British Isles. This was Stretch's Puppet Show – mentioned by Jonathan Swift (1667–1745) – in Capel Street (*c*.1721–65). Later in the century, when puppets became a more aristocratic amusement, there was the Patagonian Theatre

in Abbey Street, which brought together such literary talents as Kane O'Hara, and whose elaborate productions included the Dryden-Davenant version of *The Tempest* with music by Purcell. Through the nineteenth century we hear spasmodically of puppets in Ireland, and George Speaight, in his *History of the English Puppet*

Theatre, goes so far as to suggest that the great revival of puppetry in England in the latter part of the nineteenth century may have been a result of puppet companies operating in Ireland. In particular, he mentions Bullock's marionettes. These were *fantoccini*, probably in the manner of Holden's puppets. We do not hear of any dramatic repertoire, but rather of variety acts, which became, and remained, the staples for travelling puppet companies well into the twentieth century. We hear of various such companies in the first half of the twentieth century. One of the last of these was McCormick's, which continued until the 1960s, when their caravan burned in the town of Drogheda.

In the late 1940s, an architect, Nelson Paine, established a puppet company, using glove-puppets, but working as 'art' rather than 'traditional'. His repertoire included such pieces as Debussy's *Toybox*, as well as puppet versions of ballads. In the early 1950s he set up a travelling puppet opera company, with elaborately staged glove-puppet versions of *La Bohème*, *I Puritani*, *Carmen* and *La Traviata*, performed to gramophone records. The puppets had extended arms, which gave them a more naturalistic appearance when performing in a medium more frequently used by marionettes. Although the company lasted for barely three years, it brought opera, through the medium of puppetry, to the most remote rural areas of Ireland. Also in the 1950s, an English couple, the Cheneys, ran a marionette theatre in a basement in Mount Street, Dublin, for two years, presenting a variety show.

Most important, however, for the development of puppet theatre in Ireland was Eugene Lambert (b. 1928), whose name has become almost synonymous with the art itself, and whose family now forms a puppet dynasty. Eugene began as a variety artist in the 1950s, with exceptionally fine skills as a ventriloquist. With the establishment of Irish television in 1962, Eugene was invited to create a puppet programme for the promotion of the Irish language. The result of this was a popular series, *Murphy agus a chairde*. Later in the 1960s, he created one of the most popular children's programmes ever on Irish television, *Wanderly Waggon*, which combined human actors (including himself) and puppet figures such as Judge (the dog) and Mr Crow, who became vir-

tually national characters. At the same time, Eugene and his family toured puppet shows the length and breadth of Ireland, probably reaching larger audiences than any form of dramatic entertainment has ever done. In the early 1970s, it was decided to set up a permanent theatre as a base for the company, and the Lambert Mews Theatre opened in 1972, at the back of their home in the Dublin suburb of Monkstown. Some years later, this theatre was enlarged to seat some 300 children, giving regular performances on Saturday afternoons, and special performances for schools and other groups. The repertoire ranges from simple pieces for young children, such as *The Three Little Pigs*, to pieces for older children, such as *Pinocchio*, *The King with Donkey's Ears* (based on an Irish legend), and *Alice's Adventures in Wonderland* (the voices for which included some of Ireland's greatest actors, such as Michael Mac Liammoir). The repertoire also includes pieces from major Irish writers, such as Oscar Wilde and W.B. Yeats. In 1991, the Lambert Theatre hosted the first Dublin International Puppet Festival; in 1992, the company toured Russia, performing at the Central Puppet Theatre in Moscow. Since the early 1980s, Paula Lambert has been operating Bosco, a very popular television puppet for younger children. She also runs her own company, and her brother, Conor, is one of Ireland's most popular Punch and Judy professors.

Two important companies developed in the 1980s. Theatre Omnibus, based in County Clare, uses a mixture of masks, puppets and humanette figures, and generally performs in non-theatrical environments or the street. Its work has a strong popular slant, and its members also work with established writers. MacNas, based in Galway, has done environmental performances, including *Alice's Adventures in Wonderland*, but its main work is with large-scale street and professional puppets, including an enormous Gulliver figure, 'washed up' on one of Dublin's beaches for the city's municipal millennium celebrations in 1988. Puppetry on television continued into the 1990s with Zig and Zag, two 'Muppetish' creatures with ready repartee, who have become cult figures.

John McCormick

Design

Irish theatre has been led by its playwrights in the first instance, and its directors in the second instance. As a consequence, the work of the theatre's many talented scenographers has been undervalued, and is often difficult to assess. This relative undervaluation of the art of the scenographer in the contemporary Irish theatre can be registered by the lack of recognition granted to designer Bronwen Casson (b. 1948), who worked with director Patrick Mason, actor Tom Hickey and writer Tom MacIntyre on *The Great Hunger*. The importance of the visual aspect of the production was emphasized by all three men in interviews; yet, while acknowledging a wider collaborative circle, the resulting performance was presented as the creation of, in Mason's words, 'a writer, a director and a player' but not, significantly, a scenographer.

The situation of the scenographer is equally problematic in more conventionally scripted productions. The plays of Samuel Beckett, for instance, provide an extreme instance of authorial control over the visual aspects of a performance, and in his lifetime Beckett withdrew performing rights from several productions which contradicted the precise descriptions contained in his scripts. Hence, the scenographer of a Beckett production is presented with the challenge of working within narrowly defined parameters to create a stage environment as meticulous as the scripts themselves. One Irish scenographer to have met this challenge successfully in recent years is Robert Ballagh, best known as a painter who has developed a witty, post-modern style with affinities to American photo-realism. However, his stage designs for Barry McGovern's *I'll Go On* (1985), *Waiting for Godot* (1986) and *Endgame* (1991) have echoed Beckett's affinity for abstraction with their use of claustrophobic, enclosed acting areas in which a rigorously limited range of colours, patterns and textures are repeated with a mathematical precision which belies their apparent roughness. Similarly, Ballagh's design for English director Steven Berkoff's 1988 production of Oscar Wilde's *Salome* at the Gate Theatre gave Berkoff's heavily stylized direction a visual form through the use of strongly contrasting primary colours against a predominantly black and white background. In all of these instances, Ballagh, an artist with a distinctive personal style of his own, has adapted his vision to that of another theatre professional.

In recent years, touring has become a priority for many Irish companies seeking to reach a truly national audience – a situation that poses special challenges for the scenographer. Touring venues throughout the country vary considerably in terms of performance area and technological capabilities. Hence, while certain companies without a touring policy, notably Co-Motion, whose work has been influenced by early German expressionist theatre, have made use of projections and designs adapted to specific theatre spaces (including, in a 1990 production, a play dealing with Joan of Arc performed in a deconsecrated church), many companies are restricted in their work by demands of portability. There are thus structural similarities in the designs created by the different Irish scenographers who have worked with the Field Day Theatre Company, in so far as a number of different productions have made use of freestanding components arranged in front of a cyclorama – a mode of design which facilitates the set's adaptation to stages of varying sizes.

The wider influence of world theatre in Ireland suggests that the status of the scenographer will increase in coming years. One indication of this change of direction is to be found in the work of Iomha Illanach, a company whose Irish name means 'many crafted image'. Founded in 1985, the company's aesthetic owes much to the ideas of Jerzy Grotowski, particularly to those ideas that were developed by him in Italy. The company's work, such as its 1990 production, *Isabella, the Movie*, places a collective emphasis on ritual and startling visual imagery, using both novel and formal theatre spaces. While this visual orientation is significant in itself, it also has implications for the group's choice to present much of their work in the Irish language. While Irish-language theatres, such as An Taibhdhearc, often have difficulty reaching audiences comparable in size to those which attend the English-language theatre, the visual impact of Iomha Illanach's work makes it accessible to those with limited proficiency in the language.

Theatre Space and Architecture

The challenge of Ireland's colonial history is nowhere more apparent than in Irish theatre architecture. One of the distinguishing characteristics of Irish culture in the twentieth century has been an engagement (or its modernist opposite, deliberate disengagement) with the country's Gaelic past, extending from the revivalism of the first decades of the century to the creative and critical reassessments of recent years. In the area of theatre architecture, however, there are no earlier Gaelic models. While there was an Elizabethan theatre built in Dublin in 1637, and important Restoration and eighteenth-century stages in a number of major urban centres, they were associated primarily with the British colonial administration. Moreover, the first play in the Irish language was performed not in the distant bardic past, but in 1901 – and it appeared on the proscenium stage of a Victorian theatre building.

The home of the principal Gaelic revivalist theatre in operation today, Siamsa Tire, is an excellent example of the consequences of this discontinuity for Irish theatre architecture. The building itself, built in 1991, is designed to resemble, from the outside, an Iron Age ring-fort. The raked proscenium stage and continental-style auditorium, however, have their origins in the mainstream European theatre of the eighteenth and nineteenth centuries. The sets used by the theatre's resident company are designed to represent a rural nineteenth-century Irish kitchen, similar to that in which traditional storytelling, music and dance would have been performed. However, there is a crucial difference, not least in actor–audience relationship, between a real kitchen and the representation of a kitchen on a proscenium stage. Hence, the result of this curious mixture of architectural styles in the Siamsa Tire Theatre is an unintentional post-modern pastiche that highlights the difficulties of a revivalist approach to the fragmented Irish tradition.

In most instances, however, Irish theatre architecture has become distinctively Irish in the same way that the English language has – by adoption and reinterpretation. Almost all Irish theatres have the proscenium arch, small fore-stage, and raked auditorium which have been the norm in British theatre architecture for 300 years. These Irish theatres range in size from the four Victorian theatres which are capable of seating audiences of more than a thousand (the Gaiety and Olympia in Dublin, the Grand Opera House in Belfast, and the Cork Opera House) to Dublin's Focus Theatre, which was converted from a garage in 1967 and seats sixty-nine patrons less than a metre away from a stage only 6.7 metres wide. Between these two extremes are the more than 120 theatre venues listed in the *1992 Irish Performing Arts Yearbook* – a list that does not include many of the parish halls, gymnasiums and community centres used for amateur theatre in rural areas. Given the sheer number of theatre spaces in Ireland today, it could thus be said that if theatre building is not a native growth, it has none the less flourished.

Of the proscenium stages in Ireland, the Grand Opera House in Belfast calls for particular comment. Built in 1895, it was designed by English architect Frank Matcham, one of the leading theatre architects of his day. Its brick exterior is a distinctively late-Victorian mixture of Baroque, Flemish and Orientalist styles; its lavishly decorated auditorium has excellent acoustics, and is used as much for musical events as it is for theatre. Unlike the French rococo Olympia Theatre of 1879, or C.J. Phipp's Dublin Gaiety Theatre of 1871, the Grand Opera House has received substantial state funding, and was reopened in 1980 after extensive restoration work (although it has since suffered bomb damage). Also of considerable historical architectural interest is the 371-seat Gate Theatre in Dublin, housed in what was previously the Great Supper Room of the Rotunda Maternity Hospital, which dates from 1767. In 1930 it was transformed into a theatre with unusual sphinx reliefs in plaster above the proscenium.

The scenographic technology available in Irish theatres varies considerably from building to building. The Abbey's 628-seat main auditorium, designed by Michael Scott (b. 1905) in 1966 is a good example of the upper end of the spectrum – a situation which can be attributed to the high level of state funding that the Abbey receives. Its stage is large (15.54 metres by 10.12 metres), with a correspondingly high proscenium arch; there is a fly system with thirty-eight counterweight sets each capable of holding 300 kilograms, and five lifts, three with traps. Lighting is controlled from a booth

The Siamsa Tire Theatre, Tralee, County Kerry.
Photo: Siamsa Tire.

behind the balcony by a Rank Strand Galaxy board with 240 circuits, and the sound system is capable of accommodating eight speaker positions with input from reel-to-reel, double cassette deck, digital audio tape or compact disc. The theatre has a large backstage area, with Tannoy to six dressing rooms, a band room and quick-change rooms. At the other extreme, the Focus Theatre has a Strand twelve-way board operating five spots and ten fresnels, with sound provided by two speakers and a single cassette deck; there are many amateur theatre spaces that would lack even this rudimentary technology.

As has been the case in most countries heir to European post-Renaissance theatre architectural tradition, there have been reactions against the limitations of the proscenium arch in recent years. When the Abbey was built, for instance, it included a second stage in the form of a 157-seat flexible studio, the Peacock. While the Peacock contains an elevated proscenium stage, it is also possible to arrange the audience on three sides of a floor-level acting area. This option has been used with notable success in staging plays by Yeats, originally conceived on the model of the Japanese Noh. A recently converted Dublin cinema, the 750-seat Tivoli (1988) similarly offers the choice of an end stage or staging in the round. The Tivoli has mounted productions by the Rough Magic company, which, until 1988, worked in the Project Arts Centre (1973), a converted factory studio space which seats audiences of 180 on three sides of a floor-level acting area. Since the 1970s, under the artistic direction (1976–80) of Jim Sheridan (b. 1949), who has since won international acclaim as a director, the Project provided a focus for much of the most challenging Irish theatre outside the mainstream.

These rearrangements of the theatrical space are relatively modest, however, compared to the experiments of recent years. In 1989, for instance, Nicodemius Productions chose to explore one of the most important events in Ulster Unionist history, the Siege of Derry of 1689, by staging a pageant using techniques reminiscent of Peter Schumann's Bread and Puppet Theatre. In the course of the performance, the historically charged streets and walls surrounding the city became an acting area. Similarly, in 1992 MacNas Theatre Company of Galway staged a spectacle involving figures from Irish mythology in the streets of Galway. In the cases of these and other open-air performances, culturally resonant aspects of the landscape have been transformed into semantically rich performance spaces.

Training

Formal theatre training is among the least developed aspects of the Irish theatre, although this situation started to change in the 1980s. Until the late 1980s, there had been no full-time tuition programmes in Ireland for a number of years, with the consequence that most theatre professionals began their careers by serving an apprenticeship with amateur or semi-professional companies. This is not to say, however, that professionals who began their careers in the amateur theatre are completely untrained; the Amateur Drama League offers its members a wide range of training programmes, including a two-week summer course taught by theatre professionals, in operation since 1966, which in 1991 attracted 200 participants. More recently, the University of Ulster at Magee (in Derry) and St Patrick's College, Maynooth, introduced two-year, part-time diplomas which provide training in practical and theoretical aspects of theatre for the non-professional.

Apart from the amateur theatre, the most influential training ground for actors in the contemporary Irish theatre has been the Stanislavski Studio which has been operated in Dublin's Focus Theatre since 1963 by Deirdre O'Connell (b. 1939), who had studied with Erwin Piscator and Lee Strasberg in the United States. Like several other small part-time training organizations, it continues to attract students.

In 1987, however, director Joe Dowling opened a school of acting based in Dublin's Gaiety Theatre, which offers a one-year full-time course in performance. Around the same time, two third-level institutions, Trinity College, Dublin, and the University of Ulster at Coleraine upgraded their theatre studies departments to include a substantial training programme. The Samuel Beckett Centre for Drama and Theatre Studies at Trinity College now offers two university degrees. As part of the college's four-year Bachelor of Arts programme, it offers courses on theatre history, direction, puppet theatre, community theatre, lighting, and theatre management, with a facility for students to spend part of the period of study in one of seventeen European universities. The centre also offers a two-year intensive actor training programme, the Diploma in Theatre Studies. The University of Ulster at Coleraine offers courses in stage management, theatre administration and other areas as part of its three-year BA degree. For those not wishing to attend a university, three institutes of higher education in Northern Ireland (Belfast, North Antrim and Newtownabbey) offer two-year performance courses leading to a recognized British qualification, the BTEC National Diploma. Similarly, the Inchicore Vocational School in Dublin offers a two-year performance programme leading to a recognized diploma, and a one-year course on stagecraft and design.

Criticism, Scholarship and Publishing

There is an imbalance in Irish theatrical scholarship between the vast quantity of criticism dealing with the work of playwrights, and the relative underdevelopment of criticism relating to theatrical practice. To give but one extreme example, the number of books and articles published in 1986 dealing with the work of Samuel Beckett exceeded the total for any other playwright in the world, living or dead, including William Shakespeare. The high quality of Irish writing for the theatre this century, its centrality in Ireland's socio-cultural development, and the size of the Irish diaspora, have all contributed to the creation of a large international critical community devoted to the study of Irish writing for the stage. When the International Association for the Study of Anglo-Irish Literature (IASAIL) met in Dublin in 1992, for example, more than 200 scholars heard twenty-five papers dealing with the work of Irish playwrights read by critics from Egypt, Japan, Canada, the United States, France, Germany, Sweden, Holland, England and Ireland. However, only three of these papers dealt with performance, as one might expect from critics whose opportunities to experience live theatre in Ireland are limited.

However, the world-wide interest in Irish writing for the stage has encouraged publishers with access to international distribution networks to print the work of major contemporary Irish playwrights. The recent work of Brian Friel and Frank McGuinness, for instance, is available in editions published by Faber & Faber in London and Boston. Faber is also notable for publishing work by new writers from the North of Ireland, particularly those associated with Field Day. Similarly, several of Thomas Murphy's best known plays have been published by one of the leading script publishing houses in the English-speaking world, Methuen of London. Less highly acclaimed writers, and the more obscure work of major writers, are available only in editions published by relatively small Irish publishing houses, the most notable of which are Gallery Press and Mercier Press, located in the midlands and south of Ireland respectively.

If the international scholarly community shows a literary bias in its research into the Irish theatre, the approach of most Irish critics is socio-cultural. The work of Fintan O'Toole (b. 1958) is a prime example. In the mid-1980s, O'Toole established himself as the most perceptive theatre reviewer in the country, a position consolidated in 1987 with the publication of *The Politics of Magic*, a study of the plays of Thomas Murphy. However, in the early 1990s, O'Toole became dramaturge to the Abbey Theatre, and began writing a column in the leading Irish daily newspaper, *The Irish Times*, in which he analysed a wide range of cultural matters. This same drift from the purely theatrical to wider issues of cultural study is true of the leading scholarly critics working in the universities, to the extent that it would appear that the interrelationships between the theatre and contemporary Irish society have been so compelling that few critics wish to ignore the socio-cultural dimension. One of the few exceptions to this rule can be found in the *Irish Times* notices of David Nowlan (b. 1936), which concentrate doggedly on production values.

None the less, Irish theatrical research at all levels has become increasingly professional in recent years, prompted in part by the establishment of university departments dedicated to the study of theatre. The influence of third-level educational training can be detected in the leading Irish theatre magazine, *Theatre Ireland*, now published in Belfast, which has appeared sporadically since 1982. In its latest incarnation, it combines extensive use of visual material with sophisticated critical models, and provides a useful guide to the rapid proliferation of new Irish theatre companies. The other Irish magazine devoted to the theatre, *Irish Stage and Screen* (founded 1988), is more uneven, although it has taken a most sympathetic attitude towards the amateur movement.

Irish Stage and Screen also incorporates *Prompts*, the newsletter of the Irish Theatre Archive. Since its inception in 1982, the archive has accepted professional and amateur programmes, stage designs, posters, scripts, and other theatrical documents from the whole of Ireland. However, in spite of a Northern Ireland Arts Council grant in 1992 which established an office for the archive in Belfast, most of the collection remains housed in the civic records office in Dublin City Hall, where only 10 per cent of the material has been catalogued due to financial constraints. Although the completed cataloguing has been done on a computer, there are no immediate plans to make it publicly available in this format. More recently, *Theatre Ireland*, in conjunction with the University of Ulster at Coleraine, has initiated an Irish theatre database, which will make information on all aspects of the Irish theatre available through a subscription computer network.

The history of the Irish theatre in the early years of this century has been written about extensively, particularly in relation to the work of W.B. Yeats and J.M. Synge; indeed, even the most minor plays of the Irish Renaissance have been reprinted in the 1990s. However, one of the most challenging analyses of this period in recent years is Adrian Frazier's *Behind the Scenes at the Abbey* (University of California Press). For an overview of the Abbey's development since its inception, see Hugh Hunt's *The Abbey: Ireland's National Theatre, 1904–1978* (Gill & Macmillan). Other Irish theatres to have published histories include the Gate and the Lyric: Richard Pine and Richard Cave, *The Dublin Gate Theatre, 1928–1978* (Chadwyck-Healey) and Conor O'Malley, *A Poet's Theatre* (Elo Press). A good picture of theatre life in Ireland during the 1950s can be found in Carolyn Swift's history of the Pike Theatre, *Stage by Stage* (Poolbeg). The history of a more recent company can be found in Jerome Hynes, *Druid: The First Ten Years* (Druid Performing Arts). Anyone wishing to understand the issues motivating many contemporary Irish theatre

companies should read the first two series of pamphlets published by the Field Day Theatre Company, collected as *Ireland's Field Day* (Hutchinson).

For an accessible overview of the Irish theatre from AD 1169 to the early 1980s, read Christopher Fitz-Simon's *The Irish Theatre* (Thames & Hudson). Fitz-Simon, a working director, writes with a strong awareness of performance practice. A more history based text can be found in D.E.S. Maxwell's *A Critical History of Modern Irish Drama, 1891–1980* (Cambridge University Press). Both of these works provide good introductions to the works of Sean O'Casey and Samuel Beckett, each the subject of an extensive archive of critical commentary. In particular, if venturing for the first time into the daunting area of Beckett criticism – which includes its own journal, the *Journal of Beckett Studies* – it would be advisable to begin with Deirdre Bair's highly accessible *Samuel Beckett: A Biography* (Picador).

Articles dealing with more recent contemporary writers can be found in Irish studies journals such as *The Irish University Review* (published in Dublin) or *Eire-Ireland* (published in Minneapolis, USA). For example, a 1992 essay by playwright and critic Tom Kilroy makes a particularly good starting point: 'A Generation of Irish Playwrights' in *Irish University Review* (vol. 22, no. 1). For more sustained analysis, two of the most interesting full-length studies of Irish playwrights to have appeared in recent years are Fintan O'Toole's *The Politics of Magic: The Work and Time of Tom Murphy* (Methuen) and Richard Pine's *Brian Friel and Ireland's Drama* (Routledge). Both works are written with a subtle understanding of the contexts from which their respective subjects have emerged. Although his Third World Marxist critical model is at odds with his subject matter, Michael Etherton's contribution to Macmillan's Modern Dramatists series, *Contemporary Irish Dramatists*, provides a useful overview of the Irish theatre today. A cogent analysis of government funding for the theatre can be found in O'Hagan and Duffy's *The Performing Arts and the Public Purse: An Economic Analysis* (published in Dublin by the Arts Council). Although not comprehensive, the frequently updated *Stagecast: Irish Stage and Screen Directory* provides an extremely useful listing of performers, agents and theatrical suppliers. Finally, anyone interested in theatre companies, venues, and organizations cannot ignore the annually updated *Irish Performing Arts*

Yearbook, which includes coverage of Northern Ireland. It is edited by Sheena Barbour and is published by Rhinegold.

Christopher Morash

Further Reading

Barbour, Sheena, ed. *Irish Performing Arts Yearbook 1992*. London: Rhinegold, 1992. 97 pp.

Brinson, Peter, and Andy Ormston. *The Dancer and the Dance: Developing Theatre Dance in Ireland*. Dublin: Arts Council, 1985. 79 pp.

Etherton, Michael. *Contemporary Irish Dramatists*. Basingstoke: Macmillan, 1989. 253 pp.

Fitz-Simon, Christopher. *The Irish Theatre*. London: Thames & Hudson, 1982. 208 pp.

Fox, Ian. *100 Nights at the Opera: An Anthology to Celebrate the 40th Anniversary of Wexford Opera Festival*. Dublin: Townhouse and Country House, 1991. 151 pp.

Frazier, Adrian. *Behind the Scenes at the Abbey*. London/Berkeley, CA: University of California Press, 1990. 258 pp.

Hogan, Robert, and Michael O'Neill, eds. *Joseph Holloway's Irish Theatre*. 3 vols. Dixon, CA: Proscenium Press, 1968–70.

Hunt, Hugh. *The Abbey: Ireland's National Theatre, 1904–1978*. Dublin: Gill & Macmillan, 1979. 306 pp.

Hynes, Jerome, ed. *Druid: The First Ten Years*. Galway: Druid Performing Arts, 1985. 79 pp.

Kilroy, Tom. 'A Generation of Irish Playwrights'. *Irish University Review* 22, no. 1 (Spring/Summer 1992): 135–41.

Maxwell, D.E.S. *A Critical History of Modern Irish Drama, 1891–1980*. Cambridge: Cambridge University Press, 1984. 250 pp.

Mikhail, E.H. *An Annotated Bibliography of Modern Anglo-Irish Drama*. Troy, NY: Whitston, 1981.

O'Hagan, John W., Christopher Duffy, and T. Duffy. *The Performing Arts and the Public Purse: An Economic Analysis*. Dublin: Arts Council, 1987. 89 pp.

O'Malley, Conor. *A Poet's Theatre*. Dublin: Elo Press, 1988. 168 pp.

Pine, Richard. *Brian Friel and Ireland's Drama*. London: Routledge, 1991. 256 pp.

——, and Richard Cave. *The Dublin Gate Theatre, 1928–1978*. Cambridge/ Teaneck, NJ: Chadwyck-Healey, 1984. 124 pp.

Stagecast: Irish Stage and Screen Directory. Monkstown: Stagecast, 1992. 144 pp.

Swift, Carolyn. *Stage by Stage*. Dublin: Poolbeg, 1985. 312 pp.

Wilmer, Steve. 'Women's Theatre in Ireland'. *New Theatre Quarterly* 7, no. 28 (November 1991): 353–60.

Worth, Katharine. *The Irish Drama of Europe from Yeats to Beckett*. Atlantic Highlands, NJ: Humanities Press, 1978.

ISRAEL

Located on the eastern seaboard of the Mediterranean at the meeting point of Asia and Africa, Israel's land area is 20,700 square kilometres (8,000 square miles) and its 1988 population was 4.3 million. The State of Israel dates back only to 1948 but the links between the Jewish people and Eretz Israel (the Land of Israel) date back to about 2000 BC when Hebrews began to arrive in Canaan, as the land was then called. They became the dominant group in the area from about 1200 BC and remained so until 63 BC. From that date, the area was ruled in turn by Romans, Arabs, Crusaders, Turks and British until 1948. During that period, the Jewish community spread to many parts of the world with the majority settling in Europe. In the late nineteenth century, under the banner of Zionism, a movement back to Israel began and a Hebrew renaissance developed. Precisely because of these lengthy cultural links with Europe – especially during the modern period – it is more logical to deal with theatre in Israel as part of the European mainstream than as part of the indigenous traditions of its Arab neighbours – Lebanon and Syria in the north, Jordan in the east and Egypt in the southwest.

Throughout the modern period and certainly until the end of the nineteenth century there was no Hebrew theatre in Eretz Israel; indeed, Hebrew had almost disappeared as a living language. The restoration of the Hebrew language and the development of the Hebrew theatre itself was a phenomenon linked to the last decade of the nineteenth century in Jerusalem and to the beginning of the twentieth century in Jaffa. The Hebrew theatre grew a decade later in Moscow and Berlin, and finally made its home in Tel Aviv in the mid-1920s. With audiences that never numbered more than hundreds at first, theatre in this newly revived ancient

tongue began to flourish. It was the Hebrew language as well which was a primary justification for the establishment of a Hebrew theatre in Eretz Israel (then called Palestine). These early performances were not staged for artistic or entertainment purposes, but rather to educate, to develop the audience's knowledge of Hebrew and to mould the spirit of the Hebrew nationality, as it was then called, which was beginning to evolve in Eretz Israel. The honour of staging the first Hebrew performance in the country, in 1890, goes to the students of the Lemel School in Jerusalem who appeared before an audience composed of students and their parents. The group staged Peretz Smolenskin's Yiddish play *Zerubavel* or *Return from the Babylonian Exile*, translated into Hebrew and adapted by David Yellin. The script was directed by the principal of the school in association with a Jewish employee of the Russian consulate in the city.

In 1895 this play was staged again, this time in the colony of Rehovoth by young farmers, making it the first Hebrew play performed in the country by adults. From 1904, groups of semi-amateurs began organizing themselves into more permanent companies. In 1904, the Society of Lovers of the Dramatic Art was established in Jaffa, among whose founders and actors was the Jewish Russian director, Menachem Gnessin (1882–1951), later one of the founders of the Habimah Theatre. Most of the active members were teachers at the Jaffa School for Girls. In 1909 the group disbanded, but several months later was re-established, this time under the name Lovers of the Hebrew Stage. The amateur theatre active in Jerusalem from 1909 to 1911 had a similar name, as did an amateur theatre that existed for a short time in Petah Tikva.

After World War I, these amateur groups

were replaced by more professional companies. However, the most important steps towards the development of a professional Hebrew theatre actually took place in Moscow in 1914. There Nahum Zemach (1887–1939) invited a number of young Jews including Gnessin and Hanna Rovina (1892–1980) to set up a Hebrew theatre. The company, which from 1917 was called Habimah (Stage), overcame its initial difficulties. With the aid of the Russians Konstantin Stanislavski and Yevgeny Vakhtangov, it developed a symbolic expressionistic style of acting, first shown in David Pinski's (1872–1959) play *The Eternal Jew*. This paved the way for the international fame which Habimah's classic play *The Dybbuk* by Solomon Ansky (1863–1920) earned. A tragedy staged in a musical, expressionistic style when it was first performed in 1922, it was unique and a marked contrast to the Chekhovian realism then dominant in Moscow. In 1926, the troupe left Moscow for a world tour, which included a visit to Eretz Israel in 1928. The company travelled widely and settled permanently in Israel only in 1931.

In the mean time, during the two decades that divided the two world wars, Eretz Israel became an active centre of Hebrew culture. Hebrew literature made its home there, composers gathered there and wrote music in keeping with their nationalistic views, the first films were made, in architecture there was a transition from a traditional Hebrew style to modern housing developments. As part of all of these endeavours, theatres were also set up: Te'atron Eretz Yisra'eli (Eretz Israel Theatre), the Ohel (Tent), the Kumkum (Kettle) and the Matate (Broom). Like all the other creative artists of that period, those in the world of theatre realized they had to found not just a theatre to provide entertainment for a large public, but rather one that would participate in building the country and the people and create a new, Hebrew art form.

In 1922, the Dramatic Theatre, under the management of Miriam Berenstein-Cohen (1895–1992), attempted to put these ideals into practice by adapting scenes from the Bible and staging a production of *The Dybbuk* in which the expressionism and ritual magic of the Habimah's original production was replaced by naturalism. The Dramatic Theatre, however, closed after four of its leading actors left in 1924 to study in Berlin. Gnessin, who had left the Habimah, soon joined that group.

In 1925, when the troupe returned again to Eretz Israel, it performed the play *Belshazzar* about fifty times. In 1927, the group disbanded once more, primarily because of disagreements in selecting plays. In 1925, Moshe HaLevy (1895–1970), formerly with the Habimah in Moscow, founded the Ohel Theatre. The Russian communist revolution and socialist ideals strongly influenced the ideology and conduct of this theatre. The director advocated a proletarian theatre, one expressing the positions of working people, and he recruited his actors from among the working class. HaLevy's actor-workers organized as a collective and at first earned their living more by their work outside the theatre than in it. Ohel's opening play, *Peretz' Parties*, underscored the decadence of life in the Diaspora in contrast to the liberation of the new Jewish community living in Eretz Israel. Until the 1950s, the Ohel maintained this collective structure, operating under the auspices of Israel's General Federation of Labour.

Two years later, in 1927, the Kumkum was founded in Tel Aviv by the writer Avigdor Hameiri (1890–1970). This was a satirical cabaret theatre, a new phenomenon on the local scene. A year later it disbanded, and the Matate was founded in its place and continued its activity until the early 1950s. This was a popular theatre, which expressed local colour and life with humour, song and satire. Some of Israel's leading young poets wrote lyrics for its shows.

In 1931, the year that the Habimah finally settled in Eretz Israel, an open rivalry developed between it and the Ohel. Over the next decade, these two theatres both became well established and, in fact, began to resemble each other not only in their acting styles but also in their repertoires – classics from world literature, Jewish classics, and some original plays. In general, the style was realistic (with a bent towards pathos) but a realism influenced by the expressionism initially adopted by the Habimah. In 1940, the Ohel built its own playhouse, and in the early 1940s, the Habimah also began constructing a theatre building.

In 1944, for the first time in two decades, a new theatre was founded in Tel Aviv, one with artistic ambitions and a unique dramatic idiom. It was later to become known as the Cameri (Chamber). Its director, Yossef Milo (b. 1916), along with four young actors, staged four one-act plays in the first season. These evinced the trend of this new troupe – a concern for the Hebrew language, a chamber setting, and a Brechtian quality. Later the founders were joined by Hanna Meron (b. 1925) and Yossef

Yadin (b. 1920), who became the company's leading actors. In Goldoni's *A Servant of Two Masters*, Milo stressed what could be called 'pure' theatre in contrast to Stanislavski-styled illusionary theatre.

In the 1940s and 1950s, the culture of Eretz Israel reached its apogee, but dialectically, it also began its decline. The pioneering ethos was predominant and Eretz Israel produced the figure of the *sabras*, the native-born sons and daughters of the pioneers who came to the country in the second and third waves of immigration. This generation celebrated the victories of the Hebrew revolution. But under the surface, new currents were stirring. It was during these years that trends typifying Israeli culture first took shape: a determination to root this new society in the region, the development of a new type of individual freed of the thinking of the Diaspora Jew, and an interest in maintaining an essentially European culture. These trends were also to be manifested in the theatre.

During the struggle to create a politically independent state, the Palmachnicks, the fighting *sabras*, became part of the national mythology. In 1948, *He Walked in the Fields* by Moshe Shamir (b. 1921) became the first original Israeli play to be produced (Israeli as distinct from the plays of Eretz Israel, those written prior to the establishment of the state). It was this play that put the Cameri on the map as the theatre depicting the essence of the new Israeli reality. The audience was finally able to

Yossef Milo's 1948 Cameri production of Moshe Shamir's *He Walked in the Fields*, designed by Arie Navon.

see itself on the stage, fighting its wars, living its life in the *kibbutz* (collective farm) and experiencing contacts with Holocaust refugees. Other theatres followed in its footsteps, especially the Habimah with its production of *The Wastes of the Negev* by Yigal Mossinsohn (b. 1917).

However, the 1950s brought no new innovations to these theatres. The Habimah, the Ohel and the Cameri became almost monopolistic institutions on the Israeli theatrical scene. Their repertoires lacked any particular identity and tended towards commercialism. On the other hand, avant-garde experiments then developing in the west, particularly in France, called for alternative types of groups and these did spring up. The Zira (Arena), the first and perhaps the most important one, was founded in 1949 as an amateur company and functioned until 1959. Its founder, Michael Almaz (b. 1920), wanted to stage experimental plays in an intimate hall with a young company. The hall took the form of an arena and the seating of the audience created intimacy with the actors. Almaz, who directed most of the plays, also selected the repertoire himself. The theatre staged some sixty plays, one-third of them original works. But the Zira's importance was mainly due to the productions it staged of foreign avant-garde plays. In 1959, Almaz left the theatre and the company ceased operation. The Zira was the harbinger of a tendency that would come to the fore not only in the theatre but also in Israeli culture itself in the coming decade: a combination of an interest in western trends and a penchant for artistic experimentation with commercial objectives.

The Zira was replaced by another small theatre, the Zavit (Angle). It was founded by a group of young actors, and staged, first and foremost, modern plays in an attempt to encourage original playwriting. In addition, the Zavit mounted many vaudeville-type plays, and this trend grew stronger as the theatre's demise grew closer.

The Zuta (Little) was a small travelling theatre, founded in 1958 by Zigmund Turkov (1896–1966) and intended mainly for new immigrants and the residents of developing towns. It disbanded in 1967.

In the 1960s, the public repertory theatres – the Habimah, the Cameri, the Ohel – kept their place in the centre of Israel's theatrical life. However, the dynamic theatrical activity now moved from the centre towards the edges, to the small fringe theatres which were barely managing to subsist with their limited budgets and organizational difficulties. These theatres tried to offer an innovative repertoire, to revitalize the work of the actors, to support the creation of original drama, and to open new lines of communication with the audience and the community. At the same time, the decade also brought prosperity to several commercial theatres and brought in new audiences.

At this time as well, the pattern that now characterizes most Israeli theatrical establishments began to take shape: repertory theatres partially subsidized by public funds supplemented by income from season subscriptions. After the Six Day War of 1967, the economy began to grow, immigration to the country increased, and Israel became a consumer society dominated by a culture of affluence. Large new audiences began to frequent these institutions of art and culture.

As a new generation sprang up – graduates of an Israeli school system and not strangers to Hebrew culture as their largely immigrant parents of the 1950s had been – many actually became creative artists. Clearly, a new Israeli culture was coming into being: a secular more than a religious culture, open to the west and its innovations, cut off from the pioneering ethos of the 1930s and 1940s, and linked through complex threads of remembrance to the experiences of the Holocaust generation. During this period, new artistic institutions were established, including the Israel Museum (1965), the Batsheva and Bat Dor dance companies and many theatres.

In the wake of economic prosperity, commercial theatre also thrived and began to develop a star system. The Popular Theatre, founded by the impresario Avraham Deshe (b. 1926) and the actor-director Uri Zohar (b. 1935), staged numerous original comedies, musicals and revues.

The Godik Theatre, founded by the impresario Giora Godik, at first specialized in bringing singers and performers from abroad, and then began mounting its own musicals, both translated scripts and original works. Godik managed a theatrical enterprise that at its peak had about 200 employees and paid very high salaries to dozens of actors, singers, musicians, directors and dancers. In the end, however, the enterprise went bankrupt and Godik fled from his creditors to Germany, where he died.

From the mid-1960s, there was also revived interest in older Yiddish-language theatre. In 1967, there were five permanent companies putting on Yiddish plays. Some were built around a well-known star, like Yossef (Joseph) Buloff, who shuttled between Israel and the United States. In Israel, he performed Yiddish plays before traditional audiences – the middle-aged and the old. Because of the great success that Yiddish theatre enjoyed, popular plays from the Hebrew stage were now being translated into Yiddish.

During the same period, the *kibbutz* movement established its own company called the Kibbutz Stage, which performed mainly in agricultural settlements. Quickly, there was a flurry of dramatic activity in the *kibbutzim* by amateur groups. Theatrical activity was also organized by local councils, workers' committees and schools. About a hundred such companies, including a Jewish–Arab group from Nazareth, participated in an International Theatre Week held in 1966.

The early and mid-1950s were a period of affluence, growth and change. In 1959, the curtain fell on the Zira Theatre, but at the same time, the curtain rose on another small theatre, the Zavit. In 1961, Milo founded the first municipal theatre in Israel, the Haifa Hebrew Theatre. That same year, Dan Ben Amotz (1923–89) and Haim Hefer (b. 1925) founded the Hamam Theatre in an ancient bathhouse in Jaffa. In 1963, the playwright Nissim Aloni (b. 1926) founded the Theatre of the Seasons, which lasted only two years. A year after it closed, three young actors founded the Actors' Stage which after undergoing various transformations, became part of the Haifa Hebrew Theatre in 1970.

The Tzavta Club in Tel Aviv also staged monodramas and engaged in theatrical experiments during the 1960s, and in Jerusalem an English theatre, the Circle, staged a number of avant-garde plays. Yaakov Agmon (b. 1920) founded the Bimot and staged a number of original productions that also became box-office successes. In doing so, the Bimot, without public funds, came to be regarded as a commercial theatre.

By 1970, however, Israeli theatres had become increasingly dependent on public funds and subsidies. This economic dependence led to a concentration of many of the groups in the country's urban centres. In Tel Aviv, the Habimah, the Ohel and the Cameri were all active while the Haifa Theatre was the theatrical centre for the north. In Jerusalem, a rather weak amateur theatre was taking shape, which took on some momentum in the early 1970s. All these theatres enjoyed public, municipal and government assistance and all, in their way, merged into a single, large artistic personality. Their unique features were so diminished that by the 1990s one could say that the Israeli theatre had become a single centralized body with no real differences between performances by the Habimah, the Cameri, or even the Haifa Theatre.

In 1958, the Habimah was named the National Theatre of Israel, and over the next few years, the collective ownership of the company ceased as the theatre became nationalized. That same year, the General Federation of Labour discontinued its sponsorship of the Ohel and its longtime artistic director, Moshe HaLevy, resigned. The Ohel continued to exist until 1967, trying to sustain itself mainly from its box office. Of the social and theatrical concepts that were the basis for its establishment in the mid-1920s, nothing remained.

In 1961, Yossef Milo was appointed the artistic director of a theatre to be established by the municipality of Haifa. The new Haifa Municipal Theatre had a permanent budget at its disposal, a sumptuous building and a regular audience. In 1967, following conflicts with the actors and scandals that were widely covered in the press, Milo resigned but he left behind a considerable achievement: he had succeeded in bringing new audiences to the theatre. The theatre opened with a production of *The Taming of the Shrew* with a cast of unknown actors. The Haifa Theatre's greatest success in this period, though, was Brecht's *The Caucasian Chalk Circle*, in which two new stars were discovered – Zaharira Harifai (b. 1929) and Haim Topol (b. 1935).

Many small, experimental theatres also thrived during this decade. One of these was the Actors' Stage (1966–70), founded by a group of young people who attempted to devise a new and more natural style of acting, under the leadership of Oded Kotler (b. 1937). Despite his youth, Kotler was already a well-known actor at the Cameri and in 1967 won a prize at Cannes for his performance in the film *Three Days and a Boy*. In 1963, Kotler opened an acting studio and in 1966 he established a company which mounted fifty-one productions, including a number of modern western plays and some original plays. In 1970, the group merged with the Haifa Theatre; three of its founders received key positions while Kotler was appointed its manager. Over the next years they were able to realize the objectives they had tried unsuccessfully to achieve as an independent company: to encourage indigenous writers, to develop new actors, to draw on realistic contemporary material, to reach out to new audiences, and to offer training.

Throughout the 1970s, Kotler, as managing director of the Haifa Theatre, encouraged young playwrights. His main interest was not to mount impeccably written plays but to give the writers an opportunity to learn from seeing their plays staged. In this way, he in fact created a group of Israeli playwrights who would set the tone for Hebrew theatre in the 1970s and 1980s – Hanoch Levin (b. 1943), Yehoshua Sobol (b. 1939), Hillel Mittelpunkt (b. 1949), Danny Horowitz (b. 1941) and others.

At the same time, Kotler set up a theatrical laboratory, headed by US-born Nola Chilton, in which he assembled a group of young actors known as the Project Group. In her work with the group, Chilton created a school of docudramatic playwriting. The actors lived in a certain place, learned the local colour, became familiar with the life there, and created plays based on the things they saw and experienced.

The Jerusalem Khan Theatre was founded in 1972 under the management of British director Michael Alfreds. Its first play was an astutely directed revue based on the Book of Esther, followed by *Woyzeck*, and the documentary play *One City*, about life in Jerusalem. The latter caused a public scandal because of the one-sided and negative picture that it drew. Alfreds was interested in an experimental, multi-movement theatre, with the accent on the actors. His plays were to be created collectively.

In 1978, the young director Ilan Ronen (b. 1954) was appointed as the theatre's manager and he carried on Alfreds's approach. At the same time, Ronen strengthened the theatre's contacts with young playwrights and staged original, innovative plays as well as those based on topical events and local issues in an attempt to form strong links with the community, particularly with the inhabitants of poorer neighbourhoods. Ronen's resignation in 1982 marked the end of this chapter, not only for the Khan but also in the annals of Israeli theatre. Thanks to this work, however, the belief that there was no audience in the country for new approaches to theatre was finally shattered. This company was the closest example of a viable experimental theatre yet tried within the Israeli establishment.

Early in the 1970s, still another theatre was founded in Beersheba, in the south of the country, an area no one believed would produce an audience. Created by Gershon Bilu, who brought in actors from all parts of the country, the company mounted five plays and had 189 subscribers. In the early 1990s the Beersheba Theatre was giving more than 400 performances each year before an audience totalling tens of thousands, including 8,000 subscribers. Since its establishment, the company's major contribution has been to promote and encourage young actors and many launched their careers there. Its repertoire has consisted mainly of proven foreign plays with few artistic risks.

The 1970s marked a rather grey period for the two main established theatres – the Habimah and the Cameri. The Habimah continued to produce a balanced mix of classical and modern drama as well as some original works. Along with these, the company also staged a number of more popular plays in an effort to balance its budget. Despite this, at the end of the decade, the theatres were in difficult straits, both financially and artistically.

In 1971, after experiencing financial hardships, the Cameri officially became the Municipal Theatre of Tel Aviv and since then has been operating under the management of a Board of Trustees composed of public figures and artists and headed by the mayor of the city. At the end of the 1970s, the works of playwright Hanoch Levin began to be produced there, under his direction. Virtually all of Levin's fifteen productions to the end of the 1980s were hits, and the Cameri quickly became the leading theatre in the country.

As the 1980s began, almost all Israeli repertory theatres found themselves in dire economic straits. A national committee was then set up which ultimately recommended that the government should support these theatres up to 65 per cent of their budgets. But this was only a recommendation and due to spiralling inflation, allocations never went higher than 50 per cent; in the mid-1980s, the figure declined to below 40 per cent.

From an artistic standpoint, three important events marked the 1980s. The first was the establishment of a Fringe Theatre Festival in Acre by the still very active Oded Kotler. The second was the establishment of the Neve Zedek Theatre Group by Kotler, Nola Chilton and a group of young actors. The third was the appointment of the director Omri Nitzan (b. 1950) as artistic director and Noam Semel (b. 1946) as managing director of the Haifa Theatre.

The Acre Fringe Festival constituted an important setting for the advancement of young talent. It very quickly became a kind of annual mass happening during which new actors, directors and playwrights could show their work. It also proved the Israeli public's interest in experimental theatre.

Since 1981, Semel and Nitzan have been managing the Haifa Theatre. They formed both a company and an ideology that were centred on Israeli and Jewish drama. In 1982, the theatre produced two Sobol plays, *A Jewish Soul* and *Ghetto*, both directed by Gedalia Besser (b. 1939). The theatre earned acclaim and *A Jewish Soul* was performed at the Edinburgh Festival in 1983, at the Berlin Festival in 1985 and at the Chicago Theatre Festival in 1986. At the same time, Semel and Nitzan established a stage for productions in Arabic and both *The Island* by Athol Fugard and *Waiting for Godot* by Beckett were performed in Arabic and Hebrew.

In 1982, Kotler and Chilton's new Neve Zedek Theatre Group began performing in a run-down building on the outskirts of Tel Aviv. With scant public assistance, and mostly with funds raised through donations, they succeeded

Gedalia Besser's 1982 Haifa Theatre production of Yehoshua Sobol's *A Jewish Soul*, designed by Adrian Vaux.

in renovating the building and began to develop a group that concentrated on experimental theatre. In 1984, when Kotler was appointed director of the Israel Festival, he handed over the theatre to the young actors who then managed it as a collective. They did not, however, succeed in attracting audiences or in achieving the hoped-for artistic gains, and the group disappeared from the theatrical scene in 1988.

In 1985, something akin to an October revolution took place in Israeli theatre. It was during that month that Ilan Ronen was appointed artistic director of the Cameri theatre, and Omri Nitzan, who had left the Haifa Theatre at the end of the 1984 season, was appointed the Habimah's artistic director. Yossi Yisraeli became the manager of the Khan, while Sobol and Besser became artistic co-directors in Haifa. This meant that the artistic directors of all the major theatres suddenly had similar artistic outlooks, similar tastes, and were all adhering to a Zionist-Jewish ideology. They all agreed on the need to support and stimulate local playwriting and to approach the Jewish world from a secular-ritualistic point of view. They were also in favour of encouraging theatrical involvement in current events and strengthening theatre's links with the community.

In contrast to the years just after 1948, when the repertoire had strong nationalistic overtones, in the mid-1980s Israeli drama began to express existential despair. There was disillusionment with the fading Zionist dream; artistically, the new plays were providing much more complex artistic answers than those offered by the documentary dramas of the mid-1970s and early 1980s.

At the Cameri, challenging new plays especially met with great success. Ronen fostered many young talents in addition to Hanoch Levin, who was now the theatre's in-house director. At the Khan, on the other hand, Yossi Yisraeli was not as successful in his attempts to create a new Jewish drama, employing mystic effects and adapting Jewish stories to the stage; after two years he left the Khan and was replaced by the director Amit Gazit (b. 1946).

Omri Nitzan adopted a similar approach at the Habimah. He abandoned the ideology that he had advocated in Haifa and instead stressed a return to modern classics, world drama of the 1960s and Israeli drama of the 1970s. His aim was to make contact with a broader audience, and he achieved this objective. He also aspired to bring international prestige to the Habimah, and brought renowned directors to the theatre such as Andrzej Wajda from Poland, Yuri Lyubimov from the USSR and Jérôme Savary from France. He also produced lavish plays with large casts.

By the end of the 1980s, Israeli theatre again faced economic hardships. Although audiences were attending the theatre in large numbers and theatrical activity was on the increase, inflation was depleting the resources allocated to theatres by the government. As a result, theatres were turning to more commercial plays that they felt would be box-office hits. In 1987, the Cameri produced the musical Les Misérables. It was an unprecedented success and gave rise to the belief that public theatre ought to be run according to commercial rather than artistic standards. The fine line between the two was not always clear. The Cameri performed Les Misérables 380 times (from August 1987 to April 1989) and earned the acclaim of the critics and the cheers of its audiences. This success enabled the company to devote considerable resources to encouraging original drama, but it also had an impact on its future thinking. Other theatres tried to emulate it, but their productions were financial flops: from 1987 until the early 1990s several incurred large deficits. In the 1991 season, after the Gulf War, many plans for the production of musicals were cancelled, while efforts were diverted to the production of 'safe' plays: classical dramas of the 1950s and 1960s, some original plays, and comedies. Clearly, a period of regression and dejection was beginning. Even this supposedly cautious approach was failing at the box office. By 1992, one was witnessing a return to the ideas of the early 1980s when it seemed that encouraging local drama made the most sense.

Structure of the National Theatre Community

The theatre is the most popular of the performing arts in Israel. At its centre are the sub-sidized, public, Hebrew repertory theatres. About 70 per cent of the audiences are for plays;

the remaining 30 per cent are for dance and music. In 1988, 17 per cent of audiences were children. On average, those who attend theatre go 1.5 times a year.

Most Israeli theatres receive some public support, which is supplemented by box-office income. Although theatres are located throughout the country, Israeli theatre by its nature is urban and has one artistic centre, Tel Aviv, where the majority of theatrical activity takes place.

In December 1990, a survey conducted by the Culture Administration of the Ministry of Education on the activities of publicly supported institutions in the country for the 1988–9 season was published. The results of the survey provide an idea of the activities of Israeli theatre not only at the end of the 1980s, but also in the early 1990s, since any changes that occurred in between were not significant.

In 1988–9, fourteen public theatres (one performing in Arabic) produced 115 plays. Two theatres performed plays for children and young people specifically and one company performed in Yiddish. The rest were all public theatres performing for the broad Hebrew-speaking public.

The two largest theatres are the Habimah National Theatre and the Tel Aviv Municipal Theatre (known as the Cameri). Each of these performs concurrently in at least three halls (the Cameri frequently performs in four or five halls at the same time). In 1988–9, the Cameri employed 214 workers, and the Habimah, 173.

There are also two medium-sized theatres – the Haifa Municipal and the Beit Lessin. The larger of the two is the Haifa Municipal Theatre, which performs concurrently in two halls and employs a staff of 114. The Tel Aviv Beit Lessin Theatre also performs in two halls and has seventy-two employees.

Three smaller theatres are the Beersheba Municipal, the Khan Theatre in Jerusalem and the Kibbutz Theatre. The largest is the Beersheba with fifty-six employees, followed by the Khan with thirty-nine employees, and the Kibbutz Theatre, which does not have its own permanent building and employs nineteen people. There is also the Yiddish Theatre, which appears in rented halls in Tel Aviv and elsewhere, with about forty employees.

The survey shows that in 1988–9, these theatres gave 3,917 performances, attended by 1.8 million spectators, from a population of about 4 million. It should be noted here that the

overall population includes large numbers of people who normally do not attend theatre at all: the very old, new immigrants who do not know Hebrew, and many who stay away from the theatre for religious reasons.

In the season covered by the survey, the theatres produced fifty-one new plays and continued to perform thirty-four from previous seasons: a total of eighteen at the Cameri, thirteen at the Habimah, thirteen at the Beit Lessin, thirteen at the Haifa, thirteen at the Beersheba, seven at the Khan, six at the Kibbutz Theatre, and two at the Yiddish Theatre.

That year, the Habimah gave 896 performances, the Cameri 857, the Haifa 620, the Beit Lessin 665, the Beersheba 433, the Kibbutz Theatre 282, the Khan 219, and the Yiddish Theatre about seventy performances.

In 1988, those theatres with their own halls gave 3,635 performances, 69 per cent in their own playhouses and about 31 per cent in other cities. The Kibbutz Theatre performed in various locations while the Yiddish Theatre obtained its own hall only in September of 1991.

As for audiences, in 1988–9, nearly 1 million

Omri Nitzan's 1992 Cameri production of Shakespeare's *Richard III*, designed by Ruth Dar.

people attended performances by the large theatres – about 555,000 at the Cameri and 445,000 at the Habimah. Audiences at medium-sized theatres reached a high of 260,000 at the Haifa Theatre and about 170,000 at Beit Lessin. Performances by the Beersheba were attended by about 165,000 people, and at the Khan and Kibbutz Theatres, about 85,000 each. About 40,000 spectators attended plays by the Yiddish Theatre.

There were three other theatres which received public support and were under public management in that year: the Children and Youth Theatre, the Bimama Theatre, and the Beit HaGefen Theatre in Haifa (an Arabic theatre which also puts on adult plays, but in the year under review performed only children's plays). These three theatres produced thirty plays that ran for 1,232 performances in schools and large halls. Only the Beit HaGefen Theatre had a hall of its own. In total, these groups reached an audience of 390,000, 20,000 of whom were Arabs.

Israeli audiences tend to purchase tickets on an organized basis with the majority (71 per cent) sold to workers' committees at work-places. These sales enable theatres to cover about 62 per cent of their budgets with the rest coming from subsidy, divided between the Ministry of Education (61 per cent) and the municipalities and General Federation of Labour (about 36 per cent). Another 3 per cent comes from private and public foundations. The overall expenditure for the year was about 60 million new Israeli shekels (about US$30 million), while income amounted to about 51 million shekels.

In addition, there are several other smaller groups not supported by state budgets, but rather by allocations from local councils, private foundations, and the like. The most prominent of these is the Simta Theatre in Jaffa, which receives a tiny subsidy from the municipality of Tel Aviv. It has been in operation since 1982 and performs in several small halls in the restored old quarter of Jaffa. Its plays all have small casts, are usually original, and are performed before very small audiences.

In Jerusalem there is also a women's group, called the Jerusalem Workshop. Another group is affiliated with the School for Visual Design, which also occasionally puts on plays in Jerusalem.

Private commercial theatres are not very active in Israel, since the public theatres provide for a range of theatrical needs. Occasionally, plays are mounted by private impresarios in other languages, mainly in Yiddish, but these are temporary and fleeting events on the theatrical scene.

In 1990, a theatre for new Soviet immigrants called Gesher (Bridge) began operation. It mounted plays in small halls, before Russian-speaking audiences, and was financed jointly by the Ministry of Education and donations.

The situation is quite different in the commercial theatres for children. Here there has been a great deal of activity since 1988, giving schools an opportunity to choose between plays produced by either public or private theatres. (This is discussed further in **Theatre for Young Audiences**.)

Two quite distinctive theatrical institutions are the Acre Theatre Group and Amir Orian's (b. 1924) Chamber Theatre. The Acre Theatre Group was founded in 1987 by several young directors and actors who came to Acre from the centre of the country. They support themselves by teaching, working as tour guides, and performing specialty plays for a limited audience, usually no more than the number that would fill a room. The Chamber Theatre operates alongside the Acting Studio run by the director and theatre critic Amir Orian. It operates on a casual basis; its plays are performed as 'rehearsals in the presence of an audience'. These productions are relatively few in number and obviously without commercial aspirations.

These last two projects can be regarded as representing Israel's fringe theatres. In fact, in order to foster fringe drama in Israel a separate venue was created, which has developed since the early 1980s into Israel's main theatre festival. This is the Acre Festival for Fringe Theatre, which is held annually, usually around mid-September.

The festival first began in the autumn of 1980, under the initiative of Oded Kotler. It is hard to say that it faithfully represents the fringe, since there is no real fringe movement in Israel. The festival is really more a happening of original theatre, produced with a negligible budget on a semi-voluntary basis by young artists, most of whom hope in this way to get a footing in the more established Israeli theatre.

Over four days, the festival attracts an audience of 200,000 to 300,000 to the old city of Acre. Only about 30,000 tickets are sold to the plays put on in halls and in the alcoves of Acre's Crusader fortress. Theatre people themselves – students, actors, teachers of theatre, actors in amateur groups – make up a large part of these audiences. Since the government budget is so minute (about 300,000 shekels) most of the work is done voluntarily or for minimal payment by a group of artists who are organized on an *ad-hoc* basis before the festival. In three years, plays by thirty-seven playwrights were performed in Acre. Of the twenty-nine directors who worked in Acre during the same period, three subsequently found work in the established theatre.

Twenty to thirty premières of new plays are held during each festival, although the total number of performances is much greater. In 1989–90 there were eighty performances, in 1991 only forty. The decline was due to a decision not to include children's shows and some outdoor events.

The plays in Acre are also performed in several different locales. The most prestigious part of the festival is the competition for which only eight to twelve plays, candidates for monetary prizes and honourable mentions, are accepted. In recent years, some of the outstanding plays have been staged by the public theatres. Since 1990, there has also been a stage for inexperienced artists, called Hamama (Greenhouse) and designed for productions of monodramas or plays with very small casts. In principle, this is a distinctly local theatre festival to which international companies have sometimes been invited.

The Israel Festival, held each spring in Jerusalem, was founded in 1968. It is an international performing arts festival with a broad representation of musical, opera and dance performances as well as plays, mostly by foreign companies. The festival is usually financed by the Ministry of Education, the Jerusalem Foundation, the municipality of Jerusalem, the Ministry of Foreign Affairs and the Ministry of Tourism. It covers more than half its expenses from its own income. Some performances are actually brought to Israel by private impresarios in conjunction with the festival. Alongside the international events, sometimes local productions of high-cost shows are mounted especially for the festival.

Since 1986, a smaller theatre festival has been held in Jaffa – a festival of original drama, produced and run by the Simta Theatre. This has a much more flexible framework than the Acre Festival. It is held in an informal atmosphere without either competition or the noisy crowds that are usually part of the other festivals. It is an ideal setting for budding playwrights, some of whom are seeing their first plays staged. Between eight and ten new productions, with small casts, are usually presented.

In Tel Aviv since 1990 a festival of monodramas has been held, called Theatronto. When it was first held, fifteen actors performing monodramas participated. The producers were the Cameri Theatre and a private production company, with the top participants awarded prizes. All of the actors were professionals, and the idea of a monodrama festival proved itself viable from a commercial standpoint since some of the plays continued to run in all parts of the country a year and more after the festival.

There are two actors' unions in Israel. The largest is EMI (Union of Israeli Artists) with 1,800 members – actors, dancers, mimes, comics, circus performers and magicians. It was founded in 1979 by a group of performing artists, not salaried employees of repertory theatres, to protect their rights. EMI is affiliated with the International Federation of Actors (FIA).

The Histadrut Union of Actors and Directors is a much older organization. Founded before the establishment of the state, it now has about 1,000 members, and acts to improve their working conditions and to promote stage, television, radio and film arts. Unlike EMI, this union also includes directors and the salaried actors of the repertory theatres who, under its aegis, sign collective agreements with the theatres that employ them. The union has also signed agreements with the Israel National Broadcasting Corporation and the Educational Television Authority.

The Israel Playwrights' Association (IPA) has been active since 1975, and now has about fifty members.

AKUM is an association of composers, lyricists and publishers founded in 1936. It has 1,200 members and has signed mutual agreements with most of its affiliate associations throughout the world. It protects copyrights deposited with it during an artist's lifetime and for seventy years after the artist's death, but does not deal with stage production rights (plays, operas, ballets or musicals).

Artistic Profile

Companies

The large companies, to which all the creative energies, young and veteran talents, and stage tradition are channelled, are mainly concentrated in Tel Aviv, in the Habimah and the Cameri. Original playwriting flourished at the Haifa Theatre from the 1970s, and the Beersheba Theatre has served mainly as a training ground for young actors who have just completed their studies. The Jerusalem Khan, for several years during the 1970s, filled the role of an experimental theatre and developed a troupe with a distinctive character.

In the early 1990s, however, there were actually no differences between these theatres, neither in their aesthetic concept, nor in their style of staging or acting, nor in their stage designs or basic theatrical norms. Fundamentally, the Israeli theatre in the 1990s was motivated by artistic tendencies dictated by the need to survive in a harsh economic reality. The theatres therefore produced a variety of original and translated drama from world classics to modern plays, striving to offer a repertoire which was balanced between box-office hits and more intellectually challenging plays and which would enable them to keep their subscribers and maintain contacts with the workers' committees who were likely to fill their halls. For this reason, there was hardly a company that could allow itself the luxury of developing a specific style, unless it operated under the sponsorship of a repertory theatre. But there are almost none that fall into that category.

Due to the concentrated structure of the Israeli theatre, any innovation introduced by one company is quickly taken up by others, and actors can move from one theatre to another without having to adapt themselves to the specific requirements of the new company.

From an historical perspective, one can say that this has always been the state of affairs. Until the mid-1940s, the Hebrew theatre was dominated by playwriting, stage design and – in acting – a theatrical norm characterized mainly by pathos, an 'elevated' mode of mimesis, and the portrayal of characters who were usually larger than life. The actors' makeup, costumes, gesticulation and lofty tone of acting, even when portraying beggars, were in keeping with this norm. The Habimah's flagship plays – David Pinski's *The Eternal Jew* (1922), directed by

Vasoviad Mechdelev (1922), Ansky's *The Dybbuk* (1922), directed by Vakhtangov (1922) and Leivick's *The Golem*, directed by Boris Waroshilov – were all presented in an elevated expressionistic mode. The leading roles in these plays were filled by actors like Hanna Rovina, Aharon Meskin (1898–1974) and Yehoshua Bertonov (1879–1971). In fact, the three halls in the Habimah building are named after them. These actors were adored by generations of theatre-lovers in Israel. Their acting style was marked by an idealization that suited the taste of their audiences, who wanted to see actors on the stage through whom they could identify with the ideals of the Zionist revival. When expressionism was no longer part of the theatre's repertoire, the actors carried on with the same norm of elevated pathos, even at the end of the 1940s when original realistic drama developed in popularity.

Against this background, one can understand the revolutionary change wrought by the Cameri Theatre in the mid-1940s. Its founder, the director Yossef Milo, had a clear central European influence, in contrast to the Russian tradition that had been dominant at the Habimah and the Ohel. Milo and Hanna Meron emigrated to Israel from Czechoslovakia and Germany, Avraham Ben-Yossef (1907–80) from Romania, and Yossef Yadin was a native-born Israeli. They conformed to the image of the new Israeli figure, the *sabra*. They shaped a new theatrical norm which from the outset tended toward a lower degree of imitation than that of the Habimah, introduced Brechtian alienation, despised pathos, and preferred everyday language, irony and topical material to the elevated style of the old guard.

Hanna Meron was the antithesis of Hanna Rovina. She proved it was possible to speak on the stage in the same language spoken in the street, to use a minimum of gestures and still to be considered a star. In *He Walked in the Fields* (1948), Moshe Shamir's realistic, topical play about the War of Independence, she appeared in the role of a young immigrant girl, wearing shorts, and received resounding applause.

Directors from Europe and the United States also made an impact on the Cameri; they chose European and American plays, made sure these were translated into Hebrew, tried to break down the barrier between the stage and the audience, and avoided portraying idealized characters and classical heroes. They wanted to be topical, to sound young, and to stick close to the spoken language. While Hanna Rovina remained the leading lady at the Habimah, at the Cameri young actresses like Hanna Meron, Orna Porat (b. 1924) and Rachel Marcus (1913–85) were the stars.

Following these developments in the Cameri, things changed at the Habimah. Young voices, free of the heavy Russian accents of the founding generation, began to be heard – actors such as Shlomo Bar-Shavit (b. 1928), Shmuel Segal (b. 1924), Shraga Friedman (1924–70), Misha Asherov (b. 1924) and Nachum Buchman (b. 1917). In parallel with the Cameri's production of *He Walked in the Fields*, the Habimah staged Mossinsohn's *In the Wastes of the Negev*, also a topical war play. The Habimah also produced American and British plays, including Arthur Miller's *Death of a Salesman* (1951) and John Osborne's *Look Back in Anger* (1959). Still, the Habimah's veteran actors continued to set the tone until the 1960s. This caused a deep crisis at the Habimah from which it managed to emerge only after adopting a new style, a style opposed to the old elevated one that had dominated Hebrew theatre from its inception.

An historical play set in biblical times, *Most Cruel The King* (1953), by the young playwright Nissim Aloni, was opposed to the predominant Zionist ideology in its content, but in its level of expression still belonged to the old style. It was only in Aloni's later plays – *The King's Clothes* and *American Princess* – that irony became part of the style. But these plays were produced in Aloni's own theatre rather than by the established companies.

The trend towards alienated and ironic European plays grew stronger in the early 1950s, especially at the tiny Zira Theatre, at the time the centre of avant-garde French drama. The Theatre of the Absurd made an impact, mainly in the 1960s, on plays by Aloni, Amos Kenan (b. 1927) and Yossef Mundi (b. 1935). On the other hand, the influence of American and British theatre was felt in the mid-1960s, with the establishment of the Actors' Stage, and in the 1970s when the Jerusalem Khan and Nola Chilton's Project Groups at the Haifa Theatre were set up. They exerted an influence in the direction of 'eye-level' expression: documentary drama whose material was taken from everyday life, a style of acting that tried to reduce emotion, to remove barriers between the stage and the audience and to employ subtle gestures. In

short, a topical theatre involved in the community and which reacted to political events.

Since that time, nothing much has changed in the Israeli theatre. Only the emphases differ. Everyone seems to agree with the fundamental assumptions, but some prefer one to another. For example, in the 1980s, the Neve Zedek group showed a marked penchant for community and political involvement. It launched joint projects with children from its neighbourhood and made several attempts to stage plays of a current political nature. The most outstanding was Hanoch Levin's *The Patriot* (1986) which caused the theatre management problems with the censor and led in the long run to the abolition of all stage censorship in Israel.

In the 1980s, the Haifa Theatre followed a similar pattern of involvement with the community through a series of social and political plays. But since this was a public theatre with season subscribers, these trends were played down in its repertoire which in addition to Sobol's plays included translated and classical drama. The Cameri Theatre also undertook special projects, such as the staging of the musical *The King and I* in one of the poorer neighbourhoods of the city.

The Itim Ensemble, under the leadership of the director Rina Yerushalmi, carried the minimalist idiom to an extreme, removing all barriers between the audience and the stage and performing poetic Shakespearian monologues with the simplicity and flow of everyday conversation. Its production of *Hamlet* was performed at several foreign festivals, and earned prizes in Israel. This ensemble operates under the aegis of the Cameri Theatre.

The Acre Theatre Group selects its material from the lives of its actors and creates productions directly involving members of the audience, going so far as to have them eating with the actors on stage and participating in the production.

Dramaturgy

In 1972, director Peter Brook visited Israel. Among other things, he said that Israeli drama will never be able to compete with the Israeli reality, which is both dramatic and theatrical, fierce and compelling. Brook was certainly correct. The vibrant and harsh Israeli reality has had a profound influence on local drama. During most of the period under discussion here, this drama drew the major part of its content from political events or local sensitivities rather than from universal topics. The impact of the Holocaust on first- and second-generation Israelis, the problems of national identity, criticism of militarism, not to mention the direct influence of Israel's wars and relations between Jews and Arabs, provide the major themes of virtually all Israeli dramaturgy. But though the content is national, the forms are essentially European and range from the realism of Ibsen to the British drama of the 1960s, from the absurd theatre of Ionesco to García Lorca's lyrical Mediterranean style.

In 1948, the State of Israel was established and the War of Independence broke out, events which gave a new impetus to local dramaturgy and led to the formation of something akin to a school of drama with its own form and content. One of the most outstanding of the playwrights of the War of Independence period was Moshe Shamir, whose play *He Walked in the Fields* ushered in a new era. A realistic melodrama, this play put on the stage for the first time the figure of the *sabra*, the young native-born Israeli. Another playwright of that period was Yigal Mossinsohn who, in his play *In the Wastes of the Negev* (1950), wrote about the defence of a besieged *kibbutz* in the south of Israel. Natan Shaham (b. 1923) wrote *They'll Arrive Tomorrow* (1950). Later critics have regarded this drama as the first Israeli absurdist play although its young author obviously had never heard of the term when he wrote it.

These three plays drew enthusiastic audiences and aroused a great deal of debate. In their wake, social drama was written during the 1950s expressing disillusionment with the materialistic society of the new Israel. Mossinsohn's *Call Me Siomka* (1950) satirized an inhumane bureaucracy and in *Throw Him to the Dogs* (1958), he castigated the moral bankruptcy of Israeli society. Aharon Megged's (b. 1920) play *Hedvah and I* (1954) lamented the fact that urban society in Israel had lost its pioneering spirit. All of these playwrights began their careers as writers of fiction, and later devoted most of their energies to writing prose.

Two renowned Israeli poets also wrote plays that were more poetic in theme and form and less based on local colour and events. Natan Alterman (1910–70) wrote a neo-romantic play called *The Inn of Spirits* (1963), a symbolic lyrical drama about the relationship between the artist and society. Leah Goldberg (1915–70) was the author of *Lady of the Manor* (1954), a drama about the clash between European culture and modern civilization in which the Israeli confronts the European, the Jew the Christian, and new values are contrasted against traditional ones.

Nissim Aloni was the first Israeli playwright to devote all of his time and energy to the theatre. Although he also wrote fiction, he focused mainly on writing and directing plays and for a short time even managed his own private theatre. His plays reveal the influence of avant-garde French drama of the 1950s. His poetic language blurs the boundaries of time and space and yet, through the use of metaphor and allegory, relates to burning issues of Israeli society ranging from militarism (*Napoleon Dead or Alive*) to problems of an antisocial regime (*Most Cruel the King*). None the less, in *The Bride and the Butterfly Hunter*, his writing is given over entirely to lyrical yearnings. Aloni wrote his finest work during the 1960s.

From the 1970s, and particularly during the 1980s, Hanoch Levin stood out as a great playwright and director. He began towards the end of the 1960s as a writer of political, anti-

The 1989 Habimah production of Hanoch Levin's *The Labour of Living*, designed by Ruth Dar.

war satires which caused a public uproar, continued in the 1970s as a writer of comic absurd plays, and in the 1980s turned to lyrical dramas that drew their material from ancient myths and contended with the basic stuff of Greek tragedy, the New Testament and the Bible. In one way, most of his more than twenty plays appear as variations on the theme of humiliation. In most, he employs the same types of characters and situations, varying them only in style or theatrical approach. Through them, he systematically delves into the degradation and pain which he sees as the essence of human existence, and which to him are the most appropriate materials for a work of art. He first drew public attention with his satirical revue *Queen of the Bathtub* (1970), then with *Hefetz* (1972) and *Jacoby and Liedental* (which won an honourable mention at the Edinburgh Festival in 1980). Later, he achieved even greater dramatic note with his *The Suffering of Job* and *The Great Whore of Babylon*.

During the 1970s, another talented young playwright, Yehoshua Sobol, began to make a name for himself. Sobol's work developed from national political dramas to poetic plays that aimed for universality, although even the latter had political and social overtones. At first he critically examined the country's failure to fulfil the Zionist dream – *Sylvester '72* (1974) and *The Night of the Twentieth* (1976) – in a realistic and frequently docu-dramatic style. In the 1980s, his style became more lyrical and symbolic (*The Last of the Workers*, 1982), although the subjects of his plays did not change. His mature style was evident in the trilogy produced by the Haifa Theatre in the 1980s – *A Jewish Soul* (1982), *Ghetto* (1984) and *Jerusalem Syndrome* (1988). In these plays, he tried to observe the problems of Jewish existence through a broad historical prism, using symbolic stage devices (some of which were designed by the director, Gedalia Besser). Many of these plays were subsequently translated into other European languages and produced both in Europe and on Broadway.

Other playwrights who came to note during the 1970s included Yaakov Shabtai (1934–81) and Avraham Buli Yehoshua (b. 1936), both of whom achieved great success as theatrical storytellers, and Ephraim Kishon (b. 1924) who became known as a writer of humoresques and as a film director, though his bourgeois comedies were his greatest hits.

Others, like Yossef Bar-Yossef (b. 1933) and Hillel Mittelpunkt became known in the 1980s. Yossef Mundi and Amos Kenan introduced French absurdist theatre to local drama.

Hannan Snir's 1985 Habimah production of Yaakov Shabtai's *The Spotted Tiger*, designed by Yael Pardes.

Mundy's most important success was his sur-realistic play *It Turns*, which examines the Zionist dream and was performed hundreds of times on stages outside the established theatres. The impact of the Holocaust on the younger generation was the theme of Ben-Zion Tomer's (b. 1928) play *Children of the Shadow*. For his part, A.B. Yehoshua employed a realistic style, incorporating allegorical elements as well as elements of the Theatre of the Absurd to explore the Jewish–Arab conflict and father–son relationships (*A Night in May, Last Treatments*). Yaakov Shabtai, who later became known for his original prose style, nostalgically scrutinized the remnants of the Zionist dream in *The Spotted Tiger* (1974). Israel Eliraz (b. 1936), still another writer of this generation, wrote allegorical lyrical plays in a style reminiscent of García Lorca (*Three Women in Yellow*, and *Far from the Sea, Far from the Summer*, 1966).

Hillel Mittelpunkt is a playwright who began writing in the 1970s in the theatre of docu-dramatic realism, but he really developed in the 1980s with his plays drawn from the milieu of the lower social classes, in one case about a youth gang (*Deep Waters*, 1977), in another about a family whose existence centres on a neighbourhood shop (*Grocery Store*, 1987). At the same time, he strove to expand the boundaries of stage expression with a rock opera called *Mammy* (1987); in his play *The Girl and Death* (1986) he introduced surrealistic elements into a plot about the effects of the Holocaust on modern Israel's first and second generations.

Among the most recent group of new playwrights, Shmuel HaSafri (b. 1954), a director-playwright, had his initial work produced at the first Acre Festival in 1980. His style is a mix of realism and fantasy, and his themes vary from father–son relationships to religious tradition versus secularism. He has written of the effects of the Holocaust and many of his plays contain political criticism. *Kiddush* (1987) was a hit which played in repertory over several years at the Cameri. HaSafri has also run his own group, the Simple Theatre.

Motty Lerner, another of the late-1980s group, was born in Zichron Yaakov and began his career writing docu-drama. His later plays, no longer in that rigid form, were produced by the Cameri: *Kastner* (1986), based on a controversial historical figure from the time of the Holocaust, and *Pangs of the Messiah* (1988) about a futuristic traumatic event – the effect of a peace treaty on a small Jewish settlement in the administered territories. Another of his plays,

Elsa (1989), was a drama for two actors about the life of the German Jewish poet, Elsa Lasker-Schiller, based on her poetry and the memories of her friends.

Others who emerged in the 1980s include the novelist Shulamit Lapid (b. 1934), with her play *Abandoned Property* (1987); Ira Dvir (b. 1953), who was discovered at the Acre Festival with *Sacrifice* (1984); Benny Barbash (b. 1951), a scriptwriter, with his play *One of our Own* (1988); and Eldad Ziv (b. 1951), another writer of absurd comedies.

Directors, Directing and Production Styles

Prominent Israeli directors fall into two categories: those who engage only in directing, and those who are author-directors and also write or adapt plays.

In the past, playwrights often harshly criticized directors for their unwillingness to devote their energies to original drama. It was against this background that the Israeli version of the *auteur* developed – the director and playwright in one. Although there were several exceptions – the most striking being the Sobol–Besser team, who jointly staged a number of outstanding plays at the Haifa Theatre during the 1980s – many Israeli playwrights have directed their own work: Nissim Aloni, Hanoch Levin, Hillel Mittelpunkt and Shmuel HaSafri among others.

In the past, there was a much clearer division between playwrights and directors. The most outstanding director of the 1940s was Prague-born Yossef Milo, founder of the Cameri and Haifa theatres. He was a devotee of Brecht and of a stylized theatre of social action. In later years, the Cameri became increasingly a theatre of directors, in contrast to the Habimah, which was essentially a collective of actors. At the Habimah in the 1940s and 1950s, most of the directors were actors, and all came from eastern Europe: Zvi Friedland (1898–1967), Baruch Tschimerinski, Avraham Baratz, Shimon Finkel (b. 1905), Yehoshua Bertonov. At the Cameri, the directors were young and came from central Europe (Milo and Gershon Plotkin), the United States (Peter Frey, Hy Caylus) or from the ranks of the military entertainment troupes (Shmuel Bunin). They chose European and American plays that suited their taste and upbringing, prepared by young translators who worked closely with them (Dan Ben-Amotz, Benyamin Tamuz,

Benyamin Galai, Yair Burla, Shlomo Tanai) or to poets (Leah Goldberg, Natan Alterman).

There was no such distinction at the Ohel. There its founder, manager and leading director for many years, Moshe HaLevy, formerly with the Habimah, held sway. When HaLevy lost control of his theatre in the 1960s, its star actor, Meir Margalit (1906–74) took control and exerted influence on its production style. The 1960s brought British and American realistic theatre to Israeli stages. The main exponent was the Acting Studio, which was later to develop into the Actors' Stage. Oded Kotler was not only a leading actor during that period but also a director who applied the principles of American Lee Strasberg's Actors' Studio to plays he directed. Yossi Yisraeli began his career as the adaptor and director of *Only Fools are Sad*, a play of Hasidic songs and tales presented in a modern style. He later continued at the Habimah, working on adaptations of Jewish and Israeli fiction, based mainly on the devices of story theatre, and imparting an up-to-date style in dress and acting (*Bridal Canopy*, *Tehila*, *A Simple Story*, all based on stories by Agnon). He further refined his neo-Jewish approach in the 1980s but it never achieved either the hoped-for artistic success or a truly enthusiastic audience reaction.

Another outstanding director of the 1970s was Michael Alfreds from Britain, who founded the Khan Theatre in Jerusalem along with a company of actors to which he introduced a new style of acting, a combination of characterization and acrobatic feats in collectively created plays. Ilan Ronen continued this method of direction when he took over management of the Khan in 1978.

The Haifa Theatre brought in a director from the United States, Nola Chilton, who promoted the principles of docu-drama. Other groups went to the development towns of Kiryat Shmone and Ein Hod, where they stayed for a year, became involved in the community, and created plays whose materials and style were based on these sources.

Playwright Nissim Aloni, together with actors, Yossi Banai (b. 1932) and Avner Hez-kiyahu, produced a style characteristic of all his plays – a blend of spoken language and lyric poetry. As director, Aloni produced vibrant plays that were rich in imagination and visually beautiful. In some of his plays, he achieved this effect with surrealistic stage settings designed by artist Yosel Begner (b. 1920). If one can say that the Habimah in the 1920s was an actors'

theatre, and the Cameri in the 1940s a directors' theatre, then Aloni was the creator of a playwrights' theatre.

In this sense, playwright Hanoch Levin resembles Aloni. He also has actors who regularly appear in his plays – Yossef Carmon, Zaharira Harifai and Albert Cohen – who are among the leading actors in present-day Israel. Levin also pays close attention to design, frequently working with Ruth Dar (b. 1941). He devises stylized, nearly choreographed gesture, a mode of speech with a special lyric quality, and incorporates music into some of his plays while creating complex counterpoints or ironic contrasts that heighten the bathos of the dramatic experience. For example, the singing of angels accompanies an execution scene (in the play *Execution*) in which an angel-faced actress defecates on the face of the condemned man.

Hillel Mittelpunkt, a playwright in the realistic vein, adheres to a naturalistic, minimalist style of performance as a director. He has worked regularly with actor-director Rami Danon and Aharon Almog. Danon tends toward a naturalistic style while Almog is more poetic.

Shmuel HaSafri, Yoram Falk and Miki Gurevitz (b. 1951) are directors who also write and adapt plays. Falk is best known for his adaptation and direction of Saay Agnon's *Shira* (1989) and Gurevitz for his direction of original burlesques (*They Were All My Sons, Except for Naomi*), and classics in a modernistic form (*Macbeth*). In the 1980s the emphasis shifted from the playwright to the director and this trend became more pronounced in the plays directed by Hannan Snir (b. 1943), Omri Nitzan and Ilan Ronen. These are versatile directors, capable of staging both chamber plays in which the stress is on the work of the actors and more spectacular shows such as Brecht's *The Caucasian Chalk Circle*. Snir is a lyrical director who is meticulous about nuances and creating an atmosphere (*The Spotted Tiger*, *Uncle Vanya*). Ronen carried on the approach he began at the Khan of promoting original playwrights, in particular Shulamit Lapid and Motty Lerner, whose first plays he directed.

The trend toward a directors' theatre was further strengthened in the 1980s through the work of Rina Yerushalmi and Dudi Mayaan. Yerushalmi set up her own group (Itim) with which she staged *Hamlet* (1989) and *Woyzeck '91* (1991) employing a specific type of movement and speech that brought these classics close to contemporary reality. Mayaan, founder

Yoram Falk's 1989 Cameri adaptation of Saay Agnon's *Shira*, designed by David Sharir.

and director of the Acre Theatre Group, created original plays with his actors, taking material from the actors' own lives and creating a visual drama with audience participation.

A few words should be said here on the unique role of actors in Israeli society. During the 1930s and 1940s, actors on the Hebrew stage were the heroes of their generation. Larger than life, the objects of adoration, they all spoke with east European accents and employed a lofty tragic style. With the passage of time, their style of acting grew closer to the everyday, minimalist and subtle; at the same time, they became much more human personalities.

Aharon Meskin, Hanna Rovina, Yehoshua Bertonov, Shimon Finkel, members of Israel's founding generation, were all astonishing in the intensity of feeling they projected. When Rovina first appeared in the role of a whore on the Habimah stage in the 1930s, the audience was genuinely shocked.

Meir Margalit, the leading actor of the Ohel Workers' Theatre, was the exception who ushered in a new style of acting. All his life he portrayed anti-heroes and is especially remembered for his role as Schweyk in *The Good*

Soldier Schweyk in which he appeared until he was very old. Margalit was the antithesis of Meskin, Bertonov and Finkel, just as his co-actors on the Ohel stage, Zev Berban (1900–47), Simcha Zechovak (1901–55), Jacob Canaani (b. 1949) and Leah Deganit (1907–86) were the less glamorous counterparts of the great Habimah stars.

At the end of the 1940s and in the early 1950s, members of a younger generation made their first appearance on the Israeli stage. These were mostly native-born actors, speaking in a local accent, employing an understated, realistic style of acting. Yossef Yadin was born in Israel, while Avraham Ben-Yossef, Natan Cogan (b. 1914) and Rachel Marcus were born in central and western Europe. The German-born Hanna Meron now became a star, competing with Hanna Rovina. Orna Porat, who also came to Israel from Germany, gave stunning performances in *Jeanne d'Arc* and *Pygmalion*. All of these actors portrayed flesh and blood characters, and demonstrated an alternative to the archaic, flowery language of the Habimah.

They were followed by a still younger group of actors trained at the Habimah's acting studio and in the first military troupes. Shlomo Bar-Shavit, Misha Asherov, Shraga Friedman, Ada Tal (b. 1922) and Shmuel Segal, who became leading actors after the 1950s, all got their experience as members of entertainment troupes of the British or the Israeli armies. Shaike Ophir (1928–87), an actor who became Israel's first mime and later one of its best known comic actors, also came from the ranks of the army troupes.

The big turnabout at the Habimah took place in the 1960s when Martha's curses in Albee's *Who's Afraid of Virginia Woolf?* were first heard on its stage. Miriam Zohar (b. 1928), in the leading role, was the complete antithesis of Hanna Rovina, still queen of the Habimah stage. During that period, Lea Koenig, who began her career in the Yiddish Theatre, became a famous actress on the Hebrew stage. She and Zohar were recipients of the Israel Prize for Theatre in 1987.

In the 1960s, Gila Almagor (b. 1939) began to achieve fame not only as a versatile actress with an impressive stage presence, but also as a star in the Israeli film industry, which was then in the early stages of its development. She reached the peak of her career in the 1980s when she revealed her creative abilities as a writer and actress for stage and cinema in the monodrama and film based on her autobiographical book, *The Summer of Aviah*.

Shaike Ophir and Yossi Banai also directed the threesome known as the Pale Tracker, an entertainment troupe founded in 1965, which was still performing in the 1990s. Its actors – Gavri Banai (b. 1940), Shaike Levy (b. 1939) and Israel Poliakoff (b. 1940) – were trained by Naomi Polani (b. 1927), who established the singing troupe HaTarnegolim (Chickens). They created a style of acting and speech that endeared them to Sephardic audiences, although in the content of their sketches there is no special emphasis on ethnic differences.

The military troupes in the late 1950s and early 1960s produced a cadre of new actors that began to find employment in the commercial theatre and later moved to the repertory theatres. Two of the most outstanding of these young actors were Uri Zohar and Haim Topol. Zohar was a comic and an outstanding film director. Topol began in the established theatre, where he became a star in the Haifa Theatre's production of *The Caucasian Chalk Circle*, and then moved to Giora Godik's musical theatre. After his role as Tevya in *Fiddler on the Roof*, he worked in the British theatre and became internationally known in both film and theatre.

In the 1960s, the Actors' Stage, which stressed

Miriam Zohar, Shmuel Rudensky and Moscy Alkalay in Amit Gazit's 1987 Habimah production of Yalov Gordin's *Mirale Efrat*, designed by Eli Sinai.

an understated style of acting, was established. Its dominant member was Amnon Meskin, the antithesis of his father, Aharon, the veteran Habimah actor.

In the mid-1970s, naturalistic acting reached its peak. During those years, television drama was also developing in Israel. Conditions were then ripe for a further step in the direction of a style of acting nearly free of all emotion, but precise and rich in detail.

At the same time, other actors launching their careers in the 1980s followed a track leading from the acting school to the establishment theatres. Graduates of the Beit Zvi school or Nisan Nativ's studio often reached the main companies through the Beersheba Theatre. At the Haifa Theatre in the 1980s, Arab actors were also launching promising careers as Hebrew-language actors – Yossef Abu Varda (b. 1953), Mahram Khoury (b. 1946), recipient of the Israel Prize in Acting in 1987, and Mohammed Bakri (b. 1953), star of the film *Behind the Bars*.

Music Theatre
Dance Theatre

The Habimah Theatre was created as an attempt at 'total' theatre. *The Dybbuk*, first produced in January 1922, was realized through the cooperative work of a director (Vakhtangov), a composer (Joel Engel), a designer (Nathan Altman), a playwright (Solomon Ansky) and a translator (H.N. Bialik). Its music, dance, and stage design were all integral parts of the play, which was later introduced into the repertoire of world drama.

In the years that followed, very few attempts were made to repeat this combination. One of the few occurred in 1925 when the Hebrew Theatre of Eretz Israel produced *Belshazzar* as a combination of drama, music, stylized movement and dance. The première of this play, based on the work of the French dramatist, Henri Roche, was held in Berlin under the direction of Menachem Gnessin. A third interdisciplinary production, the biblical drama *Jacob and Rachel*, was produced by the Ohel Workers' Theatre in 1926. The designs in this instance were in a constructivist style, while the choreography was based on Bedouin dances.

In the Inbal Dance Theatre, founded in 1949 by choreographer and composer Sara Levi Tanai, and managed by her until 1991, a stage technique was created akin to earlier experiments – a combination of dance, song and speech. Israeli audiences identified this company for many years with Yemenite folklore. But although the company was active in its attempt to preserve this folklore, it also utilized it to create independent works of art.

In the 1960s musical theatre flourished, mainly on Israel's commercial stage in Giora Godik's theatre. Godik began by importing musicals translated into Hebrew, which were great successes (*My Fair Lady*, *The King and I*, *Fiddler on the Roof*), and later mounted a number of original musicals, including *Cazablan* (1967), based on a Yigal Mossinsohn drama, with Dov Zeltzer's music and Haim Hefer's lyrics. The American influence on this musical was obvious; it clearly echoed *West Side Story*. As a result of its success, musical plays became a separate branch of the Israeli theatre, and it was followed by *Eldorado* (again based on a text by Mossinsohn, with music by Yohanan Zarai); *I Like Mike*; *Five, Five* and others. With the demise of Godik's theatre in the early 1970s, however, original musicals also disappeared from the theatrical scene due to the high cost of production. In 1968, a new musical was mounted that departed from the Broadway model – *Only Fools Are Sad*, with Hasidic tales and melodies, performed by actors in jeans and strumming on guitars.

Hanoch Levin's *The Execution*, a play in song, first staged by the Cameri in November 1979 and directed by the author, attempted to use musical forms. Music was by Poldy Schatzman and designs by Ruth Dar, the cast of fourteen was accompanied by a chorus of five singers and a six-person orchestra. For the most part, actors sang their lines opera-style while the play was staged as an execution ceremony. Audiences sat around the edges of the stage on which victims were abused and slaughtered.

Hillel Mittelpunkt's *Mammy* (music by Ehud Banai and Yossi Mar-Haim) was performed in the hall of the Tzavta Centre for Progressive

Culture in 1987 as a 'rock opera'. Directed by the playwright, the play is about an Israeli girl from a development town who comes to the big city, where she is raped by Palestinian Arabs. The emphasis is on the deprived conditions of all the lower social classes, both Arabs and Jews. Innovative in form, *Mammy* was also clearly provocative in its political message. Its ultimate success, however, may well have been because the Israeli public enjoyed the combination of music and drama.

Still another drama of this kind was produced in 1989, *Picnic in Husamba*, a drama in song written by Haim Nagid (b. 1940) with computerized music by Uri Vidislevsky. Micky Ben

Canaan's setting was a housing development next to a municipal dump. The play was directed by Jack Messinger, an immigrant to Israel from Canada.

Stage works combining dance and theatre are even fewer in number. The Tmuna Theatre, founded in 1986 under the artistic direction of the choreographer Naava Zuckerman, is trying to move in this direction. While Zuckerman's first creations placed a greater emphasis on dance, some of the later ones showed a tendency towards theatre. The same trend is evident in the most recent work of the choreographer Mosha Ephrati, *A Mixed Technique on Stage – A Work for an Actor and Dancers* (1991).

Theatre for Young Audiences

Until the mid-1960s, plays for children were produced by private companies as well as by the more permanent subsidized groups. The most prominent of the private groups was the Bimatenu (Our Stage) Theatre, founded and managed by the director Eliezer A. Anski (1903–90). Active between 1948 and 1958, the company worked in conjunction with the Ohel Theatre, some of whose actors appeared in its plays. Its major productions included *Hasamba*, *Aladdin and the Magic Lamp* and *The Prince and the Pauper* in an adaptation by a youthful Oded Kotler, who also played a leading role. In 1960, Anski moved the theatre to Jerusalem, this time with young people from the poorer neighbourhoods. The group remained a socially cohesive one but did not last very long.

In 1965, the Cameri established a children's company under the management of one of its leading actresses, Orna Porat. This was the first formal attempt in Israel to establish a theatre that would regularly and professionally produce plays for children with adult actors. Its first effect was to eliminate the numerous inferior plays being done by young actors which were regularly staged during school holidays. Another important result was the fact that this theatre afforded Porat the opportunity to gain the experience that enabled her to establish the Children and Youth Theatre in 1971, with financial support from the Ministry of Education. It was the country's first public repertory theatre exclusively for children and it existed until 1990. In that year, it met with financial

difficulties from which it never recovered and in 1991, burdened with a heavy fiscal deficit, it discontinued activities.

Until that time, the Children and Youth Theatre was also the most mobile theatre in Israel. In 1988, it gave 1,000 theatrical performances and another 1,200 performances for individual groups of more than 600,000 school children throughout the country. Of this number, 4,000 were subscribers in Tel Aviv. Its subscription programme also enabled children to attend theatre performances after school hours. All of this was accomplished on an annual budget of about 2 million shekels (about US$1 million), one-third of which came from the Ministry of Education. Though its centre was in Tel Aviv, it had no building of its own, despite efforts made through the years to obtain a permanent home for the company. It also did not have a regular troupe of actors but used different actors each year. None the less, from its inception one of its major aims was to reach all the students in the country. Many young Israeli actors launched their careers from its stage.

Between 1982 and 1988, when the theatre's artistic director was Pnina Gery, about fifty new plays were produced, forty of which were original works. The plays included in the theatre's varied repertoire ranged from Shakespearean classics to documentary drama. One of the outstanding writers was the young playwright-director Hagit Rakavi.

Until 1986, the Children and Youth Theatre was the only group of its kind recognized by the

Ministry of Education as an official public theatre. As such, it performed in schools without having to meet artistic or educational criteria. In that year, its status was changed and it was obliged from then on to satisfy a new artistic-educational committee which was supervising artistic groups that wanted to be active in the school system. This change in its status caused the company hardships, since it suddenly had to compete with many private bodies, some organized by students, others set up by private impresarios. Among the best known of the private groups have been Teddy Productions, Hany Productions, Theatres for Children and Youth and, in particular, the Bimama Theatre. Bimama commenced operation in 1975 as a private theatre established by the Habimah actor Misha Asherov and his actress wife, Bilha Mass. In 1987 it became a public theatre, subsidized by the Ministry of Education.

Puppet Theatre

There are two centres for puppet theatre in Israel – Tel Aviv and Jerusalem. In Tel Aviv, the activity is more intensive and the approach more traditional. In Jerusalem, the approach is more innovative, aspiring to break the conventional definitions of the genre.

The tradition of puppet theatre in Israel goes back to the 1930s. In the early 1990s, there are about twenty puppeteers, most working in small venues, including kindergartens and schools. There is no tradition in Israel of puppet shows for adults.

The originators of puppet theatre in Israel were Paul Levy (1890–1987), and Honzo, the pseudonym of David Ben-Shalom (1911–90). Honzo was born in Czechoslovakia and emigrated to Israel in 1934. Two years later he established on his *kibbutz*, Givat Brenner, the first puppet theatre in Israel, the Bubatron (Grandma's Place). Its star puppet, Ziva, with her fresh, naïve appearance and her Israeli style of dress, reflected the Zionist-pioneering ideals of the period. Honzo moved his puppets with strings, although in the early 1980s he also introduced rod-puppets.

Paul Levy, born in Germany, came to Israel in the late 1930s and founded a puppet theatre in Tel Aviv in which Yossef Milo worked as an operator and writer of texts before establishing the Cameri Theatre.

Eric Smith (born in South Africa in 1939) emigrated to Israel in 1969 and after two years established a puppet theatre in Tel Aviv. His aim was to preserve the traditions of classical puppet theatre. Smith, an architect and set designer who had gained experience in the Little Angel Theatre in London, designed an extensive gallery of puppets for his Tel Aviv theatre. His collaborator from the start, as well as the theatre's permanent director, was the actor Yossi Graber (b. 1933). In the early 1980s the theatre merged with a private production company and soon began receiving support from the municipality as well as establishing its own premises. In 1992, the Eric Smith Company was still giving about sixteen performances a month in large halls (most sold out in advance) before a total audience of some 160,000 children a year.

The Ganei Yehoshua Puppet Theatre was founded in 1986 by the Ganei Yehoshua Company, a municipal group that runs the Yarkon Park in Tel Aviv. This group performs for a wide range of young people, holds meetings, and offers creative workshops for teachers and children. About 130,000 people attend its performances each year.

In Jerusalem, audiences are generally much smaller, with activity centred around the Karon Theatre, a group of independent artists, established in 1977. The theatre receives municipal assistance, performs for children in an old railway car, and before adults in a framework called HaBamah. Its manager is the designer Hadas Ophrat.

Connected to the Karon Theatre is an International Puppet Theatre Festival. First held in 1980, this festival takes place in Jerusalem every two years during August under the management of the Karon. It usually hosts local companies and groups from abroad. The festival has become one of Israel's major avant-garde events, with its participants attuned to new trends in both theatre and puppetry. At times, it is doubtful whether the name puppet theatre correctly describes this festival. In general the work tends towards the abstract, boasting an innovative vocabulary and syntax. Generally breaking down barriers between media, its varied performances create *tableaux vivants*, cross cultural and linguistic boundaries and speak in a universal, visual language.

Festival shows often look like moving sculptures, with animal figures fashioned from plexiglass and glass, or with a combination of dance theatre and plastic art that merges through a series of dreamlike images. Some shows are based on classical or modern stories, while others are stagings of psychological and realistic dramas using expressionless puppets which by their very nature deny any realistic characterization and lean toward social abstraction. Among the young Israeli artists who have brought such work to the festival, some of the more outstanding are Rafi Goldwasser, who creates a theatre of objects; Ilan Savir, who operates puppets while also telling a story; Marit Ben-Israel, Eliana Ashbal, and Hadas Ophrat himself, whose best known play is *Icarus*, an adaptation of Gabriel García Marquez's story, *A Very Old Man With Huge Wings*.

Design
Theatre Space and Architecture

The Habimah National Theatre building is in the centre of Tel Aviv, and is one side of a triangle which forms the city's cultural centre. On the other two sides are the Mann Auditorium, the largest in Tel Aviv, and the Helena Rubenstein wing of the Tel Aviv Museum. In 1935, four years after the Habimah made its home in Tel Aviv, the cornerstone of its building was laid. The theatre was designed in a Bauhaus style by the architect Oscar Kaufman – a large building with six large stone columns in the classic Greek style at its entrance. Its twin, the Schiller Theatre, stands in Berlin. The construction of the theatre progressed very slowly and it was not completed until 1945.

The theatre has three halls. The main space

The Habimah National Theatre of Israel.

seats 980, while the second seats 400. The Bimartef is a flexible space in the basement and seats 200.

The Cameri Theatre's building is located on fashionable Dizengoff Street in the commercial and entertainment centre of Tel Aviv. The hall, inaugurated in 1961, seats 950 and was designed as a proscenium stage with all of the technological innovations then available. As part of the preparations for the production of *Les Misérables* in 1988, modern amplification and remote control systems were added to the hall. In 1990, the hall and lobby were remodelled.

In 1961, the new building of the Haifa Theatre was also completed, at that time the best equipped and most modern theatre in the country. The main hall seats 854 and it has two other spaces, one seating 300 and the other 170.

In Jerusalem, two theatrical centres were created in the early 1970s – the Khan and the Jerusalem Theatres. The Jerusalem, opened in 1971, is a vast, sumptuous building that also contains three halls and boasts the most up-to-date electronic equipment. The largest hall seats just over 1,000; the other two halls seat 400 and 600, respectively.

The Khan Theatre, opened in 1972, operates in one of the most exotic sites in the city: a very old building that served as a caravan stop in the nineteenth century. The hall has been remodelled, although some columns remain and somewhat block the audience's line of vision, and the entrance to it is through an inner courtyard.

Training

In 1946, Zvi Friedland, the Habimah's in-house director, set up an acting studio for the younger members of the company and it was here that the future mainstays of the group learned their trade. Shraga Friedman, Misha Asherov, Shmuel Segal and Shlomo Bar-Shavit, among others, studied acting there, both theoretical and practical. One of the studio's major teachers was Fanny Luvitch (1902–90), an excellent actress and one of the Habimah's veterans. Unfortunately, the studio existed for only two years, with the War of Independence dispersing all its students. It was re-established in 1956, but lasted less than a year.

A studio was also set up at the Cameri in 1950. Its director was Yemima Milo, one of the theatre's founders. Its teachers were Cameri actors along with visiting teachers such as Peter Dogwood from the United Kingdom, and Sara Shakow from the United States who taught Lee Strasberg's method. This school, too, closed down but not before it had trained many of the Cameri's young cadre: Ili Gorlitzki (b. 1935), Zaharira Harifai and Edna Fliedel (1931–93), among others.

In 1970, under the initiative of the Ministry of Education, a new drama school was opened in Ramat Gan – Beit Zvi, headed by the influential critic Haim Gamzu (1909–82). During his youth, Gamzu had studied in French universities and the connection with France grew. The school's next director was Avraham Asao, a pupil of Friedland's, who had studied in England at the Royal Academy of Dramatic Arts. Beit Zvi was actually the first acting school in the country independent of any established theatre. It patterned its programme of studies on a naturalistic, essentially Stanislavskian base. In the early 1970s, the director David Bergman, who had also studied in France, was appointed director. Once again a French influence was felt in the school, but this was counterbalanced by the appointment in the 1980s of Gershon Bilu, one of the founders of the Beersheba Theatre. Beit Zvi today has a three-year programme of studies, the last year of which emphasizes practical work. There is especially close cooperation with the Beersheba Theatre.

Another acting school is the Nisan Nativ Acting School, opened in 1963, founded by Nisan Nativ, another student of Friedland's, who studied in France with Étienne Decroux. The school receives support from the Ministry of Education and the municipality of Tel Aviv. It stresses practical work and stage technique. The students have to earn their own living during the first two years, but in the third year they are subsidized to work on plays, the most successful of which are often produced on a private basis.

The Theatre Department of Tel Aviv University's Faculty of Arts was established in 1958. It trains students in all aspects of drama, from acting to design and directing, but with a heavy emphasis on theoretical aspects.

There are also schools of acting and theatre in the Levinsky Teachers' Seminary in Tel Aviv and in the Oranim Seminary and Tel-Hai College, the latter affiliated with Haifa University.

Criticism, Scholarship and Publishing

Theatrical criticism in Israel generally does not affect the fate of theatrical productions on a day-to-day basis. A dozen or so critics organized in a national critics' section (as part of the National Association of Journalists) influence mainly those purchasing performances on behalf of companies and many of these people often do not distinguish between preview articles, publicity profiles and reviews written by critics the morning after an opening night. As for the critics themselves, most have been writing for the same publications for ten or twenty years, and it seems that only death can come between theatre critics and their jobs in Israel.

The world of Israeli theatre also has very little in the way of large research projects. This dearth of scholarship is particularly marked in the area of recent theatrical production and playwriting.

Mendel Kohansky (d. 1982), a longtime critic for the *Jerusalem Post*, wrote a useful general book on the first fifty years of the Israeli theatre. There are also a number of memoirs of actors, such as the book written by veteran actor and director Shimon Finkel. Several monographs have also been written on Israel's most famous actors (one on Hanna Rovina, by Finkel; another on Aharon Meskin). A monograph was also published on the Habimah as part of a doctoral thesis, and several books interpreting and analysing Israeli plays have been published, as well as research studies on world drama, particularly on works by Shakespeare, psychodrama, and so on. However, theatrical research is one of the least-developed fields in the country.

One independent publisher, Oram, specializes in the publication of play texts of both Israeli and translated drama, and occasionally also of theoretical texts. This is done without any public support and without any likelihood of earning sizeable profits. The Beit Zvi School of Theatre publishes mimeographed texts.

The Schocken Publishing House also publishes play texts. It has commissioned the retranslation of a number of Greek classics by scholar and poet Aharon Shabtai, who has translated some twenty Greek tragedies into Hebrew. The Kibbutz HaMeuhad Publishing House specializes in the publication of new translations of Shakespeare, usually with an introduction by theatre scholar Avraham Oz. Samuel Beckett has been translated and interpreted, mainly by Helit Yeshurun and Shimon Levi, who also specializes in the translation of German drama, particularly modern plays.

The *Bamah* journal, founded by the late critic Israel Gur, is the only theatre periodical in Israel. It is published quarterly and contains general articles on theatre, excerpts from plays and reviews.

Haim Nagid
Translated by Haya Naor

Further Reading

Abramson, Glenda. *Modern Hebrew Drama.* London: Weidenfeld & Nicolson, 1979. 232 pp.

Bernstein-Cohen, Miriam. *Ke-tipah ba-yam.* [A drop in the sea]. Ramat Gan, 1971. 253 pp.

Ephrat, Gideon. *Israeli Drama.* Tel Aviv, 1975. 328 pp.

Feingold, Ben-Ami. *The Holocaust in Hebrew Drama.* Tel Aviv, 1990. 143 pp.

Finkel, Simon. *Stage and Wings.* Jerusalem: Israel University Press, 1969. 306 pp.

Friedman, Maurice, ed. *Martin Buber and the Theatre.* New York: Funk & Wagnalls, 1969. 170 pp.

Kohansky, Mendel. *The Hebrew Theatre: Its First Fifty Years.* New York: Ktav Publishing House, 1969. 306 pp.

Levi, Emmanuel. *The Habimah, Israel's National Theatre 1917–1977: A Study of Cultural Nationalism.* New York: Columbia, 1981. 346 pp.

Ohed, Michael. *Raphael Klatzkin.* Tel Aviv, 1989. 263 pp.

Orian, Dan. *From Test to Play.* Tel Aviv, 1988. 171 pp.

Richetti, Giorgio, and Giorgio Romano. *Teatro en Israele.* [Theatre in Israel]. Bologna: Cappelli, 1960. 131 pp.

Rosenfeld, Lulla. *Bright Star of Exile: Jacob Adler and the Yiddish Theatre.* New York: Crowell, 1977. 368 pp.

Shako, Zara. *The Theatre in Israel.* New York: Herzl Press, 1963. 143 pp.

Shoham, Haim. *Challenge and Reality in Israeli Drama.* Ramat Gan, 1975. 247 pp.

——. *Theatre and Drama in Search of an Audience.* Tel Aviv, 1989. 159 pp.

Zusman, Ezra. *After the Première.* Tel Aviv, 1981. 336 pp.

ITALY

Divided into numerous independent states until the nineteenth century, Italy unified itself into a single political entity in 1861 and since 1946 has been a democratic republic. In 1991, its population was 57.5 million living in a territory of some 301,200 square kilometres (116,300 square miles).

Though Tuscan is the language that most characterizes the nation, thanks to writers and poets such as Dante Alighieri (1265–1321), up until the first half of the twentieth century the majority of the people spoke various dialects, such as Piedmontese, Lombard, Venetian, Emilian, Roman, Neapolitan and Sicilian, while Sardinian and Friulian are two other languages spoken. Only since the development of television in 1955 has the knowledge and use of a standard Italian language been diffused throughout the population. This may partially explain why, with the exception of Neapolitan, productions of theatre in dialect have decreased significantly. Nevertheless, local and regional traditions on the cultural, artistic and theatrical level are diverse and lively in many cities from Rome to much smaller urban centres. There are even 300,000 people who speak German (in the province of Bolzano) with their own German-language theatre and some valleys where about 40,000 people speak Ladino. Along the north-eastern border there are some 50,000 Slovenes with their own theatre groups, while in Istria, divided between Slovenia and Croatia, there are theatre groups playing in Italian.

The vast majority of the population is Catholic, though only about one-third actively practise the religion.

The history of theatre in the Italian language and its dialects includes musical and dramatic creations of the *Laudi* in the late Middle Ages and successive works in the sixteenth century

– among them, plays by Machiavelli (1469–1527). It includes written texts as well as those orally transmitted in dialect, from Goldoni's (1707–93) eighteenth-century 'Venetian' to Eduardo de Filippo's (1900–84) twentieth-century 'Neapolitan'.

Since World War II, theatre has not played as major a role in Italian cultural life as it did in the society of the time preceding World War I. There are several reasons for this. Since the 1940s, audiences have been attracted by cinema and later by television. Also, the theatre clientele has changed. At the beginning of the 1940s, most Italian theatre was privately sponsored. But after the war, in several cities, starting with Milan, there grew up a network of theatres subsidized by state, regional or municipal governments. Touring companies were also significantly reduced during this time.

In the immediate post-war period, Italian theatre was revived by a new generation of directors who staged significant texts from the contemporary European theatre as well as classical texts in original ways. The two masters who emerged were Luchino Visconti (1906–76) who, while establishing himself in the neo-realist cinema, was also staging plays from Shakespeare to Beaumarchais in which he clearly asserted the director as creator and not simply as interpreter. Visconti brought to the stage works by Cocteau and Sartre, merging psychological investigation of character with a *mise-en-scène* rich in movement, meticulous care in the reconstruction of ambience and costume which he wanted to be as close as possible to reality. Later on, he turned his attention in similar ways to Chekhov and Miller.

The other master was Giorgio Strehler (b. 1921), who in 1947 founded the Piccolo Teatro in Milan with Paolo Grassi (1919–91). This unique public theatre would constitute a model for Italian theatres for many years to come. Among his many contributions were a re-examination of *commedia dell'arte*, and an unveiling to Italian audiences of German expressionism going back to Büchner and reaching moments of dramatic intensity with Brecht. His realistic revivals of Goldoni, with their elements of extreme fantasy, were especially popular.

Those were years as well in which theatre experienced a revival linked to social change and ideological and moral themes. It seemed to become imperative, in fact, for Italian writers to deal only with contemporary issues. Writers such as Leopoldo Trieste (b. 1917) in plays such as *La frontiera* (*The Border*, 1945), *N.N.* (1947) and *Cronaca* (1948), Gian Paolo Callegari (1912–82) in *Cristo ha ucciso* (*Christ Killed*, 1948) and Enrico Bassano (b. 1899) in *Uno cantava per tutti* (*One Song for Everyone*, 1969), all wrote about the experience of war. One can list here as well the early works by Luigi Squarzina (b. 1922), who displayed the misery of the Roman poor, constantly exposed to the abuses of the authorities in such plays as *Esposizione universale* (*Universal Exposition*, 1947).

Another dramatist truly affecting the development of Italian theatre with significant works was Ugo Betti (1892–1953) who expressed the malaise of Italian society in plays which invited audiences to reconsider human responsibility in the light of their traumatic and painful experiences. Between 1946 and 1949, three of his works were staged – *Il vento notturno* (*The Wind in the Night*, 1946), *Ispezione* (*Inspection*, 1947) and *Corruzione al palazzo di giustizia* (*Corruption in the Palace of Justice*, 1949). The latter play obtained large audiences, a very strong and positive critical response and many revivals.

Diego Fabbri (1911–89) developed theses of an openly Catholic nature in *Inquisizione* (*Inquisition*, 1950) and *Processo a Gesù* (*The Trial of Christ*, 1950), and moreover penetrated the subtle evolution of changing morality with *Il seduttore* (*The Seducer*, 1951) and *La bugiarda* (*The Deceitful Woman*, 1956). Silvio Giovaninetti (1901–62) closely examined the psychological implications of individual actions in works like *L'abisso* (*The Abyss*, 1948) and *Sangue Verde* (*Green Blood*, 1953), where one perceived echoes of the metaphysical allegories of J.B. Priestley. The long career of Carlo Terron (b. 1910) may be associated with the trend of problematical theatre through such

works as *Giuditta* (*Judith*, 1950), *Processo agli innocenti* (*Trial of the Innocent*, 1950) and *Lavinia tra i dannati* (*Lavinia Among the Damned*, 1959).

The works of Giovanni Testori (b. 1923) are also very Catholic in nature. They are characterized above all by the distinctive function of language and draw elements from the Lombard setting to sketch out individual actions, particularly in *L'Arialda* (*Arialda*, 1960) and *Erodiade* (*Eriodade*, 1980). The Sicilian dramatist Beniamino Joppolo (1908–65) criticized the condition of people, particularly in southern Italy, who are compelled to submit to an external force. This is evident in *I carabinieri* (*The Military Police*, 1949).

Between 1948 and 1963, severe censorship forbade the production of plays in which societal ills were represented. This was a period in which a large section of the population experienced dismal social conditions which many tried to hide with bourgeois respectability. The most sensational censorship case was Vitaliano Brancati's (1907–54) *La governante* (*The Governess*, 1952), which sharply denounced social hypocrisy. Censorship was a major issue for many authors during this period.

Franco Parenti (1921–89) is another author

Paolo Stoppa in Giovanni Testori's *Arialda*. Photo: Bosio.

of this period who threw an indiscreet gaze at reality, in his *Il dito nell'occhio* (*Finger in the Eye*, 1953), written and performed with Giustino Durano (b. 1923) and Dario Fo (b. 1925). Fo would later renounce traditional playhouses in an attempt to rediscover older theatrical forms. Using busy spaces in urban centres, he staged a series of theatrical events starting in the late 1950s, receiving his greatest popularity with *Mistero buffo* (1969), an absurdist remake of the Medieval Mystery play. His productions with Franca Rame (b. 1929) follow the unfolding of various political events in Italian life: *Morte accidentale di un anarchico* (*Accidental Death of an Anarchist*, 1960), *Settimo, ruba un po' meno* (*Seventh: Thou Shalt Steal a Bit Less*, 1964) and *Clacson, trombette e pernacchi* (*Trumpets and Raspberries*, 1978). Other authors in this period looked to history as a way to comment on the present. Federico Zardi (1912–71) proposed in his *I giacobini* (*The Jacobins*, 1957) a critical re-examination of the French Revolution. This work followed *I tromboni* (*The Trombones*, 1956) in which he attacked those who misuse power even in artistic and professional fields.

In Luigi Squarzina's *Tre quarti di luna* (*Three Quarters of the Moon*, 1953) he severely critiques idealism and the impact it had on young people during the fascist regime. In *Romagnola* (*Romagnese*, 1959) a fresco of the people in those years comes to life. During its run, the play was attacked by members of extreme right groups. Squarzina later collaborated on several historical plays with Vico Faggi (b. 1922) – *Il processo di Savona* (*The Trial of Savona*, 1965), *Cinque giorni al porto* (*Five Days at the Port*, 1969) and *Rosa Luxembourg* (1976).

Corrado Alvaro (1895–1956) wrote *Lunga notte di Medea* (*The Long Night of Medea*, 1949) in the post-war period. Other writers have left their mark on dramaturgy, albeit with varying degrees of success. Ennio Flaiano (1910–72), endowed with a refined sense of humour, wrote *La guerra spiegata ai popoli* (*The War Explained to the Masses*, 1946) and *Un marziano a Roma* (*A Martian in Rome*, 1960). Leonardo Sciascia (1921–89) gleaned his theatrical works from his prose, as with *Il giorno della civetta* (*The Day of the Owl*). Other novels were adapted for the stage by Giacomo Rizzotto with *I mafiosi* (*The Mafiosi*, 1960), by Ghigo De Chiaro (b. 1921), the author of the influential *Antonello capo brigante* (*Antonello, Prince of Thieves*), in addition to a work based

on the life of the actress Eleonora Duse (1859–1924), *Eleonora ultima notte a Pittsburgh* (*Eleonora's Last Night in Pittsburgh*, 1991). Giuseppe Fava (1925–84) devoted one play, *Ultima violenza* (*Ultimate Violence*), to the theme of the mafia in 1983. He was killed the following year by the mafiosi he had denounced.

The 1960s witnessed the appearance of new themes as well as new complacency by the bourgeoisie which had consolidated its position within Italian society. The decade's economic boom and consumerism led to a theatre of pure entertainment. The extension of compulsory schooling led to more public interest; better incomes allowed the possibility of spending greater sums for leisure. Contrary to expectation, theatre was not hurt by the competition of television (indeed, it was cinema that was most affected).

In 1964, censorship was abolished for adults though shows still had to be submitted to ministerial commissions for approval if admitting people under 18 years of age. Magistrates therefore still had the right to bring to court 'obscene' shows and eventually forbid their staging.

As the 1960s went on, musicals were particularly popular, some of them restagings of successful New York and London shows. Other musicals were original, however. Among these, the best were those written by Pietro Garinei (b. 1919) and Sandro Giovannini (1915–77) – *Rugantino* (1962), *Ciao Rudy* (*Bye Bye Rudy*, 1966) and *Alleluia, brava gente* (*Hallelujah, Good People*, 1970), all staged at the Sistina Theatre in Rome.

It was his performance in the title role of Camus's *Caligula* in October 1958 that brought the young Carmelo Bene (b. 1937) to public notice. In *Lo strano caso del dr Jekyll e del sig. Hyde* (*The Strange Case of Dr Jekyll and Mr Hyde*, 1961), Bene expressed the issue of split personality in modern times in Artaudian terms. In his interpretation of *Pinocchio* (1962) he subverted Carlo Collodi's (1826–90) story and imposed his own vision. A new type of personalized theatre was born with a clear separation between the dramatist's vision and that of the actor or director. Thus one gets not Shakespeare's *Hamlet* but rather Bene's. Outstanding productions in this style were *Salomé* (1963) and *Faust o Margherita* (*Faust or Margherita*), written in collaboration with Franco Cuomo (b. 1938). This approach constitutes an interpretation that does not aim at representing or satisfying conventional aesthetic taste but rather intends some kind of critical derision, an attack on fixed roles. As such, it can be placed between those of Artaud and Deleuze.

One could see this even in the work of a director like Luca Ronconi (b. 1933), who asked poet Edoardo Sanguineti (b. 1930) to create a new version of Ludovico Ariosto's (1474–1533) *Orlando Furioso* (1975), which he staged in a memorable fashion. In Ronconi's vision, spectators mingled with actors and the mobile wooden figures of sculptor Mario Ceroli in the same space. This and many other stagings by Ronconi created and inspired a whole school of theatrical expression in the country. Others working in this way included Roberto De Simone (b. 1933) who, with *La gatta cenerentola* (*Kitty Cinderella*, 1974), launched a new type of musical spectacle which found its roots in new interpretations of popular tunes, and Armando Pugliese (b. 1946), whose *Masaniello* was written with Elvio Porta (b. 1945), one of Naples' most important contemporary poets.

The late 1960s saw the emergence of socially critical attitudes, especially among the young. Clearly apparent among people from the suburbs and those from marginalized classes of society, this development was accompanied by a proliferation of theatre groups which reflected their feelings and opinions. These new theatre companies, comprised mainly of young people who wished to work collectively and who preferred to experiment without a predetermined text, found their focus in what they saw as abuses of power by political and institutional ruling classes as well as in family and civil environments. Their productions denounced power structures generally while at the same time praising youth and uncorrupted attitudes. These shows functioned as societal examples, expressions of the new relevant schools of thought. Few productions, however, achieved any long-term artistic significance.

Some which came close, though, were those by Giulano Scabia (b. 1930), who up until 1965 was known as Zip. His scripts, written in association with Carlo Quartucci (b. 1938), were collected in a volume entitled *Teatro nello spazio degli scontri* (*Theatre in the Midst of Battles*, 1973) and remain as testimony to a phenomenon which wedded poverty with the food of higher moral and societal values to create characters who lived outside of any rhetorical tradition.

During this same period, elementary schools also began to introduce the notion of 'theatrical animation'. The goal was not to produce theatre as spectacle but rather to encourage children to reveal feelings, states of mind, likes, dislikes and specific social attitudes.

By 1968 many of the new groups had become politically active and were deliberatley provoking the authorities and the police. Often performers would re-enact a demonstration. These events tended to place the blame for all the ills of society on capitalism, government, and social exploitation. In 1974, many groups became involved in a political campaign supporting the legalization of divorce. Typical was the work of Franco Cuomo who, from initial collaborations with Carmelo Bene, began to utilize historical material – Giacomo Matteotti (1885–1924), Antonio Gramsci (1891–1937) – or historical narrative in his plays. One of the most interesting was written with Maricla Boggio (b. 1937) – *Santa Maria dei battuti* (*St Mary of the Defeated*), which questioned conditions in psychiatric hospitals. Cuomo later looked at the lives of people such as Nero AD 37–68) and Casanova (1725–98) using illustrations from outside their own social contexts. Boggio created effective visions of the young in such plays as *Mamma eroina* (*Mama Heroine*, 1983), *Schegge* (*Splinters*, 1989) and *Rosa Delly*, the latter written with Valeria Moretti (b. 1950).

Paolo Poli (b. 1929) is an extremely original playwright, endowed with an exceptional talent for irony, whose works should be placed somewhere between the *canzone* and parody for their savoury character portrayals which veer delightfully close to insolence in order to poke fun. His best works are *Il diavolo* (*The Devil*, 1964), *Rita da Cascia* (*Rita of Cascia*, 1967), *Carolina Invernizio* (*Wintery Caroline*, 1969), *La vispa Teresa* (*Teresa the Lively*, 1970) and *Femminilità* (*Femininity*, 1975).

The works of Franco Brusati (b. 1922) – *Il benessere* (*Well-being*, 1959), *La fastidiosa* (*The Fastidious Woman*, 1963) and the later *La donna nel letto* (*The Woman in Bed*, 1984) – as well as those of Renato Mainardi (1931–76) – like *Una strana quiete* (*A Strange Silence*, 1969) and *Per una giovinetta che nessuno piange* (*For a Chick No One Misses*, 1965) – can be included in the intimate theatre current. Renzo Rosso's (b. 1926) *La gabbia* (*The Cage*, 1978), *Concerto* (*Concert*, 1980) and *Pianeta indecente* (*The Indecent Planet*, 1983) bring to the stage the idea of the destruction of ideal worlds, while Luciano Codignola (1920–87) has stressed the importance of noncompliance in a standardized and male-dominated society with *Il gesto* (*The Gesture*, 1962). Gennaro Pistilli (b. 1920) revealed the instability of the microcosm in which people seek refuge when confronted with mass society in *Le donne dell'uomo* (*Man's Women*, 1964) and *L'arbitro* (*The Arbiter*, 1961).

By the late 1970s and 1980s, feminism was becoming an important issue in the theatre. Dacia Maraini (b. 1930) was one of the eloquent voices for women who had traditionally been sacrificed to the importance of men. Finding a female voice in the transmission and development of narrative, Maraini created an impressive body of dramatic work – *La famiglia normale* (*The Ordinary Family*, 1966), *Ricatto a teatro* (*Blackmail on the Stage*, 1968), *Maria Stuart* (1977), and *Le figlie del defunto colonnello* (*The Daughters of the Dead Colonel*, 1985). Her 1991 work, *Marianna Ucria*, was based on one of her novels and became an even greater stimulus for the feminist movement in the Italian theatre. In the same vein using her own distinct dramatic personality, is Adele Cambria (b. 1931) who writes of the misogynous attitudes of well-known historical figures – *Nonostante Gramsci* (1975) and *La governante di Marx* (*Marx's Governess*, 1981).

If the works of some of these figures seem connected to events beyond simply Italian society, one must note that there were many significant influences entering Italian theatre at this time. Among them were the ideas of Peter Brook and the Brechtian plays of Peter Weiss which redirected Italian theatre and made it rethink itself. So too did the ideas of Artaud (especially as seen in the writings of Jacques Derrida) and Witkiewicz, who cautioned that cruelty and the grotesque were dominant in the modern world (as seen in the early Bene), and were destined to end in a demystification of the great figures of history.

Still another influence was the Living Theatre which evoked a profound interest in its American directors, Julian Beck and Judith Malina. From them came the exaltation and reappropriation of the body as a central medium for dramatic expressiveness.

The ideas of Polish director Jerzy Grotowski also had enormous importance. In *The Constant Prince*, Grotowski showed the value of gesture, the magic of body movement and the possibilities of a Poor Theatre. Italian director Eugenio Barba (b. 1936), a disciple of Grotowski who took the master's ideas even further, began offering through his Odin Teatret, a theatre laboratory in Holstebro, Denmark, introspection manifested through ritual body movements in productions such as *Ferai* (1989) and *Min Fars Hus* (*My Father's House*, 1972). His works also explore myth and suggestion.

The theatre that followed was born in the search for theatre as an event in and of itself, not necessarily connected to the outside world. Within this development, language became important again for its ability to be deconstructed, but without consideration for content. In this way, language no longer spoke through the written word but rather only through gesture and image. If earlier theatre was confused by mixing with life – and consequently lost its vital energy – this later version centred itself upon the materials and instruments it employed.

Still another direction was initiated in Orsoline by Mario Ricci (b. 1928) – a rediscovery of myths, characters, writers, and the way in which they created a theatre of living, vibrant signs. Involving visual artists, critics and writers, this new approach had its roots in such early experiments as *Movimento* (*Movement*, 1964), *Gulliver* (1966), *Il barone di Munchhausen* (*Baron Munchhausen*, 1967) and *Il lungo viaggio di Ulisse* (*The Long Voyage of Ulysses*, 1972). We see in this work the influence of the American Robert Wilson in the conscious expansion of time and the attempt to influence spectator perceptions in order to validate the experiences (apparent physical immobility in tandem with lights, sounds and colours creating a series of significant meaningful movements). As the 1990s began, it was this Theatre of Images that was most dominant in the country.

Structure of the National Theatre Community

Italian theatre is characterized by a mixed system that is on the one hand directly financed by the government or other public entities – regions (for example Emilia, Romagna or

Sicily), provinces (nearly ninety across the country) and municipalities. On the other hand, one also finds an active private sector run by commercial producers or individual directors (for example, the Teatro Eliseo or Lucio Ardenzi's Plexus Society), both of which also receive modest public funding because their activity follows government criteria for such performances.

During the 1970s theatrical cooperatives developed somewhere between the two models. They were initially committed to the equal distribution of income among the various participants (actors, directors and technicians). This method gradually disappeared and these groups became rather similar to other private theatres.

The public theatre's prices are normally lower than those at the private theatres and the theatrical circuits of public theatres normally include small towns and the suburbs of big cities. Born in the aftermath of World War II in a totally new political climate, this kind of theatre has had a major role in the founding of new companies and the staging of original works, as well as in the artistic growth of new directors and actors. It often built around the staging of contemporary and foreign plays. Unfortunately, interference by politicians has lowered the quality of the performances of many public theatres.

The state intervenes in favour of theatrical productions with a special Common Theatre Fund, whose endowment is set yearly by parliament. In 1993 the total amount was 900 billion lira (US$547 million): approximately 48 per cent for opera, 19 per cent for cinema, 16.5 per cent for theatre, 14 per cent for dance, orchestras and festivals, and 2.5 per cent for circuses.

State subsidies for dramatic activities are regulated according to Law 513 of 1973 and Law 410 of 1975. The figures for the three seasons 1983–4, 1984–5 and 1985–6 show the following for each respective season (in millions of lire): government subsidized theatre – 13.4, 17.4 and 20.2; private theatres – 7.95, 10.9 and 12.8; young people's theatre – 30.8, 45.4 and 61.0; magazines – 17.8, 28.9 and 39.9; Italian literary publications – 23.0, 32.0 and 33.0.

One of the foremost banks, the Banca Nazionale del Lavoro, has a special credit section for theatre companies which allows them to take out loans at favourable interest rates. These credit facilities have been used extensively.

As far as audiences are concerned, based on the experience from the immediate post-war period to 1990, theatre is a predominantly urban phenomenon. It is not, however, confined to the big cities, as similar initiatives have been taken in minor centres from Bolzano and Brescia in the north to L'Aquila and Catania in the south.

From a quantitative point of view, an analysis of the number of theatrical and operatic productions from 1951 to 1990 reveals characteristics that can be evaluated according to three criteria – cost to the public, number of paying customers and number of shows. The number of performances between 1951 and 1989 has on the whole increased from 70,000 to 100,000 and the number of tickets sold has risen from 20 million to 26 million. However, considering the increase in population and the greater spread of elementary and secondary school education, the increase is very slight. The number of performances and tickets sold was greatly reduced in the 1950s and 1960s because of the competition first with cinema, then with television. The cost has risen in numerical terms but, given the diminished value of the lira, one may consider the increase as being threefold.

Dramatic performance has improved while dialect theatre recorded first a strong decline and then a recovery from the 1970s to the 1980s (using figures that reveal only a slight increase compared to the 1950s). Whereas the audience for dialect theatre has increased only slightly, the audiences for theatre as a whole and musical productions (opera and ballet) have almost doubled.

During the 1991–2 season there were 64,000 theatrical performances and 12.7 million tickets sold. One should keep in mind that from 1970 to 1990 the theatre audience increased from 6 million to 12 million and that the audience for musical performances increased from 3.6 million to 6.5 million.

There is a clear concentration of theatrical activities in the most important cities (Rome, Milan, Naples, Genoa, Palermo, Bologna, Florence, Venice and Turin) representing the staging of two-thirds of all performances. Companies in smaller cities, however, are also involved during the winter and summer with festivals (Benevento, Caserta, Montepulciano, Fiesole, Nervi for ballet, Verona for opera, Spoleto, Parma, Volterra and Monticchiello). Among these festivals one should also mention the Maggio musicale fiorentino.

There are fifteen public production companies, ten civic, private or mixed companies, twenty-seven associations in the field of experimental and youth/children's theatre, and almost 300 private and cooperative theatrical companies.

The total number of theatres in Italy (calculated in 1993) is 615: the cities with the greatest number are Rome (almost fifty), Milan (almost thirty), Naples (seventeen), Turin (fifteen) and Florence (thirteen). There are numerous theatres in the Emilia–Romagna region (Bologna, Parma, Reggio, Modena and Ferrara), in Lombardy (Bergamo, Brescia and Como) and in the Marche (Ancona, Jesi, Sirolo, Ascoli, Macerata and Urbino). The south of Italy and the islands (Sicily and Sardinia) have far fewer; the major ones are Bari and Catania. These are mainly for theatrical and musical performances. There are about thirty theatres devoted solely to music.

In summer a number of important festivals occur across the country, even in small towns, in opera (from Verona to Rome), ballet and dance, and theatre, such as the Festival of Two Worlds in Spoleto, founded by the composer Gian-Carlo Menotti (b. 1911). Among other important festivals are the Estate teatrale in Verona (a Shakespearian festival); the Festival Fondi-La Pastora (a festival devoted to new theatre forms); an International One-Act Play Festival in Arezzo; the Muggia Festival (at the border with Slovenia – a meeting of companies from eastern and western Europe); the Orestiadi in Gibellina (directed by the critic and editor Franco Quadri, this festival researches ritual in early drama); a Pirandello Week in Agrigento;

the Taormina Arte Festival (a series of summer performances in the Taormina Greek theatre); and perhaps the most famous, the Venice Biennial (music, dance and theatre).

Established companies, especially those that are state-sponsored, usually have an artistic director, one or more staff directors, a fixed cast of actors, technicians and designers. The average number of employees at the state theatres is 300. Private companies normally hire according to the needs of individual shows. Rehearsals range from a few weeks at private theatres to several months at the public theatres.

Public funding goes to any company which meets state artistic requirements and gives a certain number of performances. The largest foundation in the country is that of the Banca Nazionale del Lavoro, which has focused on lending to the cultural sector.

Most theatre companies are members of AGIS (Italian Performing Arts Association) which represents all aspects of theatre including cinema, opera and circuses. There are also organizations specifically focusing on Italian plays (IDI), for authors (SIAD), for professional associations (ASST and SNAD), as well as unions for actors and administrators (within CGIL, CISL and UIL). Public ticket sale is monitored by the SIAE (Italian Society of Authors and Publishers); its function is of extreme importance because public funding is dependent on the number of performances and on the number of tickets sold. It also edits an *Italian Theatre Yearbook*.

Artistic Profile

Companies

In Italy artistic trends are most clearly revealed through the staging practices of directors. Some directors are attached permanently to one theatre, while others are associated with a company for only a particular period of time. Thus the history of Italian theatre companies is, in fact, the history of their directors.

This said, it should be noted that the theatre companies which have most influenced Italy's national theatre since 1945 have all tended to be state and municipal companies and are generally located in the major urban centres (Milan, Rome, Genoa, Turin, Bolzano, Bologna,

Florence and Catania). From the immediate post-war period, several private companies should also be mentioned – the Compagnia dell'Eliseo (Eliseo Company of Rome), which benefited from the directorship of Luchino Visconti and from actors like Gino Cervi (1901–74), Andreina Pagnani (1906–78), Rina Morelli (1907–76), and Paolo Stoppa; the Compagnia del teatro di Via Manzoni (Via Manzoni Theatre Company) of Milan; and the Compagnia dei Giovani (Young People's Theatre Company). This last company, founded in 1954, consisted of Romolo Valli (b. 1925), Giorgio de Lullo, Rossella Falk (b. 1926) Annamaria Guarnieri (b. 1934) and, for a time,

Tino Buazzelli (1922–80). The company, with the excellent actor-director Romolo Valli, staged many famous plays, from the Frenchman Alfred de Musset's *Lorenzaccio* (1954) to Luigi Pirandello's (1867–1936) *Il gioco delle parti* (*The Rules of the Game*).

The Teatro Stabile di Roma (Civic Theatre of Rome), after a period (1948–54) directed by Orazio Costa (b. 1911), was reformed under the name Teatro di Roma. Since the 1960s its directors have been Vito Pandolfi (1917–74), Franco Enriquez (1927–77), Luigi Squarzina and Maurizio Scaparro (b. 1932), consistently maintained a high level of production.

All these companies made use of a more-or-less permanent company supplemented by actors for particular shows. Among its most renowned actors were Valeria Moriconi (b. 1931), Anna Proclemer (b. 1923), Mario Scaccia (b. 1919), Enrico Maria Salerno (b. 1926) and Mariangela Melato (b. 1943).

The Teatro dell'Elfo (Elfo Theatre Company) made quite a name for itself in Milan in the 1970s and 1980s under the direction of Gabriele Salvatores.

Gianfranco De Bosio (b. 1924) of the Teatro universitario di Padova (University Theatre of Padua) worked with several major companies. He directed, among others, the Teatro stabile di Torino (Civic Theatre of Turin) and staged numerous plays including an adaptation of the poet Aldo Palazzeschi's (1885–1974) novel, *Roma* (*Rome*). He was also superintendent of the Arena of Verona where he directed operas.

Mario Missiroli (b. 1934) is another director who made a reputation for himself doing contemporary theatre (Gombrowicz, Witkiewicz and Osborne) and operatic works. These were staged with an inspired use of various ingredients of stage design.

The generally wordless Theatre of Images is a trend that, with Simone Carella's *Auto-diffamazione* (*Self-defamation*, 1976), was able to create a theatre event using only a single empty chair. In this type of work – popular in the 1980s and 1990s – the director, after having eliminated the author, can even dissolve the physical image of the actor. The company Il carozzone (The Caravan) very early in this period staged *I presagi del vampiro* (*The Sign of*

Anna Proclemer in her production of Pirandello's *As Well as Before, Better than Before*.
Photo: Tommaso Le Pera.

the Vampire, 1976) using this show to prepare itself for the motifs of Jack Kerouac in *Sulla strada* (*On the Road*, 1982). The company Gaia Scienza (Gay Science) also staged a remarkable performance of *La rivolta degli oggetti* (*The Objects' Uprising*, 1976) which attempted the visualization of sound as performance.

Still another company, Magazzini criminali (Criminal Warehouses) produced *Crollo nervoso* (*Nervous Breakdown*, 1980), a mixture of mime and musical elements, while Il falso movimento (False Movement) company presented *Tango glaciale* (*Glacial Tango*, 1982) which evoked an obscure feeling of longing through its use of gesture. A spectacular new form emerged in the later productions of the Magazzini troupe, especially with Federico Tiezzi's (b. 1951) *Genet a Tangeri* (*Genet in Tangiers*, 1984) which proved itself through the creation of original scenic movements, as in *Ritratto d'un attore da giovane* (*Portrait of the Actor as a Young Man*, 1985).

This trend bore different fruit with Giorgio Barberio Corsetti's *Frammenti di una battaglia* (*Battle Fragments*, 1988) and *Il legno dei violini* (*Wood for Violins*, 1990) in performances inspired by Kafka.

Giancarlo Sepe (b. 1946) founded the troupe La Comunità (The Community) in 1972. Its function as a workshop enabled it to achieve impressive visual effects in the manner of Robert Wilson but with a personal style that was enriched by the influential collaboration of the set designer Uberto Bertacca.

Dramaturgy

The influence of Pirandello on Italian theatre was somewhat stalled, as is proved by the fact that his own plays continued to be performed with traditional dramatic settings. Thanks in part to the critical essays of Adriano Tilgher (1887–1941) and other scholars, Pirandello's ideas gradually penetrated Italian culture. This led to a break with previous systems in which the search for the truly human essence by means of dialogue (which draws out problems of epistemology) was replaced by that of the frameworks prevalent in cinema.

Eduardo De Filippo introduced some elements of Pirandellian dialectic in his own rich presentation of daily life experiences. In particular he reintroduced the theme of objective madness, expressed by Pirandello in *Enrico IV* (*Henry IV*) and *Il berreto a sonagli* (*The Fool's*

Cap), especially in works where alienation leads to madness. Also to be noted in this regard are *Ditegli sempre di sì* (*Always Tell Him Yes*, 1929) and *La grande magia* (*Great Magic*, 1948).

Writing in the Neapolitan dialect, De Filippo brought fragments of everyday life to the stage with an acute sense of humanity and simplicity which immediately won over audiences. Among his many works, the most popular are *Napoli milionaria* (*Millionaire from Naples*, 1945), *Questi fantasmi* (*Fantasy Quest*, 1946), *Filumena Marturano* (1946), *Le voci di dentro* (*Inner Voices*, 1948), *Sabato domenica e lunedì* (*Saturday, Sunday, Monday*, 1959), *Il sindaco del rione sanità* (*The Mayor of the Sanità District*, 1960) and *Gli esami non finiscono mai* (*Exams Never Finish*, 1973). All are works in which aspects of family life are brought to light in performances filled with comic but also bitter moments.

Not to be forgotten is the brother of Eduardo, Peppino De Filippo (1903–80), also a capable author of farcical comedies. He, Eduardo and their sister Titina (1898–1963) formed an exceptional trio of actors. To this day their descendants continue in the best tradition of Neapolitan theatre (Luca (b. 1948) and Luigi (b. 1930) De Filippo).

Another Neapolitan writer of note is Ettore Giannini (b. 1912), author and director of *Carosello napoletano* (*Neapolitan Carousel*, 1951) which used Neapolitan songs and folklore in a composition characterized by an unequalled stylistic unity.

Pirandellian problematics in an expressionistic style were the hallmarks of Pier Maria Rosso di San Secondo (1887–1956), a Sicilian nourished with German culture, who established himself between 1918 – *Marionette che passione!* (*Puppets – What a Passion!*) – and the end of the 1930s and the beginning of the 1940s, when he wrote *Lo spirito della morte* (*Spirit of the Dead*), a work in which one perceives the self-destructive spirit that can drive society to moral suicide.

Among the most representative playwrights in the censorship years of the 1950s were Aldo Nicolai (b. 1920) who, with refined introspection and sensibility, investigated and unveiled intimate psychological mechanisms in *Teresina* (1954), *Il soldato Piccicò* (*The Soldier Piccicò*, 1958), *Le formiche* (1961), *Classe di ferro* (*Class of Iron*, 1974), ending up with *L'altro* (*The Other*), taken from a novel by C. Samonà, in 1990, and in 1991 *Amleto in salsa piccante*

(*Hamlet in Hot Sauce*), a grotesque remake of the Prince of Denmark's tragedy seen from the royal kitchen. Several of his works have been staged successfully abroad (USSR, Poland, Hungary and France), even before being performed in his mother country.

In 1958 Giuseppe Patroni Griffi (b. 1921) made his début with *D'amore si muore* (*One Can Die for Love*), an emblematic fresco of Italian society. His later works in the same style include *Anima nera* (*Black Soul*, 1960), *Metti una sera a cena* (*Someone is Coming to Dinner*, 1967), *Persone naturali e strafottenti* (*Natural and Arrogant People*, 1974) and *Prima del silenzio* (*Before Silence*, 1982). With this author there is a return to a private dimension, a need to clarify personal awareness, that in the preceding period had been sacrificed to collective values and interests.

Antonio Nediani (b. 1921) evoked the myth of cinema as it was experienced by the generation of the 1940s in *Film, soggetto e sceneggiatura* (*Film, Script and Screenplay*, 1965) which eventually became *La commedia dell'arte* (1975). He also faced the problems created by the process of decolonization in *I colori dell'Africa* (*The Colours of Africa*, 1965), as well as the individual dilemmas of great historical figures from Ovid (43 BC–AD 17) to Giovanni Pascoli (1855–1912). In *La grazia umana* (*Human Grace*, 1988) Nediani creates a subtle psychological study of impossible love.

In this period, the whimsical comedies of Giorgio Buridan (b. 1921) also appear such as *I più cari affetti* (*Dearest Affections*, 1960), scripts which have been compared to Ionesco's. Buridan was preceded in this style before the war by Achille Campanile (1900–77), an extremely original writer whose works are both successful and unmistakable – *Centocinquanta la gallina canta* (*150 Singing Chickens*, 1925), *L'inventore del cavallo* (*The Inventor of the Horse*, 1925) and *La moglie ingenua e il marito malato* (*The Ingenuous Wife and the Sick Husband*, 1960).

Alberto Moravia (1907–90) reached the stage in an adaptation of his *Gli Indifferenti* (*The Indifferents*), the novel that first brought him international recognition. Staged by Luigi Squarzina, the play was followed by a number of powerful dramatic works, including *Beatrice Cenci* (1935), *Il mondo è quello che è* (*The World is What it Seems to Be*, 1966), *Il dio Kurt* (*The God, Kurt*, 1969) and *La vita è gioco* (*Life is a Game*, 1970).

Another novelist-playwright is Dino Buzzati

Romolo Valli in Giorgio de Lullo's 1982 production of *Before Silence* by Giuseppe Patroni Griffi.
Photo: Tommaso Le Pera.

(1906–72), who first came to note with an adaptation of his novel *Un caso clinico* (*A Clinical Case*, 1953). His later plays were written directly for the theatre – *Un verme al ministero* (*A Worm at the Ministry*, 1960), *La colonna infame* (*The Infamous Column*, 1962) and *La famosa invasione degli orsi in Sicilia* (*The Bears' Famous Invasion in Sicily*, 1967).

Natalia Ginzburg (1916–91) introduced to the Italian stage a pitiless and measured language built to suit well-defined characters, and used it especially in *Ti ho sposato per allegria* (*I Married You Just for Cheerfulness*, 1966), *La segretaria* (*The Secretary*, 1967), *L'inserzione* (*The Advertisement*, 1969) and *L'intervista* (*The Interview*, 1989).

Roberto Mazzucco (1927–89) describes with a sense of irony social defects of Italians and what he perceives to be a lack of significant traditions – *Uguali a tanti* (*Just Like Others*, 1963). In other scripts, he examines the suffering of Italian society – *L'andazzo* (*The Bad Practice*, 1968), *La corruzione* (*The Corruption*, 1984) and *Tre squilli per Lola* (*Three*

Calls for Lola, 1989) which takes one back to the experiences of the individual. Mazzucco is also one of the most important fighters in the many cultural and political battles fought through the years by contemporary Italian authors.

Mario Fratti (b. 1919), an Italian author who lives in New York, has developed a real following for his musicals, political biographies and exposés. His preferred subject is representations of experiences from everyday life such as *La gabbia* (*The Cage*, 1963), *Che Guevara* (1978) and *Fuoco* (*Fire*, 1989). His musicals *Cybelle* and *Nina* were very successful in the United States.

One can trace a comic vein in Bellisario Randone's *Il califfo Esposito* (*Esposito the Caliph*, 1956) and *Bello di papà* (*Daddy's Favourite*, 1957) and a subtle sense of humour in Pier Benedetto Bertoli's (1926–87) *I diari* (*The Diaries*, 1959) and *La fama fatua* (*Fatuous Fame*, 1968) while Silvano Ambrogi (b. 1929) in *I Burosauri* (*The Burosaurs*, 1963) has dedicated himself to social satire.

Vincenzo di Mattia (b. 1932) penetrates restless consciences in *I confessori* (*The Confessors*, 1976) and *Dannata giovinezza* (*Doomed Youth*, 1983). Ermanno Carsana's (b. 1923) refined *Storie di maschere* (*Stories of Masks*, 1984) is playfully reconstructed with the characters of the *commedia dell'arte*. The established satirists Vittorio Caprioli (b. 1921) and Alberto Bonucci (1918–69) began their careers with Luciano Salce (b. 1922) in short revues. They have also written and performed *Teatro dei gobbi* (*Hunchback Theatre*, 1979) and *Cornet die notes* (1952) with Franca Valeri (b. 1920).

A sense of existential despair is clear in the works of Pier Paolo Pasolini (1922–75). His plays *Orgia* (*Orgy*, 1968), *Affabulazione* (1973) and *Calderón* (1977), rather than constituting a transposition into theatre of the artist's longings as manifested in his poetry, prose or cinema, indicate a more profound reconsideration of man's fate, his subjection, his will and his weakness.

Corrado Augias (b. 1935), after writing his Beckett-like *Direzione memorie* (*Memory Office*, 1966) and *Soluzione finale* (*The Final Solution*, 1969), offered a Machiavellian interpretation of Iago's subtle schemes against Othello in *L'onesto Iago* (*Iago the Honest*, 1984).

The critic Enzo Siciliano (b. 1934) has dedicated himself to comedy of manners with *La parola tagliata in bocca* (*The Word Cuts in the Mouth*, 1985) and *La casa scoppiata* (*The House Exploded*, 1987) in which victims of human disillusion are also restrained by words. In Fabio Doplicher's (b. 1938) *L'isola dei morti, variante* (*Variation on the Island of the Dead*, 1977) and *Il ventre del gigante* (*The Womb of the Giant*, 1986) one can see a fusion of thought, lyricism and performance where poetry reappears as a reflection of psychological change.

In this overview of recent Italian theatre one cannot overlook certain phenomena that are historically significant. These include the representations of simple human experiences in the Lombard tradition as seen in the work of the Legnanesi Company, in Neapolitan *sceneggiata* (a typical Neapolitan genre with song), and productions of other regional traditions like *Mezza femmina* (*Half Female*, 1977) by the Abruzzi playwright Alfredo Cohen (b. 1937) and the always lively Sicilian and Sardinian dialect productions.

Among the authors who established themselves in the 1980s are Vittorio Franceschi (b. 1936), who, with works that have few characters, emphasizes forms of individual alienation such as *Scacco pazzo* (*Checkmate*, 1989); Manlio Santanelli (b. 1938), author of *Uscite d'emergenza* (*Emergency Exit*, 1980) and *Regina Madre* (*Queen Mother*, 1985); and Annibale Ruccello (1956–86), author of *Weekend* (1984) and *Ferdinando* (1986), which gave birth to a whole new 'Neapolitan School'. This group also includes Enzo Moscato (b. 1948), author of *Pièce noire* (1985) and *Rasoi* (*Razors*, 1991), and Francesco Silvestri (b. 1956), author of *Angeli all'inferno* (*Angels in Hell*, 1991) and *Streghe da marciapiede* (*Sidewalk Witches*, 1992).

Of a more intimate nature are works by Giuseppe Manfridi (b. 1956) such as *Anima bianca* (*White Soul*, 1988) and *Giacomo il prepotente* (*Giacomo the Overbearing*, 1989) about the poet Giacomo Leopardi (1798–1837). Umberto Marino (b. 1952) has captured the manners of his generation, and his work has subsequently been taken up with great success by the cinema; for example *La stazione* (*The Station*, 1967) and *Volevamo essere gli U2* (*We Wanted to be U2*, 1991).

Directors, Directing and Production Styles

Prior to World War II, it was the director Luchino Visconti, the young assistant to Jean Renoir in 1936, who dedicated himself to theatre despite having already achieved his first major successes in cinema. It was Visconti who made a major contribution to the renewal of the Italian stage and its inclusion in a European discourse. He forced Italian theatre to exercise phenomenal rigour to the point of perfectionism and helped give life to stylistic experiments, unmistakable as much for the method (beginning with long rehearsals) as for the impression made on the performances.

This approach was calculated to consider the most minute realistic detail and to sharpen its tone to create intense, often acrid atmospheres. Among his most memorable productions were Cocteau's *Les Parents terribles* (*My Terrible Relations*, Rome 1945), a delightful version of *Le Mariage de Figaro* (*The Marriage of Figaro*, 1946), Vittorio Alfieri's (1749–1803) *Oreste* (*Orestes*) and a romantic version of Shakespeare's *Troilus and Cressida* (1949), of exceptional decorative splendour.

He was also very successful with Chekhov's *The Cherry Orchard* (1965), American theatrical works like Tennessee Williams's *The Glass Menagerie* and Arthur Miller's *Death of a Salesman*, as well as contemporary British theatre such as Harold Pinter's *Old Times*. He later became involved in operatic performances at Milan's La Scala and other theatres. He shaped – or at least influenced – the development of many of the most significant Italian directors and actors including the film star Marcello Mastroianni (b. 1924).

After Visconti, it was doubtless Giorgio Strehler whose influence was greatest on the modern Italian and European stages. Strehler and Paolo Grassi founded the Piccolo Teatro di Milano (Little Theatre of Milan) in 1947, one of the most important modern Italian theatres. The presence of actors like Gianni Santuccio (b. 1914) and Lilla Brignone (b. 1913) in the early years, and later the modern acting of Ottavia Piccolo (b. 1949), Giulia Lazzarini (b. 1934) and Marcello Soleri, allowed Strehler to analyse in depth both contemporary and classical theatre, from Shakespeare to Goldoni.

Strehler began in 1947 with Maxim Gorki's *Lower Depths*, which remained famous for its depiction of poverty in a veristic manner. He then turned to the epic theatre of Brecht, many of whose works he staged. *The Threepenny Opera* and *The Life of Galileo* with Tino Buazzelli rank among the most memorable modern Italian performances for their extraordinary scenic effects. A historico-critical approach allowed Strehler to capture a clear expressivity

with plays by the popular descriptive author Carlo Bertolazzi (1870–1919).

Strehler's brilliant *Arlecchino servo di due padroni* (*Harlequin, Servant of Two Masters*) was toured with world-wide success by Marcello Moretti (1910–62). Other memorable productions of Goldoni's works were *La trilogia della villeggiatura* (*The Holiday Trilogy*) and *Il Campiello* (*The Campiello*). Among the more recent productions was an outstanding version of Goethe's *Faust*. Strehler has subsequently directed in many other European theatres and was the first artistic director of the Paris-based Théâtre de l'Europe.

Orazio Costa trained as a director at the Accademia nazionale d'arte drammatica (National Academy of Dramatic Arts) and supplemented his studies in Paris where he was first a student and later an assistant to Jacques Copeau. It was during this time that he defined, in the tradition of his French master who saw theatre as a thing in which words acquire a religious significance and where each person is almost ascetically at its service, his own artistic search. His work with sacred plays and liturgical drama was particularly congenial to him. One has but to think of *Il parcello* based on Copeau's text, the Medieval *I misteri* (*The Mysteries*) and Georges Bernanos's *Dialogues des Carmélites*. Equally significant was his encounter with the later works of Ibsen – *Il piccolo Eyolf* (*Little Eyolf*) and *L'anitra selvatica* (*The Wild Duck*) – and Ugo Betti. His grand outdoor performances were meant to heighten the expressive role of the chorus. An antinaturalist director, Costa directed the first Teatro Stabile di Roma. As a teacher of the Academy of Dramatic Arts he influenced some of the major actors and directors of the contemporary Italian theatre.

From Luigi Squarzina's first theatrical productions – Arthur Miller's *All My Sons* in 1947, and his first performances of works by Gabriele D'Annunzio (1863–1938) and Pirandello – he seemed to be at the peak of his expressive ability. He stayed at this level with performances of Goldoni's works, *Una delle ultime sere di carnevale* (*The Next-to-Last Night of Carnival*) and *I quattro rusteghi* (*The Four Rustics*). Squarzina also attained good results with works he wrote himself – *Tre quarti di luna* (*Three Quarters of the Moon*, 1983) – or in collaboration with other authors (Vico Faggi, Enzo De Bernard and Ruggero Zangrandi) – *Cinque giorni al porto* (*Five Days in Port*, 1970) and *Otto settembre* (*The Eighth of*

September, 1971), both of which re-examine Italian historical events. Most of his works were staged at the Teatro Stabile di Genova, which he directed from 1962 to 1976, before taking over the Teatro di Roma, where he honed his skills further.

Squarzina is also a director of opera as well as a university professor, and one of his works, *Siamo momentaneamente assenti* (*Momentarily Absent*), winner of the 1991 IDI Award, was staged at the Piccolo Teatro di Milano.

Giancarlo Cobelli (b. 1933) also proved himself an inspired and imaginative director in his attempts to revive Goldoni and in his work on the plays of John Osborne. Alessandro Fersen (b. 1911), with his *Lea Lebowitz* and *Golem*, revived little-known characters and myths from Italian culture while Aldo Trionfo (1921–90) made a name for himself by extending the limits of classical and modern plays using the exaltation of crude and grotesque intonations.

Luca Ronconi is a graduate of the Accademia nazionale d'arte drammatica and was for many years an actor with the most important companies and with the most important directors. He made his début as a director with Goldoni's *La buona moglie* (*The Good Wife*, 1963). It was in his work on Elizabethan and Jacobean drama (especially Thomas Middleton) that he revealed a new style which would be asserted in his later productions of Shakespeare's *Measure for Measure*, *Richard III* (1967) and Giordano Bruno's (1548–1600) *Il Candelaio* (*The Candlemaker*). He burst on to the international scene in 1968 with his extraordinary production of *Orlando Furioso*, written in collaboration with Edoardo Sanguineti. One of the most important Italian performances in the post-war decades, it required audiences to move about to see simultaneous scenes.

As director of the Teatro Stabile di Torino (Civic Theatre of Turin) he staged such influential performances as K. Kraus's *Gli ultimi giorni dell'umanità* (*The Last Days of Humanity*, 1990) and Eugene O'Neill's *Strange Interlude* (1991). He has also done several operas.

From Maurizio Scaparro's first experiences at the Teatro Stabile di Bolzano (Civic Theatre of Bolzano), which ranged from popular political theatre on the one hand to Shakespearian plays on the other, he reached the position of director of the Venice Biennial, one of the country's major festivals. Scaparro later directed the Teatro di Roma where, through his direction of works ranging from Camus's *Caligula* (1983) and Cervantes's *Don Chisciotte* (*Don Quixote*,

1983) to an adaptation of Pirandello's *Il fu Mattia Pascal* (*The Late Mattia Pascal*, 1986), he established a personal style which utilized modern technological media to extend the boundaries of the stage area.

Gabriele Lavia (b. 1942) began his career as an actor in Ronconi's productions of Shakespeare's *Titus Andronicus* and Sophocles' *Oedipus Rex*, and Strehler's production of Shakespeare's *King Lear* (1973). In 1975, he began his own company and it achieved considerable success with Schiller's *Rebel Pelican* and *The Scoundrels*. These productions revealed textual research enhanced by a neo-naturalistic approach which was applied as successfully to Pirandello as to adaptations of classical works.

Besides Carmelo Bene, whose theatrical vision has already been discussed among playwrights, one must also note the director Giancarlo Nanni (b. 1941) whose production of Frank Wedekind's *Spring's Awakening* was an expression of primitive sensuousness wrapped in a romantic aura. Memè Perlini (b. 1940) showed herself to be a master of light with *Pirandello: chi?* (*Pirandello: Who?*, 1972) where the visual image was shattered and reduced to cold gesticulation. Giuliano Vasilicò (b. 1940) arrived at suggestive figurative evocations with *Le 120 giornate di Sodoma* (*120 Days of Sodom*, 1972) and his *Proust* (1976).

The Pirandellian canon was shaken by Massimo Castri (b. 1943) with an interpretation that used only certain narrative schemes of the original.

A few final words here about actors who in Italy have always had an enormous impact on production styles. After the death of Ermete Zacconi (d. 1948), who acted alongside Eleonara Duse and achieved his greatest success in Plato's *L'apologia di Socrate* (*The Trial of Socrates*), and that of the sisters Emma (1875–1965) and Irma (1870–1962) Grammatica, leading interpreters of the plays of Ibsen and Pirandello, the Italian theatre scene of the post-war period continued to boast such eminent actors as Ruggero Ruggeri (1871–1953), a renowned interpreter of Pirandello, Gino Cervi, who established himself in contemporary pieces, Renzo Ricci, in Shakespearian plays, Andreina Pagnani, a superb interpreter of Cocteau and Goldoni, Anna Magnani (1908–73), the preferred actress of Visconti for Goldoni and twentieth-century plays, Marcello Moretti, who brought to the international stage Strehler's *Arlecchino* (*Harlequin*), Sergio Tofano (1886–

1973), a refined specialist of light comedy and the classics as well as a creator of set designs for children, Totò (1898–1962), an incomparable comedian who progressed from a mere pre-show comic to classic grotesque and absurd performances in theatre and cinema, and Lamberto Picasso (1880–1962), playing Pirandello.

From the 1950s to the 1990s other actors who made an impact on theatre included Tino Car-raro (b. 1910), who distinguished himself with Shakespeare and Chekhov Turi Ferro (b. 1921), who brought Pirandello and Sciascia from his native Sicily to the theatres of Europe, Vittorio Gassman (b. 1922), for many years Italy's premier dramatic actor while in the cinema he devoted himself to light comedies, and Salvo Randone (b. 1906), an incomparable Shakespearian actor.

Music Theatre

It is not easy to trace a stylistic progression for opera companies in Italy since these are founded primarily on a plurality of experiences involving various composers, directors and sceno-graphers. To understand trends, therefore, it is perhaps more useful to follow the work of important new composers who have begun to exert some significant influence. This said, no influence would be felt without the support of Italy's major opera companies – La Scala, the Teatro dell'Opera, Teatro San Carlo and the Teatro La Fenice.

La Scala – or more correctly the Teatro alla Scala in Milan – is the most famous and important in Italy and possibly in the world. Opened in 1778 with a performance of Antonio Salieri's (1750–1825) L'Europa riconosciuta (Europe Discovered), its artistic directors have ranged from Arturo Toscanini (1867–1957) to Victor De Sabata (1892–1967). It is used for an intense concert and opera season, a school of dance, and has its own specialized school for young singers. Beside the main theatre (rebuilt after the war) there was also built in 1955 a small theatre (Piccola Scala) intended to accommodate smaller operatic performances. It was inaugurated with Domenico Cimarosa's (1749–1801) Il matrimonio segreto (The Secret Wedding). La Scala is probably best known for the extraordinarily high quality of its singers and conductors. Also of great importance to La Scala is the contribution of dance which, in recent years, has profited from the presence of ballerina Carla Fracci (b. 1936).

As for the Teatro dell'Opera (Opera Theatre) of Rome, it began in 1880 as the Teatro Costanzi (after the famous impresario) and was inaugurated with Rossini's (1792–1868) Semiramide (Semiramis). It was renamed the Teatro reale dell'Opera (Royal Opera House) in 1928 after having undergone renovations designed by the architect Marcello Piacentini (1881–1960). It assumed its current name in 1946. Boasting a flourishing school of dance, it has organized a summer season at the Terme di Caracalla (Caracalla Baths) in Rome since 1927 which is capable of accommodating thousands of spectators.

Naples' Teatro San Carlo, built in 1737, has a capacity of 3,500 seats yet has excellent acoustics. It has hosted the premières of many operas composed by Italian musicians, among them Lucia di Lammermoor (1835) by Gaetano Donizetti (1797–1848). It boasts a tradition of performances of very high and refined quality. From Maria Felicita Malibran to Maria Callas, its performers are usually among the most renowned in the world.

Finally, the Teatro La Fenice in Venice was inaugurated in 1792 with an opera by Giovanni Paisiello (1740–1816). It has played host to the greatest composers of every era since and has premièred many operas.

Other important theatres are the Teatro Olimpico of Vicenza, the Massimo of Palermo, the recently renovated Carlo Felice of Genoa, and the Bellini of Catania. In all, there are approximately eighty opera houses many of which have histories that date back to the eighteenth century, excellent operatic seasons and appreciative audiences. Most of these are in the Emilia–Romagna region.

Turning to composers, starting just prior to World War II, Goffredo Petrassi (b. 1904) achieved a high stylistic level, taking his cue from Stravinsky. During the war years and the immediate post-war period, Petrassi composed works which included pieces of a clearly spiritual nature – from the Leopardi-inspired Coro dei morti (The Choir of the Dead, 1941) to Gloria in excelsis Deo (1952). His music was also used for ballets such as La follia di Orlando

(*Orlando's Folly*, 1943) and *Ritratto di don Chisciotte* (*The Portrait of Don Quixote*, 1945). While he began to make use of new artistic forms – such as in the work *La morte nel'aria* (*Death in the Air*, 1950) which aligns itself with musical abstraction – the presence and importance of vocal aspects diminished.

The Istrian Luigi Dallapiccola (1904–75) also began to show the profound influence of new directions utilizing literature (Joyce and Proust) and the ideas of Schoenberg and Webern. With *Volo di notte* (*Flight in the Night*, 1940) he was inspired by Saint-Exupéry; in 1949 he developed his style further with *Il prigioniero* (*The Prisoner*), a didactic work located somewhere between clear formal construction and pure poetic freedom. Alfredo Casella (1883–1947) is another composer who made an important contribution to the link between Italian composer-writers and European music. His opera *La favola di Orfeo* (*The Fable of Orpheus*, 1940), his ballets, and his teaching have all been of enormous influence. His major essay, written with Virgilio Mortari (b. 1902) and published posthumously in 1950, describes the nature of modern orchestral technique. Still another composer, Valentino Bucchi (1916–70), reveals a fundamental, personal style and an attraction to the popular in his work while Luciano Chailly (b. 1930) takes inspiration for his themes from the society around him.

One of the best known opera composers is the experimentalist Luciano Berio (b. 1925), who returned to more literary texts for his inspiration – Italo Calvino (1923–87) – and to those of the poet Sanguineti. Berio studied and taught in the United States and has become one of the more notable composers to write for the theatre. The Venetian Bruno Maderna (1920–73) has also exerted influence on the Italian music sphere. Best known as a conductor, Maderna's own compositions have played an important role in musical innovation particularly in the area of electronic music.

Luigi Nono (1924–90) set the pace for the new avant-garde in the 1970s and 1980s, finding his themes in a recognizable reality while denouncing invisible and subtle forms of repression and racial discrimination. His most important operas include *Il canto sospeso* (*The Suspended Song*, 1955), *Intolleranza* (*Intolerance*, 1955) and *Al gran sole carico d'amore* (*In the Bright Sunshine Burning with Love*, 1975).

The undertakings of Italy's opera festivals are also very productive in the field. Pride of place goes to the Spoleto Festival of Two Worlds, founded and directed by composer Gian-Carlo Menotti.

From Rome's Accademia di Santa Cecilia (Saint Cecilia Academy) to the approximately sixty conservatories and other 150 musical institutes (among these are forty-odd Pontifical Institutes for sacred music), the business of musical training is intense. The 1980s and 1990s have witnessed the creation of twenty ethno-music centres as well as an intensification of musical instruction in the schools. Among the most important are the Accademia Filarmonica di Roma (Rome Philharmonic Academy), founded in the nineteenth century and reorganized in 1946; the Accademia Musicale Chigiana (Chigiana Musical Academy) in Siena, which offers master classes and an elegant festival; the Accademia Filarmonica di Napoli (Philharmonic Academy of Naples) and the Istituto Musicale A. Cherubini (A. Cherubini Music Institute).

Also noteworthy is the existence of institutions devoted to concert as well as educational activities in various cities from Bologna to L'Aquila. To this list would be added the Società Italiana di Musica Contemporanea (Italian Society of Contemporary Music), the Italian section of the Société Internationale pour la Musique Contemporaine (International Society of Contemporary Music), which has sponsored a composition competition every two years since 1958, the Fondazione Giorgio Cini (Giorgio Cini Foundation) of Venice, promoter of cultural, scientific and artistic initiatives, the Centro Internazionale di Studi Musicali (International Centre for Musical Studies) of Rome's Primavera Musicale Italiana (Italian Spring of Music), the Ravello courses in performance and musical studies, the courses in Sorrento and the Estate di Taormina (Taormina Summer).

Musical publications of wide circulation include *L'Opera* (*Opera*) of Milan; Turin's *La Scala*, *Il giornale della musica* (*The Music Newspaper*) edited by E. Perruccio; Milan's *Musica d'oggi* (*The Music of Today*), *Lo spettatore musicale* (*The Musical Spectator*), *La rassegna musicale* (*The Music Review*) and *La nuova rivista musicale* (*The New Journal of Music*, published by ERI, Rome); *Musica e dossier* (*Music and Dossier*) of Rome; and *Musica viva* (*Live Music*) of Milan.

Dance Theatre

Since 1945 the rebirth and renewal of dance in Italy has been influenced by various schools of Europe – notably French, Soviet and English – and new development in the United States. Through these influences, a new energy was injected into a form that was in danger of becoming a mere rehash of preceding models.

International exchanges – particularly those that first occurred with the New York City Ballet, Merce Cunningham, John Cage and later Pina Bausch – produced fertile seeds in the creative soil of Italian dance. Tours by the New York City Ballet played a primary role in diffusing new forms through Italy. At this time, dance, like painting and the other visual arts, began to feel the influence of the abstract: geometric designs and a stylization devoid of historical scenic references bringing a new sense of freedom.

The Hungarian choreographer Aurel M. Millos, whose Italian début was at Naples' Teatro San Carlo, lived in Italy from the pre-war period. Through his works, like the 1942 La Scala performance of *The Miraculous Mandarin* with music by Bartók, he achieved great stylistic heights and later became the official choreographer of the Opera of Rome. Thanks also to the technical skill that he displayed as a dancer, he managed to instil a new spirit into earlier models. His training, rooted in his experiences in Berlin and Budapest, translated into his active participation in major dance companies and in the creation of a refined choreography which made use of music by major composers from Casella to Vlad, Bussotti to Berio. His approach to set design was similar in that he looked to such artists as Felice Casorati (1886–1963), Giorgio De Chirico, Gino Severini (1883–1966), Filippo De Pisis, Scipione Maffei (1902–65), Renato Guttuso (b. 1912) and Ceroli.

In total, Millos created some 170 ballets. Of these the most notable are *Marsia* (1948, music by Dallapiccola) and *Follia di Orlando* (*Orlando's Folly*, 1943, music by Goffredo Petrassi (b. 1904), set design by Casorati) staged during his tenure as chief choreographer at La Scala. Also worthy of special mention are *Estri* (*Creative Inspirations*), a success at the 1978 Spoleto Festival, *Persephone* (1978, music by Stravinsky) and *Rara* (*Rare*, 1971), with music by Sylvano Bussotti (b. 1931).

In post-war Milan, La Scala was able to reopen its doors by staging very impressive ballets produced by Millos. There followed a series of performances by the Paris Opera with Serge Lifar, which also had influence on the Italian dance scene. Among the greatest successes of the following years were the ballets *Marsia* (the combination of Millos's choreography and music by Dallapiccola which made its début at Venice's La Fenice Theatre); Balanchine's *Il balletto imperiale* (*Ballet Imperial*) and *Petrushka*, complemented by the tours of the New York City Ballet; and Sadler's Wells Ballet of London (later the Royal Ballet) and Roland Petit's existential ballet *Le jeune Homme et la mort* (*Death and the Young Man*).

The year 1955 was memorable for the début of Carla Fracci and the Gluck-Angiolini production of *Don Juan*. Also memorable were the triumphs of Luciana Novaro (b. 1923) with *L'amore stregone* (*Love the Magician*) and *Le donne di buon umore* (*The Good-Natured Ladies*). From Ulanova to Plesitskaya and the entire star cast of the Bolshoi, all the major international companies have graced the stage of the Milanese theatre.

The high point of Italian dance from the 1950s to the 1990s is linked to the name of Carla Fracci, who graduated from La Scala School and later became the most important of Eric Bruhn's partners. Her 1955 success *Sleeping Beauty* preceded an international triumph in *Giselle*. After having become prima ballerina at La Scala she played the part of Gelsomina in the ballet *La strada*, inspired by the Federico Fellini (1920–93) film of the same name, choreographed by Mario Pistoni (b. 1933). Her ability also shone forth in *Swan Lake* and *Coppelia*. With the termination of the arrangement with La Scala, she performed in 'dance-plays' which possessed elements of Diaghilev and Isadora Duncan. Nineteenth-century choreography with romantic motifs, reworked by Beppe Menegatti (b. 1929), gave the artist the opportunity to take part in vibrant performances, which led to her being granted the 1991 award of New York's Stravinsky–Diaghilev Foundation for her work in *Vespro Siciliano* (*Sicilian Vespers*).

The connection between opera and dance has had a negative effect on the latter since the organizing bodies of opera look after ballet which, consequently, receives less attention. Among established choreographers there is

Paolo Bortolozzi (b. 1938) who, as a soloist, received great acclaim in Xenakis's *Nomo Alpha* (where he danced as a man 'possessed' by electronic music) as well as in his appearances with Fracci. In addition to Enzo Cosimi there is Elisabetta Terabust (b. 1949), a great ballerina who was called upon to direct the ballet corps of the school of the Rome Opera, and who achieved great success in the *pas de deux* of *Don Quixote* among other pieces.

Also included in this group are Mario Pistoni, active at La Scala in numerous productions based on the music of major contemporary composers and showing a broad range of inspiration (among others, *Francesca da Rimini* based on the music of Tchaikovsky), and Luciana Novaro, who is celebrated particularly for classical ballet and a famous *Bolero*. Cristina Bozzolini, dancer and choreographer, has organized the Balletto di Toscana (Tuscan Ballet) while Amedeo Amodio (b. 1940) is the director of Ater-balletto in Reggio Emilia.

Among smaller groups which produce dance performances, one should mention the Centro studio della danza (Centre for the Study of Dance) of Turin which stages school performances under the direction of Susanna Egri (b. 1926), as well as the Compagnia teatro danza (Theatre Dance Company), directed by Luciana

De Fanti. The latter group's choreography tends to reflect its social and political engagement, from the 1970 production of *Sotiris Petroulas* (music by Theodorakis) to the 1974 *Canti della resistenza spagnola* (*Songs of the Spanish Resistance*).

Also significant are the activities of the Accademia Filarmonica di Roma (Philharmonic Academy of Rome) and the long-term contribution made by Vittoria Ottolenghi to the knowledge and diffusion of contemporary dance. The positive results achieved through such experiments as 'dance-events' have confirmed the validity of a critical position in which the classical tradition is reconciled with modern and post-modern innovations (the latter being the fruit of stylistic borrowings from different sources).

In Rome, the Accademia Nazionale di Danza (National Academy of Dance), created in 1940 through the initiative of Jia Ruskaia (1902–70), has recently undergone renovations. This has extended to new faculty members, among them Alberto Testa, an author of important studies.

Journals devoted to dance include *Balletto oggi* (*Ballet Today*), *La danza* (*Dance*), *La danza italiana* (*Italian Dance*), *Danza & Danza* (*Dance & Dance*) and *Tutto danza* (*All Dance*).

Theatre for Young Audiences

Professional performances of productions for young people are a relatively recent phenomenon in Italy. Traditionally dealing in this area have been amateur groups, but between 1978 and 1989 the number of performances staged by professional companies for young audiences with support from the Ministry of Performing Arts increased from little more than 4,000 to over 11,000 and the number of tickets sold doubled.

In 1993 a volume was published called *Il teatro per i ragazzi, catalogo 1992–1993* (*Young People's Theatre, 1992–1993 Catalogue*). It included a list of the many small but active theatre companies and information on performances, authors, directors and actors, as well as costs, venues and subsidy levels.

The broadening of compulsory education requirements (since 1962) and the longer attendance in schools (high school and university level) by students from backgrounds that tradi-

tionally did not pursue higher levels of education have contributed generally to an increased interest in humanistic and literary studies from this new social group. However, the inefficiency of the education system which has not made possible the creation of a deep and stable link between the world of youth and the world of theatre is so acute that initiatives put forth by non-governmental agencies are more successful.

In certain cities competitions between school theatre groups have been organized. Among the various attempts at a real 'young people's theatre', one must recall those of certain public administrations like ETI (Ente Teatrale Italiano). From the 1930s to the 1960s a great number of initiatives must be attributed to the actor-director Sergio Tofano who, under the pseudonym of Sto, invented characters and staged performances of a high artistic calibre. Among undertakings of this kind are *Il teatro salvato dai bambini* (*The Theatre Saved by*

Children), a show intended to introduce young children to the world of artistic creation. The university theatre scene was very lively in the fascist period through the theatres of the Fascist Youth Organizations (Gioventù Ufficiale Fascista – GUF), by which dissent was manifested.

After a period of relative vitality in the immediate post-war period, later decades were less active. The exceptions are the university theatre of Parma and the Archivolto di Genova theatre group.

Puppet Theatre

Among the oldest forms of puppet theatre in Italy is the famous Sicilian Opera dei Pupi (Theatre of the Puppets) with its chivalric repertoire, transmitted orally. It was established in Rome in the late 1980s, where the writer Fortunato Pasqualino and his brother Giuseppe modernized it, introducing new motifs (such as the Pinocchio figure).

At the beginning of the 1920s Vittorio Podrecca (1883–1959) founded in Rome the Teatro dei Piccoli (Theatre of the Little Ones), which availed itself of the help of renowned musicians and set designers. Composers such as Ottorio Respighi (1879–1935) and Adriano Lualdi (1885–1971), as well as many designers and costume designers made their débuts in this theatre. To this day there exist throughout Italy companies which stage children's versions of works such as *Orlando Furioso* in the Podrecca style.

The activity of the marionette company of Carlo Colla (1833–1906) began in the nineteenth century and continues to this day through his descendants. Its headquarters at the Teatro Gerolamo of Milan were frequented by Igor Stravinsky, Edward Gordon Craig and other figures of the music and theatre world, some of whom actually employed his marionettes in their works. The company's repertoire spans everything from traditional fables through the Excelsior Ball to the fantastic narratives of Jules Verne.

In 1993, its main performers were Eugenio Monti Colla (b. 1939), Teresa Colla (b. 1909), Carla Colla (b. 1916) and Carlo Colla III (b. 1935). The company possesses an enormous collection (some 90,000 pieces in all) which includes marionettes (many of which are true works of art), sets, costumes, props, scripts and musical scores. Some of these are from as far back as 1699.

Maria Signorelli (1908–90) represented modern tendencies in Italian puppetry. She founded the Opera dei Burattini in Rome in 1947, with a repertoire ranging from *Little Red Riding Hood* to ballet suites with music by Monteverdi and Khachaturian, and plays written for puppets by Edward Gordon Craig. New companies such as Teatro del Burato in Milan and Otello Sarzi's company in Emilia were founded in the 1960s. Sarzi has continued a long family tradition, as has the younger generation of the Monticelli family at the Teatro del Drago in Ravenna.

Southern Italian traditions, such as *pupi siciliani* and Pulchinella street comedy (hand-puppets and portable booths), have been continued by new generations of puppet players. Among them are Mimmo Cuticchio, running his own company in Palermo, and Fratelli Napoli in Catania. In Naples in the 1970s Bruno Leone, Salvatore Gato and Maria Imperatrice, using their own styles, rejuvenated Pulchinella.

Important puppet companies since the 1970s have been Teatro Gioco Viat in Piacenza (founded in 1970), Teatro delle Bricciole (1976) in Parma and Teatro del Carretto (1978) in Lucca. Teatro Gioco Vito developed new forms of shadow theatre in such shows as *Gilgamesh* and *The Castle of Perseverance* as it demolished the traditional screen and offered the free play of light and shadows. Teatro delle Bricciole experimented successfully with scenic space, applying a sort of film framing in *Call of the Jungle* (1983) and a storytelling style in a comic version of *The Creation* (1981), Teatro del Carretto gave a series of multimedia presentations with an accent on the symbolic expression of puppets, people and props in plays such as *Snow White* (1983) and *Camelia's Lady* (1987).

Also in the 1970s several Italian puppeteers began a new form of spectacle called Object Theatre and some of them, including Claudio Cinelli, Gyula Molnar and the Assondeli e Stecchettoni company, achieved international popularity.

Design

Italian post-war designers underwent a period of disorientation. A different society (and therefore a different public) created a generation of new artists who realized that they needed to change direction regarding previous methods, both the traditional and those outlined by the Futurists. As a result, the scenic approach to performance changed radically.

Those changes, however, did take into account the experiments of director Anton Giulio Bragaglia (1890–1960), the greatest experimenter in Italian theatre in the 1930s who staged at the Teatro delle arti (Art Theatre) important innovative works of Italian and American authors with the help of the set designs of Enrico Prampolini (1894–1950). He was among the first in Italy to pay attention above all to the physical staging of works.

After the post-war resumption of work, each designer followed his own conception of scenic space. On one level was the use of only furnishings and simple painted solutions. Luchino Visconti, however, turned to designs of a naturalistic nature, rich in historical and artistic references (particularly in opera). In direct opposition, stagings dissociated from any historical reality (particularly in dance) creating imaginary settings were also done.

Luigi Nono introduced the use of projections, as well as a diverse and original use of such traditional elements as lights, fabrics, drapes, scrims, metals and wood. Mario Ceroli particularly excelled in the creative use of this last element. By the late 1960s, many directors and designers were feeling the need for new spaces beyond the traditional stage, the need to expand for the purpose of best manifesting new ideas. In the 1970s, new research and experiments in visual theatre began.

The majority of set designers work primarily with one director to achieve their results. Visconti was among the first to establish this kind of rapport in which the set designer becomes a genuine creator. Among the designers who actively worked with him in this way were Mario Chiari (b. 1903), Mario Garbuglia (b. 1927) and Franco Zeffirelli (b. 1923), who went on to become an important opera and film director.

Enzo Frigerio (b. 1930), a member of the Piccolo company, was the designer for its performances of Goldoni's *Arlecchino, servitore di due padroni* and Pirandello's *I giganti della mon-tagna* (*Giants of the Mountains*). Both productions allowed the scenic machinery to remain in view. He has also worked on operatic performances at La Scala.

Gianni Polidori (b. 1923) has exhibited a tendency to pass from the use of mangled, used materials to traditional, descriptive scenes with great attention to minute details for a production of *Don Carlos*. Misha Scandella (b. 1921) often collaborates with Gianfranco De Bosio at the Civic Theatre of Turin.

The inventive inspiration of the eclectic Emanuele Luzzati (b. 1922) manifests itself in different ways for each performance. The designs are intended to function as an extension of text and are characterized by the use of 'simple' materials: cardboard, fabric (particularly jute) and gypsum. His 'assemblages', which he often enriches pictorially, are the result of his manual dexterity and his direct rapport with these materials. These characteristics could be seen in performances of *Lea Lebowitz* by Fersen at the Nuovo di Milano as early as 1947, in Ionesco's *Rhinocéros* in 1960, Shakespeare's *Titus Andronicus* (directed by Aldo Trionfo, b. 1921) and in Walton's *Façade*, directed by Lindsay Kemp at the Nuovo di Milano in 1983.

At the beginning of the 1960s, Pier Luigi Pizzi (b. 1930) showed an extremely refined poetic realism in his careful choice of objects, following an elegant and linear aesthetic tradition. In his early work, the stage was stripped of realistic elements and enriched by lighting effects and revolving platforms. An example of this was included in the stage set-up for the director De Lullo.

The name Uberto Bertacca is linked to Luca Ronconi with whom he staged *Orlando Furioso*. This performance was endowed with a scenic structure, dislocated at various points, allowing for simultaneous scenic action without a stage. The audience was, in fact, part of each scene and the actors moved about on dollies. Also important were his later collaborations with the director G. Sepe.

In the experimental theatre of the 1960s and 1970s, the designs of S. Venditelli for the works of Carmelo Bene deserve a place of distinction. Venditelli, in tune with the ideas of Carmelo Bene relating to reconstruction of text and the union of dissonant theatrical genres, rented an old stage set from an opera and crammed it into the theatre's narrow stage space, depriving it of its supporting framework. Consequently, it fell on the actors, as intended, forcing the stagehands out during the performance to set it up again.

For his part, M. Perlini (b. 1940), oriented like the rest of the Roman school of the 1970s towards the primacy of gesture and the expressive powers of the human body, made light the protagonist of a performance dealing with the destruction of images.

Even for the post-avant-garde groups of the 1980s (Magazzini, Falso Movimento and Gaia Scienza), set design was a fundamental element of performance. This was expressed through projections, the expressive use of lighting and the movement of the actors who intersected the constructed set.

Numerous painters and sculptors have again begun to collaborate with opera and ballet. Piero Zuffi (b. 1919) is one of the great innovators of opera set design. His trademarks are the interplay of full and empty spaces, surfaces finished with large bas-reliefs, the accentuation of dramatic tones, contrasts of light and the visual dynamism of forms in scene changes.

Fabrizio Clerici in the 1940s staged his works after being inspired by the urgency of surrealistic art. By matching apparently incompatible elements, he created an atmosphere approaching unreality. This was evident in performances of Stravinsky's *Orpheus*, choreographed by A.M. Millos at the Maggio Musicale di Firenze (1948) and Henry Purcell's *Dido and Aeneas* at Rome's Teatro dell'Opera (1949).

Roberto Francia is closely linked to director Maurizio Scaparro, for whose *Cyrano* he created impressive set designs. The same can be said of the performances of the sixteenth-century *La Venexiana* (*The Venetian*) and *The Life of Galileo* by Brecht. For the latter, the scientist's study was made to resemble a globe with latitude and longitude lines that made it appear to be an enormous cage in which the actors moved, both through and around. These were also 'poor' set designs made of modest materials; costumes were often merely a few rags.

From the 1950s onward, numerous high-fashion designers have created theatre costumes, in particular for operas. A number of painters such as Enrico Job and Santuzza Calì (who took classes with Oskar Kokoschka and later became his assistant) have also done distinguished work. Calì has worked particularly with Fersen, Trionfo, De Bosio and Luzzati. With Luzzati, she enjoyed a steady and impeccable artistic understanding that led to many awards.

Theatre Space and Architecture

The increased expense for the best stage and lighting equipment has often led to the use of small venues. For example, the Roman school, which made a name for itself in the 1960s and 1970s, is closely connected with performances staged in cantinas and small theatres. Since Eugenio Barba, there is no lack of performances with limited seating.

This movement toward small venues may also be an elitist reaction by directors, or a genuine wish to explore intimate performance space (like Luciano Damiani's (b. 1922) theatre in Rome).

Changes of theatrical space may also be connected to cinema, which has broadened the space confronting the spectator. It is not unusual now to see the use of vast spaces involving many people.

As far as the construction of new theatres or the renovation of old ones, important accomplishments have been made in various Italian cities. Among these is the recent reconstruction of the Genoese Theatre Carlo Felice.

Changing a building's usual purpose has allowed not only the actors but also the audience to use unusual artistic locations. Luca Ronconi, in particular, has looked into renovated locations like the Fabricone in Prato or former sites of automobile factories in Turin.

In the 1950s theatres were created which tended to be multi-use in nature. Built as cultural complexes with many stages in a single hall or with only one circular stage placed in the middle, Milan's Teatro San Erasmo is a good example. Other complexes were built to also accommodate cinemas or even sporting events.

On the other hand, great classically designed theatres such as Milan's Teatro alla Scala must continuously update their technical systems to facilitate the new computerized approaches of designers, electricians and even stagehands.

Training

The number of training schools in both large and small cities increased significantly between the 1950s and 1990s. Initially, these schools concentrated almost exclusively on training actors. Later, directing and technical aspects, as well as film training were added.

Among the principal schools there is, first of all, the Accademia nazionale d'arte drammatica Silvio d'Amico (Silvio d'Amico National Academy of Dramatic Arts), founded in Rome in the 1930s. This school strives to combine tradition and experimentation.

La Scuola di teatro (Theatre School) in Milan, directed by Giorgio Strehler and connected to the Piccolo Teatro seeks to provide essential classical and modern techniques. In the same city the Civica scuola d'arte drammatica Paolo Grassi (Paolo Grassi Municipal School of Dramatic Art), founded by the former director of the Piccolo and managed by the city, has offered a solid classical curriculum since the 1950s.

In Turin, the Scuola del teatro stabile (School of the Civic Theatre), long directed by Luca Ronconi, made a name for itself for its ability to link both traditional and modern forms in a rigorous and consistent way. Two Florence schools of note are the Bottega teatrale di Vittorio Gassman (Vittorio Gassman Theatre Studio) and the Laboratorio internazionale dell'attore (International Actor's Workshop).

Among the private schools in Rome are the Studio Fersen (Fersen Studio), which concentrates on communication techniques; the Accademia Pietro Sharoff (Pietro Sharoff Academy); the Scuola Mario Riva (Mario Riva School); and the Laboratorio di esercitazioni sceniche (Workshop of Stage Arts) created by the actor Giorgio Proietti.

The Centro sperimentale di cinematografia (Centre for Experimental Cinematography) is a public institution which has dealt with performance studies since the 1930s.

Other important institutions are Milan's Accademia dei filodrammatici (Academy of Amateur Theatre), Renzo Casoli's Comune Baires, Bologna's Scuola di teatro (Theatre School), Genoa's Scuola di recitazione del teatro stabile (School of Performing Arts of the Civic Theatre), Sicily's Scuola del teatro stabile di Catania (School of the Civic Theatre of Catania) and the Istituto nazionale del dramma antico (National Institute of Ancient Drama), which is dedicated primarily to performances of ancient Greek and Roman theatre.

Another school, DAMS in Bologna, operates at the university level, teaching all aspects of art, music and performance with a careful examination of theatre's literary aspects as well as the mechanics of performance. The school LUISS offers courses that are focused more on the management and administrative side.

Criticism, Scholarship and Publishing

Theatrical journals abound in Italy and may at times be linked closely to either a particular school of thought and methodology or a particular area of production, such as set design. Often these publications are sponsored by schools of dramatic arts such as L'Accademia nazionale d'arte drammatica, La Scuola di Teatro del Piccolo di Milano, La Scuola del Teatro Stabile di Genova, La Scuola del Teatro Stabile di Torino, and La Civica Scuola d'arte drammatica Paolo Grassi.

The journal *Ridotto* (*Lobby*) was founded in Venice in 1949 by Vincenzo Filippone, edited first by Mario Federici (1900–75) and currently by Carlo Vallauri (b. 1925) and is published in Rome by the Società Italiana Autori Drammatici (Italian Society of Dramatic Authors) and directed by Aldo Nicolai. The journal's issues constitute the most comprehensive survey of modern and contemporary Italian theatre. Each issue contains two plays.

Sipario (*Curtain*), another important journal, was founded in Genoa by Ivo Chiesa (b. 1920), an author and administrator. It contains articles on various of the performing arts.

A newer journal is *Ystrio*, edited by Ugo Ronfani (b. 1926) and published quarterly in Milan. *Il Dramma* (*Drama*), edited by Lucio Ridenti (1895–1973) and *Scenario*, edited by the Istituto del dramma italiano (Institute for Italian Drama), have both ceased publication but played an important role in the field.

Up until the 1960s, criticism tended to concentrate on the literary value of text and ideas. With the development of a more visual, image-oriented theatre, attention was shifted to other areas and a more theoretical schema.

The sociology of the theatre became a thing of interest in the 1960s, but in different ways. From one side it was simply an interpretation of dramatic texts done with a sociological slant, and therefore can be said to have remained still within the confines of dramatic literature. From the other side, one can find a more profound link between anthropology and performance/representation. In this area, from the point of view of performance one must look at the works of Eugenio Barba.

Critics of the immediate post-war period were quite sharp in their writings and perceptions. Among the best was Renato Simoni (1875–1932) who collected his reviews in *Trent'anni di storia drammatica* (*Thirty Years of Drama History*), the last volume of which was published in 1952. Silvio d'Amico (1887–1955), the founder of Rome's Accademia nazionale d'arte drammatica, which now bears his name, was greatly committed to the acknowledgement of the role of the director and the decline of the star, as well as of the importance in the repertory of Italian works (Pirandello in particular) and major foreign writers such as Ibsen, O'Neill and French dramaturgy.

The most important of the literature-based critics have been Giorgio Prosperi (b. 1911) of the Rome newspaper, *Il Tempo* (*Time*); Guido Davico Bonino, a professor at the University of Turin; Renzo Tian and Franca Angelini (b. 1930) of the University of Rome. Historically minded critics of note include Nicola Chiaromonte, author of *La situazione drammatica* (*The Dramatic Situation*); Ruggero Jacobbi (1920–81), a director, dramatist and author of fundamental essays on the Italian contemporary theatre; and Vito Pandolfi (1917–74), an expert in Italian theatre from the sixteenth century to the *commedia dell'arte*, on which he wrote a seminal work.

Noteworthy among contemporary critics have been Paolo Emilio Poesio from Florence and Aggeo Savioli, who writes for the left-wing daily *L'Unità* (*Unity*). Following the path of Umberto Eco (b. 1932), recent years have seen the establishment of an increasing number of critics (like Ugo Volli) who are linked to the study of semiotics. Other scholars, such as Achille Mango, professor at the University of Salerno, and Franco Quadri, editor of a very

informative yearly publication *Il Pata Logo*, have demonstrated an unmistakable preference for the new theatrical styles linked to images. Not to be forgotten are the poet Giovanni Raboni (b. 1932) who writes for *Il Corriere della sera* and the Anglicist Guido Almansi (b. 1931) who contributes to *Panorama*.

Mino Vianello (b. 1932) and Elsa di Meo have published studies and research on theatrical sociology, as has Carlo Vallauri, who has dealt with areas such as audience and theatre economics. On the occasion of the third World Congress of Theatre Sociology (Lisbon, 1992), a new journal, the *Revue internationale de sociologie du théâtre* (*International Revue of the Sociology of Theatre*) began publication.

In the 1980s, an association of university teachers also began.

Important theatre libraries exist in a number of cities. The richest is Rome's Biblioteca e raccolta teatrale Burcardo (Burcardo Theatre Library and Collection) which contains manuscripts, texts and librettos of many operas as well as playbills, programmes and performance runs of the main journals. In total it has almost 40,000 volumes. The richest libraries for music are the Museo del Teatro alla Scala (La Scala Museum), full of rare materials, followed by Genoa's Museo dell'attore (Actor's Museum) directed by Alessandro D'Amico (b. 1926). Many university libraries also have valuable collections.

Carlo Vallauri
Translated by Donato Santerano and
Robert Buranello

Further Reading

Amoia, Alba. *The Italian Theatre Today: Twelve Interviews*. New York: Whitston, 1977. 136 pp.

Angelini, Franca. 'Teatri moderni'. [Modern theatre]. Chap. in *Letteratura Italiana*. [Italian literature], vol. 6. Turin: Einaudi, 1986.

——. *Il teatro del Novecento da Pirandello a Fo*. [Italian theatre of the twentieth century from Pirandello to Fo]. Bari: Laterza, 1976.

——, ed. *Scrivere il teatro*. [Writing for the theatre]. Rome: Bulzoni, 1990.

Apollonio, Mario. *Storia del teatro italiano*. [History of the Italian theatre]. 2 vols. Series Civiltà europea. Florence: Sansoni, 1981.

Barsotti, A. *Futurismo e avanguardia. Nel teatro italiano tra la 2 guerre*. [Futurism and avant-garde: Italian theatre between the two wars]. Rome: Bulzoni, 1990.

Bentivoglio, L. *La danza contemporanea*. [Contemporary dance]. Milan: Longanesi, 1985.

Bernard, E., ed. *Autori e drammaturgi. Enciclopedia del teatro italiano. Il dopoguerra (1950–1990)*. [Playwriting and playwrights. An encyclopedia of Italian post-war theatre (1950–1990)]. Rome: 1991.

Cappelletti, D. *La sperimentazione teatrale in Italia tra norma e devianza*. [Theatrical experimentation in Italy from the normal to abnormal]. Rome: ERI, 1986.

Cruciani, F. *Teatro nel Novecento. Registi, pedagoghi e comunità teatrali nel XX secolo*. [Theatre in the twentieth century: directors, teachers and the theatre community]. Florence: Mulino, 1989.

——, and C. Falletti. *Civiltà teatrale nel XX secolo*. [Theatre civilization in the twentieth century]. Bologna: Il Mulino, 1986.

——, and N. Savarese, eds. *Guida bibliografica al Teatro*. [Bibliographic guide to theatre]. Milan: Garzanti, 1991.

D'Amico, Silvo. *Storia del teatro drammatico*. [History of theatre]. 8 vols. 5th ed. Rome: Bulzoni, 1991.

Davico Bonino, Guido. *Il teatro del '900*. [Theatre in the twentieth century]. Turin: Einaudi, 1991.

——. *Identikit dell'attore italiano*. [The identity of Italian actors]. Turin: Rosenberg e Sellier, 1990.

De Marinis, M. *Capire il teatro. Lineamenti di una nuova teatralogia*. [Understanding theatre: outline of a new theatre theory]. Florence: Casa Usher, 1988.

Duecento alla Scala. [Two hundred years of La Scala]. Milan: Electra, 1978.

Duse, V. *Per una storia della musica del Novecento*. [On the history of music in the twentieth century]. Turin: EDT, 1990.

Guazzotti, G. *Teoria e realtà del Piccolo Teatro di Milano*. [Myths and realities of Milan's Piccolo Teatro]. Turin: Einaudi, 1986.

Jacobbi, Ruggero. *Teatro da ieri a domani*. [Theatre from yesterday to tomorrow]. Florence: Nuova Italia, 1972.

Livio, G. *La scena italiana*. [The Italian stage]. Milan: Mursia, 1989.

——. *Il teatro in rivolta*. [Theatre in revolt]. Milan: Mursia, 1976.

Lo spazio, il luogo, l'ambito, da Scenografie del Teatro alla Scala 1947–1983. [The space, the place, the environment: the scene designs of La Scala, 1947–1983. Milan: Silvana, Cinisello Balsamo, 1983.

Lunari, Luigi. *Cento trame del teatro italiano*. [A hundred plots from the Italian theatre]. Milan: Pirroe, 1993.

Mango, Achille. *La morte della partecipazione. Cinque studi sul teatro*. [The death of participation: five studies on theatre]. Rome: Bulzoni, 1980.

——. *Verso una sociologia del teatro*. [Towards a sociology of theatre]. Trapani: Celebes, 1978.

Meldolesi, C. *Fondamenti del teatro italiano. La generazione dei registi*. [Foundations of Italian theatre: a generation of directors]. Florence: Sansoni, 1984.

Ottolenghi, V. *La danza contemporanea*. [Contemporary dance]. Rome: Gremiese, 1990.

Pandolfi, Vito. *Regia e registi nel teatro moderno*. [Directing and directors in the modern theatre]. Bologna: Cappelli, 1973.

——. *Il teatro italiano contemporaneo*. [Contemporary Italian theatre]. Milan: Schwarz, 1959.

Puppa, P. *Teatro e spettacolo nel secondo Novecento*. [Theatre and performing arts from the 1950s]. Bari: Laterza, 1990.

Quadri, Franco. *L'avanguardia teatrale in Italia. Materiali 1960–1976*. [Avant-garde theatre in Italy: materials from 1960 to 1976]. 2 vols. Turin: Einaudi, 1977.

——. *Il teatro degli anni Settanta*. [Theatre in the 1970s]. 2 vols. Turin: Einaudi.

Ripellino, A.M. *Siate buffi. Cronache di teatro, circo e altre arti (1969–1977)*. [A chronicle of theatre, circus and other arts (1969–1977)]. Rome: Bulzoni, 1989.

Scenografia in Italia oggi. [Italian stage design today]. Foreword by Roberto Rebora. Milan: Gorlich, 1974.

Vallauri, Carlo. *Il pubblico in palcoscenico. Ricerca sugli spettatori di teatro*. [The audience in the balconies: research on theatre audiences]. Rome: Regione Lazio, 1980.

——. 'Per una Sociologia del teatro politico.' [Towards a sociology of political theatre] in *Fantasia e sovversione*. Milan: Angeli, 1979.

Verdone, M. *Teatro nel tempo futurista*. [Theatre of the future]. Rome: Bulzoni, 1988.

Vlad, Romano. *Capire la musica e le sue forme*. Florence: Giesti, 1989.

Zanetti, R. *La musica italiana nel '900*. [Italian music in the twentieth century]. Busto Arsizio: Bramante, 1989.

KAZAKHSTAN

(Asia/Oceania volume; see also USSR)

KIRGHIZIA

(Asia/Oceania volume; see also USSR)

LATVIA

The small nation of Latvia (land area: 64,590 square kilometres or 24,930 square miles) is located in northeastern Europe on the Baltic Sea, between Lithuania, Belarus, Russia and Estonia. Its capital, Riga, was established in 1201 and soon became a key trading centre. Latvia's strategic geographic position has been coveted and also controlled by many foreign powers: Germany, Russia, Sweden and Poland. By the eighteenth century, Latvia's territory had become part of the Russian Empire.

Between 1918 and 1940, Latvia was a free and independent nation. In June 1940, however, Latvia was once more occupied and forcibly annexed by the Soviet Union. In August 1991, Latvia regained its status as an independent, parliamentary republic.

The country's largest cities are Riga, Liepaja, Daugavpils and Jelgava. In 1989, a census found that of its 2.7 million population some 46 per cent were non-Latvian: 34 per cent Russian, 4.5 per cent Belarussian, 3.5 per cent Ukrainian, 2.3 per cent Polish and 1.3 per cent Lithuanian.

Latvia's advantageous geographic location was also important in its theatrical development. Riga was a midway point between western and Russian cultural centres. As far back as 1204, there were open-air performances – Christian Mystery play overtones, organized by bishops to educate the 'pagan' populace. In the following centuries, Riga became acquainted with various other Medieval theatrical forms, including mummery and later *commedia dell'arte*.

The play *The Prodigal Son*, for example, by German poet Burckhard Waldiss, was first performed in Riga in 1527. A full German Theatre and Opera Company was established in 1782 and its repertoire included such masters of the day as Schiller, Goldoni and Beaumarchais. The company's opera conductor from 1837 to 1839 was no less a personage than Richard Wagner and guest performers included such stars as Ira Aldridge and Adelaide Ristori.

A specifically Latvian theatre began developing only in the 1860s, coinciding with Latvia's 'period of national awakening'. Rooted in folklore traditions – mummery, games and rituals connected to weddings, funerals, holidays and solstices – and tempered with a strong German influence, the first Latvian-language production was Schiller's *Die Räuber* (*The Robbers*), translated and directed by Diklu estate serf Jānis Peitāns.

By 1868, regular performances were being seen in Riga. Among them was an adaptation of Ludvig Holberg's *Jeppe Paa Bjerget* (*Jeppe of the Hill*) under the auspices of the newly established Riga Latvian Society. From 1870 to 1885, the Rīgas Latviešu teātris (Riga Latvian Theatre) was headed by director Adolfs Alunāns (1848–1912), who was himself educated in the German theatre. Alunāns formed the first Latvian acting company, which initially consisted of amateurs. Alunāns is also credited with developing the early Latvian theatre repertoire (mostly farces translated from German). Alunāns himself was the author of many popular farces, among which were *Priekos un bēdās* (*Laughter and Tears*, 1871) and *Džons Neilands* (*John Neiland*, 1881) as well as the first Latvian operetta *Mucenieks un muceniece* (*The Cooper's Love*, 1872). Alunāns's comedies were filled with satiric commentary on current events, many in song. Productions of foreign plays were rare. Of particular note, though, were stagings of Gogol's *Revizor* (*The Government Inspector*, 1870) and Lessing's *Minna von Barnhelm* (1889).

The artistic director of the Riga Latvian Theatre from 1886 to 1893 was German director Hermann Rode-Ebeling (1846–1906), who also taught acting technique. Under his leadership, the Riga Latvian Theatre began performing such plays as Shakespeare's *The Merchant of Venice* (1888) and *Richard III* (1893), Schiller's *Luise Miller* (1889), as well as the Latvian playwright Rudolfs Blaumanis's (1863–1908) *Zagļi* (*Thieves*, 1890) and *Ļaunais gars* (*The Evil Spirit*, 1891). This period also brought the first generation of actors – Berta Rūmniece (1865–1953), Dace Akmentiņa (1858–1936), Jūlija Skaidrīte (1871–1942), Jēkabs Duburs (1866–1916) and Aleksis Mierlauks (1866–1943).

The Krievu drāmas teātris (Riga Russian Theatre) began operating in 1883. The 1890s brought artistic maturity and the rise of original Latvian playwriting. Director Pēteris Ozoliņš (1864–1938) and the Latvian playwright Aspazija (1868–1943) made their début with the romantic drama *Vaidelote* (1894) and the socially conscious *Zaudētās tieslbas* (*The Loss of Rights*, 1894). Also presented was Blaumanis's drama *Pazudūšais dēls* (*The Prodigal Son*, 1893). At the Jaunais Rīgas teātris (New Riga Theatre), founded in 1908, the symbolic verse dramas of Latvian Jānis Rainis (1865–1929) were given evocative life. With direction by Mierlauks and scenic design by Jānis Kuga (1876–1966), Rainis's 1911 play *Uguns un nakts* (*Fire and Night*) stood out at the time. The New Riga Theatre also performed plays by Ibsen, Hauptmann and Andreyev.

World War I caused many ensembles to disband. Others simply evacuated Latvian territory while still others continued activity on the front lines. On 18 November 1918, Latvia declared its independence. After the liberation of Riga in 1919, a National Theatre was established. Its primary goal was the promotion of original Latvian dramaturgy. Rainis was the artistic director from 1921 to 1925. In the 1920s and 1930s many new writers appeared, including Anna Brigadere (1861–1933), Andrejs Upīts (1877–1970), Aspazija, Jūlijs Pētersons (1880–1945), Mārtiņš Zīverts (1903–90) and Vilis Lācis (1904–66). Actors and directors were trained in and worked in the then-predominant style of psychological realism.

The Daile (Art) Theatre was launched on 19 November 1920, under the aegis of director-actor Eduards Smiļģis (1886–1966). Smiļģis's bold, theatrical style was much more in the tradition of the Russians Alexander Tairov and Vsevolod Meyerhold, with a new accent on music, lighting and movement. The Daile Theatre concentrated primarily on world classics and the plays of Rainis, and developed plays in the musical genre.

The forte of Latvia's Workers' Theatre (1926–34) was Russian socialistic agitprop and German expressionism. The latter greatly influenced the work of director Anna (Asja) Lācis (1891–1979), who initially worked mostly with amateur groups.

The experimental Latvju drāmas ansamblis (Latvian Dramatic Ensemble, 1935–44) put to use the teachings of Russian actor-director Mikhail (Michael) Chekhov (1891–1955).

The Soviet occupation of Latvia in June 1940 brought the Latvian theatre under the influence of socialist-realism. The German occupation (1941–4) simply added to the political directives. Despite the turmoil, Latvian theatres continued mounting world classics and each night provided a few hours of solace for war-weary playgoers.

But by 1944, the future of the country was clear and a mass exodus began of Latvian artists to the west. Many were put into displaced person camps in war-ravaged Germany. By 1945, these *émigré* theatre professionals formed theatre troupes in Meerbeck and Esslingen. They overcame many hardships and their productions were surprisingly vibrant. Latvian theatre artists later continued their activity in various *émigré* Latvian ensembles in New York, Boston, Washington, Toronto, Stockholm and other major cities.

In May 1945, Latvia came under the complete control of the Red Army and was soon incorporated into the Soviet Union. Those theatre artists who remained resumed their professions. Daile Theatre director Smiļģis, for instance, successfully continued working in the theatre he founded until 1964. The National Theatre (renamed the Drama Theatre) came under the direction of veteran director Alfrēds Amtmanis-Brieditis (1885–1966). The National Opera company was renamed the Opera and Ballet Theatre.

The Latvian Jaunatnes (Youth) Theatre, founded in 1941, resumed activity as did the main regional theatres in Valmiera, run by Pēteris Lūcis (1907–91) and Liepaja, run by Nikolajs Mūrnieks (1904–77). In 1945, all Latvian theatre companies officially became 'state' theatres, operating with significant government subsidies. All the theatres ran in repertory and evolved large resident acting companies.

The repertoire itself was controlled by the Ministry of Culture. Latvia's Communist Party particularly objected to 'patriotic' tendencies on the stage. Directors were urged – perhaps required is a better word – to reflect the 'class struggle', which caused many productions to be weak in character development and lacking in depth. Post-war playwrights and directors were also hampered by a restrictive 'non-conflict' theory that included a ban on reflecting any negative aspects of daily life. They were urged to 'discuss' problems of mass production in their plays. As a result, tragic historical events and painful contemporary issues were ignored. Among these were the mass deportations of Latvian citizens to Siberia, the exodus of 200,000 Latvians to the west, the forced collectivization of Latvian farmland and the extermination of private enterprise.

Generally, theatre in Latvia was guided by the leading Riga theatre companies and their artistic directors. Despite ideological pressure, Amtmanis-Brieditis's productions at the National were truthful and hearty, successfully avoiding naturalistic pitfalls. His stagings of Latvian classics reflected profound aspects of the national character. Noteworthy were Upīts's Zaļā zeme (The Green Land, 1950), Pāvils Rozītis's (1889–1937) Ceplis (1953) and Blaumanis's Skroderdienas Silmačos (Tailor Days in Silmachi, 1955).

Equally successful – but working in a broad-stroked, theatrical style – was Smiļģis. His guiding principles were clarity, simplicity and passion. Most successful were his stagings of classic drama – Tolstoi's Anna Karenina (1949), Schiller's Maria Stuart (1956) and Shakespeare's Romeo and Juliet (1953) and Hamlet (1959).

The 1940s and 1950s brought a heavy influx of Russian dramatic literature, material not fully explored by the Latvian theatre before the war. In many cases, the results were rewarding. Worth mentioning were productions of Ostrovsky's Bezpridaņņica (Bride Without a Dowry, National Theatre, 1948), and Chekhov's Tri sestri (Three Sisters, Daile Theatre, 1951) and Djadja Vaņja (Uncle Vanya, Valmiera Theatre, 1954).

In terms of artistic methodology, Latvian theatre artists focused on the Stanislavski system. The high priestess of his principles was Russian-trained director-teacher Vera Baļuna (1904–78), who worked at the Drama Theatre (later the National) from 1944 to 1956. Other disciples of Stanislavskian principles were guest directors from Moscow – Maria Knebel, Yuri Zavadsky and Vassily Toporkov. Unfortunately, the Stanislavski system in Latvia was the only officially acceptable one; by the 1950s its approaches seemed dogmatic and limited.

Stalin's death opened the door in the mid-1950s new plays, approaches and themes. Foremost were the plays of Gunārs Priede (b. 1928) – Jaunākā brāļa vasara (The Youngest Brother's Summer, 1955), Lai arī rudens (Even Though It's Fall, 1956) and Vikas pirmā balle (Vicky's First Dance, 1960). Priede moved away from sketchy portrayals of the class struggle in favour of a lyrical, more genuine depiction of daily strife. In tandem with Priede at the Daile Theatre came a new director, Pēteris Pētersons (b. 1923). Pētersons also put into practice Brechtian principles for his production of Der gute Mensch von Sezuan (The Good Person of Setzuan, 1958). Pētersons became the Daile's artistic director in 1964, succeeding Smiļģis.

A new generation of directors also took charge at other major Latvian theatres. The National Theatre's new artistic director was Alfrēds Jaunušāns (b. 1919). Ādolfs Šapiro (b. 1939) began a fruitful reign at the Youth Theatre and the Valmiera Theatre reached artistic maturity under the guidance of director Oļģerts Kroders (b. 1921).

At the Drama Theatre, particularly striking were Jaunušāns's stagings of works previously unknown to post-war Latvian audiences – Tennessee Williams's A Streetcar Named Desire (1969) and Sweet Bird of Youth (1977), de Musset's Lorenzaccio (1973) and Molnar's Liliom (1970).

At the Daile, Pētersons successfully tackled Dostoevsky's The Idiot (1969) and introduced modern verse theatre with a vibrant collage of the works of the popular Latvian poet Imants Ziedonis, entitled Motocikls (Motorcycle, 1967).

The 1960s also saw the advent of a new type of socially conscious drama. Harijs Gulbis's (b. 1926) play Aijā, žūžū, bērns kā lācis (Rockabye Baby, 1968), written in a journalistic style, probed one of society's growing ills – irresponsibility. Muted protest plays like these were well received by audiences and critics alike.

In 1971, Pētersons was succeeded at the Daile Theatre by director Arnolds Liniņš (b. 1930), who revived Smiļģis's tradition of colourful theatricality. Ibsen's Brand (1975), Bruckner's Elisabeth von England (1980) and Blaumanis's Īsa pamācība mī lēšanā (Short Course on Love, 1973) were triumphs.

Arnolds Liniņš's 1975 Daile Theatre production of Ibsen's *Brand*, designed by Ilmārs Blumbergs.
Photo: U.A. Ikonnikova.

Through the 1960s and into the 1970s, the Latvian theatre boasted docu-dramas, like Jerome Kilty's *Dear Liar* (Drama Theatre, 1962); intellectual fare like the verse drama *Spēlē, Spēlmani* (*Play, Player*, Youth Theatre, 1972); and musicals, like *The Prince and the Pauper* (Liepaja Theatre, 1968).

The work of new directors in the 1970s and 1980s was filled with innovative flair. Valdis Lūriņš (b. 1951) pumped new life into Upīts's tragedy *Spartacus* (Drama Theatre, 1977), Kārlis Auškāps (b. 1947) revitalized Shakespeare's *A Midsummer Night's Dream* (Daile Theatre, 1977) and Valentīns Maculēvičs (b. 1950) modernized Rainis's classic *Spēlēju dancoju* (Valmiera Theatre, 1981).

Critically acclaimed were the poetic-metaphoric ventures of Youth Theatre artistic director Šapiro into the works of Gorki – *Posledniye* (*The Last Generation*, 1967); Chekhov – *Ivanov* (1975); Ibsen – *Peer Gynt* (1979); and Brecht – *Mutter Courage und ihre Kinder* (*Mother Courage and Her Children*, 1968) and *Furcht und Elend des Dritten Reiches* (*Fear and Misery of the Third Reich*, 1986). Also innovative was the work of director Arkady Kacs (b. 1931) at the Riga Russian Theatre, especially his *Chaika* (*The Seagull*, 1983).

One must also mention here Kroders's psy-chologically and philosophically rich stagings of Shakespeare's *Hamlet* (Valmiera Theatre, 1972; Liepaja Theatre, 1984) and Dostoevsky's *Prestupļeniye i nakazaniye* (*Crime and Punishment*, Liepaja Theatre, 1977). In a similar vein but psychologically even deeper was the work of Māra Ķimele (b. 1943) at the Valmiera Theatre. Of note were Anouilh's *Medea* (1975) and Ken Kesey and Dale Wasserman's *One Flew Over the Cuckoo's Nest* (1978).

The late 1980s brought a change in artistic leadership at both the Daile and the National. Jaunušāns relinquished his post at the National to director Mihails Kublinskis (b. 1939), who was succeeded by Oļģerts Kroders in 1989. In 1988, Kārlis Auškāps became the Daile Theatre's new artistic director.

With the collapse of the Soviet Union, Latvia regained its long-sought freedom on 21 August 1991. Economic problems were, however, enormous and subsidy quickly began to vanish. In 1992, for example, the Youth Theatre was closed, victim of a government decision to withdraw subsidy. This meant that one of the most gifted and respected Latvian directors, Ādolfs Šapiro, was left without a theatre. No one could predict how many other theatres might also fall victim to the sudden changes.

Viktors Hausmanis

Structure of the National Theatre Community

In 1993, Latvia had ten subsidized theatre companies in operation, three serving the provincial cities of Liepaja, Daugavpils and Valmiera. All had between twenty and twenty-five productions in their repertoires. Performances were given in the Latvian language, except at the Riga Russian Drama Theatre. The Daugavpils Theatre and the Riga Puppet Theatre had both Latvian and Russian troupes.

In addition to the subsidized groups, Riga also had six privately funded theatres.

Amateur groups were also abundant in Latvia, with over a hundred in regular operation. The thirty-eight most active ones are categorized as Tautas teātri (People's Theatres).

The first totally independent Latvian theatre, Kabata (Pocket), founded in 1987, was supported both by the box office and by its own publishing company. Latvia had only one municipal theatre – Liepaja's Puppet Theatre, established in 1991.

For the fiscal year 1992, the ten state theatres were supported through subsidies of some 147 million rubles, 26.9 per cent of the total state expenditure for culture and education. These theatres were also relying on private sponsorship and donations, though only 9 per cent of their total income was to come from ticket sales.

State theatres on average were staging about nine new productions per season.

Staff size, creative and otherwise, ranged from 600 at the National Opera to seventy-three at the Riga Puppet Theatre. The National Theatre, for example, employed sixty actors, seventeen directors, scenic, lighting and costume designers, one composer, sixty-eight technical personnel, and eleven management and administrative personnel.

The regional state theatres were operating with smaller companies (approximately forty-five actors), had more new productions per season and a shorter rehearsal period. A special function of these theatres was to stage performances in rural communities.

Inflation in 1992 caused ticket prices to soar ten to fifteen times higher than in 1991. On average, admission cost about 50 rubles, twice the price of admission to cinemas.

The coordinating organization for theatre is the Latvian Theatre Union (LTU), whose offshoots include a Directors' Association and an Actors' Association. The LTU's Critics' Circle each season presents awards for outstanding achievement. Actors and directors are also awarded prizes by the Ministry of Culture.

Since 1956, Latvia has participated in (and also hosted) the Baltic region's annual theatre festival, Baltijas teātru pavasaris (Baltic Theatre Spring).

Amateur troupes since 1969 have also participated in the Baltic Republics' People's Theatre Festival – Draudzības rampa (Friendship Footlights) – held every two to four years.

Antra Torgāne

Artistic Profile

Companies

Latvia's government-subsidized theatre companies include the National Opera, the National Theatre, the Daile Theatre, the Riga Russian Drama Theatre, the New Riga Theatre, the Riga Musical Theatre, the State Puppet Theatre, the Valmiera Drama Theatre, the Liepaja Theatre and the Daugavpils Theatre.

The National Theatre (established in 1919) slowly but surely recovered from the loss of sixty-four company members, who had emigrated to the west in 1944, to become the most respected and most popular theatre company in Latvia. Of equal stature is Latvia's largest theatre company, the Daile, operating with an acting ensemble of seventy-one. The work of these two groups serves as a kind of national model for the direction and scope of Latvian theatre in general. The predominant style is traditional psychological realism, although more modern forms of expression are also explored.

Riga's Jaunatnes Theatre, dissolved in 1992, was considered Latvia's most innovative group. This company began production in 1941.

Vidzeme province's Valmiera Theatre (established in 1919) came into its own in the 1970s

Alvis Hermanis's 1993 New Riga Theatre production of Steven Soderbergh's *Sex, Lies and Videotape*.
Photo: Jānis Deināts.

with a series of taut and intelligent ensemble performances.

One company in the 1990s vanguard was the experimental, independent theatre, Kabata (established in 1987 in Riga), featuring an intimate performance space, a small acting company and regular guest performers and directors. Its repertoire includes three or four new productions per season.

The Kustību (Movement) Theatre was established in 1979 and is the foremost performance art group in the country and claims to 'visualize music'.

The Experimental Studio Theatre was established in 1974 and champions a form of street theatre. Also following a non-traditional path is Riga's Komediantu kompānija (Company of Comedians) established in 1991.

Guna Zeltiņa

Dramaturgy

Because of the many political changes in the country in the mid-1940s, Latvian drama in the post-war era found itself in an awkward position. Its two leading playwrights – Mārtiņš Zīverts and Anšlavs Eglītis (1906–93) – were in exile and therefore politically taboo in Latvia. Zīverts was a master of intellectual dialogue and emotional conflict, usually writing small-cast plays such as *Kāds, kura nav* (*Someone Non-existent*, 1947), *Rakete* (*Rocket*, 1959), *Kopenhāgenas dialogs* (*Copenhagen Dialogue*, 1982) and *Teātris* (*Theatre*, 1987).

Eglītis revitalized classic European comedy in such plays as *Kazanovas mētelis* (*Casanova's Cloak*, 1947), *Galma gleznotājs* (*The Court Artist*, 1948), *Omartija kundze* (*Mrs Omarty*, 1961), *Jolanta Durbe* (1967) and *Bezkaunīgie veči* (*The Shameless Old Men*, 1971). Most of these are witty, often nostalgic, character comedies about Latvians living in exile in the United States.

Given the political situation, however, companies tended to stage didactic social dramas by playwrights such as Arvīds Grigulis (1906–89). Following the directives of the Communist Party, such reflections of everyday life on stage seemed narrow-minded and heavy-handed in comparison to the popular comedies of Blaumanis, Zīverts and Eglītis.

Playwright Gunārs Priede's appearance on the scene in the mid-1950s was like a breath of fresh air. Owing much to Chekhov, Priede's plays were subdued, lyrical character close-ups. His most powerful work, *Centrifūga* (*Centrifuge*, 1985), dealt effectively with the fate of Latvians during World War II. During the 1960s and 1970s, the politically and dramatically astute plays of Miervaldis Birze (b. 1921) were also staged.

Another leading dramatist of the 1960s was Harijs Gulbis, whose plays were chronicles of familial woes – *Cīrulīši* (*The House of Cirulisi*, 1975); or of society in general – *Aijā, žūžū, bērns kā lācis* (*Rockabye Baby*, 1968). Playwright Pauls Putniņš (b. 1937) perfected Latvia's version of the realistic, 'kitchen sink' genre. Politically and socially topical were his *Paši pūta, paši dega* (*Tiny, Small Brushwood Rods*, 1972) and *Ar būdu uz baznīcu* (*From a Shack to a Church*, 1988). Playwright-director Pēteris Pētersons offered up a series of intellectually challenging, symbolic dramas, including *Bastard* (1978) and *Meteor* (1984).

Two women who moved to the forefront of Latvian dramatic literature in the 1980s were Māra Zālīte (b. 1952) and Lelde Stumbre (b. 1952). Zālīte's plays – *Pilna Māras istabiņa* (*The People in Mara's Room*, 1981) and *Tiesa* (*Trial*, 1984) – are stirring verse dramas rooted in Latvian folklore and mythology. Stumbre's best plays – *Sarkanmatainais kalps* (*The Redheaded Servant*, 1987), *Kronis* (*Crown*, 1989) and *Suns* (*Dog*, 1992) – are intricate and intriguing intellectual tugs-of-war.

Viktors Hausmanis

Directors, Directing and Production Styles

For a discussion of directing, see previous material in **Artistic Profile** and the opening, historical section.

Music Theatre

Latvia's first musical theatre entertainments were created in the late nineteenth century by one of the fathers of Latvian theatre, Adolfs Alunāns. In the 1920s and 1930s, the musical form was refined at the Daile Theatre by composer-conductor Burhards Sosārs (1890–1953) who wrote music for over 150 productions. Songs from Martins Zīverts's *Aksts* (*The*

Jester, 1938) and Selma Lagerlöf's (1858–1940) *Gösta Berlings Saga* (1934–58) are now standards. Sosārs was succeeded at the Daile by Marģeris Zariņš (1910–93) and Indulis Kalniņš (1918–86). Kalniņš's atmospheric music was an integral part of the 1956 Daile hit *Spēlēju, dancoju* (*I Played Music and Danced*).

Skroderdienas Silmačos (*Tailor Days in*

Alfrēds Jaunušāns's 1975 National Theatre production of Rudolfs Blaumanis's *Tailor Days in Silmachi*, designed by G. Zemgals.

Silmachi) by Rudolfs Blaumanis is considered to be the country's most popular musical comedy. Widely performed, this comedy has music by Aleksandrs Būmanis (1881–1937).

Latvia's most renowned composer, Raimonds Pauls (b. 1936), has also worked extensively in the theatre. His contributions are diverse, from light fare like *Isa pamācība mīlēšanā* (*A Short Course on Love*, 1973) and *Sherlock Holmes* (1979) to Ibsen's *Brand* (1975) and Bruckner's *Elisabeth von England* (1980).

Another prolific composer, Imants Kalniņš (b. 1941), is remembered for two hits, *The Prince and the Pauper* (Liepaja Theatre 1968; National Theatre, 1983) and *Liliom* (1971).

In the 1990s, music is an important part of almost every production in Latvia; most theatre companies, in fact, have their own composer-in-residence, like Artūrs Maskats (b. 1957) at the Daile.

Irēna Lagzdiņa

Dance Theatre

Until the 1920s Latvia's dance scene was strongly influenced by Russian classical ballet. Popular in the 1920s and 1930s were rhythmo-plastic dance studios – like Beatrise Vīgnere's (1903–90) school – where aspiring dancers were taught modern dance forms as developed by Jacques Dalcroze, Rudolph Laban and Mary Wigman.

For the most part, dance in the Latvian theatre has served an ornamental function. An exception was the work of Felicita Ertnere (1891–1975) at the Daile Theatre, where dance was often unified with dramatic action.

Socialist-realism in the post-war period did not recognize modern dance, therefore the development of this art form came to a halt. In response, amateur dance groups in the 1950s and 1960s began to develop performances based on folk dances and rituals.

The most successful use of dance to express character was R. Pauls's musical *Māsa Kerija* (*Sister Carrie*, 1976), choreographed by Imants

Magone (b. 1936) and performed by the folk-dance group Liesma.

On the whole, choreography has played a minimal role in the traditional Latvian theatre. Of note, though, has been the work of Tamāra Ēķe (b. 1940) on such productions as Danish playwright Astrid Saalbach's *Deju stunda* (*Ballet Class*, Liepaja Theatre, 1992) and Hans Christian Andersen and Ādolfs Šapiro's *Neglītais pīlēns* (*The Ugly Duckling*, Youth Theatre, 1991).

The sole luminary in the field of modern dance in Latvia is Ansis Rūtentāls (b. 1949), whose performance art dance group, Kustību teātris (Movement Theatre), explores many contemporary art forms, including Japanese *bhuto*.

One of the highlights of the 1991 season in Riga was the Movement Theatre's *Dejas pret vēju* (*Dances Against the Wind*, 1991) to the music of Philip Glass and Carla Bley.

Ija Bite

Theatre for Young Audiences

The leading theatre for young audiences in Latvia from its establishment in 1941 to its demise in 1992 was Riga's Jaunatnes Theatre (Youth Theatre). Originally, the company also included a children's troupe which participated in production crowd scenes and worked backstage. Many of these young people later became professional actors. The repertoire in the early 1960s consisted simply of fairytales and plays dealing with the problems of adolescence.

The Youth Theatre reached artistic maturity

and became one of the most respected theatres in Latvia under the leadership of director Ādolfs Šapiro. Assuming the directorship of the group in 1964, Šapiro expanded the repertoire and began to include works for audiences of all ages.

Virtually all theatre companies in Latvia offer special productions for children. The National Theatre, as one example, each year stages a large-scale Christmas musical.

Professional directors are at the helm of the University of Latvia's Student Theatre Group and the Latvian Agricultural Academy's Student Theatre, where non-traditional forms and themes are examined and presented.

The children's theatre Zīļuks, located in Riga Castle, was active in the immediate post-war period. The company included between seventy and eighty performers from ages 5 to 18.

A new children's theatre group, Rīgas bērnu teātris (Riga Children's Theatre), was formed in 1990. The group performed at the Kabata Theatre in the Old Town and at the Riga Latvian Society Hall under the direction of Swedish director Hanss Bertilsson.

Guna Zeltiņa

Puppet Theatre

Latvia did not have a marionette troupe until 1941 when a group of professional puppeteers began performing regularly at Riga Castle. Performances were given on an occasional basis until 1948.

Latvia's Valsts leļļu teātris (VLT: State Puppet Theatre) was formed in 1944 by Latvian refugees living in Ivanov, Russia. The company, headed by poet Mirdza Ķempe (1907–74), would later take up permanent residence in Riga. The group's repertoire included works by Latvian literary masters Jānis Rainis, Anna Brigadere, Rūdolfs Blaumanis and Kārlis Skalbe (1879–1945). Productions were primarily geared towards younger audiences, but in 1954 VLT also began mounting shows for adults. Of particular note were lively productions of Stravinsky's *Pertrouchka* and the Brecht/Weill *Die Dreigroschenoper* (*The Threepenny Opera*). In 1958, VLT puppets, staging a production of *Zelta zirgs*, received a silver medal at the Brussels World Fair. The company has subsequently toured as far as Japan, Iran and Sri Lanka. The heart and soul of VLT is designer Pauls Šēnhofs (b. 1924), whose rich imagination has inspired the company since 1946. Another company veteran and now VLT artistic director is Tina Hercberga (b. 1921).

The Valsts Leļļu teātris uses hand-puppets, marionettes and on-stage actors. Its repertoire also includes 'black box' performances and masquerades.

The Liepaja Regional Theatre had a puppet theatre troupe between 1959 and 1970. This puppet theatre was re-established in 1990 and now receives municipal funding.

A new troupe, Krūmu ezis (Bush Porcupine), was established in 1991 by a group of young puppeteers. The company works out of two trunks, the 'porcupines' are mobile, innovative and work in an intimate way with audiences young and old.

Aldis Linē

Design

The predominant style of scene painting in Latvian stagecraft had by the 1960s been almost completely replaced by sophisticated scenic design, with the designer seen as an important collaborator in the interpretation of a play.

The most respected scene painter in the post-war era was Oto Skulme (1889–1967) whose backdrops and flats were monumental in scope. Skulme developed a specific Latvian ornamental design based on ethnographic symbols. A landmark production in this style was Rainis's *Uguns un nakts* (*Fire and Night*, Daile Theatre, 1947).

Perhaps the most creative of modern scenic designers has been Ilmārs Blumbergs (b. 1943), whose concepts have visually illuminated the ideas of many important plays. In Andrejs Uplīts's *Žanna d'Ark* (*Joan of Arc*, Russian Dramatic Theatre, 1972), a snow-white stage is gradually littered with refuse, forming the heroine's funeral pyre. For Ibsen's *Brand* at the Daile Theatre (1975), an overturned pyramid-like platform symbolized aspects of Brand's mind. In the mid-1980s, Blumbergs left the theatre to concentrate specifically on painting and graphic design.

One of the most prolific and innovative scenic designers since the 1960s has been Andris Freibergs (b. 1938), who collaborated regularly with director Ādolfs Šapiro at the Jaunatnes Theatre. In Gunārs Priede's play about mass deportations, *Centrifūga* (1985), sliding doors

553

Ādolfs Šapiro's 1986 Riga Youth Theatre production of Brecht's *Fear and Misery of the Third Reich*, designed by Andris Freibergs.
Photo: E. Freimanes.

from livestock box cars, framed in a typical interior set, served as a chilling reminder of the past and a warning for the future.

In 1986, bicycles placed in grooves in the stage of the Jaunatnes Theatre symbolized the drive of youth organizations in the Third Reich in Brecht's *Furcht und Elend des Dritten Reiches*. Such striking images have become hallmarks of Freibergs-designed productions.

Theatre Space and Architecture

The most impressive theatre edifice in Latvia is Riga's National Theatre, designed and built in an eclectic style in 1901. The 941-seat main proscenium theatre contains an orchestra pit, two balconies and side boxes. The theatre has a 263 square metre stage with turntable and is regularly used for conventions, concerts and other special events. The National's building also houses a smaller Actors' Hall. Located in the basement, this theatre is a two-sided, arena-style performance space with a seating capacity of one hundred.

Similar, but smaller than the National Theatre, is the Liepaja, built in 1907. Its main proscenium theatre seats 600; the stage is 151 square metres. The complex also contains a mini-theatre with a capacity of sixty.

The largest theatre in Latvia is Riga's Daile Theatre, constructed in 1977, with a seating capacity of 1,000 and a 500 square metre proscenium stage. While the Daile's productions are generally popular, this modern facility has been criticized for acoustic deficiencies and a sterile atmosphere. The vast complex also houses two smaller theatres, the Small Hall (capacity of 200) and the Chamber Hall (capacity of seventy).

The Latvian theatre has also regularly featured open-air productions on large permanent or makeshift platforms in city squares and parks, castle ruins, lakefronts and seashores. The National's production of Rudolf Blaumanis's musical comedy *Skroderdienas Silmačos* (*Tailor Days in Silmachi*) is considered the ultimate open-air spectacle. It staged each June on the site of the actual Silmachi estate. The dwellings, nearby lake, horses and carriages always make this Latvian classic come to life. The number of spectators in this location is also almost unlimited. In these open-air productions (a speciality of regional theatre companies in particular) Latvian actors truly seem to be in their element.

The Kabata company's space is a small gem in Old Town Riga. Constructed in 1992 in a cellar, its cosy performance area is haloed by a natural stone arch. Its bleacher seats hold about eighty for theatre and pop music performances.

Altogether Riga boasts approximately thirty stages appropriate for theatrical productions. Provincial locations add another hundred or so venues, including fifty open-air amphitheatres.

Edīte Tišheizere

Training

The education and training of aspiring theatre artists in Latvia is coordinated by the Academy of Music's theatre department, which was established in 1952 after the dissolution of the Theatre Institute that same year. Many theatre companies also have their own actors' studios and workshops, usually following the guidelines of the academy's curriculum. Graduates receive diplomas from the academy and certification of competence for specific employment in either the theatre or cinema.

In most cases, actors are schooled in the Stanislavski system, although the Daile Theatre's recent studios have accented dance forms.

Distinguished instructors Vera Baļuna, Alfrēds Jaunušāns and Edmunds Freibergs (b. 1948) were and are staunch champions of psychological realism. Arnolds Liniņš, Oļģerts Kroders, Māra Ķimele and Pēteris Krilovs (b. 1949) have been influenced by trends in European theatre in the 1960s, especially experimentation by such directors as Poland's Jerzy Grotowski.

Stretching Stanislavski's theories further with Oriental forms of expression, the International New Cinema Centre's actors' training studio formed its own new theatre group, Rīgas Jaunais Teātris.

Directors have generally been trained in Moscow and St Petersburg. In Riga, the Academy of Music has a four-year training programme for stage, television and amateur group directors. The 1980s produced thirty-one graduates of this programme.

Latvia's Academy of Art offers a six-year scenic design degree programme for two or three students per year.

There are no formal programmes available in Latvia for costume designers, technical staff or administrative personnel. These people generally come into the theatre by way of other professions or, again, have been trained in Moscow or St Petersburg.

Līvija Akurātere

Criticism, Scholarship and Publishing

Along with the first Latvian professional theatre performances in the 1860s came the first press notices. Criticism as a professional literary form developed in the 1920s and 1930s. Reviews began to appear in periodicals regularly. The first monographs about Latvian actors and directors were also published during this time.

Kārlis Kundziņš (1902–92) is considered the father of Latvian theatre history. His books are,

to this day, an invaluable source on the origin and development of theatre arts in Latvia before 1940.

Latvia's Academy of Sciences' Linguistic and Literature Institute in 1968 established a Theatre, Music and Cinema Research Centre. Lilija Dzene (b. 1929), Līvija Akurātere (b. 1925) and Valentīna Freimane (b. 1922) are the leading theatre researchers who charted the course of the modern Latvian and world theatre and wrote many books.

Most critics active from the 1960s to the 1980s received their education at GITIS in Moscow. Three leading academics and critics, Jānis Kalniņš (b. 1922), Viktors Hausmanis (b. 1931) and Silvija Radzobe (b. 1950), however, came from literary circles. Hausmanis's extensive work has included books on the interpretation of Jānis Rainis's plays. He is also an expert on playwrights Mārtiņš Zīverts and Anšlāvs Eglītis.

In 1991, the University of Latvia began a formal training programme for critics, headed by Radzobe.

Another leading research centre is the Latvian Theatre Museum, housed in the former residence of the eminent director Eduards Smiļģis.

Books on theatre (plays, biographies, autobiographies, essay compilations) are printed by the publishing houses Zinātne, Liesma and Māksla, and by the Rainis Literature and Art History Museum.

Due to financial difficulties, the annual chronicle of the Latvian theatre scene, *Teātris un dzīve*, published since 1956, discontinued publication in 1992.

The first issue of the Latvian theatre monthly *Teātra Vēstnesis* (*Theatre Messenger*) appeared in 1989.

Reviews, articles, commentary and biographical material are published regularly by Latvian newspapers including *Literatūra un Māksla* (*Literature and Art*), *Diena* (*Today*), *Latvijas Jaunatne* (*Young Latvia*), *Rīgas Balss* (*Riga's Voice*) and others.

Guna Zeltiņa
Translated by Martin Parnickis

(See also USSR)

Further Reading

Akurātere, Līvija. *Aktiermāksla Latviešu teātrī.* [The art of acting in the Latvian theatre]. Riga: Zinātne, 1983. 296 pp.

——, Ligita Bērziņa, Lilija Dzene, and Silvija Radzobe. *Rīgas Krievu drāmas teātris (Krievu val.).* [The Riga Russian Dramatic Theatre (in Russian) 1940–83]. Riga: Zinātne, 1983. 359 pp.

——, Lilija Dzene, Valentīna Freimane, and Viktors Hausmanis. *Latviešu padomju teātra vēsture (1940–70).* [Soviet Latvian theatre history (1940–70)]. 2 vols. Riga: Zinātne, 1974. 500 pp.

Bērziņa, Ligita, and Janīna Brance. *Latviešu teātra hronika: 1913–17.* [A chronicle of the Latvian theatre: 1913–17]. Riga: Zinātne, 1991. 351 pp.

——, and Guna Zeltiņa. *Latviešu teātra hronika: 1909–12.* [A chronicle of the Latvian theatre: 1909–12]. Riga: Zinātne, 1988. 510 pp.

Bībers, Gunārs. *Latviešu padomju dramaturģija.* [Soviet Latvian drama]. Riga: Zvaigzne, 1976. 231 pp.

Dzene, Lilija. *Drāmas teātris.* [The Drama Theatre]. Riga: Zinātne, 1979. 380 pp.

——. *Mūsu paaudzes aktieri.* [Actors of our generation]. 2nd ed. Riga: Latvijas Valsts izdevniecba, 1964. 408 pp.

Freinberga, Silvija. *Pauls Putniņš un latviešu drāmas divi gadu desmiti.* [Pauls Putniņš and twenty years of Latvian drama]. Riga: Liesma, 1989. 287 pp.

Gessen, Elena. 'Iz ruin i pepla'. [Out of ruins and ashes]. *Teatr* 47, no. 10 (October 1984): 8–12.

Grēviņš, Māris. *Dailes teātris.* [Daile Theatre]. Riga: Liesma, 1971. 240 pp.

Hausmanis, Viktors. *Dramaturgs Harijs Gulbis.* [Playwright Harijs Gulbis]. Riga: Liesma, 1980. 151 pp.

——. *Rainis mūdienu teātrī, 1965–90.* [Rainis in modern theatre, 1965–90]. Riga: Liesma, 1990. 111 pp.

——. *Rainis un teātris.* [Rainis and the theatre]. Riga: Liesma, 1965. 240 pp.

Kundziņš, Kārlis. *Latviešu teātra hronika: 1901–08.* [A chronicle of the Latvian theatre: 1901–08). Riga: Zinātne, 1977. 228 pp.

——. *Latviešu teātra repertuārs līdz 1940 gadam.* [Latvian theatre repertoire to 1940]. Riga: LPSR Zinātņu akadēmijas izdevniecība, 1955. 288 pp.

——. *Latviešu teātra vēsture: 1. sēj.* [Latvian theatre history: volume I]. Riga: Liesma, 1968. 400 pp.

——. *Latviešu teātra vēsture: 2. sēj.* [Latvian theatre history: volume 2]. Riga: Liesma, 1972. 438 pp.

Pētersons, Pēteris. *Darbības māksla. Rakstu krājums par teātri.* [The art of activity: essays on the theatre]. Riga: Liesma, 1978. 296 pp.

——. *Drāma kā kritērijs.* [Drama as criterion]. Riga: Liesma, 1987. 340 pp.

Radzobe, Silvija. *Cilvēks un laiks Gunāra Priedes lugās.* [People and time in the plays of Gunārs Priede]. Riga: Zinātne, 1982. 287 pp.

Stepiņš, Laimonis. *Henriks Ibsens latviešu teātrī.* [Henrik Ibsen in the Latvian theatre]. Riga: Liesma, 1978. 210 pp.

Vilsons, Alfons, Biruta Gudriķe, Ingrīda Kiršentāle, and Viktors Hausmanis. *Šekspīrs latviešu teātrī.* [Shakespeare in the Latvian theatre]. Riga: Latvijas Valsts izdevniecība, 1964. 168 pp.

LITHUANIA

Situated on the Baltic Sea between Latvia, Poland, Russia and Belarus, Lithuania is a republic of some 3.7 million people with a land area of 65,200 square kilometres (25,170 square miles). About 20 per cent of the total population is composed of Polish, Russian, Jewish and other ethnic minorities with Lithuanian as the official state language. The capital city of Vilnius (577,000 inhabitants), the seaport Klaipėda (195,000) and the major cities Kaunas, Šiauliai and Panevėžys all have theatres and high schools and/or universities.

Created in the middle of the thirteenth century, the Lithuanian state eventually became the Grand Duchy of Lithuania. In 1569, after its union with Poland, Lithuania's power began to decrease and collapsed after the Russian occupation in 1795. Its independence was restored only after World War I and the country remained independent until World War II when it fell victim first to Russian, then German occupation and then again to Russian control. Incorporated into the USSR in 1944, Lithuania once more became an independent parliamentary republic in 1990.

The path of the Lithuanian professional theatre was also a winding one. Amateur theatre, rich in folklore and rudimentary dramatic elements, developed over many centuries. From the sixteenth to the end of the nineteenth century there existed in Lithuania professional or semi-professional theatres (in schools, at the residences of grand knights, and in manors) performing in Latin, Polish, Russian and other languages. The first public performance took place in Vilnius in 1570. But it was not until the last decade of the nineteenth century that a national liberation movement began giving a strong stimulus to the formation of professional theatre in the Lithuanian language.

The earliest Lithuanian-language plays were primarily focused around the ideas of liberation from czarist oppression. Stylistically, they were connected to romanticism. Between 1918 and 1940, historical verse dramas were created by prominent writers such as Balys Sruoga (1896–1947), Vincas Krėvė (1882–1954), Vincas Mykolaitis-Putinas (1893–1967), and Vydūnas (Vilhelmas Storosta, 1868–1953).

After the war, under Soviet artistic directives, socialist-realism became the required style and the free development of drama and theatre was suppressed. Despite this, poetic and historical drama with a focus on national identity remained vital. In the mid-1950s, following the death of Stalin, such plays became even more important. Many plays were written between the late 1950s and the 1970s dealing with resistance to Soviet control. Among the most significant were the tragedy *Herkus Mantas* (1957) by Juozas Grušas (1901–86), and the historical verse trilogy *Mindaugas* (1969), *Katedra* (*Cathedral*, 1971) and *Mažvydas* (1976) by Justinas Marcinkevičius (b. 1930).

By the late 1960s and right through the 1980s, ideologically correct plays were being replaced by plays concerned with real human problems and the first, still timid, modern Lithuanian plays.

In the early 1990s, as reconstruction was beginning of the once more independent republic of Lithuania, biographical plays about notable public figures of the past – many previously banned or intentionally ignored – began to be produced. One could also see links with ethnography and folklore as well as various kinds of adaptations and dramatizations.

Possibilities also began in the 1990s to form municipal and corporate-sponsored theatre companies without state permission. Among the first to be started this way was the Vilniaus mažasis teatras (Vilnius Little Theatre, 1991). Even in smaller cities such as Marijampolė and Alytus (35,000 and 46,000 inhabitants respectively) municipally sponsored semi-professional companies were beginning to appear.

As well, conditions were established for the formation of private theatre companies along with the introduction of personal contracts.

Antanas Vengris

Structure of the National Theatre Community

Lithuanian theatres may be divided into two main groups: professional (that is, state supported) and amateur. In 1992 Lithuania had twelve state theatres in five major cities. Among them were the Opera and Ballet Theatre (in Vilnius), two musical theatres (in Kaunas and Klaipėda), seven drama theatres (three of them in Vilnius) and two puppet theatres (in Vilnius and Kaunas). All these theatres were financed by the government to about 85 or 90 per cent of their budgets with ticket sales usually covering the remaining 10–15 per cent.

Ticket prices ranged from being equivalent to a cinema ticket for children's performances, to about six times more expensive for plays, to as much as ten times higher for opera.

All professional theatres play in repertory with about twenty-five productions in their repertoires at any one time. Administrative and technical staffs are usually two to three times larger than artistic staffs. In the Panevėžys State Drama Theatre, for example, there were thirty-five actors and nearly seventy staff in 1992. Rehearsals generally last from three months to a year and sometimes even more.

In 1989 the Lithuanian Association of Free Theatres was founded, uniting over fifty children's, youth, student, folk and adult theatres and studios. Since then, the association has organized biennial international children's and youth theatre festivals and regional folk festivals. In 1990 the Klojimų teatrų draugija (Society of Barn Theatres) was founded to foster the nineteenth-century amateur tradition of performing in barns for local audiences. In 1991 the Lietuvos Vaikų teatrų draugija (Lithuanian Society of Children's Theatres) was founded, uniting some fifty school theatres.

All the amateur theatres are associated with existing cultural institutions, factories or municipalities which pay wages to the director and sometimes to the stage designer. The average amateur company has twenty-five actors, producing one or two new plays each year.

The Lietuvos teatro sąjunga (Lithuanian Theatre Union) is the major professional association representing all the professional theatres, playwrights, theatre critics, theatre teachers, and radio and television performers. The Theatre Union also presents annual awards for directing and acting. Lithuania has been active in the festival Baltijas teātru pavasaris (Baltic Theatre Spring). This festival rotates annually among Lithuania, Latvia, Estonia and Belarus; since 1989 it has also included groups from other countries.

Elona Bundzaitė-Bajorinienė

Artistic Profile

Companies

The largest theatre in Lithuania in the period just after World War I was the Lithuanian State Theatre, a company with separate groups for drama, opera and ballet. Between 1920 and 1940, the State Theatre operated in Kaunas since the capital – Vilnius – had been incorporated into Poland and was under Polish occupation. A separate branch of the State Theatre was the Šiauliai Drama Theatre, founded in 1931 (from 1935 to 1939 operating in Klaipėda). After World War II the State Theatre was re-established in Kaunas as the Kaunas valstybinis dramos teatras (Kaunas State Drama Theatre). Established along with the Drama Theatre was the Kaunas valstybinis muzikinis teatras (Kaunas State Musical Theatre).

The State Theatre also gave rise to two other Vilnius theatres – the Lietuvos valstybinis akademinis dramos teatras (Lithuanian State Academy Drama Theatre, founded in 1940) and the Lietuvos valstybinis akademinis operos ir baleto teatras (Lithuanian State Academy Opera and Ballet Theatre, founded in 1948).

From their earliest days, all these theatre companies stuck to older traditions in terms of repertoire, directing and acting. Directors began to assert their primacy in the theatre during the 1930s and 1940s following the ideas of Stanislavski and Vakhtangov. Among the directors who were instrumental in this were Andrius Oleka-Žilinskas (1893–1948), Romualdas Juknevičius (1906–63) and Algirdas Jakševičius (1908–41).

One should mention here as well some of the important semi-professional companies of the pre-war period, which also made real contributions. Among them were the Karių ir Šaulių sąjungos teatrai (Soldiers' and Riflemen's Union Theatres, 1919–40), the Tautos teatras (Nation's Theatre, 1920–5), Mūsų teatras (Our Theatre, 1926–8) and the Darbo rūmų teatras (Working Palace Theatre, 1937–40).

Antanas Vengris

Dramaturgy

In the post-war period, compulsory optimism and lack of conflict in Soviet plays was first rejected by the prominent author, humanist and moralist of the pre-war generation, Juozas Grušas. Grušas rehabilitated the genre of tragedy, destroyed the notion of 'class morals' and brought back human values. Grušas wrote psychological dramas, the most important of which were *Adomo Brunzos paslaptis* (*The Secret of Adomas Brunza*, 1966) and *Meilė, džiazas ir velnias* (*Love, Jazz and the Devil*, 1976). He also wrote several historical poetic dramas and rhymed heroic tragedies – *Barbora Radvilaitė* (1972) and *Švitrigaila* (1975). His play *Cirkas* (*Circus*, 1976) dealt with odd, evil creatures who enter human worlds. Using dialogue that is aphoristic in nature, his characters are half metaphorical and half realistic, at once ironic, sarcastic and grotesque.

Grušas was followed by other writers, such as Juozas Glinskis (b. 1933), who constructs his plays as poetic visions with elements of Artaud's Theatre of Cruelty. Set in such locations as mad houses and prisons, his plays often deal with physical and moral suffering and his stories are often based on historical fact: a nineteenth-century poet and priest in the drama *Grasos namai* (*The House of Menace*, 1970); the twentieth-century Lithuanian painter and composer Mikalojus Konstantinas Čiurlionis (1875–1911) in *Po svarstyklių ženklu* (*Under the Sign of Libra*, 1976); adolescent prisoners in *Kingas* (1980); and a folk legend, *Nelabųjų raisto repeticija* (*The Rehearsal at the Swamp of the Wicked*, 1989), dealing with moral choice.

The originality of Saulius Šaltenis's (b. 1945) plays arises from a mixture of reality and myth, sarcasm and lyricism. His most important works were *Škac, mirtie, visados škac!* (*Scat, Death, Always Scat!* 1976), *Jasonas* (1978) and *Duokiškio baladės* (*Ballads of Duokiškis*, 1978). He has also written librettos for musicals and done various literary adaptations for the stage, usually working with director Eimuntas Nekrošius (b. 1952).

One other playwright of note is Kazys Saja (b. 1932), who writes comedies of everyday life – *Gaidžio pentinai* (*The Cock's Spurs*, 1964); philosophical allegories – *Oratorius. Maniakas. Pranašas Jona* (*Orator. Maniac. Prophet Jona*, 1967) and *Mamutų medžioklė* (*Mammoth Hunting*, 1968); farces – *Poliglotas. Abstinentas* (*Polyglot. Abstinence*, 1970); and even folk plays – *Devynbėdžiai* (*Men of Nine Troubles*, 1974).

Gražina Mareckaitė

Directors, Directing and Production Styles

Without doubt, the most important Lithuanian director in the post-war period was Juozas Miltinis (b. 1907), the artistic director of the Panevėžys Drama Theatre from 1940 to 1980. Influenced by the ideas of Artaud, Miltinis saw theatre not simply as a means of self-expression but rather as self-creation, both for the actors and the audience. The magic of his productions was created by energy more than anything else, energy which threw real light on text. In his *Hedda Gabler* (1957), he showed a single individual challenging a repressed society. In his 1961 *Macbeth*, he dealt with levels of consciousness. Other famous Miltinis productions include Borchert's *Draußen vor der Tür* (*The Man Outside*, 1966) and Dürrenmatt's *Die Physiker* (*The Physicists*, 1967). Miltinis's actors also starred in many films by other Soviet directors. Despite working during a difficult totalitarian period, Miltinis was able to build a bridge between modern European culture and pre-war Lithuania. By doing so, he made a strong impact on the rise of philosophical thought as well as on theatrical development in the country.

Jonas Jurašas (b. 1939) carried on Miltinis's tradition in the 1970s at the Kaunas State Drama Theatre. As political controls tightened, he used Aesopian metaphors in such masked critical works as Russian dramatist Mikhail

Shatrov's *Bolsheviki* (*The Bolsheviks*, 1970), laying the foundation for metaphoric theatre generally in Lithuania. In Jurašas's work, a strong lyrical ego is often found in conflict with itself and with the surrounding censorship – a poet locked up in an asylum in Juozas Glinskis's *Grasos namai* (*The House of Menace*, 1970). This was later transformed into the 'ego' of the nation and ultimately into the problem of identity and historical fate in Grušas's *Barbora*

Jonas Vaitkus's 1985 Kaunas State Drama Theatre production of Shakespeare's *Richard II*, designed by Dalia Mataitienė.
Photo: Vladas Žirgulis.

Radvilaitė (1972). This was Jurašas's last production in Lithuania. Persecuted by the authorities, he emigrated in 1974. In 1990, however, he returned to Lithuania to direct Smėlio klavyrai (The Sand Piquos) at the Kaunas Drama Theatre, a play based on the German novel Litauische Klaviere (Lithuanian Pianos). In 1992 Jurašas was appointed artistic director of the Kaunas Drama Theatre.

At the end of the 1970s and into the 1980s, the poetic theatre of Jurašas branched off into Jonas Vaitkus's (b. 1944) Theatre of Signs and Eimuntas Nekrošius's Theatre of Metaphors. Both these directors were similar in their struggles to reflect their own unique world outlooks.

Vaitkus produced about thirty plays at the Kaunas (1975–87) and Vilnius (1988–92) Drama Theatres in various genres. Most were concerned with analyses of evil and its various alternatives. Vaitkus used stylized costumes, scenographic trajectories, and well-defined voice modulations – Ibsen's Bygmester Solness (The Master Builder, 1980) and Shakespeare's Richard II (1985). His characters are additional elements in his system of signs, expressing laws rather than individual features. Also continuing Artaud's traditions and Miltinis's sense of the actor as 'acrobat-philosopher', Vaitkus makes his actors mediums of metaphysical power. One of the few actors to achieve this has been Valentinas Masalskis (b. 1954) with whom he regularly works. Masalskis is equally able to sink into the passions of Dostoevsky or rise to the heights of Chaplinesque comedy.

Nekrošius, as director of the Lithuanian State Youth Theatre since 1977, used literary material as a starting point. He often went on to create his own scripts where non-verbal communication was used more often than words. In his production of Kvadratas (The Square, 1980) a prison was created by four poles which became a clear metaphor for the Soviet system. The materials of Nekrošius's work are taken from nature (fire, water and stone) and from the everyday (sugar, a ladder and a suitcase). The main themes are love, creative work and death. The polyphonic structure of his work tends to reveal a dialectic connection between the temporary and the eternal, the variable and the constant. He often gave his actors the freedom to improvise, even to omit text. Nekrošius's company is an ensemble capable of performing in a musical such as Kestutis Antanėlis (b. 1951) and Sigitas Geda's (b. 1943) Meilė ir mirtis Veronoje (Love and Death in Verona, 1982, based on Shakespeare's Romeo and Juliet), in a psychological play such as Chekhov's Uncle Vanya (1986), or in a tragi-comic farce such as Nosis (The Nose, 1991) based on Gogol.

Elona Bundzaitė-Bajorinienė

Music Theatre

In the post-war period, and even earlier, Lithuanian opera had many talented soloists including the founder of the Opera Theatre in 1920, Kipras Petrauskas (1885–1963). Drama directors Juozas Grybauskas (1906–64) and Juozas Gustaitis (1912–90), working in opera, were applying the principles of realisitic theatre.

By the 1940s, opera production had become connected to the artistic ideas of scenographers of the period. Painter Mstislavas Dobužinskis (1875–1957), raised in Lithuania and returning after the Russian revolution, raised the level of opera production with an art historian's erudition combined with the refined beauty of his scenery and costumes. His scenography for Tchaikovsky's Pikovaja dama (The Queen of Spades, 1925), for Jurgis Karnavičius's (1884–1941) Radvila Perkūnas (1937) and for Mozart's Don Juan (1933), became keys in the development of the art in Lithuania. Scenographic art was again renewed by Liudas Truikys (1904–87). Paraphrasing architectural rhythms, horizontal and vertical lines and a broad combinations of forms, he attempted to create a dialogue between art and music. Truikys believed artistic creation to be 'balance in space', to which he added his own vision of opera as a blending of arts. Truikys devoted his life to the search for visual and musical unity in scenery. His visual symphonism is best represented in the scenery for Antanas Račiūnas's (1905–84) opera Trys talismanai (Three Talismans, 1935), which was awarded a diploma of honour at the Paris World Exhibition in 1937, in Aïda (1975) and in Don Carlos (1959 and 1978).

Similar high principles were brought to the opera by director Jonas Vaitkus, best known for his work in spoken drama. For opera, he focused on a musical flow of action and architectonics with the actions becoming 'musical motifs'. In his productions, connections were always being made between European arts from various epochs and Oriental arts. His major productions include Bronius Kutavičius

(b. 1934) and Sigitas Geda's *Strazdas, žalias paukštis* (*Thrush, a Green Bird*, 1984); Feliksas Bajoras's (b. 1934) *Agnus Dei* (1991); and Verdi's *Nabucco* (1992).

Edmundas Gedgaudus,
Audronė Girdzijauskaitė

Dance Theatre

The year after the State Theatre was founded in 1920, professional dancers and pupils of the ballet studio of Olga Dubeneckienė-Kalpokienė (1891–1967) found themselves participating in many of the full-length operas being performed. In 1925, the first ballet evening – *Coppelia* – was staged. Up to 1935, the company was generally led by visiting or emigrant Russian ballet masters who trained dancers first in their studios and, from 1935, at the ballet studio of the State Theatre. During this time romantic, contemporary and national ballets were staged.

In 1935 the company toured to Monte Carlo and London. In 1937 the first Lithuanian ballet master, Bronius Kelbauskas (1904–75), began his work with the company but this was interrupted by the Soviet occupation in 1944. When almost half the company emigrated, the ballet studio was closed.

In 1948 the theatre was moved to Vilnius. During the next two decades, thematic ballets by Russian and Soviet composers were staged. A choreographic section (later to become an independent school of choreography) was opened in 1952 at the Vilnius School of the Arts. The school trained for both ballet and folk dance. By the 1980s, a more contemporary choreography and a freer classical expression was being seen once again in one-act, non-thematic ballets and short programmes.

During the seven decades of its existence, the state company has performed most of the classical ballets but only a few national ballets; almost all the Lithuanian ballet masters and

choreographers were trained in Russia, while Russian choreographers quite often worked in Vilnius.

The Kaunas and Klaipėda Musical Theatres also have dance companies.

The links between modern dance and ballet can be traced to the Kaunas studios of *Ausdruckstanz* in the 1930s and 1940s. The most famous studio was that of Danutė Nasvytytė (1916–83). This was continued by the Sonata Studio in Kaunas in the 1970s and 1980s. Modern dance theatre, neither supported nor accepted by the government, had no opportunity to reach a professional level. It was only in 1980 that a modern dance theatre was founded in Kaunas – Aura. The group focuses on short pieces and one-act works. In 1989, the company began organizing festivals of modern dance from Lithuania and abroad.

As for Lithuanian folk dance, historical sources mention such work as early as the ninth century. In theatrical form, it was used in the nineteenth century for special soirées. Folk tradition remains in ritual (work, calendar and family dances) as well as non-ritual dances (thematic and non-thematic). Such dancing is done in pairs or alone. The usual accompaniment is a song or a musical instrument.

Folklore forms today are splitting into two movements: ethnographic and stylized, the two types performed equally by amateurs and professionals including the Lithuanian State Ensemble of Folk Song and Dance.

Audronis Imbrasas

Theatre for Young Audiences

Until 1940 permanent theatre companies for young audiences did not exist in Lithuania. Rather, the dramatic theatres produced chil-

dren's productions on an occasional basis. In 1930 teachers, writers and actors jointly founded the Children's Theatre Association in

Kaunas, which tried producing plays for children on a regular basis. In 1940, the Vaikų teatras (Children's Theatre) was opened in Kaunas, later changing its name to Kauno Jaunojo žiūrovo teatras (Kaunas Theatre for Young Audiences). The company remained active until 1959.

In 1965 another such theatre was opened in Vilnius, very soon becoming the State Youth Theatre, mostly producing plays for adults rather than children and teenagers. The fact is, except for Christmas performances and the occasional musical production directed by Aurelija Ragauskaitė (b. 1924), performances for younger children or teenagers were very few. One could speak of a major production of the

Eimuntas Nekrošius's 1986 Lithuanian State Youth Theatre production of Chekhov's *Uncle Vanya*, designed by Nadežda Gultiajeva.
Photo: Jonas Kernagis.

Swedish writer Astrid Lindgren's *Pippi Long-stocking* in 1971 or of the minimalist improvisational 1978 production directed by Dalia Tamulevičiūtė (b. 1938) based on a Lithuanian folk fairytale, *Bebenčiukas*, but true children's performances – even dramatizations of classical literature – were rare.

Performances for older children and teenagers were slightly more frequent. One of the most successful was the Kaunas Drama Theatre production of *Mary Poppins* which opened in 1977 and was still running in the early 1990s. Another was Benjamin Britten's *Let's Make an Opera* (1979) at the Kaunas Musical Theatre. Scenes performed by graduates of the State Conservatory of Lithuania (from 1992, the Academy of Music) were transferred to the stage of the Šiauliai Drama Theatre and were developed into full productions. Among these were Saroyan's *The Human Comedy* (1977), and *Vaikų dienos* (*Children's Days*, 1977), a collective creation.

In the 1990s, the inadequate attention paid to this area by professional theatres was being compensated for by the growth of secondary school theatre groups and the appearance of children's theatre studios. The latter are organizing local and international children's theatre festivals and working toward the creation of new companies and contacts in the field.

Gražina Mareckaitė

Puppet Theatre

Marionette performances by wandering puppeteers date back to the fifteenth century in Lithuania. By the eighteenth century, such foreign performances were being produced in the manors of the nobility.

At the same time, there was also a folk puppet tradition. At Easter, in churches around Žemaitija, puppets were used to enact the Mysteries of the Sufferings of Christ. Traces of this old form can still be found in certain churches.

The first professional marionette theatre was founded by constructivist artist Stasys Ušinskas (1905–74), a pupil of French artists Fernand Leger and Alexandra Exter. His company's first season was in Kaunas in 1936 with a performance of *Silvestras Dūdelė*. The puppets were extremely large and moved on springs. They were later used in the Lithuanian puppet film *Storulio sapnas* (*Dream of a Fat Man*, 1938). In Ušinskas's work, design was primary.

Puppet theatre became even more popular after the war. Mykolė Krinickaitė (1908–54) directed a puppet company from 1945 to 1949 and the state began to promote the formation of puppet theatres in different cities. In 1958, two professional puppet theatres were founded. The founder of the Vilnius Puppet Theatre, Balys Lukošius (1900–87), combined in its productions everyday life with the romantic. Stasys Ratkevičius (b. 1917), founder of the Kaunas Puppet Theatre, began by creating a realistic theatre.

By the end of the 1960s, a Baltic puppet theatre festival was organized and contacts with Europe became stronger. Vitalis Mazūras (b. 1934), artistic director of Lėlė (Puppet Theatre) changed the direction of the theatre entirely and by refusing to imitate dramatic theatre, revived Ušinskas's earlier tradition. Combining folk and modern forms, Mazūras's theatre became an interaction between sculptured forms in space and a free interpretation of text. Music and the actor's imagination become substitutes for words. His productions *Pelenų antelė* (*Little Duck of the Ashes*, 1971) and *Žemės dukra* (*The Daughter of the Earth*, 1981) by Marcelijus Martinaitis (b. 1936); *Baltas Niekas* (*The White Nothing*, 1974) and *Raudonligė* (*The Red Disease*, 1989) by Sigitas Geda; *Retabillo de Don Cristobal* and *El Amor de Don Perlimplín con Belisa en su jardin* (*The Love of Don Perlimplín with Belisa in His Garden,* 1986) by Federico García Lorca, took on universal meaning. With *Eglė, žalčių karalienė* (*Egle, the Queen of the Grass-snakes*, 1968) by Salomėja Nėris (1904–45) and *Zuikių mokykla* (*School of Hares*, 1968) by Bulgarian Petr Mančev, Ratkevičius's work found large audiences.

One other puppet group of note is the student political-satirical puppet theatre, Šėpa (Wardrobe). The company started in Vilnius in 1988.

Audronė Girdzijauskaitė

Vitalius Mazūras's 1981 Vilnius Theatre Lėlė production of Marcelijus Martinaitis's *The Daughter of the Earth*, designed by Mazūras.
Photo: Audrius Zavadskis.

Design

The Lithuanian theatre design school began to form in the 1930s when graduates of the Kaunas Art School, after studying in France and Germany, returned to Lithuania. With the support of director Andrius Oleka-Žilinskas, director of the Kaunas State Theatre, designers such as Adomas Galdikas (1893–1969), Stasys Ušinskas and Liudas Truikys developed design as an equal creative element in the overall performance.

In their designs, folk tradition was combined with avant-garde twentieth-century styles of expressionism and constructivism. The natural development of this work was interrupted by the war, after which the link with these artists of the 1940s was lost. Following the war, some of the designers were rejected as 'formalists' and simply stopped working. Others gave in to the aesthetic principles of socialist-realism, naturalistic scenery and mirror-like reality.

The first signs of change in this style were noticeable at the end of the 1960s with Janina Malinauskaitė (b. 1935), the first to respond to the demands of the more poetic and metaphoric theatre being done by directors Jurašas and Vaitkus. Working mostly at the Kaunas State Theatre, her best designs – Glinskis's *The House of Menace* (1970), Bulgakov's *Molière* (1968), Jarry's *Ubu Roi* (1977), Gorki's *The Last Generation* (1978) and Ibsen's *Master Builder* (1980) – were characterized by a rich Baroque-like texture, a dense atmosphere and the conceptual arrangement of space.

Another designer of note at this time was Dalia Mataitienė (b. 1936) who was active in folk theatre where she created costumes and scenery in the Lithuanian soirée and barn theatre traditions and in dramatic theatre where she worked precisely with directorial concepts.

In the 1980s, Adomas Jacovskis (b. 1948) was collaborating regularly with directors such as Gytis Padegimas (b. 1953), Nekrošius and Jurašas. Very often in his designs, objects – either real or imaginary – became visual centrepieces. For example, a long white table in Strindberg's *Miss Julie* (1977) at the Šiauliai Drama Theatre, four poles in *The Square* (1980), a shop window in *Pirosmani* (1982), or a railway in *A Day Longer Than a Hundred Years* (1982) at the Youth Theatre.

Audronė Girdzijauskaitė

Theatre Space and Architecture

All major theatre buildings in Lithuania are similar in style (proscenium houses with balconies and orchestras) and differ only in size. Since World War II, many of them have been modernized or rebuilt. In fact, only two original examples of traditional architecture remain: the Kaunas Musical Theatre and the old building of the Vilnius Opera Theatre (until 1939 called the Polish Theatre). Both theatres were built at the beginning of the twentieth century in an eclectic, neo-classical style. The other theatres were redesigned to meet modern requirements in terms of size and space.

The biggest and most modern is the State Opera and Ballet Theatre in Vilnius, built in 1972. The large stage has a revolving floor, traps, and modern lighting equipment. Some of the newer buildings also have small experimental stages.

Apart from these professional theatres, cultural centres now exist in most of the major provincial towns. Most are suitable for touring shows.

In summer, performances often take place in outdoor historical surroundings. The Kiemo teatras (Yard Theatre) performs on the beautiful campus of the old Vilnius University. The castle of Trakai is also sometimes used for historical productions. The Cellar Theatre was also active at Vilnius University for some time. Folk theatre performances are sometimes held in an old barn at the Rumšiškės Folk Museum.

Eugenijus Gūzas

Training

From the turn of the twentieth century to World War II, directors and actors were often trained in Russian theatre schools. One major exception was Juozas Miltinis, founder of the Panevėžys Drama Theatre (1940) and a pupil of Charles Dullin in France. In 1919, the Vaidybos mokykla (School of Performing Arts) was established. From 1924, it was associated with the State Theatre. The school was founded by director Antanas Sutkus (1892–1968), who had also founded the Nation's Theatre and the satire theatre, Vilkolakis (Werewolf).

Theatre critics and historians have traditionally been trained at Vytautas Didysis University. Musical theatre training was offered by the Kaunas Conservatory (1933–49), and now also at the Lithuanian Academy of Music in Vilnius. Dancers are trained at the Vilnius School of Choreography.

In Lithuania, the Stanislavski system is dominant. The only exception has been the actors' studio of Miltinis at the Panevėžys State Drama Theatre.

The main theatre training institution in the 1990s is the theatre and cinema department of the Lithuanian Academy of Music. Training actors and, since 1989, directors, the school also trains puppet theatre actors and television directors. Actors graduate in four years and directors in five. Often a whole class of ten to fifteen students is employed at a single theatre upon graduation, thus rejuvenating the company and widening its repertoire. The Klaipėda Drama Theatre company was enlarged in this way in 1980 with graduates of the Klaipėda Academy of Music.

Another centre for theatre training is Vilnius University. Many of its graduates in language and journalism have taken up theatre criticism. In 1989 the university started a course in theatrology, and in 1992 an experimental course in performing arts was begun.

The Lithuanian Academy of Art started training theatre designers in 1979. Technicians are usually self-trained, beginning in most theatres as apprentices.

In 1991, Klaipėda University was founded and began training directors for work in secondary schools. In 1992, the Vilnius College of Culture started a three-year programme training theatre and concert managers.

Elona Bundzaitė-Bajorinienė

Criticism, Scholarship and Publishing

Lithuanian theatre criticism grew along with the developing Lithuanian theatre in the late nineteenth and early twentieth centuries. Much attention was paid to the new professional theatres by prominent scholars such as Gabrielius Landsbergis-Žemkalnis (1852–1916), Sofija Kymantaitė-Čiurlionienė (1886–1958) and Vincas Krėvė. Perhaps the best known of the early scholars and critics was Balys Sruoga, a theatre and literary historian, playwright, critic and expert in Russian and western drama. Among the major figures trained by him were Vytautas Maknys (b. 1907) and Antanas Vengris (b. 1912).

After World War II, Lithuanian theatrologists studied at Moscow and St Petersburg theatre schools, most often afterwards joining the department of theatrology at the Institute of History of the Academy of Sciences. In 1990, a department of theatre and cinema research was opened at the Institute of Culture and Arts. It has published three volumes of Lithuanian theatre history, with Vengris and Markas Petuchauskas (b. 1931) as its main authors and editors.

A quarterly journal, *Teatras* (*Theatre*), was published by the Theatre Union from 1964 to 1990; an almanac, *Muzika ir teatras* (*Music and Theatre*), was published between 1962 and 1977; and a chronicle, *Teatras*, was published from 1982 by the Vaga publishing house. Theatre issues are discussed in the monthly journals *Kultūros barai* (*Domains of Culture*, from 1965) and *Krantai* (*The Shores*, from 1989), and in weekly newspapers such as *Literatūra ir menas* (*Literature and Art*, 1946), *7 meno dienos* (*7 Days of Art*, founded in 1992) and *Mūzų malūnas* (*Windmill of the Muses*), a weekly supplement to the daily paper *Lietuvos rytas* (*Lithuanian Morning*).

Audronė Girdzijauskaitė
Translated by Raimonda Sadauskienė
(See also USSR)

Further Reading

Aleksienė, Gražina. *Truikys Liudas*. Exhibition catalogue. Vilnius: Lietuvos TSR dailės muziejus, 1979. 32 pp.

Girdzijauskaitė, Audronė. 'Vitalis Mazūras'. *Teatras* 1 (1982): 23–33.

Jansonas, Egmontas. *Etiudai apie teatra*. [Sketches about theatre]. Vilnius: Vaga, 1988. 245 pp.

Kuleshova, Vera. *Stasys Ušinskas*. Moscow: Sovietskiý khudozhnik, 1973. 159 pp.

Lankutis, Jonas. *Lietuvių dramaturgijos raida*. [Development of Lithuanian drama]. Vilnius: Vaga, 1988. 454 pp.

Maknys, Vytautas. *Lietuvių teatro raidos bruožai 1570–1940*. [Features in the development of Lithuanian theatre 1570–1940]. 2 vols. Vilnius: Mintis, 1972, 1979. 554 pp.

Mažeika, Vytautas. *Opera 1940–1965*. Vilnius: Mintis, 1964. 255 pp.

Petuchauskas, Markas. *Teatro akimirkos*. [Theatre moments]. Vilnius: Mintis, 1977. 136 pp.

——, ed. *Lietuvių tarybinis teatras 1940–1956*. [Lithuanian Soviet drama theatre 1940–56]. Vilnius: Mintis, 1979. 387 pp.

Rutkutė, Dana. *Aktorius teatro veidrodyje*. [The actor in the looking-glass of theatre]. Vilnius: Vaga, 1989. 192 pp.

Ruzgaitė, Aliodija. *Lietuviško baleto kelias*. [The way of Lithuanian ballet]. Vilnius: Mintis, 1964. 116 pp.

Sakalauskas, Tomas. *Monologai*. Vilnius: Mintis, 1981. 230 pp.

Samulionis, Algis. *Balys Sruoga*. Vilnius: Vaga, 1986. 428 pp.

——, ed. *Neramios šviesos pasauliai*. [Worlds of restless light]. Vilnius: Vaga, 1976. 246 pp.

Sruoga, Balys. 'Mūsų teatro raida'. [Development of our theatre]. *Lietuva 1918–1938*. Kaunas: Šviesa, 1990. 368 pp.

Vasiliauskas, Valdas. *Teatras be iliuzijų*. [Theatre without illusions]. Vilnius: Vaga, 1989. 252 pp.

Vengris, Antanas. *Kastantas Glinskis*. Vilnius: Mintis, 1965. 131 pp.

——. *Nemuno mergaitė*. [Maid of Nemunas]. Vilnius: Vaga, 1990. 140 pp.

——, ed. *Lietuvių tarybinis dramos teatras 1957–1970*. [Lithuanian Soviet drama theatre 1957–70]. Vilnius: Vaga, 1987. 383 pp.

——, ed. *Teatrinės minties pėdsakais*. [The world and Lithuanian directors and actors]. 2 vols. Vilnius: Mintis, 1969, 1982. 688 pp.

——, Vytautas Mažeika, and Žilvinas Dautartas. *Lietuvių teatras 1918–1929*. [Lithuanian theatre, 1918–29]. Vilnius: Mintis, 1984. 336 pp.

LUXEMBOURG

(Overview)

The position of theatre in the Grand Duchy of Luxembourg is unusual as a result of its geographical situation (2,590 square kilometres or 999 square miles landlocked between Belgium, France and Germany), its cosmopolitan population of some 400,000 and its obligatory trilingualism (Letzeburgesch, French and German). The country uses Letzeburgesch in its everyday business, but the influence of French and Germanic culture is enormous.

There are two municipal theatres in the country, one in Luxembourg City (population 80,000) and one in Esch, both of which have season-long programmes. These include touring performances from across Europe, mostly performing in French and German, with occasional productions by local groups in Letzeburgesch. Also included are operas, operettas and ballets. There are no resident professional companies attached to these theatres.

For many years, touring companies from Paris made up most of the French-speaking theatre played in Luxembourg, with a repertoire of more than 80 per cent light comedy, intended for a public which tends to see theatre as more of a social occasion than anything else.

However, theatre in Letzeburgesch has been extremely vital since World War II. During the 1950s, authors such as Fernand Hoffmann, Norbert Weber, Tit Schroeder and Pol Greisch opened new routes for Letzeburgesch theatre and were followed by a series of younger writers such as Guy Rewenig, N. Helminger and J. Braun. As a result, each year several new plays in Letzeburgesch are performed in the different theatres, and can now reckon on an even larger public than the French-speaking or German-speaking performances.

Since 1970 specifically, various Luxembourg groups have been working to create a viable indigenous theatre and to reflect the newer, more nationalistic dramatic output. Of these, mention should be made of the Théâtre Ouvert Luxembourg (TOL), the Théâtre du Centaure and the Théâtre des Casemates. They have also staged performances by French, Spanish and German authors such as Guy Foissy, Fernando Arrabal, Georges Michel, Victor Haim, Robert Pinget, Claude Prin, Jean-Claude Grumberg, Jeannine Worms, Eric Estphal, Franz Xaver Kroetz and Peter Handke.

A great step forward was realized in 1985 with the formation of the Théâtre des Capucins de la Ville de Luxembourg, subsidized by the City of Luxembourg, and which has become a driving creative force, playing the role of producer or co-producer with various Luxembourg companies. Each season the Théâtre des Capucins puts on seven or eight new productions, engaging a new company for each production.

In total, it is now possible to see in one season in Luxembourg some seventy different productions – about forty in French, twenty in German and ten in Letzeburgesch. But still, few of the productions created in Luxembourg are performed under professional conditions (only the productions of the Théâtre des Capucins enjoy such a position). The small size of the territory and the necessarily limited audience mean that it is difficult if not impossible for a professional company to survive long term. For this reason there are very few professional actors in Luxembourg.

Though there is also a growing body of French- and German-language writing in

The Théâtre des Capucins of the City of Luxembourg.

Luxembourg (especially novels, essays and poetry), it has to be said that the country's dramatic output in these languages is still fairly limited. Most authors have not gone past their first or second plays, and their work has generally not been performed. Only Edmond Dune can justly claim the title of playwright, with some ten French-language plays to his credit, several of which have been performed professionally.

Perhaps the most popular phenomenon in Luxembourg is cabaret, with some half-dozen small groups appearing in cafés and equipped halls. Within this genre, the Annual Revue, essentially a political satire, attracts an audience of up to 30,000.

In sum, one can say that theatre in Luxembourg has shown a significant popularity since 1970; despite this, official structures remain inadequate to promote any sort of widespread professionalism.

Marc Olinger
Translated by Philip Murgatroyd

MACEDONIA

Situated in the south central part of the Balkan Peninsula, the Republic of Macedonia has 2 million inhabitants (65 per cent Macedonian, 21 per cent Albanian, 4 per cent Turkish, 2 per cent Serbian, 3 per cent Romany, 5 per cent Muslim, Vlach, Montenegrin and Croat). Covering an area of 25,700 square kilometres (9,900 square miles). Its capital is Skopje and its principal towns are Bitola, Prilep, Kumanovo, Tetovo, Titov Veles and Štip.

At the close of the fourteenth century, Macedonia fell under the Ottoman Empire, remaining under Ottoman Turkish rule until the Balkan Wars of 1912 and 1913. After the Second Balkan War, as a result of the aspirations of the neighbouring states, the territory of Macedonia was divided among Bulgaria, Serbia, Greece and Albania. With minimal alterations, this division was reaffirmed at the close of World War I.

Having fought on the side of the anti-fascist coalition in World War II, the Macedonian people won their national and social freedom in the Vardar part of Macedonia, which was constituted as a Macedonian national state within the framework of Yugoslavia. At the time of Yugoslavia's dissolution (1991–2), Macedonia was constituted as an independent and sovereign republic.

The proximity of ancient Greece had a crucial influence on the life of the Slavs who settled in ancient Macedonia in the sixth and seventh centuries. Dionysian bacchanalia and theatrical performances from this period have left traces which are still present today in the ethnic spirit of the Macedonian nation.

After the Hellenic and Illyro-Thracian periods, Roman domination in Macedonia lasted for several centuries. The Roman theatrical repertoire was thus added to existing dramatic forms and was performed in amphitheatres. The mingling of the old Slav pagan and the Byzantine Christian worlds signalled the beginnings of a new culture. The adoption of Christianity had its effect on the theatre, but in folk tradition the abandoned Slav pagan inheritance lingered on.

The theatre retained a presence during the period of Ottoman rule and visiting shadow theatres and *medahi*, a kind of small oriental chamber theatre, left their mark. The Macedonian cultural renaissance of the nineteenth century saw the first attempts to use the Macedonian vernacular for dramatic purposes.

Jordan Hadži Konstantinov-Džinot (1821–82), a teacher, philanthropist and playwright, was one of those who initiated school performances. However, the real founder of the Macedonian theatre was Vojdan Černodrinski (1875–1951). Thanks to his work, theatre in Macedonia opened to the world of twentieth-century drama. It was in the period before 1912 that professional companies from Belgrade and Sofia first visited Macedonia. These foreign companies influenced the followers of Džinot and Černodrinski to build a theatre in Macedonia, which had become part of the Kingdom of the Serbs, Croats and Slovenes, later to become Yugoslavia. For some thirty years, up to 6 April 1941, the official theatres in Macedonia put on plays from the classical repertoire only in the Serbian language. With the fascist occupation, which lasted until 1944, the national situation deteriorated radically.

Despite these unfavourable circumstances, Macedonians endeavoured to maintain their national identity through culture generally and theatre specifically. Soon, a whole generation of writers began to write in Macedonian. Major figures among them were Marko Cepenkov (1829–1920), Nikola Kirov-Majski (1880–1962), Anton Panov (1905–68), Risto Krle (1900–75) and Vasil Iljoski (b. 1902).

The pioneers of acting in modern Macedonia appeared at the end of the nineteenth and the beginning of the twentieth centuries when Černodrinski formed several theatre companies on a semi-professional basis. As well as Černodrinski and his wife and lifelong companion Marija Černodrinska (1885–1974), these included Milka and Vlado Milčinov, Fana Kostova, Rizo Rizov, Ivan Atanasov and Kirče Nikolov.

The first modern professional actor was Dimče Trajkovski (1888–1978) who began his acting career immediately after World War I at the newly formed People's Theatre in Skopje. In 1933 Trajkovski formed his own travelling theatre, the Little Skopje Theatre, which continued until 1939. After the end of World War II he became a member of the Macedonian National Theatre in Skopje where he worked until his retirement in 1954. The peak of his career was his interpretation of the role of Tasa in Branislav Nušić's *Suspicious Character*.

Petre Prličko (b. 1907) joined Mihajlo Lazić's travelling theatre in 1923. He later formed his own company, called the Blue Bird (later called the Bohemian). The group existed from 1931 to 1939.

Todor Nikolovski (b. 1902) made his first appearance in the Skopje People's Theatre in 1917. His acting career blossomed in the postwar years and he continued to appear on the stage even after his official retirement at the age of 85.

To meet the lack of trained acting personnel a Theatre High School was opened in Skopje in 1947 and although its existence was a short one, some of its ex-pupils have been among the leading Macedonian actors.

Since the 1970s, the Faculty of Dramatic Art has produced a large body of highly qualified actors who have gained their reputation in the theatre, in films and on television. Still others graduated from academies in the former Yugoslavia or in neighbouring Bulgaria.

During World War II, known in Macedonia as the National Liberation War (1941–5), a new and genuinely Macedonian theatre began to appear and, in fact, spread. Performances were given in the liberated territories and in partisan camps in the woods, in prison camps and elsewhere. Immediately after the liberation of Skopje, a Macedonian National Theatre was founded (November 1944). The first full-length performance was of *Platon Krechet* by the Ukrainian writer Oleksander Korniychuk, which had its première on 3 April 1945.

A performance of Mascagni's *Cavalleria Rusticana* marked the founding of the Opera Company of the National Theatre on 9 May 1947, while the company itself began to function officially on 1 January 1949. The first ballet company, led by Georgi Makedonski (b. 1925), laid the groundwork that led to the formation of the National Ballet, whose first performance was of Gounod's *Walpurgisnacht* on 30 December 1949.

From the late 1940s until 1991, Macedonian theatre grew Yugoslavia (see YUGOSLAVIA for further information). Since 1991, theatre in Macedonia has begun once more to develop its own clear identity.

Risto Stefanovski, Ivan Ivanovski

Structure of the National Theatre Community

All professional theatres in Macedonia are financed through the Ministry of Culture. The number of such theatres was at its peak in the 1950s: the Macedonian National Theatre, the Theatre of the Nationalities (with Albanian and Turkish companies) and the Puppet Theatre in Skopje, and theatres in Bitola, Prilep, Strumica, Kočani, Štip, Gevgelija, Ohrid, Tetovo, Kumanovo and Titov Veles. The Skopje Puppet Theatre grew into the Youth Drama and later the Drama Theatre, while a separate Children's Theatre was founded.

The theatres stage, on average, between five and eight new productions each season and retain about the same number from previous years in their repertoire.

There is an annual festival, the Černodrinski Theatre Festival, in Prilep; it is selective and competitive, with awards for performance, script, direction, acting, set design, costume design, music, adaptation and dramatization.

There is also the Young Open Theatre, an international festival organized by the Youth Cultural Centre in Skopje, and the May Opera

Evenings, an international festival in Skopje. There are as well indoor and outdoor performances at the annual international Ohrid Summer Festival. Kočani is host to an annual festival of amateur and alternative theatres.

Artistic Profile

Companies

The Macedonian National Theatre is the country's largest group and boasts a theatre company, an opera company, and a ballet troupe along with its own stage managers, technicians, designers, carpenters and wardrobe staff.

Between 1945 and 1985 the National Theatre staged 415 new productions with 9,200 performances to a total audience of over 2 million. The theatre company put on 232 new productions with 5,144 performances before a total audience of over 1 million; the opera, 111 new productions with 2,460 performances to an audience of more than half a million; and the ballet, seventy-two new productions with 1,596 performances to 267,000 people.

Other large theatres include the Drama Theatre in Skopje (with over a hundred on its staff), the National Theatre in Bitola and the theatre company of the Theatre of the Nationalities in Skopje. This last, with its Albanian and Turkish companies, also includes in its repertoire plays by Macedonian authors, world classics and contemporary plays. All theatres are required to stage new productions.

Among the smaller groups since World War II, the most important have been Estrada 59 (founded 1959), the Theatre of St Nicholas the Pauper (founded in the early 1970s), the Pralipe Romany Theatre and the alternative Sorrow and Consolation Theatre, which both began in the 1980s.

In addition to the theatres already mentioned there is a professional Children's Theatre in Skopje and national theatres in Prilep, Strumica, Štip, Kumanovo and Titov Veles. Their premises, with the exception of the Strumica theatre, are generally old-fashioned and ill equipped.

Risto Stefanovski

Dramaturgy

The beginnings of modern Macedonian playwriting are to be found in the mid-nineteenth century. It was then that Jordan Hadži Konstantinov-Džinot produced for the first time plays – didactic and moralistic – in the vernacular.

The next step was taken by Macedonian emigrants in Bulgaria, where Vojdan Černodrinski created a national liberation theatre reflecting the uprising against the Ottoman Empire. His most significant works – *Macedonian Blood Wedding* (1900), *The Slave and the Agha* (1902) and *Evil for Evil* (1903) – are imbued with both national and romantic emotions. He was also the founder of numerous theatre troupes in the period from 1894 to 1943.

Stylized theatrical productions reflecting the life of the people, dominated by folk elements, were developed between the two world wars. The most popular of these were Vasil Iljoski's *Eloper* (1928) and *Teodos the Rich Man* (1937), and Anton Panov's *Migrant Workers*. During the 1941–4 anti-fascist war, a theatre of resistance developed, producing plays such as *Hitler in His Death-Throes* by Marko Šulakovski (1921–92) and *Gjore of the Five Names* by Vlado Maleski (1919–84).

The rapid development of post-war Macedonian theatre has been connected to the work of a considerable number of gifted playwrights who have embraced various genres and contemporary styles. One of the most thematically and stylistically innovative is Kole Čašule (b. 1921) who began with psychological realism (*A Twig in the Wind*, 1957) and later explored the harsh fate of the country (*Darkness*, 1961; *Whirlpool*, 1968; *Judgement*, 1978). But his work also deals with more universal phenomena such as totalitarianism and dictatorship, bureaucracy and alienation (*Partitura for a Miron*, 1967; *As You Please*, 1971).

At about the same time there also appeared the prolific playwright Tome Arsovski (b. 1928), whose works were characterized by their social commitment and diagnosis of social anomalies as they affected the fate of the individual (*The Paradox of Diogenes*, 1961; *Hoops*, 1965; *A Step into Autumn*, 1969).

In contrast to Arsovski's realism, Branko Pendovski (b. 1927) has cultivated tragic farce and the grotesque; the influence of the Theatre of the Absurd is evident in such works as *Flood* (1974), *Travelling* (1978) and *Victim of the Pantheon* (1985).

The work of Bogomil Gjuzel (b. 1939) is marked by a preoccupation with demystifying history, revolution as a destructive social phenomenon (*Alexiada*, 1978; *Apocalypse*, 1987) and demythologizing universal myths and legends (*Adam and Eve*, 1971; *Job*, 1971).

Georgi Stalev (b. 1930) has a place in contemporary Macedonian theatre together with numerous other writers who have been inspired by the rich tradition of folklore; he seeks archetypal mythic nuclei while breaking the conventional forms (*The Wounded Hero*, 1971; *Angelina*, 1972).

The most significant contemporary Macedonian playwright is Goran Stefanovski (b. 1952) who established his reputation with his very first plays, *Yane Zadrogaz* (1974), *Proud Flesh* (1979) and *Flight on the Spot* (1982). His subject matter is wide-ranging and complex, but he deals mainly with the Macedonian past and present, searching through its existential forms. Among his major works are *Hi-fi* (1982), *False Bottom* (1984), *Black Hole* (1988) and *Tower of Babylon* (1990).

Another author of note is Jordan Plevneš (b. 1953) who has most often dealt with Macedonia's national past and present, as in *Erygon* (1982), *Mazedonische Zustände* (1984) and *R* (1987).

Among still later playwrights, one should mention Žanina Mirčevska (b. 1967), author of *Shuabi Up* (1989) and *Dies Irae* (1990), and Dejan Dukovski (b. 1969), author of *The Boastful Giant* (1992) and *The Balkans Are Not Dead* (1992).

Aleksandar Aleksiev

Directors, Directing and Production Styles

A number of important theatre directors emerged in Macedonia almost immediately after World War II, first on the stage of the

The 1982 Skopje Drama Theatre production of Jordan Plevneš's *Erygon*, directed and designed by Ljubiša Georgievski.

Macedonian National Theatre in Skopje and then throughout the country and particularly in Bitola.

Dimitar Kjostarov (b. 1912) is generally regarded as the first of the modern directors. He graduated from the Theatre High School in Sofia, worked for a period as an actor and in 1942, during the Bulgarian occupation, joined the Bulgarian People's Theatre in Skopje. During this period he became involved in illegal resistance activity, working for a time in the agitprop section at the headquarters of the liberation army. After the war, he began lecturing at the Theatre High School and later as a professor at the Faculty of Dramatic Art in Skopje. A representative of the realist school, he worked throughout the former Yugoslavia staging productions in Belgrade, Zagreb, Mostar and elsewhere, directing in all over a hundred productions while specializing in Russian classics and comedies by Nušić.

Dimitrie Osmanli (b. 1926) and Todorka Kondova (b. 1928), two other directors of note,

were both trained in Belgrade. Kondova was both an actress and a director, as has been the case with many other figures in the Macedonian theatre, notably Ilija Milčin (b. 1918) and Krum Stojanov (b. 1917). The former began his directing career with *The Glass Menagerie* by Tennessee Williams; the latter with *The Big Knife* by Clifford Odets; Kondova with García Lorca's *The House of Bernarda Alba* and Osmanli with *The Diary of Anne Frank*. All but Stojanov later became professors at the Skopje Faculty of Dramatic Art. Mirko Stefanovski (1921–81) worked in the theatres in Prilep and Bitola and staged memorable productions such as *Othello* at the Theatre of the Nationalities in Skopje.

In the 1970s, a new wave of directors emerged, represented first by Ljubiša Georgievski (b. 1937) who, ever searching for new means of stage expression, began his career with Nušić's comedy *The Deceased*. Like Slobodan Unkovski (b. 1948) and Vladimir Milčin (b. 1947) slightly later, Georgievski

Ljubiša Georgievski's 1977 Skopje Drama Theatre production of Kole Čašule's *Darkness*, designed by Branko Kotovski.

established his reputation largely on the basis of his productions of native Macedonian plays, such as Jordan Plevneš's *Erygon*, Kole Čašule's *Darkness* and Vladimir Kostov's *Mara's Wedding*.

Slobodan Unkovski's approach as a director was equally impressive in the folkloric *Jane Zadrogaz* by Goran Stefanovski at the Drama Theatre in Skopje and in his work on Corneille and Lope de Vega at the Yugoslav Drama Theatre in Belgrade, and on Arthur Kopit's *Nothing* in Skopje.

Vladimir Milčin was partly responsible for the discovery of new playwriting talents such as Blaže Minevski (b. 1961) and Blagoj Ristevski (b. 1949) and was a frequent guest at theatres in the Croatian cities of Varaždin, Split and Dubrovnik.

Other directors of note include Branko Stavrev (b. 1939), Dimitar Stankovski (b. 1946), Kole Angelovski (b. 1943) and Naum Panovski (b. 1950).

Ivan Ivanovski

Music Theatre

Music theatre is an inheritance from the ancient period when, before the Slavs came to Macedonia, Orphic rituals were practised. This cult, in fact, seems to have had its origins either in Thrace or Macedonia. There is a considerable amount of evidence from archaeological excavations at ancient theatres pointing to numerous Dionysian and other ritual celebrations with a rich musical accompaniment. It is difficult to evaluate the musical or scenic influence of this in the culture of subsequent periods. Cultural discontinuity unfortunately has been a recurrent feature in Macedonia.

In the Medieval period, folklore acted as a diachronic cultural bridge and it has continued to have its influence on individual artistic creativity. Medieval court theatre and musical performances differed from those in other European and non-European centres precisely because of their specific folk qualities.

During the period of Ottoman rule, culture developed along oral lines and song cycles were created. This process continued into the nineteenth century, the century of the Macedonian revival. A pioneering role was played here too by Jordan Hadži Konstantinov-Džinot, with his school theatres incorporating patriotic songs, and also by Vojdan Černodrinski, whose dramatic texts were frequently interspersed with folk music.

In the inter-war period of the twentieth century, attempts to stage operas and operettas were made both by professional and amateur enthusiasts at the Skopje Theatre and through the Society of Friends of Music. There were similar endeavours elsewhere, notably in Štip, where Sergei Mikhailov staged opera performances with local talent and a piano accompaniment in the absence of an orchestra.

The real growth of a professional music theatre began with the formation of the Republic of Macedonia after World War II. On the initiative of Petre Bogdanov-Kočko (1913–88) and Todor Skalovski (b. 1909), who organized professional music groups and soloists, *Cavalleria Rusticana* was performed in 1947. The opera company within the Macedonian National Theatre became a state institution in 1948. The initial successes of the Skopje Opera were linked to the name of one of the great conductors of the period, Lovro Matačić (1899–1985), who lived and worked in Skopje from 1948 to 1952, establishing sound foundations for the future development of music theatre and staging works by Puccini, Mascagni, Leoncavallo, Gluck, Mozart and Verdi.

There soon followed opera scores by local composers. The first was the opera *Goce* by Kiril Makedonski (1925–1984), premièred in 1954. Makedonski went on to compose the operas *Czar Samuil* and *Ilinden*, while Trajko Prokopiev (1909–79) wrote *Parting* and *Kuzman Kapidan*, and Toma Prošev (b. 1931) *Spider's Web* and *The Little Prince*.

The opera company has continued to enrich its repertoire which now includes most of the best known Italian and other European works, performing not only in Skopje but also in neighbouring cultural centres and even in smaller towns. The May Opera Evenings festival has taken place annually since 1972 with participation by local and foreign soloists, conductors and directors.

Dragoslav Ortakov

Jordan Mitrovski's 1975 Macedonian Public Theatre Skopje Opera production of Alexander Borodin's *Prince Igor*, designed by Dimitar Kondovski.
Photo: Vladimir Plaveski.

Dance Theatre

In 1948 a ballet troupe was formed in Skopje in order to meet the needs of the newly formed opera at the National Theatre and a ballet studio was opened under the leadership of Georgi Makedonski, who was the first solo ballet dancer, leader of the ballet troupe, choreographer and teacher.

Among those recruited to the troupe were members of the folk group at the Karpoš Pioneer Centre in Skopje. They – Janka Atanasova (1935–80), Emilija Džipunova (b. 1936), Magdalena Janeva (b. 1934), Svetlana Mavrovska, Olga Milosavleva (b. 1934), Elpida Pakovska (b. 1936), Natka Penušliska (b. 1934), Elica Popovska (1937–92) and Smilka Siljanova – subsequently played a major part in the growth and development of Macedonian ballet.

In 1948 the ballet sequence from the third act of Verdi's *La Traviata* was performed and in 1949 Leoncavallo's *I Pagliacci* and the *Walpurgisnacht* ballet from Gounod's *Faust*. In the course of the 1949–50 season full-length ballets by Asafiev, Tchaikovsky and Ravel, all choreographed by Georgi Makedonski, entered the repertoire.

The positive results pointed to a need for systematic training for the younger members of the troupe and in 1950 the ballet studio was transformed into a ballet high school, later a part of the Ilija Nikolovski-Luj Music and Ballet Teaching Centre, staffed by ballet artists and graduate teachers, most from the State Institute of Theatre Art in Moscow.

The names of several distinguished ballet dancers – among them Aleksandar Dobrohotov (1909–83), ballet master, choreographer and teacher, and Dimitrije Parlić (1919–86) – are also linked to the early stages of Macedonian ballet. A particular place was occupied by the eminent Russian and Yugoslav ballerina Nina Vasilieva Kirsanova (1899–1989).

The first Macedonian ballet, *Macedonian Tales* by Gligor Smokvarski (1914–74), was staged at the Macedonian National theatre in

1953. Its inspiration lay in the pastoral melodies of Macedonian folk songs and dances and it was choreographed by Parlić. There followed ballets by Rimsky-Korsakov, Mozart, Weber, Delibes and others. From 1956 onwards, larger-scale ballets such as Tchaikovsky's *Sleeping Beauty*, Adam's *Giselle* and Chopin's *Les Sylphides* were performed.

In 1958, a second Macedonian ballet received its première: *Labin and Dojrana*, composed by Trajko Prokopiev with choreography by Dobrohotov and Olga Milosavleva, later to become one of the most outstanding choreographers in Macedonia.

Macedonian ballet has always been open to experts from other centres and outstanding among the names of the numerous teachers and choreographers who have left their marks is that of Yuri Myachin, a well-known teacher from St Petersburg, who brought the wealth of his experience to the country between 1968 and 1973.

In addition to classical ballet there has also been interest in other forms of dance including neo-classical, contemporary, modern and post-modern approaches. Among such have been ballets by Stravinsky, Prokofiev, de Falla and Bizet, with choreography by Vera Kostić (b. 1925), Parlić and others. There have also been numerous performances of works by local composers such as Toma Prošev, Tomislav Zografski (b. 1934), Branko Ivanovski (b. 1921), Aleksandar Lekovski (b. 1933), Kiril Makedonski, Ljubomir Brangjolica (b. 1932) and Dimitrie Bužarovski (b. 1952). There have also been multi-media projects such as Carl Orff's *Carmina Burana* with choreography by D. Boldin (b. 1930), who also choreographed *Pink Floyd: To the Unknown* with music by Vangelis, choreographed by Dušanka Gradiški (b. 1966) and directed by Vladimir Milčin; and *Mansard*, music by Zlatko Origjanski, choreographed by Jagoda Slaneva (b. 1949) and directed by Branko Brezovec (b. 1955).

Emilija Džipunova

Theatre for Young Audiences
Puppet Theatre

The first modern performance of a puppet play in Macedonia was *Siljan the Stork* in 1946, based on a story by Marko Cepenkov (1829–1920) and dramatized by Petre Prličko. Written in Macedonian, it owed much to the work of Svetlana Malahova (b. 1919) who together with Prličko founded the first professional puppet theatre in the country.

Most professional theatres in Macedonia have at some time or other in their development experimented with puppet stages. One such theatre in Skopje developed into the Youth Drama Theatre (later the Drama Theatre) and gave puppet performances on a regular basis.

In 1990, *The Monsters from Our Town* by Rusomir Bogdanovski (b. 1942) and directed by Nikola Angelovski marked the opening of the Children's Theatre in Skopje. The opera and ballet have also included productions with young audiences in mind, such as Benjamin Britten's *The Little Sweep* and Tchaikovsky's *The Nutcracker*. There are also children's drama departments attached to both radio and television stations.

Risto Stefanovski

Design

In plays, operas and ballet performances immediately after World War II, illustrative or narrative set design was dominant. Stage sets by Vasilije Popović-Cico (1914–62) and Tomo Vladimirski (1904–71) were characteristic of this period and gave an obvious 'realism' to the actors' performances.

The appearance of designer Branko Kostovski (b. 1924) introduced a more profound significance to Macedonian design. Kostovski used

Slobodan Unkovski's 1974 Skopje Drama Theatre production of Goran Stefanovski's *Jane Zadrogaz*, designed by Vladimir Georgievski and costume design by Georgi Zdravev.

predominantly natural materials, giving them maximum functionality. Using semiotics, he wrote his own plays in space, as illustrated in his designs for *The Wall, the Water* and *Kangaroo Jump*.

In the 1980s, designs became more complex both notionally and aesthetically while incorporating experience from the other arts. The material used continues to be primarily natural. The designs by Krste Džidrov and Vladimir Georgievski have been the most significant of these.

Macedonian costume design is a relatively young branch of applied art. It began on a professional level in the mid-1950s when the first trained personnel began to appear, including Rada Petrova (b. 1930) and Jelena Patrnogić (b. 1932). This circle has widened to include Georgi Zdravev (b. 1941), Elena Dončeva (b. 1942), Lira Grabul and Meri Georgievska-Jovanovska. Before them, personnel from other theatres in Yugoslavia were regularly engaged for productions at the Macedonian National Theatre. The first costume designer in Macedonia was Sotir Naumovski (1919–87), who worked for more than thirty years in the Bitola Theatre and in theatres throughout Macedonia. His first major project was Risto Krle's *Antica* in 1950.

Vladimir Georgievski, Ivan Ivanovski

Theatre Space and Architecture

The most architecturally significant theatres in Macedonia are modern in style and date from the end of the 1970s. These include the Macedonian National Theatre, the Drama Theatre and the Theatre of the Nationalities in Skopje. All three are proscenium stages.

The main auditorium of the National Theatre has seating for 860 and a stage of 2,000 square metres with a proscenium 16 by 22 metres and with a rear and two lateral stages. The main stage is composed of four 'wagon' platforms 5 by 15 metres each. The first can be lowered below stage level. The National Theatre also contains a studio theatre with a seating capacity of about 200. There are also dressing rooms for more than 200 performers, large workshops and two ballet studios.

The Drama Theatre is a prefabricated building donated by the former German Democratic Republic after the catastrophic earthquake of 1963. It has a classical box stage with a proscenium but no apron. It has fixed lighting banks and scene changes are made by classical flies.

Other theatres in Macedonia are part of cultural centres built at various times since the end of World War II. The theatres in Kumanovo, Štip, Strumica, Prilep and Bitola thus have multipurpose concepts.

A number of theatre performances are given in the open air. Historic sites are used for this purpose: Samuil's Fortress in Ohrid and the ancient theatres at Heraclea, Stobi and Ohrid. Performances have also been given in the courtyards of old churches such as the cathedral of St Sophia in Ohrid. New spaces in non-theatrical venues exist as well, while some alternative theatres are even making use of basements in new buildings.

Vladimir Georgievski

Training

Because of the lack of national educational establishments in Macedonia up to the time of its liberation and independence after World War II, the training of theatre personnel was done on a personal and individual basis. Also certain theatrical troupes attempted to train people to meet company needs.

In this way, as early as 1904, Vojdan Černodrinski, one of the key figures in the modern Macedonian theatre, began to pay for the training of talented young Macedonians in institutions in Bulgaria where his own Macedonian theatre was then active. In the inter-war period several Macedonians studied in Belgrade, while during the Bulgarian occupation many studied acting and directing in Sofia. The main source of new artists, however, continued to be the numerous amateur or travelling companies which gave their members mastery of the craft through practical experience. Of particular importance was the contribution of the Bohemian travelling theatre, formed by Petre Prličko, the doyen of Macedonian acting, in 1932.

The situation was radically altered with the formation of a Theatre High School in Skopje in 1947. When it began the school had only a single department – acting. As professional theatres began to be established in virtually all the major Macedonian towns, though, the need for trained actors increased, while directors, playwrights and other specialists were educated in Yugoslav universities.

In 1969, a Faculty of Dramatic Art was established as a part of Skopje University. Today it has departments of acting, theatre and film direction, playwriting, camera work, montage and management. The teaching staff consists of some of the most eminent Macedonian directors, playwrights, theatre historians and other specialists. Costume design is studied at the Faculty of Fine Art and stage design at the Faculty of Architecture. There are about eighty students a year at the Drama Faculty. Graduate students frequently organize alternative theatre events which add enormously to the theatrical life of Macedonia, and many go on to find work in professional theatres, film, radio and television.

Criticism, Scholarship and Publishing

Theatre criticism appeared in a rudimentary form at the beginning of the twentieth century in

the pages of the Macedonian emigrant press in Bulgaria, linked to the activities of Vojdan

Černodrinski's original Sorrow and Consolation Theatre as well as his Macedonian Capital and Ilinden Theatres. Also written about were Hristov's Freedom Theatre and Petrov's Macedonian Revolutionary Theatre. Between the two world wars the most important theatre critic was Jovan Kostovski (1907–81) who, from 1937, regularly followed theatre life in Macedonia in the pages of the *Vardar* newspaper, which was published in Skopje. His critical writings have been collected in the volume *Works and Performances* (Kultura, Skopje, 1973).

Since World War II the most significant critics and reviewers have been Jovan Boškovski (1920–68), Ivan Mazov (1923–77), Mateja Matevski (b. 1929), Aleksandar Aleksiev (b. 1929), Ivan Ivanovski (b. 1930) and Petre Bakevski (b. 1947). Their criticism has been published in the *Nova Makedonija* (*New Macedonia*) and *Večer* daily newspapers and in the journals *Razgledi* (*Review*), *Kulturen život* (*Cultural Life*) and *Sovremenost* (*Contemporary*). Some theatre criticism immediately after the war, typified by Dimitar Mitrev (1919–76), was based on the ideas of socialist-realism as imported from the Soviet Union, while after the 1950s Macedonian theatre criticism was characterized by an aesthetic pluralism which went with an abandonment of the Stanislavski system in theatre education and production.

Theatre studies have developed in Macedonia hand in hand with critical writing. Its first task has been to reconstruct the beginnings and subsequent development of the theatre in Macedonia, to reveal and evaluate the dramatic works and activity of the past and to establish a vital and direct contact between tradition and the present moment. In so doing they have uncovered the paradox that while Macedonian theatre developed under extremely unfavourable conditions, it has been a dominant cultural form in the country since the end of the nineteenth century.

Major studies include Aleksandar Aleksiev's *Founders of Macedonian Drama* (1972), Ljubiša Georgievski's *World Dream* (1979) and *Ontology of the Theatre* (1985), Blagoja Ivanov's *Contemporary Drama and Theatre in Macedonia* (1982), a collection of writings in Serbian, Ivan Ivanovski's *On Its Own Soil* (1983), Rade Siljan's *Macedonian Drama: The Nineteenth and Twentieth Centuries* (1990), a collection of writings and *100 Years of Macedonian Drama* (1992), an anthology of plays and Risto Stefanovski's *The Theatre in Macedonia* (1990).

The first specialized periodical, *Teatar* (*Theatre*), appeared in 1952, published by the Macedonian National Theatre. The journal *Teatarski glasnik* (*Theatre Courier*) edited by Risto Stefanovski, has been appearing since 1977. Theatre criticism is regularly published in the magazines *Sovremenost* and *Kulturen život*. Plays are published by a variety of publishers as there is no specialist drama publishing house.

Aleksandar Aleksiev
Translated by Margaret Reid
and Graham W. Reid

(See also YUGOSLAVIA)

Further Reading

Aleksiev, Aleksandar. *Founders of Macedonian Drama*. Skopje: Misla, 1972.

Georgievski, Ljubiša. *Ontology of the Theatre*. Skopje: Misla, 1985.

——. *World Dream*. Skopje: Studentski zbor, 1979.

Hećimović, Branko. *Suvremene makedonske drame*. [Contemporary Macedonian drama]. Zagreb: Znanje, 1982.

Ivanov, Blagoja. *Savremena drama i pozorište u Makedoniji*. [Contemporary drama and theatre in Macedonia]. Novi Sad: Sterijino pozorje, 1982. 372 pp.

Ivanovski, Ivan. *On Its Own Soil*. Skopje: Kultura, 1983.

Siljan, Rade. *Macedonian Drama: The Nineteenth and Twentieth Centuries*. Skopje: Makedonska kniga, 1990.

——. *100 Years of Macedonian Drama*. Skopje: Matica Makedonska, 1992.

Stefanovski, Risto. *The Theatre in Macedonia*. Skopje: Misla, 1990.

MALTA

The Maltese Archipelago is in the middle of the Mediterranean Sea about 100 kilometres (60 miles) south of Sicily and 360 kilometres (220 miles) north of Libya. It is made up of a series of tiny islands, the two inhabited ones being Malta (28.2 kilometres by 13.4 kilometres) and Gozo (14.5 kilometres by 7.2 kilometres). Their combined 1992 population was 362,000; their land area is 316 square kilometres (122 square miles).

The strategic position of the Maltese islands has always attracted foreign powers; in fact, their history is one of domination. The islands passed from the Phoenicians to the Carthaginians, then to the Romans, Arabs, Normans, Angevins and Aragonese. In 1530 they were given to the Order of the Knights of St John of Jerusalem, who ruled up to 1798 when the islands were taken over by Napoleon. Two years later, the Maltese rose against the French, calling for British assistance. Malta and Gozo remained a British colony up to 1964 when the islands acquired independence. The country became a republic in 1974.

When the British assumed power in 1800, the islands bore predominantly Italian influence in all fields of culture and education. The Italian language was taught in schools, spoken by the educated classes, used in the law courts and church curia, as well as in the administrative and journalistic fields. The Maltese language, of semitic origin, was spoken by all the inhabitants but, except in rare cases, remained unwritten.

The British disapproved of this cultural situation, apprehensive lest Italian nationalistic ideas spark off Maltese fervour. Around 1880, a policy to oust the Italian language, replacing it with English, was embarked upon. Progressively, the Maltese grew more aware of the cultural importance of having a language of their own. In 1934, English and Maltese became joint official languages.

The struggle for one language to emerge as dominant, later known as the Language Question, eventually resulted in the affirmation of a national identity. The issue gathered momentum during the nineteenth century, unleashing itself in the 1920s. It was not resolved until after World War II, leaving a marked impact on Maltese theatrical reality. In fact, when dealing with Maltese theatre it is important to distinguish between 'theatre in Malta' as perhaps the culmination of European colonial culture, and 'Maltese theatre' or 'theatre in Maltese', which marks the recognition of an autonomous culture.

For many centuries efforts to capture in writing the spoken language (with its markedly semitic vocabulary, syntax and morphology) had posed considerable difficulties for Maltese scholars whose European education had given them no grounding in Arabic script. It was not until 1931 that an association of Maltese scholars finally hammered out a logical and scientific grammar for the language.

Research on theatre in Malta is still in its initial stages, the basis of a serious research programme having only recently been established. Lack of proper documentation therefore makes it difficult to affirm whether the nineteenth-century awareness of the European literary movements and the activity it sparked off in Malta also found echoes in the field of theatre. It would seem that the language for performances given in churches, private homes and public places, and later, in the two major theatres, was manifestly Italian – at least until the mid-nineteenth century. The first instance of a play in Maltese was recorded in 1847, when

Luigi Rosato's (1795–1872) play *Caterina* was staged at the Manoel Theatre.

Theatre in Maltese *might* have existed before that, but no trace has yet been found. Is this attributable to the difficulties which would have faced anybody trying to write down Maltese dialogue in Latin script? Or is it attributable to there never having been any theatre in Maltese prior to the nineteenth century?

If the first were the case, any theatre in Maltese would only have been 'constructed' orally. It would not have been written and therefore would have been lost. A document dated 1760 brought to light by G. Cassar Pullicino (b. 1921) indicates the existence of a sense of theatre in the comic celebration of *Il-Qarcilla* which took place during Carnival. A person dressed up as a notary would go through the streets carrying a basket containing a bride made out of sweet pastry and the *qarcilla*, a pastry ring, followed by a mock wedding-party. At every corner, the 'notary' would read out a mock dowry list, and at the end the bride and the ring would be eaten by the 'guests'. Another tradition described by the same author and bearing theatrical elements is the *Qarinza*. On New Year's Eve, singers would go round the village carrying straw effigies of a man and a woman, procuring invitations to people's homes. There, one of the singers would fall on the ground pretending to be dead, and rise up only after his companions had been given food and money.

If the second hypothesis were the case, explanation would have to be sought elsewhere. One possibility would be that the vast majority of the Maltese never engaged in theatrical art until the turn of the nineteenth century. Several factors may have contributed to this.

The first would be the semitic origins of the Maltese race, origins further strengthened by a period of Arab occupancy of over 200 years (AD 870–1090). This may have resulted in the Maltese sharing the Islamic inhibition of – and estrangement from – theatrical art. It may also have led to their retaining that outlook even after the European occupying powers moved in once more in 1090.

A second factor would be the smallness of the island and its early isolation from the European mainstream. This may have resulted in austerity even among the occupiers. The linguistic and cultural chasm separating occupiers from occupied may have resulted, moreover, in the Maltese people not being very aware of whatever forms of entertainment their occupiers may have indulged in – with the possible exception of a small number of educated persons (nobility, clergy, notaries).

A third possible contributing factor would be the geographical, demographic and economic nature of the archipelago. The population of the islands in the thirteenth century seems to have been only about 10,000, while by 1798 it had risen to just 100,000. This small population lived in small scattered groups, apart from one or two fortified townships. The arid harshness of the environment and its paucity of raw materials would have imposed a severe survival-level existence of an introverted nature with family groups leading a hard, severe, silent life. It would seem to have offered little scope for extroverted activity. All known celebration seems to have concentrated on events in the Christian calendar, which set off a single communal festivity every year in each village. Little else is known of private or public celebration in earlier times. Only in the time of the knights are Carnival and *Calendimaggio* known to have been boisterous affairs. Otherwise the general austerity and sobriety would have inhibited theatrical art.

One big harvest celebration, *Imnarja*, seems to have mobilized the entire population with historical records going back to the sixteenth century. Although no ancient folk dances are known, *ghana* (folk music in the form of a series of variations on one or two basic themes) was one of the central components of *Imnarja*, with night-long food, wine and song, at first in the fields around the old capital, and later, in a small torch-illuminated wood. Though certainly having undergone developments and alterations throughout the centuries, *ghana* is still very much alive today.

Ghana is sung either unaccompanied or to an accompaniment of instruments which could include guitar, accordion and percussion. In true Maltese spirit the instrumental accompaniment is manifestly European while the voice, with its texture, its placing and the micro-intervals and *glissandi*, is clearly Mediterranean with North African undertones.

In *ghana tal-fatt* (narrative) the songs could be about unrequited love, a tragedy at sea, the death of a beloved, the non-return of a soldier or a sailor, a betrayal. The sounds and moods of the Mediterranean are clearly captured but the bard evokes the drama with only his vocal prowess and verbal poetry. His outward appearance is totally restrained. He does not transform himself into the various roles. His function is that of a dispassionate observer – brought out even more clearly when a single singer presents both sides of a dialogue – with maximum restraint.

This restraint is also the case in *ghana* known as *spirtu pront* (improvised). This comic genre takes the form of a dialogue between two singers. Each hits at the other on issues ranging from family to work, status, honour, singing prowess, love or politics. Each respondent has to compose his rhyming reply to the previous shot from his opponent during an instrumental interval lasting only a few bars. Expressionless faces and relaxed bodies belie intense and vitriolic verbal exchanges, at once sharp and caustic. Once more, the medium is the word. The body is non-representative. It is but an acoustic amplifier giving access to mental activity. We are here strongly in the culture of the word, very much in the Arabic tradition.

Much as the village festivities, carnival and *Imnarja* satisfied somewhat the community's basic human need to engage collectively in theatrical art, it is easy to realize how *ghana* somehow satisfied the individual's basic human need to engage personally in the theatrical act – that is, to orchestrate one's presence in an extraordinary manner. The hypothesis is that these genres of *ghana* would have sufficed for the Maltese – until the nationalistic tremors of the romantic movement started affecting them too because of the Language Question.

At the beginning of the century, theatre in Maltese was seen primarily in parish halls and theatres all over the islands, and on certain occasions, at the Manoel Theatre. There were some dramatic companies in towns and villages such as the Alfieri from Cospicua and the I Vittoriosiani from Vittoriosa. The *teatrin* genre seems to have dominated – crowded village halls saw evenings packed with farces, sketches, variety programmes, *kummiedji brillanti*, while 'tragedies in five acts with a prologue and epilogue' drew many tears.

In 1910 the British services stationed in Malta founded a theatrical company called the Malta Amateur Dramatic Club (MADC). The actors were British amateurs. Their productions (pantomimes, musicals and light opera) were staged solely in English for British and Maltese audiences in the two major theatres.

The amateur Compagnia Carlo Goldoni was founded in 1928 by two Italian professors. Another amateur company, the Giacosa, was created to prepare inexperienced actors for the Goldoni Company. In fact, great efforts were made to train actors within the Goldoni, to the extent that the services of Italians residing in Malta were enlisted to help budding Maltese actors acquire proper diction. The repertoire was solely Italian, ranging from Goldoni to Pirandello. The company also staged one play in Italian written by a Maltese – Vincenzo Maria Pellegrini's (b. 1911) *La Predestinata* (*The Chosen One*) in the early 1950s. Soon operas and plays in Italian were competing with plays in English and Gilbert and Sullivan operettas.

As plays in Maltese started gaining popularity, the plays and translations of Mikiel Ang Borg (1868–1939) – vaudevilles and parodies of operas adapted to the local situation – began to be staged at the Royal Opera House in the 1920s and 1930s. Borg's company of actors was aptly called L-Indipendenza, and this at the height of the political crisis which had been brought on by the Language Question.

Lesser companies also developed: the Anici Dramatic Company (1936), the Ghaqda Talent Teatrali (1936), the Salesians Filodramatic Company San Genesio, which produced plays in Maltese, English and Italian with an all-male cast, and the Cittadini in Vittoriosa, Gioventù Cattolica in Valletta, for whom a prolific playwright, the Reverend Salv Laspina (1903–81), wrote a great number of plays.

Thus before World War II the situation was that of three main companies, each performing exclusively in English, Italian or Maltese and lesser companies performing mainly in Maltese.

During the war, theatrical activity was almost completely suspended. The exceptions were troop entertainments by such actors as Johnny Navarro (b. 1912), Johnny Catania (1926–92)

Charles Clews as the groom in his *The Wedding of Karmena Abdilla*, the longest playing comedy in Malta.

and Charles Clews (b. 1919). Their company, the Stage Commandos, would, after the war, present ribald and quasi-anarchic performances, particularly radio theatre, with the seemingly simple locals always outwitting their British army superiors.

In the early 1950s new companies were formed and new actors came to the fore. Theatre in Maltese gradually gained in importance, both on stage and on the radio.

All through the post-war period, foreign dramatic, dance and operatic companies regularly performed in Malta. Among them were performers such as Tito Gobbi, Ram Gopal, Anna Galina, Donald Wolfit and Margaret Rutherford. The wind of independence from British rule in the early 1960s gave rise to new forms of theatre, and marked improvement in the quality of theatre in Maltese.

Theatremaking also took to the streets: squares, promenades, seafronts, towns, villages and summer resorts saw performers meeting the public on its own ground.

Structure of the National Theatre Community

The importance of theatre as a major socializing factor in Malta at the beginning of the twentieth century is unquestionable. The Manoel Theatre, built in 1732 by the Grand Master de Vilhena, was the only theatre in Malta up to 1866 when the new and much larger Royal Opera House was inaugurated. The name itself shows the popularity of the operatic genre at the time. In fact the operatic season lasted from November to Lent, followed by a much shorter season of prose and operetta. Enthusiasm for theatregoing was such that when the inside of the new theatre was destroyed by fire in 1873, it was completely refurbished and enlarged within five years, only to be bombed in World War II. It was never rebuilt. Its former site, at the very entrance to the capital city, stands empty to this day.

In its heyday, the Theatre Royal, as it was known, housed world premières of operas by such Italian composers as Respighi and Zandonai and saw some of the best directors and singers, as well as major British and Irish dramatic companies such as the Old Vic and the Gate from Dublin. Professional acting was always 'imported'. Up to 1939, this was done very extensively. Maltese theatre companies, however, have always been amateur. The country is too small to allow anybody to earn an income solely from theatre; thus even the most dedicated actors do theatre in their free time.

Drama festivals were launched immediately after the war. In 1945 Jimmy Allen (an Irishman) started a drama festival limited to British services personnel. The following year Michael Kissaun (1898–1972) set it up so that Maltese dramatic companies could participate but all the plays had to be in English.

That same year, Nikol Biancardi (1904–69) founded an association, Ghaqda Maltija Bajda w Hamra (The White and Red Maltese Association, red and white being the colours of the Maltese flag), to organize drama festivals in Malta, and in April/May of that year the First Maltese Drama Festival was founded. This initiative sparked off the creation of various new companies specifically established to participate in the festival. One of these was the prize-winner: the Maltese Amateur Light Entertainment Theatricals (MALETH), which included experienced Maltese actors who had acted with the Carlo Goldoni Company or with the Salesians, particularly Nosi Ghirlando (1908–64), famed for his larger than life rendering of female roles.

Other festivals of all-Maltese plays in 1950–1 were organized by the Malta Drama League, also founded in 1946. During the same period, the Ministry of Education set up a committee for Maltese Educational Theatre which organized a competition of Maltese one-act plays. One of the entries was written by the first Maltese female playwright, Giuseppina Attard Montaldo (1896–1970), who later adapted and translated many European plays. Children's drama festivals were also organized in 1947–8, and included plays in Maltese and English.

This need for performance, a post-war *joie de vivre*, found a fast and effective outlet in a flurry of activity on the radio. As in many other countries whose theatres were destroyed during the war, radio turned out to be an important contribution to the development of theatre. An enormous number of radio plays, radio sketches, serialized dramas and religious plays filled the air. Actors and writers wrote, adapted or translated plays for radio. Standards were constantly upgraded, generally through competitions. The broadcasts aroused the curiosity of many who had never been to the theatre, thus attracting new theatregoers.

The steady development of the theatre in the 1950s and the new experimentations in the 1960s led to the organization, by university students, of an annual festival, Xsenuru ('what are we going to show'), in the late 1960s. The students were also the first to stage Greek plays translated into Maltese.

Artistic Profile

Companies

Of the three main pre-war companies, L-Indipendenza, whose company had been depleted during the war, simply ceased operation. Tribute was paid to the company by asking the surviving actors to stage a special appearance on the last day of the First Maltese Drama Competition, which saw the setting up of new companies. The Compagnia Carlo Goldoni reappeared under the directorship of Carlo (1908–67) and Bice (b. 1909) Bisazza, but British political strategies and especially the war, with Italian planes bombing Malta, had curbed Maltese enthusiasm for things Italian, and the company was dissolved in 1958 after the players had valiantly tried to keep it alive. After its disappearance it was only the Società Dante Alighieri which on rare occasions staged plays in Italian. Bice Bisazza, together with Nosi Ghirlando, later founded a new company, La Ribalta, staging plays in Maltese.

Faced by post-war drops in service personnel stationed on Malta and consequently by a lack of British nationals who were interested in acting, the MADC started to admit Maltese into its ranks. With productions of plays by Coward, Milne, Priestley, and later Anouilh, Camus, Miller, Chekhov, García Lorca and Giraudoux, MADC's standards rose progressively, and it is today the oldest dramatic company in Malta with the bulk of its productions still staged in English.

The MADC was also the first company to own large premises which served as club rooms and rehearsal rooms, as well as for the construction and storage of sets, props, costumes, light and sound equipment. The premises were later to be used as a playhouse. Other British and Maltese companies appeared. The British Institute Players, founded in 1944 by Major Cathcart Bruce, had a mixed cast of Maltese and English actors. In 1946 university students formed the Fergha Drammatika Ghaqda tal-Malti (Università) – the Drama Branch of the Maltese Language Association. The Ariel Players from the Royal Air Force relaunched pantomime. In the 1950s, the Banks Sports Association and the Civil Service Sports Club joined forces to produce musicals, including *The Belle of New York* as well as *The Maid of the Mountains*, with a cast of over 300 people each.

Dramaturgy

Throughout the nineteenth century, up to the beginning of the twentieth, the romantic influence on the Maltese literary movement was also felt in the theatre. Romantic themes and certain theatrical forms, especially melodrama, prevailed. Various successful novels of the time, such as those of Guze Muscat Azzopardi (1853–1927) were adapted for the theatre. In 1913 Nino Cremona tried to raise theatre to levels that had been gradually attained in other literary fields. His work *Il-Fidwa tal-Bdiewa* (*The Peasants' Redemption*) was the first serious effort to exploit the literary potential of the Maltese language on stage. Poetic form and literary narrative were used to depict an historical event, the revolt of the Maltese against their Spanish overlord in 1426.

In the 1950s the taste for historical themes was abandoned and realism was introduced into Maltese playwriting. This new trend can be seen in Guze Chetcuti's (b. 1914) work *Il-Kerrejja* (*The Slum Dwellings*, 1963) dealing with social structure and rank, but is developed more extensively in the works of Guze Diacono (b. 1912). In his sharp observations of society, Diacono tries to provide a truthful, objective account of a situation taken from everyday life, seen through the eyes of the passive spectator. His best known play, *Il-Madonna tac-coqqa* (*The Madonna in the Black Mantle*, 1978), raised much controversy at the time because of its story, depicting a monk lured away from his monastery by a beautiful woman. (Diacono, also a critic, examined nineteenth-century theatre and published a collection of essays called *It-teatru wara Ibsen – Theatre After Ibsen*, 1972.)

At the beginning of the 1960s, Francis Ebejer (1925–93), Malta's greatest playwright to date, introduced the Maltese public to a new kind of theatre, with a distinctive literary quality. His plays, where narrative is markedly absent, depict personalities in moments of turbulent inner crisis and conflict with one another. The author's extensive use of symbols and metaphor is extended to the settings. His universal themes are at times applied specifically to the Maltese context, and show a concern for the influence of the past upon the present which, according to the author, 'might provide glimpses of alternative futures'. The Maltese public, although initially startled by this new theatrical form, eventually acclaimed it. Among his plays are *Menz* (1967); *Il-Hadd fuq il-bejt* (*Sunday on the Roof*, 1971); *L-Imwarrbin*, first played in an English version called *The Cliff Hangers*; *Hitan* (*Walls*), originally written for television and first broadcast in 1970; and *Meta morna tal-Mellieha* (*When We Went to Mellieha*, 1976).

The new trend set by Ebejer was taken up by a number of young writers, including Oreste Calleja (b. 1946), Alfred Sant (b. 1948) and Doreen Micallef (b. 1949). Calleja's works portray characters striving vainly for fulfilment which they never attain because of social and psychological hurdles. His themes are at once highly allegorical and ironic and, like Ebejer's, encompass a world both universal and local. A collection of his four main plays was published in 1972, and his play *Ghasfur tan comb* (*The Bird of Lead*) was published in 1993.

In his plays, Alfred Sant is concerned with the psychological aspects of human behaviour. His pessimistic visions are built through precise language. He is best known for his radio plays, published in 1979 under the title *Min hu Evylin Costa? u drammi ohra* (*Who is Evylin Costa? and Other Plays*). The plays of Doreen Micallef – published under the titles *Wicc imb'wicc u drammi ohra* (*Face to Face and Other Plays*) and *Fit-tielet cerkju* (*Within the Third Circle*) – show the author's efforts to introduce poetry into playwriting.

The innovations of collective dramaturgy appearing in Europe and the United States in the late 1960s found reverberations in Malta in

Francis Ebejer's 1971 Manoel Theatre production of his *Sunday on the Roof*.

1968 with Teatru Workshop (eventually to call itself Teatru tal-Bniedem/Theatre of Man) and Teatru Henri Dogg launching their first such productions.

Directors, Directing and Production Styles

New Maltese directors came to the fore in the 1960s, some from the acting ranks: Albert Marshall (b. 1947), Mario Azzopardi (b. 1944), John Schranz (b. 1942), Joe Friggieri (b. 1946), Lino Farrugia (b. 1947) and Mario Vella (b. 1953) engaged in an eclectic search, trying to merge elements from Maltese popular theatre, Maltese cultural traditions, the Maltese language and the new energies of European theatre of the time. Most performances, however, were built around translations of English, American, Italian and French works.

The Maltese penchant for comedy and farce has never flagged. Adaptations, translations as well as many original works depicting Maltese everyday life and poking fun at Maltese habits and traits continued to be produced right through this period, launching a commercial

form of theatre which also became very popular on television.

The theatrical movement launched in the mid-1960s did not sustain the promise of its original accelerated growth and in the late 1970s it suffered a marked decline.

A new company, the Atturi Theatre Group, was formed in 1974 and included several well-established actors. Karmen Azzopardi, one of the co-founders, was one of Malta's leading actresses. The aim of the company was to create a Maltese organization presenting quality productions of major authors, whether in the original English or in English translations, occasionally also in Maltese.

The Atturi Theatre group twice set up a playhouse in the 1970s to stage its own performances, once outside Valletta and once in Sliema. Each effort was, however, not very longlived, although memorable performances were staged. Once more, financial burdens proved too big to be met from the income from tickets sold to Malta's limited theatre audience.

In November 1982, A-Teatru (Anti-Theatre) was founded, using for its premises a converted barracks in Sliema. It became a regular venue for alternative theatre. Young directors and

Michael French's 1984 A-Teatru production of Alfred Jarry's *Ubu Roi*.

actors, mostly coming out of MTADA, were given the space to try out their ideas.

The movement's aim was threefold: to present original works by Maltese playwrights, to show classic and contemporary European theatre in translation, and to stage experimental adaptations of classical texts in unconventional settings. Plays by Maltese authors such as Alfred Buttigieg (b. 1956) and Immanuel Mifsud (b. 1967) and works by Arrabal, Beckett, Brecht, Dario Fo and others were staged.

In 1984 the theatre was gutted by arson: it is assumed because of the controversial nature of the plays shown there, the last of which, *Ara Gejja il-Mewt Ghalik* (*Death is Knocking at Your Door*), had been staged only half an hour before the theatre was set on fire. The perfor-

mance had been built on children's games which adults keep on 'playing', only much more seriously. The theatre reopened with undiminished verve, but closed down permanently in May 1987 when it was ransacked and all its equipment stolen or destroyed. The group tried to relocate to the more conventional stage of the Manoel Theatre but suspended its activities after a few productions.

In 1988, the General Workers' Union launched another group, Politeatru, with Narcy Calamatta (b. 1939) and Mario Azzopardi among its directors. Politeatru eventually opted also to put on some of its productions at the Manoel Theatre.

John J. Schranz, Vicki Ann Cremona

Music Theatre

When the war ended, the opera public and scores of people previously connected with operatic productions, mainly chorus singers and orchestral players, found themselves without either an opera house or the resources needed to engage foreign artists. This led to a decision by two groups, which eventually amalgamated, to mount their own productions at two cinemas in the town of Sliema, and in a new cinema-cum-theatre hastily built in the town of Hamrun toward the end of the war.

Operas in the 1950s often included Maltese singers in the main roles, such as Antoinette Miggiani (b. 1937), Oreste Kirkop (b. 1923), Giuseppe Satariano (1895–1992) and Paul Asciak (b. 1923) who were also to perform abroad. In the 1960s, however, operatic tradition in Malta lost ground, later to be taken up in Gozo, where it is still very much alive today.

The works performed included not only old favourites like *La Traviata* and *Tosca* but also a revival of a native Maltese opera, Carlo Diacono's (1876–1942) *L'Alpino* (1918). The soloists were mostly experienced chorus singers or concert recitalists as well as new singers like Oreste Kirkop, a handsome tenor with a splendid voice, who was to go on to a brief but impressive career in Britain and the United States.

By the early 1950s this native movement, with its strongly nationalistic flavour, had spent itself and Maltese productions were replaced by Italian ones presented by Italian impresarios

such as Luigi Cantoni. Occasionally leading foreign singers appeared in full productions while others gave recitals. Subsequently, the Manoel Theatre and private bodies in Gozo acted as impresarios, using performers usually from Italy or Bulgaria.

With very few exceptions, opera seasons are now reduced to a few weeks' duration, and have tended to be restricted to not more than two or three productions. As in pre-war years, works performed are predominantly Italian and sung in Italian; even Mozart was ignored completely until the 1991 bicentenary. Also entirely absent were works by contemporary foreign composers. However, a few contemporary Maltese composers have had works performed, all of them in more or less traditional idioms. Soon after the war Mario Cirillo (b. 1897) presented his *Il figlio del Sole* (*The Child of the Sun*, 1950), with a libretto that is a sequel to *Madame Butterfly*, while between 1965 and 1976 Carmelo Pace (1906–93) produced a series of operas with librettos in Italian but based on Maltese history or legend, starting with *Caterina Desguanez* (1965), his most appealing work. More recent works are Charles Camilleri's (b. 1931) *Il-Weghda* (*The Vow*) and *Il-fidwa tal-bdiewa*, the first two operas with librettos in the Maltese language by Joe Friggieri.

Since 1980 there has been a revival of interest in opera, one not limited to people who could still remember the pre-war years. This was partly fuelled by the availability of a few enthusiastic teachers of singing. An Opera Studio, formed by singers aiming to become professional, has presented operatic concerts and productions, while the Strauss School of Music has stimulated interest in Malta's operatic tradition by presenting the first production in Malta since 1799 of a work by Nicolò Isouard (1715–1818), *Jeannot et Colin*. Today's most successful singer in the operatic field is the acclaimed soprano Myriam Gauci (b. 1957).

Paul Xuereb

Dance Theatre

Malta has no native dance tradition. Both its folk dances and its theatre dance followed developments in Europe from the seventeenth century onwards. Dance interludes, in both the Italian and French styles, were performed during opera performances and intervals, certainly from the time the Manoel Theatre was opened in 1732. Folk dances have generally been limited to two basic melodies, one of which is a typical eighteenth-century European court minuet.

Ballet seems to have been introduced to Malta by Princess Nathalie Poutiatine, who gave charity performances during her short stay on the island between 1919 and 1921 and who eventually opened the first school of classical ballet in 1929, shortly after she returned to settle permanently in Malta. The first local shows were necessarily school shows but they seem to have achieved a reasonably high standard. Today it can be said that practically all the ballet schools in operation – about ten of them – have evolved from the Poutiatine Academy of Classical Ballet.

Possibilities for further training are still limited and opportunities to perform at the professional level scarce. Male dancers are still rare, and the handful of trained female dancers mostly open their own ballet schools and present school concerts. It was only in the 1990s that dancers like Tanya Bayona (b. 1945) and Daphne Lungaro (b. 1948) were invited, either as soloists or with their group of dancers, to perform abroad. The former also set up the first part-time professional company in Malta, a group which specializes in modern dance.

Maltese composers also only in the 1990s started composing music for ballet. Among the pieces worth mentioning are Carmelo Pace's *Air de Ballet*, Charles Camilleri's *Elements*, and Joseph Vella's (b. 1942) *Hagar Qim*. Tanya Bayona has also produced a very interesting ballet to the music of Camilleri's *Unum Deum* (*One God*) which though not written expressly as dance music, proved to be a most happy medium for this mode of expression.

The Maltese audience's love of ballet has also encouraged impresarios to invite foreign soloists and companies to perform either during the theatrical season or during the summer festivals that have become annual events. The size of the performances has necessarily been limited by the size of the stage at the Manoel Theatre. Practically every season since 1961 has seen at least one performance by a foreign company. The preference of the Maltese remains mostly with the classical and romantic repertoire.

Cecilia Xuereb

Theatre for Young Audiences
Puppet Theatre

There are no specific companies operating in Malta dealing with theatre for young audiences nor are there any professional puppet troupes.

Design
Theatre Space and Architecture

When theatre was resumed after the war, the first problem that had to be faced was that of theatre space: the main and most popular theatre – the Royal Opera House – having been destroyed by enemy action, alternative spaces had to be created. Performances were first housed in the knights' *auberges* and *sacra infirmeria* that had survived the bombing. Village halls and cinemas acquired new importance. Even the Empire Football Stadium was used as a venue for open-air operas and operettas.

In the 1950s, two new theatres were built by the church: the Catholic Institute in Floriana and the De Porres Hall in Sliema. The Manoel Theatre, which had been sold after the building of the Royal Opera House, was bought back by the government in 1957.

Open-air plays continue to be presented in summer at the Teatro Melita in St Julians.

The 1991 production of Francis Ebejer's symbolic drama *Menz*.

Training

The need for theatre training was always felt in Malta and various efforts have been made in that direction. As already stated, the Carlo Goldoni Company had devoted much energy to training its actors. In 1946, Cathcart Bruce instituted a drama study circle where classes and lectures in dramatic instruction were organized. The Third Drama Festival in 1947 offered a drama course (open to competitors and their guests). In the 1950s and 1960s, actors such as Ethel Farrugia (who trained with the Bristol Old Vic), as well as Johnny Navarro and Karmen Azzopardi, were sent abroad for training. In 1969, one finds for the first time actors working exclusively and regularly together in a group to research training methods. The year 1972 saw the creation of the Manoel Theatre Academy of Dramatic Art (MTADA) which teaches theatre on a part-time basis.

The first of the experimental groups to have its own theatre studio was Teatru Workshop, running a centre for research in training and performance montage between 1970 and 1975.

Criticism, Scholarship and Publishing

In spite of its inability to provide artists with a means of living, theatre in Malta today engages the interest, attention and energy of a great number of people. It is researched and studied at university level, it is learned in drama schools, it is investigated by groups of actors working together on contemporary techniques, it is discussed with expert practitioners from many countries, it is shared in festivals in Malta and beyond, it is fruitfully employed in certain classroom situations, it is presented and sought after by many and it is discussed and reviewed, and also (though insufficiently) published.

The Biennial Festival for Group Theatre, as well as certain other theatrical events in the Malta International Arts Festival, are helping to create an awareness of current theatre forms beyond Malta's shores, aiming for a wider exposure to transculturalization.

This interest is perhaps embodied in the theatre studies programme which Peter Serracino Inglott (b. 1936) set up in 1988 within the Mediterranean Institute of the University of Malta. Research is being organized to reconstruct the history of the development of theatre in Malta, investigating the possibility of its constituting a point of convergence of Mediterranean culture and of its ongoing dialogue with cultures beyond.

John Schranz, Vicki Ann Cremona

Further Reading

Blouet, Brian. *The Story of Malta.* London: Faber & Faber, 1967.

Calleja, Oreste. *4 Drammi.* [4 plays]. Blata l-bajda: Union Press, 1972.

——. *Ghasfur tac-comb, Haz Zabbar.* Gutenberg Press, 1993.

Cassar Pullicino, Guze. 'Il-bidu tal-palk malti'. [The origins of the Maltese stage]. *Analizi* (October 1966, May–June 1990, January 1991).

——. 'Fête des Lumières à Malte'. [The festival of light in Malta]. *Littérature Orale Arabo-Berbère* 14 (1983).

——. *Guze Muscat Azzopardi: Studju.* [Guze Muscat Azzopardi: a study]. Pieta: Indipendenza, 1991.

——. *Il folklore malti.* [Maltese folklore]. Msida: Malta University Press, 1975.

——. 'Il-Qarcilla – Bejn Drawwa u Drama f'Malta'. [The *Qarcilla* – between custom and drama in Malta]. *Il-Malti* (December 1954).

——. 'Maltese Ballads'. *The Sundial* 4 (1944).

Ebejer, Francis. *The Bilingual Writer as Janus.* Valletta: Foundation for International Studies, 1989.

Eynaud, Joseph. *Il teatro italiano a Malta (1630–1830).* [Italian theatre in Malta (1630–1830)]. Sta Venera: Lux Press, 1979.

Frendo, Henry J. 'Language and Nationality in an Island Colony: Malta'. *Canadian Review of Studies in Nationalism I* 3 (1975): 22–32.

Friggieri, Oliver. 'Il-kwistjoni tal-lingwa – Gharfien ta' Identita' Nazzjonali'. [The Language Question – the recognition of a national identity]. *Perspektiv* 16 (1981): 25–41.

——. 'In Search of a National Identity: A Survey of Maltese Literature'. *Durham University Journal* (December 1985).

——. *Kittieba ta' Zmienna.* [Contemporary authors]. Valletta: A.C. Aquilina, 1976.

Fsadni, R. 'The Wounding Song: Honour, Politics and Rhetoric in Maltese Ghana'. Diss., University of Cambridge, 1989.

Ganado, H. *Rajt Malta Tinbidel.* [I saw Malta change]. Malta: 1977.

Kirkpatrick, O.L., ed. 'Francis Ebejer' in *Contemporary Dramatists.* London: St James Press, 1986.

Kissaun, Michael. 'Post-war Amateur Theatre (1944–51)'. *Malta Yearbook 1956.* Sliema: De la Salle Brothers, 1958.

Luttrell, Anthony. *Approaches to Medieval Malta.* London: British School at Rome, 1975.

Mompalao Depiro, Joseph C. *The MADC Story 1910–85.* Sta Venera: Imprint, 1985.

Schiavone, Michael, ed. *Il-Purcissjonijiet tal-Gimgha l-Kbira f'Malta w Ghawdex.* [The Good Friday processions in Malta and Gozo]. Blata l-Bajda: Indipendenza, 1992.

Wettinger, Godfrey, and M. Fsadni. *L-Ghanja ta' Pietru Caxaru.* [The singing of Pietru Caxaru]. Fgura: Printwell, 1983.

MOLDAVIA

(see **MOLDOVA**)

MOLDOVA

(Overview)

The Republic of Moldova, formerly known as Moldavia, came into being as a result of the disintegration of the Soviet Union in 1991. A parliamentary republic, it is situated in southeastern Europe in the Black Sea basin and borders on Romania in the west and Ukraine in the east. It covers 33,700 square kilometres (13,000 square miles) and has a population of 4.5 million people. Just over one-third of the population are minorities: 14 per cent Ukrainian, 13 per cent Russian, 4.5 per cent Gagauz (Turkish) and 2 per cent Bulgarian. The majority of the population has Romanian roots and contacts with Romania have remained strong. Romanian, in fact, is the country's official language.

Moldova's main cities and cultural centres are Chişinău – the capital of the country (700,000 people) – Tiraspol (230,000) and Bălţi (220,000). Those who practise religion generally belong to the Eastern Orthodox Church.

Other religions practised include Protestantism, Catholicism and Islam.

Medieval history knew another state named Moldova which existed until 1859, when it joined with Wallachia and created the Romanian Kingdom. Moldovan theatre traditions also date back to the Medieval period when rituals and mysteries began to be linked to religious drama. As well, folk forms and carnival shows had, by the late eighteenth century, evolved into a distinctive form of folk theatre known as *gaiduk* (brigand) drama.

The present territory of the Republic of Moldova was part of the old Moldavia and its fate was separated from that of the rest of the country in 1812. In that year, one of the numerous Russian-Turkish wars ended. As part of the cessation of hostilities, the territory of the present Republic of Moldova – which was at the time, like all Medieval Moldavia, under Turkish domination – was yielded to Russia. The

Russian czar promoted a policy of national discrimination in Moldova and conscious Russification, forbidding the Romanian language and blocking connections with the other part of Moldova which later became a part of Romania.

The territory of present Moldova turned into a backwater of the Russian Empire and the only cultural events were rare sporadic tours by Russian, French and German troupes. Only in the second part of the nineteenth century did tours by Romanian troupes become possible.

At the beginning of the twentieth century, the first Romanian newspaper was launched and the native language was again spoken publicly. From 1908 to 1912, an amateur troupe gave performances in Chişinău and other localities, led by the writer and folklorist Gheorghe Madan (1872–1944).

World War I, the Russian Revolution and Moldova's National Liberation Movement all developed at the same time, promoting a new geopolitical division. Most of the territory of the present Republic of Moldova, with Chişinău as its centre, became part of Romania in 1918, while the territory on the left bank of the Dniester, with Tiraspol as its centre, remained under Russian influence.

In both Chişinău and Tiraspol there existed a Romanian cultural movement, but its quality and effects were quite different. In Chişinău a cultural effervescence began in 1921 and the first state theatre, Teatrul Naţional din Chişinău (Chişinău National Theatre), was opened; in Tiraspol, however, Russification became more blatant. The ideological offensive of Bolshevik authorities was manifested in two ways: by denying any connection with Romanian cultural traditions, and by putting the arts into the service of communist ideology. As a consequence, the Latin alphabet was replaced by the Cyrillic one, and the literary Romanian language, which was declared a creation of the Romanian aristocracy and bourgeois, was replaced with a dialectal surrogate. The theatre which opened in Tiraspol in 1933 was compelled to propagate that dialect on stage. Only Soviet plays with a distinct dogmatic character were allowed to be staged. The few classical plays to appear were interpreted from the point of view of the class struggle theory and the theory of inevitable conflict between rich and poor.

These tendencies greatly influenced the evolution of the theatre in Moldova after 1945. In 1944 Chişinău was occupied by the Soviet Union and the Tiraspol Theatre company was moved there. The policy-making centre of the Bolshevik Ministry of Culture was also transferred there. Theatre, as well as other arts, began to be subjected to even more severe censorship. The repertoire was ideologized to the maximum. More than half of the plays praised the communist regime and its leaders, the rest were anti-capitalist dramas and musical comedies. Connections with Romanian culture were forbidden and the supremacy of Russian and Soviet culture was declared. From that time, the National Theatre took on the name of the Russian poet Pushkin and became known as Teatrul de Stat Puşkin (Pushkin State Theatre).

Marxist-Leninist ideology proclaimed people as primary and spirit as secondary and, according to that postulation, in the theatre content was declared primary and form secondary. The form, in fact, was unified: all theatres in the Soviet Union staged the same plays in the same socialist-realism style. Content was also subjected to unification: all theatres had to promote only one idea, the inevitable victory of socialism over capitalism. So no independent theatre existed during that period. Theatre was simply an instrument for propaganda.

Soviet occupation caused the reduction of Romanian-language audiences, replacing them with Russian-speakers. The Romanian language, however, remained a language of the people and the Pushkin Theatre took its plays on tour to the country. That practice was still in force in the 1990s and gave birth to the curious phenomenon of one art for the city and another for the village, in which the same plays had more sophisticated and polished productions in the city and less sophisticated ones for villages. An important role in both styles, though, was given to folk songs and dances. One should also mention here the Likuritch National Puppet Theatre, which was opened in 1945 and had both Moldovan and Russian companies, and the Prikindel, another puppet company, which started in 1967.

After Stalin's death in 1953 Soviet policies were liberalized to some extent, which influenced culture and theatre in Moldova in a positive way. The staging of Romanian plays suddenly became possible as well as an exchange of tours with Romanian theatres. These early contacts with the maternal theatrical tradition had a beneficial influence on Moldovan theatre, supplying it with both new energy and theatrical ideas. An important place was given to the plays of Vasile Alecsandri (1821–90), one of the major classical Romanian authors. A new theatre was opened in Bălţi in 1957 and took on his name. The new Alecsandri Theatre was created first as an amateur troupe, the repertoire of which had mainly been plays of Moldovan authors mostly for village audiences.

Another Romanian-language theatre, Luceafărul (Bright Star), was also created in Chişinău through the initiative of a group of young actors who had graduated from the Shchukin School for Actors in Moscow. This group promoted a new style in the Moldovan theatre, a style which emerged from the carnival theatre of the *commedia dell'arte*. The 1960s were years of hope, when the possibility of political reform, of democratization of Soviet society and freedom of speech and creation seemed real. Luceafărul voiced those hopes, giving birth to a dynamic art, highly romantic and bright. It was the first time in Chişinău that a theatre wasn't offering a socialist-realist copy of reality, but rather was creating an artistic reality, reinventing life and improvising upon it.

The Luceafărul Theatre began the true theatrical revolution in Moldova and developed the interest and admiration of both the public and specialists, not only at home, but also across the Soviet Union.

The political liberalization also permitted the opening in 1958 of a theatrical faculty at the Chişinău Institute of Arts, which went on to train a large number of actors for Moldovan theatres.

During the 1960s and 1970s the plays of Ion Druţă (b. 1928) also began to appear. One of the few authors in Moldova to create a dramaturgy with a strong religious subtext, his works focused on the life of the Moldovan peasant and the historical fate of Moldova. Although staged in Moscow, Paris and Warsaw, Druţă's plays were unfortunately forbidden in Chişinău, and their author was declared to be an anti-Soviet Moldovan nationalist.

The Czechoslovak revolution of 1968 put an end to political liberalization and marked a further ideological hardening of the Soviet system. The struggle against influences from the west, against nationalism and formalism became even more active. In the Ministry of Culture, a Censorship Commission was created to look at all plays before they were shown to the public, to exclude ideological deviations. Interference in text, stagings and even gesture and intonation took place. Whatever looked 'anti-Soviet' or formalistic was excluded. The KGB even recruited informers from among actors, who reported on company opinions. Those with 'unfit thoughts' were ostracized, while those who 'had the right opinions' and staged communist plays were given awards and various privileges. In these conditions, theatre people attempted to maintain professional dignity and fight censorship, but the forces were uneven and the fight was both exhausting and demoralizing. The impact was so strong that with the coming of *perestroika*, when the liberty of creation became real, Moldovan theatres simply could not overcome their own deficiencies.

As in other regions of the Soviet Union, *perestroika* (restructuring) in Moldova also promoted the appearance of new theatres. While during the 1945–87 period only three Romanian-language theatres appeared in Moldova, seven more were opened during the 1987–92 period. Among them, the Eugène Ionesco Theatre proved to be the most remarkable. With a troupe of mainly young actors, this theatre was the first in Moldova to stage plays from the Theatre of the Absurd and achieved great success in its work. Beckett's *Waiting for Godot* (1992) was also staged by the Ionesco Theatre and toured abroad.

Perestroika also led to the end of censorship. But since totalitarianism had managed to remove a whole generation of actors and directors, all hopes for a future Moldovan theatre lay with young people. Theatre art in Moldova in the 1990s was without question the art of the young and it was an art which was still developing. They had the possibility of speaking Romanian and experiencing world theatre influences denied their older colleagues.

During the process of democratization and the transition to a market economy, Moldova is, like other eastern European countries, trying to come back to the general humanistic traditions of Europe.

Constantin Cheianu

(See also USSR)

Further Reading

Bryžinky, V.S. *Narodnyj teat'r mordvy.* [Popular theatre in Mordovia]. Saransk: Mordovian Publishing House, 1985. 168 pp.

Lat'eva, Lidiia V. *Litso i maska.* Chişinău: Lit-ra artistikă, 1980. 212 pp.

NETHERLANDS

Located in northwestern Europe, the Kingdom of the Netherlands is bounded on the north and west by the North Sea, on the east by Germany and on the south by Belgium. The country's overall land area is some 41,500 square kilometres (16,000 square miles) which includes more than 1,600 square miles of inland water, much of it reclaimed from the sea. The densely populated coastal areas, in fact, are almost entirely below sea level.

With an immigration that regularly exceeds emigration, the Netherlands had a 1990 population of approximately 15 million. Turks and Moroccans make up the country's largest group of cultural minorities although there has long been significant immigration from the former colony of Dutch Guiana, now Suriname, and other islands of the Dutch Antilles in the Caribbean.

The original inhabitants of the Netherlands were Celts and Germans who were annexed by successive European imperial states. In 1579 they disengaged themselves from Spain, and the Republic of the Netherlands was founded. During the seventeenth century, it became Europe's leading commercial nation, due mainly to its colonial trade. In 1795, during the reign of Napoleon, the country became a French protectorate.

In the nineteenth century, a new Kingdom of the Netherlands was founded including Belgium and Luxembourg, which were later given their independence. During World War I, the Netherlands remained officially neutral; during World War II it was occupied by the Germans. This occupation cost the lives of many people, particularly among its Jewish population.

During the war, German occupation troops, convinced that Dutch artists could form an important link in the dissemination of Nazi ideology, increased subsidies to most artistic institutions. Over a period of four years, theatre subsidies alone increased sixtyfold. While this finally gave artists the security they had longed for but had never known, it also required them to join the *Kultuurkamer* (a grouping of Nazi cultural organizations). Those who failed to do so were not allowed to work. The majority of actors gave in and accepted that certain (Jewish) colleagues and certain (Jewish and 'degenerate') writers were taboo. Those who did not join wound up having to work underground and gave secret performances in private homes.

A number of underground artists, intellectuals and politicians even then began planning for after the war. In a manifesto recognizing art's social function, they wrote:

> it is the responsibility of the state to foster the development and prosperity of the arts, to support artists and artistic institutions financially. It is the task of artistic institutions to ensure that everything made by artists can be seen and heard throughout the country (horizontal distribution) and by all levels of the population (vertical distribution).

These two notions would make their mark on artistic policy in the Netherlands for several decades after World War II.

Ideas of the corporate state were also included in those plans for a reorganization of the artistic world. According to this pre-war concept, each industrial branch of society would be guided by its own democratic organization with far-reaching powers. Such corporate organization would also take place in the arts with each individual artistic discipline forming its own professional association, all coming together as part of one large federation.

It would be this federation which would then

provide the membership for a Raad voor de Kunst (Arts Council) which, though independent, would include members of parliament. This Arts Council would, as the theory went, have money at its disposal from the government.

After the war, these plans were only partially realized. An Arts Council was brought into being, as was a Federation of Artistic Associations. The Arts Council, however, was no more than an advisory body for government while the Federation was only one of many organizations dealing with the government on arts-related issues.

This interest in getting government involved in the arts stemmed in great measure from the basically *laissez-faire* policies towards the arts that were in effect prior to the war. At the time, with theatre production generally operating on commercial principles, bankruptcies were common.

During the war, a number of theatre managers – Albert van Dalsum (1889–1971), Johan de Meester (1897–1986) and Cor Hermus (1889–1953) among them – argued that there should be state-subsidized companies in operation across the country. All, they said, should be located in the urban agglomeration known as the Randstad (Amsterdam, Utrecht, Haarlem, Rotterdam and The Hague) with one each in Amsterdam, The Hague and Rotterdam; one operating between Haarlem and Utrecht; and one doing a repertoire of popular plays for 'everyday folk'. This was realized after the war. In Amsterdam and Rotterdam (later operating just in Amsterdam), van Dalsum and August Defresne (1893–1961) were given control of a new group called Amsterdams Toneelgezelschap (Amsterdam Stage Company). Operating in the period 1947–53, the company performed in the municipal theatres there and gave shape to an expressionistically focused, socially committed type of theatre.

In Haarlem and Utrecht, Hermus was put in charge of the Comedia, founded in 1945. The company functioned until 1953. Of these two groups, audiences seemed to have a clear preference for Comedia's livelier and more explosive acting style and the raw realism of the American writers such as Tennessee Williams that director Johan de Meester was producing.

The first decades after the war were years of economic growth in the Netherlands, which made it possible to increase the number of theatre companies. In the Randstad, new companies included De Haagsche Comedie (The Hague Comedy Theatre) which operated from 1947 to 1988 under the direction of Cees Laseur (1899–1960) and Paul Steenbergen (1907–89); the Rotterdams Toneel (Rotterdam Stage Company) which operated from 1947 to 1962, first under the direction of Ko Arnoldi (1883–1964) and thereafter under Ton Lutz (b. 1919); the Nederlandse Comedie (Dutch Comedy Theatre) which operated in the Amsterdam Municipal Theatre from 1950 to 1971 under the direction of Han Bentz van den Berg (1917–76), Johan de Meester and Guus Oster (1915–84); and Puck (1950–61) – the first subsidized youth theatre company – which later called itself Centrum, becoming a repertory company (1961–87), and which operated under the direction of Cas Baas (b. 1918) and Egbert van Paridon (b. 1920) among others.

Companies sprang up as well in other parts of the country. In the east, it was Toneelgroep Theatre (Theatre Stage Company) which operated from 1953 to 1988 and started under the direction of Rob de Vries (1918–69) and Kees van Iersel (b. 1912), who was quickly replaced by Richard Flink (1903–67). In the south it was the Zuidelijk Toneel (Southern Stage) which operated between 1956 and 1958 under the direction of Louis Saalborn (1891–1957) and under the name Ensemble from 1958 to 1968, mostly under the direction of Karl Guttman (b. 1913).

In the far north of the country, the Noorder Compagnie (Northern Company) operated from 1966 to 1979 under Manon Alving (b. 1923) and Jaap Maarleveld (b. 1924) while in the extreme south the Groot Limburgs Toneel (Great Limburg Stage) operated from 1966 to 1975 under Cas Baas and Willy van Heesveld (1933–83).

A beginning was made as well at this time on horizontal distribution across the country with money being made available for the first time to construct theatre spaces even in small towns, without companies. Most became regular stops for touring repertory companies as well as dance and music groups.

Despite differences in style, all the post-war repertory companies believed that theatre had a role to play in society and saw the repertoire from Aeschylus to O'Neill as a pyramid of masterpieces in which universal human problems were looked to for debate on the moral and philosophical problems of war and on individual responsibility. The pre-war French theatrical philosophers were most often turned to for advice on human failings.

It should be noted here that there was up to

Joan Remmelts's 1958 Dutch Comedy Theatre production of N.C. Hunter's *A Touch of the Sun*.
Photo: F.L. Lemaire.

this time no real tradition in the Netherlands of a predominantly home-grown repertoire. Just as the Dutch economy was based primarily on foreign trade and the manufacture of raw materials from all over the world, the Dutch stage produced mainly foreign plays and showed influences.

In the mid-1950s, however, the first signs began to appear questioning this approach to drama generally and to indigenous drama specifically. It was Kees van Iersel who made the first attempt at producing a more contemporary repertoire (Beckett, Ionesco, Adamov; later Pinter and Arrabal) at the Theatre Stage Company. When the public failed to respond, he went further and began producing *only* contemporary plays. Working with a small group of actors who rehearsed after normal performances ended, he called his new group Test; it played from 1956 to 1962 in various small spaces in and around Amsterdam.

This initiative struck a chord with existing companies and in 1960, Paul Steenbergen of the Hague Comedy Theatre gave his young actors and directors an opportunity to experiment with a more contemporary repertoire in a small, upstairs auditorium in the Koninklijke Schouwburg (Royal Playhouse) in The Hague. In the same year, Centrum began presenting a series of modern pieces in a small auditorium above an Amsterdam art cinema, the Hypokriterion. In all these cases, the audience was seated close to or even around the stage action.

In 1962, van Iersel was given the directorship of Studio along with money to transform it into a company that would produce only contemporary theatre. A new, small and flexible space was adapted for the purpose called the Brakke Grond (Wasteland). In 1965, Centrum under director Peter Oosthoek (b. 1934) eventually moved into a smaller auditorium in Amsterdam, the Bellevue. Fairly quickly, a new audience was created at all these theatres – young, intellectual, and artistically elitist.

During the later 1960s, the Provo-Movement came into being. This movement, which attracted young people from across the country, attempted to undercut traditional authority through comic challenges thereby opening up serious issues for discussion. Attempts to repress the movement through strong-arm measures simply made the campaigns more aggressive. The movement gained even more strength when student uprisings in Berlin and Paris in 1968 brought Dutch students to their feet demanding greater democratization.

Parallel to this growing social engagement was a developing interest in the work and ideas of both Bertolt Brecht and Antonin Artaud by Dutch theatre artists. At the same time, touring avant-garde groups such as the Living Theatre were proving that topical social realities were fit subjects for both plays and discussions. In 1965, the first unsubsidized, politically focused theatre company was created, Teater Terzijde (Theatre Aside) which would operate for the next four years under the direction of Annemarie Prins (b. 1932).

Using improvisation as well as physical and visual forms of expression, Theatre Aside became one of many such groups to find an audience in Amsterdam. Other foreign companies which were influential on Dutch theatrical thinking at the time were the Bread and Puppet Theatre, the Open Theatre, La Mama and Jerzy Grotowski's Theatre Laboratory from Poland.

The Netherlands had always led the way in importing foreign plays. Now the Netherlands was leading the way as well in importing foreign experimental companies. The Mickery Theatre, during 1965–91 under the direction of Ritsaert Ten Cate (b. 1938), and the Universiteitstheater (University Theatre) played a central role in this development, bringing these and other avant-garde groups to Amsterdam from all over the world.

The use of mixed media entered Dutch theatre in the late 1960s and early 1970s. Coming from areas such as mime, modern dance and the plastic arts, practitioners of the new mixed forms included Frits Vogels of the Bewth Company (founded in 1965); Koert Stuyf (b. 1938) of Eigentijdse Dans (Contemporary Dance, operating 1964–74); Bart Stuyf (b. 1944) of Multimedia (1971–7); and Adri Boon (b. 1933) of Scarabee (1965–83).

Attempts to give substance to these new developments within the framework of the major existing repertory companies failed. The new ideas were simply too extreme or too deviant for established stage directors. Not only was the repertoire itself being questioned but so too were interpretations of the role of theatre, theatre history and the nature of theatrical collaboration.

In October 1969, two student directors threw tomatoes at actors taking a curtain call at the Dutch Comedy Theatre following a performance of Shakespeare's *The Tempest*. Other student artists soon joined their ranks. Over the next few months various protests took place in other theatres, with bread, eggs and tomatoes the basic theatrical ammunition.

Artists on the receiving end were understandably indignant and shocked. Memories of the intimidation against them practised by Hitler's supporters shortly before World War II were still strong.

Some of the protests, in fact, were politically inspired. A performance of Tankred Dorst's *Toller* was disrupted by smoke bombs and pamphlets tossed by several young anarchists involved in the production as walk-ons. On 1 January 1970, a performance for Amsterdam's political and cultural elite was seriously sabotaged by the circulation of forged tickets.

Aktie Tomaat (Tomato Action) is the name under which this campaign generally has gone down in Dutch theatre history. Its goal – to some extent achieved – was the creation of socially critical theatre and the creation of a new 'people's theatre' to replace the traditional bourgeois theatre.

In Amsterdam over the next few years, the two major companies were, in fact, replaced by three smaller companies. Taking over the municipal theatre from the Dutch Comedy was the Publiekstheater (Audience Company), which operated from 1973 to 1987 under the direction of Hans Croiset (b. 1935). Also introduced were the Centrum (recently arrived in the city) and Baal, a company which operated in the city from 1973 to 1988 under the direction of Leonard Frank (b. 1942).

In Rotterdam, the Ro Theatre was founded in 1976 by Franz Marijnen (b. 1943). Two collectives which also started at about the same time were Onafhankelijke Toneel (Independent Stage), founded in 1973 by Jan Joris Lamers (b. 1942), and Diskus, which operated from 1976 to 1985. Two existing companies which catered for younger audiences were quickly politicized – Proloog (Prologue), which operated 1964–83, and the Nieuwe Komedie (New Comedy), which operated 1961–85.

Even extra subsidies were suddenly made available for companies such as the Werkteater (Work Theatre, 1970–85); the Appel (Apple, 1970– under the direction of Erik Vos (b. 1929); and Sater (1971–85) under Peter de Baan (b. 1946).

A number of companies also began to work at this time on the principle of almost complete democratization: the right of all collaborators to participate in all decisions and the de-emphasizing of specializations (including those of the actors, directors, dramaturges, technicians and administrators). Where specialization was necessary, decisions were made by the collective as a whole. The companies thus created rarely performed in traditional theatres and sometimes they did not 'perform' at all. They sought their audiences in schools, institutions, clubs, community centres or on the street. The Work Theatre made an international reputation for itself in this way and the political youth theatre Prologue became the model for similar companies abroad. Several of these new companies also decided to write their own plays

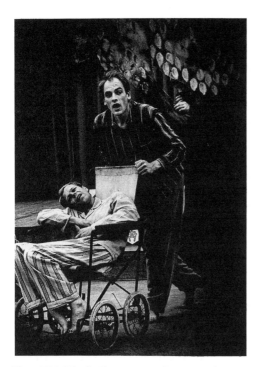

The 1978 Work Theatre production of *Gabbers*.
Photo: Johan Vegeveno.

collectively in an attempt to deal more directly with social and political realities.

At the same time, the nurturing of Dutch playwrights was becoming a serious matter. The Instituut voor Theateronderzoek (Institute for Theatre Research) was founded in 1970 by Jan Kassies (b. 1920) and worked with established novelists and poets interested in trying their hands at playwriting. Working closely with director Johan Greter (b. 1927), the writers were able to hear professional actors read their work. It was in this way that poet Judith Herzberg (b. 1934) began writing for the theatre. In 1973, the Centre Stage Company decided to produce only new Dutch plays and over the next decade, a number of Dutch dramatists slowly emerged including Wim T. Schippers (b. 1942), Guus Vleugel (b. 1933) and Ton Vorstenbosch (b. 1950).

The Work Theatre, Baal, Prologue, Sater, the New Comedy, Diskus and Hauser Orkater also took up Studio's commitment to contemporary work generally and Dutch work in particular. When they found such a repertoire unavailable, they set out to create it themselves.

New independent studio spaces also began to appear at this time, all without subsidy, for the new companies to perform in. In Haarlem it was the Toneelschuur (Theatre Shed); in Amsterdam, the Shaffy; in Rotterdam, the Lantaren (Lantern).

The model for all of these new spaces was the Wasteland where the Studio company performed. Over the next few years, such studios were even constructed within the larger playhouses.

One company which significantly differed from most of the other small groups was Hauser Orkater, founded in 1972 as a centre for multimedia theatre. The company included elements of movement theatre, the plastic arts, pop music, songs, acrobatics and slapstick. The founders had no ambitions to reform society. To them, society was both inscrutable and out of control. As far as they were concerned, theatre practitioners should practise theatre while remaining committed to the new ideas of youth culture.

In the eyes of some practitioners, this group was the real 'fringe', attracting audiences under the age of 30 and performing wherever the possibility offered itself. This style of work spread rapidly. In Amsterdam, the Festival of Fools, first organized in 1975, became a meeting-place for similarly inclined companies from the United States, Britain, Germany, Belgium and the Netherlands.

Ritsaert Ten Cate, founder of the Mickery, was among the first to recognize the importance of television and video for theatre. He investigated not only the influence of television on perceptions of reality but also the possibilities for television as a means of theatrical expression. His television experiments continued well into the 1980s.

The mainstream theatres, meanwhile, inspired by the work of foreign artists such as Giorgio Strehler, Peter Zadek, Peter Stein, Claus Peymann and Jean-Pierre Vincent, began to contemporize the classics. Among the first Dutch directors to do this was Franz Marijnen at the Ro Theatre in Rotterdam. Others began dramatizing even more personal visions of both humanity and society.

Among those working in this way at the time were Jan Joris Lamers at the Independent State Theatre, Gerardjan Rijnders (b. 1949) and Paul Vermeulen Windsant (b. 1943) at the Globe, and Frans Strijards (b. 1952) at Projekttheater, a company which operated from 1975 to 1982.

The late 1970s saw the Dutch economy start to decline and the notion of solidarity with the underprivileged began to loose its appeal for the cultural community. Meanwhile, younger people – punks and squatters – did not hesitate to adopt violence as a method of social change.

The socially engaged theatre of only a few years before seemed to stop developing artistically at this point and became locked into political discussion. The result was the collapse, one after another, of many of these groups.

One of the few social groups to survive into the 1980s were the feminist groups, whose development was explosive both within existing theatre companies and without. The Spiegeltheater (Mirror Theatre, 1980–4) and Theatre Tachtig (Theatre Eighty, 1980–5; later renamed Persona, 1985–8) came into being as protests against the choice of plays by other theatres as well as against the manner in which they saw women represented. By the end of the 1980s, however, even these companies had vanished.

Mainstream audiences began to look for more traditional plays again and when they did not get them, they stayed at home. Few young directors, however, were willing or interested in working in traditional styles. By the end of the decade, public opinion and artistic interests were clearly moving in separate directions. Fewer and fewer people were going to the theatre.

It was at this point that the government decided to intervene by appointing, in 1987, Gerardjan Rijnders as director of the Toneelgroep Amsterdam (Stage Company Amsterdam); in 1988, the Hague Comedy Theatre became the Nationale Toneel (National Theatre) under the direction of Hans Croiset. Unfortunately, even then, the work that was going on in the studios of the mainstream theatres did not really make its way onto the main stages. Additional subsidy was offered but most of the theatres became little more than facilities for various other independent groups. Even the notion of 'ensemble' began to fall away.

In the early 1990s one could clearly see two distinct streams of contemporary Dutch theatre thinking beginning to emerge: the strand that wished to see classical theatre albeit in updated and contemporized versions and the strand that wanted to see a contemporary but heavily national repertoire of plays.

In performance terms, the Zomerfestijn (Summer Festival, 1986–90) was the last international alternative theatre festival in the country. One could find there everything from the neo-fascist symbolism of the squatters to the most extreme examples of 'aggressive' theatre. In the early 1990s, groups working in this way formed a kind of alternative circuit where 'everything was possible that was not possible elsewhere'. Among the varied styles and subjects (often textual collages) were works about consumerism, housing shortages and the welfare state. Most groups were working without any direct subsidy although many small theatres with their own studios were making space available to them and occasionally subsidizing the work. Authorities accepted this situation by classifying such productions as workshops and have even modestly helped in their support.

Structure of the National Theatre Community

In theory, all towns in the Netherlands with a population of 75,000 or more have their own theatre buildings. This means that most groups in the country are able to tour and they do. In fact, touring has been an almost necessary part of Dutch theatre survival since the seventeenth century. Even when a city has a resident company, the group will rarely be given more than one-third of the theatre building's programming time.

Amsterdam, the Dutch centre of both art and culture, has the largest number of theatres and the most companies.

Most Dutch theatre groups receive subsidy. This reaches as high as 9 million guilders (US$5,150,000) for the largest in Amsterdam and The Hague, which operate both large mainstage and studio stages.

Another ten to twenty studio groups receive between 1 and 2 million guilders each (US$570,000 to US$1,140,000) and keep between five and ten actors under contract.

About ten subsidized groups exist across the country exclusively producing theatre for young audiences. These groups each receive about 1 million guilders in support and keep about five actors per company under contract. Rehearsals at Dutch theatres generally last about two months.

Most subsidy in the Netherlands comes from the state, with the larger groups in Amsterdam, The Hague and Rotterdam receiving substantial amounts from municipal governments as well (as much as 60 per cent of their budgets can come from municipalities). Support for youth theatre groups, on the other hand, comes primarily from provincial authorities (60 per cent) with the state contributing the rest.

Each year, there are about ten commercial productions staged in the large centres, most often small-cast successes from abroad.

The major subsidized groups generally sell their productions on season subscriptions. Amsterdam has its own theatre ticket organization, which sells subscriptions for all the large theatres and publishes a regular newsletter. No other city has such a sales organization, although Rotterdam and The Hague do have similar newsletters.

The normal admission cost for a major production in 1992 was about 30 guilders (US$17), about twice the price of a ticket to a film. Studio production ticket prices, however, were about equal to cinema prices.

The Holland Festival is the country's largest arts festival and is held annually in Amsterdam, usually during the month of June. Though the largest portion of the programme consists of traditional opera and music performances, the festival also serves as a showcase for successful contemporary theatre, dance, music and opera performances.

Since 1984, there has also been an annual theatre for young audiences festival held in Den Bosch where companies are able to stage their productions and discuss new developments and problems in the field.

Since 1987, there has also been an annual Flemish–Dutch theatre festival held in late August or early September where the year's ten most interesting productions are restaged. The productions are selected by a jury of leading Flemish and Dutch theatre critics and the festival alternates between major cities in Holland and Flanders (Belgium).

The best production at the festival wins a 50,000 guilder prize – the Dommelsch Theatre Prize – while the best new Dutch play wins a 20,000 guilder prize (US$11,430). In addition to these prestigious prizes, the Association of Playhouse Directors also gives out awards for best actors in leading and supporting roles as well as for best productions in both adult and youth theatre. Amsterdam's municipal council also awards a prize for the best production of a play written in Dutch.

The country has a general trade union for all artists with separate departments for individual disciplines. There is also a national organization for the subsidized companies.

The Theater Instituut Nederland (Dutch Theatre Institute), based in Amsterdam, keeps archives on virtually everything in the field of Dutch theatre. Its library and theatre museum are both open to researchers as well as the general public.

Tom Blokdijk

Artistic Profile

Companies

In the early 1970s, a schism in the Dutch theatre world – the first signs of which were seen in the mid-1950s – finally became clear. Alongside the large playhouses with their traditional repertoires, proscenium stages and a tendency toward Ibsenian realism, many small groups were emerging playing in non-traditional venues with flat floors and makeshift stages. In these new theatres, stage and auditorium merged and behind-the-scene trappings were largely visible. In the large theatres, the traditional repertory groups were continuing to stage world classics; the small stages, on the other hand, seemed generally reserved for experimental work.

In the 1990s, the distinctions between these two types of companies could not be made so easily. Then, directors moved back and forth between the large and small groups putting their individual stamp first on one company and then another. Experimental work could occasionally be seen even on the large stages, while classics were also done in the studios. All Dutch directors have their own vision of reality, life and humanity and these varying visions are now regularly worked out at almost any of the venues.

As an example, between 1962 and 1971, Hans Croiset was the artistic director of the Stage Theatre in Arnhem, a mid-sized repertory company of the more traditional type; in 1973, he founded the Publiekstheater (Audience Theatre), a company based on the ideas of French director Jean Vilar, which he ran for the next twelve years. The most important productions staged by Croiset at these two theatres included *A Midsummer Night's Dream* in 1973, Chekhov's *Ivanov* in 1974, Brecht's *The Good Person of Setzuan* in 1975, the seventeenth-century Dutch classic *Lucifer* by Joost van den Vondel (1587–1679) in 1979, *Groß und klein* (*Big and Little*) by the German dramatist Botho Strauss in 1981, and another classic van den Vondel work, *Adam in Ballingschap* (*Adam in Exile*) in 1983.

After 1981, Croiset slowly lost control of the Publiekstheater and failed as well to keep up with any of the approaches being taken by other repertory companies. In 1985, he left the Publiekstheater and from that point on devoted himself almost exclusively to work with the smaller studio theatres. Between 1985 and 1987, he staged several productions at the Apple in The Hague including Goethe's *Faust*, Heinrich von Kleist's *Amphytrion* and van den Vondel's *Faëton*. All these productions were dramaturgically controversial but also spectacular and very successful. In 1988, Croiset again started a company, this one in The Hague, which he called (once more inspired by Vilar) the Nationale Toneel (National Theatre).

Another artistic director of note who put his stamp on several different types of groups is Erik Vos. Vos studied with Étienne Decroux in Paris and in 1956 became artistic director of the Nieuwe Jeugdtoneel (New Youth Theatre) in The Hague which he quickly renamed Arena and later reshaped into a company for adults under the name the Nieuwe Komedie. He ran the group until 1965. His major production during this time was a spectacular circus version of Aeschylus' *The Persians* done at Carré, a circus theatre built originally as an amphitheatre. The production involved the use of masks, music and choreography.

From 1965 to 1972, Vos chose to work with many different groups across the country. In 1972, he established the Apple in Amsterdam (in 1974 it moved to The Hague) to give himself and his actors greater creative freedom. Similar to both the Work Theatre and the Independent Stage, the Apple produced work that was initially based on actor improvisation. Over the next few seasons, the company developed its work into a strongly physical and often musical style.

The company soon began taking on a number of world classics to produce in this new style along with original works. The group's breakthrough with the public came with Shakespeare's *The Tempest* in 1976 and Aeschylus' *Oresteia* in 1977. Other productions which achieved great audience approval included an evening of two short Brecht plays, *Mahagonny* and *Burgerbruiloft* (*Die Kleinbürgerhochzeit/A Civil Wedding*) in 1980; *King Lear* in 1981; *Uncle Vanya* in 1984; and the Israeli play *Ghetto* by Joshua Sobol in 1988. Through the years, the Apple has won a large and loyal following for its work. The company now has its own flexible-space theatre in The Hague.

Leonard Frank's Baal Company has also developed a unique and appropriate acting style for its politically topical studio theatre. The company, named after its first production, Brecht's *Baal*, has been directed by Frank for many years. Frank has often quoted Brecht, saying that unusual matters that have become ordinary must somehow become unusual again for an audience.

Besides Brecht, the company has also staged the work of many other modern German-language dramatists including Peter Handke, Botho Strauss, Albert Bronnen and Thomas Bernhard. The work consistently moves away from realism in its approach toward something more theatrical and dynamic. Normal human behaviour is consistently enlarged and costumes exaggerated (actors, in fact, often change costumes in full view of the audience). Designs tend to be artistically independent with music normally playing a significant role. Baal has, in fact, worked on several occasions with established jazz and classical musicians and the company has collaborated from time to time with writers to create texts.

In 1981, the company moved from the Shaffy Theatre to other theatres ending up in a converted auction room called Frascati in Amsterdam. This move also marked a turning point in Frank's development as a director. From this point, he focused increasingly on Jewish themes. In 1982 he staged *Leedvermaak* (*Malicious Pleasure*) by Judith Herzberg using all available spaces in the auction room. This episodic play about the post-war Jewish generation caused a sensation.

In the mid- to late 1980s, the Baal Company and Frank himself both let go of their specific styles and Frank directed only occasionally. In 1984, he staged Ansky's *The Dybbuk* and in 1987, Brecht's *Mother Courage*. Over the years,

his vision became more and more pessimistic and the company's course became unclear. In 1988, Frank decided to dissolve the company. In the years since, Frank has most frequently been a guest director at the National Theatre and at Theatre in the East, among others.

Still another approach has been seen over many years at both the Independent Stage and Discordant Society in the work of director-actor-designer Jan Joris Lamers. Right from the beginning of his career, Lamers has concentrated specifically on the relationship between style and content in his work. Initially inspired by the ideas of Vladimir Mayakovsky, he wanted to introduce elements from other media feeling that only in this way could new forms be given shape. His production of Mayakovsky's *Banya* (*The Bath House*) in 1974 was one of his first experiments in this direction.

Slowly, his attention turned more and more to the relationship of actor to text. This was developed in a season of seven plays done with the Independent Stage in 1977: Ibsen's *Hedda Gabler*, de Musset's *Fantasio*, Herzberg's *Cranky Box*, Chekhov's *The Seagull*, Wilde's

The 1986 Discordant Society production of Oscar Wilde's *Lady Windermere's Fan*, directed and designed by Jan Joris Lamers.
Photo: Bert Nienhuis.

The Importance of Being Earnest, Shakespeare's *Hamlet* and Beckett's *Waiting for Godot*.

Lamers's *mises-en-scène* are generally based on a thorough but constantly evolving analysis of text. Relations between characters are analysed through geometrical visualizations, with actors often working against an obvious textual reading. The performance itself is very often unfinished, a suggested interpretation only, a commentary crystallized visually but still hesitant, often with actors carrying scripts.

At Discordant Society, Lamers worked most closely with Matthias de Koning (b. 1954) and Titus Muizelaar (b. 1949), attempting in the work to bring about both an ideological and artistic iconoclasm. Among their artistic peaks have been their *mises-en-scène* for Thomas Bernhard's *Am Ziel* in 1982 and *Ritter Dene Voss* in 1986; Handke's *Über die Dörfer* (*Among the Villages*) in 1983; *Das Spiel von Fragen* (*The Question Play*) in 1990; and Herzberg's *Krass* (*Crass*) in 1988.

Lamers and his company have also developed a remarkable way of weaving plays together. The most successful example was *Sardou, Wilde, Shaw* in 1987, in which Sardou's *Divorçons*, Wilde's *A Woman of No Importance* and Shaw's *Mrs Warren's Profession* were quite brilliantly interwoven to explain and comment upon one another.

The largest repertory company in the country is the Amsterdam Stage Company, successor to the Audience Theatre. The company's early topical reinterpretations of classical plays were hotly debated by both press and public. When Gerardjan Rijnders became its artistic director in 1987, a more eclectic approach began to be seen.

Rijnders himself has directed the classical repertoire – *Hamlet* (1986), Racine's *Andromache* (1991), von Kleist's *Penthesilea* (1992) – with an eye towards the spectacular. He has also done a number of what he calls 'assembly' performances involving large groups of artists of often disparate backgrounds: *Bacchanten* (based on Euripides' *The Bacchae*) in 1986 in collaboration with the National Ballet; *Bakeliet* in 1987–8 in which thirteen actresses and a drummer performed fragments from a book by Steven Anderson called *Savage Grace*; and *Titus, Geen Shakespeare* (*Titus, Not Shakespeare*, 1988), a study in shamelessness in which Shakespeare's play was interwoven with material culled from popular confessional talk shows.

The diversity of genres in Rijnders's staging is bounded by his ever-present black-edged vision of the world with human beings always compulsively lusting for freedom and life but simply degenerating into restless wandering. For Rijnders, sex and death are the fuel of art. Stylistically, much of the work seen in Rijnders's productions shows a tendency toward abstraction. For each production, he consciously chooses a specific acting style which is then explicitly played, serving also as a commentary on the piece.

The company Artikelen en Projekten (Articles and Projects) was founded in 1985 and its long-time director, Frans Strijards, has spent most of his career investigating theatrical convention as a way of investigating life itself. Human beings each create their own fictional worlds, worlds that defy anyone outside to distinguish personal illusion from personal reality. Jealousy of the fictional worlds of others becomes an important theme in Strijards's work.

Each of his characters has to decide whether to act or be acted on. His characters are slaves to their own feelings, cherishing false images of reality. The result is a grotesque and physical acting style staged at a rapid-fire pace; a cynical commentary on the notion of the theatrical lie. This can be seen even in his choice of plays – Pirandello's *Naked Masks* (1985), Chekhov's *The Cherry Orchard* (1987), Handke's *Ride Across Lake Constance* (1988) and *De laatsten der onverstandigen* (*The Last of the Ignorant*, 1989), and Ibsen's *Hedda Gabler* (1990). Strijards also writes plays himself.

Since the 1970s, there has been a clear compulsion toward innovation in the Dutch theatre with many practitioners heavily influenced by experiments in the visual arts, especially sculpture. There has also been a separation between a role and the actor playing that role on stage. Women often play male roles today and it is no longer seen as something unique. When the female director Matin van Veldhuizen (b. 1942) wanted to do Beckett's *Waiting for Godot* with an all-female cast in 1988, the author banned the performance. In the ensuing court case, a Dutch judge ruled that the piece was universal in human terms, not merely male, and that if women play male characters it should no longer be seen as 'a provocative statement'.

By way of illustrating this point, in 1989 the North Holland-based Hollandia Company staged *Prometheus Bound* outdoors with both Prometheus and the Chorus played alternately by different groups of actors and actresses.

Dramaturgy

The Dutch-written *Abel Cycle* from the second half of the fourteenth century is arguably the oldest Medieval secular drama in Europe and there are Dutch-written farces that are contemporaneous with it. Perhaps the most famous play of the Medieval period is *Elkerlyc* (*c*.1495) by Peter Dorlant from Diest in Flanders. The play was later translated into English as *Everyman* and has been produced steadily ever since. Playwrights' organizations – Chambers of Rhetoric as they were called – go back to the fifteenth century. Yet from the Medieval period to the 1970s productions of plays by Dutch dramatists (with the possible exception of the seventeenth century) were rare in Dutch theatres.

Probably the earliest Dutch dramatists of real importance were Pieter Corneliszoon Hooft (1581–1647) and Joost van den Vondel. Each came from the Chambers of Rhetoric where they were trained in the use of strict classical rules. Van den Vondel concentrated on tragedy with classical, biblical or historical subject matter, striving to find links to his own century. *Lucifer* (1654), a tragedy, is set entirely in heaven but the political and moral implications were so clear that the play was banned by the church. Other well-known plays from his hand are *Gijsbreght van Aemstel* (1637) and *Jeptha* (1659).

From the second half of the seventeenth century until the nineteenth century, theatre was generally considered to be an inferior art in intellectual and literary circles: the elite geared itself to foreign literature and, at the same time, Calvinism began to play a dominant role in Dutch culture. Even exemplary theatre, for the entertainment and instruction of the people, was considered to be the work of the devil by the righteous Calvinist.

Even in modern Dutch literary history, room was seldom made for playwrights. Herman Heyermans (1864–1924) is one of the few playwrights from the recent past who still receives at least some recognition. Heyermans was a naturalist motivated by strong political and social concerns. Among his best known plays is *Op Hoop van Zegen* (*The Good Hope*, 1900) in which poor fishermen become victims of the malpractice of ship owners and are sent out to sea in dilapidated boats. A sentence from the play – 'The fish are dearly paid for' – has come into common usage.

After World War II, a number of companies consciously set out to convert Dutch poets and novelists into dramatists. One such was Hugo Claus (b. 1929), who had ongoing success with such works as *Suiker* (*Sugar*, 1958) and *Vrijdag* (*Friday*, 1969). Most of his plays are set in a Flemish working-class environment. His characters tend not to be eloquent or reflective but beneath the seemingly broad dialects and apparently banal situations gleam profound universal issues. Claus is a virtuoso and very musical writer with an authentic ear for language.

Due to the general lack of writers after the war, it was very often the theatre practitioners themselves who wrote most effectively for the stage. This tendency grew out of many attempts at collective creation based on improvisation.

Among the most important of the later generation of Dutch dramatists has been Lodewijk de Boer (b. 1937), a writer renowned for his comic theatre-serial in four parts, *The Family*, about a couple living in a vacant building. All of de Boer's plays are moralities, the Dutch equivalent of tragi-comedies. In many of his plays, two friends land in a strange environment in which their friendship is put at risk. Women usually are catalysts in the conflict.

Frans Strijards also both writes and directs his own work. Comic elements in his plays usually mask the tragedy in his characters' lives. Just as his staging tends to play with conventional theatrical notions, his plays, too, toy with dramatic traditions. The well-made play with its cause-and-effect relationships was the form satirized in *Hitchcock's Driesprong* (*Hitchcock's Three-Forked Road*, 1987). Psychological realism was taken to its less than logical extreme in two plays – *Gesprekken Over G* (*Discussions About G*, 1988) and *Toeval. Voorval* (*Coincidence. Incident*, 1991).

Gerardjan Rijnders is another writer-director who has staged most of his own dark comedies. In *Tulpen/Vulpen* (*Tulips and Fountain Pens*, 1988), he deals with keeping relationships alive, while in his television series *De Hoeksteen* (*The Cornerstone of Society*, 1988) the pretence of social responsibility and understanding is attacked. Rijnders has also written a number of more serious plays such as *Schreber* (1977) and *Wolfson* (1984). In both these pieces, a young man is driven to madness by his parents and relatives. The dream of a happy and free life is systematically destroyed in most of his works, often simply by an inability to communicate.

Matin van Veldhuizen, also a writer-director, often revises already existing material for her own dramatic purposes. She has written plays based on material by writers such as Jane Bowles (*Jane*, 1983), Anna Blaman (*Affaire B*, 1985) and Dorothy Parker (*Dorothy Parker*, 1987). In these plays, women challenge existing reality while in their own work they create an alternative existence. In her plays different dramatic techniques are combined and the perspective is continually shifting.

Still another writer of note who deals with changing theatrical perspectives is Rob de Graaf (b. 1952) who writes very personal plays for the New West company based on incidents from the lives of company members themselves. These have included *Rinus* (1987), *Pygmalion* (1989) and *Nichus* (1990).

At the beginning of the 1970s, Centre Stage began to commission young playwrights. Working under the supervision of a dramaturge, were the writers Ton Vorstenbosch, Guus Vleugel, Wim T. Schippers and Paul Haenen (b. 1946).

The Instituut voor Theateronderzoek (Institute for Theatre Research) and Theaterwerkplaats Independence (Theatre Workshop

Independence) both also offer workshops where inexperienced playwrights have the opportunity to work under the direct supervision of dramaturges, directors and actors.

The institute's major success has been with poet Judith Herzberg who started her playwriting career in the 1970s at the institute and has since amassed an impressive body of dramatic work. Many of her plays are now part of the established repertoire. Among them are *Leedvermaak* (*Malicious Pleasure*, 1982), *En/Of* (*And/Or*, 1985), *De Caracal*, based on Copeau's *La Voix Humaine* (1988), and *Een Goed Hoofd* (*A Good Head*, based on Wedekind's *Lulu*, 1991). She has also done an adaptation of Schnitzler's *Reigen (La Ronde)* called *Cranky Box*.

Herzberg's plays have dealt with a range of subjects from Jewish identity to the problems of dying. Her characters rarely speak directly but in a roundabout way hoping that those things they are unable to speak about will somehow surface.

Marien Jongewaard's 1982 New West production of Rob de Graaf's *Prae*, designed by Dik Boutkan.
Photo: Ben van Duin.

**Directors, Directing
and Production Styles**

For a discussion of directing, see previous material in **Aristic Profile** and the opening, historical section.

Music Theatre
Dance Theatre

In the early 1970s, a number of young pop musicians and plastic artists founded the Hauser Orkater company. Pop music was an essential ingredient in the group's work, which included rapid scene changes, a fast-paced style, acrobatics and surprising visuals with fairly simple, straightforward texts. The company had its strongest appeal for those under 30 who traditionally had no real interest in either theatre or dance.

Slightly earlier, dance was freed from the rigid conventions of classical ballet through the experiments of the brothers Bart and Koert Stuyf who had been inspired by the examples of Anthony Tudor, Martha Graham, Merce Cunningham and Alwin Nikolais. Pauline de Groot (b. 1942) later added contact improvisation to the mix.

Because of this work, attention began to be paid to the visual aspects of dance, particularly images and the use of space. The Stichting Eigentijdse Dans (Contemporary Dance Foundation) operated from 1964 to 1975. Created by Koert Stuyf and dancer Ellen Edinoff (b. 1942), the group produced a series of performances in which set and props were essential parts of the experience. Its members argued that movement itself was essentially theatrical, a notion that led to a controversial but vital form of image theatre. Movement, by their definition, meant all movement including that of the audience. This led to audience provocations, including one event which took place *outside* the Stedelijk Museum (Civic Museum) in 1969.

Mime too was part of the new approach to movement. No longer rooted in mime, the new Dutch Mimetheater Will Spoor – which operated between 1963 and 1973 under the direction of Will Spoor (b. 1927) – and the School voor Bewegingstheater (School of Movement Theatre) in Amsterdam established by Frits Vogels, brought new attention to the form. It was from Vogels's school that the Bewth company came into being in 1965. Members of this group collectively created movement theatre in various unusual locations including factories and churches. In their performances, movement, lighting and sound interacted with architectural forms.

During this same period, a new company in The Hague began to concentrate on blending visual and music theatre with the plastic arts. Scarabee began its life in 1967 under the direction of painter and graphic artist Adri Boon. Boon assembled his performances with a series of images in which the actors became part of a fast-moving, complex, visual entity. When text was used it was generally narrative and subordinate to the spectacle as a whole.

Bart Stuyf's Multimedia company put together productions in which objects and complex, technical, spatial constructions played the major role. Justa Masbeck's Beeldend Theatre (Pictorial Theatre, 1973–83) concentrated on what was called locational theatre, while Frits Vogels's Griftheater (founded in 1975) explored the possibilities of producing a pictorial theatre in which movement, space, sound and design cohered.

The Shaffy Theatre in Amsterdam was founded in 1968 by Steve Austen (b. 1945) and gave many of these groups the opportunity to put their experiments into practice. This theatre became the home for the fringe in the field of dance, music theatre and mime. In 1975, the Festival of Fools gave these experiments an international outlet.

Younger theatre practitioners brought these experiments into even closer contact with the mainstream by adding elements of music, movement and visual design. One of the leaders in this was the Independent Stage of Jan Joris Lamers, essentially a collective for actors and visual artists who shared with several other groups the desire to transcend the boundaries between theatre and other media.

The mime company Nieuw West (founded in

1977) showed mimes as central in a movement-oriented art that paid attention to text.

Leonard Frank's Baal was equally interested in music as a theatrical element and works were often created to the music of Louis Andriessen among others.

It was clear by the 1980s that interdisciplinary attitudes were bringing actors into dance and music, and musicians and dancers into roles traditionally reserved for actors. The boundaries between the various disciplines were becoming increasingly blurred by the end of the decade, and independent concepts of theatre, music theatre and dance theatre were becoming indistinguishable on Dutch stages.

Janny Donker

Theatre for Young Audiences
Puppet Theatre

Until the twentieth century, Dutch children's theatre was all but non-existent and Dutch puppetry was generally composed of two local Punch and Judy-type figures – Jan Klaasen and Katrijn – who were seen in glove-puppet form on streets or at fairs. Several puppeteers used these figures in short, slightly vulgar or politically oriented sketches. Because of these approaches, the tradition was often treated as an object of contempt by both artists and intellectuals.

During the 1920s, children's theatre generally and puppet theatre specifically took a turn toward professionalism with trained performers trying their hands at shadow and/or marionette forms. After World War II, glove-puppetry itself was rediscovered. Among the early innovators in the field was Jan Nelissen (b. 1918), whose work directly involved children. Nelissen also created musical productions for adults using puppets, among them adaptations of Marlowe's *Faust* and Ravel's *L'Heure espagnol*. Since this time, Dutch puppeteers have been experimenting with the form in extraordinary and versatile ways.

Partly under the influence of pop art, all sorts of materials and objects became part of the puppeteer's equipment – umbrellas, paper napkins, brushes, even the puppeteer's hands. Over time, a more abstract imagistic language was created by such innovators as Feike Boschma (b. 1920), a master of the form, who gave life and movement to the simplest of objects and helped to bring about what was subsequently called Object Theatre.

The true revolution came when puppeteers literally came out of the closet, the portable cubicle in which Punch and Judy had traditionally been performed. In 1958 Henk Abbing (b. 1931) did exactly this, and this step, which coincided with the general movement toward social democratization of the early 1960s, put an end to the isolation of the puppeteer and opened the door to numerous new artistic possibilities. Direct contact with audiences became possible.

Depiction of perspective, introduced at the same time by Abbing, could be perfected: the same character could appear in or out of the traditional cubicle as successively larger or smaller figures, from glove-puppet to marionette to actor and vice versa. The acting area was enlarged. During the early 1970s, all sorts of new forms for the cubicle were tried out so that the cubicle itself came to function as part of a larger setting.

In the work of Hinderik de Groot (b. 1939), the most important innovator up to that time, there came a moment when one had to speak of the form as an art of setting rather than of manipulation. The highlight of this work was his production of *Schillen* (*Peel*, 1980). Although the traditional cubicle has not fallen entirely into disuse, it is rare to see it used in the older way today.

During the 1970s and 1980s, audiences could also see a blending of all these new elements as objects merged with images to create a much more pictorial form. With boundaries continuing to blur in the 1990s, puppeteers seemed to be moving even further toward the visual arts and the form was even attracting the interest of sculptors such as Jeroen Henneman (b. 1942), whose 1988 performance *Hinderlaag* (*Ambush*) was built almost entirely around the set itself.

With this growing complexity of performance came a parallel growth in the creative team needed to generate the work – writers, directors, set designers and costumiers. Working with a fantasy world conjured up by

Lidwien Rothaan's 1991 House of Amstel production of Heleen Verburg's *Voyeurs I*.
Photo: Bas Mariën.

sets and scraps of text, the sculptor Frans Mals-schaert (b. 1939) and his company Sirkel (Circle) founded in 1979, has proved convincingly that such theatre is indeed an art form to be taken seriously. In such productions as *Vuurrood* (*Scarlet*, 1984) and *Lot* (1991), Malsschaert showed that visual metaphor could be much more eloquent than realistic narrative.

Important artists of that time were Henk Boerwinkel, Damiet van Dalsum and Neville Tranter. Boerwinkel, an artist and sculptor, founded with his wife, Ans, the Figurentheater Triangel in 1971 in Mepel. Their shows often include a series of surrealistic items and use all kinds of puppets, which present a pessimistic but humorous view of human existance. Van Dalsum, an adherent of stylized puppetry, developed surrealistic shows for adults and sensitive, poetic plays for children, such as the famous *Hollebollebeer*. Tranter, an Australian, settled in the Netherlands in 1976 with his 'Stuffed Puppets'. As a solo player, he used sophisticated puppets, manipulating them in view of the audience. His usual subjects are human psychological problems and the relationships between all sorts of manipulators and their manipulated

subjects, in such shows as *The Seven Deadly Sins* (1984), *Manipulator* (1985), *Underdog* (1985), and *Kamer 5* (1988).

Children's theatre as a whole took a major leap forward in the 1980s with theatre practitioners seeing new possibilities in it. Utilizing elements from all the arts, Dutch children's theatre found itself connected to dance, music, literature and sculpture as well as traditional puppetry. In its 1991 and 1992 productions, *Voyeurs I* and *Voyeurs II*, the House of Amstel company directly linked these various forms in effective and unique collaborations.

Many contemporary directors have shown a genuine gift for translating literary and dramatic classics into clear cut and recognizable image performances for children. Among the major productions in this genre have been *Soria Moria* (1985), an adaptation of Ibsen's *Peer Gynt*, directed by Ted Keijser (b. 1947); and *Het Vervolg* (*The Follow-up*, 1982) and *Ifigenia Koningskind* (*Iphigenia the Royal Child*, 1989), based on Euripides' plays, directed by Liesbeth Coltof (b. 1954).

A number of writers have emerged in recent years working regularly in the form, among them, Paulin Mol (b. 1953), Suzanne van Lohuizen (b. 1953), Roel Adam (b. 1935), Heleen Verburg (b. 1964) and Ad de Bont (b. 1949). In 1991, children's dramatic texts also began to be published for the first time.

Hanny Alkema

Design

At the close of World War II, stage settings in the Netherlands were conventional in the extreme. Off-the-rack sets were still used although sets could also be made in studios to a director's specifications. Most were nothing more than an illustration of the dramatic text and left little room for the audience to use its imagination. Theatre architecture, by this time considerably dated, was not exactly an invitation to innovation in set design. A proscenium with wings was a standard feature; flexible theatres were few and far between.

With the introduction of theatrical subsidies in the Netherlands, money finally began to be available to hire designers to work on specific productions. However, the limitations of the architecture, the conventionality of the space and the need to tour most productions after an initial run meant that sets still had to follow fairly strict guidelines and forms. The result was that only rarely was artistic innovation attempted.

Earlier in the century, sculptors had begun to try their hands at stage design and the attempt to include designers in productions increased. The unchallenged leader in this work was the hyper-realist Nicolaas Wijnberg (b. 1918). In his wake came many others – Hans van Norden (b. 1915), Friso Wiegersma (b. 1925) and Herman Berserik (b. 1921) to name just three. All were adept realists who tried to epitomize the spirit of the play in visual form. The results were stage images that, especially in the 1950s, were characterized by pictorial excess. These painters, aided by developments in stage lighting, set out to conquer the entire space.

This continued until the 1960s, when a new generation of plastic artists – among them, Roger Chailloux (1931–77), Herman van Elteren (b. 1928), Herman Gordijn (b. 1932) and Niels Hamel (b. 1933) – adopted the motto 'clarity and simplicity'. In their sets, they tried to visualize spatial tensions as they related particularly to the stage floor. In doing this, they drew a somewhat hesitant parallel with recent developments in the plastic arts.

This parallel, particularly with regard to pop art, was rendered more explicit by a group of plastic artists from The Hague, known as Studio Scarabee and founded by Adri Boon. They took the plastic arts, rather than drama, as their point of departure and developed projects in museums and later in their own theatres in which plastic art, literature, music and movement became inextricably linked.

After the Tomato Action (see opening section), it seemed that the days when Dutch theatre could drink exclusively from its own wells were gone forever. The collaboration between plastic artists and theatre practitioners flourished; the designer came to be regarded as equal to the director. This could be seen in certain productions where lighting was the only structural element (Chailloux's work and Peter Oosthoek's) or in productions where the stage picture was like a giant collage of disparate objects and projections (as in the work of Niels Hamel and Annemarie Prins).

These collaborations often began in theatre school. It was there, for example, that Jan Joris Lamers and Gerrit Timmers (b. 1949) met each other and it was there that plans for the establishment (1972) of the Independent Stage in Rotterdam were born. Without any strict division of labour, they set about creating what they called 'shams on a wooden structure with the help of artefacts'. They performed almost anywhere, except in an established theatre. Their structural elements varied from *objets trouvés* to video monitors and backdrops which were sometimes painted as part of the performance. Their innovative approaches were rapidly adopted by other companies.

Attempts were also made to increase the theatre space itself. Designers here were concerned with creating not only functional settings but also space for movement by the actors. The most important of these designers was Wim Vesseur (1919–77) who used ingenious constructions to achieve this end. The pragmatism of these non-painters was frequently regarded with suspicion since their sets were usually less colourful. During the 1950s and 1960s, however, the pioneering work of these

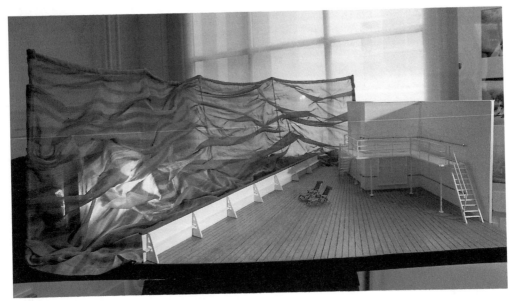

Mirjam Grote Gansey's design for the 1986 Toneelgroep Centrum production of Peter te Nuyl's *Het Vergeten*.
Photo: Roel Bogaards.

'functionalists' was put to good use in designs involving reduction, abstraction and suggestion.

In order to go even further in the creation of abstract space, theatres looked to industrial designers and architects such as Benno Premsela (b. 1920), Floris Guntenaar (b. 1946) and Paul van den Berg (b. 1945). These designers had the advantage over the pure functionalists in that their designs were not only functional and spatial but also aesthetic. This latter element quickly gained in importance.

Paul Gallis (b. 1943) was one of the most important exemplars of the 'new aesthetics'. Gallis drew extensively on pictorial archives as well as new developments in architecture and the plastic arts. From these elements, he created spatial stage pictures in which seemingly unimportant details were thrown into relief by the *mise-en-scène*. Later Peter de Kimpe (b. 1951), Judith Lansink (b. 1951) and Mirjam Grote Gansey (b. 1952), among others, worked along similar lines.

Theatre Space and Architecture

The majority of Dutch theatres have been built since World War II, which means that the Netherlands has been in a unique position to profit from the many revolutionary developments that have taken place since that time in theatre architecture.

During the 1950s, theatre architecture tended toward bringing the stage itself closer to the auditorium so that audiences could literally be drawn into the action. Johan de Meester and Nicolaas Wijnberg went so far as to bring audiences both close to and around the performance by staging Euripides' *Iphigenia* in a former circus building in Amsterdam, the Theatre Carré.

Another experiment in theatre-in-the-round during the late 1950s was tried by director Kees van Iersel whose company Test experimented with the French absurdists in a small dance-hall above the art-deco cinema Tuschinsky in Amsterdam. As artistic director of the Studio Stage Company, he worked most often at Amsterdam's Wasteland Theatre. This space had earlier functioned as a coffee market and dance-hall and in 1964 became the first totally flexible theatre space in the country.

The Wasteland was the first in a long line of alternative performance spaces to begin operation. The Dutch fringe was also expanding at this time to include the Mickery (first in Loenersloot, later in Amsterdam) and the Shaffy Theatre in Amsterdam. These new spaces offered theatre artists and scenographers possibilities for experimentation which often appeared impossible in the more traditional venues.

During the 1970s and 1980s, the very notion of a fixed stage was replaced by the more modern idea of a theatrical space. Performances moved increasingly into spaces not initially designed for the purpose – streets, trains, stables, swimming pools, factories. These locations needed no sets; in fact, they were the sets.

Lia Gieling

Training

Before 1945 the only professional school for acting was located in Amsterdam. It tended to be exclusively rooted in the ideas of Stanislavski, a text-based approach. In the post-war period similar acting schools were established in Arnhem and Maastricht. In Amsterdam all kinds of theatre training facilities emerged, as the diversity of modern theatre forms grew. In the late 1960s most of them were brought together under a single academy offering training in a variety of disciplines and faculties – the Amsterdam Theatre School.

The Amsterdam School for Mime also developed during this period as a laboratory for the study of more physical and plastic forms of theatre.

During the 1970s and 1980s, training possibilities at the Amsterdam Theatre School became greater. As design grew in importance, students at many of the art academies were given opportunities to specialize in the art.

During the 1980s, still another branch was added: Object Theatre, a programme geared exclusively towards this experimental element of plastic theatre. Since the technical side of the work required skilled craftspeople, courses for theatre technicians were also added into the mix.

In 1989, an actor's training programme was begun in Utrecht. The programme was not specifically focused on text but rather on the physical training of actors.

Much Dutch actor and theatre training was linked to the training of drama teachers in the schools. These courses were established in the belief that every child should have some familiarity with the theatre since the theatrical arts were seen as liberating forces in the formation of opinions. During the late 1960s, a school exclusively for directors was formed along with professional schools for the training of mime, dancers, visual artists and musicians.

Criticism, Scholarship and Publishing

Dramatic literature has long been a part of literary studies at most Dutch universities but it was not until after World War II that separate departments for theatrical studies began to be set up with the aim of dealing with more than just the literary aspects of the art.

The first university-level programme was established in 1964 by Ben Hunningher (b. 1903) with the Institute for Dramatic Art at the University of Amsterdam. Originally offering only post-graduate work, in the 1980s the institute was remodelled into a full faculty offering both undergraduate and graduate-level courses. Its students are generally trained as researchers

with course material shaped by studies in theatre history.

The department of theatre research at the University of Utrecht provides similar training, though its programme is geared towards investigation of the theatrical experience itself including audience reception. Since 1984, Utrecht and Amsterdam have published their own *Journal of Theatre Research*.

Virtually all the regional and national daily newspapers, along with the weeklies, contain sections on theatre criticism. The dailies predominantly review the work of mainstream companies and established practitioners from the fringe. Most of the critics are journalists specializing in the field. The most trend-setting reviews appear in *The Volksrant* (*People's Paper*) and the *NRC Handelsblad* (*NRC Tradepaper*).

Reviews of greater depth can usually be found in the journal *Toneel Theatraal* (*Theatrical Stage*), a continuation of the theatre magazine *Het Toneel* (*The Stage*) founded in 1875 by the Dutch Stage Society. The present name was adopted in 1966. The journal closely follows developments in the Dutch theatre on both the artistic and technical levels. It tends to restrict itself to more established practitioners with its writers concentrating particularly on innovations in textual theatre, television drama and the influences of other arts on performance and design. *Toneel Theatraal* is published by the Dutch Theatre Institute.

In 1951 an annual called *Theaterjaarboek* (*Theatre Yearbook*), documenting the previous season's productions and events, began publication (since the 1970s published by Toneel Theatraal). The volumes now include a number of essays dealing with the season's artistic trends and developments.

The Dutch Institute for Dance publishes a journal called *Notes* geared toward developments in dance, mime, movement theatre and its various offshoots.

Because of the lack of tradition in modern Dutch playwriting, the publication of Dutch plays has never been a priority with publishers. It was only towards the end of the 1950s that the publishing firm Bezige Bij (Busy Bees) began to publish mass paperback editions of prose, poetry and drama. These were mostly translations of world classics and the drama section was heavily weighted toward Shakespeare in translations by Bert Voeten (1918–93) but it did also include original plays by Hugo Claus and Lodewijk de Boer.

Most other publishers limit themselves to occasional editions of classics, specific anniversary editions of plays or company histories. Quite often these are state subsidized.

In 1971, the Amsterdam Stage Company, under Hans Croiset, began the practice of publishing its own plays in a low-priced paperback format to accompany performances. Other companies later followed suit.

Since 1982, the initiative has been strengthened with the help of the International Theatre and Film Book Shop which has itself published a large number of play texts. The company has also begun marketing anthologies of works by

Dutch writers such as de Boer, Frans Strijards, Gerardjan Rijnders and Judith Herzberg, as well as important foreign dramatists such as Heiner Müller from Germany. There is now also a series of books dealing with theory and drama-in-education. Many of these works are also subsidized by the state.

Jackelien van Deursen, Pol Eggermont
with Hanny Alkema, Tom Blokdijk,
Janny Donker, Lia Gieling
Translated by Jackie Fletcher

Further Reading

Abbing, H. *Een economie van de kunsten: Beschouwingen over kunst en kunstbeleid.* [The economics of the arts: views on art and arts policy]. Groningen: Historische uitgeverij, 1989. 273 pp.

Alkema, Hanny. *Kijk op jeugdtheater.* [A view of youth theatre]. The Hague: 1977.

——, and Christine Boer. *Poppen-, object-, en beeldend theater in Nederland.* [Puppet, object and pictorial theatre in the Netherlands]. Amsterdam: Dutch Theatre Institute, 1991. 157 pp.

Austen, Steve, ed. *10 jaar margetheater in Nederland.* [Ten years of Dutch fringe theatre]. Utrecht/Antwerp: Spectrum, 1980. 160 pp.

Bevers, A.M., and S.J. Doorman. *In ons diaconale land. Opstellen over cultuurspreiding.* [In our diaconal land: essays on cultural dissemination]. Amsterdam: Boekmanstichting/Van Gennep, 1988. 183 pp.

Deddes, Ingrid, ed. *Tomaat documentation: een documentair verslag van een actie, 9 oktober 1969–28 februari 1970.* [Tomato documentation: a documentary account of a protest, 9 October 1969–28 February 1970]. Amsterdam: Instituut voor Theateronderzoek/Holland Festival, 1979. 333 pp.

De Voogd, G.J. *Facetten van vijftig jaar Nederlands toneel 1920-70.* [Facets of Dutch theatre from 1920 to 1970]. Amsterdam: Moussault, 1970. 236 pp.

Dieho, Bart. *Theater op de bres. Vormingstheater in Nederland en Vlaanderen.* [Theatre in the breach. Socio-developmental theatre in the Netherlands and Flanders]. Amsterdam: Dutch Theatre Institute, 1979. 96 pp.

Erenstein, Robert. *Jeugdtheater geen kinderspel.* [Children's theatre not child's play]. Amsterdam: International Theatre Bookshop, 1981. 115 pp.

——, and Joost Sternheim, eds. *Baal: 15 jaar toneelhistorie, 1973–88.* [Baal: 15 years of theatre history, 1973–88]. Amsterdam: International Theatre Bookshop, 1988. 179 pp.

Frey, Martin. *Kreatieve Marge: die Entwicklung des niederländischen Off-Theaters*. [The creative fringe: the development of Dutch Off-Theatre]. Vienna: Böhlau, 1991. 166 pp.

Gieling, Lia. *Toneelbeeld: vanaf 1945 in Nederland*. [The stage set in the Netherlands since 1945]. Amsterdam/The Hague: SDU, 1990. 176 pp.

Hollenberg, Inez, and Rob Klinkenberg. 'Mickery in Amsterdam. De geschiedenis van januari 1972 tot juni 1979 met een analyse van de voorstellingen'. [Mickery in Amsterdam. The history from January 1972 to June 1979 with a performance analysis]. *Mickery dossier 1–2*. [Mickery file 1–2]. Amsterdam: Instituut voor Theateronderzoek. 302 pp.

Hunningher, B. 'Toneelverzet en toneelplan'. [Stage resistance and stage planning]. *Maatstaff* 10, no. 6 (1962). 10 pp.

Kassies, J. *Op zoek naar cultuur*. [In search of culture]. SUN-schrift, Nijmegen: SUN, 1980. 376 pp.

Ogden, Dunbar H. *Performance Dynamics and the Amsterdam Werkteater*. Berkeley/Los Angeles/London: University of California Press, 1984. 261 pp.

——. *Das 'Werkteater' von Amsterdam: Geschichte, Inszenierungen, Spieldynamik*. [The Amsterdam Werktheater: history, stagings, performance dynamics]. Würzburg: Königshausen und Neuman, 1993. 290 pp.

Roseboom, Koos, and Marleen Sikker, eds. *Eenoneindig circuit: de theaterzucht in Nederland*. [A never-ending circuit: the craving for theatre in the Netherlands]. Amsterdam: Alligator/Instituut voor Theateronderzoek, 1986. 79 pp.

Stroman, B. *De nederlandse toneelschrijfkunst: verklaring van een gemis*. [Dutch playwriting: an explanation of an absence]. Amsterdam: Moussault, 1973. 240 pp.

NORTHERN IRELAND

(see both **IRELAND** and **UNITED KINGDOM**)

NORWAY

Occupying the northern and western sides of the Scandinavian Peninsula and lying west of Sweden and north of Denmark, Norway boasts one of Europe's highest standards of living and lowest population densities. As of 1992, 4.1 million people lived in Norway with some 450,000 living in and around the capital, Oslo. Norway's land area is 324,000 square kilometres (125,000 square miles).

Norway became a unified country under King Harold the Fairhaired (880–940). Christianity was finally accepted in 1030. By 1262, Norway was at the height of its power with all the far-flung Viking territories from Europe to Greenland swearing allegiance to the Norwegian king. A little more than a century later the country and its possessions were joined to Denmark. Danish domination continued to 1814, when it had to accept a union with Sweden. In June 1905, the Norwegian parliament voted to end the union with Sweden and four months later this was ratified by both parliaments. In 1940, Norway was occupied by the Germans; the

country did not regain its freedom until the end of the war.

The Norwegian language operates with two official linguistic variants, standard Norwegian and new Norwegian. In addition, the Sami language is spoken, mostly in the north.

If there were any religious dramas in Norway it has not been proven, but there were travelling theatre groups and later the humanistic dramatic traditions were popular all across Scandinavia, in the sixteenth and seventeenth centuries.

It was in fact Denmark that most influenced Norwegian theatre development. It was the leading theatre country in Scandinavia because of its geographic proximity to the rest of Europe as well as because of its political and cultural strength, Denmark's political centre was located in Copenhagen; all Norwegians who wished to have influence in either the political or cultural life of the united countries had to come here. This also meant that many Norwegians influenced Danish theatre development and made names for themselves in European theatre. Probably the best known and the most influential was Ludvik Holberg (1684–1754) from Bergen, an important writer of comedy who was the principal representative of Scandinavian classicism. He was also influential in opening the first Danish theatre in Lille Grønnegade (Little Green Street) in 1722.

Because Norway did not have its own monarch, the country did not develop a court theatre tradition as did other Scandinavian countries. It was the travelling Danish theatre companies therefore which most influenced the development of Norwegian cultural and theatre life in the seventeenth and eighteenth centuries.

Towards the end of the eighteenth century in Norway another theatre form grew which also was a factor in the development of a professional theatre. Wealthy merchants and those from the civil service laid the foundation for the establishment of permanent drama companies. These private groups had strict rules for membership. The companies also built impressive theatre houses in the larger cities. Kristiania (Oslo) got its first company by 1780, Kristiansand in 1787, Bergen in 1794, Trondheim in 1802 and Stavanger in 1823. Some of these buildings are still in use today.

Between 1830 and 1880 Norway enjoyed a period of prosperity and saw the growth of a middle class in the cities and among farmers in the country. Both groups had power in the economy, in politics and in culture. A new audience was also developing for a more popular theatre and this was taken advantage of by the still active travelling companies. Professional theatre became accessible to anyone who could pay.

Several attempts were made to create permanent theatre groups in Kristiania before 1850 but the effort did not succeed because of a lack of funds. Most of these theatres, however, had employed Danish actors and had a repertoire that was mostly based on comedies and light farces of German and French origin. As part of a national attempt to break free from Danish dominance, a new interest evolved in the Norwegian language using Norwegian actors and Norwegian plays. The first specifically Norwegian theatre was opened in Bergen in 1850. The inspiration came from the internationally known Bergen violinist Ole Bull (1842–1916). This company, Det Norske Theater (Norwegian Theatre), moved into the building that Det Dramatiske Selskab (The Dramatic Company) had built in 1800.

Bull employed Henrik Ibsen (1828–1906) as stage director and playwright from 1851 and this is also where Ibsen started his career as a dramatist. Ibsen stayed in Bergen until 1857, then Bjørnstjerne Bjørnson (1832–1910) took over leadership of the theatre until 1859 but by 1863 Bergen was again without a permanent company for financial reasons. In 1876, the city started still another theatre now called Den Nationale Scene (The National Stage). Bull's initiative inspired similar theatre undertakings in both Trondheim and Kristiania.

Ibsen became artistic director of the Kristiania Norske Theater (Kristiania Norwegian Theatre) in 1857 and this is where the world première of his play *Hærmændene på Helgeland* (*The Vikings of Helgeland*) took place in 1859. The theatre closed because of poor finances in 1863 and most of the actors moved to the Christiania Theater which became the basis for the establishment of the Nationaltheatret (National Theatre) in 1899.

By the start of the twentieth century, Norway, in fact, had two established national theatres, Den Nationale Scene in Bergen and Nationaltheatret in Oslo. In spite of a consistently weak economy and without support from government, both managed to keep dramatic art alive. It was these two theatres that would set the tone for Norwegian theatre over the next few generations.

Det Norske Teatret (The Norwegian Theatre) began in 1913; it put emphasis from the beginning on staging new Norwegian drama and became particularly important both before and after 1945 and particularly in the 1960s. In 1985 the company moved into a newly built house, one of northern Europe's most modern theatres.

The range of development of Norwegian theatrical art could probably best be illustrated by looking at what happened at the Nationaltheatret in the years before 1945. Its first director, Bjørnstjerne Bjørnson, was trained as an actor and director with the company of the Duke of Saxe-Meiningen and became familiar there with the company's unique crowd scenes, realistic designs and long rehearsal periods. It was Bjørnson – with his productions first at the Christiania Theater (1884–93) and later at the Nationaltheatret – who introduced these ideas into Norwegian theatre and helped introduce the so-called 'golden age' at the Nationaltheatret. He built a solid ensemble there with some outstanding actors, including Johanne Dybwad (1867–1950), who became one of the most prominent actresses and directors of her

Kjetil Bang-Hansen's 1982 Den Nationale Scene production of *Raskolnikov*.
Photo: Trygve Schønfelder.

generation. From 1907 to 1923 Dybwad deve-loped her own directorial interests. Among other elements, she introduced the chamber play to Norway and an impressionistic style associated with monumental realism.

Inspired by Dybwad's ideas, the Norwegian theatre developed quickly in the decades before World War II and a group of strong directors emerged: Agnes Mowinckel (1875–1963), Halfdan Christensen (1873–1950), Hans Jacob Nilsen (1897–1957), Knut Hergel (1899–1982) and Stein Bugge (1896–1961). They all offered productions influenced by the latest trends in Europe but usually focused around Norwegian plays, most often those of Ibsen.

German occupation during World War II interrupted this development and had a signifi-cant impact on Norwegian culture even after-ward. The director of the Trondheim theatre, for example, was killed by the Nazis for opposing them through theatre. Though finan-cial resources had never been large before the war, the roots of government support were clear from 1935 when the theatres in Norway were included in the national budget for the first time and the government participated on theatres' boards of directors. The government's goal was

to make theatre part of the common experience and give the entire nation access to the values and knowledge that theatre represented. This was also the seed for the later development of regional theatre in the country. After the war, these ideas developed to an even greater extent.

In the years before 1940 there had been much debate about the role of theatre and repertoire policies as part of ongoing ideological debates on the social role of the arts generally. Theatre still did not have a clear place in the cultural pic-ture for large parts of the country and many expressed scepticism over government support of theatre. The fact was that theatres were located only in the largest cities and were basi-cally patronized by a middle-class audience. Should culture be part of the political education of the people? The government's answer was 'yes' and cultural subsidy quickly grew. By 1960, a stable foundation for theatre operations was established and among other things, chil-dren's theatre was recognized as a part of the process. Supplementary grants became linked to audience size at this point.

During the 1970s, government expenditure for culture increased significantly. Up to this time, grants had mostly gone to established

Stein Winge's 1986 Det Norske Teatret production of Ghelderode's *Pantagleiz*.
Photo: Leif Gabrielsen.

theatres, which left little room for new development. As a result of the new funds a number of new theatres emerged.

Entering the 1990s, budget cuts were once again causing problems at every level, including in the major theatres in Oslo. The Nationaltheatret, as a result, closed its studio theatre despite its high reputation and solid audience following.

Structure of the National Theatre Community

In Oslo there are three established theatres: the Nationaltheatret, Det Norske Teatret and Oslo Nye Teater (Oslo New Theatre, 1929). Added to these are Den Nationale Scene in Bergen, the Rogaland Theatre (1947) in Stavanger and the Trøndelag Teater (1937) in Trondheim. During the 1970s, five regional theatres began: the Hålogaland Theatre (Tromsø, 1971), Teatret Vårt (Our Theatre, Molde, 1972), Teater Ibsen (Skien, 1975), Sogn og Fjordane Teater (Førde, 1977) and the Nordland Teater (Mo i Rana, 1978). These theatres also receive government and local support, and have touring responsibilities. Most of the 'free' regional theatres were connected to the 'group' or theatre movement of the 1970s and most operated by collective

decisions. During the 1980s, these companies moved back to a more traditional model by hiring artistic directors. Teatret Vårt in Molde, however, retained its collective model until 1991.

During the 1980s several new regional theatres were created – the Hedemark Theatre (Hamar, 1987), the Haugesund Theatre (Haugesund, 1986), the Hordaland Theatre (Bergen, 1988) and the Agder Theatre (Kristiansand, 1991). There has also been a regularly producing Sami theatre – the Beaivvas Sami Theatre (Kautokeino). The company was established in 1981 as an independent theatre and in 1987 began receiving government funds.

The Agder Theatre operates on a production-by-production basis while the Hordaland Theatre is Norway's first institutional theatre for children and youth.

Riksteatret is the country's national touring company and was established in 1948. In addition to its own productions, Riksteatret works closely with government-funded theatres in Oslo, Bergen, Stavanger and Trondheim, with various project theatres, theatre workshops and local groups in the regions and gives technical and artistic support. Riksteatret's administration is located in Oslo.

All of these theatres have regular companies, musicians, dancers and full technical staffs. They also generally have their own theatre buildings with one or more stages as well as their own administrations. All are financed by government funds and from box-office income.

Funding also comes from the regional counties and municipalities. The federal government, however, contributes the largest amounts. The total federal budget for theatres (including Den Norske Opera) in 1991 was over 375.4 million Norwegian kroner (approximately US$68 million). This represents about 60–80 per cent of each theatre's budget.

Sizes of the companies vary widely. At Nationaltheatret 247 people are employed, sixty of them actors. The theatre's director is usually hired for three to five years.

The Norske Teatres Forening (Norwegian Theatre Association) functions as a national association of theatre companies and is responsible for negotiating terms of employment and salaries with the unions. Other key organizations are the Norske Skuespillerforbund (Norwegian Actors Association), Norsk Sceneinstruktørforening (Norwegian Directors Group) and the Norske Dramatikeres Forbund (Norwegian Dramatists Association). Salaries and terms of employment at theatres are at the same level as for other professionals.

The largest theatres stage between twelve and sixteen productions a season (usually from the end of August to the beginning of July). The average rehearsal period for a production is eight to ten weeks and most shows for run forty to fifty-five performances. At regional theatres, five or six productions per year are mounted. Most theatres offer a varied repertoire ranging from classical dramas to international modern plays to new Norwegian dramas. Performances for children and youth have a high priority with the theatres in the province. In Oslo the Oslo Nye Teater has the largest and best variety shows for young people.

Ticket prices average 100 Norwegian kroner (approximately US$20) and vary from 80 to 250 kroner. Through workplaces and schools, all theatres promote their productions via printed materials and guest visits. Most theatres attempt to sell seasons on subscription which reduces prices by up to 30 per cent.

The economic situation for Norwegian dramatists has improved significantly since 1965 when the Norsk Kulturråd, the Norske Teatres Forening and Norske Dramatikeres Forbund joined together to create more positive working conditions for playwrights. In the 1970s and 1980s, the theatres all had temporary writers-in-residence positions. This was in addition to royalties that the dramatist received from the theatre. In 1977, 60 per cent of each writer's fee was covered by the Kulturfondet for three-month residencies, with the balance covered by the theatres themselves. The commissioning fee for a new play in 1974 was 12,000 kroner (approximately US$2,100); by 1992, that had increased to 108,000 kroner (US$19,600).

Through such programmes there was a considerably larger desire in the 1990s to do new Norwegian plays than there had been previously. One of the pioneers in this area was Den Nationale Scene in Bergen, especially under the direction of Tom Remlov (b. 1949). A Norwegian drama festival took place for the first time in Oslo in 1985 and was well received. A second festival took place in Bergen in 1990 and a third one at Det Norske Theatret, Oslo, in 1994.

Det Åpne Teater (Open Theatre, Oslo) also started in 1985 as a workshop specifically for contemporary Norwegian dramatists and has become a centre for new play development. The theatre also offers training, readings, private showings and open rehearsals. Another educational offering for Norwegian writers is the Skrivekunstakademiet (Writers Academy) in Hordaland.

One of the major theatre events since its establishment in 1990 is the Ibsen Festival at the Nationaltheatret in Oslo, while the Bergen Festival has been devoted to various themes and styles through the years.

Artistic Profile

Companies

Norwegian theatres were, in the 1960s and 1970s, characterized by cultural and political engagement, an inheritance from Brecht. The start of the regional theatre movement took place in the 1970s, and a wave of travelling theatres grew from the large institutional theatres. The groups at this time wanted to find a collective working method which could reach as wide an audience as possible. This was even felt at the Nationaltheatret in productions by Janken Varden (b. 1938). Productions such as *Svartkatten* (*The Black Cat*, 1971) and *Pendlere* (*Commuters*, 1972) were the result of strong political consciousness and the group around Varden ended up in opposition to the activities of the Nationaltheatret.

Towards the end of the 1970s, the companies became even more consciously theatrical. They focused on the visual and poetic with classical texts, this approach was led by director Kjetil Bang-Hansen (b. 1940). As early as 1972 at the regional Teatret Vårt in Molde, Bang-Hansen had demonstrated what proved to be one of his most characteristic features as a director – the conscious use of formal tableau arrangements. His production of Ibsen's *Peer Gynt* at the Rogaland Teater in 1978 was the beginning of this new direction in Norwegian theatre. It was, however, in Bergen in 1982 with *Raskolnikov* (based on Dostoevsky) that Bang-Hansen established himself in this new expressionistic context.

In 1972 Bang-Hansen also helped create a regional theatre for Møre and Romsdal; from 1976 to 1982 he directed the Rogaland Teater in Stavanger, and from 1982 to 1986 he ran Den Nationale Scene in Bergen. In 1986, he took over the Nationaltheatret for a year. Wherever Bang-Hansen was his theatres quickly became creative centres. However, he also tended to have regular budget overruns and when this occurred at the Nationaltheatret he withdrew as its director. He subsequently worked as staff director at Det Norske Teatret in Oslo and did some experimental work at Den Nationale Scene in Bergen.

Another Norwegian director of note is Stein Winge (b. 1940). His performances have also been characterized by a consciously theatrical production style with emphasis on the physical. He has worked this way at Det Norske Teatret, Teatret på Torshov and the Nationaltheatret. In his search for theatrical emotion (as in his production of Shakespeare's *King Lear* in Bergen, 1978) Winge showed the influence of German directing styles from the 1960s and 1970s and he was one of those who introduced this approach to the Norwegian theatre. His theatrical style was particularly strong in his *Faust* at Det Norske Teatret in 1986 where the performance was staged as a kind of grotesque sex comedy involving the use of video, and his production of *Merlin* by Dorst in 1989. From 1990 to 1992, he was artistic director at the Nationaltheatret and worked on new stagings of Ibsen and even launched an annual Ibsen Festival. It was also Winge together with a group of actors who started Teatret på Torshov in 1977 after a group of artists from the Nationaltheatret felt the need for a more experimental and open stage.

Both Bang-Hansen and Winge have been instrumental in reinterpreting classical texts. Earlier, ideological motivation and content were at the root of production; in their work, it was the aesthetics that were more in focus. Classics became a new development and perhaps even an easy way to find new plots.

Despite these exceptions, it is fair to say rhat psychological realism and naturalism continue to dominate the largest theatres. As for the provincial and regional theatres, they have begun to find new audiences by commissioning and staging new Norwegian drama. Eugenio Barba's Odin Theatre – an offshoot of Jerzy Grotowski's early experiments – was established in Oslo in 1964. Because of the lack of funds in Norway, however, the theatre moved to Denmark in 1966 to continue its work. This was a real loss to Norway's free theatre movement and has bothered the Norwegian cultural conscience ever since. However, several small local groups were inspired by Barba's working methods: the Saltkompagniet (Salt Company) and the Grenland Fritheater (Grenland Fritheater), in particular. The latter is still giving performances and course activities.

During the 1980s, project theatres became particularly active, serving as home for such free groups as Baktruppen, Passage Nord (Passage North) and Verdensteatret (World Theatre). All these groups seem to have had a positive influence on the more established theatres which had become rather conservative in both programming and production. Creating an imagistic theatre and a fragmentary dramaturgy, these groups were seen all across the country and often toured abroad. Even within the larger institutions, new models for production began to be examined at this time with project theatres as models in terms of operation. At Den Nationale Scene in Bergen, for example, experiments aimed at developing new Norwegian drama were done. It has consistently been the free project groups which have been the most artistically creative in this area.

Teatersentrum (Theatre Centre) has acted as a kind of umbrella-group for all the independent professional theatres, dance groups and project theatres. The organization has its own theatre in Oslo, the Black Box, which started its activities in 1985. In 1991, Teatersentrum had thirty-one member companies.

The amateur theatre movement in Norway also has long and deep roots as a counter-culture movement. It was initially connected to the workers' movement, partly as agitation, partly as entertainment. In the years after 1945 a network of those groups developed throughout the country. It was from this movement that interest grew in staging large outdoor historical pageants such as *Spelet om Heilag Olav* (*Play About St Olav*), which had its world première at the St Olav's Day Celebration at Stiklestad in 1954 and has been presented annually since 1960. In the 1980s this tradition grew again with several new plays staged in the form of combined efforts between amateurs and professionals.

The Norsk Amatørteaterråd (Norwegian Amateur Theatre Council – NAT) was founded in 1980 and is the coordinating body for the amateur groups in Norway. In fact, Norway has the largest amateur theatre activity in Scandinavia with approximately 1,800 groups and had some 45,000 active members registered in NAT in 1991.

Dramaturgy

The 'golden age' of Norwegian drama dates from about 1880 to World War I and includes the plays by Ibsen and Bjørnson. The development of this tradition paralleled the growth in Europe of the *drame bourgeois* or middle-class drama. It developed from national romantic literature through historic to what became clearly realistic.

Bjørnson particularly put Norwegian theatre on the same level as theatres in the rest of Europe. Building on his experiences with the Meiningen players, he demanded realism in costumes and props, stimulated actor's research and defined the work of Ibsen for Norwegian audiences. Though the Ibsen tradition was established earlier both in form and content, it was Bjørnson who introduced it to Norwegian theatres.

One of the first to break from the realistic tradition in Norway was Johanne Dybwad with her production of the German expressionist Ernst Toller's *Hoppla vi lever* (*Hurrah, We are Alive*, 1927) at the Nationaltheatret in 1928. Her production immediately connected her to the avant-garde German theatre in which the visual arts merged with the more traditional forms of psychological realism.

In the 1930s, Hans Jacob Nilsen's productions at Den Nationale Scene in Bergen represented a move in the direction of political theatre with inspiration from both Russia and Germany. With his production of Nordahl Grieg's (1902–43) plays *Vår ære og vår makt* (*Our Honour and Our Power*) in 1935 and *Nederlaget* (*The Defeat*) in 1937, the terms political theatre and documentary-realism became part of the stage vocabulary. The introduction of theatre-in-the-round and revolving stages added to the sense of the modern. Nilsen also formed a creative tie with the Swedish director Per Schwab, who brought with him an even stronger expressionistic orientation. Nilsen gave expression to a kind of stage choreography with a monumental spaciousness.

In terms of artistic vision, one must also mention the ideas of dramatist, teacher and theorist Stein Bugge. Bugge sought poetry in the theatre and wanted to move away from the realistic and naturalistic traditions of psychological drama. He wanted to create a theatre which brought back style, a theatre which did not build on everyday occurrences but on the fantastic, the visionary and the theatrical. Bugge's approach began to be realized in his production of Grieg's *Barrabas* at Den Nationale Scene in 1946. As a director, Bugge was also very successful with comedies such as Gogol's *Revizor* (*The Government Inspector*) and in several productions of Holberg's comedies. Bugge was clearly ahead of his time. His ideas, first articulated at the end of the 1920s, were in the 1990s still relevant in discussions about form and aesthetics.

Norwegian dramaturgy from 1945 to about 1965 can hardly be described as innovative.

Looking at the repertoire from this period, most plays varied within a realistic style. This essentially Aristotelian methodology began to change toward a more modern and symbolic drama of ideas in the work of Tore Ørjasæter (1886–1968) and Tarjei Vesaas (1897–1970). Ørjasæter's play *Cristophoros* (1948) is a dream play about split personalities wavering between constructive and destructive elements. Vesaas wrote, among others, *Morgonvinden* (*The Morning Wind*, 1947), a symbolist play focusing on the resistance movement of World War II.

In the 1950s there was little new or innovative, and experiments quickly vanished as the 1960s began. Later developments moved toward fantasy, making political points as in the plays of Tor-Åge Bringsværd (b. 1939). During the 1970s a new realistic approach evolved: documentary realism as seen in *Svartkatten* and *Pendlere* at the Nationaltheatret, group works which got their inspiration from Brecht and were built on the ancient exchange between episode and choir but done as protest songs. This was developed further by, among others, Klaus Hagerup (b. 1946) at Hålogaland Teater, and by Edvard Hoem (b. 1949) at Teatret Vårt. Here the theatre moved into everyday life and created the foundation for a new realistic drama, as originated in the 1930s by Nordahl Grieg.

Hagerup made his début with *Alice i underverdene* (*Alice in the Underworld*, 1970) at Den Nationale Scene and the Nationaltheatret and continued with *Kuler i solnedgang* (*Bullets at Sundown*, 1971) which was a parody on a western romance with rough ballads in a Brechtian style. Hagerup is one of the few Norwegian writers who has managed to show the contemporary world with a humorous perspective while managing to retain the true satirist's sting. He developed his style with the Hålogaland Teater where he also showed a talent for writing folk comedy. During his career, he moved from local political problems to a more international perspective as with *I denne verden er alt mulig* (*In this World Everything is Possible*, 1978) about the growth of fascism in Germany. In *Heartbreak Hotel* (1987) he focuses on the idolization of Elvis Presley and how it is possible to lose one's own identity by borrowing from an idol.

Edvard Hoem is a writer who has turned back to Norwegian history for storyline and conflict. In his plays, it is often an historical change which creates the plot: *Der storbåabryt* (1979) concerns 1814 and Norway's constitution; in

God natt, Europa (*Good Night, Europe*) the historic reference is to World War II; the Reformation is the subject of *Sankt Olavs skrin* (*St Olav's Chest*, 1989). As a dramatist Hoem has been inspired by writers such as Ludvik Holberg and Jens Bjørneboe (1920–76) as well as by foreign traditions. When *Musikken gjennom Gleng* (*The Music Through Gleng*, 1978) was performed at the Nationaltheatret, Hoem was compared to Brecht.

The plays of director and writer Sverre Udnæs (1939–82) have lively, poetic dialogue and are powerful on stage. His works tend to deal with family conflict – hatred and the yearning for love – much the same as the works of the Swede Lars Norén and the American dramatist Sam Shepard. His four major plays are all about middle-class families and how they deal with outsiders – *I dette hvite lyset* (*In This White Light*, 1976), *Vinger* (*Wings*, 1977), *Kollisjon* (*Collision*, 1978) and *Tidsnød* (*Pressed for Time*, 1980).

The plays of Cecilie Løveid (b. 1951) have been played in theatres in Bergen and Oslo as well as on radio and television. Her scripts are

Annette Grønneberg's 1990 Oslo Nye Teater production of Cecilie Løveid's *Double Pleasure*.
Photo: Leif Gabrielsen.

lyrical, fragmented and associative in structure. The dialogue is composed of short sentences. Breaking with traditional middle-class realism, her play *Vinteren revner* (*The Winter Splits*, 1983), which had its world première at Den Nationale Scene in Bergen, is a poetic and humorous drama with a classic triangle: mother/daughter/lover, while *Fornuftige dyr* (*Sensible Animals*, 1986) and *Balansedame* (*Tightrope Walker*, 1986) can be compared with the plays of German dramatists Heiner Müller and Botho Strauss. Eschewing chronological development, the plays are stylized fragments. One of her latest plays, *Dobbel nytelse*

(*Double Pleasure*), had its world première at the Oslo Nye Teater in 1990 and was produced again in Vienna in 1992 under the title *Rokokko*. Produced as well in both Sweden and Germany, she is considered a daring and provocative dramatist in Norway.

Yet for all these dramatists, realism still lives on in Norway in such writers as Arne Skouen (b. 1913), Bjørg Vik (b. 1935) and Knut Faldbakken (b. 1941). Still written and still played, the realistic problem drama is tenacious in its hold and still lived on in the 1990s.

Kirsten Broch

Music Theatre

Music has long been an integral part of Norwegian theatre. One reason, perhaps, is that the very first Norwegian theatre, in Bergen, was established by the renowned violin virtuoso Ole Bull, during the national cultural and political renaissance of the 1850s. One result was the national romantic search in historical plays by Bjørnson and Ibsen, in the music of Edvard Grieg (1843–1907), and in the paintings of Hans Gude (1859–1908) and Adolph Tidemand (1814–76).

One of the most revolutionary theatre productions in the immediate post-war period was Det Norske Teatret's anti-romantic *Peer Gynt* with music by Harald Sæverud (b. 1897). Traditionalists were generally upset, believing that Grieg – whose original *Peer Gynt* music was and is a national treasure – would turn in his grave. Sæverud's comment on the opening night in 1948: 'Yes, if he's sleeping on his good ear, he will turn; Edvard Grieg was always interested in innovation.'

This comment may well serve as an introduction to contemporary Norwegian theatre music. All major Norwegian theatres originally had small orchestras, and springtime operettas were standard fare at most theatres. Most major Norwegian composers of the twentieth century at some point or other worked in or for the theatres. But with a few noteworthy exceptions, the status of music in Norwegian theatre started building during the expansive 1960s.

Arne Nordheim (b. 1931) – the country's best known contemporary composer and certainly the one most responsible for teaching Norwegians to listen with joy to modern music –

has a large body of theatre music to his credit, including works for radio and television drama (and best known of all: the music to Glen Tetley's ballet version of Shakespeare's *The Tempest*, today the signature ballet of the Norwegian National Ballet Company). Finn Ludt (1918–92) – for many years musical adviser at the National Theatre – was responsible for musicals, songs, incidental music and full scores. Modern composers like Kåre Kolberg (b. 1936) and Eyvind Solås (b. 1937) have also made distinctive contributions.

Several theatres now have composers on staff, as permanent members of the artistic ensemble. Among the most noteworthy in recent years have been Håkon Berge (b. 1954), Henning Sommerro (b. 1952) and Guttorm Guttormsen (b. 1950). They have all worked across a range of musical expressions, often testing new forms, new approaches and new ways of integrating music into the total concept of a production.

Another important aspect has been the partnership that has developed between composers and directors: Ketil Hvoslef (b. 1939) and Stein Winge represent one such team. They have worked together in a number of theatres – with classical as well as modern plays – and have developed a stage language together that is quite distinctive and different.

Synne Skouen (b. 1950) has formed a different kind of partnership with playwright Cecilie Løveid. Through a number of productions they have developed a fusion of forms in language and music that is unique.

Among the most versatile musical voices in contemporary Norwegian theatre is Olav Anton

Thommessen (b. 1948). His range is extraordinary, his intuitive understanding of theatre rare. He moves with apparent minimalist Asian tones, always finding a deep musical resonance for words and action. Bjørn Kruse (b. 1946), another noted composer, comes from a background of pop and jazz and teaches composition at the State Academy and has a keen sense for the theatrical while spanning a wide range of musical language.

One additional name of note in this field is Egil Monn-Iversen (b. 1928), musical director of Det Norske Teatret in Oslo. As a composer, he has been responsible for some of the country's most successful original musicals, often based on well-known works from Norwegian literature. During his tenure, he has made Det Norske Teatret pre-eminent among national theatres in the musical field.

Halldis Hoaas

Dance Theatre

The Ballet Company at Den Norske Opera was for a long time the only professional dance company in Norway, but its repertoire and approach were extremely traditional. Anything new in the field or even vaguely experimental has tended to take place in the country's independent professional dance groups. The oldest of these, Høvik Ballett, was started in 1969 with the Collage Dansekompani (Collage Dance Company) and the Dansekompaniet Kantarellen (Chanterelle Dance Company) both beginning in the 1970s and the Danse Design company beginning in 1978.

The first groups were inspired by modern dance as developed in the United States by Martha Graham and later in London by the Contemporary Ballet. Others found their inspiration in the experiments of Merce Cunningham, Trisha Brown and Molissa Fenley in American post-modern dance. Several other small groups began in the 1980s and took their inspiration more from new European dance theatre and creators such as Pina Bausch, Reinhild Hoffman and the Belgian Jan Fabre. Unfortunately, all the groups have regularly been in financial difficulty because of poor government funding. It is remarkable that any of the groups have managed to bring forward so many performances both in Oslo and on tour.

Of the four modern groups, the Collage Dansekompani has the strongest artistic sense. Inger Buresund (b. 1954), Sølvi Edvardsen (b. 1951) and Lise Nordal (b. 1950) – its primary choreographers and dancers – are responsible for most of the group's production. However, they also regularly bring in choreographers from outside the group and from other countries, for example, Jorma Uotinen from Finland.

Danse Design is led by the husband-and-wife team of Anne Grethe Eriksen (b. 1953) and Leif

Hernes (b. 1952). Both were trained at the Laban Centre in London. The group tends to work in multimedia. A smaller multimedia group is Huldra (Nymph) which uses improvisation as its primary form. Bergen also has its own dance group, the Riss Dansekompani (Riss Dance Company) established in 1982. This group experiments with dance in relation to the visual arts. Riss also produces dance works for children. In addition to modern

Sølvi Edvardsen's 1990 Nye Carte Blanche Danseteater production of *Kurios*, Bergen.
Photo: Øystein Klakegg.

dance, its members have also experimented with the use of objects and installations.

Scirocco was founded in Oslo by choreographer Ina Christel Johannessen (b. 1959) and scenographer Kristin Torp (b. 1950). The group has also worked with visual installations. Zakraz dance company was founded in 1987 by the dancers and choreographers Ingun Bjørnsgård (b. 1962), Øyvind Jørgensen (b. 1960) and Karen Foss (b. 1957).

Imago Danseteater was founded in 1983 with Lise Eger (b. 1946) as artistic director and received a prize in 1988–9 for its performance, *Men jorden drømmer* (*The World is Dreaming*).

A number of freelance choreographers have also distinguished themselves with specific projects. Best known is Kjersti Alveberg (b. 1948), whose work often starts in Norwegian folklore. A television production by her – based on *Peer Gynt* – won first prize in a TV-video competition for dance. She also created the

major ballet *Vollen* for Den Norske Opera-balletten.

Other choreographers of note include Lise Ferner (b. 1946) and Jane Hveding (b. 1952) whose poetic ballets are deeply rooted in pantomime.

Det Norske Teatret is the only theatre in Norway with its own company of dancers. Its longtime resident choreographer is Runar Borge.

The Norsk Ballettforbund (Norwegian Ballet Association) is a national organization for dancers, choreographers and teachers and has done much to improve dance conditions in Norway. The association is now actively working toward expansion of dance instruction for children and young people in connection with schools and universities. It is also trying to develop regional dance companies and to increase the status of dance generally.

Kirsten Broch

Theatre for Young Audiences

Every Saturday, almost 50,000 Norwegian youngsters listen to *Barnetimen* (*Children's Time*), a programme of the Norwegian Broadcasting Corporation which has produced weekly children's radio theatre since 1945. These productions have been, on the whole, of excellent quality. *Barnetimen* has also become an important purveyor of children's theatre generally in Norway with its many classical and modern plays. For many children, this form of theatre is the only one they will ever be exposed to; even televised children's productions are rare.

It can be fairly said therefore that the staging of theatre for children and teenagers in Norway has been somewhat arbitrary. Although most theatres put on a few such plays, children's scripts have never been staged as part of any consistent policy. Most theatre companies have – ever since the Nationaltheatret started putting on comedies for children – staged one major production each year, normally a Christmas play. And even this has not always been the case. Ironically, since they have been so rare, most productions have been tremendous commercial successes. The theatres often put on the same play for several consecutive ears. *Hakkebakkeskogen* (*Hakkebakke Forest*, 1992) by Thorbjørn Egner (1912–90) and

Pippi Langstrømpe (*Pippi Longstocking*) by Sweden's Astrid Lindgren are two of the most popular.

Egner and Lindgren, as well as Anne-Cath Vestly (b. 1920) and Alf Prøysen (1914–70) have been the major names in children's dramaturgy with their plays performed again and again, partly because there have been so few Norwegian plays for children and young people. The fact is that theatres have not actively sought new material and only from 1976 did authors of children's plays receive the same fees as other dramatists. Obviously, reputable authors could not afford – or did not have the time – to work for little pay. Increased remuneration itself did not lead to an immediate surge in Norwegian productions but it certainly changed the spirit in the field. Renowned authors such as Peder W. Cappelen (1931–92) and Tor-Åge Bringsværd wrote several plays which were staged by the touring Riksteatret and the Oslo Nye Teater, the two companies with the most generous children's repertoire. The Rogaland Theatre headed by Bjørn Endreson (b. 1922) has also created a unique programme for and by children.

Both Riksteatret and the Oslo Nye Teater have also had their own puppet theatres: Riksteatret for a short period of time in the 1970s,

The 1991 Oslo Nye Puppet Theatre production of Jesper Halle's *King Oscar of Nothing.*
Photo: Leif Gabrielsen.

and the Oslo Nye Teater since the beginning of the 1950s, first in collaboration with Folketeatret (People's Theatre, a popular theatre modelled after the Volksbühne in Berlin), then with Julian Strøm (b. 1901) and later with his daughter Birgit (b. 1931), both of whom are pioneers of puppet theatre in Norway.

Thanks to Birgit Strøm, Norwegian theatres were to also benefit from the extraordinary talent of the Czech Karel Hlavaty (1919–88). Hlavaty came to Norway in 1968 and created some of the finest productions – both regular and black light presentations – ever staged in Norway (for Riksteatret, Den Nationale Scene and Det Norske Teatret). However, due to the rather lukewarm attitude and poor remuneration for children's plays, Hlavaty had to supplement his income by extensive freelancing when he should have had his own theatre. His death in 1988 cost Norwegian children's theatre much. He also improved the quality of the New Theatre Company's Puppet Theatre.

Nationaltheatret staged its first production for teenagers in 1969, *Et spill om pugg* (*All About Memorization*) – still one of the few plays written for this age group. At about the same time, the company started taking its own children's productions on tour.

Swedish theatre, and specifically the company Unga Klara in Stockholm, has been a source of inspiration and motivation for Norwegians producing socially engaged theatre for children and teenagers. The radicalization of ideas and values in the 1960s contributed considerably to the genre. In its wake, several independent children's theatres emerged (there are presently sixty in Norway) challenging the meaning of the term children's theatre and the requirements needed to perform for both children and young people.

The first independent company to produce high-quality shows in this style and to make headlines was Musidra. Musidra, and other independent companies, introduced new ideas by staging innovative and committed productions; however, they also produced numerous under-rehearsed pieces and, consequently, the quality of the work varied tremendously.

Traditionally, newspaper critics have not paid much attention to children's productions; they started doing so only in the 1980s.

A new trend emerged in the early 1990s with an increasing number of established theatres putting on high-budget children's productions.

A major step was also taken when children's theatre was made part of the curriculum at Statens Teaterhøgskole (State Theatre College). All students there now take part in a children's play in Vigeland Park at the end of the second year of their three-year studies.

Harriet Eide

Puppet Theatre

The art of puppetry in Norway had a major breakthrough in 1952 when Jane and Agnar (b. 1915) Mykle, in collaboration with the Folketeatret, founded Norsk Dukketeater (Norwegian Puppet Theatre). In 1954, Julian Strøm became the manager of the theatre and in 1959 the puppet theatre became affiliated with the Oslo Nye Theater. In 1991, Kjersti Germetsen (b. 1942) became artistic director of the company.

The first puppet theatre to be associated with a major theatre company, its productions were first and foremost aimed at children. Presentations using hand-puppets or rod-puppets were most common, but plays demanding interaction between the puppet and the puppet master were also done. The interactive form was developed and elaborated from the early 1980s on.

Riksteatret, the touring theatre, operated its own puppet theatre from 1976 to 1981 and – on the initiative of Mona Wiig (b. 1944) – started a school for puppeteers. The theatre started using types of puppets hitherto little known in Norway – marionettes and humanettes – and called upon internationally acclaimed puppet artists, such as Margareta Nicolescu from Romania, for advice and assistance. When Riksteatret's puppet theatre disappeared as an autonomous unit in 1981, most of the puppeteers joined Riksteatret's regular ensemble which began staging puppet productions on a regular basis.

Hordaland Theatre, founded in 1988 under the auspices of Karel Hlavaty, has also given prominence to puppet theatre and it is now an integral part of the theatre's repertoire. The theatre offers classes in puppetry in cooperation with Riksteatret, and in 1991 Dukkeakademiet i Fredrikstad (Fredrikstad Puppetry Academy) began a training programme under the direction of Mona Wiig. Nordland Dukketeaterverksted (Puppet Theatre Workshop of Nordland) in Lofoten was also inaugurated that same year. The workshop operates as a project theatre, and tours throughout its region.

A number of independent professional puppet theatres also emerged during the 1970s. Most use a variety of types of puppets, and their presentations include solo shows as well as productions for larger ensembles. Petrusjka Theatre, founded in 1978 in Trondheim, is one such group which presents puppet theatre for adults.

The Norsk Dukketeaterforening (Norwegian Association of Puppet Theatres) organizes events for both amateurs and professionals. The association is the national branch of UNIMA (International Puppeteers Union) and included in 1992 thirty-five ensembles and 200 individuals. The association also publishes a periodical entitled *Ånd i hanske* (*Spirit in a Glove*).

Kirsten Broch

Design

Norwegian theatre has long been built on realism. Though the style is still dominant, Norwegian scenographers since World War II have made many attempts to break away from its restrictions and sets have often become somewhat abstract.

Two scenographers who contributed substantially to the form were Per Schwab (1911–70) and Arne Walentin (b. 1915). Both started in theatre before 1940 and were active for a long period after the war. Walentin's designs for Det Norske Teater's productions of *Peer Gynt* in 1948 and 1962 used projections to give the scenes an abstract character. Guy Krogh (b. 1917) – a painter of the same generation – also deserves special mention.

Norwegian scenography today is flexible and promotes such innovations as the use of abstract scenery, the use of new types of stage spaces and differing relationships between actors and audience. Innovative approaches are found alongside more conventional solutions.

Norwegian scenography has been especially influenced by Czech theatre, mainly through the work of Lubos Hruza (b. 1933), who settled in Norway toward the end of the 1960s and worked at many theatres but primarily at the Nationaltheatret. Helge Hoff Monsen (b. 1942), another of Norway's more prominent contemporary scenographers, trained in Poland and brought back a number of original ideas and notions.

Other important scenographers are Kari Gravklev (b. 1944), Tine Schwab (b. 1947), Anna Gisle (b. 1941) Kathrine Hysing (b. 1953) and John Kristian Alsaker (b. 1949); Alsaker has worked mainly for the opera.

Trine Næss

François Rochaix's 1989 Den Nationale Scene production of Ostrovsky's *The Thunderstorm*. Photo: Hans Jørgen Brun.

Theatre Space and Architecture

The first permanent theatres in Norway were built in the major cities starting at the beginning of the nineteenth century. The model was the European Baroque theatre with its proscenium arch and the orchestra pit as a physical barrier between stage and audience, with horseshoe-shaped balconies helping to separate the social classes. This type of theatre – the panoramic box – became the frame for Ibsen's plays from the middle of the century on. In 1899, the Nationaltheatret left the Christiania Theater (built in 1837) while in 1909 Den Nationale Scene in Bergen moved from the Komediehuset (built in 1800). The Trøndelag Theatre Company still uses the same 1816 building it started in.

Though many of the older theatres are still in use, they have all been modernized. Most added smaller stages during the 1960s and were upgraded again during the 1970s to accommodate more spectators and more sophisticated technical equipment.

After World War II, most of the natural energy went into rebuilding the country: infrastructures and industry had to be reconstructed and there was also an urgent need for housing. Apart from the activities of Folketeatret in Oslo – built during the 1930s when the social democratic ideology of 'enlightenment of the masses' was on the agenda – little was done in the area of theatre building. This 1,200-seat functional-style theatre is of impressive proportions and has been the home of the National Opera since 1959. It can accommodate complex designs and an orchestra; however, the theatre has several technical shortcomings.

Older Norwegian theatres generally compare well with their European counterparts although, with respect to exterior ornamentation and materials used for interior decoration, they are relatively spartan. Most theatres were equipped with raked stages (now replaced) though the Trøndelag Theatre still retains its original 1816 stage. Little by little, revolving stages were also added to the bigger theatres; some of them, however, like the one at Nationaltheatret, were removed at the beginning of the 1980s. In the 1990s, a new generation of revolving stages, with machinery occupying only a fraction of the space required by the older types, were again being installed.

It was only during the 1960s that the general economy of the country permitted a reinvigoration of the older theatres. There was an unmistakable increase of interest in technical experimentation and computer technology led to the development of more powerful, visual stage productions demanding even more space and better trained technicians.

The major theatres have for many years catered to the regions with touring productions with Riksteatret playing the key role in bringing theatre to less urban parts of the country. State policy on cultural affairs has also led to the construction of community centres which organize and host a variety of cultural events for the local population. Today, virtually every Norwegian village and community has its own such centre. Unfortunately, they are not always well suited for theatre. Nevertheless, Riksteatret has classified every one of them so as to keep track of technical installations and audience capacity. It has even renovated an old equestrian centre at Akershus Castle and Fortress in Oslo with a brand new stage and rehearsal rooms.

Most regional theatres use these cultural centres which are of little architectural interest in and of themselves. An exception is Teater Ibsen in Skien, which moved into the old Festiviteten – a prestigious ballroom of the nineteenth century. Most towns have such a ballroom (almost always called Festiviteten) which can be used for many different grand occasions. The Skien building has been completely renovated and can handle most requirements of modern stage productions.

Perhaps the most unusual theatre in the country is in Sogn og Fjordane County. In the early 1980s, a company purchased an old commercial ship and transformed it into a floating theatre. This theatre has become extremely popular in an area characterized by fjords and the sea and where boats and ferries are the common mode of transportation. The theatre can accommodate a hundred spectators.

Det Norske Teatret's new house was inaugurated in 1985. Now the largest theatre in northern Europe, it has two stages which can both be used conventionally (proscenium) or as amphitheatres. Performances have also taken place in the rehearsal room.

The 1960s and 1970s saw numerous historic factory buildings and workshops left vacant and these offered a unique opportunity to construct

Jos Groenier's 1991 Sami Theatre Company production of Brecht's *The Good Person of Setzuan*, designed by Aage Gaup.
Photo: Ola Røe.

new commercial and cultural centres. The old wharf at Åker Brygge (Åker Quay), for example, was converted into a shopping and cultural centre that included the country's first black box stage. Many independent theatre companies now work in these spaces.

In addition to the cultural centres and various small theatres, nature itself has often proved a functional setting for historical plays presented in different parts of the country. The most original production so far has been a play presented by the Samiske Teatret (Sami Theatre Company) on the heathery northern tundra of Finnmark where ice constructions were used as scenery for Brecht's *The Good Person of Setzuan*.

Steinar Vestlie

Training

Most performing arts students are trained at Statens Teaterhøgskole (State Theatre College). While the bigger theatres formerly trained their own students through apprenticeships, today (apart from Det Norske Teatret, which in collaboration with Sogn og Fjordane Teater still trains a small group of students in the art of acting in the New Norwegian linguistic variant), few theatres get involved in training on any level.

Statens Teaterhøgskole is the official educational institution for the dramatic arts. Founded in 1953, it is a three-year school admitting only seven to ten students per year. Working in cooperation with the actors' and directors' union, students study movement, voice, acting and fencing, along with regular curriculum studies in Norwegian, theatre history, literary history and drama. In 1979, the school began a degree programme in directing and in 1982 it was given university status.

In addition to Teaterhøgskole, some of the large companies, particularly at the provincial level, also have their own schools. Many of Norway's most prominent actors were trained after the war at the Studioteatret (Studio Theatre). This was an experimental group for young actors run from 1945 to 1951 by Claes Gill (1910–73) in Oslo and based on the ideas of Stanislavski. Gill, one of Norway's important actors and directors of the post-war period, gave new insights into a wide range of plays from Shakespeare to Chekhov, Brecht, Wilder, O'Neill, Sartre and Miller.

A private theatre school in Oslo called Teaterverkstedet (Theatre Workshop) also offers a one-year training course, while several county colleges (*Folkehøgskole*) also offer introductory courses in theatre. However, these courses, though decidedly above amateur level, do not provide students with professional training. The classes offered by Romerike Folkehøgskole (Romerike County College), for instance, function partly as a preparatory course for the Statens Teaterhøskole's admission examination, and partly as preparation for other jobs within the world of professional and amateur theatre.

An executive committee for cultural affairs in northern Norway (Nordnorsk Kulturråd) sought in the early 1990s to establish local training facilities for actors and theatre technicians in the north, especially for the Sami Theatre.

Students aspiring to other professions and crafts connected with the operation of theatre receive very little formal training. There is, for example, no organized training for scenographers, although a few students at Kunst og Håndverksskolen (National College of Art, Crafts and Design) and Arkitekthøgskolen (Norwegian School of Architecture) in Oslo have specialized in scenography.

There is no school for playwrights though Skrivekunstakademiet i Hordaland (Hordaland Writers' Academy) offers courses in playwriting. Those who want to become theatrical composers mainly study at Musikkhøgskolen (College of Musicology) although no specific classes in dramatic composition are offered.

Dramaturges find themselves in the same position. However, the department of theatre studies (Oslo) and the department of theatre research (Bergen) are now offering postgraduate programmes of admirable quality. In collaboration with the department of drama, film and theatre at Trondheim University, they also offer theoretical courses in many fields related to the operation and management of theatres.

Kirsten Broch

Criticism, Scholarship and Publishing

Inspired by contemporary periodicals in Germany and Denmark, Ole Rein Holm started publishing a theatre review called *Critica* in Kristiania (Oslo) in 1829. At about the same time, newspapers started featuring columns discussing theatre and the dramatic arts. The actual written play was usually treated separately from performance and the quality of the acting.

Toward the end of the century, a new naturalistic perception of the arts emerged in Norway, represented by, among others, Johan Irgens Hansen (1854–95) who wrote reviews for both Kristiania's *Intelligenseddel* and *Dagbladet* (a centre-liberal paper). He supported the Danish critic Edvard Brandes and believed that criticism should fight against the traditional declamatory style of acting. He also firmly believed that criticism should be based on clear, precise criteria.

Hansen's criticism was in many ways the extension of an analytical tradition which toward the turn of the century had to make room for a more impressionistic style, well suited to the emergence of the rotary press and penny papers. This trend found an advocate in Gunnar Heiberg (1857–1929) of *Dagbladet*, and later, with more force and conviction, in Sigurd Bødtker (1866–1928) who had a column in several newspapers; first in the right-wing *Morgenbladet* (Kristiania), then in *Verdens Gang*, *Tidens Tegn* and *Aftenposten*. His articles appeared regularly over a period of thirty years and were subsequently published in three volumes (1923–4).

Even though critics like Kristian Elster Jr (1881–1947) and Anton Rønneberg (1902–89) were interested in what was going on abroad and informed readers about new trends in theatre, impressionistic criticism persisted until well after World War II. Odd Eidem (1913–88) of *Verdens Gang* and Jan E. Hansen (b. 1959) of *Aftenposten* were representative of this school. Other critics, such as Erik Pierstorff (1926–84) of *Dagbladet*, and to some extent Odd-Stein Andersen (b. 1915) of *Aftenposten* and Bengt Calmeyer (b. 1932) of *Arbeiderbladet* (a social democratic paper), adopted a more analytic approach to theatre. Certainly, the penny press and the tabloid newspapers influenced to a great extent the more established newspapers' attitude towards theatre and criticism, although Bjørg Vindsetmo (b. 1950) and Edvard Hoem of *Dagbladet* tried to cover the more conventional theatre forms in depth.

More analytical criticism has been given consideration in the smaller newspapers, such as *Klassekampen* (a left-wing paper) by younger critics such as Janne Kjellberg (b. 1960) and Trond Aglen (b. 1957). The emergence of theatre research as an independent academic discipline at the major universities during the 1960s further encouraged the development of analytical criticism.

The only national magazine devoted to theatre has been *Spillerom* (*Open Space*) originally published by Grenland Friteater, then by Teatersentrum, and finally by the department of theatre studies at the University of Oslo. The review first concentrated on the independent theatre companies and their achievements but later – under the direction (1984–7) of Gunnar Nyquist (b. 1951) and Jon Nygaard (b. 1946) – *Spillerom* developed into a magazine for Norwegian theatre in general and has given much space to analytical, systematic criticism and discussion. *Spillerom* also writes about international trends and ideas. Theatre has also been dealt with in other literary and cultural journals such as *Kontrast* and *Dyade*.

Norwegian drama critics as far back as 1927 formed an association – Kritikerlaget for teater, musikk og ballett. The three sections of the association award an annual prize for outstanding artistic achievement. The prizes, first presented in 1939, have dealt only with activities in Oslo, something that has caused controversy in light of later theatrical activity outside the capital.

Methodological studies of theatre and theatre-related disciplines started when professorships were created at the University of Oslo in 1965 and the University of Bergen in 1975. Hans Midbøe (b. 1915) and Berit Erbe (b. 1923) were instrumental in the constitution of the new departments. The department of theatre studies and the music department at the University of Oslo later merged into a single department of music and theatre studies.

Trondheim University created a department of drama, film and theatre under the auspices of Viveka Hagnell (b. 1940). The department concentrates mainly on theatre and the pedagogy of drama and film.

During the 1980s, the University of Oslo concentrated on a sociological approach, whereas the University of Bergen focused on aesthetics and contemporary theatre. Theatre pedagogy and children's theatre has been central to the department of drama, film and theatre at Trondheim University. The different universities have tried to come to some sort of agreement as to methodology, but much has yet to be clarified.

Despite the fact that the publishing of literature about theatre has received very little monetary support, two major works have been published: Berit Erbe's study *Bjørn Bjørnsons vej mot realismens teater* (*Bjørn Bjørnson's Progression Towards Realism in Theatre*, Oslo-Bergen 1976) and Hans Midbøe's studies of *Peer Gynt* productions (*Peer Gynt, Teatret og Tiden*, Oslo, 1980). A comprehensive history of Norwegian theatre has not yet been written though such a project continues to be discussed.

Universitetsforlaget (Oslo University Press) and a few smaller publishing companies, such as Solum and Tell, have published several books about theatre, for example Tell's *Skuespillerkunst* (*The Art of Acting*) and *Regikunst* (*Stagecraft and Production*, edited by Helge Reistad, 1991). Kunnskapsforlaget in Oslo published an encyclopedia of theatre and film in 1991 covering both national and international events, theatre history and definitions. Works by Erbe and Midbøe were both published by Oslo University Press.

This meagre output can be ascribed to the fact that publishers are hesitant to invest in specialized literature in a restricted market. For a survey of Norwegian and Nordic literature on theatre research one should consult *Nordic Theatre Studies: Yearbook for Theatre Research in Scandinavia*.

Knut Ove Arntzen
Translated by Cathrin Bowen
and Elizabeth S. Rasmussen

Further Reading

Aarseth, Asbjørn. *Den Nationale Scene 1901–31*. [The National Stage 1901–31]. Oslo: Gyldendal Norsk Forlag, 1969. 499 pp.

Anker, Øyvind. *Scenekunsten i Norge fra fortid til nutid*. [Theatrical art in Norway from the beginning to the present]. Oslo: Studier i Norge, 1968. 123 pp.

Arntzen, Knut Ove. 'New Theatre in Norway: From Group Theatre to Project Theatre'. *Scandinavica* 31 (1993): 187–202.

——, and Siren Leirvåg, eds. *Vestlandsmodernismen i norsk teater*. [Western modernism and its influence on Norwegian theatre]. *Teatervitenskapelige Studier* no. 3. Bergen: University of Bergen, 1992. 113 pp.

Bringsværd, Tor Åge, and Halldis Hoaas, ds. *Norsk teaterårbok 1975*. [Norwegian theatre yearbook 1975]. Oslo: Aschehboug, 1976.

Kulturpolitikk i 1980–årene. [Cultural policy in the 1980s]. Stortingsmelding [White paper] no. 23. Oslo: 1981.

Mæhle, Leif, ed. *Det Norske Teatret: 75 År*. [The Norwegian Theatre: 75 years]. Oslo: 1988. 464 pp.

Nordic Theatre Studies: Yearbook for Theatre Research in Scandinavia, 5 vols. Copenhagen: Munksgaard, 1989–.

'Norges Offentlige Utredninger' [Report prepared by a parliamentary commission on planning and research] in *Dramatic Art*. Oslo: 1988. 245 pp.

Norsk Kulturråd. *Utredning om barneteaterarbeid i Norge*. [Report on children's theatre in Norway]. Oslo: Norsk Kulturråd, 1974.

Ny kulturpolitikk 1974. [New cultural policy 1974]. Stortingsmelding [White paper] no. 52. Oslo, 1974.

Nygaard, Knut, and Eiliv Eide. *Den Nationale Scene 1931–1976*. [The National Stage 1931–76]. Oslo: Gyldendal Norsk Forlag, 1977. 518 pp.

På norske scener. [On Norwegian stages]. Annual yearbook. Oslo: Det Norske Teatres Forening, 1987–.

Rønneberg, Anton. *Nationaltheatret gjennom femti år*. [The National Theatre: through fifty years]. Oslo: Gyldendal Norsk Forlag, 1949. 514 pp.

——. *Nationaltheatret 1949–1974*. [The National Theatre 1949–74]. Oslo: Gyldendal Norsk Forlag, 1974. 339 pp.

Sletbak, Nils, ed. *Det Norske Teatret 50 År: 1913–1963*. [The Norwegian Theatre: 50 years: 1913–63]. Oslo: Det Norske Samlaget, 1963. 487 pp.

Teaterutvalgets innstilling om dans 1973. [A committee report on dance 1973]. Oslo, 1973.

POLAND

A country of some 38 million people located in central Europe, Poland through most of the twentieth century was bounded by Germany to the west, Czechoslovakia to the south and the Soviet Union to the east and found itself regularly subject to the political pulls of both its eastern and western neighbours. By 1993, Poland still found itself bounded on the west by Germany but its southern border was now split between the Czech Republic and the Slovak Republic, and to the north and east by several different republics of the former Soviet Union – Russia, Lithuania, Belarus and Ukraine. A Slavic country itself with a history going back to the tenth century, Poland in 1993 had a land area of 311,700 square kilometres (120,300 square miles).

Historically, Poland has long found itself in complicated political situations. In 1772, for example, most of Poland was, in fact, divided up geographically among its powerful neighbours. Russia, Prussia and Austria took large pieces of Polish land and in 1792, Russia invaded what was left of the country. Poland was partitioned once more in 1793. A third partition in 1795 wiped the country off the European map entirely. Until 1918, Poland did not exist except as a piece of history, a language and a culture.

In 1918, however, with the end of World War I, the Polish state was restored to Europe, with the pianist Jan Ignacy Paderewski (1860–1941) serving as its prime minister from January to November 1919. In September 1939, German armies once more invaded Poland, this time without declaring war; a few weeks later, Soviet troops entered the country from the east. In 1941, Poland came completely under German control and between 1939 and 1945 lost nearly 20 per cent of its population, some 6 million

people. Some of the war's fiercest fighting eventually took place in and around Warsaw, the capital and cultural centre of the nation, during the Warsaw Uprising of 1944. By the end of the war, Warsaw lay in ruins.

Clearly, theatre in Poland after World War II had to re-establish itself under extremely difficult circumstances. The German occupation had brought heavy losses across the country, both in human and material terms. Virtually every theatre in the country had been destroyed and members of most theatre companies were living wherever they could. Many artists were living abroad at war's end.

Given that situation, the speed with which the theatres reopened across the country in 1945 was truly astounding. Even as the war raged elsewhere, theatre spaces were found and re-opened as German troops left city after city. The first official première of the period was actually on 1 August 1944, the very day the Warsaw Uprising broke out. A performance of *Śluby panieńskie* (*Maidens' Vows*) by Aleksander Fredro (1793–1876) was performed in Lublin by the theatre group of the First Polish Army, which had only recently arrived home from the Soviet Union. Immediately after this production, many outstanding Polish actors moved to Lublin and it was there that the first permanent, official theatre of the period was established. Plays were also being produced in Warsaw, where fighting was still going on in October.

By May 1945, when war in Europe actually ended, a dozen theatres were already functioning in Warsaw, Lublin, Kraków, and Łódź, often in buildings with broken windows, no heating and with damaged equipment. Very shortly after that, the Union of Polish Theatre Artists (ZASP) began to operate in the open once again and even theatre magazines were launched: *Teatr* and *Łódź Teatralna* (*The Theatre World in Łódź*).

In actuality, Polish theatre had never really ceased to exist under Nazi occupation and was an active part of the underground, despite being banned and despite severe repression by occupation authorities.

During the war itself, several variety theatres and a number of dramatic companies officially supported by the Nazis were actually encouraged to remain open but their repertoire had an obvious propaganda side – to show Polish culture in as primitive a light as possible. However, few people attended. These theatres were boycotted by almost the entire artistic community as well as the public at large.

During the Nazi occupation, real theatre life in Poland was clandestine. This included the activities of ZASP and a secret national Theatrical Council. The teaching of drama was organized, as were underground performances. One such was a Medieval spectacle staged by the great director Leon Schiller (1887–1954) and played in the Convent of the Samaritan Sisters in Henryków. Clandestine theatres also performed in private homes. In Kraków, Mieczysław Kotlarczyk's (1908–78) Teatr Rapsodyczny (Rhapsodic Theatre) gave several performances as did Tadeusz Kantor's (1915–90) Teatr Niezależny (Independent Theatre), a prototype for his later Cricot 2 company.

Even competitions for playwrights were clandestinely organized. Among the plays written – many of them valuable continuations of pre-war currents and trends – were *Aby podnieść różę* (*To Pick a Rose*, 1943) by Andrzej Trzebiński (1922–43); *Święto Winkelrieda* (*Winkelried's Feast*, 1944) by Jerzy Andrzejewski (1909–83) and Jerzy Zagórski (1907–84); *Orfeusz* (*Orpheus*, 1943) by Anna Świrszczyńska (1909–84); and *Homer i Orchidea* (*Homer and the Orchid*, 1944) by Tadeusz Gajcy (1922–44).

Only when the occupation came to an end could the general public openly return to theatres for the first time since 1939. As a result, these first post-war performances took on an even greater importance than usual.

Soon after the war, the state officially took over the role of sole patron of the arts. On the positive side, this meant that theatres did not have to worry about popularity at the box office; on the negative side, this also placed major limitations on artistic expression and political criticism. In accordance with principles laid down in the state's new socialist cultural policy, realism was favoured, closely following the idea of 'art for the masses'. Everything that disagreed with that ideology and philosophy was received with mistrust.

This was soon reflected in the repertoire, particularly in the absence of Polish romantic drama which had flourished as a symbol of Poland during the more than twelve decades that the country had ceased to exist as a political entity. More specifically, authorities actually banned certain of the most well known of the poetic romantic plays including *Dziady* (*Forefathers' Eve*) by Adam Mickiewicz (1798–1855); *Kordian* and the so-called 'mystical dramas' of Juliusz Słowacki (1809–49); and *Wyzwolenie* (*Deliverance*, 1903) by Stanisław Wyspiański (1869–1907). In their place, directors turned to contemporary poetic dramas which used Greek mythology as a base, among them plays by Jean Giraudoux and modern Polish writers such as Gajcy and Świrszczyńska.

It was Polish romantic drama, however – particularly the works of Mickiewicz, Słowacki, Zygmunt Krasiński (1812–59) and the neoromantic Wyspiański – which formed the backbone of the national repertoire. It was this genre too which had developed into what was probably the most important Polish performance style before the war: *Teatr Ogromny* (Monumental Theatre). Directors such as Schiller, Wilam Horzyca (1889–1959), Edmund Wierciński (1899–1955), Wacław Radulski (1904–83) and Leopold Pobóg-Kielanowski (1907–88) all shared Schiller's opinion that the plays of the romantics, as well as of Cyprian Kamil Norwid (1821–83) and Wyspiański, were the most effective works for the realization of Polish monumentalism on the stage.

The concept derived from a lecture that Mickiewicz gave in the Collège de France in 1842. In this lecture (the so-called Lesson 16), Mickiewicz anticipated that Slavic drama – represented, for example, by Krasiński's *Nie Boska komedia* (*The Undivine Comedy*, 1835) – needed to go beyond the proscenium. The concept was taken up again at the turn of the century and was used in both theory and practice by Wyspiański in such plays as *Deliverance* and *Legion* (1900), *Warszawianka* (*The Varsovienne*, 1898), *Wesele* (*The Wedding*, 1901), in productions he directed (including the world première of Mickiewicz's *Dziady*) and in designs he created for new stages and buildings (including a blueprint for an amphitheatre in Kraków).

The concept was further developed in political dramas staged by Schiller in the early 1920s. Unlike Craig, with whom he shared a number of ideas on the primacy of the director in the theatre, Schiller believed that theatre should not be separated from text. As part of his approach, he reintroduced Medieval drama into the contemporary theatre and promoted the ideas of 'the Polish Molière', Wojciech Bogusławski (1757–1829), who was considered, even by the romantic writers, to be the father of Polish national theatre. Together with set designer Andrzej Pronaszko (1888–1961), Schiller's stagings of Monumental theatrical performances utilizing romantic dramas clearly influenced the thinking of most of Poland's theatre artists at the time.

After the war, Schiller and other directors of his generation were unable to continue work in this direction because of, among other reasons, the banning of the key romantic plays.

The history of Polish theatre after 1945 can be divided into four stages, all closely related to the country's changing political situation: the transitory phase (1945–9); the period of socialist-realism and full Stalinization (1949–55); a period of relative artistic independence (1955–80); and, from 1980 to 1989, a new phase of repression and resistance culminating in the gradual destruction of the communist system and a new-found political independence in the 1990s.

Throughout these years, Poland's theatre played a key social role as artists across the country fought a quiet war and played a dangerous and daring game with political authorities. Looked at as a whole, the situation was also extremely paradoxical in that Polish theatre artists found themselves in a stable material situation during this same time thanks to the country's realization of certain socialist ideals. The tension between socialist security on the one hand, and the need to find a free dramatic voice on the other, combined to create a theatre during these decades of genuine international significance. It is clear as well that the shape of that theatre was itself a direct result of the quiet war being waged during this period against both the regime and the censors.

Though the politicization of theatrical art was not strictly enforced until about 1948, preferences in terms of repertoire could clearly be seen even earlier. Modern plays from western Europe and North America were rarely staged. Among the few western authors whose works were done at this time beside Giraudoux were Jean-Paul Sartre, J.B. Priestley, Tennessee Williams and Maxwell Anderson.

By the late 1940s, the cultural authorities, now suspicious of all foreign plays from non-socialist countries, also began to voice their concern over the dearth of contemporary Polish dramas being written and staged under the new socialist guidelines. They even suggested preferential treatment for national authors but the appeal brought little interest. The only new plays of note from this period were *Dwa teatry* (*Two Theatres*, 1946) by Jerzy Szaniawski (1886–1970) and *Niemcy* (*Germans*, 1949) by Leon Kruczkowski (1900–62).

Clearly, the main interest of Polish directors at this time continued to lie in the classics, with Shakespeare being especially favoured. Shakespeare also turned out to be a favourite author of the authorities and in 1947 the Festival of Shakespeare's Works was organized by the Ministry of Culture and Art. Virtually every company had a Shakespearian play in its repertoire since it was an acceptable opportunity to satisfy the large-scale production ambitions of directors still cut off from the Polish romantics.

One of the more original (though also marginal) companies operating during the first phase was Mieczysław Kotlarczyk's Teatr Rapsodyczny in Kraków. Founded during the Nazi occupation and operating as part of the underground, the company was initially described as 'mystical' because of its non-realistic approach and it was this lack of realism which brought it considerable difficulties in the immediate postwar period. However, Teatr Rapsodyczny – a company in which the future Pope John Paul II, Karol Wojtyła (b. 1920), actually played – did plays that were, in fact, not tolerated elsewhere, including *Król Duch* (*King Spirit*) and *Samuel Zborowski*, both by Słowacki. The theatre's aesthetics were based on the notion that the 'word' was primary with performances being musical recitations more than anything else.

To move from this rather loose first post-war period into the second stage of Poland's postwar theatre is to focus on the year 1949, when Polish authorities officially proclaimed socialist-realism as the *only* approved style in art (in the USSR it had actually been compulsory since 1934). Virtually every artists' organization quickly held a congress to discuss the new guidelines. In actuality, every one of these meetings had the same purpose: to publicly support the new edicts. Almost all the congresses issued statements denouncing trends which did not fit the new convention. It was in this way that cultural authorities essentially eliminated anything that could be considered avant-garde, patriotic, mystical, romantic or psychological. These forms were soon under attack for their 'formalism' or for being bourgeois. The only valid criterion for art at this point was its ability to help build socialism. Socialist-realism was therefore defined and then redefined many times in terms of both subject matter and style.

For example, situations and characters had to be 'typical'. There had to be a clear-cut division between 'positive' characters (workers, peasants, party intellectuals) and 'negative' ones (bourgeois capitalists, saboteurs, urbanites). The focus had to be laid on society rather than the individual. Conflict had to be 'class' oriented and had to have a positive ending so as not to discourage the public. The model was to be Soviet drama and Russian-style realism since the second half of the nineteenth century. Plays corresponding to these categories would receive state support. Later, theatres were actually required to play them.

From 1949 with the first Polish Festival of Russian and Soviet Drama, these plays constituted the largest percentage of the repertoire. And as a result, an inordinate number of plays began to appear set in factories, shipyards, cooperatives, and sometimes, as in the case of 'anti-imperialist' productions, in the offices of capitalists. Some authors, to be fair, did try to break from the style, which was perceived by most to be a rather one-sided rewriting of history. But most companies followed the new principles and all their productions became part of the class struggle.

Design, directing and even acting suddenly became drastically uniform. The most adventurous companies took the opportunity to stage classics such as *Hamlet*, Racine's *Phèdre*, and even some Shaw (*Mrs Warren's Profession*). But many individuals chose to give up their careers; those who complained publicly were simply removed from artistic life. A number of artistic directors actually lost their theatres. Actors and directors were harassed until serious work was rendered impossible.

Interestingly, a number of young directors made their débuts during this difficult period, directors who would influence the Polish theatre for years to come. Among the most important of these were Lidia Zamkow (1918–82), Kazimierz Dejmek (b. 1924), Ludwik René (b. 1914), Janusz Warmiński (b. 1922), Krystyna Skuszanka (b. 1924) and Jerzy Krasowski (b. 1925). It was this group which was most directly involved in creating the 'thaw' in Poland after Stalin's death in 1953 and which soon replaced Schiller's generation, a generation that would never again play a significant role.

Over the next few years as the schematic nature of socialist-realism started to be criticized, repertoires slowly evolved and it was possible to see both greater subtlety in performing and a new openness in staging. Design also became more fluid and realism somewhat more stylized.

Following Stalin's death, there was an almost total lifting of all stylistic guidelines and restrictions. Polish theatre became more like the European mainstream. During the next few seasons, the most important European and American plays of the previous twenty years were staged. Also staged were works by two of Poland's most avant-garde dramatists – Stanislaw I. Witkiewicz (1885–1939) and Witold Gombrowicz (1904–69).

The rules of theatrical performance were revalued and transformed, a process that also led to significant stylistic changes involving new developments in theory and practice. Brecht, Artaud and Meyerhold, for example, became subjects for renewed debate, as did Witkiewicz's theatre aesthetics.

One of the first signs of these changes was a production of Mayakovsky's *Banya* (*The Bath House*) at the Teatr Nowy in Łódź, directed by Dejmek in December 1954. A political satire by nature which diverges from most theatrical norms, it was played in a colourful futurist set. Three weeks later, the first Brecht play to be performed in Poland after the war, *Der kaukasische Kreidekreis* (*The Caucasian Chalk Circle*), was staged at Teatr Słowackiego in Kraków by Irena Babel (b. 1914).

At the Teatr Polski in Warsaw in 1955, Aleksander Bardini (b. 1913) directed a new production of *Dziady*. Fragments of *Dziady* were also staged that same season by Tadeusz Byrski (1906–87) in Kielce. The following season, Erwin Axer (b. 1917) staged another romantic tragedy, Słowacki's *Kordian*, a play of enormous patriotic and historical significance. Dejmek then turned to the world première of the play *Winkelried's Feast*, which provided a unique opportunity to look critically at the decade since 1945.

The première of *Mątwa* (*Cuttlefish*) by Witkiewicz in 1956 was the starting point for Tadeusz Kantor's Cricot 2 theatre in Kraków while Henryk Tomaszewski (b. 1924) began his Studio Pantomimy (later known as Teatr Pantomimy/Pantomime Theatre) in Wrocław that same year. Playwright Sławomir Mrożek (b. 1930) made his début in 1958 with *Policja* (*The Police*) at the Teatr Dramatyczny (Dramatic Theatre) in Warsaw, while in 1960, Tadeusz Różewicz (b. 1921) started out with *Kartoteka* (*Card Index*) at the same theatre.

The first issue of *Dialog*, the most important of Poland's many theatre magazines, was published in May 1956 under the editorship of Adam Tarn (1902–75).

This third phase – beginning in 1955–6 – was one in which all professional theatres were to undergo transformations. Everywhere, new repertoire and new approaches to staging, design and performance prevailed. Gombrowicz's *Iwona księżniczka Burgunda* (*Iwona, Princess of Burgundy*) had its première in 1957; the first performance by Jerzy Grotowski's (b. 1933) new company, Teatr 13 Rzędów (Theatre of the 13 Rows) in Opole took place in 1959; the work of poet Miron Białoszewski (1922–83) with his Teatr Osobny (Separate Theatre) in Warsaw started in 1955. During this same period one could find many daring forms of political cabaret being staged by Poland's semi-professional student theatres.

One theatre of particular importance during these years was the Teatr Domu Wojska Polskiego (Polish Army House Theatre) which began in 1955 but was taken over two years later by the Warsaw authorities and renamed the Teatr Dramatyczny (Dramatic Theatre).

Tadeusz Kantor's 1975 Cricot 2 production of *The Dead Class*.
Photo: W. Szperl.

Until 1963, it operated under the joint artistic management of Marian Meller (1905–74), Ludwik René, Jan Kosiński (1916–74) and Jan Świderski (1916–88). Its activities reflected almost everything that characterized Polish theatre of this particular phase.

Especially important at this point was the development of a new brand of political theatre in which Brecht's works played a major role. It was thanks to Teatr Dramatyczny's performances of plays such as *Der gute Mensch von Sezuan* (*The Good Person of Setzuan*, 1956) and *Schweyk im Zweiten Weltkrieg* (*Schweik in the Second World War*, 1957), directed by René and designed by Kosiński, that Brecht's plays made a decisive entry into Polish theatre.

Another theatre of importance at this time was Warsaw's Teatr Ateneum (Atheneum Theatre), run by Janusz Warmiński since 1952. The Ateneum's varied repertoire ranged from classics to modern works, from drawing-room dramas to literary adaptations. Besides Warmiński himself, the Ateneum offered regular opportunities to directors such as Konrad Swinarski (1929–75), Aleksander Bardini (b. 1919) and Andrzej Wajda (b. 1926).

After 1954, a number of important theatres were also established outside Warsaw, led by Dejmek's Teatr Nowy (New Theatre) in Łódź. Another theatre of significance at this time was the Stary Teatr (Old Theatre) in Kraków, the country's second most important city in terms of culture.

Although companies had considerable artistic freedom in style and selection of repertoire, politicians often had a decisive and destructive influence on them. Such was the case, for example, with the 1967 production of Mickiewicz's *Dziady* at the prestigious Narodowy (National) Theatre, which had been led since 1962 by Dejmek. Conservative elements within the Communist Party used this production as a pretext for political provocations which in turn led to student protests. In consequence, Dejmek was dismissed from his position at the theatre, which was forced to abandon his ambitious long-term artistic policy. This effectively marked the end of the significance of this once prestigious theatre.

Provocations of a clearly anti-semitic nature led to other changes in Warsaw at this time. The staff of Teatr Żydowski (Yiddish Theatre), including actor-director Ida Kamińska (1899–1980), Marian Melman (1900–78) and Chewel Buzgan (1897–1971), all resigned in protest and Kamińska soon after left the country. Thus, the company, perhaps the best Yiddish theatre in the world, deteriorated quickly, lost its relevance within the country and its artistic focus.

Similar experiences took place with other directors and theatres. The Teatr Dramatyczny lost direction because of political interference in the mid-1960s. When Gustaw Holoubek became its artistic director a decade later, however, audiences began to return and a number of other outstanding directors began to work there, including Jerzy Jarocki (b. 1929), who did world premières of several Mrożek works, including *Rzeźnia* (*Slaughterhouse*, 1975) and *Pieszo* (*On Foot*, 1980), and the Polish première of *Ślub* (*The Marriage*, 1974) by Gombrowicz. This situation continued for nearly a decade until the management was changed yet again.

During this period a significant number of theatres also began to take on 'alternative' characteristics. Not only Jarocki, who often worked with students, but also Swinarski, Wajda and many other directors, attempted to break with traditional staging and draw audiences directly into the performances, to make them participants, to treat time and space freely. Swinarski's production of *Dziady* in 1973 was performed not on the stage but throughout the theatre itself. Jarocki's 1979 performance, dedicated to the anniversary of Polish independence, of *Sen o bezgrzesznej* (*Dream of the Sinless One*) lasted well into the night as did Wajda's *Z biegiem lat, z biegiem dni* (*As the Years Pass, As the Days Go By*) also in 1979.

Generally speaking, 'the directors' theatre' that flourished in this phase represented a truly exceptional era in the history of the Polish stage. A whole new model of dramatic performance was developed at this time which spread throughout the country – anti-realistic, spectacular, dynamic, impressive and visually rich. This style was also amenable to literature from all periods, easily conveying current issues and relating directly to the demands of its time, however dogmatic those demands might seem in retrospect.

Perhaps the decisive factor in the shape of Polish theatre at this point was stage design. In the breakthrough of the 1950s, it not only became a visual element in performance, but was itself an interpretation of the text, a group of signs that were sometimes more meaningful to an audience than words and acting. Because of this, set designers achieved an exceptionally privileged position in Poland.

In a theatre dominated by directors and set designers, the art of acting too underwent fundamental changes. On the one hand, acting tradition in the romantic repertoire worked well in the metaphorical, anti-naturalistic theatre. On the other hand, acting styles for traditional comedy had to evolve into something more related to the new grotesque/absurdist plays being written and staged. A large, firmly established group of actors emerged to take up all these challenges and, in the process, laid new stress on the very nature of the actor's art.

The position occupied by artists and companies outside the prevailing institutionalized theatre became known as 'the second avant-garde' and, from the 1960s, as alternative theatre. The Polish theatre at this point was associated primarily with theatrical alternatives and experiments in which language barriers were insignificant.

From the very outset, the second avant-garde was not a negation of the lavish style of production introduced into Polish theatre from the mid-1950s. Rather, it was a reaction to the whole idea of theatre as something that required technological sophistication (not in great supply in Poland anyway), to theatre which needed traditional actor–audience relationships, settings, performers and recognized dramaturgical approaches. The argument went far beyond simple innovation and transformation of existing performance styles towards a search for alternative locations even outside the theatre buildings themselves.

There were other initiatives as well. Kotlarczyk and his Teatr Rapsodyczny resumed their activities during the thaw and continued until 1967 basing their work almost entirely on words, while the Teatr Pantomimy of Tomaszewski kept to the classical rules of pantomime but expanded to full evenings of dramatic plays and later created a uniquely blended type of ballet-mime performance.

At the other end of the spectrum was Miron Białoszewski's small Teatr Osobny, which functioned (in his apartment) between 1955 and 1963. His was a poetic theatre. Plays performed there constituted the materialization of dramatic miniatures based on linguistic associations. Yet it was also an extremely sophisticated theatre using only ordinary household objects.

By the mid-1970s, however, avant-garde aesthetics had evolved to a new point: the continuation of artistic research was leading away from the realm of art altogether. It had become clear that going beyond the existing conventions

Henryk Tomaszewski's 1978 Wrocławski Teatr Pantomimy production of *La Dispute*, designed by Kazimierz Wiśniak.
Photo: Marek Grotowska.

might no longer mean simply creating a new type of theatre but rather actually doing away with theatre altogether. When Grotowski decided in 1970 to break with the theatre and instead do what he referred to as para-theatrical events, the Polish avant-garde as a whole had clearly reached a turning point in its development.

Still another phenomenon of Polish theatrical life has been the student theatre, a unique form of what might in other countries be termed semi-professional theatre. The earliest student companies in the 1950s were mainly cabarets which quickly developed their own style of condensed, metaphorical sketches, often based on panto-mime. They dealt more directly than the pro-fessional theatre with political and social issues, not having to worry about subsidies or careers in the same way. The most interesting among them were Bim Bom in Gdańsk; STU (Studencki Teatr Uniwersytecki/Student University Theatre) in Kraków; Kalambur in Wrocław;

and the STS (Studencki Teatr Satyryków/Students' Satire Theatre) and the Stodoła (Barn), both in Warsaw.

In the 1960s, student companies proliferated in the country until their number reached some 200. Meanwhile, they became stylistically diver-sified with outstanding professional directors often working with them (in 1960, Jarocki directed the première of Gombrowicz's *Ślub* for the STG Company in Gliwice). The fact is that many directors and playwrights who later became famous started out in these student theatres.

By the late 1960s, several of the student groups stood apart and, in fact, became pro-fessional. Teatr Ósmego Dnia (Theatre of the Eighth Day) was created in 1964 in Poznań and has been managed by Lech Raczak (b. 1946) since 1968. The group developed its own Grotowski-influenced style of performance and quickly became the most radical and dissident group of the period. Kraków's STU, founded in

1966, initially looked for new means of expression in acting, but later, under the influence of its director Krzysztof Jasiński (b. 1943), STU performances became more and more spectacular, depending heavily on lighting effects and scenography. STU also dealt with political issues, and like Teatr Ósmego Dnia, based many of its performances on Polish contemporary poetry.

Teatr 77 in Łódź (created in 1969) became known for its environmental performances – poetic in style and topical in content. And the oldest of the student groups, Kalambur, founded in 1957, began as a more traditional cabaret group but eventually turned to experimental forms of drama. The group actually premièred *Szewcy* (*Shoemakers*) by Witkiewicz in 1965. Eventually, Kalambur became the organizer of a Festival of Student Theatres (from 1967 it was called a Festival of Open Theatre), an important biennial international gathering of alternative companies under the director of Bogusław Litwiniec (b. 1931).

All the student theatres have traditionally been interested in new methods of performance and new modes of expression. All have generally eschewed proscenium stages and written text utilizing instead various forms of collage, poetry and documentary forms. Much of it has also been derivative – the Grotowski style taken up most frequently – and on occasion productions in the style of major directors such as Swinarski and Jarocki or works in the Różewicz absurdist style can be seen. In the late 1960s and early 1970s, the Polish student theatre movement was one of the main centres of Polish counter-culture.

It was at this same time that a number of even newer student companies emerged. Among the most interesting was the Akademia Ruchu (Academy of Motion) based in Warsaw. The group, led by Wojciech Krukowski (b. 1944), based its work in movement and staged a number of almost dance-like events. It also organized several street happenings. Another student company of interest was the Scena Plastyczna (Plastic Stage) which began in 1970 at the Catholic University in Lublin. Based on the work of Leszek Mądzik (b. 1945), the group's performances have existed on the very edges of theatre – mobile, three-dimensional compositions, involving shapes and figures, light and darkness. The productions have also involved music with the performers serving the director's vision as living sculptures.

Still another group of note stemming from the student movement is the Stowarzyszenie Gardzienice (Gardzienice Association) founded in 1977 by Włodzimierz Staniewski (b. 1950). Based in the village of Gardzienice near Lublin, the group combines anthropological research in the region with its own style of actors' training. The resulting performances involve elements of the local folklore.

Up to 1980, Poland underwent a series of massive social protests aimed at changing the political direction of the country. Led by the Solidarity movement and union leader Lech Wałęsa (b. 1943), actors, directors and stage designers found themselves caught up in these national protests. It was not unusual during this period to find artists aiding significantly in the staging of national events or even reciting protest poetry in factories and shipyards. In 1981, martial law was imposed; as a result both theatrical and political protest activities moved inside the still powerful Catholic Church. Although theatres soon resumed public production, church productions continued to hold on strongly to audiences. At the height of these protests, theatre people were even refusing to appear on television or radio, a boycott that lasted from December 1981 well into 1983.

Few stage performances at this time could match the events happening in the streets. Those that did clearly reflected contemporary events – a documentary collage directed by Izabella Cywinska (b. 1935) at Teatr Nowy (New Theatre) in Poznań focusing on a 1956 workers' uprising, and massive stagings by student directors of *Dziady* and *Kordian* in a Katowice sports stadium each attracted more than 4,000 spectators in a kind of patriotic happening. Certainly, it was a clear example of mass performance, in which Mickiewicz's dreams of a Monumental Theatre quite unexpectedly began to be realized.

The events of 1980–2 did not, in and of themselves, have a direct influence on the artistic side of Polish theatre, but they did have an impact on its structure. The aforementioned 'church theatre' continued to be produced while at the same time the student theatre movement shrunk in size and significance. And there were frequent changes of directors in the professional theatres which caused much chaos.

Polish subordination to the Soviet Union ended in 1989 with the collapse of communism in Poland. With independence came significant changes to the system in place since the war and a sudden switch to a market economy.

The long struggle against censorship, the domination of political issues in the theatre – issues in the foreground for more than forty years – was finally over. With it came the end of an era during which theatre fulfilled political as well as artistic aims and had a special place in the life of the nation.

Freed of patriotic duties and of monitoring imposed by communist authorities, Polish artists since 1989 have been attempting to concentrate on purely aesthetic matters. However, every artist in the country had benefited socially from state aid in the past. The rapid reduction of such patronage has forced many theatrical groups to virtually give up artistic ambitions in their search for audiences.

The period after 1989 saw the quick growth of those acting companies and artists such as Cricot 2 who had established positions earlier. Many of the stage directors who had made their débuts in the mid-1980s entered the new decade with completely different attitudes. And there was a return to realism in many of the theatres. Tadeusz Bradecki (b. 1955), manager of the Stary Theatr since 1991, Rudolf Zioło (b. 1952) and Krzysztof Babicki (b. 1956) are probably the most outstanding representatives of this increasingly prominent neo-realist trend. This movement back to relatively simple, traditional means of expression on the part of directors is obviously linked to changes in repertoire at the majority of Polish theatres, where contemporary plays of manners, comedy and farce have begun to dominate.

At the same time, alternative theatre has, interestingly, retained its significant position. Teatr Ósmego Dnia returned from abroad in 1990 and began attracting audiences. The work of Stowarzyszenie Gardzienice, particularly its *Carmina Burana* in 1991, has remained popular and the company has continued to participate in international festivals. Towarzystwo Wierszalin (Wierszalin Association), still another new group, has been building on the anthropological programme of Gardzienice, and has based its work on the folk culture of Poland's eastern regions. The Scena Plastyczna and other avantgarde groups from Lublin also continue their work – Provisorium, Grupa Chwilowa (Temporary Group) and Scena 6 (Stage 6).

As one indication of this new direction, in 1992 the annual Warsaw Festival of theatres from outside the capital was nearly wholly devoted to alternative theatre for the first time. One could see in groups such as the Witkiewicz Theatre from Zakopane – founded in 1985 by Andrzej Dziuk (b. 1954) – stage production styles of many generations. In this, it was creating still another original kind of spectacle, both ambitious and popular and attracting a broad audience. This was perhaps the clearest indication of where the rich and complex structure of contemporary Polish theatre was headed in the 1990s.

Structure of the National Theatre Community

The structure of the modern Polish professional theatre was formed in the late 1940s and early 1950s. Its essential shape was decided – though there were initiatives and ideas from the theatre community – by the internal political policies of the state and was heavily influenced by the Soviet Union. Other than the clear need to rebuild cultural life after years of war and occupation, this policy focused on the nationalization of theatre companies and the dissemination of cultural products as defined by the Polish Communist Party.

The importance of theatre to the new communist government was clear even before the war ended. The Polish Committee for National Liberation, itself created in territory occupied by the Soviet army, established a special department for theatre during the war. Later subsumed by the Theatre Department of the Ministry of Culture in the new Provisional government, the policies between 1944 and 1954 saw about thirty buildings and theatres set up for new cultural purposes. By 1947, over forty dramatic theatres were operating in Polish territory including new theatres in the expanded western part of the country (for example, in Wrocław and Jelenia Góra).

Opera theatres were set up in Poznań, Bytom, Wrocław and Warsaw with two additional operetta theatres in Lublin and Łódź.

The majority of these theatres were already receiving subsidies from various sources (including local authorities and social organizations). However, in 1945, the formal process of nationalization began, a process which took about ten years to complete for most theatres (in the case of puppet theatres, almost twenty). One of the first stages was the clear separation of amateur theatre groups from professionals. Next, all professional theatres were to be financially supported directly by the Ministry of Culture and Art. By government decree in 1950, professional theatres were all given official status as state enterprises with guaranteed funding which was to come directly from the state treasury.

By 1949, the state effectively had full control over the theatres. The Ministry of Culture's various agencies approved not only budgets but also the choice of employees as well as repertoires. Policies for choosing plays were actually worked out at the central level. After 1955, some of these prerogatives were delegated to local authorities and later to the theatres themselves but the Theatre Department of the Ministry of Culture retained supervisory and advisory functions as well as the final say in disputes. In practical terms, the new decentralization was not always effective but it did ensure an active censorship system, a system that operated through the mid-1970s.

In 1975, Polish theatres gained some control of their own budgets and in the 1980s, controls were modified still further with the State Fund for the Promotion of Culture becoming the principal conduit for state support. On average, the fund covered up to 80–90 per cent of each theatre's budget. At the same time, professional theatres were granted new tax status. Not only was the tax burden lessened but also the directors of the theatres were given even more autonomy.

With the many political changes at the end of the 1980s, the strings loosened still further with only the largest theatres still connected to the Ministry of Culture. In Warsaw, only the Teatr Narodowy (National Theatre), and in Kraków only the Stary, remained tied to the ministry and among the musical theatres Teatr Wielki (Grand Theatre). Others operated under local administrative authorities. In 1991, large subsidies were to be given only to the 'national theatres', such as the Narodowy and the Teatr Wielki, with another forty theatres receiving only partial subsidies from the state. It was up to provincial governments to find the remaining funds. Some other theatres became charges of municipal authorities.

These changes partly corresponded to suggestions from the theatre community. There was a sense, for instance, that the state was maintaining theatres that were artistically dead.

No one could judge the likely effect of privatization and the other political and economic changes that Poland was experiencing in the early 1990s.

In 1992, there were in total sixty-nine dramatic theatres operating (most with more than one stage) in thirty-six cities. There were another thirty puppet theatres operating in twenty-two cities, most of them with technical workshops and their own auditoriums. The largest number of dramatic theatres (sixteen) was located in Warsaw, while Kraków had five and Łódź four. There were also seventeen musical theatres.

Members of all professional theatrical companies – actors, directors, and in the case of musical theatres, singers, dancers and conductors – were generally operating on renewable one-year contracts.

All theatre professionals in the 1990s were members of the Union of Polish Theatre Artists (ZASP). ZASP, founded in 1918, was actually dissolved twice (in 1950 and 1982) for political reasons, and for a long time existed under the name SPATIF-ZASP. Its formal and actual functions have evolved through the years, since it was never a trade union in the strict sense. But it has consistently been the only professional organization truly representing the theatre community.

In addition to these large professional theatres, there have also been theatres since the late 1950s much less institutional in nature. Frequently ephemeral, these alternative groups have appeared on the margins through the initiative of specific individuals or groups, most often student groups. The largest numbers of these theatres emerged in the late 1950s, again in the late 1960s and early 1970s, and then again in the 1980s.

In the 1990s, many new small theatres sprang up, functioning sometimes under the auspices of the state, sometimes privately, sometimes under the aegis of youth organizations. Another 1990s phenomenon was the increase in jobbing (that is the hiring of individual performers for specific productions).

Festivals of various sorts have long played an important role in theatrical life. The first festivals organized after the war were in fact national competitions with the finals taking place in Warsaw. Since 1959, most of these national festivals have tended to be held annually in the same cities, with the number rapidly increasing in the 1960s and 1970s.

Most professional theatres are encouraged to

perform regularly outside their home cities. Guest performances on an exchange basis are also quite popular. Since 1982, the Teatr Rzecz-pospolitej (Theatre of the Republic), in 1991 renamed Krajowe Centrum Teatralne (National Theatre Centre), came into being specifically to coordinate such national exchanges. Formalities connected with performing abroad have traditionally been handled by the state agency, PAGART.

Artistic Profile

Companies

When socialist-realism held sway in Poland, all companies found themselves under an obligation to comply with its political and artistic strictures. One company, however, embraced them willingly and recognized them as its own. It was the Teatr Nowy in Łódź, run by the director Kazimierz Dejmek. Composed of young and generally unknown actors, the company wanted to serve 'political reality and be its creators . . . we do not want to answer needs of an elite of intellectuals, snobs, and petit-bourgeois'. Eschewing the classics, they staged only contemporary, politically involved plays.

After the 'thaw' of 1956 (known in Poland as the October Breakthrough), socialist realism was immediately rejected by everyone. The drive to innovate in terms of repertoire and means of expression was spearheaded by Warsaw's Teatr Dramatyczny. In 1957, for example, it produced *Les Chaises* (The Chairs) by Eugène Ionesco, directed by Ludwik René, with designs by Jan Kosiński. Over the coming years, the Dramatyczny would become the centre for a whole new style of acting. That same year, 1957, Halina Mikolajska (1925–89) directed the première of Gombrowicz's *Iwona, Princess of Burgundy* there and Świderski directed Mrożek's *Police*.

In both these productions, the new style could be seen, a much more metaphoric style rooted in Stanislavski but clearly connected to the Polish romantic tradition. The style was extended in Wanda Laskowska's (b. 1925) production of *W małym dworku* (In a Small Country House) and *Wariat i zakonnica* (The Madman and the Nun), both by Witkiewicz (1959), and in *Kartoteka* (Card Index, 1960) by Różewicz with a set by Kosiński. The same can be said of productions by René and Kosiński, especially *The Good Person of Setzuan* (1956) by Brecht, Sartre's *Le Diable et le Bon Dieu* (The Devil and the Good Lord, 1960) with Gustaw Holoubek

(b. 1923), one of the country's brightest young actors, in the leading role of Goetz. The whole Polish theatre seemed to follow Teatr Dramatyczny's lead. The result was a period in which hundreds of new, interesting and ambitious performances, styles and approaches could suddenly be seen.

During this same period, Konrad Swinarski returned home from a training period at the Berliner Ensemble and directed Brecht's *Herr Puntila* at the Dramatyczny, and *Der Dreigroschenoper* (The Threepenny Opera) at Warsaw's Teatr Współczesny (Contemporary Theatre), another group which would become one of the important companies in the capital over the next decades. Like René and Kosiński, who had pioneered productions of Brecht in Poland, Swinarski did more in directing the two plays than imitate the Berliner Ensemble style. An eager student, he quickly began to diverge from the established Brecht acting traditions, providing yet another fresh alternative to the entrenched Stanislavski system.

The Teatr Współczesny, run by director Erwin Axer and Jerzy Kreczmar (1902–85), began to turn their company into what can be described as a literary theatre with a unique visual style. A teacher at the Warsaw Theatre School for many years, Axer quickly became a major figure in terms of contemporary Polish staging. His imaginative productions were moderated only by his belief that production was ultimately subordinate to text. The Współczesny prided itself on being the home of the most interesting new drama in Poland.

In 1957, the Polish première of Beckett's *En attendant Godot* (Waiting for Godot) was performed there directed by Kreczmar. Also produced were plays by Thornton Wilder, Max Frisch, Eugène Ionesco, John Osborne, Harold Pinter, Edward Albee and Peter Weiss, all directed by Erwin Axer. His psychologically grotesque version of Brecht's *Der aufhaltsame Aufstieg des Arturo Ui* (The Resistible Rise of

Arturo Ui, 1962) with Tadeusz Łomnicki (1918–92) in the title role, was arguably the definitive interpretation of the play. Perhaps most important of all, Teatr Współczesny, became the home for new plays by Mrożek of which *Tango* (in 1965) was the most renowned.

Outside Warsaw, the most important company in the country has been the Stary Theatre in Kraków. First under Władysław Krzemiński (1907–66) and then under Zygmunt Hübner (1930–89), the Stary was perhaps the outstanding theatre in Poland between 1955 and 1989, a reputation earned through its core of excellent actors and directors, including Hübner, Jerzy Jarocki, Swinarski, Andrzej Wajda and Lidia Zamkow. At the Stary Teatr in Kraków, Wajda directed a modern version of Sophocles' *Antigone* in 1983 and then returned to Dostoevsky's prose, staging an adaptation of *Prestupleniye i nakazaniye* (*Crime and Punishment*) in 1984, a production later seen at many international festivals. At the same theatre, Jarocki mounted a powerful production of Calderón's *La vida es sueño* (*Life is a Dream*, 1983), a positive return to the best traditions of the Stary.

Another important company outside the capital has been the Teatr Ludowy (People's Theatre), opened in a suburb of Kraków called Nowa Huta, an entirely new, 'model' city built around a large steel works in 1955. From the beginning it was run by directors Jerzy Krasowski and Krystyna Skuszanka with Józef Szajna (b. 1922) as the theatre's designer. Intended as a true 'popular' theatre, Krasowski, Skuszanka and Szajna focused their attention not only on developing a new type of repertoire but particularly on the development of new staging methods which were, in fact, closely related to experiments by the Soviet avant-garde of the 1920s.

When Skuszanka and Krasowski left the theatre in 1963, Szajna took over as managing director, remaining in the position until 1966. Under his leadership, the theatre took Szajna's unique artistic vision, making it the first major designer's theatre in the country. Everything, in fact, became subject to Szajna's extraordinary vision of neo-expressionist performance.

One of the largest companies in Poland was the Warsaw-based Naradowy Theatre, the official Polish National Theatre, a title that should have made it the most important company but often made people suspicious about its approaches.

In 1962, Kazimierz Dejmek became the artistic director of Teatr Narodowy. Until his dismissal in 1968, he pursued a policy of continuing Schiller's style of work, especially in his choice of plays and staging methods. Together with stage designer Andrzej Stopka (1904–73), Dejmek even developed a new specific style for Medieval plays, so as to make them meaningful to present-day audiences. He returned to the romantic tradition and staged many contemporary plays as well.

From 1968 to 1982, the Narodowy was run by the controversial Adam Hanuszkiewicz (b. 1924) who had run the Teatr Powszechny from 1963. His productions were rooted (as so many were) in the notion of the director's omnipotence, a predilection for effects, novelty and originality with a deliberately simplified meaning. Hanuszkiewicz's period of work was marked by a series of particularly heated arguments and discussions about this approach. In 1982, he was sacked by the authorities. In 1984, the building itself was destroyed by fire.

Among the more unusual groups was Jerzy Grotowski's Actors' Lab Theatre, originally established in Opole and eventually settling in Wrocław. Among his many goals was research on the actor and development of a new relationship between actor and audience. His Poor Theatre experiments became world famous in the late 1960s and 1970s.

In 1982, he left Poland as did many members of his state supported research group. His longtime dramaturge, Ludwik Flaszen (b. 1930), took over the Lab but two years later – after twenty years of existence – the company officially ceased operation. A year later, one of the Lab actors, Zbigniew Cynkutis (1938–87), created a company called Drugie Studium Wrocławskie (Second Wrocław Studio) but this undertaking ended with his untimely death in a car crash.

In 1981, Dejmek, for several years *persona non grata* because of his provocative theatrical challenges to the state, returned to Warsaw to take over the Teatr Polski, a company that had been in decline for many years. Dejmek brought with him a repertory programme that he had devised for the Teatr Narodowy many years before – the staging of Polish drama first and foremost, both neo-romantic and contemporary. He also directed world premières of several Mrożek plays – *Ambasador* (*Ambassador*, 1981), *Letni dzień* (*A Summer Day*, 1983), *Kontrakt* (*Contract*, 1986) and *Portret* (*Portrait*, 1987). During this period, the Polski achieved genuine note.

The Teatr Ateneum under Janusz Warmiński

Jerzy Jarocki's 1991 Stary Teatr production of Witold Gombrowicz's *The Marriage*, designed by Jerzy Juk-Kowarski.
Photo: Wojciech Plewiński.

has been still another company of importance in the decades since the 1960s. Boasting a wide-ranging international repertoire at this time and a stylistic uniqueness, the Ateneum staged everything from a contemporary *Hamlet* directed by Warmiński in 1983 to adaptations of Gombrowicz's *Pornografia* (*Pornography*, 1983) and *Trans-Atlantyk* (*Trans-Atlantic*, 1984) directed by Andrzej Pawowski (b. 1953). In 1988, the company staged the Polish première of *Samoubiytsa* (*The Suicide*) by Russian writer Nikolai Erdman and, from time to time, has even tried its hand at musicals.

After Axer retired from Teatr Współczesny in 1981, his successor, Maciej Englert (b. 1946) began staging both Brecht and Bulgakov – *Mahagonny* (1982) and *Master i Margerita* (*Master and Margarita*, 1987). Another company that deserves mention is Teatr Powszechny in Warsaw, taken over in 1975 by Zygmunt Hübner. The first production under his management was that of *Sprawa Dantona* (*Danton's Case*) by Stanisława Przybyszewska (1901–35), directed by Andrzej Wajda. It established its position as a leading Warsaw company, renowned particularly for the political importance of its productions, its ability to make intellectual statements through its choice of Polish and foreign plays and its ensemble style of acting.

During the 1970s and 1980s, Cricot 2 attracted attention both nationally and internationally with a series of unique productions created by its founder, Tadeusz Kantor. Among them were *Dead Class* and *Wielopole, Wielopole* (see **Directors, Directing and Production Styles**), *Niech szczzną artyści* (*Let Artists Die*, 1986) and *Już nigdy tu nie powrócę* (*I Will Never Come Back*, 1988). The death of Kantor at the end of 1990, during rehearsal of a performance entitled *Dzisiaj są moje urodziny* (*Today Is My Birthday*), however, meant the end of the company, even though this production was staged by the group in 1991. Controversies quickly arose over the work of Janusz Wiśniewski (b. 1949), who tried to follow the style of Cricot 2 in his stage productions, from *Koniec Europy* (*The End of Europe*, 1983) to *Olśnienie* (*Dazzle*, 1991).

Perhaps the most original of the Warsaw theatres during the 1980s and into the 1990s was the Studio Theatre. Under Józef Szajna the theatre reached national and even international note with a series of visually spectacular productions. Jerzy Grzegorzewski took over as manager in 1982 and has developed his own original style of impressionist and 'post-modern' staging in such works as *Powolne ciemnienie malowideł* (*The Slow Dimming of Paintings*), after Malcolm Lowry in 1988; and *Miasto liczy psie nosy* (*The Town Counts Dogs' Noses*), his own script, in 1991.

Dramaturgy

Romanticism has been the most important style in Polish theatre since the nineteenth century but another dramatic form developed in the 1920s which has come to rival the romantic. Known within the country as 'the Polish grotesque' and outside eastern Europe as the 'Polish Theatre of the Absurd', the form, developed decades earlier, came to real prominence in the decade after 1955 when many new styles were allowed to be played for the first time.

An offshoot of tragi-comedy, its most important feature has been the parabolic nature of the events presented and its utilization of specific signs, metaphors and pseudonyms for reality, speaking in an indirect, allusive way with a kind of black humour. Links to Ionesco and Dürrenmatt are obvious but because of its political and historic nature (relating to Poland's political and geographic situation in the twentieth century) this specific approach to dramaturgy and its developing popularity with writers, directors and audiences has made it unique.

The movement toward the grotesque originated, for the most part, in Stanisław Ignacy Witkiewicz's first plays as well as in his essays on 'pure form'. In these works, Witkiewicz expressed his arguments for an extreme, anti-realistic concept of drama which would render both the plot and character motivation absurd. In essence, Witkiewicz was creating a specific kind of tragi-comedy with an obvious historical meaning connected to his own experiences and attitudes to such events as the Russian Revolution of 1917.

Witold Gombrowicz later utilized and developed the basic tenets of Witkiewicz's new poetics but without the theoretical orthodoxy. Dramatists working in the country from about 1955 on were discovering the works of both Witkiewicz and Gombrowicz at about the same time they were first seeing foreign works by such writers as Ionesco and Beckett.

Sławomir Mrożek, one of these young Polish writers, created a still newer version of the grotesque which was in a way the reverse of the traditional well-made thesis play. In Mrożek's work, the action is absurd and real meaning is hidden under a bizarre and grotesque story.

Tadeusz Różewicz, another writer working in this style, took a different approach again. His basic practice was to use elements from newspapers, radio and everyday language as 'ready-made' theatrical objects, giving them the status of art simply by choosing them.

A similar trend could be observed in the works of other playwrights who also emerged at this time – Jarosław Abramow-Newerly (b. 1933), Janusz Krasiński (b. 1928) and Stanisław Grochowiak (b. 1934) – constituting a second wave of the Polish grotesque. Others followed including Zbigniew Herbert (b. 1924) and Ireneusz Iredyński (1939–85) whose works were based on much more brutal subjects yet still retained a metaphoric and stylistic sophistication.

By the mid-1970s, the prevailing Polish grotesque style began to fade away. Both Mrożek in *Emigranci* (*The Emigrants*, 1974)

and Różewicz in *Do piachu* (*Six Feet Under*, 1979) turned to forms of neo-realism.

Attempts to revive poetic drama were made by such writers as Jarosław Marek Rymkiewicz (b. 1935) and Ernest Bryll (b. 1935) whose play *Rzecz listopadowa* (*November Case*, 1968) achieved particular attention. Other important trends characterized by the use of historico-political parables and quasi-historical themes to comment more or less subtly on contemporary events have been represented by Tomasz Łubieński (b. 1938), Władysław Terlecki (b. 1933) and Jerzy S. Sito (b. 1934).

By the late 1980s, relatively few works were being created by a new generation of dramatists but among those who were developing in notable ways were Jerzy Żurek (b. 1946), Tadeusz Słobodzianek (b. 1955) and Tadeusz Bradecki (b. 1955). Some were dealing with political themes much more openly. The most interesting play of the period was probably *Polowanie na karaluchy* (*Hunting Cockroaches*,

Laco Adamik's 1991 Teatr Ateneum production of Janusz Głowacki's *Hunting Cockroaches*, designed by Barbara Kędzierska.
Photo: Z. Rytka.

1986) by Janusz Głowacki (b. 1938), a play written in the USA and staged on Broadway. Audiences, however, were still looking to the old masters like Różewicz (*Pułapka/The Trap*, written in 1982) and Mrożek (*Portret*, 1987) for insight into their rapidly changing society.

Directors, Directing and Production Styles

Leon Schiller, without doubt the most influential, famous and controversial director during the first half of the twentieth century, headed the Teatr Wojska Polskiego (Polish Army Theatre) in Łódź just after World War II. An advocate of Monumental Theatre and the use of Polish romantic plays on the stage, Schiller's inclination toward the political could also be seen in his post-war production of *Krakowiacy i Górale* (*Krakovians and Highlanders*), a play by Wojciech Boguslawski (1767–1829) which, as interpreted by Schiller, was full of recognizable topical references. A later production of Shakespeare's *The Tempest* (1947) was seen by Schiller as 'an intellectual morality play'. In Schiller's interpretation, Prospero was portrayed as Shakespeare himself and was, to some extent, Schiller's own spokesman.

Many Schiller productions from this time were staged as clear moral parables of good and evil – Fernando de Rojas's *La Celestina* (1947) and Gorki's *Lower Depths* (1949) among others. In *Kram z piosenkami* (*A Stall Full of Songs*, 1945) and *Gody Weselne* (*Wedding Ceremony*, 1945), Schiller even turned to musical folk forms to make his points.

Another major pre-war actor and director of significance was Juliusz Osterwa (1885–1947) who in the 1920s and 1930s wanted to create a company that would be bound together by a rebirth of the 'human' factor in the theatre. Unfortunately, his ideas were considered by the new regime after the war to be useless and alien. Nevertheless, his Reduta company had influence far beyond its time.

Still another director of note during this period was Edmund Wierciński (1899–1955), who before the war was a member of the Reduta Theatre. Fond of classical plays such as Corneille's *Le Cid* (produced in 1948) and Slowacki's *Fantazy* (also in 1948), but responsive as well to current issues, his production of Giraudoux's *Electre*, prepared during the war but not staged until 1946, was legendary. In it, he argued that sacrifices were important if made in the name of truth, an obvious reference to the Warsaw Uprising of 1944. Much praised for its artistic values, *Electre* was, unfortunately, also the first post-war performance to be banned by the state censor. At the same time, the experimental Scena Poetycka (Poetic Stage) in Łódź where *Electre* was produced, was also closed down.

One must also speak here of the post-war work of Iwo Gall, a director and set designer with the Reduta, author of several books on theatrical architecture, teacher and wartime manager of a secret studio for actors. In his productions, Gall stressed theatricality and did not try to disguise the fact that his plays were themselves theatrical events. He was one of the first in Poland to use open set changes. His functional stage designs (often with 'good' and 'evil' sides as in Medieval Mystery plays) and his clearly recognizable style of directing emphasized ensemble over individuals.

Erwin Axer, a student of Schiller before World War II at Warsaw's State Institute of Theatrical Art, was active both in Poland and abroad, particularly at the Burgtheater in Vienna. He owed his position as a stage director in Poland to his ability to combine traditional literary and acting traditions with modern set designs and repertoire. A longtime lecturer at the Drama Academy in Warsaw, he educated many generations of Polish stage directors. In turn, Kazimierz Dejmek, whose career in the Polish theatre also spanned many decades, was a main link to pre-war traditions: Monumental Theatre (in which he combined Medieval and romantic motifs with folkloric ones) and neo-realism, reflected particularly in his productions of contemporary drama.

Konrad Swinarski was arguably the most brilliant of all Poland's many outstanding directors since World War II, despite the fact that he never actually ran his own theatre nor even attempted to establish a company of his own. After working in Warsaw at all the major theatres – the Współczesny, Dramatyczny and Ateneum – and after training with the Berliner Ensemble, Swinarski worked most often with the Stary Teatr in Kraków and was tremendously influential in developing its reputation, style and method of work.

Swinarski also directed abroad with some regularity – especially in Austria, Switzerland, Italy, Israel and the USSR – generally doing productions of plays by Dürrenmatt, Mayakovsky and Peter Weiss. In Poland, his most important productions were of plays by romantic and neo-romantic writers, and his work was compared to Leon Schiller's forty years before. Essentially, Swinarski's directorial genius lay in his ability to combine the many different and often contradictory trends of Polish and foreign traditions – the political and poetic tradition of the Polish romantics, for example – with a kind of Brechtian historical analysis/social interpretation of a play. His style also reached back to German expressionist traditions as well as forward to the contemporary 'anti-aesthetics' of such writers as Witkiewicz and Gombrowicz.

Another important director closely linked to the Stary Teatr was Jerzy Jarocki. Like Swinarski's, Jarocki's productions were unusually lavish, well composed and meticulously planned. However, the most crucial element was his ability to translate text into physicality and his use of movement and mime in particular styles for each play. Jarocki played an exceptional role as an interpreter of Polish playwrights such as Gombrowicz, Mrożek and

Różewicz. Especially important was his work on Witkiewicz. It was Jarocki who gave them a special theatrical shape which revealed both their unique styles and meanings.

Zygmunt Hübner first came to attention as the innovative director of Gdańsk's Teatr Wybrzeże (Seashore Theatre) with such plays as Witkiewicz's *Szewcy* (*Shoemakers*, 1956), which was later banned by the censors. He continued along the same provocative political lines when he moved to Kraków's Stary Teatr in 1963. When the authorities dismissed him from there in 1969, Hübner returned to Gdańsk, where he staged an immensely popular production based on James Joyce's *Ulysses* in 1970. In 1975, he became director of the Teatr Powszechny in Warsaw where he continued to explore contemporary Polish and foreign drama through cleverly camouflaged anti-totalitarian productions. The ongoing work by both Dejmek and Hübner was closely followed by large audiences not only for artistic innovation but also for their political links to current issues.

Andrzej Wajda's 1975 Teatr Powszechny production of Stanisława Przybyszewska's *Danton's Case*, designed by Wajda and Krystyna Zachwatowicz.
Photo: R. Pajchel.

Still another important Polish director is Andrzej Wajda, known abroad primarily as a film director. Wajda began to direct in theatre as early as the mid-1950s. His stage style was easy, somewhat eclectic, visually attractive, but always based on precise psychological analysis. Of particular importance were his work with the Stary Teatr, his experiments in direct contact with the audience and his productions of Dostoevsky adaptations: *Biesy* (*The Possessed*, 1971) and *Nastasya Filipovna* (based on *The Idiot*, 1977), which was first performed in 'open rehearsals'. Some of Wajda's productions were later filmed – *Wesele* (*The Wedding*, 1963) by Wyspiański and *Sprawa Dantona* (*Danton's Case*) by Stanisława Przybyszewska, first seen at the Teatr Powszechny in Warsaw in 1975.

Also outside Warsaw, a number of attempts at transferring avant-garde trends and styles into the professional mainstream were tried by director Kazimierz Braun (b. 1936) in Lublin and in the Teatr Współczesny in Wrocław. In two of his major productions, both based on Różewicz plays – *Stara kobieta wysiaduje* (*Old Woman Broods*, Lublin, 1973) and *Przyrost naturalny* (*Birth Rate*, Wrocław, 1979) – elements of happenings, environmental events, improvisation, chance, games, and even Grotowski-inspired projects (including links between actors and viewers) were introduced.

Jerzy Grzegorzewski, a director-designer, made his début in 1967, working first in Łódź, then Warsaw at the Ateneum and then as director of Teatr Polski (Polish Theatre) in Wrocław. Like Braun, Grzegorzewski leaned toward the avant-garde in his productions – *Le Balcon* (*The Balcony*, 1972) by Genet along with adaptations of Kafka, Joyce and plays by Różewicz. He usually designed his own sets often using ready-made objects such as old machinery and musical instruments. His performance spaces were also non-traditional (cloakrooms, foyers and even the auditorium seating area). His work slowly evolved toward auteur-style creativity in which – adopting either a literary text, or simply some literary motif as his point of departure – he would single-handedly develop all aspects of a production.

Grzegorzewski's performances were consistently delicate in mood, sometimes almost abstract in composition and heavily dependent on lighting for their effects.

Similar evolution may be observed in the work of Krystian Lupa (b. 1943), a stage director working regularly with the Stary Teatr in Kraków. In his productions (his own adaptations of prose, such as *The Brothers Karamazov* by Dostoevsky, *The Dreamers* by Musil and *Kalkwerk* by Thomas Bernhard), stage design is less important than in Grzegorzewski's work. He has developed for his actors a subtly emotional style of acting while still allowing them to render psychological truth.

In 1956, director and stage designer Tadeusz Kantor, with a group of his friends (most of whom were visual artists), opened Cricot 2 in the basement of a sixteenth-century Kraków palace. The originality of Kantor's approach was apparent from the beginning as he began to create a new type of performance based not on theatrical ideas but on ideas prevailing in the visual arts.

In the first stage of Cricot 2's operation (1956–75), Kantor used the plays of Witkiewicz (and Witkiewicz's concept of pure form). Although the aesthetic principles pursued in subsequent Cricot 2 productions derived directly from abstraction, action painting, constructivism and the anti-aesthetics of Marcel Duchamp's dada experiments, Kantor's performances were always rooted in the theatre. They were also, however, rooted in a minimalist acting style, a simplified type of actor interpretation which was subordinate to the overall vision. Kantor created with Cricot 2 essentially plotless compositions in which dramaturgy was reduced to a mere guideline for movement based on a 'playing' with things – usually visual objects.

In 1965, Kantor organized the first happening in Poland and after that he loosened the structure of his shows even more. But he never confused happenings with his other theatre performances. In fact, while organizing happenings, Kantor would often simultaneously devise other performances, even some in which text played a role.

His 1975 production of *Umarła klasa* (*The Dead Class*) was, for example, both a spectacular event and a thoughtful and literate dramatic poem, at once metaphysical and symbolic. The work was clearly an emotional release for audiences as well as a source for reflection. From an historical point of view, the international acclaim for *Umarła klasa* and his 1980 production *Wielopole, Wielopole* seem important. But from the point of view of theatrical aesthetics, the synthesis of concepts found in these two pieces led to a new belief in the ultimate possibilities of theatre as a whole, an artistic activity *par excellence*. Kantor opposed trends that led other avant-garde artists away from theatre as a whole and towards areas such as cultural anthropology.

One major director-teacher who moved precisely in such a direction was Jerzy Grotowski. After finishing his studies in Moscow and working for several years at various Polish theatres, Grotowski founded in Opole in 1959 a company devoted more to research in performance than to performing. Rooted in his own interpretations of Stanislavski's theories, Grotowski's ideas coalesced into what he called Poor Theatre, an idea based on the notion that the actor was the centre of the theatrical event and that the event itself was simply a confrontation between actor and spectator. Eschewing everything that was not essential in this relationship, Grotowski argued against the traditional theatre's dependence on buildings and technology as well as on the traditional actor's dependence on script, character, costume and makeup.

Grotowski gradually reduced his own theatrical work to focus only on the work of actors. From the late 1950s onward, Poland's rapidly growing directors' theatre and the influence of spectacular stage design on the performance event became examples for Grotowski of roads *not* to be taken.

Elements of Grotowski's artistic search can probably also be found in the famous lecture of Adam Mickiewicz at the Collège de France referred to earlier. Besides his vision of Monumental Theatre, Mickiewicz also argued for a theatre connected directly to people, a theatre rooted in folklore, linked to the village storyteller tradition, the magician of primeval ritualistic theatre, a theatre that was literally 'poor'. Many of Grotowski's major performances were, not surprisingly, based on texts by Polish romantic writers, including Mickiewicz (*Dziady*, 1961), Słowacki (*Kordian*, 1962; *Książę Niezłomny/The Constant Prince*, 1965) and Wyspiański (*Akropolis*, 1962).

As a director, Grotowski seemed most inspired by Osterwa whose Reduta Theatre was also essentially an 'actors' commune' as was his own Actors' Laboratory, which operated for many years in Wrocław. Grotowski's ideas quickly won followers – probably more outside Poland than in – and his work began to be seen and discussed in other countries.

It was not until publication of his book *Towards a Poor Theatre* in English in Denmark in 1968 (with a preface by Peter Brook), however, that his theories became well known. Even then, the fact was that the ideas included in the book were not so far from those which were pervading Polish theatre as a whole at this time. It can be said, in fact, that the ideas of both Grotowski and Kantor were neither accidental nor fragmentary but were rooted in reactions to elements at the very root of Polish theatrical performance and connected to its deepest socio-cultural structures.

Yet another important director who should be mentioned here is Józef Szajna, originally a designer, who worked closely with Grotowski for a time and who, in 1972, became manager of the Studio Theatre in Warsaw. At the Studio, which he ran until 1982, he directed performances based on his own film-like scenarios, combinations akin to Kantor's linkings of visual arts and acting. These ranged from the pantomimic *Replika* (*Replica*, performed for the first time at the Edinburgh Festival in 1971), to dramatic 'monographs' on particular artists (*Witkacy*, 1972; *Dante*, 1974; *Cervantes*, 1976).

Szajna created theatre through his own unique attitude towards the world, an attitude clearly influenced by his personal experiences in the Nazi death camp at Auschwitz. From his first production in Nowa Huta, Szajna remained faithful to what can be described as a neo-expressionist model, an extreme version of yet another trend of the Polish avant-garde.

*Jan Kłossowicz, Marta Fik, Paweł Konic,
Elżbieta Wysińska, Edward Krasiński*

Music Theatre

At the turn of the twentieth century, Poland could boast of having produced some famous opera stars but as late as 1939 only three opera companies (based in Warsaw, Poznań and Lvov) had actually achieved not only stability but also a notable level of performance. After World War II the number of companies opening across the country increased rapidly. The first were opera theatres in Poznań, Bytom, Wrocław and Warsaw, and operetta theatres in Łódź and Lublin.

In the early 1950s in Warsaw alone three new

music theatres appeared. These included the Opera Objazdowa (Travelling Opera) which later became the Opera Kameralna (Chamber Opera), and two operetta theatres. By the late 1950s, new opera troupes had opened in Gdańsk, Bydgoszcz, Łódź and Kraków, while five new operetta troupes had opened in Gliwice, Wrocław, Poznań, Szczecin and Gdynia. Three of these theatres (Bydgoszcz, Kraków and Sczcecin) actually played a mixed repertoire of operettas and operas.

Throughout the post-war period, the repertoires of Poland's seventeen operating opera/operetta companies consisted mainly of classical works with particular emphasis on the Italian and Slavic traditions. Because of the special interest shown in musical theatre by directors and writers from the mid-1950s, there have also been an unusually large number of contemporary Polish operas staged.

The native repertoire has tended to rest mainly on the works of three composers – Stanisław Moniuszko (1819–72), Karol Szymanowski (1882–1937) and Krzysztof Penderecki (b. 1933). Moniuszko's works, still performed regularly, contain recognizable national music such as the *mazurka* and the *polonaise*. His works have been particularly popular with directors such as Leon Schiller and Maria Fołtyn (b. 1924), a former opera singer.

Szymanowski's works tend to focus on folkloric elements (as in his ballet *Harnasie*, written between 1923 and 1931), though directors generally stage them along modernist lines, bringing out the composer's philosophical and religious themes. Examples of these latter elements include Szymanowski's Medieval-styled *Król Roger* (*King Roger*, written between 1918 and 1924) and a dramatized oratorio entitled *Stabat Mater*, 1925–6). These works, particularly popular between the 1960s and the 1980s, offered unique opportunities for designers.

Among later composers, Penderecki is the author of four major operas – *Diabły z Loudon* (*Devils of Loudon*, 1968), *Raj utracony* (*Paradise Lost*, 1978), *Czarna maska* (*Black Mask*, 1987) and *Król Ubu* (*Ubu Roi*, 1991).

During the 1980s, many composers were inspired by the plays of Witkiewicz. Works based on his plays have included a chamber opera called *Sonata Belzebuba* (*The Beelzebub Sonata*, 1977) by Edward Bogusławski (b. 1940), *W małym dworku* (*In a Small Country House*) by Zbigniew Bargielski (b. 1937) and *Nowe Wyzwolenie* (*New Deliverance*, 1986) by Krzysztof Baculewski (b. 1950).

Teatr STU in Kraków staged a musical based on Witkiewicz themes in 1977 entitled *Szalona lokomotywa* (*The Crazy Locomotive*) with music by Marek Grechuta (b. 1945) and Jan Kanty Pawluśkiewicz (b. 1942), and directed by Krzysztof Jasiński (b. 1943). In 1987, a Witkiewicz-inspired jazz ballet called *Nienasycenie* (*Insatiability*) was staged at the Teatr Wielki by choreographer Zofia Rudnicka (b. 1948) to music by Tomasz Stańko (b. 1942).

One of the major successes of the 1980s was a chamber opera called *Manekiny* (*Mannequins*, 1982) based on a work by Bruno Schulz (1892–1942), with words and music by Zbigniew Rudziński (b. 1935). Staged in Wrocław in 1981 and in Warsaw in 1983 by Janusz Wiśniewski (b. 1949) and Marek Grzesiński (b. 1949) as a type of marionette theatre, its unique style was consistent with Schulz's poetic and visual imagination. Schulz himself was a remarkable writer and graphic artist of Jewish extraction who was killed by the Nazis during World War II. The opera has been presented abroad on several occasions.

In the 1960s, conductor Bohdan Wodiczko (1912–85) was one of the first in Poland to develop a modern style of opera theatre. Working at the Teatr Wielki in Warsaw, Wodiczko based the theatre's repertoire almost exclusively on twentieth-century works, attracted younger audiences and even launched a periodical, *Opera Viva*. His premières of Stravinsky's *King Oedipus* in 1962, as staged by Swinarski with a Monumental setting by Jan Kosiński, was an immediate success with both critics and audiences, as were his productions of Honegger's *Judith* that same year and Stravinsky's *Orpheus* in 1963 (starring the Polish ballet star Stanisław Szymańsi – b. 1930). He worked with such major designers as Andrzej Majewski (b. 1936) and Tadeusz Kantor, who designed Bartók's *Zamek Sinobrodego* (*Bluebeard's Castle*, 1963), and such major directors as Aleksander Bardini and Ludwik René.

Of the opera directors who emerged in the 1970s and 1980s, Ryszard Peryt (b. 1947) has been among the most prominent. His stagings have been characterized by rich imagination, intellectual inquisitiveness and genuine skills in translating drama and music into a single vision. He directed many contemporary operas during this period in Poznań including Honegger's *Joan of Arc at the Stake* (1979), Prokofiev's *The Fiery Angel* (1983), Verdi's *Requiem* (1985), Britten's *Death in Venice* (1987) and Rossini's *Moses*

(1989). Between 1987 and 1993, Peryt staged at Warsaw's Opera Kameralna (Chamber Opera) all the dramatic works of Mozart (twenty-four in total including several unfinished operas and sketches such as *Le sposo deluso* and *L'Occa del Cairo*) shaping them into original, beautiful and coherent theatrical works.

Over this same period, the most highly subsidized company in the country has been Warsaw's Teatr Wielki. The Wielki has staged a number of important and seldom-done works such as Wagner's *Ring* cycle, Berg's *Wozzeck*, the thirteenth-century work *Ludus Danielis*, da Gagliano's *Daphne*, Handel's *Amadigi di Gaula* and operas by Britten, Menotti, Romuald Twardowski (b. 1930), Zygmunt Krauze (b. 1938) and Joanna Bruzdowicz (b. 1943).

The Teatr Wielki company in Poznań has long been an exceptionally stable organization noted for its high level of musicianship while the

Marek Grzesiński's 1982 Warsaw Teatr Wielki production of Zbigniew Rudziński's *The Mannequins*, costumes by Irena Biegańska.
Photo: Juliusz Multarzyński.

Teatr Muzyczny (Musical Theatre) in Kraków has specialized in the Baroque and Enlightenment repertoire (Purcell, Handel, Gluck, Scarlatti and Pergolesi).

Łódź's Teatr Wielki is the second-largest opera theatre in the country and its repertoire is dominated by the major romantic operas of Beethoven, Donizetti, Bellini and Verdi. Opera Śląska (Silesian Opera) in the industrial city of Bytom has, from its very beginning, concentrated on vocal talents. It was from Opera Śląska that some of the country's most eminent singers first emerged – baritone Andrzej Hiolski (b. 1922) and tenor Bogdan Paprocki (b. 1919) to name just two.

Warsaw's Opera Kameralna started out in 1961 as an alternative musical stage created by the musicologist and oboist Stefan Sutkowski (b. 1932). Apart from an orchestra and singers the Kameralna also used to include two separate companies – the Scena Mimów (Mime Stage) and Operowa Scena Marionetek (Marionette Opera Stage). Before moving into a permanent home in 1986, the company performed in churches, palaces and museums. It specializes in sixteenth- and eighteenth-century music and opera.

As for non-operatic works, in the political and social system adopted after 1945 most light musicals were denounced by Marxist ideology as symbols of 'capitalist and bourgeois culture'. As a result, the few operetta theatres that existed at the time found it difficult to survive. Librettos were constantly being adapted to socialist-realist concepts of art with Soviet operettas prevailing. The situation began to change after 1956. In 1958 director Danuta Baduszkowa (1919–78) founded the Teatr Muzyczny (Musical Theatre) in Gdynia, focusing on the contemporary Polish and foreign repertoire.

American-style musicals simply could not be played before 1956 for ideological reasons. Later, productions were held back for lack of sufficient funds even for foreign royalties. The first Polish premières of large-scale musicals wound up taking place in the dramatic theatres starting in 1958. Eventually, funds were found to produce them in the operetta theatres as well with Poznań, Warsaw, Gdynia and Łódź taking the lead.

In 1983, film and television director Jerzy Gruza (b. 1932) became artistic director of Teatr Muzyczny and made a breakthrough of sorts when he began staging such popular musicals as *Fiddler on the Roof* (1984), *Jesus Christ Superstar* (1987) and *Les Misérables*

(1989). He also staged several Polish musicals on contemporary issues such as Korzyński's *Drugie Wejscie Smoka* (*Enter the Dragon for the Second Time*, 1984) and *Czarna Dziura* (*The Black Hole*, 1985), and Kofta and Rychter's *Kompot* (*Compote*, 1984).

Other popular Polish musicals of note during this period include Bryll's *Na szkle malowane* (*Painted on Glass*, 1969) with music by Katarzyna Gaertner (b. 1942), and *Kolęda nocka* (*Christmas Carol Night*, 1980) with music by Wojciech Trzciński and *Cień* (*The Shadow*) based on a work by Yevgeny Svarts with music by Maciej Małecki (b. 1940) and lyrics by Wojciech Młynarski.

In Warsaw, Teatr Rampa (Ramp Theatre) has also attracted much attention. Created in 1987 by a young director named Andrzej Strzelecki (b. 1953) who hired a group of recent graduates from the Warsaw Theatre Academy, Teatr Rampa quickly developed an excellent performance style which was clearly seen in *Złe zachowanie* (1984), based on excerpts from the American musical, *Ain't Misbehavin'*. The theatre utilizes renowned actors and humorists, and its performances have maintained not only a high technical level but a political point of view as well.

In Wrocław, the Teatr Instrumentalny (Instrumental Theatre) developed from a jazz base out of the student theatre movement. Unique in form and language, it was created by jazz performer Ryszard Misiek, who created the concept of 'musi-actor', an actor-musician who could create a broad range of music as well as narrative theatre. In some of his works, Misiek has included ideas from the works of Strindberg, Kafka and Roland Topor. In 1981, he moved with his theatre to Gdańsk where it eventually affiliated with Gdynia's Teatr Muzyczny.

From the pre-war activities of Leon Schiller, a unique tradition of specifically Polish performances based on popular songs has also developed. Since 1960, these pieces have been important elements in the repertoires of many theatres and have always been performed to nearly full houses. Among the most popular have been *Kram z piosenkami* (*A Stall Full of Songs*, 1949), *Pastorałka* (*Christmas Carol*, 1939) and new compositions in the style such as *Niech-no tylko zakwitną jabłonie* (*Let's Wait for the Apple Blossoms*, 1964) by Agnieszka Osiecka. These are essentially evenings of nostalgic war songs, popular student songs and even church-connected pieces.

More than simple nostalgia, however, these songs both reveal the past and articulate feelings and ideas which, for many years, could not be even hinted at because of state censorship. After 1980, a new type of 'song' performance was developed by Młynarski at the Teatr Ateneum involving pieces done in the styles of major international performers such as the popular Russian folksinger Vladimir Visotski and the Belgian writer Jacques Brel. Because these performances offered actors an opportunity to take on specific vocal challenges, a number of singer-actors emerged, many of them quite eminent. At the same time, the National Festival of Actors in Song began in the city of Wrocław.

One should also mention the use that dramatic theatres have made of music in their work. Going all the way back to the 1950s, many of the country's best composers have been commissioned to do music for dramatic theatres. As examples, Erwin Axer collaborated on several occasions with Zbigniew Turski (1908–79) while Konrad Swinarski and Bohdan Korzeniewski (1905–92) both collaborated with Penderecki. Music for productions by Bardini and René has been written by Tadeusz Baird (1928–81). And in 1981, Stanisław Radwan (b. 1939), who composed music for the Stary Theatre, actually became artistic director of the company, a post he held until 1990.

Małgorzata Komorowska

Dance Theatre

Polish dance theatre has always been linked to opera or drama theatre. This has been the case from its beginning in Warsaw in 1785. A number of eminent Polish choreographers did try to set up independent dance ensembles – Jan Ciepliński (1900–72) in 1922–4 and 1937, Feliks Parnell (1898–1980) in 1935–9 and 1945–7, and Eugeniusz Papliński (1908–78) in 1955–8.

The pre-war Ballet Polski – managed by Bronisława Niżyńska (1891–1972) during 1937–8 and Leon Wójcikowski (1899–1975) from 1938 to 1939 – became known for its dance theatricalization of national folklore supported by original Polish music. Based on both classical dance forms and Polish folk dances, the company was modelled after the achievements of Diaghilev's Ballets Russes as well as on the discoveries of German expressive dance.

After the war, Polish dance again became part of the opera theatres; from 1945 in Poznań and Wrocław, from 1946 in Warsaw and Bytom, from 1949 in Gdańsk, from 1956 in Bydgoszcz, from 1957 in Łódź, from 1958 in Kraków, and from 1974 in Szczecin. Opera company ballet ensembles presented both the classical repertoire and original works by Polish choreographers.

Janina Jarzynówna-Sobczak (b. 1915) played an important role in the development of Polish dance theatre as the manager and choreographer of the Baltic Opera Ballet in Gdańsk from 1949 to 1976. A dancer, actor and teacher of dance, she was a student of Ruth Abramowitsch Sorel (formerly a dancer with the German ensemble of Mary Wigman) and Leon Wójcikowski, a former soloist of Diaghilev's ensemble. Both instilled in her a love for expressive dance theatre, despite the then obligatory aesthetic model of Soviet ballet. Among her most important works were *Dafnis i Chloe* (*Daphnis and Chloe*, music by Ravel, 1958), *Cudowny Mandaryn* (*The Miraculous Mandarin*, music by Bartók, 1960), *Syn marnotrawny* (*The Prodigal Son*, by Prokofiev, 1963), *Niobe* (by Łuciuk, 1967), *Tytania i osioł* (*Titania and the Ass*, by Turski, 1967) and *Pancernik Potiomkin* (*Battleship Potemkin*, by Łuciuk, 1967). The creator of what has been called 'anti-ballet', 'theatre of gesture set to music', 'pantomime of events' and 'theatre of vision and movement', her works clearly introduced a creative ferment into Polish ballet, encouraging other choreographers to conduct their own original quests and to defend themselves against the strong influence of Russian classical dance under conditions of restricted contact with achievements by American and western European dance theatre.

Another Polish choreographer of note is Conrad Drzewiecki (b. 1926), who went even further. After training in Poland, he moved to France and between 1958 and 1963 danced with various French ensembles. He learned both modern and jazz dance there and after returning to Poland began to popularize them, both as choreographer and as teacher. In 1972 he studied American modern dance in New York. Between 1963 and 1973 Drzewiecki was director of the ballet ensemble and choreographer at the Poznań Opera. In 1973 he established Poland's first autonomous dance theatre in Poznań under the official name Polski Teatr Tańca (Polish Dance Theatre). He headed the company till 1987 and it regularly toured abroad. He was held in especially high regard in eastern European countries as the propagator of the aesthetic model of western ballet and dance theatre.

Drzewiecki's choreographic work was extremely eclectic, taking as its models such artists as Balanchine (*Divertimento*, music by Bartók, 1970); Béjart (*Pieśń o nocy*/*Song of the Night*, music by Szymanowski, 1977); Cranko (*Jezioro łabędzie*/*Swan Lake*, music by Tchaikovsky, 1969); German dance theatre (*Pawana na śmierć infantki*/*Pavane pour une infante défunte*, music by Ravel, 1968); and *Cudowny Mandaryn*/*The Miraculous Mandarin*, music by Bartók, 1970).

But his best works were patterned after American modern dance, in which he expressed himself most freely. Examples of this are visible in works ranging from his *Wariacje 4:4* (*Variations 4:4*, Woźniak, 1966) and *Modus vivendi* (Kuźnik, 1975), to his *Nokturny* (*Nocturnes*, Chopin, 1982). Drzewiecki's greatest achievement was probably *Krzesany* (Kilar, 1977), a kind of choreographic ritual based on the dances and customs of Polish highland dwellers. Some of Drzewiecki's works have been included in the repertoire of foreign ballet ensembles: the Dutch National Ballet in Amsterdam, the German Opera Ballet in Berlin as well as theatres of Havana, Prague, Sofia and Malmö.

In 1988 Drzewiecki's place at Polski Teatr Tańca was taken over by Ewa Wycichowska (b. 1949). A dancer with the Wielki Theatre Ballet in Łódź, she later studied jazz dance in Paris and modern dance in London. An outstanding choreographer, her most important works include *Stabat Mater* (Szymanowski, 1982), *Faust Goes Rock* (The Shade, 1986), *Samontność Fauna* (*Loneliness of the Faun*, Kuźnik, 1989), *Święto wiosny* (*Le Sacre du printemps*, Stravinsky, 1989) and *Skrzypek opętany* (*The Demented Fiddler*, Kuźnik, 1991).

There are two other equally eminent Polish choreographers – Emil Wesołowski (b. 1947), formerly a soloist with Drzewiecki's ensemble, later a choreographer with the Wielki Theatre in Warsaw, and Waldemar Wołk-Karaczewski (b. 1954), formerly a soloist with Béjart's ensemble and with the opera theatres of Berlin and Munich. He works for both the Wielki Theatre in Warsaw and the Polski Teatr Tańca in Poznań.

Zofia Rudnicka's 1987 ballet *Insatiability*, Teatr Wielki, Warsaw.
Photo: Juliusz Multarzyński.

Since the 1970s a number of famous foreign choreographers have worked with Polish ensembles, among them Kurt Jooss, Birgit Cullberg, Anna Sokolov, Erich Walter, John Neumeier, Maurice Béjart, John Butler, Hans van Manen, Gray Veredon, Antal Fodor, Alberto Méndez and Lorca Massine.

In Poland, dancers are educated at five state ballet schools – in Warsaw, Poznań, Gdańsk, Bytom and Łódź. Since 1968, an international festival has been organized in Łódź every two years – the Łódź Ballet Meetings. Since 1973, National Choreographic Competitions have also been held in Łódź, aimed at promoting the work of young choreographers. Dance theatre and ballet has had its special magazine in Poland since 1974 – *Taniec* (*Dance*), published by Polski Teatr Tańca in Poznań till 1986. This publication was revived in 1992 in Warsaw and is now published as a quarterly by the Teatr Wielki.

Pawel Chynowski

Theatre for Young Audiences

The earliest attempts at creating theatre for children and young people in Poland were by Halina Starska (1888–1957) and Janina Strzelecka (1890–1937), who together led the Jaskółka Theatre in Warsaw from 1929 to 1933. In the 1930s, Warsaw's Reduta Theatre also began an ambitious programme, the Reduta Institute's Theatre for Children, which operated from 1934 to 1939. The work of both groups was based on the idea of trying to combine artistic and educational elements in their performances.

After World War II, theatre for young audiences became a responsibility of the puppet theatres (see **Puppet Theatre**). One exception was the Young Audience Theatre, set up in 1947 and closed in 1956, where work was modelled on that of similar theatres in the Soviet Union. The group presented mainly didactic plays and dramatizations.

Clearly, performances for children and young people were being marginalized in the state drama theatres and treated as artistically unimportant. After 1955, however, the repertoire of theatres playing for young audiences began to be varied and state authorities stopped forcing theatres to stage propaganda pieces. In the 1990s, stage adaptations of various kinds of children's stories can be seen ranging from traditional folk tales through classics, from contemporary poetic tales to rewrites and adaptations of comic books and science fiction stories. Other dramatic and stage genres are also regularly attempted such as opera, folk opera and musicals.

Among the important post-war figures working in the field was Jan Dorman (1912–86), a director who sought inspiration in children's folklore, in the rhythms and structures of children's games, as well as in folk art, the twentieth-century avant-garde, and the whole varied tradition of puppet theatre. Dorman was the founder and director of Teatr Dzieci Zagłębia (Silesian Children's Theatre) in the Silesian town of Będzin. Remaining at the theatre through to his retirement in 1979, his performances often upset adult audiences with their lack of plot, unexpected associations, and their unconstrained composition. The author rightly assumed that children were able to accept any rules proposed and would always play the game with him.

Among Dorman's most significant productions were Kornel Makuszyński's *Krawiec Niteczka* (*Niteczka the Tailor*, 1958), Maeterlinck's *The Blue Bird* (1963), Shakespeare's *A Midsummer Night's Dream* (1965), *Don Quixote* (1966) based on Cervantes, his own *Kaczka* (*The Duck*, 1968) and *Kandyd – optymizm* (*Candide – Optimism*, 1974) based on Voltaire.

Leokadia Serafinowicz (b. 1915), stage director and scenographer, was director of the Teatr Lalki i Aktora 'Marcinek' (Marcinek Puppet and Actor Theatre) in Poznań from 1960 to 1978 and was followed there by Wojciech Wieczorkiewicz (b. 1934), director from 1978 to 1981. Both tried to reveal to young audiences the language of art and the secrets of the stage. Treating their audiences seriously, they asked young people to fill in a general structure with their own imaginations and minds.

The most significant of their stage productions include Wojciechowski's *Która godzina?* (*What Time Is It?*, 1964), Wyspiański's *Wesele* (*The Wedding*, 1969), Kownacka and Kurczewski's folk opera *O Kasi, co gąski zgubiła* (*The Tale of Kate, Who Lost Her Geese*, 1967) and Wieczorkiewicz's *Co z tego wyrośnie?* (*What Will Grow from This?*, 1988).

Jan Wilkowski (b. 1921), artistic director of the Lalka Theatre in Warsaw from 1950 to 1969, was one of the first to reject didacticism and infantilism as elements of children's theatre. As both playwright and stage director, he offered young audiences an imaginary world enabling them to play roles which suited them best, to enter situations which could never exist in reality. His famous stage productions include Wilkowski and Moszczyński's *Guignol w tarapatach* (*Guignol in Trouble*, 1957), *O Zwyrtale myzykancie* (*The Tale of Zwyrtal the Musician*, 1959), Januszewska's *Tygrys Pietrek* (*Pete the Tiger*, 1962) and Wilkowski's *Spowiedź w drewnie* (*Confessions in Wood*, 1983).

Włodzimierz Fełenczak (b. 1941) creates performances in both puppet and drama theatres. Never avoiding difficult or painful topics, he nevertheless leaves young viewers with hope for a world of sense and justice. A mixing of forms is characteristic of his work; live actors are combined with shadow theatre, puppets, marionettes and huge dolls.

Bogusław Kierc (b. 1943), another important director in the field, creates a theatrical world in which reality is combined with myth and ritual, in which the rituals of childhood and adulthood reveal areas normally concealed by routine attitudes. His work with the Wałbrzych Puppet Theatre in 1982–7 was especially productive. Among his important stage productions have been Mickiewicz's *Dziady* (1982), his own *Tajemnica* (*The Secret*, 1983), Andrzejewski's *Złoty lis* (*The Golden Fox*, 1986) and his own *Pan Lusterkorilke* (*Mr Lusterkorilke*, 1987).

Among other directors, one should mention Piotr Tomaszuk (b. 1961), who has worked at the Białystok Puppet Theatre, the Miniatura Puppet and Actor Theatre in Gdańsk and at the Towarzystwo Wierszalin, a company he co-directs; and Andrzej Maleszka (b. 1955), who directs his own plays in Poznań's Teatr Nowy and on television with child performers.

A number of independent theatrical groups became active in the 1980s, timidly at first, then more and more intensively. They were usually established by puppet actors, but performances

Szczepan Szczykno's 1991 Opole Teatr im. Jana Kochanowskiego production of Andrzej Maleszka's *Giants*, designed by Leszek Ołdak.
Photo: Marek Szyryk.

have not been limited to puppet theatre techniques alone.

The bimonthly *Sztuka dla Dziecka* (*Art for the Child*), together with other periodicals and non-periodical journals published by the National Centre of Art for Children and Young People in Poznań, is a forum for the exchange of experiences between creators of children's and young people's theatre. Issues concerning theatre for young audiences are often discussed in the magazine *Teatr Lalek* (*Puppet Theatre*).

Festivals also play a significant role in Poland.

In addition to the exclusively puppet theatre festivals in Opole and Białystok, important events include the Biennial of Art for Children in Poznań (first organized in 1973), the National Festival of Art for Children and Young People in Wałbrzych (since 1979, with mainly drama theatres participating), and the International Fair of Theatrical Initiatives in Piła (first organized in 1991 with an open formula, organized mainly for independent groups).

Juliusz Tyszka

Puppet Theatre

Before World War II, major puppet theatres were already active in cities such as Warsaw, Kraków, Katowice, Poznań and Wilno, performing for both children and adults. In Warsaw, the Baj Theatre was well known for its educational programmes and its courses in

puppetry for students. The company was founded in 1928 by Szczepan Baczyński (1901–89) and Jan Wesołowski (b. 1901). Wesołowski led the company from 1930 to 1939.

As well, folk productions called *szopka* (nativity scenes) were popular in both villages and towns during Christmas holidays. At the beginning of the century, amateur productions of the *szopka* were regularly seen.

Even during the war, puppet performances were organized (often *szopki* for the armed forces, and clandestine performances for children in prisoner of war camps, concentration camps, in ghettos and prisons).

After the war, puppet theatre became an important element in the revival of theatrical art. Organized by puppeteers, artists and teachers, it very quickly became part of private or municipal theatres and was often subsidized by the Workers Society for Children. The move to a socialist system of government resulted in the withdrawal of personal patronage and its replacement by state patronage. In 1949, three puppet theatres were nationalized; in 1950 the number rose to eleven. Between 1954 and 1962 an additional eight theatres were nationalized and in the following years even more theatres were started. As of 1993, there were twenty-eight puppet theatres operating.

The majority of companies (twenty-four) had their own theatre spaces/auditoriums with state subsidy covering running costs. Puppet theatres, like drama theatres, are required to adhere to a repertoire schedule with at least two to four premières each year, and a performance schedule averaging 300 performances per season.

Puppet theatres also fulfil a function as theatre for children, although most also give performances for adults. The children's repertoire is comprised of both old and modern fairytales, animal tales, folk and poetic works. The works of such authors as Maria Kownacka, Maria Kann, Hanna Januszewska, Leon Moszczyński, Natalia Gołębska and Jan Wilkowski dominate the Polish scene. Dramatic pieces and adapted prose works – classic and contemporary – are performed for adult audiences and range from Fernando de Rojas and Giovanni Boccaccio to Michel de Ghelderode and Franz Kafka, from Jan Kochanowski to Stanisław Ignacy Witkiewicz and Sławomir Mrożek.

Puppet theatres have generally been subject to the same regulations as drama theatres: only licensed professionals could work in them. Each company traditionally employed its own directors, designers, puppeteers, stagehands, mask and puppet designers, and administrators. An average of forty people were employed in most state puppet theatres.

Training between 1947 and 1951 first came from the Studio and then from the State School of Puppet Theatre in Warsaw. In 1954 a pup-

petry department was started at the PWST (State Drama School) in Kraków, and in 1967 an Actors' Studio of Puppet Theatre was begun in Wrocław. In 1972 the Kraków school moved its puppetry department to Wrocław while in 1975 the Warsaw School moved its puppetry faculty to Białystok. Between 1980 and 1990, it included a puppet theatre directing department.

This growing circle of puppeteers regularly exchanged experiences and knowledge at gatherings both in Poland and abroad. From 1966, the International Festival of Puppet Theatres began to be held in Bielsko-Biała and played an important role in disseminating information and showcasing new developments in the field. The specialist journal *Teatr Lalek* was another important factor in integrating Polish puppetry into the larger theatre community.

From immediately after the war Polish puppet theatre searched for its own individual style, experimenting with various means of expression. Many types of puppets were used – marionettes, Javanese dolls, hand-puppets, mannequins – together with masks and live actors. Socialist-realism, the required form of art in the years 1949–55, was a clear hindrance to development, however. Even puppet theatres were forced to present productions in accordance with official ideology. Authorities, in recommending that Soviet plays be performed, effectively eliminated folk plays, including the *szopka*. The theatres attempted to overcome these restrictions by focusing on sets and performances with particular Polish allusions. During this period, in fact, several outstanding productions were realized: *The Emperor's New Clothes* (1951) by Hans Christian Andersen, *Games with the Devil* (1952) by Jan Drda in the Groteska Theatre in Kraków managed by Zofia (b. 1919) and Władysław (1896-1976) Jarema, and Molière's *Le Médecin malgré lui* (1954) in the Arlekin Theatre in Łódź, under the management of Henryk Ryl (b. 1911).

After 1955, poetic and folk productions were once again allowed, among the first being the productions of *Babcia i wnuczek* (*Grandmother and Grandson*, 1955) by Konstanty Ildefons Gałczyński at the Teatr Groteska in Kraków and *Guignol w tarapatach* (1956) by Leon Moszczyński and Jan Wilkowski at the Teatr Lalka in Warsaw, directed by Wilkowski himself. In later years, these styles were developed further by Leon Schiller's *Pastorałka* (*Pastoral*, 1957) at the Poznań Marcinek Theatre, and *O Zwyrtale myzykancie* (1958) after Kazimierz Przerwa-Tetmajer at the Lalka Theatre and

Zofia Jarema's 1979 Groteska Theatre production of Sławomir Mrożek's *Home on the Border*, designed by Kazimierz Mikulski.
Photo: J. Wolski.

Młynek do kawy (1959) after K.I. Gałczyński in the Arlekin Theatre in Łódź. These productions opened the way for a more experimental puppet theatre, for a return to a Polish repertoire and the traditions of folk plays and the *szopka*.

These directions dominated the Polish puppet theatre for many years and resulted in many productions of works from the poetic and absurdist repertoires. The Groteska, for example, did such plays as *Męczeństwo Piotra Oheya* (*The Martyrdom of Peter Ohey*) by Sławomir Mrożek in 1959, *Kartoteka* (1961) by Tadeusz Różewicz and *Ubu Roi* (1965) by Alfred Jarry, while the puppet theatre in Poznań staged *Mątwa* (*The Cuttlefish*) and *Szalona lokomotywa* (*The Crazy Locomotive*) both by Witkiewicz in 1968. There were also many folk productions which served as an instrument of cultural identification for children. This idea resulted in the development of the Miniatura Theatre in Gdańsk, managed by Ali Bunsch (1925–85), Natalia Gołębska (b. 1911) and Michał Zarzecki (b. 1929). Another work representative of this tendency was the production of *Bo w Mazurze taka siła* (*Such is the Mazovian's Spirit*, 1962), containing both folk and national motifs.

Jan Wilkowski, working closely with the set designer Adam Kilian (b. 1923) at the Lalka Theatre, expanded the artistic possibilities of puppet theatre even within the folk tradition. Applying different methods of staging for virtually every production, he took his cues from the theatre itself in *Guignol* (1956), from film in *Tygrys Pietrek* (1962), and from rehearsals in *My i nasze krasnoludki* (*We and Our Dwarfs*, 1967).

The Poznań Puppet Theatre experimented with and developed new means of expression under the direction of Leokadia Serafinowicz and Wojciech Wieczorkiewicz, putting on everything from classical plays (*Wesele* by Wyspiański in 1969) to contemporary opera for children (with Krzysztof Penderecki) to poetic plays for children using live actors (written by Krystyna Miłobędzka).

Attempts to break away from traditional techniques of puppetry were also being seen at other theatres in the 1960s. This was very obvious at the Teatr Dzieci Zagłębia, managed by the great Jan Dorman, who shaped his productions around the rhythm of children's games composing collages of specific literary and theatrical motifs.

During the 1960s, the importance of the Wrocław Puppet Theatre increased as it turned to performances for adults. Andrzej Dziedziul (b. 1939) brought the concept of one-person shows to the theatre in *Stan losów Fausta* (*Faust's Fate*) in 1968. Wiesław Hejno (b. 1936) put on plays by Bertolt Brecht and de Ghelderode and, in the 1980s, staged Kafka's *The Trial* (1985) and *Gyubal Wahazar* by Witkiewicz (1987).

In the 1970s, the theatre in Białystok led by Krzysztof Rau (b. 1937) became an important centre of puppetry with productions of Różewicz's *Kartoteka* (1972) and *Before the Third Cock Crows* (1983) by Vasili Shukshin. The puppet theatre was generally also sensitive to old Polish works, and presented a large number of Medieval Mystery plays such as *Tryptyk staropolski* (*Old Polish Triptych*) at the puppet theatre in Lublin which met with great popularity. A poetic theatre *d'auteur* also developed at a fast pace.

In the 1980s there was a return to classical and Mystery plays which in the early 1990s led a number of young directors to a search for links with image theatre and the theatre of objects.

Henryk Jurkowski

Design

Poland's most renowned stage designers were active in the period immediately following World War II. They included Andrzej Pronaszko (1888–1961), who combined the otherwise contradictory constructivist and expressionist styles (characteristic of the avant-garde group from the 1920s, known as formists), Karol Frycz (1877–1963), who perceived sets as providing a stylistically appropriate setting for the drama, and Władysław Daszewski (1902–71), a typical representative of neo-realism. Their followers, who made their débuts after the war and came into their own in the mid-1950s, played a major role in creating, together with stage directors, what has been called 'the Polish school of stage design'. Those who are part of this group are generally divided into two groups, a breakdown evolving from the two stage design departments at the Warsaw and Kraków Fine Arts Academies.

The most prominent representative of the Warsaw School was Jan Kosiński, one of the founders of Teatr Dramatyczny. As a designer, Kosiński departed from the popular neo-realism of the period and, in the late 1950s, developed his own architectonic concept of setting, a concept which brought his work close to surrealism. Younger representatives of the Warsaw School – Andrzej Sadowski (b. 1925), Andrzej Majewski (b. 1936), Krzysztof Pankiewicz (b. 1933), Franciszek Starowieyski (b. 1930) and Zofia Wierchowicz (1924–78) to name just a few – used sculptural forms, architectonic shapes, or followed non-geometrical abstractions and, like Kosiński, often touched upon surrealism. Ewa Starowieyska (b. 1930), on the other hand, referred back to the neo-realistic tradition in her designs and pastiches, which parodied various realistic techniques.

In Kraków, a series of unconventional designs were created by Tadeusz Kantor. Although design composed only a small part of his career (he stopped designing in 1963), Kantor played a crucial role in shaping the trends of the period. He introduced abstract geometrical forms to the stage on a large scale, as well as what he called 'soft abstraction'. He also initiated the idea that sets could be seen as an independent interpretation of and commentary on the play at hand. Józef Szajna, another designer-director, followed a similar path, though his designs ultimately evolved towards a kind of neo-expressionism.

Characteristics of some of the other designers of the Kraków School included the fantasy of Wojciech Krakowski's (b. 1927) large-scale designs; the humour found in the works of Kazimierz Wiśniak (b. 1931); Jerzy (b. 1924) and Lidia (b. 1920) Skarzyński's skill in finding forms and styles appropriate to a literary text; Krystyna Zachwatowicz's (b. 1930) mock-naturalism; and Andrzej Cybulski's (1926–71) vivid and imaginative approaches. All these styles contributed to the productions of such distinguished Polish directors as Konrad Swinarski, Jerzy Jarocki, Andrzej Wajda and Zygmunt Hübner.

Contrary to these dominant styles and

Laco Adamik's 1983 Warsaw Teatr Wielki production of Karol Szymanowski's *King Roger*, designed by Andrzej Majewski.
Photo: Zbigniew Feliksiak.

fashions were the designs of Andrzej Stopka (1904–73) and Adam Kilian, both inspired by folk art.

By the 1970s, the importance of design in the Polish theatre began to diminish. The old trends were being continued and even developed by such designers as Marian Kołodziej (b. 1924) and Andrzej Markowicz (b. 1942), who practised aggressive, colourful and lavish stage setting. But the painterly and sculptural nature of the earlier work was gradually replaced by something much more functional. Designers were again becoming subordinate to directors, and the Polish theatre as a whole after 1980 was becoming much less lavish, a trend which was even more clearly seen in the 1990s. However, sets by Jerzy Juk-Kowarski (b. 1944) and Wiesław Olko (b. 1948) were noted for their original style – a naturalistic treatment of objects, props and costumes and an attempt to do away with the traditional proscenium stage. The rich traditions of the Warsaw School could also be seen at this time in the work (in both theatre and opera) of Andrzej Majewski. He remained faithful to the painterly style of Polish stage design, combining abstract expressionism with surrealism.

Jan Kłossowicz, Marta Fik, Paweł Konic,
Elżbieta Wysińska, Edward Krasiński

Theatre Space and Architecture

During World War II, twenty-eight of Poland's theatre buildings were destroyed, many of them of historical significance. Warsaw suffered the greatest losses, being systematically demolished by the Nazis after the 1944 uprising. Included in this group was Teatr Wielki, containing both the opera and the Narodowy. Altogether, 90 per cent of theatres and cinemas were destroyed.

Simply because of the availability of suitable premises, two cities became centres of post-war theatre life: Kraków, where the buildings of the Słowacki and Stary theatres had survived the war, and Łódź. In the western territories, which Poland received after Yalta in exchange for lands lost in the east, eight theatre buildings were destroyed in the war.

In all the theatre buildings, those which had survived and those which were quickly adapted, the traditional stage–audience relationship was maintained. Experiments with flexible space that had taken place in the inter-war decades (for example, at the Reduta or the Żeromski Studio in Warsaw) were not continued with most simply accepting the proscenium arch. Between 1949 and 1954, the period of socialist-realism, such experiments were not even allowed.

The majority of theatre buildings which survived the war unscathed became important architectural features in city centres, among them the theatres in Bielsko-Biała and Cieszyn and the *fin-de-siècle* theatre in Katowice. The neo-Renaissance Polski Theatre in Poznań, built during the Prussian partition of Poland and inaugurated in 1875, had found itself later squeezed between apartment blocks for political reasons. The blocks came down after the war. Both of Kraków's preserved theatres, the Słowacki Theatre (opened in 1893) and the Stary Theatre (opened in 1799 and remodelled three times), both began operating again in 1945.

In Warsaw, the Polski Theatre was the first to start working (in January 1946). Completed in 1913, it survived the war in a state requiring only small renovations. The Narodowy and Wielki theatres, however, had to be rebuilt. The Narodowy was opened in 1949 (designed by Romuald Gutt), and the Wielki in 1965 (designed by Bogdan Pniewski). The mass of the latter, and particularly its façade, was similar to the original concept of Antonio Corazzi built in 1833. The restoration of this building, designed to host both opera and ballet, was supervised by Arnold Szyfman, the first director of the Polski Theatre.

One of the first completely new theatre buildings after the war was the Polski Theatre in Bydgoszcz (1949). Several culture centres with theatre halls were built in the early 1950s, and the exceptionally decorative Komedia Theatre in Warsaw was erected in the same period. Socialist-realism was represented mainly by the Palace of Culture and Science – another political symbol – which housed three theatres: the 'empire-modernistic' Dramatyczny (seating 642), the more modest Klasyczny (now the Studio, seating up to 350), and the puppet theatre Lalka (seating 284); there was also the Ludowy Theatre in Nowa Huta, built for the 'new workers' audience', seating 400. These theatres were opened in 1955, when socialist-realism was nearing its end.

The Monumental style of the late 1940s and early 1950s was preserved to a certain degree in the Wielki Theatre in Łódź. Opened in 1967, this theatre was excellently equipped and became famous for its acoustics. The theatre has a box stage, as does Teatr Wybrzeże (opened in Gdańsk in the same year) and the Żydowski Theatre in Warsaw (opened two years later).

At this time, attempts were being made to create theatres with flexible performing space, organizing the performing and viewing area differently for each performance. Director Jerzy Grotowski undertook the most radical attempts in this field, first in Opole with the help of architect Jerzy Gurawski, then from 1965 in Wrocław.

A stage in the round was built in Warsaw's Ateneum Theatre in 1961, and in the late 1960s student theatres merged actors and audience into one common area for ideological reasons.

These trends were reflected in the way new theatres were designed or old ones modernized in the 1970s. The idea of changeable space was incorporated into the Mały Theatre (designed by Zbigniew Wacławek) built in Warsaw and opened in 1972, and into the Teatr na Woli (designed by Jacek Jedynak, Anna Kapitaniak and Marek Wojciechowski) which was opened

Jerzy Grotowski's 1965 Teatr Laboratorium production of Słowacki's *The Constant Prince*, architecture by Jerzy Gurawski.
Photo: Teatr Laboratorium.

in 1975. The Mały Theatre was built under an arcade in the city centre, while the Teatr na Woli was adapted from a former cinema. The Mały has movable floor modules and an acoustic ceiling with a free choice of lighting suspension; the performing area can also be reshaped. In the latter, the hall is divided into a fixed space for the audience and a changeable area for the stage. One of the possible alternatives to the proscenium stage is the theatre auditorium in Łask near Łódź (designed by Wiktor Jackiewicz, 1968), where the stage partly surrounds the audience, who sit on swivel chairs.

Theatres with two halls – usually a larger proscenium one and a flexible smaller one – have been the model for several new buildings: the Kochanowski Theatre in Opole (1975), the Muzyczny Theatre in Gdynia (1979), and a new theatre in Kielce. This model is also present in the Muzyczny Theatre in Bydgoszcz (designed by Józef Chmiel, co-designer of the Gdynia theatre) which was under construction in 1993, and in many modernized theatre interiors. Some older theatres have managed to add small auditoriums in their buildings (the Dramatyczny in Warsaw, for example) while the Słowacki in Kraków was connected by an underground passage to the small Miniatura Theatre situated nearby. Those who modernize existing theatre buildings have generally avoided significant changes both inside and out.

The best known of the experimental groups are theatres without theatres (Akademia Ruchu, Stowarzyszenie Teatralne Gardzienice, Teatr Osmego Dnia). The Witkacy Theatre in Zakopane arranges its performances in several rooms it has access to in one of the city's historical buildings. Leszek Mądzik's Scena Plastyczna of the Lublin Catholic University creates a theatrical space mainly through the use of light.

The opera theatres in Warsaw and Łódź have the largest houses (1,900 and 1,300 respectively); the opera theatres in other cities have houses seating fewer than 1,000, but have extended orchestra pits. The Narodowy Theatre, reconstructed in 1993 after the fire of 1985, seats 681. Generally speaking, the houses of most drama theatres, both in new and historical buildings, seat 300–700 people (exceptions are the Polski Theatre in Warsaw with 967 and the Polski Theatre in Wrocław with 1,212). In theatres with two halls, the smaller house usually seats 150–300 people.

Paweł Obracaj

Training

The State Institute of Theatrical Art, founded in 1932 in Warsaw, closed down during the war (although it functioned as part of the underground). Almost as soon as the country was liberated, three new drama schools opened. These were the Zelwerowicz Drama Academy in Warsaw, the Solski Drama Academy in Kraków and the Schiller State Theatre Academy in Łódź (which later became the Schiller State Film, Television and Theatre Academy).

In the 1990s these three academies, which all have university-level status, run four acting departments (one is a branch of the Kraków academy and is located in Wrocław), two directing departments (in Kraków and Warsaw) and three puppet theatre departments (Warsaw's puppet theatre directing department is in Białystok, while Kraków's puppet theatre department is in Wrocław).

Education in the theatre academies lasts four years. Besides specialist practical training, the courses also encompass lectures on the history and theory of theatre and drama as well as on culture in its broadest sense. Graduates receive

a Master's degree in arts and all the rights and privileges the state offers to licensed professional actors and directors.

Designers, for their part, are trained in specialist fine arts academies in Warsaw and Kraków. In Warsaw's Theatre Academy there is a separate department of theatre studies, which trains theatre researchers, critics and dramaturges. This programme, like that for actors and directors, lasts four years. Theatre academies also train theatre administrators.

Since 1990, private schools of acting have also begun to operate.

The idea of courses organized directly by theatres was cultivated by teacher-artists such as Iwo Gall in Kraków and Irena (b. 1901) and Tadeusz (1906–87) Byrski in Warsaw. Grotowski's training at his Actors' Lab in Wrocław was perhaps the best known of these studios. Others have since been opened in Gdańsk and Gdynia. A separate theatre studio also existed at Państwowy Teatr Żydowski (Yiddish Theatre) in Kielce (1955–8).

Criticism, Scholarship and Publishing

Theatre is a frequent subject for books published by various state publishing houses, a few of which even have autonomous theatre sections. There are serial editions of biographies of theatre artists, a series called *Teorie współczesnego teatru* (*Theories of Contemporary Theatre*), Polish contemporary plays and monographs on Polish student theatres. On a more casual basis, volumes are regularly published of memoirs of theatre people and collections of reviews, essays and photographs.

Polish theatre criticism itself basically divides along two lines. The first one, inspired by two longstanding editors – Edward Csató (1915–68) of *Teatr* and Konstanty Puzyna (1929–89) of *Dialog* – treats theatre as a diverse kind of art involving various aspects of performance. The second one tends to focus almost exclusively on the literary aspects of theatre.

The works of the country's best known theatre critic, Jan Kott (b. 1914), though heavily of the 'literary' school, are excellent examples of

the mutual interpenetration of politics and theatre criticism. Kott's *Shakespeare Our Contemporary* (1965), his best known work, has influenced a whole generation of critics and theatre practitioners. Equally influential among the generation of critics writing in the 1960s and 1970s has been the critical work of Puzyna, particularly in his editorial decisions relating to *Dialog*, a monthly.

Theatre specialists connected with *Pamiętnik Teatralny* (*Theatre Diary*) and the Arts Institute – Zbigniew Raszewski (1925–92), Bohdan Korzeniewski (1905–92), Barbara Król-Kaczorowska (b. 1921), Stanisław Marczak-Oborski (1921–87), Edward Krasiński (b. 1933) and others – are the authors of studies that have had genuine influence on Polish theatre culture. Grzegorz Sinko (b. 1923), also a professor at the Arts Institute, has dealt extensively with the theory of theatre from a semiotic standpoint.

People from the institute have also prepared

Słownik biograficzny teatru polskiego (*A Biographical Dictionary of Polish Theatre*) and *Dzieje teatru polskiego* (*The History of Polish Theatre*) which have appeared in several editions. Another book that is considered possibly the best guide to the history of Polish theatre is *Krótka historia teatru polskiego* (*A Short History of Polish Theatre*) by Zbigniew Raszewski (published in 1977).

Works dealing with the history and theory of theatre are regularly published by universities in Warsaw, Kraków, Wrocław, Łódź, Katowice, Poznań and Gdańsk. Theatre studies have developed, thanks to scholars such as Irena Sławińska (b. 1913) and Stefania Skwarczyńska (1902–88). In 1957, a classic publication appeared, Roman Ingarden's (1893–1970) *O funkcjach mowy w widowisku teatralnym* (*On the Functions of Speech in Theatrical Performance*). Later on, research into the semiology of theatre was further developed by Tadeusz Kowzan (b. 1922) who worked in France. Henryk Jurkowski (b. 1927), longtime president of UNIMA (the International Puppeteers' Union), has done extensive research on the history of puppet theatre.

Research and popularization work is also done by theatre museums in Warsaw and Kraków.

In the 1940s and 1950s, the most important polemics on theatre – often of an ideological and programmatic nature – appeared on the pages of literary weeklies such as *Kuźnica* (*Ironworks*), *Odrodzenie* (*Revival*), *Przegląd Kulturalny* (*Cultural Review*) and *Współczesność* (*This Age*). A number of theatres also published their own magazines.

The only independent specialist magazine, and for several years after 1950 the only one at all, was the monthly *Teatr*, founded in 1945 and for some time published as a biweekly. The characteristic feature of this publication is its reluctance to express opinions and its attachment to traditional literary theatre; the publication's goal has always been simply to observe and analyse contemporary theatre life.

In 1956, the monthly journal *Dialog* was launched under the editorship of Adam Tarn. In its first thirty-five years of publication it published approximately 1,400 Polish and foreign scripts. Besides essays and editorial discussions about contemporary drama and theatre, the journal has attempted to offer detailed documentation of outstanding performances both in Poland and around the world. In the 1970s, *Dialog* also played a significant role in promoting the achievements of Polish and foreign avant-garde theatre.

Another monthly, *Scena* (formerly *Teatr Ludowy*), founded in 1969, deals with amateur theatre. The Polish Centre of the International Theatre Institute has been publishing its own monthly, *Théâtre en Pologne/Theatre in Poland*, since 1958. In 1991, it became a bimonthly publication. The Polish Centre of UNIMA also publishes the quarterly, *Teatr Lalek*.

One of the most valuable annuals is the *Almanach Sceny Polskiej* (*Polish Stage Annual*), a yearbook listing all premières in the professional theatres including numbers of performances, cast lists and a detailed diary of major events in Polish theatre life. Updated information is gathered by ZASP and the Institute of Art at the Polish Academy of Sciences.

The Institute of Arts also publishes a scholarly quarterly devoted to theatre history called *Pamiętnik Teatralny* (*Theatre Diary*) containing documents and source material on Polish theatre history and, to a lesser extent, foreign theatre history.

Information and more general commentaries are published in both the national and local daily press. Cultural weeklies and monthlies, such as *Tygodnik Powszechny* (*Popular Weekly*), *Przekrój* (*Cross Section*), *Polityka* (*Politics*) and *Wprost* (*Outright*) and literary monthlies such as *Twórczość* (*Creativity*) and *Odra* (*The Oder River*) also regularly publish reviews, interviews, discussions and critical essays.

In Kraków, there is a documentation centre for the work of Tadeusz Kantor and his Cricot 2 company while in Wrocław, a similar centre is devoted to the work of Jerzy Grotowski and his Actors' Lab.

Jan Kłossowicz, Marta Fik, Paweł Konic,
Edward Krasiński, Elżbieta Wysińska
Edited by Małgorzata Semil and WECT staff

Further Reading

Csató, Edward. *The Polish Theatre*. Translated by Christina Cenkalska. Warsaw: Interpress, 1968. 191 pp.

Czerwinski, E.J. *Contemporary Polish Theater and Drama: 1956–1984*. New York: Greenwood Press, 1988.

——. 'The Polish Theatre of the Absurd'. In *Studies in Polish Civilization: Selected Papers Presented at the First Congress of the Polish Institute of Arts and Sciences in America*, ed. Damian S. Wandycz, 199–213. New York:

Institute on East Central Europe, Columbia University and the Polish Institute of Arts and Sciences in America, 1971.

Drozdowski, Bohdan, and John Calder, eds. *Twentieth Century Polish Theatre*. London: J. Calder, 1979.

Fik, Marta. *Trzydzieści pięć sezonów*. [Thirty-five seasons]. Warsaw: Wydawnictwa Artystyczne i Filmowe, 1981.

Filler, Witold. *Contemporary Polish Theater*. Translated by Krystyna Deplicz. Warsaw: Interpress, 1977. 147 pp.

Gąssowski, Szczepan. *Współcześni dramatopisarze polscy*. [Contemporary Polish playwrights]. Warsaw: Wydawnictwa Artystyczne i Filmowe, 1979.

Gerould, Daniel C. *Twentieth Century Polish Avant-Garde Drama: Plays, Scenarios, Critical Documents*. Ithaca, NY: Cornell University Press, 1977. 287 pp.

—— Bolesław Taborski, Steven Hart and Michał Kobiałka. *Polish Plays in Translation: An Annotated Bibliography*. New York: City University of New York, 1983.

Goldfarb, Jeffrey C. *The Persistence of Freedom: The Sociological Implications of Polish Student Theatre*. Boulder, CO: Westview Press, 1980. 159 pp.

Grodzicki, August. *Reżyserzy polskiego teatru*. [Polish theatre directors. Warsaw: Interpress Publishers, 1979. 185 pp.

——, and Roman Szydłowski. *Teatr w polsce ludowej*. [Theatre in people's Poland]. Warsaw, 1975.

Hartmann, Karl. *Das polische Theater nach dem zweiten Weltkrieg*. [Polish theatre after the Second World War]. Marburg, 1964.

Kłossowicz, Jan. *Tadeusz Kantor. Teatr*. Warsaw: Państwowy Instytut Wydawniczy, 1991.

Kumiega, Jennifer. *Theatre of Grotowski*. London: Methuen, 1985.

Marczak-Oborski, Stanisław. *Teatr czasu wojny*. [Theatre during the war]. Warsaw: Państwowy Instytut Wydawniczy, 1967.

Misiołek, Edmund. *Bibliographie théâtrale polonaise, 1964–1972*. [Polish theatre bibliography, 1964–1972]. Warsaw: Centre Polonais de l'ITI, 1974. 154 pp.

Osiński, Zbigniew. *Grotowski i jergo Laboratorium*. Warsaw: Państwowy Instytut Wydawniczy, 1980. Published in English as *Grotowski and His Laboratory*. New York: PAJ, 1986.

Puzyna, Konstanty. *Burzliwa pogoda*. [Stormy weather]. Warsaw: Państwowy Instytut Wydawniczy, 1971.

Semil, Małgorzata, and Elżbieta Wysińska. *Słownik wspołczesnego teatru*. [Dictionary of international theatre]. Warsaw: Wydawnictwa Artystyczne i Filmowe, 1980. 423 pp.

Sławinska, Irena. *The Slavic Contribution to the Great Reform*. Warsaw, 1972.

Strzelecki, Zenobiusz. *Wspólczesna scenografia polska*. [Contemporary Polish scenography], 2 vols. Warsaw: Arkady, 1983–4.

Sztaundynger, Jan, Henryk Jurkowski and Henryk Ryl. *Od szopki do teatru lalek*. [From Nativity scenes to marionette and puppet theatre]. Łódź, 1961.

Szydłowski, Roman. *Theatre in Poland*. Translated by Christina Cenkalska. Warsaw: Interpress, 1972. 176 pp.

Wolicki, Krzysztof. *Gdzie jest teatr?* [Where is theatre?]. Kraków: Wydawnictwo Literackie, 1978.

PORTUGAL

Located on the southwest Atlantic coast of Europe, Portugal shares the Iberian peninsula with Spain. Portugal has a population of 10.4 million people and a land area of 92,000 square kilometres (35,500 square miles). Since 1147, Lisbon has served as the country's political and cultural centre as well as its capital. The country's second city, Oporto, occupies the site of an ancient seaport known as Portus Cale (Door of Cale or Door of Gaul) from which the country itself takes its name.

The earliest known people in the area were the Lusitanians, who resisted Roman occupation for nearly two centuries. About the time of the birth of Christ, however, they were finally conquered. The Romans added new blood to the country as well as their language and religion. Modern Portuguese is closely linked to the dialect of northwestern Spain.

Historically, the country's theatre traces its roots back to the Middle Ages and the popularity of the *arremedilhos* (little farces) and the richness of the *momos* (jesters) of the court. The country's golden age of theatre was in the first half of the sixteenth century. In performance, the period was highlighted by the company of playwright, actor and director Gil Vicente (1465–1536); in dramatic writing, by works such as the tragedy *Castro* by António Ferreira (1528–69).

From the seventeenth century to the early nineteenth century, inquisitorial censorship dimmed the bright lights of early Portuguese theatre. The revolution of 1820, however, opened the way to genuine change. In 1837, a theatre school was started; in 1846, the Teatro Nacional (National Theatre) was created and quickly a new repertoire began to emerge in which Almeida Garrett's (1799–1854) *Frei Luís de Sousa* proved to be the masterpiece of romantic drama. Theatre, always popular in the capital, spread once again across the country. Between 1870 and 1900, some seventy-five theatre buildings went up in Portugal to house the many groups in existence and the many tours they were undertaking.

In 1910, the modern Portuguese Republic was declared. By 1926, however, a military *coup d'état* toppled the regime. A year later, the new government imposed official censorship on plays and productions. The reason given was 'to protect public opinion from perversion' and to help defend 'the fundamental principles of society'. For the next half century, Portugal's theatre activity was tightly controlled and managed to survive only outside the mainstream of contemporary theatrical movements and even then with great difficulty. The censorship was severe not only for Portuguese writers whose prohibited plays could be counted in the hundreds but also for other theatre artists who were forbidden to stage anything that could be considered in the least bit political. Included in this group were such plays as Shakespeare's *Julius Caesar*, Machiavelli's *La Mandragola*, Lope de Vega's *Fuente ovejuna* as well as all plays by Brecht, Sartre and Peter Weiss. Even performances of Witkacy's *The Mother* and Feydeau's *La Dame de chez Maxim* (*The Lady from Maxim's*) were disallowed.

Other factors also contributed to the deterioration of theatre practice in the country. Especially damaging was the high level of illiteracy and the low level of the economy. Few people could even afford to go to the theatre and it quickly became a fiefdom for the upper classes whose tastes and interests it clearly espoused. The economy also affected the choice of repertoire which had to be chosen in terms of potential profitability. Outside Lisbon, there was almost a total absence of professional companies. From a creative standpoint, Portugal was a desert with only a single oasis – and that a very circumscribed one – in the capital.

In 1945, the defeat of Nazi fascism threatened other fascist regimes still remaining in Europe, including Portugal's. A liberalization of sorts occurred at this time allowing Portuguese theatre artists at least some opportunity to catch up with theatrical events in other countries. Very quickly, both amateurs and professionals began to experiment with new forms and ideas. Though clearly limited in appeal and aimed at small audiences, these new approaches began to influence the repertoires of the large establishment companies which, with few exceptions, had been both cautious and dull since 1927. Among the few exceptions were the Teatro Nacional, which had been imaginatively managed since 1929 by the actress Amelia Rey-Colaço (1898–1990) and her husband Robles Monteiro (1888–1958); and the Comediantes (Comedians) de Lisboa, founded in 1944 by the actor-director Francisco Ribeiro (1911–84). From 1945 on, both companies were producing such authors as Anouilh, Cocteau, García Lorca, Pirandello, O'Neill, Giraudoux and Priestley.

The beginning of this new movement came from the Teatro Estudio Salitre (Salitre Theatre Studio) which began in 1946 and staged some twenty formally innovative productions by 1950. A number of similarly minded companies quickly appeared including the Casa da Comédia (Playhouse) in 1946; the Pátio das Comédias (Play Patio) in 1947; the Manuela Porto Company in 1949; the Teatro Experimental do Porto (Oporto Experimental Theatre) in 1953, the only regularly producing theatre group in the city of Oporto; and the student theatre at the University of Coimbra under the direction of Paulo Quintela (1905–87) which had started its own search for a new stage language in 1938.

In 1950, a national Theatre Fund was created by the state to assure finances for the development of national dramatic art. Modified in 1971, this fund had as its first obligation the 'promotion and regulation of theatrical activity as an artistic expression, as a cultural instrument and as public entertainment.' In practice, however, these noble intentions were minimized, even contradicted, by a bureaucratic network of prohibitions and over-centralization. Rather than freeing the Portuguese theatre, it actually held it back in a number of ways and in 1973 operation of the fund was condemned in petitions signed by a large number of leading theatre professionals.

A political revolution in the country in 1974 changed both government and culture. Theatre took an active role in the changes that occurred in the post-1974 period. In the years that followed this revolution, the country slowly moved toward a mixed economy and a growing sense of democracy. A national commission was established in 1974 to study the needs of theatre (including critics and audiences). Its report proposed new policies in areas such as decentralization and subsidy. Unfortunately, its findings were never enacted.

Nevertheless, the revolution redirected the activities of the many experimental and independent groups which had begun operation in the late 1960s and early 1970s. Founded by young actors and directors for the most part, these groups – the Teatro Moderno de Lisboa (Lisbon Modern Theatre) founded in 1961; the Teatro-Studio de Lisboa (Lisbon Studio Theatre), founded by Luzía María Martins (b. 1926) in 1964; the Teatro Experimental de Cascais (Cascais Experimental Theatre) founded in 1965; Casa da Comédia (1963); Grupo 4 (Group 4) founded in 1967; A Comuna and A Cornucopia, founded in 1973 – suddenly found themselves able to match both their ideological and aesthetic positions.

By the 1990s, despite occasional lapses into arbitrariness and despite only modest state subsidy (the Portuguese cultural budget was, in fact, the lowest in the European Community), theatre life was healthier than at almost any point in its recent history. Portuguese artists have managed to cross extraordinary boundaries both in cultural and political terms and have found new audiences in this country. Perhaps most tellingly, the commercial theatre – with the exception of musical revues – has practically disappeared.

Structure of the National Theatre Community

In 1945, Lisbon had 800,000 people and there were ten professional companies operating. Two were state supported – the Teatro Nacional, operated by Rey-Colaço and Robles Monteiro, and the Teatro São Carlos, which exclusively played opera and music.

Four other groups were privately run and played a fairly traditional repertoire of national and international comedies and dramas with an emphasis on plays from Spain and France – the Apolo, the Avenida, the Ginásio and the Trindade. Four other theatres, also privately operated, were doing strictly commercial seasons of comedies, farces, revues and light musicals. There were no professional companies existing anywhere else in the country, although many tours were being made to the city of Oporto where two theatres were operating regularly.

By the early 1950s, two new theatres had been erected in Lisbon – the Monumental (1951) and the ABC (1957). Oporto also opened its first modern company at this time (1953), the 100-seat Teatro Experimental under the direction of Antonio Pedro (1909–66). During the 1960s, three more theatre spaces were added in the capital – the Villaret (1965), the Vasco Santana (1964) and the Maria Matos (1969), while in Cascais, about 30 kilometres from Lisbon, another Teatro Experimental

opened in 1965, operating under the direction of Carlos Avilez (b. 1937).

In 1964, fire destroyed Lisbon's original Teatro Nacional; three years later, the Avenida also went up in flames. By the end of the 1960s, the Ginásio and the Apolo, and later the Monumental, were gone as well. Rather than causing a diminution in theatrical activity, however, the loss of so many spaces forced the independent companies coming along at this time to simply rethink the nature of their work and the kind of theatrical space they wanted. Most chose to move into non-traditional venues which fitted quite well with the work they were attempting.

They adapted existing buildings, as was the case with Os Bonecreiros (1971) in Moscavide, A Comuna (1973) in Praça de Espanha, Teatro da Cornucópia (1973) in Bairro Alto, and the Grupo de Teatro Hoje in Graça (1975), while Grupo 4 had a new building erected, the Teatro Aberto (Open Theatre), in 1976.

Another change after the revolution was a movement towards decentralization. The first regional cultural centre began operating in Évora in 1975, occupying the beautiful Teatro García de Resende, directed by Mário Barradas (b. 1931), but the companies in Oporto – the Teatro Experimental do Porto and the Seiva

The 1979 Teatro Experimental do Porto production of García Lorca's *Yerma*.

Trupe (1973) – could not boast of the same space facilities.

Other experiments outside Lisbon, though begun with a considerable enthusiasm, did not last long as subsidies began decreasing, as was the case with Faro, Leiria, Caldas da Rainha and two other companies in Oporto: TEAR (Teatro Estúdio de Arts Realista/Studio for Realist Art) and Os Comediantes. However, a change of policy in the late 1980s made it possible for some city councils to support municipal theatres, and a number of them began operating in restored theatres with proscenium arch stages or in formal theatres built for the purpose. Most

receive state subsidies, though modest, and the Teatro Nacional, which resumed its activity in 1978 after being restored, also began receiving direct state subsidy.

By 1992, Lisbon had a population of 1 million and could again boast ten regularly producing companies plus the Teatro Nacional and a half-dozen experimental or fringe groups. On the other hand, commercial theatre in the capital had been reduced to three groups – the Villaret for boulevard comedies and the ABC and the Maria-Vitória for musical revues.

Luiz Francisco Rebello

Artistic Profile

Companies

Among the companies that came into being in the 1960s only the Teatro Experimental de Cascais, directed by Carlos Avilez, continued operation into the 1990s. Its building – Teatro Marita Casimiro – in the outskirts of Lisbon, is a studio, not very large and with about 130 seats. Its repertoire includes Portuguese contemporary playwrights like Bernardo Santareno (1920–80), Jaime Gralheiro (b. 1930) and Miguel Rovisco (1959–87), as well as Brecht, Genet and Shakespeare, and its artistic direction tends to stress an emotional tone in the acting, together with a dynamic handling of stage space.

The two leading companies formed in the early 1970s and still operating in the 1990s were A Comuna and the Teatro da Cornucópia. Independent theatre groups, they tend to set themselves against both commercial theatre and the dominant political situation. The director of A Comuna, João Mota (b. 1942), who studied with Peter Brook, tends to stress corporality in his acting style and has developed a kind of ritualistic performance. The company originally did collective creations, but today Mota mainly directs the performances and designs the sets, while Carlos Paulo (b. 1951), the leading actor, creates the costumes. Its productions tend toward political satire (sometimes in the form of café-theatre or cabaret) or toward a kind of poetic celebration and they attract vast young audiences. It was particularly so with *A Viagem* (*The Voyage*, 1982) by Helder Costa (b. 1939), director of *A Barraca*, and *A Pécora* (*Drab*,

1990), by Natália Correia (1923–93), a distinguished poet, as well as with *Oedipus* or the Frenchman Richard Demarcy's *Um estrangeiro em casa* (*A Stranger in the House*) and *Dois corcundas e a lua* (*Two Hunchbacks and the Moon*). Since 1985 the company has a new building which has allowed it to experiment with space, even in-the-round, but the old building (right beside the new one) is still operating as a café-theatre. The space is also used for productions by visiting groups.

The Teatro da Cornucópia developed from a student theatre group at the University of Lisbon which made its first appearance in the late 1960s with the eighteenth-century play *Anfitrião* by Antónia José da Silva (1705–39). It was founded in 1973 by two young actor-directors, Luís Miguel Cintra (b. 1949) and Jorge Silva Melo (b. 1948). The latter left the company in the early 1980s to engage in film direction. The company's artistic focus is based on three major beliefs: first, the primacy of text (a passionate belief in the word, so as to construct and deconstruct meaning); second, theatre as analysis of life 'tortured by the idea of truth' and meaning in the world; and third, theatre which accepts and shows its own theatricality (a theatre of 'comical illusion').

Cintra, an intelligent and sensitive director, and one of the best Portuguese actors, plans his repertoire very carefully, often going against the grain of popular taste with an uncompromising accuracy and inventiveness. His space – the Teatro do Bairro Alto – is a large studio which resident designer, Cristina Reis (b. 1945), arranges differently for each performance. She always brings one or two elements (sometimes just props) from one production to the next in an attempt to confirm a living identity and continuity. Most of da Cornucópia's productions are done by its company of about twelve and many have been milestones in Portugal's theatre life: *E não se pode exterminá-lo?* (*And Couldn't We Exterminate It?*) by the German Karl Valentin, *Ah Q* (still with Melo in the company), *Auto da Feira* (*Pageant of the Fair*) and *Comédia de Rubena* (*Comedy of Rubena*) by Gil Vicente, *Der Auftrag* by Heiner Müller (1984 and 1992), *O público* (*The Public*) by Federico García Lorca and Shakespeare's *Much Ado About Nothing*.

Out of Grupo 4 came Novo Grupo (New Group) in 1982, directed by João Lourenço (b. 1944). With its own space, built in 1976, the company boasts a varied repertoire and is especially known for its productions of Brecht.

The Grupo de Teatro Hoje (Today's Theatre Group), operating in Graça and formerly directed by Carlos Fernando (d. 1992), plans its repertoire in cycles. One season saw several plays by Joe Orton, another by Tennessee Williams and another from Russian theatre. It is best known for its precise acting style and its focus on an essentially tragic universe.

Formed in 1975, A Barraca is run by Helder Costa and María do Céu Guerra (b. 1943), its leading actress. The Brazilian Augusto Boal directed some of its early productions and it has often produced works by the sixteenth-century playwright Gil Vicente.

In 1990, still another company came into being around the well-known comic actor Mário Viegas (b. 1948) – Companhia Teatral do Chiado, which operates in a studio at the municipal theatre.

Outside Lisbon, Évora has proved to be the most important theatrical centre since 1974, operating in a proscenium arch house – the municipally run Teatro García de Resende. In addition to its extensive seasons, the company includes a training school for actors, the puppet theatre Bonecos de Santo Aleixo, and editing of the review *Adágio*. Directed by Mário Barradas, it began to call itself CENDREV when it joined with another company, Teatro da Rainha, from Caldas da Rainha. Barradas studied in Strasbourg, France, and is now one of Portugal's leading directors, imaginatively creating a Brechtian style in such productions as *Auto da Lusitânia* (*Play of Lusitania*) by Vicente.

With the closing of TEAR and Comediantes, the Seiva Trupe became the only active company in Oporto. In addition to its regular performances, it also stages a very important annual festival for Spanish- and Portuguese-speaking companies, the FITEI.

The 1988 Grupo de Teatro Hoje production of Tennessee Williams's *Suddenly Last Summer.*

The major company in Almada is the Teatro Municipal de Almada, formerly the Teatro de Camnpolide. Directed by Joaquim Benite (b. 1943), best known for his work on historical plays, the company staged a brilliant play entitled *1383–1385*, about the dynastic succession crisis that occurred in Portugal at that time, written by resident dramaturge and playwright Virgílio Martinho (b. 1928). The group has also had success with the plays of José Saramago (b. 1922), *A noite* (*The Night*) and *Que farei com este livro* (*What Shall I Do With This Book?*).

On the outskirts of Lisbon, the Centro Dramático Inter-municipal Almeida Garrett (CDIAG) plays at the Teatro da Malaposta. Directed by José Peixoto (b. 1942), its work has been growing in quality with productions such as *A Midsummer Night's Dream* (1990) and *Kennedy's Children* (1993) by Robert Patrick, both directed by Rui Mendes (b. 1937).

After resuming activity in 1978, the Teatro Nacional found itself inviting guest directors such as Mário Feliciano, who directed an outstanding *Casa de Bernarda Alba* (*House of Bernarda Alba*) by García Lorca in 1983, and João Lourenço, who directed Brecht's *Mother Courage and Her Children* in 1986, with Eunice Munoz (b. 1928) in the leading role. But it was in productions by director Ricardo Pais (b. 1945) that the National finally reached its heights in productions of plays such as *Anatol* and especially *Fausto-Fernando-Fragmento*, a reflection on the Faust story by the Portuguese poet Fernando Pessoa (1888–1935).

Pais later became manager and artistic director of the Teatro Nacional and began planning a new repertoire, which included *Minetti* by Thomas Bernhard, performed by the great actor Ruy de Carvalho (b. 1927). Unexpectedly, the Minister of Culture personally invited director Filipe la Féria (b. 1945) to stage a spectacular production of *Passa por mim no Rossio* (*Pass by Me in Rossio*) at the National. A collection of some of the most famous and popular sketches from Portugal's *revista* (a combination of music hall and political satire) it proved such an overwhelming success that it ran for two years (1991–3), effectively closed down the National as an active repertory space and led to the resignation of Pais. Ultimately, it created a tremendous artistic emptiness in a company that was supposed to be at the centre of the country's theatrical art.

Maria Helena Serôdio

Dramaturgy

Most of the major Portuguese playwrights of the early part of the century had died by 1946 – Raul Brandão (b. 1867), António Patrício (b. 1878), Vitoriano Braga (b. 1888) and Alfredo Cortez (b. 1880). The only two major writers still working for the theatre at the end of the war were Ramada Curto (1886–1961) whose naturalistic formula comedies remained popular, and Carlos Selvagem (1890–1973), the author of the Teatro Nacional's 1944 masterpiece, *Dulcineia ou a última aventura de Don Quixote* (*Dulcineia or the Last Adventure of Don Quixote*).

The late 1940s and early 1950s saw a blossoming of new voices, some avant-garde. These were writers whose plays had been kept off Portuguese stages and who were not even able to have their works published until after the war; among them, the poet José Régio (1901–69) whose play *Jacob e o Anjo* (*Jacob and the Angel*) actually premièred in Paris in 1952; the painter José de Almada Negreiros (1893–1970); and novelist Branquinho da Fonceca (1905–74).

A new generation of playwrights emerged over the course of the 1950s. The result was plays such as *Um dia de vida* (*Barely a Day*, 1958) and *Os desesperados* (*The Desperate Ones*, 1961) by Costa Ferreira (b. 1918); *O vagabundo das mãos de ouro* (*Vagabond with Golden Hands*, 1960) by Romeu Correira (b. 1917); *O dia seguinte* (*The Day After*, 1953) and *Condenados à vida* (*Sentenced to Life*, 1963) by Luiz Francisco Rebello (b. 1924); and *A promessa* (*The Promise*, 1957) and *O crime da Aldeia Velha* (*The Crime of Aldeia Velha*, 1959) by Bernardo Santareno.

In 1960, a touring Brazilian troupe was given special permission to stage Brecht's *Der gute Mensch von Sezuan* (*The Good Person of Setzuan*), the first Brecht to be done in the country. The production attracted enormous attention especially when it was closed after only five showings for 'disturbing public order'. The fact was, however, that Brecht's Epic Theatre style along with the discovery of the Theatre of the Absurd began to exercise influence over the country's younger dramatists.

Playwrights began to deal in new ways with national history extracting from it alternative approaches to contemporary problems. It seemed possible at this time to actually affect society through the theatre and writers fashioned their plays with this aim in mind.

This was seen clearly in the work of José

Cardoso-Pires (b. 1925), particularly in *O render dos heróis* (*Relief of the Heroes*, first published in 1960 but not performed until 1965). Cardoso-Pires led the way for still other dramatists such as Luis Sttau-Monteiro (b. 1926) in his play *Feliz hente há luar* (*Praised be the Moonlight*, 1962); Santareno's *O Judeu* (*The Jew*, 1966); Luzía María Martins in *Bocage* (1967); and Luso Soares (b. 1924) in *Antonio Vieira* (1968). Miguel Franco (1918–88) approached this new activism from a naturalistic standpoint in his 1965 drama *O motim* (*The Riot*) while Jaime Gralheiro approached it from the style of expressionist realism in his 1972 play, *O fosso* (*The Ditch*).

Those working in a more absurdist and satirical style include Jaime Salazar Sampaio (b. 1925) whose major works include *As sobrinhas* (*The Nieces*, 1967) and *A batalha naval* (*The Naval Battle*, 1970); Prista Monteiro (b. 1922), author of *A rabeca* (*The Violin*, 1961) and *A bengala* (*The Cane*, 1962); Miguel Barbosa (b. 1925), author of *Os carnívoros* (*The Carnivores*, 1965); Augusto Sobral (b. 1933), author of *O borrão* (*The Stain*, 1962) and *Os degraus* (*The Steps*, 1964); and the poet Natália Correia, whose sumptuous language is reminiscent of Genet in her play *A pécora* (1966). Almost all of these writers, it should be noted, encountered censorship problems at one time or another in their careers.

Among the playwrights emerging in the 1980s, two stand out: first, the well-known novelist José Saramago, author of *A noite* (1979), a play about the 1974 revolution, *Que farei com este livro* (1980), a discussion about the relationship between art and power; and *A segunda vida de Francisco De Assis* (*The Second Life of St Francis of Assisi*, 1987); and second, Miguel Rovisco (1959–87), who committed suicide at 27 years of age yet left a considerable number of plays on historical themes including *Trilogia dos heróis* (*Heroes Trilogy*) and *Trilogia Portuguesa* (*Portuguese Trilogy*). One should also mention the work of Helder Costa, Virgílio Martinho, Carlos Coutinho (b. 1943), Júlio Valarinho (b. 1948) and particularly Norberto Ávila (b. 1936), a prolific and versatile playwright who wrote many modern works on classical themes: *Don João no jardin das delícias* (*Don Juan in the Garden of Delights*, 1987), *O marido ausente* (*The Absent Husband*, 1990) and *Arlequim nas ruinas de Lisboa* (*Harlequin in the Ruins of Lisbon*, 1992).

Among foreign authors, the works of Brecht have been most widely played in the period after the revolution. João Lourenço, in particular, staged two memorable Brecht productions during this period – *Der kaukasische Kreidekreis* (*The Caucasian Chalk Circle*) with the Grupo 4 in 1976 and *Mutter Courage und ihre Kinder* (*Mother Courage and Her Children*) at the Teatro Nacional in 1986.

Luiz Francisco Rebello

Directors, Directing and Production Styles

For a discussion of directing, see previous material in **Artistic Profile** and the opening, historical section.

Music Theatre

In contrast to development in many other European countries since 1945 (especially the concepts propounded by the German director Walter Felsenstein at Berlin's Komische Oper after World War II), Portuguese music theatre has remained attached to the most conservative traditions, particularly in opera. The reduction of the form to its purely musical elements could still be found in the 1990s at the Teatro São Carlos in Lisbon with its repertoire of Italian, German and French works.

Under the dictatorship (1932–68) of António de Oliveira Salazar (1889–1970), the eighteenth-century Teatro São Carlos had its foyers redesigned but not much else was done to breathe life into it. An ornament for politicians, the São Carlos, except for the chorus, was essentially an import house. Its singers were brought in from abroad for each production as were both the musical and stage directors and even designers. The orchestra came from the National Radio. Despite some modest changes, the situation essentially maintained itself even after the 1974 revolution. While there is today, for example, a resident company of singers and a resident orchestra, the repertoire is still foreign, as are the key artists and directors.

One of the few exceptions at the São Carlos

was a 1984 production of the Brecht–Weill opera *Aufstieg und Fall der Stadt Mahagonny* (*The Rise and Fall of the City of Mahagonny*) performed in Portuguese by a resident company under the direction of João Lourenço.

One of the most unusual musical theatres is the Marionetas de São Lourenço Teatro de Opera founded in 1972 under the name of the Companhia de Opera Buffa (the name was changed in 1974). Its goal was the revival of the Portuguese tradition of puppet opera which reached its height in the musical works of António José da Silva. Da Silva, known historically simply as 'The Jew', combined traditional narrative and stage techniques with musical forms in his work. The São Lourenço company has reconstructed both da Silva's work and the form generally while attempting to evolve a new form of music theatre with puppets. The company also tries in its work to bridge the gap between formal, educated speech and that which is used every day. The company combines professional singers, puppets and musicians on the stage. Run by puppeteer Helena Vaz (b. 1944) and composer José Alberto Gil (b. 1949) the São Lourenço company has had popular success both at home and abroad with such shows as *Don Quixote* in 1980 (based on da Silva's original text), Stravinsky's *L'Histoire du soldat* in 1982, *Salome* in 1982 (based on the folk forms of the province of Tras-os-Montes) and the revue *Barnum* in 1985.

For whatever reason, traditional opera does not seem to have attracted the interest of most Portuguese composers. Among the few who have written for the form are Ruy Coelho (1892–1986); Joly Braga Santos (b. 1924), author of a musical version of the neo-classic tragedy *Merope* in 1959 and a new version of Vicente's *Barcas Trilogy* in 1970; and Vitorino D'Almeida (b. 1939), author of the controversial *Canto da praia ocidental* (*Song of the Western Beach*, 1979). One should also mention here the 1970 stage cantata of the great composer Fernando Lopes-Graça (b. 1906), based on an *auto-sacramentale* by Vicente called *Don Duardos et Flerida*.

Another distinct and separate branch of Portugal's music theatre is represented by the *revista*, a Portuguese musical revue whose appearance on the stage dates back to the second half of the nineteenth century. It was in 1851 that the *revista Lisboa em 1850* (*Lisbon in 1850*) opened at the Teatro Ginásio (Gymnasium Theatre); it was a show combining satirical songs and sketches about the previous year in the capital. The style was imported from France and the production was an enormous popular success.

Similar revues, each becoming increasingly more Portuguese in flavour, have been produced regularly ever since. The *revista's* popularity was enormous even under pre-1974 censorship, when everyone was curious to see just how far its critical barbs would be allowed to go. Its popularity is still such today that even 'serious' authors contribute material and willingly link themselves to the tradition.

Mário Vieira de Carvalho,
Luiz Francisco Rebello

Dance Theatre

In the years following the war, Portuguese dance theatre was represented almost exclusively by the Companhia Verde Gaio (Green Jay Company). The company, created in 1940 by the state and operated under the aegis of the national Propaganda Department, was directed by dancer and choreographer Francis Graça (1902–80). The company had what could most kindly be termed an unfocused repertoire and it was difficult to know exactly what it was trying to be, a folk group or a classical ballet.

It was only with the creation in 1965 of a formal ballet troupe by the Lisbon-based Gulbenkian Foundation that dance theatre took a step forward in the country. Directed in the beginning by British-born Water Gore, then by Yugoslav-born Milko Sparemblek and from 1976 by Jorge Salavisa (b. 1939), the Gulbenkian Ballet has become widely known as Portugal's foremost dance company. The company has made particular contributions in the field of choreography, introducing the world to such innovative choreographers as Armando Jorge (b. 1938), Carlos Trincheiras (1940–92) and especially Olga Roriz (b. 1955).

In the late 1980s, a number of young choreographers began to be seen, including João Fiadeiro (b. 1965), Barrilaro Ruas (b. 1967, a former student of Corsetti), Vera Montero and Joana Providência, among others.

Luiz Francisco Rebello

Theatre for Young Audiences

One cannot speak about a theatre movement for young audiences prior to the revolution of 1974. Though there have been exceptions, most productions have been commercial in character. During the 1950s and 1960s, a company for children – Gerifalto – produced, with government support, a number of free performances, some of interest but most quite conventional in terms of repertoire and staging.

After 1974 came a vast and creative growth in shows for young audiences although they were and still are not as important as theatre for adults.

The work produced in this field can be divided into two sectors: performances by non-specialized groups and performances by specialized groups. Among the first, one finds productions by some of the important independent groups such as A Comuna, Teatro da Cornucópia, Casa da Comédia, Grupo de Camnpolide (currently Companhia de Teatro de Alamada), Centro Cultural de Évora (later the Centro Dramático de Évora) and the Teatro Experimental do Porto. The work of many of these groups is based on the ideas of French director Catherine Dasté, who has directed in Portugal.

Among the specialized groups, O Bando (founded in 1974) is the most important. Others of note include TIL (Teatro Infantil de Lisboa, 1976), Máscaras (1981) and Papa-Léguas (1983).

The first performances of O Bando were exclusively for children but grew into creations for all ages. The group was founded by João Brites (b. 1947). Brites lived for some years in Brussels as a political exile and studied scenography at the École des Beaux Arts as well as taking part in street theatre performances there.

The 1991 Teatro da Cornucópia production of Gil Vicente's *Comédia Rubena*.

A playwright, stage director, scenographer and actor, Brites has become one of the major artists in the Portuguese theatre. Turning generally to non-theatrical texts for his productions, Brites combines imaginative stagings with innovative scenic approaches. In his works, he has experimented with elements such as the façades of buildings, the surface of water, and forests, always trying to create a direct relationship between production and space while pointing out the openness of his scenic devices.

Some of Brites's productions for O Bando have become historical landmarks of the Portuguese theatre – *Afonso Henriques* (1982), adapted from Medieval texts; *Nós de um Segredo* (1986), a traditional text; *Viagem* (1987), after a tale by Sophia de Mello Andresen (b. 1922); *Montedemo* (1987), after a novel by Hélia Correia (b. 1949); *Estilhaços* (1989), after a text by Mário de Carvalho (b. 1944); *Terceira Margem do Rio* (1990), after a text by João de Guimarães Rosa; *Bichos* (*Beasts*, 1990), after tales by Miguel Torga (b. 1907); and *Boda d'Água* (1992), after poems by António Ramos Rosa (b. 1924).

In such a stocktaking, one should also note the work of other artists in this field such as José Caldas and Fernando Gomes (b. 1944) with TIL. Caldas, a Brazilian artist, has lived in Portugal since 1974 and, like Brites, chooses to adapt literary works, mainly by Brazilian authors. Among them are *Ou Isto ou Aquilo* (1979), after poems by Cecília Meireles; *A Vida Íntima de Laura* (1981), after a tale by Clarice Lispector; *Corda Bamba* (1983), after a story by Lygia Bojunga Nunes (with CCE); *Pleurer pour rire* (1984), by the Canadian author Marcel Sabourin (with Teatro Experimental de Cascais); *O Gato Malhado e a Andorinha Sinhá* (1984) by Jorge Amado (with Teatro Amador da Infância, Oporto); *A Mulher que Matou os Peixes* (1986), after a text by Clarice Lispector; and *Acende a Noite* (1988), after a text by Ray Bradbury.

His productions stand out not only for their dramatic poetry but also for their psychological investigation. In 1993, he staged a new work based on *A Vida Íntima de Laura* in French with the Théâtre des Jeunes Années from Lyon, presented at the Biennial of Theatre for the Young.

The young people's theatre of Fernando Gomes, generally based on his own texts, is

João Brites's 1990 Teatro O Bando production of Miguel Torga's *Beasts*.
Photo: Christian Altorfer.

both formally simple and conventional but instantly communicable.

Among other groups, Joana and Pé de Vento in Oporto (directed by João Luis) stand out.

Groups like O Bando, TIL and Papa-Léguas produce two or three shows per year, normally with government and/or local support, and these are shown mostly in schools. They also have their own modest premises.

Puppet Theatre

The tradition of marionette theatre in Portugal dates back to the sixteenth century. The most important and influential of its creators was António José da Silva, also a major playwright. His puppet operas were performed at Teatro do Bairro. A Jew, he died at the hands of the Inquisition.

The group Marionetas de São Lourenço, directed by José Gil and Helena Vaz, claims to be the successor of da Silva and has shown several of his operatic puppet works. With the assistance of musicians and singers, the company's performances stand out for their originality and modernity. The group has also set up a small but interesting museum of marionettes.

Another group which inherited a puppet tradition is the Bonecos de Santo Aleixo (Alentejo), a company of string marionettes which are accompanied by music and singing. Their performances reveal connections, on the one hand, with religious dramatic pieces of the Middle Ages and, on the other, with urban vaudeville. The Bonecos de Santo Aleixo, whose form was recovered by Mestre Jaleca and then Mestre Talhinhas, is now part of the Centro Dramático de Évora whose directors follow the old traditions. The group has been very successful both locally and abroad and is considered one of the most authentic forms of popular theatre still practised in Europe.

Still another group with intense activity in this domain is the Teatro da Branca-Flor, directed by Lília da Fonseca (b. 1916), whose performances were focused on children during the company's existence in Lisbon between 1963 and 1983.

The Marionetas de Lisboa (founded in 1985) is directed by costume designer José Carlos Barros (b. 1944) and uses various techniques of manipulation. The company has presented performances of great complexity, based on literary works such as *O Romance da Raposa* by Aquilino Ribeiro, *O Auto da India* by Vicente and *Don Quixote* adapted by Norberto Ávila. A newer group in Lisbon is the Lanterna Mágica.

Various individuals and amateur groups were instrumental in recovering these traditions. In Oporto it was João Paulo Seara Cardoso (b. 1956), an artist working on puppets of a popular character. Performances such as *A Vida de Esopo* (1987) and *Miséria* (1992) made his name known across the country.

Design
Theatre Space and Architecture

The most interesting examples of theatre architecture in Portugal date from the nineteenth century. Though many were pulled down or converted into cinemas, some rather worthy examples still exist. Among them are the Teatro Nacional de São Carlos – originally intended for opera, music and dance – and the Teatro da Trindade, devoted to drama. In Oporto, the Teatro Nacional de São João and the Auditório Nacional Carlos Alberto are still used for various types of theatrical activities. There are also the Teatro García de Resende in Évora, the Teatro-Circo in Braga, and the Teatro Sá de Miranda in Viana do Castelo. Each have their own companies.

All these theatres are in the Italian style and have capacities between 500 and 1,000 seats. In the 1970s and 1980s, independent groups converted a variety of open spaces into theatres, seldom exceeding 200 seats with most having between eighty and 150 seats.

There has been as well a real revolution in the field of stage design with a number of young artists working with directors to create superbly imaginative environments. The work of Cristina Reis, especially with the actor-stage director Luís Miguel Cintra, resulted in a series of designs at the Teatro da Cornucópia that were beautiful, inventive and modern in their use of shapes, images and materials.

Training

The teaching of drama in Portugal formally began on 5 May 1836 (the date of the decree for its establishment) and was due to the efforts of playwright Almeida Garrett. Garrett was a poet, novelist, minister and deputy, as well as a fighter for liberalism. He paid for the latter by jail and exile. Garrett, author of *Frei Luís de Sousa*, a masterpiece of romantic theatre, established a base for the teaching of drama with the creation of the Teatro Nacional and the National Conservatory of Lisbon.

In 1911, after the creation of the modern republic, positive reforms put the school on a level with those of most European countries. However, the 1926 dictatorship, with its dislike and distrust of theatre, transformed the school into a bureaucratic and inefficient teaching institution. It remained that way for nearly five decades.

In 1971, the Ministry of Education invited Mário Barradas, a stage director who had graduated from the theatre school in Strasbourg, France, to redesign the school and he did so with very positive results. With the support of Madalena Perdigão (1923–89), its director, new teaching methods were introduced along with new areas of apprenticeship and renewed attention was given to subjects such as physical expression, voice and acting skills.

After the revolution of 1974, the school went through another period of turbulence. By the end of the 1980s the school of drama – together with a school of cinema – had become autonomous and it is now known as the Higher School of Drama and Cinema. With about a hundred students, the school functions as a polytechnic institute.

There are as well several private schools – the Centro Dramático de Évora, the Instituto de

Formação, Investigação e Criação de Teatro in Lisbon, the Academia Portuguesa Contemporânea de Espectáculos and the Ballet-Teatro Contemporâneo in Oporto.

Academic study of drama is offered by the Faculty of Letters of the Universidade de Coimbra with post-graduate studies offered at the Faculty of Letters at the Universidade de Lisboa.

Carlos Porto

Criticism, Scholarship and Publishing

The first *Historia de Teatro Português* (*History of Portuguese Theatre*) was published in Lisbon in 1870–1 by the scholar Teófilo Braga. It was not until the 1960s, however, that other studies began to be published: both the Italian Luciana Picchio's *Storia del Teatro Portoghese* (1964) and Luiz Francisco Rebello's *História do Teatro Português* (1967) were important statements in the field.

Despite this long gap between histories, the modern period has been an active one for Portuguese criticism and scholarship. It is during this period that the country's classical writers have been rediscovered and studied (particularly Vicente, Garrett and da Silva) and much work has begun to be done on the contemporary theatre.

Yet despite this growth in interest, the publication of theatre books (both plays and books on theatre generally) is still extremely limited. One of the few regular sources of play publication is the Portuguese Society of Authors which, since 1970, has issued more than forty plays by contemporary Portuguese dramatists. Publication by commercial houses is occasional at best.

Most plays have traditionally been reviewed in local newspapers but rarely with more than a plot synopsis and a basic description of the event. Exceptions to this style of review have been rare with just a few names standing out – Jorge De Faria (1888–1960), a man whose writings showed a connoisseur's knowledge of Portuguese theatre history; Eduardo Scarlatti (1899–1990), one of the country's few theorists of dramatic art (his seminal 1928 essay *A Religião do Teatro* was reissued in 1945); and poet Adolfo Casais Monteiro (1908–72), musician Fernando Lopes-Graça and João Pedro de Andrade (1902–74), all of whom were especially attentive to literary aspects of the plays they wrote about. Today, the leading critics in the country deal with text as only one element of many in the theatrical experience.

One should also note the existence of a number of collections of reviews by leading critics, such as Junior Redondo (1914–91), Luis Forjaz Trigueiros (b. 1915), Urbano Tavares Rodrigues (b. 1923), Jorge De Sena (1914–91) and Carlos Porto (b. 1930).

Portugal's first national association of theatre critics was founded in 1980 and is linked to the International Association of Theatre Critics.

Luiz Francisco Rebello
Translated by Charles-Antoine Rouyer

Further Reading

Barbosa, Pedro. *Teoria do Teatro Moderno, axiomas e teoremas*. [Theory of the modern theatre, axioms and theorems]. Oporto: Edições Afrontamento, 1982.

Cruz, Duarte Ivo. *Introdução ao Teatro Portuguesa do Século XX*. [An introduction to the Portuguese theatre of the twentieth century]. Lisbon: Espiral, 1969.

França, José-Augusto. *Notícia duma Morfologia Dramática*. [Notes on a dramatic morphology]. Lisbon: Confluência, 1953.

Mendonça, Fernando. *Para o Estudo do Teatro em Portugal*. [Towards a study of theatre in Portugal]. Rio de Janeiro: Assis, 1971.

Pedro, António. *Pequeño Tratado de Encenação*. [A short treatise on the scene]. Lisbon: Confluência, 1962.

Picchio, Luciana. *Storia del Teatro Portoghese*. [History of the Portuguese theatre]. Rome: Edizioni dell'Ateneo, 1964. Republished in Portuguese, Lisbon: Portugália, 1969.

Porto, Carlos. *Em busca do Teatro Perdido*. [In search of the lost theatre]. 2 vols. Lisbon: Plátano Editora, 1973.

——. *10 Años de Teatro em Portugal*. [10 years of theatre in Portugal]. Lisbon: Caminho, 1985.

Rebello, Luiz Francisco. *100 Años de Teatro Português*. [100 years of Portuguese theatre]. Oporto: Brasília, 1984.

——. *Combate por um teatro de combate*. [The struggle for a theatre of struggle]. Lisbon: Seara Nova, 1977. 233 pp.

——. *História do Teatro Português*. [History of

the Portuguese theatre). Lisbon: Publicaçoes Europa-America, 1967. 141 pp.

——. *História do Teatro de Revista em Portugal.* [History of the Portuguese theatrical revue]. 2 vols. Lisbon: Dom Quixote, 1984–5.

——. *History of Theatre.* Translated by Candida Cadavez. Europalia '91 series 'Synthesis of Portuguese Culture'. Lisbon: Imprensa Nacional-Casa da Moeda, 1991. 112 pp.

——. *Teatro Moderno: Caminhos e Figuras.* [Modern theatre: trends and personalities], 2nd ed. Lisbon: Prelo, 1964.

Redondo, Junior. *Panorama do Teatro Moderno.* [An overview of modern theatre]. Lisbon: Arcádia, 1961.

Saviotti, Gino. *Filosofia do Teatro.* [Philosophy of the theatre]. Lisbon: In Quérito, 1945.

Soares, Fernando Luso. *Teatro, Vanguarda, Revolução e Seguança.* [Theatre, vanguard, revolution and bourgeois security]. Lisbon: Afrodite, 1973.

Tabucchi, António. *Il Teatro Portoghese del Dopoguerra.* [Portuguese theatre since World War II). Rome: Abete, 1976. 124 pp.

ROMANIA

Located on the Balkan Peninsula in southeastern Europe, Romania is bounded by the Ukraine and Moldova to the north and northeast, the Black Sea to the east, Bulgaria to the south, Serbia to the southwest and Hungary to the northwest. The country's official language is Romanian, a neo-Latin language, mother tongue to about 89 per cent of the population. Among other languages spoken in the country are Hungarian, German, Yiddish and Greek. The country's 1991 population was 23.2 million, with just over 2.3 million people living in the capital city of Bucharest.

First settled northeast of the Danube river over 2,000 years ago by the Geto Dacian people, the country has changed its size many times through the millennia as a result of invasions, occupations and wars. In 1991, it consisted of some 237,500 square kilometres (91,700 square miles). In the second century, Roman legions conquered and settled the region and the language and customs of the Romans took root. As the Roman Empire began to crumble in the third century, Dacia was overrun by various invaders including the Goths, Huns, Gepidae, Avars, Slavs and Tartars. At the beginning of the thirteenth century, the Hungarian Kingdom conquered Transylvania, inhabited by a Romanian population, but this province conserved its political individuality. During many centuries, Romanians lived separated into three states – the principalities of Wallachia, Moldavia and Transylvania – but economic, political and cultural links remained strong thanks to their common language and spiritual traditions.

During the sixteenth century, the three principalities were forced to accept Ottoman domination, but again preserved their autonomy. In 1858 Wallachia and Moldavia won some degree of independence from the Ottoman Empire and in 1859, the two provinces united under Alexandru Ioan Cuza (1820–73), who was elected prince. The new country was named Romania, gained its independence in 1877–8 and in 1881 became a kingdom under the Hohenzollern dynasty.

In World War I, Romania fought alongside France, Great Britain, Italy, Russia and the United States against the Central Powers and their allies. At the end of the war, in 1918, Bessarabia and Bucovina as well as Transylvania – territories which had been under foreign domination – decided to unite with Romania, at the time a constitutional monarchy.

In 1940, Romania was forced to cede Bessarabia and Northern Bucovina to the Soviet Union, the northern part of Transylvania to Hungary, and the southern part of Dobruja to Bulgaria. In June 1941, Romania entered World War II as an ally of Germany against the Soviet Union in order to recover the territories lost in 1940. In 1944, Romania switched to the side of the Allied armies and again liberated Transylvanian territories.

The new government established after the war included several members of the Communist Party. In 1945, backed by the Soviet army, the communists took control of the country and in 1947, the king was forced to abdicate. A socialist political system was quickly installed, ruled by the Communist Party. Within a year, the country's principal enterprises and cultural institutions were nationalized. In 1965, Nicolae Ceauşescu (1918–89) became president of the State Council and in 1974, he was elected president of the republic, a position he held with an iron grip until he was deposed by a popular revolution in December 1989. The end of the Ceauşescu regime opened the way to the establishment of a more democratic, constitutional system, one more favourable to creativity in the country.

Theatrical performances have an equally long history in Romanian territory with evidence of such events dating back to the sixth century BC. Documents attest to the existence of theatrical events in various languages during the Middle Ages, though it seems clear that the most significant contribution to the performing arts at the time was a developing folk theatre. Most such performances developed out of pre-Christian rituals and magic practices over which Christian meanings were superimposed as time went by.

The development of a more formal drama in the Romanian language was clearly hampered by the long-term political instability of the territories. The earliest performances in the Romanian language, in fact, were not staged until the eighteenth century when seminary students staged such performances in Blaj, Oradea and Beiuş (Transylvania). The Oradea text (dating from 1770–80) was, in fact, discovered only in 1900 – *Occisio Gregorii in Moldavia Vodae, tragedice expressa* (*Prince Gregorii's Killing in Moldavia, Expressed in Tragedy*). It is unusual in that it was written in both Latin and Romanian but appears in a Cyrillic script. The play was staged in 1970 at the State Theatre in Oradea. In 1982, it was staged again at the Bulandra Theatre in Bucharest as part of a double bill with another early Romanian play, *Barbul Văcărescul, vînzătorul ţării* (*Barbul Vacarescul, Traitor to His Country*), written about 1828 by Iordache Golescu (1768–1848).

In the nineteenth century, Romanian theatrical life was energized by a growing national consciousness, a movement which came to fruition in 1848. In Moldavia, it was animated by young intellectuals, the most important of whom was Gheorghe Asachi (1788–1869), a playwright, director, designer and producer. Asachi was responsible for the production of a pastoral called *Mirtil si Hloe* (*Myrtle and Chloe*) staged in Iaşi in 1816, in Romanian.

In 1819 in Bucharest, the Theatre at Cişmeaua Roşie (itself built only two years before) presented its first Romanian-language performance, an adaptation of Euripides' *Hecuba*. By 1833, Bucharest had established a Philharmonic Society and it was there that the first generation of Romanian actors was trained under the guidance of Constantin Aristia (1800–80). Asachi was involved in the estab-

lishment of still another Philharmonic Dramatic Conservatory in Iaşi in 1836; in Transylvania, the scholar Gheorghe Bariţiu (1812–93) laid the foundations for a 'troupe of dilettanti' in Blaj and another later in Braşov.

Vasile Alecsandri (1821–90) wrote a number of plays in Romanian, establishing in a way the basic directions and styles of Romanian dramatic literature. Among his works are satiric comedies, historic dramas, musical fantasies and verse satires. Founder of the National Theatre in Iaşi, a theatre which today bears his name, his plays can still be seen more than a century after their creation.

Generally regarded as Romania's greatest playwright is the writer who inherited Alecsandri's mantle but surpassed his predecessor, Ion Luca Caragiale (1852–1912). A prose writer, journalist, theatre manager and theatre theorist, Caragiale's reputation rests on four major comedies, one drama and a large number of 'flashes and sketches'.

Barbu Stefănescu-Delavrancea (1858–1918) and B.P. Haşdeu (1838–1907) further developed the genre of historical drama while great actors and directors such as the realist Matei Millo (1814–96), the more romantic Mihai Pascaly (1830–82) and the actor-director-teacher Constantin I. Nottara (1859–1935) advanced the art of performance still further, as well as Alexandru Davila (1862–1929), a playwright, director and theatre manager, founder of the first private theatre company in Romania and promoter of a more complex concept of a realistic modern performing art.

By the turn of the century, Romanian theatre could be seen as following the basic trends and developments of European theatre as a whole. It

The Vasile Alecsandri National Theatre in Iaşi, built in 1896.

came to play a leading part for a time in the period between the two world wars, when culture generally was given real recognition. Evidence of this can be found in many arts, ranging from the internationally admired sculptor Constantin Brâncuşi (1876–1957) to the musician and composer George Enescu (1881–1955); from writer and philosopher Mircea Eliade (1907–86) to poet, playwright and philosopher Lucian Blaga (1895–1961). In the theatre, it was the period of great directors and producers such as Soare Z. Soare (1894–1944), Victor Ion Popa (1895–1946), Ion Sava (1900–47) and George Mihail Zamfirescu (1898–1939).

After World War II, Romania had four well-established companies operating – the National Theatres in Bucharest, Iaşi, Cluj and Craiova – and a number of more or less stable private troupes, mostly in Bucharest. In 1948, all the theatres in the country were nationalized and a network of state institutions was created in both large and small centres. In a few years, the number of theatre companies increased across the country with new National Theatres established in Timişoara and Tîrgu-Mureş while some two dozen new companies came into being at district and municipal levels in various cities. Separate companies were created for ethnic minorities in their own languages – six in Hungarian, two in German and two in Yiddish. State subsidy went as high as 80 per cent of each theatre's budget.

Since that time, it is possible to identify at least four different periods in Romanian theatre development. The first period runs from 1948 to about 1960. During this time, the newly nationalized and the newly founded theatres were directed consciously to move their repertoires away from what were called bourgeois concerns and to try to build a new repertoire based on the ideas of humanism and socialist-realism. While this occurred to some extent, full-blown socialist-realism proved a utopian dream.

Nevertheless, writers who wanted their plays produced had to grapple with socialist-realism for many years. For some, the most imaginative, it was taken as a kind of neo-romanticism, realized dramatically by presenting uncompromising 'positive characters'. Comparing their heroes to those of the *Sturm und Drang* tradition, this was the only positive approach that writers seemed willing or able to take in response to the new ideological requirements.

Some others were unable to find a way through the ideology, however, and found themselves, at the very least, unproduced during this period. This was particularly true between 1950 and 1960, years that came to be called the 'haunting decade', with writers often finding themselves *persona non grata*.

Between 1960 and 1971, the next period, dependence on the Soviet Union and Soviet models gradually decreased in both social and cultural life and a certain amount of liberalization set in. This could be seen in the theatre in the widening of the repertoire, in the flourishing of many trends of 'theatrical' theatre, and in outspoken new plays by Dumitru Radu Popescu (b. 1935) who passionately anatomized the Stalinist period. In the 1970s, flouting official conventions, he created a series of plays which ranged from fantasy and surrealism to the absurd.

A third period of development can be seen starting in about 1971 and continuing to the people's revolution and the fall of Ceauşescu in 1989. During this time, theatrical styles as well as the general cultural situation changed once more with many artists feeling a need to do more than simply mirror life. Rather, they wanted to debate the very meaning of existence.

In this period, many of Romania's greatest directors – feeling constrained in their creative freedom – simply left. Among them were Liviu Ciulei (b. 1923), who became active first in West Germany, then in the United States and Australia; Lucian Pintilie (b. 1933), who worked both in France and the United States; David Esrig (b. 1935), who worked mostly in West Germany; Lucian Giurchescu (b. 1930), who worked in Denmark and Sweden; Radu Penciulescu (b. 1930) in Sweden; Vlad Mugur (b. 1927) in West Germany; and Andrei Şerban (b. 1943) in the United States. A few of these directors later returned, but the overall loss to Romanian theatre was enormous.

Nevertheless, despite the loss of so many important artists, the theatre moved to even deeper issues with official positions often rejected, though subtly. A split personality of sorts began to emerge on the Romanian stage at this time – an amiable external image which would be acceptable to those in authority but one which often masked disturbing social questions. This public image and its polemical counterpart created a clever duplicity which went to the heart of Romanian life. It was this double level, in fact, which helped Romanian theatre to survive the Maoist-style cultural revolution which wreaked heavy damage on all the arts during this difficult period.

In 1990, the situation changed once again.

With the fall of Ceauşescu and a general loosening of dogma throughout eastern Europe in the wake of the collapse of the Soviet Union, theatres began to recover their artistic independence. A whole range of new regulations for the functioning of theatres began to be drafted, this time in consultation with artists themselves.

The network of state theatres was kept alive, but the relations between theatres and authorities – central or local – changed, becoming simply administrative. All kinds of ideological censorship and central direction were abolished.

Also in 1990, an independent theatre organization called UNITER (the Romanian Theatre Union) came into being whose aim was to foster creativity and international exchanges, stage festivals, arrange tours and set up colloquia. UNITER (Uniunea Teatrală din România) replaced the former ATM (Association of Theatre and Music Artists). One other association for music and dance artists was also created, replacing the musical branch of the ATM, called UICCM (Uniunea Interpreţilor, Coregrafilor şi Criticilor Muzicali – Union of Performers, Choreographers and Music Critics).

Many directors were fired and new ones elected at this time by company members. Several private companies also came into operation, some commercial in approach, others still supported by the state.

Structure of the National Theatre Community

In Romania in 1993, there were forty-two dramatic companies in operation, along with five opera companies, nine music theatres of various types, three dance companies (besides the dance troupes of the operas and other music theatres) and seven private groups. There were also nineteen puppet and marionette theatres.

Bucharest had the largest concentration of companies in the country. In addition to the National, there were at least a half-dozen other regularly producing troupes, several with more than one auditorium, as well as the Opera Română company and the Ion Dacian Operetta Theatre. Other national companies were operating in Cluj-Napoca, Craiova, Iaşi, Timişoara and Tîrgu-Mureş. Theatres also existed in at least twenty smaller cities across the country, among them Arad, Brăila, Braşov, Constanţa, Piatra Neamţ, Oradea, Galaţi and Sibiu.

As well, the country had six groups working in the Hungarian language – in Cluj (where the first Hungarian theatre began in 1792), as well as in Sfântu-Gheorghe, Timişoara, Tîrgu-Mureş, Oradea and Satu-Mare; and two in German – in Sibiu (a city with a German-language theatre tradition going back more than 200 years) and in Timişoara. Bucharest also had one Yiddish-language company carrying on the tradition of the Yiddish theatre founded in Iaşi in 1876.

Most Romanian theatres have permanent troupes ranging from fifteen to seventy-five actors, up to three directors, one or two resident designers as well as technical and administrative staff. Most also have their own buildings.

State subsidies cover 80–90 per cent of company budgets and are distributed through the Ministry of Culture (to the national theatres, the State Hungarian Theatre in Cluj-Napoca and

Gábor Tompa's 1992 Cluj Magyar State Theatre production of Eugène Ionesco's *The Bald Soprano*, designed by Judit Kothay Dobre.

the Romanian Opera in Bucharest) and through district and municipal authorities according to programmes proposed by the theatres. For special activities – festivals or national or international tours – additional subsidies can also be granted.

Most Romanian theatres are repertory companies, staging an average of four to six premières each season in addition to a number of productions carried in their basic repertoires. Some of them stage even more. Most seasons therefore see between 150 and 200 openings representing a mix of Romanian and world drama, both classical and contemporary.

In addition to professional troupes, there are also a large number of non-professional groups operating. These include groups doing folk plays, others doing more or less the same repertoire as the professional theatres and still others committed to more experimental work.

Among the major festivals in the country are the annual I.L. Caragiale National Festival based in Bucharest and gathering the best productions from across the country; the annual International Festival in Piatra Neamţ; the annual Image Theatre Festival in Satu-Mare; the Contemporary Theatre Festival which from 1993 was to be known as the International Festival of Contemporary Theatre in Braşov; the Week of Short Forms of Theatre in Oradea; and

the Gala of Young Actors in Costineşti. All these festivals have international participation and are competitive.

The most important national prizes in theatre and drama each year include the Caragiale National Festival Prizes – the Festival Prize and the Bucharest Trophy (for Best Production), the Best Production of a Romanian Play, the UNITER Prize for Original Creation, the Toma Caragiu Prize for Best Début, the Ion Sava Prize for Best Director, the Best Design Prize, the Lucia Sturdza Bulandra Prize for Best Performance by an Actress, the Costache Aristia Prize for Best Performance by an Actor; and the annual Critics Association Prizes, along with UNITER Prizes for Best Production, Best Actor, Best Actress, Best Director, Best Designer, Best Critic, as well as its Life Award, Theatre Schools Production Award and the Year's Best Romanian Play Award.

Before 1990, ticket prices at Romanian theatres were kept low but were still twice that of films. Since 1990, ticket prices have risen and become variable, but they are still relatively low because of state subsidies. Sometimes theatre tickets are only half the price of film tickets (which have also risen) but occasionally, for special productions, they surpass film ticket prices, and can cost the same as three or four loaves of bread.

Artistic Profile

Companies

The largest number of companies in Romania can be found in Bucharest, the country's cultural and political capital. The Bucharest companies' prestige constantly attracts the best actors, directors and designers and most are contracted for life, although some are contracted only for a season or even just for a production.

The largest and oldest of the Bucharest companies is the National (set up in 1852) which has seventy-five actors and works on four stages. It has carried on the realistic traditions inherited from its nineteenth-century forerunners and the duty to foster and promote national Romanian drama. Its style expanded under directors Ion Sava and Soare Z. Soare, who sought more visual effects. It was run after 1944 by major writers and cultural personalities including

Victor Eftimiu (1889–1972), Tudor Vianu (1897–1964) and Zaharia Stancu (1902–74). After 1948, director-producer Sică Alexandrescu (1896–1973) created within the National what became known as the 'Golden Company of Comedy' with a group of extraordinary actors, counterbalanced by the work of the subtle and analytical director Mony Ghelerter (1905–79) and the romantic Alexandru Finţi (1910–72). From 1969 to 1989 the National was run by actor Radu Beligan (b. 1918). In 1973 the National moved into a new building, after years of wandering caused by the destruction of its beautiful original building (dating from 1852) which had been bombed by the Nazis in 1944.

The new building required even more spectacular productions, an approach that fitted with the work of Horea Popescu (b. 1926), whose Monumental style was effective on the proscenium stage of the large auditorium (1,187 seats). After Radu Beligan's retirement in 1990, Andrei Şerban was named director-general and proceeded to redevelop the troupe by hiring many young actors and actresses and diversifying the production styles through both his own stagings and others by invited young directors. The country's 'first stage' under Şerban was quickly going from simply restaging scripts to doing the most up-to-date experiments in a wide variety of styles.

Another company of significance in Bucharest is the Bulandra. Founded in 1947 as the Municipal Theatre, it bears the name of its first director, Lucia Sturdza Bulandra (1873–1961), a great actress and teacher with a majestic deportment, whose personality imprinted a style of high artistic rigour on the company. Under the later leadership of Liviu Ciulei, the Bulandra Theatre achieved fame through its overtly theatrical style. Its artistic boldness was often at odds with the authorities and some of its productions were banned after just a few performances. In 1990, its manager was Ion Caramitru (b. 1942), a leading actor who had taken an active role in the people's revolution of December 1989 and who had also been elected in 1990 president of the newly created Romanian Theatre Union (UNITER). The Bulandra works in two houses – one with a large proscenium stage, the other with a 385-seat thrust stage (the Toma Caragiu Auditorium).

The Mic Theatre, another company of importance, was created in 1961 by Radu Penciulescu through a merger of two other troupes. It is still noted for its bold explorations of the Romanian and world repertoire. Even after Penciulescu's departure, under the management of writer Dinu Săraru (b. 1932), it has regularly encouraged young directors with poetical imagistic approaches, among them Cătălina Buzoianu (b. 1938), Silviu Purcărete (b. 1950), Cristian Hadjiculea (b. 1952) and metaphorical playwrights such as Romulus Guga (1939–83).

The Comedy Theatre, created in 1961 by Radu Beligan, who was followed by director Lucian Giurchescu, aimed at presenting on stage the 'human comedy' of all times and forms, from the ancients and Shakespeare to various styles of contemporary poetic, satirical, absurdist or dramatic comedy. The company has been extremely popular with audiences.

Located in an outlying district of Bucharest, the Giuleşti Theatre was created in 1946 through a blending of professional and amateur actors as the Theatre of Railway Workers, with

The 1961 Bulandra Theatre production of Shakespeare's *As You Like It*, directed and designed by Liviu Ciulei.

a popular repertoire and largely accessible performance style. Thanks to the young directors who started their careers there – among them Horea Popescu, Lucian Giurchescu and Dinu Cernescu (b. 1935), encouraged by manager Elena Deleanu (b. 1920) – the company acquired a special place in Bucharest's artistic life through its large, theatrical productions highlighting the political meanings of Brecht, Mayakovsky and Shakespeare. Receiving a second building in the city's centre (the Majestic Hall), its activity became more diverse. After 1990, it changed its name to the Odeon Theatre, and under the leadership of director Alexandru Dabija (b. 1955) has focused most of its work on the Majestic, doing mainly experimental stagings. It has had particular success in exploring stage space. The Giuleşti house is dedicated mostly to multimedia activity. In 1992, the Odeon also started to stage experimental work in a small attic hall.

The Nottara Theatre was created in 1946 as the Army Theatre and later became a civic theatre run by the great actor George Vraca (1896–1964) who created its classical style. In 1965, the company became known as the Constantin Nottara Theatre. Under the leadership of playwright Horia Lovinescu (1917–83), it also developed experimental activities, encouraging young playwrights and promoting new works. Its repertoire is generally eclectic, ranging from boulevard comedies to high tragedy and musicals. It works in two auditoriums in the same building and has also been run by the theatre scholar, Victor Ernest Masek (b. 1937).

Among the new companies that emerged in Bucharest after 1990 is Masca (Mask), created and run by the actor-mime Mihai Mălaimare (b. 1950). It has a most original style, mixing mime and body expression with masks, in a repertoire based on folk and Medieval farces or adaptations of world classics. It has a permanent troupe, is state subsidized, but has no building of its own, so it operates in various spaces, both in the open air and indoors. It has a special interest in international activities.

Outside Bucharest, the other National Theatres, located one in each province, serve as national cultural centres, producing classics as well as contemporary works by both Romanian and foreign authors.

The National Theatres in Iaşi and Craiova have traditions going back to the early 1800s, but their styles follow the most advanced trends of today's theatre and change as their directors change. The National Theatre in Craiova, for example, owes its fame to director Silviu Purcărete, who worked regularly with the company as a guest director. The National Theatre in Cluj-Napoca, on the other hand, was created in 1919, to represent Romanian cultural spirituality in the capital city of Transylvania. The particular national character of these theatres is given by their various historical backgrounds and geo-cultural positions. That is also the case with the National Theatre in Timişoara and with the National in Tîrgu-Mureş (a National Theatre with two troupes in the same building, one working in the Romanian language and the other in Hungarian).

Other companies of note outside Bucharest have been the Youth Theatre in Piatra Neamţ and the Drama Theatres in the cities of Braşov, Brăila, Constanţa, Oradea and Satu-Mare.

Dramaturgy

Lucian Blaga was one of Romania's greatest poets and thinkers and also the author of a number of dramatic works, most of which are at least partly based in expressionism. Rooted in national folk traditions, his work utilized legends and myths and was indebted as well to the dramatic ideas of the nineteenth-century poet Mihai Eminescu (1850–89). Though Blaga pointed the theatre in new directions, few of his ideas came to fruition in production although

many have experimented with his works, especially since the 1960s. Marginalized for a time after 1945, his most important works are from the pre-1945 period and include *Zamolxe* (1921), *Tulburarea apelor* (*Turgid Waters*, 1923), *Meşterul Manole* (*Master Builder Manole*, 1927) and *Cruciada copiilor* (*Children's Crusade*, 1930).

Another writer whose work was primarily from the pre-war period but who continued to exercise real influence in the years after World War II was Camil Petrescu (1894–1957). A prose writer, essayist, dramatic theorist as well as a playwright, his plays tend to focus on the tragic destiny of the intellectual, the professional seeker of ideas, the doubter searching for the absolute. Among his most important plays are *Jocul ielelor* (*The Fairies' Dance*, published in 1919, first performed in 1964), *Act veneţian* (*Venetian Act*, 1964), *Suflete tari* (*Strong Characters*, 1938) and *Danton* (published in 1931, premièred in 1975).

Still another pre-war dramatist whose classical tragedies and satirical comedies bear the imprint of a school of drama untouched by official dogma was Victor Eftimiu.

The post-war period also inherited a lot of comedies which had been written earlier but were still produced often after 1948, many in the Caragiale tradition. Perhaps the most popular of the comic dramatists was Tudor Muşatescu (1905–70) whose one-line quips became known as 'muşatisms' and were hugely enjoyed in their time. Muşatescu wrote witty and delicate satires with romantic characters who strongly opposed middle-class pragmatism. The most often produced of his plays was *Titanic-Vals* (1932).

Trained like Muşatescu in the French tradition of the well-made play, Mircea Ştefănescu (1898–1982) wrote both sentimental comedies and dramas which dealt with the tragedies of everyday living. Still another writer in this tradition was Alexandru Kiriţescu (1888–1961) whose masterpiece was *Gaiţele* (*Jay Birds*, 1932), an Ibsenesque study of a rootless aristocracy.

Gheorghe Ciprian (1883–1968) is the author of a series of unusual comedies anticipating the absurdist style of Romanian-born dramatist Eugène Ionesco (1912–1994). Among Ciprian's major plays are *Omul cu mârţoaga* (*Man With a Jade*, 1927) and *Capul de răţoi* (*The Duck's Head*, 1940). Mihail Sebastian (1907–45), another of the pre-war sentimentalists, is the author of, among other plays, *Steaua fără nume* (*A Nameless Star*, 1943), still another play which has been an ongoing part of the repertoire of most post-war Romanian theatres.

During the post-war years, playwrights struggled with the concept of socialist-realism. The plays of Mihail Davidoglu (1910–88) were literally swarming with the working class and those of Lucia Demetrius (1910–92) effectively dealt with the impact of communism on middle-class families. Davidoglu's *Minerii* (*The Miners*, 1949) and *Cetatea de foc* (*City of Fire*, 1950) ushered in Romania's new drama of a more industrial milieu.

Horia Lovinescu, despite official dogma, created important works at this time in a realistic/symbolic style. One of the most prominent playwrights in the country, Lovinescu's *Citadela sfărâmată* (*The Crumbling Citadel*, 1955) was a powerful family drama showing both a conflict of ideas within the home and a society in decline outside. Among Lovinescu's important later plays were *Moartea unui artist* (*Death of an Artist*, 1964), a drama about self-denial and the conflict between existential anguish and classical harmony, and *Omul care şi-a pierdut omenia* (*The Man Who Lost His Sense of Humanity*, 1965). His 1979 parable,

Jocul vieţii şi al morţii în deşertul de cenuşe (*A Game of Life and Death in the Ashen Desert*) was a reconstruction of the Cain and Abel myth with the background of a planetary nuclear catastrophe.

Aurel Baranga (1913–79) ushered in a new generation of social satire in the 1950s and 1960s. His earliest success was with *Mielul turbat* (*The Mad Lamb*, 1954). Other important plays by Baranga include *Siciliana* (1960), *Opinia publică* (*Public Opinion*, 1967) and *Interesul general* (*General Interest*, 1971). Other satirists of note include Alexandru Mirodan (b. 1927) and Tudor Popescu (b. 1930). Some of Mirodan's plays were quite realistic such as *Ziariştii* (*The Pressmen*, 1956) while others contained elements of fantasy such as *Şeful sectorului Suflete* (*Head of the Heart Department*, 1962). Popescu's originality lay in a unique mixture of satire and cruel farce sweetened by a compassionate outlook. It could be seen clearly in such plays as *Paradis de ocazie* (*Second Hand Paradise*) and *Concurs de frumuseţe* (*Beauty Contest*), both written and produced in 1979.

Working in a different genre was Paul Everac (b. 1924) who treated with equal skill issues of

Dan Micu's 1979 Nottara Theatre production of Horia Lovinescu's *A Game of Life and Death in the Ashen Desert.*

689

industrialization, and civil and moral awareness in such plays as *Camera de alături* (*The Adjoining Room*, 1970) and *A cincea lebădă* (*The Fifth Swan*, 1979). He also dealt with these ideas in the historical drama *Urme pe zăpadă* (*Snow Tracks*, 1969) and two 1982 plays, *Salonul* (*The Drawing Room*) and the epic drama *Costandinestii* (*Costandin's Kind*). In the latter play he reflected on history as cultural destiny.

Alexandru Sever (b. 1921) patiently and resolutely built an *oeuvre* of contemporary tragedies, ignoring official positions. A concern over fascist terror became the basis for an earnest meditation on the tragic condition of twentieth-century humanity in his play *Ingerul bătrîn* (*The Elderly Angel*, 1980). Language generally is the strength of his works with the best known being *Descăpățînarea* (*Beheading*, 1977) and *Leordenii* (*Leordeni's Kind*, 1984).

Dumitru Radu Popescu broke with the established styles in the late 1960s and 1970s in such plays as *Cezar, măscăriciul piraților* (*Caesar, the Pirates' Jester*, 1969), a fantasy hovering between surrealism and the absurd; *Acești îngeri triști* (*The Sad Angels*, 1969), a drama of poetic realism and dissent; and *O pasăre dintr-o altă zi* (*A Bird of Another Day*, 1972), a play of political crime aimed at the excesses of the Stalinist period. His dramatic socio-historical frescoes were equally powerful, plays of epic grandeur such as *Muntele* (*The Mountain*, 1977) and *Studiu osteologic al unui schelet de cal dintr-un mormînt avar din Transilvania* (*The Grave of the Avar Horseman in Transylvania*, 1981). He showed skill as well in creating unmitigated tragedy in his 1974 play, *Piticul din grădina de vară* (*The Dwarf in the Summer Garden*). In the 1980s he developed his metaphorical style in other plays such as *Dalbul pribeag* (*The Wanderer*, 1987).

Comedies turned dark once more in the 1960s and 1970s in the hands of innovators such as Teodor Mazilu (1930–80) whose paradoxical satires – *Proștii sub clar de lună* (*The Moonlit Fools*, 1964), *Sărbătoare princiară* (*Princely Feast*, 1969), *Acești nebuni fățarnici* (*These Hypocritical Madmen*, 1970) and *Mobilă și durere* (*Furniture and Grief*, 1979) – created a whole new audience.

The plays of Dumitru Solomon (b. 1932) are distinguished by an unusual blending of dramatic ideas and refined humour. Neither dramas nor comedies, he himself has referred to his works as 'dramedies'. His philosophical trilogy – *Socrate* (*Socrates*), *Platon* (*Plato*) and

Diogene Câinele (*Diogenes the Dog*), written between 1974 and 1976 – is an intense intellectual debate. Concerned with the intricate, tragic connections between life and philosophy in most of his work, Solomon has also shown himself to be an adept writer of satire in his 1985 comedy *Noțiunea de fericire* (*The Idea of Happiness*) and *Fata Morgana* (1971).

Poet Marin Sorescu (b. 1936) is a philosophical absurdist who has written a series of what were called 'dramas of cognition' – *Iona* (*Jonas*, 1969), a parable of gnostic captivity; *Paracliserul* (*The Verger*, 1971), a parable of sacrifice in the quest to create and *Matca* (*Matrix*, 1974), a poem with folk references about life and hostile nature. Others of his plays are bitter-comic meditations on history – *Răceala* (*A Cold*, 1977) and *A treia țeapă* (*The Third Stake*, 1979), mixing tragedy with sparklingly witty humour.

Among writers who have emerged in the late 1960s and 1970s, one should note the plays of Iosif Naghiu (b. 1933), author of the anti-totalitarian parable *Intunericul sau Gluga pe ochi* (*Darkness or the Hood Over the Eyes*, 1971); and Ion Băieșu (1933–92), an absurdist who specialized in 'cruel farces' such as *Iertarea* (*Forgiveness*, 1969), *Dresoarea de fantome* (*Trainer of the Ghost*, 1971), *Chițimia* (1974) and the parable *In căutarea sensului pierdut* (*In Quest of the Lost Meaning*, 1978).

In the early 1980s, Romulus Guga asserted his powerful dramatic personality in such plays as *Evul Mediu întîmplător* (*The Accidental Middle Ages*, 1980) and *Amurgul burghez* (*Bourgeois Twilight*, 1983). In both these dramas, he denounces human devaluation under terrorizing social systems. Mihai Ispirescu (b. 1940) is noted for his satires such as *Trăsura la scară* (*Carriage at the Door*, 1983) and *Intr-o dimineață* (*One Morning*, 1989).

New playwrights of the younger generation emerged after 1990, rejecting all kinds of realism and neglecting the traditional rules of dramatic structure. Among them, Matei Vișniec (b. 1956), produced in many theatres, made a name for himself with *Angajare de clovn* (*Clown for Hire*, 1991), awarded Best Play of the Year in the 1991 UNITER competition, *Spectatorul condamnat la moarte* (*The Spectator Sentenced to Death*, 1992) and *Omul care vorbește singur* (*The Man Who Speaks to Himself*, 1992), parables about the human condition written in an absurdist style. Since 1987 Vișniec has been living in France.

Among several important Hungarian-language dramatists writing in Romania, the best known is András Sütö (b. 1927). A tetralogy by Sütö examining the idea of revolt was produced beginning in 1975 – *Egy lócsiszár virágvasárnapja* (*A Horse Dealer's Palm Sunday*), *Csillag a máglián* (*A Star on the Pyre*), *Káin és Ábel* (*Cain and Abel*) and *Szuzai mennyegzö* (*The Wedding in Souza*).

Other skilful Hungarian-language dramatists include János Székely (b. 1929), author of the historical drama *Caligula helytartoja* (*Caligula's Deputy*); István Kocsis (b. 1940), author of an effective parable about power called *Korona aranybol van* (*The Golden Crown*, 1972); and Geza Páskándi (b. 1933), author of an absurdist comedy, *Külsö zajok* (*Distant Noises*, 1967).

Among the German-language dramatists of note in Romania, the best known is Hans Kehrer (b. 1913), author of *Zwei Schwestern* (*Two Sisters*, premièred in 1980).

Directors, Directing and Production Styles

Romania has had a long tradition of outstanding directors and actors. As one generation has slowed down, another has always seemed to come along to pick up the slack. So it was in the immediate post-war years. A number of the country's leading directors and producers died at this time – Paul Gusty (1859–1944) and Soare Z. Soare in 1944; Victor Ion Popa in 1946; and Ion Sava in 1947. In 1946 Sava, an admirer of the ideas of Edward Gordon Craig, had achieved a *succès de scandale* with a masked production of *Macbeth*. The production was a milestone in the movement to 'retheatricalize' the theatre, a movement that began in earnest in the country after 1956.

Arguably the most important of the directors working just after the war was Sică Alexandrescu, doyen of the realistic tradition which had dominated Romanian theatre to that time. Working at the National Theatre in Bucharest, he successfully staged all of Caragiale's comedies, starting in 1948 with *O scrisoare pierdută* (*The Lost Letter*), a production which has come to be regarded as a landmark of Caragiale's works. Other major productions by Alexandrescu were Gogol's *Revizor* (*The Government Inspector*) and Goldoni's *I rusteghi* (*The Tyrants*). His prestige also helped introduce several new plays by the dramatist Aurel Baranga.

Most other major directors who began their careers prior to World War II followed stylistically in Alexandrescu's footsteps, aiming for realistic fidelity to text and classical balance in production.

One of those who began to challenge what had become narrow realism (under the influence of a formal assimilation of the Stanislavski system) was Radu Stanca (1920–62). Working at the State Theatre in Sibiu which now bears his name, Stanca, a poet and playwright, began to create a series of productions which took clear steps away from visual verisimilitude in the mid-1950s.

The battle for the retheatricalization of the theatre had clearly begun and it found willing supporters in young graduates from the drama schools as well as in graduating designers from the fine arts academies. Among the dominant figures emerging at this time was Liviu Ciulei – actor, designer, architect as well as stage and film director – who argued effectively for the 'theatricalization of stage design' in 1956 as well as for a new type of realism in performance ('realism to the bone'). Ciulei believed that stylistic elements which were apparently discordant could be blended into a theatrical synthesis.

Working most closely with the Bulandra Theatre, Ciulei staged Shakespeare's *As You Like It* (1961), Büchner's *Danton's Death* (1966) and *Leonce and Lena* (1970). In 1972 he staged Caragiale's *Lost Letter* in a production that rivalled Alexandrescu's famous 1948 version. His productions of both Gorki and Brecht, as well as of Shakespeare's *The Tempest* (1979) were equally significant for the new Romanian theatre – rethinking established classics in relation to contemporary events and usually finding highly imaginative visual ways of realizing each production.

Another pioneer of the new theatricalized approach was Horea Popescu whose production of *Domnişoara Nastasia* (*Miss Nastasia*, 1956) by George Mihail Zamfirescu was considered to be a kind of manifesto for the movement. Popescu's work at both the Giuleşti Theatre and the National Theatre in Bucharest, showed an obvious preference for monumentalism. He continued to work over the next decades staging such epic dramas as Mayakovsky's *Banya* (*The Bath House*), Brecht's *The Resistible Rise of Arturo Ui*, Shakespeare's *Richard III*, Buero-Vallejo's *Fundacion* (*Foundation*), Camus's *Caligula* and Petrescu's *Danton*.

David Esrig scored huge successes through the 1960s with his inventive productions – most often at the Comedy Theatre in Bucharest – of plays by Ciprian (*The Duck's Head*), Yevgeny

Svarts (*Teni/The Shadow*), Shakespeare (*Troilus and Cressida*) and Diderot (*Le Neveu de Rameau/Rameau's Nephew*). Still another polished and highly inventive 'theatrical' director was Vlad Mugur, who achieved a major reputation with his grotesque imagistic productions at the National Theatre in Cluj, especially Camus's *Caligula* (1969) and Shakespeare's *A Midsummer Night's Dream* (1970).

Other directors of note who emerged in the pre-1971 period included Crin Teodorescu (1926–70), who had success with both Petrescu's and Ionesco's work, and Lucian Giurchescu, who worked mostly at the Comedy Theatre and achieved note with a wide range of authors including Ionesco, Brecht, Popescu and Caragiale.

Still another major director from this period was Radu Penciulescu, who created a theatre of austere means in his unique stagings of plays by Mrożek (*Tango*, 1968), Shakespeare (a free-form *King Lear* in 1970 at the National in Bucharest) and by Hochhuth (*Der Stellvertreter/The Deputy*, 1972, at the Bulandra).

One could see this movement as well at Romania's Hungarian theatres in the work of

György Harag (1925–85). Harag had a special gift for image which he turned into refined pictorial effects at the National Theatre in Tîrgu-Mureş and at the Magyar Theatre in Cluj. Especially effective were his productions of Sukhovo-Kobylin's *Smerti Tarelkina* (*Death of Tarelkin*, 1976), Gorki's *Lower Depths* (1979), András Sütö's works (1975–8) and, most poetically, Chekhov's *The Cherry Orchard* (1985).

After the political events of 1971, directorial experiments went on, although party control over culture became all-powerful. Lucian Pintilie was one of the first victims of this new cultural revolution. Known throughout the 1960s for his satirical approaches to plays and performances as well as for his ability to create a sense of stage poetry, Pintilie had successfully staged at the Bulandra Theatre a wide range of plays from Max Frisch to Caragiale. In 1972, however, his version of Gogol's *The Government Inspector* hit a bit too close to home and was banned by government authorities. Clearly times were changing.

Also banned in 1972 was the production of Iosif Naghiu's *Gluga pe ochi* (*The Hood Over the Eyes*) directed by Valeriu Moisescu

Andrei Şerban's 1990 Bucharest National Theatre production of Euripides' *The Trojan Women*, designed by Dan Jitianu and Lucu Andreescu.

(b. 1932). In 1989, however, Moisescu was able to stage a powerful production of Molière's *Misanthrope* at the Bulandra, a clear warning against the abuses of totalitarianism.

More subtle approaches to the politicization of classical plays emerged in the productions of Dinu Cernescu, especially his interpretations of Shakespeare's *Measure for Measure* (1971) at the Giuleşti, *Hamlet* (1974) and *Timon of Athens* (1978) at the Nottara and *Coriolanus* (1979) at the Mic. In his *Hamlet* especially, all the murders were politically motivated and the audience was closely involved in the criminal interplay. Cernescu was also influential in the new recognition of the plays of Lucian Blaga.

Gradually, dramatic art was forced to become an art of political allegory and scenic metaphor. Paradoxically, the period produced many works of high artistic value. These ranged from carefully articulated productions of foreign dramas – such as Dürrenmatt's *Romulus the Great* staged by Sanda Manu (b. 1933) at the National Theatre in Bucharest in 1974) – to productions of refined psychological realism by such authors as Gorki (*Vassa Jeleznova*) and Eliade (*Iphigenia*) as staged by Ion Cojar (b. 1931). Cojar had earlier been known also for a more overtly theatrical style and had enormous success with his fantasy production of Ecaterina Oproiu's (b. 1931) play *Nu sunt Turnul Eiffel* (*I Am Not the Eiffel Tower*, 1965, in Piatra Neamţ), a play which later had a long international career.

Perhaps the most important of the 'lost' generation of directors was Andrei Şerban. Şerban made a brilliant début in the late 1960s with two visually extraordinary productions in the Youth Theatre in Piatra Neamţ – Brecht's *Der gute Mensch von Sezuan* (*The Good Person of Setzuan*) and the early English play, *Arden of Faversham*. He followed this a year later with a spectacular production of *Iona* by Marin Sorescu at the Mic Theatre in Bucharest. Shortly thereafter, however, he left Romania and began achieving even greater note in the United States. Happily, Şerban returned to Bucharest in 1990 to become director-general of the National Theatre. Very quickly, he restored real energy to what had become a tired company with his *Ancient Trilogy* – *Medea*, *The Trojan Women* and *Electra*; *Our Country's Good* by the British dramatist Timberlake Wertenbaker; a collectively created piece called *The Audition*; Shakespeare's *Twelfth Night*; and Chekhov's *The Cherry Orchard*.

Among the many talented directors who stayed in Romania during this period, several stand out: Cătălina Buzoianu, whose productions, especially of Pirandello but also of novels by Romanian and foreign authors in her own scenic adaptations became essays in stage imagery; Dan Micu (b. 1949), who followed Ciulei's approaches although much more subtly; Alexa Visarion (b. 1947), who used a harsh and laconic idiom to express his often severe views of the world, views that shock by their polemic energy; Alexandru Tocilescu (b. 1946), one of the directors with a real gift not only for comedy but also for suggestive visual images with political meanings, as in his polemical *Hamlet* at the Bulandra Theatre (1985) with Ion Caramitru (b. 1942) in the title role; and Aureliu Manea (b. 1944), who projects his own obsessions on to texts in strongly visual images.

Among the later directors, Silviu Purcărete distinguished himself for his daring exploration of theatrical space producing a *son et lumière* in his *Atrides' Legends* and Euripides' *Hecuba* (on the seashore) and by his taste for violent images in Sartre's *Le Diable et le Bon Dieu* (*The Devil*

The 1991 Craiova National Theatre production of *Ubu Roi with Scenes from Macbeth*, directed and designed by Silviu Purcărete.

and the Good Lord) at the Mic Theatre. Other important productions included a grotesque epic *Ubu Roi with Scenes from Macbeth* after both Jarry and Shakespeare (1991) as well as Shakespeare's *Titus Andronicus* (a Romanian première) with the National Theatre in Craiova (named Best Production in 1992).

Other highly personal visions involving text and topical ideas have come from Gábor Tompa (b. 1957) – with the Magyar Theatre in Cluj-Napoca, fresh and insightful readings of Sigmond István's *Szerelemesö* (*A Downpour of Love*, 1989) and Ionesco's *La Cantatrice chauve* (*The Bald Soprano*) in a puppet theatre style (1992); Mihai Măniuţiu (b. 1954) – an intellectual and imagistic exuberance in Shakespeare's *Taming of the Shrew* (1986), *Antony and Cleopatra* (1988) and Ionesco's *La Leçon* (*The Lesson*, 1992) all of them at the National Theatre in Cluj; Victor Ioan Frunză (b. 1958) – theatrical poetry in Svarts's *Dragon* (Youth Theatre in Piatra Neamţ); Alecsandri's *Iaşii în carnaval* (*Carnival in Iaşi*, 1989, at the National in Cluj) and Blaga's *Cruciada copiilor*

(*Children's Crusade*, at the National in Tîrgu-Mureş in 1992).

The art of acting has also had a significant development in the post-war period, going from a 'true to life' realism, which highlighted psychology and social background, to a wider sense of expressiveness often involving movement. Without giving up the emotional, actors have acquired a deeper intellectual insight while making visual their feelings and states of mind.

A final word about a unique figure in the Romanian theatre – Radu Beligan, actor, theatre essayist and former artistic director of the Comedy Theatre and the National in Bucharest. An extraordinarily subtle, lyrical and ironic actor, Beligan spent many years attempting to keep Romania's theatrical channels to the rest of the world open. For six years (1971–7) he served as president of the International Theatre Institute and was later named its honorary president.

Mircea Ghiţulescu

Music Theatre

Prior to the war, the country had two major opera houses, in Bucharest and Cluj. Following nationalization of the theatre companies in 1948, five opera troupes went into operation. These included one each in Bucharest, Iaşi and Timişoara and two in Cluj-Napoca (one working in Romanian and the other in Hungarian).

In addition, there was one other theatre in Bucharest exclusively staging operettas while two 'lyric' theatres in Constanţa and Craiova and two other 'musical' theatres began operating in Braov and Galaţi. Three additional 'revue' theatres also operated in Bucharest, Constanţa and Deva while several dramatic companies in the country also had their own revue sections.

Certain of the drama companies also began to try their skills in the musical theatre field. Bucharest's Mic Theatre, for example, had genuine success with its 1979 musical adaptation of *Nu sunt Turnul Eiffel* (*I Am Not the Eiffel Tower*) by Ecaterina Oproiu, with music by Ion Cristinoiu (b. 1942) and staged by Cătălina Buzoianu, and with a musical version of Petrescu's play *Mitică Popescu*, with music by Nicu Alifantis (b. 1954) and staged by Cristian Hadji Culea. The Bulandra in 1988 also had

success with its rock musical version of Lope de Vega's *The Gardener's Dog*, adapted by actor Florian Pittiş (b. 1943).

Most of the theatres exclusively devoted to musical theatre – especially the opera houses – generally keep a large repertory going, each season adding three or four new productions to those ten to twenty already in the repertoire. Of this number, about one-third are usually by Romanian authors. Subsidy, as with other theatres, is at about the 80 per cent level although during the 1980s that percentage was reduced. After 1989, it was raised again. All the music theatres have permanent troupes, with soloists, choir, orchestra and ballet ensemble, administrative and technical personnel.

Most musical productions are staged by resident directors, although directors from the dramatic theatres, some of whom have become specialists in the field, regularly work as guest artists.

From a theatrical point of view, notable successes have been *Secretul lui Don Giovanni* (*Don Giovanni's Secret*) by Romanian composer Cornel Ţăranu (b. 1935), directed by Mihai Măniuţiu in the Gheorghe Dima Conservatory in Cluj-Napoca (1970); a Romanian work, Aurel Stroe's (b. 1932) *Orestia II (The Choephores)*, staged by Lucian Pintilie in 1979 at the Avignon Festival in France with an international troupe; and Verdi's *Falstaff* staged by Dinu Cernescu with the Romanian Opera House in Cluj.

Perhaps the greatest national success in the field has been the musical tragedy *Oedipus* by George Enescu. Premièred at the Paris Opera in 1936, it was subsequently produced in Brussels and in other European cities. It opened in 1958 in a new version at the Romanian Opera House in Bucharest directed by Jean Rânzescu (b. 1909), an outstanding director and teacher who succeeded in theatricalizing opera performances. This version was still playing to packed houses in 1990. The libretto, written by Edmond Fleg, is based on Sophocles' *Oedipus Rex* and *Oedipus at Colonus*. Enescu's music has been recognized for its originality since its first production.

Romania's most important man of music, Enescu was a versatile artist, working as a violinist, pianist and conductor. As a composer, he contributed significantly to the international recognition of Romanian music. Many of his symphonic works have served as musical bases for folk-inspired ballets or for modern, abstract dance pieces (such as the poem *Vox Maris*). A newly staged version of his *Oedipus* was produced by Cătălina Buzoianu at the Bucharest Opera House in 1991.

Pascal Bentoiu (b. 1928) is another composer who achieved international fame for a musical adaptation – *Hamlet*. Awarded the Guido Valcarenghi Prize in Italy in 1970, the opera was staged four years later in Marseille and in Bucharest in 1975 by George Teodorescu (b. 1922). Bentoiu also wrote the libretto.

Director Dimitrie Tăbăcaru (1929–87) has carved out a special niche for himself with his staging of Romanian operas such as *Răscoala* (*Uprising*) by Gheorghe Dumitrescu (b. 1914) and *Petru Rareș* by Eduard Caudella (1841–1924), the first Romanian opera. Tăbăcaru worked mostly at the Opera Română in Iași.

George Zaharescu (b. 1927) is a director who has argued that the complete actor must be able to sing as well as dance and act. His views were realized in a series of operetta productions between 1975 and 1990 which showed actor-singers working in a wide range of styles. These included *West Side Story*, *Die Fledermaus* and *Lysistrata*, the latter a musical version by Gherase Dendrino (1901–73).

One of the most popular forms of music theatre in the country is the revue. With roots going back to the eighteenth century, Romanian revue theatre took its modern form at the end of the nineteenth century through the work of such writers as Vasile Alecsandri, Matei Millo and I.D. Ionescu (1833–1900) who was also a performer. Even Caragiale tried his hand at creating for revues.

Perhaps the most famous name in the field is the performer Constantin Tănase (1880–1945), founder of the Cărăbuș Revue Theatre, and master of the satirical couplet. After 1948, this company became known as the Constantin Tănase Theatre. Another of Romania's important revue companies is the Fantasio in Constanța.

Dance Theatre

Traditionally, Romanian ballet troupes have existed as part of opera companies, participating in opera productions as well as producing independent works on their own. After 1948, the country's first independent ballet company was created in the city of Constanța. Known as Fantasio, the company was founded by choreographer Oleg Danovski (b. 1917) who had previously been the ballet master at the Romanian Opera in Bucharest. Danovski created a range of works there, both classical and modern.

One of the key figures in the development of Romanian dance is Floria Capsali (1900–82), an outstanding dancer and teacher who taught many generations of dancers and choreographers. Capsali, like many in the field, often worked from folk sources.

Among Romanian composers, Mihail Jora (1891–1971) devoted much of his work to the ballet, aiming to create the musical basis for a genuine Romanian style of dance. From his picturesque *La piață* (*At the Marketplace*, 1932) to *Hanul Dulcinea* (*Dulcinea's Inn*, 1966), his musical creations for dance included a wide range of works in various styles: *Demoazela Măriuța* (*Miss Mariutsa*, 1940), *Curtea Veche* (*Ancient Courts*, 1948), *Când strugurii se coc*

(*When the Grapes are Ripe*, 1953), *Intoarcerea din adâncuri* (*Coming Back from the Depths*, 1959), some folk inspired, some symbolic, their music serving as a vivacious, lyrical, often humorous base to dance productions in both classical and modern styles. Jora is generally considered the father of Romanian modern ballet.

Since the 1960s, Romania has seen a continuous series of attempts to bring theatre and dance even closer together. A number of choreographers have gone so far as to write their own libretti (often based on world dramatic classics) and compose their own scores (often a collage of fragments from varied sources) to go with their choreographic creations.

One choreographer working in this way has been Mihaela Atanasiu (b. 1944), first with the dance troupe of the Operetta Theatre in Bucharest and later with the Romanian Opera in Bucharest. With the Operetta Theatre she created *Viaţa, dragostea omului* (*Life, Man's Love*) and later *Băiatul si paiele fermecate* (*The Boy and the Miraculous Straw*). With the opera company, she created new dance versions of *Peer Gynt* and *A Midsummer Night's Dream*.

Two of the country's major dancer-choreographers are Alexa Mezincescu (b. 1936) and Ion Tugearu (b. 1937), both principal soloists with the Romanian Opera in Bucharest. Mezincescu created a series of highly personal

ballets based on the Tristan and Isolde and Medea stories, both to music by Bruckner. She also did a *Cinderella* to music by Rossini and mounted a definitive version of *Curtea Veche* (*Ancient Courts*).

Tugearu has explored the dramatic aspects of dance in such pieces as *Bodas de sangre* after García Lorca's *Blood Wedding* and *Femeia îndărătnică* after Shakespeare's *The Taming of the Shrew*. In 1990, he founded the Orion Ballet in Bucharest, an independent dance company. In 1992, he became artistic director of the ballet troupe of the Romanian Opera in Bucharest.

An outstanding ballet master and choreographer, Vera Proca Ciortea (b. 1915) is a disciple of Floria Capsali and creator of folk-inspired rhythmic dance. Sergiu Anghel (b. 1953), co-founder with Adina Cezar (b. 1941) of the dance group Contemp, tends to explore the more philosophical aspects of dance expression in his choreography.

Noteworthy also are the dancer-choreographers Miriam Răducanu (b. 1924), who gained acclaim for her dance-miniatures on dramatic subjects to jazz music, and Francisc Valkay (b. 1940) working mostly in Timişoara, where he created many productions in an original blend of neo-classical and modern styles.

Petre Codreanu

Theatre for Young Audiences

Productions exclusively for young audiences date back to the 1920s and 1930s in Romania, when Victor Ion Popa began staging such shows in Bucharest. After 1948 and the development of a state system, the form developed rapidly.

It was agreed in 1948 that each subsidized theatre would be required to present at least one new production for young audiences each season. Three years later, a group of actors from the National Theatre in Bucharest formed a troupe specifically for the production of children's plays, the Young People's Company, the first Romanian theatre of its type.

This new group presented classic stories from both Romanian and world literature and was soon renamed the Ion Creangă Theatre in honour of Creangă (1837–89), a great Romanian children's story writer. The company

created work for a variety of age groups, from pre-school children to teenagers.

Among its directors have been Ion Lucian (b. 1924), an actor, director, author and probably the country's main producer of children's theatre; Ion Cojar, a director and a professor of drama; Alecu Popovici (b. 1927), a noted writer of puppet plays; Emil Mandric (b. 1937), a director and theatre critic; and Cornel Todea (b. 1935), a director. The Creangă Theatre, in addition to its many productions, also offers courses for children to introduce them to theatrical art generally.

In 1961, a second company for young audiences was formed in the city of Piatra Neamţ. Calling itself simply the Youth Theatre, the group was founded by a group of young actors after their graduation from the Theatre Institute in Bucharest. Very soon, the company

Ion Cojar's 1965 Piatra Neamṭ Youth Theatre production of Ecaterina Oproiu's *I Am Not the Eiffel Tower*.

became famous in the country not only as a company for young audiences but also as a company of young people, always in quest of new means and devices, playing for audiences of all ages. In addition to producing seasons of plays, the company has also hosted a biennial festival of theatre for young audiences. Directing the troupe over the years have been Ion Coman (1925–70), Eduard Covali (b. 1930), Gheorghe Bunghez (b. 1936), Cornel Nicoară (b. 1938) and (since 1991) Nicolae Scarlat (b. 1940), a founder of the International Festival of Piatra Neamṭ.

In Iaşi, the Theatre for Children and Youth,

established in 1948 as a puppet theatre, decided in 1973 to bring together a mix of both live actors and puppets. In 1987, the company moved into a new modern building equipped with several auditoriums of varying shapes and sizes. In the new house, the company has been able to mount performances in a wide range of styles, from musicals to animation theatre. Two of its major contributors since 1987 have been writer Natalia Dănăilă (b. 1936) and director Constantin Brehnescu (b. 1934).

In 1990, Ion Lucian founded another children's group, Excelsior, in Bucharest. The company's first production was based on an Ionescu children's story, *Nu treziṭi un copil care visează* (*Don't Wake a Child Who is Dreaming*).

Over the years, a national repertoire of popular children's plays has been developed. Among them are *Nota zero la purtare* (*Black Mark for Conduct*) by Virgil Stoenescu (b. 1915) and Octavian Sava (b. 1928) (premièred in 1956); *Cocoşelul neascultător* (*Naughty Little Rooster*) by Ion Lucian (premièred in 1965); *Băiatul din banca a doua* (*The Little Boy at the Second Desk*) and *Afară-i vopsit gardul, înăuntru-i leopardul* (*A Painted Cat Outside, a Leopard Inside*) both by Alecu Popovici and premièred respectively in 1961 and 1968.

Apart from those by these specialized theatres, about forty to fifty additional productions are staged each year for children by the country's other subsidized theatres.

Romania was one of the co-founders of ASSITEJ, the International Association of Theatre for Children and Young People.

Ion Lucian

Puppet Theatre

Puppet Theatre is one of the oldest of the performing arts in Romania with folk origins going back into antiquity. Initially the work of village artisans, puppetry evolved into a professional art by the nineteenth century.

Between World Wars I and II several attempts were made to establish permanent puppet troupes but it wasn't until 1945 with the founding in Bucharest of the Țăndărică Theatre that a permanent puppet theatre finally came into existence. Its founders were Lucia Calomeri (1883–1955) and Elena Pătrăşcanu (1914–85), the latter a well-known set designer.

In 1949, Țăndărică became a state theatre

and several other subsidized companies were established outside the capital. By the mid-1950s, the country boasted nineteen state puppet companies, five of which had two troupes, one working in the Romanian language and the other working in one of the national minority languages.

Țăndărică, however, has retained its position as the largest and most prestigious of the puppet companies producing for both children and adults. The troupe has not only encouraged the development of new plays for the genre but also trained puppeteers from Romania and abroad. Among Romanian writers who have created plays for Ţăndărică are such noted authors as Nina Cassian (b. 1924), Gellu Naum (b. 1915) and Alexandru Popescu (b. 1921).

Early on in the modern development of Romanian puppet art, it was naively believed that the puppet needed only to imitate reality and realistic attitudes. By the 1960s, however, explorations of expression through the puppet became more essential and this revealed modes and styles which transformed the puppet – whether worked by hands, strings or other techniques – into an essential visual expression of humanity, making it a suggestive rather than a representational art.

From the 1970s on, the art of puppetry came to include poetry, humour and even the absurd in productions which became scenic metaphors for sophisticated philosophical concepts. At this point, the work of the designer became crucial and again Ţăndărică led the way by working with leading designers (puppet as well as scenic) such as Lena Constante (b. 1909), Ioana Constantinescu (1907–90), Ştefan Hablinski (1915–74), Ella Conovici (b. 1920) and Mioara Buescu (b. 1926).

Ţăndărică's most important artistic director was Margareta Niculescu (b. 1926), who ran the troupe between 1949 and 1985. The company's work under her was highly refined and innovatively explored the art – *Mâna cu cinci degete* (*The Five Fingered Hand*, 1958) by Mircea Crişan (b. 1924), Penciulescu's *Cartea cu Apolodor* (*The Book with Apolodor*, 1962) by Gellu Naum, *Cele trei neveste ale lui Don Cristobald* (*Don Cristobald's Three Wives*, 1965) by the prolific puppet play writer Valentin Silvestru (b. 1924) and *Făt Frumos din lacrimă* (*The Tearful Prince Charming*, 1982) her own adaptation of a tale by Romanian poet Mihai Eminescu. In 1985, Niculescu became director of the International Marionette Institute in Charleville-Mézières, France. Replacing Niculescu at Ţăndărică was Mihaela Tonitza-Iordache (b. 1942), a theatre scholar.

Outside Bucharest, puppetry has also flourished. In Cluj-Napoca and Sibiu, director Ildyko Kovács (b. 1927) and her co-workers, designers Alexandru Rusan (b. 1926) and Edith Bothar, produced a number of highly imaginative adaptations of world classics using a

Christian Pepino's 1992 Ţăndărică Theatre production of *The White Negro*.

combination of puppets, masks and mime. These ranged from *A Midsummer Night's Dream* in 1960 to *Ubu Roi* in 1980.

In Craiova, Horia Davidescu (b. 1921) explored the art's folk roots in *Domnul Goe* (*Master Goe*, 1959) after Caragiale, and *Cinci săptămâni în balon* (*Five Weeks in a Balloon*, 1960) after Jules Verne's novel.

Antal Pál (b. 1925) in Târgu-Mureş created a number of highly original shows in Hungarian using both Romanian and Szeckler folklore as well as creating several large-scale productions based on Maeterlinck and Saint-Exupéry.

Other puppeteers of note include Florica Teodoru (1910–84) in Timişoara and Cristian Pepino (b. 1950), a brilliant poet of animated objects, working first in Constanţa and later in Bucharest with Ţăndărică, where he continues to explore with fantasy and the manifold abilities of puppet expression.

Mihai Crişan

Design
Theatre Space and Architecture

Design, theatrical space and directorial vision have long been linked in Romanian theatre tradition and it is difficult to speak of one area without considering the others. Most of the major theatre buildings in the country were created in the nineteenth century and were, more or less, traditional proscenium houses. These theatres required realistic pictorial backup which was provided by nineteenth-century theatre designers, genuine professionals by this time. Design remained true to its painterly roots until the 1930s.

It was then that major directors began to rethink both the nature of the visual aspects of theatrical art and the very nature of theatrical space itself. Two of the earliest to explore the relationship were artist Victor Ion Popa and director-designer-scholar Ion Sava.

After World War II, in an attempt to follow political dictates calling for socialist-realism in the arts, designers began to 'reconstruct reality', which lead to an almost mimetic form of realism. But by the mid-1950s, directors began to argue again for a 'retheatricalization' of the theatre which led to the development of a new interpretation of the designer's responsibilities. Very quickly, the term 'scenography' came into wide usage.

Important theoretical discussions began to take place led by scenographers, directors and critics such as Eugen Schileru (1916–68), Liviu Ciulei and later on Dan Jitianu (b. 1940). Young graduates of the theatre institutes and of the Grigorescu Fine Arts Institute took sides in these debates with most discarding realism and aiming instead for suggestiveness and poetic imagery. 'Recognizable' was replaced by 'plausible' as a working concept for the designer. Ciulei argued that 'scenography is the spiritual space of the performance'.

The logical conclusion of the argument was that the very spaces themselves needed to be rethought to foster a closer interrelationship between performer and audience. It was in this spirit that Ciulei, Jitianu and Paul Bortnovschi (b. 1922) created a thrust stage at the Bulandra Studio Theatre and at the Davila Theatre Studio in Piteşti. About this same time, architect-designer Toni Gheorghiu (1926–61) restored the Mic Theatre and Traian Niţescu (b. 1924) redesigned one of the stages of Bucharest's National Theatre.

Other studio spaces were soon created in the National Theatres in Iaşi, Timişoara and Cluj-Napoca. New modern buildings also went up at the National Theatres in Craiova and Tîrgu-Mureş (both in 1973). That same year, the National Theatre in Bucharest also got a new building which, in addition to a 1,200-seat proscenium house, has a variable proscenium-arena-thrust stage in a smaller auditorium, a multifunctional experimental workshop space, a hall with a platform stage, and a ninety-nine-seat studio.

As well, there have been a number of successful attempts at creating outdoor spaces for summer performances. Amphitheatres holding between 2,000 and 4,000 people now exist in Bucharest parks, and directors and designers have begun to utilize both historical sites and seashore areas.

Scenography in the 1990s tends to place the emphasis on sculptural design which, with the help of sophisticated lighting techniques, creates

György Harag's 1985 Tîrgu-Mureş National Theatre production of Anton Chekhov's *The Cherry Orchard*, designed by Romulus Feneş.

a symbolic interpretation of the text. Scenery, as a result, has become metaphoric; picturesque decoration and architectural settings sometimes coexist on the stage, creating striking effects.

As for designers, during the immediate post-war years it was the poetic realism of Alexandru Brătăşanu (1901–70) at the National Theatre which attracted the greatest attention. He was the teacher of those who achieved the retheatricalization of set design.

At the Bulandra Theatre during the same period the designs of Wladimir Siegfried (1909–82) created visual effects through an ingenious use of harmonious and disharmonious colours. Siegfried left the country in 1957 and spent the rest of his life working in Paris.

A third designer of note in this period was Tony Gheorghiu (1925–61), who conceived design as 'directing theatrical space'. Gheorghiu avoided naturalism, favouring instead a discreet symbolism while utilizing principles of sculptural composition in productions such as Machiavelli's *La Mandragola* (1956), Miller's

The Crucible (1957) and Maxwell Anderson's *Winterset* (1957).

Director Liviu Ciulei achieved particular note as a designer for his productions of Shaw's *St Joan* (1958), a symbolically linked *Macbeth* and *Julius Caesar* in 1968 and 1969, Büchner's *Leonce and Lena* (1970), *The Tempest* (1979) and *A Midsummer Night's Dream* (1991), where he used reds and blacks to create not so much a dream but rather a nightmarish atmosphere. Ciulei is a master of symbolic spatial structures, always seeking an imaginative visual device to communicate and highlight contemporary meanings within the plays being staged and designed.

Another designer of note is Paul Bortnovschi, who uses dynamic structures in his work – often visible stage machinery. Among his major productions are *Danton's Death* (1966), Chekhov's *The Cherry Orchard* (1967), Ionesco's *Victims of Duty* (1968) and Gogol's *The Government Inspector* (1972), all at the Bulandra. For the National in Bucharest, he also designed important productions of Petrescu's

Danton, Camus's *Caligula* and Vallejo's *Foundation*.

Dan Jitianu is a teacher of design whose work has been distinguished by its synthesis of elements from both visual arts and architecture. His functional, constructive organization of theatrical space is often unconventional and usually involves the audience very directly in the theatrical environment. Among his major productions at the Bulandra were O'Neill's *Long Day's Journey Into Night* (1976), Sorescu's *Răceala (A Cold,* 1977), Molière's *Tartuffe* and Bulgakov's *Molière* (visually linked productions), plus *Hamlet* (1985) and *An Ancient Trilogy* (1990) at the National in Bucharest.

Mihai Mădescu (b. 1937) is a poet of scenic space who has worked with distinction at many theatres including the National in Bucharest and the National in Iaşi. His works are often large in scale while boasting an organic stylistic unity. His outstanding productions range from Ibsen's *Peer Gynt* in Piatra Neamţ in 1972 to Şerban's 1992 production of *The Cherry Orchard* at the National in Bucharest.

One final designer to be mentioned here is Emilia Jivanov (b. 1938), who designs both sets and costumes. Working most often with the Timişoara National Theatre, she gained fame for her use of symbolic chromatics and central sculptural elements in such plays as *King Lear* and Popescu's *The Grave of the Avar Horseman.*

Traian Niţescu

Training

Dating from the middle of the nineteenth century, theatre training in Romania has a rich tradition. From 1864, conservatories in Iaşi and Bucharest were state subsidized. In 1948, such training was given university-level status. Subsequently, two institutions of higher education emerged: the Caragiale Institute of Theatre and Film in Bucharest and the Szentgyörgy István Institute of Theatre in Tîrgu-Mureş (the latter with separate sections for actors in Romanian and Hungarian).

Until 1990, the Caragiale Institute offered programmes in acting, stage and film directing, science and theory of theatre and film, and film and television production. In 1990, the institute was renamed the Theatre and Film Academy and established separate faculties for theatre and film. Independent departments were also established for theatre and film directing, theory of theatre and film, and script writing. The new academy also increased the number of students that it accepted each year. Also in 1990, the Tîrgu-Mureş Institute became the Theatre Academy and added a directing department.

Added to these major theatre training institutions are smaller programmes in Iaşi (acting and puppetry) and in Bucharest (puppetry, directing and choreography). A theatre school was also created in Cluj. These programmes, like the others, are also recognized as university-level equivalents.

At these institutes, student actors regularly perform with established professional companies. The schools also offer their own particular seasons. The Cassandra Studio at the Bucharest Institute, as one example, has focused on the production of new and experimental plays utilizing avant-garde scenic techniques.

At all the schools, teaching is done by established professionals. Trained in a deeply rooted, traditional psychological realism, students are also taught other acting styles from the *commedia dell'arte* to modern forms, as well as musical theatre. Courses generally include training in improvisation, singing, mime and acrobatics. Students must also take a range of history and theory as well as courses in Romanian and world dramatic literature and aspects of technical theatre.

The training of theorists and critics includes courses in history, theory and aesthetics along with research techniques and practical work in drama and film, radio and television. Courses are also offered in dramaturgy for theatre and film.

Admission to the institutes is on a competitive basis involving both intellectual skills and talent. About 400–500 students apply each year for a total of thirty places in Bucharest, ten to twenty in other cities. Acting programmes last four years while directing and theoretical programmes last five and four years respectively. Upon graduation, students are awarded the degree of Master of Arts.

In the field of musical theatre, until 1989 three conservatories offered specialized university-level training in Bucharest, Cluj and Iaşi. In 1990, all three changed their titles to music academies and have expanded their training to include singing, acting for the musical theatre and dance.

For professional dancers, university-level training did not exist until 1990 when the Theatre and Film Academy in Bucharest added a choreography department to the school. The academy also offers occasional post-graduate courses for musical theatre directors and choreographers.

In 1990, a number of private drama and music schools also began to operate offering training at a variety of levels.

Criticism, Scholarship and Publishing

The tradition of drama criticism in Romania goes back to the nineteenth century and is linked to many of those same people who helped create indigenous theatre in the country, particularly poet Mihai Eminescu and playwright Ion Luca Caragiale, both of whom wrote theatre criticism at the time. In those early years, criticism tended to be theoretical, the productions serving as the basis for extensive essays in theatre theory. One of the major writers in this style was Tudor Vianu, a scholar and professor of aesthetics who tended to specialize in acting theory.

One can still find a tendency towards theory in Romanian criticism, even late into the twentieth century. After 1920, this found its way into newspapers and periodicals. In the 1950s, critics tended to focus their attention mostly on scripts examining how the plays and their production fit or did not fit with the tenets of socialist-realism.

In the 1960s and 1970s, many critics joined forces with proponents of new ideas in the theatre, with innovative directors such as Liviu Ciulei and Radu Stanca, with those who sought to discourage dogmatism and naturalism and who fought for the retheatricalization of the theatre.

Many of these debates could be found in the weekly journal *Contemporanul*, and in the monthly *Teatrul*, the latter founded in 1956 and in 1990 renamed *Teatrul Azi*, and in *România Literară*. These publications argued for the importance of the director in the theatre and about the relationship of script to staging. Also appearing were debates about the creative nature of acting, the relationship of plot and character in contemporary drama, the nature of theatre generally, the relationship between theatre and life, and audience reception among other subjects.

Journalistic criticism – including criticism in Hungarian – has long been available in the major cities. Running alongside reviews of new productions are usually longer analytical pieces relating the specific event to larger trends either in Romania or abroad. Though criticism often reflected the prevailing ideology, genuine artistic issues were dealt with as well, issues of aesthetics and evaluation.

Scholarly research since World War II has concentrated mainly on the history of Romanian theatre. Many of these studies have taken place at the theatre department of the Institute of Art History and within the theatre institutes in Bucharest and Tîrgu-Mureş. Individual scholars such as Ioan Massoff (1904–85) contributed significantly to the field with his eight-volume history of theatre in Romania.

Valuable studies of international theatre history have been done by Ion Marin Sadoveanu (1893–1964) and Ion Zamfirescu (b. 1907), outstanding researchers as well into the general field of Romanian theatre history.

A number of scholarly periodicals publish research in the field regularly. Among them, *Studii şi cercetari de Istoria Artei* (*Studies in Art History*) and *Revue Roumaine d'Histoire de l'Art* (*Romanian Revue of Art History*), both supported by the Art History Institute. Editura Academiei has regularly published volumes on Romanian theatre history.

During the 1970s and 1980s, a number of major publishing houses issued collections of reviews or essays. Editura Eminescu in Bucharest published a series of such volumes under the imprint Masca; Editura Junimea in Iaşi did the same type of publishing under the name Arlechin; as did Editura Dacia in Cluj.

Eminescu has also regularly published plays and essays in its Rampa and Teatru comentat series; Editura Cartea Românească has issued plays from time to time.

Until 1989, the Association of Theatre and Music Artists (ATM; since 1990, UNITER) has sponsored regular professional forums on various subjects for people working in the field.

The result has been the development of what has come to be called 'action-criticism', the active involvement of criticism in theatre, close cooperative contact of critics with theatre practitioners stimulating initiatives and innovative approaches. One of the major promoters of this kind of criticism has been Valentin Silvestru, one of the country's most prolific writers in the field.

Other noted critics who have also undertaken theatre research include Marian Popescu (b. 1952), who distinguished himself with an essay-style approach to the relationship between drama and literature and performing art; Constantin Măciucă (b. 1927), who made essential contributions to the theoretical aspects of drama and theatre structures; and Maria Vodă Căpuşan (b. 1940), who worked mostly in Cluj-Napoca as a teacher and as editor of the university periodical *Thalia*.

Ileana Berlogea
Translated by Angela Rianu

Further Reading

Alterescu, Simion, ed. *An Abridged History of Romanian Theatre*. Bucharest: Academiei Republicii Socialiste România, 1983. 192 pp.

——, ed. *Istoria Teatrului in România*. [History of theatre in Romania]. 3 vols. Bucharest: Academiei Republicii Socialiste România, 1965, 1971, 1973.

——, and Ion Zamfirescu, eds. *Teatrul românesc contemporan 1944–1974*. [Contemporary Romanian theatre: 1944–1974]. Bucharest: Meridiane, 1975. 332 pp.

Association of Theatre and Music Artists. *Aspects du théâtre roumain contemporain*. [Aspects of contemporary Romanian theatre]. 2 vols. Bucharest: Arta Grafica, 1967 and 1971.

Berlogea, Ileana. *Teatrul românesc, teatrul universal*. [Romanian theatre, universal theatre]. Confluenţe, Iaşi: Junimea, 1983. 230 pp.

——. *Teatrul şi societatea contemporană*. [Theatre in contemporary society]. Bucharest: Meridiane, 1985. 340 pp.

Brădăţeanu, Virgil. *Istoria dramaturgiei româneşti şi a artei spectacolului*. [History of Romanian playwriting and the performing arts]. 3 vols. Bucharest: Didactică şi Pedagogică, 1966, 1979, 1982.

Deleanu, Horia. *Elogiu regizorului*. [Praise to the director]. Bucharest: Meridiane, 1985. 300 pp.

Ghitulescu, Mircea. *O panoramă a literaturii dramatice române contemporane: 1944–1984*. [An overview of contemporary Romanian dramatic literature: 1944–1984]. Cluj-Napoca: Dacia, 1984. 316 pp.

Gitza, Letitia, Iordan Chimet, and Valentin Silvestru. *Teatrul de Păpuşi in România*. [Puppet theatre in Romania]. Bucharest, 1969.

Măciucă, Constantin. *Motive şi structuri dramatice*. [Dramatic motifs and structures]. Bucharest: Eminescu, 1986. 278 pp.

——. *Viziuni şi forme teatrale*. [Theatrical visions and forms]. Bucharest: Meridiane, 1983. 272 pp.

Masek, Victor Ernest. *Literatură şi existenţă dramatică*. [Literature and dramatic existence]. Bucharest: Meridiane, 1983. 212 pp.

Massoff, Ioan. *Teatrul românesc. Privire Istorică*. [Romanian theatre: a historical review]. 8 vols. Bucharest: Editura Minerva, 1961–81.

Popescu, Marian. *Chei pentru labirint*. [Key for the labyrinth]. Bucharest: Cartea Românească, 1986. 252 pp.

——. *Teatrul ca literatură*. [Theatre as literature]. Bucharet: Eminescu, 1987. 230 pp.

Râpeanu, Valeriu. *O Antologie a dramaturgiei româneşti: 1944–1977*. [An anthology of Romanian plays: 1944–1977]. 2 vols. Bucharest: Eminescu, 1978.

Sever, Alexandru. *Iraclide. Esseuri despre teatru si dramaturgie*. [Essays on theatre and drama]. Bucharest: Eminescu, 1988. 170 pp.

Silvestru, Valentin. *Elemente de Caragialeologie*. [Introduction to the study of Caragiale's work]. Bucharest: Eminescu, 1979. 256 pp.

——. *Ora 19,30: Studii critice asupra teatrului dramatic din deceniul opt al secolului douăzeci*. [Ora 19,30: critical studies of theatre and drama in the 1980s]. Bucharest: Meridiane, 1983. 486 pp.

Zamfirescu, Ion. *Drama istorică universală şi natională*. [Universal and national historical drama]. Bucharest: Eminescu, 1976. 279 pp.

RUSSIA

Known since 1991 as the Russian Federation and for most of the twentieth century as the Russian Soviet Federated Socialist Republic, Russia is located in both eastern Europe and the northern part of Asia. It has been an independent state since 1991. Its vast land area is 17 million square kilometres (6.6 million square miles). Its 1991 population was estimated at 148.4 million people, 70 per cent of whom were city dwellers. Russians comprise 82.6 per cent of the population. More than a hundred different nationalities live in the Russian Federation, which consists of sixteen autonomous republics, five autonomous national regions, ten autonomous national districts, six counties, forty-nine regions, 997 cities and more than 2,000 towns. Russia was the largest united republic and the seat of government of the Soviet Union.

During the time of what was known as 'Kievan Russia' (ninth to twelfth centuries) a single ancient Russian nationality was formed; based on this nationality the Russian, Ukrainian and Belarussian peoples formed in the thirteenth, fourteenth and fifteenth centuries. In the twelfth century, the Vladimir-Suzdal territory, and the Novgorod feudal republic, occupied the area now known as the Russian Federation. In the thirteenth century, these people repelled Swedish and German attacks in the battle at Neva (1240) and the so-called *Ledovoie poboische* (Combat on the Ice, 1242). They later fell to Tataro-Mongolian attacks and lived under Tataro-Mongolian rule for 250 years.

From the fourteenth to the sixteenth centuries, the Russian state was forming around Moscow. In the sixteenth and seventeenth centuries it became multinational (including at this time the territories along the Volga river, the

people of the Urals and the people of Siberia). Eventually a union with Ukraine occurred.

The reforms of Peter the Great (1672–1725) and the fight for access to the Baltic Sea (1700–21) resulted in the formation of a mighty naval empire. Ties with European culture grew strong after the war of 1812 with Napoleon. A defeat in the Crimean War in 1856, however, led to crisis – not least in the system of serfdom – and in 1861 the Christian Reform was passed giving support to a growing capitalism.

On 27 February 1917, during World War I, the czar, Nikolas II, abdicated the throne. A non-czarist, democratic republic existed until October 1917. A Soviet government was established in November 1917 under the leadership of Vladimir Ilyich Lenin (1870–1924). At this point, other republics in the region began to unite around Russia leading to the creation of a socialist society known as the Union of Soviet Socialist Republics. (*See* USSR *for additional background on this period.*)

A Russian professional theatre was established by decree of Catherine the Great (1729–96) in 1756, on the model of the Yaroslav Lubitelskaya Troopa (Yaroslav Amateur Company), under the leadership of Fyodor Volkov (1729–63). Serfdom was abolished in 1861 but until that time serf theatres existed widely alongside the imperial public theatres – the Marianski and Alexandrinski in St Petersburg (founded in 1756) and the Bolshoi and Maly Theatres (founded in the late 1750s). In the 1860s, a network of provincial private theatrical enterprises expanded substantially, and private theatres also began to appear in Moscow and St Petersburg. Companies of Russian actors began to work in Kiev, Minsk, Tbilisi, Kazan, Riga, Vilnius, Tallinn and other large cultural centres within the Russian empire.

By the late nineteenth century, two main schools of Russian theatre had developed. First, the Petersburg school followed the traditions of classicism, its academic manner defined and determined by its leading artists. Second, the Moscow school was involved with the aesthetics of the more contemporary romanticism, and the development of a domestic everyday realism. The founder of the Russian realist tradition was Mikhail Shepkin (1788–1863), an artist and teacher who had trained several generations of students, many of whom later determined the aesthetics of the Moscow Maly Theatre. His artistic and ethical principles were extremely influential for Konstantin Stanislavski (1863–1938), the creator of a system of acting which has had world-wide influence on the theatre.

The founding fathers of Russian theatrical culture were also major figures in Russian literature – Alexander Pushkin (1799–1837); Nikolai Gogol (1809–52), author of the comedy *Revizor* (*The Government Inspector*, 1836) and the novel *Dead Souls* (1842); Alexander Ostrovsky (1823–86), the creator of much of the nineteenth-century Russian repertoire and who was also closely connected with the Maly Theatre; and Anton Chekhov (1860–1904), who was associated with the birth of the Moscow Art Theatre in 1898.

Stanislavski and Vladimir Nemirovich-Danchenko (1858–1943), the founders of the Moscow Art Theatre (Moscovski Khudozhestvenny Academicheski Teatr – Moscow Academic Art Theatre, known to Russians simply as MXAT) brought together a group of prominent artists to further the development of new Russian drama, to introduce Russian audiences to the accomplishments of modern world literature, and to further the role of the director and playwright. The influence of MXAT on both the theatre of Russia as well as on world theatre was due primarily to the theatrical experiments of its founders as well as to their innovative methodology of working with actors. The aggregate fundamental ideas known today as the Stanislavski system – related to avant-garde experiments of the nineteenth century – developed on the edge of realistic art and a new psychophysical way of working with the actor.

But Stanislavski was not the only one seeking new directions. Others, who were in their way equally revolutionary, approached theatre from other directions – politically, symbolically, futuristically and expressionistically. They included actor-directors such as Vsevolod

Konstantin Stanislavski.

Meyerhold (1874–1940), Yevgeny Vakhtangov (1883–1922), Mikhail Chekhov (1891–1955) and Alexander Tairov (1885–1950), the creator of a Kamerni (Chamber) Theatre (founded in 1916), uniting classicism with the latest trends in world art. These artists also determined the development of theatre in Russia in the two decades that followed the October Revolution of 1917.

Immediately after the revolution, the construction of a new Soviet culture began. Censorship of theatres became stricter and by the mid-1930s theatrical affairs right across the country were fully centralized. After the first Congress of Soviet Writers in 1934, a full-scale confirmation of 'Soviet state aesthetics' occurred throughout the country. This meeting established socialist-realism as the literary method for all new art, a method which forced the artist to view the world through a Communist Party prism, as a struggle between classes. Using totalitarian methods, the state engaged in an epic battle with aesthetic thought.

When ideas differed, the state stepped in. In 1937 the Meyerhold Theatre was closed and by 1940 its founder had been arrested, subjected to various forms of torture, and then shot. The principles of the realistic MXAT turned it into the favourite theatre of Joseph Stalin (1879–1953), both artistically and organizationally. Soon all theatres in the USSR were required to follow its form.

This universal model of theatre established right across the Soviet system a single approach to art. Until it began to break down in 1987 under the ideas of *perestroika* (restructuring) and *glasnost* (openness), every company followed the same system. At least ten different plays had to be in each theatre's repertoire. All had to have a permanent troupe, headed by a manager and a chief director. Because actors' positions were guaranteed by the state, companies became static and the number of actors in

leading theatres would often exceed a hundred people. (It was due to this situation that the huge troupe of the Moscow Art Theatre, which consisted of close to 200 actors in the mid-1980s, divided into separate groups in 1987 – the Chekhov Company of MXAT and the Gorki Company.) In regional companies troupes of actors usually numbered sixty while in smaller towns troupes rarely went above thirty to thirty-five people. With the change-over to a market economy in the early 1990s, the Russian system found itself undergoing enormous changes: theatres and theatre artists all across the country were finding themselves once again in totally new circumstances with their futures totally unpredictable.

Structure of the National Theatre Community

As of 1993 there were about 400 state-subsidized professional drama theatres in the Russian Federation, along with another eighty puppet theatres, about forty theatres for youth, and close to fifty musical theatres. About forty of the state drama theatres were in Moscow with another twenty in St Petersburg (formerly Leningrad). As a rule, each regional centre with a population close to 1 million has a drama theatre, a musical theatre, a puppet theatre and a theatre for youth. In the autonomous republics of the Russian Federation and the regions, there are both theatres with performances in the local language and theatres working in Russian.

State theatres run almost year-round and all have their own buildings which they are given to use without charge. They receive a subsidy from the government through both the Federation Ministry of Culture and the Ministry of Culture of the republic. Part of the subsidy may also be given by the municipality. State subsidy rarely exceeds 50 per cent of the budget and is traditionally given to support ideological and administrative control of the theatres. The appointment of managers and chief directors by local authorities had to be confirmed in any event by the State Ministry of Culture, as did the selected repertoire on a yearly basis. Ticket prices were kept low in the same manner, especially on plays for children.

In the mid-1980s prices for tickets to a drama theatre did not exceed 3 rubles, and did not exceed 1.5 rubles for children's plays, approxi-

mately double what it cost for a film ticket. The increase in prices for film tickets was actually greater than the increase in prices for theatre tickets in the late 1980s and early 1990s. By 1992, the prices for tickets for cinema and theatre were approximately the same.

Rehearsals in Russian theatres traditionally occurred without any interruptions to other plays in the repertoire. Large theatres staged about four new shows per year; theatres in smaller cities staged up to eight new shows annually. In provincial areas, rehearsal time rarely exceeded ten to twelve weeks while in the larger cities rehearsal time could take up to a year.

In 1986 reform of this system began, and after the removal of censorship in 1987 this progressed into a process whereby central influence dissipated. Theatres received new economic and artistic freedom while actually maintaining government subsidies. Under the new system, they could formulate their own budgets, consider commercial aspects of productions, and had the right to solicit sponsorship capital from various commercial structures.

A much more simplified licensing procedure led to an increase in the number of studios and other theatrical groups structurally analogous to western fringe or alternative companies. Towards the end of the 1980s there were almost 200 such studios, but only a few of them survived longer than a season.

At the end of the 1980s, independent production companies began to emerge which began to gather artists for productions based on Broadway or West End models.

An important place in the theatrical life of the federation was held for many years by the Vserosiikoe Teatralnoe Obshchestvo (VTO – All-Russian Theatrical Society), founded in 1877 as a relief fund for disabled and elderly actors. In time VTO began to conduct a wider range of consultative services including artistic lobbying and festivals. Its 30,000 members included both practitioners and theoreticians of theatre, technical workers, as well as managers at various levels. VTO owned copyrights, various productions, art houses, retirement homes and even did charity work. When VTO ceased to exist in 1986 all of its work and many projects were taken over by the Soyuz Teatralnikh Deyatelei (Union of Theatre Workers).

One of Russia's largest theatrical festivals is now the Chekhov International Theatrical Festival in Moscow (founded by the International Confederation of Theatrical Unions in 1992, in cooperation with the Ministry of Culture). In the second half of the 1980s, with the cooperation of the Union of Theatre Workers of the USSR and the Union of Theatre Workers of the Russian Federation, several theatrical study centres were created including the Stanislavski International Theatrical Centre and the Meyerhold International Theatrical Centre.

The centres of theatrical life in the Russian Federation have long been Moscow and St Petersburg, where the leading theatres were concentrated, as well as the schools, research institutes, and theatre people themselves.

Artistic Profile

Companies

There are literally dozens of important companies working across the Russian Federation, the largest concentration being in Moscow. The Moscow Academic Maly Theatre (founded in the late 1750s) is Moscow's oldest drama theatre, and the cradle of the Russian school of realistic stage art. In its early days, when it was known as the Aktiorski Teatr (Theatre of the Actor), it had a troupe consisting of outstanding actors and a large audience. This tradition was followed from the 1930s to the 1950s with actors such as Igor Ilinski (1901–90) and Mikhail Tsarov (1903–89) who replaced earlier stars such as Alexandra Yablochkina (1866–1964), Varvara Rizhova (1871–1963) and Vera Pashena (1887–1962). Throughout its history one could count on the Maly for realism as well as romanticism, always paying strict attention to the tradition of Moscow speech. Its repertoire included Russian and western classics. With the exception of Boris Ravenski (1914–80), a student of Meyerhold who directed the Maly from 1970 to 1976, the theatre has always been headed by leading actors.

The Moscow Academic Art Theatre, founded in 1898 by Stanislavski and Nemirovich-Danchenko, was the first Russian directors' theatre. From 1945 to 1970, its so-called 'second generation' took charge (mostly those who had made their débuts on the main stage in the mid-1920s), actors such as Boris Dobronravov (1896–1949), Alla Tarasova (1898–1973), Olga Androvskaia (1898–1975), Claudia Elanskaia (1898–1972), Angelina Stepanovna (b. 1905), Mark Prudkin (b. 1898), Victor Stanitsin (1897–1976), Alexei Gribov (1902–77), Mikhail Yanshin (1902–76) and others.

The repertoire during this period retained plays originally staged by the founders of MXAT, but by the 1950s the theatre was experiencing a crisis in that its directors were rather weak. It wasn't until 1971 that Oleg Efremov (b. 1927), a graduate of MXAT's own school and the founder of the Sovremenik (Contemporary) Theatre, was invited to become the theatre's artistic director. Efremov brought to the theatre well-known stars from both stage and film and attracted leading dramatists. He also restaged the plays of Anton Chekhov and helped MXAT to restore the theatre to the position of being the country's leading theatre.

In 1987 MXAT was divided into two separate companies: the Chekhov Company, headed by Efremov, and the Gorki Company, headed by actress Tatiana Doronina (b. 1933). The Chekhov group continued the traditions of the Art Theatre with the Gorki going in newer directions.

A school also exists at the theatre, teaching actors, directors, administrators and dramatists. It was founded in 1943.

Oleg Efremov's Moscow Art Theatre production of Chekhov's *The Seagull.*

Moscow's Vakhtangov Theatre was founded in 1921 by Yevgeny Vakhtangov. Growing out of the ideas of the third experimental Studio of MXAT, the theatre developed the notion of a theatricalized theatre, celebrative and poetic, as well as notions of the tragic grotesque. This work was carried on even during the years of changes to MXAT's system (1930–50).

From 1939 to 1968 the theatre was headed by Ruben Simonov (1899–1968), a student of Vakhtangov, who continued his mentor's experiments involving expressionism, the grotesque, and celebrative plays during the thaw period (1954–64). Also active were the co-founders of the theatre – Anna Orochko (1898–1965) and Cicily Mansurova (1897–1976) – along with a number of younger actors and directors such as Ulia Borisova (b. 1925), Mikhail Ilianov (b. 1927), Nikolai Gritsenko (1912–79), Yuri Lyubimov (b. 1917) and Yuri Yakovlov (b. 1928). Between 1968 and 1987, the theatre was headed by Yevgeny Simonov (b. 1925) with Mikhail Ilianov running it from 1987. Its directors during this time included Piotr Fomenko (b. 1932), Arkady Katz (b. 1931), Roman Viktuke (b. 1940) and Garrei Cherniakhovski (b. 1944). The theatre also has its own school, the Boris Shchukin Theatrical College (also founded in 1921).

The Mossoviet Theatre was founded in 1923. From 1940 to 1977 it was headed by Yuri Zavadski (1894–1977), a student of both Stanislavski and Vakhtangov. His style of directing tried to bring together internal and external reality. Since 1978, the head of the theatre has been Pavel Khomski (b. 1925).

A group of young actors founded the Sovremenik Theatre in 1956. Headed by Oleg Efremov, the group focused on plays connected to psychological and social realism, the social role of individuals, humanitarian issues and democracy. The theatre took a generally anti-Stalinist view, and spoke out against totalitarianism. It was the centrepoint for the best new plays for many years and attracted dramatists whose civil and artistic views were close to those of the company. Among its playwrights were Victor Rozov (b. 1913), Alexander Volodin (b. 1919), Mikhail Shatrov (b. 1932) and Mikhail Roschin (b. 1933), all of whom played a role in the development of Russian drama from the 1950s to the 1970s with their harsh questioning productions.

In the 1970s and 1980s, many of the actors trained by the Sovremenik moved on to MXAT and formed the nucleus of the Chekhov Company there. Among them were Yevgeny Yevstignaev (1926–92), Oleg Tabakov (b. 1935),

Tatiana Lavrova (b. 1938) and Igor Kvasha (b. 1933). Galina Volchek (b. 1933), a director and actress, took over as head of the Sovremenik in 1972.

The Taganka Theatre of Drama and Comedy (located on Tagansky Street in Moscow) was founded in 1946 and was reorganized in 1964. It was in that year that a group of recent graduates of the Shchukin Theatrical College, headed by their teacher Yuri Lyubimov of the Vakhtangov Theatre, came to Taganka as a group.

Like the Sovremenik, it became one of the most important centres for free thought in the country. Lyubimov revived the principles of Vakhtangov, Meyerhold and Brecht with his young actors and staged plays with a political bent, often based simply on initial scenarios. Lyubimov's closest associate in this work was Davyd Borovskyi (b. 1934), a co-author and designer of some of the theatre's best plays, usually poetic and/or metaphoric. Another major figure connected to the Taganka was Vladimir Visotski (1938–80), an actor, singer and poet. Trained at the Taganka, he expressed a personal ethic and a rebellious spirit. Repressed by the totalitarianism of the time, he

inspired various social groups and the younger generation by his presence and his work.

The Lenin Komsomol (Young Communist League) Theatre was founded in 1927 and since 1991 has been called the Moscovski Teatr Lencom. Ivan Bersinov (1889–1951), a student of Stanislavski, was the artistic director of the theatre from 1938 to 1951. A leading actor and director of the second MXAT Studio, he rooted the theatre on the ideas of the psychological grotesque. From 1963 to 1967 the theatre was directed by Anatoly Efros (1925–87), one of the leaders of post-war Soviet theatre, a director who tried to unite principles of psychological realism and the ideas of Meyerhold. Since 1973 the theatre has been directed by Mark Zakharov (b. 1933), whose goal has been to bring together the aesthetics of the dramatic and the musical theatres. The theatre has actively worked with some of the country's new dramatists including Grigori Gorin (b. 1940), Ludmila Petroshevskaia (b. 1938), Dimitri Lipskerov (b. 1963) and Alexander Galin (b. 1947).

The Malaya Bronnaya Drama Theatre was founded in 1946. The theatre attained fame during the period that Andrei Goncharov (b. 1918) was its artistic director. It became one of

Mark Zakharov's Moscow Lencom Theatre production of Konstantin Simonov's *Boy From Our City*.

the leading theatres of the country in 1967 when it hired Anatoly Efros – then in disgrace with the political authorities – to work there. Efros created some of his best productions there.

The artistic director from 1957 of Moscow's Satire Theatre (founded in 1924) was Valentin Pluchek (b. 1909), a student of Meyerhold. Pluchek resurrected the principles of Meyerhold and gave new energy to the traditions of stage satire while working on both classical and modern plays. The troupe included stars of theatre, television, film and stage such as Vladimir Lepko (1898–1963), Giorgi Menglet (b. 1912), Anatoly Papanov (1922–87), Andrei Mironov (1941–87), Vera Vasiliova (b. 1925), Alexander Shirvind (b. 1934) and Mikhail Der-zhavin (b. 1936).

The Mayakovsky Theatre (founded in 1922) became the Theatre of the Revolution in 1943, and in 1954 reverted to its original name again. In the 1920s and 1930s, its leading directors were Vsevolod Meyerhold and Alexei Popov (1892–1961). From 1944 to 1966, its artistic director was Nikolai Okhlopkov (1900–67), a student of Meyerhold. In 1967, Andrei Goncharov took over. Boasting a style that can be called bright and emotional, this has long been one of the best troupes of actors in Moscow.

The Central Theatre of the Soviet Army was founded in Moscow in 1929. Alexei Popov was its artistic director from 1935 to 1960. Bringing to the theatre stage monumentalism, poster expressionism, and experimentation in the realm of musical shows, the company used two stages – one the biggest drama stage in the country. Popov and Maria Knebel (1898–1985), while developing the Stanislavski methodology, also developed a 'study method' for rehearsing, which ended up having a huge influence on Soviet and eastern European theatres in the post-war period. From 1988, the artistic director of the theatre was Leonid Kheifits (b. 1936), a student of Popov and Knebel.

Other companies of note in Moscow in the period between 1945 and 1990 included the Stanislavski Drama Theatre (founded in 1946) and the Alexander Pushkin Theatre (founded in 1916 and called the Chamber Theatre until 1948.) In 1948, Alexander Tairov, one of Russia's major experimental directors and one of the founders of the Chamber Theatre, along with his wife, the great Russian actress Alisa Koonen (1889–1974), were thrown out of the theatre in the state's fight against 'modernism

and cosmopolitanism'. The somewhat moderate rebirth of the theatre at the end of the 1950s was due in great part to the artistic director at the time, Boris Ravenski, one of the last students of Meyerhold, who had kept his devotion to the aesthetics of his master.

One of the newer companies to emerge in Moscow was the Theatre Studio under the directorship of Oleg Tabakov, in 1984. The nucleus of this theatre was made up of Tabakov's students at the MXAT Theatre School.

The oldest Russian professional theatre is the Pushkin Academic Theatre, founded in 1756 in St Petersburg. The period from the 1940s to the 1960s was the theatre's brightest period when it was headed by Leonid Vivien (1887–1966) who had worked in productions of Meyerhold, the director of the theatre in the first decade of the century. Vivien also began a theatre-school in 1918, the present St Petersburg Institute Theatre of Music and Cinematography.

The most important of the St Petersburg theatres in the period since the 1940s has been the Bolshoi Drama Theatre, now called the Giorgi Tovstonogov Bolshoi Dramatic Theatre. Founded in 1918 with the support of Maxim Gorki (1868–1936) and Alexander Blok (1880–1921), it was known as the Maxim Gorki Bolshoi Dramatic Theatre until 1991. The artistic director of the theatre from 1956 until his death was Giorgi Tovstonogov (1915–89), one of the leaders of Russian Soviet directing. An innovator though based in the methodology of Stanislavski, his productions reflected humanitarian and democratic ideologies for which his company, along with the Sovremenik and the Taganka, were subjected to regular quasi-official Soviet criticism. His major productions were of Russian classics – Dostoevsky (1821–81), Chekhov, Alexander Griboedov (1794–1829), Tolstoi (1817–75) and Gorki – and very problematic modern plays by Victor Rozov, Alexei Arbuzov (1908–87), Alexander Volodin, Alexander Gelman (b. 1934) and Alexander Vampilov (1937–72) among others. Tovstonogov also trained a group of artists who ultimately came to hold leading positions in theatre, film and television: Vitaly Politseimako (1906–67), Efim Kopelian (1912–75), Pavel Luspekaev (1927–70), Inokentei Smoktunovski (b. 1925), Kiril Lavrov (b. 1925), Vladislav Strzhelchik (b. 1921), Sergei Urskei (b. 1935), Yevgeny Lebedov (b. 1917), Oleg Basilashvili (b. 1934) and Tatiana Doronina. In 1989 Lavrov was named artistic director of the theatre.

Other theatres of note in St Petersburg include the Maly Dramatic Theatre (founded in 1944) with its most important work done in the 1980s when it was headed by Lev Dodin (b. 1944); the Comedy Theatre (founded in 1929 as the Theatre of Satire) whose most interesting work was done from 1955 to 1968, when it was headed by director Nikolai Akimov (1901–68) and in the second half of the 1970s when Piotr Fomenko was its director; the Petersburg New Theatre (founded in 1933 and called the Petersburg Soviet Theatre from 1953 until 1992); the Vera Komissarzhevskaia Theatre (founded in 1942) whose best work was done in the 1970s and 1980s under the leadership of Ruben Agamerzian (1922–91), a director of historical drama as well as modern dramatists; and the Lenin Komsomol Theatre (founded in 1936), a theatre for youth.

Some of the most important companies outside Moscow and St Petersburg include the Yaroslav Drama Theatre (founded in 1750), Russia's oldest provincial professional theatre; the Gamzat Tsadasi Avarian Theatre (founded in 1935 and operating in Makhachkala, Republic of Dagestan in the northern Caucus, since 1943); the Adygei Drama Theatre (founded in 1933 and operating in Maikop, a Krasnodar city, since 1941); the Arkhangelsk Drama Theatre (founded in 1846, Arkhangelsk); the Balkarian Drama Theatre (founded in 1939 in Nalchic, the capital of Kabardino-Balkaria, northern Caucus); the Bashkir Academic Drama Theatre (founded in 1919 and now operating in Ufa, the capital of the Bashkir Autonomous Republic) which saw the premières of plays by Mustai Karim (b. 1919) and Azat Abchulin (b. 1934), who attained fame throughout the Soviet Union in the 1950s and 1960s; the Namsaraeva Buryat Drama Theatre (founded in 1950 in Ulan-Ude, the capital of the Buryat Autonomous Republic); the Gorki Vladivostok Drama Theatre (founded in 1931 in Vladivostok) which performs in Russian; and the Koltsev Voronezh Drama Theatre (founded in 1802, called the Bolshoi Soviet Theatre from 1919, then after 1937 called the Voronezh Government Drama Theatre).

The Jewish Theatre was founded in 1919 in Petrograd under the direction of A. Granovski (1890–1937) and it led to the establishment in Moscow in 1921 of the Jewish Chamber Theatre, the latter renamed the Moscow Jewish Theatre. The Moscow Jewish Theatre was closed down in 1949 during a period of anti-semitism and the theatre's leaders were killed. A

Jewish Drama Concert Ensemble worked during the 1960s, 1970s and 1980s with a repertoire that included plays by Sholom Aleichem Rabinovich (1859–1916). The company worked in both Yiddish and Russian.

Other provincial theatres of note in the Russian Federation include the Gorno-Altaisk Theatre (founded in 1937 in the capital of Siberia's Gorno-Altaisk Autonomous Region), the first professional theatre of the Altaian people, performing in both Altaian and Russian; the Gorki Nizhny-Novgorod Drama Theatre (founded in 1798); the Darginsk Theatre (founded in 1961 in Izberbash, Dagestan, northern Caucus), the first professional theatre of the Dargin people, founded with the help of graduates of the Darginsk Studio of the Armenian Institute of Theatre Arts; the Ivanovo Drama Theatre (Ivanovo Bolshoi Drama Theatre, founded in 1852); the Irkutsk Drama Theatre (established in 1934, in the centre of eastern Siberia) which staged the premières of some of the first works of Alexander Vampilov; the Kabardino Drama Theatre (founded in 1737 in Nalchic, the capital of Kabardino-Balkari); the Kazan Bolshoi Drama Theatre (founded in 1791, it has borne the name of Vasili Kachanov since 1948), the largest drama theatre in the Tatar Republic; the Tver (Kalinin) Drama Theatre (founded in 1922), a Russian-language company which did some strong work under the directorship of Giorgi Giorgovski (1907–72) in the 1950s and 1960s; and the Kalmitsk Drama Theatre (founded in 1936 in Elista, the capital of the Kalmitsk Republic).

Other provincial companies of note are the Komi Drama Theatre (founded in 1919, Siktivkar); the Komi-Permiatsk District Drama Theatre (founded in 1931 in Kudimkar, the capital of the Komi-Permiatsk National District); the Ostrovsky Kostroma Drama Theatre; the Pushkin Krasnoyarsk Drama Theatre of eastern Siberia; the Krasnei Fakel (Red Torch) Theatre (founded in 1920 in Odessa and operating in Novosibirsk, the capital of Siberia, since 1932); the Samarsk (Kuibeshevsk) Drama Theatre (founded in 1930); the Kumik Musical Drama Theatre (founded in 1930 in Makhachkala, the capital of the Republic of Dagestan); the Lacsk Drama Theatre (founded in 1935 in aul Kumukh, Republic of Dagestan); the Lesginsk Drama Theatre (founded in 1935 in the Akhta Dagestan Republic); the Mareisk Drama Theatre (founded in 1919) in Ioshkar-Ola; the Mordovsk Drama Theatre (founded in 1930 in Saransk, the capital of the Mordovsk

Autonomous Region); and the Omsk Russian Drama Theatre (founded in 1876).

Also significant are the Rostov-na-Donu (Rostov on the Don) Drama Theatre (founded in 1917) with a building in the form of a tractor, by the architects Vladimir Shchuko (1878–1939) and Vladimir Gelfreich (1885–1967); the Saratov Drama Theatre (founded in 1865) which in the 1980s attained note thanks to its productions by director Alexander Dzekun (b. 1944) of plays by Andrei Platonov (1899–1951) and Mikhail Bulgakov (1891–1940); the Ekaterinburg Drama Theatre (known as the Sverdlovsk Drama Theatre from 1924 to 1990, founded in 1845) which performs in the largest industrial centre of the Ural region; the Severo-Osetinski Drama Theatre (founded in 1935); the Kamal Tatar Drama Theatre (founded in 1906 in Kazan), the national drama theatre of the Tatars and which performs the major playwrights of Tataria: Kamal, Isanbet, Tinchurin, Usmanov, Valeiv, Husni, Vakhit and others; the Tuva Drama Theatre (founded in 1936 in Kizil, the capital of the Republic of Tuva) specializing in Tuvan dramatists such as Toka, Sarig-oola, Sagan-oola, Kudazhi and Seureun-oola; and the Udmurtia Drama Theatre (founded in 1931 in Izhevsk, the capital of Udmurtia) which stages drama as well as opera, ballet and musical comedy.

There is also a Finnish Drama Theatre (founded in 1932 in Petrozavodsk, the capital of the Republic of Karelia) performing in Finnish. Its repertoire includes the works of Karelian and Finnish dramatists, as well as Russian and world drama.

The Khabarovsk Theatre of Drama (founded in 1896 in Khabarovsk, eastern Siberia) is one of the largest Russian theatres in the far east and in eastern Siberia. Its repertoire also consists of Russian and world drama.

Other provincial theatres include the Khakassk Drama Theatre (founded in 1939 in Abakane, the capital of the Khakassk Autonomous Region, in eastern Siberia); the Cheliabinsk Drama Theatre (founded in 1921 in Cheliabinsk); the Chuvash Drama Theatre (founded in 1918 in Kazan, the theatre moved in 1920 to Cheboksari, the capital of the Chuvash Autonomous Republic); the Checheno-Ingush Drama Theatre (founded in 1931 in Groznei, the capital of the Checheno-Ingush Autonomous Region in the northern Caucus) which has two troupes, one performing in the Chechen language, the other in Ingush (in 1990 the theatre split into the Chechen Drama Theatre and the Ingush Drama Theatre); the Oiunski Yakutsk Musical Drama Theatre (founded in 1925 in Yakutsk); the Volokov Yaroslav Drama Theatre (founded in 1750); and the Lipetski Drama Theatre (founded in 1937) which attained fame in the 1980s, and 1990s thanks to the efforts of the director Vladimir Pakhomov (b. 1941), who turned the theatre into a laboratory of classical drama, especially the plays of Anton Chekhov.

Dramaturgy

Russian dramatists from the 1930s on worked within the context of socialist-realism which preached collectivist communist ideals. Certain writers stood out for their ability to deal within these structures with the individual person, the psychological problems of individual minds, and the personal problems of existence.

Alexei Arbuzov was one such writer. Melodrama and light irony made his plays popular among theatre professionals as well as theatre patrons and his works were immensely popular from the 1950s to the 1980s. He was also the first Soviet-Russian dramatist whose plays were staged in the west. In the 1970s and 1980s, he spent a great deal of his time working with younger dramatists. The Arbuzov Studio turned out a number of well-known dramatists such as Ludmila Petroshevskaia and Victor Slavkin (b. 1935). Among Arbuzov's most important plays are *Tanya* (1935), *Gorod Na Zaree* (*The City at Dawn*, 1940), *Godi Stranstvei* (*The Years of Wandering*, 1954), *Moi Bednei Marat* (*My Poor Marat*, 1964), *Schastliveii Dni Ne Schastlivogo Cheloveka* (*The Fortunate Days of an Unfortunate Person*, 1967), *Zhestokie Igri* (*Cruel Games*, 1978), *Skazki starogo Arbata* (*Fairytales of Old Arbat*, 1970) and *Irkutskaya Istoriya* (*Irkutsk Story*, 1964).

Among other influential dramatists, two stand out – Alexander Vampilov and Alexander Volodin. Vampilov was a journalist from Irkutsk, a Siberian city, who drowned in Lake Baikal on his 35th birthday (in 1972). One of the legends of Russian theatre, Vampilov worked within the traditions of Chekhovian drama with its undetectable shifts from comedy to tragedy. He paid special attention to the lives of young people in the second half of the 1960s. Vampilov's influence on later dramatists has proved to be unusually important with many terming themselves the 'post-Vampilov generation'. One of the most popular dramatists of the 1970s and 1980s, his best plays are *Svidanie v Predmeste* (*The Meeting in a Suburb*), also called *Starshei Sin* (*The Elder Son*, 1967), *Proshlim Letom v Chulinske* (*Last Summer in Chulinsk*, 1972) and *Utinaya Okhota* (*Duck Hunting*, 1967).

Alexander Volodin, from St Petersburg, is a poet and fiction writer. After serving in World War II, he had his first successes as a playwright in the mid-1950s, during the time of the thaw of Nikita Khrushchev (1894–1970). His plays are linked to the Russian sentimentalist tradition and defend the rights to individual thoughts and feelings. It was no surprise that they were disapproved of by many communist critics. Due to censorship, he was forced to stop writing for both theatre and film in the mid-1970s. Like Arbuzov, he was subjected to criticism for his 'narrow specialization' and his alleged lack of interest in the Communist Party. Among his important plays are *Fabrichnaya Devochka* (*The Factory Girl*, 1955), *Piat Vecherov* (*Five Evenings*, 1956), *Naznachenie* (*The Appointment*, 1961), and *S Lubimimi Ne Rostavaitece* (*Do Not Part With Loved Ones*, 1969).

Two of the so-called classics of Soviet drama are Nikolai Pogodin (1900–62) and Alexander Shtein (b. 1906). Pogodin attained wide fame in the 1930s, 1940s and 1950s by writing plays about the joys of new industrial work and plays about Vladimir Lenin. Pogodin was also a great public figure and became manager of the magazine *Teatr* (*Theatre*) in the 1950s. In his plays he battled for the destalinization of Soviet society. Among his best works are *Mi Vtoriom Poekhali Na Tselinu* (*Our Second Trip to the Virgin Lands*, 1957) and *Tretya, Patetichiskaya* (*The Third, Pathétique Speech*, 1957).

Shtein attained wide fame in the 1930s and 1940s for his historical and historical-revolutionary plays. In the 1950s and 1960s his best plays were also dedicated to destalinization of the armed forces. In the 1970s he created a number of stage biographies of cultural figures and writers. His important plays include *Personalenoe Delo* (*Personal Process*, 1954), *Gostinitsa Astoria* (*The Hotel Astoria*, 1956), *Okean* (*Ocean*, 1961) and *U Vremeni V Plenu* (*Imprisoned By Time*, 1967).

Several other writers dealt with the nature of 'work' within Soviet society and the problems of industrialization. Among the most influential were Ignacy Dvoretski (1919–88) and Alexander Gelman.

Dvoretski was a St Petersburg playwright who attained wide fame as an author of dramas based on the conflicts which occur in the industrial environment – plants, factories and mines. This type of journalistic genre, as a rule, described the conflict between conservatives and innovators in both production and socialist life. It was in a way the only possible method of expressing opinions on these issues during the period of totalitarian rule, within the rigid guidelines of the censors. Dvoretski set up his own studio of young dramatists in St Petersburg which, like Arbuzov's studio in Moscow, helped to form the 'post-Vampilov generation'. His best play is *Chelovek so Storoni* (*A Person From the Side*, 1974).

Gelman, a former naval officer, construction worker and journalist, first involved himself with drama in the early 1970s, and quickly became a leader among those writing 'industrial plays'. Examining conflicts in production, he looked at the highest echelons of power and made a number of statements which criticized the regime. In the 1980s, he focused on the social and psychological nature of heroes. Gelman's plays invariably led to serious sociopolitical discussions. In the mid-1980s he became a publisher and in so doing, a participant in the larger political battles. His significant plays are *Premiya* (*Bonus*), previously titled *Zasedania Partcoma* (*The Party Committee Meeting*, 1975), *Obratnaya Sviaze* (*Feedback*, 1977), *Na Idine Sa Vsemi* (*In Private With Everyone*, 1980), and *Skameika* (*The Bench*, 1983).

Victor Rozov was one of the leaders of Russian Soviet playwriting in the post-war period. An actor, he made his début as a writer after the war, orienting himself toward the tradition of Russian critical realism. Maxim Gorki was his model and Rozov was probably the most famous author of problem plays in the 1950s and 1960s. He looked at problems of relationships between generations and the morality of political establishments. He was involved with the best directors in Russia – Oleg Efremov (at the Sovremenik and MXAT) and Anatoly Efros. Rozov's best plays are *V Poiskah Radosti* (*In Search of Happiness*, 1956), *Vechno Zhivie* (*Alive Forever*, 1943), *Traditsionei Sbor* (*Traditional Gathering*, 1966), *Brat Aliosha* (*Brother Aliosha*, based on Fyodor Dostoevsky, 1969) and *Kabanchik* (*Piglet*, 1987).

Afanacy Salinski (1920–1993) was also a journalist. His first success as a playwright came in the mid-1950s when he wrote a number of plays which defended human dignity in a communist society and which confirmed the principles of destalinization. With a philosophical understanding of reality, he created philosophical democratic dramas with elements of melodrama in some of the more popular plays. He was interested in the behaviour of heroes in extreme situations. From 1973 to 1983, and from 1987 to 1992, he was chief editor of the magazine *Teatr*. His best plays include *Barabanschitsa* (*The Drummer Girl*, 1957), *Lozh Dlia Uzkogo Kruga* (*A Lie for a Narrow Circle*, 1962), *Maria* (1967), *Letnie Progulki* (*Summer Walks*, 1973) and *Molva* (*Rumour*, 1983).

Mikhail Roschin is a writer who developed during the time of the thaw, 1956–64. He compared and contrasted totalitarian ideological doctrine with interest in the life of private citizens and private problems. He defended a liberal approach to solving social problems. He was also the author of a dramatic epic in which he defended the necessity of humanism in all extreme situations. His important plays are *Valentin and Valentina* (1971), *Eshelon* (*Troop Train, 1975*) and *Speshite Delat Dobro* (*Hurry To Do a Good Deed*, 1982).

In the 1960s and 1970s, three writers emerged who began to challenge their society in many new ways – Mikhail Shatrov, Edward Radzinski (b. 1936) and Grigori Gorin. Shatrov, a playwright and a public figure, created historical political drama which was, on a deeper level, supposed to be giving lessons to the rulers and politicians of the 1960s, 1970s, and 1980s. Freely discussing the facts of the October Revolution of 1917 in his biographies of political figures, Shatrov tried to humanize the Bolshevik doctrines while actively battling with the Stalin heritage. He tried to maintain a position of 'socialism with a human face'. His significant plays include *Bolsheviki* (*The Bolsheviks*, 1967), *Brestskei Mir* (*The Peace at Brest*, 1965), *Shestoie Iulia* (*The Sixth of July*, 1965), *Revolutsionei Etude* (*Revolutionary Exercise*, 1977) and *Tak Pobedim* (*This Is How We Will Beat Them*, 1981).

Radzinski also wrote historical theatrical parables. He began as a creator of plays with modern themes, written under the influence of 'confessional literature' in the 1960s, and became an author of intellectual historical drama focused on the problems of modern Soviet life. Plays for various star actresses took a special position within his creative work, the best of which includes *104 Stranitsi Pro Lubove* (*104 Pages About Love*, 1964), *Besedi s Socratom* (*Conversations With Socrates*, 1978),

Lunin (1981), *O Zhenshine* (*About Women*) and *Staraya Aktrisa Na Rolle Zheni Dostoevskogo* (*An Old Actress for the Role of Dostoevsky's Wife*, 1985).

Gorin, in his turn, began as an author of humorous prose and satirical comedy about modern life. In the mid-1970s, his work evolved into Aesopian satire, which in the twentieth century was practised in Russia only by Yevgeny Svarts (1897–1958). Using well-known plots, almost acting as a co-author of particular classics, Gorin produced very original works which reflected the social and philosophical problems of contemporary life. His plays were usually romantically ironic and included elements of the absurd. Gorin's constant partner in his work in theatre and film was the producer Mark Zakharov, artistic director of the Moscow Lencom Theatre. His important plays include *Ubitte Gerostrata* (*The Killing of Herostrates*, 1971), *Tille* (*Tile*, 1974), *Tot Samei Munhauzen* (*That Same Munchhausen*, 1976), *Dom Katorei Postroil Swift* (*The House That Swift Built*, 1983), *Pominalnaya Molitva* (*Memorial Prayer*, 1988) and *Kot Domashnei Srednei Pushistosti* (*The Standard Fuzzy House Cat*, co-authored with Vladimir Voinovich (b. 1932), 1989).

The post-Vampilov generation moved even closer to grotesque and absurdist forms of theatre. Three important members of this group were Victor Slavkin, Ludmila Petroshevskaia and Alexander Galin.

Slavkin was a humorist, the manager of the department of humour in one of the most popular magazines of the 1950s, 1960s, 1970s and 1980s, *Yunost* (*Youth*). A participant in the studio of Alexei Arbuzov, he began as an author developing a Russian Theatre of the Absurd and created two plays, *Vzsroslaya Doch Molodogo Cheloveka* (*The Grown-up Daughter of a Young Man*, 1977) and *Serso* (*The Ring*, 1982), which were produced by Anatoly Vasiliov (b. 1942) in this style. They became in their own ways manifestations of the late 1960s. The elements of absurdism in these plays were later absorbed by the traditions of Russian lyrical film-making.

Petroshevskaia began as a prose writer, an author of tales and scenarios for animated films. One of the more outstanding representatives of post-Vampilov drama, she built on the traditions of Gogol and Mikhail Saltykov-Schedrin (1826–89), combining them with elements of the absurd. One sees in her work hyperbolic, grotesque theatrical images. Petroshevskaia's best plays were forbidden by the censors for a long time and their theatrical life began only in the 1980s. She writes many one-act dramas and comedies which often unite into various theatrical cycles. Her most significant plays are *Chinzano* (1975), *Tri Devushki V Golubom* (*Three Girls in Blue*, 1981), *Dene Rozhdenia Smirnovoi* (*Smirnova's Birthday*, 1976), *Uroki Musici* (*Music Lessons*, 1974), *Moscovski Khor* (*The Moscow Choir*, 1985), *Kvartira Colombini* (*Colombine's Apartment*, 1976), and *Lestnichnaya Kletka* (*The Staircase*, 1977).

Galin, a playwright and director who started on his artistic path in St Petersburg in Ignacy Dvoretski's studio, strove to combine raw realism with the well-made play. A psychologist who paid special attention to images of women and old people, he was one of the most reputable dramatists between the 1970s and early 1990s. His best plays include *Retro* (1977), *Vostochnaya Tribuna* (*Eastern Tribune*, 1979), *Groupa* (*Group*, 1988) and *Sorry* (1991).

Leonid Zorin (b. 1924) is the author of several sharply satirical comedies and social melodramas as well as satirical and lyrical prose. He possesses a masterful literary style in his best plays – *Dobriaki* (*The Kind Ones*, 1962), *Dion* (1964), *Varschavskaya Melodia* (*The Warsaw Melody*, 1966) and *Tsitata* (*Quotation*, 1986).

Another writer who stands out is the Moldovan Ian Drutse (b. 1928). He moved to Moscow in the early 1970s to escape persecution, entered into Russian drama and became one of the major authors of the 1960s, 1970s and 1980s. He unites poetic metaphor with sharply socialist problems. He is especially interested in the preservation of national traditions and philosophical individualism. His best plays are *Kasa Maree* (1961), *Ptitsi Nashei Molodosti* (*Birds of Our Youth*, 1977) and *Vozvroschenia Na Krugi Svoia* (*Resurrection in One's Self*, 1981) about Lev Tolstoi (1828–1910).

Directors, Directing and Production Styles

In the nineteenth century, Russian realism moved toward psychological realism, a movement that can be seen in the dramaturgical changes apparent in the works of Gogol on the one hand and Chekhov on the other. Though realism continued to dominate through most of the twentieth century – including socialist-realism – directors from Stanislavski and Nemirovich-Danchenko to Vakhtangov and Meyerhold searched in other areas for alternative approaches. Stanislavski's ideas have remained strong in the period since 1945 while the approaches of Vakhtangov and Meyerhold have been the subjects of new examinations in Russia especially in the 1980s and 1990s.

Among those influential Russian directors who have followed the Stanislavski system in their work in the post-1945 period – and who have helped to evolve new understandings of it – one must speak of Alexei Popov, Maria Knebel, Oleg Efremov, Çiorgi Toustonogov, Leonid Kheifits, Anatoly Vasiliov and Anatoly Efros.

Popov was a student of Stanislavski and began his theatrical career in 1912. He later worked in the Vakhtangov Theatre and the Revolution Theatre (presently the Mayakovsky Theatre), among others. From 1935 to 1960 he was the artistic director of the Central Theatre of the Soviet Army. Together with Maria Knebel he helped establish a new 'method of active analysis' or the 'study method' in work on plays. Later, Popov was a professor in the Government Institute of Theatre Arts and taught several generations of directors. He did some of his best work on classics such as *Romeo and Juliet* (1935), *The Taming of the Shrew* (1937) and *The Dancing Master* (1946) by Lope de Vega. These productions showed something of the monumentalism and epic proportions which became hallmarks of his work on the stage of the Central Theatre of the Soviet Army, upon which even tanks could enter. Nevertheless, his handling of actors included very deep and sensitive psychological insight.

Maria Knebel was also a student of Stanislavski and Mikhail Chekhov and worked for many years at the Moscow Art Theatre. In 1948, she was dismissed in what became known as the 'battle against cosmopolitanism' and later worked in the Central Children's Theatre. Together with Alexei Popov, she helped evolve the 'method of active analysis' which had influence on the development of Russian, Soviet and European theatre in the second half of the twentieth century.

She also trained several generations of directors in the Government Institute of Theatre Arts (presently known as the Russian Academy of Theatre Art) and wrote books and articles dealing with problems facing directors and theatre teachers. Among her more important productions were *Gore Ot Uma* (*Woe from Wit*) by Alexander Griboedov (Central Children's

Meyerhold's 1922 Moscow production of Fernand Crommelynck's *The Magnificent Cuckold*, designed by Lyubov Popova.

Theatre, 1951), *Ivanov* by Anton Chekhov (Alexander Pushkin Theatre, Moscow, 1956), *Vishniovi Sad* (*The Cherry Orchard*) by Chekhov (Central Theatre of the Soviet Army, 1967), *Tot, kto poluchaet poschiochini* (*He Who Gets Slapped*) by Leonid Andreev (1871–1919) (Central Theatre of the Soviet Army, 1971).

Kheifits, in his turn, was a student of Popov and Knebel and was one of the best directors in utilizing the 'active analysis' approach. In his work, he united psychological insight with a genuine sense of the theatrical. He was pushed in this latter direction by his work in the Central Theatre of the Soviet Army where he made his début in the mid-1960s. From the late 1960s, he moved to the Maly Theatre in Moscow, then from the early 1980s he worked at MXAT. In 1987 he moved back to the Central Theatre of the Soviet Army. Among Kheifits's major productions are *Czar Ivan Groznei* (*Czar Ivan the Terrible*) by Alexei Tolstoi (1883–1945) (Central Theatre of the Soviet Army, 1967), *Svadba Krechinskogo* (*Krechinski's Wedding*) by Alexander Sukhovo-Kobylin (1817–1903) (Maly Theatre, 1970), *Letnie Progulki* (*Summer Walks*) by Afanacy Salinski (Maly Theatre, 1973), *Fiesko's Plot in Genoa* by Schiller (Maly Theatre, 1976) and *Pavel I* by Dimitri Merezhkovski (1866–1941) (Central Theatre of the Soviet Army, 1990).

Vasiliov was also a student of Knebel and Popov and also followed the principles of Stanislavski's system using the 'methods of active analysis'. Vasiliov has also regularly experimented in the area of the psychology of acting, trying to link Russian psychological theatre with the experiences of Artaud and Grotowski. Vasiliov's most important productions have included *Pervei Variant Vassi Zheliznovoi* (*Vassa Zheleznova, the First Version*) by Maxim Gorki (Stanislavski Theatre, Moscow, 1975), *Vzroslaya Doch Molodogo Cheloveka* (*The Grown-up Daughter of a Young Man*) by Victor Slavkin (Stanislavski Theatre, 1976), *Serso* by Slavkin (Taganka Theatre School, Moscow, 1983) and *Six Characters in Search of an Author* by Luigi Pirandello (School of Dramatic Arts, Moscow, 1986). Vasiliov has devoted many years to teaching in the School of Dramatic Arts and its various studios.

Anatoly Efros also studied with Popov and Knebel and was one of the leaders of the 'theatre revolution' of the mid-1950s. Rooting his work in Stanislavski and the 'method of active analysis' as well as the 'study method', he was a director with an incredibly lyrical gift who united the traditions of the psychological theatre with principles of Meyerhold's montage approach. Subjective in his work, he has often expressed modern problems in his productions. From 1954 to 1963 he directed for the Central Children's Theatre and from 1963 to 1967 he was the artistic director of the Moscow Komsomol Theatre. He later moved to Malaya Bronnaya Drama Theatre and from 1984 he was artistic director of the Taganka. Major productions by Efros include *V Dobrei Chas* (*At a Good Time*) by Victor Rozov (Central Children's Theatre, 1955), *104 Stranitsi Pro Lubove* (*104 Pages About Love*) by Edward Radzinski

(Komsomol Theatre, 1964), *Moi Bednei Marat* (*My Poor Marat*) by Alexei Arbuzov (Komsomol Theatre, 1965), *Molière* by Mikhail Bulgakov (Komsomol Theatre, 1966), *Tri Sestri* (*Three Sisters*) by Chekhov (Malaya Bronnaya Drama Theatre, 1968), *Na Dne* (*Lower Depths*) by Gorki (Taganka Theatre, 1984), *Eshelon* by Mikhail Roschin (MXAT, 1975) and *Vishniovei Sad* (*The Cherry Orchard*) by Chekhov, (Taganka Theatre, 1977).

Productions at the MXAT in the 1950s and 1960s renewed the importance of psychological realism generally and Stanislavski's ideas in particular. Younger directors such as Galina Volchek and Lev Dodin and established masters such as Efremov and Tovstonogov moved the art forward with their basically realistic approaches.

Volchek was actually a graduate of the Moscow Art Theatre School and was involved with the Sovremenik Theatre for most of her career. The Sovremenik tried to develop psychological realism in the MXAT sense in the 1950s and 1960s. She worked there first as an actress and then as a director from the mid-1960s. In

Galina Volchek's Sovremenik Theatre production of Eugenia Ginzburg's *Bad Road*.

1971, after the departure of Efremov to the Moscow Art Theatre, Volchek became the Sovremenik's artistic director, a position that she still held in 1993. Volchek's socially active and psychologically profound art brought her success in productions such as *Na Dne* (1968), *Obeknovenaya Istoria* (*The Same Old Story*) by Victor Rozov, based on a Goncharov novel, in 1964, *Eshelon* (1975) and *Murlin Murlo* (1990).

Lev Dodin, a graduate of the St Petersburg Institute of Theatre, Music and Cinematography, began his career in the St Petersburg Theatre for Young Viewers in the mid-1970s. Dodin later became artistic director of the St Petersburg Maly Theatre and did a cycle of plays in the 1980s based on the works of Fyodor Abramov (1920–84) from the life of Pekashino, a village in the Russian north, *Kak Molodi Mi Bily...* (*How Young We Were...*), *Stroibat*, based on the prose of Sergei Kaledin (b. 1946), in 1988, and *Besi* (*Devils*) based on the novel by Fyodor Dostoevsky, in 1991.

Oleg Efremov's name is related to the 'theatrical revolution' of the mid-1950s. A disciple of the Moscow Art Theatre School trained under the influence of 'the method of physical actions', Efremov tried to further develop Stanislavski's system which had been rejected by dogmatists of the 1940s and 1950s, who were caught up in their zealous concern for official ideologies. Efremov connected his work on Stanislavski's system with a move towards new social meaning in art. These ideas became part of the Sovremenik, whose very creation was due to the political destalinization of society after Stalin's death in 1953. The Sovremenik opened in 1956 and defended the new approaches. Efremov headed the Sovremenik until the summer of 1971, when he was offered the directorship of the Moscow Art Theatre. He made major changes at MXAT, inviting into it stars of both theatre and film.

Efremov's important productions include *Vechno Zhivie* (*Alive Forever*) by Victor Rozov (Sovremenik, 1956), *Goli Korol* (*The Naked King*) by Yevgeny Svarts (Sovremenik, 1959), *Traditsionei Sbor* (*Traditional Gathering*) by Rozov (Sovremenik, 1965), *Piat Vecherov* (*Five Evenings*) by Alexander Volodin (Sovremenik, 1963), *Bolsheviki* (*The Bolsheviks*) by Mikhail Shatrov (Sovremenik, 1968), *Chaika* (*The Seagull*) by Chekhov (MXAT, 1979), *Na Idene Sa Vsemi* (*In Private with Everyone*) by Alexander Gelman (MXAT, 1980), *Diadia Vanya* (*Uncle Vanya*) by Chekhov (MXAT, 1985) and

Gore Ot Uma (*Woe from Wit*) by Alexander Griboedov (MXAT, 1992).

The last of the great realists was Giorgi Tovstonogov, who began his stage career in 1931 in Tbilisi. From 1938 to 1946 he was artistic director of the Tbilisi Russian Drama Theatre and from 1956 to the end of his life was the artistic director of the Bolshoi Drama Theatre in St Petersburg. Tovstonogov played one of the most important roles in the theatrical revolution of the mid-1950s, leading the decisive battle against a dogmatic view of Stanislavski's system. In fact, he renewed and deepened the ideas of Stanislavski. He also united MXAT-style realism with St Petersburg's traditional academism and Georgian romanticism. The St Petersburg Bolshoi Theatre under Tovstonogov became one of the centres of spiritual opposition to totalitarianism. His major productions included *Optemisticheskaya Tragedia* (*The Optimistic Tragedy*) by Vsevolod Vishnevski (1900–51) (Pushkin Theatre, 1956) and, for the Bolshoi Drama Theatre, *The Idiot* based on Dostoevsky (1957, 1966), *Gore Ot Uma* (1958), *Varvari* (*Barbarians*, 1959) by Gorki, *Meschanie* (*Narrowmindedness*, 1966) by Gorki, *Dachniki* (*Summer Folk*) by Gorki in 1976, *Istoria Loshadi* (*The Horse's Story*) based on Lev Tolstoi in 1975, *Protocol Odnago Zasedania* (*Minutes of the Meeting*) by Alexander Gelman in 1975, *Tikhii Don* (*And Quiet Flows the Don*) by Mikail Sholokhov (1905–87) in 1977 and *Diadia Vanya* by Chekhov in 1982.

Five directors of note developed various aspects of the non-realistic Vakhtangov tradition: Ruben Simonov, Piotr Fomenko, Garrei Cherniakhovski, Andrei Goncharov and Yuri Lyubimov.

Ruben Simonov was actually a student of Yevgeny Vakhtangov, having arrived at his studio in 1920. A painter and a director, he became the artistic director of the Vakhtangov Theatre in 1939. He maintained Vakhtangov's traditions of theatre as celebration and the aesthetics of the theatrical grotesque. Similarly, in his work with actors, he used images uniting them with the principles of 'transformations into images'. His important productions included *Front* (1942) by the Ukrainian Oleksander Korniychuk, *Zhivoi Troop* (*The Living Corpse*, 1962), *Mademoiselle Nitouche* (1946), *Princess Turandot* by Carlo Gozzi in 1965 and *Konarmi* (*Red Cavalry*) by Isaac Babel (1894–c.1940) in 1967.

Piotr Fomenko had great knowledge of the

laws of psychological theatre and brought this to his work at the Vakhtangov. He also worked in the Taganka and at the St Petersburg Comedy Theatre. As a teacher, he trained several generations of actors and directors at the Government Institute of Theatre Arts in Moscow (now the Russian Academy of Theatre Arts). Fomenko's major productions include *Scandalnoie Prishestvie s Misterom Ketlom i Missis Moon* (*A Scandalous Incident with Mr Kettle and Mrs Moon*, Taganka Theatre, 1963), *Tiger at the Gates* by Jean Giraudoux (St Petersburg Comedy Theatre, 1974), *Delo* (*The File*) by Sukhovo-Kobylin (Vakhtangov Theatre, 1989) and *Bez Vini Vinovatie* (*Guilty Without Guilt*) by Ostrovsky (Vakhtangov Theatre, 1993). In 1993, Fomenko created his own Theatre-Studio, one of the brighter new groups in Russia.

Garrei Cherniakhovski graduated from the Vakhtangov School and tried to combine Vakhtangov's traditions with the psychological theatre.

Andrei Goncharov has been a public stage figure since 1942. He worked in the Satire Theatre and became artistic director of the Moscow Drama Theatre in 1958. In 1967 he took over the Mayakovsky Theatre where he was still artistic director in 1993. Goncharov unites traditions of the Russian actors' theatre with the control of the director's theatre. He is another ally of the brightly emotional theatre of the grotesque.

Yuri Lyubimov began his career as an actor in the Vakhtangov Theatre and then continued as a teacher in the Vakhtangov Theatre School. In 1963, at the age of 46, he staged the graduating play there – *The Good Person of Setzuan* by Bertolt Brecht. The success of this production set Lyubimov on a new career as a director and a year later he was named head of the Moscow Theatre of Drama and Comedy (later known as the Taganka Theatre). He reorganized the theatre and made substantial changes to the troupe bringing in many of his former students.

Lyubimov's productions gave new life to the traditions of Vakhtangov, Meyerhold and Brecht: from the 1930s to the 1980s, Vakhtangov and Meyerhold were under an ideological ban. Lyubimov's productions attracted immediate attention for their daring poetic metaphors and their obvious political meanings.

Yuri Lyubimov's Taganka Theatre production of Boris Mozhaev's drama about forced collectivization in the 1930s, *Alive*.
Photo: N. Zvjasinzeb.

In the 1960s, 1970s and 1980s, the Taganka Theatre was both politically and aesthetically running counter to the ruling regime and the orthodoxy of socialist-realism. After two of his productions – *Boris Godunov* by Pushkin and *Vladimir Visotski* (based on the songs and poems of his leading actor-singer, Vladimir Visotski) – were banned in 1982, Lyubimov left the country and immediately had his citizenship taken away (it was not returned until 1988). In 1990, he returned to Moscow as artistic director of the Taganka though he has also worked in Italy, the United States and Israel. One of Russia's major directors, his most significant productions include *Antimiri* (*The Antiworlds*) by Andrei Voznesenski (b. 1933) in 1965, *10 Dnei kotorie potriasli mir* (*10 Days that Shook the World*) based on John Reed in 1965, *Poslushaite!* (*Listen!*) by Vladimir Mayakovsky (1894–1930) in 1967, *The Life of Galileo Galilei* by Brecht in 1968, *Akh Zori Zdese Tikhie...* (*The Dawns are Silent Here*) based on Boris Vasiliov (b. 1924) in 1971, *Hamlet* (1971), *Tri Sestri* (*Three Sisters*) by Chekhov in 1978, *Vladimir Visotski* (1980), *Boris Godunov* (1982 and 1988) and *Zhivoi* (*Alive*, 1968 and 1988) based on Boris Mozhaev (b. 1923).

Also working in more non-realistic areas – but in the Meyerhold style – were Nikolai Okhlopkov and Valentin Pluchek. Okhlopkov made his début in 1918 and worked at the Meyerhold Theatre from 1923. From 1930 to 1937 he headed the Realistic Theatre and, from 1943 to 1966, the Mayakovsky Theatre. He strived to save the aesthetics of Meyerhold at the time of harsh persecutions of the master. Okhlopkov's best productions were *Molodaya Gvardia* (*The Young Guard*) based on Alexander Fadaev (1901–56) in 1947, *Hamlet* (1954) and *Medea* by Euripides (1961).

Pluchek worked as an actor in the Meyerhold Theatre from 1929 and after 1950 became a director. In 1957, he became artistic director of the Satire Theatre in Moscow, a position he still held in 1993. His very bright style of production is based on knowing the secrets of both comedy and satire. In the 1950s, his best productions involved him with Vladimir Mayakovsky and 'leftist' foreign drama. Pluchek's productions include *Banya* (*The Bath House*) by Mayakovsky (1953 and 1967), *Klop* (*The Bedbug*) by Mayakovsky (1955 and 1974), *Mystère Bouffe* by Mayakovsky (1957), *Revizor* (*The Government Inspector*) by Gogol (1972), *Beg* (*Flight*) by Bulgakov (1977) and *Vishniovi Sad* (*The Cherry Orchard*) by Chekhov (1983).

Two other directors of note are Mark Zakharov and Roman Viktuke. Zakharov, working in several areas including political cabaret, was a graduate of the Government Institute of Theatre Arts and later worked as an actor. His first notable accomplishment as a director was *The Resistible Rise of Arturo Ui* by Bertolt Brecht for the Student Theatre of the Moscow Government University (1965). Zakharov was the director of the Moscow Satire Theatre from 1966 to 1973 where he put on several notable plays of the 1960s – *Dokhodnoe Mesto* (*A Profitable Job*, 1967) by Alexander Ostrovsky (forbidden by the censors), *Temp–1929* (*The Pace of 1929*) based on Nikolai Pogodin, and *Banket* (*The Banquet*, 1968) by Arkady Arkanov (b. 1933) and Grigori Gorin (forbidden by the censors).

Zakharov's production style is almost completely expressed in the plays of the Moscow Lencom Theatre, which he took over in 1973. He made this theatre the most popular one in the capital by the beginning of the 1990s. Zakharov was the youngest of the 'revolutionaries of the theatre' of the 1950s and 1960s. He created Russian versions of several modern musicals. Among his important productions were *Zvezda i Smerte Hoakino Muretti* (*The Life and Death of Joaquin Murieta*) based on Neruda (1977), *Yunona i Avose* (*Juno and Avos*, 1981), a rock musical by Andrei Voznesenski and Alexei Ribnikov (b. 1945), *Pominalnaya Molitva* (*Memorial Prayer*) by Grigori Gorin based on Sholom Aleichem (1987) and *The Marriage of Figaro* by Beaumarchais (1993).

Zakharov worked with playwright Mikhail Shatrov on *Revolutsionei Etude* (*Revolutionary Exercise*, 1977). He also paid special attention to the 'new wave' of Soviet drama – *Three Girls in Blue* (1985) by Ludmila Petroshevskaia and *A School for Immigrants* (1985) by Dimitri Lipskerov, where he united his knowledge of psychology with a Vakhtangov-style theatre poetry. A professor in the Russian Academy of Theatre Arts, Zakharov is also an author of both books and articles.

Roman Viktuke began his career in Ukraine and Lithuania. He attained some success in Moscow in the early 1970s on both professional and amateur stages. His production of *Music Lessons* by Ludmila Petroshevskaia was done in 1976 and became one of the brightest events of the 'new drama'. By the mid-1980s Viktuke had developed his own style in which techniques of the psychological theatre are united with elements of cabaret theatre. He has also shown interest in themes dealing with sexual minorities. In the late 1980s, together with a local bank, he established the Roman Viktuke Theatre to which he has brought such productions as *The Maids* by Jean Genet, *M. Butterfly* by David Henry Huang and *Lolita* by Edward Albee and Vladimir Nabokov (1899–1977). Viktuke has worked with many Moscow theatres, but most often with the Vakhtangov Theatre and the Sovremenik.

Music Theatre

The development of contemporary Russian music theatre is based on the traditions of classical Russian opera of the nineteenth century – Glinka (1804–57), Dorgomyzhski (1813–1969), Mussorgsky (1835–81), Borodin (1833–87), Rimsky-Korsakov (1844–1908) and Tchaikovsky (1840–93) – as well as on Russia's rich folk heritage and Russian orthodox musical tradition.

The energy of musical experiments of the 1910s and 1920s was in a sense cut off by the theoreticians and practitioners of socialist-realism in opera who proclaimed, in particular, the principles of 'song' opera which made poor musical dramaturgy. The official ideologists' demands to 'fill the opera with a new Soviet content' narrowed the area of each composers' creative search. There were, however, some creations of an innovative character appearing at that time: *Semion Kotko* (1940) by Sergei Prokofiev (1891–1953); *Ledi Makbet Mtenskogo Uyezda* (*Lady Macbeth of Mtenšk*, 1932, revised in 1962) by Dimitri Shostakovich (1906–75); *Kola Brugnon* (*The Master from Clamsey*, 1938, revised in 1968) by Dimitri Kabalevski (1904–86); and a comic opera by Prokofiev, *Obruchenie v Monastyre* (*Betrothal in a Monastery*, 1940).

During World War II, Prokofiev created the epic opera *War and Peace* in which the heroic and epic layers were united with the lyrical and dramatic. In the first post-war decade (1945–55), several significant operas on the subject of the Great War of the Fatherland were created. Among those were *Semya Tarasa* (*Taras's Family*, 1947, revised in 1950) by Kabalevski; *Povest o Nastoyaschem Cheloveke* (*The Story of a Real Man*, 1948) by Prokofiev; and *Molodaya Gvardia* (*The Young Guard*, 1947, revised in 1950) by Julius Meitus (b. 1903). At the time, simplified perceptions of realism and ethnicity dominated in opera.

Fresh impulses came to opera after the 1951 debates during which the high value of operatic creations by Prokofiev and Shostakovich was reaffirmed, after being for a number of years unfairly condemned. From the second half of the 1950s dogmatism began to be overcome. In Russian opera of the 1970s and 1980s, different types of musical structures and writing techniques abounded and the topics for opera broadened. Concerned with the close unity of word and music, some composers began writing librettos for their operas themselves. An important place in opera compositions was taken by the oratorio. Chamber and one-person operas were also being widely explored.

A distinctive place in contemporary Russian music has been taken by historical opera: *Piotr I* (*Peter the Great*, 1975) by Andrei Petrov (b. 1930), a musical-dramatic fresco about the beginning of the Petrine period in Russia's history. A folk background is seen in Vladimir Kobekin's (b. 1947) opera *Pugachov* about the hero of the peasant uprising of the eighteenth century while epic intonations are characteristic of the opera-ballad *Maria Stuart* (1981) by Sergei Slonimski.

Ideology dictated the appearance of operas on revolutionary-historical topics: *Mate* (*The Mother*, 1957) by Tikhon Khrennikov (b. 1913), after the novel by Gorki; *Oktiabr* (*October*, 1964) by Vano Muradeli (1908–70); *Optimisticheskaya Tragedia* (*The Optimistic Tragedy*, 1965) by Alexander Kholminov (b. 1925); *Virinea* by Sergei Slonimski (1967); *Grigori Melekhov* (1967) by Ivan Dzerzhinski (1908–78), after Sholokhov's novel *Tikhii Don*.

New operas were also driven by the events of World War II, some reaching the heights of tragedy: *Neizvestny Soldat* (*The Unknown Soldier*, 1967) and *Ah Zori Zdese Tikhie* (*The Dawns are Silent Here*, 1977) by Kiril Molchanov (1922–82); *Letyat Zhuravli* (*The Cranes are Flying*, 1970) and *Sovremennaya Pastoral* (*The Modern Pastorale*, 1985) by Arkady Nesterov (b. 1918); *Zhivi i Pomni* (*Live and Remember*, 1984) by Kiril Volkov

(b. 1943); and a 'vocal-symphonic poem' by Valery Gavrilin (b. 1939), *Voyenniye Pisma* (*The War Letters*, 1972).

One of the most outstanding modern operas is *Ne tolko liubov* (*Not Only Love*, 1961) by Rodion Schedrin which incorporates folk instrumentals and songs. Similarly original for the 1990s was the opera *Zhizn s idiotom* (*Life with an Idiot*, 1993) by Alfred Shnitke (b. 1934), after a short story by Victor Yerofeev (b. 1947). It premièred in Amsterdam under the musical direction of Mstislav Rostropovich (b. 1927).

Composers seemed to enjoy their creative freedom most when working on musical versions of Russian and world classics: *Miortvye Dushi* (*Dead Souls*, 1977) by Schedrin, after the epic novel by Gogol; *Fyodor Protasov* (1979) by Boris Gribalin, after a play by Leo Tolstoi; and *Kashtanka, Istoriya Klouna i Sobaki* (*Kashtanka, the Story of a Clown and a Dog*, 1989) by Vladimir Ruben (b. 1924), after a short story by Chekhov.

Between 1957 and the mid-1970s, comic opera also progressed. Among the most interesting were *Taming of the Shrew* (1957) by Vissarion Shebalin (1902–63), after Shakespeare; *Bezrodny Zyat* (*Son-in-Law from Nowhere*, 1967) by Tikhon Khrennikov; and *Dvenadtzataya Seriya* (*The Twelfth Episode*, 1977) by Alexander Kholminov, after a short story by Vasili Shukshin (1929–74).

In the 1970s and 1980s there was a noticeable increase in chamber opera, in many ways related to the opening of the Moscow Chamber Musical Theatre in 1970, founded by director Boris Pokrovski (b. 1912) and conductor Gennady Rozhdestvenski (b. 1931). Composers, such as Yuri Butzko (*A Madman's Diary* after Gogol, 1967; *The White Nights* after Dostoevsky, 1970); Grigori Frid (b. 1922) (*The Diary of Anne Frank*, 1969; *Van Gogh's Letters*, 1975); Alexander Kholminov (*An Overcoat*, 1971; *A Carriage*, 1975, after Gogol; *Vanka*, 1984, and *The Wedding*, 1984, after Chekhov), and Vladimir Kobekin (*Diary of a Madman*, 1980, after Lu Sin; *The Swan Song*, 1980, after Chekhov; and *The Game About Maks-Yemeliyan, Aliona and Ivan*, an opera round dance, 1990) are all actively working in the field of chamber opera.

There have also been a number of operas created for children and young people: *Maksimka* (1976) by Boris Terenlov (1913–89), *Lopushok U Lukomoria* (*Burdock Leaf at Lukomorie*, 1977) by Mikhail Ziv (b. 1921),

The Bolshoi Theatre production of Rodion Schedrin's *Dead Souls*.
Photo: G.F. Soloveva.

and *Istoriya Kaya i Gerdy* (*The Story of Kai and Gerda*, 1981) by Sergei Banevich (b. 1941). Operas for radio and television are rare but do exist: *Vedma* (*The Witch*, 1961) by Vladimir Vlasov (1903–86) and Vladimir Fere (1902–71); and *Anna Snegina* (1970) by Vladislav Agafonnikov (b. 1936).

There were in 1993 fifty opera-ballet theatres operating all across the country. The highest level of work exists in the capitals. The most famous is the Bolshoi Teatr Rossii (Bolshoi Theatre of Russia, founded in 1766, Moscow). This internationally famous company has been in its present building since 1825 (architect Osip Bove (1784–1834)). From the beginning of the 1920s, the Russian Vocal School – Fyodor Chaliapin (1883–1938), Antonia Nezhdanova (1873–1950), Leonid Sobinov (1872–1934) and others – has received wide recognition. In the second half of the twentieth century the opera troupe grew under the direction of various conductors including Alexander Melik-Pashaev (1905–64), Boris Khaikin (1904–78), Yevgeny Svetlanov (b. 1928), Gennady Rozhdestvenski and Alexander Lazarov (b. 1946); and of directors Leonid Baratov (1895–1964), who staged at the Bolshoi such productions as *Boris Godunov* (1948) and *Khovanshchina* (1950) by Mussorgsky, and *War and Peace* (1957) by Prokofiev; Iosif Tumanov (1909–81), who staged *Don Carlos* (1963) by Verdi and *The Saga of the Invisible Town of Kitezh* (1966) by Rimsky-Korsakov and finally, Boris Pokrovski, who staged *Eugene Onegin* (1944), *Sadko* (1949), *Aida* (1951), *War and Peace* (1960) and *The Gambler* (1974).

Four other important companies in the field are the Stanislavski and Nemirovich-Danchenko Musical Theatre in Moscow, the Chamber Music Theatre in Moscow, the St Petersburg Opera Ballet and the St Petersburg Maly Opera Ballet.

The Muzikalny Teatr imeni Stanislavskogo i Nemirovicha-Danchenko (Stanislavski and Nemirovich-Danchenko Musical Theatre) was founded in 1941 as a merger between the Stanislavski Opera Theatre and the Nemirovich-Danchenko Musical Theatre. The theatre follows principles of the Moscow Art Theatre, applying them to the art of opera and ballet (as opposed to the Bolshoi, where an actor's vocal abilities prevail over his or her dramatic ones). It is characteristic of this theatre to strive for a synthesis of music and action. Work by directors such as Lev Mikhailov (1928–80) and Alexander Titel (b. 1950) and conductors such as Samuel Samosud (1884–1964) and Yevgeny Kolobov (b. 1946) have played an important role in the theatre's existence.

The Kamerni Muzikalny Teatr (Chamber Music Theatre) was founded in 1970 by director Boris Pokrovski for the purpose of experimental research in chamber opera form. The theatre's repertoire is both classical and contemporary and has included works such as *The Nose* by Dimitri Shostakovich, *Let's Compose an Opera* by Benjamin Britten, and *Rostov's Action*, based on folk music.

The Peterburgski Gosudarstvennyi Teatr Opery i Baleta (St Petersburg State Theatre of Opera and Ballet) was the Kirov Theatre until 1990; then the Mariinski. Founded in 1783, in its present building since 1860 (architect Katerino Cavos (1775–1840)), it was the czar's 'show' theatre, similar to the Bolshoi. On Mariinski's stage have been such outstanding singers as Fyodor Chaliapin and Leonid Sobinov. Directors who have worked there include Vsevolod Meyerhold and Sergei Radlov (1892–1958). The opera troupe reached its prime in the 1970s and 1980s when Yuri Temirkanov (b. 1938), one of the great musicians of Russia, was artistic director of the theatre, and also in the 1990s when, after Temirkanov's departure, the orchestra was headed by Valery Gergiov (b. 1950).

The St Petersburg Maly Teatr Opery i Baleta (Maly Theatre of Opera and Ballet) was founded in 1918 as an affiliate of the Mariinski Theatre in the building of the former Mikhailovski Theatre. From 1920 known as the Theatre of Comic Opera and from 1926 as the Leningrad State Academic Opera Theatre, it has been known as the Maly since 1964. The theatre was long a laboratory for contemporary opera and not-so-well-known opera classics. Composers such as Shostakovich, Ivan Dzerzhinski and Dimitri Kabalevski worked there. After 1945, conductors such as Alexander Gauk (1893–1963), Kurt Zanderling (b. 1912) and directors Boris Pokrovski, Boris Soloviov-Sedoi (1907–79) and others worked with the theatre. The artistic director of the theatre in 1993 was Stanislav Gaudasinski (b. 1935).

Strong opera troupes can also be found in Nizhni-Novgorod, Perm, Samara, Novosibirsk and Sverdlovsk.

Contemporary Russian operetta has basically been an attempt to reinterpret traditions of foreign operetta which has been seen in Russia since the 1860s. Also connected to Russian comic opera of the seventeenth century, Russian

Boris Pokrovski's Moscow Chamber Music Theatre production of *Rostov's Action*.

vaudeville of the nineteenth century, and Russian and Soviet comedy and satire, indigenous operetta had its contemporary start in the 1920s and 1930s with the work of Isaac Dunaevski (1900–55) and Nikolai Strelnikov (1888–1939). Utilizing national folk songs in their work and elements of mass song, they strove to create a light musical dramaturgy while bringing operetta closer to opera. Many operettas in Russian are in fact called musical comedies, the terms often taken as being the same.

Between the 1950s and the 1990s, a number of well-known composer-songwriters began to work in the genre: Yuri Milutin (b. 1903) – *Kiss of Chanita* (1957) and *The Circus Turns Its Lights On* (1960); Konstantin Listov (1900–83) – *Sevastopol's Waltz* (1960); Anatoly Novikov (1896–1984) – *Levsha* (1957) and *Vasili Tiorkin* (1971); Soloviov-Sedoi – *Olympic Stars* (1962); Nikita Bogoslovski (b. 1913) – *Spring in Moscow* (1972); and Oscar Feltzman (b. 1921) – *Let the Guitar Play* (1975), *Old Buildings* (1978) and *Terrible Girl* (1985).

Even the great masters of opera and symphony music tried the genre: Dimitri Shostakovich – *Moscow, Tcheriomushki* (1959); Dimitri Kabalevski – *The Spring Sings* (1957); Tikhon Khrennikov – *One Hundred Devils and One Girl* (1962); and Vano Muradeli – *The Girl with Blue Eyes* (1966).

Other well-received operettas and musical comedies were written by Semion Zaslavski (1910–78), Vladislav Kazenin (b. 1937), Alexander Kolker (b. 1933), Mikhail Ziv, Alexander Fliarkovski (b. 1931), Yevgeny Ptichkin (1930–93) and Alexander Zhurbin (b. 1945). Despite ideological pressure, which is reflected in the librettos of both operettas and musical comedies, many of them are delightfully melodic with well-developed dramaturgy.

In the 1970s and 1980s, the first Russian musicals began to appear – *Svadba Krechinskogo* (*Krechinski's Wedding*) and *Delo* (*The File*) by Alexander Kolker; *Zakat* (*Sunset*) by Alexander Zhurbin, after prose by Isaac Babel; and even rock-operas – *Yunona i Avos* (1982) by Alexei Ribnikov and Andrei Voznesenski; and *Liturgiya Oglashonnykh* (*Liturgy of the Insane*, 1992) by Ribnikov.

Mikhail Ziv, Ludmila Lyadova (b. 1925), Giorgi Portnov and Sergei Banevich all specialize in writing operettas and musicals for children.

By 1990 in Russia, there were nearly thirty operetta and musical comedy theatres in operation.

Dance Theatre

Traditions of Russian choreography date back two and a half centuries. The classical school was formed during the nineteenth century along with the notion of the full-length, large-scale ballet. It was the Frenchman Marius Petipa (1819–1910) who created multi-act spectacles with storylines, ballets which included solo and ensemble dancing, character dances and narrative pantomimes. Among the major works in this style were *Don Quixote*, *La Bajadère*, and ballets to the music of Tchaikovsky and Alexander Glazunov (1865–1936) in the period from 1870 to 1890. Around World War I, Mikhail Fokine (1880–1942) created a series of one-act ballets – dramatically tense, action-filled, based on a synthesis of music (often not written for the dance), scenography and choreography, enriched with classical elements.

Organizationally, most Russian ballet troupes have permanent companies, usually belonging to an opera-ballet theatre which performs repertory seasons of about ten months. Such famous theatres as the Bolshoi or the Mariinski do no more than two new productions in a given year, preferring to keep alive the classical heritage such as *Giselle* and *Swan Lake*. Dance troupes vary from thirty to as many as 150–80 (as in the Bolshoi or the Mariinski).

The first decade after the 1917 Revolution was filled with experiments in the field of dance theatre in Russia. Similar to those conducted in the dramatic theatre by Meyerhold and Tairov, in cinema by Sergei Eisenstein (1898–1948) and Vsevelod Pudovkin (1893–1953), in architecture by the constructivists, and in literature by the futurists, these were a stark contrast to the political and ideological changes of the 1930s when socialist-realism flourished and there was a rapid return to tradition. Nevertheless, a number of productions created during the 1930s and early 1940s continue on in the repertoires as a kind of Soviet classic. Among these are *Krasnyi Mak* (*The Red Poppy*, 1927) composed by Rheingold Glière (1905–67) and choreographed by Vasili Tikhomirov (1876–1956) and Lev Laschilin (1888–1955); *Plamya Parizha* (*The Flame of Paris*, 1932) composed by Boris Asafiov (1884–1949) and choreographed by Vasili Vayonen (1910–64); *Bakhchisaraisky Fontan* (*The Fountain of Bakhchisarai*, 1934) composed by Asafiov and choreographed by Rostislav Zakharov (1907–84); and *Romeo and Juliet* (1940) composed by Sergei Prokofiev and choreographed by Leonid Lavrovski (1905–67). During this period, choreographers created dance works which progressed and showed real characters on the stage. These works required performers who not only could dance but also had to act. The outstanding dancer from this period was Galina Ulanova (b. 1909).

In the first decade after World War II, even less of significance was produced. With most choreographers happy to simply reproduce older works, the level of dance fell although some good ballet music was created (*Cinderella* by Prokofiev and *The Copper Horseman* by Glière).

A turning point occurred in the mid-1950s when the tenets of socialist-realism eased and choreographers and researchers such as Yuri Slonimsky (1902–78) and Vera Krasovskaia (b. 1915) returned to more innovative forms and dance became more than an interlude once more. Important new productions began to be seen in Leningrad created by Yuri Grigorovich (b. 1927) – *Kamennyi Tzvetok* (*The Stone Flower*, 1957) composed by Prokofiev, and *Legenda o Liubvi* (*The Legend of Love*, 1961) composed by Arif Melikov; by Igor Belski (b. 1925) – *Bereg Nadezhdy* (*The Shore of Hope*, 1959) composed by Andrei Petrov, and *Leningradskaya Simfoniya* (*The Leningrad Symphony*, 1961) to music from Shostakovich's Seventh Symphony. In these productions, new ideas were revealed in the development of musical-choreographic images.

At the same time, masters from the 1920s and early 1930s slowly began to return to work: Fyodor Lopukhov (1866–1973), Kasian Goleizovski (1892–1970) and Leonid Yakobson (1904–75) to name just three. Working with younger choreographers such as Oleg Vinogradov (b. 1937), Natalia Kasatkina (b. 1934) and Vladimir Vasiliov (b. 1931), they revived forgotten genres and forms. New life was given to one-act ballets and symphonic ballets. As sources, they turned to literary classics, history and legend and interpreted them from a contemporary point of view, searching for immediately recognizable metaphors. Stravinsky's music returned to the repertoire (*The Rite of Spring*, produced by Kasatkina and Vasiliov) and attempts were made to reconstruct earlier works by Fokine that had not been seen since the 1920s. Progress in this direction continued throughout the 1970s at major companies across Russia.

Among them was the Bolshoi Ballet from Moscow, headed by Grigorovich from 1964. Bringing many of his Leningrad productions to the Bolshoi repertoire, he staged such major works as *Spartak* (*Spartacus*, 1968, by the Armenian composer Aram Khachaturian (1903–78)), *Czar Ivan Groznei* (1975, Prokofiev), *Angara* (1976, Andrei Eshpai (b. 1925)), *Raimonda* (Glazunov) and *The Golden Age* (Shostakovich).

Grigorovich's productions boasted the stylistic unity of Fokine as well as the cohesion of Petipa's major ballets. This was a new type of spectacle – a dance-based drama, monumental and theatrical in which the choreographer's personal ideas, clearly defined, grow away from the purely lyrical and acquire a social sensibility. In the centre of a Grigorovich ballet is usually a hero struggling with opposing passions. Among his many dramatic dancers were Natalia Bessmertnova and Maya Plisitskaia (b. 1925), the

Sergei Radchenko and Maya Plisitskaia in her Bolshoi Theatre production of *The Seagull*.
Photo: G.F. Soloveva.

latter creating several dramas featuring powerful and individualistic women in her work for the Bolshoi. Plisitskaia's pieces include *The Carmen Suite* to music by Bizet (choreographed by Alberto Alonso) and some of her own choreography such as *Anna Karenina*, *The Seagull* and *Lady with a Dog* (music for all these by Rodion Schedrin).

In the 1980s, a number of significant Bolshoi works were staged by Vladimir Vasiliyev (b. 1940): *Ikar* (music by Sergei Slonimski), *Macbeth* (Kiril Molchanov) and *Aniuta* (Valery Gavrilin).

As the country's main dance theatre, the Bolshoi sees its responsibility not as following any particular style or trend but rather as reflecting the best of the art for its large audiences. It has consciously refrained from being a centre of experiment in choice of repertoire, interpretation, or means of expression. Hence, it has developed a popular audience for its spectacular, vivid productions, its talented and expressive dancers and its ability to address a large public with a full firm voice.

The Stanislavski and Nemirovich-Danchenko Musical Theatre is another important company which has had a ballet troupe since the mid-1930s. From 1941 to 1971, it was headed by Vladimir Bourmeister (1904–71) who staged many dramatic ballets there including *Vindzorsliye Prokaznitzy* (*The Merry Wives of Windsor*, 1942, composed by Victor Oranski); *Lola* (1943, music by Isaac Albenis and Enrique Granados), *Bereg Stchastia* (*Shore of Happiness*, 1948, Antonio Spadaveccia), *Joan of Arc* (1957, Nikolai Peiko) and *Snegurochka* (*Snow White*, 1963, Tchaikovsky). Bourmeister, a director-choreographer, staged ballets using the ground rules of dramatic theatre, usually giving acting priority over dance. His performers followed the tradition of the Moscow Art Theatre which made very specific demands on these 'dancing actors'. The same direction was taken by Bourmeister's successor, Alexei Chichinadze (b. 1917).

In 1985, Dimitri Briantzov (b. 1947) took over the company and changed its approach. Among his first works with the troupe was *The Optimistic Tragedy* (1986), which affirmed his reputation as a choreographer with a rich sense of fantasy. The most interesting dancers who have worked at the theatre in the 1970s and 1980s included Margarita Drozdova (b. 1948), Vadim Tedaev (b. 1946), Svetlana Smirnova (b. 1952) and Svetlana Tzoi (b. 1957).

The Kirov Opera and Ballet Theatre in St

Petersburg (since 1991 called once more the Mariinski Theatre) has been headed by many choreographers since 1945. Among them have been Piotr Gusov (b. 1904), Fyodor Lopukhov, Konstantin Sergaev (1910–92), Boris Fenster (1916–60) Igor Belski and (from 1977) Oleg Vinogradov (b. 1937). The theatre has long attempted to combine tradition and innovation with special attention paid to the Russian and Soviet ballet heritage as well as foreign classics (ballets by the Dane August Bournonville, for instance). Among the many important works staged here have been *Tropoyu Groma* (*By the Path of Thunder*, 1958, by the Azerbaijani composer Kara Karaev (1918–82)) and *Hamlet* (1970, Nikolai Chervinski), both choreographed by Sergaev; and *Sotvoreniye Mira* (*Creation of the World*, 1971, Andrei Petrov) choreographed by Kasatkina and Vasiliov; *Gorianka* (1968, Murad Kazhlaev (b. 1931)), *Revizor* (*The Government Inspector*, 1980, Tchaikovsky), *Vityaz v Tigrovoi Shkure* (*The Knight in Tiger Skin*, 1985, Alexander Machavariani (b. 1913)) and *Bronenosetz Potiomkin* (*Battleship Potemkin*, 1986, Tchaikovsky).

The St Petersburg Ballet has long been known for its classical performing style and its noble strictness. Among its best known dancers have been Natalia Makarova (b. 1940), Olga Moisaeva (b. 1928), Rudolf Nureyev (1939–93), Mikhail Baryshnikov (b. 1948) and Valeri Panov (b. 1940).

The Maly Opera and Ballet Theatre St Petersburg was created as a 'laboratory for Soviet opera and ballet'. Among the major post-war choreographers working there have been Boris Fenster – *Mnimyi Zhenikh* (*Would-be Groom*, 1946, music by Mikhail Chulaki (1908–87)) – and Piotr Gusov – *Sem Krasavitz* (*Seven Beauties*, 1952, music by Kara Karaev). Several important one-act ballets were premièred at the theatre, including *The Lady and the Tramp*, staged by Konstantin Boyarski (1915–74) in 1962, and *The Eleventh Symphony*, staged by Belski in 1966.

One of the most significant productions of the theatre was *Yaroslavna* (1974), composed by Boris Tishtenko (b. 1939) and choreographed by Vinogradov. The whole production was under the direction of Yuri Lyubimov, who utilized the principles of suppositional construction of the stage action, typical of drama of the 1960s and 1970s.

The theatre had prided itself on introducing new choreographers. Among those making their débuts at the Maly have been Nikolai Boyarchikov (b. 1935) with *The Three Musketeers* (1964, composed by Benjamin Basner) and Igor Tchernystchov (b. 1937) with *Antony and Cleopatra* (1968, Eduard Lazarov (b. 1935)).

Since 1977, the troupe has been headed by Boyarchikov. Working in an imaginative style, his works are based on an interaction of poetic metaphors with a sculptural vocabulary. He has staged a number of literary ballets based on tragedies by Pushkin (*Czar Boris*, 1978, music by Prokofiev); Schiller (*The Robbers*, 1983, music by Mark Minkov (b. 1944)); Shakespeare (*Macbeth*, 1984, music by Shandor Kalash); and Mikhail Sholokhov (*And Quiet Flows the Don*, 1988, music by Leonid Klinichov).

In the late 1960s and early 1970s, a number of independent dance troupes not associated with opera-ballet theatres emerged. Most worked as touring companies. The most interesting of these were the Choreographic Miniatures Ensemble created in 1969 by Leonid Yakobson; the Moscow Classical Ballet (now called the Moscow Theatre of Russian Ballet) which was founded in 1971 and run until 1976 by Yuri Zhdanov (b. 1925), and then by Kasatkina and Vasiliov; and the Leningrad Theatre of Modern Dance (from 1990 called the St Petersburg State Ballet Theatre) founded in 1977 by Boris Aifman (b. 1946).

Several other small companies have begun operating on a commercial basis since the late 1980s and early 1990s. Most are created for touring, some outside Russia. Experimental companies have also begun to appear at this time: Experiment (headed by Yevgeny Panfilov) based in Perm, Pirouette based in Sverdlovsk, the Moscow Art Ballet (headed by Yuri Puzakov) and the Independent Troupe (headed by Alla Sigalova). Other interesting small troupes are run by Olga Vavdilovich, Leonid Lebedov (b. 1946) and Vakil Usmanov.

Since 1969 an International Competition of Ballet Artists and Choreographers has been held in Moscow every four years. There are sixteen dance schools in Russia and since 1981 one important dance magazine, *Ballet* (until 1991 *Soviet Ballet*).

Theatre for Young Audiences

Professional theatres for children and young people were widely created after the October Revolution of 1917, and became part of an overall state educational programme in 1918. In 1920, the Pervyi Gosudarstvenny Teatr dlia Detei (First State Theatre for Children) was created in Moscow, and a year later the Moskovsky Teatr dlia Detei (Moscow Children's Theatre) was formed. The Leningradsky Teatr Yunogo Zritelei (Leningrad Theatre for the Young Viewer) began in 1922, founded by Alexander Briantzov, (1883–1961); and the Moskovsky Teatr Yunogo Zritelei (Moscow Theatre for the Young Viewer) in 1927. In 1936, the Central Children's Theatre of Natalia Satz (1903–93) began, probably the best known group in the country.

Known generally by the initials TUZ, these theatres for the young established in the 1920s and 1930s a general model for a Russian and Soviet children's theatre: a varied repertoire which addressed all children of varying age groups. At the same time, Briantzov, while acknowledging the dual – didactic and aesthetic – nature of children's theatre, insisted on the priority of the artistic in these theatres. Most operate similarly to other Russian repertory theatres: that is, they have permanent troupes, their own buildings and, traditionally, a generous state subsidy.

Through the years, this form of theatre has shown remarkable stability and has developed its own dramatists. Among them are Leonid Makariov (1892–1975), Alexandra Brushtein (1884–1968), Samuel Marshak (1887–1964), Lev Kassil (1905–70), Sergei Mikhalkov (b. 1913) and Yevgeny Svarts, whose works have been staged throughout the Soviet Union and all across eastern Europe. These authors in many ways defined the first post-war decades in Russian children's theatre. During World War II, the number of children's theatres understandably declined, but by war's end it quickly began to rise and by the 1990s surpassed the pre-war number with over forty such theatres in operation in Russia.

From the mid-1950s, theatres no longer saw childhood and adolescence separately from the world of adults. 'Problem' productions were being staged more and more often by TUZ companies and a significant number of TUZ shows addressed both children and parents, or sometimes even only adult audiences. It was no coincidence that many children's theatres eventually changed their names to youth theatres, supposing the majority of their audience to be teenagers, young adults and even adults. On the other hand, children are not forgotten. These theatres still feature all the world's fairytale classics – from folk tales to fairytales by Pushkin, Tolstoi, Andersen, Perrault and Kipling. Even the 'new' fairytales of Janush Korchak (1878–1942), Lindgren, Carroll and Saint-Exupéry are regularly staged. Certainly a special place is taken in the repertoire by Russian literary classics from Fonvizin (1744–92) to Chekhov. Scripts based on classic foreign works are also regularly seen, from adaptations of Molière and Shakespeare to Gozzi, Dickens, Schiller and Lope de Vega. Prose classics too are done – Tolstoi, Saltykov-Schedrin, Victor Hugo, Alexandre Dumas père and Mark Twain. They also stage Voltaire, and modern plays by Brecht, Williams and Anouilh.

During the Soviet period, TUZ companies paid special attention to historical and revolutionary themes, but even under heavy censorship they strived to maintain a certain level of moral uprightness. In the 1980s and 1990s, the children's theatres even staged productions of works by Bulgakov, Platonov, Nabokov, and other writers whose works were simply inaccessible under censorship. The history of the country, as presented on these stages, is more often than not being revealed as a history of major works of literature.

Two well-known directors played a special role in the development of children's theatre – Maria Knebel and Anatoly Efros. Both worked at the Central Children's Theatre where, along with classical children's plays, they staged works by Victor Rozov whose plays discussed contemporary issues (*Alive Forever*, *All the Best*, *In Search of Happiness*, *Unfair Fight* and *On the Road*). In these, as well as in his later plays, Rozov talked about morality and standards of decency in any, even the most difficult, situations. They also staged other issue-oriented plays by Alexander Khmelik (b. 1925) and Anatoly Alexin (b. 1924). In the 1970s and 1980s, more plays written for adults, by authors such as Alexei Arbuzov, Mikhail Roschin (b. 1933) and Alexander Vampilov, made it to the TUZ stages.

In the 1960s and 1970s, psychology entered

children's theatre – both for the actor and the child – as did principles of issue-oriented theatre (*Stop Malakov!* by Valery Agranovski at the Moscow and Leningrad TUZ, *Trap No. 46, Level 2* by Yuri Shchekochikhin at the Central Children's Theatre) and parodies of fairytales especially in the work of Zinovy Karagodski (b. 1921), the head of the Leningrad TUZ.

Also extremely important for Russian children's theatre was a developing synthesis of music, scenography and spectacle. Well-known composers and scenographers began to work with the many TUZ groups. This influx of outstanding figures from adult theatre was partly to do with the requirement for artists to fit 'party' criteria. Those who were considered risks were as often as not allowed to work with the TUZ companies. Among these were Boris Naravtzevich, who for many years headed the TUZ in Nizhni-Novgorod; Yuri Kopylov, who headed the children's theatre in Oriol; and Adolf Shapiro (b. 1939), who headed the TUZ in Riga which for many years had been a leader in the TUZ movement.

Over the decades after World War II, all the theatres for young audiences worked hard to free themselves from school programmes and strictly pedagogical requirements. Those theatres which have been most successful at doing this have been the Central Children's Theatre (from 1992 called the Russian Youth Theatre), the Moscow Theatre for the Young Viewer, the Leningrad Theatre for the Young Viewer, and similar theatres in Saratov, Krasnoyarsk, Novosibirsk, Irkutsk, Sverdlovsk, Cheliabinsk, Rostov, Oriol, Voronezh, Perm, Kazan and Lipetzk.

The Rossiisky Molodiozhny Teatr (Russian Youth Theatre) was founded in 1936. Its acting style was developed by directors Piotr Fomenko and the Ukrainian Les Taniuk. In the early 1980s Alexei Borodin (b. 1941), a student of Yuri Zavadski, became its director. Among Borodin's important works have been *Otverzhennye* (*Les Misérables*) after Hugo's novel (1984), *Banya* (*The Bath House*) by Mayakovsky (1987), *King Lear* (1990) and *Our Town* by Thornton Wilder (1993).

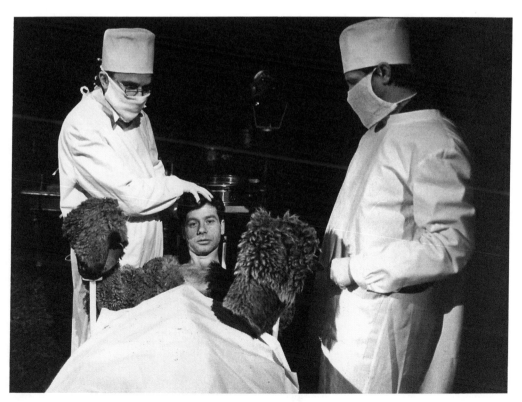

Henrietta Yanovskaia's 1985 Moscow Theatre for the Young Viewer production of *Heart of a Dog*.

The Moskovsky Teatr Yunogo Zritelei (Moscow Theatre of the Young Viewer) was founded in 1927. After World War II, such directors as Pavel Tzetnerovich (1894–1963), Rolan Bykov (b. 1929) and Boris Golubovski (b. 1919) helped the theatre to achieve real note. It was, however, most successful during the second half of the 1960s, when it was headed by Pavel Khomski (b. 1925), and at the end of the 1980s and the beginning of the 1990s, when the artistic director was Henrietta Yanovskaia (b. 1941) and Kama Ginkas (b. 1941) a director. Yanovskaia's *Sobachie Serdtze* (*Heart of a Dog*) after Mikhail Bulgakov's novel (1985), *Goodbye, America!* (1988) and Ginkas's *Igrayem v Dostoevskogo* (*Playing Dostoevsky*, 1990) were remarkable for their energy and imagination.

The Leningradsky Teatr Yunogo Zritelei (Leningrad Theatre for the Young Viewer) was in the 1960s and 1970s, as well as in the 1920s and 1930s, a leader of the TUZ movement thanks to the work of its principal director, Zinovy Karagodski. Karagodski stood for a festive theatre while keeping all the best that TUZ was known for in the past. A strong troupe came together under him – Giorgi Taratorkin (b. 1945), Olga Volkova (b. 1945) and Antonina Shuranova (b. 1936) among others.

The Saratovsky Teatr Yunogo Zritelei (Saratov Theatre for the Young Viewer) was founded in 1918. Its highest achievements are connected with productions by Yuri Kiselov (b. 1914), who staged plays by Chekhov and Gorki and other contemporary plays including the first plays of Victor Rozov.

A Central Children's Musical Theatre was opened in Moscow in 1965 headed by Natalia Satz. It has offered a wide repertoire of operas and ballets for children as well as musical adaptations of major classics. At the beginning of the 1970s, similar theatres were opened in Leningrad and other cities.

Both the Ministry of Culture and the Theatre Workers' Union always paid special attention to children's theatre. Over the years they have sponsored special workshops for children's theatre directors, seminars for writers and laboratories on the problems of TUZ workers.

Briantzovskiye chteniya (*The Briantzov Readings*) is a Russia-wide review of children's and puppet theatres. Many regional festivals are also held, some under the umbrella of the Russian National Centre of the International Association of Theatre for Children and Young People (ASSITEJ). Among the presidents of the Soviet Centre of ASSITEJ through the years have been Konstantin Shakh-Azizov (1903–77), Natalia Satz and Adolf Shapiro.

Puppet Theatre

Russian (and Soviet) puppet theatre has a tradition that is over 300 years old. The first evidence of Russian puppet theatre – found in the notes of the German scientist Olearius (1636) – is related to the activities of the *skomorokhs* (folk entertainers at markets and fairs) which are inseparable from traditional family events such as pageants. Later Russian puppet theatre moved closer to uncensored folk-satire.

The most vivid Russian puppet character is Petrushka, the centre of the puppet folk market plays.

During the early Soviet period, puppetry developed as both theatre for children and as agitprop theatre. In 1918, with *The Legend of Czar Saltan*, the Petrograd State Marionette Theatre opened, headed by Lubov Shaporina-Yakovlova (1877–1967). In the same year in Moscow, another State Puppet Theatre opened under Nina (1877–1948) and Ivan (1878–1959) Efimov with two groups: one following the glove-puppet Petrushka tradition, the other working in shadow theatre.

Agitprop puppet theatre was widespread during the Civil War of 1918–22, especially at the front lines. Standing out among these groups was the Children's Theatre Book, organized in 1929. Another important puppet theatre was the Petrushka in St Petersburg, founded by Yevgeny Demmeni (1898–1969) in 1924. In 1930, the Petrushka merged with the Petrograd Marionette Theatre and was renamed the Leningrad Puppet Theatre. In 1931 in Leningrad, still another group – the Bolshoi Puppet Theatre – was created.

In the 1930s, a great number of new puppet theatres opened all across the country staging plays for both children and adults.

A new era in the development of Russian puppet theatre began with the opening in 1931 of the Central Puppet Theatre in Moscow, under the direction of Sergei Obraztsov

(1901–92). This was a truly artistic puppet theatre, bringing together puppetry and principles of dramatic art. Even in the 1990s, the Central Puppet Theatre remained a unique company and a kind of methodological research centre for Russian puppet art. At the Central Puppet Theatre, there is also a Museum of Puppetry, founded by Andrei Fedotov (1901–68).

Demmeni was the first puppeteer to use a multilevelled stage, close-ups (directing light on a certain character) and a non-frontal type of staging. Rod-puppets were introduced by Nina and Ivan Efimov while Obraztsov, in his personal cabaret show, popularized more symbolic puppets (ball-heads with barely defined facial features). At the Central Puppet Theatre in Moscow, he came back to realistic puppets, both hand-puppets and rod-puppets. He also experimented with backscreens and space, even using cinema and mechanical recordings. After World War II, Obraztsov gathered around him a very strong troupe of artists who remained with the theatre until nearly the end of the 1970s. Productions such as *Obyknovenny Kontzert* (*The Ordinary Concert*, 1946), *Tchiortova Melnitza* (*The Devil's Mill*, 1953), *Bozhestvennaya Komediya* (*Divine Comedy*, 1961) and

Don Juan (1977), all stayed in the repertoire for decades. Among those who worked with the theatre were Yevgeny Speranski (b. 1903), Semion Samodur (1911–91) and Zinovy Gerdt (b. 1916).

A new movement in puppet theatre began in the 1970s grafting on to itself modern experiences, involving live actors and puppets and the experience of new forms of marionette theatre. As a rule, such experiments were conducted outside the walls of traditional puppet academies – the Central Puppet Theatre in Moscow or the Bolshoi Puppet Theatre in St Petersburg.

Among the experimental puppet theatres were groups in Magnitogorsk under the direction of Victor Shraiman (b. 1946) and Valery Volkhovski (b. 1944), who redefined the vocabulary of the puppet stage in various peripheral theatres, especially in Teheliabinsk and Voronezh.

In 1993, there were nearly eighty state puppet theatres in Russia, and another 10,000 amateur puppet groups. The appearance of small private companies has also been important as has a school for puppetry founded in Mikhail Korolyov (1913–83) in St Petersburg.

Design

The first decade after 1945 was a period of crisis in Russian scenography. Many of the masters of the art of design from the 1930s had died, including Vladimir Dmitriov (1900–48), Piotr Williams (1902–47) and Fyodor Fyodorovski (1883–1955). In their place came designs that were dull, lifeless and domestic. Exceptions were works by Alexander Tishler (1898–1980) – *Freilekhs* by Shneyer (State Jewish Theatre, 1945); Vadim Ryndin (1902–74) – *The Young Guards* by Fadaev (Mayakovsky Theatre, 1947) and *Hamlet* (Mayakovsky Theatre, 1954); and Nikolai Akimov (1901–68) – *The File* by Sukhovo-Kobylin (Lensoviet Theatre, 1954).

The mid-1950s saw the beginning of renovation in stage design. Initially it was related to the older masters – Tishler, Ryndin, Nisson Shifrin (1892–1961), Anatoly Bosulaev (b. 1904) – going back to their experiences of the 1920s and 1930s. Recognizable and specific images were replaced by more generalized images and the use of metaphor, all leading toward a more active scenography. Alexander Vasiliov (1911–90)

developed at this time methods of projection which would later replace painted backdrops. Simon Virsaladze (1908–90) argued for 'painted symphonism' and 'dynamic light scores' in ballet.

Designers of the 1950s and early 1960s brought a new expressiveness of line, contour, silhouettes and contrast to their work with an abundance of local colour. The most outstanding representatives of this ethnographic trend were Enar Stenberg (b. 1929) and Boris Messerer (b. 1938).

By the mid-1960s, another group of young artists, mostly graduates of the All-Union Institute for Cinematography, began to be seen – Marina Sokolova (1939–93), Valery Levental (b. 1938), Vitaly Serebrovski (b. 1938) and others. They opposed the graphic trend with its principles of symbolism and understatement and offered in its place a sense of design as an aesthetic reality with its own value. Their means of expression once again became painting which gradually unfolded in the space of the stage.

Boris Ravenski's Bolshoi Theatre production of Rimsky-Korsakov's *Snowgirl*.
Photo: G.F. Soloveva.

In opposition to the new decorative trend came a series of productions of Russian classics in which mood and atmosphere became all important. These were seen in the second half of the 1960s and were done by the older generation of masters such as Sofia Yunovich (b. 1910) – *Three Sisters* by Chekhov (1965); Iosif Sumbatashvili (b. 1915) – *Czar Ivan Groznei* by Alexei Tolstoi (1966); and Alexander Vasiliov – *Petersburg Dreams* after Dostoevsky (1968). Adherent to the more traditional values, they sought new methods of symbolism while creating images that were deeply emotional.

In the late 1960s, another trend emerged which in the 1970s played a determining role in Russian scenography. Davyd Borovskyi, Edward Kochergin (b. 1937) and Mart Kitaev (b. 1925) all began turning to natural textures and real objects in creating stage images. These objects became active components in their designs which became known as Active Scenography. The designer's task as they saw it was to create not so much a place of action, but rather action itself, action that could reveal content, a sculptural realization of each play's issues. They

strove to create environments as visual realizations, expressing the characters' spiritual worlds. This developed through the 1970s into visualizations of real landscapes and real interiors through painting on back and front curtains (this was done by Alexander Vasiliov), or through lifelike design of spaces, as in Serebrovski's works.

Collage manifested itself in the late 1970s in creations by Kitaev and Sergei Barkhin (b. 1939), who emerged as conscious eclectics. But one could still see the principles of Active Scenography in the work of David Borovskyi, especially in his works with director Yuri Lyubimov at the Taganka Theatre. In *Hamlet*, for example, the curtain itself became a ghostly and frightening figure. This style seemed especially successful in the classics.

The masters of the 1980s were Oleg Sheintzis (b. 1948), Ksana Shimanovskaia (b. 1952), Maria Rybasova (b. 1951) and Stanislav Benediktov (b. 1949), all fluent in several styles of the past and rejecting, for the most part, post-modern irony.

Throughout these decades, Russian scenographers have worked much more closely than their predecessors with directors. Their contributions, such as the living curtain in *Hamlet*, helped define each show's actions. In the 1990s, the scenographer had clearly replaced the designer in the Russian theatre.

It should be noted here that Russian scenographers were subject to the same ideological control as those working in other areas of the system. Nevertheless, the best of them showed some kind of creative braveness and artistic dignity.

Theatre Space and Architecture

Until the twentieth century Russian theatre troupes tended to spend much of their time touring but by the end of the 1930s, they settled in particular cities and became attached to particular buildings. In 1993, the number of state theatre troupes was exactly the same as the number of theatre buildings which, in Russia, means more than 600. These buildings, of course, differ in quality and size and range from the classic Bolshoi to a modest puppet theatre situated in the basement of a theatre.

A significant number of companies still operate in buildings constructed in the late nineteenth or early twentieth centuries. This is especially true of the eastern and central parts of Russia. Theatres from the nineteenth century are semicircular in the Italian style with a certain adjustment for Russian amplitude.

After 1917, groups were using buildings owned by the former nobles or commercial halls operated by various clubs. In the 1930s, new buildings went up reflecting the hoped-for socialist utopia. In Moscow the new Central Theatre of the Soviet Army was completed – a huge building constructed in the shape of a five-pointed star (seen clearly from the air) with a capacity of 2,200. It also had a small auditorium for 600 people. In its main house was a huge stage on which real ships and tanks could appear. Even the interior was monumentally decorated (architects Karo Alabian (1897–1959) and Vasili Simbirtzov (1901–82); artists Alexander Deineka (1899–1969) and Vladimir Favorski (1886–1964) among others).

In Rostov-na-Donu, a theatre building was constructed in the form of a tractor, to symbolize the country's industrialization (architects Shchuko and Gelfreich). After World War II, in regions destroyed by the fascists, theatre buildings were reconstructed in a pseudo-classical, imperial style – referred to generally as the Stalinist style – with columns and other architectural excesses. Most of these theatres were also inconvenient for actors and had

virtually no technical or storage space. At the same time, a number of former cinemas and club buildings were given over to various theatres.

Corbusier-style theatre buildings were being built from the beginning of the 1960s, during a period of steel-and-concrete construction for community cultural centres. Constructed all over the country, these were often built with mass performances in mind, rather than normal plays: their capacity was usually over a thousand seats like the ones built in Cheliabinsk and Oriol, the TUZ in Novosibirsk and Omsk, and the musical theatres built in Omsk and Krasnoyarsk. One could say that these were copies on a smaller scale of the type of building used by the Communist Party Central Committee in Moscow for big social functions – the Kremlin Palace of Congresses (1959, architects Mikhail Posokhin (b. 1910), Mdoyantz, Alexander Stamo (1899–1969) and Pavel Shteller (1910–77)) which was added to the much more traditional Kremlin buildings. The new style was seen as a type of universal spectacle building suitable for opera, ballet, concerts or party congresses.

Approaches to theatre construction were defined by the Ministries of Culture of both the USSR and Russia through the research organization in the field of performance architecture, GIPROTEATR (State Institute for Projects on Theatre and Spectator Events). GIPROTEATR was founded in 1934 with its mandate to create projects for new performance buildings and to assist in the reconstructions of existing buildings. One of the essential shortcomings of such theatre construction in Russia was its constant dependency on what was available in the way of materials to the construction industry. On the positive side, no work was ever started without consultation with directors and designers of the company for which the building was being constructed.

Among the theatres created this way were the

Central Puppet Theatre (Sergei Obraztsov himself was the head of the project); the new building of the Taganka Theatre in Moscow (Yuri Lyubimov and Davyd Borovskyi were supervisors on the project along with the architects); and the Moscow Art Theatre (Oleg Efremov).

In the 1980s and 1990s, new theatre building construction in most cases was in the hands of regional and municipal authorities.

From the 1970s, second-stage and foyer theatres also became wide spread. Many productions now take place in non-theatrical venues – empty rooms, arenas and basements.

Training

During the Soviet era (1917–91), Russia had an impressive system of theatre education. Training was provided for virtually every profession in the theatre and entertainment industry. All education establishments, whether considered advanced (university equivalent) or secondary/specialized (college equivalent) were and still are state owned. All graduates receive a qualifying diploma which guarantees them job security and placements through ministry and regional culture authorities.

One of the changes since 1991 has to do with paid studies at these institutions. Most have now expanded to include an extra 30 per cent in their numbers who pay full tuition costs. Tuition remains free, however, for those in the acting, directing and choreography programmes.

There were in 1993 some twenty theatre education establishments in Russia (higher and secondary combined) where students in drama, puppetry, musical theatre, acting and directing (including variety and circus) were trained; seven schools of choreography trained dance artists.

Training in professional areas is never done in universities. Theatre education institutions therefore belong to the Ministry of Culture rather than the Ministry of Higher Education. However, in 1993 the Russian State Humanitarian University accepted students for theatre criticism courses in its Faculty of History and Philology.

Most of the leading theatre education institutions are located in Moscow and St Petersburg. They include the Russian Academy of Theatre Arts (until 1991 known as the Lunacharsky State Institute for Theatre Arts) which was founded in 1878 and in 1886 became a conservatory. In 1918 it was called the Music and Drama Institute, in 1925–6 the Central Technical School of Theatre Arts, and from 1935 – the Lunacharsky State Institute. Most theatre people know it by its Russian initials, GITIS.

The school has always attracted the country's leading actors, directors, theatre critics and specialists as teachers. Major programmes at the Russian Academy of Theatre Arts include acting (with students from other nationalities of Russia receiving training in their own languages), directing, criticism, musical theatre, choreography, music theatre directing, scenography, variety and circus directing, theatre management and theatre economics. Studies generally last five years (four for actors). All students take classes in such subjects as the history of literature, history of theatre, fine art, music, state history and the history of philosophy.

The Nemirovich-Danchenko School-Studio at the Moscow Art Theatre was founded in 1943 to train actors for MXAT following the ideas and artistic principles of the Stanislavski system. The school trains specialists for other theatres as well. Besides actors, it also trains stage designers and production managers. The training system is similar to the one at the Russian Theatre Arts Academy. The school's teachers include leading actors from MXAT. Again, most courses run four or five years. Both the GITIS and MXAT schools are on the university level.

The Boris Shchukin Theatre School is connected to the Vakhtangov Theatre in Moscow. Founded in 1913 to train actors in the Vakhtangov style, it became a higher educational establishment in 1945. Graduates of the Shchukin school are known for their sense of style and their ability to create a festive theatre (having at the same time managed the principles of psychological theatre). Programmes exist for actors and directors (including actors from the various national theatres of the Russian Federation).

The higher education institution at the Maly Theatre in Moscow is the Shchepkin School. Its roots date back to the Moscow Theatre School, founded in 1809. The school was created as a training programme for the Maly troupe and in

1943 it became an institution of higher education. Keeping to the traditions of Russian realism, it trains actors for all Russian theatres including those of other nationalities within the federation. Training lasts four or five years.

The Moscow School of Choreography (from 1984 called the Academy of Dance) began as the Ballet Department of the Moscow Education House in 1773. From 1920 it became connected to the Bolshoi Theatre. Besides choreographic and general subjects, training is also provided in dance and musical criticism.

The School of Circus and Variety Arts was founded in Moscow in 1927. Besides providing training for all types of circus professions, it also trains variety artists. It is recognized as a secondary school, with a training programme of four years.

Moscow's Technical School of Theatre Arts was started in 1931 and has long provided training for makeup specialists, electricians, radio specialists, dressers and artist-decorators.

The Leningrad (St Petersburg) Institute of Theatre, Music and Film was founded in 1961 after a merger between the Ostrovsky Leningrad Theatre Institute and the Leningrad Institute of Art History. It is a higher education institution with a university equivalency programme. Its training system is similar to that of the Russian Academy of Theatre Arts. The institute's roots go back to the Acting Skills School opened in 1918. Today, the institute has departments of acting, directing, criticism, puppet acting, musical theatre and theatre management.

Finally, Leningrad's (St Petersburg's) Vaganova School of Choreography was

Yuri Grigorovich rehearsing Shostakovich's *The Golden Age* at the Bolshoi Theatre.
Photo: G.F. Soloveva.

founded in 1738 as the Dance School. In 1918 it was reorganized and became the Petrograd Theatre Ballet School. In 1921, Agrippina Vaganova (1879–1951) took over the school and developed a whole system for classical ballet education. The dance pedagogy department opened in 1934, and in 1937 a choreography department was opened.

Other higher theatre education institutions operate in Voronezh, Yaroslav and Vladivostok. Secondary theatre schools exist in many of the larger theatre centres of the country. Russian higher education institutions in theatre and choreography have also trained hundreds of specialists from foreign countries through the years.

Criticism, Scholarship and Publishing

Theatre aesthetics and the social meaning of a work of art were the key elements of critical thought during Russia's Soviet period. Supported through strong ideological pressure by the Communist Party, these two ideas were taught at major centres of theatre science and criticism in Leningrad and Moscow. In Leningrad, critical scholars were known for their strict, somewhat dry academism and scientific purism; in Moscow the critical scholars were inclined toward a more active public role.

Besides departments of theatre history in educational establishments, the two critical studies centres in post-World War II Russia were the Moscow Institute of Art History (now called the Russian Institute for Artistic Sciences) and the Leningrad Scientific Research Institute for Theatre, Music and Cinematography (now called the St Petersburg Russian Institute for Art History).

The Moscow Russian Institute was founded in 1944 and remains under the control of the Ministry of Culture and the Russian Academy of Sciences. Its goal is the creation of fundamental works on a wide range of artistic subjects. It has nearly twenty sections and departments: history of theatre, the classical arts, the contemporary arts of developed capitalist countries, the arts of eastern Europe, the arts of Latin American countries, the arts of Asian countries, the economics and sociology of culture, and so on. The institute issues a regular series of scientific publications on various kinds of artistic endeavours – *Questions of Modern Aesthetics* and *The World of Arts* as well as fundamental academic works such as *The History of Soviet Theatre, 1917–1967* (in six volumes), works on scenography and even the history of music. Among leading researchers in theatre who worked in the past with the institute are Pavel Markov (1897–1980), Alexei Dzhivilegov (1875–1952), Stefan Mokulski (1896–1960), Alexander Anikst (1910–89) and Grigori Boyadzhiov (1909–74). Among those working there through the early 1990s were Melitina Kotovskaia (1929–93), Boris Zingerman (b. 1928), Yuri Ribakov (b. 1931), Elena Poliakova (b. 1926), Mariana Stroeva (b. 1917), Vitas Siliunas (b. 1939) and Alexei Bartoshevich (b. 1940), among others.

The Leningrad Institute is one of the oldest theatre research centres in Russia. Founded as part of the Moscow State Academy of Arts and Sciences and transferred to Leningrad in 1933, the institute has one of the major theatre library collections in the country. Leading Leningrad theatre scholars associated with the institution have included Raisa Beniash (1914–87), Vadim Sakhnovski-Pankaev (1927–79), Sergei Tzimbal (1907–79), Naum Berkovski (1901–74) and Anatoly Yufit (1928–78). The institute issues scientific studies, does various academic research as well as research on the history of Russian culture.

The Stanislavski and Nemirovich-Danchenko Heritage Commission is a research group connected to MXAT. It does research on and acts as an archive of the founders of the Moscow Art Theatre and other leading MXAT artists. Two collections of works by Stanislavski and several volumes of Nemirovich-Danchenko's works, along with other publications, have been published by the group. Among the commission's key associates have been Anatoly Smelianski (b. 1942), Vitaly Vilenkin (b. 1911) and Inna Soloviova (b. 1924), among others.

Scholarly and research work is also done by groups of scholars in all the regions and republics of Russia. All are connected to either the Institute for History, the Institute for Language and Literature or the Institute for Culture.

As well, similar work is being done at leading theatre museums – the Moscow Theatre Museum, the St Petersburg Theatre Museum, the Stanislavski House Museum, the Meyerhold House Museum in Penza, the Ermolova House Museum in Moscow, and in leading theatre libraries in Moscow, St Petersburg and Nizhni-Novgorod among others.

Critics and theatre scholars have also traditionally been associated with leading Russian theatre publications. From the 1950s to the 1980s the centre of national criticism was *Teatr*, a glossy, high-circulation monthly published under the auspices of the Ministry of Culture and the Writers' Union of the USSR since 1930. Until 1962, the magazine was headed by Nikolai Pogodin, who brought together in the magazine some of the most progressive theatre critics, dramaturges and literary minds. Under Pogodin, *Teatr*'s critics took liberal-democratic positions and supported new directions in the field. In the 1970s and 1980s, the magazine paid more attention to aesthetic issues.

Another widely read magazine has been *Teatralnaia Zhizn* (*Theatre Life*), founded in 1956. Until the early 1980s it tended to take a very orthodox communist view of the arts.

Many new publications began to appear in the 1980s offering alternative points of view including post-modern readings of recent theatre activity. Among them have been *Contemporary Dramaturgy* (founded in 1981), which publishes new scripts and reviews (it appeared quarterly until the mid-1980s, bimonthly until 1993, and then again quarterly); *Moscovski Nabliudatel* (*Moscow Observer*) (founded in 1989) brings together writings on theatre by former members of the editorial board of *Teatr*; *St Petersburg Theatre* (founded in 1992) attempts to provide an outlet for new writing by Leningrad–Petersburg critics; *Culture*, a weekly newspaper, founded in 1956 and until 1991 called *Soviet Culture*; and *Screen and Stage*, a weekly newspaper published since the mid-1980s.

Books on theatre history, theatre memoirs, photo books and other publications were most often published by two venerable publishing houses – Nauka (Science) and Iskusstvo (Arts). Since 1991, books on theatre subjects have also been published by Culture Editorial Complex, a publishing venture supported by the Russian Ministry of Culture.

The Federation of Theatre Unions has its own publishing house as has the Union of Theatre Workers of Russia. A publishing house also exists within the commercial organization Soyuzteatr. There are publishing groups as well at the Russian Theatre Academy (Moscow), and at the St Petersburg Institute for Theatre, Music and Cinematography.

Mikhail Shvidkoi
Translated by Oleg Ginzburg and
Roman Koudriavtsev

(See also USSR)

Further Reading

Agamerzian, Ruben. *Vremya. Teatr. Rezhisser.* [Time. Theatre. Directors]. Leningrad: Iskusstvo, 1987.

Akimov, Nikolai. *Teatralnoye naslediye.* [Theatre legacy]. 2 vols. Moscow/Leningrad: Iskusstvo, 1976.

Anastasiov, Arkady, Grigori Boyadzhiov, Anna Obraztsova, and Konstantin Rudnitski. *Novatorstvo sovetskogo teatra.* [Novatorship in Soviet theatre]. Moscow: Iskusstvo, 1963.

Balet Entziklopediya. [Ballet encyclopedia]. Moscow: Sovetskaya entziklopediya, 1981.

Benedetti, Jean. *Stanislavski.* London: Methuen, 1988. 340 pp.

Braun, Edward, ed. *Meyerhold on Theatre.* London: Methuen Drama, 1969.

——. *The Theatre of Meyerhold.* New York: Drama Book Specialists, 1979. 299 pp.

Dal, Oleg. *Vospominaniya. Materialy iz arkhiva.* [Memories. Materials from an archive]. Moscow: Arts Publishing Culture Editorial Complex, 1992.

Davidov, Mike. *People's Theatre from Box Office to the Stage.* Moscow: Progress, 1977.

Edwards, Christine. *Stanislavsky Heritage: Its Contribution to the Russian and American Theatre.* New York: New York University Press, 1965. 346 pp.

Efros, Anatoly. *Prodolzheniye teatralnogo romana.* [Continuation of the theatre romance]. Moscow: Iskusstvo, 1985.

Gaevski, Vadim. *Divertisment.* [Divertissement]. Moscow: Iskusstvo, 1981.

Goncharov, Andrei. *Rezhisserskiye tetradi.* [Director's notebooks]. Moscow: All-Union Theatre Society, 1980.

Green, Michael. *The Russian Symbolist Theatre: An Anthology of Plays and Critical Texts.* Ann Arbor, MI: Ardis, 1986.

Houghton, Norris. *Moscow Rehearsals: An Account of Methods of Production in the Soviet Theatre.* New York: Octagon Books, 1975.

Iofiov, Moisei. *Profili iskusstva.* [Arts' profiles]. Moscow: Iskusstvo, 1963.

Istoriya russkogo sovetskogo dramaticheskogo teatra. [History of Russian Soviet dramatic theatre]. 2 vols. Moscow: Prosvestcheniye, 1984–7.

Istoriya sovetskogo dramaticheskogo teatra. [History of Soviet dramatic theatre]. 6 vols. Moscow: Nauka, 1966–71.

Kalish, Victor. *Teatralnaya vertikal.* [Theatre vertical]. Moscow: Union of Theatre Workers of Russian Federative Socialist Republic, 1991.

Kholodov, Yefim. *Piesy i gody.* [Plays and years]. Moscow: Sovietsky pisatel, 1967.

Knebel, Maria. *Poeziya pedagogiki.* [Poetry of pedagogics]. Moscow: All-Union Theatre Society, 1984.

Komissarzhevski, Viktor. *Moscow Theatres.* Translated by Vic Schneierson & W. Perelman. Moscow: Foreign Languages Publishing House, 1959.

Krymova, Natalia. *Imena.* Moscow: Iskusstvo, 1971.

Lemâitre, Maurice. *Le Théâtre futuriste italien et russe.* [Italian and Russian futurist theatre]. Paris: Centre de Créativité, 1967.

Macleod, Joseph Todd Gordon. *The New Soviet Theatre.* London: George Allen & Unwin, 1943.

Obraztsov, Sergei. *Maya professiya.* [My profession]. Moscow: Iskusstvo, 1981.

O khudozhnikakh teatra, kino i televideniya. [On artists of theatre, film and television]. Leningrad, 1988.

Otcherki istorii russkoi sovetskoi dramaturgii. [Essays on the history of Russian Soviet dramaturgy]. 3 vols. Leningrad/Moscow: Iskusstvo, 1963–8.

Poliakova, Elena. *Stanislavski.* Translated by Liv Tudge. Moscow: Progress, 1986.

Pyžova, O.V. *Fragmenty teatral'noj sud'by.* [Fragments of a theatrical destiny]. Moscow: Soviet Russia, 1986. 336 pp.

Reeve, F.D., ed. *An Anthology of Russian Plays. Vol. 2: 1890–1960.* New York: Vintage Books, 1961.

——. *Contemporary Russian Drama.* New York: Pegasus, 1968.

Rudnitski, Konstantin. *Spektakli raznykh let.* [Shows of different years]. Moscow: Iskusstvo, 1974.

——. *Teatralnye siuzhety.* [Theatre plots]. Moscow, 1990.

Rühle, Jürgen. *Das Gefesselte Theater: von Revolutionstheater zum sozialistischen Realismus.* [The enchained theatre: from theatre of the revolution to socialist-realism]. Köln: Kiepenheuer & Witsch, 1957.

Russell, Robert. *Russian Drama of the Revolutionary Period.* Basingstoke: Macmillan, 1988.

——, and Andrew Barrat, eds. *Russian Theatre in the Age of Modernism.* Basingstoke: Macmillan, 1990.

Shvidkoi, Mikhail. *Dramaturgiya. Teatr*. [Drama. Theatre]. Moscow: Znaniye, 1987.

Simonov, Ruben. *Stanislavski's Protégé: Eugene Vakhtangov*. Adapted and translated by Miriam Goldina. New York: Drama Book Specialists, 1969. 243 pp.

——. *Tvorcheskoye naslediye*. [Creative legacy]. Moscow: All-Union Theatre Society, 1981.

Slonim, Mark L'lovich. *Russian Theatre from the Empire to the Soviets*. Cleveland, OH: World, 1961.

Smirnova, Natalia Ilinichna. *Teatr Sergeia Obraztsova*. [Sergei Obraztsov's theatre]. Moscow: Izdatelstvo-Navka, 1971.

Sovetskaya literatura po stzenographii (1917–1983). [Soviet literature on scenography (1917–1983)]. Moscow/Prague: 1983.

Sovetskii muzykalny teatr. Problemy zhanrov. Sbornik statei. [Soviet music theatre: issues of the genre. A collection of essays]. Moscow: Nauka, 1982.

Sovetskii teatr. [Soviet theatre]. Moscow: Iskusstvo, 1967.

Sovetskii teatr dlia detei. Ukazatel literatury. [Soviet theatre for children. An index of literature]. 4 vols. Moscow, 1978–9.

Sovietskiye khudozhniki teatra i kino. [Soviet theatre and film artists]. Issues 6–7. Moscow, 1984–6.

Sovremennaya sovetskaya opera. Sbornik. [Contemporary Soviet opera. A collection]. Leningrad, 1985.

Svobodin, Alexander. *Teatralnaya Plostchad*. [Theatre square]. Moscow: Iskusstvo, 1981.

Teatralnaya entziklopediya. [Theatre encyclopedia]. 5 vols. Moscow: Sovetskaya entziklopediya, 1961–8.

Tovstonogov, Giorgi. *Krug myslei*. [Scope of thoughts]. Leningrad: Iskusstvo, 1972.

——. *O professii rezhissera*. [On the director's profession]. Moscow: All-Union Theatre Society, 1965.

——. *Zerkalo stzeny*. [Mirror of the stage]. 2 vols. Leningrad: Iskusstvo, 1980.

Vysotzki, Vladimir. *Chelovek. Poet. Aktior. Sbornik*. [Human. Poet. Actor. A collection]. Moscow: Pogress, 1989.

Warner, Elizabeth. *The Russian Folk Theatre*. The Hague: Mouton, 1977.

Worrall, Nick. *Modernism to Realism on the Soviet Stage: Tairov-Vakhtangov-Okhlopkov*. Cambridge: Cambridge University Press, 1989.

Yevstignaev, Yevgeny. *Vospominaniya, statyi*. [Memories, essays]. Moscow: Culture Arts and Editorial Complex, 1993.

Zakharov, Mark. *Kontakty na raznykh urovniakh*. [Contacts on different levels]. Moscow: Iskusstvo, 1988.

SCOTLAND

(see **UNITED KINGDOM**)

SERBIA-MONTENEGRO

Formerly part of Yugoslavia and maintaining 'the Federal Republic of Yugoslavia' as a joint name for the two republics, Serbia and Montenegro are situated on the Balkan Peninsula in southeastern Europe on an area of 102,375 square kilometres (39,500 square miles) (Serbia: 88,563 square kilometres; Montenegro: 13,812 square kilometres). Their 1993 population was 10.4 million (Serbia: 9.7 million; Montenegro: 616,300). Ethnically, the largest number are Serbs (6.5 million) but there are also Albanians (1.7 million), Montenegrins (520,500), Hungarians (345,300) and Muslims (327,200) with another 407,600 declaring themselves simply as Yugoslavs, and 523,600 others. The official language of both republics is Serbian, while national minority languages are also in use (Albanian and Hungarian particularly) in areas where they are in the majority. The Serbian capital is Belgrade; the Montenegrin capital is Podgorica. Other political and cultural centres are found in Novi Sad, Priština, Cetinje, Subotica, Sombor, Niš, Kragujevac, Nikšić and Kotor.

Present-day Montenegro – historical Duklja (Zeta) – became an independent state in the eleventh century, when it gained the status of a kingdom. In the twelfth century, Serbian territories northeast of Zeta became dominant when they gained independence through their struggle against Byzantium and Hungary. By the end of the twelfth century, Zeta and Raška joined together to form a new unified Serbian state headed by the Nemanjić dynasty. It became a kingdom in 1217 (when it received a crown from the Roman Pope), and during the thirteenth and fourteenth centuries, by extending its territories south (as far as the Peloponnesus), it became an empire under Dušan. Despite Turkish occupation for the next four centuries, the national consciousness of the Serbian people continued to develop, rooted both in its Orthodox faith and the traditions of its Medieval states. During this period, many Serbs also migrated north across the Danube where, on the territory of present-day Vojvodina, an independent Serbian region was established within the Austro-Hungarian Empire.

In the nineteenth century, there were two great Serbian uprisings (1804 and 1815). Serbia finally gained its independence in 1878 following the Congress of Berlin and was accorded the status of a kingdom in 1882. Liberation of the entire national territory was achieved during the Balkan Wars 1912–13.

Montenegro, also an independent state by the nineteenth century, supported Serbia in its struggle for liberation which finally ended in 1918 with the establishment of the Kingdom of Serbs, Croats and Slovenes (from 1929 known as the Kingdom of Yugoslavia). The new state was created, on the one hand, as a result of the collapse of the Austro-Hungarian Empire; on the other, as a consequence of the notion of a Yugoslav state, spoken of since the second half of the nineteenth century.

Following World War II, communists established a regime in Yugoslavia with the help of the Soviet Union and the king was banned from returning to the country. Under the government of Josip Broz Tito (1892–1980), six federal republics were created (Bosnia-Herzegovina, Macedonia, Slovenia, Serbia, Croatia and Montenegro) while within the framework of Serbia two autonomous provinces were established (Vojvodina along with Kosovo and Metohija). With the collapse of communism in the eastern bloc countries in the late 1980s, national dissolution also began as Slovenia, Croatia and portions of Bosnia-Herzegovina seceded. In 1991, war broke out in the region. In 1992 Serbia and Montenegro joined together to form what they called the Federal Republic of Yugoslavia, a federal state with a multi-party parliament.

Theatre in Serbia and Montenegro has a tradition which goes back more than nine centuries, although its development has not been continuous. Records of the Medieval theatre among Serbs can be found in the religious literature of the epoch; believers were forbidden from attending events in which actors took part. Teodosije (1264–1328), a monk in the Serbian monastery of Hilandar on Athos and an author, juxtaposes in his *Žitije Svetog Save* (*The Life of St Sava*) – a manuscript exists from 1336 – the heavenly beauty of the church and the evil theatre of travelling players which is performed in the streets, 'where the gathered crowds, in all kinds of weather, come to watch and listen, to the very end, the harmful devilish songs and unseemly, ugly words'. Memories of earlier performances seen and even of old sports events

lived on in the Serbian community until the fourteenth century. (This is confirmed by Medieval Serbian painting. In the fresco, *The Mocking of Christ*, in the monastery of Staro Nagoričane and painted between 1317 and 1318, one can see three figures with long sleeves and others with unusual instruments mocking the Saviour. The motif was, quite certainly, taken from some Byzantine stage presentation.)

The rulers of Serbia and Zeta (present-day Montenegro) were determined to maintain good neighbourly and diplomatic relations with Dubrovnik and would regularly send companies of musicians and entertainers for the holiday of St Vlaho (the patron saint of Dubrovnik). In September 1395, artist-musicians came to Zeta from Dubrovnik and performed at the church festival of the Holy Virgin of Ratac, while artists from Zeta and Dubrovnik visited Serbia in 1412 and 1413.

Their programmes were made up of music, pantomime, and clown shows. Among the Serbs, the long period of Turkish rule (from the second half of the fifteenth to the beginning of the nineteenth century), arrested the development of cultural pursuits, so that there were only sporadic performances of a religious character, while the other regions were either under Mediterranean influence (regions of Montenegro on the Adriatic Sea) or under central European influence (Vojvodina).

In 1734, a Serbian school production was staged in Sremski Karlovci. Regular school performances lasted until 1813 when amateur companies began to be founded. The first professional theatre troupe was founded in 1838, and the first professional theatre in 1861.

The entire second half of the nineteenth century was noted for its adaptations by Serbian playwrights to the demands and tastes of the audience. Two permanent Serbian professional companies came into being at this time – the Srpskog narodno pozorište (Serbian National Theatre, founded in 1861 in Novi Sad on territory which was under Austrian and later Austro-Hungarian rule) and the Narodno pozorište (National Theatre, founded in 1868 in Belgrade in the free principality, that is the Kingdom of Serbia). Both had a primarily national-patriotic function and were in continuous financial difficulty. Both were also oriented towards the spiritual and the hierarchical principles of a patriarchal society and were just barely touched by some of the ideas, culture and morals that were being consolidated by middle-class society in other parts of Europe. For this reason, Serbian theatres were dominated by two principal types of dramatic works: historical plays and late romantic tragedies (at that period most often based on mythical themes and national history) which fostered national feeling and awakened Serbian historical consciousness. Also popular were comic plays of village life with 'songs and dancing'.

More generally, the repertoire of world drama featured an average central European repertoire (a mix of classics, melodrama, vaudeville, drawing-room plays and middle-class drama). By the end of the nineteenth century, German influence began to dominate: the Burgtheater of Vienna was at that time the leader in new theatrical trends including organizational models, repertoire selection, directing, acting and stage décor. This said, it was actually the Budapest theatres which were the transmitters of this influence.

By the early twentieth century, the influence of the French theatre began to be felt more and more since new generations, educated in France, were returning home, especially to Belgrade. It should also be pointed out that up to World War I it was not the new theatre currents in France (the Théâtre-Libre of André Antoine, for instance) but rather the Comédie-Française and the Paris boulevard theatres that were most influential. The newer styles of European dramaturgy (naturalism, symbolism and expressionism) also began to be felt at that time: Branislav Nušić (1864–1938), considered the national master of comedy, wrote such plays as *Narodni poslanik* (*The Member of Parliament*), *Sumnjivo lice* (*A Suspicious Character*), *Gospodja ministarka* (*The Cabinet Minister's Wife*) and *Ožalošćena porodica* (*The Bereaved Family*). His works are still produced today as are those by some of his early-twentieth-century contemporaries – Vojislav Jovanović Marambo (1884–1968), Milutin Bojić (1892–1917) and others.

Between the two world wars, theatre professionals in the country were fascinated by guest performances of the Moscow Art Theatre (1920–1 and 1924), which became their model. In practice, however, various styles appeared: from expressionism and symbolist stylization, to naturalism and psychological realism, all parallel with romantic diction in acting. In the first post-war decade, natural urban speech and a more modern stage sensibility began to make their appearance. At that time, Belgrade and Novi Sad had companies of outstanding actors.

After World War II, the theatre began to expand even further, because the Communist Party considered it a powerful means of political propaganda. A network of professional theatres was established, made up of state, regional and municipal theatres. In Serbia, it was decided that the state theatres would be the National Theatre in Belgrade, the National Theatre in Niš and the newly founded theatres in Kragujevac, Užice and Šabac; in Vojvodina, state theatres were to be the Serbian National Theatre in Novi Sad, the Madjarsko narodno pozorište (Hungarian National Theatre) in Subotica and the National Theatre in Pančevo; in Kosovo and Metohija, the Oblasno narodno pozorište (Territorial National Theatre) in Prizren.

Regional national theatres were established in the Serbian cities of Kruševac, Čačak, Vranje, Leskovac, Pirot, Zaječar, Prokuplje and Požarevac; the Hrvatsko narodno pozorište (Croatian National Theatre) in Subotica, and the Vojvodina theatres in Sombor, Zrenjanin and Sremska Mitrovica.

A number of professional and semi-professional city theatres were opened in Smederevo, Kraljevo, Valjevo, Bor, Knjaževac, Jagodina, Negotin, Paraćin, Ćuprija, Novi Pazar, Vrnjačka Banja and Vršac, while in Kosovo and Metohija, where there was no native theatre tradition, about 120 amateur theatre groups were formed in 1945. In 1949, the state Teatri popullor krahinor (Provincial National Theatre) was opened in Priština, while in the period 1953–6 the Gradsko pozorište (City Theatre) was active in Kosovska Mitrovica, and from 1977 the Teatri popullor (National Theatre) in Djakovica.

The social status of theatre artists was defined by an Act for State Employees (based on the Constitution of the People's Federal Republic of Yugoslavia of 31 January 1946) which meant that the Serbian Ministry of Education could simply determine positions and salaries by decree. It was not a rare event that actors, even the most prominent, were transferred from one theatre to another, based not on their artistic achievement, but rather on the characteristics of their ideological orientation (in which their 'behaviour' during World War II was crucial). From 1947 to 1951, all of the theatres received lists of plays for their repertoire from whichever ministry was in charge of culture, and they were required to stage only plays that were on the list. It was also required, especially in the provinces, that the repertoire should be chosen only following analyses of the political and cultural situations in each community for it was believed that only in this way could its influence be a creative one.

In Montenegro, in the five years following World War II, the National Theatre in Cetinje was revived and three additional theatres were established (in Kotor, Nikšić, Pljevlja). In 1953, the Crnogorsko narodno pozorište (Montenegrin National Theatre) was opened in Podgorica (formerly Titograd, the capital of Montenegro). These theatres began their activities in quite unfavourable conditions: their companies were small, consisting mainly of young and inexperienced actors, while in Pljevlja and Nikšić the facilities were simply inadequate. In the early 1960s, when economic criteria began to be applied to social development in Montenegro, of the five existing theatres, four were closed. In the only remaining theatre, the Montenegrin National Theatre in Podgorica, half of the actors received notice. Almost all of the noted actors of the closed theatres joined the company which was given the status of a state theatre.

A similar process took place in Serbia between 1954 and 1958. At that time, the Serbian theatres of Valjevo, Prokuplje, Požarevac, Vranje, Kruševac, Kraljevo and Smederevo along with the theatres of Vojvodina – Sremska Mitrovica, Pančevo, Bačka Topola and the Rumunsko narodno pozorište (Romanian National Theatres) in Vršac and Kosovska Mitrovica were closed. At the same time, a law was passed stating that in future theatres did not have to be founded and financed only by the state but could also be supported by social organizations.

For the first time, it was possible for theatre companies to be formed by groups of citizens and even artists. In such new organizations, principles of social management and self-management were applied. Theatre councils, which up to that time had been formed in all theatres as a form of state (that is party) control, could now decide independently on matters of programme orientation and repertoire policy

and make decisions on internal organization.

An important evolution in the relationship between theatres and government bodies came with the passing of the constitution of 1963, when communities were allowed to decide on the financing and activities of existing theatres and the creation of new ones. The most important feature was the change in the status of the actors: they gained permanent contracts along with the same rights as those at state institutions. These measures proved a double-edged sword: they provided actors right through the 1990s with work and financial security and enabled theatres to formulate long-term repertory policy, but they led to poor repertoire selection and enabled uncreative individuals to make it difficult for young actors to gain professional engagement since the number of positions was always limited by the amount of subsidy. Financing was done through so-called self-management communities of interest (funds were appropriated from the earnings of each employed citizen), but it was soon evident that these financial means were not sufficient and by 1990 theatres had to find other sources of financing (often by direct contracts with economically powerful companies).

One final word here about the amateur drama movement, which has also had a long tradition. Originating in village and urban communities in the first half of the nineteenth century, it later spread to national minority communities and is today very developed among Hungarians, Slovaks, Ruthenians, Romanians, Albanians and Gypsies. The plays performed are most often from the national dramaturgy – the most popular playwrights are Dušan Kovačević, (b. 1948) Branislav Nušić and Aleksandar Popović (b. 1929) – while productions are most frequently directed by professional directors. The Festival dramskih amatera Srbije (Festival of Dramatic Amateurs of Serbia – FEDRAS) has been held continuously since 1972 in the village of Malo Crnuće (near the town of Požarevac).

Structure of the National Theatre Community

In 1993, there were thirty-eight professional companies operating in Serbia and Montenegro – thirty-five in Serbia, three in Montenegro. All received subsidy from either state, regional or municipal levels.

Throughout the period after World War II, the state aided virtually all theatres financially, while at the same time, it controlled the repertoire selection. Whenever a production was to be staged which the authorities judged to be menacing to the regime, it was censored. Of interest here is the fact that censorship was never official: there were never any written documents legally banning productions. Nor was it ever known who the originator of any ban was. In fact, such bans were usually carried out by the theatres themselves as a form of self-censorship. Theatres which did not cooperate could find themselves in financial trouble later on. There was no essential change in this process even during the 1960s, 1970s or 1980s when the great influence in theatres was allegedly that of 'socially conscious self-management'.

Two instances of such self-censorship had a particularly negative effect on theatre life: one was the Yugoslav Dramatic Theatre's production of *Kad su cvetale tikve* (*When Gourds Were in Bloom*) by Dragoslav Mihailović (b. 1930) directed by Boro Drašković (b. 1935). The subject of this play was the relationship between the communist parties of Yugoslavia and the Soviet Union. Banned in 1969, its director, one of the most talented in Yugoslavia, has refused to direct in the country ever since as a protest. Another banned production was at the Serbian

National Theatre – *Golubnjača* by Jovan Radu-lović (b. 1951) directed by Dejan Mijač (b. 1934). This play's subject was the relationship between Serbs and Croats. Banned in 1982, attacks on the play were accompanied by fierce denunciation campaigns in both political forums and the media.

In 1956, Sterijino pozorje was founded in Novi Sad and quickly became the most important theatre institution in Yugoslavia. Under its auspices was the annual Jugoslovenske pozorišne igre (Yugoslav Theatre Festival), a competition for theatre productions of Yugoslav works which became a valuable stimulus for the growth of national dramaturgy. The Sterija Awards – given each year for the best performances at the festival as well as for script, directing, stage design, costumes and stage music – have long been the most distinguished theatre honours in Yugoslavia.

Special mention should be made here also of the annual autumn festival, BITEF (established in Belgrade in 1969) which gave Yugoslav theatregoers the opportunity to see the latest innovations in world theatre.

Artistic Profile

Companies

Despite the numerous negative effects of government regulation of theatres in the first years following World War II, many managed to develop a more self-conscious and serious attitude toward creativity, and their artistic ambitions also grew. Immediately after the war, Soviet influence increased and there was a dogmatic approach taken to Stanislavski's acting system. The exception to this was the Jugoslovensko dramsko pozorište (Yugoslav Dramatic Theatre) which had been founded in Belgrade in 1947 by the country's best actors. Owing to its director, Bojan Stupica (1910–70) and to the joint determination of its company not to swerve from attaining creative results and perfection in theatre art, in the first decade of its activity it became one of the major theatres in Europe.

At that time, the company had a repertoire of both Yugoslav and foreign classics, along with several modern works. Realism was the credo of this theatre, while its interpretations were struggles against stereotype, banality and vulgarization. Within the company 'the actor was

an artist, the scenographer a master craftsman, the director a maestro, rehearsals were festivities, the première a historical event'.

After 1951, when the opening of Yugoslavia towards the west began, a more tolerant and artistically more productive climate was established in the arts. Among Serbian theatres, the repertoire was renewed, and the Beogradsko dramsko pozorište (Belgrade Dramatic Theatre) made a name for itself from 1951 to 1956 by producing Arthur Miller's *Death of a Salesman*, *The Crucible* and *A View from the Bridge*, Tennessee Williams's *The Glass Menagerie* and *Cat on a Hot Tin Roof*, John Osborne's *Look Back in Anger*, and other western playwrights. Based on these texts, a new type of acting emerged, a much less classical approach and a personal means of expression.

After the banning of Beckett's *Waiting for Godot* (Belgrade Dramatic Theatre, 1956), a new era began in Serbian theatre. By perseverance and some luck, the director, Vasilije Popouić (b. 1926), and the actors managed to transfer this production on to the newly opened stage of the Atelje 212 Theatre in Belgrade.

Branko Pleša's 1973 Belgrade Yugoslav Dramatic Theatre production of Alexander Sukhovo-Kobylin's *Tarelkin's Death*, designed by Vladislav Lalicki.

From 1956 to 1960, the Atelje 212 performed plays by Sartre (*No Exit*), Ionesco (*The Chairs*), Mrożek (*The Police*), Camus (*Le Malentendu*), Pinter (*The Caretaker*) as well as other works of modern world drama, both from the west and the east. The Atelje 212 Theatre liberated itself from a simple striving after verism and became a stage (without concealing this, but rather, revealing it to its audience), while its company began to cultivate a style of acting resembling what William Butler Yeats termed 'objectivism'. This emerged in a sense of acting persiflage and a system of anti-indicated technique (or, as actors say, 'counter acting'). The leading representative of this style was the very popular actor Zoran Radmilović (1933–85).

After the establishment in 1967 of the Belgrade International Theatre Festival (BITEF), whose *spiritus movens* were Mira Trailović (1924–89), director of the Atelje 212 Theatre, and Jovan Ćirilov (b. 1931), dramaturge and artistic director of BITEF, the Atelje 212 Theatre turned itself toward the national

dramatic repertoire by staging the work of new playwrights or by dramatizing the fiction of well-known national writers, and this remained a dominant feature of its repertoire policy.

A major role in theatre events from the 1950s to the 1970s in Yugoslavia was played by the Serbian National Theatre from Novi Sad. Its 'heyday' was from 1953 when it brought together a group of young directors headed by Dimitrije Djurković (b. 1925) to 1974 (when this 'team of directors' broke up). It will long be remembered for its search into new forms of stage expression within the framework of Yugoslav theatre space. It was an ironic, lyrical theatre with an insistence on the physical aspects of acting expression and a repertoire directed toward the sensibility of the young, educated theatregoer. It believed that the actor and the acting space were the fundamental elements of theatre language and it was a theatre striving for some form of intervention in society, representing the darker side of the contemporary period and socialist society.

Vasilije Popović's 1956 Atelje 212 Theatre production of Samuel Beckett's *Waiting for Godot*, designed by Stojan Celić.

During the 1980s and into the early 1990s, one should mention the activity of the Nepszinhaz (National Theatre) in Subotica, whose unique principles derived from the multinational character of Vojvodina (a region inhabited by Serbs, Hungarians, Bunjevacs, Croats, Ruthenians, Slovaks and Romanians) and from the variety of religions practised there (Eastern Orthodox, Catholic and Protestant). This theatre's productions were based on the theatre experience of its artistic director, Ljubiša Ristić (b. 1947). Rather than from focusing on a precisely conceived and executed repertoire (it has put on the works of Shakespeare, Molière, the classics of the avant-garde, noted Yugoslav writers and little-known poets from Subotica) its distinction comes from its commitment to creating a multi-national company, the bringing together of different languages and the interweaving of different cultural influences and traditions. This has had an important effect on the character of its productions, variously judged in different parts of the country.

Dramaturgy

After 1945, Serbian playwrights found themselves in a society which had been radically changed by the war and which began to deny its previous traditions. Forced to accept socialist-realism as the only theatrical style, in the first post-war decade plays were written with major discrepancies between theatrical art and reality. The turning point for post-war Serbian dramaturgy was the play *Nebeski odred* (*Heaven's Detachment*, 1956) by two new writers, Aleksandar Obrenović (b. 1928) and Djordje Lebović (b. 1928). Despite programmatic allegiance to 'realism' in the official style, this was really the first realistic play in Serbia in the post-war period. The work dealt with seven prisoners in Auschwitz who, in November 1944, agreed to kill and cremate their fellow prisoners in order to gain three more months of life. Not judging the action ethically, the writers had the courage to open up a discussion on the nature of ethics and the nature of humanity, a discussion that did not follow the official and optimistic doctrine of socialist-realism.

In the following decade, the characters and situations in the works of Serbian playwrights became more flexible and more realistic, but they continued to employ the approaches of traditional middle-class theatre. Slowly, symbolic stylization and historical analogy began to be used along with an Aesopian language in order to make connections with the contemporary social situation and current historical processes. A turning point, in the 1970s, was brought about by Aleksandar Popović, at a time when the poetic and reflective drama of the previous period was beginning to show clear signs of exhaustion and fatigue.

Popović, along with Ljubomir Simović (b. 1935) and Dušan Kovačević, created a series of original and valuable plays. Serbian theatre studies have affirmed the belief that Popović was the first Serbian writer to question seriously the assumptions of Aristotelian dramaturgy. In Popović's plays, as various critics have pointed out, almost nothing remains of plot and characters. The structure of Popović's plays is reduced to an insistence on the phenomenon of play, the phenomenon of the performance, and the final communication to the audience is essentially anti-illusionist, for it is a repetition of the theatre itself. Sensitive to the ideas of his time (in his youth he was a road-builder, painter, tinsmith, glass-cutter and travelling salesman), he is an exceptionally prolific writer (more than 100 plays for the theatre, 300 television plays and numerous plays for children). He has also written works in which he is severely critical about the social reality of socialist Yugoslavia.

In one of his best known comedies, *Razvojni*

put Bore Šnajdera (*The Development of Boris Tailor*, 1967), he takes a satirical view of three specific elements of the politically managed socialist economy: lack of professional expertise on the part of people appointed to managing positions (a tailor becomes the director of a tin-smith cooperative); the easy fall into hedonism by rigid, puritan party morality; and the blindness of politicians (interested not in production but rather in the system of organization; unmoved by the fact that everything is going wrong in a state-owned enterprise and worrying only about destroying the competition, a private company). Popović's major works include *Ljubinko i Desanka* (*Ljubinko and Desanka*, 1964), *Čarapa od sto petlji* (*The Hundred Loop Stocking*, 1965), *Mrešćenje šarana* (*The Spawning of Carp*, 1984), *Kus petlić* (*The Rooster Without a Tail*, 1990) and *Bela kafa* (*White Coffee*, 1991).

Ljubomir Simović's humorously imaginative work is filled with moral sensibility, melodiousness and rich language. His works are based on both folk and written tradition though they are also filled with images of modern life. In his first, and perhaps his most important play, *Hasanaginica* (*Hasanaga's Wife*, 1973), he uses elements of a folk ballad about the tragic conflict between a man and his wife (after they divorce, she dies) a tale which originated in the second half of the seventeenth century in a patri-archal Muslim society. The play focuses on con-temporary society and modern marital relations and its style reflects the influence of Strindberg. In his play, the conflict between husband and wife is psychologically motivated and inevitable, stemming from essential misunderstandings between the sexes, and marked by the partners' lack of sexual fulfilment, guilt, and the man's fear that he will lose dominance. Simović points out that even today, despite state and social laws, individuals can still be deprived of their rights by those who are socially more powerful. Simović's free verse and extraordinary language effectively convey his ideas.

In his tragi-comedy *Čudo u Šarganu* (*The Miracle in Šargan*, 1975) Simović constructs two plot lines – one taking place today, the other dealing with a soldier from World War I. Both plots are linked by a poor beggar who believes that he can save people by taking on their troubles. The play offers an authentic image of the life, thought and manners of socially rejected, insufficiently educated and morally unstable people who find themselves torn between rural and urban environments.

Simović's third play, *Putujuće pozorište Šopalović* (*The Travelling Troupe Šopalović*, 1985), takes place in Serbia during World War II and follows a troupe of travelling actors who, while armies march by and blood flows, try to per-form and convey the eternal beauty and poetry of the theatre. One of them dies both from the bullets of German soldiers and by a grotesque, absurd re-enactment of the Orestes myth.

The early comedies of Dušan Kovačević already confirmed him as a writer able to expose social shortcomings, delusions, meanness and stupidities. His first play – *Maratonci trče počasni krug* (*The Marathon Runner's Honorary Lap*, 1973) – was staged at the Atelje 212 Theatre. Perhaps his best comedy is *Balkanski špijun* (*The Balkan Spy*, 1983) which portrays a minor office worker Ilija Čvorović, a former prisoner, who gradually becomes obsessed with the idea that it is his role to spy on and to bring to justice enemies of the state.

The heroes of Kovačević's other comedies attempt to get as much as they can out of life, although all of them, borne on the wings of the author's irresistible talent for the comic, are thwarted and defeated. The rhythm of self-preservation and self-confirmation at any cost, therefore, is both the form and the content of Kovačević's comedies.

There are two other Serbian authors – both originally from Montenegro – who should be mentioned here. The first is Borislav Pekić (1930–93), the author of the dramatic grotesque *Generali ili srodstvo po oružju* (*The Generals or a Kinship-in-Arms*, 1971). Its heroes are a retired general of the Yugoslav Royal Army and a colonel of the Wehrmacht quartermaster corps who, far away from the battlefront, bent over military maps, with flags representing the warring armies in their hands, like children playing a game, give vent to their obsession to shape history. Pekić's characters substitute fiction for fact and in doing so lose awareness of the absurdity of their own position.

The second author is Veljko Radović (b. 1940), a writer of enormous sarcasm and an exceptional sense of language. His play *Medalja* (*The Medal*, 1975) takes as its hero a former Olympic boxing champion who brings to his native village an air of success which causes envy in his fellow villagers. His fame oppresses them and makes them feel even smaller than they are. Radović is a writer-moralist who has no illu-sions about the society in which he lives and works. He places his characters in a world in which it is impossible for them to achieve any ideal or to live with any integrity.

Probably the most frequently performed Yugoslav dramatic works abroad have been the plays of Nušić, Simović and Kovačevic. A large number of Nušić's comedies and plays have been performed in the former Soviet Union (*The Cabinet Minister's Wife* was performed in Moscow and twenty-six other Soviet cities), and in other eastern European countries. Simović's *The Travelling Troupe Šopalović* is his most produced play. Kovačević's comedies have been performed in theatres in Germany, Poland, Hungary, Great Britain, the USA, Ukraine and Czechoslovakia.

Directors, Directing and Production Styles

Mata Milošević (b. 1901) is one of Serbia's leading directors. His creative personality was influenced by the great actors of the Serbian National Theatre – Pera Dobrinović (1853–1923) and Žanka Stokić (1887–1947) – by the visits of the Moscow Art Theatre and by his professional visits abroad (Munich, Berlin, Prague, Paris and London) during which he was able to see productions by Reinhardt, Dullin, Jouvet, Baty, Pitoëff and other great names in European theatre. His life and work are connected with several Belgrade theatres, especially the National (from 1922 to 1947) and the Yugoslav Dramatic Theatre (from 1947 to 1974). His productions were studious, oriented towards eternal truths, measured, rational, rich and refined, lucid and innovative. Patient and experienced in his work with actors, he was able to realize acting of the highest realistic levels. His most powerful productions included Shakespeare's *King Lear*, Gorki's *Yegor Bulychov*, Sartre's *Les Sequestrés d'Altona* (*The Condemned of Altona*) and the classical works of Yugoslav dramatic literature – Jovan Sterija Popović's (1806–56) *Rodoljupci* (*The Patriots*), Nušić's *The Bereaved Family* and Miroslav Krleža's (1893–1981) *Na rubu pameti* (*At Wit's End*).

Dejan Mijač is another of the leading directors in Serbia. Mijač studied directing at the University of Belgrade, and developed his style at the Serbian National Theatre in Novi Sad between 1962 and 1974. He later became a professor of directing at the Faculty of Dramatic Arts in Belgrade, working at the same time as a guest director in the country's most important theatres. His directing is marked by simplicity and credibility and his stage solutions derive from movement and stillness, sometimes even from silence. Several of his performances have been entirely based on music.

His most important productions have been Gorki's *Vassa Zheleznova*, *Pokondirena tikva* (*The Stuck-Up Woman*), *Ženidba i udadba* (*Weddings and Marriages*) and *The Patriots* by Sterija Popović, whom he has brought back to the stage in a new, modern way. Other notable Mijač productions were Chekhov's *Uncle Vanya*, García Lorca's *La Casa de Bernarda Alba* (*The House of Bernarda Alba*) and several modern Yugoslav plays – Aleksandar Popović's *The Spawning of Carp* and Ljubomir Simović's *The Travelling Troupe Šopalović*.

Bojan Stupica, a Slovenian director, was one of the most important and controversial directors in Belgrade after World War II. He also helped found the Yugoslav Dramatic Theatre in Belgrade for whom, between 1947 and 1955, he directed brilliant productions of Goldoni's *La Baruffe Chiozzotte* (*The Chioggian Squabbles*), Chekhov's *Uncle Vanya*, Ostrovsky's *Talents and Suitors*, and his most important achievement in the Yugoslav theatre in the first post-war decade, the Renaissance comedy *Uncle Maroje* by Marin Držić (1508–67). This last production was later seen by audiences in Paris, Vienna, Budapest, Warsaw, Moscow, St Petersburg, Venice and other European cities.

His productions were challenged by official, Marxist-oriented, dogmatic critics who accused him of 'formalism', an extremely negative label at that time. Following a short stay in Zagreb (1955–9), he returned to Belgrade, where he was a director at the National Theatre, artistic manager of the Atelje 212 and manager of the Yugoslav Dramatic Theatre until the time of his death. Important productions during this period of his life were Dostoevsky's *The Idiot*, Leonov's *The Thief*, Sardou's *Mme Sans-Gêne*, Ionesco's *Rhinocéros* and Marceau's *L'Oeuf*. Stupica was essentially a director with a luxuriant and inventive stage imagination. For him, theatricalization was the manifestation of a life principle and not simply an abstract artistic law.

For their exceptional and recognizable contribution to Yugoslav acting style, special mention should also be made here of Milivoje Živanović (1900–76), Mira Stupica (b. 1923) and Branko Pleša (b. 1926). Živanović's acting was powerful and all-embracing. Blessed with a striking appearance and a sonorous voice, he created with broad lines of inspiration and elementary power. Best in the Slavic and national repertoire, if one could speak of acting which is Yugoslav in its style, Živanović would be one of its originators and most prominent representatives. He starred in a wide range of plays by writers such as Nušić, Shakespeare, Gorki, Ibsen and O'Neill.

In the first two post-war decades the most distinguished actress in Yugoslavia was Marija Crnobori (b. 1919), a tragic actress with a repertoire of classical roles (Sophocles' Antigone, Racine's Phèdre, Goethe's Iphigenie), while the entire post-World War II period was marked by Mira Stupica. Stupica was an actress with a luxurious natural talent whose foundation was a sincere emotionality that coloured all her creations on stage. This made her acting both intimate and suggestive, and contributed to her enormous popularity with audiences. Along with many roles from the national repertoire she starred in plays by Ostrovsky, Goldoni, Dostoevsky, Sardou and Kohout.

Branko Pleša's acting marked a turning point in the Yugoslav theatre. Pleša introduced Yugoslav acting to modern trends of stage expression in the period after World War II. He began his career at the Croatian National Theatre in Zagreb (1945–6) and in the theatre of the same name in Split (1946–7), while his great talent came to its fullest expression at the Yugoslav Dramatic Theatre in Belgrade, in which he was, since its founding in 1947, a permanent member and leading actor. His flawless diction inspired a faster and more modern pace of speech than had been heard on the Yugoslav stage while his considerable education enabled him to communicate on profound levels. Known for playing a wide range of authors – Schiller, Dostoevsky, Sartre, Wilde and Shaw – he interpreted many of Shakespeare's leading characters including Romeo, Hamlet, MacDuff and Edgar.

Several actors originally from Montenegro also performed successfully on Belgrade stages during the post-war period. Among them, one should mention Neda Spasojević (1941–81), an actress with a special sensibility for her time, and Slobodan Perović (1926–78), an outstanding actor capable of interpreting characters from George in *Who's Afraid of Virginia Woolf?* to the beggar in Simović's *The Miracle in Šargan*.

Petar Marjanović

Music Theatre

Rudimentary forms of music theatre have had a long tradition among Serbs. Plays with song – usually inspired by themes from folk life – have been present since the second half of the nineteenth century. The basis for these works are generally melodramatic events to which song and dance can be easily added. Most often they take place in the village, and the dramatic scheme is a stereotypical one: the love of a boy and girl, quarrels between their families, weddings and religious holidays. Most have simple plots, lack powerful dramatic conflicts and have obligatory happy endings in which the young couple triumphs, without going against patriarchal morals. The most popular of these works can be seen from time to time even today.

The national repertoire also involves plays with music, usually performed in a traditional style (improvised folk or even urban songs). Among the most noted of these works is the Serbian drama *Koštana* by Borisav Stanković (1876–1927) which has remained in the repertoire of Serb theatres since 1901.

Following the great success of foreign musicals such as *Hair* (Atelje 212 Theatre, Belgrade, 1969), and *Fiddler on the Roof* (Savremeno pozorište/Modern Theatre, the Terazije Stage, 1972), which in their time exerted a significant influence on theatres in Yugoslavia, modern Serbian composers wrote similar popular musicals which were also successful with audiences. The most successful of these works were by composers Aleksandar Ilić (1921–71) and Vojislav Vojkan Borisavljević (b. 1947).

Within the dramatic theatre, the most important composer of incidental stage music has been Vojislav Kostić (b. 1931), known particularly for his daring harmonies.

Raško Jovanović, Petar Marjanović

Dance Theatre

In the late 1980s, dance theatre and choreo-drama began to appear in the projects of a group called KPGT (an acronym from the first letters of the words for theatre in the various languages of the former Yugoslavia). The group was founded by Ljubiša Ristić and the choreographer-director-ballerina Nada Koko-tović (b. 1944), who was educated in Zagreb, Italy and the United States. In her independent projects (*Othello*, *A Midsummer Night's Dream* and *Anita Berber*), she has used dance parallel with the spoken word, in an effort to enhance speech with stage movement, 'to continue to speak in the stylized action of the body, when words are no longer enough'. In the National Theatre in Subotica, Kokotović and Ristić organized in 1986 and 1991 an International Festival of Dance Theatre called Emergency Exit and managed to bring together some of the most prominent names in dance theatre in Europe.

The most interesting of the later generation of dance theatre artists is the choreographer-director Dejan Pajović (b. 1960), founder of the theatre company Signum. Pajović created several productions – *The House of Bernarda Alba*, *The Picture of Dorian Grey* and *Magbet traži Magbeta* (*Macbeth in Search of Macbeth*) – in which speech was almost completely eliminated or reduced to simple sound. His productions are all based on a dramatic structure in which speech is simply translated into movement.

Aleksandar Milosavljević,
Petar Marjanović

Theatre for Young Audiences

Young people's theatre is present in two forms in Serbia and Montenegro: there are professional theatres (three in Belgrade, and one each in Novi Sad, Subotica and Podgorica) and hundreds of amateur school drama groups. All of them prepare young people and amateur actors to become theatregoers in the adult theatre.

National achievement in this field is best characterized by the Boško Buha Theatre in Belgrade, a repertory children's and young people's theatre, founded in 1950, which presents about five premières a year. With a permanent company of actors and a large staff of stage, technical and organizational personnel, the company's directors are guests and it is they who determine the style of acting. In the first decade of work on its traditional proscenium stage, most performances were representational – realistic presentations of fairytales along with musical and poetic visions, often adaptations of great works of world fiction.

Since the 1960s, the style has been replaced by a more emphatic theatricalization – essentially non-realistic, ironic and connected to theatrical illusion. Many plays during this period have been heroic comedies or even *commedia dell'-arte*, the latter developing an improvised style of acting while retaining the universal moral messages of all fairytales: that the triumphs of evil are only temporary.

There has long been a plentiful and developed children's literature in Serbian which has been very present on this stage. Many original texts, plays or adaptations have been staged of works by Dušan Radović (1922–84), Ljubivoje Ršumović (b. 1939) and Ljubiša Djokić (b. 1929). The theatres focusing on teenagers have also presented productions of Shakespeare's comedies.

Mira Santini, Petar Marjanović

Puppet Theatre

The origins of puppet theatre go far back into Serbian folk tradition as well as that of the other former Yugoslav nations. Theatre with puppets – from symbolic performances to anthropomorphic puppets – has been preserved in folk customs to this very day. Modern puppets appeared among the Serbs in the early nineteenth century, through travelling puppet theatres at village fairs.

The first modern Serbian puppet play was written by Jovan Jovanović Zmaj (1883–1904), the great children's poet. This was the playlet *Nesrećna Kafina* (*Unfortunate Kafina*, 1881), whose absurdist elements represent an anticipation of the surrealist approach. Following World War II, puppet theatres with professional companies were organized in Serbia, with a permanent repertoire and audiences of young people.

By applying various puppet techniques (marionette, Guignol, shadow and black light theatre), the puppet theatres managed to draw together numerous authors, directors and actors interested in the creative possibilities of this ancient art and its modern expression.

In Serbia and Montenegro in the early 1990s there were ten professional puppet companies (in Belgrade, Zemun, Novi Sad, Niš, Zrenjanin, Subotica and Podgorica) among which the leading ones are the Dušan Radović Little Theatre in Belgrade (founded in 1948) and the Toša Jovanović National Theatre in Zrenjanin (a puppet theatre working in Serbian and Hungarian and founded in 1956).

An annual festival of puppet theatres of Serbia was founded in 1967 in Belgrade.

Radoslav Lazić, Petar Marjanović

Design

Between the world wars a circle of stage and costume designers was formed in Belgrade whose members began to free themselves from the influence of European illusionistic stage design. Most prominent among them was the painter Jovan Bjelić (1884–1964), who was among the first to make the transition from the art of painting to something more scenographic.

Also, technical innovations at the National Theatre (particularly the rotating stage and the nature of the backdrop) required designers to solve the problems of stage space in a more modern way. In Belgrade, this meant a sculptural plastic relationship between the dramatic work and the stage space. This period is therefore characterized by a wealth of design solutions (impressionism, cubism, new realism and expressionism), while costume became more adaptable.

In the immediate post-war decades, the prominent names in stage design were Miomir Denić (b. 1913) the creator of realistic stage designs (both literally illusionistic and subtly stylized) which were characterized by an effective use of stage space; and Vladimir Marenić (b. 1921) whose stage designs were characterized by monumental yet functional solutions which created suggestive stage environments. In the 1950s and 1960s, Milica Babić-Jovanović (1909–68) was a major figure in costume design. Her creations revealed a refined sense of style, a feeling for proportion in the use of colour, and the utilization of authentic folk elements and ornaments.

The trend in the 1980s and 1990s has been toward designers who take responsibility for the entire visual effect of the productions they work on.

Miodrag Tabački (b. 1947), one such figure, entered the world of the theatre in the 1970s as a mature and already formed artist. He graduated from the Faculty of Architecture in Belgrade and the Academy of Fine Arts (department of stage design, 1972). From 1978, he was a professor of stage and costume design at the Faculty of Dramatic Arts in Belgrade.

Dejan Mijač's 1977 Belgrade Yugoslav Dramatic Theatre production of Branislav Nušić's *The Crowd*, designed by Miodrag Tabački.

Active throughout Yugoslavia, he makes no distinction between drama, opera and ballet designs and has received all the most important Yugoslav awards including a silver medal at Novi Sad in 1990. His work was seen at the Prague Quadrennial in 1979, 1983 and 1987. He is daring in his choice of materials, simply marking out stage spaces suggestively. His designs are dramaturgically layered: a basic daring idea with a subtext of its own.

The leader in costume design, Božana Jovanović (b. 1932), graduated in stage design at the Academy of Fine Arts in Belgrade and entered the world of costume design theory and practice through her work at the Yugoslav Dramatic Theatre in Belgrade (1955–7), the Serbian National Theatre in Novi Sad (1957–65) and the National Theatre in Belgrade (from 1966). Her artistic shapes, tones and colours help coordinate the overall design with the personality or 'tonality' of the characters. She has taken part in both the Novi Sad International Triennial Exhibition of Stage and Costume Design and the Prague Quadrennial in 1967 and 1983.

Milenko Misailović, Petar Marjanović

Theatre Space and Architecture

The majority of theatre companies in Serbia and Montenegro give performances in buildings which were specifically designed as theatres (most often with proscenium stages which have been improved by advancements in stage technology in the twentieth century). There are in total thirty-eight theatre buildings (thirty-five in Serbia and three in Montenegro). Furthermore, a number of small groups are housed in facilities which have simply been adapted for theatrical purposes.

The largest stage space is that of the Serbian

The main hall of the Serbian National Theatre in Novi Sad.

National Theatre in Novi Sad, with a width of 18 metres and a height of 8 metres. The smallest stage is in the basement of the Atelje 212 Theatre in Belgrade (a total of 25 square metres).

The National Theatre in Subotica is the most unconventional in its use of stage space. The company, in fact, uses several municipal buildings: a former Jewish synagogue which was left without worshippers and holy objects during World War II and which the Jewish community later opened to the city; the City Hall – a wonderful *fin-de-siècle* building on the main city square; the shores of the nearby Lake Palić and Lake Ludoš; Kelebija – a sand quarry, near the Yugoslav–Hungarian border, where nature has brought together in one place a wood, sand dunes and a small, artificial lake; in the woods by Lake Palić where a monstrous globe – a gigantic 'devil's wheel' – has been set up, an enormous barrel along whose sides motor cyclists ride their bikes at daredevil speed, and in which the Subotica actors once performed their version of Shakespeare's *Titus Andronicus* directed by Dušan Jovanović.

The moving spirit behind the Subotica theatre is the controversial director Ljubiša Ristić whose unconventional use of stage space was best illustrated by his project *Madač – komentari* (*Madách – Commentaries*) based on the work *Az ember tragediaja* (*The Tragedy of Man*) by the classical Hungarian author Imre Madách and adapted very freely by Dragan Klaić (b. 1950) and Laszlo Vegel (b. 1941). This performance inaugurated specific concepts of theatre for the country – aesthetically, spatially and ideologically.

The first part of the performance began in the building of the National Theatre with stage images of Adam and Eve's expulsion from Paradise and the beginnings of human history. The actors then proceeded to the theatre courtyard. The second part took place on the city square with camels passing by, harem women, a *gusle* player singing of Miltiades (a *gusle* is a traditional pear-shaped folk instrument, one-stringed and played with a bow, widespread among the Balkan peoples), and Danton, who was guillotined according to Büchner's interpretation. Later, Aldo Moro was kidnapped as part of a Red Brigades plot. This was accompanied by the stoning of an Arab princess in Riyadh.

The third part took place in the City Hall, in the form of twenty-seven simultaneous scenes interpreted by subtitles in two languages. The audience walked through City Hall and its courtyard following Adam and Eve and their guide Lucifer, taking routes of their own choice. In a neighbouring courtyard, two football teams were assembled (the Yugoslav Olympic team and the Hungarian Puskas) and national anthems were played for an hour, while in another courtyard six people were executed by a firing squad for a full hour (the commands were shouted in Spanish); in still another yard there was a showing of the old Hollywood movie, *The Queen of Czardas*.

The fourth part, set in the Subotica synagogue, began with a scene between the spirit of an old rabbi and the spirit of Anne Frank (the first words spoken in the temple were in Hebrew). There was a scene of the Last Supper at which were seated the spirit of the old rabbi, Anne Frank and the spirits of the European revolutionaries from 1848, Hungarian, Russian, German, French and Italian, Daniel Cohn-Bendit, Verdi, Marx and, in the same portion of the performance, there was a meeting in 1988 in West Berlin between Cohn-Bendit and the little girl Uhlrike Meinhoff.

In the ancient coastal city of Budva in Montenegro, dating from Roman times, the City-Theatre offers seasonal performances. Since its productions are on only for the summer, it supports itself mainly from a tourist tax. Budva productions are performed mainly in natural surroundings, and the city itself is also the stage for outdoor performances: the Citadel, a stone plateau in front of the Orthodox monastery in Stanjevići, and even Miločer beach on the outskirts of Budva in the vicinity of the old city centre.

Petar Marjanović

Training

The highest institutions of theatre education in Serbia are the Faculty of Dramatic Arts (Belgrade), the Academy of Arts (Novi Sad) and the Faculty of Arts (Priština).

The Faculty of Dramatic Arts is part of the University of Arts in Belgrade. It was opened in 1937 as the theatre department of the Academy of Music, and since 1948 it has been an independent institution. In addition to departments for film and television, it has departments for acting, theatre and radio directing, dramaturgy, theatre and radio production, along with a chair for theory and history.

The Academy of Arts, which is part of the University of Novi Sad, was founded in 1974 and has departments for drama, music and fine arts. At the drama department there is a section for acting (with subsections in Serbian and Hungarian) and a group for directing (multimedia, theatre, film, radio and television).

The Faculty of Arts is part of the University of Priština. It has departments for music, fine arts and drama, and it was opened in 1989. At the drama department there is a section for acting.

All of these academies are university-level institutions, and upon their completion graduates receive a BA, while the Faculty of Dramatic Arts and the Academy of Arts also offer MA and PhD degrees. All of these schools are state subsidized as part of the state system of university education; they are also strictly selective in their admission policies and studies are vocationally oriented. Graduates find employment in cultural institutions (theatre, television and radio stations) or freelance as artists.

The curriculum consists of thirty hours of teaching a week. Of this, approximately one-third is classes in major subjects, one-third in related artistic subjects (movement, voice, scenography and the like) and one-third in theoretical subjects (theatre history, psychology, aesthetics). Studies take four years. A large portion of the students' practical training is realized through cooperation with professional theatres and television studios.

Svetozar Rapajić, Petar Marjanović

Criticism, Scholarship and Publishing

The most important books on theatre studies in Serbia and Montenegro have traditionally come about through individual efforts by authors outside academic institutions. Since the early 1980s two faculties (the Academy of Arts in Novi Sad and the Faculty of Dramatic Arts in Belgrade) have organized team research projects, which have resulted in twenty books in various areas of theatre studies (history and aesthetics of directing, dramaturgy, and the history of theatre and drama).

There are two theatre museums – the Museum of Theatre Arts of Serbia in Belgrade and the Theatre Museum of Vojvodina in Novi Sad – and a Centre for Theatre Documentation of Sterijino pozorje in Novi Sad, where a variety of materials are collected (books, articles from newspapers and periodicals, videotapes of theatre performances, photographs, theatre records, tape recordings, play manuscripts, letters, personal objects and donations from theatre artists and others).

Theatre book publishing is done by Sterijino pozorje – publishers of seven books and the periodical (in Serbian and English) *Scena*; the Museum of Theatre Arts of Serbia – four books and the periodical *Teatron* to its credit; the Belgrade publisher Nolit – publishers of *Srpska književnost: Drama* (*Serbian Literature: Drama*) in twenty-five volumes, and Prosveta, also in Belgrade, specializing in books of theatre criticism by writers such as Eli Finci (1911–80), Jovan Hristić (b. 1933) and Vladimir Stamenković (b. 1928).

Among other journals of note have been *Pozorište* (*Theatre*), published monthly from 1871 to 1910 and then again from 1969; *Ludus: Pozorišne novine* (*Ludus: A Theatre Magazine*) and *Teatron*, a journal of theatre history. The most important occasional and annual publications have been *Godišnjak jugoslovenskih pozorišta* (*Yugoslav Theatre Yearbook*), published annually since 1981 by Sterijino pozorje in Novi Sad, and *Zbornik Matice srpske za scenske umetnosti i muziku*, an annual review of the performing arts published since 1986.

One of the major problems with theatre criticism in Yugoslavia in the period after World War II has been the failure by most critics to move away from text-based criticism and their inability to write with the same expertise and talent about acting, directing and the visual aspects of production. The first two post-war decades were marked prominently by the work of Eli Finci, drama critic for the widely circulated Yugoslav daily *Politika* (Belgrade), a writer with a refined taste and a broad knowledge. A materialist and a Marxist, his approach to dramatic work could best be described as sociological as he passed through all the phases of development which socio-political and theatre life in Yugoslavia dictated. When necessary, he was also a critic with a 'mission': those were probably his weakest moments. Finci was the only theatre critic of real authority in Yugoslavia during this time.

In the 1970s and 1980s, the most reliable and authoritative critic was Jovan Hristić, poet, playwright, essayist and professor of dramaturgy at the Faculty of Dramatic Arts in Belgrade. Though he has contributed mostly to a monthly periodical with a small circulation (*Književnost*, Belgrade, since 1971), his regular column has been one of the most valued and quoted pieces of theatre writing in Yugoslavia. Knowledgeable and unconventional, Hristić's critiques are marked by an unobtrusive erudition and a rejection of everything that he sees as false avant-gardism in the modern theatre. Unafraid of bearing the label traditionalist, he defends conservativism as a socially and creatively productive principle with spirit and nerve. In his critiques and studies, *Čehov dramski pisac* (*Chekhov the Dramatist*, 1981) and *Studije o drami* (*Studies on Drama*, 1986), which both featured a poetic and philosophical concern about the world and a breadth of insight into professional literature on the theatre, Hristić has remained consistent in presenting his views and his love for the theatre, which has been widely eclectic.

Petar Marjanović
Translated by Vladislava Felbabov

(See also YUGOSLAVIA)

Further Reading

Cvetković, Sava V., ed. *Repertoar narodnog pozorita u beogradu 1868–1965*. [Repertoire of the National Theatre in Belgrade 1868–1965]. Belgrade, 172 pp.

Drašković, Boro. *Paradoks o reditelju*. [The paradox of the director]. Novi Sad: Sterijino pozorje, 1988. 247 pp.

Finci, Eli. *Više i manje od života I-V*. [More and less than life I-V]. Belgrade: Prosveta, 1955–77.

Hristić, Jovan. *Pozorište, pozorište I–II*. [Theatre, theatre I–II]. 2 vols. Belgrade: Prosveta, 1977–82. 332 and 340 pp.

——. *Pozorišni referati. Pozorište, pozorište III*. [Theatre essays. Theatre, theatre III]. Belgrade: Nolit, 1992. 332 pp.

Lešić, Josip. *Istorija jugoslovenske moderne režije*. [The history of modern Yugoslav directing]. Novi Sad: Sterijino pozorje & IRO Dnevnik, 1986. 470 pp.

Marjanović, Petar, ed. *An Anthology of Works by Twentieth Century Yugoslav Playwrights*. Scena, Theatre Arts Review, 7,8. Novi Sad: Sterijino pozorje, 1984–5. 272 and 239 pp.

Milanović, Olga. *Beogradska scenografija i kostimografija 1868–1941*. [Belgrade stage and costume design 1868–1941]. Belgrade: Muzej pozorišne umetnosti SR Srbije and Univerzitet umetnosti, 1983. 396 pp.

Miočinović, Mirjana. *Eseji o drami*. [Essays on drama]. Belgrade: Vuk Karadžić, 1975.

Misailović, Milenko. *Dramaturgija scenskog prostora*. [The dramaturgy of stage space]. Novi Sad: Sterijino pozorje & IRO Dnevnik, 1988. 457 pp.

Perović, Sreten. *Darovi scene. Studije i kritike I. Pozorišne kritike II*. [Gifts of the stage: studies and criticism I, drama reviews II]. 2 vols. Titograd: Leksikografski zavod Crne Gore, 1986. 467 and 367 pp.

——, and Radoslav Rotković, eds. *Savremena drama i pozorište u Crnoj Gori*. [Contemporary drama and theatre in Montenegro]. Novi Sad: Sterijino pozorje, 1986. 311 pp.

Selenić, Slobodan, ed. *Antologija savremene srpske drame*. [An anthology of contemporary Serbian drama]. Belgrade: Srpska književna zadruga, 1977. 722 pp.

Stamenković, Vladimir. *Kraljevstvo eksperimenta. Dvadeset godina BITEF-a*. [The kingdom of experiment. Twenty years of BITEF]. Belgrade: Nova knjiga, 1987. 272 pp.

Stojković, Borivoje S. *Istorija srpskog pozorišta od Srednjeg veka do modernog doba. Drama i opera*. [The history of the Serbian theatre from the Middle Ages to modern times. Drama and opera]. Belgrade: Muzej pozorišne umetnosti SR Srbije, 1979. 1,031 pp.

Volk, Petar. *Pozorišni život u Srbiji 1944–1986*. [Theatre life in Serbia 1944–86]. Belgrade: Fakultet dramskih umetnosti, 1990. 1,416 pp.

SLOVAK REPUBLIC

Slovak theatrical traditions stem from dramatizations of early pagan myths, evolve through Medieval farce, religious and scholastic theatre and culminate in a rise of amateur theatre in the nineteenth century at a time of growing national self-awareness. The most significant authors of this later period were comic writers such as Ján Chalupka (1791–1871), Ján Palárik (1822–70) and Jonáš Záborský (1812–76), the latter also writing historical tragedies. A major exponent of realistic drama at the end of the nineteenth century and in the first two decades of the twentieth century was Jozef Gregor-Tajovský (1874–1940) who wrote strongly emotional plays with a village setting.

Before the creation of Czechoslovakia in 1918, the area of what is now the Slovak Republic was one in which national, linguistic, cultural, political and economic elements and trends of diverse European provenance intermingled and influenced one another. The general development of Slovak theatre was most directly influenced by touring companies from German-speaking areas (German-speaking groups, in fact, played in the region from the seventeenth century), Italian-speaking companies and, during the nineteenth century, by Hungarian-speaking groups. The most direct and greatest influence on the development of a professional theatre in the Slovak Republic, however, was from Czech-speaking companies.

The period between 1918 and 1945 saw regular guest appearances in Bratislava, the Slovak capital, and other cities by important Czech companies and individual performers such as Prague's National Theatre, the D34 Theatre and the Osvobozené divadlo. Of importance too in the development of Slovak theatrical style was a visit by the Moscow Art Theatre to Bratislava in 1921.

Slovak professional theatre emerged with the Slovak National Theatre, the first stable professional theatre group in Slovakia. Created in Bratislava in 1920, the company still performed during its first few seasons in the Czech language due to a lack of trained Slovak actors. In 1932, however, there emerged within this theatre, an independent Slovak-language drama group led by the director Ján Borodáč (1892–1964). The years up to 1945 gave birth to a whole generation of artists who, after World War II, were to shape Slovak theatre more clearly. In the years leading up to World War II, the social comedies of Ivan Stodola (1888–1977) enjoyed particular popularity in Slovakia, while the plays of Július Barč-Ivan (1909–53) clearly anticipated European symbolism and expressionism.

As an expression of the new communist regime's concern just after the war for the development of national minorities, a touring Hungarian company called the Hungarian Regional Theatre was created in 1950, based from 1952 in Komárno. A second Hungarian-language group, the Thália, was started by the Hungarian Regional Theatre in 1969 in the city of Košice. In 1991, the Hungarian Regional Theatre's name was changed to the Jókai Theatre, and, at the same time, the Thália became autonomous.

In 1945 in Prešov, a Ukrainian National Theatre was formed on a cooperative basis and in 1954 the Poddukelský Ukrainian Folk Company (a professional folkloric song and dance company) began to work under its aegis. Since 1991, the Ukrainian National Theatre has been called the Alexander Duchnovič Theatre (Duchnovič was a Ruthenian freedom fighter) and has begun to perform in the Ruthenian language as well.

In 1992, still another minority theatre – this one performing in Romany – was founded in Košice.

Prior to the dissolution of the Czech and Slovak Federal Republic in January 1993, the country's 5.5 million Slovaks had twenty-nine permanent theatres (ten of them in Bratislava) – fifteen for drama (of which two were specializing in plays for young audiences), four for opera, two for musical theatre, two for ballet and six puppet groups.

By way of comparison, in 1950 there were nineteen Slovak professional companies (five in Bratislava); in 1960, twenty-six (seven in Bratislava); in 1970, twenty-five (eight in Bratislava); in 1980, twenty-five (seven in Bratislava).

Structure of the National Theatre Community

See CZECHOSLOVAKIA for structure 1945–92.

Artistic Profile

Companies

Foremost among Slovakia's theatrical institutions is the Slovak National Theatre. Still the showcase of Slovak theatrical life, the National has companies for drama, opera and ballet. The period between 1923 and 1930 was the most significant in the opera group's history and is linked with the names of the conductor-composer-impresario Oskar Nedbal (1874–1930) and his nephew Karel (1888–1964). During this period, its operatic repertoire was of the highest European standard and the company regularly toured abroad.

Between 1932 and 1938, the dramatic theatre at the National was led by Ján Borodáč, whose approach was more traditional though he did produce many Slovak authors (Gregor-Tajovský, Stodola, Chalupka, Palárik). He also staged many Russian and world classics. His realistic – often naturalistic – productions, however, appeared anachronistic in comparison to those of the expressionist Viktor Šulc (1897–1944) who was at that time working with the Slovak National Theatre's Czech-language group.

At the end of the 1930s, more modern approaches reached the Slovak company through the work of Ferdinand Hoffmann (1908–66), Ján Jamnický (1908–72) and, above all, Jozef Budský (1911–89). Between 1939 and 1945, they transformed this group into an artistically important company which, through its choice of repertoire, maintained a dialogue with the fascist ideology then dominating the European political scene and was able, moreover, to transcend Borodáč's traditionalism and show itself worthy of comparison with more modern European theatres.

In the immediate post-war years, the company staged a number of ambitious productions from the contemporary international repertoire along with modern dramas by Slovak authors. However, the political climate following the socialization of theatres in 1948 meant that the artistic potential of many talented individuals was ruined on meaningless works of socialist-realism and many leading artists simply emigrated. It was only with the thaw that followed the communist changes of 1956 that artistically demanding work again became possible.

After years of being accused of 'formalism', Budský once more emerged as a leading figure on the artistic scene with productions in 1957 of Tyl's *The Court of Blood* and Vishnevski's *The Optimistic Tragedy*; in 1958 with Čapek's *Power and Glory* and in 1960 with Arbuzov's *Incident on the River Bank* and Chekhov's *Ivanov*. He fostered a tradition of metaphorical-poetic theatre while his productions also had a strongly topical orientation.

During the same period, Tibor Rakovský (1922–81) specialized in philosophically demanding works such as Brecht's *Galileo* (1958), Imre Madách's *The Tragedy of Man* (1969) and Ibsen's *Peer Gynt* (1979).

The National's drama section was also able to keep in close contact with developments in contemporary world drama by producing works by

Jozef Budský's 1958 Slovak National Theatre production of Čapek's *Power and Glory*, designed by Ladislav Vychodil.

Sartre, Hochhuth, Miller, Beckett, Albee and Mrożek.

In 1944, a group called the Slovak Theatre was founded in the city of Prešov and other Slovak theatres began in Košice (where a company had existed as early as 1924) and in the city of Martin (the Slovak Chamber Theatre).

The 1950s and 1960s also saw the birth of professional Slovak drama companies in Nitra, Trnava, Zvolen and Spišská Nová Ves, an opera company in Banská Bystrica, and five professional puppet theatres. Performances in the Ukrainian/Ruthenian language were regularly staged in Prešov at the Alexander Duchnovič Theatre (known prior to 1990 as the Ukrainian National Theatre); at the Jókai Theatre in Komárno (until 1990 the Hungarian Regional Theatre, with a subsidiary theatre in Košice); and at the Thália in Košice. Both Hungarian-language companies directed their efforts predominantly to locating themselves within the context of contemporary Hungarian 'village' theatre; in recent years the Duchnovič Theatre, thanks to some very adventurous experiments in

collaboration with leading Slovak directors such as Jozef Pražmári (b. 1943) and Blahoslav Uhlár (b. 1951), has made a significant impression on the overall Slovak theatre scene.

After a number of not entirely successful attempts at supplementing this network of state theatres, 1967 witnessed a significant development with the establishment of Slovakia's first independent theatre (an experimental chamber theatre). Divadlo na korze (Korzo Theatre) was formed by a group of graduates of the Academy of Performing Arts, some of whom gave up contracts with larger theatres. Martin Porubjak (b. 1944), later to become a deputy prime minister in the government of the Slovak Republic (1991–2), was the theatre's dramaturge, Vladimír Strnisko (b. 1938) and Miloš Pietor (1933–91) its directors, and the company of actors included many of the next generation's leading Slovak players: Martin Huba (b. 1943), Magda Vášáryová (b. 1948), Marián Labuda (b. 1944), Milan Kňažko (b. 1945), Milan Lasica (b. 1940), Stano Dančiak (b. 1942), Július Satinský (b. 1941), and others. The theatre's repertoire ranged from absurdist drama (Beckett, Ionesco, Mrożek) to Russian realist comedy (Gogol, Ostrovsky, Chekhov).

In the period of communist 'normalization' that followed the invasion of Czechoslovakia in 1968, every theatre's repertoire became based almost exclusively on ideological works mostly of Slovak, Czech or Soviet provenance. A system of censorship and other restrictions targeted prominent creative individuals and artistic celebrities. Very quickly, the work of all the companies began to look the same – grey and lifeless.

Paradoxically, this period of uniform and conformist theatre – unpropitious for both society and artistic activity – produced a whole stream of work which at the end of the 1980s had proven significant throughout Slovak society. Directors such as Pietor, Strnisko, Uhlár, Jozef Bednárik (b. 1947) and Ľubomír Vajdička (b. 1944) consistently found in classic dramatic texts hidden historical parallels and used them to echo the fundamental problems of the time.

Particularly important in this respect was Strnisko, whom the regime only allowed to return to directing five years after the closure of the Korzo Theatre and who managed to work with a group of former Korzo actors in creating at the Nová Scéna (New Scene) a theatre of political opposition, openly taking issue with the ideology of the communist government through classic plays even by such writers as Molière, Schiller, Gogol and Goethe. Pietor used topical parallels in the plays of Chekhov and Shakespeare, producing a whole cycle of the latter's plays during the 1970s and 1980s initially at the New Scene and later at the Slovak National Theatre.

All these artists combined their individual talents to give back to the theatre some of its artistic freedom and aesthetic values. In the second half of the 1980s, it was this movement which gained ascendancy and its protagonists began to be given official recognition.

Following the revolution of 1989 and the abandoning of communist ideology, new attempts began to be made towards dismantling the ossified structure of the state theatre network. The state monopoly on theatre licensing disappeared and theatres acquired greater creative freedom. On the other hand, they could no longer count on guaranteed state subsidies. For these reasons, major changes in the map of Slovak theatre were beginning to be seen in the 1990s.

On the minority language side, both Hungarian-speaking companies, the Jókai and the Thália, have traditionally received the same type of subsidies as Slovak groups. As well, they have been able to receive support from the government's various minority programmes, which has given even more solidity through the years. The Jókai, for example, is one of the few groups in the Slovak Republic to perform in a modern facility, a theatre built in 1986. Even at the Slovak Academy of Performing Arts, there is a Hungarian-language performance section.

Both companies have concentrated on a mixed repertoire of classic and contemporary works including plays by Hungarian-language writers living in Slovakia such as Egri, Dávidová and Lovicsek. The company has also performed works by Slovak, Czech and Soviet authors.

Dramaturgy

In the immediate post-war period, original works of Slovak drama very closely reflected the dominant European currents. The post-war atmosphere, including its emotional aridity and the loss of human value systems, found expression in plays by Leopold Lahola (1918–68) such as *Bezvetrie v Zuele* (*Becalmed at Zuela*, 1947) and *Štyri strany sveta* (*The Four Sides of the World*, 1948); and in plays by Štefan Králik (1909–83) such as *Veľrieka* (*The River*, 1943), *Trasovisko* (*Marshland*, 1945), *Posledná prekážka* (*The Final Obstacle*, 1946), *Hra bez lásky a smrti* (*A Game Without Love*, 1946) and *Hra o slobode* (*A Play About Freedom*, 1948); and in works by Peter Karvaš (b. 1920) such as *Meteor* (1945) and *Návrat do života* (*Return to Life*, 1946).

After 1948, development was violently interrupted by the political and social changes within the country. As a result, the only plays that stood any chance of getting into the repertoires of theatres were those accepting the Stalinist model of a simplistic ideologized aesthetic. Even Karvaš, Slovakia's foremost post-war dramatist, a writer whose comedies were close to the irony and sarcasm of Bernard Shaw's, paid his dues to propagandist writing. Only with *Polnočná omša* (*Midnight Mass,* 1958) and *Antigona a tí druhí* (*Antigone and the Others,* 1962) could he display his brilliance in studying heroes at moments of extreme psychological pressure. With *Veľká parochňa* (*The Big Wig,* 1965), *Experiment Damokles* (*The Damocles Experiment,* 1967) and *Absolútny zákaz* (*Strictly Forbidden,* 1970) he again approached modern currents in world drama. Karvaš was, however, classified as an undesirable author (between 1971 and 1988) because his plays were deemed to be absurdist in nature. Throughout the period, it was therefore impossible for his plays to be staged in the country. Alongside his creative writing, Karvaš was also a teacher specializing in dramatic theory and one of Slovakia's leading theoreticians.

Like Karvaš, Ivan Bukovčan (1921–75) also went through a period when he was forced to pay his dues to the poetics of socialist-realism. In his best works – *Pštrosí večierok* (*The Ostrich Party*, 1967), *Kým kohút nezaspieva* (*Until the Cock Crows*, 1969) and *Zažeň vlka* (*Repulsing the Wolves*, 1970) – he dealt with morality and the problem of individual freedom. The plays are an unsettling testament to humanity's moral devastation by a repressive social system. Later, anticipating possible repression, he abandoned Slovak settings and located his plays in exotic contexts, always maintaining, however, a Slovak metaphorical image.

Osvald Zahradník (b. 1932) was originally a radio producer and writer. His individual poetics and sensitive analyses of questions of human existence were most effectively demonstrated in the play *Sólo pre bicie hodiny* (*Solo for Grandfather Clock*, 1972). Another frequently performed author is Ján Solovič (b. 1934).

Of the next generation of playwrights, Stanislav Štepka (b. 1944) was the leading figure in Bratislava's Radošinské Naivné Divadlo (Naïve Theatre Company of Radošina) which started as an amateur group. He tended to create freely constructed, cabaret-style plays which exploited the individual charm of his actors effectively. His trilogy – *Ako som vstúpil do seba* (*How I Entered Myself*, 1981), *Ako sme sa hladali* (*How We Tried To Find Ourselves*, 1983) and *Ako bolo* (*The Way It Was*, 1984) – is the only attempt in Slovak drama to focus specifically on the nation's history, consciousness and uniqueness. The plays are full of self-irony and tender understanding. A later play, *Vygumuj a napíš* (*Rub It Out and Start Again*, 1989), deals with the self-examination of someone growing up in the desolate ethical context of a communist society.

Karol Horák (b. 1943) was active for many years as an organizer of student theatre. His first plays were written in the 1970s for the needs of his own student company and were characterized by their visual imagery, elements of biomechanics and non-verbal expression. His début in professional theatre came with his play *Medzivojnový muž* (*The Inter-War Man*, 1984) in which he looked at the emotional spectrum of a man living in a world devoid of humanity. In *Evanjelium podla Jonáša* (*The Gospel According to Jonáš*, 1987) he examined the life of the Slovak dramatist Jonáš Záborský (from the period of national reawakening). This became the basis for a tract on the problem of individual liberty as well as an investigation of the relationship between the creative individual and the limitations of society. In *Skaza futbalu v meste K* (*The Destruction of Football in the Town of K*, 1991), he developed a theme comparing a man on the threshold of old age and a community experiencing its own demise.

Andrej Ferko (b. 1956) spent his formative years as a writer with student cabaret. His plays – *Proso* (*Millet*, 1986) and *Noc na zamrznutom jazere* (*Night on a Frozen Lake*, 1988) metaphorically portrayed the hopeless situation of individuals manipulated by society.

Directors, Directing and Production Styles

As a director, Miloš Pietor utilized the ideals of psychological realism in the preparation of roles but maintained a more poetic than naturalistic portrayal of reality. In much of his work, he attempted to transpose social tension and inner feelings, and to argue questions related to the social struggle. Particularly in his productions of Russian classics – Gorki's *Lower Depths* (1967); Chekhov's *Three Sisters* (1967, 1972), *Uncle Vanya* (1974) and *Platonov* (1979) – he tried to deal with such large themes as the meaning of life, human communication and the contrast between verbal idealism and passive vegetation. With his production of *Hamlet* (1974), he achieved a stylistic purity and a de-emotionalizing tragic majesty. In 1978 Pietor began a systematic presentation of Shakespearian plays with *Love's Labours Lost*. He followed this with *Richard II* (1980), *Henry IV* (1984) and *Richard III* (1987).

Ľubomír Vajdička is a director with an exceptional capacity for thinking in terms of dramaturgy, which enables him to interpret classical texts in untraditional and surprisingly topical ways while fully respecting his authors. He has specialized in Russian classics (Gorki, Chekhov) as well as in classical Slovak dramas, for example *Kubo* by Jozef Hollý (1879–1912),

Miloš Pietor's 1974 New Proscenium production of Shakespeare's *Hamlet*.

produced in 1981; *Najdúch* (*The Foundling*) by Ján Záborský, produced in 1973; *Čaj u pána senátora* (*Tea With the Senator*) by Ivan Stodola, produced in 1974; *Kocúrkovo* by Ján Chalupka, in 1978. The productions of these plays were like minutely and brilliantly composed musical scores in which the dominant elements were bitter, ironic and sarcastic. Their new tones transposed the original genre into tragi-comedy. In 1983, Vajdička became staff director at the Slovak National Theatre.

Vladimír Strnisko brought to perfection the theatre's ability to express in elaborate circumlocution officially forbidden truths about the state of society under dictatorship. His productions have been continuous reports on the manipula-

tion of individuals by totalitarian regimes. He guides his actors towards very precise portrayals and helps them to grasp their characters' essence through non-verbal action and finely chiselled detail. He tends to specialize in classical German, Russian and French drama and was a leading figure in the company Divadlo na Korze between 1967 and 1971.

Jozef Bednárik is another director of unusual invention and theatrical fantasy. His projects for the theatre go beyond any concise and clearly formulated aesthetic programme: they are theatrical happenings in which all is subordinated to the aim of maximum emotional impact on the spectator. The epithet 'brilliantly eclectic' is often used in discussing his work. He achieved notable success with his production of García Lorca's *House of Bernarda Alba* (1979) which the Andrej Bagar Theatre from Nitra staged at Sofia's Theatre of Nations Festival in 1980, and with Shakespeare's *Titus Andronicus* in 1981. Although he was still working with dramatic companies in the 1990s, it is in opera and musical theatre that his individuality has found its greatest expression.

Between 1974 and 1989, Blahoslav Uhlár mounted a series of productions at Trnava's Theatre for Children and Youth dealing allegorically with the destruction of moral values in a totalitarian society. Working with a number of professional and amateur companies, he developed what he called 'decomposed theatre', conceived in collaboration with the artist Miloš Karásek (b. 1960) and created a number of productions articulating in untraditional but authentic ways the emotions of contemporary humanity. These productions tend to be created collectively without reference to a prepared text. Among his major works in this style are *Kde je sever?* (*Where is North?*, 1987), *Predposledná večera* (*The Next To Last Supper*, 1989), *Sens, nonsens* (*Sense, Nonsense*, 1988), *Ochotníci* (*The Amateur Thespians*, 1987), *A čo?* (*So What?*, 1988) and a series referred to simply as 'company projects' between 1990 and 1992.

Music Theatre

Slovak musical theatre is generally considered to have begun with the founding of the opera company of the Slovak National Theatre in 1920. In 1926, conductor Oskar Nedbal premièred the

first Slovak-authored opera – the neo-romantic *Kováč Wieland* (*Wieland the Blacksmith*) written by Ján Levoslav Bella (1843–1936).

Nedbal's successor, Karel Nedbal, helped to

create a whole generation of Slovak opera stars in the 1930s and a repertoire of works never seen before in the country including Prokofiev's *Love of Three Oranges* (1931) and Shostakovich's *Lady Macbeth of Mtenšk* (1935). In the years just prior to World War II, director Viktor Šulc and Czech designer František Tröster worked together on a number of modern and contemporary operatic productions in Bratislava.

The development of Slovak opera after 1945 is closely linked to the development of original Slovak works, which reached a peak in the 1960s. Leading exponents include Eugen Suchoň (b. 1908) and Ján Cikker (1911–89). The classic work of modern Slovak opera is Suchoň's *Krútňava* (*Whirlpool*, 1949). His 1960 opera *Svätopluk* is an important historical work dealing with Slovakia's past. Of Cikker's ten operas, the most significant are those based on great humanist works of European literature including *Mister Scrooge* (1963), *Hra o láske a smrti* (*Play of Love and Death*, 1969) and especially *Vzkriesenie* (*The Resurrection*, 1962) based on the novel by Lev Tolstoi.

The stylized and anti-illusionist operatic theatre of Juraj Beneš (b. 1940) constitutes a consistent attempt to reject the traditional opera aesthetic. Many of his works such as *Cisárove nové šaty* (*The Emperor's New Clothes*, 1969) and the biblical epic *Hostina* (*Banquet*, 1984) have been seen as allegorical political protests.

The mid-1950s saw the emergence of several young directors who were to shape the opera of the Slovak National Theatre in the following decades. The very analytical Branislav Kriška (b. 1931) working with designer Ladislav Vychodil (b. 1920) staged an extraordinary production of Janáček's *The Makropoulos Affair* in 1973. Another director of note is the emotional and full-blooded realist Miroslav Fischer (b. 1932), who first brought Berg's *Wozzek* to the Slovak stage in 1989. More daring interpretations and more metaphorical expression are to be found in productions by Marián Chudovský (b. 1959) and especially in Jozef Bednárik's *Faust and Marguerite* (1989).

The long-term programming by the National's opera company has been marked by a sense of balance in its selection of national

The 1962 opera company of the Slovak National Theatre production of Ján Cikker's *The Resurrection*, directed by K. Hájek.

works, world classics, and twentieth-century foreign opera. The fact that Italian romantic and *verismo* works are well represented is a reflection of the breadth and depth of singing talent available in recent years, and of the quality of soloists of earlier generations. Major artists who began their careers with the opera of the Slovak National Theatre include Lucia Popp (1939–93), Edita Gruberová (b. 1946), Gabriela Beňačková (b. 1947) and Peter Dvorský (b. 1951).

Outside Bratislava, smaller opera companies have operated in the cities of Košice since 1945 and in Banská Bystrica since 1960. In 1979, the latter company organized the first Slovak international opera festival – the Zvolen Castle Plays. In 1987, Bratislava's Chamber Opera company was formed and has produced operas ranging from Gluck and Paisiello to works by young Slovak composers.

The rich operetta tradition in Bratislava between the two wars was obviously influenced by the city's proximity to both Vienna and Budapest. During World War II, this tradition reached its peak in the works of Gejza Dusík (1907–88). In 1946, an independent operetta company was established at Bratislava's New Scene, which initially staged musical comedies, then traditional operetta, and, until 1971, ambitious productions of American musicals such as *My Fair Lady* (1965), *West Side Story* (1965), *Hello Dolly* (1966), *Man of La Mancha* (1967), *Fiddler on the Roof* (1968) and *Zorba* (1970). The company was also responsible for many premières of Slovak musicals, the most successful of these being *The Suburban Cyrano* (1978) by Alta Vášová (b. 1939).

At the beginning of the 1990s, there were three opera groups and two musical and operetta groups, with the most important opera theatre based at the Slovak National Theatre in Bratislava.

Dance Theatre

Between the founding of the Slovak National Ballet Company in 1920 and the many changes that occurred after World War II, the most significant period was the war years, when its leader was Maximilian Froman (b. 1889), a former member of Diaghilev's famous Ballets Russes. After the war, the company received substantial reinforcement in the form of Czech choreographers Rudolf Macharovský and Stanislav Remar. They alternated in heading the troupes of the Slovak National Theatre in Bratislava and the State Theatre in Košice. It was under them that the first generation of Slovak professional dancers emerged, headed by the dancer and choreographer Jozef Zajko (1923–91).

The dominant programming element in the decade after the war was Russian and Soviet ballet. The first original Slovak ballet was *Orpheus and Eurydice* by Tibor Andrašovan (b. 1917), produced in 1949. The second full-length Slovak ballet, *A Ballad of Chivalry* by Šimon Jurovský (1912–63) was not staged until 1960. Nevertheless, this ushered in a rich repertoire ranging from world classics to Soviet ballets, from the most modern western pieces to new domestic works.

In the 1970s, choreographer and director Boris Slovák (b. 1926) brought a new impetus to the company's dramaturgy, choreography and production. Leading figures to have emerged in Slovak ballet in the latter half of the 1980s include the choreographers Robert Balogh (b. 1960), Ondrej Šoth (b. 1960) and Libor Vaculík (b. 1957), who is also a major dancer.

In Slovakia, the important area of mime became associated mostly with the mime artist-director-theatre manager Milan Sládek (b. 1938). Sládek gave his first one-man performance in 1958; between 1962 and 1967 he worked with the Slovak National Theatre. In 1967, he became director of the Theatre Studio, which had its own mime group. Following the occupation of 1968, he left the country and settled in Germany where he founded the Kefka Theatre as well as a mime festival and school. He subsequently returned to Slovakia and in 1992, he was named manager of the Arena Theatre in Bratislava.

Theatre for Young Audiences

The tradition of staging plays for young audiences in Slovakia is a clear continuation of a form that had its modern beginnings in Russia. Slovak performances, however, vary greatly from naturalistic retellings of classic children's fairytales and often include original poetic works which may or may not have didactic purposes.

Throughout Slovakia, all repertory companies routinely stage one or two plays each season exclusively for children. The first Slovak attempt at establishing a children's company, however, was at the New Scene at the end of the 1950s; in 1974, a Theatre for Children and Youth was established in Trnava and in 1980 a second company was established in Spišská Nová Ves. Performance quality has varied widely and styles have ranged from illusionistic interpretations of classic stories to modern poetic work involving audience participation. Perhaps the two most famous productions both took place at the Trnava Theatre – Blahoslav Uhlár's *Princess Maru* (1979) and *The Night of Miracles* (1982).

Unfortunately, staging only material for young audiences in Slovak territories did not satisfy the artistic ambitions of most of those involved. Gradually, all of the youth theatres turned to a more traditional dramatic repertoire although they have continued to give special emphasis to productions for young people.

Blahoslav Uhlár's Theatre for Children and Youth première production of his play *The Night of Miracles*.

Puppet Theatre

The Slovak professional puppet theatre is almost exclusively a post-1945 phenomenon. Though there was an earlier tradition based on religious folk theatre or on visits by touring foreign groups, the family puppet theatre of Ján Stražan (1856–1939) was perhaps most significant in setting the stage for a more modern puppet repertoire.

Between 1950 and 1960, five professional companies were created, the most important being the State Puppet Theatre in Bratislava under the direction of Bohdan Slavík (1917–74). In the 1970s, the activities of the Regional Puppet Theatre in Banská Bystrica attracted national attention thanks to its extensive repertoire and its work in blending live actors and puppets on the stage.

There are three authors of significance in the modern Slovak puppet theatre. Ján Kákoš (b. 1927) was in the 1950s and 1960s one of the first to take a contemporary view of Slovak fairytales. Ľubomír Feldek (b. 1936) became popular in the 1960s and 1970s for his unique comic productions for children. Ján Uličiansky (b. 1955), for his part, achieved special note in the 1980s, for his poetic approach to puppet plays.

The 1979 Regional Puppet Theatre in Banská Bystrica's production of Carlo Gozzi's *The Stag King*, sets and puppets designed by Jozef Ciller.

Design

Stage design in Slovakia began to emerge as a professional discipline in its own right after 1945, thanks primarily to Ladislav Vychodil, who brought Czech designer František Tröster's ideas to Bratislava. Following in these new directions, Vychodil and costume designer Ludmila Purkyňová (1928–90) developed several generations of Slovak stage and costume designers.

The first graduates of the Academy of Performing Arts in the 1950s rid stage design of its illusionistic and representational tendencies. The same anti-illusionistic approach was also reflected in Slovak stage design from the 1960s to the 1980s. Those gradually to emerge as key figures were the costume designer Helena Bezáková (b. 1936), Jozef Ciller (b. 1942), Ján Zavarský (b. 1948), Peter Čanecký (b. 1952), Tomáš Berka (b. 1947), and the costume designer Ľudmila Várossová (b. 1956) among others. All seemed to be seeking new theatrical possibilities in untraditional places. Most also worked as teams with their designs evolving from a close-knit collaboration between directorial, dramaturgical and performance components.

Theatre Space and Architecture

The beat known theatre buildings in Slovakia are the opera house of the Slovak National Theatre built in Bratislava in 1886 and the empire theatre of Count Erdödy in the city of Hlohovec, built in 1802.

The Dramatic Theatre in Bratislava was

completed in 1955 and followed the recent trend to eliminate the strict division between stage and auditorium. Other versions of this more modern style can be found in the Studio S theatre in Bratislava (built in 1982) which also allows for a maximum of theatre–auditorium flexibility. As the 1990s began, new buildings were scheduled for construction in the cities of Nitra and Prešov. Both were expected to express even more modern architectural thinking in the field.

Training

The first Slovak theatre school was the Hudobná škola pre Slovensko (Music School for Slovakia) founded in Bratislava in 1919. In 1928, the Hudobná a dramatická Akadémia (Music and Drama Academy) was formed with its own chair in drama. In 1941 the Music and Drama Academy was turned into a State Conservatory. In 1949 Vyskoá škola múzickych umení (Academy of the Performing Arts) took over all tertiary training in the field. Specialized training is done there for music theatre, radio, film and television as well as traditional areas of dramatic theatre. Design training is also done at the school, for many years under the direction of designer Ladislav Vychodil.

Secondary-level conservatories exist in the towns of Košice and Žilina as well as in the capital.

Criticism, Scholarship and Publishing

The development of theatre reviewing in Slovakia is linked to the appearance of the first Slovak newspapers and periodicals. A pioneer theoretician was Mikuláš Dohnány (1824–52), who published in 1845 a work entitled *Slovo o dramate slovanskom* (*On Slavonic Drama*) in the context of the movement for national emancipation.

Right up to 1949 and the founding of Bratislava's Academy of Performing Arts, with its own department of theatre studies, theory and criticism courses were undertaken by specialists in literature, translators, dramaturges and journalists. Though many achieved high standards, their work in this sphere remained essentially a sideline. A great influence, however, was exercised by the Czech structuralist Ján Mukařovský who, through his seminars at Bratislava University in the first half of the 1940s, shaped the first generation of Slovak theatre theoreticians such as Rudolf Mrlian (b. 1916), Peter Karvaš and Zoltán Rampák (b. 1920). The first structuralist-oriented studies dealt with the unchanging state of theatrical form – Mrlian's 1940 study *Štruktúra javiskového umenia* (*The Structure of Stage Art*), Karvaš's 1947 study *Úvod do základných problémov divadla* (*Introduction to Basic Problems of Theatre*) and Rampák's 1948 study, *Znak v umeleckej výstavbe divadla* (*The Symbol in the Artistic Construction of Theatre*).

Since 1952, research on theatre history has been the province of the department of theatre and film at the Slovak Academy of Sciences which publishes the theoretical review, *Slovenské divadlo* (*Slovak Theatre*, beginning in 1953, four issues annually). From the 1950s, works have been published from time to time on the history of theatre. A culmination of this research was the publication in 1967 of a work entitled *Kapitoly z dejín slovenského divadla* (*Chapters from the History of Slovak Theatre*). Since the beginning of the 1960s, theatrical life has been documented by the Národné Divadelné Centrum (National Theatre Centre) in Bratislava (until 1984, the Theatre Institute; until 1990, the Institute of Art Criticism and Theatre Documentation).

Historical research and text-based criticism is also done at the department of theatre and film research of the Slovak Academy of Sciences in Bratislava. The Matica Slovenská in Martin researches and provides documentation on amateur theatre activities.

Since 1970–1, the National Theatre Centre has published the *Ročenka slovenského divadla* (*Yearbook of Slovak Theatre*) with a complete record of professional events. In addition, it publishes monographs on distinguished artists, catalogues of stage designers and occasional specialist publications. It also provides basic material on all professional productions in Slovakia (programmes, clippings, scripts, video and audio cassettes, visual documentation and photographs).

The 1960s and 1970s saw publication of a rather large number of historical and theoretical studies in specific areas as well as important overviews such as Rampák's *Dráma, divadlo, spoločnosť* (*Drama, Theatre, Society*, 1976) and *Cesta drámy* (*The Path of Drama*, 1984). Another major work is the *Encyklopédia dramatických umení Slovenska* (*Slovak Encyclopedia of Dramatic Arts*, 1989) which gives a comprehensive account of the facts, events and people which make up the Slovak theatre.

Theatre criticism is regularly featured in most Slovak daily and weekly newspapers as well as in specialized periodicals such as the monthly *Javisko* (*Stage*), which was known from 1925 as *The Slovak Amateur Player* and later underwent a series of name changes before adopting its present name in 1969. Other publications of note include *Slovenské Divadlo* (*Slovak Theatre*), a quarterly published since 1953; *Film a Divadlo* (*Film and Theatre*), a fortnightly founded in 1957; and *Kapitoly z dejín slovenského divadla* (*Studies in the History of the Slovak Theatre*), founded in 1967.

Jaroslav Blaho, Andrej Maťašík
Translated by Martin R. Ward

(See also CZECHOSLOVAKIA)

Further Reading

Boor, Ján. *Dialektika dejín divadla*. [Dialectic of the history of theatre]. Bratislava: Tatran, 1977. 196 pp.

Čavojský, Ladislav, and Vladimír Štefko. *Slovenské ochotnícke divadlo 1839–1980*. [Slovak amateur theatre 1839–1980]. Bratislava: Obzor, 1983. 508 pp.

Karvaš, Peter. *Priestory v divadle a divadlo v priestore*. [Space in theatre and theatre in space]. Bratislava: Tatran, 1984. 587 pp.

——. *K problematike estetickej kategórie komična*. [Towards the problematic of the aesthetic category of the comic]. Bratislava: Výskumný ústav kultúry, 1980. 166 pp.

——. *Reštrukturácia umeleckých potrieb a premeny dramatických umení*. [The restructuring of artistic needs and changes in dramatic art]. Bratislava: Výskumný ústav kultúry, 1982. 170 pp.

——. *Úvod do základných problémov divadla*. [Introduction to the basic problems of theatre]. Bratislava: Ústredie slovenských ochotníckych divadiel, 1948. 236 pp.

——. *Zamyšlení nad dramatem*. [Reflections on the drama]. Prague: Čs. spisovatel, 1964. 136 pp.

——. *Zamyšlení nad dramaturgií*. [Reflections on dramaturgy]. Prague: Čs. spisovatel, 1969. 138 pp.

——, and Ladislav Lajcha. *Súčasná slovenská scénografia*. [Contemporary Slovak stage design]. Bratislava: Pallas, 1977. 244 pp.

Kret, Anton, Jaroslav Blaho, Dagmar Hubová, and Ladislav Lajcha. *Slovenské národné divadlo*. [The Slovak National Theatre]. Bratislava: Tatran, 1990. 158 pp.

Pašteka, Július. *Estetické paralely umenia*. [The aesthetic parallels of art]. Bratislava: Veda, 1976. 432 pp.

Rampák, Zoltán. *Dráma, divadlo, spoločnost.* [Drama, theatre, society]. Bratislava: Tatran, 1976. 438 pp.

——. *Cesta drámy*. [The path of drama]. Bratislava: Tatran, 1984. 344 pp.

Ursínyová, Terézia. *Cesty operety*. [The paths of operetta]. Bratislava: Opus, 1982. 198 pp.

Various. *Encyklopédia dramatických umení Slovenska*. [Slovak encyclopedia of dramatic art]. Bratislava: Veda, 1989. 700 pp.

Various. *Pamätnica Slovenského národného divadla, Slovenské vydavateľstvo Krásnej literatúry*. [The scrapbook of the Slovak National Theatre]. Bratislava: Vydavateľstvo Krásnej literatúry, 1960. 522 pp.

SLOVENIA

One of the newest and smallest countries in central Europe, Slovenia is a former Yugoslav republic bordering Austria, Hungary, Croatia, Italy and the Mediterranean Sea. Covering some 20,250 square kilometres (7,800 square miles), it has a population of just over 2 million, of which 91 per cent are native Slovenes, just over 0.5 per cent are Hungarian, 0.1 per cent Italian and the remainder are mostly immigrants from other republics of the former Yugoslavia. The capital of the republic is Ljubljana (300,000 inhabitants), a city with all the usual national foundations – an Academy of Sciences and Arts, a university, theatres, opera house, two philharmonic orchestras and various art galleries. Other major cities are Maribor, Celje, Kranj, Koper, Novo mesto, and Nova Gorica.

The Slavic forebears of today's Slovenes settled in the area between Vienna, Salzburg, Linz, Trieste and Zagreb some time after AD 500; the first Slovene state of Carantania (with its centre in Klagenfurt in today's Austria) dates from AD 620. The Slovenes accepted the overlordship of the Frankish Empire and the Christian religion, and for a thousand years were submerged in the Holy Roman Empire of Charlemagne until its fall in the early nineteenth century, and then, until the end of World War I, in the Austro-Hungarian Empire. In 1918, they joined the Croats and Serbs in forming the Kingdom of Yugoslavia which existed until 1941. During World War II, Slovenia was occupied by the Germans, Italians and Hungarians. After the war, Slovenia remained part of Yugoslavia, which, following the example of the Soviet Union, became a socialist federal state. After the disintegration of Yugoslavia in 1991, Slovenia declared its independence and in 1992, with its acceptance into the United Nations, its international sovereignty. A year after the first free,

multi-party elections, Slovenia obtained its first constitution under which it became a democratic republic with a multi-party, bicameral parliament.

The ninth-century Freising manuscripts are the earliest preserved writings in Slovene history. The first Slovene printed books (catechisms, grammars and translations of the Bible) date from the mid-sixteenth century. The earliest Slovene writer was Primož Trubar (1508–86), a Protestant, though Slovenia remained for the most part Catholic. The beginnings of Slovene theatre date back to the seventeenth century – plays performed by students of the Jesuit college in Ljubljana between 1657 and 1670, among which *Igra o paradižu* (*A Play about Paradise*) is particularly well known. The highpoint of Slovene Passion plays is considered to be *Škofjeloški pasijon* (*The Škofja Loka Passion*, 1721).

Slovene secular theatre and drama was born in 1789 when the Enlightenment writer and historian Anton Tomaž Linhart (1756–95) presented *Županova Micka* (*Mary the Mayor's Daughter*), a translation of the German comedy *Die Feldmühle* (*The Mill in the Field*) by playwright Franz Richter on the stage of the Stanovsko gledališče (Guild Theatre) in Ljubljana, with the help of amateur actors. Linhart was also the author of the first original Slovene play, *Ta veseli dan ali Matiček se ženi* (*Oh What a Happy Day or Little Matthew Marries*), inspired by Beaumarchais's *La Folle Journée ou le mariage de Figaro*.

In 1867, the poet, writer and literary critic, Fran Levstik (1831–77), founded the Dramatic Society in Ljubljana, an institution which combined concern for indigenous drama, theatre training and professional performance. Its head was Ignacij Borštnik (1858–1919), an actor and

Janez Pipan's 1992 Ljubljana Municipal Theatre production of Goethe's *Stella*, designed by Dušan Milavec and Boris Benčič.
Photo: Tone Stojko.

director. After the turn of the century, other theatres were founded in Trieste (1902), Maribor (1909) and Celje (1911).

The years between World Wars I and II saw the emergence of Slovene professional theatre. After 1945, an Academy for the Art of Acting was founded in Ljubljana (now the Academy for Theatre, Radio, Film and Television). A number of other theatres were founded at the same time: Prešeren Theatre in Kranj (1945), Mestno gledališče ljubljansko (Ljubljana Municipal Theatre, 1951), Slovensko mladinsko gledališče (Slovene Youth Theatre, 1955) and two puppet theatres. A series of fringe theatres were also established, first in the 1950s and then in the 1970s – Eksperimentalno gledališče (Experimental Theatre, 1955), Oder 57 (Stage 57, 1957), Ad hoc Theatre (1958), Glej (1970, still working) and Pekarna (1972).

During the 1980s and early 1990s, there was a steady growth of independent productions.

Vasja Predan

Structure of the National Theatre Community

In 1993, there were nine theatres with permanent companies, technical staffs and administrators maintained by the state. These included two puppet theatres in Ljubljana and Maribor. There was also a tenth professional Slovene theatre in Trieste, Italy, serving the Slovene minority there and having close creative links with theatres in Slovenia. This company, however, was operating in the organizational and administrative framework of the Italian state.

Most of these institutional theatres operate as repertory companies with subscription systems of four to six premières each season. The

Slovene Youth Theatre, and Drama Slovenskega narodnega gledališča v Mariboru (Drama Company of the Slovene National Theatre in Maribor), however, abandoned repertory in favour of limited-run productions.

All the national theatres are organized along a similar model varying in size from twenty full-time actors and fifty employees to the Drama Company of the Slovene National Theatre in Ljubljana which has a permanent acting company of forty to fifty and 130 employees.

The state guarantees each theatre's entire budget and, with only one exception (Kranj), this is their only source of funding. In 1992, theatres received the equivalent of US$7.5 million with the smallest theatre receiving some US$200,000 and the largest – the Drama Company of the Slovene National Theatre in Ljubljana – receiving US$1.7 million. In addition to its normal budget, the state also allows all theatres to use the entire income from the sale of tickets, and this provides an additional 5 to 10 per cent on top of state subsidies.

Since 1980 Slovenia has seen more and more independent theatre productions created outside the state institutions. These have been brought together mainly by directors and choreographers who hire actors, dancers and performers – sometimes freelance artists, sometimes students from theatre school, sometimes even actors from the national theatres – for varying periods of time. This form of theatre production is primarily concentrated in Ljubljana. Some of these *ad-hoc* groups have their own, more or less regular space available; others must rent stages and auditoriums. Projects sometimes even take place in non-theatrical venues.

In the early 1990s the state tried to provide more planned and intensive support for these independent productions through subsidies which cover 50 per cent of the costs. Individual projects which must be registered in advance in an annual competition. In 1992, state subsidies for independent theatre, dance theatre, puppetry and multimedia projects ranged from US$2,000 to US$20,000, a total of US$170,000.

Since the early 1960s, there has been a regular annual festival of all Slovene theatres in Maribor called the Borštnik Meeting. At this festival, a series of national awards is also given out. As well, a Ring of Honour is bestowed on an actor for lifetime achievement. Another major festival is the Week of Slovene Drama in Kranj – focused on Slovene plays – and a prize is given for the best original Slovene play.

There are about 250 working actors in Slovenia, the majority permanently employed in individual theatres. Once hired, they are guaranteed long-term professional, social and material security. Less than 10 per cent of the country's actors work freelance. The state also guarantees funds for their social security. This does not apply to other theatre creators (directors, playwights, scenographers and costumiers), who, according to theatre regulations, are not permanently employed and are contracted by theatres for individual productions.

Actors, directors and other arts professionals have their own associations, as do technicians. There is also a Society of Theatre Critics and Theatre Science. Playwrights do not have their own association; many work in other professions and may also be members of the Writers' Association.

The price of theatre tickets is intentionally kept low and only rarely exceeds US$5. Theatre tickets are twice as expensive as those for cinemas.

The image of Slovene theatre would not be complete without a mention of the 600 or so permanent and occasional amateur groups. For the most part, they are organized and linked through the Union of Cultural Organizations, which also arranges a number of annual festivals.

Albert Kos, Simon Kardum

Artistic Profile

Companies

Slovenia has two 'national' companies – one in Ljubljana and the other in Maribor. Both are large institutional, state-supported groups. The Slovene National Theatre in Ljubljana is the older of the two, founded in 1867, while the Maribor company was founded in 1919. In both cases, the sense of 'national' has been very strong. Both have kept to traditional 'national' theatre repertoires – equal shares of domestic and foreign plays, modern plays and classics.

The Slovene National Theatre in Maribor's 1991 production of Slavko Grum's *An Incident in the Town of Goga*, directed and designed by Damir Zlatar-Frey.

The Ljubljana company has been the larger and more traditional of the two, especially since World War II. Usually boasting the country's best actors, the company's most creative period was between 1961 and 1969 when it was headed by Bojan Štih (1923–86). During that time, the company was adventurous in its explorations of new forms of expression. Primarily moving toward greater theatricality and stylization and away from psychological realism, the company even experimented with the ideas of Peter Brook and the Theatre of the Absurd. Its production of Brendan Behan's Irish play, *The Hostage* (1963) was one of its highpoints, while its most innovative director was Mile Korun (b. 1928).

The Maribor company was at its strongest after 1989, under the direction of Tomaž Pandur (b. 1963), when it began to stage huge spectacles in which dramatic literature is pushed aside and monumental, fantastic, inventive scenic elements become dominant. Music and dance have become part of its dramatic approach which tends to focus around well-known myths. Perhaps its best production during this latter period was a spectacular version of *Faust* (after Goethe).

Other institutional groups of note include the Stalno slovensko gledališče v Trstu (Trieste Permanent Slovene Theatre, founded in 1902), the Slovensko ljudsko gledališče v Celju (Celje Popular Slovene Theatre, 1911), the Mestno gledališče ljubljansko (Ljubljana Municipal Theatre, 1951) and the Prešernovo gledališče v Kranju (Kranj Prešeren Theatre, 1945).

Among the most interesting of the non-institutional companies is a group currently calling itself the Kozmokinetični kabinet Noordung (Noordung Cosmo-kinetic Cabinet). The company regularly changes its name, often from production to production. Hosted for periods of time by the institutional theatres, the group's continuity is provided by both its artistic director – Dragan Živadinov (b. 1960) – and its ongoing mystic, mythic, almost cult-like atmosphere.

The Noordung group is very much part of what is known as the Neue Slowenische Kunst (New Slovenian Art) movement, created in the early 1980s. The name was deliberately chosen to be provocative. Because it is a German name, it sets up a defensive reaction in Slovenes and sets off traumatic memories of both Nazi and Austrian occupation. Its goal was to encourage debate about nationalism, the relationship between art and authority. Structured in a kind

of military hierarchy into three artistic areas – music, visual arts and theatre – Neue Slowenische Kunst music tends to be heroic, militant and barbaric punk while its visual arts aspects tend towards the heroic and officially optimistic mentality of both Nazi and communist art. In its theatrical manifestation it ranges from Wagnerian *Gesamtkunstwerk* to patriotic Slovene machismo, from Appian and Craigian concepts to futurism, constructivism and the theatre of Robert Wilson.

Probably the most interesting performance of this unique genre has been *Krst pod Triglavom* (*Baptism Beneath the Mountain of Triglav*, 1986) dealing with the Christianization of Slovenia.

Another explicitly provocative, sharply focused company is Koreodrama (established in 1987). Inspired by the Pole Tadeusz Kantor's Theatre of Death and stressing physicality, mime, fantasy, the grotesque and even psychoanalysis, Koreodrama stages major European plays, usually quite radically interpreted. Among its most interesting productions have been Genet's *Les Bonnes* (*The Maids*, 1989) and *Prihajajo* (*They're Coming*, 1992) after Ionesco's *Les Chaises* (*The Chairs*).

The Betontanc Company (currently calling itself the Intrusion of Reality Theatre, founded in 1988) uses dance to evoke an explosive, even dangerous atmosphere. Its most interesting production has been *Za vsako besedo cekin* (*A Gold Coin for Every Word*, 1992). Another independent group is Helios (founded in 1988). Using unusual, bizarre and very complicated sets in an environmental style, its strongest production was *Brigade lepote* (*Brigades of Beauty*, 1990). The Ana Monro Company (established in 1981) is another group which deals with popular forms including circus. The company does a kind of contemporary *commedia dell'arte* in such shows as *San Remo* (1992).

The history of fringe and alternative groups is much more recent than the history of institutional theatres. Groups such as Oder 57 (established in 1957) began to emerge in the 1950s. In 1964, the communist regime shut it down when it was determined that its performance of *Topla greda* (*Hotbed*) by Marjan Rožanc (1930–90) began to move away from the Theatre of the Absurd in favour of a more direct criticism of the authorities. Another group, the Glej Company, was founded in 1970 and quickly moved away from text. Its most productive period was in the 1970s and its most successful production

The 1990 Betontanc Company production of Matjaž Pograjc's *Poets With No Pockets*, directed and designed by Matjaž Pograjc. Photo: Diego Andrés Gómez.

was *Grenki sadeži pravice* (*Bitter Fruits of Justice*, 1974) by Milan Jesih (b. 1950). In the 1990s, it functioned mainly as an independent producer offering its organization to other groups. One last group that should be noted is the Pekarna Company (1972–7) which during its short existence dealt primarily with ritualistic theatre and was influenced by the ideas of Jerzy Grotowski. Its most interesting production was *Tako tako* (*Just So*, 1974), after a short story by the Serbian author Mirko Kovač.

Lado Kralj

Dramaturgy

Dušan Jovanović (b. 1939) established himself as one of Slovenia's major playwrights in the late 1970s. He writes from an explicitly theatrical perspective, as a result of being both a playwright and a director. Because his plays are devised with a view to their practical staging, they tend to be unusually condensed in language. They also retain a concreteness, a

vividness of individual scenes and situations and thus, even in entirely rhetorical passages, work effectively in performance. Jovanović often takes his own earlier stories and reworks them for the stage. *Znamke, nakar še Emilija* (*Stamps, and then Emily*, 1969), the first work which established his name as a playwright, is a detective story parody, reminiscent of Theatre of the Absurd. His play, *Norci* (*Lunatics*, 1970), parodies political plays in which revolutionaries are blasphemously substituted with clinical lunatics. This trend in Jovanović's dramatic approach is given final shape in a play with the long title, *Igrajte tumor v glavi ali onesnaženje zraka* (*Play Out the Tumour in the Head*, 1971). All the author's interests are gathered here: absurdity, parody, sensitivity, lunacy, magic and theatricality. The subject of this script is the theatre itself in which the theatre's organization, creativity and, finally, its very essence comes into crisis. The theatre here is clearly the author's metaphor for society, for life. All these scripts show the author's hidden revolt against communist single-mindedness. The basic nihilism with which these texts are imbued is the author's answer to the false, forced and unconvincing 'constructiveness' of the prevailing regime.

Jasnovidka ali dan mrtvih (*The Clairvoyant Woman or All Saints' Day*, 1989) is similar in its approach. A new dimension is added in *Zid, Jezero* (*A Wall, A Lake*, 1989), in which the author, apparently sincerely, looks into the genre of sentimental comedy.

There is another side to Jovanović's dramaturgy, a side without any kind of ironic or nihilistic distance. A kind of documentary drama, using Brechtian techniques, it attempts to expose the crimes of a particular social system directly. Its best example is *Osvoboditev Skopja* (*The Liberation of Skopje*, 1977), about the terrors of occupation during World War II, and *Karamazovi* (*The Karamazovs*, 1980), based on Dostoevsky's novel, which deals with the fate of people accused of political crimes under the former Yugoslav state.

Drago Jančar (b. 1948) is equally critical of the system, although by other means. His plays are built on historical or biographical material, mostly from the nineteenth and twentieth centuries. The protagonists are usually intellectuals who deliberately antagonize the totalitarian regime they are living under. Society is symbolized by a pig farm in *Disident Arnož in njegovi* (*Dissident Arnož and His Followers*, 1982), by a lunatic asylum, in *Veliki briljantni valček* (*The Great Brilliant Waltz*, 1985) and by a prison in

Dedalus (1988). He explores the ethical attitudes of intellectuals in terms of their fragility and dubiousness in *Klementov padec* (*Klement's Fall*, 1988), based on the life and death of a well-known mountain climber and university philosophy lecturer.

Another playwright of note is Rudi Šeligo (b. 1935). Mainly concerned with the idea of the eternal woman, he attributes to her special characteristics. He sees woman as self-willed, nonconformist, irrational and full of mystical energy. His powerful women try to survive, unsuccessfully, at the edge of the male world in such plays as *Čarovnica iz Zgornje Davče* (*The Witch from Upper Davča*, 1977), *Svatba* (*The Marriage*, 1980), *Ana* (1984) and *Volčji čas ljubezni* (*The Wolfish Time of Love*, 1988).

Dominik Smole (1929–92) was long considered the best of Slovenia's post-World War II playwrights and in some ways the estimate was still holding in the 1990s. Most of his major works were published in the 1960s. He started off as a romantic of sorts in *Potovanje v Koromandijo* (*Journey to Coromandia*, 1956), which at the same time was existential in nature. He achieved his power, however, in highly poetic works closer to the grotesque in dramatic expression. Among the most important of Smole's plays are *Antigone* (1960), a provocative variant on the classical myth with clear references to post-revolutionary Slovene experience; *Krst pri Savici* (*Baptism by the Savica*, 1969), which paraphrases and extends the poem of the same name by France Prešeren (1800–49), a famous Slovene poet who wrote of the forced Christianization of the Slovenes; and an important short play about suicide, *Zlata čeveljčka* (*Little Gold Shoes*, 1982).

Primož Kozak (1929–81) came from the same critical generation as Smole and was also connected with the magazine *Perspektive* (founded in 1960, suppressed in 1964). Kozak was a political playwright researching the tragic conflict between history and the individual, necessity and freedom. His ideas are similar to those in the existentialist dramas of Sartre. In some of his plays, Kozak deals with the internal struggles of Stalinism, as in *Dialogi* (*Dialogues*, 1961), with liberation fighters during World War II, as in *Afera* (*The Affair*, 1961), professors of a university in a communist regime, as in *Kongres* (*Congress*, 1968) or rebels gathering around a charismatic Latin American leader, as in *Legenda o svetem Che* (*The Legend of Saint Che*, 1969).

Lado Kralj

Directors, Directing and Productional Styles

Mile Korun is without doubt Slovenia's most important director. Working continuously from the 1950s through to the 1990s, Korun has directed virtually every major Slovene play of the period as well as a steady stream of Slovene and world classics. Slovenia's greatest dramatist, Ivan Cankar (1876–1918), whose works date back to the beginning of the twentieth century, is one of Korun's favourites and Korun has become Cankar's foremost interpreter. Many of his productions of Cankar's works have, in fact, provoked angry responses and even accusations of committing literary blasphemy.

Korun is essentially a poetic director with a tendency to create a somewhat melancholic atmosphere in his work. At the same time, he is able to provide an intellectual, ironic or even psychological interpretation to many plays. His sets are often filled with symbolic props (such as umbrellas) to the point of being somewhat obsessive. Probably his best known production is Cankar's *Hlapci* (*The Bondsmen*) staged in 1980.

Playwright Dušan Jovanović has been directing since the early 1970s when he started in the fringe theatre Glej. The radical aesthetics and ideas of the fringe became familiar in all his later works, even his 'institutional' productions. There is, for example, a marked influence of Artaud's Theatre of Cruelty and, associated with it, the study of extreme psychological states (dreams and hallucinations). Jovanović builds his productions around his actors' psychophysical abilities and he has the capacity to take them even along the borders of hysteria. He has also become known for his interpretation of classic world drama as well as the work of Slovene playwrights. His most important production is *Blodnje* (*Wanderings*, 1986) after Dostoevsky's novel, *Possessed*.

The front man of Slovenia's neo-avant-garde theatre is Dragan Živadinov, whose radical aesthetic and political approaches in the 1980s began a fundamental transformation of the Slovenian theatre. Connected to the Neue Slowenische Kunst movement, he tends to work on the frontiers of theatre aesthetics, following the lead of Ferdo Delak (1905–68), the head of the Slovene avant-garde in the 1920s. In his early work, he tried to create a monumental and critical union between theatre and the state, an approach which was not deeply appreciated by the state. In the early 1990s, his cosmic obsession

Tomaž Pandur's 1990 Slovene National Theatre in Maribor production of Goethe's *Faust*, designed by Marko Japelj.
Photo: Andelo Božac.

has been Space Theatre based on his own studies and those of the Slovene pioneer of space studies, Herman Potočnik-Noordung (1892–1929).

Croatian-born Damir Zlatar-Frey (b. 1955) began his career in the 1980s as a choreographer, later developing a directing style similar to that of Tadeusz Kantor. It is thus essentially non-verbal. In the process of creating a production, he gradually moves further and further away from text. It is for this reason that he chooses works that are generally well known to the audience. His work with actors is rooted in mime and he often works on psychologically profound levels in fields such as the erotic, the aggressive and the pathological. Thematically, his productions evoke a personal, morbid view of a crumbling central Europe. His most characteristic production was *Dogodek v mestu Gogi* (*An Incident in the Town of Goga*, 1991) by Slavko Grum (1901–49).

Janez Pipan (b. 1956) began his efforts towards 'total theatre' at the end of the 1970s, introducing dance, singing, elements of mime, and even acrobatics. He later added an interest in existential and ethical questions to the mix. Because he sees theatre as an ethical institution on the one hand, and as a purveyor of sensual theatrical autonomy on the other, his productions create an interesting and very exciting tension, a verification of the immediate, of the spirit of the time. This could be seen in his productions of contemporary works as well as Slovene and world classics, among them his 1988 staging of *Klementov padec* (*Klement's Fall*) by Drago Jančar.

Still another director of note is Vito Taufer (b. 1959) who began his career as a director in the Slovene Youth Theatre. One of his first important productions was *Class Enemy* by Nigel Williams, produced in 1982. From this realistic beginning he moved into the poetic, imaginative world of dreams and children's stories using music (*Alice in Wonderland*, 1986, based on Lewis Carroll). Taufer's directorial approach has a comic-book spirit and a critical, amused distance even when he deals with adaptations of classical texts. It is typified by irony, black humour and playfulness.

The iconographic fantasy of Tomaž Pandur is unusually luxurious, imaginative and unbridled. It is necessary to understand his productions above all as monumental, gigantic movable icons, in which the stage machinery, the sumptuousness of the materials, colour and light are most important. The actor's contribution as well as the text tend to be pushed into the background. Pandur produces mega-projects based on well-known mythical texts (*Faust*, *Hamlet* and *The Divine Comedy*). He also has a unique grasp of aggressive marketing and promotion and a real capacity to lure the public into the theatre.

Other important directors of note are Slavko Jan (1904–87), Jože Babič (b. 1917), France Jamnik (1921–92), Žarko Petan (b. 1929), Dušan Mlakar (b. 1939) and Zvone Šedlbauer (b. 1944). Among the younger directors, Matjaž Berger (b. 1963), Emil Hrvatin (b. 1964) and Vlado Repnik (b. 1961) should be mentioned.

Vasja Predan, Lado Kralj, Simon Kardum

Music Theatre

A number of theatres began to use music in the 1980s, as it is used in film, while the Noordung Cosmo-kinetic Cabinet and a number of other companies have used music more autonomously, as if performances were taking place in a concert hall or in a disco (this mainly applies to two rock groups, Laibach and Boghesia).

Variety theatre has always used music to create a 'subculture social atmosphere'. The Ana Monro Theatre is quite typical in this respect.

Frane Milčinski-Ježek (1914–63) was the earliest modern Slovene cabaret artist, performing as a comic singer in the 1950s and 1960s. The tradition has been continued by Jerca Mrzel (b. 1945) and Vita Mavrič-Ruič (b. 1965) among others.

Simon Kardum

Dance Theatre

Ballet has existed in Slovenia since 1918 as an autonomous performing art. From 1960 to 1972, the Ballet Ensemble of the National Theatre in Ljubljana was led by choreographer Henrik Neubauer (b. 1929), a period notable for productions of *Firebird* (1962), *Romeo and Juliet* (1968), *Othello* (1960) and *Spartacus* (1972).

The coupling of dramatic theatre and dance/movement is a relatively new phenomenon, however, experiencing a real upsurge only in the 1980s. Such dance theatre forms developed in two directions. The first was the intrusion of dramatic narration into dance structure and this goes back all the way to the strong tradition of Slovene dance expressionism in the 1920s and 1930s, especially by Meta Vidmar (1899–1975) and the couple, Pia (b. 1908) and Pino (b. 1907) Mlakar, who transmitted the experience gained with Jacques-Dalcroze, Laban and the Wigmans. It was their students who introduced movement into explicitly dramatic media and had a direct influence on the prosperity of dance theatre in the 1980s.

Slovene theatre began to be more intensively creative in this area at the end of the 1970s when directors and choreographers began to work together. This applied equally to productions at the national theatres and independent productions. Kinetic modes of expression were first and most clearly established in the Slovene Youth Theatre where the specific approach of a choreographer to a play enabled closer contact between words and movement. The cooperation between director Ljubiša Ristić (b. 1947 in Serbia) and choreographer Nada Kokotović (b. 1945 in Croatia) in the pivotal post-modern production of *Missa in A-Minor* (1981) is typical of the approach.

The whole image of Slovene theatre began to be fundamentally transformed by dance in 1985 when a group of choreographers and dancers founded Plesni teater Ljubljana (Dance Theatre Ljubljana). The majority of choreographers and directors who dominated the dance theatre scene of the 1990s staged productions. Perhaps the best known is Ksenija Hribar (b. 1938), one of the founders of Dance Theatre Ljubljana and for many years a dancer and associate of the London School of Contemporary Dance and a movement consultant in more than a hundred dramatic productions. Her production *Alpsko sanjarjenje* (*Alpine Dream*, 1986) parodied the Slovene Alpine folk mentality.

Damir Zlatar-Frey was originally a dancer and a student of the Zagreb dance teacher Ana Maleti. Later a choreographer of such productions as *Metastaza Laibach* (*Metastasis Laibach*, 1985) – a production performed in mud and dust to the raucous music of the group Laibach – he entered the world of dramatic theatre with the founding of Koreodrama in 1986. He relies heavily on a dark expressionist style and symbolism in his search for acting expression.

Another choreographer working in this way is Maja Milenović-Workman (b. 1959), who choreographed *Adaggio ma non tropo* (1987), based on Beckett, for the Dance Theatre Ljubljana. Her work with director Tomaž Pandur has been extensive: *Scheherazade* (1988), *Faust* (1990) and *Hamlet* (1991), establishing an equality between choreographer and director, even in the text-based institutional theatres.

Dragan Živadinov brings together many elements of the historical avant-garde – Meyerhold's constructivist biomechanics, futurist mechanical and plastic ballet, and Bauhaus. His work has turned Slovene modern theatre heavily toward the use of visual, spectacular and non-verbal means, especially his 'retrogradist happenings' and his 'drama and ballet observatories'.

Matjaž Pograjc (b. 1967) founded the Betontanc company in 1990 and from their first production brought together contemporary dance and theatre in a dynamic, explosive and dangerous way. Utilizing the narrative characteristic of dramatic theatre, Betontanc productions are marked by a childlike freedom, a playfulness and a simple and direct dramaturgical treatment. Among their major works are *Pesniki brez žepov* (*Poets With No Pockets*, 1990), *Romeo and Juliet* (1991) and *Za vsako besedo cekin* (*A Gold Coin for Every Word*, 1992). The company has drawn considerable critical acclaim both at home and on tour.

Among more recent creators, Matjaž Farić (b. 1965) combines pure dance with elements such as speech, projection and singing, most explicitly in his production of *Veter, pesek in zvezde* (*Wind, Sand and Stars*, 1991), based on the novel *Terre des hommes* (1939) by Saint-Exupéry. As movement consultant, he co-created a number of productions with Vito Taufer: *Odisej in sin* (*Odysseus and Son*, 1991), written by his father Veno Taufer (b. 1933), *Kraljevo* (1992) and *Timon of Athens* (1992).

Tanja Zgonc (b. 1959) put her experience in mime, contact improvisation and *Butoh* dance into practice as a choreographer in her production of *Pot* (*The Way*, 1991), as well as cooperating in a number of productions in the national theatres. Her application of *Butoh* is most resounding in *Don Juan na psu* (*Don Juan Defamed*), written and directed by Dušan Jovanović in 1991.

The use of live singing and music, in addition to dangerous acrobatic elements and other movement and acting skills is typical of the work of Iztok Kovač (b. 1962) in such productions as *Kako sem ujel sokola* (*How I Caught a Hawk*, 1991).

Simon Kardum, Henrik Neubauer

Theatre for Young Audiences

Interest in theatre for young audiences started in Slovenia in the early nineteenth century with a presentation of *Tinček Petelinček* (based on the German author August von Kotzebue) performed in 1803 by Ljubljana amateurs. From then until the end of the century, though, only three more 'fairytales with singing' intended for children appeared. In the early twentieth century, Christmas shows by professional theatres became very popular and were most often aimed at young audiences. In the years between World Wars I and II, theatres also began to provide for teenage audiences, mainly calling on scripts by domestic authors such as Fran Milčinski (1867–1932) and Pavel Golia (1887–1959).

After World War II, however, this development became systematic, and it took two directions: first, an amateur-based and government-supported series of educational performances organized by both Pionirski dom in Ljubljana, directed by Draga Ahačič (b. 1924), and the Association of Cultural Organizations of Slovenia; and second, the creation of a professional theatre for young audiences in 1955, that is the Slovene Youth Theatre, with a permanent company.

The Slovene Youth Theatre has greatly changed its concept since 1975: the focus has shifted from performances for children to performances for teenagers and, at the same time, for adults. It has developed an individual, provocative style of performance, based mainly on strictly disciplined collective acting, as well as on a studied exploration of contemporary sensibilities. The most interesting productions have been *Alice in Wonderland* (1986, based on Lewis Carroll) and *Scheherazade* (1989) by Ivo Svetina (b. 1948).

Vito Taufer's 1986 Slovene Youth Theatre production of *Alice in Wonderland* (based on Lewis Carroll) designed by Rae Smith. Photo: Tone Stojko.

Since the late 1980s, other professional theatres have been including productions for children in their repertoires as well.

Rapa Šuklje

Puppet Theatre

Though the first professional Slovene puppet theatre was founded in 1910 by Milan Klemenčič (1875–1957), the real flowering of puppetry activities came only after World War II. In 1948, the Lutkovno gledališče Ljubljana (Ljubljana Puppet Theatre) was founded and in 1993 was still the most important Slovene puppetry institution. It has its own theatre with three stages ranging from sixty to 210 seats. It also boasts a large puppet museum. Jože Pengov (1916–68) ran the theatre in the 1950s. From the 1970s, the company staged many specially written scripts by Slovene writers, often poets.

The Jože Pengov Puppet Theatre was founded in 1954 and has been a professional group since 1968. Led by Helena Zajc (b. 1944), it does not have its own premises and spends most of its time on tour. The inclusion of live actors along with puppets is a characteristic of this theatre.

The Maribor Puppet Theatre has been operating since 1974 and has its own 200-seat auditorium. TV-Slovenia has also regularly programmed puppet broadcasts as part of its children's programming. In the 1960s, it even had a special puppet studio which was run by the popular puppeteer, Nace Simončič (b. 1918).

The most important contemporary puppet director is Edi Majaron (b. 1940). All elements of his productions (animation, script, music, design, even live actors) are rooted to his artistic vision of the value of the puppet in theatre. Majaron also directs a great deal outside Slovenia.

The couple, Maja (b. 1954) and Brane (b. 1951) Solce, are the only members of the Papilu Puppet Theatre; they work with paper-puppets as a kind of 'object theatre'.

Helena Zajc tends towards experimental work; in particular, she tries to achieve effective interaction between puppets and live actors. Other important directors in this field are Cveto Sever (b. 1948), who also builds on the interaction between puppets and players; Jelena Sitar (b. 1959) and Sašo Jovanović (b. 1965).

Slovene puppeteers took part in the creation of the world puppet organization UNIMA in 1929 and a number of professional meetings have since taken place in Ljubljana. Mention should also be made of puppetry on an amateur level, which is widespread. There was a creative puppetry workshop in the 1960s in Pionirski dom in Ljubljana run by Lojze Kovačič (b. 1928), who also happens to be one of Slovenia's best contemporary novelists. Many professional puppeteers got their start in that workshop.

Edi Majaron

Design

Slovene theatre began to deal with set design as an autonomous element only in the period after World War I. It was then that directors began to comprehend that the set had its own conceptual dimension and from that time scenographers began to appear. The years between World Wars I and II were marked in this area by the work of painters Ivan Vavpotič (1877–1943) and August Černigoj (1898–1985) and architects Ernest Franz (1906–81) and Bojan Stupica (1910–70). The latter two were also active after World War II and their example motivated many younger designers. The most prominent of these were Viktor Molka (b. 1923; also a director), Uroš Vagaja (1920–70), Niko Matul (1928–88), Sveta Jovanović (b. 1927) and Meta Hočevar (b. 1942).

Molka and Matul, along with Stupica, were the first to abandon realistic spatial reality and use only indicated interiors and exteriors with suggestions, ingenious details and much styliza-tion. Vagaja added humorous or gently ironic stresses to his sets while Jovanović broke the stage area into sections achieving rather unconventional expressions.

Designer Meta Hočevar has covered a wide range of theatrical activities. She has very successfully directed, taught at the Academy of Theatre, Radio, Film and Television in Ljubljana, and, as an architect, has designed several theatres. Her scenography is expressive and distinct, consistently avoiding the traditional principles of the Italian stage. She uses unusual materials, including aluminium foil. Other designers who have turned to a metaphoric treatment of the total stage area include Marko Japelj (b. 1961) and Tomaž Marolt (b. 1953).

Monumental sets are a popular phenomenon in Slovene theatres since *Baptism Beneath the Mountain of Triglav* in which director Dragan Živadinov included huge retrogradist paintings. Japelj is an architect who has consistently implemented the boldly conceived neo-rococo visions of Tomaž Pandur through a variety of spatial approaches. In *Scheherazade*, for instance, there was a movable central stage which withdrew from or approached the auditorium; in *Faust*, the frame of the set was a leaning frontal section of a castle (with rooms as scenes/stages), while in *Carmen* (1992) an extended oval covered the orchestra pit and a large part of the stalls.

Marolt worked with Vito Taufer on a cinematographic *Timon of Athens*, creating fast scene changes by the simulation of film/video spot techniques. Marolt regularly achieves a relatively quick building of his sets through a combination of revolving stage, movable horizontals (tracks) and verticals (lifts).

Lighting design has been established as an important conceptual, symbolic and visual element since the 1970s, above all with the very visual theatre of the 1980s and 1990s, and in dance theatre. Among the most important lighting designers are Igor Berginc (b. 1957), Franci Safran (b. 1943) and Miran Šušteršič (b. 1960).

In mask design, one of the few to reach beyond the usual illustrative convention is the film and theatre mask-maker, Aljana Hajdinjak (b. 1961). She replaces the faces of the actors and dancers with painted canvases which are often painted as poster artifacts.

There are also several important designers of posters and theatre programmes – Matjaž Vipotnik (b. 1944), the group Novi kolektivizem (New Collectivism), and the group Imitacija života (Imitation of Life).

Vasja Predan, Simon Kardum

Theatre Space and Architecture

The proscenium stage is the basic form of Slovene theatre space. The first public theatre building, the Guild Theatre, was built in 1765 in Ljubljana. This was followed by theatres in other towns (Idrija, Maribor, Ptuj, Koper, Celje, Piran). The Deželno gledališče (Provincial Theatre) in Ljubljana (today's Opera House, seating 550), built in 1892 in the representative neo-Renaissance style, embodied the peak of Slovene theatre architecture in the period of the Habsburg monarchy. Toward the end of the nineteenth century, amateur auditoriums and *narodni domovi* (national houses) began to be built along with professional theatre buildings, which, as focuses for the national awakening, played an important role in the development of Slovene theatre art.

A new flowering was seen only after World War II. Newly founded professional theatres adapted some of the existing amateur auditoriums; the professional theatre of the Slovene minority in Italy obtained a new 'cultural centre' (550 seats) in Trieste in 1964; a number of new municipal cultural centres sprang up intended for amateurs, and in 1978–82, Cankarjev dom (Cankar House) was built in Ljubljana according to the designs of architect Edvard Ravnikar (b. 1907). A multipurpose cultural and congress centre, it features five auditoriums, including a 250-seat 'round hall', constructed as a typical theatre-in-the-round.

In 1993, new theatre buildings in Maribor (850 seats) and in Nova Gorica (370 seats) became the most modern cultural facilities in Slovenia.

Summer theatres (in Ljubljana and Ruše) appeared in the period between World Wars I and II and multiplied after 1945. The most important is the Festival Ljubljana hall (1,200 seats), built in 1955, which is also fitted with a movable canvas roof in case of rain.

In addition to these architectural spaces, there is also a variety of forms of environmental theatre: street theatre, such as is performed by the Ana Monro Theatre; amateur productions of ethnic Slovenes in Austrian Carinthia on a folk stage; and various 'happenings' which border between theatre and the plastic arts. The neo-avant-garde group, OHO, began this latter work at the end of the 1960s and became established in the 1980s. Performers also regularly use non-theatre environments, mainly Ljubljana art galleries.

Smaller theatre buildings are located across Slovenia, in both large (Ljubljana, Maribor) and small towns (Celje, Nova Gorica, Kranj) and have very varied capacities (from 180 to 550 seats). Because of old and inappropriate building design, their auditoriums are relatively modest and their stages small and inadequately equipped. None of them provides what could be considered contemporary standards. Apart from the Trieste cultural centre, only buildings erected since 1980 can be considered to be satisfactory theatre spaces.

The large hall of Cankar House (1,500 seats) is the largest auditorium, while temporary and permanent auditoriums of independent theatre companies range between twenty and 200 seats.

Since 1955, Slovene theatre art has used its theatre spaces in a variety of ways. In traditional theatres, the playing area has been increased by extending over the orchestra pit and even over seats in the stalls. The spaces of some of the institutional theatres, however, are unique: the vaulted lower auditorium of the Slovene Youth

Theatre, which directors often use as a simultaneous stage, and the second stage of the National Theatre in Maribor – a Minorite Church. Independent theatre productions were the first to implement and develop alternative performance technologies and create non-traditional relationships between acting areas and the auditoriums. Adapted cellars and warehouses (such as those used by Koreodrama and Glej) require chamber performances while some smaller centres (France Prešeren Cultural Art Society and Klub K4), force a kind of intimacy on the audience.

Viktor Molka, Simon Kardum

Training

There is only one regular theatre school in Slovenia. Part of the University of Ljubljana, it is called the Academy for Theatre, Radio, Film and Television and was founded in 1945. Study is organized over four departments: acting, theatre and radio directing, film and television directing, and theory of drama. Subsidiary subjects under the rubric of acting include speech and movement as well as courses in singing, ballet and acrobatics. Under theory of drama, personnel are trained who will provide theoretical and historical backup for productions in the theatres.

Training on all four levels is closely connected with practical work both within the framework of the school and outside it in regular theatres. A system of scholarships also exists so that

students can be provided with monthly financial support by regional theatres in return for a commitment to spend a specified number of years with the company after graduating. That said, it is difficult to get financial support, and even more difficult to get an engagement from theatres in the capital. Occasional classes are also organized by specific theatres.

In the field of dance, there is a chronic lack of continuity in training. This is made up for in part by the dance-theatre workshop of Dance Theatre Ljubljana and smaller studios in other centres such as Celje and Maribor. The development of a future network of private schools and studios will be dependent on the form allowed under privatization legislation.

Andrej Inkret

Criticism, Scholarship and Publishing

Two centres are primarily involved in the study of theatre: the Slovene Theatre and Film Museum (established in 1964) and the theatre magazine *Maske* (established in 1985). The museum mostly focuses on theatre history and publishes studies in a periodical called *Documents of the Slovene Theatre Museum* (begun in 1964). The bimonthly *Maske*, in addition to criticism of current productions, deals mainly with theoretical, as well as managerial and organizational questions relating to contem-

porary theatre, domestic and foreign. Its focus is mainly on non-institutional and independent productions.

The recording and publishing of data on productions by all Slovene theatres is a very important permanent project of the Slovene Theatre and Film Museum. Called *Repertoire of Slovene Theatres Since 1867*, the first such documentation came out in 1967 and dealt with work of the previous hundred years. Since then, documentation has been published every five years. It includes listings of the author, title of play, director, scenographer, costumier, date of première, number of performances and cast.

A specialized theatre publishing house is based in the Ljubljana Municipal Theatre, and takes its name from it – Knjižnica MGL (Library of the Municipal Theatre of Ljubljana). This house (established in 1958) publishes historical and theoretical research on Slovene theatre, selections of critical writings by theatre critics, and translations of well-known historical and contemporary books by such people as Stanislavski, Grotowski, Lyubimov, Brook and Spolin among others. By 1993, this publisher had issued 115 books. One of its important publications is a three-volume study of all Slovene theatre houses between 1945 and 1970. Entitled *Živo gledališče* (*Live Theatre*), it was published in 1975 and edited by Dušan Tomše (1930–86).

Among the important contemporary critics are Andrej Inkret (b. 1943), author of *Milo za drago* (*Measure for Measure*, 1978), Vasja Predan (b. 1930), author of *Kritičarevo pozorište* (*The Reviewer's Theatre*, 1983) and Aleš Berger (b. 1946), author of *Ogledi in pogledi* (*Surveys and Aspects*, 1984). All three deal with script as well as performance. Earlier critics of note who focused much more on text include Vladimir Kralj (1901–69) – *Pogledi na dramo* (*Aspects of Drama*, 1963); Josip Vidmar (1895–1992) – *Gledališke kritike* (*Theatre Reviews*, 1968); and Filip Kalan (1910–89) – *Odmevi z ekrana* (*Echoes from the Screen*, 1969). Younger critics and theoreticians have gathered round the journal *Maske*, such as Emil Hrvatin, author of *Ponavljanje, norost, disciplina* (*Repetition, Madness, Discipline*, 1983), a book on Jean Fabre.

Among contemporary authors of scientific theatre research, mention should be made of Andrej Inkret, author of *Drama in gledališče* (*Drama and Theatre*, 1986). The most important historical and theoretical research was done by writers such as Filip Kalan – *Essais sur le théâtre* (*Essays on Theatre*, 1961), Vladimir Kralj – *Dramaturški vademekum* (*Theory of Drama, a Vade-Mecum*, 1984) and Dušan Moravec (b. 1920) – *Temelji slovenske teatrologije* (*Elements of Slovene Theatre Studies*, 1990).

Denis Poniž, Lado Kralj
Translated by Martin Cregeen

(See also YUGOSLAVIA)

Further Reading

Berger, Aleš. *Ogledi in pogledi*. [Surveys and aspects]. Ljubljana: Knjižnica Mestnega gledališča ljubljanskega, 1984. 312 pp.

Erjavec, Aleš, and Marina Gržinić, eds. *Ljubljana, Ljubljana*. Ljubljana: Mladinska knjiga, 1991. 156 pp.

Filipič, Lojze. *Živa dramaturgija*. [Live theory of drama]. Novi Sad: Sterijino pozorje, 1979. 410 pp.

Hečimović, Branko. *Izabrane slovenske drame*. [Selected Slovene plays]. Zagreb: Znanje, 1982. 345 pp.

Inkret, Andrej. *Drama in gledališče*. [Drama and theatre]. Ljubljana: Državna založba Slovenije, 1986. 133 pp.

——. *Milo za drago*. [Measure for measure]. Ljubljana: Knjižnica Mestnega gledališča ljubljanskega, 1978. 527 pp.

Kalan, Filip. *Essais sur le théâtre*. [Essays on theatre]. Ljubljana: Édition de l'Académie d'art dramatique, 1961. 252 pp.

——. *Odmevi z ekrana*. [Echoes from the screen]. Maribor: Obzorja, 1969. 181 pp.

Kralj, Vladimir. *Dramaturški vademekum*. [Theory of drama, a vade-meckum]. Ljubljana: Mladinska knjiga, 1984. 197 pp.

——. *Pogledi na dramo*. [Aspects of drama]. Ljubljana: Cankarjeva založba, 1963. 412 pp.

Moravec, Dušan. *Temelji slovenske teatrologije*. [Elements of Slovene theatre studies]. Ljubljana: Cankarjeva založba, 1990. 237 pp.

Predan, Vasja. *Kritičarevo pozorište*. [The reviewer's theatre]. Novi Sad: Sterijino pozorje, 1983. 238 pp.

——, ed. *Savremena drama i pozorište u Sloveniji*. [Contemporary drama and theatre in Slovenia]. Novi Sad: Sterijino pozorje, 1986. 491 pp.

Repertoar slovenskih gledališč 1867. [Repertoire of Slovene theatres since 1867]. 6 vols. Ljubljana: Slovenski gledališki muzej, 1967–93.

Tomše, Dušan, ed. *Živo gledališče. Pogledi na slovensko gledališče v letih 1945–70*. [Live theatre. Aspects of Slovene theatre 1945–70]. 3 vols. Ljubljana: Knjižnica Mestnega gledališča ljubljanskega, 1975.

Vidmar, Josip. *Gledališke kritike*. [Theatre reviews]. Ljubljana: Cankarjeva založba, 1968. 361 pp.

Zinaić, Milan, and NK, eds. *Neue Slowenische Kunst*. [New Slovenian Art]. Los Angeles: AMOK Books, 1991. 283 pp.

SOVIET UNION

(see USSR)

SPAIN

Since joining the European Community in 1986, Spain has had one of Europe's fastest growing economies due largely to increased foreign and domestic investment. On the negative side, Spain has also had one of the highest unemployment rates in Europe.

Spain's two largest cities are Madrid, the capital, and Barcelona, an ancient Catalonian seaport. Other major cities across the country's 504,750 square kilometres (194,900 square miles) include Valencia, Seville, Zaragoza, Bilbao and Málaga. Occupying most of the Iberian peninsula with Portugal, Spain borders France on the north and is surrounded by the Bay of Biscay, the Atlantic to the west and southwest, and the Mediterranean to the east. It is separated from north Africa (Morocco) by the Strait of Gibraltar. The country includes the Balearic and Canary Islands, two enclaves in Africa and three other island groupings.

Castilian (Spanish) is spoken by nearly 75 per cent of the population but other languages have official status in their respective areas:

Catalonian (spoken by 17 per cent of the population), Galician (7 per cent) and Basque (2 per cent). In 1991, Spain boasted more than a hundred daily newspapers for its population of over 40 million, more than 90 per cent of whom are Roman Catholic.

Throughout its history, Spain has been the subject of invasions from Asia, Europe and Africa. By the fifteenth century, however, Spain had itself grown powerful enough to begin to spread its own language, culture and traditions throughout Europe, Africa and the Americas. It was, in fact, for a time the wealthiest power in the world.

Modern Spanish history is marked by one very important date – April 1939, the end of the Spanish Civil War. The major consequence of this war was the establishment of a new political regime, a military dictatorship led by General Francisco Franco (1892–1975) which would last until 1975. The changes in the country during this period were as dramatic as they were enormous.

Politically, a new kind of state emerged: one that withdrew from the rest of Europe and the world and set out to live in its own past. Culturally, the Civil War meant the end of a rich intellectual period, a period in which movements such as the Institución Libre de Enseñanza (Free Teaching Institution), the Junta para la Ampliación de Estudios e Investigaciones Científicas (Committee for Scientific Study and Research) as well as the so-called 'Generation of 1898', 'Generation of Philosophers of 1914' and the 'Literary Generation of 1927' had clearly established a Spain committed to renovation, openness and cultural progress. All this began to wither away after 1939.

It was these intellectual forces which, together with political forces of a similar ideology, were most active in the establishment of a democratic and enlightened political regime – the Second Spanish Republic (1931–6). This republican government was intent on freedom and social progress and stood out as a promoter of education and culture. During the short life of the Second Republic, literature, the arts and education all reached glorious heights and there were attempts – both officially and unofficially – to popularize the cultural experience and take it to all levels of society. By the time the Civil War ended in 1939, though, most of the intelligentsia from this period had been removed, killed, exiled, or otherwise silenced.

Because the new regime established itself through the armed overthrow of a legally elected government, Spain soon found itself subject to an international blockade with few exceptions. Adding to this new sense of international isolation was the regime's determination to withdraw generally from the modern world and from the disasters of recent wars. As a result, national life – including theatre and cultural life generally – collapsed.

Some of the country's best modern playwrights died during this period – Miguel de Unamuno (1864–1936), Ramón María del Valle-Inclán (1866–1936), Federico García Lorca (1898–1936), Miguel Hernández (1910–42), Pedro Muñoz Seca (1881–1936) and Honorio Maura (1886–1936) among them. Others found themselves in exile – Alejandro Casona (1903–65), Max Aub (1903–72), Joaquín Grau (b. 1928), Rafael Alberti (b. 1902), Rafael Dieste (b. 1899), Pedro Salinas (1892–1951), José Bergamín (b. 1895) and Francisco Ayala, to name just a few. Actors too left Spain, such as Margarita Xirgú (1888–

1969) and María Casares (b. 1922), as did major designers such as Rivas Cheriff, Enrique Díez Canedo (1879–1944) and Alberto Custodio (b. 1912). On the other hand, there were playwrights who actually embraced the regime including Jacinto Benavente (1866–1954), the Nobel Prize-winner for Literature in 1922, and José Martínez Ruíz (1873–1967) who wrote under the pen-name Azorín.

All post-war periods are hard and difficult and the national priority must always be recovery and reconstruction. Reviving a destroyed theatre was certainly not a priority but it did enter the political guidelines of the new regime. It was the taste of the bourgeoisie – a social class psychologically wounded but politically victorious – which dominated in these years and which restricted everything from playwriting styles to theatre criticism and scholarship. Because of this unexpected interest in the arts, political and commercial interests very quickly became one and the same.

Spain was, in fact, a right-wing totalitarian state during this time, traditional and conservative, subject to the desires of a government determined to direct and control all spheres of Spanish life. Theatre policy was meant to assure both the presence and intervention of the state apparatus in all stages of artistic creation. The official philosophy was clearly stated in 1943 by Patricio González de Canales, secretary-general of the state propaganda office:

> theatre's goal is to be a leader in the new social order.... The function of the State must be to guide morality as it must be to guard literature and grammar, in order to guarantee the basic public good.

Indeed, the new government saw to it that playwrights and theatre activity in general became tools for socio-political and aesthetic purification, the control of social behaviour, education and the improvement of national customs within the organization of the new society. Theatre activity was put under the control of the Department of Press and Propaganda, early on a branch of the Ministry of the Presidency (Internal Affairs) and later part of the Vice-Secretariat of Popular Education of the Ministry of National Education. New theatre activity commenced but it was carried on under severe censorship though rules were not written down or verbalized until years later when the blatant subjectivity of the decision-making process forced the establishment of arbitrary criteria.

Confusion and injustice were the norm

through the 1940s and 1950s. Ethics were confused with aesthetics, Catholic moral standards being the guides. Any work which was perceived to threaten official religious, social or political principles was quickly repressed.

Theatre policy was implemented in three major ways. First, by direct intervention of the state. The government could buy, rent or lease theatre spaces, maintain official theatres, establish companies or organize festivals as it saw fit. By this policy, during the 1940–1 season, the Teatro Español (Spanish Theatre) in Madrid, known as Teatro del Príncipe (Theatre of the Prince) before 1849, was converted into a state-owned space rented by the municipality. Its repertoire focused on classical theatre. The Teatro Nacional María Guerrero (María Guerrero National Theatre), another such theatre and previously known as Teatro de la Princesa (Princess Theatre), was also converted into a state-owned space in the same year and placed under the direction of Luis Escobar (1908–91) and Humberto Pérez de La Osa (b. 1897). It specialized in modern foreign plays. Finally, the Teatro Español Universitario (Spanish University Theatre) was established in Madrid under this policy of direct intervention in 1948 under the leadership of Modesto Higueras (1910–85). In 1952 the Teatro Popular Universitario (Popular University Theatre) was established under the leadership of Gustavo Pérez Puig (b. 1930), who would become the artistic director of the Teatro Español in the late 1980s.

Second, theatre policy was implemented by indirect intervention of the state. Through a system of grants and sponsorships not only to traditional theatres but also to commercial companies, political groups, unions, universities and other cultural organizations, the state apparatus supported groups which were sympathetic to its ideology. The commercial companies, always safe and harmless, benefited enormously from their alliance with the state. But even these groups had to surrender much of their independence if they accepted support, especially in the regime's first years.

Third, theatre policy was implemented by grants to playwrights. In fact recipients of the grants generally shared the ideology of the regime anyway and were the same ones considered first for appointments and prizes, including political missions and diplomatic postings. Ironically, some of the prize-winning plays were themselves later censored and forbidden.

Those who were not supported by the system found themselves unable to succeed commercially. Companies out of favour had to rely on the favoured writers, classics or contemporary authors who were willing to deal only with the past. Companies and audiences gradually fell into a theatre of pure nostalgia.

Even independent criticism quickly became part of the system. Operating without academic foundation, it quickly turned petty and shy. In many cases, the critics interpreted, judged or condemned either directly or indirectly on behalf of the state and there was virtually no difference between the roles of critic and state censor.

Quite clearly, in the years following World War II, even Madrid and Barcelona lacked any kind of serious theatre and certainly had no political theatre. What existed were theatrical showcases emphasizing an empty patriotism or classical plays which praised the most traditional national values. There was a return to the *costumbrista*-styled folk theatre of the brothers Serafín (1871–1938) and Joaquín (1873–1944) Álvarez Quintero and the easy-going comic sketches (*sainetes*) of Carlos Arniches (1866–1943). Also staged were plays by Jacinto Benavente (usually his poorest works) taking advantage of his past popularity as a Nobel Prize-winner. The dominant theatrical forms were the dubious farces (*astracán*) of Muñoz Seca, Antonio de Lara Gairláu (1896–1978, who wrote under the pen-name Tono), Jorge (b. 1919) and Carlos (1913–79) Llopis, Teodoro Llorente (1836–1911) and Luis Tejedor (b. 1903) – and the light melodramas of Adolfo Torrado (1904–58) and Leandro Navarro (1900–74).

The *costumbrista* and other folkloric genres such as *zarzuela*, musical revue, Spanish *variétés* and Andalusian folk music were also revived and great stars were created. There were attempts as well at real satire by such people as Enrique Jardiel Poncela (1901–52) and Miguel Mihúra (1903–77) but their theatre was not understood at the time and was generally ignored. The best established playwrights of the time – José María Pemán (1898–1981), Juan Ignacio Luca De Tena (1897–1975), Joaquín Calvo Sotelo (b. 1904), José López Rubio (b. 1903) and Víctor Ruíz Iriarte (1912–82) – all created historical sentimental plays, evasive comedies, *costumbristas* and domestic psychological dramas. At their best, their plays could be called literary and poetic. One of the best studies of state control over Spanish playwriting during this time is *Condicionantes para el dramaturgo y su obra en el Madrid de la post-guerra, 1939–1969* (*Conditions for the Playwright and their Effect on Post-war Madrid, 1939–1969*), a doctoral dissertation written by Víctor Valembois.

As for the state's interest in classical writers, it virtually appropriated the playwrights of the Spanish golden age. This return to the theatrical Baroque – a time of Spanish imperialism – meant a clearly imperialistic kind of theatre in the 1940s and 1950s. Interestingly, the playwrights of the golden age were reinterpreted in an effort to re-establish a national popular theatre as well as a theatre in the service of the state, as they were in the golden age itself. Official interpretations of these golden age classics were always true to the original and always remained conservative. It was these productions that were exported to Latin America as part of a movement to improve the image of the Franco regime overseas.

As well, the state used writers known before the Civil War for propaganda purposes. Included in this group was Miguel de Unamuno, whose life was of more interest to the government than his work as a playwright. The brothers Álvarez Quintero, on the other hand, were highly promoted because of the popularity of their socially and politically harmless plays. The same could be said about many second-rate authors from the late nineteenth century, the 'belle epoque', and from the time of General Primo de Rivera's dictatorship (1923–30). Many other important living playwrights were simply silenced at this time and found themselves totally unable to publish or produce their work.

Through such pressure, Juan Ignacio Luca De Tena and Emilio Romero (b. 1917) actually shifted from writing political theatre to writing partisan theatre for the regime. Calvo Sotelo and Pemán, as well, actively encouraged audiences to embrace the regime's ideology. Their theatre, like that of Luca de Tena, was especially important to the state because of its willingness to deal with historical reconstruction and its belief in the permanent relevance of ideas from the golden age. All of these playwrights were part of the post-war Spanish theatre and their work is collectively marked by its strong anti-republican sentiment.

As for foreign influences, the state opened up first to its wartime supporters – Italy and Germany particularly – and later to Argentina and France as well, but only the lightest and mildest of their plays were imported. Among these countries, Argentina stood out as the most important. Official relations between Perón (the Argentine military dictator) and Franco were centred not only on wheat and meat but also on culture. Of special interest were popular Argentine vaudevilles and melodramas. Later, US imports began to appear – action movies and musicals.

In short, theatre was used to evade reality, to quickly forget the recent past. Theatre of social criticism all but disappeared. As early as the 1950s, however, a growing restlessness was becoming apparent among certain theatre professionals, particularly those uncomfortable with both the official theatres and the commercial theatres. New independent and university groups began to be created which would offer a very different form of theatre. Among the first to move in this direction were the Arte Nuevo (which had been founded in 1945), an aggressive collection of talented young people. Many of them went on to become outstanding directors and playwrights during the 1970s and 1980s including Alfonso Sastre (b. 1926) and Alfonso Paso. Many even abandoned their university studies to pursue the theatre.

As the 1950s drew to a close, Spain found itself with a proliferation of groups working in many different styles – from chamber theatre to issue-oriented theatre – while others set up lecture series on theatrical and other issues and still others became involved in the publication of theatre manifestos demanding a break with past forms and advocating modernity. All these elements struggled to balance the emptiness of the commercial and official theatres. If 1949 marked the beginning of this transition between political isolation and cultural openness, 1955 was its climax as Spain was finally admitted to the United Nations. After sixteen years of looking inward, the doors were finally opening and the production of foreign plays increased considerably.

New schools of writers emerged – the Grupo de Teatro Realista (Realism Theatre Group) – as well as individual writers with their own unique voice such as Antonio Buero Vallejo (b. 1916), Miguel Mihúra and Alfonso Sastre. Plays such as Buero Vallejo's *Historia de una escalera* (*The Story of a Stairway*, 1949), Mihúra's *Tres sombreros de copa* (*Three Top Hats*, 1952) and Sastre's *Escuadra hacia la muerte* (*Squad Doomed to Die*, 1953) opened the way to a whole new kind of theatre in Spain: a theatre of social and political criticism, of aesthetic innovation, and of social commitment. With productions of these plays, Spanish theatre once again was linked to playwrights of both the Generation of 1898 (Valle-Inclán and Unamuno) and the Generation of 1927 (García Lorca and Alberti).

Scholars such as Maria Pilar Pérez-Stansfield in *Direcciones del teatro español de post-guerra* (*Directions in Post-War Theatre in Spain*, 1983) and Francisco Ruíz Ramón in his *Historia del teatro español. Vol II: Siglo XX* (*History of Spanish Theatre. Vol II: 20th Century*, 1980), identify these three plays as crucial to the literary and socio-historical changes that were clearly beginning. For both, these plays are at once representative and paradigmatic, for they contain the roots of the entire modern Spanish theatre. Pérez-Stansfield, in fact, argues that these three plays created a new form of

> committed psychological realism, full of anti-heroes; a denunciatory theatre of the absurd, based on the irrational as an aesthetic proposal to discover and explain the rational; a revalorization of absurdist tragedy; and a new form of social-realism not just as an easy political label but as a testimonial and denunciatory tool in which social commitment does not exclude quality.

While Buero Vallejo and Sastre continued to work in these directions, Mihúra ended up 'honourably' fitting into the system and serving bourgeois audiences.

There were other efforts as well to renew the theatre at this time. One of the most important was the *Manifiesto del Teatro de Agitación Social* (*Manifesto of Theatre for Social Agitation*) written in 1950 by Sastre and José María De Quinto (b. 1925). In it, these two playwrights defended the social and political function of theatre, rejecting not only the 'theatre establishment in vogue' but also the general Spanish vision of the time. Another important effort was the *Documento de Conclusiones de las Jornadas sobre Teatro de la Universidad Internacional Menéndez Pelayo* (*Concluding Notes From the Theatre Congress at the International University Menéndez Pelayo*), written in Santander in 1955, a document which presented all of the problems of the theatre profession at the time while offering a particular solution to each of them.

Theatre also began to appear within various workers' unions, which organized and sponsored annual competitions in cooperation with the Teatro Móvil (Itinerant Theatre), sponsored by the cultural section of the Ministry of Education. Important as well was the birth of the Teatro Popular Universitario (Popular University Theatre), created in the style of the University Theatre La Barraca (Thatched Farmhouse), founded by García Lorca during the years of republican government; and the creation of the Real Escuela Superior de Arte Dramático (Royal Higher School for the Dramatic Arts) in 1954. That same year also saw the creation of the Teatro Nacional de Cámara y Ensayo (National Chamber Theatre), financed and sponsored by the government. Its goal was to produce new plays whose ideas or approaches were deemed not to be commercial. In fact, most of the plays produced at this theatre were by foreign playwrights.

As this new 'independent' movement flourished and as the number of groups increased, the works of the most important Spanish playwrights of the century – Valle-Inclán, García Lorca and Unamuno – were resurrected. Despite the strictness of producing plays by the independent groups – only three performances of a play, one location and a limited audience – these independent groups had a long-term effect on Spanish theatre generally and an enormous relevance for theatre in Madrid during the latter part of the Franco era.

There were still many writers who refused to work even within these structures, whose work still transgressed the limits of censorship and who were forced into or chose exile. Among them were Francisco Arrabal (b. 1932), José Ruibal (b. 1925), José Martín Elizondo (b. 1922), José Guevara (b. 1928) and José García Lora. Ironically, their works were generally produced abroad before they were produced in Spain.

In comparison not even the theatre of Buero Vallejo or Sastre was truly 'committed'. Rather, theirs was a theatre that gave testimony to current situations, a theatre of protest that denounced the painful reality of the time, a reality that had little to do with the image the state wanted to spread. It is unquestionable, however, that Buero Vallejo and Sastre first sowed the seeds which grew later into a more realistic theatre, one committed to its time and to the truly important national issues.

Another key year for Spanish politics was 1959, a year that marked the end of two political phases: the first which set out to achieve internal stability while gaining international recognition for the regime and the second which continued to seek Spain's integration into the wider European community. Because of these desires, the government was forced to begin to change its internal policies; it was this change that began to bring about a new cultural openness. Combined with an increase in tourism, the seeds of change were beginning to grow.

In 1962 the Spanish government applied to become part of the European Economic Community (EEC), an application that was not accepted until 1986. In 1966 the government established new laws relating to the press, laws with wider margins for cultural expression. As a consequence of these two steps, there was another new influx of plays and theoretical work from abroad. Many of the plays were fully produced in the 1960s while others were presented simply as staged readings.

It was in this context of relative political and cultural openness that the state set out to get its many exiled writers back home and Madrid's stages slowly began to produce more contemporary works.

Perhaps the most typical example was that of Alejandro Casona, an exiled playwright with whom the Spanish state was particularly 'generous' and indulgent from 1962 onwards. The state saw in Casona's work a new style of nostalgic theatre, poetic and politically harmless. Thus Casona was welcomed back with open arms and his plays found success in productions staged by José Tamayo (b. 1928). Casona's work, in fact, came back to Spain in major productions by the commercial theatres. Interestingly, because of his commercial success and official favour, his plays were rarely produced by university or independent theatres.

The works of García Lorca, however, a playwright connected to the 'Generation of 1927', were accepted *only* in the small theatres while Valle-Inclán, the great Spanish playwright of the 'Generation of 1898', took even longer to be recognized. His work – opinionated, critical and non-conformist – remained off the stage until very late in the Franco regime. Writers like Bergamín and Max Aub were not accepted back in Spain until the 1970s.

The university theatres at this time grew considerably in number and in quality, expanding through many of Spain's fourteen regions (reorganized into seventeen autonomous communities in the 1980s). When official censorship diminished still further in 1966, these groups lost their *raison d'être* and soon closed down. Independent theatre groups, however, continued growing, as they had in the previous decade. These groups knew how to adapt to

change and transformed themselves, improving training and quality, especially after 1969.

Despite this growth, however, the commercial theatre still dominated and the state continued to control all the major theatres and spaces. Small theatres, nevertheless, continued to open in Madrid where plays had even longer runs and audiences grew.

It was still the work of Buero Vallejo and Sastre which was the most advanced and challenging to the new audiences. In 1960, the Grupo de Teatro Realista (Group for Theatre Realism), playwrights who shared Buero and Sastre's ideas, was constituted. The group issued a manifesto signed by Sastre and José María De Quinto calling for the full elimination of censorship and national prizes, the decentralization of theatrical resources, the reduction of national bureaucracy, and the withdrawal of rules limiting professionals to one show per day. Later that year, Sastre demanded confrontation with those who controlled the theatres. As a result, his plays were not produced again.

Between 1960 and 1964, a number of other 'realist' authors were produced. Among them were José María Rodríguez Méndez (b. 1925), Ricardo Rodríguez Buded (b. 1928), Carlos Muñiz (b. 1927), Lauro Olmo (b. 1927) and José Martín Recuerda (b. 1925). Though their forms were very different, all shared a belief in theatre as a form of social commentary, a form involving commitment and protest. For them, this was more of an ethical attitude than an aesthetic one.

Historian Ruíz Ramón has seen three clear styles within the realist theatre of the time – 'realism-naturalism, neo-expressionism and popular farce' (this last is rooted in *esperpento*, a term coined by Valle-Inclán about his own quasi-absurdist works).

All the realist authors also adopted 'Iberismo', that is Hispanism, as a common approach of both content and form. One could find in the work of these writers the results of Valle-Inclán's experiments as well as the formal experiments of both García Lorca and Alberti. It was not surprising to find many of these new authors officially silenced at this time.

With Franco gravely ill from 1969 to his death in 1975 and with Juan Carlos de Borbón (b. 1938) officially named Franco's successor, a new cultural openness began to ensue. In 1969 there was a cultural amnesty and writers like Aub and Ramón J. Sénder (1901–82) came back from exile. The year 1969 also marked the culmination of Spain's thirty-year-long desire to

José Sanchis Sinisterra's Teatro Fronterizo production of Samuel Beckett's *First Love.*

break with the past. Suddenly, new ideas could be looked at openly. Critical independent theatres such as Els Joglars and Tábano enjoyed enormous success at this time. Café theatres opened as part of an attempt to create new forms and to experiment with new spaces. Madrid's own municipal theatrical monopoly also started to break down as a new independent organization called Teatros Nacionales y Festivales de España (National Theatres and Festivals of Spain) began to encourage theatre production in other cities.

The New Spanish Theatre, as it was called, saw itself, for various reasons, as subversive, as a transgressor of traditional Spanish values, an attitude that made it appear to be dangerous and, not surprisingly, rejected by those who controlled the large theatres. Its aesthetics, impregnated by the most avant-garde European theories and connected to the most socially crit-

ical Spanish theatre artists of the time, were too new and difficult to be generally understood by most audiences. These new playwrights built complex symbolic worlds for their new concepts.

Produced by the growing independent theatre groups (now numbering approximately 150), these younger writers, directors and actors joined with institutions such as the Royal Higher School for Dramatic Arts to challenge the government's cultural policies at every level, demanding both explanations and solutions for official failures. Among the areas the state is now involved in are equal access to theatre for all strata of the population; increased integration of playwrights into the production process; revival of national classics; and the recognition of theatre as a vital and important profession within society.

Structure of the National Theatre Community

The year following Franco's death marked the real beginning of transition to a full democratic regime in Spain, a liberal one until 1982 and later a social-democratic one. The new political systems significantly affected the old cultural policies.

First, a Ministry of Culture was established with a special section for theatre and the performing arts. On 1 April 1978, the censorship laws were repealed and a law of Freedom of Speech put into place. Additional laws guaranteeing Freedom of Theatrical Representation as well as Guidelines for the Classification of the Performing Arts were also introduced that year.

In 1985, the former National Directorate was transformed into the Instituto Nacional de las Artes Escénicas y de la Música (INAEM: National Institute for the Performing Arts and Music) and a number of organizations were officially linked to it: the Centro Dramático Nacional (National Drama Centre), first directed by Adolfo Marsillach (b. 1928), later

by the actress-director Núria Espert (b. 1935), then José Luis Gómez (b. 1940), Ramón Tamayo and director Lluís Pasquale (b. 1951); the Centro Nacional de Nuevas Tendencias Escénicas (National Centre of New Stage Trends); the Centro de Documentación Teatral (Centre for Theatre Documentation), which publishes the journal El Público (The Public); and the Compañía de Teatro Clásico (Classical Theatre Company). The new administration has also published guidelines and regulations for the establishment and operation of festivals, both at the national and international levels, as well as new guidelines for the creation of grants and scholarships.

Spain itself was politically reorganized into comunidades autónomas (autonomous communities) and municipalities. Centres for the production and study of theatre were also established at these new levels of government. Most of the seventeen autonomous communities today have their own regional drama centres, as

José Carlos Plaza's Centro Dramático Nacional production of Shakespeare's *Hamlet*.
Photo: Antonio de Benito.

well as their own theatre companies and festivals. Likewise, most of the municipalities already have or are in the process of forming their own drama centres, as they also organize their own campaigns to popularize theatre. One should mention here the Centro Cultural de la Villa de Madrid (Cultural Centre of the Municipality of Madrid) and the Teatro Español, both run directly by the municipal government of Madrid.

In 1982, when the Socialist Party took power in Spain, life began to resemble that of most other social-democratic European countries. With a renewed interest in having Spain's 40 million people become part of the European Community, the central government has finished the process of transferring power to the autonomous communities, in accordance with a new Spanish constitution approved in 1978. Culture in its entirety, for all intents and purposes, has now been transferred to the communities and most municipal governments already have their own guidelines for the regulation and production of theatre. Because the state does not want wide variations in cultural support, the central government passed a decree on 24 April 1985 under which the National Institute for Performing Arts and Music was created as a completely autonomous organization. The institute would operate in an arm's-length relationship with the Ministry of Culture but would clearly be a way to implement the cultural policy of the central government. The institute's main functions are to promote, protect and disseminate theatrical and musical activities both nationally and internationally and to support communication among autonomous communities.

In order to fulfil these goals, the institute was empowered by law to develop those theatrical and musical production companies which belong to the state; to support the organization, dissemination, and investigation of research on Spain's theatrical and musical heritage; and to encourage theatrical and musical production through the subsidizing of theatrical and musical professionals.

The creation of the institute was a clear attempt at ensuring the decentralization of cultural resources. Legally independent, the institute has its own regulations and budget. Under the institute's direct responsibility are the Centro Dramático Nacional, the Teatro Nacional María Guerrero, the Teatro Nacional de la Zarzuela (Zarzuela National Theatre), the Centro Nacional de Nuevas Tendencias Escénicas (National Centre of New Stage Trends) and the Compañía de Teatro Clásico, all located in Madrid.

The institute's music department coordinates musical activities generally and supervises two companies which work under the generic name of Ballet Nacional (National Ballet), a classical and modern ballet company, and a company for Spanish dance. As well, the institute has responsibility for the two national documentation centres – one for theatre and the other for music – including their various publications.

Even though Madrid and Barcelona have always been the cultural centres in Spain, the decentralization process has also meant that major productions now can première on regional stages and regional drama centres can prepare their own seasons with their own local shows.

In general, the main goal of the central government, as stated in 1985, has been 'to open up new possibilities of cooperation between public institutions and theatre professionals, to guarantee the existence and independence of theatre companies and theatre spaces, and to promote the highest degree of decentralization for the administration of the public theatres'.

Theatre was considered by the Spanish state in the 1990s as a 'basic cultural activity' for society. Because of this, the government saw itself as being empowered to eradicate problems in the Spanish theatre and to offer solutions.

Eduardo Huertas Vázquez

Artistic Profile

Companies

Spanish theatre during the 1980s and 1990s was characterized by confrontations between the private theatre and the hegemony of the public theatre, a new emphasis on commercial criteria, the connections between the large theatres and the independent companies, and a growing support for the work of national playwrights.

Connections between the large theatres – private and public – and the smaller independent groups as well as the impact of government institutions constitute the political framework within which other practical developments took place in the closing decades of the twentieth century. These relationships explain the important presence of the theatre of images in the large theatres.

In the four years from 1982 to 1986, for example, many new independent groups were formed and other groups from previous decades were reorganized. As a result, collective creation enjoyed a strong revival, and the number of productions by national authors increased significantly. The collectively created works were often of outstanding quality and attracted both critics and audiences. Among the most important of the independent groups working this way were La Fura dels Baus, La Cuadra, Els Comediants and Els Joglars.

La Cuadra, from Seville, directed by Salvador Távora during this period, had several successes with works drawn from Andalusian folklore and works dealing with contemporary social problems in the region. Among its successes were *Nanas de Espinas* (*Lullabies of Thorns*,

1985), *Las Bachantes* (*The Bacchae*, 1987), *Alhucema* (1988), *Crónica de una muerte anunciada* (*Chronicle of a Death Foretold*, 1990) and *Picasso Andaluz: La Muerte del Minotauro* (*Andalusian Picasso: The Minotaur's Death*, 1992). Practitioners from the independent groups of the 1960s and 1970s were also influential in stimulating theatre production throughout the country in the 1980s. It is of interest to note here that many of the official institutions from the autonomous communities, the regional dramatic centres (such as the Centro Dramático in Valencia, whose on-stage work has consistently been high), along with most of the public theatres which belong to the National Network of Theatres and Public Spaces are now run by people who were earlier involved in the independent theatre movement. Many of the festivals too are now being influenced by practitioners who started in the independent theatre movement.

Though the independent theatres did some of the most interesting work, the large regional public theatres were active as well in the 1980s and 1990s. It is of interest to note

Salvador Távora's 1987 La Cuadra adaptation of Euripides' *The Bacchae*.
Photo: Conxita Cid.

here that very significant funding has gone to them as well as to the production of regional festivals. Funds have also gone into the restoration of theatre buildings in Alicante, Almagro, Avilés, Bilbao, Cádiz, Las Palmas, Murcia, Oviedo, Segovia, Seville and Toledo. Theatres in many of these cities have also hosted tours from major Madrid and Barcelona companies which have shown interest in decentralization. Some of these groups now regularly tour the regions.

One can see this in the policies and work of the Núria Espert Company whose production of Inoue's *Makeup* was done in Valencia; José Luis Alonso de Santos's *Trampa para pájaros* (*Bird Trap*) premièred in Toledo; Antonio Gala's *Los buenos días perdidos* (*The Lost Good Days*) premièred in Córdoba; Adolfo Marsillach's *Feliz Aniversario* (*Happy Anniversary*) in Seville; Francisco Nieva's *Los españoles bajo tierra* (*Spaniards Under Ground*) in Bilbao; and Vol-Ras's *Pssssh* in Albacete.

In the context of the relatively recent geographical and political division into such autonomous communities, some theatre work has also been used as a tool to explore the historical past and present identity of a region. This has been especially true in Andalucía, Galicia and the Basque Country (Euzkadi). A good example of this type of production is Ignacio Amestoy's *Durango, un sueño 1439* (*Durango, a Dream 1439*), performed by the group Geroa, a thought-provoking theatre piece of great plasticity which dealt with social events in Durango during that time.

At the Festival Iboamericano in Cádiz, Spanish audiences have seen the work of some of the best Latin American theatre companies. Among them are the Compañía Nacional de México, the Compañía de Teatro Argentino, the Laboratorio de Teatro Campesino e Indígena, Ornitorrinco, Rajatabla from Caracas, Sportivo Teatral from Buenos Aires, Teatro Circular from Montevideo, Teatro de la Campaña, Teatro Municipal General from San Martín, and the Teatro Popular from Bogotá.

Among small groups of import from Madrid and Barcelona, one should note the work of the Cambaleo Teatro, Cocktail Teatro Pirata, Espacio Cero, Corral del Principe, La Cubana Dagull-Dagom, La Gàbia, GAT Companya Teatral, Guirigay, El Talleret de Salt, La Tartana, El Tricicle, Teatro Fronterizo, Vol-Ras, Zampanó, Zascandil and Zotal Teatro.

Given the recent interest in Spanish work it may be surprising to some that very little

Spanish classical theatre has been produced in recent decades. The exceptions to this have been on the occasions of centenaries – those of Calderón (1600–81) or Lope de Vega (1562–1635), for example – or as part of a festival. Another exception here has been the Compañía Nacional de Teatro Clásico (National Classical Theatre Company) whose mandate is to produce such works. Under Adolfo Marsillach and Rafael Pérez Sierra, the company has enjoyed great popularity since its founding in 1986. Though many of its productions are faithful to the originals, some have actually parodied the classical style or taken a modern psychological approach. It has had particular success with *La verdad sospechosa* (*Suspicious Truth*, 1991) by Juan Ruis de Alarcón, directed by Pilar Miró. At their permanent home in the Teatro de la Comedia, they have staged strong productions of Calderón's *Antes que todo es mi dama* (*Before Anything Else She's Mine*), a production done in a cinematographic style directed by Rafael Pérez Sierra; and *El alcalde de Zalamea* (*The Mayor of Zalamea*, 1988) and *La dama duende* (*The Goblin Lady*, 1990), both directed by José Luis Alonso.

The company also co-produced a play by Tirso de Molina (1571–1648) with the Teatro Municipal of San Martín, *El burlador de Sevilla* (*The Seducer of Seville*, 1988).

Its major successes with Lope de Vega have included *El caballero de Olmedo* (*Gentleman from Olmedo*, 1990) directed by Miguel Narros and *El castigo sin venganza* (*Punishment Without Revenge*, 1985) with designs by Narros.

Dramaturgy

The National Theatre Law gave official support to theatres and companies committed to the production of Spanish playwrights. The result was the production of a large number of writers and plays which had not been produced previously. This was the case for such writers as Fernando Arrabal, Angel García Pintado, Agustín Gómez Arcos, Jerónimo López Mozo, José Martín Recuerda, José Martínez Mediero, Luis Matilla, Domingo Miras, Francisco Nieva, Lauro Olmo, Luis Riaza, José Rodríguez Méndez, Alfonso Vallejo and José Ruibal among others.

At this same time, plays by Antonio Buero Vallejo and Antonio Gala were also staged – in some instances, remounted under the direction of Gustavo Pérez Puig – to great acclaim. Important works of Buero Vallejo staged during this period include *Diálogo Secreto* (*Secret Dialogue*, 1984) at the Teatro Infanta Isabel; *Lázaro en el laberinto* (*Lazarus in the Labyrinth*, 1986) at the Teatro Maravillas; and *Música Cercana* (*Familiar Music*, 1989) at the Teatro Arriaga in Bilbao.

Gala's *Samarkanda* (1985) premièred at the Teatro del Príncipe, directed by María Ruiz; *El hotelito* (*The Small Hotel*, 1985), a reflection of the problems of the autonomous communities, was presented at the Teatro Maravillas; *Séneca o El beneficio de la duda* (*Seneca or The Benefit of the Doubt*) premièred at the Teatro Reina Victoria; while *Carmen, Carmen* (1988) was directed by José Carlos Plaza at the Teatro Calderón with music by Juan Cánovas.

Because of this new interest in Spanish plays, a number of productions had long runs (in Spain anything over a hundred performances qualifies in this regard). Among these commercial successes were Manuel Canseco and Pérez Mateos's *Proceso a Besteiro* (*The Trial of Besteiro*, 1986) about the prosecution of a socialist leader staged at the Teatro Pavón; *Las bicicletas son para el verano* (*Bicyles are for Summer*, 1982) directed by José Carlos Plaza at the Español; *Historias de la puta mili* (*Army Stories*, 1990) by Ramón Ivá, a collection of comic tales about Spain's compulsory military service at the Teatro Villarroel; Alberto Miralles's *Comisaría especial para mujeres* (*Police Station for Women*, 1992), a *costumbrista* approach to feminist issues produced at the Circulo Cultural de Madrid; and Alfonso Sastre's *La taberna fantástica* (*Fantastic Tavern*, 1985) at the Centro de Bellas Artes.

Among women writers to have a hundred performances of their plays, one should note the work of Ana Diosdado and María Manuela Reina, both of whom have had several long-run successes.

The works of Fernando Arrabal, though important, have never had commercial success in Spain. Among his most important works for the stage produced in Spain have been *El rey de Sodoma* (*Sodom's King*, 1983) and *El arquitecto y el emperador de Asiria* (*The Architect and the Emperor of Assyria*, 1983) at the Teatro Martín.

It is of interest to note that many of the writers who worked exclusively for the independent groups in the 1960s and 1970s are now being regularly produced, with some success,

by the large companies. Among the writers in this category are José Luis Alonso de Santos, Josep Maria Benet i Jornet, Fermín Cabal, José Sanchis Sinisterra, whose *Ay, Carmela!* (1988) for the Teatro Fígaro was later turned into a major film by Carlos Saura and whose *Lopé de Aguirre, Traidor* (*Lopé de Aguirre, Traitor*, 1992), explored the role of the Spanish state in the conquest of the Americas, and Rodolf Sirera, whose *El veneno del teatro* (*Theatrical Venom*, 1983) at the María Guerrero was a play-within-a-play about theatrical life.

The work of Spanish playwrights from the early twentieth century has been mostly remounted by the large public theatres, a development aided by the ideological proximity those playwrights and contemporary directors. The works of García Lorca fall into this category along with the works of Alberti, Arniches, Casona and Valle-Inclán.

García Lorca's work has also been the focus of several exhibitions, congresses and books. This has led to renewed interest in his work on-stage. Among his plays produced with success have been *La casa de Bernarda Alba* (*The House of Bernarda Alba*, 1984) directed by José Carlos Plaza at the Teatro Español; *La Zapatera Prodigiosa* (*The Shoemaker's Prodigious Wife*, 1985) directed by Alfredo Mañas; *Bodas de sangre* (*Blood Wedding*, 1985) directed for the Teatro Cervantes in Andalucía by José Luis Gómez who emphasized the social dimensions and treated the text as mythic; *Yerma* (1986) staged by the Núria Espert Company as a remount of the 1971 production directed by Víctor García and *El Publico* (*The Public*, 1987) and *Comedia sin titulo* (*Untitled Play*, 1989), directed by Lluís Pasqual at the María Guerrero.

Valle-Inclán has also been staged with some frequency by the public theatres. *Luces de Bohemia* (*Bohemian Lights*, 1984) has been staged at the María Guerrero and his *Tirano Banderas* (1992) has been done at the Teatro Lope de Vega in Seville under the direction of Lluís Pasquale. José Luis Alonso's production of *La enamorada del rey* (*The King's Lover*) was staged in 1968 at the María Guerrero. José Carlos Plaza directed *Comedias bárbaras* (*Barbaric Comedies*) in 1991 at the María Guerrero and it quickly became one of Spanish theatre's greatest successes.

Three plays by Jacinto Benavente had strong productions in the late 1980s and 1990s – *La Malquerida* (1987) directed by Miguel

Narros at the Teatro Español, *Rosas de Otoño* (*Autumn Roses*, 1990) directed by José Luis Alonso at the Teatro Alcázar, and *Los intereses creados* (*Created Interests*, 1992), directed by Gustavo Pérez Puig at the Español. José Bergamín's *La risa en los huesos* (*Laughter in the Bones*, 1989) was staged by Guillermo Heras at the Sala Olimpia using evocative textual images and a complex semiotic recreation of myth. The production was framed by sound and colour along with an accomplished choreography, a beautiful example of post-modern theatre.

A number of important Catalonian writers were staged by theatres in Barcelona. Among these were plays by Àngel Guimerà (1845–1924), Joan Oliver, Josep Plá, Santiago Rusiñol and Josep Maria de Sagarra.

It should be noted here that there are six major Spanish prizes for playwriting – the National Theatre Prize, the Legismundo Prize, the Mayte Prize, the Marques de Bradomin Prize, the Tirso de Molina Prize and the Calderón Prize.

Directors, Directing and Production Styles

The growth of Image Theatre and the use of empty stages characterized many of the most daring productions seen in Spain in the 1980s and early 1990s. Emphasizing visual elements rather than text, this style was first seen as early as the 1960s but became one of the major styles through the work of independent groups.

Audiences in the 1990s, even the most conservative, had come to accept some of the complex semiotic codes utilized by this theatrical style. Some of the most successful Image Theatre productions have been *Azaña, una pasión española* (*Azaña, a Spanish Passion*, 1988), a text based on the life and writings of Manuel Azaña (1880–1940), president of Spain (1931–3), which was directed by José Luis Gómez at the María Guerrero; and Pier Paolo Pasolini's *Calderón* (1988) produced at the Sala Olimpia, a complex reflection on the Spanish character accomplished almost exclusively by visual images. One of the most successful bare

The 1992 Centre Dramàtic de la Generalitat de Catalunya production of Josep Maria de Sagarra's *L'hostal de la Glòria*.
Photo: Teresa Miró.

The 1989 Companyia Teatre Lliure production of Beaumarchais's *The Marriage of Figaro*, directed and designed by Fabià Puigserver.
Photo: Ros Ribas.

stage productions of the period was *Ara que els ametllers ya estan batuts* (*Now That the Almond Trees Have Been Picked*, 1990), based on texts by Catalonian writer Josep Plá, directed and performed by Josep Maria Flotats at the Teatro Poliorama. It utilized a series of cinematic projections by Alain Poisson.

Women directors are still a minority in Spanish theatre. However, directors such as Carmen Portacelli and María Ruíz have produced some outstanding work. Portacelli has staged several modern French and German plays (Koltès and Strauss, for example) at the Mercat, while Ruíz has directed Shelagh Delaney's *A Taste of Honey* and David Mamet's *Edmond* (1990) at the María Guerrero.

María Francisca Vilches de Frutos

Music Theatre

When one speaks of music theatre in Spain one is generally speaking of opera and *zarzuela*.

Opera has become fashionable since the 1960s and has become part of the consumer society. At the same time, opera has had a legitimate revival as part of Spanish cultural life thanks in part to the development of an infrastructure. Organizations such as the Association of Friends of the Opera have brought genuine attention to the form and have helped to solve traditional problems in both its creation and perception. Traditional classical opera along with its Spanish counterparts, could be regularly seen in the 1990s at many theatres but especially at the Teatro de la Zarzuela in Madrid and at the Teatro Liceo de Barcelona (destroyed by fire in 1994). Other important music theatres are the new and highly sophisticated Teatro de la

The 1991 Teatro de la Zarzuela production of Händel's *Rinaldo*.
Photo: Chicho.

Maestranza in Seville the Arriaga in Bilbao, the Campoamor in Oviedo, the Perez Galdós in Las Palmas and the Palau in Valencia.

Madrid and Barcelona continue as the major centres of activity in both music and dance theatre but more and more productions from these cities are touring across the country and have often appeared in regional festivals.

The music magazine *Scherzo* has since 1988 organized a Festival Mozart in and around Madrid. A number of well-known theatre directors have also begun to explore the operatic form with new productions in the period since 1982. Among them are José Luis Alonso, Lluís Pasquale and Francisco Nieva. Simón Suárez has, as a director, focused on contemporary opera, while others such as Núria Espert, José Carlos Plaza, Emilio Sagi and Gerardo Vera have experimented with the form.

Opera has also begun to be seen regularly on television and heard on radio. Beside regular broadcasts, there have also been a number of specially commissioned premières. Such premières were relatively rare prior to 1987 although there were some by composers such as

Xavier Montsalvatge, Lleonard Balada, Luis de Pablo and Tomás Marco to name a few.

Since 1987, the Ministry of Culture has begun to commission new operas annually with many of them staged at the Sala Olimpia, not traditionally known as an opera venue. Despite generally good results, the critical reception of these works has continued to point to a confrontation between old and new aesthetics. The same confrontation exists in the works being done outside the Olimpia, works such as Josep Soler's *Edip i Yocasta* (*Oedipus and Jocasta*, 1986), Alberto García Demestres and José María Prats's *Para tí, soledades sin sombra* (*For You, Solitude without Shadows*, 1989), Antonio Gala and Lleonard Balada's *Cristóbal Colón* (*Christopher Columbus*, 1989), Vicente Molina Foix and Luis de Pablo's *El viajero indiscreto* (*Indiscreet Traveller*, 1990) and Antonio Gallego and Miguel Angel Coria's *Belisa* (1992).

Official support has even been extended to opera designers through a National Competition for Set Design held in Oviedo in 1991 while parallel activities such as panels, conferences, public forums, courses and publications are also rapidly expanding across the country.

A number of recent productions have moved away from traditional forms and have begun to explore the point where opera *per se* and music theatre meet. These have ranged from experiments based on Debussy by Peter Brook and Marius Constant (*Impressions of Pelléas*, 1992) at the Teatro de la Comedia and plays by Charles Santos (*Tramuntana/Tremens*, 1989), to *Very Gentle* and *Berceuse* by Luis de Pablo and *Melodrama* (1988) by Luciano Berio at the María Guerrero.

The *zarzuela* is a form of musical comedy dating back to the days of Calderón. Named for the outdoor performance location at the Palacio de la Zarzuela near Madrid, these musical plays often took the form of allegories. The form was revived in the nineteenth century and though it is still performed at the Teatro de la Zarzuela in Madrid the form is gradually disappearing despite the efforts of groups and individuals such as Antonio Amengual, the organization of special congresses to discuss it, and seminars, prizes and the establishment of organizations devoted to its survival.

Yet *zarzuela* always sells. The annual production by José Tamayo, *Antología de la Zarzuela* (*Zarzuela Anthology*) is always a commercial success. Other productions contained within the seasons of theatres in large urban centres are equally popular. Those who look down on the form argue that it is often done in poor taste, that it is too traditional or too old or too populist.

Dance Theatre

Much of the present interest in traditional dance theatre genres can be traced to successful tours abroad made by Spanish artists. The first was La Argentina (1888–1936), who has been considered the founder of the renaissance of Spanish dance in the twentieth century. Her concert repertoire, though based on folk forms, was brilliantly theatricalized, and this approach was maintained by her successors. La Argentinita (1895–1945), who founded her Ballet de Madrid with Federico García Lorca in 1927, was praised for the purity of her classical style. Carmen Amaya (1913–63) choreographed in the vibrant, passionate Gypsy style of flamenco. The partnership of Rosario (b. 1918) and Antonio (b. 1922) travelled with a wide repertoire of dances – classical, flamenco and regional. Pilar López (b. 1912) formed her own Ballet Español in 1946 with José Greco (b. 1919). From them came Antonio Gades (b. 1936), who later concentrated on flamenco and also made films. All of these dancer-choreographers had companies that toured extensively.

The first government sponsored company was founded in 1970. In 1979 the Ballet Nacional Clásico de España was formed, with Víctor Ullate as its first director. He was succeeded in 1983 by María de Ávila, who acquired ballets by George Balanchine and Antony Tudor. In 1987 Maya Plisitskaia took over, bringing with her works from the Russian repertoire. In 1990 the company was renamed Compañía Nacional de Danza. Its director, Nacho Duato, aims to preserve the classical legacy but also to develop a more contemporary style, largely based on his own work with the Netherlands Dance Theatre.

Cesc Gelabert in *Solos* by the Gelabert/Azzopardi Dance Company.
Photo: Ros Ribas.

Among the most critically acclaimed classical dance productions done in Spain in recent years have been the *Laberinto* (*Labyrinth*) to music by Xavier Montsalvatge and *Don Juan*, both choreographed by José Antonio, *Sueños Flamencos* (*Flamenco Dreams*), choreographed by Cristina Hoyos for her company, and *Allegro Brillante* (*Bright Allegro*), choreographed by Víctor Ullate for his company.

On the modern side, important productions have included *Destiada* choreographed by Edison Valls for Ananda Dansa; and for the same company, his *Crónica Civil 36/39* (*Civil Chronicle 1936–39*), a piece about the effect of the Spanish Civil War on a group of children from Valencia. Other significant works included *Homenaje a K* (*Homage to K*) by the Avelina Argüelles Company and *Alhambra*, *Five to Two* and *Belmonte* by the Gelabert/Azzopardi Dance Company. A number of groups are working in classical, modern and folk forms.

Elena Santos Deulofeu

Theatre for Young Audiences

One of the most neglected areas of theatre during the Franco regime was that of theatre for young audiences. In this respect, both national and municipal governments started to take action beginning in 1976 followed by the autonomous communities. It was in 1976 that the national government organized the Jornadas de estudio sobre teatro escolar, teatro para niños y teatro de títeres (Conference on the Study of School Theatre, Children's Theatre and Puppet Theatre) and the Congreso de teatro para la infancia y la juventud (Children's and Youth Theatre Congress) at the national and international levels.

Also organized was the Centro Nacional de Iniciación del Niño y el Adolescente al Teatro (National Centre for the Introduction of Children and Adolescents to Theatre) which has organized various activities in schools, streets and parks. The municipal government of Madrid has also established a permanent children's theatre at the municipal cultural centre.

In this area, it has, however, most often been the independent theatres that have worked most effectively, even rediscovering classical characters such as Cristobica, Popelim and Aunt Norica. Nevertheless, there are still relatively few productions available for young people even in Madrid and Barcelona.

Among the most important of these centres in 1993 are four in Madrid (El Mirador, San Pol, Pradillo and the Centro Cultural), three in the Valencia area (Escalante, Los Duendes and El Teatre), two in Catalonia (Teatro Regina and Teatro Malic) and one each in Asturias (Teatro Quinquilimón), Aragón (Arbolé), Castilla/León (Teatro Los Gigantillos), and in the Canary Islands (Teatro de Maese Guillermo).

Though festivals of children's theatre have occurred in Bilbao, Seville, Segovia and Tolosa, they still tend to be isolated events.

In terms of content, most companies either utilize classic stories or collective creations, although some modern plays have been written specifically for children. Most of the shows are participatory and have minimal design elements and technical support. Circus techniques are regularly utilized. Street theatre for children outdoors has also been tried in recent years.

Puppet Theatre

There are some companies in Spain that focus exclusively on work for children; some have experimented with shadow theatre, *bunraku* techniques and even black light. In Madrid the most important are the Teatro Permanente de Títeres del Retiro (Retiro Park Permanent Puppet Theatre), La Deliciosa Royale, Los Títeres de Horacio, La Tartana, Sol y Tierra and La Bicicleta. The most important in Catalonia are the Centro de Titelles de Lleida (Lleida Puppet Centre), Els Aquili nos Titelles, Els Farsants, and L'Estaquirot. The most significant in the Basque region are Bihar, Bobaya, Tanxarina and Txotxongillo Taldea. Teatro de I. Medianoche, Achiperre, Arbolé, Bambalma Titelles are important in other regions.

Most of these groups have two objectives – education of the audiences and the spread of regional languages, especially in the Basque country (which has a long history of using puppets in carnivals and fairs) and in the Comunidad Valenciana. Frequently many of these companies have their own shops in which they can build their own puppets utilizing everything from wood to rubber, from cardboard to corrugated metal and clay.

The work of Francisco de Porras stands out as a pillar of puppet theatre in Madrid, where he has created his own theatre in Retiro Park. One must also mention the work of La tia Norica in Andalucía and of the group Titelles Vergès (founded in 1910 by the Vergès family) who work with both glove-puppets and rod-puppets. La Claca, founded in 1968 in Barcelona by Joan Baixas and his wife Terése, had special importance. They considered puppetry to be an animated fine art and invited the cooperation of important painters such as Antonio Saura, Roberto S. Mata and Joan Miró. It was with Miró that La Claca produced its well known *Mori el Merma* (1978). La Fanfarra was founded in 1976 by Toni Rumbau, who was also the founder of the company Malic in Barcelona in 1984 and the founder of the annual journal *Malic*. The company specializes in traditional Catalonian puppets and Chinese shadow-puppets. Its whole repertoire is based on a character named Malic.

There is also a Centro de Documentación de Títeres (Puppetry Documentation Centre) in Bilbao.

Some of these groups have consciously tried to revive Spain's historic folk puppet tradition which has been nearly lost in the modern period.

Design

Spain's growing interest in design is a relatively recent phenomenon created to a very great extent by the visually oriented generation that emerged after the 1960s. Again, it was mostly the many independent groups which led the way in this field partly because of the limitations created by small spaces and partly their need to keep shows inexpensive.

One of the most important designers working in these new areas is Fabià Puigserver. For his production of García Lorca's *El Publico* (*The Public*), one of the great productions of the decade, he simply created a floor of blue grains which gave the stage both a sense of colour and sound while still allowing the actors freedom to move easily.

A number of designers, however, continue to work in the realistic mode reproducing precise environments in furniture, costumes and props; among them are Gerardo Vera and Tony Cortés. Directors of the 1980s and 1990s have tended to ignore realism, preferring instead bare stages and the symbolism of objects rather than the objects themselves. This trend has now found its way even into the work of the major public theatres.

Projections are now used with some regularity in both large and small theatres because of their ability to easily suggest space, time and experience, something which has also been accomplished by using light more imaginatively than in the past. One of the best examples of designing with light was a production by the Basque group Oráin based on Valle-Inclán's *Divinas Palabras* (*Divine Words*) directed by José Carlos Plaza. Similar elements were seen in Plaza's production of another Valle-Inclán work, *Comedias Bárbaras* (*Barbaric Plays*), for the Centro Dramático Nacional.

The increased use of movement in many productions has also led many designers to simply choose bare stages in both the large and small venues. One of the masters of creating bare stage environments has been Andrea d'Odorico, an architect who has a classical and often monumental sense of space. He is most interested in the relationship between mass and emptiness and often utilizes chiaroscuro and imitations of marble. His work was at its best in the extremely beautiful designs he created for Lope's *El castigo sin venganza* (*Punishment Without Vengeance*) and in Benavente's *La Malquerida* (*The Unloved*) as well as his production of *A Midsummer Night's Dream*, all directed by Miguel Narros for the Teatro Español.

Yet despite the attractiveness of the open stage, some designers have also managed to create designs with a visual suggestiveness, often through lighting. Again, one must acknowledge here the work of Puigserver in Brecht's *Mother Courage* and Tony Córtes in Rudolf Sirera's *El veneno del teatro* (*Theatrical Venom*). One of the best known productions in this style was a merry-go-round designed by Frederic Amat for *Tirano Banderas* directed by Lluís Pasquale, and a ship created by Montse Amenós and Isidre

Fabià Puigserver's design for Lluís Pasquale's Centro Dramático Nacional production of García Lorca's *The Public*.
Photo: Ros Ribas.

Prunés for *Mar i cel* (*Sea and Heaven*), a production by Dagoll-Dagom based on the work of Àngel Guimerà.

In many other instances, companies have simply chosen to use the house area rather than the stage. One can even see this now in commercial theatres. This breaking of the proscenium was obvious in such productions as García Lorca's *Comedia sin título* (*Untitled Play*) designed by Puigserver and directed by Lluís Pasquale in which the actors freely mingled with the audience, and in *Un hombre de cinco estrellas* (*Mr Perfect*) by María Manuela Reina in which the actor Arturo Fernández regularly stepped into the house to share his words with the audience.

This tendency to surprise audiences can perhaps also explain the reintroduction of real animals on stage which was a normal practice in the Spanish theatre of the 1920s and 1930s but which has only lately been reclaimed with great success by designers such as d'Odorico in *La malquerida* and in Salvador Távora's *Alhucema*.

Designers were also working with colour much more in the 1980s and 1990s than in years before. In this area, the work that stands out is again mostly that of d'Odorico and Carlos Cytrynowski especially in productions with the Teatro Clásico Español such as *El médico de su honra* by Calderón in which the designer played with chiaroscuro, *Los locos de Valencia* in which the designer used extremely bright tones to suggest the Mediterranean part of the country, and *El vergonzoso en palacio* with a design based on cubes and moving mirrors.

Francisco Nieva and Pedro Moreno are two designers who have regularly worked with textiles in both set and costume design. Nieva particularly has utilized fabrics for special visual and acoustic effects – to suggest the sea or the sky or blood. Among his best shows have been *Coronada y el toro* (*Coronada and the Bull*) and *Corazón de arpia* (*Heart of the Shrew*). Moreno has played with chromatic ranges in his costume

and set designs both for productions of classics such as *El alcalde de Zalamea* (*The Mayor of Zalamea*) and *La dama duende* by Calderón directed by José Luis Alonso and even in more modern plays such as *La risa en los huesos* (*Laughter in the Bones*) by José Bergamín.

Influenced by oriental aesthetics, some designers have played with the expressive possibilities of the human body. Cytrynowski did this in his designs for *El vergonzoso en palacio*, utilizing them as rugs, trees and tables. Gerardo Vera transformed bodies into a fence in García Lorca's *Don Perlimplín*.

Theatre Space and Architecture

One of the most significant achievements of recent Spanish theatre has been the process of decentralization which has allowed for theatre productions outside Madrid and Barcelona. In smaller cities, theatre was traditionally only done in the summer or for various festivals. Given the growth in productions outside the main centres, new venues were obviously required. In most cases towns and small cities simply restored much older buildings, often nineteenth-century theatres which had been turned into cinemas or which were being used for other less interesting functions. This occurred as well even in the larger centres.

Most Spanish theatres built in the nineteenth and twentieth centuries were, of course, built in the Italian style with proscenium arch stages, but they are all modern in terms of size, machinery, rehearsal space, green rooms, storage and administrative space.

In the wake of these various architectural reconstructions came the creation of an organization called Red Nacional de Teatros y Espacios Públicos (National Network of Theatres and Public Spaces). Begun in 1990 and managed by the Ministry of Culture, this network has been one of the best initiatives of the socialist government. Its first result has been the organization of a Showcase of Contemporary Spanish Theatre.

Some groups have made it clear that they prefer non-traditional venues – old factories, funeral homes, markets, subway platforms, garages and warehouses. The group Els Comediants had great success with *Dimonis*, a collective creation that they performed outdoors in the Parque del Retiro in Madrid, as did La Fura dels Baus company, which performed

Accions in the old Galileo Funeral Home in Madrid. In the case of Els Comediants, the use of the space allowed the director to include fireworks, races and masks, while in the case of Fura dels Baus, the use of the funeral home provoked public outrage through its connection with the dead.

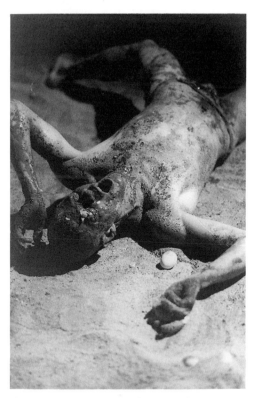

The Fura dels Baus production of *Accions*.
Photo: Gol.

Training

Traditionally, training in the Spanish theatre was done by families of actors on the apprentice system but in the 1990s Spain had two large and important schools – the Institut de Teatre de Barcelona (Theatre Institute of Barcelona) and the Real Escuela Superior de Arte Dramático de Madrid (Royal Higher School of Dramatic Art of Madrid).

The Institut de Teatre (with centres in Vic and Terrasa) operates through the Universidad Autónoma de Barcelona and offers programmes in acting, design, mime, puppetry and directing. The Escuela de Arte Dramático in Madrid offers a three-year programme in acting and one year of directing. Under the most recent reorganization of the general education system, it too can offer graduates a university degree.

Other schools in other parts of Spain such as the Instituto del Teatro de Sevilla, the Escuela Superior de Arte Dramático y Danza de la Comunidad Valenciana, Escuela de Arte Dramático y Danza de Euzkadi, the Instituto del Teatro de Asturias, the Escuela Municipal de Teatro de Santa Cruz de la Palma, and the Escuela Provincial de Teatro in Valladolid (to which should be added schools created recently in Santander, Pamplona and Toledo) are not university level and are directly connected to the Ministry of Education and Science and the autonomous communities. These schools specialize in the training of actors.

Aside from these public schools, there are also private schools, some funded publicly, which appear from time to time. In Barcelona, for example, there are more than thirty schools; in Madrid the number is similar and some are quite prestigious, such as the Laboratorio William Layton and the Proyecto Piamonte. One should also mention the Taller de Zulema Kats, La Cuarta Pared, Triángulo, Ensayo 100, Pradillo, and Teatro Estudio de Madrid.

There are also a number of public institutions such as the Centro Nacional de Nuevas Tendencias Escénicas, El Centro Dramático Nacional and the Compañía Nacional de Teatro Clásico, (all created by the Ministry of Culture) and the Instituto de la Juventud (Youth Institute) which offers the possibility to study playwriting, dramaturgy, directing and set design and which holds literary competitions and offers prizes.

Criticism, Scholarship and Publishing

The old argument around the question of theatre as production or literary genre is still present in Spanish criticism. While some critical voices are in favour of emphasizing text in production – and most of these come from academic fields – other voices push for a re-evaluation of the role of staging, normally the view of practitioners. These two views have created an enmity of sorts between the two camps. In regular critical practice, however, there is a balance between these tendencies, mainly because there are so many critics each representing a different point of view.

Even at the beginning of the 1980s when there was a genuine rebirth of Spanish theatre, critical practice did not seem to change at all although there continued to be important contributors. One even saw a reduction in the number of published collections of theatre reviews and essays coming from such publishers as Escelicer, Sociedad General de Autores, Aguilar, Taurus, Vox, Akal, Cuadernos para el Diálogo, Nueva Cultura, Ediciones Almar, Godoy, Júcar and Prometeo.

By the 1990s, the publishing of such theatre materials had come to depend almost exclusively on the ability of publishers to find public subsidy and even then only a few publishing houses risked on anything other than classics. It has been almost exclusively state institutions, the autonomous communities, and local governments which have taken up the publishing of theatre documentation – detailed registries of dates and credits as well as explaining creative processes. Along this line are several volumes published by the Centro Dramático Nacional, El Centre Dramatic de la Generalitat de Catalunya, El Teatre Lliure and Teatro Español.

Important play anthologies are still published and include *Nuevo Teatro Español* published by the Centro Nacional de Nuevas Tendencias Escénicas and those of the Centro de

Documentación Teatral and the theatre department of the University of Murcia (*Cuadernos de Teatro de la Universidad de Murcia*).

Among the important private publishing houses for theatre are still Fundamentos (Colección Espiral – living authors); La Avispa, a bookstore which has begun its own publishing programme called Colección Teatro; Espasa-Calpe (Colección Austral, inexpensive pocket editions), Cátedra (Letras Hispánicas), and the Sociedad General de Autores de España.

If the offering of theatre collections has been revitalized thanks to support from public institutions that of theatre journals has not. After *Yorick* (1965–71) and *Pipirijaina* (1966–82) ceased operation, only the publications of the Centro de Documentación Teatral of the Ministry of Culture – *El Público* (founded in 1983) and *Primer Acto* (founded 1957) – still exist. Other journals are published but tend to cover very specialized areas – *Estudis Escenics* (founded 1957) and *Estreno* (1973).

María Francisca Vilches de Frutos
Translated by Mayte Gómez

Further Reading

Alvar López, Manuel. *El teatro y su crítica: Reunión de Málaga de 1973*. [Theatre and criticism: the Málaga Conference, 1973]. Málaga: Diputación Provincial de Málaga, 1975. 520 pp.

Amorós, Andrés, Marina Mayoral, and Francisco Nieva. *Análisis de cinco comedias: teatro español de post-guerra*. [Analysis of five comedies: post-war Spanish theatre]. Colección Literatura y Sociedad. Madrid: Castalia, 1977. 218 pp.

Arias de Cassío, Ana María. *Dos siglos de escenografía en Madrid*. [Two centuries of set design in Madrid]. Madrid: Mondadori, 1991.

Asociación de Amigos de la Opera de Madrid, XXV años (1964–1988). [Association of Friends of the Madrid Opera, twenty-five years (1964–1988)]. Madrid: Banco Exterior, 1988.

Berenguer, Angel. *Teoría y Crítica del teatro. Estudios sobre teoría y crítica teatral*. [Essays on the theory and criticism of theatre]. Alcalá de Henares: Universidad de Alcalá, 1991.

Borel, Jean Paul. *El teatro de lo imposible: Ensayo sobre una de las dimensiones fundamentales del teatro español contemporáneo*. [Theatre of the impossible: essays on one of the fundamental dimensions of twentieth-century Spanish theatre]. Translated by Gonzalo Torrente Ballester. Colección Guadarrama de Crítica y Ensayo. Madrid: Ediciones Guadarrama, 1966. 304 pp.

Buero Vallejo, Antonio. *Teatro español actual*. [Spanish theatre today]. Madrid: Fundación Juan March, 1977. 297 pp.

Cabal, Fermín, and José Luis Alonso de Santos. *Teatro español de los 80*. [Spanish theatre in the 1980s]. Colección Arte, Serie Teatro no. 94. Madrid: Fundamentos, 1985.

Centro de Documentación de Títeres de Bilbao. *Anuario de Títeres y Marionetas*. [Yearbook of puppetry]. Bilbao, 1991.

The Contemporary Spanish Theater: A Collection of Critical Essays. Lanham, MD: University Press of America, 1988. 261 pp.

'La Danza en España'. [Dance in Spain]. *Scherzo* 21 (January–February 1988): 51–65.

Dougherty, Dru, and María Francisca Vilches de Frutos. *El teatro en España entre la tradición y la vanguardia*. [Theatre in Spain between tradition and the avant-garde]. Madrid: Consejo Superior de Investigaciones Científicas/Fundación García Lorca, 1992.

Edwards, Gwynne. *Dramatists in Perspective: Spanish Theatre in the 20th Century*. Cardiff: University of Wales Press, 1985. 269 pp.

La escritura teatral a debate: nuevas tendencias escénicas. [Playwriting under debate: new stage trends]. Madrid: Ministerio de Cultura, Dirección General de Música y Teatro, Centro Nacional de Nuevas Tendencias Escénicas, 1986. 275 pp.

Fernández Cambria, Elisa. *Teatro español del siglo XX para la infancia y la juventud*. [Spanish theatre in the twentieth century for children and young audiences.] Madrid: Escuela Española, 1987.

Fernández Cid, Antonio. *Cien años de teatro musical en España 1875–1975*. [One hundred years of musical theatre in Spain 1875–1975]. With a foreword by José Luis Gallardón. Madrid: Real Musical, 1975. 610 pp.

Fernández Torres, Alberto. *Documentos sobre el teatro independiente español*. [Documents on independent theatre in Spain]. Madrid: Centro Nacional de Nuevas Tendencias Escénicas, 1987.

Ferreras, Juan Ignacio. *El teatro en el siglo XX: desde 1936*. [Theatre in the twentieth-century: since 1936]. Madrid: Taurus, 1988. 144 pp.

Gallén, Enric. *El teatre a la ciutat de Barcelona durant el régim franquista (1939–1954)*. [Theatre in Barcelona during the Franco regime (1939–54)]. Barcelona: Institut del Teatre, 1985. 440 pp.

——. *Estudios sobre teatro español clásico y contemporáneo*. [Studies in classical and contemporary Spanish theatre]. Madrid: Fundación Juan March, 1978. 252 pp.

García Lorenzo, Luciano, ed. *Documentos sobre el teatro español contemporáneo*. [Documents on the contemporary Spanish theatre]. Colección Temas no. 17. Alcobendas, Madrid: Sociedad General Española de Librería, 1980. 449 pp.

Giuliano, William. *Buero Vallejo, Sastre, y el teatro de su tiempo*. [Buero Vallejo, Sastre and the theatre of their time]. New York: Las Américas S.A., 1971. 264 pp.

Gordon, José. *Teatro experimental español: Antología e historia*. [Spanish experimental theatre: an anthology and history]. Madrid: Escelicer, 1965. 211 pp.

Hormigón, Juan Antonio. *Teatro, realismo y cultura de masas*. [Theatre, realism and mass culture]. Edición de Bolsillo, Literatura y Ensayo no. 340. Madrid: Cuadernos para el Diálogo, 1974.

——, ed. *Teatro de cada día de José Luis Alonso*. [The everyday theatre of José Luis Alonso]. Madrid: Asociación de Directores de Escena, 1991.

Huerta Calvo, Javier. *El teatro en el siglo XX*. [Theatre in the twentieth-century]. Colección Lectura Crítica de la Literatura española. Madrid: Playor, 1985. 140 pp.

Isasi Angulo, Armando C. *Diálogos del teatro español de la post-guerra: entrevistas*. [Conversations about post-war Spanish theatre: a collection of interviews]. Madrid: Ayuso, 1974. 547 pp.

Marcus, Maury Hal. *Freedom and Tyranny in the Theatre of Late Franco Spain*. Ann Arbor, MI: University Microfilm International, 1984.

Mariscal, Ana [Ana Arroyo]. *Cincuenta años de teatro en Madrid*. [Fifty years of theatre in Madrid]. Madrid: El Avapiés, 1984. 146 pp.

Medina Vicario, Miguel Angel. *El teatro español en el banquillo*. [Spanish theatre on the stand]. Valencia: Fernando Torres, S.A., 1976. 483 pp.

Monleón, José. *Cuatro autores críticos: J.M. Rodríguez Méndez, J. Martín Recuerda, Francisco Nieva y Jesús Campos*. [Four critical authors: J.M. Rodríguez Méndez, J. Martín Recuerda, Francisco Nieva and Jesús Campos]. Granada: Secretariado de Extensión Universitaria, Gabinete de Teatro, 1976. 162 pp.

——. *Treinta años del teatro de la derecha*. [Thirty years of right-wing theatre]. Barcelona: Tusquets, 1971. 155 pp.

Oliva, César. *Cuatro dramaturgos 'realistas' en la escena de hoy: sus contradicciones estéticas. Carlos Muñiz, Lauro Olmo, Rodríguez Méndez, Martín Recuerda*. [Four 'realist' dramatists today: their aesthetic differences]. Murcia: Universidad de Murcia, Departamento de Literatura Española, 1978. 172 pp.

——. *Teatro desde 1936*. [Theatre since 1936]. Colección Estudios, no. 42. Madrid: Alhambra, 1989. 496 pp.

'Opera en España'. [Opera in Spain]. *Scherzo* 46 (July–August 1990).

Pérez de Olaguer, Gonzalo. *Teatre Independent a Catalunya*. [Independent theatre in Catalonia]. Barcelona: Bruguera, 1970.

Pérez-Stansfield, María Pilar. *Direcciones del teatro español de post-guerra*. [Directions in post-war Spanish theatre]. 1st edition. Colección Ensayos. Madrid: Porrúa Turanzas, 1983. 361 pp.

Primer Acto: 30 Años. [Thirty years of First Act]. Madrid: Centro de Documentación Teatral, 1991.

Rodríguez Lloveras, J. *Treinta y cinco años de teatro tras la cortina*. [Thirty-five years of theatre behind the curtain]. Barcelona: By the author, 1970. 306 pp.

Rodríguez Méndez, José María. *Comentarios impertinentes sobre el teatro español*. [Some impertinent comments on Spanish theatre]. Barcelona: Península, 1972. 216 pp.

——. *La incultura teatral en España*. [Theatre illiteracy in Spain]. Barcelona: Laia, 1974. 215 pp.

Ruíz Ramón, Francisco. *Historia del teatro español. Siglo XX*. [History of the Spanish theatre. Twentieth-century]. 8th edition. Madrid: Cátedra, 1989. 576 pp.

Salvat, Ricard. *El teatro como texto, como espectáculo*. [Theatre as text and as spectacle]. Biblioteca de Divulgación Temática no. 17. Barcelona: Montesinos, 1984. 152 pp.

Sastre, Alfonso. *Drama y Sociedad*. [Drama and society]. Madrid: Taurus, 1956. 213 pp.

Vilches de Frutos, María Francisca. 'La temporada teatral española'. [The Spanish theatre season]. *Anales de la Literatura Española Contemporánea*. [Yearbook of contemporary Spanish literature]. 1983–92.

——. 'Panorámica de la escena española en la década de los ochento: Algunas reflexiones'. [A panorama of the Spanish stage in the 1980s: some reflections]. *Anales de le Literatura Española Contemporánea* 17 (1992): 207–20.

Villegas, Juan. *Ideología y discurso crítico sobre el teatro de España y América Latina*. [Ideology and critical discourse in the theatre of Spain and Latin America]. Minneapolis: Prisma Institute, 1988.

Wellwarth, George E. *Spanish Underground Drama*. University Park: Pennsylvania University Press, 1972. 169 pp.

SWEDEN

Part of the Scandinavian peninsula, Sweden is situated in the northernmost part of Europe. The country is large (450,000 square kilometres or 174,000 square miles), but sparsely populated (its 1990 population was 8.6 million). Sweden's capital is Stockholm with a population of 1.5 million, which together with the second largest city Göteborg (Gothenberg, population 731,000) and the university towns Lund, Uppsala and Umeå constitute the main cultural centres. Malmö (population 475,000) is Sweden's third largest city, with a flourishing theatre scene.

Sweden is constitutionally a kingdom but has a parliamentary system of long standing; the king and royal family execute solely ceremonial functions. Sweden also has a state church of the Protestant denomination. A highly developed industrialized nation with an extensive social welfare system, Sweden has one of the world's highest standards of living.

The fact that Sweden has not been at war since 1814 has favoured a political and cultural development more secure and shielded than nearly all other western nations. Until the end of the nineteenth century, Sweden was a sparsely populated agricultural country but during the first decades of the twentieth century it was rapidly transformed into a highly industrialized parliamentary democracy. In 1932 the social democrats won the national elections and were to govern the country until 1976. During this period the party's policy was oriented towards building a so-called 'people's home', that is a social welfare state administered by the national government and municipalities, and financed by high taxes. In foreign policy, Sweden has traditionally maintained strict neutrality which continued through the two world wars.

Culturally Sweden was for a long period dominated by an aristocratic culture associated with the royal court. At the end of the eighteenth century King Gustavus III instigated the founding of the Swedish Academy (1786), as well as two national theatres: the musical theatre Kungliga Teatern (Royal Theatre), commonly called Operan (1773), and the Kungliga Dramatiska Teatern (Royal Dramatic Theatre), called Dramaten (1788). These still-existing institutions have been state supported since the beginning of the twentieth century, and continue to exercise a considerable influence on the theatrical arts of Sweden.

Nineteenth-century liberalism, followed by parliamentary reforms in the 1840s and 1850s, led to the bourgeoisie taking over cultural influence from the court. This led to a significant growth in literature, with August Strindberg (1849–1912) and Selma Lagerlöf (1858–1940, Nobel Prize-winner 1909) the leading figures.

An economic boom brought about by industrialization made it possible to build several new theatres at the turn of the century and the expansion of the railway system brought travelling theatre companies to all parts of the country.

In the 1910s two specific cultural characteristics emerged – *folkparkerna* (people's parks) and *Folkets Hus* (people's houses). Both were gathering places for a wide range of audiences who demanded popular entertainment: in the summertime, theatre and concerts in the parks; during the winter, in the *Folkets Hus*.

The driving force behind this development was the so-called 'people's theatre movement' born in Germany at the end of the nineteenth century. This movement was given other concrete expressions in the founding of the

Skådebanan (1910), an organization for making theatrical performances available to new audience groups, and in the rapid expansion of radio theatre from the 1920s on.

During the 1920s and 1930s, the first municipally supported theatres were founded in Helsingborg (1922) and in Göteborg (1934); before them the music theatre Stora Teatern was founded in Göteborg (1920). The year 1934 also saw the founding of Riksteatern (Swedish National Theatre Centre) whose function was to make theatre available all over the country. In the beginning, this was done by touring productions by major companies; later, Riksteatern mainly did its own productions.

In the 1920s, leading directors Per Lindberg (1890–1944) and Olof Molander (1892–1966) introduced a number of modernistic ideas to the theatre taken mainly from Germany and France. It was at this time as well that the director's pre-eminent position in Swedish theatre was established.

Before 1945, Swedish theatre, like Swedish society, was essentially traditional and only moderately modernized. In the field of theatre, traditions were also firmly rooted, mainly in the form of nineteenth-century psychological realism stemming in part from the plays of Strindberg. The more modern aspects of theatre found their expression in a visionary but intellectually controlled, modestly experimental style of directing and set design.

The urbanization of the country accelerated rapidly after 1945 and people's access to culture in various forms increased drastically. Since 1976 conservatives/liberals and social democrats have alternately governed Sweden, but there had, up to the beginning of the 1990s, been a broad consensus between right-wing and left-wing parties on the main lines for Swedish society: neutrality, generous and widespread support for export and high technology, as well as a continuous refinement and expansion of the social welfare system.

Throughout the post-war period, theatre has also been extremely favoured by massively growing state and municipal subsidies. Right through to the end of the 1980s, theatre audiences grew steadily despite an increasingly severe competition from expanding state television, a vigorous sports scene and new leisure activities created in conjunction with a shortening of working hours and longer vacations. The early 1990s turned out to be a period of

Alf Sjöberg's 1951 Dramaten production of C.J.L. Almqvist's *Amorina*.
Photo: Drottningholm Theatre Museum.

uncertainty, marked by difficult economic conditions and disorientation in cultural areas.

In the 1940s new municipal theatres were founded in Malmö (1944) and Norrköping (1947) and many studio stages also emerged, chiefly used for the presentation of new international drama, mainly Anglo-American and French plays. Private theatre enterprises also abounded offering a broad range of genres to growing audiences. The leading modern directors – Alf Sjöberg (1903–80) and Ingmar Bergman (b. 1918) – rose to fame in the late 1940s. They were, each in his own area of activity – Sjöberg at Dramaten, Bergman in Göteborg, Malmö and at Dramaten – to dominate Swedish theatre (and film) right into the 1990s.

The 1950s was a decade of aesthetic invigoration in Swedish arts: in dance it was Birgit Cullberg (b. 1908) and Birgit Åkesson's (b. 1908) boldly grandlinear choreography; in the theatre it was the concept of 'theatrical theatre'. Inspiration for this movement came from many sources: France brought the actor-focused theatre of Jean-Louis Barrault, the mime of Marcel Marceau, Antonin Artaud's Theatre of Cruelty, and French cabaret. Germany brought Bertolt Brecht's epic theatre. Italian *commedia dell'arte* was also rediscovered during this time. Sjöberg's productions at Dramaten of the Swedish nineteenth-century writer C.J.L. Almqvist's (1793–1866) *Amorina* (1951) and *Drottningens juvelsmycke* (*The Queen's Trinket*, 1957) – both originally novels – signified a national breakthrough for the new theatrical theatre.

The prevalent tradition of psychological realism, however, continued to be strong, and it brought forth a landmark production in the Swedish theatre – the world première at Dramaten of Eugene O'Neill's *Long Day's Journey into Night* in 1956.

At the Malmö Stadsteater, Bergman staged a long series of highly personal interpretations of classical plays, for example *Peer Gynt* and Franz Kafka's *Das Schloß* (*The Castle*). It was here that he began his collaboration with many of the actors – Max von Sydow (b. 1929), Bibi Andersson (b. 1935) and others – who have since played important parts in Bergman's films.

Ideas typical of the 1950s – the aesthetic renewal of forms and an intellectual orientation towards the future – came to a magnificent synthesis in Operan's production of *Aniara* (1959), the libretto of which was based on a suite of poems by Swedish writer Harry Martinson (1904–78, Nobel Prize-winner 1974). Directed by Göran Gentele (1917–72), with music by Karl-Birger Blomdahl (1916–68) and choreography by Birgit Åkesson, the production gave a poetic and at the same time horrifying picture of life after a nuclear holocaust.

One of the new municipal theatres of the 1950s was the Folkteatern (People's Theatre) in Göteborg, financially supported by the city and owned by workers' syndicates and educational institutions. The year 1952 was also the start-up year of the Pionjärteatern (Pioneer Theatre), which played in prisons, mental hospitals and nursing institutions; in 1965, it was incorporated into Riksteatern.

The 1960s was a period of great turbulence in Swedish cultural life. World events, above all the Vietnam War, fused the cultural and political debate into an inseparable entity. For the theatre this also meant an astounding rise in artistic quality and audience support; from the latter part of the decade, theatre became a centre for cultural life as never before or since.

This development proceeded along four distinct lines: a growing interest in the avant-garde; changing working conditions for artists; politicization; and new forms for the 'distribution' of theatre.

Happenings, pop art, concrete music and other new forms, mostly imported from the United States, created opportunities for an avant-garde theatre in unusual and often hitherto unused locales – cellars, museums and the streets, among others. A new and lively discussion of the role of labour and democracy spilled over into the theatre. In practical terms, this meant that actors and other elements of the artistic staff began exercising a greater influence over repertoire and working conditions. Many 'free' groups – aesthetically as well as politically radical – were formed. A number of them would dominate Swedish theatre well into the 1970s. State television's theatre production was also radicalized and many socially committed plays dealing with contemporary Swedish issues were broadcast. A new interest in Brecht's drama and theories of theatre was also emerging especially in the field of training.

Making theatre available to underprivileged groups and previously untapped audiences became one of the main concerns of Swedish cultural life. This led, among other things, to the founding of the first regional theatre in the country, Norrbottensteatern (1967), north of the Arctic Circle, and many regional companies which would operate within Riksteatern –

Västerås (1967), Örebro (1969) and Skellefteå (1969).

In Stockholm, the municipal theatre – Stockholm's Stadsteater – was founded (1961); it was to play a leading role in Swedish theatre in the coming decades. The economically prosperous climate also favoured the building of new theatre houses, often with two or more stages, throughout the country.

The 1970s, especially the first part of the decade, saw a strong consolidation and expansion of publicly supported culture and arts activities with a new state cultural policy implemented in 1974. In the theatre this led to the creation of new regional institutions, new free groups (some of which were later given the status of regional theatres) and a tremendous expansion of theatre for children and *uppsökande teater* (literally 'call-in', 'call-on' or 'visiting' theatre), small and cheap productions which could be performed in various places not primarily designed for theatre. In 1970 the Dramatiska Institutet (Dramatic Institute) was founded, a state-supported training institution for directors, set designers and other professionals in theatre, film, television and radio. Along with this came an increasing concentration on new Swedish drama on state television, the large theatre institutions and the free theatre groups.

Leading theatres in the 1970s were Göteborg's Stadsteater, the Folkteatern in the same city, and Stockholm's Stadsteater, the latter led from 1969 to 1979 by Finnish director Vivica Bandler. Still another important company was Unga Klara (Young Klara, founded in 1975 as a part of Stockholm's Stadsteater). Led throughout its existence by the innovative director Suzanne Osten (b. 1944), Unga Klara has offered a steady series of extremely innovative and advanced theatre productions always collaborating with children as its primary reference group.

In Göteborg director Lennart Hjulström (b. 1938) – one of the creators of collective or group theatre in the 1960s – offered a number of new interpretations of classics by writers such as Strindberg, Ibsen and Kafka at the Stadsteatern and later at the Folkteatern. At the same time Finnish director Ralf Långbacka staged a series of politically radical and theatrically innovative productions of Shakespeare, Chekhov and Brecht at the Stadsteatern in the same city.

In Stockholm, Dramaten also showed its strength in stagings of classics – Sjöberg's productions intellectually razor-sharp, Bergman's emotionally high-strung. Bergman, however, left Sweden for several years after a dispute with the internal revenue authorities and Sjöberg died in 1980.

Among the institutional theatres it was Stockholm's Stadsteater that attracted the liveliest interest: it stood for a theatrical art fostered in the spirit of group theatre, often with collectively written dramas dealing with contemporary social issues. Together with radical and broadly epic productions of classical plays for large audiences, many spectators met theatrical arts for the first time in their lives.

However, towards the end of the decade it became clear that the radical theatre had spent its innovative energy. In fact, the majority of leading free groups came together – after many a long discussion – to stage an enormous touring production, *Vi äro tusenden...* (*We Are Thousands*, 1977), which treated the history of Swedish workers' struggles. But instead of being a step forward for the group theatre movement, this so-called Tältprojektet (Tent Project – the play was performed in a large tent) became something of a terminal point.

A similar point was reached in the institutional theatre when Dramaten made a tremendous effort with *Stormen* (*The Storm*, 1978), an all-pervading project attacking the use of nuclear technology in particular and technocratic rule in general. A growing opinion now came to criticize socially committed theatre which, to many people, seemed frozen in time.

The 1980s became in many respects an era of reassessment. The heavy public financial support of theatre became an object of increasing doubt and criticism and the notion of private sponsorship turned out to be a quickly passing hope. A number of smaller regional theatres were founded (for example, the Folkteatern in Gävle, 1983) but for the first time in Swedish theatre history a regional theatre had to close (the Blekinge Länsteater, 1988). This modest dismantling of what was seen hitherto as a firmly structured, publicly supported theatrical life accelerated in the 1990s.

Throughout the 1980s aesthetic fragmentation and uncertainty was the characteristic feature both in free groups and in the institutions. What was left was eclecticism, meta-theatre and 'art-for-art's-sake'. Several of the most spectacular productions used spectacular spaces – factories, hangars and gasworks. Where the theatre of the 1960s and 1970s had striven to move out of theatres to play for workers, the

Peter Oskarson's 1988 Gävleborgs Folkteater production of *The Great Wrath*.
Photo: David Skoog.

theatre of the 1980s began using the workers' now closed-down work places.

The new free groups that were added to the theatre scene at this time mainly devoted themselves to experiments in form, marked by visually striking design and strict control by directors. Collectively created drama was replaced by more entertainment-oriented stage forms such as vaudevilles and cabarets. Yet the 1980s became an outstanding epoch for new Swedish plays, above all through writers such as Lars Norén (b. 1944) and Staffan Göthe (b. 1944).

One saw many more productions by private theatres and private production enterprises, successfully producing international musicals, farces and comedies. This became a trend which established itself even further in the early 1990s and heavily influenced the repertoire at both the institutional theatres and certain of the free groups. The theatre as a whole also experienced steadily growing influence from commercial television, a form introduced in Sweden towards the end of the 1980s.

A counterbalance to both art theatre and commercial theatre in the 1990s was the revived phenomenon of 'summer spectacles', outdoor productions created by professionals and amateurs working together. The 1990s also saw growing interest in opera and music theatre, dance and mime, pantomime and movement theatre, especially among young audiences.

Structure of the National Theatre Community

Riksteatern and the two national theatres in Stockholm – Dramaten and Operan – base their operations to a large extent on state support, which is decided annually by parliament. In addition, Dramaten and Operan supplement their state subsidies with revenues from ticket sales. In the 1980s Operan also became involved with heavily criticized private sponsorship agreements but these have had only a marginal effect on its financing.

Riksteatern, on the other hand, sells its productions to various arranging bodies across the country. The majority of these are local theatre associations connected to Riksteatern and this makes Riksteatern a very typical model for twentieth century Swedish society generally, with its centre and periphery united by common interests. This parallels the building of workers' unions and other national, popular associations. In their turn, the local theatre associations are subsidized by their own municipal and rural authorities with ticket revenues again constituting another source of income for them. It is, however, the state subsidies to Riksteatern centrally which guarantee Riksteatern's economic viability and that of its local theatre associations.

State cultural policy beginning in 1974 formalized a development that had started in the late 1960s aiming to establish a regional theatre in every province of Sweden. At the same time, Riksteatern's role was formulated as supplementary. That is, when the creation of a full regional theatre network had come about, Riksteatern was to function mainly as a producer of large productions or for theatrical styles not feasible at the regional theatres. The completion of this network has not taken place: some provinces still do not have their own regional theatre. In other places, the regional theatres are very small, employing fewer than ten actors. Only a few regional theatres have economic and staff resources enabling them to offer a broad range of productions for different types of groups, thereby lessening the need for touring productions from Riksteatern.

One idea that will be tested in the late 1990s is the feasibility of redistributing the funds and assets of Riksteatern among existing (and possibly new) regional theatres. Such a re-evaluation would be consistent with Sweden's early 1990s policy of dismantling centralist institutions and authorities. Riksteatern is also considered to be one of the most characteristic examples of social democratic construction, a type which the more ambitious right-wing policies of the 1990s actively seeks to thwart. This could possibly mean that the Swedish model of a national touring theatre, admired for years as a matrix for advanced cultural policy and with direct imitators in Norway and Denmark, could soon turn out to be more history than reality.

Ironic in this context is that a majority of the regional theatres founded since the late 1960s have started out as companies established by Riksteatern itself in various parts of Sweden. Other such regional theatres were municipal ventures which after 1974 were restructured to work in wider geographic areas. Still other theatres have been founded thanks to local political efforts. Regional theatres receive financial support from the state and administrative province, a system created by cultural policies instituted in 1974.

Management structures in the regional theatres are also of various types. Common to them all is that regional and local authorities work together in an economic organization which is given state subsidies, traditionally calculated by the number of staff positions at each theatre. Some of the regional theatres employ – thanks to generous local financial support – larger staffs than would be possible with state subsidies alone.

The regional theatres, as well as Dramaten, Operan and the municipal theatres (which still mainly function locally) have another feature in common: they work under a politically or community-appointed board which selects the theatre's management, usually for a renewable period of three years. In Sweden, the artistic director is also normally the managing director.

The regional theatres receive ticket revenues directly in their home towns, where they autonomously decide the number of performances and such things as extensions of playing periods. However, outside their home cities they, as well as Riksteatern, count on local theatre organizations and other arranging bodies to buy their productions. This makes a predominant part of Swedish theatre life dependent on theatre arrangers other than the initial producing theatres themselves; this also applies to the free groups, unless they have a stage of their own.

There are obvious drawbacks connected with this indirect relationship between producers and audiences, a permanent issue of debate. But there are also advantages in this system which are part and parcel of specific Swedish qualities: each professional theatre can be confident that in practically every town or city in the country there *is* a theatre arranger, someone who interacts with the local community and who, voluntarily and out of their own interest, works for the general good of theatre there.

More than fifty free groups in the early 1990s were receiving direct production support from the state, support which went far toward guaranteeing their survival. The largest amounts were nearly equal to the subsidies of the small regional theatres. Nearly as many free groups were also receiving project grants, funds designated for specifically defined projects and generally quite modest. All appropriations to the free groups are reassessed annually, though the more established groups can generally count on continued subsidy. From the late 1980s, the state also made an effort to ensure local support for groups mainly working in municipal or rural communities or groups working in a defined region in order to give them support analogous to grants given to regional theatres.

Some examples of state support in 1992–3 include Dramaten – 145.8 million Swedish kronor (Skr) (US$18 million); Riksteatern – Skr212.7 million (US$26 million); Operan – Skr251.6 million (US$31 million); Östergötland's Länsteater (the biggest regional theatre, earlier the municipal Norrköping-Linköping's Stadsteater) – Skr17.9 million (US$2 million); Malmö Stadsteater (the biggest theatre institution outside Stockholm) – Skr41.2 million (US$5 million); Norrbottensteatern (the northernmost regional theatre) – Skr6.4 million (US$0.8 million); Älvsborgsteatern (one of the smallest regional theatres) – Skr2.4 million (US$296,000); Skånska Teatern (one of the most established free groups) – Skr2.6 million (US$321,000); Teater UNO (a renowned free group particularly oriented towards children's theatre and with an extensive touring business) – Skr600,000 (US$74,000).

Commercial theatre in Sweden is mainly concentrated in Stockholm. The most important private theatre producer has for a long time been Sandrew Film & Teater AB, a company which runs several theatres in the capital, among them Oscars, a stage for musicals and operettas. Two theatres, China and Folkan, which offer musicals and farces respectively, are Sandrew's main competitors. In the late 1980s and 1990s, efforts were also made to establish private theatres in Malmö (Galateatern) while in Göteborg a small number of private producers have managed to keep up a continuous business.

Economic developments in the 1980s have blurred the previously clear boundaries between different forms of theatre production. A lack of sufficient financial public support and a general tendency towards a more commercially oriented repertoire have made an increasing number of free groups look like small private theatres. Many groups have chosen to try their luck with

permanent houses in Stockholm. Parallel to this development, new independent producers have come into the picture – some out of idealism, some for commercial profit. For audiences in the large cities this has meant a heavily increased offering of theatre.

Professional theatre in Sweden is also *organized* to a very high degree. Actors, directors, dancers, choreographers, designers and other groups are part of the union Svenska Teaterförbundet (Swedish Union of Theatrical Employees) while certain other professional categories are part of the Svenska Musikerförbundet (Swedish Musicians' Union). Playwrights have their own organization – Svenska Dramatikerförbundet (Swedish Playwrights' Union). Theatre critics have a more informal forum – Svenska Teaterkritikers Förening (Swedish Theatre Critics' Association). There are also Swedish sections of several international organizations such as UNIMA, SIBMAS, FIRT, ASSITEJ and IATC among others. Representing theatre managements is Teatrarnas Riksförbund (Association of Swedish Theatres and Orchestras).

All these organizations together compose the Svensk Teaterunion (Swedish Theatre Union), which houses the International Theatre Institute Centre of Sweden. Individual theatres are also members of the union.

Swedish theatre critics annually award two prizes for innovative or especially important achievements in Swedish theatre. One of these is specifically for achievements in children's theatre. A number of the biggest daily newspapers also award annual theatre prizes.

The Swedish government annually awards a prestigious prize for important work in the children's theatre field while the Swedish section of ASSITEJ annually awards one or more children's theatre prizes. As well, the Sveriges Dramatikerförbund awards its August Prize (after Strindberg) for achievements which have especially advanced Swedish drama. Other prizes are connected to activities at specific theatres or to certain parts of the country.

One must also say a few words here about Swedish amateur theatre, which has a vigorous life alongside professional theatre. Amateur theatre associations with more or less continuous operations exist in practically every Swedish town or large village. The more established are members of the national organization ATR – Amatörteatrarnas Riksförbund (National Union of Amateur Theatres). ATR organizes important activities including a central library of plays, courses and consulting programmes with cooperation and partial economic support from Riksteatern.

The amateur theatre also rose conspicuously, artistically as well as politically, during the 1970s and 1980s, thanks to a series of 'workers' plays' and other significant productions. These mainly took place outdoors during the summer (when Swedish theatres are generally closed). There have also been efforts by amateur theatres to establish contacts with interested professionals for appearances and collaboration, something which also has led to similar contacts the other way. This interaction has to a high degree stimulated both the professional as well as the non-professional theatre in Sweden and has led to a number of new initiatives.

One specific form of amateur theatre with a strong local appeal is the New Year's vaudeville which in many places is an annual event. Poking fun at local issues, politicians and celebrities, these are often tremendous box-office successes, even though their artistic qualities are often dubious.

Artistic Profile

Companies

In Sweden it is unusual for a theatre to build on the talents of a single individual. An exception to this rule is the extremely intimate cellar theatre, Brunnsgatan 4, in Stockholm. There one of Sweden's most prominent actors, Allan Edwall (b. 1924), an excellent director and playwright as well, has given himself and several colleagues the opportunity to create intimate, actor-centred productions since the 1980s. Edwall's own one-man stagings – such as *Oedipus* (1987) – are artistic landmarks in Swedish theatre and have also toured internationally.

But Edwall also still occasionally performs at Dramaten, the Swedish national stage, a theatre that has always guaranteed performances of the highest standards in all areas. Through the entire post-war era, Dramaten has represented stability in its professionalism, even if it has not always been the country's artistic leader. Periodically Dramaten has seemed to be in the doldrums, an ancient relic of sorts surrounded by a vigorous theatre life. Its forcefulness partly stems from the various legitimate protests against it, protests aimed at creating an alternative to the artistic level of the company.

In the 1980s and 1990s, Dramaten consciously accentuated its unique position as the national theatre and strengthened its renown as a guarantor of theatrical quality. During this same time Swedish theatre as a whole sought new inspiration, after the political and artistic radicalism of the 1960s and 1970s. With a skilful management at the helm, Dramaten's mighty ship has had fair winds. Even mediocre stagings of classics and what earlier would have been unthinkable commercial productions have sailed along with tremendous success.

In the field of music theatre, Operan plays a similar role as the main upholder of the quality of the art. This, however, has not always automatically meant the same thing as being the most exciting company or the one with the most artistically important output. During the 1980s and 1990s Operan's artistic status was often hotly debated, while bolder endeavours by other music theatres in the country had greater success.

In Göteborg, the music theatre is Stora Teatern (Grand Theatre), which besides opera also produces musicals, operettas and ballet. In the 1980s Stora Teatern successfully produced works of music theatre for young audiences on a special stage. Stora Teatern's future would be linked to the building of a larger house in the mid-1990s.

Göteborg's Stadsteater has during several long periods been among the country's most artistically important. This is also true of Göteborg's smaller dramatic theatre, Folkteatern, whose administrative structure links it to the labour movement in that city, a fact that affects both its repertoire and artistic attitude. Both these theatres have thriving specialty groups: Stadsteater runs a children's and youth theatre, Backa Teater, as well as the suburban stage, Angereds Teater, while Folkteatern does *uppsökande* theatre for both children and adults with almost all its productions being new Swedish plays.

Malmö Stadsteater has a multiple mandate – music and dramatic production – which for years has caused it severe problems. In 1993, the theatre began a reorganization in which the music and dramatic companies became two separate institutions, each with its own stage, ensemble and artistic management.

The third largest municipal theatre in Sweden, Stadsteater in Stockholm, was in the early 1990s at the centre of Swedish theatre debate as a consequence of serious threats posed to it by local politicians. Conservative powers argued that one large dramatic theatre (Dramaten) should suffice for the capital, a position that would also mean that only the state would be involved in financing such theatre in Stockholm.

The artistic profile of Stockholm's Stadsteater has always been rather extroverted with a repertoire directly engaged in political discussion, something that certainly has contributed to the many attacks on it. Stockholm's Stadsteater has several stages in the modern Kulturhuset (House of Culture) in the city's commercial centre – among them the children's and youth theatre stage Lagret (Storeroom) used by Unga Klara.

The regional theatres and the smaller municipal theatres in Sweden are, roughly speaking, of two kinds: one is the mainly traditional 'all-round' model, with a varied repertoire – in Sweden often condescendingly called *smörgåsbordsteater* – rarely doing anything artistically audacious. This policy is not necessarily due to a lack of vision and will, but rather a natural consequence of the theatre being extremely dependent on its audiences.

The other model is represented by theatres which because of their administrative and economic construction feel freer to break new ground in their work. One of these is Norrbottensteatern, the northernmost theatre of Sweden, covering a region the size of Switzerland. Norrbottensteatern has been a source of inspiration for many new regional theatres (also in adjacent countries) thanks to the clearly local character and validity of its repertoire, as well as the democracy of its internal structure. The slogan of Norrbottensteatern, 'Stockholm may be all right, but it's a bit far', is a good summary of the attitudes behind the massive decentralization of Swedish theatre in the late 1960s.

A number of free groups have also managed to establish themselves as locally and regionally important in similar ways. The most prominent example of the early 1990s style is Västanå Teater based in the western province of Värmland, close to Sweden's border with Norway.

This small group very consciously works with material indigenous to the region (its authors and folklore), and it has also been inspired by local storytelling, folk dance and music.

In Södertälje (35 kilometres south of Stockholm), the music theatre group Musikteatergruppen Oktober has become an important cultural and artistic focus. Oktober is one of the pioneers of free groups in Sweden and has had huge successes with its highly personal mix of theatre and music; for example, Ibsen's *En folkfiende* (*An Enemy of the People*, 1978), where the current debate on environment was placed in a bourgeois salon milieu with the help of music characteristic of the period. Oktober also ranks among the chief exponents of fruitful cooperation between professionals and amateurs. In several productions immigrant problems have been treated in an artistically fertile way, as in *Södertäljebor* (*The People of Södertälje*, 1981) and other productions, cast with actors employing different mother tongues (in this production, Swedish, Finnish and Arabic).

Some of the more recently created professional theatres – mainly in Stockholm – have experimented with different companies for each show rather than using permanent groups. Their intention has not been to reach new audiences, or to perform for children as in previous decades. Their work has often been inspired by other art forms, predominantly dance, mime and music. Among the more successful groups have been Teater Galeasen, Teater Aurora and Teater Bouffons.

Many older free groups have, after several years of touring, chosen to try and work from permanent houses in the capital. The most successful is Boulevard Teatern with an impudent and brazen style of acting and a drastically personal attitude in its productions of classical plays such as Gogol's *Revizor* (*The Government Inspector*, 1990) and of comedies such as Alan Ayckbourn's *Season's Greetings* (1991).

Dramaturgy

August Strindberg is Sweden's foremost dramatist with a reputation as important internationally as it is nationally. With his psychologically penetrating naturalistic dramas such as *Fröken Julie* (*Miss Julie*, 1888) and *Dödsdansen* (*Dance of Death*, 1900), Strindberg opened new paths for the modern theatre. With his boldly outlined yet fragmented expressionistic plays such as *Ett drömspel* (*A Dream Play*, 1901) and

Spöksonaten (*The Ghost Sonata*, 1907), he also renewed the drama's formal language.

Strindberg – and virtually all Swedish drama after him – has swung widely between extreme realism (particularly in descriptions of interpersonal conflicts) and a 'drama of the mind', where inner processes have been expressed in advanced poetic and dramatic form.

After 1945, the young Stig Dagerman (1923–54) reflected the two aspects of Strindbergian style in plays tinted with existentialism such as the family drama *Skuggan av Mart* (*The Shadow of Mart*, 1948) and the slightly surrealistic drama of ideas, *Den dödsdömde* (*Sentenced to Death*, 1947). In the 1950s Lars Forssell (b. 1928) showed himself as an advocate of the 'theatrical theatre' with *Kröningen* (*The Coronation*, 1956), a satire of the ancient myth of Alcestis. Forssell later came to follow another line drawn by Strindberg, the historical drama, in *Christina* (1968).

The 1960s and 1970s saw the development of many new forms: linguistic experiments, political agitation drama (agitprop), collectively created plays, formally advanced children's theatre, narrator's theatre, and socially committed television drama.

In the 'talkies' of Sandro Key-Åberg (1922–91), as well as in many productions with small avant-garde theatres, one found deconstructed language reassembled in absurd new combinations resembling comic strips and stilted poetry. Similar tendencies could be seen in some of the dramas of the 1990s, most often under the influence of television and rock videos.

Peter Weiss (1916–82) was born in Czechoslovakia, wrote in German and from the 1940s made his home in Sweden. The works of Weiss are based, not to say steeped, in Marxism with a high theoretical level of consciousness. His plays were the subject of much attention in the 1960s and 1970s for their sophisticated form in dealing with historic processes of key importance, for example, *Jean-Paul Marat förföljd och mördad så som det framställs av patienterna på hospitalet Charenton under ledning av herr de Sade* (*The Assassination and Persecution of Jean-Paul Marat as Performed by the Inmates of the Asylum of Charenton Under the Direction of the Marquis de Sade*, 1965), commonly called *Marat/Sade*; the Auschwitz drama *Rannsakningen* (*The Investigation*, 1965); *Hölderlin* (1971); and the Kafka-adaptation *Nya Processen* (*The New Trial*, 1982).

Per Olov Enquist (b. 1934) treated Swedish

Ingmar Bergman's 1965 Dramaten production of Peter Weiss's *The Investigation*.
Photo: Beata Bergström.

history and social experiences in a similar vein, though Enquist's work is more family-oriented in such plays as *Tribadernas natt* (*Night of the Tribades*, 1975), a play about August Strindberg's marital tribulations.

Collectively created drama most frequently emerged from the free groups and dealt with the social issues of the 1960s and 1970s: the Vietnam War, workers' strikes and municipal politics among other subjects. Many plays from this period were created by two or more playwrights and were staged as group productions within institutional theatres. Leading playwrights Kent Andersson (b. 1933) and Bengt Bratt (b. 1937) scrutinized the decay of the Swedish welfare state in plays such as *Flotten* (*The Raft*, 1968), and *Hemmet* (*The Home*, 1970) in cooperation with a group of actors led by Lennart Hjulström at Göteborg's Stadsteater. Margareta Garpe (b. 1944) and director Suzanne Osten wrote the feminist comedy-drama *Jösses flickor* (*Gee Whiz, Girls*, 1975), about a collective of working-class women; it was a formidable success. Garpe later

went on to treat other women's issues – often intergenerational – in plays such as *Till Julia* (*To Julia*, 1987) and *Alla dagar, alla nätter* (*All Days, All Nights*, 1992).

The most prominent representative of poetic drama is Staffan Westerberg (b. 1937) who in his plays and stage productions, mostly for children, looks at the problems of human existence with an absurdist eye, for example in the Strindberg-adaptation *Ett litet drömspel* (*A Little Dream Play*, 1981).

Two names dominate Swedish drama from the 1980s on: Lars Norén and Staffan Göthe. Norén's dramas deal with problem-ridden family relations and love affairs, and his extreme, often unexpected verbal violence along with the lyrical qualities of his dialogue make his plays strikingly effective on stage.

After a successful career as a poet, Norén made his breakthrough as a playwright in the early 1980s, with terrifying and yet paradoxically humorous portraits of urban intellectuals – *En fruktansvärd lycka* (*A Terrible Bliss*, 1981) and *Underjordens leende* (*Smile of the*

Lennart Hjulström's 1970 Göteborg Stadsteater production of Kent Andersson's *The Home*.
Photo: Werner Goldbach.

Underworld, 1982). In later years he returned to these themes in more broadly shaped, polyphonic dramas such as *Endagsvarelser* (*Creatures of One Day*, 1989) and *Tiden är vårt hem* (*Time is Our Home*, 1993).

The family has always been at the centre of Norén's works, markedly so in his 1980s trilogy *Modet att döda* (*The Courage to Kill*, 1980), *Natten är dagens mor* (*Night is the Mother of Day*, 1982) and *Kaos är granne med Gud* (*Chaos is the Neighbour of God*, 1983). Without being autobiographical, these tragic yet irrepressibly optimistic dramas draw on the author's own experiences and are usually placed in an easily recognizable Swedish social milieu. A variation on this theme is found in Norén's play about Eugene O'Neill and his family, *Och ge oss skuggorna* (*And Give Us the Shadows*, 1991).

Sweden and the transformation of the Swedish welfare state are at the heart of Staffan Göthe's plays. Beginning in the 1970s as an actor and writer of children's plays, Göthe tinted the hearty optimism and radicalism of the epoch with a poetic sadness entirely his own.

Since the early 1980s Göthe has devoted himself to plays for adults, and few writers have reached his excellence in depicting the tragic side of the welfare state: pulling people up by the roots and replanting them in a soil of material wealth and spiritual poverty. Born in sparsely populated northern Sweden, Göthe paints pictures of life in small towns as both bleak and dreamy, a suffocating prison as well as a longed-for idyllic refuge. His trilogy most clearly testifies to this vision: *La Strada dell'amore* (1985), *En uppstoppad hund* (*A Stuffed Dog*, 1986) and *Den perfekta kyssen* (*The Perfect Kiss*, 1990); the last a portrait of a modern inferno where the big city deforms the weak, where 'poets' are de-stroyed by 'murderers'.

Among the younger playwrights who have given voice and body to the 1980s' often desperate pursuit of substance in life, one of the most successful is Stig Larsson (b. 1955), whose plays, films and television dramas – such as *VD* (*Executive Director*, 1987) are stark in language and puzzling in content with a mixture of gratuitous cruelty and longing for contact. Finnish-born Barbro Smeds (b. 1950) offers bizarre portraits of the *nouveaux riches* in their fumbling quest for identity in such plays as *Klättrarens röda öron* (*The Climber's Red Ears*, 1992).

Directors, Directing and Production Styles

The director holds a very strong position in Swedish theatre. Even efforts at developing collective modes of creation have failed to undermine this. A counter-reaction in the early 1990s, in fact, was a call for new, strong directors.

Dramaten plays an important part in this scheme of things: this national company has shaped and supported a long tradition of powerful directors since 1945. At the same time this tradition has constituted a challenge: since the 1910s new performance ideas, aesthetically and democratically founded, have arisen as a counterpoint to the directorial rule at the company.

Alf Sjöberg spent his entire working life at Dramaten. Analytical poignancy, scenic concreteness, formal consciousness, social commitment and an utterly keen ear for contemporary intellectual currents are hallmarks of his directorial achievements. More than fifty years of unbroken activity at one theatre made him unique among western directors. Sjöberg was also a film director and his *Miss Julie* (1950), after the Dramaten production in 1949, brought his work to an even larger audience. He was as well a prolific theoretical essayist, dealing mainly with the relation between theatre and society.

During the late 1940s Sjöberg introduced new international playwrights and philosophical ideas to the Swedish theatre in his stagings, for example, of Sartre's plays. In the 1950s he turned towards the 'theatrical theatre' with his aforementioned Almqvist productions while in the 1960s he was mainly responsible for Brecht's breakthrough in Sweden. During the 1970s he not only staged contemporary interpretations of classical plays but also put 'forbidden areas' of the world – dictatorships and social crises – on stage with his productions of new drama from South Africa, Latin America and eastern Europe. His influence on Swedish theatre was immense, incalculable and indispensable.

Ingmar Bergman came to fame as a theatre director in the 1940s in Helsingborg where he was director of the municipal theatre between 1944 and 1946, as well as in Göteborg. He achieved genuine mastery at the Malmö Stadsteater between 1952 and 1956. A high emotional temperature, black humour, a precise, formal stage language as well as a predilection for theatre magic have long been characteristic of Bergman's directorial style. Alongside his stage and film directing, Bergman has also written plays and film scripts, done radio and television productions – for example, the renowned series *Scener ur ett äktenskap* (*Scenes from a Marriage*, 1973) and *Ansikte mot ansikte* (*Face to Face*, 1975) – and he has also turned out autobiographies.

In 1963 Bergman was appointed manager of Dramaten, the theatre where he has since worked in Sweden. Succeeded by actor-writer Erland Josephson (b. 1923) in 1966, Bergman staged productions there as varied as Edward Albee's *Who's Afraid of Virginia Woolf?* (1963), plays by O'Neill and Peter Weiss's *Rannsakningen* (1966).

Bergman's 1970s stage productions included Strindberg's *Ett drömspel* (1970) and Ibsen's *Vildanden* (*The Wild Duck*, 1972); both variations on Bergman's enquiries into the hardships of human relations; both intimately and tautly staged, devoid of all external splendour and machinery.

This striving towards an appearance of greater simplicity, bordering on austerity, was characteristic of many of Bergman's 1980s productions including *Fröken Julie* (1985), perhaps the most furiously angst-ridden version of Strindberg's erotic drama that has ever been staged in Sweden. This outer simplicity also applies to the remarkable *Markisinnan de Sade* (*Marquis de Sade*, 1990), by Yukio Mishima, a chamber play about unimaginable human passions under an extremely controlled, beautiful surface.

But Bergman has also been drawn towards the spectacular, fragmented and fantastic: *Hamlet* (1986) became a mystifying and many-splendoured voyage in time and history as well as in the human mind. His production of *Peer Gynt* (1991) was Ibsen's life frieze reimagined as a scenic saga, carried by magic, humour and compassion as dominant narrative elements.

The new tendencies in Swedish theatre from the 1960s have followed different lines but common to them has been an opposition to the 'demon director'. This protest has been most

Suzanne Osten's 1975 Unga Klara production of her and Per Lysander's *Medea's Children*, designed by Anita Kajaste.
Photo: André Lafolie.

strongly articulated by actor Keve Hjelm (b. 1922) – a distinguished director in his own right – who as professor at Teaterhögskolan (National School of Theatre) in Stockholm has striven to reinstate the actor's predominance on the stage.

At Stadsteater in Göteborg, actor Lennart Hjulström first worked as 'coordinator' for group productions; he was to go on developing his non-authoritarian directing method in politically accentuated but also associatively theatrical productions of new Swedish plays as well as of classical drama. Among the latter were Strindberg's *Gustav Vasa* (1975) and Ibsen's *Peer Gynt* (at Folkteatern, 1986).

From the free groups have emerged directors such as Suzanne Osten and Peter Oskarson (b. 1951); both made their breakthrough in the 1970s, both are permeated by a feeling for intricate scenic expression and illusion-smashing ironies.

Osten has, with her group Unga Klara (from 1975), taken Swedish theatre for children and youth to hitherto unreached heights, using bold form as well as an intellectually sophisticated literary approach. She has consistently sided with the defenceless, vulnerable child and scrutinized family relations from a psychoanalytical point of view as in her own and Per Lysander's *Medeas barn* (*Medea's Children*, 1975) and

Niklas Rådström's (b. 1952) *Hitler's barndom* (*Hitler's Childhood*, 1984). As a director of plays for adult audiences (and films) Osten has moved towards an increasingly uninhibited but strongly intellectually controlled scenic language.

Peter Oskarson began his career in the 1970s as director of a free group, politically propagandist but formally undogmatic. From the 1980s on, Oskarson has – in Peter Brook's spirit – researched indigenous, popular narrative forms in projects such as *Den stora vreden* (*The Great Wrath*, 1988), a bountiful performance in a closed-down ironworks, with the myths of northern Sweden as the drama's theme and its vast wilderness as its playing space. In *Amledo* (1990), produced in a disused gas bell in Gävle, he approached the traditional Hamlet theme with a multitude of ethnic expressions.

The powerful young directors in Sweden of the 1990s were found mostly in free groups or in small independent productions. However, when these young up-and-coming directors were given the chance to work in institutions, their originality and creative force seemed to be suffocated in a most peculiar way. New trends in Swedish directing during the 1990s – apart from a flaring interest in what has been called 'movement theatre' – were not easy to discern.

Music Theatre

Swedish music theatre had a strong start in 1773 when King Gustavus III urged the founding of the music theatre Kungliga Teatern (Royal Theatre). Known as Operan, the theatre's aim was to promote Swedish theatrical arts. This was, in fact, fifteen years before the Kungliga Dramatiska Teatern, Dramaten, was inaugurated. In 1792, the king was murdered at a masked ball at Operan and thereafter the performing arts in Sweden declined significantly. Music theatre experienced a slow development, especially in terms of its on-stage realization. This fact is partly true of the national music theatre even in the 1990s.

Singers of international magnitude have probably been Sweden's foremost contribution to the art of music theatre, above all since the 1940s with names such as Jussi Björling (1911–60), Birgit Nilsson (b. 1918), Nicolai Gedda (b.

1925), Elisabeth Söderström (b. 1927) and Ingvar Wixell (b. 1931) becoming well known in many parts of the world.

Productions at Operan since the 1920s have often been praised for their set designs (colourful and original specimens of 'painter's theatre' influenced by continental modernism) rather than for their dynamic and psychologically truthful directing style or for delving into the opera's inner qualities.

Two exceptions as directors have been Göran Gentele and Göran Järvefelt (1947–89). Gentele's aforementioned production of *Aniara* (1959), after Harry Martinson's suite of poems, with set designs by painter Sven Erixson (1899–1970), united painter's theatre and artful directing in a music theatre staging of rare poetic stature and intellectual consciousness of contemporary moral problems. Operan's

Göran Gentele's 1959 Operan production of Karl-Birger Blomdahl's *Aniara*, designed by Sven Erixson.
Photo: Enar Merkel Rydberg.

production of Martinson's visionary image of humanity coasting in empty space after a nuclear holocaust was a luminous monument in Swedish music theatre.

Theatrically and dramatically, perhaps the most interesting opera productions have been done by Ingmar Bergman. Stravinsky's *The Rake's Progress* (1961) suited Bergman perfectly, with its grotesque, ironic story of human suffering and humiliation while Mozart's *The Magic Flute* (1975) was a *Singspiel*-film, striking an easy-going and compassionate note, true to the spirit of the composer. Bergman's production of Daniel Börtz's (b. 1943) *Backanterna* (*The Bacchae*, 1991) featured the sophisticated expressionism of painter's theatre (set design by Lennart Mörk, b. 1932) as well as a refined modernist tonal language in its retelling of Euripides' myth.

During the 1980s, Göran Järvefelt staged a series of theatrically imaginative, deeply penetrating Mozart productions, effective musically as well as psychologically, with conductor Arnold Östman (b. 1939) at the historic Drottningholmsteatern. In 1986, Järvefelt also staged Hans Gefors's (b. 1952) nuance-rich opera *Christina* (after Lars Forssell's play) in a production where the modern fragmented ego was integrated with music of complexity and creative eclecticism.

Since the late 1960s a number of music theatre companies have opened outside major cities, theatres with often bold repertoires, playing to audiences previously unfamiliar with opera. These include Norrlandsoperan in Umeå (founded 1974), Musikteatern in Värmland (founded 1975), Ystadoperan (founded 1978) and Vadstena Akademien (founded 1964).

One music theatre company of note in Stockholm is Folkoperan. Starting out as a free group in 1976, it constituted a vital alternative to traditional opera in the capital.

During the early 1990s, the musical generally, with all its possibilities, attracted more and more attention (especially audience-wise) and efforts to give a national Swedish slant to this form have also increased.

Dance Theatre

Modern Swedish dance drama was born with Birgit Cullberg's version of *Fröken Julie* in 1950. A student of the German Kurt Jooss in the late 1930s, Cullberg subsequently created over a hundred ballets. Other important works by her include *Månrenen* (*The Moon Reindeer*, 1957, in Copenhagen) and *Adam och Eva* (*Adam and Eve*, 1961, for the American Ballet Theater).

Distinctness of movement and musical clarity are hallmarks of Cullberg's ballets. The storyline is always strong and crammed with emotions, most often love (seen from a woman's point of view). But her works are also filled with humour, satire and a passion for justice. One prominent example is *Eurydike är död* (*Eurydice is Dead*, 1968) created for her own company, Cullbergbaletten, founded at Riksteatern in 1967. A pioneer in choreography for television, Cullberg twice won the Prix Italia: in 1961, with *Den elaka drottningen* (*The Evil Queen*) and in 1971, with *Rött vin i gröna glas* (*Red Wine in Green Glasses*).

Birgit Cullberg's 1950 dance drama *Miss Julie*.
Photo: Sallstedt.

Cullberg's son, Mats Ek (b. 1945), is also a major choreographer and had resounding successes with three of his first four ballets – *Sankt Göran och draken* (*St George and the Dragon*, 1976), *Soweto* (1977) and *Bernarda* (1978, after García Lorca's play). All were done for Cullbergbaletten. His 'remakes' of classical ballets such as *Giselle* (1982) and *Swan Lake* (1987) have made him and his company (whose artistic director he became in 1985) internationally famous. Indeed, Cullbergbaletten has for several years been Sweden's best known ballet troupe.

Ek's best creations are passionate and persuasive, rarely leaving spectators indifferent. From the very start, he succeeded in achieving three things simultaneously: accentuating the outline of well-known ballet plots, commenting on them (in a Brechtian manner), and giving them a new interpretation, often with extreme dramatic effects. In his close studies of the mechanisms of oppression he has consistently found surprising ways to embody the situation of the underdog.

Ek's movement style is also unconventional – a solid base of classical ballet but usually twisted and turned. His dancers are often found screaming, engaging in slapstick routines or performing in the nude. An incomparable aide in his endeavours has been the eccentric set and costume designs of Marie-Louise Ekman (b. 1944).

Birgit Åkesson, a former student with the German Mary Wigman in the 1940s, developed a unique movement style of her own particularly in her use of the stage floor. During the 1950s she depicted inner worlds and created a series of vitally important works in cooperation with prominent modernists such as poet Erik Lindegren and composer Karl-Birger Blomdahl. Åkesson later turned her attention to researching African dance. Over the years, she has exercised a lasting influence on modern Swedish dance, becoming a revered model to the post-modern generation.

Leading in this latter movement has been Margareta Åsberg (b. 1939) who in 1992 was appointed Sweden's first professor of choreography (at Danshögskolan, the National College of Dance in Stockholm). Some of her creations are based on literary texts including *Atlanten* (*The Atlantic*, 1989) after Marguerite Duras's *Les Yeux bleus, cheveux noirs* (*Blue Eyes, Black*

Hair), and *Bildbeskrivning* (*Description of a Picture*, 1991), a hilarious staging of Heiner Müller's *Bildbeschreibung*.

In Göteborg, Ulf Gadd (b. 1943) was the ingenious director of the ballet at Stora Teatern from 1976 to 1988, the Göteborg Ballet. Teaming up with set and costume designer Svenerik Goude (b. 1945), he created a dazzling series of dance theatre evenings: *Kristina* (1978), *Diaghilevs ryska balett* (*Diaghilev's Ballets Russes*, 1980) and *Gösta Berlings saga* (*The Saga of Gösta Berling*, 1981, after Selma Lagerlöf's novel). Perhaps the greatest of them all was his *Ringen* (*The Ring*, 1983), a three-act, four-hour fresco based on Wagner's *Nibelungen* saga and the story of its conception. Still another major work was his *Tango, Buenos Aires 1907* (1985).

These were glorious years for the Göteborg Ballet, at its best in creations where dance, mime and wordless theatre combined to form extraordinary works of art. Gadd's last works in Sweden (he later moved to Bali to take an active part in the dance community there) were a dramatic *Harmageddon* (1987, this time without Goude), and *Gallos* (1988), for Riksteatern, a sequel to his *Tango*.

Kungliga Baletten (Royal Swedish Ballet, a company within Operan) is Sweden's largest dance company (seventy-five strong) and regularly stages pre-romantic, romantic and modern pieces. One unusual feature of the company is

its yearly summer seasons at Drottningholms-teatern, where the repertoire consists of recreated historical ballets covering the years 1650 to 1815. The first ballets in the series, commencing with *Then fångne Cupido* (*Cupid out of Humour*, 1956), were created by Mary Skeaping (1902–84). Important later creations were done by Regina Beck-Friis (b. 1939) and Ivo Cramér (b. 1921). The latter led his own company, Cramérbaletten, from 1967 to 1986. Also a prolific director of drama, musicals, opera and operetta, Cramér staged *La Dansomanie* (1976) at the Paris Opera and he made the first serious reconstruction of a Noverre ballet, *Jason et Medée* (*Jason and Medea*, 1992), for the Ballet de Nantes and thus helped France to rediscover parts of its own dance history.

The avant-garde Ballet suédois worked in Paris from 1920 to 1925 and scored three of its greatest successes with folk ballets. By 1990, folk dance again entered the scene. A remarkable example of dance's means to develop drama was shown by the Västanå Teater working out in the countryside of western Sweden. In their dramatic version of *Gösta Berlings saga* (1992), the three-beat rhythm of the polka became a point of departure for the entire staging of the play which was directed by folk music and folk dance expert Leif Stinnerbom (b. 1956).

Theatre for Young Audiences

The development in the late 1960s and 1970s of Swedish theatre for young audiences was explosive and brought forth an impressive advancement in both quantity and quality. In many ways theatre for the young became a leading force in Swedish theatre and the progress made in this field was also to influence the theatre as a whole.

This rise of children's theatre was also closely connected to the social situation of the time: at the centre of a radicalized discussion of society were questions concerning the roles and rights of women and children. In cultural discussions the main issues were decentralization and reaching audience groups other than the traditional culturally refined adults. One such group consisted of children and adolescents.

This process was also taking place in a period

when state and municipal support of culture was increasing as a consequence of the tenor of the social debate and Sweden's relative affluence. Later ideological shifts in this debate, together with an extended recession starting in the late 1980s, had an impact on theatre for young audiences too: in the early 1990s its position was once again weakened. Much of its economic subsidies, social opportunities and focus were lost.

Until the middle of the 1960s, the larger Swedish theatres as a rule staged one major family production annually, most often around Christmas when the ordinary repertoire was suspended. The main genre was fairytales, usually staged with a generous display of the theatre's technical resources. Directors and actors in these contexts fulfilled their duties without excessive effort fully conscious of the near impossibility of making one's name in theatre for children.

There were, however, exceptions to the rule: special school productions created with greater and more genuine interest in the special problems of children's theatre were regularly created by Riksteatern as early as the 1950s. In Stockholm, Skolbarnsteatern (School Children's Theatre) was founded, to play with its own ensemble in all the schools of the capital. In the early 1950s Michael Meschke (b. 1932) had also begun to produce marionette and puppet plays in Stockholm, many of them also for young audiences.

As the climate changed in the mid-1960s, a new situation for children's theatre emerged, closely related to the birth of several free theatre groups, most of which were focusing on younger audiences. Soon even the established larger theatre institutions created special ensembles, departments or even stages for the young. Riksteatern formed a special central unit, now named Unga Riks (Young Riks); it is still a powerful factor in the children's theatre scene in Sweden. Göteborg's Stadsteater lets young actors come together in a special ensemble for school theatre. The new regional theatres, in some instances, had theatre for young audiences as their sole mission; among these, ensembles in Växjö (now Kronobergs-teatern) and in Skellefteå (now Västerbottensteatern).

Among the free groups, Narren (Jester) and Fickteatern (Pocket Theatre) were among the leading companies to emerge, with director Suzanne Osten as the most prominent figure. In 1975 she was given the opportunity to form a special ensemble for children's theatre, Unga Klara, within the framework of Stockholm's Stadsteater; it is still an internationally acclaimed centre of theatre for the young.

The guiding star in Osten's work with children's theatre is absolute focus on the child; at the same time, modern psychological and sociological research is actively used for Unga Klara's strongly intellectual work behind the productions. In the late 1980s and into the 1990s Unga Klara alternated between children's theatre and productions aimed at adults, the latter mostly unveiling the inner and outer world of children and adolescents.

Unga Klara's work has become a source of inspiration for many other children's theatre groups but alternative aesthetic attitudes have also developed. For example, Staffan

Westerberg has since the beginning of the 1960s, as actor, director, puppet-maker and playwright, been a representative of a poetic, in all respects playful but at heart extremely serious, children's theatre.

A number of leading playwrights also emerged with the new children's theatres. Many of these writers later wrote plays for adult audiences, plays where experiences drawn from their work in children's theatre are obvious. The most successful, in the area of both theatre for the young and for grown-up audiences, has been Staffan Göthe. An actor and director as well, several of Göthe's plays for children have become classics, often recurring in repertoires across the country and even abroad, most often in Germany – En natt i februari (A February Night, 1972) and Den feruketansvärda semällen (The Horrible Bang, 1978). The seriousness of the new children's theatre, its abhorrence of meaningless entertainment, is well summed up in Göthe's definition of his plays – 'tragedies for children'.

This attitude was also coupled with an exploration of the fairytale's formal aspects. In this, American psychologist Bruno Bettelheim's theories strongly contributed to the formation of a children's theatre seeking new dimensions.

Swedish children's theatre developed mostly in playing areas other than ordinary theatres. Performances often took place in the schools' own spaces, most frequently in gymnasiums, in broad daylight. The theatre went to visit its audiences and it wished to create theatrical miracles without the technical resources of the large theatres. Concentration was kept on dramaturgy and the actors thus created a kind of Poor Theatre which showed even adult groups a way to go beyond traditional illusion-making. Swedish children's theatre became for two decades an experimental centre which gave the entire Swedish theatre a new orientation and outlook.

Because of the need for so much touring – often with several performances a day in different spaces – a need also grew for opportunities to work on a stationary basis as well. That Unga Klara settled in central Stockholm is but one example. Another is the Backa Teater, the children's theatre ensemble of Göteborg's Stads-teater created by director Eva Bergman (b. 1945). Backa Teater has won international acclaim for its informal, showy Shakespeare productions for young audiences such as Twelfth Night (1991). Another important playwright for children, Börje Lindström (b.

1952), has had several of his plays produced by Backa Teater; his chamber play *Åtta år* (*Eight Years*, 1987) about three children's dreams and fantasies, was one of the most influential children's plays of the 1980s.

Lindström has also written plays for Unga Riks, a theatre which through the years has always stimulated the creation of new drama. Another important tale of childhood is *Min store tjocke far* (*My Big Fat Father*, 1989) by Magnus Nilsson (b. 1948), produced by Unga Riks.

Nilsson, Lindström and Göthe, as well as Staffan Westerberg, can be described as stage poets. This vein in Swedish children's theatre is probably more genuinely Swedish in character than the more intellectually analytic, consciously avant-garde theatre, where the leading name continues to be that of Suzanne Osten. Together, these two attitudes represent the meaning of the prodigious and impressive Swedish children's theatre.

Economic and ideological development during the 1980s and early 1990s was unfortunately not so favourable to theatre for young audiences as children themselves do not really pay to go to the theatre. Their visits, rather, are entirely dependent on subsidies and choices made by adults. As children's theatre groups find themselves unable to afford experiments or extensive cooperation with playwrights, stagnation and impaired reputation set in leading to even more unfavourable economic conditions.

This then was the sombre situation Swedish children's theatre found itself in during the 1990s. The negatives continued to grow as the national stage, Dramaten, one of the few artistic organizations with great resources, staged once again exactly the type of grandiose Christmas family theatre against which the entire children's theatre movement originally protested.

Puppet Theatre

Puppet theatre has no strong national tradition in Sweden. Yet, puppet theatre in various forms has been a vital part of the Swedish theatre scene since the 1960s mainly due to a number of artistically fecund experiments featuring combinations of puppets and live actors performing together.

The pioneer in this area was Michael Meschke, who in 1958 founded the small avant-garde Marionetteatern in Stockholm. Meschke has with great perseverance explored puppet theatre's aesthetic possibilities in productions for children as well as for adults. His personal and sophisticated stagings have included both classical and modern drama. Perhaps his best known production was Alfred Jarry's *Ubu Roi* (1964) in which a single human actor in the title role played against a series of puppets. Meschke has also been an important inspiration and teacher for a great number of theatre artists and his theatre in Stockholm still functions as a centre for puppet theatre in Sweden.

Staffan Westerberg started out as a creator of puppet theatre with Meschke but has since evolved his deeply original style at theatres in many parts of the country. Westerberg is a poetic surrealist who can playfully handle almost any conceivable object and transform it into a living figure on stage or television.

The free group Byteatern (Village Theatre) works out of Kalmar in southern Sweden and was designated in 1992 as an official regional theatre. The group was formed by a number of painters, sculptors and textile artists, a fact that has contributed greatly to Byteatern's unique formal language where various objects are given scenic life together with live actors in extremely elaborate productions. Noteworthy examples have been *Den flygande geparden* (*The Flying Cheetah*, 1985), *När valarna försvann* (*When the Whales Disappeared*, 1988) and *Äventyret Peer Gynt* (*Peer Gynt, the Adventure*, an adaptation of Ibsen's play, 1990).

A number of puppet theatres around the country work with a form of storytelling production known as 'usable theatre'. Being mainly for small children, most of them have no discernible artistic profile but their specialty is gentle, quiet narrative productions with live actors and puppets appearing together. The most prominent of these groups is Dockteatern Tittut (Puppet Theatre Peek-a-boo), a pioneer in performing for children under 4 years of age.

Design

Set design after 1945 evolved along two paths analogous to the development of Swedish theatre in general: the realistic/mimetic line building on nineteenth-century standards, and the modernist line – stylish and simplified, following trends in continental theatre movements from the turn of the twentieth century on.

An important, vital side-path from the 1920s has been the so-called 'painter's theatre' in which prominent painters and sculptors have created daring set designs and costumes, mainly at Dramaten and Operan.

From the late 1960s, set design in Sweden has more and more been a question of formation of theatrical space rather than images *per se*. This trend has also thrived thanks to the technological and architectural progress of theatre construction. Such design usually has a strong inclination towards instrumentalism or functionalism, seldom constituting an autonomous world.

As a consequence of the director's domination of Swedish stages, set designers most often have to subjugate themselves to the director's interpretation of the plays. This has generally been the case at the municipal theatres in and outside Stockholm, the regional theatres, and the free groups. At the national stages, with their greater financial resources, set design has adapted to the general pattern though it is indulged in terms of variation, complexity and size.

Leading among technically advanced designers in the country since the 1960s has been Sören Brunes (b. 1938) who, not surprisingly, was trained as an engineer. Mostly working in Stockholm, he began his career with free groups and later worked mainly at Stadsteater. Among the painters who have devoted themselves to set design, Gunilla Palmstierna-Weiss (b. 1928) has been widely acclaimed for her austerely balanced style. She has also created important designs for the plays of her husband, Peter Weiss, and worked extensively with Ingmar Bergman.

The rapid expansion of children's and particularly *uppsökande* theatre since the 1970s has also favoured the growth of cheap, simple scenic solutions. Designers have been required to create economical, flexible and technically inventive works which suggest more than depict. Scenic space has also become narrative following the predominant conception of children's and *uppsökande* theatre's basic functions.

Through the 1980s and into the 1990s, the goal was often simply to find new playing spaces, most frequently for one production only, such as hangars, schoolyards, culverts and so forth, and further accentuated the prevalence of space over the scenographic picture. Moreover, the increasing number of summer plays outdoors has given nature a hitherto unheard-of role in the scenic arts.

Late-twentieth-century ideas in the visual arts – conceptualism, post-modernism and installations – have seldom been brought to Swedish stages. When this has been the case, it has most often occurred in dance or other forms of movement theatre.

Theatre Space and Architecture

Swedish theatre architecture in the twentieth century was concentrated in three distinct periods: the turn of the century, the 1930s and 1940s, and the 1970s.

At the turn of the century, an economic boom and a culturally conscious bourgeoisie combined to create opportunities for the construction of traditional proscenium theatre houses in many Swedish towns and cities: Operan (1898) and Dramaten (1908) in Stockholm, and across the country in towns of various sizes such as Göteborg, Norrköping, Linköping, Kristianstad, Karlstad, Skara, Halmstad, Landskrona, Ystad, Sandviken, Bollnäs, Umeå and Luleå. The majority of these houses still stand; they have been modernized and are continually used by institution theatres and touring companies.

During the 1930s and 1940s modern functional architectural ideals broke through leading to the construction of theatres without balconies, circles or galleries, but with flexible stages. These can be seen in theatres such as the Malmö Stadsteater (1944), which also has Sweden's largest auditorium, some 1,500 seats.

During this period the larger institutional theatres also added small chamber stages – for example, Göteborg's Stadsteater (1937) and Dramaten (1945).

By the 1970s, when regional theatre spread rapidly, came the construction of functional yet flexible houses, where acting areas were often nothing but empty spaces, black boxes, which could be varied in terms of scenic solutions, the use of technology and the placement of audiences. These spaces were also frequently used for non-theatrical purposes such as concerts and conventions.

The new permanent stages, as well as the *uppsökande* theatres, have profited particularly from the revolutionary technical solutions developed by AVAB, Sweden's major electronics company: extremely compact, computerized, portable lighting devices which have won international renown.

Outdoor theatre became popular in Sweden around World War II with productions done on the stages of 'people's parks' and in other locations. After a certain slackening of interest, outdoor theatre has, since the late 1980s, had a renaissance with hundreds of productions each year by professional companies and amateur groups doing 'workers' plays' and co-productions of dramatic, musical and dance performances in places as different as old ships, beaches, ancient monuments, islands, or simply under the sky. One unique feature of Stockholm is the municipally subsidized Parkteatern (Park Theatre), which for more than fifty years has staged free productions in the city's park areas.

Not far from Stockholm at the Royal Palace of Drottningholm (the home of the royal family), the Drottningholmsteatern (1766) is situated; it is the world's only theatre with completely preserved machinery from the eighteenth century. Each summer, Drottningholmsteatern gives performances of Baroque and rococo opera, musical evenings, ballet and pantomimes.

In total, Sweden has more than 3,000 premises used for theatre and other stage purposes; of these, some 350 are stages of more or less permanent status.

Training

Theatre training has, for a long period, been the business of the theatres themselves, mainly at the national stages, Dramaten and Operan. In the 1960s, their two schools were made autonomous institutions and in 1977 all theatre training was integrated into the college system. This includes training for actors, opera singers, directors, set designers, dramaturges, producers, makeup artists, stage technicians, dancers, choreographers, pantomime artists and dance teachers.

Actors are now trained at Teaterhögskolor (National Theatre Schools) in Stockholm, Malmö and Göteborg, each of which accepts ten to twelve students a year. The college in Göteborg has a special training programme for opera singers as well as other musical artists, while Teaterhögskolan in Stockholm also trains deaf actors.

Actors' training takes three and a half years, of which six months are at one of Sweden's professional theatres. Basic training consists of technique training (body and voice), stage presentation and theory. Training is similar at all three schools although certain methodological differences exist between them. Revisions of the curriculum are frequent.

Opera singers have their own school, Musikdramatiska skolan (Music Theatre School) in Stockholm, which annually admits six to eight students. A major part of the curriculum is devoted to individual voice training but in other respects Musikdramatiska skolan has a basic structure similar to the other schools.

Dancers are trained from 7 years of age at Svenska balettskolan (Swedish Ballet School) which has succeeded and replaced the dance school at Operan. Dance teachers, choreographers and pantomime artists are trained at Danshögskolan (National Dance College) founded in 1970. The dance course covers three years and trains dance teachers and choreographers, twelve and three per year, respectively. The pantomime course admits twelve students every third year and trains them for both stage and teaching careers.

Other professions are trained for at the Dramatiska Institutet (Dramatic Institute), founded in 1970.

Since the late 1980s an increasing number of

private schools also offer theatre, opera and musical training, most often high priced and of low status.

All state theatre training is free with students often receiving scholarships and grants as well as state-guaranteed study loans.

Criticism, Scholarship and Publishing

As the number of theatres in Sweden is large, there is more or less continuous theatre criticism and reviewing in most Swedish dailies as well as on the state radio's Channel One. In the early 1990s, however, for economic reasons, the media reduced coverage.

Theatre criticism in the two major national dailies – *Svenska Dagbladet* and *Dagens Nyheter* – exercises a not insignificant influence on the theatre preferences in the country. The two important evening tabloids, *Expressen* and *Aftonbladet*, mostly focus on spectacular productions.

The local press deal with 'their' regional theatres, often extensively, as well as with visits from Riksteatern. Theatre criticism and continual coverage of theatre events are non-existent on both state and commercial television.

Sweden has two independent theatre journals. The quarterly *Entré* produces journalistic and/or theoretical issues devoted to a single theme, plus nation-wide coverage of all new Swedish dramas, operas and children's plays. *Entré* is also the only publishing house in Sweden entirely devoted to issuing books on theatre. Annually, since 1982, it has issued *Teaterårsboken* (*Theatre Yearbook*). *Teatertidningen* (*Theatre Review*), for its part, is a magazine that appears five times a year; it has a more popular image than *Entré* and is oriented towards young and avant-garde theatre. *Teatertidningen* also publishes a separate magazine called *Danstidningen* (*Dance Review*).

Theoretical training for critics and scholars is given at the Institutionen för teater- och filmvetenskap (department of theatre and cinema studies) at Stockholm University. Theatre history and science have been academic disciplines in Sweden since 1946. There are also courses in drama offered by the literature departments at universities in Lund, Göteborg, Uppsala and Umeå.

The Drottningholms Teatermuseum near Stockholm has one of Europe's largest collections of theatre books (approximately 62,000 volumes). The museum also has collections on art and music history, dance and mime.

Claes Englund and Leif Janzon
with Peter Bohlin (Dance Theatre)
Translated by Leif Janzon

Further Reading

Ambjörnsson, Gunilla, and Annika Holm, eds. *Barnteater – en klassfråga.* [Children's theatre – a matter of class]. Stockholm: Rabén & Sjögren, 1970. 144 pp.

Bergman, Gösta M., ed. *Svensk teater. Strukturförändringar och organisation 1900–1970.* [Swedish theatre. Structural changes and organization 1900–70]. Uppsala: Almqvist & Wiksell, 1970. 125 pp.

Dahlström, Gil, *et al.*, eds. *Kungliga Dramatiska Teatern 1788–1988. Jubileumsföreställning i fyra akter.* [The Royal Dramatic Theatre 1788–1988. Jubilee performance in four acts]. Höganäs: Bra Bok, 1988. 280 pp.

Ek, Sverker R. *Spelplatsens magi. Alf Sjöbergs regikonst.* [The magic of the playground. Alf Sjöberg's art of directing]. Stockholm: Gidlunds, 1988. 390 pp.

Engdahl, Horace. *Swedish Ballet and Dance. A Contemporary View.* Stockholm: Svenska Institutet, 1984. 32 pp.

Engel, Ann Marie. *Teater i Folkets Park 1905–1980.* [Theatre in the people's parks, 1905–80]. Göteborg: Akademilitteratur, 1982. 314 pp.

Engel, P.G., and Leif Janzon. *Sju decennier. Svensk teater under 1900-talet.* [Seven decades. Swedish theatre in the twentieth century]. Lund: Forum, 1974. 212 pp.

Englund, Claes, ed. *Teaterårsboken.* [Theatre yearbook]. Stockholm: Entré, annually since 1982.

Fridell, Lena, ed. *Children's Theatre in Sweden.* Stockholm: Swedish Centre of the International Theatre Institute, 1979. 96 pp.

Hägglund, Kent. *Theatre for Children in Sweden.*

A Contemporary View. Stockholm: Svenska Institutet, 1986. 32 pp.

Liljenberg, Bengt. *Svenska stycken efter Strindberg. Anteckningar kring den svenska scendramatiken och dess författare 1910–1960*. [Swedish plays after Strindberg. Notations on the Swedish stage drama and its authors 1910–60]. Stockholm: Carlssons, 1990. 271 pp.

Marker, Lise-Lone, and Frederick Marker. *Ingmar Bergman: A Life in the Theatre*. Revised edition. Cambridge: Cambridge University Press, 1992. 262 pp.

Näslund, Erik. *Birgit Cullberg*. Stockholm: Norstedt, 1978. 369 pp.

Ralf, Klas, ed. *Operan 200 år. Jubelboken*. [The Royal Opera's 200 years. The jubilee book]. Stockholm: Prisma, 1973. 252 pp.

Sjögren, Henrik. *Ingmar Bergman på teatern*. [Ingmar Bergman in the theatre]. Stockholm: Almqvist & Wiksell, 1968. 316 pp.

——. *Stage and Society in Sweden. Aspects of Swedish Theatre Since 1945*. Stockholm: Svenska Institutet, 1979. 182 pp.

Sparby, Monica, ed. *Unga Klara. Barnteater som konst*. [Unga Klara. Children's theatre as art]. Stockholm: Gidlunds, 1986. 208 pp.

Teater i Göteborg. [Theatre in Göteborg]. 3 vols. Umeå: Acta Universitatis Umensis, 1978.

Teater i Stockholm. [Theatre in Stockholm]. 3 vols. Umeå: Acta Universitatis Umensis, 1982.

SWITZERLAND

Set in the centre of western Europe and bordering on Austria, France, Germany, Italy and Liechtenstein, Switzerland has a population of 6.6 million people and a land area of 41,300 square kilometres (15,900 square miles). Switzerland has a complex cultural structure related directly to its equally complex linguistic structure: its largest single linguistic area – representing nearly three-quarters of the population – lies in the northwest, north and northeast, is German-speaking and is adjacent to Germany and Austria. In the west, next to France, 20 per cent of the Swiss population speak French; in the area south of the Alps near the border with Italy, 4 per cent speak Italian. A minority of 1 per cent in the east speak Romansh. The country as a whole is a federation of twenty-six autonomous cantons which have enormous independence especially in cultural and educational matters.

Due to the differing regional identities, there is no such thing as a 'national' Swiss theatre, despite several modern attempts to create one. The rich theatre tradition in the German-speaking part of Switzerland goes back to the Middle Ages; in the French-speaking part, an aristocratic theatre tradition started in the eighteenth century and was discontinued before an entirely new form of theatre life emerged in the twentieth century.

Rooted in religious drama from the tenth century, a much more popular type of Swiss drama began emerging in the nineteenth century after the appearance of German, French and Italian touring companies in the eighteenth century. Eventually, the big cities of Basle, Berne, Geneva, St Gallen and Zürich started building theatres and establishing permanent companies following the model of German court theatres.

The first modern municipal theatre (Stadttheater) was created in Lucerne in 1839. To this day, these theatres have remained typical institutions of professional theatre in Switzerland. In general, they are operated by cooperatives, joint-stock companies or associations, and financed mainly by municipalities. In their programmes, they offer plays as well as operas, operettas and ballet. From the beginning, the new Stadttheater primarily presented the German classics, which meant that High German was the stage language rather than Swiss German, and that German and Austrian actors were regularly invited to perform. Many other German intellectuals came to Switzerland as exiles in the nineteenth century: Georg Büchner, for example, lectured at Zürich University between 1835 and 1837, and Richard Wagner conducted the orchestra at the Stadttheater Zürich from 1849 to 1858.

Up to the mid-twentieth century, in fact, the urban tradition, heavily influenced by Germany, was the only form of drama and theatrical life of any importance in Switzerland. Patronized in the beginning by the upper middle class, the professional stage was directed mainly by foreigners despite being heavily subsidized by public funding.

Arguments for the development of a truly national theatre were put forward as early as the beginning of the nineteenth century when it was suggested that there should be two 'official' companies: one German-speaking and one French-speaking. Even though this remained an unfulfilled dream, a new type of popular Swiss drama began to appear by the end of the nineteenth century. In 1858, the Quodlibet company in Basle revived the tradition of Carnival plays as well as that of Pamphilus Gengenbach's (1480–1525) political dramas.

Gymnastic and rifle clubs, as well as the choral and music societies that mushroomed all over Switzerland at the time also produced monumental festival performances illustrating either historical themes or the facts of everyday life (work, harvest or trade). The amateur theatre groups in Altdorf and Interlaken are particularly well known for their regular productions in High German of Schiller's play *Wilhelm Tell* (focusing on the legendary Medieval Swiss hero). In Vevey, in the French part of the country, it was the unique Fête des Vignerons (Wine Harvest Festival), produced every twenty-five years since 1797 in the market-square by thousands of local performers, that helped develop a strong amateur tradition. The Fête des Vignerons, rooted in popular custom, is centred on the theme of the four seasons.

After Hitler's coup in Berlin in 1933 and his subsequent annexation of Austria, the theatre in the German-speaking part of Switzerland, particularly in Zürich, profited a great deal from the political situation: during this period, many outstanding German-speaking actors and stage directors (mostly Jewish and communist emigrants) fled to Switzerland as political exiles. Their centre was the Schauspielhaus Zürich, a private theatre whose director, Ferdinand Rieser (1886–1947), organized seasons according to available finances. The presence of such stage directors as Leopold Lindtberg (1902–84) and Leonard Steckel (1901–71), of the stage designer Teo Otto (1904–68), and of a strong company, induced Emil Oprecht (1895–1952), Richard Schweizer (1900–65) and Rolf Langnese (1904–68) to found the Neue Schauspiel AG in 1938. Directed by Oskar Wälterlin (1895–1961), who had years before broken new ground in the opera while working as a director in Basle and Frankfurt, and assisted by dramatic adviser Kurt Hirschfeld (1902–64), the Neue Schauspiel AG was the cornerstone of what was to become the most important German-speaking theatre in Europe during World War II.

Bertolt Brecht's plays *Mutter Courage und ihre Kinder* (*Mother Courage and Her Children*, 1941) with the unforgettable German actress Therese Giehse in the leading part, *Der gute Mensch von Sezuan* (*The Good Person of Setzuan*, 1943) and *Leben des Galilei Galileo* (1943) all had their premières at the Schauspielhaus Zürich. Even smaller theatres such as the Stadttheater Chur contributed to the international impact of Swiss theatre in the 1930s and 1940s. In 1947, Hans Curjel (1886–1974), director of the

company, invited Brecht to direct the first performance there of his new play, *Antigone*.

Small anti-establishment theatres in Switzerland started appearing in 1949 when the Compagnie des Faux-Nez in Lausanne and the Theater am Zytglogge in Berne were founded. Since then, over a hundred such small theatres were gradually created and established in basements, lofts, barns and other, often scantily equipped premises.

The significance of the early 'cellar' or basement theatres (Kellertheater) differed according to their location. Programmes consisted not only of traditional and non-traditional scripted plays but also of folk music, mime and cabaret. None of the individual companies was long-lived: most of them appeared for only a few productions and then disappeared again.

In the 1950s and 1960s, these companies – particularly the Rampe in Berne and Maria von Ostfelden's (1896–1971) productions at the Theater an der Winkelwiese in Zürich – offered enriching alternatives to the programmes of the German-language Stadttheater by presenting experimental works by authors such as Ionesco, Beckett, Arrabal and Sartre. Berne, located in the German-speaking part of Switzerland and capital of the country, quickly became the centre for many of these groups, and between 1972 and 1986 an annual International Festival of Small Theatres was held in the city each summer.

Before 1945, national consciousness in the French-speaking part of Switzerland expressed itself in the same way as in the German-speaking part: through folk drama, particularly in the large open-air festivals, for example, the Fête des Vignerons in Vevey. In this production, amateurs played substantial parts instead of just appearing on the stage as supernumeraries. Further examples of these large-scale events were the 1903 Festival vaudois in Lausanne, in which a chorus of 1,800 amateurs sang, and the Fête de juin in Geneva in 1914, in which 1,500 people acted under the direction of Émile Jaques-Dalcroze (1865–1950); Adolphe Appia (1862–1928), famous for his renewal of stage directing, also assisted with the preparations. Inspired by this kind of popular drama, René Morax (1873–1963) founded the Théâtre du Jorat in 1908 in Mézières, a village near Lausanne. Morax wrote popular plays for his wooden theatre, for example *Le Roi David* (*King David*, 1921), with music by Arthur Honegger (1892–1955). In 1918, Charles-Ferdinand Ramuz (1878–1947) wrote the text for Stravinsky's *Histoire du Soldat* (*A Soldier's Story*), performed for the first time in Lausanne.

In the larger cities, French-speaking theatre companies found it difficult to establish a permanent foothold. Until the beginning of World War II in 1939, the Théâtre municipal de Lausanne (founded in 1871) did, however, offer brief seasons, with its own small company of actors and ballet dancers. Due to financial difficulties, both the Théâtre municipal and the Grand Théâtre de Genève (founded in 1879) were reduced to functioning as premises for guest performances only. After the war, the Galas Karsenty Agency presented guest performances by French companies (mainly from Paris); the agency also arranged for these companies to perform in French in other linguistic areas of Switzerland.

In French-speaking Switzerland, the many Théâtres de Poche (Pocket Theatres), which started to appear after 1945, were not really perceived as an alternative but rather as an avant-garde part of the development of French-language theatre life generally.

There was no permanent professional company in the Italian-speaking part of Switzerland (that is in the Canton of Ticino and some valleys of the Canton of Grisons) until the end of the war in 1945. However, an annual *Sacra rappresentazione* (religious performance) had been produced by the inhabitants of the town of Mendrisio since the end of the seventeenth century, and at the end of the nineteenth century, there were regular seasons at the Teatro Apollo in Lugano. Apart from this, though, theatre life in the Italian-speaking part of Switzerland has generally been animated mainly by guest companies from Italy and visiting artists and groups from German-speaking Switzerland.

In the 1970s, the dominant position of the Stadttheater across the country began to be challenged by the many new *Freie Gruppen* (free groups – see **Structure of the National Theatre Community**) formed by actors and directors who were dissatisfied with the conditions at the municipal theatres: the Spilkischte, for example, a free group established in Basle, devoted itself to the production of plays for children, while Norbert Klassen's (b. 1941) experimental Studio am Montag in Berne also offered training to young performers. Zampanoo's Variété in Berne became known for its street performances, while the Theater Momo in Etzgen experimented with masks and mime; in Baden the small company Claque, founded by Paul Weibel (b. 1943) and the Theater 1230 in Berne, tended to deal with socio-political issues. Coprinus in Zürich experimented with literary texts. Federico Emmanuel Pfaffen (b. 1948) created the Komedie Zürich in 1976, a company that was wise enough to look for premises that related to its plays (ships, factories, public squares or parks).

Most of these free groups, including those still existing in the 1990s, have tended to work collectively and many of their productions, like Theater 1230's, have been critical of society at large. On several occasions, this has led to political difficulties and eventually to the cancelling of financial support. Some of these collective creations were done in collaboration with Swiss playwrights while others departed from literary forms almost entirely.

By the 1980s, all these groups began to feel the need for collaboration and organization. In 1983, they formed the Vereinigte Theaterschaffende der Schweiz (VTS – United Swiss Theatre Creators) which promotes this type of theatre, organizes meetings, initiates training programmes, and conducts negotiations in areas of cultural and social policy. The VTS has also developed a national network of performance premises and has helped these groups to attract an ever-increasing public.

In 1982, the first Swiss convention of dramatists was organized in Berne and attended by some thirty Swiss playwrights, publishers and critics. Among the major resolutions passed at the convention was one calling for the appointment of playwrights-in-residence at the Stadttheater, and another demanding more commitment to the production of contemporary drama.

The federal government took special interest in these demands and helped to set up a national Hausautorenmodell (Theatre and Dramatists' Agreement). By 1983–4, this programme made it possible for eighteen playwrights to be involved in fourteen different projects at theatres all over the country for full seasons; the playwrights thus gained an immediate understanding not only of production conditions but also of literary management, public relations and even directing. Because of a lack of financial support, this programme lasted only a few years. However, in the 1990s, several cantons began supporting workshops for dramatists or were giving special writing bursaries. In the 1980s, the Pro Helvetia Foundation, (Swiss Council for the Arts) organized regular meetings for playwrights from all areas of the country.

A number of attempts have also been made

over the years at developing a comprehensive national cultural policy. The federal Clottu Report of 1975, in fact, contained eleven wide-ranging recommendations on the subject. Essentially, the report argued that the federal government should take financial responsibility in cultural matters, that theatre groups should choose areas of specialization rather than trying to be all things to all people, and that theatre exchanges between the different linguistic and cultural areas of the country should be supported by the government.

The report went on to suggest that theatre could be further promoted by the federal government's involvement in the development of national awards, the inclusion of theatre and drama in school and university programmes, and the creation of formal theatre schools for the training of artists in all areas of theatrical endeavour.

Unfortunately, except for increased financial support by the federal government for the exchange of productions between the linguistic areas, the report was largely ignored. Because no constitutional foundation for federal support of cultural activities exists to date, the federal government has carefully avoided extending its involvement in these areas, arguing that municipalities and cantons could best deal with the issues.

After calling together several groups of theatre specialists under the direction of Charles Apothéloz (1922–82) in 1982, the Swiss Centre of the International Theatre Institute advanced fifteen theses for a Swiss national theatre policy. Essentially supporting the Clottu Report and making its recommendations even more specific, the new proposals were accepted in Fribourg in 1985 and published the same year.

Calling on all levels of governments to take responsibility for national theatre life, the new proposals demanded that the federal government coordinate the efforts of both municipal/local and cantonal authorities, regulate copyright conditions and rights of interpretation, and guarantee the social security of theatre professionals. Unfortunately, once again little was done and the debate itself was more or less concluded in 1986 when a proposal to write federal support for the arts into the constitution was defeated in a national referendum.

It should be noted as well that between 1980 and 1985, the seasons' most interesting productions all over the country were brought together in Winterthur, a city near Zürich, at the annual Winterthurer Theater-Mai Festival. Sponsored by various theatre organizations and funded by the Federal Department of the Interior, the event culminated in a series of prizes. In 1986, Swiss theatre schools were invited to join in the festival.

Other theatre festivals of note in Switzerland include the Internationales Festival Kleiner Bühnen, held annually for small theatres in Berne; the Biennale du Théâtre, a festival designed for free groups and held in La Chaux-de-Fonds; the Festival de la Cité and the Festival du Théâtre Contemporain in Lausanne; and the Theaterspektakel held annually in Zürich. During the 700th anniversary of the Swiss Confederation in 1991, numerous theatre events took place; among these, the Canton of Schwyz – one of the three founding states of the Confederation – offered *Das Mythenspiel* (a play based on Swiss myths) by Herbert Meier (b. 1929) as its official contribution to the festivities. As well, the musical *Hop-là* by Jörg Burth (b. 1944), a critical analysis of Switzerland's history, was staged in the Roman amphitheatre in Avenches.

Structure of the National Theatre Community

Because there is no clear-cut national policy for the arts in Switzerland to support professional theatres, virtually every type of theatrical structure can be found. Privately supported commercial enterprises exist side-by-side with highly subsidized non-profit companies as well as barely subsidized free theatres. Support may come from regional authorities or municipalities, from the cantons and – exceptionally – from the federal government. In general,

municipalities carry the largest part of the financial burden. In 1981, for example, the nationwide public expenditure for the arts amounted to some 149 million Swiss francs. Regional and municipal governments contributed 67 per cent of the total, while the cantons contributed barely 30 per cent. The federal government contributed only one-quarter of 1 per cent. The remaining funds came from the SRG, the Swiss Radio and Television Corporation, and specifically from DRS, TSR and RTSI, which represent the three main linguistic areas.

According to the 1990–1 annual report on theatre life in Switzerland, *Szene Schweiz* (*Swiss Stage*, no. 18), a total of 146 institutions offered theatrical productions during the year, ranging from drama to opera, from operettas and musicals to ballet. Ninety-two institutions were in operation in the German-speaking part of Switzerland, forty-eight in the French-speaking part and six in the Italian-speaking part. A further breakdown shows that the municipal theatres (which produced in each of the genres) existed only in the German-speaking part of the country. Specifically, in Basle, the Basler Theater has three premises – Grosse Bühne (1,015 seats), Komödie (579) and Kleine Bühne (150) offering thirty productions per year and employing 600 people; in Berne, Stadttheater Bern (789 seats; eighteen productions), Lucerne, Stadttheater Luzern (558 seats; seventeen productions) and St Gallen, Stadttheater St Gallen (771 seats for operas, 855 for plays; twenty-seven productions).

Apart from these multi-stage, multi-genre enterprises, Switzerland has thirteen additional companies which specifically produce spoken drama. They are all major companies, supported by public funds, and seat from 300 to 1,000. Among them are the Schauspielhaus Zürich – Grosse Bühne (820 seats; eleven productions) and the Schauspielhaus-Keller (100–200 seats; seven productions). Nine of these playhouses are in the German-speaking part of Switzerland, four in the French-speaking part.

There is only one building designed specifically for opera in German-speaking Switzerland, the Zürich Opernhaus (1,100 seats; nine productions and four philharmonic concerts) and two in the French-speaking part, Geneva's Grand Théâtre (1,488 seats; ten productions, as well as recitals and concerts) and Lausanne's Théâtre municipal/Opéra de Lausanne (890–923 seats; five productions and concerts).

Szene Schweiz also lists 110 free groups. They offer their productions (two to five per year) in premises that can hold audiences of fifty to 200 people. Sixty-four free groups were operating in the German-speaking part of Switzerland, forty-one in the French-speaking part, and five in the Italian-speaking part. Twenty-two of these groups devote their work to theatre for children and youth (fourteen German-speaking, seven French-speaking, and one Italian-speaking).

In 1990–1, there were six free dance companies (four of which were in the German-speaking part, one in the French- and one in the Italian-speaking part of the country). Ten touring companies operate in German-speaking Switzerland; eight offering plays and two offering operas. The opera groups include Zürich's Opera Factory and Unterlunkhofen's Schweizer Gastspieloper. The large stages (the Stadttheater, the Schauspielhäuser and the opera houses) receive public funding, mainly from the municipalities in which they are located. In recent years, larger regional communities and the cantons have also offered financial support. In the 1987–8 season, for example, the Opernhaus Zürich had an annual budget of 59 million Swiss francs (SFr). Of this figure, the City of Zürich contributed SFr21 million while the Canton of Zürich contributed SFr17 million. In the same year, the Stadttheater Bern had an annual budget of SFr21.5 million with the City of Berne contributing SFr8.4 million, the Canton of Berne SFr6.5 million and regional communities another SFr1.5 million. (SFr1 million = US$660,000.)

All publicly funded premises are controlled by supervising bodies that are also responsible for the election of directors. The directors have freedom of choice for their programmes and may employ whatever artistic, technical or managing personnel they need.

The electronic media have also influenced both the range and structure of the country's theatres. Television in particular has enticed performers away from long-term contracts at theatres and raised their financial expectations. However, television productions of stage plays help to bring theatre to larger audiences than would otherwise be possible; but it must also be pointed out that the national television corporation records far fewer theatrical productions than its counterparts in neighbouring countries.

Among the positive examples in this regard, during the 1982–3 season, the Schauspielhaus Zürich and DRS-TV jointly commissioned four dramatists to write one play each in a Swiss-German dialect. The plays were then staged at the theatre and recorded on tape for DRS. But cooperative ventures of this kind are the exception rather than the rule.

Radio drama has also been produced consistently since the 1930s. On average, some fifty plays are produced by the national radio company each year.

An extensive infrastructure protects the interests of virtually all persons involved in theatre matters. The Schweizerischer Bühnenverband (SBV – Swiss Theatre Union) represents most theatre managements. Performers are represented in the German-speaking part of the country by the Schweizerischer Bühnenkünstlerverband (SBKV – Union of Swiss Stage Artists) and in the French-speaking part by the Syndicat Suisse Romand du Spectacle (Swiss Romand Theatre Union).

The Charles Apothéloz-Stiftung is a foundation whose mandate is to provide insurance protection for theatre personnel working with small companies or as soloists who might not have insurance plans of their own. Covering illness, accident, disability and death, it takes into account the special needs of freelance theatre artists and provides this insurance at special rates. It should be noted here as well that the subsidized theatres all have their own insurance and pension plans.

The Schweizerische Kleintheater-Vereinigung (KTV – Association of Swiss Small Theatres) brings together authors, actors and promoters of the arts and organizes two meetings per year during which artists have an opportunity to publicly announce and discuss their seasons.

The aim of the Vereinigte Theaterschaffende der Schweiz (VTS) is to unite solo performers and the free theatre groups which generally do not have their own permanent premises. The VTS works in the fields of cultural and social policy; it organizes national theatre conventions and promotes professional training.

In 1986, an association called Teatri Associati della Svizzera Italiana (TASI – Theatre Association of Italian Switzerland) was founded. It represents the interests of theatres, free groups, and solo performers working in all the genres in the Italian-speaking part of Switzerland.

The Schweizerische Vereinigung für Puppenspiel (Swiss Puppet Theatre Association) is the national branch of UNIMA (the International Puppeteers Union) and promotes the interests of audiences, mass media and public authorities in the puppet theatre field.

The Schweizerische Vereinigung technischer Bühnenberufe (SVtB – Swiss Union of Stage Technicians), the Swiss Centre for OISTAT (the international organization for scenographers, theatre architects and technicians) promotes elementary and advanced training for those working in technical areas.

The Zentralverband Schweizer Volkstheater (ZSV – Swiss Folk Theatre Federation) is comprised of German- and Romansh-speaking amateur groups and offers both courses and advice. The Fédération suisse des sociétés théâtrales d'amateurs (FSSTA – Swiss Federation of Amateur Theatre Societies) is its counterpart for the French-speaking part of Switzerland. The Post da Teatr of Lia Rumantscha specifically encourages and supports Romansh amateur theatre.

All of these organizations have their own bulletins published between four and ten times per year aimed at keeping their members informed of new developments in these areas.

The Schweizer Theatervereine (Swiss Theatre Association) promotes interest in the theatre in the widest possible circles and tries to encourage theatregoing in general. Like youth theatre clubs, they belong to the International Association of Theatrepublic Organizations (IATO).

The country's most prestigious theatrical prize is the Hans Reinhart-Ring, awarded each year by the Schweizerische Gesellschaft für Theaterkultur (Swiss Association for Theatre Studies). It has been awarded to a wide range of artists including actresses Margrit Winter (b. 1917) and Anne-Marie Blanc (b. 1919), actor Bruno Ganz (b. 1941), choreographer Heinz Spoerli (b. 1941), director François Rochaix (b. 1942) and the female clown, Gardi Hutter (b. 1953).

Amateur theatre societies that are members of the ZSV exist in approximately 300 towns and cities and often have very old traditions. During the season of 1983–4, for example, more than a thousand productions were presented; this does not include the several thousand theatrical events offered by associations that are not members of the ZSV. Amateur theatricals are mostly presented in dialect. Time and again, stage directors have felt the attraction of working with amateurs: in earlier times this form of collaboration appealed to Oskar Eberle (1902–56) and Charles Apothéloz, and later to Charles Joris (b. 1936), Gian Gianotti (b. 1949) and Louis Naef (b. 1943). From the artistic point of view, amateur theatre has been markedly successful, in particular the Emmentaler Liebhaberbühne whose production of Friedrich Dürrenmatt's (1921–90) *Der Besuch der alten Dame* (*The Visit*, 1956) was recorded on television. Another very successful amateur company is the Volkstheater Wädenswil near Zürich which produces classical plays in the Zürich dialect.

Artistic Profile

Companies

There are three principal bases upon which theatre life in the German-, French- and Italian-speaking parts of Switzerland exist today: the large municipal theatres, the independent theatres (including independent dance companies), and the so-called 'small artistic scene' involving cabarets, pantomime groups, puppet theatres and *chansonniers*.

In the German- and French-speaking parts of the country, the municipal theatres (Stadttheater) usually have at least two stages and offer a wide range of programming including spoken theatre, opera, operetta/musical and dance. The independent theatre and dance companies, on the other hand, often spend a great portion of their seasons touring.

In addition, amateur theatres (especially in the Romansh-speaking part of the country) are of real import offering in some instances performances of plays which might not otherwise be seen, or even such events as outdoor performances. Many of the amateur groups also organize regular festivals.

The Schauspielhaus Zürich is probably the most renowned of Switzerland's larger, publicly funded theatres. The theatre's fame dates back to the 1940s when it became the centre for German-language theatre in Europe and the home of many famous German writers, directors and actors. The atmosphere created then still persists. Many Brecht plays were performed there for the first time during the war; in 1948, the theatre, in fact, premièred Brecht's *Herr Puntila und sein Knecht Matti* (*Puntila and His Man Matti*). All of Max Frisch's (1911–91) plays, from 1945 when *Nun singen sie wieder* (*Now They Sing Again*) was premièred, through to 1967, had their first nights at the Schauspielhaus; so did many of the plays of Switzerland's other internationally known contemporary dramatist, Friedrich Dürrenmatt, whose first play *Es steht geschrieben* (*All As It Is Written*) created a scandal in 1947. In 1938, Carl Zuckmayer's (1898–1977) *Bellmann* was staged in Zürich for the first time, and in 1939 it was the turn of *Der schwarze Hecht* (*Fireworks*) by Paul Burkhard (1911–77). First performances in German of the plays of major French, Italian, Spanish, American and English playwrights – Claudel, Sartre, Giraudoux, Pirandello, García Lorca, O'Neill, Wilder,

Williams and T.S. Eliot – also took place there. Just before the end of the war, Ignazio Silone's *Und er verbarg sich* (*And He Hid*) was shown in German.

Under the artistic direction of Oskar Wälterlin, many of the most important actors from German-speaking Europe contributed to the legendary fame of the Schauspielhaus Zürich: Therese Giehse, Maria Becker (b. 1920), Heinrich Gretler (1887–1977), Gustav Knuth (1901–87), Ernst Ginsberg (1894–1964) and the German Wolfgang Langhoff among others.

After Wälterlin's death in 1961, Kurt Hirschfeld, the theatre's literary adviser since 1938, became director for a short but important period that included the premières of Frisch's *Andorra* in 1961, Dürrenmatt's *Die Physiker* (*The Physicists*) in 1962 and the Austrian poet and dramatist Hugo von Hofmannsthal's *Der Schwierige* (*The Difficult Man*) in 1962. Leopold Lindtberg – who emigrated from Austria and became one of the most important directors at the Schauspielhaus as well as an outstanding film director – took over the company in 1964 and began to introduce modern playwrights such as Genet, Pinter, Shaffer, Mercer and Mrożek in seasons that also contained traditional classics.

Peter Löffler (b. 1926) followed Lindtberg in 1969 after having been the longtime dramatic adviser and colleague of both Wälterlin and Hirschfeld. He appointed the German director Peter Stein as his stage director and German dramaturge Klaus Völker as his dramatic adviser. By setting up a programme centred on 'particularly anti-bourgeois' themes, Löffler intended to give new impetus to the Schauspielhaus. His production of Edward Bond's *Early Morning*, a very successful play in London, triggered a tumultuous rejection, however, by the theatre's 'establishment' public. Frightened authorities put an end to the experiment after one season.

The Schauspielhaus presented more traditionally mixed seasons under the German Harry Buckwitz from 1970 to 1978, and under the Austrian Gerhard Klingenberg from 1978 to 1982. Avant-garde and experimental theatre was offered only outside the main house (in warehouses such as the Tramdepot Tiefenbrunnen, or in the Keller-Studio after 1978).

In 1982 the German Gerd Heinz became the

The 1956 Schauspielhaus Zürich première of Dürrenmatt's *The Visit*, directed by Oskar Wälterlin, starring Therese Giehse and Gustave Knuth. Stage and costume design by Teo Otto.
Photo: W.E. Baur.

director of the Schauspielhaus; he and Werner Düggelin (b. 1929) sought inspiration in Peter Löffler's model and tried to bring new life to the company. With the Austrian Achim Benning, the Schauspielhaus appointed a former director of the Vienna Burgtheater for the second time – the aforementioned Gerhard Klingenberg having been the first. Benning was employed as a director in 1989, but his vision of how the programme could be improved seemed incompatible with the general financial restrictions of public expenditure that became necessary all over Switzerland in the early 1990s; Benning terminated his contract prematurely at the end of the 1992–3 season.

From the mid-60s, the most important avant-garde company in Zürich was the Theater am Neumarkt, under the direction of Felix Rellstab (b. 1924). The company quickly became known for its staging of such writers as Ionesco, Mrożek, Gombrowicz and Handke.

In Basle, the major playhouse is still the Stadttheater; founded in 1873, it became famous between 1925 and 1932 when the young Oskar Wälterlin was its director. The Stadttheater Basel received new energy in 1968 when Werner Düggelin became its director and secured Friedrich Dürrenmatt's close cooperation. At the same time, the Komödie Basel merged with the Stadttheater Basel to form a new enlarged group called the Basler Theater. The Komödie Basel was founded in 1950 by Egon Karter (b. 1911); it achieved early recognition through its ambitious programming and the quality of its actors: the young Maria Schell (b. 1926), for instance, was an early member of the company. Düggelin directed the Basler Theater until 1975. Among his goals was the widening of the scope of programming at the theatre and the commissioning of authors to do modern adaptations of world classics (for example, Dürrenmatt's *König Johann*, adapted from Shakespeare's *King John*).

The theatre also became known for its 'Montagabende', a series of Monday night discussions on topical social issues, aesthetics and experimentation. The Austrian Hans Hollmann, Düggelin's successor in 1975, inaugurated the theatre's new building by presenting a spectacular production of Austrian writer Karl Kraus's (1874–1936) *Die letzen Tage der Menschheit* (*The Last Days of Mankind*) in the theatre's foyer. The German Horst Statkus, who took over the management of the theatre in 1978, extended the Monday night programmes to fill entire weeks focusing on themes such as

peace, psychiatry, youth unrest, foreign policy and political asylum, and using as well film material, readings and conferences. Frank Baumbauer (b. 1945) was appointed director of the Basler Theater in 1988 and restored its international reputation: several times, dramatic productions that were created while he was director were included in the programme of the annual Berliner Theatertreffen der zehn besten deutschsprachigen Inszenierungen (Berlin Meeting of the Ten Best Productions in German).

During his nineteen years as director of the Stadttheater Bern, Walter Oberer (b. 1911) achieved note for presenting forgotten and rarely produced operas such as *The Coronation of Poppea* by Monteverdi (1963–4); he also opened the theatre to a wider audience. His dramatic adviser, Walter Boris Fischer (b. 1940) tried to win young audiences by producing theatre at the youth centre Gaskessel including works by Brecht and Weill. Fischer was later responsible for the arts (especially theatre) at the Migros-Genossenschafts-Bund (Federation of Migros Cooperatives) and was president of the Swiss Centre of the International Theatre Institute.

Since 1972, the Städtebundtheater Biel/Solothurn has been doing important work under the direction of Alex Freihart (b. 1933). In an untiring effort to produce new plays from all the linguistic areas of the country, Freihart formed a project called CH-Dramaturgie (Swiss Dramaturgy) in the late 1970s: he commissioned young dramatists to create modern counterparts to well-known plays. The newly created plays were produced immediately following their 'originals' and, after the two productions, an open discussion was held involving the author, the director and the audience. In 1981, for example, the theatre offered new versions of Ibsen's *Doll's House* by Manfred Schwarz (b. 1932) – *Nora '81*; of Schiller's *Die Räuber* by Manfred Züfle (b. 1936) – *Weitergeräubert* (*Further Robbed*); and of Osborne's *Look Back in Anger* by René Regenass (b. 1935) – *Arme, arme Bären* (*Poor Old Bears*).

In the 1970s, the director of the drama section at the Stadttheater Luzern, Jean-Paul Anderhub (b. 1942), also adopted the policy of addressing a wider audience, especially in the Mobiles Studio where he presented modern anti-establishment plays. The Stadttheater St Gallen pursued the same aim by establishing its Studiobühne.

The artistic and economic model established by the Theater für den Kanton Zürich (TZ) makes it an interesting theatre for the German-speaking part of Switzerland. Founded by Reinhart Spoerri (b. 1930) and based in Winterthur, since 1972 it has toured not only the Canton of Zürich but also other regions, offering a wide palette of productions ranging from popular plays in dialect to demanding classics. It is supported by a cooperative whose paying members are, among others, the municipal authorities of the Canton of Zürich.

In Geneva, the Théâtre de la Comédie has long been the Swiss home of well-known foreign artists including director Jacques Copeau from France, the Pitöeffs from Russia and director Giorgio Strehler from Italy. In its early years, it offered mainly popular boulevard comedies. It began moving away from light entertainment in 1972 when Richard Vachoux (b. 1933), artistic director of the Théâtre de Poche, started cooperating with the Théâtre de la Comédie. In 1982, Benno Besson, a colleague of Brecht's and a former director of the Berliner Volksbühne, took over its artistic direction. During his seven rich and varied years with the company, one production especially needs to be noted – L'Oiseau vert (The Green Bird) after Carlo Gozzi in 1983. The production not only remained in the repertoire for many years but also played in France and in Canada. He also staged various productions with both the Théâtre de la ville in Paris and the Théâtre National in Strasbourg. His successor in 1989 was Claude Stratz (b. 1946).

Another Geneva company, the Théâtre de Carouge/Atelier de Genève, has tended to focus on the work of Swiss writers and has a distinguished record of premières in this area. The company was founded in 1957 by François Simon (1917–82, son of film actor Michel Simon) and Philippe Mentha (b. 1933). In 1979, Mentha founded the Théâtre Kléber-Méleau in an old gas plant in Lausanne-Renens.

In Lausanne, the Centre Dramatique controlled three theatres for many years – the Théâtre de Vidy, the Passerelle de Vidy and the Théâtre Municipal. Each theatre staged its own productions while the centre itself also invited Swiss and foreign companies to perform. In 1989, the German Matthias Langhoff was appointed director of the Théâtre de Vidy and began staging plays by writers seldom seen in Lausanne such as Strindberg, Schnitzler and Heiner Müller. He left in 1991. In the late 1980s, the Théâtre Municipal became essentially an opera house, under the artistic direction of Renée Auphan (b. 1941).

The Lausanne Compagnie des Faux-Nez, an alternative company founded in 1948 by Charles Apothéloz, has since its inception offered a range of theatrical work from avantgarde to street theatre. It has also made a substantial contribution to the translation of plays from German into French, and has encouraged many French-speaking Swiss authors to write for the stage in their own language.

In the 1960s the city of La Chaux-de-Fonds, situated in the French-speaking part of Switzerland where no professional theatre existed, became the home of the Théâtre Populaire Romand (TPR). The company, founded in 1959 in Neuchâtel, was reactivated in 1961 by Charles Joris, who gave it its own unique character: Joris and his group have managed to keep producing collective creations with a great deal of enthusiasm that survives despite tremendous financial difficulties. In their view, theatre is 'an important part of life, a means of understanding our world'. The company performs also for young audiences (see **Theatre for Young Audiences**) and spends much of its time touring not only in Switzerland but also in France and French-speaking Africa.

In the Italian part of Switzerland, the Teatro PAN (formerly Teatro Panzinis) offers regular seasons for both adults and children in Lugano. The stage director Alberto Canetta (b. 1924) has made an important contribution to theatre in the Canton of Ticino by founding and directing the Teatro La Maschera. On Peter Bissegger's (b. 1932) initiative, the Teatro della Svizzera Italiana came to life in 1983 as a professional theatre with neither permanent premises nor a permanent company. Its aim is to perform professional theatre in remote areas of the Italian parts of Switzerland and to introduce Italian theatre in the other linguistic areas of the country. In Verscio, the mime and clown Dimitri (Dimitri Müller, b. 1935 in Berne) founded not only a theatre school but also a playhouse that presents a wide range of domestic and guest productions.

The small Romansh area has too limited a population to support its own permanent professional theatre. However, people who work for the theatre are intent on maintaining a continuity that is vital for the Romansh cultural identity, and an office for the promotion of theatre was created, affiliated since 1977 with the Lia Rumantscha/Ligia Romontscha (the parent organization of the Romansh people) in Chur. Its primary aim is to support critical popular drama.

One of the more unusual theatres in the country is the Goetheanum-Bühne (Goetheanum Stage) in the city of Dornach; it was founded by the German theosophist Rudolf Steiner. Professional actors, eurhythmists and teachers of eurhythmy use the premises to express their interpretations of Steiner's ideas through dramatic techniques inspired by anthroposophy; their performances of Goethe's complete *Faust* have led to new interest in Steiner's work.

Dramaturgy

Switzerland's cultural identity was significantly boosted after World War II by the work of a number of young playwrights, in particular Max Frisch and his junior by ten years, Friedrich Dürrenmatt. Throughout their long careers on the Swiss and international stages, their work increasingly addressed themes and motifs of particular interest to their fellow Swiss.

When Dürrenmatt and Frisch began writing their first relevant plays in the 1940s, they were clearly affected by the Nazi atrocities of World War II. Dürrenmatt's theatrical methods – his witty dialogue, cabaret-like ideas, and his grotesque or tragi-comic plots – were an effective reflection from this period upon the questionable nature of humanity. He argued that burlesque was the only adequate form in which to present such horror since

> tragedy implies an awareness of guilt, of deprivation, of the measure of all things, of perspective and of responsibility. In the muddle of our times, in this last dance of the white race, no one feels guilty any more, no one feels responsible. Everybody just can't help it and didn't want it to happen.

In his plays, Dürrenmatt examines the behaviour of society at large and its reactions to exceptional individuals, as is particularly obvious in *Der Besuch der alten Dame* (*The Visit*, 1956).

Frisch, on the other hand, shows more interest in individual characters and questions the conditions under which individuals can realize their potential when influenced by a society that has preconceived ideas about what a person must be, thereby defining the individual from the outside. The best example for this central problematic in Frisch's work is the play *Andorra* (1961). In *Biographie: Ein Spiel* (*Biography: A Game*), Frisch tries out a variant of his main theme: he asks whether individuals would be able to live differently and better if they could revise and relive their lives. Frisch does not allow his test character to succeed and intentionally leaves the causes of the failure unexplained.

In their early years at the Schauspielhaus, both Dürrenmatt and Frisch received developmental support from both Oskar Wälterlin and Kurt Hirschfeld. It was Wälterlin, Hirschfeld and Leopold Lindtberg who directed most of the premières of their plays.

Among other Swiss writers, only a few dramatists have succeeded in making it on to the stages of playhouses at home and abroad. Among them are the German-speaking authors Herbert Meier, Adolf Muschg (b. 1934), Hansjörg Schneider (b. 1938), Urs Widmer (b. 1938) and Thomas Hürlimann (b. 1950); and the French-speaking dramatist Michel Viala (b. 1933).

Meier was commissioned to write *Das Mythenspiel* for Switzerland's 700th anniversary. Muschg, who lectures on the history of literature at the Swiss Federal Institute of Technology in Zürich, has written plays based on his literary criticism, for example, *Die Aufgeregten von Goethe* (*Goethe's Revolutionaries*, 1971). In his play *Der Schütze Tell* (*The Archer Tell*, 1982), Schneider debunks Switzerland's national hero by presenting him as a 'guy like you and me'.

Widmer's play *Nepal* – premièred in 1977 in Frankfurt-am-Main and staged repeatedly in playhouses all over German-speaking Europe – is a paraphrase of *Waiting for Godot*: Beckett's tramps have moved into town, into an abandoned warehouse. They're no longer hoping, no longer waiting. They just exist, and merely stage their dream of travelling to Nepal. *Grossvater und Halbbruder* (*Grandfather and Half-brother*, premièred in 1981 at the Schauspielhaus Zürich) is Hürlimann's best known drama; it deals with the opportunism of the Swiss middle class during Nazi times.

Viala, a native of Geneva, writes plays for small groups of actors; the play *Séance* (*The Meeting*, Geneva, 1974) presents an old man who holds a general assembly in a bar for an association of which he is the only remaining member; alternately, the old man plays the president, the secretary and the treasurer.

Many Swiss dramatists have also been involved in the writing of plays for radio and television. Approximately forty radio plays are produced annually in either High German or Swiss German for DRS; about the same number are broadcast in French. The Italian-speaking radio for its part broadcasts up to sixty plays annually. In addition, there have been occasional radio versions of films and readings of novels in serial form.

Directors, Directing and Production Styles

Pantomime and Satirical Cabaret

Two forms of theatrical activity that are particularly important in Switzerland should be mentioned here – pantomime and satirical cabaret.

The Swiss have always had a predilection for mimes and mime-clowns. One of the greatest Swiss mime-clowns was Adrien Wettach (1880–1959) who performed under the name Grock. His stage was the circus-ring or the variety theatre. After Grock's death, Dimitri Müller became the most popular mime in the country; he is known simply as Dimitri. After many years of touring, Dimitri settled down in Verscio where he founded his own school to which the Compagnia Teatro Dimitri and a little theatre

are connected. The theatre is host to both the Teatro Dimitri and guest performances.

Other Swiss mimes and mime groups which have won fame in recent years include the female clown Gardi Hutter and the group Mummenschanz. Mummenschanz, founded in 1972 by Andres Bossard (1944–92), Bernie Schürch (b. 1944) and Floriana Frassetto (b. 1950), takes the usually staid mime form into new areas with the performers slipping into fantastic shapes and becoming figures twice normal human size. Often they represent figures such as giant jellyfish, huge amoebae or over-sized human hands. Their precise sketches play on very human themes from sexual union to life and death.

From the 1970s, pantomime entered the streets, squares and other public places. Mixed mime/dance forms emerged, too, and it is has now become difficult to distinguish clearly between mime, dance, drama and even musical-drama.

As for satirical cabaret, it is said to have been created by Swiss-born Rodolphe Salis (1851–97), the founder of the Chat Noir (Black Cat)

The 1991 première of the collective creation *Baguala* by the independent company Teatro delle Radici in Lugano.
Photo: Giuliana Pelli.

cabaret in Paris in 1881. One of the major satirical cabaret companies before World War II was Klaus and Erica Mann's Pfeffermühle (Peppermill) based in Zürich. The Manns emigrated from Munich in 1933 and quickly began employing Swiss artists. Another company of note during the war period was Cornichon (Pickle), founded in Berne by songwriter Walter Lesch (1898–1958). The company's work was enormously critical of Nazi Germany. In Lausanne, the cabaret group Le Coup de soleil (Sunburn) pursued the same goals as Cornichon.

Elsie Attenhofer (b. 1909), Voli Geiler (b. 1920), Emil Hegetschweiler (1887–1959), Margrit Rainer (1914–82), Zarli Carigiet (1907–81), Walter Morath (b. 1918) and Ruedi Walter (1916–90) are among the most important individual exponents of satirical cabaret since 1945. Working as soloists, in pairs or in small groups, further cabaret artists continued the tradition of satirical cabaret while touring throughout the country. Among the memorable performers are the virtuosos César Keiser (b. 1925) and Margrit Läubli (b. 1928), the biting humorist Alfred Rasser (1907–77) with his presentation of *Soldat Läppli*, a Swiss figure akin to *Soldier Schweyk*, and Walter

Roderer (b. 1920), who used caricature and farce. The Basle comic actor Rudolf Bernhard (1901–62) also produced cabaret in his Zürich theatre.

Among the younger generation, Franz Hohler (b. 1943) is well known throughout the German-speaking countries. The Lucerne comic Emil Steinberger (b. 1933, simply called Emil) even achieved international success with his grotesque imitations of everyday social types that remind one of the famous German mime, Karl Valentin.

Whereas in German-speaking Switzerland the theatrical setting for satirical cabaret and mime has been quite important, in the French-speaking part of the country the artists concentrated mainly on the effect of words, music, and interpretation. The Compagnie des Faux-Nez and the Théâtre Boulimie belong to the most important French-speaking cabaret companies in Switzerland since 1945; the Swiss Jean Villard (1895–1982) and Albert Urfer (1914–85) (Gilles et Urfer) and the solo artists Bernard Haller (b. 1933) and Zouc (Isabelle von Allmen, b. 1950) have also been very successful both in Switzerland and France.

Music Theatre

Since publication of the Clottu Report in 1975, the role of music theatre has been the focus of much debate in Switzerland. What is usually discussed is the question of opera programming and opera audiences: most people prefer traditional musical forms and especially traditional operas. Do companies, though, have a responsibility to produce new works in new styles? What if audiences stay away? Opinions differ greatly about whether adherence to the traditional repertoire is in the public interest or not. The Swiss experiences of the late 1970s and 1980s showed that opera is still very popular with audiences of all ages. There is even interest in unconventional productions such as those by the American Robert Wilson and the German Ruth Berghaus in Zürich, or by the Frenchman Jérôme Savary and Matthias Langhoff in Geneva.

However, this positive attitude towards music theatre cannot be found among all classes. In 1980, renovations to the Opernhaus Zürich became the object of a local referendum. Before the vote, there were several demonstrations,

some of them quite violent, in which young people (who belonged mainly to vigorous anti-establishment groups) protested against the project. One group demanded that funds go toward the funding of an autonomous centre for young people. Local authorities agreed to partially finance the centre on condition that the city keep a certain control over its operations, but the petitioners demanded full autonomy or nothing. As a result, the referendum approved renovations to the Opera House. But the riots did move the City of Zürich to fund the Youth Centre for the Arts in the Rote Fabrik (Red Factory). Anti-establishment and avant-garde cultural events had already been taking place in this red-brick industrial complex that had belonged to the municipality since 1972; the range of cultural events there, including many musical events, widened considerably after 1980.

Apart from the Opernhaus Zürich, only one other major opera house exists in the country – the Grand Théâtre de Genève (Geneva Opera House). The Opera House in Zürich has its

The Grand Théâtre de Genève's 1987 production of Rolf Liebermann's opera *The Forest*, designed by William Orlandi.
Photo: Marc Van Appelghem.

own resident company and presents approximately 300 performances per year, whereas the Grand Théâtre stages only about a hundred performances a season (usually of seven different operas and two ballets) and has adopted the system of the *stagione* that is normally used in Italy and France: for each production, actors and members of the production team (usually internationally known figures) are jobbed in, that is appointed as guest personnel. The chorus and the ballet ensemble are the only ones in the company to be permanently employed.

Despite these differences in approach, both institutions have managed to maintain their international reputations. For example, while the German Claus Helmut Drese was the director of the Zürich Opera House in the 1970s, the Frenchman Jean-Pierre Ponnelle and the Austrian Nikolaus Harnoncourt created a remarkable Monteverdi cycle. This production became a model for the staging of other early baroque operas because of its stylistic unity, sensual baroque decorations and costumes, and its musical authenticity. During the 1991–2 season, Alexander Pereira from Vienna was appointed director of the Zürich Opera House. His determination to create an ensemble with

first-class international singers who were employed for more than one role quickly showed its advantages. The supplementary funds necessary to finance this new concept came, on the one hand, from a massive price increase for top seats and, on the other hand, from contributions made by sponsors, thus allowing the Opera House to maintain low prices for the cheaper seats.

Under the management of Hugues Gall (b. 1940), the Geneva Opera House has often been the subject of debate because of its unconventional modes of artistic direction, for example with Rolf Liebermann's (b. 1910) staging of Wagner's *Parsifal* in 1982 or Matthias Langhoff's interpretation of Mozart's *Don Giovanni* in 1991.

Among the numerous internationally known Swiss artists who have worked in these Opera Houses, some have attained world fame. Lisa Della Casa (b. 1919, particularly brilliant in works by Mozart and Strauss) and Edith Mathis (b. 1938), for example, were both very convincing winners of the Reinhart-Ring Award. After Salzburg, Glyndebourne and Berlin, Mathis made her American début in New York in 1970. The tenor Eric Tappy (b. 1931), well known for his interpretations of Mozart, also belongs to this group; as does Fernando Corena (1916–84), the virtuoso interpreter of Italian basso-buffo parts; also the tenor Ernst Haefliger (b. 1919), who was appointed as 'Berliner Kammersänger', and the conductor Nello Santi (b. 1931), a specialist in Italian opera.

In order to introduce contemporary opera to the public, theatre managers have also occasionally offered new works by modern Swiss composers such as Heinrich Sutermeister (b. 1910) with *Die schwarze Spinne* (*The Black Spider*, St Gallen, 1948) and *Die Füße im Feuer* (*The Feet in the Fire*, St Gallen, 1949–50); Willy Burkhard (1900–55) with his only opera, another version of *Die schwarze Spinne*; Rolf Liebermann with his internationally known operas, *Leonore 40/45* (Basle, 1952), *Penelope*

(Salzburg, 1954), *Die Schule der Frauen* (*School for Wives*, Salzburg, 1957) and *La Forêt* (Geneva, 1987); and Rudolf Kelterborn (b. 1931) with *Errettung Thebens* (*The Rescue of Thebes*, Zürich, 1963), *Ein Engel kommt nach Babylon* (*An Angel Comes to Babylon*, Zürich, 1977) and *Der Kirschgarten* (*The Cherry Orchard*, Zürich, 1984).

Finally, a special note about Paul Burkhard, the composer of the musical *Der schwarze Hecht* (*Fireworks*, Zürich, 1939). Burkhard has also created religious lyrical plays for children. Among them, *Zäller Weihnacht* (*Christmas in Zell*, 1960) and *De Zäller Josef* (*Joseph of Zell*, 1964), both of which were created for the children of his home town, Zell, in the Canton of Zürich. These scripts were later used in many Swiss schools.

Dance Theatre

Ballet companies connected to Swiss Opera Houses/Stadttheater were originally engaged only to perform in the theatre's operas or operettas. Actual ballet evenings took place only rarely though attempts at staging them date back to the first decades of the century. It was only after World War II that ballet companies connected to the subsidized theatres in Basle, Berne, Geneva, Lucerne, St Gallen and Zürich succeeded in actually establishing regular ballet seasons. Those in Basle, Geneva and Zürich even began to achieve international note.

From the mid-1950s to the early 1960s, two Soviet ballet masters left their mark on Swiss ballet – Vaslav Orlikovsky (b. 1921) and Nicholas Beriozoff (b. 1906). Orlikovsky began his work in Basle in 1955 with the first staging of an original, full-length ballet in the country, *Swan Lake*. In the following years, he brought many other nineteenth-century classics on to the stage with a particular emphasis on Russian works.

By 1973, one of the Basle company's dancers, Heinz Spoerli began to choreograph as well and working with the company to 1991 took it from one with virtually no international recognition to one known both across Europe and in other parts of the world. Spoerli himself became a frequent guest choreographer and his versions of *Giselle*, *La Fille mal gardée*, *Swan Lake* and *Dead End* have joined the repertoires of many

major ballet troupes. Spoerli's successor was Hungarian-born Youri Vamos.

In 1964, Beriozoff became ballet master at the Zürich Opera House and began staging both classic and modern works ranging from *Sleeping Beauty* (Tchaikovsky) to *The Red Cloak* (Luigi Nono). Ballet audiences began to develop rapidly in Zürich, with the British-born ballerina Gaye Fulton becoming the city's adored star over the next thirteen years.

The next distinguished ballet director was the American Patricia Neary in 1978, formerly an assistant to George Balanchine at the Geneva Opera, who built up an impressive Balanchine repertoire together with a wide range of other works from *Don Quixote* (Nureyev) and *Giselle* (Spoerli) to *Love Songs* (Forsythe). In 1985, she was replaced by a young German choreographer, Uwe Scholz (b. 1958). Scholz began developing the repertoire in still other directions doing his own stagings to works by Schubert, Rachmaninoff and Stravinsky. His first ballet in Zürich – danced to the Haydn oratorio *Schöpfung* (*The Creation*) – was an immediate success and began attracting newer audiences.

The ballet company in Geneva was advised by George Balanchine from 1973 to 1978 and the repertoire was centred around his works. In 1980, the Argentine-born Oscar Araiz (b. 1944) was appointed ballet director. Araiz considered movement to be only one part of theatrical

The Basler Theater's 1983 production of Gluck's *Orpheus and Eurydice*, choreographed by Heinz Spoerli.

dance and he created a series of choreographic works which effectively utilized the dancer within a larger space involving setting and lighting as well.

The director of the Geneva company since 1991 has been Gradimir Pankow (b. 1938). Not a choreographer himself, he has regularly invited guest choreographers (Kylian, Bruce) who have helped to develop the company into one with a distinguished repertoire of experimental modern and classical dance.

All of these troupes have between thirty and forty dancers, which makes them large for Switzerland but only medium-sized in comparison with leading companies in other countries. All have a classical base. The companies connected to the Stadttheater of Berne, Lucerne and St Gallen – also classical – are smaller still, averaging between ten and twenty dancers. Nevertheless, Riccardo Duse (b. 1937), director of the Berne and Lucerne companies in the 1980s, proved that even with severely restricted resources, vivid and serious ballet work could still be done.

Besides these more or less official companies are a number of free companies, all working in areas of modern dance and only barely subsidized (if subsidized at all). The key figure in this movement is Jean Deroc (b. 1925), director of the Schweizer Kammerballett from 1967 into the 1990s, whose work has helped the Kammerballett to achieve genuine note in Europe.

Most of the other small companies – despite their occasional distinguished soloists – have come and gone, exhausted by the combined difficulties of artistic problems and always having to search for money. All these groups have focused exclusively on the development of new work and have been important in expanding audiences for dance across the country.

In 1987, the Belgian Maurice Béjart's Ballet du XXième Siècle moved from Brussels to Lausanne and regularly performed short seasons there between international tours. Among the important productions staged there by the Ballet Béjart Lausanne (since 1992 Rudra Béjart Lausanne) are *La Révolution de 1789 et nous* (*The French Revolution and Us*) in 1989 and *Tod in Wien* (*Death in Vienna*) in 1991.

Major public events which have helped to support dance and dancers in the country include the annual Concours international de choréographie de Nyon (Nyon International Choreography Competition) which operated from 1977 to 1987; the annual Festival de la danse contemporaine de Vernier, founded in 1983; the annual Festival de la Cité de Lausanne; the annual Berner Tanztage (Berne Dance Days); as well as a festival created by Spoerli, Basel tanzt (Basle Dances). Since 1988, the Department for Cultural Events of the Migros-Genossenschafts-Bund has been organizing the biennial international dance festival STEPS. Invited ensembles tour major Swiss cities.

Between 1981 and 1991, study opportunities for young dancers both at home and abroad also increased significantly: in 1980, special classes for talented 14- to 16-year-old dance students and top-class gymnasts were created in the secondary schools in Geneva; this initiative was copied in 1989 in Zürich. These classes are intended to allow pupils to receive their basic education while having special training in private ballet schools or sports centres.

In 1988, the Schweizerische Ballett-Berufsschule Zürich (SBBZ – Swiss Professional School for Ballet) was founded in Zürich. This is the first publicly funded school in the country to offer professional ballet training (funding comes from the City and Canton of Zürich). The Migros-Genossenschafts-Bund awards up to ten scholarships annually to young Swiss dancers. The Prix de Lausanne also gives young dancers an opportunity to perfect their art through a year of free study at an international school.

Several associations concerned with problems of dance generally and dancers specifically united over the years into two national organizations: Schweizerischer Dachverband der Fachkräfte des künstlerischen Tanzes (SDT – Swiss Union of Teachers of Artistic Dance) founded in 1974; and, more recently, Schweizerische Vereinigung der Berufsverbände Tanz (SVBT – Swiss Union of Dance Professionals) founded in 1992.

Theatre for Young Audiences

The cultural meaning of the term 'animation' comes from the French-speaking countries where the word has come to refer to the many activities in which theatres interact with audiences. It can include such things as after-performance discussions, exhibitions, courses, preparation of educational pamphlets and even street theatre productions. In no area is 'animation' as important in Switzerland as it is in the area of theatre for young audiences.

In 1967, the Théâtre Populaire Romand, founded eight years earlier in Neuchâtel as a company for adults, created its first play for young audiences, *Molière et Nous*, as an introduction to theatre. Played 361 times for students, the production led TPR to regularly stage one production per year specifically for school audiences. As an indication of the importance of this work in the company's thinking, it should be noted that more than a dozen issues of the *Journal du TPR* have been devoted to youth theatre subjects. In 1976, the company also held an international conference (the Fifth Biennial of TPR) on the theme, 'Young People and Theatre'.

Also in 1967, Zürich's Theater am Neumarkt initiated another 'animation' event which was repeated over several years. Entitled *Wie eine Aufführung entsteht* (*Birth of a Production*), and originally created by the Schauspielhaus Zürich for its own audience, it was adapted to give young people an insight into the theatrical process as a whole.

The first company for young audiences in German-speaking Switzerland to have its own building was the Spilkischte in Basle. The company – founded in 1974 by Fredy Heller (b. 1943), Gerhard Imbsweiler (b. 1941), Ruth Oswalt (b. 1946) and Fridolin Zaugg (b. 1950) – developed a form somewhere between the fairytale and educational drama.

Geneva's Théâtre Am Stram Gram was created in 1974 by Dominique Catton (b. 1942). Its repertoire ranges from *Beauty and the Beast* and Molière to collectively created works based on the music of Prokofiev and Saint-Saëns. The company also performs in a 'story bus', a small mobile theatre with a tent; in 1992, the country's first theatre built specifically for young audiences was constructed for the Am Stram Gram group.

Two other theatres of note working in the field are the Théâtre Tel Quel from Lausanne which performs in both French and German, and Zampanoo's Variété in Berne, founded in 1976, which presents political questions in a critical light. Another Bernese company, Theater 1230, presents its productions in hospitals, parish halls and gymnasiums.

One special form of 'animation' which has developed in Italian-speaking Switzerland is Ettore Pellandini's (b. 1935) Atelier Mimo which is connected to the cantonal psychiatric clinic. The company consists of a group of patients, ex-patients, clinic employees and theatre professionals who work on mime-mask drama for therapeutic purposes.

Jean Grädel (b. 1943) founded the children's theatre Spatz & Co. in 1976 in Baden (Canton of Argovy). Influenced by the concerns of the 1960s, many of the company's plays deal with problems of growing up. The company is a particular favourite among parents. Spatz & Co. was also instrumental in organizing the first convention of Swiss children's theatres in Bremgarten in 1979. Subsequently, other conventions were organized, with debates often focusing on whether companies should be working for education or entertainment.

Another form of theatre for young audiences is represented by the Basler Jugendtheater (Basle Youth Theatre), founded in 1977. The company consists not of professional actors but of young people themselves.

Most of the newer companies established in the 1980s, such as Theater Smomos in Etzgen, Theater M.A.R.I.A. U.N.S.E.R. in Aarau and Theater Octopus in Berne, tour as a regular part of their work and are always struggling for their very survival.

For years, the Schauspielakademie Zürich ran a programme called Theater im Schulhaus (Theatre in the School); in continuation of this project, the Kinder- und Jugendtheater Zürich (KJTZ – Children's and Youth Theatre) was founded in 1986. It is funded by both the City and the Canton of Zürich, has its own premises (Depot Hardturm), and tours to schools and other facilities in German-speaking Switzerland; its director from 1986 was Henrique Köng (b. 1950).

Two organizations which support the work of youth theatre in Switzerland are the Swiss centre of ASSITEJ (International Association of Theatre for Children and Young People) and the Schweizerische Arbeitsgruppe für das darstellende Spiel in der Schule (SADS – Swiss Working Group for Plays in Performance in

The Theater Spatz & Co. 1980 collective creation *Strititis*, directed by Jean Grädel.

Schools) which promotes school theatre and animation, and organizes courses.

As for the relationship between theatre and education, it is as varied as the different school systems in the country's twenty-six cantons. Historically speaking – and this remained true in many parts of the country right into the 1960s – children were not taken to the theatre by their schools until they were about 14 years of age. Even then, it was usually only to see a production of Schiller's *Wilhelm Tell* in order to improve their literary skills and patriotic education. But this has changed considerably since the 1970s, at least in the larger cities: besides the great classics of Goethe, Schiller, Lessing and Molière, the plays of Brecht, Frisch, Dürrenmatt and many more modern authors have been performed for school classes.

The integration of theatrical techniques in the Swiss educational system began only after the end of World War II; but it was not until 1973 that the Schauspielakademie in Zürich started training teachers for educational drama (the same year that SADS was founded). Since then, many teacher training colleges have begun offering a wide variety of courses. Some of the larger cities even have information centres for teachers working in the field.

Now that creative drama has been recognized as an important pedagogical device, and acting itself is thought to impart creative impulses, theatrical events for students have increased, the production of plays has been encouraged and even week-long workshops for students have begun to be held. Similar efforts are also being made for students in the field of opera.

Professionals from the Stadttheater Luzern have had some of their personnel working at various schools since 1980, and the Stadttheater Basel has regularly made its facilities available to schools for plays performed by students, as well as for workshops. Similar initiatives have also taken place in other cantons.

Puppet Theatre

Puppet theatre in Switzerland evolved for the most part from casual performances given by amateur puppeteers at parish fairs in the late nineteenth century. Puppets eventually made their way into schools where children tried their own hands at creating plays with them. Only in the latter part of the twentieth century has the form evolved to the point that it can be said to have its own professional life and identity. The first permanent playhouses for puppet theatre were actually established in the 1940s and the genre really began to develop only after 1945.

For 1991, *Szene Schweiz* mentions twelve puppet companies with permanent premises and season-long programmes; also listed are about thirty travelling groups. Some of the major permanent companies are the Basler Marionetten-Theater which produces classic plays such as Lessing's *Nathan der Weise* (*Nathan the Wise*), Carl Orff's *Die Kluge* (*The Clever Wife*), Rostand's *Chantecler*, Dürrenmatt's *Romulus der Grosse* (*Romulus the Great*) and Chekhov's *The Bear*; and the Theater für die Chlyne in Biel which favours traditional fairytales.

Les Marionnettes de Fribourg focuses on religious plays and legends while the Marionnettes de Genève ranks as the oldest continuing puppet theatre in the country. Founded in 1929 by Marcelle Moynier (1882–1980), the Marionnettes de Genève offers productions in a wide range of styles. Two companies that are particularly interested in puppet operas are the Berner Puppentheater, which has staged puppet productions of Mozart's *Die Zauberflöte* (*The Magic Flute*) and *Die Entführung aus dem Serail* (*The Abduction from the Seraglio*), and the St Gallen Puppentheater, which has produced both traditional operas and musical plays by Swiss composers such as Heinrich Sutermeister and Armin Schibler (b. 1920).

Among noteworthy touring companies are the Puppenbühne Monika Demenga (b. 1949)/Hans Wirth (b. 1948) in Berne; the Zürcher Puppentheater, with Peter (b. 1919) and Trudi (b. 1928) Loosli; Michèle (b. 1941) and Michel (b. 1943) Poletti's Théâtre Antonin Artaud in Ascona; the Puppentheater Bleisch in Henggart, founded by Hanspeter (b. 1945) and Elisabeth (b. 1954) Bleisch; and Czech ex-patriot Jiri Prochazka's Schwarzes Theater (Black Theatre) in Zürich.

In 1947, Fred Schneckenburger (1912–66) created a rarely seen form of the genre – puppet cabaret. His puppets were expressionistic burlesques of known figures. Utilizing witty and humorous texts, the form brought him rapid international recognition.

Annual or biennial puppet festivals regularly take place in Lugano, Zürich and Lausanne. The interests of puppeteers in the country are taken care of by the Schweizerische Vereinigung für Puppenspiel, founded in 1959. This associ-

ation has a large collection of documents on puppet theatre at its disposal. The Swiss Puppet Theatre Museum (Musée suisse de la Marionnette) was founded in 1985 in Fribourg; it presents a variety of contemporary and historical puppets from both Switzerland and abroad.

Design

Swiss-born Adolphe Appia probably did more than anyone else in the country to modernize both stage design and stage directing at the turn of the century. After seeing a performance of Wagner's *Meistersinger* in 1888, Appia resolved to reform the art of staging. In 1892, he wrote his most important work, *La Musique et la mise en scène* (*Music and the Art of the Theatre*) which was first published in German as *Die Musik und die Inszenierung* in Munich in 1899. In 1906, he met Émile Jaques-Dalcroze, the creator of *la rythmique* (rhythmic movements, a forerunner of expressionistic dance), and the two men worked on plans for a school and festival.

In his work, Appia called for non-naturalistic and symbolic sets and argued for the connection of music and action, body and spirit. He also

defended the idea of lighting as a dramaturgical device: in his view, beams of light should emphasize the three-dimensionality of actors and scenery. Furthermore, light should be 'mobile'. As with music on the stage, changes in intensity should underline the emotional development of the plot. Appia believed that lighting could give a spiritual quality to the stage and should therefore be considered very carefully.

Few people understood the importance of Appia's ideas during his lifetime and he was rarely given opportunities to try them out on stage. It was only in the 1950s that Wieland and Wolfgang Wagner in Germany began applying Appia's ideas consistently; since then, his concepts of stage directing and designing have become a basis for contemporary stagecraft.

Theatre Space and Architecture

From 1945 on, many existing theatre buildings in Switzerland began to be renovated, transformed and extended. Generally, the buildings were fitted with the latest stage technology. While renovations were carried out – often over several years – companies were forced to find alternative premises. For example, the Opernhaus Zürich performed in the Hallenstadion, a local sports stadium, as well as in a church. Performing in such non-traditional venues generally meant finding new staging and designing methods.

A number of these makeshift premises have now become permanent theatres, thus proving how strongly audiences were interested in these experiments. Examples are the Depot Hardturm, the Rote Fabrik and the so-called Theaterhaus Gessnerallee in Zürich, and the

Altes Schlachthaus (Old Slaughterhouse) in Berne (which was used while the Stadttheater was under renovation).

After 1945, a number of new theatre premises were built. In St Gallen, architectural innovation was important while in Basle attempts were made to compete with the ambitious new buildings of Germany. In Winterthur, concrete and glass were used to build a new facility for guest performances, the Theater am Stadtgarten. In every new building special attention was given to audience perspective, as most of the premises erected before 1945 featured picture-frame stages and auditoriums with horseshoe rows, according to the model of the traditional Baroque stage. In the seventeenth and eighteenth centuries, this structure fulfilled social expectations: people had to see the stage

The 885-seat Stadttheater St Gallen, designed by the architect Claude Paillard, completed in 1968.

as well as one another. In this area, the traditional structure of Swiss theatres never actually corresponded to the country's social structure: Switzerland has been a democracy for many centuries and has never had a royal court since its founding in 1291.

Training

Four public theatre training academies exist in Switzerland. The largest is the German-language Schauspielakademie Zürich (SAZ), founded in 1937 and directed from 1960 to 1992 by Felix Rellstab (b. 1924), and later by Peter Danzeisen. The Schauspielakademie Zürich offers a three-year programme for actors and directors, and a related four-year programme for teachers of theatre (theatre pedagogues) who will be working in theatre-in-education. Students at the SAZ follow an initial common programme for one year, after which they are offered separate curricula depending on their interests: actors train for two years, including practice and stage productions; stage directors complete two years including a course in film and video directing, and do their own projects with groups within the school; theatre pedagogues complete three years of training in theatre pedagogics and animation; they also play in the school's own productions, have individual training outside school, and participate in theatre work in youth centres, centres for refugees and prisons. Most of those working in Switzerland's German-language theatres have been trained here, including many of those working in free theatres and other alternative venues.

The drama programme at the Konservatorium für Musik und Theater in Berne, directed since 1965 by Paul Roland (b. 1931), was opened in 1942. In addition to a traditional four-year curriculum for actors seeking to enter the profession, it also offers courses in physical expression, linguistic interaction and new approaches to theatre for those intending to work in amateur drama. In 1991, the drama department of the conservatory began using new premises that include two well-equipped stages.

In the French-speaking part of Switzerland, there are two major schools which offer theatrical training. The École supérieure d'art dramatique (part of the Conservatoire) in Geneva, directed since 1971 by Leyla Aubert (b. 1934), offers a three-year programme in acting. Students in their second and third years take part in productions at a professional theatre in Geneva. At the Section professionnelle d'art dramatique of the conservatory in Lausanne, professional training for actors also lasts three years. The school offers a one-year, 'pre-professional' preparatory course for very young students. It was founded in 1960 and has been directed since 1984 by director and actor André Steiger (b. 1928).

Since the early 1990s, a number of companies have also been offering training adapted to their own needs, especially in French-speaking Switzerland. Rather than following the more traditional curricula for actors, these company-oriented training programmes tend to focus on actors as 'creators' rather than as 'interpreters' of dramatic texts and spend considerable time working on collective creations and animation.

In the Italian-speaking part of Switzerland, the Scuola Teatro Dimitri in Verscio, a private school, has been offering training in mime and clown work, dance, acrobatics, speech techniques, breathing and improvisation since 1975. This, too, is a three-year curriculum.

Since 1961, the International Opera Centre (IOC) of the Zürich Opera House has offered training to singers who have already completed voice studies. Usually the course lasts one year, in certain exceptional cases two years. Admission to the course is restricted by a demanding competition. A major part of the training programme is participation in the productions of the Opera House. Director of the IOC since 1974 has been American-born Marc Belfort.

Basle also has an Opera Studio connected with the Academy of Music. Before being admitted, students must again have completed voice studies. The Basle course lasts two years and also offers basic training in performing; a related studio has been inaugurated in Bienne. Both studios are directed by Martin Markun (b. 1942).

The Kulturmühle Lützelflüh, founded in 1972 by Yolanda Rodio (b. 1914), offers a three-year private course called Totales Theater focusing on the following questions: under what conditions are ideas generated? How can one express them and how can they be given a theatrical shape? The Kulturmühle also offers one-week advanced courses in theatre and music. Major financial difficulties were facing the centre in 1992.

Those interested in eurhythmy as well as the speech and dramatic techniques developed by the German educator Rudolf Steiner can take up either a four- or five-year study programme at the Goetheanum in Dornach. The school is located in the Freie Hochschule für Geisteswissenschaft.

Stage technicians can also do both elementary and advanced training in special programmes offered by the Schweizerische Vereinigung technischer Bühnenberufe (SVtB).

Criticism, Scholarship and Publishing

There are two important organizations in Switzerland involved in theatre research and publishing – the Schweizerische Gesellschaft für Theaterkultur (SGTK) and the Schweizerische Theatersammlung (STS – Swiss Theatre Documentation Centre) in Berne. Both organizations have made enormous national contributions to the field.

Among other functions, the SGTK is the publisher of research and documents on the theatre. It has issued studies of theatre subjects ranging from Italian-speaking Swiss theatre in the 1970s to comparative studies of such companies as the Théâtre Populaire Romand and the Theater für den Kanton Zürich. It has also published volumes on music theatre, Swiss folk forms and the influence of Swiss theatre on other German-speaking countries. The SGTK has also been the publisher of Szene Schweiz which is compiled annually by the SGTK and the STS and documents events of the previous year in Switzerland; it includes a complete bibliography of

Swiss publications on theatre. Furthermore, the SGTK has been issuing *Mimos*, a report on theatre research, two or four times a year since 1948. The SGTK is the basic support organization for the STS and coordinates the awarding of the national Hans Reinhart-Ring.

As for the STS, it is essentially a public library and a documentation centre for the theatre. As early as 1927, the former chairman of the SGTK, Oskar Eberle, began to build up a theatre collection for research purposes. It was this collection which became the basis for the present STS library. In addition to books, the STS collection comprises newspaper articles, theatrical photos, slides, posters, advertisements, prints, costumes, masks, puppets, toy theatres, stage and production designs. It has the largest collection in the world of Appia materials including autographs and stage designs. In 1987, the STS set up a permanent exhibition on both the contemporary Swiss theatre and the history of theatre in Europe: *Theater in Gegenwart und Geschichte* (*Theatre Today and in the Past*), created by Martin Dreier (b. 1942), director of the STS since 1979.

The work of these two organizations – especially the presence of the STS materials – has played a decisive role in the advancement of theatre research in Switzerland in the absence of a university institute for theatre studies. The establishment of such an institute has remained an important goal on the SGTK's agenda since its creation in 1927. In a major step forward for the field, the government of the Canton of Berne finally decided to introduce a chair of theatre studies at the University of Berne in 1989. Andreas Kotte (b. 1955), from the Berlin Humboldt-Universität, was appointed first chair-holder in 1991; he began lecturing in the summer term of 1992.

Most theatres – especially the subsidized ones – regularly publish their own journals, bulletins and programmes. This has long been an important source of information.

General information on theatre activities across the country can be found in the magazine *Musik & Theater* published in St Gallen ten times per year; in the French-speaking part of the country, *Voir* (*Look*) and *Scène Magazine* have a similar function. The weekly periodical *L'Hebdo* from Lausanne also offers a large section on the arts with regular theatre reports.

There is also a large amount of theatre reviewing and reportage in the daily and weekly papers, though few of the writers have a significant background in the field. One of the few informed writers was Elisabeth Brock-Sulzer (1903–81, from Zürich), the first Swiss critic to recognize the importance of Dürrenmatt's work.

Christoph Reichenau
Editorial revisions by Martin Dreier and
Bibi Gessner
Translated by Ann Zimmermann

Further Reading

Ausgangspunkt Schweiz – Nachwirkungen des Exiltheaters: Schweizer Theaterjahrbuch 50. [Switzerland as starting point – the influence of political exiles on the theatre: Swiss theatre year-book no. 50]. Willisau: SGTK, 1989.

Bissegger, Ursula. *Puppentheater in der Schweiz.* [Puppet theatre in Switzerland]. Zürich: Theater Kultur-Verlag, 1978.

Clottu, Bericht, et al. *Beiträge für eine Kulturpolitik in der Schweiz. Bericht der eidgenössischen Expertenkommission für Fragen einer schweizerischen Kulturpolitik.* [Proposals for a cultural policy in Switzerland. Report of the Federal Commission of Experts on a Swiss policy for the arts]. Berne: Swiss Federal Government, 1975. pp. 47–94.

Duvanel, Blaise. *Théâtre pour les Jeunes en Suisse: Annuaire du Théâtre Suisse no. 42.* [Swiss theatre yearbook no. 42: theatre for young audiences in Switzerland]. Zürich: SGTK, 1979.

15 Thesen zu einer Schweizerischen Theaterpolitik. Über Situation und Zukunft des Theaters in der Schweiz. [Fifteen proposals for a Swiss theatre policy: on the situation and future of theatre in Switzerland]. Berne: Swiss Centre of the International Theatre Institute, 1985.

Jotterand, Franck. 'Das Theater in der Schweiz'. [Theatre in Switzerland]. In *Die Schweiz vom Bau der Alpen bis zur Frage nach der Zukunft.* [Switzerland from the creation of the Alps to the question of the future]. Zürich: Migros-Genossenschafts-Bund, 1977. pp. 469–75.

Keiser, César. *Herrliche Zeiten 1916–1976: 60 Jahre Cabaret in der Schweiz.* [The glorious years 1916–76: sixty years of cabaret in Switzerland]. Berne: Benteli Verlag, 1976.

Der Kritiker als Theater und Kulturpolitiker. [Theatre critics as politicians for the arts]. Boswil: Stiftung Künstlerhaus, 1985.

Maurer, Roland. *Die Schweizer Theaterszene.* [Theatre in Switzerland]. Zürich: Schweizer Kulturstiftung Pro Helvetia, 1983. 86 pp.

Muggler, Fritz. *Zum Musikleben in der Schweiz.* [Towards musical life in Switzerland]. Zürich: Schweizer Kulturstiftung Pro Helvetia, 1982.

Müller, Eugen. *Schweizer Theatergeschichte.*

[History of the Swiss theatre]. Zürich: Oprecht Verlag, 1944.

Musiktheater: Schweizer Theaterjahrbuch no. 45. [Swiss theatre yearbook no. 45: music theatre]. Bonstetten: SGTK, 1983.

Pastori, Jean-Pierre. *Tanz und Ballett in der Schweiz.* [Dance and ballet in Switzerland]. Zürich: Schweizer Kulturstiftung Pro Helvetia, 1985.

Schweizer Theaterbuch. [Swiss theatre book]. Zürich: SBV, 1964.

Szene Schweiz/Scène Suisse/Scena Svizzera: Eine Dokumentation des Theaterlebens in der Schweiz. [Swiss stage: a yearbook of Swiss theatre life]. Zürich: SGTK, annually since 1973.

Theater in der Schweiz/Théâtre en Suisse/Teatro in Svizzera: Schweizer Theaterjahrbuch no. 40. [Swiss theatre yearbook no. 40: theatre in Switzerland]. Zürich: SGTK, 1977.

Das Theater – unsere Welt/Le Théâtre – notre monde. Das Schweizer Theater/Le Théâtre suisse 1970–80. [The theatre, our world: Swiss theatre 1970–80]. Lucerne: SBV, 1980. 303 pp.

TADJIKISTAN

(Asia/Oceania volume; see also USSR)

TURKEY

Turkey has long been a cultural bridge between east and west. Located at the junction of Europe and Asia, Turkey is at once a Balkan, Middle Eastern and Mediterranean country and is also part of the Islamic world. The centre of great historical civilizations, modern-day Turkey is a republic of 60 million people with a land area covering some 780,000 square kilometres (301,000 square miles).

Theatrically, Turkey traces its history back to the shamanistic rituals of central Asia as well as to the fertility rites of ancient Mesopotamia and Anatolia. Theatre historians have found dramatic dances, comic dialogues, interludes and mimetic narrations by early Turkish nomads dating from long before the rule of the Seljukian Empire in the eleventh century.

When the early Turks migrated from central Asia and settled in the part of Turkey now called Anatolia in the tenth century, they assimilated the influences of many of the great civilizations that had preceded them there, including the Hittites, the Phyrigians, the Lydians, the Assyrians,

the Persians, the Greeks, the Romans, the Byzantians and the Arabs. Music, singing, dance and comedy seem always to have been part of life in Anatolia and these activities were encouraged by trade guilds, religious sects, the army and the court. Groups which developed were, in fact, invited to perform during the occasional court-sponsored festivals. These events brought together people from every social class.

Until the birth of the modern Turkish theatre in the middle of the nineteenth century, three main traditional performance forms dominated the theatrical landscape: *meddah* (storytelling), *karagöz* (shadow theatre) and *orta oyunu* (improvised folk performances).

The *meddah* was essentially a storyteller who impersonated various characters through gesture and voice, relating comic scenes from life and old tales. More an actor than a narrator in his suggestion of various character types, the *meddah* improvised, re-created and reacted to the responses of his audience. Generally, the *meddah* used two props to produce the audible and the visible – a cudgel and a handkerchief (sometimes a napkin). For the most part, the story was acted from memory; on occasion it was read.

It is of interest to note here that the word for mime in Turkish tradition is also the word for story (*hikâye*). To be a storyteller (*hâki*) is to be a mime: the words are synonymous. During the period of the Ottoman Empire – from the fourteenth to the twentieth centuries – more than 200 such master storytellers were identified and acknowledged.

Turkish shadow theatre, *karagöz* (literally, black-eye), takes its name from its principal character. It came to Turkey from either Java, China or India via Egypt in 1517 when Sultan Selim I, the ninth Ottoman emperor, brought shadow artists to Turkey after incorporating Egypt into the Ottoman realm. It reached its height of popularity in the eighteenth and nineteenth centuries. This shadow theatre was heavily influenced by Turkish puppetry (see **Puppet Theatre**).

Orta oyunu, in its turn, is an improvised folk theatre which has similarities to shadow theatre but uses live actors rather than puppets. *Orta* means middle and refers to a play performed in the centre of a programme as well as in the centre of an audience. As early as 1582, in the royal festival of Murat III, groups of actors performed such pieces.

In *orta oyunu*, there is neither a curtain nor a changing area. Actors don costumes in view of the audience and wait among the musicians for their turn on a simple, folding-frame stage. As musicians play, the actors enter dancing and whirling. As in the shadow play, there can be dozens of different characters and –a hallmark of traditional Turkish theatre – a great deal of improvisation.

From the middle of the nineteenth century, a clear European influence began to develop: European-style plays began to be performed and proscenium arch stages were built to house them. This new European influence can be traced directly to a series of social, political, economic, cultural and military reforms – the *tanzimat* (reorganization) – which took place in 1839 and did much to turn the country's institutions towards the west.

The earliest proscenium theatres were built in İstanbul and İzmír for foreign performances sponsored by embassies and the court. In 1860, the first public European-style theatre – Gedikpaşa Tiyatrosu (Gedikpaşa Theatre) –

was built in İstanbul by a French circus company. In 1867, a wealthy Armenian, Güllü Agop (1840–1902) bought the theatre to produce European plays and musicals. A year later, he announced that plays in Turkish would also be performed there, both translations of foreign plays and original plays by Turkish authors. Since this style of theatre was basically new for Turkish audiences, Agop (who later became a Muslim and took the name Yakup) applied to the government and received what was to become a ten-year monopoly on the production of Turkish-language plays, including vaudevilles. In return for the monopoly, Agop agreed to open additional theatres in other parts of the city.

In 1879, a new proscenium playhouse was built in Bursa by Ahmet Vefik Pasha (1823–91), the former Grand Vizier and a great fan of Molière and other French writers. Over the next four years, thirty-four of his own adaptations and translations of Molière's plays would be produced, many directed by him.

The presence in İstanbul of the Gedikpaşa Theatre had a great influence on other companies even before it was operative. Sultan Abdülmecit (1822–61) ordered a 300-seat court theatre to be built near the Dolmabahçe Palace on the Bosphorus in 1858; torn down in 1889, it was replaced that same year by another court theatre at the Yıldız Palace in which the famous Italian actor Ernesto Rossi played *Othello* and *The Merchant of Venice*. Other prominent European actors who appeared on its stage included Salvini, Bernhardt and Coquelin.

Not to be outdone by these new forms, *orta oyunu* performers soon began adapting to the western style and began creating their own improvised versions of the plays, particularly the melodramas. This new hybrid became known as *tuluat* (improvised theatre) and quickly created its own stock characters.

In 1908, a constitutional monarchy was established in the country, headed by the sultan. In 1914, nine years before the proclamation of the Turkish Republic, André Antoine, the celebrated French director, was invited by the prefect of İstanbul to establish a European-style theatre conservatory in the country. Nearly 200 students applied for entrance to the new school and sixty-three were selected. The outbreak of World War I, however, kept the school from opening and Antoine left Turkey after only a month's stay.

For some years after the war, İstanbul was occupied by the British and French, and most parts of Anatolia (including the Aegean coast) were occupied by the Greeks, French and Italians. In 1922, Turkish General Mustafa Kemal (1881–1938) expelled the occupying forces, deposed the sultan and in 1923 established a Turkish republic with its new capital at Ankara. Discarded at this point was the former name of the country – the Ottoman Empire.

Mustafa Kemal introduced many reforms, especially in industry, language, alphabet, education and culture. One reform that was to affect everyone had to do with names. Until that time, family names were not normally used but from this point on every Turk was to select and use a surname. Mustafa Kemal took for his own name Atatürk, meaning Father of the Turks.

With these reforms, the arts also developed a new vitality. In theatre, this manifested itself in a desire by the state to create a theatre that would be at once both popular and educational. Primary emphasis was laid on improving Turkish culture and the Turkish language. Ottoman Turkish was the primary spoken form of the language during the Ottoman period, a highly sophisticated and formal language spoken by the upper classes and the court artists. Heavily influenced by Islam and the Persian and Arabic languages, it used the Arabic alphabet in its written form. Atatürk, however, wanted to create a nationalistic and non-Ottoman culture, a pure Turkish culture, and he selected Anatolian Turkish as the primary spoken form of the language. Theatre artists from that time on were expected to use it and encourage its use among audiences.

It was at this point as well that Muslim women were allowed to appear on stage for the first time and to attend the theatre and sit in the same sections as men.

Atatürk's strongest supporter in theatre was Muhsin Ertuğrul (1892–1979), an actor, director, administrator and zealous reformer as well as an enthusiastic apostle of contemporary Turkish theatre. Ertuğrul was appointed the artistic director of what would become the İstanbul Belediyesi Şehir Tiyatroları (İstanbul municipal theatres) in 1927. Under his management, this first municipal theatre became a truly influential, efficient and disciplined artistic organization. Ertuğrul encouraged Turkish playwriting and Turkish authors were regularly produced.

As well, the theatre began its own training programmes and even opened the country's first children's theatre in 1935. In 1936, Ertuğrul and the famous German actor-director Carl

Muhsin Ertuğrul, the foremost figure in the history of Turkey's modern theatre.

Ebert gained state support for the theatre school to become Turkey's first State Conservatory (Devlet Konservatuvarı) offering training in acting (a five-year programme), opera (seven years), ballet (nine years) and music (six years). Training was offered free to students who, on graduation, were to join the Tatbikat Sahnesi (Theatre Workshop) which offered a wide range of public performances. In 1947 the Theatre Workshop began to gradually transform itself into the Devlet Tiyatro ve Operası (State Theatre and Opera).

In 1949, the State Conservatory was separated from the State Theatre and Opera and, with Ertuğrul as its director, what was once only a scenery dock was turned into a well-equipped 605-seat playhouse called the Küçük Tiyatro (Small Theatre). In 1948, the company's 762-seat Büyük Tiyatro (Big Theatre) opened. Designed by the German architect Paul Bonatz, the Büyük Tiyatro officially opened on 2 April with Turkey's first major opera, *Kerem*, written by the prominent composer Adnan Saygun (1907–91). In 1949, the Büyük Tiyatro began performing repertory seasons including both opera and non-musical plays.

In 1951, Ertuğrul left the State Theatre and Opera to establish a private theatre called the

Küçük Sahne (Small Stage) in İstanbul but in 1954, he returned to the State Theatre and Opera. Over the next four years, as the general director of the State Theatre and Opera, he renovated an old building, turning it into a play-house called the Üçüncü Tiyatro (Third Theatre) with a capacity of 590 seats and created a sixty-five-seat Oda Tiyatrosu (Chamber Theatre) for experimental work. By his retirement in 1958, he had founded a total of eight theatres not only in İstanbul but also in İzmír, Bursa and Adana.

Ertuğrul's successor at the State Theatre and Opera, Cüneyt Gökçer (b. 1920), a celebrated actor and director, added two more playhouses to the growing chain of Devlet Tiyatroları (State Theatres) – the Yeni Sahne (New Stage) seating 205 and the Altindağ Tiyatrosu (Altindağ Theatre) seating 310.

In 1966, the administration of the Devlet Tiyatroları was officially separated from the administration of the Devlet Opera ve Balesi (State Opera and Ballet).

As the 1990s began, state theatres were either in residence in one of seven major cities or touring to most of Turkey's seventy-one provinces. In addition, five municipal theatres were operating in İstanbul, the country's most densely populated city as well as Turkey's most important cultural centre. About forty private companies were also staging major productions each season in İstanbul and Ankara.

Structure of the National Theatre Community

There are three main groupings of professional companies in Turkey today – the Devlet Tiyatroları (state theatres), the İstanbul Belediyesi Şehir Tiyatroları (İstanbul municipal theatres) and the private companies.

Of these, İstanbul's five municipal theatres are the country's oldest. Heavily subsidized by the Municipality of İstanbul, they are centrally administered and operate in various parts of the city. During the 1980s, many smaller munici-palities also began to sponsor local theatres and municipal companies also now exist in Ordu, Giresun, Trabzon, İçel, İzmír, Kocaeli and Ankara.

The chain of state theatres is the largest grouping in Turkey, reaching audiences in most parts of the country. Currently operating twenty-three different stages in seven major cities (Ankara, İstanbul, İzmír, Bursa, Adana, Trabzon and Diyarbakır), the state theatres operate under the General Directorate of State Theatres, which is connected to, subsidized and controlled by the Ministry of Culture. These theatres are fully subsidized by the state and can afford to sell tickets at extremely low prices.

Private companies also receive small subsidies from the state but traditionally have been depen-dent on box-office income. In recent years, major corporations, newspapers and banks have also begun regular financial sponsorship of specific private productions. It was again Muhsin Ertuğrul who set the style for modern private theatres in the country when, in 1952, he convinced a bank to partly sponsor his new Küçük Sahne (Small Stage) in İstanbul. Catering to all tastes with a varied repertoire of high-quality productions, the major companies today have more or less followed his model.

The private Dormen Theatre in İstanbul first established the practice in 1958 of giving out awards for the season's Best Play, Actor, Actress, Director, Translator, Designer and Composer. The major awards as the 1990s began were those of the Ankara Sanat Kurumu (Ankara Arts Institute) given for the Best Actor, Actress, Director, Playwright, Translator, Designer and Composer; the Avni Dilligil Award, for Best Actor, Actress, Director, Playwright and Designer; and the Ulvi Uraz Theatre Award given to a national playwright. Additional awards are the Kültür Bakanlığı Tiyatro Ödülleri (Ministry of Culture and Tourism Theatre Awards), the MEKSAV Tiyatro Ödülleri (Mersin Foundation of Culture and Arts Theatre Awards) and the Tiyatro ve TV Yazarları Tiyatro Ödülleri (Theatre Awards of the Association of Theatre and Television Writers).

In 1989, the Turkish Association of Theatre Critics also established an award for contri-butions to national theatre life. Among the early recipients were AÇOK (the Anatolian Children's Theatre Troupe), the Company Theatre, the Dostlar Theatre, the Bakirköy Municipal Theatre and the Bursa National Theatre.

One of the highest individual honours in Turkey was for a long time to be named a State Artist. In the field of theatre, three actors –

Cüneyt Gökçer, Vasfi Rıza Zobu (1902–92) and Bozkurt Kuruç (b. 1938) – and four actresses – Yıldız Kenter (b. 1928), Bedia Muvahhit (b. 1897), Ayten Gökçer (b. 1938) and Macide Tanir (b. 1924) – have been so honoured. In 1992, controversy surrounded this honour when some forty people were named State Artists.

There are three international culture and arts festivals held annually in Turkey. The oldest is the International İstanbul Festival, established in 1973 by the İstanbul Kültür ve Sanat Vakfı (Culture and Arts Foundation of İstanbul). Under the direct patronage of the Ministry of Culture and Tourism, the festival, until 1989,

tended to emphasize music. In 1989, however, a theatre festival – the International İstanbul Theatre Festival – was established within its overall framework.

The İzmir International Festival, established in 1987, holds concerts in the ancient theatre in Ephesus near İzmir, but is also now adding theatre performances as well.

Since 1989, the state theatres have begun to hold an annual festival bringing together their own productions from different cities across the country. In addition, there are about twenty cities which also organize annual amateur theatre festivals.

Artistic Profile

Companies

Since organization of the municipal and state theatres is centralized and artistic personnel move from theatre to theatre within these large groupings, it is difficult to speak of particular companies.

The İstanbul municipal theatres, for example, have 110 actors on their payroll and operate on five stages in four different sections of the city. These stages include the Musahipzade Theatre, the Muhsin Ertuğrul Theatre, the Oda Tiyatrosu (Chamber Theatre), the Reşat Nuri Güntekin Theatre and the Haldun Taner Theatre. The repertoire ranges from classics to the avant-garde, from musicals to dramas and popular comedies. The productions generally reflect various acting styles ranging from those of the self-taught older masters to those of graduates of recognized theatre schools.

Each season, these theatres present some 900 performances of approximately twenty Turkish and foreign plays to a combined audience of 300,000 people. Box-office sales represent 20 per cent of the overall budget, the remainder being guaranteed by the municipality. The İstanbul municipal theatres now tour annually.

The state theatres have their own general directorate in Ankara. A Literary Committee decides the plays to be included in the repertoire for all state theatres across the country and the administrative directors of different regions determine their own yearly repertoire. The general director of the Turkish State Theatre, a political appointee, has the ultimate decision on

play selection. The general directorate is also responsible for selecting artistic personnel and technical staff. Generally, the state theatres try to encourage the production of plays by Turkish writers while keeping up to date with the world repertoire of classical and modern drama as well as popular Broadway musicals. State theatres also try to introduce theatre to various parts of the country through extensive touring programmes.

With few exceptions, the actors and directors of the state theatres are graduates of the State Conservatory based at Hacettepe University in Ankara. Unlike the İstanbul municipal theatres, the state theatres, from the start, have been based on the work of an artistic staff which has settled on a unified style of acting.

Country-wide, the state theatres employ 450 actors, with the largest number working in Ankara, İstanbul, İzmir and Bursa. The oldest and most established of all, the Ankara State Theatre, has seven stages of various sizes. The Büyük Tiyatro is the largest and best equipped and it also shares its stage with the State Opera and Ballet. The others are the Küçük Tiyatro, the Yeni Sahne, the Oda Tiyatrosu, the Altındağ Tiyatrosu, the Şinasi and the experimental İrfan Şahinbaş Atölye Tiyatrosu (Workshop Theatre). The İstanbul State Theatre has three theatres in the Atatürk Kültür Merkezi (Atatürk Cultural Centre), known as AKM. The largest auditorium seats 1,330 and the second one 618; the third one is a chamber theatre. A fourth State Theatre stage in İstanbul is called the Taksim Sahnesi (Taksim Stage).

Mustafa Avkıran's 1991–2 İstanbul Municipal Theatres' production of Aeschylus' *Oresteia*, designed by Nurettin Özkönü.

State theatres produce an average of seventy plays each season for adults and young audiences. In total, some 3,000 performances are given annually with approximately 2 million people attending.

As for the companies which operate privately, they can also be divided into three groupings: those that follow the state and municipal theatres in terms of general style, quality and repertoires; those that provide light entertainment; and those that focus on social and political issues.

The most important of the private theatres are in İstanbul and are owned and directed by prominent actors, actresses and directors. The Dormen Tiyatrosu was founded in 1957 by Haldun Dormen (b. 1928), a graduate of the Yale University Drama School in the United States. Through the years, Dormen proved himself an efficient producer, director and actor through his productions of Broadway hits, popular French comedies, original Turkish plays and musicals. This company produced more 'stars' than any other private company in the country and enjoyed extreme popularity in the 1960s. The theatre closed in 1972 because of financial problems but opened again in 1983.

The Kent Oyuncuları (Kent Players) was established in 1958 by Yıldız Kenter and her brother, Müşfik Kenter (b. 1931), both graduates of the State Conservatory in Ankara and former performers with the state theatres. Two of Turkey's leading actors, the Kenters charmed audiences with their performances and by 1958–9 had already made their company one of the most admired private theatres in İstanbul. Among their major productions early on were *Hamlet*, Chekhov's *Three Sisters*, Brecht's *The Threepenny Opera*, Albee's *Who's Afraid of Virginia Woolf?* and Ionesco's *The Chairs* and *The Lesson*. In the late 1960s, they built their own playhouse, one of the best equipped in Turkey.

Another important private theatre founded at this same time was that of Gülriz Sururi (b. 1929), a musical star and former actress at the Dormen Theatre, and her husband Engin Cezzar (b. 1935), a one-time student at New York's Actor's Studio, Yale University, and a former actor at the İstanbul Municipal Theatres. For six years, the Gülriz Sururi-Cezzar Company enjoyed great popularity. Its life was highlighted by the world première of Haldun Taner's (1916–86) epic musical,

The 1989–90 Orta Oyuncular production of Ferhan Şensoy's *The Abstract Soltan*, directed and designed by Ferhan Şensoy.

Keşanlı Ali Destanı (*The Ballad of Ali of Keshan*), which was performed 1,400 times in Turkey, Lebanon and in various European cities.

The Ali Poyrazoğlu Theatre was founded in 1972 in İstanbul. Ali Poyrazoğlu (b. 1943), a graduate of the İstanbul Municipal Conservatory and a well-known television performer, worked with several companies before starting his own group. The company has produced a wide range of Turkish and international contemporary plays including a number that have challenged the country's middle-class morality, such as Canadian playwright John Herbert's *Fortune and Men's Eyes*, directed by US novelist James Baldwin.

Orta Oyuncular was founded in 1980 by Ferhan Şensoy (b. 1951), a popular playwright, actor, director and television performer with a penchant for the controversial. The company has produced many of Şensoy's own plays, which tend towards the grotesque and the fantastic and which also include significant social and political criticism.

Other private companies producing work of note during the 1960s and which later ceased activities include the Arena Tiyatrosu (Arena Theatre) which, in a way, was the offspring of Genç Oyuncular (Young Players), a prominent amateur company established in 1957 which specialized in collective creations and performed in eleven different towns during its six years of existence; the Gen-Ar Theatre, an experimental company; the Ulvi Uraz Theatre, which concentrated on national plays and social issues; and the Meydan Sahnesi (Arena Stage), the only private company of this kind in Ankara.

The second grouping of private companies – those focusing on light entertainment – tend to produce comedies, either foreign or Turkish. The scripts are usually used more as an outline upon which, according to Metin And's (b. 1927) book, *A History of Theatre and Popular Entertainment in Turkey,* 'the actors superimpose their own inventions and improvisations in attempts at political and social satire, social oddities, topical comments and pungent jokes'.

During the 1950s and early 1960s, the leading company doing this type of work was the Karaca Theatre founded by Muammer Karaca (1906–78), a former actor with the İstanbul Municipal Theatre and a master of improvisation. When Karaca himself performed, his productions often enjoyed long runs. The company ceased operation in 1978 after Karaca's death.

The three major companies working in this genre as the 1990s began included the Devekuşu Kabare (Ostrich Cabaret), the Ülkü-Özcan Theatre and the Levent Kırca Theatre. The Devekuşu was founded in 1967 by playwright Haldun Taner and two young actors, Zeki Alasya (b. 1943) and Metin Akpınar (b. 1941). Its first performances were in small nightclubs but Taner's cabaret sketches proved so popular that the company began to perform them in full-size theatres. Taner left the company in the early 1970s while Alasya and Akpınar became television idols for their satires. When they perform live, they often sell out sports arenas seating up to 7,000 people. Their uniqueness and popularity has much to do with their ability to combine elements of traditional Turkish theatre (particularly satire and improvisation) with modern acting and production styles.

The Nisa Serezli-Tolga Aşkıner Theatre was another popular company in this category. Nisa Serezli (1928–92), a former actor with the Dormen Theatre, was a fine comedian who could skilfully add tragic nuances to her comic acting.

Improvisation around popular comedy scripts is also a feature of the Ülkü-Özcan Theatre, founded by the husband-and-wife performing team of Gazanfer Özcan (b. 1931) and Gönül Ülkü (b. 1929). The popularity of the company owes much to Özcan's ability to adapt traditional Turkish styles to representations of modern common people.

The Dostlar Theatre (Friends Theatre) in İstanbul and the Ankara Sanat Theatre (Ankara Art Theatre) are private companies led by artists who are both socially and politically committed. Dostlar was founded in 1969 by Genco Erkal (b. 1938), an actor, director, dramaturge and translator, who has had great success with the plays of Bertolt Brecht and has created a Brechtian presentational style of performance in his theatre.

Two private İstanbul companies which have been successful in the 1990s at combining theatrical research and reaching new audiences have been the Bilsak Theatre (founded in 1989) and the Kumpanya Tiyatrosu (founded in 1990). True alternatives to the subsidized and more traditional private groups, they have experimented with space, actors and new dramaturgy.

The Ankara Art Theatre (known as AST) was founded in 1963 by Asaf Çiyiltepe (1934–67), a talented French-trained director. AST based its early repertoire on the Théâtre National

Populaire in Paris. For many years, AST was Turkey's leader in introducing modern foreign plays with social or political ideas and served as a genuine alternative to both the choice of plays and the styles of acting and production found in the established state theatres. The company has continued operating, despite major changes of personnel, into the 1990s.

İzmír, Turkey's third-largest city, has not had any ongoing private theatres. Private companies from İstanbul and Ankara, however, regularly perform there during the annual İzmír International Fair each August/September.

Dramaturgy

Turkish theatre tradition, whether in the form of puppet plays or arena plays, depends much on the craft of actors in improvisation. The mosaic structure of these plays is made of loosely connected episodes. The characters are stock types. The rough outline of the written plot is elaborated by realistic as well as fantastic details most of which are created by the actors on the spot to produce humour which tends towards satire. This longlived tradition was interrupted when the Turkish theatre began to follow the line of western drama with its closely knit, more organic form.

The first original Turkish play in the European style was *Şair Evlenmesi* (*The Marriage of the Poet*) written in 1859 by İbrahim Şinasi (1826–71). This short play was followed by others in the romantic style, the best of which were written by Namık Kemâl (1840–88), a well-known poet. His play *Vatan yahut Silistre* (*Fatherland or Silistria*) is a sentimental drama about young lovers who prove to be patriots before they marry. When the play was first performed in 1873, spectators demonstrated in the streets after the performance and Kemâl was sent into exile. Patriotism and a strong sense of nationalism were the main characteristics of plays written in the period.

The only other dramatic styles of significance at this time were the many adaptations (mostly by Ahmet Vefik Pasha) of Molière's plays. These adaptations incorporating Turkish customs and manners are still done by many theatres.

After the declaration of the constitution in 1908, playwrights turned to historical themes and complicated plots. Among the hundreds of plays written between 1908 and the proclamation of the republic in 1923, very few are worth mentioning. Musahipzade Celâl (1870–1959) was the most successful playwright of the 1920s and 1930s, criticizing Ottoman institutions in his plays as well as making clever allusions to contemporary problems.

Materialism, the loss of traditional moral values, political conflict, snobbishness and bigotry became topical themes for writers in the 1930s and 1940s, providing them with dramatic situations easy to deal with in both tragic and comic terms. Cevat Fehmi Başkut (1908–71), a prolific playwright and journalist, created comic situations in which older generations find themselves unable to deal with the changes taking place around them. These same ideas were treated more seriously by Ahmet Kudsi Tecer (1901–67) and Reşat Nuri Güntekin (1889–1956), who accepted the situation as being the inevitable result of rapid social development.

Most of the plays of the 1930s and 1940s were melodramas and domestic comedies moulded into well-established dramatic forms and recognizable character types. From the 1950s on, new themes and new characters were introduced. Although writers still depended on realism and domestic drama, they tended to go deeper in their search for motivations of both social and individual behaviour. Social harmony was no longer accepted as the necessary norm and playwrights challenged traditional structures and pointed out contradictions. Refik Erduran's (b. 1928) play *Cengiz Han'ın Bisikleti* (*Ghengis Khan's Bicycle*) is a notable example, as it deals with individual dilemmas caused by social change. Many plays dealt with the struggle of individuals to retain self-respect in the midst of a corrupt society, while others blamed intellectuals for personal selfishness and social irresponsibility.

During this period, mythological and historical material was reinterpreted on stage. Selâhattin Batu's (1905–73) *Güzel Helena* (*Fair Helena*) is a typical example of the humanistic tendency prevailing in Turkish drama of the 1950s. In this play, Menelaus and his fellow commanders are so intent on making war that they forget that their real aim is to bring Helen home. Helen, understanding this, finally refuses to go back and chooses to remain in conquered Troy to help those who have been defeated.

In the 1960s, a new generation of politically committed playwrights began dealing with social problems, most especially poverty. The current economic order was severely criticized in such plays as *Ayak Bacak Fabrikası* (*Factory of Orthopaedic Feet and Legs*) by Sermet Çağan (1929–70). In this play, all the inhabitants of a village become crippled after eating chemically treated wheat. A factory is then built with foreign capital to produce orthopaedic feet and legs for the cripples, who find themselves having to feel grateful.

Another important play from the period is Güngör Dilmen's (b. 1930) *Kurban* (*Sacrifice*), a modern version of the Medea story. In this play, a village woman kills her children and herself rather than yielding to her husband's wish to bring a second wife into the house (since Islam permitted a man to have four wives, having two wives was a common practice in Turkish villages and provincial towns, though strictly forbidden by law). In *İçerdekiler* (*Those Within*) Melih Cevdet Anday (b. 1915) focuses on the psychological breakdown of a prisoner who, kept in seclusion, becomes obsessed by sex. Other plays, including Turgut Özakman's (b. 1930) *Ocak* (*Hearth*), deal with the strains of family relationships breaking down under the pressures of difficult social conditions.

Stories of mythical figures like Gilgamesh and King Midas were also dramatized from a contemporary viewpoint. The court life of the Ottoman period too proved popular material for producing stage spectacles. Turan Oflazoğlu (b. 1932) and Orhan Asena (b. 1922) went further and dealt with the psychological problems of Ottoman emperors.

By dealing with historical material, plays enabled audiences to make comparisons between past and present events and between similar events in other parts of the world. Many playwrights, in fact, preferred to express their ideas about current political situations on the safe ground of history. Eroy Toy's (b. 1936) *Pir Sultan Abdal*, Mehmet Akan's (b. 1938) *Şeyh Bedreddin*, and Orhan Asena's *Atçalı Kel Memet*, all named after Turkish folk heroes, were typical of this trend.

Plays dealing with the daily life of village people came into vogue in the 1960s. Peasant costumes and the design of rural houses provided rich visual material. Local dialects also began to be used, most often for comic effect but even in plays dealing seriously with provincial problems. Among the best plays in this style are Recep Bilginer's (b. 1922) *İsyancılar* (*Rebels*); Yaşar Kemâl's (b. 1922) *Teneke* (*Tin*); Necati Cumali's (b. 1921) *Nalınlar* (*The Clogs*) and *Susuz Yaz* (*Dry Summer*); and Hidayet Sayın's (b. 1929) *Pembe Kadın* (A *Woman Called Pembe*).

The problems of living in Turkey's shanty towns provided playwrights such as Haldun Taner, Oktay Rifat (1914–88), Orhan Asena, Dinçer Sümer (b. 1938), Ülker Köksal (b. 1931) and Cahit Atay with rich material while other writers looked at prison conditions, poor housing, mines and the injustices faced by factory workers.

Haldun Taner was one of the first Turkish playwrights to include social criticism in his plays. In his twelve plays, he linked individual behaviour with socio-political and economic changes. In *Keşanli Alı Destani* (*The Ballad of Ali of Keshan*), *Gözlerimi Kaparim Vazifemi Yaparim* (*I Close My Eyes and Do My Job*) and *Günün Adami* (*Man of the Day*), he places his anti-heros into societies where the reactions are either negative or lacking. He questions human values and how those values change. Taner was also a poineer in using traditional theatre forms such as *karagöz* in his plays.

In the 1970s, Turkish playwriting showed an increasing interest in political questions and the influence of European political drama was obvious. Brecht's theory of epic theatre was taken for a time as the only valid approach to politically committed drama. The similarity between the episodic form of the Brechtian epic and the open, presentational form of traditional Turkish drama was used at this point to good effect.

Vasıf Öngören's (1938–84) play, *Asiye Nasıl Kurtulur?* (*How Can Asiye Be Saved?*) in which the story of a poor girl who tries to escape her fate is presented alongside reactions of a comfortable, middle-class woman, was a noteworthy example of this trend which extended even into the private companies with some collectively written documentary plays. Tuncer Cücenoğlu (b. 1945), Başar Sabuncu (b. 1943), Oktay Arayıcı (1936–85) and Bilgesu Erenus (b. 1943) were other playwrights who dealt with similar social and political themes in a good number of plays, mostly experimental in form.

In the 1980s, four new writers with their own special voices emerged: Oğuz Atay (1934–1979); Memet Baydur (b. 1951), who produced nine plays in nine years; Murathan Mungan (b. 1955), who achieved note with two poetic tragedies, *Mahmut ile Yezida* (*Mahmut and Yezida*) and *Taziye*; and Ferhan Şensoy, who continuously writes and adapts plays in the style of his company, Orta Oyuncular.

Most Turkish plays are realistic dramas. Playwrights seem to be interested in social problems rather than individual psychology and usually avoid dealing with human relationships in an abstract way. Some exceptions are Aydın Arit (b. 1928), Melih Cevdet Anday, Yıldırım Keskin (b. 1932), Adalet Ağaoğlu (b. 1929), Sabahattin Kudret Aksal (b. 1920) and to some extent Aziz Nesin (b. 1915), whose plays can be grouped as Theatre of the Absurd. The most obvious achievement of modern Turkish dramatic writing and production has been the conscious effort to create a native drama by adapting traditional European styles and forms to indigenous traditional forms. Most regard the traditional form of Turkish drama as of simply historical value. Yet others have seen strong links in both style and content.

For example, the *orta oyunu* plays always begin with the line, 'I undertake the imitation'. This obviously indicates both the realistic story being told and the playfulness of the performance. This double approach clearly parallels the anti-illusionistic alienation devices used in many modern plays. The use of humour and satire is another link between traditional and modern Turkish drama. Furthermore, what one tends to find in Turkish drama is vigorous dialogue rather than complicated plots and the traditional practice of showing a cross-section of society on stage. It is these links that may well be examined further by Turkish theatre artists in the years to come.

Directors, Directing and Production Styles

Anatolian peasant plays have long provided contemporary artists with models for the integration of dance and music with dramatic texts, and numerous Turkish directors have aimed at creating a truly national style by working this way in their productions.

In the area of acting, the possibilities of this blend have already been achieved by actors such as Genco Erkal, Ferhan Şensoy and Münir Özkul (b. 1925). Since the mid-1930s, most actor training has favoured the Stanislavski approach, which is most obvious in performances by the state theatres. This is doubly reinforced since most state theatre directors are former actors themselves trained to be faithful to text and behavioural authenticity in the Stanislavskian way.

Younger directors have been more open to new approaches and have been more inclined towards experimentation and making clear their own interpretations. Ergin Orbey (b. 1935), for example, was among the first to try episodic forms and anti-illusionistic styles in his productions, while Yücel Erten (b. 1945) has staged several classical pieces in a clearly Brechtian style.

Beklan Algan (b. 1933) was among the first directors in the country actually to create a company committed exclusively to new approaches. In 1974, he created his Experimental Theatre (the company ceased operation in 1980) to work with young artists in examining new relationships between space, audiences, actors and text, In 1988, he founded TAL, the Tiyatro Araştrma Labarotuvari (Theatre Research Laboratory), which has worked ever since as a branch of the İstanbul Municipal Theatre.

Another director of note is Mehmet Ulusoy (b. 1944), who formed the Street Theatre as an alternative group in the 1970s. Performing in various outdoor locations as well as in factories and at political events, the company has had great influence on younger theatre artists.

The influence of traditional popular entertainment is more obvious in the private theatres, where earlier conventions still retain their attraction for many theatregoers. These include a loose structure, a fragmentary plot and an anti-illusionistic style of acting. Directors with political tendencies such as Genco Erkal, Başar Sabuncu and Rutkay Aziz (b. 1947) have used these forms to good advantage in many of their productions.

Music Theatre
Dance Theatre

Music and dance in Turkish theatre, with the exception of some Anatolian folk songs, developed as part of comedic devices which also included mime and impersonation. Linguistic evidence has proven that the origins of dance in Turkish theatre can be traced back to the shamanistic rituals of central Asia. The shaman who has the power to exorcise (an action that requires a great deal of dance) is called *oyun* – a term which in modern Turkish means 'to play', 'theatre', 'game' or 'dance'. The imitation of animals through dance is another eastern influence that can still be found in various Anatolian folk dances.

As Turkey expanded to become an empire and came to rule over large parts of Europe, Asia and Africa, elements from these sources integrated into what is today called the dance of Anatolian Turkey. Turkish folk dances, exceedingly rich in their variety of instruments, costumes, rhythms and steps, were also an integral part of processions and festivals in the Ottoman Empire. In these processions, trade guilds marched before the Sultan accompanied by giant puppets, buffoons and dancing boys.

As early as the seventeenth century, mime companies called *kol* included dancers and musicians of non-Islamic origin. Female dancers and mimes (also non-Muslims) had their separate companies. Both dancing girls and boys were called *çengi*. The boy dancers, whose appearance suggested femininity, were called *köçek*. Normally, the boys played female roles and the girls played male roles to add to the sense of comedy. Comic dancing by clowns, jesters and buffoons was called *curcuna*, which means 'drunken rebel', and their performances were called *curcunabaz*.

Grotesque dances were an important element in the development of *orta oyunu*, the Turkish *commedia dell'arte*, which also employed music. For the *orta oyunu*, as well as for shadow theatre, the style of music ranged from the classical *gazel* – an extemporaneous song chanted to various rhythms of Turkish music – to popular folk songs and fashionable songs from İstanbul.

Classical ballet dates back in Turkey only to 1945. It was in that year that the government invited Dame Ninette de Valois from England to help start a ballet school in İstanbul. In 1947, this became the Devlet Bale Okulu (State Ballet School) and was connected to the Devlet Konservatuvarı (State Conservatory) in Ankara. From this school grew the Devlet Balesi (Turkish State Ballet Company) which gave its first full-length performance (*Coppelia*) in 1960. In 1963, Dame Ninette choreographed what has come to be recognized as the first Turkish ballet with patterns based on Turkish folk dances, *Çeşmebaşı (The Fountain)* with music by a Turkish composer, Ferit Tüzün (1929–77).

In the 1960s and 1970s, native work in musical composition for ballet and choreography flourished. One of the earliest Turkish choreographers was Sait Sökmen (b. 1942), a student of Dame Ninette and a celebrated dancer, who also studied modern dance in England and the USA. *Cark (The Wheel*, produced in 1970), was the first work in modern international idioms to be choreographed by a Turk and Sökmen's first experience in choreography. The first native story to be choreographed in Turkey was *Pembe Kadın (A Woman Called Pembe)*, a play by Hidayet Sayın, which was composed by Necil Kâzım Akses (b. 1908) and choreographed by Oytun Turfanda (b. 1947), a celebrated Turkish dancer, in 1973. In 1977 Turfanda choreographed *Hurrem Sultan (Hurrem the Queen)*, the first full-length Turkish ballet, composed by Nevit Kodallı (b. 1924). In the 1980s, Duygu Aykal (1943–88) took the lead as the head choreographer of the State Ballet. She preferred to work on relatively short pieces in which she emphasized themes concerning human existence in the universe and social pressures upon individual freedom. Her most popular and most produced works include *Çoğul (Plural)*, *Oluşum (Formation)*, *Bulutlar Nereye Gider? (Where Do the Clouds Go?)*, *İnsan... İnsan (Man... Man)*, *Biz, Siz, Onlar (We, You, They)* and *İnsancık (The Little Creature: Man)*, all created in the late 1970s and 1980s in a poetic style which combined modern dance with classical ballet.

Today the Turkish State Opera and Ballet has established regularly operating stages in Ankara, İstanbul and İzmír. There is also a general interest in modern dance and several modern dance groups have been formed.

Classical European opera as a form was first attempted by Turkish artists in the early 1900s.

Regular performances of operas, both by European composers and by Turkish composers following European styles, are given today by the State Opera and Ballet.

Perhaps the most popular form of music theatre in Turkey for many decades early in the twentieth century was *operet* (operetta). Essentially, Turkish operetta was adapted from European vaudeville to which comic songs and dances were added. The text on which the libretto is based is usually either an adaptation of a foreign play or a Turkish one.

From the late 1890s through to about the 1930s, mostly due to the productions of Dikran Çuhaciyan (1840–98) and the librettos of Muhlis Sabahattin (1890–1947), the form achieved immense popularity and many private operetta companies existed. Even the İstanbul municipal theatres produced operettas, many of them by librettist Ekrem Reşit Rey (1900–59) and his brother, composer Cemal Reşit Rey (1904–85). As proof of the form's ongoing popularity, *Lüküs Hayat* (*Life in Luxury*), the most widely known of the Rey's works, was revived in 1986 and the production ran for several seasons at the İstanbul Municipal Theatre.

Since the 1960s, American and British musicals have become immensely popular and state theatres have reached large audiences with such shows as *Kiss Me Kate*, *Man of La Mancha*, *My Fair Lady*, *Fiddler on the Roof*, *West Side Story* and *A Funny Thing Happened on the Way to the Forum*, while the İstanbul Municipal Theatre has successfully produced *Evita*.

In the late 1970s, Egemen Bostanci (1938–86), an experienced entrepreneur, began bringing musical stars, well-known singers and leading directors together on a production-by-production basis to produce both native and foreign musicals. Though not always of the highest production quality, the shows were enormous hits with audiences. Two of the longest-running of these musicals, *Yedi Kocalı Hürmüz* (*Hürmüz With Seven Husbands*) and *Kanlı Nigar* (*Bloody Nigar*) were adapted from original texts by Sadik Şendil (1913–86), a playwright who wrote comedies about daily life in Ottoman times utilizing elements of traditional Turkish theatre. Another major musical hit was Haldun Dormen's *Hisseli Harikalar Kumpanyasi* (*Joint Company of Wonders*, 1980).

Theatre for Young Audiences
Puppet Theatre

Puppet theatre – or as it is called in Turkey, *kukla* – is among the oldest types of theatre for young audiences in the country. Beginning in ancient Turkistan (from where the original Turks emigrated), both *kol korçak* (hand-puppets) and *çadır hayal* (marionettes) were used. These two general groupings evolved into four specific types – the *iskemle kuklası* (jiggling puppet), presented by gypsy puppeteers on the streets; the *el kuklası* (hand- or glove-puppet); the *ipli kukla* (marionette); and the *ayak kuklası* (foot-puppet), about which little is known. All these puppet forms attracted the interest of both children and adults.

In the second half of the sixteenth century, the shadow theatre, *karagöz*, came into vogue and these performances were highlights of public entertainment on religious holidays and other festivals. *Karagöz* uses two-dimensional figures made of camel's hide, the shadows of which are cast on a translucent screen about 2 by 2.5

metres (later reduced to about 1 metre by 0.5 metres). The screen is stretched and tightened on to a wooden frame.

The figures in *karagöz* are operated from behind the screen with each of the coloured puppets held against it with rods. Oil lamps are preferred as a light source since they create more effective shadows by flickering, giving the puppets a more lifelike appearance.

The Turkish shadow theatre, which almost disappeared as a folk entertainment, is being restored today by the state and a number of private institutions. Today the Ministry of Culture is the official sponsor of the Devlet Karagöz Tiyatrosu (State Shadow Theatre) and even banks sponsor private shadow companies.

The idea of utilizing theatre in schools was first considered in 1908 when the Second Constitution came into effect. Educators had observed its use in private foreign schools and by 1910 the Ministry of Education authorized its use in Turkish schools. Authors quickly became interested in writing plays for theatre-in-education.

The first professional children's theatre was established by Muhsin Ertuğrul in 1935 as part of the İstanbul Municipal Theatre. Before launching the company, Ertuğrul had spent time in the Soviet Union looking at children's theatres and even working for a time with Soviet children's theatre expert Natalia Satz. The first children's play to be produced, in 1935, was *İlk Tiyatro Dersi* (*The First Lesson in Drama*) by Kemal Küçük (1901–36), an actor. In the early 1990s, this municipal children's theatre was still in operation. At about the same time, a periodical began to be published about theatre for young audiences called *Çocuk Tiyatrosu Mecmuasi* (*Children's Theatre Magazine*).

The country's second subsidized children's theatre was established in İzmír in 1946, also by the municipality. The company operated until 1950 and then was reopened in 1957 as part of the state theatre network. It too continued to function in the 1990s.

A third children's theatre began operations in Ankara in 1948, also as part of the state theatre network. A fourth was added in Bursa in 1958. Three additional companies were later established by the state in İstanbul, Adana and Trabzon.

In the 1950s, there were several attempts to open additional children's theatres. These included the Karagöz ve Kukla Tiyatrosu (Shadow and Puppet Theatre) sponsored by the Children's Charity Organization in Ankara, and the Keloğlan Çocuk Tiyatrosu (Keloğlan Children's Theatre) and Akbank Çocuk Tiyatrosu (Akbank Children's Theatre), both sponsored by private banks.

After 1960 in Ankara, almost all of the private companies organized children's drama sections and children's groups began to outnumber theatres for adults. At least two private groups were founded at this time specifically to produce for children – Dünya Çocuk Oyuncuları (World Children's Players) and the Afacan Çocuk Tiyatrosu (Naughty Children's Theatre).

In the 1970s, changes began to be initiated

Ziya Demirel's 1971–2 State Theatres production of Rabindranath Tagore's *The Post Office*, designed by Hūseyin Mumcu.

aimed at reforming Turkish children's theatres which had been doing essentially the same type of work for nearly four decades. Meetings were held for the first time involving dramatists, directors, actors and teachers focused on renewal of the repertory and staging. A new children's company, AÇOK (Anadolu Çocuk Oyuncuları Kolu – the Anatolian Children's Theatre Troupe) was established in İstanbul by Muhsin Ertuğrul and Haldun Taner. The first play performed by the company, founded in 1973, was called *Mutluluk Ülkesi* (*The Land of Happiness*). In 1975, the company appeared at the World Festival of Children's Theatres held in Hamburg, Germany, with its production of *Keloğlan*, a show filled with audio-visual effects which appealed to the collective images of children without undue emphasis on language. One other company worth noting is Salih Kalyon's (b. 1942) AÇT (Ankara Çocuk Tiyatrosu – the Ankara Children's Theatre). This company has operated in direct cooperation with schools and has had a positive effect on the education of young people in Ankara. Additional children's groups have also recently sprung up in Anatolia.

Design
Theatre Space and Architecture

The western and southern coasts of Anatolia are crowded with ancient amphitheatres, some of which have been reconstructed and used regularly for both national and international theatre festivals.

In most major cities and even in many of the smaller towns, there used to be community halls or folkhouses (*halkevleri*) which served the function of modern cultural centres. Although few of them retain their original purpose, the stages in many of them are still used by visiting companies and local amateur groups.

As for modern playhouses in Turkey, a good deal has already been explained in the opening section of this article. It may be added here that since theatrical activity is concentrated in İstanbul and Ankara the majority of the country's modern theatre buildings are to be found there. As the 1990s began, the state theatres were expanding once again into major Anatolian cities.

The capacity of most Turkish theatres ranges from 200 to 1,300 and almost all have proscenium stages. Technical equipment in most of them is generally insufficient since almost all were built for other purposes and only later turned into playhouses. The opera house in Ankara (Büyük Tiyatro) is one of Turkey's most successfully converted buildings and is also technically well equipped. Among the best equipped modern playhouses are the two in the Atatürk Cultural Centre in İstanbul and the Kent Players' theatre.

There is a tendency both in the construction of new theatres and in the adaptation of existing spaces to move away from traditional proscenium stages. This can be seen clearly in a multifunctional stage (Irfan Şahinbaş Atölye Tiyatrosu) recently built in a warehouse on the outskirts of Ankara.

Design for traditional plays used to rely on a few permanent and multifunctional stage properties. Contemporary production, however, depends heavily on more specifically designed elements. Since most theatres have conventional proscenium stages, designers either provide a realistic environment or a modified realistic decoration. Refik Eren (b. 1922), master designer of the state theatres, contributed greatly to the success of several historical plays with his highly stylized designs.

A less realistic trend in Turkish stage design was created by Turgut Zaim (1906–74), a famous painter who used elements from traditional miniature painting and folk art in his stage work. Osman Şengezer (b. 1941), a designer for ballet and opera, has created expressive as well as decorative stage designs, which range from stylized decoration to an elaborate mixture of traditional and modern motifs in an effort to achieve a harmony of line and colour.

There have been as well a number of more recent attempts to create formalist stage designs. Designers such as Metin Deniz (b. 1938), Erkan Kirtunç (b. 1939) and Yücel Tanyeri (b. 1937) have tried to surpass the limitations of the proscenium by adding to it a portable

Rutkay Aziz's 1976–7 Ankara Art Theatre production of Brecht's *Days of the Commune*, designed by Haldun Ertekin and Cengiz Kabaoğlu.

thrust stage. Creative rather than conventional, their non-realistic and expressive work tends to support the ironies possible in the dramatic imagination.

Training

Since 1982 when a new law concerning higher education was passed, all the institutions which provide formal education in theatre have been reorganized as departments of various universities in Ankara, İstanbul and İzmír. Previous to this, only two universities provided formal training in theatre – the University of Ankara and the University of Dokuz Eylül in İzmír.

The theatre department at the University of Ankara was originally established in 1958 exclusively as an institute for theatre research and the bulk of theatre research in Turkey was produced here by professors Melahat Özgű (b. 1911), Sevda Şener (b. 1928), Özdemir Nutku (b. 1931) and Metin And. The institute was reorganized in 1962 into a fully operative theatre history, theatre research and dramatic literature section. When the new programme opened in 1964, the section was given full department status. Including a four-year Bachelor of Arts programme, the department was the only academic centre for theatre research in Turkey. Today it offers three different streams: theatre history, criticism, theory, and dramaturgy; playwriting; and acting. BA, MA and PhD degrees are offered in all areas.

The department of theatrical and cinematic arts at the University of Dokuz Eylül in İzmír was established in 1976 by Özdemir Nutku. Its aim is to train theatre professionals in acting, playwriting, set, costume and lighting design as well as in dramatic research. To achieve this, it has established ties with experienced theatre professionals who teach in the university and direct student productions.

At Mimar Sinan University in İstanbul, there is a Faculty of Fine Arts with a department of theatre and cinematic arts. Its main focus is stage design, cinema and photography.

The theatre section of the State Conservatory in Ankara (discussed in the opening section of this article) was reorganized at Hacettepe University in the same city. Despite this change in location and status, its primary aim is to offer professional training in performance and to provide actors for the state theatre system.

The theatre section of the Conservatory of the

Municipality of İstanbul has also been incorporated into a university, the University of İstanbul. Its main focus is also in performance. Mimar Sinan University, in its turn, now runs the theatre section of the İstanbul State Conservatory. Bilkent University in Ankara and Anadolu University in Eskişehir have also started four-year teaching and training programmes in theatre.

Aside from these totally state-subsidized institutions, there are also a number of private acting studios in İstanbul which offer professional training. As well, a number of the private theatres both in İstanbul and Ankara provide introductory courses in acting.

Criticism, Scholarship and Publishing

Theatre criticism in the modern sense has existed in Turkey since the late nineteenth century. Following the founding of the Turkish Republic, Nurullah Ataç (1898–1957) began writing in newspapers and journals on both productions and issues in the Turkish theatre and basically set the standards for contemporary theatre criticism. The playwright Reşat Nuri Güntekin also wrote regularly at this time on ways to reform the theatre in Turkey while Muhsin Ertuğrul wrote on virtually every aspect of the art. The writings of all three have been collected and published.

Today, theatrical criticism can be found in daily newspapers as well as in weekly and monthly magazines. Most of the writers are journalists, some are scholars and a small number are actually working in the theatre community or even in other professions. A Turkish Theatre Critics' Association was founded in 1972.

The country's first theatre journal, *Darül-bedayi*, was founded by Muhsin Ertuğrul in 1930. *Devlet Tiyatro Dergisi (State Theatre Magazine)* was founded in 1949 and remained the country's leading theatre journal until 1980. Another important journal, *Tiyatro Araştırmaları Dergisi (Journal of Theatre Research)* began publishing in 1970 from the University of Ankara. The university has since published several important books on Turkish and foreign theatre.

The İstanbul municipal theatres and the state theatres eventually began to publish occasional monographs. Monthly and biweekly literary

magazines devote regular space to theatre articles, especially *Milliyet Sanat Dergisi (Milliyet Arts Magazine)*, founded in 1972 and edited since 1980 by Zeynep Oral (b. 1946), and *Gösteri (Spectacle)*, edited since 1980 by Doğan Hizlan (b. 1937).

Books on theatre are now being published by a wide variety of companies but none specializes just in publishing theatre material. Plays have been published by private publishing houses, private theatres and state theatres, as well as by the Ministries of Culture and Education.

Scholarly work in the field is carried out by researchers at various university drama departments. The theatre department at the University of Ankara, being the oldest in the country, has produced several theatre scholars of note. These include Meláhat Özgű, an expert in German drama and one of the country's pioneers in the field of scholarly writing on drama; Bedrettin Tuncel (1910–80) in the field of French drama; and Irfan Şahinbas (1912–90) in English and American drama.

Metin And is an internationally known figure in the field of Turkish and Far Eastern theatre having published numerous books and more than a thousand articles on theatre. Özdemir Nutku has also written extensively on various aspects of theatre and drama while Sevda Şener is the author of four important books on Turkish and world theatre history as well as on dramatic theory. Sevinç Sokullu (b. 1927) has written on Turkish comedy while Ayşegül Yüksel (b. 1941) has written two books on playwrights Melih Cevdet Anday and Haldun Taner. Two books on Muhsin Ertuğrul have been written and edited by Efdal Sevinçli (b. 1949), while other scholars have written on various subjects ranging from theatre history to Shakespeare.

Özdemir Nutku, Sevda Şener,
Ayşegül Yüksel

Further Reading

Akı, Niyazi. *Çağdaş Türk Tiyatrosuna Toplu Bakış, 1923–1967*. [A general survey of the contemporary Turkish theatre, 1923–1967]. Ankara: Atatürk Üniversitesi Yayınları, 1968.

And, Metin. *Culture, Performance and Communication in Turkey*. Tokyo: Institute for the Study of Language and Cultures of Asia and Africa, 1987.

——. *Cumhuriyet Dönemi Türk Tiyatrosu*. [Turkish theatre in the republican period]. Ankara: Türkiye İş Bankası Kültür Yayınları, 1983.

——. *Drama at the Crossroads*. İstanbul: Isis Press, 1991.

——. *Geleneksel Türk Tiyatrosu*. [Traditional Turkish theatre]. Ankara: Bilgi Yayınevi, 1969.

——. *A History of Theatre and Popular Entertainment in Turkey*. Ankara: Forum Yayınları, 1963–4.

——. *Karagöz: Théâtre d'ombres turc*. [Karagöz: Turkish shadow theatre]. Ankara: Dost Yayınevi, 1977.

——. *A Pictorial History of Turkish Dancing*. Ankara: Dost Yayınevi, 1976.

——. *Türk Tiyatrosunun Evreleri*. [The phases of Turkish theatre]. Ankara: Turhan Kitabevi, 1983.

Ay, Lütfi. 'Relazione e influenze del teatro occidentale nel campo delle arti dello spettacolo in Turchia'. [The influence of western theatre on the performing arts in Turkey]. In *Teatro Oriente/Occidente*, ed. Antonella Ottai, 395–414. Rome: Bulzoni, 1986.

Halman, Talât Sait. *Modern Turkish Drama*. Chicago: Bibliotecha Islamica, 1976.

Landau, J.M. *Shadow Plays in the Near East*. Jerusalem: Palestine Institute of Folklore and Ethnology, 1948.

——. *Studies in the Arab Theatre and Cinema*. Philadelphia: University of Pennsylvania Press, 1958.

Martinovitch, N.N. *The Turkish Theatre*. New York: B. Blom, 1968.

Nutku, Özdemir. *Darülbedayi'nin Elli Yılı*. [Fifty years of darülbedayi]. Ankara: Ankara Üniversitesi, Dil ve Tarih Coğrafya Fakültesi Yayınları, 1969.

——. *Meddahlık ve Meddah Hikâyeleri*. [*Meddah* and *meddah* stories]. Ankara: Türkiye İş Bankası Kültür Yayınları, 1976.

——. 'The Transformation of Turkish Culture'. In *A Panorama of the Turkish Republic Under the Leadership of Atatürk. A Collection of Essays*, eds. Gülsen Renda & C. Max Kortpeter, 165–78. Princeton, NJ: Kingston Press, 1986.

Özgü, Meláhat. 'L'influenza dell'oriente e dell'occidente sul concetto turco di teatro'. [The influence of east and west on the Turkish concept of theatre]. In *Teatro Oriente/Occidente*, ed. Antonella Ottai, 415–20. Rome: Bulzoni, 1986.

Şener, Sevda. 'Contemporary Turkish Drama'. In *A Panorama of the Turkish Republic Under the Leadership of Atatürk. A Collection of Essays*, eds. Gülsen Renda & C. Max Kortpeter, 249–66. Princeton, NJ: Kingston Press, 1986.

——. *Çağdas Türk Tiyatrosunda Ahlâk Ekonomi Kültür Sorunları, 1923–1973*. [Moral, economic and cultural problems in contemporary Turkish drama, 1923–1973]. Ankara: Ankara Üniversitesi Dil ve Tarih Coğrafya Fakültesi Yayınları, 1971.

——. *Çağdaş Türk Tiyatrosunda İnsan 1923–1972*. [Man in contemporary Turkish theatre, 1923–1972]. Ankara: Ankara Üniversitesi Dil ve Tarih Coğrafya Fakültesi Yayınları, 1972.

Sevengil, Refik Ahmet. *Yakın Çağlarda Türk Tiyatrosu*. [Turkish theatre in recent years]. İstanbul: Kanaat Kütüphanesi, 1934.

Siyavusgil, S. Esat. *Karagöz: Its History, Its Characters, Its Mystic and Satiric Spirit*. İstanbul: Turkish Press Broadcasting and Tourist Department, 1961.

Sokullu, Sevinç. *Türk Komedyasının Evrimi*. [The evolution of Turkish comedy]. Ankara: Kültür Bakanlığı Yayınları, 1979.

Yüksel, Ayşegül. *Haldun Taner Tiyatrosu*. [The theatre of Haldun Taner]. Ankara: Bilgi Yayınevı, 1986.

——. 'The Role of Theatre in Transforming the Small Ottoman Town of Ankara into the Westernized Capital of Modern Turkey'. In *Ankara Üniversitesi Dil ve Tarih Coğrafya Fakültesi Degrisi 35*, No. 1, 1991.

TURKMENISTAN

(Asia/Oceania volume; see also **USSR**)

UKRAINE

An independent east European republic, Ukraine was part of the Soviet Union until proclaiming its independence in August 1991. It shares borders with Russia, Belarus, Poland, the Slovak Republic, Hungary, Romania and Moldova. Some 603,700 square kilometres (233,028 square miles) in size, it had a 1992 population of approximately 54 million, of which 73.6 per cent were ethnic Ukrainians, 21.1 per cent were Russians, 1.3 per cent were Jews; others included Belarussians, Moldovans, Hungarians, Germans, Tartars, Poles and Greeks. Its capital is Kiev with a population of 2.5 million. The dominant religion is Christianity although in the 1990s there was a revival of Islam in the Crimea.

The ancient history of this territory reaches back to the Cimmerians (1150–750 BC), Scythians (750–250 BC) and Sarmatians (250 BC to AD 200). Historically, Ukraine descended from the Kievan Rus. The Kievan Rus (eighth to thirteenth centuries) flourished in the reigns of Prince Volodymyr (AD 980–1017) and Prince Yaroslav the Wise (1019–54). In the thirteenth and fourteenth centuries this area was ruled by the Mongol invaders of the Golden Horde. Eventually, parts of it were annexed by Lithuania and Poland.

During the wars with the Turks and Crimean Tartars in the fifteenth and sixteenth centuries and the struggle with Ukrainian, Lithuanian and Polish feudal lords, there developed a democratic model of social order with specific freedoms and rights, known as the Kozak Republic of the Zaporizhian Sich that had important impact. Further history is marked by hundreds of uprisings within the borders of the Russian Empire, to which Ukraine was annexed after the destruction of the Kozak State. During the civil war that occurred after the October Revolution in 1917, Ukraine tried to separate from Russia, forming a Ukrainian National Republic (1918–20). This republic ultimately fell to the Bolsheviks and from 1922 Ukraine became part of the USSR.

Ukraine's access to the Black Sea, its rich

farmland and its variety of mineral deposits make this country potentially one of the richest in Europe, but its long history of colonialization has left many scars. During the Soviet period, most decisions about industry, finance and prices were made in Moscow and everything was organized centrally. In the 1920s and 1930s Ukraine suffered almost total destruction of its intellectual class; in 1933 millions of peasants died in what is now perceived to be a genocidal famine. There were as well political repressions in the 1960s and 1970s. Since its declaration of independence, Ukraine has been evolving towards a market economy, and now has mixed forms of ownership. Laws have also been newly written to create the basis for banking, financial and price reforms.

As for Ukrainian theatre, it has existed since the sixteenth century while a professional Ukrainian theatre emerged at the end of the nineteenth century. Throughout its history, Ukrainian professional theatre has often functioned as a challenge and even an alternative to the regime in power. Since political channels of expression were closed in the Russian Empire, during the nineteenth century educated Ukrainians turned to literature and the arts as their means of critical social expression. When in 1863 it became illegal to publish most books in Ukrainian, attention was focused on the theatre. The Teatr koryfeiv (Theatre of the Coryphaei) was formed at the end of the nineteenth century and united the intelligentsia around its artistic and democratic ideals. The playwrights and directors of this theatre included Mykhailo Starytskyi (1840–1904), Marko Kropyvnytski (1840–1910), Panas Saksahanskyi (Panas Tobilevych, 1859–1940), Mykola Sadovskyi (Mykola Tobilevych, 1856–1933) and Ivan Karpenko-Karyi (Ivan Tobilevych, 1845–1907). The plays of this era were mostly folk dramas, because all other forms were forbidden by law. The heroes were usually strong, free and emotional and were always presented in a romantic style.

At the beginning of the twentieth century these works were replaced by neo-romantic intellectual plays which synthesized new philosophical ideas and psychology with findings in the natural sciences. Major writers included Lesia Ukrainka (Larysa Kosach, 1871–1913), Ivan Franko (1856–1916) and Volodymyr Vynnychenko (1880–1951). They created the basis for major changes in Ukrainian theatre which began to be seen between 1910 and the early 1930s, confirming Ukrainian art

as independent, self-regulating and relatively autonomous.

One of the first important examples of this can be found in the work of Les Kurbas (Oleksander Kurbas, 1887–1937). Kurbas was an actor, director, writer, theatre theoretician and translator; he studied at universities in Vienna and Lvov. Almost singlehandedly, he brought into being a Ukrainian avant-garde theatre and his ideas are still of interest today.

When Kurbas began his reforms, folk dramas still dominated the repertoire, even though new and far more interesting plays were being written by Lesia Ukrainka, Ivan Franko and Volodymyr Vynnychenko. Kurbas declared his opposition to the earlier folk theatre, which he felt prevented the 'theatricalization' of theatre. He wanted to change both the repertoire and the prevailing ideas on set decoration and acting style.

Kurbas based his ideas on the work of Swiss designer Adolphe Appia and English director, designer and theorist Edward Gordon Craig. For example, Kurbas replaced the standard single locale sets with stage designs that employed architectural elements (*Oedipus Rex*, 1918), painterly parodies (*Weh dem der lügt!/Woe to the Liar!*, by the Austrian Franz Grillparzer, 1918) and light designs influenced by Byzantine icons (*Iyola*, 1918, by the Polish writer Jerzy Zulawski and *Jan Huss*, 1919, a play based on the Ukrainian poem by Taras Shevchenko (1814–61)). He also used totally neutral stage space to provide freedom of movement in his 1920 production of *Haidamaky*, again based on Shevchenko's poetry. Designers who worked with Kurbas at this time included Anatol Petrytskyi (1895–1964) and Mykhailo Boychuk (1882–1939) who both later became artists of national importance.

Kurbas founded the Molodyi teatr (Young Theatre 1916–19) in order to stage new Ukrainian plays and world classics in Ukrainian. Kurbas was, in fact, the first to stage an ancient Greek play and Shakespeare in Ukrainian. It should be noted here that translations into Ukrainian had been forbidden by law until 1905. Kurbas consciously declared the Molodyi teatr to be open to all aesthetic tendencies – expressionism, sentimentalism, intellectualism, neo-romanticism, Greek revival, *commedia dell'arte*, Medieval Miracle plays and even eastern artistic influences. The Molodyi was to become an anthology of periods and styles where the best achievements of world culture were to be brought together. His productions of *Oedipus Rex*, *Weh dem der lügt!*, the Shevchenko evenings, *Vertep* (a Nativity play staged in 1918) and *U pushchi* (*In the Wilderness*, 1918, by Lesia Ukrainka) constituted an original and dazzling start to the dream. These were followed in 1920 by Kurbas's productions of *Macbeth* and *Haidamaky*, a Ukrainian classic.

In 1922 Kurbas founded the Berezil (the name is derived from the word *berezen*, the month of March in Ukrainian). At first it was the Mystetske Obiednannia Berezil (Berezil Artistic Association), a veritable academy of theatre with departments in charge of developing various forms – dramatic, musical, children's, cabaret, revue and comedy. There was also a directors' laboratory, an experimental workshop, a repertoire committee, and a centre which studied the audience (questionnaires were analysed and audience preferences examined). Also included were a theatre museum and a committee that looked into the organization of labour at the theatre. At one point over 400 people worked in the Berezil, which managed to initiate many activities in the country. Circumstances, however, did not allow it to pursue further its work, which was attracting the best young poets, writers, painters and composers in Ukraine.

At the Berezil, Kurbas continued his open approach to a broad range of styles. During its early days (1922–6) he favoured expressionism, evident in his productions of *Gas I* (1923) by the German writer Georg Kaiser; *Jimmie Higgins* (1923), based on a novel by the American writer Upton Sinclair and dramatized by Kurbas himself; and *Naperedodni* (*On the Eve*, 1926), dramatized by Kurbas, Stepan Bondarchuk (1886–1970) and others. The eclecticism of this period points to the fact that a new synthesis had not yet been achieved. Later, the Russian poet Osip Mandelshtam would write that at the core of the Berezil there seemed to exist a number of theatres.

Berezil in its first phase was a political theatre, but unlike the political theatres of Erwin Piscator or Bertolt Brecht, Kurbas's theatre avoided propaganda. Although the agitprop approach was popular in Soviet art, *Jimmie Higgins* explored the tragedy of a 'small man', his individuality from the mass. Kurbas focused on the individual consciousness, peering into the subconscious. This was the first example of such experimentation in the Soviet theatre.

During its second period (1926–33) Berezil became the leading theatre in Ukraine. In 1925

Les Kurbas's 1923 Berezil production of his dramatization *Jimmie Higgins*, designed by Vadym Meller.
Photo: Natalia Kuziakina, University of St Petersburg.

it won a gold medal for a set design at the Paris Exposition of Decorative Arts. In 1926 it was named National Theatre and transferred to Kharkov, which was then the capital of Ukraine. A philosophical theatre, Kurbas's Berezil now incorporated the plays of Mykola Kulish (1892–1937) and the designs of Vadym Meller (1884–1962). Meller was educated at Kiev University, the Academy of Art in Munich and had studied sculpture with Antoine Bourdelle in Paris. Meller was invited to exhibit at the Salon d'Automne together with Picasso, Braque, Derain, Metzinger, Delaunay and Gris. Later he taught at the Art Institute in Kiev.

In such shows as *Narodnyi Malakhii* (*The People's Malakhii*, 1928), *Myna Mazailo* (1929) and *Maklena Grasa* (1933) by Mykola Kulish and *Dyktatura* (*Dictatorship*, 1930) by Ivan Mykytenko (1897–1937) as well as in his directorial concept for *King Lear* for a production at the Jewish State Theatre (eventually staged in 1935 with Solomon Michoels in the lead), Kurbas achieved a synthesis of national culture with European theatrical values. His theatrical poetics tended towards a fantastic realism that combined the rational with the irrational, employed 'alienation' and 'estrangement' with profound psychological examinations, and blended the grotesque with the theatrical and poetry with biology.

His work in this period was influenced by the European literary avant-garde and examines 'the world as reflected through the consciousness of a character' (for instance in *Narodnyi Malakhiy* and *Maklena Grasa*). He deformed the outer world to reflect the inner turmoil while examining the illusion of harmony and breaks in consciousness. Folk traditions such as keening and religious icons, embroidered cloths, ribbons and bishop's staffs were used in his theatre as semiotic signs both in tragedy and tragi-comedy.

Kurbas, Kulish and Meller built a model theatre which synthesized the mystical with traditions of the carnival where the world is seen upside-down, where everything freely transforms into everything else, where the metonymical aesthetic principle juggles both the part and the whole, where the individual is at once the microcosm and the universe.

Kurbas's theory of 'transformed image' was actually taught during his time. It evolved from an individual transformed gesture (a conscious image used to express the essence of a phenomenon, a metaphor or a symbol) into the grand transformation when the entire production became a metaphor. The development of this 'transformed image' in time and space was to evoke in the spectator a large number of associations which would cause an elevation of the level of perception and reveal the philosophical aspects of the moment.

In September 1933, after resisting increasing political pressure, Kurbas was summarily dismissed as director of the Berezil and all of his existing productions were banned. In December he was arrested and sentenced to five years for participating in what were called terrorist activities. Sent to the Solovetskyi Island prison on the White Sea, he also created a theatre there and staged shows by Bernard Shaw and the Russian writer Nikolai Pogodin. Although it was called a 'model' theatre by local officials, Kurbas was executed in 1937.

In the 1920s and 1930s most theatres in Ukraine were headed by students of Kurbas. The leading directors of the time were Marian Krushelnytskyi (1897–1963), Hnat Yura (1888–1966), Vasyl Vasylko (Vasyl Myliaiv, 1893–1972), Borys Tiahno (1904–64), Leontiy Dubovyk (1902–52), Volodymyr Skliarenko (1907–84), Faust Lopatynskyi (1899–1937) and Yanuariy Bortnyk (1897–1939). They headed such companies as the Kyivskyi akademichnyi dramatychnyi teatr im. Ivan Franka (Franko Academic Dramatic Theatre in Kiev), Kharkivskyi akademichnyi dramatychnyi teatr im. T. Shevchenka (Shevchenko Academic Dramatic Theatre in Kharkov), Lvovskyi akademichnyi dramatychnyi teatr im. Maria Zankovetskoi (Zankovetska Academic Dramatic Theatre in Lvov) and Odeskuyi ukrainskyi muzychno-dramatychnyi teatr (Ukrainian Dramatic and Musical Theatre in Odessa).

The actors of Kurbas's theatre were also leaders in the arts. Kurbas trained thinking actors, who were to be 'wise Harlequins' or 'intellectual Pierrots'. The training included 'duration in the assigned rhythm', 'mechanics of emotion' and exercises based on Rudolf Steiner's eurhythmy. Five of Kurbas's actors – Iosyp Hirniak (1895–1989), Krushelnytskyi, Oleksander Serdiuk (b. 1900), Borys Balaban (1906–59) and Ambrosil Buchma (1891–1957) – were particularly remarkable.

With Kurbas's exclusion from theatrical and cultural life, Ukrainian theatre lost its leader. (Kurbas's era is now called the Executed Renaissance.) The demand for a theatre of truly profound artistic analysis disappeared and once again Ukrainian theatre saw a narrowing of vision. The traditional theatre, which had absorbed certain experimental forms from the theatrical avant-garde, turned back to folk dramas and in the 1930s provided some brilliant examples of acting but not much more.

Throughout the 1930s and 1940s, Hnat Yura – an 'actor's director' who was the founder and artistic director of the second most important theatre in Ukraine, the Franko Theatre (founded in 1920) – created an ensemble theatre to stage traditional Ukrainian drama and contemporary Soviet plays. Yura himself was a brilliant comedian and character actor. The best shows of this theatre were *Beztalanna* (*The Unfortunate Girl*, 1937) by Karpenko-Karyi, *Marusia Bohuslavka* (1941) by Starytskyi, *Don Carlos* (1936) by Friedrich Schiller, *Zahybel eskadry* (*Destruction of a Squadron*, 1933) by Oleksander Korniychuk (1905–72) and *Ukradene shchastia* (*Stolen Happiness*, 1940) by Franko with Buchma in the leading role. Other directors included Kost Koshevskyi (Kost Shkliar, 1895–1945) and V. Vilner.

Among the most interesting directors was Marian Krushelnytskyi, who headed the former Berezil, which was renamed the Shevchenko Theatre after Kurbas's dismissal. Krushelnytskyi's best work included *Eugenie Grandet* (1940) based on the French novel by Honoré de Balzac, *Dai sertsiu voliu, zavede v nevoliu* (*Give the Heart Freedom and It Will Lead You into Slavery*, 1936) by Kropyvnytskyi, *Hroza* (*The Storm*, 1938) by the Russian writer Alexander Ostrovsky, *Bohdan Khmelnytskyi* (1939) by Korniychuk and *Yaroslav Mudryi* (*Yaroslav the Wise*, 1946) by Ivan Kocherha (1881–1952).

The 1930s and 1940s were a time of restructuring under pressure from the increasingly totalitarian system. In self-defence, the theatre retreated into well-tried, stable artistic traditions, abandoning experimentation and drifting into socialist-realism as demanded by the state. This style required a drastic simplification of style, genre, tone and psychology. The state required that the theatre be agitational, didactic, educational and full of false recognition.

The audience of the Ukrainian theatre of the 1910s to the mid-1930s included of a small number of peasants and workers (never more than 4 per cent), but primarily it was the intellectuals and the students who attended. From the mid-1930s this audience changed – even fewer peasants, workers and students and increasing numbers of lumpen intellectuals and bureaucrats.

All outward signs show that there was a clear decline in the theatre of the time (however, more complex processes were taking place on the inside, as is true in every self-regulating system). The high social status which the theatre enjoyed till then (with all of its fans, ritual acknowledgements and titles) eroded. But the theatre did not become socially peripheral. Rather it temporarily took on other functions and joined those forces who would educate the conformist.

The leading Ukrainian dramatic theatres – Franko Theatre, Shevchenko Theatre, Zankovetska Theatre and the Odessa Theatre of the October Revolution – continued to develop the traditions of folk and psychological theatre (romanticism and sentimentalism increased measurably after World War II and the victory over fascism). As a result, the play *Yaroslav the Wise* by Kocherha, for instance, was presented by the theatres as a celebration of a strong leader, in which one could read a reflection of 'the leader of the people' – Stalin. A historical character (Yaroslav) was romanticized and made to resemble the leader of the Soviet Union.

The subjects of plays – like *Heneral Vatutin* (*General Vatutin*) by Lubomyr Dmyterko about a World War II military commander; *Za druhym frontom* (*Behind the Second Front*) by V. Sobka; *The Young Guard* by Alexander Fadaev about the young during the war and *Naviky razom* (*Forever Together*) by Dmyterko, about the friendship and unity of Ukraine and Russia – all reveal that the theatre was becoming increasingly politicized. Aesthetic criteria were being replaced by socio-political concerns.

During World War II theatres and theatrical brigades performing near the front lines and in the trenches were primarily concerned with lifting the spirits of the soldiers with romantic and heroic portrayals. In the post-war years they simply retained this task.

Unfortunately, society's jubilation with the victory did not yield worthy plays or productions about the tragic aspects of the war and the true price of victory. Ukrainian theatre, as well as Soviet theatre in general, continued to present productions that maintained the national myth more than anything else. The plays previously mentioned – and many more like them – were now presented by the theatres as oratorios and odes, not so much to the people who won the war but to the leader and to the state.

Dazzling, monumental, celebratory productions of these plays aesthetically resembled mass spectacles and state concerts. However, they were often full of emotion and sincerity. The success of shows like *Yaroslav the Wise* at the Shevchenko Theatre directed by Krushelnytskyi, confirmed the power of art at the service of the state. The shows of the late 1940s and 1950s are vivid examples of how a conceptual 'illusion' can fuse with excellent acting and elegant stage design. (The Ukrainian School of Scenography was, in fact, considered to be one of the best in the Soviet Union.) Kurbas's avant-garde ideas were found only in experimental elements in the works of his students and in the works of artists schooled by Meller. Alternative theatre or underground theatre simply did not exist.

The situation changed somewhat in the late 1950s and early 1960s. With the thaw in political and social life after Khrushchev's destalinization speech in 1956, there appeared a new generation. There was an explosion in Ukrainian poetry and national consciousness which led to an attempt to create a new Ukrainian theatre based on Kurbas's theories. This took place at the Kliub Tvorchoi Molodi (Creative Youth Club) which was led by Krushelnytskyi and Les Taniuk (b. 1938).

The state took advantage of the conservative position of the classical academic theatres in the aesthetic polemic that suddenly arose between them and the young experimental group at the Creative Youth Club. The club's productions of *Nizh u sontsi* (*Knife in the Sun*) by Ivan Drach, *Patetychna sonata* (*Sonata Pathétique*) by Kulish, *Mutter Courage und ihre Kinder* (*Mother Courage and Her Children*, 1961–3) by Brecht (all staged by Taniuk) were banned. Nevertheless, theatre artists, as well as young composers, musicians, painters and sculptors found a home at the Creative Youth Club which created an intellectual environment that was as close as anyone had come to an alternative theatre with its own standards and aesthetic language.

New political repression in the 1970s, which started with a series of arrests in 1972, was mainly directed against the leaders of this alternative culture. When in the 1980s the process of reviving the theatre and the nation began again, it was headed by many of these same leaders of the 1960s.

Ukrainian theatre started to change steadily in the 1980s and early 1990s. It became more varied, differentiated and dynamic. Hundreds of avant-garde productions appeared, predominantly in the post-modern style. These experiments were based on Kurbas's theory of the 'transformed image' and the contemporary experimentation of Jerzy Grotowski, Eugenio Barba, Peter Brook, Antonin Artaud, Anatoly Vasyliov and Roman Viktuke.

An especially active segment of the contemporary theatre is the studios. In the two years 1987–9, more than a hundred theatre-studios emerged with various styles and direction. The most prominent among them were the Lvivsky Molodizhni teatr im. Lesia Kurbasa (Kurbas Young Theatre of Lvov) directed by Volodymyr Kuchinskyi; Teatralny klub (Theatrical Club) directed by Oleg Liptsun in Kiev; Hydke kachenia (Ugly Ducking) directed by V. Savinov in Mykolaiiv; Teatr na Podoli (Theatre on the Podol) directed by V. Malakhov in Kiev; and Budmo! (Let's Be!) headed by Sergei Proskurnia in Kiev.

Musical theatre has been developed by I. Stoliarskyi's Odesky kamerny teatr (Odessa Chamber Theatre); H. Melskyi's Yevreisky teatr Mazeltov (Mazeltov Jewish Theatre); and O. Nikolaev's Dnipropetrovsky Teatr-studia baletu Demos (Demos Ballet Theatre Studio in Dnipropetrovsk).

Among the important movement-oriented groups are Mimikrichi led by V. Kriukov in Kiev, O. Belskyi's Theatre in Kryvy Rih, M. Milmeister's Theatre in Uzhhorod, and V. Huhnin's Mimohraf Theatre in Lvov.

Performances by various writers of their own songs have become popular as well. The best of these theatre-studios are V. Morozov's Ne zhurys! (Don't Worry!) in Lvov, and S. Rubchynskyi's Akademiia (Academy) in Kiev. The student theatre movement has not only created its own youth subculture but also started to create its own artistic experiments.

The more traditional theatres in the 1990s found themselves in an unfamiliar situation with a multiplicity of aesthetic trends to choose from

E. Molostova'a production of A. Shcherbak's *To Hope*, designed by Danylo Lider.
Photo: Victor Marustschenko.

and a new role within a new sovereign democratic nation. Most have reacted in one of three ways: first, returning to the classics of the 1910s and 1920s and presenting them in new interpretations; second, trying to reconstruct a more spiritual folk culture by stressing the national cosmology; third, expressing a cautious interest in contemporary young writers experimenting with a new aesthetic (studio work and chamber pieces that aren't always shown publicly).

In the 1990s, for the first time, one can speak of a genuine Ukrainian theatre with a real multicultural setting. In past decades, Russian-language theatres in Ukraine led all new developments in the theatre and presented definitive productions of any play they chose (indeed, they had a greater choice in repertoire and directors). By 1993, these same theatres had sunk into a state of crisis, and remain in that state. Other ethnic groups have now formed their own theatres – Crimean Tartar, Jewish, Hungarian, Greek, and so on. Despite economic difficulties, the new government is now establishing a legal base for the support of Ukrainian theatre. At the same time, it has accepted proposals to support the cultures of the other ethnic groups in Ukraine and hopes to help develop their theatres as well.

Structure of the National Theatre Community

In Ukraine today there exist eighty-eight state theatres. There are eleven musical theatres – six theatres offering both opera and ballet, one operetta, two musical comedy theatres, one children's musical theatre and one classical ballet company. There are forty-three dramatic theatres – sixteen dramatic, twenty-four musical-dramatic, three drama and musical comedies. Of these twenty-nine are Ukrainian language companies, thirteen Russian language and one in Crimean Tartar. Six of these theatres are classical. There are thirty-four theatres for children and young audiences, of which eight are for teenagers, and twenty-seven puppet theatres, most of which are bilingual. There is also a student theatre at the Karpenko-Karyi National Theatre Institute in Kiev, and an opera studio at the Tchaikovsky National Conservatory in Kiev.

The above-mentioned theatres are all state supported. Because governments have been undergoing vast changes since 1991, there are no reliable statistics available on the number of municipally supported theatres.

All large and medium-sized cities certainly have their own theatres – Kiev, Kharkov, Lvov, Dnipropetrovsk, Odessa, Symferopil, Sebastopol, Donetsk, Luhansk, Mykolaiiv, Kryvy Rih and Zaporizhia. Even smaller cities like Nizhyn and Bila Tserkva have theatres.

Opera theatres exist in Kiev (home of the National Opera), Kharkov, Lvov, Odessa, Donetsk and Dnipropetrovsk.

There are about a hundred studio theatres, which work in Ukrainian, Russian, Hebrew, Hungarian and Greek.

Each theatre is headed by an artistic director, a leading stage director, and a manager. The division of labour between the three varies widely.

Most dramatic theatres have staffs ranging from fifty to 115 creative personnel which includes actors, singers, dancers and orchestra members. They also have over 300 technical staff which includes costume shop personnel and construction crews. The National Opera in Kiev has close to 500 on its creative staff. In theatres for young audiences there are usually around forty-five creative personnel, with twenty to forty in the puppet companies.

The mounting of new productions takes from several months to a year at the classical theatres and two to three months at others. A restructuring is now taking place which will allow greater flexibility in these areas.

In addition to national and municipal theatres, there are also now a number of private theatres. Even single theatre projects have been financed in recent years by various sponsors.

In 1993, support also came from both a Presidential Cultural Fund and also a National Culture Fund.

The most prestigious prize in the country is the Shevchenko National Prize. Individual artists are also awarded the titles of Honoured Artist of Ukraine, People's Artist of Ukraine, Honoured Art Worker and Honoured Cultural Worker. The Nechui-Levytskyi Prize is given by the Union of Theatre Workers for work which best reflects the national character. Awards are also presented at various theatre festivals.

Artistic Profile

Companies

Among the most important companies – based on artistic merit, choice of repertoire, and their invitations to international events – are the Franko National Theatre in Kiev, the Shevchenko National Theatre in Kharkov, the Zankovetska National Theatre in Lvov and the Lesia Ukrainka Russian Language Theatre in Kiev.

Among the theatre-studios are the Theatrical Club, Kurbas Young Theatre in Lvov, Mimikrichi in Kiev, V. Morozov's Ne Zhurys! in Lvov, and Rubchynskyi's Akademiia Theatre Studio in Kiev.

The most important opera company is the National Opera in Kiev.

Dramaturgy

The 1920s and 1930s provided numerous

examples of plays with revolutionary ideas – Myroslav Irchan's *Buntar* (*The Rebel*, 1920) and *Platsdarm* (*Place d'Armes*, 1932), Korniychuk's *Shturm* (*Attack*, 1930) and *Na hrani* (*On the Verge*, 1928), Ivan Mykytenko's *Kadry* (*Cadres*, 1930) and Y. Yanovskyi's *Zavoiovnyky* (*Conquerors*, 1932).

There were also lyrical epics, philosophical-poetic dramas, psychological and naturalistic plays – Ivan Kocherha's *Feia hirkoho myhdaliu* (*Fairy of the Bitter Almond*, 1926), I. Dniprovskyi's *Iablunevy polon* (*The Apple Blossom Captivity*, 1926), Mykola Kulish's *97*, *Narodnyi Malakhiy*, *Maklena Grasa*, *Patetychna Sonata*, (1924–33), V. Pluzhnyk's *Professor Sukhorab* (1928) and *Zmova u Kyievi* (*Conspiracy in Kiev*, 1933).

By combining the traditional romantic style with irony, poetry and philosophy, and using the symbolism of folk beliefs and fairytales, the playwrights of the new stage provided theatre with the opportunity to examine artistically more complex conflicts. The poetic philosophical plays by Mykola Kulish suggested that this conflict was a tension between the individual, seen as a microcosm, and history seen in through a socialist lens. The plays of the Executed Renaissance created a new aesthetic and a new theatrical language.

After 1933, when political repression began in Ukraine, a number of playwrights tried to separate themselves from their immediate predecessors. The leading writer of this period was Oleksander Korniychuk. His early plays – *Zahybel eskadry* (*Destruction of a Squadron*, 1933), *Pravda* (*Truth*, 1927) *Bohdan Khmelnytskyi* (1938) and *Front* (1943) – focused on dramatic and heroic moments in history which he presented in a heroic-romantic style. Later he wrote comedies and dramas about collective farm life and also on moral-ethical themes – *Makar Dibrova* (1948), *Kalynovyi hai* (*The Berry Grove*, 1950) and *Pamiat sertsia* (*Memory of the Heart*, 1971). His drama *Bohdan Khmelnytskyi* was made into an opera of the same title by the composer K. Dankevych.

Korniychuk's plays were performed by all the theatres in Ukraine and later in many theatres in the other Soviet republics and in other nations of the eastern bloc. He was awarded six Soviet Prizes. Except for *Zahybel eskadry*, his plays are talented illustrations of the theory of socialist-realism, the idyllic form of 'conflictless drama', which reigned at the time across the Soviet Union.

Since so many Ukrainian playwrights of the 1920s and 1930s were simply erased from theatre history after 1933, the playwrights who dominated in the post-war era, in addition to Korniychuk, were those who were willing to follow the required form. That is, they would assign heroic qualities to the protagonist who was usually struggling with westerners who would tempt honest Soviet citizens into dishonest collaboration or spying, or who would struggle with rich peasants and traitors. Good examples of such plays are Yaroslav Halan's *Pid zolotym orlom* (*Under the Golden Eagle*, 1947) and *Liubov na svitanni* (*Love at Dawn*, 1949).

At the time there were many plays which presented contemporary reality as idyllic. There are better and worse examples, but their tendency to idealize the difficult reality of post-war life under Stalin and their low artistic qualities force one to categorize them as quasi-dramas. Such conflictless and idealistic plays only strengthened the social myth. It was a fairytale, something that could be fully understood only in the post-Soviet era. Their artistic purpose was to distract attention from real conflicts while providing both relaxation and hope.

Most playwrights used theatrical devices to create mythologized space but, also wanting to enter into a dialogue with their contemporaries, they searched for an Aesopian language, which would conceal their real intentions. A number gave up trying to write dramas and turned to comedy and satire which, less suspect, allowed sharper conflicts. Plays such as V. Mynko's *Ne nazyvaiuchy prizvishch* (*Not Naming Names*, 1953), Y. Yanovskyi's *Dochka prokurora* (*The Procurator's Daughter*, 1954) and O. Kolomiyets's *Faraony* (*Pharaohs*, 1961) examined careerism, subserviency, and ethical slavery in society. They provoked unusual interest because they addressed society's hidden need to change values and orientation.

Another Aesopian solution was to turn to historical subjects. Kocherha's *Prorok* (*Prophet*, 1948) was about the Ukrainian poet Shevchenko, as was O. Ilchenko's *Peterburzka osin* (*Petersburg Autumn*, 1954). L. Smilianky's *Muzhytsky posol* (*Peasant Envoy*, 1956) was about the novelist Ivan Franko while *Chervona troianda* (*Red Rose*, 1955) was about the playwright Lesia Ukrainka, and Kolomiyets's *Za deviatym porohom* (*After the Ninth Rapid*) was about the Zaporizhians.

Plays which portrayed Ukraine's heroic past too positively were often banned, however: this happened to *Na dni morskomu* (*On the Bottom of the Sea*, 1963) by Mykola Rudenko, who would later become a human-rights dissident. One statistical note: between 1952 and 1956, of eighty plays written, sixty were banned.

There were attempts to address real issues but they were usually not allowed to have a voice. Such plays as M. Stelmakh's *Pravda i Kryvda* (*Truth and Injustice*), despite its faults (unnecessary pathos) and the critics' attempt to reinterpret it solely according to the party line, nevertheless appealed to contemporary audiences as a national tragedy.

There was as well an attempt to revive the folk genre by the acclaimed film director Oleksander Dovzhenko, who in 1953 wrote a play *Potomky zaporozhtsiv* (*Descendants of the Zaporizhians*) which was not staged until 1961. O. Levada, on the other hand, attempted to create a philosophical phantasmagorical 'cosmic' drama in his *Faust i smert* (*Faust and Death*, 1961). The play – about humanity's flight into space – was ahead of its time and questioned the human cost of following this direction.

With Mikhail Gorbachev's *perestroika* in the 1980s, more creative models of cultural behaviour appeared. Plays written by young authors still in their 30s and 40s also started to be produced once more. The most popular were the plays by O. Shypenko (*Archaeology* and *Five on the Elevator*) and by A. Diachenko, a Russian-language playwright.

Directors, Directing and Production Styles

In Ukraine, as elsewhere, it was the directors who defined the direction of any particular theatre. After Kurbas, the foremost director in the country was Marian Krushelnytskyi, who in 1933 agreed to head the Berezil after Kurbas was dismissed. From 1954 to 1963 Krushelnytskyi headed the Franko Theatre in Kiev.

In his directing, he tended towards Kurbas's 'transformed image', the metaphorical blending of physical reality. The most distinctive features of his productions were their brilliantly organic tragi-comic qualities, and their musical eccentricity. His best known productions included *Dai sertsiu volius, zavede v nevoliu* (*Give the Heart Freedom and It Will Lead You into Slavery*, 1936) by M. Kropyvnytskyi; the Russian classic *Hroza* (*The Storm*, 1938) by Ostrovsky; *Yaroslav Mudryi* (1936) by Kocherha; and the opera *Bohdan Khmelnytskyi* (1953) by K. Dankevych. He was also the

subject of several films, sculptures and paintings and was awarded three National Prizes.

Another leading director was Hnat Yura, one of the founders of the Franko Theatre in 1920. At first a period of experimentation marked his directing style, but later he worked in the traditional psychological folk style. His best known productions included *Ivan Hus* and *Haidamaky* (1921) based on Shevchenko's poetry, *Don Carlos* (1936) by Schiller and *Duma pro Brytanku* (*Song About Brittany*, 1957).

Vasyl Vasylko, who directed folk comedies and romances, was another Kurbas student. His productions of *Za dvoma zaitsiamy* (*Chasing Two Rabbits*, 1925) by Mikholo Starytskyi, *Dyktatura* (*Dictatorship*, 1929) by Ivan Mykytenko, Shakespeare's *Macbeth* (1938), and *Haidamaky* (1961) based on Shevchenko's poetry were highly regarded by both critics and audiences.

Leontiy Dubovyk, Borys Balaban and Borys Tiahno were other directors with distinct individuality but who also tended to work using the Berezil aesthetic.

Of the directors who started working in the 1960s the foremost was Sergiy Danchenko (b. 1937), a People's Artist of the Soviet Union. Working at the Zankovetska Theatre in Lvov as a director from 1965 to 1967, and as its artistic director from 1970 to 1978, he was from 1978 the artistic director of the Franko Theatre in Kiev. Danchenko favoured a somewhat stylized psychological theatre. His important productions include *Maklena Grasa* by Kulish; *Kaminyi hospodar* (*The Stone Guest*, three versions) by Lesia Ukrainka; Shakespeare's *Richard III* (1974); Franko's *Ukradene shchastia* (*Stolen Happiness*, 1977 and 1979); *Diadia Vanya* (*Uncle Vanya*, 1980) by Anton Chekhov; *Eneiida* (*Aeneid*, 1986) a dramatization by Ivan Drach of Ivan Kotliarevskyi's poem; *Tevya-Tevel* based on Sholom Aleichem (1989); and *Bila vorona* (*White Crow*, 1991) by Y. Rubchynskyi with music by H. Tatarchenko. He was awarded several National Prizes.

Fedir Stryhun (b. 1939) is an actor and director. From 1965 he worked at the Zankovetska Theatre in Lvov, where he became the artistic director in 1987. He is an actor's director and his most distinctive traits are attention to folk detail, romantic emotions and a taste of irony. He has directed outstanding productions of *Beztalanna* (*Unfortunate Girl*, 1987) by Karpenko-Karyi; *Marusia Churai* (1988) based on the poetry of Lina Kostenko,

Sergiy Danchenko's production of Ivan Franko's *Stolen Happiness*, designed by Danylo Lider.
Photo: Victor Marustschenko.

the leading poet of Ukraine; and *Natalka Poltavka* (1991) by Kotliarevskyi.

Other important directors have included Mykola Ravytskyi (b. 1921) who from 1979 to 1992 was the artistic director of Teatr Druzhba; Ihor Borys (b. 1952), former artistic director of the Musical and Dramatic Theatre in Ivano-Frankivsk and from 1991 the artistic director of the Shevchenko Dramatic Theatre in Kharkov. In his work he searches for a synthesis of poetic theatre, spiritual folk symbolism and ethics as well as a fine psychological understanding. He is one of the most interesting directors working in traditional theatre today.

Volodymyr Ohloblin (b. 1915) is a director who works in the realistic psychological style. Sergiy Smiian (b. 1925) works in dramatic theatre as well as in opera and operetta; he tends towards a dazzling, celebratory style favouring romantic elements.

Another director of import is Les Taniuk, who is also a translator and poet. From 1961 to 1965 he worked in theatres in Kiev, Lvov, Odessa and Kharkov. Favouring a metaphoric theatre of 'transformed images' with avant-garde elements, he experimented with poetic theatre and Theatre of the Absurd. In the 1980s his theatre became more political. From 1965 to 1986 he worked in Russia, staging fifty productions in leading Russian theatres including the Moscow Art Theatre, the Pushkin Theatre, the Central Children's Theatre and the Mossovet Theatre.

Acting styles in Ukraine generally take two distinct directions. In western Ukraine (which for historical reasons more closely reflects trends in Europe) actors were trained to be flexible, to play in comedies, dramas, operas and operettas. They were trained to dance, play instruments and acquire various other skills. Eastern Ukrainian actors, on the other hand, were trained almost exclusively in psychological acting, although many individuals had talents in music, singing and could play various instruments. At the core of the national renaissance during the 1920s and 1930s were the western Ukrainian theatre artists who moved to eastern Ukraine.

The main characteristic of the 1940s and 1950s acting style was a new interest in the psychological approach. Metaphorical, poetic theatre or intellectual plays were, in fact, rare events. Over 200 playwrights, both foreign and Ukrainian, were banned in Ukraine during this period. Actors were also trained with material of quite low artistic quality but originality revealed itself even under these circumstances.

From the 1960s to the 1980s there were greater differentiations in acting styles. The political 'thaw' in the mid-1950s had its impact. Banned directors and actors were rehabilitated and their theories and practices were studied. This was most evident in the growth of scenography as an art form.

Today, one can see in Ukraine everything

B. Kozmenko-Delinde's production of Brecht's *The Resistible Rise of Arturo Ui.*
Photo: Victor Marustschenko.

from the plays of Shakespeare, Molière, Ukrainka and Pushkin to folk spectacles, from the psychological dramas of Chekhov and Vynnychenko to the plays of Friedrich Dürrenmatt and Jean Anouilh, from folk drama to the absurd.

Nelli Kornienko

Music Theatre

In 1945 there were five opera and ballet theatres located in Kiev, Kharkov, Odessa, Lvov and Donetsk. Each had its own building several of which were important architectural monuments: the Odessa Opera (1884–7, architects F.V. Honsiorovskyi, Ferdinand Fellner and Hermann Helmer); the Lvov Opera (1897–1900, architect Z. Horholevskyi) and the Kiev Opera (1899–1901, architect V.O. Shreter). In 1974, a sixth Ukrainian Theatre of Opera and Ballet was founded in Dnipropetrovsk. In 1982 the Kiev Children's Musical Theatre opened. In addition, theatres attached to musical institutes also produce operas while training their students.

Created in 1938, the Opera Studio at the Tchaikovsky National Conservatory in Kiev has its own theatre buildings, soloists, orchestra and chorus and functions as an independent professional company.

The Opera Studio at the Kotliarevskyi Institute of the Arts in Kharkov also regularly stages operas. It was created in 1939 as an independent training theatre but in 1958 it became a division of the institute, headed by a dean of opera and solo voice training. This studio has its own orchestra and chorus as well as soloists which allows it to constantly work on the repertoire and stage not only classics but also works by contemporary composers.

The Opera Studio at the Niezhdanova National Conservatory in Odessa (founded in 1958) and the National Conservatory in Lvov (today the Lysenko Musical Institute) founded in 1959 are of more modest means.

In 1945 there were four operetta theatres in Ukraine located in Kiev, Kharkov, Lvov and Odessa. In 1954 the Lvov and Odessa theatres were united into one troupe which was renamed the Odessa Theatre of Musical Comedy and a new theatre was constructed for them in 1981 (architects H.V. Topuz and V.V. Krasenko).

The Kiev National Operetta Theatre (founded in 1934, but till 1967 known as the Theatre of Musical Comedy) works in the building known as the Troiitsky National Home (1901–02, architects V.A. Osmak and H.M. Antonovskyi). This theatre, which seats 1,006, was restored in 1976.

The Kharkov Theatre of Musical Comedy (founded in 1929) worked in the ill-suited Mussuri circus building during the post-war years and still does not have its own premises.

All Ukrainian musical theatres have their own repertoires which are renewed very slowly. Five to six new shows are usually added each year to the existing repertoire of thirty to fifty shows. This means that sometimes shows remain in the repertoire for over ten years. By then all of the original performers have been replaced, the designs have lost much of their original look and the original musical and artistic interpretations have usually disappeared. Such productions are responsible for a drop in public interest.

The current repertoire of most companies relies on standard nineteenth-century classics and limits itself to only a few well-known works and authors: Verdi and Puccini head the list which also includes Rossini (*Il barbiere di Siviglia*), Gounod (*Faust*) and Bizet (*Carmen*). This standard list is augmented with operas by Donizetti (*Lucia di Lammermoor*, *La Favorita*, *L'Elisir d'amore* and *Don Pasquale*). In rare cases a work will be chosen which will actually enlarge the otherwise stereotypical repertoire.

Wagner is almost never heard in Ukraine (the exceptions being a production of *Lohengrin* in Kiev during the 1957–8 season and a 1977 production of *Tannhäuser* in Lvov, remounted in 1986). In choosing Mozart's operas, Ukrainian theatres and opera studios usually turn to *Le nozze di Figaro* and *Don Giovanni*. The most mature and independent production of a Mozart opera in terms of music was the 1966 Kiev presentation of *Die Zauberflöte*, in which the renowned Ukrainian conductor V.S. Tolba (1909–84) displayed a deep understanding of Mozart's style. The production was remarkable for its brilliant ensemble work.

Russian classics have long had an honoured place in the repertoire and they have resulted in some dazzling directorial interpretations, important performances and interesting stage design. M. Hryshko (1901–73), who commanded a full-voiced and richly coloured dramatic baritone was an important performer of the title roles of *Prince Igor* (Borodin) and *The Demon* (Anton Rubinstein), as well as Gregory Griazny in *The Czar's Bride* by Rimsky-Korsakov.

The dramatic baritone M.D. Vorvulev (1917–67) was distinguished by the beauty of his timbre. In his ten years at the Kiev opera he appeared in a varied repertoire, and was outstanding as Onegin (in Tchaikovsky's *Eugene Onegin*). A worthy successor in this role in the 1980s was I. Ponomarenko (b. 1945).

Boris Godunov and *Khovanshchina* by Mussorgsky (in Rimsky-Korsakov's versions) remained on the Kiev stage for many years. The Kiev Opera prefers to adhere to the established classical tradition in its productions of Mussorgsky's operas. When it replaces the performers, it does not encourage new stage interpretations.

However, the operas in Lvov, Odessa and Kharkov have taken bolder approaches in order to reveal the tragic conflicts in Russian history and the complex characters presented in the music. In order to give life to their concepts they have had to overcome many obstacles because these groups have much more modest financial, technical and artistic resources than the Kiev Opera.

In 1978 the Lvov Opera was the first in Ukraine to present *Khovanshchina* in Dimitri Shostakovich's version. This production was remarkable for the reflective interpretation of the score by the conductor I. Lutsiv (b. 1931), the accuracy of the work with the relatively small chorus and the clear images created in the mass scenes. Its remarkable design was created by Eugene Lysyk (1930–91), in a stylized symbolist manner. The central images of the set were a charred forest, great tree trunks which formed a road, and ruined wooden structures in a winter landscape.

In addition to Russian operas, works by Polish and Czech composers have also been successfully done. Among them are *Halka* and *Enchanted Castle* by Stanislaw Moniuszko, *The Bartered Bride* and *Dalibor* by Bedrich Smetana, and *The Devil and Kate* by Antonin Dvořák.

There have been many difficulties in establishing a Ukrainian repertoire within Ukrainian opera companies. Only three Ukrainian operas from the nineteenth century even qualify for production today. They are *Zaporozhets za Dunaem* (*The Zaporizhian Beyond the Danube*) by Semen Hulak-Artemovskyi (1813–73), *Natalka Poltavka*, based on Ivan Kotliarevskyi's play with music by Mykola Lysenko (1842–1912), and *Taras Bulba* by Lysenko (revised by L. Revutskyi and B. Liatoshinskyi). The first two works are lyrical comedies that structurally alternate musical numbers with prose dialogue. Both were important in the formation of Ukrainian professional theatre and have always appeared in the repertoires of both opera companies and musical-dramatic theatres. They are even staged by amateur troupes.

Historically, they are connected to performances by stars of the Ukrainian stage and the unique vocal and performance style of such masters as I. Patorshynskyi who was unsurpassed as Ivan Karas, the colourful and ingenious hero of Hulak-Artemovskyi's opera, or M. Lytvynenko-Volhemut (dramatic soprano), who performed both female roles in this opera and in her eighteen years in the Kiev opera also played both Natalka and her mother Terpelykha in *Natalka Poltavka*.

However, there is a negative aspect to this great popularity. These works have become overgrown with performers' clichés and countless additions and revisions. The problem of revisions is also critical in other Ukrainian operas. Some of them were created under great pressure when composers could not count on a full orchestra. Some were also not written by professional composers but by talented amateurs or semi-professionals. These must be revised in order to be presented by opera companies today. However, such revisions are not always correctly done and inconsistencies in style are introduced.

During the post-war era, Ukrainian operas were created under difficult circumstances as well, depending on each composer's relationship to the Soviet government and the command system of administration. The Ministry of Culture of Ukraine often commissioned works with an ideological bent and during the process of creation made sure that the artist adhered to this emphasis which had to celebrate revolutionary heroism, or communist values and ideals. This control was tightened as the commissioned work was brought to life. The party bureaucrats oversaw not only the content of the libretto but also the musical style because in accordance with Stalin's cultural policies all branches of art had to adhere to the methods of socialist-realism.

Classical nineteenth-century Russian operas were presented as the standard model to be emulated. As a result of this pressure, Ukrainian opera was even more separated from contemporary international trends than Russian opera, which produced such important twentieth-century innovators as Prokofiev and Shostakovich. Familiarity with the art of these great masters did have a positive influence on Ukrainian opera art in the post-Stalin era.

Two Kiev productions became important events in Ukrainian cultural life: *War and Peace* by Prokofiev (1956, conductor O. Klymov, director Volodymyr Skliarenko, designer Anatol Petrytskyi) and *Katerina Izmaylova* (1974, conductor K. Symeonov, director I. Molostova and designer Davyd Borovskyi, b. 1934). This production was awarded the Shevchenko National Prize and was highly regarded by the composer Shostakovich.

At the end of the 1950s, a number of Ukrainian operas were written. The operas of Julius Meitus (b. 1903) are distinguished by their variety of themes and genres. They are operas with total symphonic development of their key musical themes and tonal sources. The most popular was his opera *Moloda hvardii* (*Young Guard*, written in 1947, second version in 1950), about the young heroes of the resistance in the mining town of Krasnodon during World War II.

The Meitus opera which is most interesting in terms of its development of folk motifs and images is *Ukradene shchastia* (*Stolen Happiness*, composed in 1959), based on the harshly expressive social-ethnographic drama by the well-known Ukrainian writer Ivan Franko. *Lisova pisnia* (*The Forest Song*), a unique philosophical fairy drama by Lesia Ukrainka, was made into an opera with the same title by V. Kyreiko, a composer who, like H. Maiboroda (1913–92), the author of four operas produced by the Kiev opera, orients himself to the classical period of the Slavic school of opera. He combines this tradition with the specifics of the folk style and successfully uses folk songs and dance tunes from the various regions of Ukraine.

A more contemporary style of thinking and a more active attempt to renew the style of Ukrainian opera is characteristic of the work of V. Hubarenko (b. 1934). Among his best works are *Mamai* (1969), a folk drama from the time of the revolution created as a harsh epic story about the fate of three generations of a Ukrainian peasant family; *Nizhnist/Lysty kokhannia* (*Tenderness/Love Letters*, 1970), a refined chamber mono-opera; *Pamiatai mene* (*Remember Me*, 1980); and *Alpiiska ballada* (*Alpine Ballad*, 1984); the opera ballet *Vii* based on a short story by Gogol; and the monumental choral piece, the opera oratorio *Zhadaite bratiia moia* (*Remember My Dear Brothers*) based on the poetry of Shevchenko.

As for operetta theatres, both the party and government officials in charge of the politics of art were constantly wavering about the validity of the form. At one point even the word 'operetta' became suspect and was forbidden, so these theatres had to be renamed musical comedy theatres.

The constant emphasis on the ideological purpose of theatre, on the propaganda of political ideas and communist morality that was to emanate from the stage, obviously placed the proponents of 'light entertainment' in a difficult position. They constantly risked being accused of condoning the essentially bourgeois taste of the Viennese-style operetta which was quite foreign to Soviet audiences, and/or superficially representing Soviet reality. When they went in a more political direction, they were accused of subverting the genre.

The texts of classical operettas were reinterpreted to fit official ideology. This did not help to create dazzling shows, search for new theatrical styles or present interesting new productions. But even under such circumstances the adherents and former pupils of Ukrainian

director Les Kurbas – particularly directors Borys Balaban, Volodymyr Skliarenko and O. Zavyna, the designer Vadym Meller, the composer and conductor Bohdan Kryzhanivskyi (1894–1955) and actor I. Ponomarenko – continued to develop the genre.

Kurbas and his followers saw actors in operettas as contemporary versions of the classical buffoons, masters of a synthetic theatre with a brilliant command of movement and voice as well as acrobatic and circus skills. They understood the genre as a boisterous display of sheer theatricality. But the supporters of the old folk theatre, which also had its requisite divertissements and entertaining musical numbers, did not see it this way and it was they who carried the day in the 1950s.

This tendency was reflected in the work of composer and conductor O. Riabov (1899–1955) who was really the founder of the Ukrainian form of Soviet operetta because he created *Sorochynsky iarmarok* (*Sorochynsky Market*) based on a story by Gogol, as well as *Vesillia u Malynivtsi* (*Wedding in Malynivka*) about events during the Civil War in Ukraine in which the heroic-romantic and comedic veins were developed simultaneously. If the models for Riabov were the musical shows of the Ukrainian Teatr koryfeiv of the end of the nineteenth and beginning of the twentieth centuries, then for director V. Behma (b. 1938) and composer I. Poklad who created *Druhe vesillia u Malynivtsi* (*The Second Wedding in Malynivka*, 1971) and who wanted to renew the musical style and make it more contemporary, the models were various devices of popular revue.

V. Behma supported the expansion of both the genre and its subject matter. As the director of the Kiev operetta theatre (1976–81), he brought in composers of various stylistic orientations. At the same time the musical level of the shows improved significantly thanks to the famous Ukrainian opera and symphony conductor I. Dushchenko (b. 1925) who later took part in the creation of Dytiachy muzychny teatr (Children's Musical Theatre) and became its first conductor.

In the immediate post-war years, the Kharkov teatr muzychnoi komedii (Kharkov Musical Comedy Theatre) was remarkable for its strong acting ensemble. Some of them later joined the Kiev operetta.

Dance Theatre

Unlike the opera, Ukrainian ballet does not have its own classics since it came into being only in the 1920s. The repertoires of the various ballet companies therefore tend to differ in their balance of well-known works created by past and present Russian choreographers such as Petipa, Gorksy, Ivanov, Goleizovsky, Lopukhov and Yuri Grigorovich, along with the occasional new work.

An important role in this area was played by V. Vronskyi (1905–88) who choreographed for a number of different Ukrainian ballet companies. He was the head ballet master in both Odessa (1940–54) and at the Kiev Theatre of Opera and Ballet (1954–69), and later became the artistic director and choreographer of the artistic-sport ensemble Balet na lodu (Ballet on Ice, 1961–73). Between 1980 and 1986, he was artistic director of the Kiev Theatre of Classical Ballet. It was Vronskyi who created two of the most popular Ukrainian ballets, *Lilea* (*Lily*, 1945, 1956) and *Lisova pisnia* (*Forest Song*, 1958).

Also important was the work in Lvov from 1962 to 1976 of the ballet master M. Zaslavskyi, trained in Moscow, who collaborated with composers A. Kos-Anatolskyi on *Orysia* and with M. Skoryk on *Kameniari* (*Stone Cutters*). At the same time he sought to create his own choreographic versions of interesting new works by composers from the various republics of the former Soviet Union.

A similar direction was characteristic of the work of A. Shykera (b. 1935). His most interesting work was in reinterpretations of well-known ballets by Soviet composers in conjunction with Ukrainian scenographers such as Fedir Nirod (b. 1907) (Prokofiev's *Romeo and Juliet*, 1971, at the Kiev Theatre of Opera and Ballet) and Eugene Lysyk (Khachaturian's *Spartacus*, 1977 also in Kiev). With these designers he also premièred new works to music by Ukrainian composers which helped renew Ukrainian ballet – V. Hubarenko's *Kaminyi hospodar* (*The Stone Guest*, 1969) based on the philosophical drama by Lesia Ukrainka and designed by Lysyk; and Eugene Stankovich's historic ballet *Olha* (1982) with scenography by Nirod.

The young collective called the Children's Musical Theatre was of interest from its very first steps: a classical concert programme and two works by the ballet master V. Lytvynov, who had been one of the leading soloists of the Kiev Opera and Ballet Theatre and who was educated at the Leningrad conservatory. In his *Little Hump-Backed Horse* by Rodion Schedrin and *Pannochka i Khulihan* (*The Young Lady and the Hooligan*) which used the music of Shostakovich) a classical choreographic lexicon was combined with elements of contemporary movement, a dynamic sense of action and colourful divertissement numbers.

The creative growth of the Donetsk ballet collective in the 1980s and 1990s is connected with the appearance of a new star of Ukrainian ballet, V. Pysariev (b. 1965), who heads the touring collective Interbalet which grew out of the Donetsk company.

Maryna Cherkashyna

Theatre for Young Audiences

Theatres for young audiences exist in Lvov (First Ukrainian Theatre for Children and Youth, originally established in 1920 in Kharkov), in Kiev (established in 1924 by I. Deieva and O. Solomarskyi), in Odessa (established in 1931), in Kharkov (established in 1960), in Dnipropetrovsk (established in 1962), in Donetsk-Makiivka (established in 1971), in Zaporizhia (established in 1972) and in Sebastopol (the Sebastopol Municipal Theatre for Children and Young People, established in 1988 as a theatre-studio).

There are also two theatres that combine drama and puppetry: the Sumy Theatre for Children and Youth (established in 1975) and the Chernihiv Theatre for Children and Youth (1962).

The artistic quality of these theatres has improved from the 1960s to the early 1980s thanks to the work of directors O. Barsegian, M. Merzlikin, V. Patsunov and designer Mykhailo Frenkel (b. 1937) at the Kiev Theatre for Younger Audiences; director H. Kononenko in Dnipropetrovsk; director O. Beliatskyi and designer T. Pasichnyk in Kharkov; directors Sergiy Danchenko and A. Kunyts and designer Nirod in Lvov.

By the 1990s, the level of work began to decline and some opted to simply turn them into adult theatres. There are several reasons for this: the low social status of these theatres, their repertoires, and the unwillingness of directors to stay with theatres that have such a low status.

Puppet Theatre

The source of Ukrainian puppet theatre is the *vertep* (Nativity puppet show) which first appeared in the sixteenth and seventeenth centuries. The *vertep* was staged in a puppet booth with two levels; religious Christmas scenes were staged on top, while very broad folk satires were staged on the bottom. The puppets of the traditional *vertep* were usually carved out of wood and could not move their limbs. They had one frozen gesture which had to convey the essence of the character. The *vertep* was periodically banned because the folk scenes were usually improvised and often commented on current events.

In the early 1920s during the Civil War, propagandistic puppet theatres became popular. A favourite was the Arlekin Theatre (Harlequin Theatre) in Kiev. This type of puppet theatre was revived during World War II.

In the post-war period, naturalistic puppet theatres prevailed. Stylization and metaphor, so essential to the art of puppetry, were criticized for political reasons.

But there were gradual changes and Ukrainian puppet theatre started to expand its possibilities. Theatres started to use screens in the style of Edward Gordon Craig, changing the frontal staging to a more coordinated one suitable for the stylized and mechanized puppets.

The revival of the art in the 1950s and 1960s was closely related to the work of the Kharkov Puppet Theatre, headed by director V. Afanasiev and designer O. Shchehlov. In the 1970s, puppet theatres became more interested in experimentation and in international trends. The number of theatres increased and as did their quality.

The innovators of the 1970s and 1980s have included director I. Sikalo and designer M. Sapozhnikova at the Kiev National Puppet Theatre; director V. Buhaiov and designer V. Nikitina at the Dnipropetrovsk Puppet Theatre; director B. Azarova at the Crimean Puppet Theatre; director M. Yaremchuk and designer T. Torbenko at the Kiev Marionette Theatre; director A. Martuishova and designer E. Ledniova at the Sumy Theatre for Children and Youth.

In the 1990s, puppet theatre is one of the more experimental forms. Puppets are less 'life-like' and more metaphoric. Marionettes have also made a comeback, as has the *vertep*.

Design
Theatre Space and Architecture

Perhaps as a compensation for the limits placed on written dramas and performance, scenography has developed in Ukraine as an important, almost independent art form.

The most important representatives of what has become an acclaimed Ukrainian avant-garde include Mykhailo Boychuk, Anatol Petrytskyi, Vadym Meller, Alexandra Exter (1882–1949) and Oleksander Khvostenko-Khvostov (1895–1968).

Among the leading contemporary scenographers are Danylo Lider (b. 1917), Eugene Lysyk, Myron Kyprian (b. 1930), Fedir Nirod, Mykhailo Frenkel, Davyd Borovskyi, who has worked in Russia and abroad most often with the director Yuri Lyubimov, formerly of the Taganka Theatre in Moscow, and Andriy Alexandrovitch (b. 1958).

There are two trends in contemporary scenography that are related to architecture. The first is the use of the entire theatre building including the stage, auditorium and foyer. In utilizing the

Danylo Lider's design for Sergiy Danchenko's production of Friedrich Dürrenmatt's *The Visit*.
Photo: Victor Marustschenko.

theatres this way, image structures can be created which are less dependent on the actual architecture of the stage. Second, many designers prefer to create stage space outside traditional theatre buildings. This has developed into both outdoor scenography (in parks or on streets) and indoor scenography which exists outside traditional stage space but within architecturally enclosed spaces (sports stadiums, ruins of ancient theatres or basements).

The result today is varied combinations of stage and auditorium. Most break with the notion of frontality and bring together everything from constructivist models to naturalistic set painting, from the reconstruction of décor as space to the simple accentuation of objects, costumes and the point of view in single planes. In other instances the set exposes itself as part of the theatrical event, coming alive in a sense with the appearance of the actor who enters into a dialogue with it, uncovering endless possibilities of associative thinking. As designers such as Lider and Borovskyi show, it can create its own inner rules of 'dialogue'.

Lighting design also became more complex as colours and shafts of light started to function as forms in space.

In the 1990s costumes too functioned as an element within the director's overall semiotic system. Today a costume is defined by its dynamics, its ability to transform and its syncretic use effective of symbolism, surrealism, naturalism, impressionism and abstraction.

There are ninety theatre buildings in Ukraine. The largest is the Odessa Theatre of Opera and Ballet, which seats 1,574; the smallest the Vinnytsia Puppet Theatre, which seats eighty-five. Most of the major buildings – many discussed in earlier sections – were built in the nineteenth century or the early part of the twentieth.

Nelli Kornienko

Training

Till 1964 there were two theatre institutes in Ukraine – The Karpenko-Karyi Theatre Institute in Kiev and the Kharkov Theatre Institute. In 1964, the Kharkov Institute became the theatre division of the Kotliarevskyi Institute of Art. Both institutes train actors, directors and critics with Kiev also training theatre administrators. A musical theatre directing programme also began there in 1993.

In Kharkov there is also a division that trains actors and directors for puppet theatres. All actors study for four years, while directors, critics and scholars study for five years.

Opera singers are trained at conservatories in Kiev, Lvov, Odessa and Donetsk as well as the Kharkov Institute of the Arts. The musical institutes in Kiev and Lvov also train opera directors.

Other training schools include the Kiev School of Choreography, which has classical and folk dance departments, the Dnipropetrovsk Theatre School which trains actors for dramatic and puppet theatres and the Odessa Theatre School which does technical training.

Maryna Cherkashyna

A 1985 production at the Karpenko-Karyi Theatre Institute in Kiev.
Photo: Yuri Vladimirovich Petrov.

Criticism, Scholarship and Publishing

Theatre criticism as a national institution developed at the same time as the professional theatre and in the twentieth century continued to reflect and form the aesthetic ideas of the public. As elsewhere in Europe, theatre criticism has active contact with theatre studies and literary criticism.

Between the 1940s and the 1970s criticism, with rare exceptions, was systematically ideological. It served to censure and be politically didactic in order to stimulate an art which was supposed to serve the socialist state. Influential critics were M. Yosypenko (1912–83), Y. Kyseliov (1905–80), I. Voloshyn (b. 1908) and Yuri Stanishevskyi (b. 1936). A number of critics – interested in the ideas of Les Kurbas – found themselves unable to work during this period. Among them were Natalia Kuziakina (b. 1928), Nelli Kornienko (b. 1939), Mykola Labinsky and Raisa Scaliy.

From the 1970s to the 1990s those who were active in the field worked both within the old ideological criteria and with new approaches to theatre. A number of Ukrainian theatre historians now live and work outside the country. Among them are Valerian Revutskyi (b. 1911), Bohdan Boychuk (b. 1927), Larissa Onyshkevych, and Virlana Tkacz (b. 1952).

A number of awards exist for working critics. These include the Critics Prize awarded by the Union of Theatre Workers, the Kotliarevskyi Prize, the Biletskyi Prize and the Lysenko Prize (awarded in the musical field). The Shevchenko National Prize is awarded in all artistic fields including criticism. There are also prizes awarded by various newspapers and specialized journals such as *Ukrainsky teatr* (*Ukrainian Theatre*), *Ukrainska kultura* (*Ukrainian Culture*) and *Muzyka* (*Music*).

Major publishing houses with cultural divisions include Mystetstvo (Art), Nauka (Science), Ukrainskyi pysmennyk (Ukrainian Writer), Lybid, Smoloskyp im. V. Symonenka (Symonenko's Torch) and Dnipro. Among the important collections and almanacs are *Teatralna kultura* (*Theatre Culture*), *Teatralno-kontsertny Kyiv* (*Theatre and Concerts in Kiev*), *Nauka i kultura* (*Science and Culture*) and *Mystetstvo i etnos* (*Arts and Ethnology*).

Nelli Kornienko
Translated by Virlana Tkacz

(See also USSR)

Further Reading

Bahry (Bahrij), Romana. 'The Expressionist Experiment in Berezil: Kurbas and Kulish'. *Canadian Slavonic Papers* 14, no. 2 (1972): 324–44.

Berezkin, Viktor. *Daniil Lider*. [Danylo Lider]. Kiev: Mystetstvo, 1988. 199 pp.

Boboshko, Yuri. *Hnat Yura*. Kiev: Mystetstvo, 1980. 186 pp.

——. *Rezhyser Les Kurbas*. [Director Les Kurbas]. Kiev: Mystetstvo, 1987. 192 pp.

Chabanenko, Ivan. *Zapysky teatral'noho pedahoha: zbirnyk statei*. [Notebooks of the theatrical pedagogue: a collection of essays]. Kiev: Mystetstvo, 1980. 189 pp.

Dnepropetrovskii Gosudarstvenyi teatr opery i baleta. [Dnipropetrovsk State Theatre of Opera and Ballet]. Dnipropetrovsk: Oblpoligrafizdat, 1980. 72 pp.

Frenkel, Mykhailo. *Plastyka stsenichnoho prostoru*. [The plasticity of stage space]. Kiev: Mystetstvo, 1987. 183 pp.

——. *Suchasna stsenohrafiia*. [Contemporary scenography]. Kiev: Mystetstvo, 1980. 132 pp.

Horbachov, Dmytro. *A.H. Petrytskyi. Radianskyi khudozhnyk*. [A.H. Petrytskyi. Soviet artist]. Kiev: 1971. 152 pp.

Istoria ukrainskoi radianskoi muzyky. Uchbovyi posibnyk. [The history of Ukrainian Soviet music. A teaching guide]. Kiev: Muzychna Ukraina, 1990. 296 pp.

Kornienko, Nelli. *Teatr sohodni – Teatr zavtra*. [Theatre today – theatre tomorrow]. Kiev: Mystetstvo, 1986. 221 pp.

Kovalenko, Georgiy. *Khudozhnyk teatra Daniil Lider*. [Theatre artist Danylo Lider]. Moscow: Iskusstvo, 1980. 199 pp.

Kulish, Mykola. *Tvory v 2-x tomakh*. [Works in two volumes]. Kiev: Dnipro, 1990. Vol. 1 508 pp. Vol. 2 874 pp.

Kurbas, Les. *Les Kurbas: Staty i vospominaniia o. L. Kurbase. Literaturnoe nasledie*. [Les Kurbas: Articles and memoirs about L. Kurbas. Literary heritage]. Edited by Mykola Labinskyi and Les Taniuk. Foreword by Natalia Kuziakina. Moscow: Iskusstvo, 1987. 462 pp.

——. *Les Kurbas: U teatralnii diialnosti, v otsinkakh suchasnykiv – documenty*. [Les Kurbas: Articles on theatre, essays by his contemporaries – documents]. Edited by Valerian Revutskyi. Compiled by Osyp Zinkewych. Baltimore, MD: Smoloskyp Publishers, 1989. 1,026 pp.

Kuziakina, Natalia. *Stanovlenie ukrainskoi sovetskoi rezhissury*. [The beginnings of Ukrainian Soviet theatre directing]. Leningrad: Leningradskii gosud. institut teatra, muzyki i kinematograhii, 1984. 79 pp.

——. *Ukrainska dramaturhiia pochatku 20 stolittia. Shliakhy onovlennia*. [Ukrainian dramaturgy in the beginning of the twentieth century. Directions of renewal]. Leningrad: Leningradskii gosud. institut teatra, muzyki i kinematograhii, 1984. 79 pp.

Kyselov, Yosyp. *Dramaturhy Ukrainy*. [Playwrights of Ukraine]. Kiev: Dnipro, 1967. 378 pp.

Kysil, Oleksandr. *Ukrainsky teatr*. [Ukrainian theatre]. Edited by Pavlo Perepelytsia and Rostyslav Pylypchuk. Kiev: Mystetstvo, 1968. 258 pp.

Rulin, Petro. *Na shliakhakh revoliutsiinoho teatru*. [The direction of revolutionary theatre]. Edited by Pavlo Perepelytsia. Kiev: Mystetstvo, 1972. 354 pp.

Shliakhy i problemy rozvytku ukrainskoho radianskoho teatru. [The directions and problems of the development of Ukrainian Soviet theatre]. Edited by M.K. Yosypenko. Kiev: Mystetstvo, 1970. 344 pp.

Stanishevskyi, Yuri. *Baletnyi teatr Radianskoi Ukrainy*. [Ballet theatre of Soviet Ukraine]. Kiev: Muzychna Ukraina, 1986. 236 pp.

——. *Barvy ukrainskoi operety*. [The colours of Ukrainian operetta]. Kiev: Muzychna Ukraina, 1970. 140 pp.

——. *Internatsional'nyi pafos ukrains'koho radians'koho muzychnoho teatru: ohliad vystav za tvoramy kompozytoriv bratnikh respublik URSR*. [International pathos of the Ukrainian Soviet Musical Theatre: an overview of performances of works by composers from other Soviet Republics]. Kiev: Muzychna Ukraina, 1979. 156 pp.

Stefanovych, M. *Kyivskyi teatr opery ta baletu*. [The Kiev Theatre of Opera and Ballet]. Kiev: Derzhvydav obrazotvorchoho mystetstva i muzychnoi literatury URSR, 1960. 208 pp.

Taniuk, Les. *Marian Krushelnytskyi*. Moscow: Iskusstvo, 1974. 223 pp.

Tereshchenko, Alla. *Lvivskyi derzhavnyi akademichnyi teatr opery ta baletu imeni Ivanan Franka*. [The Ivan Franko National Academic Theatre of Opera and Ballet in Lvov]. Kiev: Muzychna Ukraina, 1989. 207 pp.

Timofejev, V. Vozroždenijé. ['Renaissance']. *Theatre Magazine* 47, no. 10 (October 1984): 4–7.

Ukrainskyi dramatychnyi teatr. [Ukrainian dramatic theatre]. 2 vols. Vol. 1 Kiev: Naukova dumka, 1967. 518 pp. Vol. 2 Kiev: Vydavnytstvo Akademii nauk URSR, 1959. 648 pp.

Ukrajinska Avangarda 1910–1930. [Ukrainian avant-garde 1910–30]. Exhibition catalogue. Zagreb, 1991. 144 pp.

Verykivs'ka, Iryna M. *Stanovlennia ukraïns'koï radianskoï stsenohrafiï.* [Development of Ukrainian Soviet scenography]. Kiev: Nauk dumka, 1981. 205 pp.

Zahaikevych, M.P. *Dramaturhiia baletu.* [The dramaturgy of ballet]. Kiev: Naukova dumka, 1978. 259 pp.

UNITED KINGDOM

The third largest country in the European Community with a population of 57.6 million in 1991, the United Kingdom is composed of four national regions – England, Scotland, Wales and Northern Ireland – with a land area of 244,000 square kilometres (94,200 square miles). Of the four, England is the largest both in geographical size and in population. London has been the administrative capital of England for nearly 1,000 years, and of the whole United Kingdom since 1801; it has been the UK's main theatrical centre since the days of William Shakespeare (1564–1616). The first buildings constructed to house theatre companies were erected in Shakespeare's time. None has survived, although in 1991 the foundations of the Rose Theatre (built in 1587), where Shakespeare's *Henry VI* and *Titus Andronicus* were first performed, were discovered by chance during excavations on a building site on London's South Bank.

Apart from the Commonwealth period (1649–60), when theatre was banned, the United Kingdom has had a rich if chequered theatrical history, enjoying patronage and censorship from the court, but with a strong basis in popular support. When the monarchy was restored after the Commonwealth, Charles II (1630–85), not only to control the theatre but also to reward his supporters, issued Letters Patent to two playwright-managers, Sir William Davenant (1606–68) and Thomas Killigrew (1612–84), allowing them to build public theatres in Drury Lane and Lincoln's Inn Fields, London. Other patents were issued, and sometimes withdrawn, but this method of licensing theatres lasted until the Theatres Act of 1843. In London today, three nineteenth-century theatres occupy the sites of the Patent Houses – the Royal Opera House (Covent Garden), the

Theatre Royal (Drury Lane) and the Theatre Royal (Haymarket). Some regional theatres were granted patents, as in York and Bath. The word 'royal' in their titles provides a clue to their ancestry.

In the late nineteenth century, a thriving entertainment industry sprang up around the new commercial centres of Britain. Most proscenium arch theatres were built in the forty years from the mid-1870s to the start of World War I. These include theatres in Piccadilly, Shaftesbury Avenue and Leicester Square, the area known as London's West End. Because they were built in the shopping areas, where land values were expensive, they were constructed on small sites but built high with several circles and galleries, often with highly decorative plaster work and elaborate stage machinery. One architect alone, Frank Matcham (1854–1920), designed and built 150 such theatres between 1879 and 1912. These imperial pleasure domes provide the traditional images of 'theatre' in Britain, although the two large post-war buildings which provide the London homes of the Royal National Theatre (on the South Bank) and the Royal Shakespeare Company (in the Barbican Centre) are constructed in another vein, encased in grey concrete, free from decoration, functional but austere.

This theatre boom at the turn of the century was productive in other ways. It saw the development of such popular traditions as Christmas pantomimes and music halls; the growth of society drama with such writers as Arthur Wing Pinero (1855–1934), Oscar Wilde (1854–1900) and Somerset Maugham (1874–1965); a new wave of politically alert writers including George Bernard Shaw (1856–1950) and Harley Granville Barker

(1877–1946); actor-managers such as Sir Henry Irving (1838–1905), the first British actor to receive a knighthood; and their opposites, visionary rebels such as Edward Gordon Craig (1872–1966), whose views on the role of the director were more heeded in mainland Europe than in Britain.

This period also saw the first challenge to the hegemony of England within the British Isles and the dominance of London in the theatre system. Irish theatre was the most significant of the nationalist movements. Ireland was then part of the United Kingdom. Theatres were built in Dublin during the seventeenth century, but their programmes often depended upon English touring companies and their leading stars were drawn away to the wider firmament of London. For two centuries, Ireland was a source of theatrical talent for the rest of Britain to enjoy, for example the actress Peg Woffington (1714–60) and the dramatists William Congreve (1670–1729), George Farquhar (1677–1707), Oliver Goldsmith (1728–74) and Richard Brinsley Sheridan (1751–1816) as well as Wilde and Shaw.

The founding of the Irish Literary Theatre in 1899 by two poet-playwrights, Lady Augusta Gregory (1852–1932) and William Butler Yeats (1865–1939), with George Moore (1852–1935), who was primarily a novelist, had two main aims: to assert the separate identity of Irish culture by promoting the ancient legends and to establish an Irish 'new theatre' movement, akin to naturalism elsewhere in Europe. But Yeats disliked naturalism and a split developed in the Irish Literary Theatre. Moore left for London, where he became a noted literary figure. Yeats stayed in Dublin and formed the Irish National Theatre Society in 1903, which took premises in Abbey Street. With financial help from an English heiress, Annie Horniman (1860–1937), the Abbey Theatre was established, a writers' theatre which became the *de facto* national theatre after the partition of Ireland in 1922. Its dramatists, who included John Millington Synge (1871–1909) and Sean O'Casey (1880–1964), laid the foundations for what was to become a distinctive new movement in western drama, blending naturalism with symbolism, commitment with compassion, local themes with universal ones.

But their plays were not always well received in Dublin, where Synge's *The Playboy of the Western World* (1907) caused riots. The Abbey Theatre refused to stage *The Tinker's Wedding* during his lifetime because of its supposed anti-clericalism: it was not produced there until 1971. O'Casey's pacifist play about World War I, *The Silver Tassie* (1928), was rejected and O'Casey spent the last half of his life mainly in England. After partition, for different reasons, the Irish and English theatres were still entwined. Some Dublin writers, such as Brendan Behan (1923–64), a Borstal boy and an IRA (Irish Republican Army) supporter, came to Britain partly to escape the cloying influence of Ireland. 'Mother Ireland,' he once said, 'get off my back'. Other artists, such as the actor Michael Mac Liammoir (1899–1978), who was born, as Alfred Lee Willmore, in Willesden, north-west London (and not in Cork, as previously supposed), and dramatist John Arden (b. 1930), also born in England, embraced the anti-British and anti-imperialist sentiments in Ireland.

Six northern counties stayed within the United Kingdom after partition and developed their own identity. The Ulster Literary Theatre (1904–34) was primarily an amateur movement, but two repertory theatres were founded in Belfast after World War II, the Lyric Theatre and the Group Theatre, complementing the city's largest theatre, the Opera House, a late-nineteenth-century architectural masterpiece designed by Frank Matcham. The widespread distrust between the larger Protestant community and the Catholic minority, the background of violence and the failure to find political solutions to deep-set difficulties provide the special circumstances of Ulster's life. Despite, or perhaps because of, these pressures, its drama has developed its own tradition, less lyrical and perhaps less sentimental than in the south, with strong actors, including Colin Blakely (1930–87) and Kenneth Branagh (b. 1960), and forceful dramatists, such as Sam Thompson (1916–65) and Brian Friel (b. 1929). (See also IRELAND.)

There were also nationalist drama movements in Scotland and Wales. While it is sometimes said that theatre in Scotland lies in its music halls, a Scottish Repertory Theatre was founded to promote Scottish plays in 1909, lasting until 1914. Its spirit, if not its name, was maintained after World War I by the Scottish National Players (1921–48), the forerunner of several repertory theatres which still exist. The most celebrated was founded by playwright James Bridie (1888–1951) in 1943, the Citizens' Theatre in Glasgow, although at times companies at the Lyceum Theatre in Edinburgh have laid claim to being the true Scottish national theatre. Repertory theatres were also established in Dundee, Perth and St Andrews to join the music halls, touring and seaside theatres. The summer holiday theatres of the 1930s provide the tradition to which two post-war success stories of Scottish theatre belong, Pitlochry's Festival Theatre (founded in 1951) and the Edinburgh International Festival, established in 1947, which with its various fringe festivals has grown to become the biggest arts festival in the world, with as many as 2,000 separate companies taking part each year.

During the inter-war years, Scottish theatre was marked by a number of small, left-wing and mainly amateur companies, such as the Fife Miner Players (1926–31) and the Glasgow Workers' Theatre Group (1937–40), which provided the background to the growth of fringe and alternative theatre companies during the 1960s, of which the Traverse Theatre in Edinburgh (founded in 1963) and the Close Theatre in Glasgow (1965–73) are notable examples. At the same time, there was a sharp decline in the music hall circuits for which Scottish theatre was once renowned. Dundee once had three

music halls and an opera house: now it has one repertory theatre. With the loss of the halls, those Scottish stars who were household names north of the border, but unknown and incomprehensible south of it, are now rare indeed.

Modern Welsh theatre developed slowly from similar roots: nineteenth-century nationalism, a romantic fascination with folk origins, left-wing amateur theatre societies in mining towns, and a resentment of the English and Londoners in particular. Welsh music and the bardic tradition were celebrated in *eisteddfods* (ancient bardic festivals of music, poetry and verse plays) but Welsh-speaking theatre was harder to establish, despite the efforts of the playwright Saunders Lewis (1893–1985) to do so. In 1968, a major touring company was founded, Theatre Cymru, to produce Welsh- and English-language plays. A Welsh Arts Council report in 1991 stated that 'theatre in the Welsh language is of surprising diversity for a minority language', but the figures suggested that despite the diversity, there was not much of it.

In Scotland and Ireland, there is little theatre in Gaelic either but the scarcity of Welsh-

Ian Brown's 1991 Traverse Theatre production of Sue Glover's *Bondagers*, designed by Stewart Laing.

language drama does not mean that Wales lacks a theatre tradition. There are turn-of-the-century touring theatres in such cities as Cardiff, Carmarthen and Swansea, while building-based production companies have been established in Cardiff (Sherman Theatre), Mold (Theatre Clwyd), Bangor (Cwmni Theatre Gwynedd) and Dyfed (Torch Theatre). There are fringe and alternative theatre groups in university towns as well as in the main cities. The contributions to British theatre that were recognized as being most distinctively Welsh in the 1950s were the voice of actor Richard Burton (1925–84) and a play by the poet Dylan Thomas (1914–53), *Under Milk Wood* (1953).

Too much stress can be laid on the ethnic authenticity of these nationalist movements. British theatre is, and always has been, composed of many strands, hard to disentangle. But there can be little doubt that the romantic search for the origins of the folk, a Europe-wide phenomenon, left its mark on British theatre, encouraging the use of regional accents and themes. Before World War I, it was assisted by the political movements towards federalism and democracy which treated the centralization of government around London as its common enemy. When there were no nationalist causes to which regional theatres could become attached, there was a tendency to promote a county or city. Edwardian theatre was composed of local managements, some owning only one or two theatres. Major theatre centres developed in such cities as Birmingham, Liverpool, Manchester and Bristol. The number of theatres in Britain before World War I was impressive in itself. It has been calculated at between 2,000 and 3,000, but some were little more than barns and for these, figures are unavailable.

During World War I, many smaller managements went out of business. The introduction of an entertainments tax in 1917, a source of wartime revenue that lasted until 1958, was a financial burden which few could carry; but the stronger or more wily managements joined together in theatrical chains, stemming from London's West End. The Number One, Two and Three touring circuits were the familiar feature of the inter-war theatre scene, which had the effect of standardizing tastes around Britain. The same cut-glass, home counties accents could be heard from Land's End to John O'Groats. Some determined repertory companies survived, such as the Birmingham Rep and the Liverpool Playhouse, but touring West End

productions provided the staple theatrical diet in most towns. The numbers of theatres declined, although those run by such managements as Howard and Wyndham were improved in standards of comfort and theatrical polish.

World War II caused so much damage to the theatre that for a time it seemed as if this important part of the British cultural heritage would never revive. At least one-third of the theatres in the West End had suffered bomb damage, as had theatres in other major cities. Many had closed during the war years and there was some doubt, as they faced the new challenge of television, whether they would open again. They were more valuable as real estate than as theatres.

Unlike the systems in France and Germany, where the state had subsidized the theatre for 150 years, British theatre had lived mainly in a free market economy. Private charitable trusts were established in the nineteenth century to support companies such as the Old Vic whose purpose was to bring classical drama and opera to the poor; but these were the exceptions rather than the rule. State subsidies were not a significant factor in the financing of theatres until the mid-1960s, although small sums of money were granted to non-profit companies through the Arts Council of Great Britain (ACGB), established in 1946.

The role of the ACGB greatly increased over the next four decades, but it was established by Royal Charter to be 'at arm's length' from government. It was an example of a 'quango', a quasi-autonomous, non-governmental organization, which received money from the public purse but whose decisions were considered not to be influenced by political considerations. Similar but smaller Arts Councils were established for Scotland and Wales, while the Arts Council of Northern Ireland was funded separately by the province's education office. Arts authorities to cover twelve major regions in England and Wales were also established after the war; their purpose was to coordinate arts funding from various sources (including commerce, private patronage, town and district councils) and to be independent sponsoring agencies in their own right. Governments were reluctant to establish a Ministry of Culture, because the phrase reminded them of examples of the totalitarian control of culture from continental Europe. For the same reason, grants were small. In 1958–9, after being in existence for twelve years, the ACGB received only £985,000 from the Treasury, of which £74,834 was spent on the theatre. Its committees in Scotland and Wales were allocated £82,176 and £42,910 respectively from the total grant.

The commercial managements of the late 1940s and 1950s had other handicaps. They were still subject to the entertainments tax, which sometimes took as much as 20 per cent from their gross box-office revenues, and all plays were subject to censorship through the Lord Chamberlain's Examiner of Plays, a quaint official post which lasted for more than 200 years. Stage censorship was not at this time intended primarily as a means of suppressing political debate. Its official object was to protect religion, the monarchy, the family and the British way of life, but these criteria were so vaguely and ambiguously interpreted that the Lord Chamberlain became a target for left-wing radicals and right-wing libertarians alike.

Under censorship, theatre in the UK was prudish rather than propagandist. Swearing and 'bad language' were banned together with the discussion of such subjects as homosexuality. Nakedness was not entirely banned, but women without clothes were not allowed to move on stage. This forced restraint affected London's musicals in particular. The gap between Sandy Wilson's (b. 1924) pastiche 1920s musical *The Boy Friend* (1953) or Julian Slade's (b. 1930) *Salad Days* (1954) and an exuberant Broadway hit such as Frank Loesser's *Guys and Dolls* (1950) was wider than the width of the Atlantic.

Some commercial managements favoured censorship, for it gave them protection against some populist forms of theatre such as American-style burlesque shows. In comparison with much US theatre such as Broadway musicals and the new realism of writers such as Arthur Miller and Tennessee Williams, British theatre seemed tame and inhibited. Miller described it as 'hermetically sealed from life' and major European plays, such as Frank Wedekind's *Spring's Awakening* (1891), could not be performed in Britain except in private theatre clubs. Samuel Beckett's *Waiting for Godot* was revised to suit the censor in 1955.

Over-taxed, arbitrarily censored, struggling to rebuild the theatre industry after the war, the commercial managements had an unenviable task. But the signs were not all gloomy. Despite the complaint that there were few new plays, the dramatists of the early 1950s included Terence Rattigan (1911–77), Noël Coward (1899–1973) and J.B. Priestley (1894–1984), who were, at worst, skilful craftsmen and, at best, major writers. The dramas of T.S. Eliot

(1888–1965) and Christopher Fry (b. 1907) were highly rated by critics and British actors were internationally renowned, particularly those who had made film careers in Hollywood.

By a strange quirk of fate, the last years of the war had provided London audiences with an unfamiliar glimpse of what might have been a great classical acting company. In 1944, the Old Vic company, whose own theatre had been bombed, moved into the West End where, under the leadership of Laurence Olivier (1907–91) and Ralph Richardson (1902–84), some of the finest productions seen in London were staged. Olivier's Richard III and Oedipus, Richardson's Falstaff and Edith Evans's (1888–1976) Ranevskaya are still remembered with awe. These triumphs led to renewed calls for a national theatre, which Britain had always lacked, although a long-drawn-out campaign to establish one began in 1834. When Olivier and Richardson were foolishly dismissed from their positions at the Old Vic in 1948, the campaign suffered another major blow.

Almost equally significant was the revival after the war of the Shakespeare Memorial Theatre at Stratford-upon-Avon under the Birmingham actor-director Sir Barry Jackson (1879–1961). Jackson brought into the company some startling young talents, including the director Peter Brook (b. 1925), who was barely 20, and the actor Paul Scofield (b. 1922). In the 1950s, the Old Vic and the Shakespeare Memorial Theatre conducted a rivalry as to which was the leading British classical company. Brook's *Titus Andronicus* at Stratford (with Olivier as Titus) in 1955 ranks as the outstanding Shakespearian production of the decade; the Old Vic, however, introduced such actors as Richard Burton and John Neville (b. 1925) to stardom. Both theatres were elevated in the 1960s to the status of national theatres – the Royal Shakespeare Company (RSC) and the National Theatre (NT).

The country's still-numerous commercial theatres operated on several levels from the local and populist to the cosmopolitan and sophisticated. Most cities after the war had music halls and variety halls which not only took in touring London companies but also staged their own shows. Christmas pantomimes, with comedians in 'drag' dressed up as 'dames' and with women in long tights as 'principal boys', are part of many British families' theatregoing experiences. For the rest of the year, these local theatres provided mixed programmes of vaudeville and farces. John Osborne's (b. 1929) play, *The*

Entertainer (1958), is a study of a run-down touring variety company, but not all comics were as seedy as Osborne's Archie Rice. There were some clowns among them, such as Max Wall (1908–91), who had worked with the great clown Grock and became known later for his performances in Samuel Beckett's plays.

On a more genteel level, this was also the age of the intimate revue with such performers as Joyce Grenfell (1910–79), Dora Bryan (b. 1924), and Michael Flanders (1922–75) and Donald Swann (b. 1923), who wrote and performed songs at the piano. In addition, there were small repertory companies which staged seasons of plays, ranging from Agatha Christie's (1891–1976) murder stories to works by Ibsen and Shaw. The heart of the commercial theatre system, however, still lay with the major touring circuits, One, Two and Three, established in the 1930s.

These circuits were largely controlled by a few London-based managements known as The Group. The Group owned or controlled about half the theatres in central London and more than half of the regional theatres on the three main touring circuits. It controlled actors' agencies, sheet music and record companies, which led the British actors' union, Equity, in 1952 to accuse it of possessing a near monopoly over British theatre. The leading management for staging straight plays was H.M. Tennant Ltd, whose managing director, H.B. Beaumont (1908–73), had the reputation of being the most powerful man in the British theatre.

Beaumont, who was born in Cardiff, was a meticulous showman who employed many of the most famous stage names at the time: the dramatists Terence Rattigan, N.C. Hunter (1908–71) and Christopher Fry; the actors John Gielgud (b. 1904), Alec Guinness (b. 1914) and Margaret Rutherford (1892–1972), and the designers Oliver Messel (1905–78) and Cecil Beaton (1904–80). Beaumont produced the London version of the Lerner/Loewe musical, *My Fair Lady*, in 1958 and his association with Noël Coward lasted for more than thirty years. He was the first impresario to turn a West End theatre into a theatre club to avoid the censor and to avoid paying the entertainments tax by setting up a charitable company which could try out new plays before presenting them commercially. He had powerful friends in parliament – and both friends and enemies outside it. Equity accused him of blacklisting actors and destroying their careers, charges that surfaced in a parliamentary debate in 1954.

Beaumont's influence cannot be measured by the number of his successful productions. On the positive side, he specialized in British boulevard drama, cool, witty and urbane, whose origins lay in Edwardian theatre and whose stylistic legacy could be felt in the plays of Michael Frayn (b. 1933), Alan Ayckbourn (b. 1939) and Simon Gray (b. 1936) in the 1980s and beyond. He was a cosmopolitan, producing the London premières of plays by Arthur Miller and Jean Anouilh. Negatively, Beaumont encouraged a snobbery often associated with the West End. He liked elegant drawing rooms on stage and elegant dress on members of both sexes in the audience.

By the mid-1950s, however, British society was changing rapidly. London was no longer the centre of an empire and welfare state legislation since the war had eroded some of the division between the rich and the poor. Snobbery fell out of fashion and Beaumont's influence came to be challenged by several small and out-of-the-centre theatre managements which specialized in producing new plays. He was also a target for a talented generation of young actor-directors then emerging from two major university centres in Britain, Oxford and Cambridge. These included Peter Hall (b. 1930), who took over the Arts Theatre Club in London, Jonathan Miller (b. 1934), who was a member of the satirical revue team *Beyond the Fringe* (1959) with the actor-dramatist Alan Bennett (b. 1934), and dramatist Michael Frayn.

These university wits quickly found their place in a theatre system which was rapidly changing. Of the new-play theatres opposed to Beaumont's Tennant companies, two London companies and one regional management were of particular importance. Joan Littlewood's (b. 1914) Theatre Workshop at Stratford-atte-Bowe in East London was the first British company to win an award at the International Theatre Institute's prestigious Théâtre des Nations Festival in Paris in 1955. In the 1930s, Littlewood had launched a theatre collective which specialized in staging socialist documentaries with the robust vigour of music hall. In 1953, she brought her team down from Manchester to occupy an old variety hall in the unfashionable East End of London.

Here they developed a unique style of performance in which teamwork, improvisation, political idealism and strong texts played almost equal parts. Their best known musical documentary was *Oh! What a Lovely War* (1963), but Littlewood also produced the first plays of Brendan Behan, Shelagh Delaney (b. 1939) and Alun Owen (b. 1926), pioneered Brecht in Britain and inspired a generation of regional directors with her local documentaries.

Less politically committed but no less idealistic was the English Stage Company (ESC), formed in 1955 under the artistic directorship of George Devine (1910–65), which took over the Royal Court Theatre – away from the traditional West End – in Sloane Square in London. The aim of the ESC was to promote new plays and its first major success was John Osborne's *Look Back in Anger* (1956), the symbol of the British 'new wave'. Jimmy Porter, the hero of Osborne's play, was a bright but frustrated product of post-war Britain, educated but wasting away in a frivolous job, venting his anger on all who came into contact with him.

The Royal Court became associated with what was eventually called 'kitchen sink drama', to distinguish it from Beaumont's drawing-room plays. But the ESC's record in promoting new plays was more varied than this label suggests. It pioneered French absurdist theatre in London, including plays by Eugène Ionesco, Jean Genet and Samuel Beckett (who, although Irish by birth, settled in Paris in the 1930s). The Royal Court Theatre witnessed the first plays from such writers as David Storey (b. 1933), Edward Bond (b. 1934) and the English absurdist N.F. Simpson (b. 1919). It provided a London home for plays from a regional powerhouse for new drama, the Belgrade Theatre, Coventry. Arnold Wesker's (b. 1932) plays were first staged in Coventry and came to the Royal Court, among them *Chicken Soup with Barley* (1958) and *Roots* (1959).

The resilience of British theatre is illustrated by the fact that in 1956, when the ACGB was predicting the imminent collapse of the theatre system and The Group were selling their theatres to invest in commercial television, there were so many small independent companies keen to take over. The number of theatres declined in Britain during the 1940s and 1950s from about 1,000 to fewer than 500, but there were signs of a renewed growth. New West End managements made their presence felt, such as Michael Codron (b. 1930), one of Beaumont's natural successors.

Codron pursued what must be considered a bold policy for any management, commercial or subsidized. He began as a producer by promoting a university revue, *Share My Lettuce* (1956), but moved on towards adventurous and even avant-garde theatre. He produced Harold Pinter's (b. 1930) *The Birthday Party* in 1958, against the advice of everyone except Pinter's agent. It was a box-office failure, but Codron persevered and produced Pinter's first commercial and critical success, *The Caretaker*, in 1960. Codron also produced the first plays of Joe Orton (1933–67), Ayckbourn and Gray and helped to transfer work from smaller try-out theatres to the main stages of the West End, including plays by David Rudkin (b. 1936) and David Mercer (1928–80). He ran new play seasons at the Arts Theatre and is a rare example of a commercial producer who never went bankrupt but did not lower his standards for profit.

As a result of these initiatives, British theatre became within ten years (from 1956 to 1966) one of the most exciting adventure playgrounds in Europe, open to influences from abroad but still maintaining and developing its own traditions. This revival has sometimes been attributed to state subsidies through the ACGB and these certainly became more significant. But Littlewood received little or no state help whereas the grant to Devine's ESC rose from £5,500 in 1955 to £32,500 in 1965, the year of Devine's death. The Shakespeare Memorial Theatre received no grants until 1961 while, in the same year, the Old Vic was the most generously subsidized dramatic theatre in Britain with grants totalling £40,000. State aid was no more than a small proportion of any theatre's income. The total Arts Council funding to fifty-eight companies in 1963–4 amounted to only just over £500,000, an average sum of less than £10,000 per company.

State subsidies were thus only a marginal factor in the post-war revival. Of greater economic significance was the abolition of the entertainments tax in 1958 and the provision of services through the local authorities, many of whom bought the theatres that The Group were eager to sell. The relaxation of censorship encouraged the production of new plays and the Lord Chamberlain's Examiner of Plays was declared redundant in 1968. But the key to the changes that transformed British theatre lay in the conjunction of the emergence of a varied group of outstanding talents with a turning point in history when it was necessary for Britain to examine many cherished beliefs. The theatre became the British way of overcoming its mid-life crisis; and close to the heart of the national turmoil lay its anguish over the class system.

'Class' was a word that evoked many different associations in Britain, of which the Marxist's was only one. Few British theatres could claim to be working class, apart from the music halls, which were in decline. One exception may have been Littlewood's Theatre Workshop, but her productions attracted audiences from all over London and from all sections of the public. However, she did encourage other companies to look for local audiences and she stimulated a revival of pub music halls and of British musicals. Frank Norman (b. 1930) and Lionel Bart's (b. 1930) *Fings Ain't Wot They Used T'Be* (1959) led to Bart's *Oliver!* (1960), the most successful British musical of the decade 1956–66.

H.M. Tennant Ltd was considered to be right wing despite the fact that Beaumont produced playwrights (like Miller) with left-wing views. But many of the new, regional and supposedly avant-garde managements claimed to be socialist, though their audiences came from the middle rather than the working classes. But 'class' could mean other things than 'class conflict'. It could mean a sense of style, a feeling for social order or an etiquette, an awareness of how people should behave to one another. The nuances of accent, dress, education and voting were all affected by the class system, which was both a force for social cohesion and a source of bitter resentment.

During the 1950s and 1960s, the theatre played a central role in examining the complex mixture of inhibitions, envies, prejudices, prides and tribal loathings that had sheltered under the umbrella of 'class'. Whereas, for example, the older generation of actors were renowned for their social poise and upper-class accents (Gielgud, Coward and Guinness), the younger ones were tough, vigorous and working class – Albert Finney (b. 1936), Tom Courtenay (b. 1937) and Glenda Jackson (b. 1936). Many of the new writers came from the left and, apart from attacking capitalism, agonized (with Storey and Mercer) about losing their class roots with their success in swinging London.

This change of image was not quite what it seemed. The writers, actors and directors of the post-1956 revival came from class backgrounds not too dissimilar from those of the former generation. Neither Beaumont nor Coward came from privileged families, but whereas they cultivated a languid, upper-middle-class style, the new wave specialized in seeming downwardly mobile. Some actors went through a startling change of image. Olivier was Osborne's first Archie Rice, while the elegant John Neville, tipped as Gielgud's successor, played the cockney anti-hero of Bill Naughton's (1910–89) black comedy *Alfie* (1963).

Two political turning points in particular hastened this transformation. The Anglo-French invasion of Suez in 1956 resulted in a débâcle that removed any latent longings to restore the empire. A series of sex and spy scandals in 1963 brought down Harold Macmillan's (1894–1987) Conservative government. His successor, the Earl of Home (b. 1903), was the last prime minister with aristocratic connections; from then on, the style in British politics became more managerial than Olympian, more internationalist than imperial. Most of the values defended by the Lord Chamberlain came under attack: sexual restraint was mocked as inhibition, Christianity derided as superstition, the monarchy reviled as archaic.

Joe Orton, Giles Cooper (1918–66) and Frank Marcus (b. 1928) were among those many comic dramatists in the 1960s who tried to unveil British sexual habits in the cause of a cultural *glasnost*; but a more startling illustration of the changes in taste occurred with a workshop season staged by the RSC under the direction of Brook and the American director Charles Marowitz, at a studio attached to the London Academy of Music and Dramatic Art (LAMDA) in 1963. This Theatre of Cruelty season took its title from an essay by the French actor, dramatist and theorist Antonin Artaud, whose play *A Spurt of Blood* was part of the programme. The public workshops contained short sketches which illustrated many of the major avant-garde theories of the time, including themes from Genet, the Actors' Studio and spur-of-the-moment improvisation.

The Theatre of Cruelty season proved to be a seminal event. It provided the RSC actors with the experience necessary for two major Brook productions – Peter Weiss's *Marat/Sade* (1964) and a collage-documentary about the war in Vietnam, *US* (1965). It inspired a new generation of fringe theatres across the country in which a mixture of French, Polish and American influences all played their parts. But the season was distinctly British in that, while many of the theories may have come from abroad, its target was the supposed stuffiness of the British way of life. British norms of taste, decency and deference were all derided.

The Theatre of Cruelty season provoked what became known as the 'dirty plays' controversy. Some members of the RSC's board resigned in protest and questions were asked in parliament. It was also one of several events that produced a split between the left and right in British theatre, although a better labelling might be between conservative and radical wings. Each wing had triumphs and disasters, but it was the conflict between them that produced the stimulating atmosphere of the 1960s. It was symbolized by the rivalry between the two national companies, Olivier's National Theatre, brought into being at the Old Vic in 1963, and Hall's RSC, transformed from the Shakespeare Memorial Company in 1961, whose London home was at the Aldwych Theatre.

Olivier's NT was thought to be an 'actor's' company, as opposed to the RSC, a 'director's' theatre, although Kenneth Tynan (1927–80), Olivier's literary manager, once said that the real difference was between the 'show-business' of the NT and the 'art' of the RSC. There can be little doubt, however, that Olivier wanted to preserve the centrality of the actor in NT productions and, in particular, to hand down to the younger generation of actors those skills of which he was a supreme example. British theatre in the 1960s is celebrated for many qualities, but rarely enough for the fact that many already well-established actors at the height of their powers, such as Olivier, Gielgud, Richardson, Guinness and Peggy Ashcroft (1907–91), were challenged to seek out new ideas by the aggressive, younger radicals.

Although it was considered to be the more conservative of the two national companies, the NT's record during the 1960s was impressive. Apart from Olivier's own performances (among them Othello), the NT produced major new plays by writers who were then little known: Peter Shaffer's (b. 1926) *The Royal Hunt of the Sun* (1964), John Arden's *Armstrong's Last Goodnight* (1965) and Tom Stoppard's (b. 1937) *Rosencrantz and Guildenstern Are Dead* (1967). These proved that the NT could produce dazzling teamwork, as well as star performances. John Dexter (1925–90) and William Gaskill (b. 1930) were Olivier's associate directors while the young actors included Colin Blakely, Maggie Smith (b. 1934), Joan Plowright (b. 1929) and Robert Stephens (b. 1931).

In contrast, the RSC stressed its company style, which included Jan Kott-inspired interpretations of Shakespeare, such as Brook's *King Lear* (1962) with Scofield and Hall's *Hamlet* (1965) with David Warner (b. 1941) as the student prince. More radical productions came with the already mentioned *Marat/Sade*, *US*, and Pinter's disturbing play, *The Homecoming*,

where home turned out to be a battleground of male fantasies coolly presided over by a dominant mistress. The RSC excelled in the boldness of its ideas and was held to be the more left wing of the two companies. Both national theatres took over as producers of new plays. With Codron in the West End and Devine (succeeded by Gaskill) at the Royal Court, few decades can have been more responsive to young playwrights than the 1960s. Christopher Hampton's (b. 1946) first plays were successfully produced in London when he was in his early 20s – *The Philanthropist* (1968) and *Total Eclipse* (1968). A pivotal year was 1965 when Beaumont produced Coward's last plays, *A Suite in Three Keys* in the West End, while the Royal Court transformed itself into a club to stage Bond's *Saved*. The contrast between the two sides of British theatre was never more marked.

Saved was the most shocking play in an age of stage scandal, a study of a south London urban society whose inhabitants (downtrodden from centuries of class oppression) behaved little better than animals. In one scene, a baby was stoned to death in a pram. It became a *cause célèbre* in Britain and was prosecuted unsuccessfully, thus helping to bring stage censorship to an end in 1968. The violence of Bond's plays became characteristic of a new wave of left-wing British writers, including Howard Brenton (b. 1942), Howard Barker (b. 1946), Heathcote Williams (b. 1941) and, to a lesser extent, David Hare (b. 1947).

After the world-wide demonstrations against the Vietnam War in 1968 and the Soviet repression of the 'Prague Spring' in the same year, the hopeful socialism of Wesker and Littlewood seemed old-fashioned. It had failed either to tame western imperialism or to produce a society that was better than its capitalist alternative. A militant socialism took its place, promising to 'disrupt the spectacle' of bourgeois democracy, along with the plays of Bond and his successors which reflected the mood of open revolt. 'I'll be a one man crime wave when I get going', threatened Hepple, the anti-hero of Howard Brenton's early play, *Revenge* (1969).

Brenton and David Hare were co-founders of a small fringe company, Portable Theatre. But the vigour of their writing took them quickly towards what was now a mainstream for new writing, the Royal Court, the new subsidized repertory theatres and the national theatres. They collaborated on such plays as *Brassneck* (1973) at the Nottingham Playhouse whose director, Richard Eyre (b. 1943), was sympathetic to the left-wing writers. Eyre also produced Trevor Griffith's (b. 1935) play *Comedians* (1975) and his blend of stylish show-business and aggressive polemic became part of Hall's NT, where Eyre was appointed an associate director in 1982. He was later joined by Hare, who became an NT associate director in 1984.

While the lyricism of Brenton's writing is idiosyncratic, Hare's plays rely upon wit rather than poetic images and disdain rather than violence. Both were 1968 rebels, embraced by the cultural establishment, unlike, for example, Arden or John McGrath (b. 1935), two able socialist writers who came from a dourer stock and struggled to make their voices heard from the community centres of Ireland and Scotland.

Not all of the avant-garde theatres during the 1960s were so narrowly political. In the wake of the Theatre of Cruelty season, 'black box' theatres sprang up in pubs and cellars in most major British cities. In 1964, the Traverse Theatre Club was founded in Edinburgh by a US entrepreneur, Jim Haynes. The Traverse

became the leading theatre for promoting the work of Scottish dramatists, among them Stanley Eveling (b. 1925) and Cecil Taylor (1929–81). With Richard Dimarco (b. 1930), who ran an Edinburgh art gallery, the Traverse brought over modern Polish companies to the Edinburgh Festival such as Jerzy Grotowski's Theatre of the 13 Rows from Opole and Tadeusz Kantor's Cricot 2. These were powerful influences on the many small fringe companies that had begun to tour universities and the studio theatres attached to repertory companies. Some of these troupes specialized in agitprop, some in multimedia shows with rock music, while others, such as the People Show, developed their own surrealist comedy.

The most significant development of the late 1960s, however, was probably the growth of the regional repertory theatres which reflected the new importance attached to state subsidy. When Harold Wilson's (b. 1916) Labour government took over from Sir Alec Douglas-Home's Conservatives in 1964, Wilson appointed Britain's first Minister for the Arts, Jennie Lee (1904–88), who introduced the first

The 1992 Tron Theatre production of Cecil P. Taylor's *Good*.
Photo: Alex Tug Wilson.

state plan for developing the arts in Britain. This envisaged a steady rise in state aid to the arts through the Arts Council, a promise that was to some extent fulfilled. In 1970, for example, nearly a hundred theatre companies, including twenty-nine fringe groups, received nearly £2 million between them. This did represent a growth in state funding although the amounts of money still fell far short of what, for instance, German municipal theatres routinely expected.

The actual rise in state funding was less significant than the expectation of growth or the choice of companies to whom state aid was given. Many local authorities, for example, knocked down their existing theatres and built new arts centres in the confident belief that more state subsidies would became available to run them. From 1965 to 1973, there was a rapid growth in theatre building, which concentrated on the regional repertory theatres and important new theatre centres came into being at Nottingham, Sheffield, Liverpool, Manchester, Leeds, Glasgow, Cardiff and Exeter. By 1970, there were sixty subsidized repertory theatres across the UK which successfully challenged the remains of the commercial touring system. In addition, major new theatres were promised in London for the NT, which was still occupying the Old Vic, and for the RSC.

At first, these new 'reps' took the lead in promoting local writers and directors. They also encouraged 'community' theatre, which meant not only local documentaries in the style of Joan Littlewood, but also theatre-in-education and some limited experiments in social engineering through drama seeking, for example, to combat racism and sexism. One model was Peter Cheeseman's (b. 1932) company at Stoke-on-Trent, which pioneered the community plays of Peter Terson (b. 1932). Most reps, however, followed Sir Barry Jackson's principle of a varied repertoire, 'each play good of its kind'; unlike most continental repertory theatres, British reps rarely had permanent companies or kept several plays running together throughout a season. They mainly presented productions in three-weekly or monthly runs.

Among the many directors who emerged through the reps were Terry Hands (b. 1941) from the Liverpool Everyman and Bill Bryden (b. 1942) from the Lyceum Theatre in Edinburgh. To develop an all-round competence, the new reps were excellent schools. But they were not always so good at nurturing those artists with sharp, individual visions. To prove their grant-worthiness, the new reps had to provide

some moral reason for their existence other than mere entertainment and sometimes a pall of artistic respectability descended to stifle creativity. Some reps used their grant money to keep ticket prices low and thus to undercut their unsubsidized rivals. Despite the growth in state aid to the theatre therefore, the theatre industry as a whole really did not grow as anticipated but even declined.

The key year was 1973, when the abrupt rise in the world price of oil caused severe inflationary problems for all western economies and had a particular impact on the new repertory theatres. Unlike the commercial theatres which they replaced, the new reps were lavish, non-cost-effective buildings, built to demonstrate civic pride. They had fulsome foyers and glass windows which were expensive to clean and poor for retaining heat. Within weeks of the price rises, the costs of running these theatres had escalated. Although funds to the Arts Council rose as well – by 1977–8 more than £10 million was being given to the subsidized theatres – these did not compensate for the rising overheads due to inflation.

The reps economized in every way they could, among them by restricting the amounts spent on productions. The originality and sense of purpose which had inspired the repertory movement since the late 1950s began to drain away. While some companies survived without any loss of dynamism, such as the Glasgow Citizens' Theatre and the Stephen Joseph Theatre at Scarborough, others drifted towards an insolvency not solely of money but of spirit as well. Even the two national companies were affected. During the 1960s, the NT and RSC had laid substantial plans for new theatre buildings, receiving the approval and allocation of money from parliament. But the NT did not move into its complex on the South Bank until 1976, while the RSC had to wait until 1982 for the opening of its Barbican Theatre.

In neither case was the move easy or untroubled. Hall resigned as director of the RSC in 1968, handing it over to his protégé, Trevor Nunn (b. 1940), who was in his 20s. Olivier wanted to lead the NT into their South Bank home but a combination of building delays and his own ill health prevented him from doing so. In 1973, the NT board appointed his successor without consulting him, choosing Hall. Hall's management style and tastes were thus reflected in both the RSC and NT. He was given more power over British theatre than any producer since Beaumont. This created some ill will among his fellow professionals, to which Hall was highly sensitive. One source of discontent lay in the disparity in funding between the two 'national' theatres and the sixty regional reps (not to mention the growing number of alternative theatre companies) which felt that their needs had been ignored. In 1983–4, the two national companies received £11.5 million between them, as opposed to the £9 million given to the fifty-six other repertory theatres and the £2 million given to the twenty-eight touring companies in Britain. An original intention of state subsidies was to spread the provision of the arts around the country, but their effect in the theatre was to concentrate the resources in London.

The once stimulating rivalry between the NT and the RSC changed into something more akin to Tweedledum and Tweedledee. When the RSC told the story of the fall of Troy in an eleven-hour epic, *The Greeks* (1980), based on plays by Aeschylus, Euripides and Sophocles, the NT responded with Aeschylus' *The Oresteia* (1981), both productions seemingly influenced by Peter Stein's *Oresteia* at the Schaubühne

in ¯Berlin. Both offered musicals from Shakespeare's early comedies in the style of US director Joe Papp. Both revived American musicals from the 1950s which transferred profitably to the West End; both had mixed fortunes with new musicals. Hall's production of a Marvin Hamlisch musical, *Jean Seberg* (1983), was a flop, while one successful collaboration between the RSC and a commercial management, Cameron Mackintosh, was the Nunn/Caird production of *Les Misérables* (1985). Nunn took time away from the RSC to direct the commercial musicals *Cats* (1981) and *Starlight Express* (1984).

The concentration of state funding on the national companies and their collaborations with the commercial sector changed the lines of argument which had brought them into being. Originally, the roles of the NT and the RSC were conceived to be limited but of high seriousness. They were to concentrate on the heritage of British dramatic literature and classical repertoire in general. They were not expected to rival either the commercial theatres or the avant-garde, but to offer 'a touchstone of excellence'.

Trevor Nunn and John Caird's 1985 Royal Shakespeare Company production of *Nicholas Nickleby*, designed by John Napier and Dermot Hayes.
Photo: Chris Davies.

These lofty ideas were somewhat simplified by Hall, who wanted the NT to be a 'shop window for the best in British theatre'. The NT should be allowed to stage anything 'good of its kind' which meant that farces, boulevard drama, alternative comedy and musicals could be included in its repertoire together with plays by Shakespeare and Aeschylus. One effect of this policy was to draw the national theatres into the kind of uneven competition with other theatres that the NT's pioneers had been anxious to avoid.

The national companies most fulfilled the expectations of their creators perhaps in the studio theatres, the RSC's Swan Theatre and Other Place and the NT's Cottesloe Theatre. Here they undertook what might be called small-scale research productions on classical texts, successful in themselves and inspiring to others, as William Archer (1876–1924) and Harley Granville Barker recommended in their blueprint for a national theatre published in 1904. The RSC's studio Shakespeares included *Hamlet* (1975), directed by Buzz Goodbody (1940–75) and *Macbeth* (1976), directed by Nunn, with Judi Dench (b. 1934) and Ian McKellen (b. 1939). In the larger and more flexible Cottesloe Theatre, Bill Bryden explored the possibilities of what were dubbed 'promenade' productions where the audience stood or walked around rather than sat. Two such productions were *Lark Rise* (1978) and *The Mysteries* (1985).

At the other extreme, the RSC and the NT staged classical and modern productions on their main stages with a visual splendour rarely seen in Britain since the days of Sir Henry Irving, such as the RSC's epic version of Charles Dickens's (1812–70) *Nicholas Nickleby* (1982). Terry Hands was appointed as Nunn's co-director in 1978, bringing his striking visual imagination to his Shakespearian productions which included *Henry V* (1975) and *Coriolanus* (1977), with Alan Howard (b. 1937) in the leading roles. In the NT's main theatres, there were successful Hall productions of *Tamburlaine* (1976), Ayckbourn's *Bedroom Farce* (1977) and particularly Peter Shaffer's *Amadeus* (1979).

The national companies formed lucrative associations with commercial managements on both sides of the Atlantic, a practice which in the early days of subsidized theatre would have been deemed unethical. Not only did the contrast in work and styles between the two national companies diminish, but also the gap between the commercial and subsidized sectors across the country. Nor were the benefits of state subsidy as clear as they had once seemed. Much could be blamed upon inflation and the reluctance of governments to provide more money to the arts than seemed necessary at the time. But it was hard to explain why – while subsidies to the theatre given through the ACGB had risen from £504,000 (1963–4) to £23.38 million (1983–4) – the system was still starved of cash. Some repertory theatres closed in the regions, unemployment rose still higher among actors and some directors who had helped to bring about the post-war theatre revival sought employment outside Britain.

Peter Brook, a central figure in that renaissance, was an early *émigré*. In 1970, he left for Paris to establish his International Centre for Theatre Research, objecting to the bureaucratic ways in which grants were given in Britain. He directed a dazzlingly inventive *Midsummer Night's Dream* for the RSC as a farewell present. He was not the only director of note to leave. Others included John Dexter, Neville and Robin Phillips (b. 1942); the latter two spent extended periods in Canada. In economic crises, the smaller fringe theatres tended to be sacrificed and through the 1970s and early 1980s, the inventiveness that once characterized the fringe and studio theatres in Britain started to decline.

It was obviously hard to devise a funding system fair to all claimants. No national aesthetic standards could be imposed nor, without moving towards a totalitarian control of culture (which all British governments in theory resisted), could there be an arts policy except that of responding to initiatives. The only theory of state support came from the nineteenth-century critic Matthew Arnold (1822–88), who believed that the public should be kept in touch with what the 'great minds of the past' had thought. In practical terms, the ACGB supported the repertory movement, leaving the choice of repertoire to the artistic directors concerned, and kept some small amounts of money aside for experimental theatre. But there had developed a hierarchy in the repertory movement itself, with two national companies at the top, whose standards the lesser reps were expected to imitate. This stress in the subsidized sector on broad-ranging repertoires failed to give adequate help either to companies which wanted to specialize in particular forms of drama or to talented individuals – such as actor-writer-director Steven Berkoff (b. 1937) – who stood outside the system.

Another unforeseen flaw with the subsidized system came with the problem of profits. For many decades, British theatres have been part of a world-wide English-speaking arts market which meant that while the initial production of a new play might require state support, there was a chance that if it became successful, substantial profits might result. Since most subsidized theatres were non-profit companies, eligible as charities for grant aid, profits were of little use. They might even be an embarrassment in that the Arts Council could decide to give them less money in the next year. Companies budgeted, if possible, for a 'containable deficit', a small loss on the current account suggesting that more subsidy would be needed in future.

This was one reason why British subsidized theatres often failed to take advantage of their achievements. One example was *Amadeus*, whose rights were owned by the Shubert Organization, an American commercial management, which reaped the financial rewards from the NT's successful first production of the play. Other examples were the Lyric Hammersmith, whose commercial successes included Michael Frayn's *Noises Off* (1982), and the Leicester Haymarket, which revived old musicals.

The profits from hit productions also went to directors and leading actors in many cases rather than back to the company, a point not wholly lost on Margaret Thatcher's (b. 1925) ministers. When Thatcher became prime minister in 1979, she made it clear to the electorate that her government did not favour the principle of state subsidies to any sector of British economy. Her first Minister for the Arts, Norman St John Stevas, warned the Arts Council that while the government might maintain existing levels of subsidy, further increases would have to come from business sponsorship, rather than the state.

In fact, during Margaret Thatcher's period of office, which ended in 1990, subsidies to the ACGB were maintained at a level slightly above that of the rate of inflation. Although business sponsorship remained a relatively small part of the theatrical economy, more money did come from this source. The financial losses to the theatre during the 1980s actually came through the 'rate-capping' of local authorities, a government-imposed measure which was intended to restrict their spending and prevented them from supporting the theatres as they had before, while the metropolitan authorities, which also funded the arts, were abolished as an unnecessary tier of local government. These measures particularly affected regional repertory theatres and one of several reports on the state of subsidized theatre, *Theatre for All* (1988), called for eight new 'national' theatres to be established in the regions, to redress the balance which had tilted toward London.

Nor was there much money left over in the 1980s to support the fringe and studio theatres, although several which had become established in the late 1960s, such as the Bush Theatre, the Hampstead Theatre, the Young Vic and the Traverse in Edinburgh, survived and even flourished. With the relative decline of the regional reps, they were now the pioneering managements for new writers, joining the two national theatres and the Royal Court. Hampstead and the Bush Theatre staged the first plays of such writers as Stephen Poliakoff (b. 1952), Robert Holman (b. 1952) and Dusty Hughes (b. 1947), while the Royal Court pioneered the work of Caryl Churchill (b. 1938) and Timberlake Wertenbaker. In the early 1990s, the Gate Theatre, west London, under its artistic director Stephen Daldry, became well known for promoting plays from central and eastern Europe.

In the late 1980s, there was agreement among the three main political parties about two obvious flaws in the subsidy system. The arts were handled by too many government departments, which led to confusing decisions, and too much grant-giving power was centred around the ACGB. In 1992, after a May general election, the Conservative government led by Prime Minister John Major (b. 1943) established a Ministry of National Heritage, whose role embraced films, broadcasting and cultural tourism, as well as what had previously been defined as the arts.

One of its first acts (December 1992) was to redefine the role of the ACGB, limiting it to the national and major touring companies and delegating most grant-giving powers to strengthened regional arts boards. The argument against this decision was that it might lead to a two-tier theatre system with the regions again losing out to London, but its aim was the reverse, to enhance the independence of the regional subsidizing authorities. Other interest groups than the geographical regions were defined, such as the ethnic and religious communities, who may not have been exactly ignored, but were considered to have been at a disadvantage to the white Anglican majority.

These supposedly liberalizing measures broadened the role of the ministry, the regional arts boards and even the ACGB, whose authority might seem to have diminished. In the light of the early fears that a single ministry might lead to a dictatorial control of culture, the politicians seemed remarkably sanguine that this would not happen in the 1990s. It requires a certain political daring to seek to allocate grants on the grounds of artistic merit, geographical distribution and religious and ethnic origins throughout the United Kingdom. The complexity of this task helps to account for the wide-ranging but hard-to-pin-down pronouncements of the ACGB's discussion document, *Towards a National Arts and Media Strategy* (1992).

In one area during the 1980s, British theatre discovered a strange new expertise – the staging and marketing of mega-musicals. Until the mid-1970s, British musicals were always, at best, the impoverished cousins of Broadway shows. The change began with the London production of *Jesus Christ Superstar* (1970), by the composer/librettist team, Andrew Lloyd Webber (b. 1948) and Tim Rice (b. 1944), both in their 20s. Their first musical, *Joseph and His Amazing Technicolour Dreamcoat* (professionally produced in 1968), was written while they were still at school and picked up by director Frank Dunlop (b. 1927), who staged it at the Young Vic. Both musicals played their part in a fashion for religious rock shows, of which the US musical, *Godspell* (1971), was another example.

Neither show could match the sophistication of a Stephen Sondheim musical, but Lloyd Webber had the apparently effortless knack of writing tunes which provided memorable theatrical moments, a skill which Sondheim never fully seemed to acquire. The next Lloyd Webber/Rice musical, *Evita* (1976), was launched on the back of one such song, 'Don't

Barry Stanton as Falstaff in Michael Bogdanov's 1989 English Shakespeare Company production of *Henry IV, Part I*.
Photo: Laurence Burns.

Cry for Me, Argentina', which was a hit single even before *Evita* itself became a transatlantic hit show. Lloyd Webber went on to write other hit musicals, including *Cats* (1981), *Song and Dance* (1981), *The Phantom of the Opera* (1988) and *Aspects of Love* (1989), all of which later transferred to Broadway and could subsequently be seen in many large theatres around the world. He became the most successful composer, in financial terms, of light British musicals before he reached his fortieth birthday.

Partly because of Lloyd Webber, London became a centre for major show-business musicals in the 1980s and made fortunes for such commercial producers as Cameron Mackintosh, whose resources were far beyond the dreams of even the national theatres. After the success of *Cats*, Lloyd Webber floated his own company (the Really Useful Theatre Company) on the London Stock Exchange at £35 million, an amount which was quickly found and subsequently produced healthy profits for its investors. It was as if British theatre had responded to Thatcher's faith in private enterprise by seeking the kind of commercialism for which it had previously blamed Broadway. The truth, however, was somewhat more complicated. Steeply rising costs on Broadway had tempted some US producers to look towards London, where new productions could be tried out with less risk, sometimes with the assistance of the subsidized companies; while subsidized theatres, to supplement their grants, looked towards the West End and Broadway for further investment.

When the RSC moved into the Barbican Theatre in 1982, it found itself sharing the building with the Guildhall School of Music and Drama. Nunn, as head of the RSC, wanted to develop a relationship between the RSC and the school which would produce a new generation of actors who could sing, dance and act. The rise of the British musical, the most astonishing feature of the 1980s, thus came from an odd combination of factors which finally erased the folk memories of the 1950s when the British theatre could do everything but sing and dance.

Another development in the 1980s was the return to the 'actor's' theatre, of which Kenneth Branagh's Renaissance Theatre Company was an example. Branagh, sometimes compared with Olivier, spent his apprenticeship with the RSC but like Simon Callow (b. 1948), who also came from Belfast, he became impatient with the habit of subjecting his actor's vision to that of his director. Branagh and Callow became actor-directors, like the actor-managers of the past, favouring independence above the security of working with the major companies, and they were helped by a new national and international touring circuit.

The national touring circuit was partly caused by the decline of the reps, which found it difficult in the 1980s to provide the repertoire of classic productions for which they had been brought into existence. They began to rely on touring productions to fill the gaps in their programmes and, as a result, companies like the Renaissance and the English Shakespeare Company (founded in 1986) were much in demand. Because the productions were not 'director's' theatre, the sets tended to be less elaborate and easier to tour.

Branagh also followed in the footsteps of Olivier by directing and starring in the film of *Henry V*. On a much smaller scale than the Renaissance, other companies developed with classical rather than modern repertoires, such as Shared Experience, Cheek by Jowl, and Théâtre

Street theatre at the 1992 Edinburgh Festival Fringe.
Photo: Iain Stewart.

de Complicité. The compactness of these companies often allowed them to be more adventurous in choice of repertoire. Shared Experience's adaptation of Dickens's *Bleak House* (1978) and Gotthold Lessing's *Miss Sara Sampson* (1990) proved how exciting these low-cost, high-performance companies could be.

Another factor in the growth of touring companies was the development of an international festival market, of which in Britain the Edinburgh International Festival was the prime example. The Edinburgh Festival still provides an accurate gauge of the strength of UK theatre, particularly at its fringe level. Taking place annually each August/September, it was at the Edinburgh Festival that university wits from Jonathan Miller to Rowan Atkinson (b. 1952) made their names, that Tom Stoppard was discovered, that many young directors tried out their ideas and that Grotowski, Kantor and Şerban made their primary impact on the UK theatre scene.

The 1980s merged into the 1990s in a cascade of symbolic endings – with the deaths of Olivier, Richardson and the last great star of the music halls, Max Wall. In 1986, Hall handed over to Eyre as the NT's director and the NT itself sought royal approval, becoming the Royal National Theatre. The RSC's directors, Nunn and Hands, passed their batons to the next director, Adrian Noble (b. 1950).

In March 1991, a report published by British Invisibles, a non-arts agency which compiles statistics on foreign 'invisible' trade, revealed that theatrical performances provided the British economy with over £80.8 million in foreign earnings in 1988–9 (a figure which did not take into account the West End's impact upon arts-related tourism). Hugely profitable at one level and starved of funds at another, theatre in the UK can perhaps best be celebrated as a triumph of the human spirit over various schemes for its better organization and improvement.

Structure of the National Theatre Community

There are about 500 theatres in the United Kingdom and about 300 centres or venues visited on a regular basis by professional theatre companies. According to the *British Theatre Directory*, the indispensable handbook for performing arts managements, there are 102 theatre buildings in Greater London, with thirty-eight fringe or 'alternative' theatre clubs and forty-one arts centres with studio theatres attached. Outside London, there are 374 regional theatres and about 100 arts centres, of which Scotland has thirty theatres and thirty arts centres, while Wales has twenty-three theatres and eighteen arts centres. This directory lists five theatres and three arts centres in Northern Ireland and the summer theatres in the islands around the coastline, such as Mull, Jersey and the Isle of Wight.

These figures, which are not comprehensive, reveal several features of the British scene. Although there has been a decline in the number of theatres since World War II, many new ones were built in the late 1960s and 1970s and the theatre still has a widespread popularity throughout the UK. Most towns have theatres, which may not always be professionally run but have regular seasons of professional entertainment, if only Christmas pantomimes. London may be the focal point, but there are thriving theatre centres in the English regions, Scotland, Wales and Northern Ireland. Edinburgh, with six theatres (including the Lyceum Theatre and Traverse Theatre Club), and Glasgow, with seven theatres (including the Citizens' Theatre and the Theatre Royal, home of the Scottish Opera), are the leading theatre cities in Scotland and both offer major festivals, the Edinburgh International Festival and the Glasgow Mayfest. Cardiff, with three, and Swansea, with five theatres, could be regarded as centres in Wales, although Theatre Clwyd in Mold is the Welsh repertory theatre which is best known within the UK and received most subsidy in the early 1990s.

Among the English regional theatre centres, Birmingham has four theatres, Leeds five, Liverpool five and Manchester eight. Some of the most influential theatres, however, are not in the major cities but in smaller towns, such as Stratford-upon-Avon (home of the Royal Shakespeare Company), Scarborough (whose Stephen Joseph Theatre boasts Alan Ayckbourn as its artistic director) and Lewes in Sussex (home of the Glyndebourne Opera). There are fifty-five principal festivals in England, four in Scotland and seven in Wales, but many towns and even villages stage local arts festivals.

London has the most (and the largest) theatres per head. With the West End at the heart of a world-wide entertainment industry, the presence of the two national drama theatres and two national opera houses as 'centres of excellence' for the subsidized sector in Britain, London ranks as one of the world's great theatre cities.

British theatre has three main sources of income: box office, state patronage and business sponsorship, although some might add that the low wages paid to most artists also constitutes a form of indirect subsidy. British theatre survives through the dedication of those who work for it. The British actors' union, Equity, established in 1930, has tended to be more flexible in its requirements from managements than its older American counterpart, Actors' Equity Association (1913). It has allowed more freedom to actors to appear in non-Equity fringe theatres than is the case in New York, where the unionization of Off-Broadway theatres led to their being mainly try-out venues for commercial managements.

This flexibility has had many advantages. It has supported the growth of small groups, allowed a relatively easy entry into the profession and promoted an atmosphere of compromise rather than confrontation. But it has also led to problems, among them the number of unemployed actors on their books and the low wages paid to all but the stars. The rise in state subsidies since the war has been of little benefit to actors, a factor in a struggle between the hard-left and centre-right factions for the political control of Equity during the 1970s, which the centre-right won.

For most British theatres, the box office is the main source of income. The UK may be the last country in Europe where it is still possible to become very rich through theatrical promotions. In January 1992, it was revealed that of the ten richest men in Britain, no fewer than three (Paul Raymond, Cameron Mackintosh and Andrew Lloyd Webber) won their early fortunes from the theatre. Raymond, who started as a conjurer in the music halls and became a leading promoter of strip clubs, ousted the Duke of Westminster as the richest man in Britain. Lloyd Webber and Mackintosh owe their position to such musicals as *Cats*, while a fourth man who figures in this list is Richard Branson (b. 1950), whose music empire also owes a debt

to the international popularity of British musicals.

These, however, are the exceptions which prove the rule that while it may be possible to be a wealthy commercial impresario in Britain, only a few very lucky or determined people actually are. Thirty-five theatres in London's West End can be considered 'commercial' in that they receive no state subsidies or business sponsorship. These have no resident companies and receive productions, brought together by outside impresarios, which run for as long as the public will come. Some impresarios, such as Michael Codron, run their own theatres and some commercial shows receive indirect state support through partnerships with subsidized companies. After 1979–80, it became usual for subsidized companies to cooperate with West End impresarios in order to receive the benefit of royalties and to demonstrate to Thatcher's government that they were capable of earning income from the market-place.

The major centres outside London have commercial theatres; one notable feature of the 1980s was the revival of the touring circuits, which led to a new lease of life for such theatres as the Palace in Manchester and Theatre Royal in Norwich. In an economy as thoroughly mixed as that of British theatre, it is not easy to separate the various sources of income and the two main management associations – the Society of West End Theatres (SWET) for London and the Theatre Managers' Association (TMA) for the regions – are not always frank about box-office figures. But the scale of commercial theatre operations in Britain can be illustrated from various sources. According to a research study conducted by John Myerscough for the Policy Studies Institute, the arts in general earned £4 billion (US$8 billion) in foreign currency for Britain in 1984–5. This figure was increased to more than £6 billion in 1988–9 in a survey conducted by British Invisibles, a business research company independent of the arts and government. This survey calculated that Britain earned £1.9 billion from arts-related tourism in the same year and that box-office income from foreign visitors amounted to £80.8 million. Another survey from the Performing Rights Society indicated that £137 million was earned in 1991 by British artists from royalty payments.

While such figures provide only a rough guide, they indicate that the arts are a major source of income to Britain, second only (according to British Invisibles) to oil. It is not easy, however, to calculate how much money has been lost in theatre promotion and while the overall picture may be one of an industry which has remained profitable despite the recession, there are always more business failures than successes.

The instability of the commercial system has always been a powerful argument in favour of state subsidy. Without taking the collaborations with commercial companies into account, British subsidized theatres have always been alert to the potential of the box office. Few theatres receive as much as 50 per cent of their income from grants, which come from two main sources, the Arts Council of Great Britain and the local authorities, but the ratios of box-office to subsidy incomes differ greatly.

The national companies and, relative to their size, some small theatres, such as the Bush and Hampstead Theatres in London which have good reputations for staging new plays, benefit most from subsidy; however, none of them can ignore ticket sales as a source of revenue. Even the national companies often require additional business sponsorships for major productions. One such company, the English National Opera (ENO), ran a special appeal to its members to raise £100,000 for one production of Janáček's *The Adventures of Mr Broucek* (1992).

Four London theatres house national companies: the Royal Opera House (Covent Garden), the Coliseum (ENO), the Royal National Theatre (RNT), which has three auditoriums, and the Barbican, with two auditoriums used by the Royal Shakespeare Company. The RSC also has a home at Stratford-upon-Avon with three theatres – the main Shakespeare Memorial Theatre, the Swan and the Other Place. The national companies account for a large slice of the ACGB's expenditure and the fact that they all have homes in London, and thus tilt public spending on the arts toward the metropolis, has been a source of controversy since the ACGB was established by Royal Charter in 1946. The conflict which is supposed to exist between 'high standards' and 'regional spread' can be said to have shaped the pattern of grant-giving in Britain, for there have been many schemes to decentralize the ACGB and almost as many to streamline and centralize it.

In 1992, for example, the Royal Opera House (Covent Garden) received £10 million from the ACGB, whose subsidy for the Welsh National Opera amounted to £2.3 million. The subsidy to the Royal Opera House was more than half the amount given to the Scottish Arts Council (£19.7 million) and nearly as much as that given to the Welsh Arts Council (£11 million). Major opera houses have, of course, always been costly items on any arts council's shopping list, but the metropolitan bias extends to straight drama too. The RNT (£9.8 million) and the RSC (£7.9 million) received between them nearly half the grant income (£36 million) given by the ACGB to English drama in general in 1992, which included thirty-one repertory theatres, sixteen touring companies, twenty-two 'annual clients', seventy-nine 'project grants', fourteen small touring companies and 108 other items.

Such figures may exaggerate the metropolitan bias in that the ACGB also gives subsidies in the form of 'matching' grants to encourage local authorities to support the arts and provided £37 million to the Regional Arts Boards and Associations (RAA). The RAAs were established to achieve a measure of devolution in grant-giving. When the ACGB was first established, it opened its own regional offices around the UK. These closed in the 1950s and were replaced by the RAAs, which were supposed to coordinate and stimulate grant-giving from the local authorities. It has been government policy since 1979 to increase the powers of the RAAs as alternative sources of arts funding to the ACGB, despite the fact that they received so much of their income from the ACGB. In 1992, a Ministry of National Heritage was established and the ACGB's grant-giving powers were defined to apply particularly to the national companies, with twelve RAAs responsible for the arts in the regions. It is too soon to tell how this reorganization will affect the arts in practice.

The ACGB has been the main means through which public money has been given to the arts, although in some years more money in total has been given by the local authorities. Its income from the state has steadily increased under Labour and Conservative governments, from £230,000 in 1946 to £205 million in 1992. This progress has taken place in three distinct phases: 1946–64 (when it was responsible to the Chancellor of the Exchequer, received little money but claimed to speak for the fine arts); 1965–79 (when it was responsible to the Ministry of Education, received more money and claimed to be building a British arts system); and 1979–92 (when it was responsible first to a Ministry of Arts and Libraries and then to a Ministry of National Heritage). It has been characteristic of British governments that they have wanted to avoid establishing a Ministry of Culture, which has a totalitarian ring to British ears, and the

ACGB has mostly claimed to be 'at arm's length' from governments, receiving money from the state but free to distribute this income as it chooses.

Since 1979, it has been government policy to decentralize grant-giving where possible. Devolution to the RAAs is one example and the growth of business sponsorships is another. The Association for Business Sponsorship of the Arts (ABSA) was founded in 1976 to encourage and coordinate sponsorship. The ABSA has no grant-giving powers but it offers awards and incentives to business sponsors. It administers the government-backed Business Sponsorship Incentive Scheme (BSIS) whereby grants from new business sponsors of the arts are matched pound for pound from public funds. In 1990–1, the level of contribution to this scheme from the Exchequer was set by the then Minister for the Arts, Richard Luce, at £3.5 million.

The *British Theatre Directory* lists 344 producing managements, which range from small-time impresarios arranging entertainments for pubs to international companies such as Cameron Mackintosh Ltd. A similar diversity can be found elsewhere in the theatre system and particularly in the range between large, prestigious companies, and small local ones. There are twenty-four ballet and opera companies, of which perhaps ten have the resources to be counted as major companies while the others lead more precarious existences. But it would be a mistake to assume that the smaller companies are less good than the bigger or that the major are more adventurous than the minor.

There are also 144 theatre clubs and associations listed in the *British Theatre Directory*. They include societies devoted to Shakespearian and Shavian research, first-night clubs, the Green Room Club (for professional theatre artists, as opposed to the more prestigious Garrick Club, which has members from all professions), critics' circles, management associations, artists' benevolent funds, the Independent Theatre Council (a management association for small or medium-sized theatres), design consultancies, song and playwriting clubs, theatre museums, the British Music Hall Society and several writers' guilds. There are also societies for African, Caribbean and Indian theatres, for feminist theatre and theatre-in-education. The social value of the theatre is reflected in the number of bodies which support drama therapy, drama for disabled people, drama for unemployed people, and drama in prisons.

Many of these organizations are small and underfunded, but they reflect much energy, time and dedication. Not all of them, however, are so small. The trade unions – Equity, the Musicians' Union and the Broadcasting and Entertainment Trades Alliance (BETA) – the guilds, professional societies and organizations concerned with copyright protection (the Performing Rights Society) are well organized and, within their fields, fairly strong. Some are government backed, including the British Council, the cultural wing of the Foreign Office, which has offices around the world and acts as both a sponsor and an agent for British companies visiting festivals and similar events abroad. It has a Visiting Arts office, semi-independently run, which helps companies coming to Britain.

Since the mid-1980s, the distinctions which used to provide separate categories in British theatre have changed, either by merging or by being dropped as old-fashioned. There is no longer the sharp division between the subsidized and commercial sectors, and the concept of building-based repertory theatres has been in part replaced by touring repertory companies and building-based production companies. The former distinction between London and the regions has been supplemented, rather than replaced, by the recognition of different ethnic and religious communities within a multicultural United Kingdom.

Some small theatres which were called fringe or alternative are better established than some supposedly mainstream companies. The opposition between the left-wing and avant-garde (the British version of east European dissidency) and the right-wing mainstream is no longer so marked. The national companies, whose purpose was once to offer classical repertoire and serious alternatives to the trivial West End, now excel in staging American musicals from the 1950s, such as *Carousel* (RNT, 1992).

This is partly because definitions of theatrical excellence have changed but it is also a consequence of government policy. By seeking to break up the grant-giving powers of the ACGB, which were thought to verge upon the monopolistic, and by trying to decentralize the theatre system, the Ministry of Arts and Libraries encouraged collaborations with business sponsors, with RAAs, with commercial managements, with audio and video companies. This trend may well continue under the Ministry of National Heritage, with the additional bonus of a National Lottery. While this quintessentially Conservative and managerial approach to

Jonathan Miller's 1990 Old Vic production of Shakespeare's *The Tempest*.

the arts may bring many benefits, it is opposed in character to the high-minded zeal which the Liberal and Labour pioneers brought to the founding of the ACGB. Perhaps the greatest change of all is that the subsidized sector of British theatre can no longer lay claim to the artistic high ground but is simply one element of many in the complex, art-funding mixture of a pluralistic society.

Artistic Profile

Companies

British theatre has certain characteristics which seem to resist time and fashion. Despite the 1990s popularity of British musicals and the influence of contemporary dance, it remains primarily a text-based theatre. The bias towards literature is coupled with a suspicion of 'intellectuals' and words like culture. Despite the growth of state subsidies, particularly since the mid-1960s, no company can ignore its box-office income or popularity. There are few coterie theatres and while the two national companies, the RSC and the RNT, are intended to be centres of excellence, the claim is based more upon the confirmation of middle-brow opinion than the defiance or re-examination of it.

A third characteristic is the streak of anarchy that cuts through all levels of British theatre from the pub variety shows to classical revivals. It could be described as Shakespearian, in that it was present in Shakespeare's plays and embodied in such characters as Thersites, Falstaff and Caliban. It shocked eighteenth-century French critics with its irreverence towards authority and its denial of classical restraint.

Some post-war plays have outraged their publics to a notable degree, such as Edward Bond's *Saved* (1965), Peter Barnes's (b. 1931) *Laughter* (1978) and Howard Brenton's *The Romans in Britain* (1980), but the trait is not limited to such examples. It is as familiar a feature of British culture as gun fights are of Hollywood westerns.

British contemporary theatre has largely been shaped by these habits. Its post-war revival is usually considered to have begun in the mid-1950s with the establishment of the English Stage Company (ESC) at the Royal Court Theatre, the Arts Theatre Club, Joan Littlewood's Theatre Workshop at Stratford-atte-Bowe in East London and, in the regions, the Belgrade Theatre, Coventry. All were renowned for the production of new plays and while they may not have set out to shock, they did grate against West End tastes. In their time, John Osborne's *Look Back in Anger* (at the ESC), Brendan Behan's *The Hostage* (at Theatre Workshop) and Samuel Beckett's *Waiting for Godot* (London première at the Arts Theatre Club) were thought to be blasphemous, anarchic or seditious.

The dominance of the text has made its impact elsewhere. British acting training often concentrates on the speaking of lines and interpretation, although some drama schools (such as the Joan Littlewood-inspired East 15) now have different priorities. Shakespearian verse-speaking is an example and most British actors would doubt that their colleagues in other countries could handle iambic pentameters with such death-defying skill. John Gielgud represented an eloquence of diction which can be traced back to Henry Irving and the Victorian actors but he has admitted that his body language is much less expressive. Peter Hall said in the 1960s that the RSC was in danger of becoming a collection of talking heads, although he himself did much to encourage the better verse-speaking in the company.

This vocal skill can be observed in the performance of such actors as Alec Guinness and Judi Dench, whose voices not only are wonderfully expressive but also are often accompanied by a stillness of stage presence which intensifies every nuance. Such actors encourage playwrights to write subtle dialogue. There have been some supremely successful partnerships of British acting and writing skills, such as Gielgud's and Sir Ralph Richardson's performances in David Storey's *Home* (1970) and Harold Pinter's *No Man's Land* (1975), or Nigel

Hawthorne (b. 1929) in Alan Bennett's *The Madness of George III* (1991, RNT). The West End is one of the few places in the world where two middle-aged men and two women talking brightly for three hours can constitute a popular hit, a privilege which has sometimes been abused by the less talented.

Despite the changes in theatre organizations since World War II and the transformation of social life, there is a stylistic continuity linking such writers as Arthur Wing Pinero, Terence Rattigan, Michael Frayn, Storey, Bennett, Simon Gray, Alan Ayckbourn, Christopher Hampton and Doug Lucie (b. 1953). They write well-made comedies and dramas, have an epigrammatic turn of phrase and an ear for social ironies. While the affinity of the modern playwrights with Edwardian social drama may seem to be belied by their lack of snobbishness and their left-wing sympathies, these were also the stances of some Edwardians as well, as the names Bernard Shaw and Harley Granville Barker will testify.

Such actors and writers have been promoted by impresarios, skilled at bringing together theatrical 'packages', appealing to the West End public and to similar-minded audiences in other parts of the UK. A management tradition connects Sir George Alexander (1858–1918), who ran the St James's Theatre at the turn of the century, H.B. Beaumont of H.M. Tennant Ltd, the leading drama promoter of the 1940s and 1950s, and Michael Codron today. They all excelled in staging small-cast plays.

Large, permanent companies akin to the Comédie-Française are relatively new to Britain. The first conceived on this scale were the Shakespeare Memorial Company in the early 1960s, which became the RSC, and the National Theatre, but the funding required to sustain such companies and the motives to do so have rarely been present in the same place at the same time. The national companies are poorly funded when compared with German state theatres but they have the advantage of being able to enter into partnerships with impresarios on both sides of the Atlantic.

This commercial streak distinguishes the British national companies from their continental counterparts. It is reflected in their programming, the still prevalent star system and their philosophy (or lack of it). State companies in mainland Europe have usually been established for reasons of national pride, personality or aesthetics. Some came into being when the old royal court theatres were transformed into national theatres following the downfall of monarchies. Some were built around the enthusiasm of a leader and some around an artistic creed such as naturalism.

These motives scarcely apply to the British experience, whose national theatres were late developers and established partly because so many other countries had them. While Laurence Olivier (RNT) and Peter Hall (RSC), the first directors, were certainly both artists and leaders, they were the figureheads of movements that started in the nineteenth century and resulted in two less well-endowed classical companies, the Old Vic and the Shakespeare Memorial Company at Stratford-upon-Avon. During the 1930s, Olivier had worked in the Old Vic company while Lilian Baylis (1874–1937), the pioneer of the company, was still alive. The philosophies of the two companies were once summarized by Sir Barry Jackson and echoed by Kenneth Tynan, the critic and Olivier's first literary manager, as 'the best of everything', a kind of pan-aesthetics. As a result, both national companies have been umbrella companies for many talents, notably Peter Brook at the RSC and the group of younger directors by whom Olivier was surrounded at the RNT – John Dexter, William Gaskill, Jonathan Miller and Michael Blakemore (b. 1928).

Neither Olivier nor Hall was doctrinaire. It has been said of them both that they listened to so many other people's ideas that they had little time to formulate any of their own. In most other respects, they differed. Olivier, acknowledged to be the finest actor of his remarkable generation, had the instincts of the actor-manager which he once (successfully) was. Hall led a younger generation scornful of the old values. The 'dirty plays' row in 1965–6, in which Hall was accused by some members of his board of bringing the RSC into disrepute, is an example of how the British anarchic streak sometimes determines who will be the next establishment, for Hall's victory over his board in this controversy secured his place not only as the RSC's director but also as the man to succeed Olivier at the RNT.

Hall conducted a very broad-based policy after leading the RNT's company into its new building on the South Bank in 1975, with classical plays, boulevard drama, musicals, polemic drama and even some 'promenade productions', notably directed by Bill Bryden in the flexible Cottesloe Theatre. Hall wanted the RNT to be a 'shop window' for talents, an aim which uncontroversially he can be said to have achieved. His successor, Richard Eyre, has also blended modern and classical plays in a popular, if not populist, programme. But the RNT has never had the reputation for being intellectually challenging. Its most popular success in Hall's time was Peter Shaffer's *Amadeus* (1979).

When Hall retired from the RSC in 1968, he helped to appoint his successor, Trevor Nunn, who has become the director with the best all-round skills in Britain, proficient at staging studio Shakespeares, historical spectacles (*Nicholas Nickleby*, 1980; *Les Misérables*, 1985) and musicals (*Cats*, 1981). From 1978 to 1987, Nunn shared the RSC directorate with Terry Hands, whose stagings often seemed more impressive than his interpretations. They were succeeded in 1989 by Adrian Noble, who also excels in visual theatre. Since the end of the 1950s, the RSC's reputation has been based upon the work of young directors, none of them 'intellectuals'. The standards of acting and staging over the years have remained high, but the RSC's weakness has been an ideological naïvety, in which new ideas are snatched up and then discarded arbitrarily.

The kind of company, symbolized by the Berliner Ensemble or the Moscow Art Theatre, where the actors are trained to work as a company and are motivated by a coordinating philosophy, is rare in Britain, except with smaller groups. Littlewood's company at Stratford during the 1950s was an exception and was imitated by such regional theatres as the Victoria, Stoke-on-Trent. The subsequent management, under Philip Hedley, is still inspired by Littlewood, not least by her love of old music-hall traditions. Its success with *One Mo' Time* (1991) had a similar vitality to the Littlewood–Lionel Bart musicals, such as *Fings Ain't Wot They Used T'Be* (1959), although it lacked the satirical brilliance of the compilation of World War I songs in *Oh! What a Lovely War*. In Scotland, the Citizens' Theatre in Glasgow was also once influenced by Littlewood although it has acquired its own, highly distinctive style with a triumvirate of directors led by Giles Havergal (b. 1938).

Most British repertory theatres have either no permanent company or what is sometimes called a 'nucleus', four or five company members, with additional actors hired as necessary. Nor do they usually have an artistic policy beyond wanting to please their public with a wide variety of plays which, apart from at the major companies, are presented in runs of three or four weeks.

The Posse's 1991 collective creation *Armed and Dangerous*, Theatre Royal, Stratford East.

Dramaturgy

Even in the 1990s, the prevailing text-based theatrical genre was still the naturalistic 'well-made' play, as it had been for most of the twentieth century. It may appear in different disguises, from detective stories to religious allegories, or set in places as diverse as high-society drawing rooms and coal-miners' parlours; sometimes the attempts may seem to be neither naturalistic nor particularly well made, but familiar outlines can often be perceived even in plays that purport to be experimental.

Most British writers write plays with 'beginnings, middles and ends', using the time-honoured devices of 'pace' and 'suspense'. They tell stories whose dilemmas are solved at 'crises', observe (however loosely) the unities of time, place and action, and in other ways respect their classical upbringings. The British public may not always 'identify' with the tragic hero or heroine, but their dramatists often start from that assumption.

This dominance has never been without its challengers. The different examples of Shakespearian drama and family pantomimes stand as reminders that there are other ways of writing plays. W.H. Auden (1907–73) and Christopher Isherwood (1904–86) wrote three expressionist verse plays in the late 1930s, of which *The Ascent of F6* (1937) is best known. T.S. Eliot devised a modern, Medieval Mystery pageant with *Murder in the Cathedral* (1935), but his attempts to develop a theatre of religious ritual were less than convincing and his later plays, including *The Cocktail Party* (1949), were society dramas written in discreet blank verse. Other poet-dramatists of the period included Christopher Fry and Dylan Thomas, whose *Under Milk Wood* (first performed posthumously in 1954) escaped from the restrictions of well-made plays, perhaps because it was originally written for radio.

During the 1960s, the influences of Artaud, Beckett, Brecht and the Off-Off-Broadway movement from New York all made their impact, while in the 1970s, agitprop, documentary theatre and performance art companies sought to do without writers altogether; but even when the plays have been improvised by actors under such a director as Mike Leigh (b. 1943), the results tend to look like well-made plays, as Leigh's *Abigail's Party* (1977) indicates.

The continuity of this tradition is notable. There have been many political, cultural and economic changes in Britain since the days of Queen Victoria, but at least within the sphere of playwriting, the process has been more evolutionary than revolutionary. Arthur Wing Pinero's *The Second Mrs Tanqueray* (1893) is similar in construction to Terence Rattigan's *The Deep Blue Sea* (1952) and Alan Ayckbourn's *Woman in Mind* (1985), however much the social habits may have altered. There is a formal continuity between the plays of Oscar Wilde, Noël Coward, Joe Orton and Doug Lucie. It is not only that they are all witty writers, but also that they are witty in similar ways, ironic, poised, outrageous and, at best, subversive of bourgeois manners which they pretend to flatter. Modern political dramatists still seek to emulate Bernard Shaw and, for example, the tycoon in David Hare and Howard Brenton's *Pravda* (1985) resembles Shaw's Boss Mangan in *Heartbreak House* (1920).

If this sounds as if British dramaturgy represents a triumph of tradition over innovation, paradoxically it needs to be stressed that since World War II, playwrights have led the way in what can only be described as a cultural revolution. This began in the early 1950s, when Rattigan was at the height of his reputation, and a representative of the middle- or upper-middle-class values of a West End dominated by the impresario, H.B. Beaumont. In an unguarded interview, Rattigan mentioned that he wrote for audiences of 'Aunt Edna', whom the critic Kenneth Tynan derided as the sort of person who went to matinées to admire the hats.

Rattigan may have been too modest, self-deprecating in the British manner. He was a successful writer of light comedies and romances, whose first play, *French Without Tears* (1936), ran for three years in the West End, but his range was much wider than that record suggests, including wartime patriotic films and plays (*Flare Path*, 1942), historical epics (*Ross*, 1960) and the social/family dramas which can now be recognized as his great achievement. Few writers have matched the subtlety, tact and emotional power of Rattigan's one-act plays, *The Browning Version* (included in *Playbill*, 1948) or *Separate Tables* (1954), although Simon Gray, Alan Bennett and Ayckbourn can all be said to have inherited his mantle.

During the 1950s, Rattigan and what he was considered to represent about British theatre was under attack, partly on class grounds and partly because of the apparent security of his assumptions. There were several vantage points from which these challenges were mounted. One was the converted music hall in London's East End which Joan Littlewood had turned into her headquarters. The new dramatists whose work she pioneered included Brendan Behan, Frank Norman and Shelagh Delaney, whose *A Taste of Honey* (1958) was written while she was only 17 and angered by a touring production of a Rattigan play. They were all as much against the British establishment as Rattigan was rumoured to be for it. Behan was a member of the IRA who had been sent as a child delinquent to Borstal (*The Quare Fellow*, 1956; *The Hostage*, 1958); Norman had a criminal record, which helped him to write about low life in Soho with first-hand authority (*Fings Ain't Wot They Used T'Be*); and Delaney was the first British dramatist to describe in intimate detail what it was like to be an unmarried mother.

Another sniping post against the West End came from the regions, particularly Coventry, where Bryan Bailey pursued a 'new plays' policy at the newly built Belgrade Theatre. He discovered Arnold Wesker, whose autobiographical trilogy – *Chicken Soup with Barley* (1958), *Roots* (1959) and *I'm Talking About Jerusalem* (1960) – transferred to the Royal Court Theatre in London, run by the English Stage Company, which under George Devine had become a 'writers' theatre'.

The English Stage Company has been credited with the transformation of post-war British theatre, notably with the surprising success of John Osborne's *Look Back in Anger* (1956). Its hero, Jimmy Porter, came to typify the 'angry young men' who were frustrated not only by being over-educated and under-employed, but also by belonging to a nation which had lost its empire but had yet to discover its global role, as one American politician cruelly pointed out. Osborne's subsequent plays for Devine's Royal Court included *The Entertainer* (1958), *Luther* (1961), *Inadmissible Evidence* (1964) and *A Patriot For Me* (1965), in which Devine played his last acting role. Devine's death robbed Osborne of his most perceptive champion and while he has continued to write plays (*Déjà vu*, 1992), somewhat intermittently, the zest for battle that infused his early plays has become a more predictable tetchiness.

Osborne, however, was less of a rebel than Behan, Norman or Delaney, and a comparison between his themes and those of Rattigan reveals the continuity. Rattigan wrote about the theatre's seedy side (*Harlequinade*, 1948), as did Coward (*Red Peppers*, 1936) and Osborne (*The Entertainer*). Rattigan wrote about a soldier who was also a suppressed homosexual (*Ross*), as did Osborne (*A Patriot For Me*). Osborne tackled themes which were usually handled with discretion in the West End, but did so with an emotional boldness and lack of restraint. He enlarged what might have been human interest stories into parables for Britain.

It could be argued, however, that the real challenge to Aunt Edna's West End came from another direction. Beckett's *Waiting for Godot* was first produced at a small theatre club, the Arts, in 1955, but it transferred to the West End. It was received at first as an anti-religious allegory, with Godot as a diminutive of God, but gradually its other meanings became more apparent. Its denial of progress, its logical unreason and Beckett's playful contradiction of a 'crisis' which is not being faced up to made a profound impact on a theatre in which all crimes were supposed to be solvable and problems were rarely set to which there were no answers.

The British dramatist who most rapidly responded to the challenge of Beckett, though the influence may seem to be more superficial than profound, was Harold Pinter. Pinter's general debt can be seen by comparing his one-act play, *A Slight Ache* (1959), with the second part of Beckett's novel, *Molloy* (1951): one is like a dramatization of the other. But Pinter, who like Osborne was trained as an actor, was never a true absurdist and shied away from philosophical queries. His strength lay in writing naturalistic well-made plays in the British tradition, but with the certainties removed. In place of problems solved, he offered anxieties increased, and 'Pinteresque' dialogue, with long pauses and inconsequential replies, was widely imitated in the 1960s, although no other dramatist could match Pinter's precise theatrical instinct, his controlled alarm and knack for concealed threats.

His early plays, *The Room* (1957) and *The Birthday Party* (1958), were received with interest but without enthusiasm, apart from one review by the critic, Harold Hobson (1904–92), who prophetically declared that here was a 'first-class' new talent. *The Caretaker* (1960) was his first major success, a study of a tramp offered shelter by two brothers who employ him as a caretaker for their house. The title holds several layers of meaning. Who is taking care of what or whom? And are the brothers caring for or exploiting the 'caretaker'?

This kind of ambiguity became a feature of Pinter's writing. In *The Homecoming* (1965), there are many versions of 'home' and its ending, where the only woman in the house lets herself be established as a Soho call-girl, caused a scandal when the play was first performed by the RSC. But Pinter is not often a controversial writer in this sense. His plays are disturbing and thoughtful, not sensational, and *The Caretaker*, *The Homecoming*, *No Man's Land* (1975) and his later one-act plays, including *A Kind of Alaska* (1982), are among the most subtle, as well as the most enduring, of modern British drama.

Beckett and Pinter in their different ways undermined the underlying social confidence of the West End, but, in general, British theatre in the 1960s resisted the kind of absurdism or abstract non-logical drama associated with French, Polish or Romanian writers. Apart from relatively minor figures such as N.F. Simpson, Barry Bermange (b. 1933) and Stanley Eveling, absurdism has been more of a feature of fringe groups which emerged during the 1960s, than of its dramaturgy. Brecht's Epic Theatre made more of an impact, but its effect was more to loosen the bonds of the well-made play, and thus to provide a vehicle for documentary dramas with left-wing messages, than to offer the thinking man's socialist theatre of which Brecht might have approved.

In this sub-Brechtian vein, there were several notable achievements, such as *Oh! What a Lovely War* (1963), Joan Littlewood's concert party account of World War I, which set a pattern for local documentaries in repertory theatres around Britain; but Brecht's wider usefulness for British writers was to offer a stock of technical ideas, some workable and others not, which could be introduced piecemeal into the established traditions. Peter Shaffer's development illustrated this tendency.

Shaffer, whose twin brother Anthony (b. 1926) is also a writer, began by writing such stage plays as *Five Finger Exercise* (1958), which were well made and naturalistic, but his television scripts of the period (*The Salt Land*, 1955; *Balance of Terror*, 1957) reveal his longing to tackle epic subjects. His first major stage play in this vein was *The Royal Hunt of the Sun* (1964), based on William Prescott's (1796–1859) account of the Spanish conquest of Peru. John Dexter's NT production was highly influential, in that it demonstrated how an open stage, mime, and an effective use of dance, music and narration could provide a disciplined storytelling that could dispense with some of the well-made play rules. The episodic

nature of the adventure was contained within a formal contrast between the God-King, Atahuallpa, and the leader of the Spanish conquistadores, Pizarro, or 'instinct' versus 'logic'.

Similar oppositions provide the structures for his other best known dramas, including *Equus* (1973), *Amadeus* (1979) and *The Gift of the Gorgon* (1993), but *The Royal Hunt of the Sun* set the pattern for what was to become a feature of 1960s playwriting, a more ambitious use of the stage and of visual symbolism. This was demonstrated in two early plays by John Arden, *Serjeant Musgrave's Dance* (1959) and *Armstrong's Last Goodnight* (1964), but the new flexibility is better illustrated by the work of two writers, Peter Nichols (b. 1927) and Tom Stoppard, whose plays featured in the programmes of the two national companies, the RSC and the NT.

Nichols, often underrated, has two main theatrical styles, which might be dubbed 'intimate' and 'public'. He can write powerful domestic dramas, tightly knit, well made and naturalistic, of which the best known examples are *A Day in the Death of Joe Egg* (1967) and *Forget-me-not Lane* (1971), but his plays for the national companies were broad-ranging parables for our time or historical plays, such as *The National Health* (1969), *The Freeway* (1974) and *Privates on Parade* (1977). Stoppard's successes were more immediate. His first play, *Rosencrantz and Guildenstern Are Dead* (1966), was picked up by the NT from the Edinburgh Fringe Festival, where it was performed by a university company. This told the story of *Hamlet*, as seen through the uncomprehending eyes of the two courtiers; its British success was partly due to the way in which it represented the relative impotence of Britain in the Cold War. Stoppard defended liberal values, while noting that they were under threat from the outside world, comically vulnerable, as in *Jumpers* (1972), *Travesties* (1976) and *Arcadia* (1993); but his verbal wit and naggingly iconoclastic mind dazzled audiences more than his themes or ideas. Like other British dramatists, he came to be employed more as an adapter of other writers' plays (*On The Razzle*, 1981, from Johann Nestroy) than as an original playwright.

Christopher Hampton is another example of a dramatist who translated and adapted European plays for the national companies. His version of *Les Liaisons dangereuses* for the RSC is bettern known than his original plays, which include *Total Eclipse* (1968) and *Tales from Hollywood* (1983). The national companies offered dramatists the opportunity to adapt foreign classics and provided them with longer rehearsal periods, open stages and, for those lucky enough to be chosen, more opulent resources. A gap opened in the late 1960s and the 1970s between those plays intended for West End audiences, well made and traditional, and those for the major subsidized companies, which tended to be more cosmopolitan, expansive and innovative. Part of this state-subsidized radicalism was political. The RSC and the NT were both brought into being during a transition between Conservative and Labour administrations, while the English Stage Company considered itself to be by definition anti-establishment. The main subsidized 'new-plays' theatres all considered themselves to be left wing and a new wave of socialist dramatists emerged whose presences were felt even before the events of 1968 added an impetus to their cause.

Among the left-wing writers established in the mid-1960s were David Storey, David Rudkin, David Mercer and Edward Bond, while among those who found their voices with the student revolutionaries after 1968 were Trevor Griffiths, David Edgar (b. 1948), David Hare, Howard Brenton and Howard Barker. Of the former group, Mercer was the most funny, Rudkin the most poetic, Storey the most convincing in his naturalistic studies of northern British life (*The Restoration of Arnold Middleton*, 1967; *In Celebration*, 1969; *Home*, 1970) and Bond the most visionary. Bond's *Saved*, a bleak and terrifying study of south London life, in which a baby is stoned to death, connected street violence with the effects of capitalism; his later plays come close to justifying terrorism as the solution to class warfare.

Violence, which socialist writers of another generation (such as Wesker) would have regarded with horror, became a feature of the new wave. In Brenton's *Magnificence* (1973), young terrorists plot to blow up a cabinet minister, while his *The Romans in Britain* (1980), which drew a parallel between the Roman invasion of Britain and British troops in Northern Ireland, was shocking in another way, by presenting buggery on the NT's stage for the first time. Of the latter group, Hare is the most polished and writes witty, drawing-room dramas with left-wing messages (*Plenty*, 1983; *The Secret Rapture*, 1988), Edgar the most prolific and inclined towards Brechtian epics (*Maydays*, 1983) and Barker the most demonic, black, angry and obscure. Griffiths is the most politically correct and writes naturalistic well-made plays. His *Comedians* (1975) is a telling analysis of the racism and sexism in popular humour, but other plays debate searchingly the directions which the socialist movement should take (*Occupations*, 1970; *The Party*, 1973).

This left-wing dominance had certain consequences. Some talented writers did not fit into either the West End or the subsidized sector and were accordingly neglected, like Nichols or older dramatists like Bill Naughton, John Mortimer (b. 1923) and Keith Waterhouse (b. 1929). While the national companies may have seemed more cosmopolitan, the world-view presented through their new play programmes was rather odd. Judging from Edgar's *Maydays*, Brenton's *Weapon of Happiness* (1976) or Griffiths's film *Fatherland* (1986), eastern Europe under communism was the repository of civilized values, despite its economic backwardness, whereas the west disguised its facism behind a consumerist façade. The collapse of international communism and the discovery of what life was actually like behind the former Iron Curtain meant that several plays hailed as masterpieces in the 1970s were revealed to be at best prejudiced and parochial. It is hard to read Hare's *Fanshen* (1976) without a painful smile.

The election of the Conservatives under Margaret Thatcher in 1979 hastened the transformation of mood. Her government did not cut subsidies, as expected, but managements were urged to seek commercial sponsorship and to enter into partnership with private impresarios for support. Consequently, some of the creativity was diverted towards the production of major musicals for the West End and its tourists, while young writers had to be content with seeing their work on smaller rather than larger stages. With a few exceptions, the young dramatists who emerged during the 1980s lacked not only the political causes which enthused the previous generation but the production opportunities as well. Especially unlucky in this respect were Stephen Poliakoff and Robert Holman, who saw their plays repeatedly staged in studios, without often making the grade to the main stages.

If the socialist theatre of the 1970s represented a form of modernism, the postmodernism of the 1980s has been marked by disillusion and political correctness, rather than the quest for utopia. The plays of Martin Crimp (b. 1956) and Nick Dear (b. 1955) are acidly witty, commenting on a Thatcherite Britain with disdain. Caryl Churchill's *Serious Money* (1987) derided the get-rick-quick society of the

Playwright Caryl Churchill.

Stock Exchange. Churchill was a left-wing writer whose first plays (*Owners*, 1972; *A Light Shining in Buckinghamshire*, 1976) were performed in the mid-1970s, but who survived the turmoils of the 1980s with conviction. With *Cloud Nine* (1979) and *Top Girls* (1982), she became a leader of a small but convincingly talented group of women who were dubbed by journalists as feminist. This also included Pam Gems (b. 1925) and Timberlake Wertenbaker, whose *Our Country's Good* (1988) and *Three Birds Alighting in a Field* (1991) convincingly bridged the ideological gaps between the left-wing Royal Court and the West End.

As a result of the cooperation between the public and private sectors, it could be argued that the differences in the programming apparent in the 1970s and early 1980s started to disappear. The subsidized companies became more populist, while the commercial impresarios were readier to take shared gambles. The popular northern playwrights – Willy Russell (b. 1947), Alan Bleasdale (b. 1946), John Godber (b. 1956) and Jim Cartwright (b. 1958) – found their places in the West End, television or the national companies, where the deals were most attractive. The argument in favour of Richard Eyre's NT, as opposed to Hall's or Olivier's, was that neither intellectual nor social snobbery ever stopped the public from having a good time. The argument against it was that its play policies could barely be distinguished from those which might have been provided by any other impresario backed by £10 million in public money. Within this newly ecumenical establishment, the traditional virtues of British theatre surfaced once more, although they had never been fully submerged.

The fact that Ayckbourn, Frayn, Gray and Bennett write well-made comedies and dramas in a genre that has flourished for a century is less important perhaps than that they do so very well. Ayckbourn is not only the most prolific comedy writer in British theatrical history, with around fifty plays to his credit, but also one of the most subtle and versatile writers in any genre. *The Norman Conquests* (1973) is an intricate trilogy which so observes the unities that the three plays take place in the same house over the same weekend but in different rooms. *Joking Apart* (1979), *Suburban Strains* (1981) and *Invisible Friends* (1991) reveal the dark side to his talents, the sense of loss and loneliness that haunts even his apparently most light-hearted scripts. He is a convincing student of human nature and, as a director and actor as well, he lays claim to being the most versatile man of the theatre in Britain.

Frayn's most successful comedy was the farce, *Noises Off* (1982), but, like Ayckbourn, the range of his work is belied by the fame of this single hit. *Clouds* (1976) is a perceptive study of journalists in Cuba observing and reporting only on what they want to see. Gray is less wedded to comedy than other writers in the group and is the most obvious successor to Rattigan, but with less snobbery. His *Quartermaine's Terms* (1981) has much in common with *The Browning Version*, while *The Common Pursuit* (1984) is a telling study of how the fortunes of some assorted Oxbridge arts graduates changed over their careers and lifetimes.

The strength of these dramatists lies not so much in their originality, although they can be innovative, as in the assured command of their medium. There are few dead lines in an Ayckbourn play and you do not find half-drawn characters littering the stage carelessly. Of the group, Bennett has a distinct command of ironic nuance and his *A Question of Attribution* (1988) is memorable as an essay in the art of one-upmanship, in which the Queen gets the better of Sir Anthony Blunt, art connoisseur, spy and keeper of the Queen's pictures.

This enjoyable play illustrates the strengths and the limits of the well-made play genre. The control over language and diction is expressive in itself, an elegant discipline that allows wit and careful observation of manners to emerge in a heightened form. But Blunt was a traitor whose activities could have destroyed or damaged the country. *A Question of Attribution* seems to be more concerned with treachery as a human weakness and as a failure in manners, than as an act of war.

It has been said that talent is the death of genius and few countries can boast of so many talented dramatists as Britain has discovered since the 1940s. This is an impressive achievement which spans many communities, age groups and classes. What British theatre lacks, however, is a sense of philosophical depth, of urgency, of compulsion. That was Osborne's great, and perhaps his only, strength. Plays are too neatly written to fit the demands of the impresarios and the tastes of their audiences. A professionalism, admirable in itself, obscures the passion to be profound or even honest. British theatre thrives as much on its limitations as its strengths, but that was always so, even in the days of Shakespeare.

Directors, Directing and Production Styles

For a discussion of directing, see previous material in **Artistic Profile** and the opening, historical section.

John Elsom

Music Theatre

The text-based traditions of British theatre have been shaken but not shattered by attempts in recent years to raise the status of the differing elements within the dramatic whole, among them music. With opera maintaining its cultural significance independent of major developments in the theatre, the two forms have remained quite separate. It is, however, the case that most of the innovative directors and designers of the post-war theatre have worked occasionally and often extensively in the opera house, from Peter Hall and Peter Brook in the 1950s and 1960s to Richard Jones and Tim Albery in the 1980s and 1990s. The large classical companies, the Royal National Theatre and the Royal Shakespeare Company, are committed to live music and have developed a number of talented composers, although often providing an incidental rather than integral contribution to the overall performance and production. Thus composers like the former National Theatre head of music Dominic Muldowney, or the Royal Shakespeare Company's Stephen Oliver, eventually both turned to the opera houses to create their major works.

The cost of producing theatre with music, even at a modest scale, has limited musical developments for some companies, although the potential of electronic instruments to provide the scale of effects required without prohibitive salary and transportation costs has inspired some new work. One feature of the burgeoning fringe theatre in the 1970s was a desire to utilize music, particularly folk or contemporary popular song, as an asset for socialist-inspired companies. In the 1980s performance art-influenced groups often used existing or specially composed music as an element equal to or surpassing the status of the spoken word.

Rock music made forays into theatrical form, particularly where the pretensions of its performers transcended concert presentation and demanded ever more sophisticated staging.

From one-off events to full-scale musicals, notably *Tommy* by the rock group The Who, these were a regular – if sometimes variable in quality – feature in the careers of ambitious bands or solo artists.

It remains the case, however, that commercial musical theatre is the most significant art form of the period to combine these two elements. It is the only genre to depend on music for its effect, and accounts for the largest volume of theatregoing as well as the longest-running entertainments.

When assessing the developments and current state of the British musical there are two names that cannot be ignored – Trevor Nunn and Andrew Lloyd Webber. Lloyd Webber's successes have been marked by shrewd use of the pop business, with pre-released singles establishing the songs well beyond the intended theatre audience. The 1980s saw a complementary development with the establishment theatre taking the previously little-regarded genre seriously. Thus the world-wide hit *Les Misérables* by Alain Boublil and Claude-Michel Schönberg was originally produced in London by the Royal Shakespeare Company, and a long-awaited staging of Frank Loesser's Broadway hit *Guys and Dolls* appeared at the National Theatre.

A director from the establishment theatre can now have his or her name linked with commercial musicals. After years of working in the classics, Trevor Nunn staged one of the most financially lucrative musicals of all time – Lloyd Webber's *Cats*. After this initial success, Nunn and Lloyd Webber, in various collaborations, have been responsible for virtually all the international British musical smash hits, from *The Phantom of the Opera* to *Evita* and *Chess*. These works – though of questionable lasting significance – have been skilfully marketed and have enjoyed world-wide success.

Carl Miller

The 1993 Young Vic Youth Theatre production of Euan Smith and David Roper's *Promised Land*.
Photo: Gordon Rainsford.

Dance Theatre

In the theatre of late-twentieth-century Britain, dance theatre implies a genre in which the meaning of the danced work predominates over the danced element alone. The American choreographer Merce Cunningham and the English choreographer Richard Alston (b. 1948) both advocated, however, that dance be performed as movement for its own sake. In opposition to them the English choreographers Kenneth Mac-Millan (1929–92) and Christopher Bruce (b. 1945) and choreographers of musicals and music theatre like Gillian Lynne (b. 1926) advocated that narrative meaning or emotion should be conveyed through dancing. Thus there are two forms of dance theatre: the subsidized dance form (ballet or contemporary dance), which presents meaning through dance without words, and the commercial dance form (musical or music theatre), which presents its meaning through a combination of such elements as dance, words and scenery. Criticism emphasizes this distinction, with subsidized dance judged by a dance critic, and the commercial form judged by a drama critic.

Today's dance theatre – irrespective of form – is rooted in French seventeenth-century *ballet de cour* and the English Stuart *masque* where words and elaborate scenery dominated. The latter vanished with the elimination of absolute monarchy in seventeenth-century England, but in France the words and music developed into opera while the dance and music became classical ballet. In popular theatre music, speech, song, dance and design combined into the extravaganzas of the Alhambra and Empire theatres in central London and remain united in the pantomimes of today.

The essence of music theatre, therefore, lies in communication and appeal – elements seen in the modern or 'free' dance of central Europe pioneered by Rudolf Laban and Kurt Jooss. Laban brought the principles of this dance to the UK, exerting a profound influence in education from the 1940s onwards, and Jooss – with his assistant Sigurd Leeder – influenced the theatre, most notably with his dance drama *The Green Table* first seen in Paris in 1932. From 1939 to 1950 the Jooss–Leeder experience trained a generation of British dancers and dance directors, including Peter Wright (b. 1926), director of the Birmingham Royal Ballet, and dancers who entered music theatre or musicals.

This emphasis on meaning and communication informed the work of contemporary dance pioneers in the United States, from Isadora Duncan and Martha Graham to today's British form of Graham dance theatre, the London Contemporary Dance Theatre Company, founded in 1967. Subsidized dance theatre in the UK in the 1990s thus comprises choreographic influences from Diaghilev and the Russian classic tradition, central Europe and the United States, always aiming to convey meaning without the use of words. Examples include Kenneth MacMillan's *Mayerling* (1978) for the Royal Ballet, Christopher Bruce's *Swansong* (1987) for the English National Ballet, and David Bintley's *Hobson's Choice* (1989) for the Birmingham Royal Ballet.

British dance theatre in its commercial form descends from English musical comedy after World War I. Shows like *Rose Marie* (1925) and *Showboat* included dance, spectacular effects and songs. In the 1930s and 1940s this formula combined with other influences from the United States (*Oklahoma*, 1943; *Carousel*, 1945), professional classical dance, strong plots and quality music. The combination of words, songs, dance, design and a social message were choreographed by Agnes De Mille (b. 1909), who studied with Ballet Rambert and Antony Tudor in London.

British music theatre developed a strong home tradition of style, local colour and integrated plot, words, music, design and dance. Examples include *The Boy Friend* (1953), *My Fair Lady* (1956) and *Oliver!* (1960). In the 1960s and 1970s the cultural influence of flower power and rock musical productions like the American *Hair* (1967), and the growth of rebel rock were reflected in shows like *Joseph and His Amazing Technicolour Dreamcoat* (1968) and *Cats* (1981). *Cats*, with its emphasis on danced story, was choreographed by Gillian Lynne, who had trained with Sadler's Wells Ballet. Through her, and others like her, the two wings of British music theatre – the commercial and the subsidized – have come together. The former, once despised, is now rated equal to the latter, and all major dance schools (including the Royal Ballet School, London Contemporary Dance School and the Laban Centre for Movement and Dance) prepare some of their students for a career in popular music theatre. There are, however, specialist schools offering training in drama and singing as well as dance specifically for commercial music theatre. Leading schools are the London Studio Centre, Doreen Bird College, and Laine Theatre Arts.

Peter Brinson

Theatre for Young Audiences

In the UK, theatre for young audiences includes young people's theatre (sometimes known as educational theatre), theatre-in-education (TiE), children's theatre and youth theatre. Although these are distinct traditions, the terms are fluid and one company may undertake several different types of work.

The Arts Council of Great Britain also recognizes puppetry and individual theatre performances by building-based companies which appeal to children, such as plays that appear on examination syllabuses.

The growth of theatre performances as a social and educational force for young people is largely a post-war phenomenon. Until then theatre for the young tended to concentrate on the literary classics within the context of English teaching. From 1945 onward, Britain saw a growing acceptance of theatre in many forms as a valuable tool for the educational and spiritual development of young people. This, coupled with local authorities' new powers under the Education Act of 1944, resulted in extra funding for theatre designed for young audiences.

Initially two groups led the way – the Young Vic and the Glyndebourne Company, the latter hired by local education authorities. In 1948 Caryl Jenner (1917–73) founded the Unicorn Theatre for Children, which still thrived in the 1990s. Over time, trained actors adapted to their new role as teachers, instructing through their acting skills.

An important stimulus in the 1950s was the appointment of county drama advisers, first funded by the Carnegie UK Trust, a charitable trust which, since 1913, has been supporting community services, arts and conservation projects. The drama advisers were able to assume the responsibility of theatre for school children. The relative autonomy of local education authorities, then and now, accounts for the peculiar patchwork of provision across the UK.

Another important development was the establishment of the Theatre Centre in 1953 by Brian Way, who researched and developed new methods for providing theatre for young people.

In 1958 Coventry was the first city to build a municipal theatre, the Belgrade. Supporters of children's theatre had been lobbying the Arts Council to increase funding for regional theatres to enable them to set up small companies to play to children. In 1965 Coventry provided a direct subsidy for the Belgrade to enlist a group of actors to perform in local schools. The experiment was called 'theatre-in-education': the name has stuck and groups have multiplied, with performances developing into workshops. By the 1970s, graduates of further education colleges and drama schools provided the labour for these TiE companies.

TiE work aims to use theatre and drama to create a range of learning activities across the whole curriculum. The actor-teachers use teaching methodology within the context of the performance, utilizing Augusto Boal's technique of forum theatre where the action of the play is halted to enable the audience to discuss a particular issue. Noteworthy groups have included Belgrade TiE, Pit-Prop and Leeds TiE.

Young people's theatre differs in that a performance by professional actors is used to some educational end, either in a school or any other forum where young people make up the audience. The audiences are usually of secondary school age (11–18) and performances are based on social themes.

Children's theatre, in comparison, primarily seeks to entertain and increase children's appreciation of the theatre as an art form. Many children's dramatists, such as David Wood (b. 1944), also write for television and adult writers are increasingly encouraged to write for children, for example, Alan Ayckbourn's *Invisible Friends* (1991).

Since 1990 the Royal National Theatre has offered a permanent mainhouse production for children in its repertory. There is also a Children's Theatre Association with some sixty members, and an international grouping (ASSITEJ) with 150 members from the UK.

Youth theatre is theatre performed by young people themselves. There are an estimated 6,000 young people (aged 15–25) in 700 youth

Children's theatre at the 1992 Edinburgh Festival Fringe.
Photo: Iain Stewart.

theatres throughout the UK. The National Youth Theatre was founded in 1956 by Michael Croft (1922–86) against the hostility of Youth Services, which favoured multipurpose projects and felt that young people should not perform in public. Today the National Youth Theatre has some 2,500 applicants per year and derives its funding from private sponsorship. In the 1960s similar ventures were set up in the regions and a National Association of Youth Theatres exists to coordinate and promote this work.

Although direct funding of youth theatre falls outside the Arts Council's terms, in 1984 the council participated in the establishment of the New Initiatives Fund, supported by the charitable trusts, the Calouste Gulbenkian Foundation and Paul Hamlyn Foundation. The scheme finances innovative new youth theatre projects and is proof of a growing commitment to theatre for young audiences in the UK.

David Prosser

Puppet Theatre

In the early part of the twentieth century puppetry fell into a decline alongside the growth of cinema, but the 1950s and 1960s saw puppetry reclaiming its place in British theatre. There have been vast developments in style and the use of materials, and puppeteers have chosen to follow diverse avenues in pursuit of their art.

The traditional Punch and Judy show suffered most from the advent of television and cinema.

Punch and Judy 'professors' performed mainly at fairs, with the art handed down through families, but in the 1950s, as television stole popular entertainment, it was a dying art. In the 1960s, however, it became fashionable for middle-class families to hire Punch and Judy shows for children's parties and local authorities booked shows in parks. With the opening of the Covent Garden Piazza in London for street entertainment in the 1970s, Punch and Judy professors gained a permanent performing site, and the Punch and Judy Fellowship was founded in 1980 as a focus for performers. Percy Press was the best-known professor, performing on Hastings Pier every summer until his death in 1980. The violence and sexism of the show is increasingly questioned, and performers now omit the black puppet while producing a fast-moving, comic-grotesque show with audience/puppet interaction.

In Britain the television industry has provided continuing employment for puppeteers since the war. On 20 October 1946 the marionette, Muffin the Mule, appeared on BBC television for the first time, created and operated by Ann Hogarth of Hogarth Puppets, a well-known touring company. Eight years of success for Muffin encouraged programmers to include more puppets on screen throughout the 1950s and 1960s. Some of these are now considered classics of early British children's television: Andy Pandy, Bill and Ben, the Magic Roundabout, and Sooty and Sweep.

Puppetry was also used as a tool for education, due to the efforts of the British Puppet and Model Theatre Guild (founded in 1925 by W.H. Whanslaw and Gerald Morice) and the Educational Puppetry Association (founded in 1943 by A.R. Philpott, a puppeteer known as Pantopuck).

The advancement of film and television technology extended to puppets, and a series of television programmes with mechanical puppets appeared on the screens, for example *Thunderbirds* and *Supercar* by Garry Anderson. During the 1950s and 1960s variety, ventriloquist and music hall performers used puppets in their acts, as in the shows of Peter Brough (with Archie Andrews) and Rod Hull's Emu.

Since the late 1970s new techniques have developed known as animatronics and supermarionation, where puppets are controlled, from inside or outside, by computer-linked programmes. The Henson Organization, founded by the American Jim Henson (1936–90), creator of *The Muppets*, mastered this technique and, though originally from the USA, the organization has had considerable influence on British television puppetry. It clearly influenced Fluck and Law who created the 1980s satirical adult puppet show, *Spitting Image*, which uses latex caricatures of public personalities. The American film *Teenage Mutant Ninja Turtles* was a 1990s example of animatronics.

Unlike state-funded puppet theatre in eastern Europe, puppetry in Britain has always been a struggling art and so is characterized by small companies. John Wright, a travelling South African puppeteer, arrived in Britain in 1946 and established the famous Little Angel Theatre in London in 1961. The Norwich Puppet Theatre (founded in 1980), Midland Arts Centre, Polka Children's Theatre and the Garratt Mask and Puppet Centre in Glasgow (founded in 1987) are key puppet venues which use a wide range of techniques from string-marionettes, glove-puppets and rod-puppets to black theatre and ultra-violet lighting techniques. All perform for children. John Blundall, at the Midlands Arts Centre in Birmingham, adopted artistic trends from eastern Europe. Jane Philipps, in Cardiff starting in 1965, was interested in native cultural traditions; her production of *Pilgrim's Progress* (1967) by John Bunyan was an excellent example of multimedia theatre. Barry Smith (d. 1989), who founded Theatre of Puppets in 1969, undertook much

The Norwich Puppet Theatre's 1993 *Harlequin in Trouble.*
Photo: Stephen Lorenc.

puppet work for adults. Most notable was his production of Christopher Marlowe's (1564–93) *Dr Faustus* with glove-puppets.

During the 1970s in Britain there was a revival of community celebration in theatre and two important groups have survived: Welfare State International and Horse and Bamboo, both based in northern England. In 1987 Faulty Optic was formed by Liz Walker and Gavin Glover to explore 'the weird and grotesque' through the use of surrealist sets and objects. Their experimental work has received international acclaim.

The Puppet Centre in Battersea, London (founded in 1974) is the reference point for British puppetry and is the UK centre of UNIMA (International Puppeteers Union). During the 1980s funding for puppetry was severely cut, and the future of the centre was uncertain into the 1990s.

British puppeteers today are less challenging and experimental than their European counterparts, and the mediocre repetition of classical fairytales is dogging the trade. Britain is one of the few European countries which has no university course in puppetry. In 1990 a conference examined the possibility of establishing a three-year training course, but without funding for the course the future looks set to leave British puppetry lagging behind.

Caroline Astles

Design
Theatre Space and Architecture

Since British theatre is itself a hybrid of nineteenth-century conventions, European experimentalism and a reworking of ideas from Graeco-Roman classical origins, its theatrical architecture has also produced a variety of performance spaces – proscenium arch, thrust, traverse and 'in-the-round' stages, in large and small, conventional and deliberately unconventional theatres, ranging from major opera houses to wagons, tents, factories and dockyards. The economic pressures of the times have also influenced design and some makeshift theatres have survived better than more elaborate and costly ones.

Until the mid-1960s, most British theatres were built on the nineteenth-century town model, sited on relatively small plots of land and therefore built tall. Each would have several circles or galleries and a proscenium arch placed high in one wall for easy visibility, providing a picture frame through which the events on stage could be seen. Continental single-tier seating was at that time rare in Britain, as were cycloramas in the style of Adolphe Appia, but most stages had good if antiquated machinery for hoisting flats, revolves or sub-stage lifts. The Victorian equipment installed beneath the stage at the Theatre Royal, Drury Lane, London, for spectaculars can still be seen in its complicated glory.

Most set designers in the immediate post-war period were therefore accustomed to designing box sets for proscenium arch stages, where there could be set changes between scenes and acts, but where the fluid transformations of the stage picture were rarely used and expensive. Among these designers, Cecil Beaton and Oliver Messel were pre-eminent. Both were as much concerned with films and fashion as with the theatre. Beaton was a society photographer whose flamboyant costumes and sets for *Lady Windermere's Fan* (1946) and *My Fair Lady* (1958) provided a dash of romantic nostalgia to a Britain under austerity.

As part of post-war reconstruction, some city centres were being rebuilt after the Blitz and new theatres were included in the plans. The Belgrade Theatre, Coventry, which opened in 1958, was the first of these, an austerity model with a traditional hall and proscenium arch stage, but an untraditional regard for community involvement, including a foyer for school children's artwork. Over the next twenty years, many civic theatres and arts centres were built with similar aims but a more adventurous use of space. The director, Tyrone Guthrie (1900–71), was one of the first to call for open stages and his makeshift production of *The Three Estates* (at the Edinburgh International Festival, 1948) became a small landmark in the history of British stage and theatre design. Because there was no theatre suitable for Sir Robert Lindsay's (*c*.1500–*c*.65) Medieval Morality play, Guthrie decided to stage it in the Assembly Hall of the Church of Scotland: the effects of using a large open stage (a debating hall) with the audience surrounding the actors on three sides so pleased him that he wanted to use similar configurations for Shakespearian and classical productions. This type of thrust stage inspired the building of the Stratford Festival Theatre in Ontario, Canada, which began in 1953, the Guthrie Theatre in Minneapolis, USA (1963) and, in Britain, the theatres at Chichester (1962), Sheffield (the Crucible, 1971) and Leeds (the Playhouse, 1970).

A large open stage, though much changed from the Guthrie model, was also planned for the new National Theatre complex on the South Bank of the Thames, designed in the late 1960s by the architect Sir Denys Lasdun (b. 1914) and finally completed in 1976. The Olivier Theatre in the NT complex was inspired partly by the ancient Greek theatre at Epidaurus, although Lasdun likened its auditorium to an 'armchair', 'hugging' the open stage. Certainly, the severe lines of the Edinburgh Assembly Hall or the somewhat dogmatic arena-shaped open stage of Chichester have been left behind. The other NT theatres have different configurations. The Lyttleton has a proscenium arch stage and a rather plain auditorium with continental seating, while the Cottesloe is like a large 'black box' studio, flexible in its staging and seating, and can be used for in-the-round, 'end-stage' or 'promenade' productions. The NT, like the RSC's Barbican Theatre, which opened in 1983, was intended to be equipped with the latest and best stage equipment. The computerized lighting board in the Olivier and the sound systems throughout the complex were well in advance of the stage technology elsewhere and worked from the beginning, but the 'spot-line' flying system in the Olivier and the large revolving split-level stage proved unreliable and to some extent unnecessary. They were intended to shift around large built sets, but by the time the new NT complex had been completed, such sets had become unfashionable.

Changes in the aesthetics of set design began in the 1950s. While Beaton and Messel were lavishly adorning West End stages, a young designer recently demobbed from the army, John Bury (b. 1925), was building three-dimensional constructs for Joan Littlewood at the Theatre Royal in East London from objects found in scrap-yards. He had no alternative. Littlewood's company had no money to spend on sets in the mid-1950s, but Bury built effective naturalistic images from bricks, wooden frames and scrap-metal.

Whether he intended to or not, Bury broke a 'glamour' barrier in set design. Sets were no longer expected to look expensive: they could look rough, street-wise and casual. In time, this style spread to the auditoriums as well, so that some of the new theatres provided a classless image suitable for the politics of the mid-1960s, with Harold Wilson's Labour government in office. A director, Stephen Joseph (1927–65), pioneered theatre-in-the-round in which stage props took the place of sets in an open arena, where the public sat on all four sides of the stage, and not simply on three, as in the Guthrie-style theatres. The Studio Theatre in Scarborough, later to be run by the actor-dramatist Alan Ayckbourn and renamed the Stephen Joseph Theatre, and the Victoria Theatre, Stoke-on-Trent, were important regional in-the-round theatres.

Under these new conditions, lavish scenery was less valuable than the telling but authentic object, selected by a keen social observer (such as Bury) and during the 1960s, many 'black box' studios were established around Britain, sometimes in disused brothels, such as the Traverse Theatre, Edinburgh, in its first Royal Mile home, and sometimes in the function rooms of pubs (such as the Bush Theatre in London). Whereas the little theatre movement of the 1940s and 1950s usually tried to imitate the West End, the fringe and alternative theatres of the 1960s explored their differences from the normal theatregoing experiences, sometimes plunging their audiences into 'total' theatre (where the public was surrounded by theatrical effects) or by staging plays in old industrial buildings, such as the Victorian train-dock in Camden Town which became known as the Roundhouse.

The 1980 *Alternative Theatre Guide* listed no fewer than 319 such alternative spaces around Britain, together with seventy-four performance spaces in community arts centres, although these numbers had dwindled by the early 1990s. Bury, who was the head of stage design at the RSC from 1963 to 1973 and at the NT from 1973 to 1985, not only introduced new materials into stage design but discovered a way of handling natural objects in a manner both realistic and abstract. Not the least of his influences lay in his stress upon the visual logic of stage proportions, so that each part of the cubic space was in use. This led to such startling sets as Sally Jacobs's (b. 1932) metallic gymnasium for Peter Brook's *A Midsummer Night's Dream*; but in the early 1960s, it was her colleague at Littlewood's Theatre Royal, the architect Sean Kenny (1932–73), who most attracted public attention.

In contrast to Bury's, Kenny's sets were complicated constructions that tended to fill the cubic stage area with many small stages and playing levels. The house in Brendan Behan's *The Hostage* (1958) was one example, but the massive revolving construction which dominated the Lionel Bart musical *Oliver!* (1960) or the underground station used as an air-raid shelter in Bart's *Blitz!* (1962) were more startling. Kenny brought a new sense of physical movement to set design. He loathed box sets and picture-frame theatres; in 1967, he delivered a paper on *The Visual Concept and the New Theatre* in which he claimed that

> the entire space should be always fluid, always flexible. A space that you couldn't even call a theatre until these boys came in and started to do something and then it would become a theatre...we need a clean white canvas place, in which we can begin to tell a story.... There should be no architectural statements made before we begin, no statements at all.

This sounded odd from a designer who tended to put more objects on the stage than anyone else, but it was in line with the view expressed by Peter Brook in *The Empty Space* (1968) and with the dramaturgical theories current at the time. It led, however, not only to the kind of improvised playing in various spaces, which characterized Brook's Centre for International Theatre Research in Paris, where a quarry would do as well as a tram-shed to stage *The Mahabharata* (1985), but also to the rapid growth of official non-theatres, playing spaces specifically chosen because nobody could confuse them with real theatres, such as dockyards and demolition dumps.

The revolt against theatricality was also expressed in the elaborately functional surfaces that characterized the new wave of British repertory theatres. Lasdun's NT was likened by one democratically elected councillor to the Greater London Council to a 'concrete bunker', whose concession to decoration lay in the woodgrained concrete blocks turning white with age.

Such modernist minimalism came at a convenient time for the growing fringe theatre movement, for so few resources were required

Richard Hudson's design for Jonathan Miller's 1988 Old Vic production of Leonard Bernstein's *Candide*.
Photo: Simon Annand.

to stage a play. Under the influence of the happenings movement, a play could be any place, any time and (it should perhaps be added) anything. But this ultimate form of free expression had its disadvantages. The RSC's Studio Theatre at Stratford may have been, as the critic Michael Billington (b. 1939) remarked, 'the most productive tin shed in history', but it seated only 140 people in any comfort. Makeshift theatres might be easy to build, but they are not necessarily cheap to run. Fifteen years after its establishment in the 'functions' room of a pub, the Bush Theatre (seating 100) was receiving an annual subsidy of more than £100,000, while the RSC's mix of conventional, unconventional and makeshift theatres would have required uncommon organizational skill to be handled cost-effectively.

There was an aesthetic argument against the makeshift theatres, 'empty spaces', of the late 1960s and 1970s. All formal theatres of whatever design carry with them visual and acoustic 'languages', which encourage their publics to look in certain directions and to cut out distractions. The sightlines of the Victorian town theatres and the acoustic properties of the ceiling were among the architects' prime considerations, as a study of the theatres of C.J. Phipps (1835–97) or Frank Matcham would reveal. But in the makeshift theatres there were no such refinements unless they happened by accident. A vast battery of lights and an elaborate amplification system had to be brought into the Avignon quarry where Brook staged *The Mahabharata*, and loudspeakers were often expected to overcome poor acoustics by sheer volume. They did not compensate for the loss of subtlety from the spoken, non-amplified voice. Companies using makeshift stages needed luck, directors sensitive to places and able to improvise solutions to unusual problems and, at best, elaborate technical equipment. Even the RSC's cut-down productions, such as its *Richard III* (1991), intended to tour school halls cheaply, were accompanied by a caravan of lorries with high-tech equipment.

The weakness of the old Roundhouse, London's equivalent to the Mickery Theatre in Amsterdam, and for which there is still understandable nostalgia, was that it had no focal point and poor acoustics, with the result that audiences did not know where to look or what to hear. It was seen at its best for such companies as Jérôme Savary's Grand Magic Circus, but when the experienced theatre administrator, Thelma Holt, took charge of it in the late 1970s,

she turned it into a normal theatre-in-the-round, replacing charm and novelty with a more functional theatrical space.

When the RSC replaced the Other Place with a new studio theatre in 1991, the New Other Place (architect: Michael Reardon), it reverted to a more conventional plan with more seats (260) and better technical facilities; but its most startling success in theatre building came with the Swan, a reconstruction of an Elizabethan playhouse (architects: Michael Reardon and John Napier), which opened in 1986 and proved itself to be more sympathetic to Elizabethan and Jacobean plays than its modern competitors.

As the makeshift theatres of the 1960s started to fall out of fashion during the 1980s, so did another feature of the post-war theatre reconstruction, the presence of large, purpose-built, civic repertory theatres. The rise in oil prices in 1973 made several of them singularly expensive to heat and run, while the emphasis in Margaret Thatcher's Britain (1979–90) was upon partnerships with the private sector and with business sponsors. Commercial touring and transfers to the West End took precedence over providing a well-balanced repertoire to the local community, the 'library' of good plays, which was the aim of the repertory movement.

As a result, the remaining Victorian town theatres, which had been badly neglected during the 1960s and 1970s, and even knocked down to make way for development schemes (as was the case with the Lyric Theatre, Hammersmith) came to be restored. The Belfast Opera House and Richmond Theatre (both designed by Matcham) were lovingly returned to their former glories, only (in the case of the former) to be bombed out of them again. In contrast, the plain and functional façades of the civic reps at Nottingham, Coventry and Colchester, trendleaders in their times, started to look not just old-fashioned but rather dowdy. The NT's complex on the South Bank, whose campaign for establishment began in the 1830s and was completed only in the 1970s, turned out to be in one sense the first and last of its kind, although the RSC's Barbican Theatre was placed within an even more grandiose modernist development.

Post-modernism in the British context has thus meant the restoration of old buildings and the revival of old theatre stocks-in-trade, such as companies touring Shakespeare and musicals. None the less, the variety of possible theatres has been greatly enlarged since World War II, with modernist and makeshift buildings jostling for recognition with arts centres in old churches,

The Royal Shakespeare Company's Swan Theatre Auditorium, Stratford-upon-Avon.
Photo: Simon McBride.

maltings and warehouses, and with restored Victorian and even Georgian theatres (such as Bath's Theatre Royal).

This diversity has been reflected in stage design. There may not seem to be too much difference between John Napier's set for Victorian London in *Nicholas Nickleby* (1980) and Kenny's *Oliver!*, both being large and complicated, but whereas the latter filled the stage, the former filled the entire theatre. If there is one predominating aesthetic theory within modern set design, it could be summarized in the Brechtian phrase of 'rich minimalism', a careful selection of props, objects and costumes which collectively provide a framework of imagery for the production. Such designers as Farrah (b. 1926), born in Algeria and an associate artist of the RSC, have brought an instinct for oriental exoticism to British theatre, which influenced such designers as Ultz, Timothy O'Brien and Napier. Rich minimalism characterized the little theatres that emerged at the end of the 1980s,

such as the Gate Theatre, whose director Stephen Daldry became the artistic director of the Royal Court in 1993, and of small touring companies such as Cheek by Jowl, whose main designer, Nick Ormrod, was joint artistic director with Declan Donnellan.

At the other end of the scale, however, is what might be dubbed the 'maximalism' of the grand musicals, such as *Cats* (1981, designed by Napier), *The Phantom of the Opera* (1986, designed by Maria Bjornson) and *Miss Saigon* (1989, designed by Napier). In *Starlight Express* (1984), Napier designed a wrap-around-the-punters roller-skating track; indeed, it may be a kind of reflection on post-modern theatre that Laurence Olivier's last West End appearance should be as a hologram in the musical *Time* (1986). The sophistication of modern theatre technology, led by a company established in the 1960s, Theatre Projects, has transformed the opportunities of theatres, large and small, across Britain. While good and ambitious design may not necessarily result in good productions, it does at least provide directors with a range of possibilities for them to explore, if imaginatively they are capable of doing so. The achievements of British theatre design have resulted from a mixture of innovation, inherited skills and imaginative speculation; and have enhanced poor and rich theatres alike. They have contributed in a major way to the renaissance of British theatre after World War II.

John Keefe,
with additions by John Elsom

Training

There are fifty-four drama schools in the UK, of which sixteen belong to the Conference of Drama Schools (CDS). Twenty-three universities have graduate and post-graduate drama departments. The CDS contains such famous institutions as the Royal Academy of Dramatic Art (RADA), the London Academy of Music and Dramatic Art, the Guildhall School of Music and Drama and the Central School of Speech and Drama (all in London) and the Bristol Old Vic Theatre School, the Royal Scottish Academy of Music and Drama and the Welsh College of Music and Drama. It has been argued that too many young people train for the theatre, which helps to explain the high unemployment rate among actors, but in this system, wastage is not always what it seems. Many of those trained to be actors become teachers, social workers or broadcasters instead, or move into the fields of advertising and even politics. Britain is in many respects a theatrical country. Margaret Thatcher, when prime minister, was coached by an actor; her speeches were rephrased by a playwright. The standards of British broadcasting and the dramatic debates in the House of Commons owe a debt, in part, to a theatre culture that is widespread and traditional.

Among professional actors it is generally agreed that, though such training is not essential to be a good actor, it certainly helps in the search for work. Those wishing to enter the acting profession often attend drama school from the outset of full-time education or apply to drama colleges on completion of their normal schooling. In addition, many universities offer three-year drama courses, but the majority of serious graduates from these course then progress to post-graduate courses at drama colleges.

To the continual lamentation of Irish actors, Ireland has no national theatre school to reflect its own culture and identity. Likewise, would-be actors from the north of Britain tend to turn to the plethora of schools based in southern England. These offer many varying methods of approach and teaching, and the best of them enjoy international acclaim.

The Royal Academy of Dramatic Art is probably the best known, as well as one of the oldest schools, founded in 1904. Its teaching method is based on the Stanislavski system and the work is aimed at enhancing individual skills and the application of those skills to work on group and public performance projects. Because of the small number of students on the course, 'the physical and vocal skill of the actor can be taught at an intense level'.

Founded in 1906, the Central School of Speech and Drama has a speech therapy course and a teaching course, as well as an acting course. The school has 'a definite body of principles: acting, movement and voice are all different aspects of one activity, and there is an avoidance of the extreme'.

The Guildhall School of Music and Drama is a conservatory for the drama and music professions. Founded in 1880, the school follows a policy of classic theatre training and, housed as it is at the Barbican Centre, has close links with the Royal Shakespeare Company and the London Symphony Orchestra. It also has a junior department for younger students. The London Academy of Music and Dramatic Art was founded in 1861 and, in addition to its acting course, also offers an overseas course with an emphasis on Shakespeare and the classics for foreign students. Its principles are 'to train people to meet the demands of contemporary theatre, and to give a strong technical base for the craft'.

There has always been a tension within the acting profession in the UK between the traditionalists with their emphasis on technique, and those who feel that this robs the performance of its soul and spontaneity. During the 1960s, several theatre training schools were founded which reflected this move away from traditional acting methods and embraced improvisation as a preferred teaching method in the training of actors.

The Drama Centre, founded in 1963, is an example of this shift in training methods in the UK. Set up by a group of teachers who broke away from the Central School of Speech and Drama, a more radical approach was established. The aim of the centre is for students to think of acting 'as a trade or a craft', and much improvisational work is carried out with careful study of Stanislavski, Grotowski and Brecht.

In 1961 the actress and director Joan Littlewood spoke out against the traditionalists, declaring 'I do not believe in the supremacy of the director, designer, actors or even of the writer. It is through collaboration that this knockabout art of theatre survives and kicks.' Littlewood went to RADA but left without completing the course, reacting against the teaching and West End theatre in general. She went on to establish the Theatre Workshop in London and was one of the first directors to make extensive use of improvisation. In 1961 the East 15 Acting School was founded to explore Littlewood's work: its methods focus on improvisational work and the desire to see acting 'as a creative art'.

Many repertory companies in the UK serve as a training ground for actors; the recent expansion in independent television production companies, commercial training videos and pop music videos offers further opportunities for actors.

Most of the drama schools in the UK offer courses in stage management and teaching, as well as scenic design or carpentry. A few offer options in directing, but training for this aspect of theatre work remains inadequate. The training of directors is sparsely catered for by the main television companies but for would-be theatre directors apprenticeship with established directors is much sought after. The Battersea Arts Centre in London has an annual Young Directors Award which encourages new directors but there is a need for greater support in this area of theatre training. Almost the only outlet for the training of playwrights is an MA course established at Birmingham University by the British dramatist David Edgar.

Olivia Eisinger

Criticism, Scholarship and Publishing

While newspaper and magazine reviewing extended its concerns beyond the boulevard in post-war Britain, a profound separation continued, and still persists today, between theatre criticism as practised in the press and the academic study and consideration of theatre. The establishment of new university and polytechnic drama departments in the 1960s led to an increased demand for books of critical theory and play and/or production analysis, as well as the more familiar theatre anthologies and memoires. With the deaths of Bernard Shaw, Max Beerbohm (1872–1956) and James Agate (1877–1947), the ghostly figures of Edwardian theatre criticism were laid to rest and the stage was clear for young writers to document post-war revolutions.

Harold Hobson was Agate's successor at *The Sunday Times* and, like him, a 'touchstone' critic. Neither was a theorist but relished memories of great theatre experiences against which they matched the present. His rival during the 1950s was the more flamboyant and politically motivated Kenneth Tynan of the *Observer*, who became Laurence Olivier's literary manager at the NT (1963–70). Both championed new playwrights, but whereas Hobson was inclined towards poetic drama and the West End (his lone support for Harold Pinter becoming a notable coup), Tynan favoured new-wave drama at the Royal Court. Tynan's review of John Osborne's *Look Back In Anger* (13 May 1956) ranks among the most quoted critical essays of the decade.

Among the critics who emerged in their wake, Irving Wardle (b. 1929), John Elsom (b. 1934), Michael Billington and Benedict Nightingale (b. 1939) were influential. As journalists, authors, broadcasters and university teachers, they sat on juries and drama panels for the Arts Council or similar bodies and carried many along in their tide. Jack Tinker (*Daily Mail*) has a wide following while among recent critical appointments to major papers, those of Michael Coveney (*Observer*), Nicholas de Jongh (London's *Evening Standard*) and Paul Taylor (*Independent*) can be deemed the most significant.

Despite the crossover between journalism and academic life, the main contribution of the reviewing critics to universities has been as observers rather than theorists or semioticians. The best known drama schools and literature departments in Britain are still those which date from the nineteenth century or before. But in the 1960s drama departments were established in many new or expanding universities such as Durham, Essex, Exeter, Hull, Kent, Lancaster and Warwick, joining the existing departments at Birmingham, Bristol, Glasgow, Leeds, Manchester, Ulster and Wales. There is a drama department in London University and the City University's department of arts policy and management (in London) established an arts criticism course in 1986. The tendency in Britain is to concentrate upon traditional methods of academic criticism, but semioticians and feminist critics have emerged from the universities since the mid-1960s, as the names Germaine Greer, Catherine Belsey and Terry Eagleton indicate.

Among the theatre periodicals, *Encore* (1954–66), *Plays and Players*, *Plays International*, *Theatre Quarterly* (under Simon Trussler and Cathy Itzin from 1970 to 1980) and its successor (*New Theatre Quarterly*, from 1985) have had periods of influence before settling down to a relatively small but loyal readership. Of the trade newspapers, *The Stage and Television Today* contains a comprehensive critical review section and a news service indispensable to actors, directors and managers. The *London Theatre Record* (founded by Ian Herbert, b. 1939) provides reprints of current reviews (not only from London but from regions as well) on a fortnightly basis, providing the best overall guide to what is happening in theatre. The listings magazines, *Time Out*, *What's On* and *City Limits*, are influential, containing summary reviews for most performing arts events in London or the towns where they are published. There are about twenty theatre annuals including the casting directory, *Spotlight* (founded in 1927), and *The British Theatre Directory*, an information handbook for the British theatre profession.

The publishing house Samuel French still dominates one area of the play publishing market, providing acting texts for amateur companies. Other imprints carry more selective lists, among them Faber & Faber and John Calder, which made its name during the 1960s by publishing Samuel Beckett and French absurdist dramatists, but their reputation for publishing new playwrights passed to Methuen and its long-time drama editor, Nick Hern, who later left Methuen to establish his own imprint. Among the more academic publishers, Routledge, B.T. Batsford, Macmillan, Cambridge University Press and Oxford University Press have all developed substantial lists, while Thames & Hudson excel in large illustrated books. There are also small houses with programmes directed towards particular topics, such as Ulster's Blackstaff Press or Edward Arnold, publishers of the Regents Restoration Drama Series and Stratford-upon-Avon Studies.

The diversity among publishers can be said to reflect the general variety in British theatre. A recession that began in the late 1980s had a devastating effect especially on small publishers; those which have survived have usually done so by joining conglomerates or by being taken over by larger companies.

It might be added that the theatre no longer commands the same coverage in the daily or weekly press as it once did. Although many theatre books are still published, and some record good sales, the degree of interest seems to be diminishing, although whether this is a fashion or a more permanent state of affairs is still an open question.

John Elsom

Further Reading

Ansorge, Peter. *Disrupting the Spectacle: Five Years of Experimental and Fringe Theatre in Britain*. London: Pitman, 1975. 87 pp.

Barnes, Philip. *Companion to Post-War British Theatre*. London: Croom Helm, 1986. 288 pp.

Belsey, Catherine. *Critical Practice*. London: Methuen, 1980.

Bigsby, C.W.E., ed. *Contemporary English Theatre*. London: Arnold, 1981.

Billington, Michael. *One Night Stands: A Critic's View of the London Stage from 1971 to 1991*. London: Nick Hern Books, 1993.

Bramble, Forbes. 'The Barbican Theatre'. *Theatre Quarterly* 1, no. 1 (1971): 29–40.

Brinson, Peter, and Clement Crisp. *The Pan Book of Ballet and Dance*. London: Pan Books, 1981.

Brown, John Russell. *Modern British Dramatists*. New York: Prentice-Hall, 1968.

Bull, J. *New British Political Dramatists*. London: Macmillan, 1984. 244 pp.

Cabochel, L. *Le Théâtre en Grande-Bretagne pendant la seconde guerre mondiale*. [Theatre in Britain during World War II]. Paris: Didier, 1969. 409 pp.

Chambers, Colin. *Other Spaces*. London: Methuen, 1980.

Craig, S., ed. *Dreams and Deconstructions: Alternative Theatre in Britain*. London: Amber Lane, 1980.

Currell, David. *The Complete Book of Puppet Theatre*. London: A. & C. Black, 1985.

Davies, Andrew. *Other Theatres*. London: Methuen, 1987.

Elsom, John. *Cold War Theatre*. London: Routledge, 1992.

——. *Post-War British Theatre*. London: Routledge & Kegan Paul, 1979.

——. *Post-War British Theatre Criticism*. London: Routledge & Kegan Paul, 1978.

——, and Nicholas Tomalin. *The History of the National Theatre*. London: Cape, 1978.

Emmett, A. 'The Long Prehistory of the National Theatre'. *Theatre Quarterly* 21 (1976): 55–62.

England, Alan. *Theatre for the Young*. London: Macmillan, 1990.

Esslin, Martin. *The Theatre of the Absurd*. Rev. ed. London: Pelican, 1968. 463 pp.

Findlater, R. *Banned: A Review of Theatrical Censorship in Britain*. London: MacGibbon & Kee, 1967. 238 pp.

Hinchliffe, Arnold. *British Theatre, 1950–1970*. Oxford: Basil Blackwell, 1974. 205 pp.

Hunt, H., K. Richards, and J.R. Taylor. *The Revels History of Drama in English*. Vol. II: *1880 to the Present Day*. London: Methuen, 1978. 297 pp.

Itzin, Catherine. *Directory of Playwrights, Directors and Designers*. London: John Offord, 1983.

——. *Stages in the Revolution: Political Theatre in Britain Since 1968*. New York: Methuen, 1981.

Koegler, Horst. *The Concise Oxford Dictionary of Ballet*. Oxford: Oxford University Press, 1988.

Lawson, Robb. *The Story of the Scots Stage*. New York: B. Blom, 1971. 303 pp.

Leach, Robert. *The Punch and Judy Show*. London: Batsford Academic & Educational, 1985.

Maiorana, Salvatore. *Lo spazio diviso. Teoria e practica del teatro politico inglese contemporaneo*. [The divided space: theory and practice of contemporary English political theatre]. Venice: Marsilio, 1984. 208 pp.

Mikhail, E.H. *Contemporary British Drama 1950–1976: An Annotated Critical Bibliography*. Totowa, NJ: Rowman & Littlefield, 1977.

Morley, Sheridan. *Spread a Little Happiness*. London: Thames & Hudson, 1987. 221 pp.

Rabey, David Ian. *British and Irish Political Drama in the 20th Century*. London: Macmillan, 1986.

Roberts, P. *The Best of Plays and Players*. Vol. I: *1953–1968*. London: Methuen, 1988. 253 pp.

Rosenfeld, Sybil. *A Short History of Scene Design in Great Britain*. London: Basil Blackwell, 1973.

Spaight, George. *The History of the English Puppet Theatre*, 2nd ed. London: George Harrap & Co. Ltd, 1990.

Taylor, J. Russell. *Anger and After*. London: Methuen, 1962. 350 pp.

——. *The Second Wave*. London: Methuen, 1971. 236 pp.

Thorpe, Matilda. *Stage Struck*. London: Hodder & Stoughton, 1990.

Trussler, Simon, ed. *Political Developments on the British Stage in the Sixties and Seventies: Symposium of September 17/18, 1976 at the University of Rostock*. Rostock: Wilhelm-Pieck-University, 1977. 135 pp.

——, and Roger Hudson, eds. 'The State of the Nation's Theatre'. *Theatre Quarterly* 11 (July–September 1973): 29–70; 12 (October–December 1973): 4–59.

Tynan, Kenneth. *A View of the English Stage, 1944–1963*. London: Davis-Poynter, 1975. 386 pp.

Vinson, James, ed. *Contemporary Dramatists*. London: Macmillan, 1982.

Wilson, Sheila. *The Theatre of the Fifties*. London: Library Association, 1963.

Woddis, Carole, and Trevor Griffiths. *Bloomsbury Theatre Guide*. London: Bloomsbury, 1988.

Wright, John. *Rod, Shadow and Glove: Puppets from the Little Angel Theatre*. London: Robert Hale Ltd, 1986.

UNION OF SOVIET SOCIALIST REPUBLICS

(Historical Overview)

The Union of Soviet Socialist Republics (USSR, or the Soviet Union) was the first socialist country in history to attempt to realize in practice an ideological utopia. The creation of this new state, based on the teachings of Karl Marx (1818–83) and Vladimir Ilyich Lenin (1870–1924), was announced in Moscow in December 1922 and ended in December 1991 when the presidents of the Russian Federation, Belarus and Ukraine signed the Belovezhsky Agreement restoring political independence to these and other republics which formed the union. Located in eastern Europe, as well as in the northern and central parts of Asia, the USSR occupied one-sixth of the world's land area – 22.27 million square kilometres (8.6 million square miles). The population (according to 1990 statistics) was 285 million, with the capital in Moscow (population 9.2 million).

By the end of World War II the makeup of the USSR consisted of fifteen republics, nine in Europe – Armenia, Azerbaijan, Belarus (Byelorussia), Estonia, Georgia, Latvia, Lithuania, Moldova and Ukraine; five in Asia – Kazakhstan, Kirghizia, Tadjikistan, Turkmenistan and Uzbekistan; and one – the enormous Russian Federation – which spread across both continents. In addition, there were twenty smaller national groupings (autonomous republics), eight autonomous regions, ten autonomous districts, and 127 regions and districts. The principle of the administrative division was to be 'nationally territorial'. In total, over a hundred different ethnic groups and nationalities resided within the USSR.

According to the 1970 census there were 129 million Russians, 40.7 million Ukrainians, 9.2 million Uzbeks, 9 million Belarussians, 5.9 million Tartars, 5.3 million Cossacks, 4.4 million Azerbaijanis, 3.6 million Armenians, 3.2 million Georgians, 2.7 million Moldovans, 2.7 million Lithuanians, 2.1 million Jews, 2.1 million Tadjiks, 1.8 million Germans, 1.7 million Chuvashes and 1 million Estonians. Other groupings comprised fewer than 1 million people.

The USSR came into existence as a result of the October Revolution of 1917, on the territories of the former Russian Empire (with the exceptions of Finland, Poland, parts of Bessarabia, and parts of the western Ukraine). The constitution of the USSR, in 1937 and in 1977, declared it a free union of national states, a federation, with the building of a communist society uniting it in a common goal, with a single political and defence strategy, a single national currency, a single economic plan, and so on. The right of a republic to secede was also included but there was never a clear mechanism for separation in place. A division of powers was also part of the constitution with legislation to be the responsibility of councils at various levels. Executive duties were to fall upon the councils of ministers and executive committees in the various regions, cities, and districts. However, even during the October Revolution and the Civil War (1917–22), the Communist Party of the Soviet Union had already risen beyond the official government structure. This was reinforced in the constitution of 1977. By that time the party's Central Committee had taken over both legislative and executive powers within the country.

Characteristic traits of the government of the USSR during its history were overcentralization in all aspects of activity including economic and spiritual areas (such as culture, sports and religion). As well, ideological and political decisions were usually given priority over economic ones. Government dictatorship was personified in the Central Cabinet of the Communist Party as well as in its general secretary, who eventually accumulated almost unlimited power. The result was a state that tended to devour its citizens under the protection of slogans promising the creation of a socialist heaven on earth. During the years when Joseph Stalin (1879–1953) was in power (1922–53), the Soviet state's tendency to be 'anti-people' showed itself most obviously when a system of concentration camps was developed. Over 20 million people passed through these camps, which served as a device of both suppression and repression. In reality, this system continued to operate, although not on the same scale, during the years of official destalinization (1954–64), as well as during the so-called Period of Stagnation (1964–85) reflecting the country's growing economic and social problems.

Even though the USSR had a relatively low standard of living compared to the west, and often violated the rights and freedoms of its citizens, it nevertheless created a militarily powerful and industrially mature state, much of it at great cost to the environment. Over 80 per cent of the economy was, in fact, connected in some way to the military.

After World War II, the USSR, having occupied much of eastern Europe, and having supported revolutionary movements in several parts of the world, became the leader of world socialism and a superpower on whose shoulders, it was argued, rested the fate of the world. Great achievements in military and aerospace technologies were attained, paid for primarily through the export of crude oil during the 1960s and 1970s. Because it was said that 'developing socialism' could not compete with the market economy of the developed western countries, a policy of peaceful but socially competitive coexistence (the Cold War) began in the late 1950s. Towards the mid-1980s the state's depleting resources, however, had brought the country's socialist system into clear crisis. *Perestroika* (restructuring), along with the political

and economic positions taken by Mikhail Gorbachev (b. 1931), general secretary of the Central Committee of the Communist Party from March 1985 to December 1991, led to rapid political changes in the republics, the eventual dissolution of the USSR, and movement towards a new democratic social order built on the ruins of this enormous social experiment.

As the socialist state grew, so too did a Soviet socialist culture. Like the new Soviet citizen whose rights and freedoms could be revoked by the state, the individual Soviet cultural worker was subordinate to the collective. In the field of theatre, this meant companies, not stars. It also meant creating art that was part of the social struggle.

It was immediately after the October Revolution of 1917 that conflicts regarding the appropriate development of Soviet culture first arose. Left-wing radicals, working through an organization called Proletarian Culture (Proletcult), urged the new state to reject the historical legacy of world culture which they declared was elitist. The most educated leaders, however – including Lenin, Anatoly Lunacharsky (1875–1933, the first People's Commissar of Enlightenment), Lev Trotsky (1879–1940), Nikolai Bukharin (1888–1938) and others – declared the country to be the inheritor of all that was best in world culture. When Stalin came to power, though, he urged the rejection of classical culture as well as modern western culture. Cultural authorities upheld the previous notion, however, although they battled against non-realistic styles and 'abstract' humanism while demanding the creation of works loyal to and glorifying the official order. Clearly, ideological and political interests determined the country's culture.

The USSR understood early on that artists could have a huge influence on public consciousness and set out to attract writers, philosophers, artists, composers and theatre people to their side. Many, such as Alexander Blok (1880–1921), one of the founders of the Bolshoi Drama Theatre in St Petersburg in 1918, were outstanding poets. Yevgeny Vakhtangov (1883–1922), the foremost student of Konstantin Stanislavski (1863–1938), was another. These people accepted the revolution with sincerity and enthusiasm and took its utopian character to heart.

In 1918 Vsevelod Meyerhold (1874–1940) became head of the Theatrical Division of the Ministry of Culture – the People's Commissariat of Enlightenment – and all theatres were put under his supervision. Inspired by the new revolutionary ideas, he and many others fought against those who thought differently in fields of ideology, art and literature. Many new organizations were formed specifically to define these ideas. In 1922 more than 200 eminent scientists, philosophers, artists and writers – on direct orders from Lenin – were exiled for their unwillingness to accept the new regime.

The conflict between revolutionary utopia and the revolutionary reality of a totalitarian socialist regime would continue in Soviet art for the duration of the USSR's existence. The same was true in the ongoing conflict between world cultural heritage and revolutionary art based primarily on Marxist and Leninist theories. Creative activities, according to the orthodoxy, had to be part of the social structure and the Communist Party's actions, and one had to be part of the Communist Party if one wanted to participate in the struggle.

The building of a multinational culture in a huge Eurasian state also caused enormous difficulties. Partly, this was due to the fact that existing cultural traditions were often connected to existing religious traditions. The development of these various cultures – supposedly 'socialist in content' – had to be separated from religion. To achieve this, culture was harshly regulated with various punitive structures put into effect between the 1920s and the 1950s. Those who did not go along with the changes were attacked as 'bourgeois nationalists' and their careers – and on occasion their lives – were put in danger.

Under Nikita Khrushchev (1894–1971) came a period of liberalism starting in 1955 which was connected to a massive separation of government policies from Stalin's approaches. Despite continued support for the formulaic ideas of socialist-realism in art, the time was ripe for change and Soviet artists began to seek new approaches to culture.

In trying to assess the overall contribution of the USSR to world culture, one must first acknowledge a lack of respect for individuals throughout its history and one must recognize as well the immense human cost of its attempts – at home and abroad – to maintain ideological control. Nevertheless, much significant art was created by and in reaction to these policies; it can be argued that the Soviet Union, despite many failures, produced one of the most individual responses to culture ever seen and one of the liveliest and most active periods of culture in the twentieth century.

Mikk Mikiver in his Estonian Drama Theatre production of John Arden's *Serjeant Musgrave's Dance*.
Photo: G. Vaidla.

Structure of the National Theatre Community

The roots of the Soviet Union's professional theatre structure are to be found in the nineteenth-century Russian Empire, with Russian professional theatre itself dating back to at least a hundred years earlier. At the turn of the twentieth century, there were numerous inter-relationships among prominent figures in theatre from various nationalities within the empire. As well, from 1898 the work of the Moscow Art Theatre (Moscovski Khudozhest-venny Academicheski Teatr, known to Russians simply as MXAT) had a huge influence on the emerging professional theatres. The work of Konstantin Stanislavski and Vladimir Nemirovich-Danchenko (1858–1943), origi-nators of what was originally called the Moscow Art and Publicly Accessible Theatre, grew from the greatest achievements of the Russian and world stages.

Immediately after the revolution, the Moscow Art Theatre created 'studios' for other republics in the union which in large part determined the development of the professional theatre in Belarus, Armenia and Turkmenistan, to name just three. A network of professional theatres soon developed along with the creation of spe-cial theatres for young people. In 1919 a decree to 'unite the theatrical field' was enacted and a Central Theatrical Committee was created as part of the People's Commissariat of Enlightenment.

Towards the end of the 1920s and the begin-ning of the 1930s, the move toward centraliza-tion of theatre began drawing to an end. In its place, a committee was charged with monitoring and approving all plays for produc-tion. After World War II the Ministry of Cul-ture, carrying out the directives of the Central Committee, took upon itself control of theatres in the country. The structure of all theatres was to be based on the organizational model of the Moscow Art Theatre which, in the second half of the 1930s, had become a benchmark for the development of other Soviet theatres. Subsidized by the government, all theatres were to have permanent companies staging ten different shows each month. This single model remained in effect through to the mid-1980s.

Geographically, each district was to have a dramatic theatre as well as a puppet theatre. In major cities – those with populations close to 1 million – musical theatres and theatres for young people were also to be in operation. Tour-ing theatres would exist as well to perform in rural areas. Across the country, theatres were to play in the various national languages, though at least one theatre performing in Russian was to be kept in operation in each republic.

At the time of the dissolution of the USSR, there were over 600 professional theatres per-forming in fifty-five languages. The theatres were subdivided into categories one, two and three, based on the level of subsidy they received, the level of their box-office income and ticket prices. Outside these categories were the academic theatres – classical companies financed directly by the Ministry of Culture and/or by the various republics. Among the aca-demic theatres were Moscow's Bolshoi Theatre (founded in 1776), the Maly (founded in 1824), the Moscow Art Theatre, the Bolshoi Drama Theatre in St Petersburg, as well as groups in the capitals of the various republics and other major cities. All theatres were under the control of the official cultural bodies of each city or district.

It was the Ministry of Culture which bought the rights to plays from the national play-wrights' association, which represented writers. Theatres were allowed to sign contracts with writers only through the ministry or one of the other cultural bodies. The inclusion of a play, even a classic, in a theatre's repertoire could occur only after permission was received from the appropriate cultural body, whose decisions in turn had to be approved by the Department of Defence and ultimately the Council of Ministers of the USSR. All were in effect mechanisms for censorship.

Until 1988, it was the policy of the state and its ideological advisory groups that no less than 50 per cent of each theatre's repertoire should be modern Soviet plays, and that no less than 25 per cent should be plays from the national republics, ideally including several Russian classics.

In 1986 a series of reforms were put into place aimed at changing the economic model while still keeping government control of the artistic process. Several layers of censorship were removed in 1987 and this proved far more radical than its initiators had envisioned. Indi-vidual theatres were finally able to formulate their own repertoires, and experimental studios, previously working semi-officially, began to rise above ground. There was, in fact, an almost spontaneous creation of new theatrical groups that did not fit the official model. In Moscow alone, this new 'Soviet fringe' numbered over 200 companies by the late 1980s. Groups cons-tantly appeared and then disappeared, with municipal authorities as well as arts unions and commercial organizations acting as sponsors for them. At the same time, the first independent Soviet production firms began to appear financing specific theatrical projects. Groups of actors also started to assemble for single produc-tions, usually with commercial backing.

Artistic Profile

By the beginning of the 1930s, the revolutionary romantic period in Soviet art was drawing to an end. This period had seen the promotion of new ideas as well as a number of artistic experiments. It was from this period that one finds the classics of Soviet literature, including the works of Maxim Gorki (1868–1936) whose method of writing was hailed at the first Congress of Soviet Writers in 1934. Socialist-realism was proclaimed to be the logical evolution of Gorki's realistic style.

But rather than artistic considerations, it was usually one's agreement with the largely class-based system of the Communist Party and one's ability to confirm a communist perspective on human development which became the primary criteria for determining talent. It was argued that the world was in a constant social competition, a battle for the attainment of communist ideals. It was also assumed that the communist victory was historically inevitable. In this respect, a play by Vsevelod Vishnevski (1900–51), *Optemisticheskaya Tragedia* (*The Optimistic Tragedy*, 1933), was a typical play of the 1930s. In this work, a commissar sacrifices her own life to ensure the Baltic Fleet's victory during the Civil War.

In the second half of the 1930s, the ideological organs of the Communist Party and of the state, which fulfilled both the social orders of the Central Committee and the personal orders of Stalin, took steps to weed-out non-realistic elements in Soviet art. The quickly rigidifying principles of the Moscow Art Theatre were reconfirmed as the correct aesthetic system for the development of Soviet art. Shut down were the Meyerhold Theatre (1937), the experimental theatre of Les Kurbas (1887–1937) in the Ukraine and the theatre of Sandro Akhmetili (1886–1937) in Georgia. Theatre groups were urged 'to study at MXAT', which answered primarily to the Conference of Soviet Directors (1939) and which in turn converted the system of Stanislavski from a living art form into dogma and seriously restricted the development of directors, dramatists and other theatre artists.

During World War II – known in the USSR as the Great War of the Fatherland (1941–5) – while facing the threat of fascism, the future of the Soviet state and its people was being decided. Many of the best known artists were later referred to as patriotic heroes. In the years following the war, it was this feeling for people who endured the hardships of war which would become one of the most important themes in Soviet theatre. Yet even here the harsh regulating of art remained active, although the celebration of the end of the war was obvious in many plays and productions.

The immediate post-war years also marked the start of new attacks on artists trying to move in new directions – among them many prominent theatre people – and leading Russian writers such as Anna Akhmatova (1889–1966) and Mikhail Zoschenko (1895–1958). Rather than attacking their art, they were personally attacked for being anti-Soviet. Others were attacked for being 'nationless' and this was blatantly expressed in increased anti-semitic attacks. It was no surprise that Goset (the State Jewish Theatre) in Moscow was closed and the Kamerni Theatre destroyed. Literally thousands of people wound up in work camps as a result of such accusations and thousands more simply lost their careers.

At about this same point, socialist-realism became the model for works of art and this led to the concept of the 'conflictless play', that is the kind of play that reflected only the conflict of 'good versus even better' within a Soviet reality. It was this concept that led to the creation of a series of very poorly written plays which tried to follow this ideological recipe. Despite their weaknesses, many of these plays were performed at theatres throughout the country, including the Moscow Art Theatre, which in the years following the war became a kind of official laboratory for new Soviet plays.

Ideology influenced everything related to the arts in the second half of the 1940s and the first half of the 1950s and, in fact, influenced every aspect of Soviet culture to the mid-1980s, and the beginning of *perestroika*. By the mid-1950s, it was also argued that the artist had to produce works which could be easily understood by the people. Between the 1950s and the 1980s this doctrine would continue to exist along with a multitude of other regulations. Artists officially had the right to experiment but only within strict Marxist–Leninist ideology.

In 1972, during the celebration of the fiftieth anniversary of the creation of the USSR, a new historic society – the 'Soviet People' – was announced along with the creation of a new

939

multinational Soviet culture. Soviet culture was in its own way a product of Soviet reality with all its many complications. And this did produce some important work, even by 'official' creators such as Sergei Mikhalkov (b. 1913), one of the writers of the Soviet national anthem and also a poet and children's dramatist, as well as unofficial creators such as Mikhail Bulgakov (1891–1940), author of *The Days of the Turbines* and *The Master and Margarita* (1940).

After Stalin's death in 1953, as the Cold War began in earnest, Soviet culture began to present to the world many artists of international repute in dramatic and musical theatre, in dance, literature, the visual arts and film, artists whose creations – though full of ideological restraints – nevertheless expressed human experience in humanitarian terms. The battle for democratization and destalinization in Soviet art was promoted as a return to pure values, revolutionary values, and the realization of ideological declarations by the Communist Party. Soviet cultural workers in the 1950s and 1960s defended humanitarian ideals including the right for individuality in both decision-making and self-examination and for the right to challenge communist orthodoxy.

The utopian ideals of socialism were therefore re-established along with a recognition of the importance of artistic creation, just as they had existed in the first decade after the revolution. The 1950s and 1960s again became a time of debate and ferment, a re-examination of the future of Soviet theatre, of the Stanislavski system, of the ideas of Meyerhold and Vakhtangov. Some attention was even paid to those artists who were experimenting – and were unaccepted – in the immediate pre-revolutionary and post-revolutionary period and who were rejected again in the 1930s and 1940s. It was finally recognized that such art did have value and could help create on the stage Stanislavski's ideal: the 'life of a human soul'. In these discussions one could also hear more and more dissatisfaction with the Moscow Art Theatre. At MXAT and at the Maly Theatre, some of the most prominent actors had been pupils of Stanislavski and of Nemirovich-Danchenko. But no one emerged as MXAT's leader who could artistically endure the pressure of having to follow official ideology.

Unable to easily change the existing theatres, the period saw the birth of a number of new theatres, new dramatists and new directors. Already established masters expanded the breadth of their artistic searches. Some new

Valentin Pluchek's 1955 Moscow Satire Theatre production of Vladimir Mayakovsky's *The Bedbug*.

plays openly challenged the cult of personality created by Stalin and examined events related to his regime. These included *Personalenoe Delo* (*Personal Process*, 1955) by Alexander Shtein (1906–93) and *Wings* (1955) by Oleksander Korniychuk (1905–72), dramatists who began to write in the 1930s. Even much earlier anti-totalitarian plays by Vladimir Mayakovsky (1894–1930) were staged. Plays were performed at the Moscow Satire Theatre by protégés of Meyerhold and Sergei Eisenstein (1898–1948). Among them, *Banya* (*The Bath House*, 1953) directed by Nikolai Petrov (1890–1964), Valentin Pluchek (b. 1909) and Sergei Utkevich (1904–85) with designs by Alexander Tishler (1898–1980); *Klop* (*The Bedbug*, 1955) directed by Pluchek and Utkevich; and *Mystère Bouffe* (1957) staged by Pluchek. Plays by Nikolai Pogodin (1900–62), Alexei Arbuzov (1908–87), Victor Rozov (b. 1913), Afanacy Salinski (b. 1920), Alexander Volodin (b. 1919), Leonid Zorin (b. 1924), Ian Drutse (b. 1928) and others contained within them clear reaffirmations of human individuality.

In the late 1950s and 1960s, the early

revolutionary period and the civil war held a particular fascination for writers: plays about this period were regularly in the repertoires. Attempts were made to re-examine accepted orthodoxies, subjects and portrayals, to reconsider history by filling the stages with humanistic values and a sense of the common people. These works also tried to portray anti-totalitarian attitudes though they avoided certain historical facts and did not touch on the revolution's tragedies from the 1910s to the 1940s. Among the major productions of this nature one should mention *The Third Pathétique* (1956) by Nikolai Pogodin, staged at the Moscow Art Theatre by Maria Knebel (1898–1985) with Boris Smirnov as Lenin, and *The Optimistic Tragedy*, which played at the Pushkin Theatre in Leningrad and was staged by Giorgi Tovstonogov (1915–89) with designs by Anatoly Bosulaev (b. 1904).

Attempts were also made to re-evaluate the experiences of the war, to challenge the official version of national triumph, and to speak of the tragic price which people had to pay in order to achieve victory over fascism. Such plays included *Vechno Zhivie* (*Alive Forever*) by Victor Rozov, which played at the Sovremenik (Modern) Theatre in 1956, staged by Oleg Efremov (b. 1927); *The Golden Carriage* by Leonid Leonov, which played at the Moscow Art Theatre (1957), directed by Pavel Markov (1897–1980) and Boris Stanitsin with designs by Leonid Silich; and *Barabanschitsa* (*The Drummer Girl*, 1957) by Afanacy Salinski (1920–93), which played at the Central Theatre of the Soviet Army (1959), directed by Abram Okunchikov with designs by Nisson Shifrin (1892–1961).

By the late 1950s, leading theatres were reinterpreting both national and world classics in new ways. For a decade, classical plays were untouched by censorship, while modern masters attempted to solve the problems of contemporary existence. The right to search for a personal way of life and individual choice appear again and again in plays from this period despite ideological censorship. Even plays such as *Hamlet* (1954) took these views in a production at the Mayakovsky Theatre staged by Nikolai Okhlopkov (1900–67), himself a student of Meyerhold; Chekhov's *Ivanov* was directed in this style by Maria Knebel at the Pushkin Theatre in Moscow; *The Power of Darkness* by Lev Tolstoi (1828–1910) played in the Maly Theatre (1956) and was directed by Boris Ravenski (1914–80), another pupil of

Meyerhold (the production starred Igor Ilinski (1901–90), the leading actor of the Meyerhold Theatre in the 1920s and 1930s).

Many stylistic experiments that had been prohibited in the late 1930s re-emerged in the 1950s and 1960s. A student of Vakhtangov, Ruben Simonov (1899–1968), attempted to resurrect in full the non-naturalistic teachings of his mentor, developing an Aesthetics of Celebration and the notion of tragi-comedy. Other Meyerhold-style directors emerged – Boris Ravenski, who worked in Moscow in the Maly and Pushkin Theatres, and Valentin Pluchek, director of the Moscow Satire Theatre. At the same time, the famous Leningrad (St Petersburg) director and artist, Nikolai Akimov (1901–68), pushed satirical traditions in cycles of performances of Russian classics.

Similar developments were taking place in other republics of the USSR as well: re-evaluations of national traditions and attempts to include national styles in the repertoires. Leonid Varpakhovski, another student of Meyerhold, returned from exile and worked mostly in Kiev, while the Georgian director Dimitri Alexidze was active in Ukraine. Directors from Moscow who received their training at MXAT and the Maly also found themselves working with theatres in various republics.

As theatre increased across the country, however, the older theatres in Moscow and Leningrad were becoming even more conservative. Stanislavski's system ironically became a theatrical equivalent of the political decrees of Marx and Lenin. Official promoters of Stanislavski's system spent their time trying to eliminate any contradictions and weaknesses they could find in it. Attempts to build on the Stanislavski system could be made only beyond the Moscow Art Theatre. Even then, one had to show connections with the system. This was the approach taken by people who had worked with Stanislavski such as Alexei Popov (1892–1961), head of the Central Theatre of the Soviet Army from 1935 to 1960; Maria Knebel, who left MXAT for the Central Theatre for Children; and Yuri Zavadski (1894–1977), manager of the Mossoviet Theatre from 1940 to 1977.

The Sovremenik Theatre was still another group which began as an attempt to revitalize the *true* theatre of Stanislavski. Oleg Efremov, a graduate of the MXAT school, later became director of the theatre.

Still another of its directors was Anatoly Efros (1925–87), whose many productions attest to the development of the artistic traditions of

MXAT. His shows were brash and cynical, theatrical poetry which defended the internal independence of people and artists. Other productions of his were staged at the Lenin Komsomol Theatre and the Theatre on Malaya Bronnaya Street in Moscow. The art of director Giorgi Tovstonogov tried to unite Stanislavski's 'life of the human soul' with Georgian expressionism and the classical style of Leningrad. His work was primarily done at the Leningrad Bolshoi Theatre and he was later head of the Leningrad Theatre School. In 1990, the Leningrad Bolshoi Theatre was renamed in honour of this important director.

From the mid-1950s, directors generally played an important role in the Soviet theatre. Across the country, they daringly united various national traditions with elements of classic theatre renewing the language of theatre as a whole. Among the most important working in this way were the Lithuanian Juozas Miltinis (b. 1907), director of the Ponivezhsky Theatre; Estonian director Voldemar Panso (1920–77), head of the Youth Theatre as well as the National Theatre; Estonian Kaarel Ird

(1909–86), director of the Vanemuine Theatre in Tartu, where drama, opera and ballet operated under one roof; Georgian directors Mikhail Tumanishvili (b. 1921) and Grigori (Giga) Lordkipanidze (b. 1927); the Azerbaijani producer Mekhit Mamedov (1918–85); and the Armenian director Hrachia Ghaplanian (1923–90).

The Theatre of Drama and Comedy in Moscow was also part of this general restructuring and rethinking. In 1964, Yuri Lyubimov (b. 1917) was hired as its director. An actor at the Vakhtangov Theatre and a teacher of theatre at the Boris Shchukin School (under the direction of the Vakhtangov Theatre), he and his students established at the theatre a new company that would follow the traditions of Meyerhold, Vakhtangov and Brecht, a theatre of poetic metaphor with open political expressions.

By the end of the 1960s this movement for renewal also came in contact with both ballet and opera. In ballet the fight was against the form being treated as simply choreographed drama, for the confirmation of dance as dance.

Yuri Lyubimov's 1977 Taganka Theatre production of Mikhail Bulgakov's *The Master and Margarita*.
Photo: V. Plotnikova.

Experiments in this area were analogous to those of Meyerhold in theatre, and Eisenstein in film. Fyodor Lopukhov (1886–1973), Kasian Goleizovski (1892–1970) and Leonid Yakobson (1904–75), together with the young masters Oleg Vinagradov (b. 1937), Natalia Kasatkina (b. 1934) and Vladimir Vasiliov (b. 1931), revived forgotten genres and forms of ballet – one-act ballets, symphonic ballets and other styles. Still newer approaches tried to join modern dance with classical ballet and this could be seen in the Leningrad and Moscow performances of Yuri Grigorovich (b. 1927), from 1964 head of the ballet of the Bolshoi Theatre. In the 1960s and 1970s, the Kiev Ballet choreographer Henryk Maiorov (b. 1936), the Minsk Ballet choreographer Valentin Yelizarov (b. 1938), the Georgian Ballet choreographer and former star dancer Vakhtang Chabukiani (1910–90), the Estonian Ballet choreographers Mai Murdmaa (b. 1938) and Ülo Vilimaa (b. 1941), as well as Boris Aifman (b. 1946) and Leonid Lebedov (b. 1943) all gained fame for their innovative work throughout the Soviet Union. In the mid-1980s, Dimitri Briantzov (b. 1947), head of the ballet troupe of the Stanislavski-Nemirovich-Danchenko Musical Theatre in Moscow, joined this important group of innovators.

The language of opera also became much more open at this time. Perhaps the major names in this field were Boris Pokrovski (b. 1912), head of the Bolshoi Theatre on several occasions and in 1970 founder of the Kamerni Theatre, and Lev Mikhailov (1928–80), director of the Novosibirsk Opera Theatre and then head of the Stanislavski-Nemirovich-Danchenko Musical Theatre.

All of the aforementioned masters, although they differed in artistic methods and aesthetic beliefs, were united in their goal of articulating through their art democratic values seeking to tell the truth about modern life no matter how difficult it was to do that. It can be fairly said that changes in the national political situation partially came about as a result of their artistic actions, even though their productions remained under strict censorship through the 1980s and producers and dramatists who worked with them often received severe criticism from the official press and various cultural organs.

Among writers, a number in the 1960s stood out for their frank expressions of experiences in the period after Stalin: Edward Radzinski (b. 1936), Mikhail Shatrov (b. 1932), Alexander

Gelman (b. 1933), Ignacy Dvoretski (1919–88), Grigori Gorin (b. 1940), Enn Vetema (b. 1936), Vasili Aksenov (b. 1932), Mikhail Roschin (b. 1933), Andrei Makaenok (1920–82), Vladimir Voinovich (b. 1932), Nodar Dumbadze (1928–84) and Kazis Sayia (b. 1932) among others. The success of their plays was related to productions by directors such as Efremov, Efros and Galina Volchek (b. 1933), the latter an actress and director at the Sovremenik. She took over this troupe after Efremov became the artistic director of the Moscow Art Theatre in 1971. Others whose work heralded significant changes in Moscow in the 1980s included Mark Zakharov (b. 1933), the innovative head of the Lenin Komsomol Theatre in Moscow; Andrei Goncharov (b. 1918), head of the Mayakovsky Theatre after the death of Nikolai Okhlopkov, Leonid Kheifits (b. 1936) and Piotr Fomenko (b. 1932).

Outside Moscow, important directors were also emerging: Zinovy Karadgodski (b. 1926), Igor Vladimirov (b. 1919) and Ruben Agamerzian (1922–91) in Leningrad; Mikk Mikiver (b. 1938), Evald Hermaküla (b. 1941) and Jan Tooming (b. 1946) in Estonia; Adolf Shapiro (b. 1939) in Latvia; Ionas Uroshas (b. 1938) in Lithuania; Robert Sturua (b. 1940) at the Rustevali and Temur Chkheidze (b. 1942) in Georgia; and Azerbaijan Mambetov (b. 1932) in Kazakhstan, all began to play an important role in the production of new work in these locales.

In the 1970s three important themes could begin to be seen in Soviet writing: first, a critical examination of the years of the revolution and the Great War of the Fatherland (mostly in works by Mikhail Shatrov (b. 1932), Salinski, Shtein, Dudarov and Drutse); second, an analysis of the problems of modern economic life (plays by Ignacy Dvoretski (1919–88), Alexander Gelman, Alexander Misharin and Anatoly Grebnov); and third, a serious look at the private lives of people, life's bitter truths, daily reality, and the absurdity of daily survival. Works by many of these writers ran into heavy censorship.

The third approach came closest to continuing the traditions of Chekhov's drama. The most influential writer in this style was Alexander Vampilov (1937–72). Others who followed him in the 1970s included Ludmila Petroshevskaia (b. 1938), Alexander Galin (b. 1947), Semion Zdotnikov (b. 1945) and Victor Slavkin (b. 1935). Interestingly, many participants in playwriting workshops run by

Alexei Arbuzov (1908–87) in Moscow and Ignacy Dvoretski in Leningrad after this time called themselves 'post-Vampilov dramatists'. Perhaps the important director of post-Vampilov drama was Anatoly Vasiliov (b. 1942), whose productions were seen in the 1970s and 1980s at various Moscow theatres including MXAT, the consistently daring Taganka, and even at leading theatre schools. Other directors of note at this time included Lev Dodin (b. 1944), a teacher at the Leningrad College of Theatre, Music and Cinematography and head of the Leningrad Maly Drama Theatre from the beginning of the 1980s, Henrietta Yanovskaia (b. 1941) and Kama Ginkas (b. 1941).

In the area of children's theatre – a USSR specialty – over ninety groups were in operation. There were as well more than 100 puppet theatres. Between the 1960s and the 1980s, these theatres were extremely active, although it must be said that many talented people unable to work in 'adult' theatres for various reasons were pressured to work in these specialized areas.

Theatrical criticism, too, had an especially important effect on theatre especially from the 1950s to the 1980s. Many of the most important critics were associated with the Vsesouzni Institute Iscustvoznania (Soviet National Institute for Arts Research), the Academy of Sciences of the USSR, the Leningrad Institute of Theatre, Music and Cinematography, even the Ministry of Culture. The publication *Teatr* (founded in 1932), a monthly magazine, dealt with the key issues of drama, history, theory and criticism during this period. In 1956 a more conservative magazine, *Teotralnaia Zhizn* (*Theatrical Life*), also began publication. In 1982, the magazine *Sovremenaia Dramaturgia* (*Modern Drama*) started while *Moscovski Nabliudatel* (*Moscow Observer*) began in 1990.

Among the important theatre schools during the Soviet period were GITIS (the State Institute of Theatre Arts) founded in 1878, the Moscow Art Theatre School (founded in 1944), the Shchepkin Theatre School (founded in 1822) and connected to the Maly Theatre, the Shchukin Theatre School (founded in 1918) and connected to the Vakhtangov Theatre in Moscow, the Leningrad Institute of Theatre, Music and Cinematography (founded in 1918), the Karpenko-Karyi Theatrical Institute (founded in 1918), the Tashkent Institute of Theatre (founded in 1945), the Tbilisi Institute of Theatre (founded in 1939), the College of Choreography at the Bolshoi Theatre, the Vaganova College of Choreography (founded in 1756) in Leningrad, the Yaroslav Theatrical Institute (founded in 1984) and the Vladivostok Institute of the Arts (founded in 1957).

Over the seven decades of Soviet rule a large network of theatrical museums and libraries was developed. Some of these include the Bahruschin Central Museum of Theatre (founded in 1894), the Museum of the Moscow Art Theatre, the House Museum of Konstantin Stanislavski in Moscow and regional theatrical museums in Leningrad, Kiev, Tbilisi, Riga, Vilnius, Tallinn and other cities. There were also government theatrical libraries in Moscow and Leningrad, the Central Educational Library of the Union of Theatrical Leaders of Russia in Moscow and other theatrical libraries in large regional centres.

The democratic movement of the 1980s and early 1990s involved a number of talented people from various theatrical professions. Many of them understood the harshness of ideological censorship. However, theatre was under less stringent censorship than the mass media and because of this advantage many generations of Soviet people viewed theatre as more than just an art. Indeed, for many, theatre took the place of a parliament, religion, university, and even an independent press. Major dramatists, directors and actors often became public leaders, thanks largely to the privileged position of theatre in society. It was in art and literature in the USSR that many felt that they could dispute official ideological doctrine and influence politicians, the same politicians who started *perestroika* in March 1985. It was not by accident that after the return from exile in 1986 of Andrei Sakharov (b. 1921), an exceptional defender of human rights and a scholar, that one of his first public appearances was at a theatre – the Moscow Theatre of the Young Viewer where he saw the play *Heart of a Dog* based on a Bulgakov work (directed by Henrietta Yanovskaia). Sakharov's first public words in the Soviet press after a decade of silence, in fact, was his review of this production in *Teatr*.

After the elimination of censorship in 1987, the organizational, economic and social positions of the theatre again changed profoundly. The theatres with the highest reputations not only had their subsidies guaranteed but also were assured of their creative independence. With the important state theatres remaining as official models until the dissolution of the USSR, a number of new national organizations

Eimuntas Nekrošius's 1991 Lithuanian State Youth Theatre production of Gogol's *The Nose*.
Photo: Stanislovas Kairys.

emerged during this last confusing period. One of the largest was in Russia and was composed of almost all the republic's theatrical leaders. Based on the Vserosiikoe (All-Russian) Theatrical Society which had been in existence for a hundred years, this new organization became the model for unions being formed in other republics. There was as well a National Union of Theatrical Leaders formed which served as an umbrella organization for all the other unions. It was, in a way, the formation of these organizations which finally destroyed the government monopoly on theatre and allowed a more active and effective defence at this crucial time of the creative and social rights of theatre workers.

In the late 1980s, works by both Soviet and foreign authors as well as many who emigrated from the USSR and were previously banned by the censors, again began to appear. The theatre was slowly freeing itself.

The main concern in the late 1980s and early 1990s – as the country was collapsing – was to save the culture, not an easy challenge at a time of uprisings by various national movements across the USSR. In the end, however, it became obvious that the processes of history would not permit any kind of continuation of Soviet concepts. In January 1992, on the territory of the former USSR, a Commonwealth of Independent States (CIS) was declared. With it came the end of a single, dominant, all-controlling Soviet theatrical culture both at home and abroad. Despite this ignominious end, it was clear that the directors and leaders who were continuing to work in the new national entities, those whose works had been a part of a rich and complicated multinational theatrical culture, those who had developed interrelations and intercommunication among these complicated communities, those who were now uniting to fight totalitarian systems, and those who were beginning to build and develop new theatrical cultures, would never be able to forget their past experiences nor would they be able to give in to the temptation of isolationism as they began to build and develop new theatrical cultures on the still-warm ashes of the experiment called the USSR.

Mikhail Shvidkoi
Translated by Oleg Ginzburg

(See also ARMENIA, AZERBAIJAN, BELARUS, ESTONIA, GEORGIA, LATVIA, LITHUANIA, MOLDOVA, RUSSIA and UKRAINE)

UZBEKISTAN

(Asia/Oceania volume; see also **USSR**)

WALES

(see **UNITED KINGDOM**)

YUGOSLAVIA

(Historical Overview)

Located on the Balkan Peninsula in southeastern Europe, the modern nation of Yugoslavia came into being in 1918 when a group of states joined together under the name of the Kingdom of the Serbs, Croats and Slovenes. In 1929, the name was changed to the Kingdom of Yugoslavia. In 1945, six primarily Slavic republics – Serbia, Croatia, Bosnia-Herzegovina, Slovenia, Macedonia and Montenegro – agreed to come together to create a federation to be known as the Federal People's Republic of Yugoslavia (land area: 255,800 square kilometres or 98,800 square miles). This federation disintegrated into civil war in 1991 with declarations of independence by Slovenia and Croatia. These republics, and Bosnia-Herzegovina, were recognized as independent countries by the United Nations in 1992.

From the earliest days of 1918, the new state was troubled by disagreement among the various peoples who made up the kingdom. So weak was the country by 1941 that in April of that year, the Germans bombarded several Yugoslav cities and invaded the country without even declaring war. The Yugoslav government and its army collapsed with minimal resistance.

Between 1941 and 1945, while the country was under occupation, a civil war began between the communist-led Partisans and the Chetniks. Both fought against the occupying Axis troops and against the Ustaši, Yugoslavia's fascists. Under the leadership of Tito (Josip Broz, 1892–1980), the communists won control of Yugoslavia's government and in 1945 a new Federal Republic was established.

Ironically, it was also during the war that the country began to develop a rich cultural life. Many theatre artists, in fact, joined the Partisans and formed theatre troupes which played a key role in helping to develop the new society. These groups, varying in number and repertoire, created an important left-leaning theatre at the time. Even before 1943, when the Anti-Fascist Council for the National Liberation of Yugoslavia (the body that preceded the official government) was formed, many theatres were already active. Theatre courses were also being offered to prepare young soldiers for artistic and technical professions. The repertoire of these theatres was an eclectic combination of classical plays, Slavic plays with patriotic tendencies (mostly from nineteenth-century romantic drama), satires by such writers as Gogol, and political plays written by the soldiers themselves. Besides these army groups, there was also a diverse theatrical life continuing in several of the major cities including productions of some pro-fascist plays as well as a few that criticized fascist authority. The liberation of the country – along with its new government – was welcomed therefore by an already active theatrical community. The fact that the vast majority of theatre buildings were not damaged by the war was also of significance at the time.

The overall organization of the former state theatres remained more or less the same in the immediate post-war period and there was relatively little censorship. The theatrical enthusiasm that characterized the years after the war gave the theatre a special, even a privileged status. Generous financial help from the government elevated cultural life generally to an especially important level. The government, in fact, endeavouring to promote its democratic cultural policies, established many professional theatres in towns where they had never before existed.

Not surprisingly, many of them lasted for only a short time, mostly due to insufficient artistic quality.

By 1949, the country boasted four times as many theatres as there had been in 1939. Among other things, this meant that new training facilities were needed to provide skilled theatre professionals, and ultimately these new schools had a major effect on the nation's theatre life. Because the national film industry was only in its infancy and television was not yet available, the theatre was clearly at the centre of the public's focus. In fact, theatres were rarely able to satisfy the demand for tickets, which, during the late 1940s, were often impossible to obtain at the box office. Going to the theatre was, as in the Soviet system, organized through unions and factories, a system that remained in place until the mid-1950s.

Programming showed little variety among the various theatres. It ranged from ideologically correct national classics by such writers as the Croatian Marin Držić (1508–67), the Slovenian Ivan Cankar (1876–1918), the Serbian Branislav Nušić (1864–1938) and the Croatian Miroslav Krleža (1893–1981) to Russian and Soviet playwrights such as Griboedov, Ostrovskyi, Leonov, Shkvarkin and Simonov. Notably absent were the more avant-garde Soviet writers such as Mayakovsky, Bulgakov and Nikolai Erdman. For variety, there were some international classics (Shakespeare, Molière, Goldoni and Balzac) in productions which emphasized, sometimes bizarrely, leftist social tendencies. Contemporary playwrights from the west were also included but only those who criticized their own society's political and social problems (for example, Arthur Miller). Opera and ballet were not so strict in adhering to ideology but they also tended to draw on Soviet models and avoided works which could be interpreted as being ideologically suspect (Wagner, for example, did not appear in the repertoire until 1952).

This post-war ideological orientation in programming, where even the smallest vagueness or doubt led to severe criticism in the newspapers and, on occasion, even to cancellation of contracts, reduced the repertoire to mostly romantic plays. Even here protagonists and antagonists were clearly identified by costume and makeup. Directors were forced into simplified interpretations, often turning away from the real issues of the play. The result was theatre as history lesson or as picturesque explanation of some simplified psychological

state. The director was clearly limited to the most basic blocking within a strictly realistic design, while the work of the actors was reduced to simply 'identifying' and 'experiencing', according to simplistic interpretations of Stanislavski. In sum, though, this was a period of enthusiasm and restoration for the country as a whole, its theatrical reflection was often only energetic and naïve.

The period was notable for other events as well. Macedonia and Montenegro, which were not allowed to have their own theatres under the centralist hegemonistic systems of the past, opened professional theatres at this time. Croatian theatres too were opened in the parts of the country where the Italian language had previously dominated the stage (Rijeka and Zadar). As well, numerous minority ethnic groups living within the Yugoslav borders were also finally allowed to speak their native tongues on stage.

Probably the most crucial political moment occurred in 1948. The Communist Party of Yugoslavia at that time rejected Soviet accusations of straying from the correct path in building a socialist system. Practically speaking, this meant that Yugoslavia would no longer allow Stalin and the Soviet leadership to interfere with its domestic and foreign policy. Breaking away from the so-called 'socialist bloc', Yugoslavia truly gained its independence at this point, laying the groundwork for future development in both politics and economics. Cultural policies too evolved with a new awareness and led to the gradual abandonment of strict canons of socialist-realism in aesthetic questions. At a Congress of the Writers' Association in Ljubljana in 1952, one of Yugoslavia's leading writers and playwrights, Miroslav Krleža, began a call for pluralism in artistic and creative attitudes.

Very quickly, radical changes began to occur. In theatres across the country, simplified and ideologized dramas by Soviet playwrights, together with their domestic replicas, began to vanish. In their place, contemporary European and American writers began to be seen such as Giraudoux, Anouilh, Williams and Miller. They were quickly followed by representatives of the new avant-garde, including Ionesco and, at first somewhat suspiciously, Beckett. The first performance of *Waiting for Godot*, for example, was secretly presented in a painter's atelier in Belgrade in 1956. Eventually, other theatrical restrictions also vanished and the Yugoslav stage began welcoming virtually all contemporary writers and trends. From the mid-1950s, the Yugoslav theatre reflected such diverse influences as the French existentialists, Broadway, Artaud, Brecht and the Living Theatre. Successful plays from many European centres including the satirical and critical dramatic views of Polish and Czech writers were also produced (the world première of Mrożek's *Tango* was, in fact, held in Belgrade in 1952).

Thematic changes were occurring as well in the national dramatic repertoire. New questions about human existence in society and reflections about historical and political problems, opened up a whole range of themes for Yugoslav writers. Ethnic problems were examined through mythology while experimentation with language followed various avant-garde models and styles including the grotesque and the fairy-tale. Criticism and analysis of the recent past became increasingly important as dramatic themes.

The mid-1950s also brought organizational changes and a diminution of the influence of centralized institutions as the only places for important dramatic achievement. New theatres were founded in unconventional locations and less tightly controlled organizational models were sought. This startling evolution completely changed Yugoslav theatre life and its effects were felt for the next four decades. One must again mention here the influences from abroad on performance styles. Thanks to visits by numerous foreign artists during the 1950s and early 1960s, European approaches to both acting and design were being clearly felt. Among those whose influence was notable during this time was the Théâtre National Populaire from France with Jean Vilar and Gérard Philipe (seen in Yugoslavia in 1955), Giorgio Strehler's production of Goldoni's comedy *Arlecchino, servitore di due padroni* (*The Servant of Two Masters*, also 1955), the Comédie-Française from Paris, the Burgtheater from Vienna, the numerous visits by leading Moscow and Leningrad theatres, Polish and Czech groups, and various avant-garde companies.

The new political openness of the country in the 1960s and 1970s along with the encouragement of free artistic research resulted in a heterogeneous theatrical life which, in spite of Yugoslavia's multinational community with its many different cultural and historic traditions and despite the use of many different languages, somehow managed to coalesce into what can be called a Yugoslav style.

As the 1990s began – and the six nationalities that had come together to form Yugoslavia were once again pulling apart in bloody fighting – the theatre was clearly unable to exercise any particular influence, a genuine loss since it really had reached some maturity in its ability to deal not only with basic human themes but also with modern and even politically controversial viewpoints.

Structure of the National Theatre Community
Artistic Profile

The complex organizational structure of the Yugoslav theatre community was developed as a result of the nation's history, its federal constitution, and specific legislative and financial institutions. Even in the names of the more than one hundred Yugoslav theatres in existence as the 1990s began, one could find virtually everything but the word 'Yugoslavia'. The one theatre that did call itself Yugoslav was the Jugoslovensko dramsko pozorište (Yugoslav Dramatic Theatre) founded in Belgrade in 1948, a period strongly affected by centralist tendencies. Formed as a blending of artists from all the republics, by the mid-1950s, this theatre – mainly because of a conscious attempt by the federal government to decentralize political and cultural life – lost its often privileged 'supranational' status. By the 1960s, it had evolved into an ensemble structure and style of programming very similar to other theatres.

What was perhaps unique about Yugoslav theatres was the strong sense of independence shown by the various republics in terms of each national theatre's choice of repertoire, a repertoire which encouraged specific language traditions and very different aesthetic ideals formed by history and culture. These differences could be seen as well among both professional and semi-professional troupes operating in minority languages such as Hungarian, Albanian, Turkish, Italian and Slovak. One must include here as well the Slovensko gledališče (Slovenian

Haris Pašović's Yugoslav Dramatic Theatre production of Wedekind's *Spring's Awakening*.

Stage) from Trieste which, since its founding in 1902, also had its own clear vision of a national theatrical identity.

On the organizational level, Yugoslav theatres inherited many characteristics from the previous states that existed in the territory (the Austro-Hungarian Empire, the Serbian monarchy and the Yugoslav monarchy, among others). Each ethnic grouping quickly developed, within its 'national' theatre, companies for drama, opera and ballet. The oldest of these theatres (the Croatian, Serbian and Slovenian National Theatres) were, in fact, founded in the 1860s as the result of a perceived need for national, cultural and political identification. In the organizational sense, these theatres were simply adaptations of the Narodno divadlo (National Theatre) from Prague and the Burgtheater from Vienna and their primary goal was as much the development of the national language and literature as it was theatre. Despite problems of operation and space, this model of a central national theatre embracing all the performing arts remained active into the 1990s.

The oldest theatres of this type were the Hrvatsko narodno kazalište (Croatian National Theatre) in Zagreb, founded in 1860; the Srpsko narodno pozorište (Serbian National Theatre) in Novi Sad, founded in 1861; the Slovensko narodno gledališče (Slovenian National Theatre) in Ljubljana, founded in 1867; and the Narodno pozorište (National Theatre) in Belgrade, founded in 1868. The Narodno pozorište in Sarajevo (Bosnia-Herzegovina) was founded in 1921. Although earlier attempts at fully developing their own theatrical expression had been dictated by history and politics, the Macedonians and Montenegrins founded their national theatres just after World War II, when they gained national rights for the first time. The national theatre of the special district of Kosovo, which performed in both the Serbian and Albanian languages, differed from the other 'national models' in that it had only a dramatic and a dance troupe while the Montenegrins were represented only by a dramatic troupe. At the beginning of the twentieth century, still other similar theatres were founded in some of the regional centres, mostly in Croatia and Slovenia, in such cities as Osijek (1907), Maribor (1909), Split (1920) and Rijeka (1945). All, in fact, had centuries-old theatre histories which had been created originally under foreign influences, mainly Austrian, Hungarian and Italian.

Through the 1960s, all these national institutions were joined by a growing number of new regional theatres and later by touring companies, especially in Serbia, with most under federal control. Independent operetta and cabaret troupes date from the liberation army period and were still operating up to 1991 in most large centres, with the most famous in Zagreb and Belgrade. It was in these theatres that Broadway-style musicals tended to be played.

Interestingly, in the mid-1950s, at the height of liberalization of political and cultural thought, this general structure began to change. Ambitious young actors and directors started to leave the 'national' theatres to form their own experimental theatres, challenging the traditional institutions. This was a crucial turning point in the theatre life of the whole country. Among the new theatres were the Mestno gledališče ljubljansko (Ljubljana City Stage), founded in 1951; the Beogradsko dramsko pozorište (Belgrade Dramatic Theatre), 1951; the Zagrebačko dramsko kazalište (Zagreb Dramatic Theatre), 1953–4, later called Dramsko kazalište 'Gavella' (Dramatic Theatre 'Gavella'); Kamerni teater 55 (Chamber Theatre 55) in Sarajevo, 1955; Atelje 212 (Atelier 212) in Belgrade, 1956; and Oder 55 (Scene 55) in Ljubljana, 1957. At the same time, many professional ensembles in some of the smaller, regional cities such as Zadar, Karlovac and Pula ceased to exist because of financial problems. As the 'national' theatres began to fade in importance, some of the newer companies took on their national and linguistic mandates.

At the end of 1949, a new method of theatre management began to be implemented. Workers' Self-Management, as it was called, was introduced throughout the country's businesses as well as in education and culture. In the theatres, this meant that directors, actors and designers were selected through a kind of public tender, usually for a period of four years with a second term option. But under this system, directors did not have the power to make independent decisions regarding choice of repertoire, hiring or financial policy. Their function essentially was to execute decisions reached by artistic committees drawn from the theatre's personnel or by councils of theatre representatives which would include social and political representatives. This form of management, based on political models, was not easily applied to the theatre, as it did not allow any individual power in the making of artistic decisions. It was also difficult to end someone's employment with a theatre before their term was up, even if they did not make significant contributions through their work. An artist's engagement with a theatre, therefore, could be ended only through old age, death or retirement. Over the decades, the system began to break down but many groups were still operating this way into the 1990s.

In the mid-1960s, other types of theatres began to appear, most often consisting of strong directorial and dramaturgical managements, but without permanent acting ensembles. Hiring directors, designers and actors from other institutions for a single production, these theatres remained mobile and unencumbered by an administrative apparatus, allowing them to set and maintain relatively high standards of performance as well as a challenging repertoire. The most distinguished among them included Atelje 212, Teatar itd. (Theatre Etc.), founded in 1966 in Zagreb and, from Ljubljana, Glej (Look) formed in 1970 and Pekarna (Bakery Theatre) formed in 1972.

In the 1970s and 1980s, still newer groups formed with more divergent artistic visions. Some, in fact, came together knowing in advance they would cease operation after reaching a specific artistic goal – the Ljubljana group Sestre Scipiona Našice (Sisters of Scipion Našica), for example, operated between 1983 and 1986 – and then closed down having 'achieved' their artistic goals. Post-modern theatrical events of the mid-1980s were marked by

an array of outstanding directorial interpretations, usually with an urban landscape as setting.

On the financial side, almost all theatre activity in Yugoslavia was paid for by the state. Until the mid-1950s funds came directly from a centrally allocated budget. After that time, theatre and culture gradually changed over to financing through a so-called 'self-managing interest centre'. These centres collected about one-third of 1 per cent of all personal income in each region for cultural activities. Certain expenses were also paid for at community, regional, municipal and republican levels. Within these self-managing interest centres, it was the programme that was subsidized rather than the particular institution.

Subsidy for the various independent groups could go as high as 90 per cent of projected expenses, while the remainder would be covered by box-office income. Prices of theatre tickets were consistently kept low in this way with tickets for festival performances generally costing three times as much as normal theatre tickets. All theatres in the country offered discounts to students and organized various subscription programmes. This was especially true for the national institutions.

The normal theatre season in Yugoslavia operated from 1 September to 30 June each year with dramatic theatres performing four or five plays, opera theatres performing three operas, and ballet theatres performing two ballets.

Festivals too were a special part of the theatre scene in Yugoslavia, with over thirty annually during the 1970s and 1980s covering all genres. Most took place every year, some every other year. Most international festivals would include meetings of theatre experts, symposiums and exhibitions of set designs, costumes, poster designs, books, and so on. Like other theatre activities, they were financed either by the particular republic, the region, municipal sources or sometimes a combination of all three.

Among the most prominent were the Dubrovačke ljetne igre (Dubrovnik Summer Festival) founded in 1950 and famous for its outdoor performances and the Sterijino pozorje (Sterija's Theatre) which took place in Novi Sad every year from 1956. This competitive festival was dedicated exclusively to national dramatic literature and was named in honour of the Serbian playwright Jovan Sterija Popovič (1806–56). The festival brought together eight to ten selected productions in the various Yugoslav languages with emphasis on contemporary

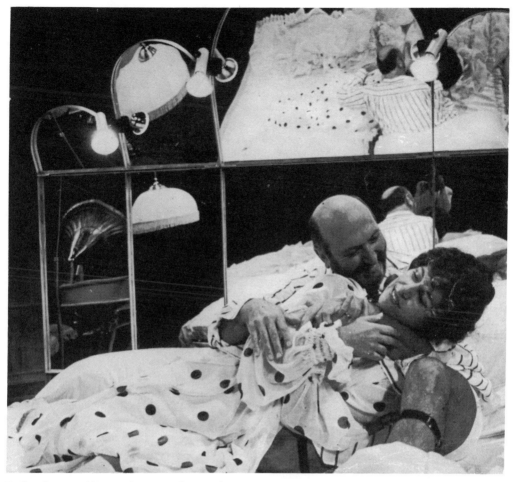

Dušan Jovanović's production of Branislav Nušić's *A Supicious Person* at the Permanent Slovenian Theatre, Trieste.

drama. The festival also developed a series of ancillary activities, one of the most important being an international symposium for critics and theatre publishers including specialized exhibitions of theatre books. A national theatre documentation centre also operated under the festivals's auspices.

The Festival malih i eksperimentalnih scena Jugoslavije (MES – Festival of Small and Experimental Yugoslav Theatres) took place in Sarajevo every year from 1960 to 1991. Its goal was to present the best productions in the country regardless of where the dramatist came from. Also competitive, the festival began as a forum for directors and actors with an emphasis on the avant-garde. Over the years, this specific criterion was abandoned but the festival remained a showcase for the latest theatre trends.

Among the best known festivals was BITEF – Beogradski internacionalni teatarski festival (Belgrade International Theatre Festival) – which took place in Belgrade every year from 1967. Founded by artistic director Mira Trailovic and dramaturge Jovan Ćirilov, BITEF was one of Europe's leading showcases for the international avant-garde.

Among other Yugoslav drama and opera festivals of note have been the Splitsko ljeto (Split Summer Festival), founded in the city of Split in 1954; Ohridsko ljeto (Ohrid Summer Festival) in the city of Ohrid, Macedonia, founded in 1961; Jugoslavenski operni bienale (Yugoslav Opera Biennial) in Ljubljana, Slovenia, founded in 1953; Osječki operni bienale (Osijek Opera Biennial) in Osijek, Croatia, founded in 1970 and dedicated to contemporary opera; and

Majske operne večeri (Operatic Evenings in May) in Skopje, Macedonia, founded in 1972.

Ballet artists competed at the Jugoslavensko baletno takmičenje (Yugoslav Ballet Competition) in Novi Sad, from 1958. An annual international festival of children's theatre began in 1958 in the city of Šibenik under the name Jugoslavenski festival djeteta. Puppet theatres were also represented at several festivals. Among the most important were the Medjunarodni festival kazališta lutaka/Pupteatra internacia festivalo (International Puppet Theatre Festival) held annually in Zagreb from 1968 (the festival was almost entirely in Esperanto); and the festival in Bugojno, Bosnia-Herzegovina, which took place annually beginning in 1971.

In demographic terms, of the fifty-eight dramatic theatres that were operating in Yugoslavia in 1990 (not counting freelance groups) nineteen were based in Serbia, twelve in Croatia, seven groups each in Slovenia and Macedonia, six in Bosnia-Herzegovina and one in Montenegro. Six additional dramatic theatres operated in what were called the special territories – five in Voivodina and one in Kosovo.

There were also nine minority language theatres: three operating in Hungarian (in Voivodina), three in Albanian (two in Kosovo and one in Macedonia) and another three operating in Croatia (Italian), Macedonia (Turkish) and Voivodina (Slovak).

In the years immediately after the war, it was the Družina mladih (Young People's Company) of Vlado Habunek and Radovan Ivšić in Zagreb which advanced puppet theatre most actively. With their unconventional repertoire (Chekhov, Merimée), they made people understand that the form had a validity of its own.

Among the leading modern directors and animators in Yugoslav puppetry were Zlatko Bourek (b. 1929) and Edi Majaron (b. 1940). Bourek was a challenging and unconventional author who utilized both actors and puppets together in the same works. He was also an excellent creator of masks as well as a costume designer, painter, graphic artist and animator. One of his most famous productions was his actor-puppet adaptation of Tom Stoppard's *Dogg's Hamlet* for Zagreb's Teatar itd. in 1982.

Theatre Space and Architecture

Since the majority of Yugoslav republics founded their professional theatres in the nineteenth century either under the Austro-Hungarian Empire or within independent Balkan countries such as Serbia and Montenegro, a great number of theatre buildings in the territory of Yugoslavia were built in the same period. But there were theatre buildings, some still in use, that originated in earlier periods. The theatre in the city of Hvar in Croatia, for example, was adapted from an armoury building created in 1612. In 1786 this theatre received its present neo-classical style. The theatre in the Slovenian city of Ptuj was built in 1786, and also still functions.

Since the middle of the nineteenth century, a number of classical, neo-classical, neo-Baroque or stylistically eclectic theatre buildings were built in Yugoslavia and most of these also still function as theatres. Almost all of Yugoslavia's major theatres, in fact, functioned in such nineteenth-century buildings and during the 1980s many were renovated and modernized.

Special attention was paid at that time to modernizing stage equipment, lighting and improving audience comfort while at the same time maintaining their original architectural integrity.

Among the many historic buildings in the country, the most architecturally interesting are to be found in Subotica (1854, neo-classical); Dubrovnik (1864, neo-classical, designed by architect Emil Vechietti, the first southern Slav theatre architect, renovated 1987); Maribor (1865); Osijek (1866, radically renovated in 1986); Belgrade (1863, neo-classical, several reconstructions, the last one in 1988); Šibenik (1870); Varaždin (1873, neo-classical, the first theatre building by the famous Viennese architect Hermann Helmer); Sombor (1882); Rijeka (1885, architects: Helmer and Fellner); Ljubljana (1890); Split (1883, architects Vechietti and Ante Bezić, renovated after a fire by Božidar Rašica in 1979); Zagreb (1895, neo-Baroque, Helmer and Fellner); Cetinje (1896, ruined during the earthquake of 1979);

Sarajevo (1898, radically reconstructed in 1939 and 1984); Ljubljana (1912); Skopje (1922, ruined during the earthquake in 1963); Banja Luka (1935); and in Niš (1939).

After 1945, therefore, theatre architecture experts were dealing mostly with adapting, improving and reconstructing already existing buildings. Their challenge was to find new artistic and urban solutions. In a few cases modern, functional and, in some details, extraordinary buildings exclusively devoted to theatrical purposes were created.

The most interesting of these were the Narodno pozorište Zenica (Zenica National Theatre) in Bosnia-Herzegovina, 1978 (architects: Jahiel Finci and Zlatko Ugljen); Srpsko narodno pozorište Novi Sad (Serbian National Theatre of Novi Sad), 1981 (architect Viktor Jackiewich of Poland); and Makedonski naroden teater (Macedonian National Theatre) Skopje, 1983 (architect: Jurij Princes, leading a group of Slovenian architects). Another Skopje theatre of note was the Teater narodnosti (Theatre of the People).

Training

Yugoslav theatre academies, like all other schools, were the sole responsibility of the state and as such were organized within state educational regulations. The education of all young artists was therefore officially organized and existed at elementary, secondary and university levels.

Before 1945, educational institutions for actors on an advanced level did not exist at all. Schools for actors were organized and structurally connected to national theatres and functioned on the secondary level over a two- or three-year period. The oldest of these was founded in Zagreb in 1896.

After the war, theatre academies (with specific departments for actors and directors) were founded in Ljubljana (1945), Belgrade (1948) and Zagreb (1950). Training at all these institutions generally lasted four years although in the late 1940s some academies insisted that those studying directing and radio broadcasting could enter only after completion of four years of higher education, usually in the humanities. Training in directing and radio would then last only two years. Through the 1960s, with the new demands of media technologies, new departments for film, television, dramaturgy and theatre administration were created.

Advanced training in set and costume design was generally organized within the Faculty of Design in Belgrade, and the majority of Yugoslav artists in those specialties gained practical experience by assisting in theatres after having completed training as painters, sculptors, graphic artists and architects.

In the early 1990s, theatre academies existed in Skopje (founded in 1969), Novi Sad (1974), Sarajevo (1981), Zagreb and Belgrade. Training was done in all of the major national languages as well as in minority languages such as Hungarian (taught at the Academy in Novi Sad). The academies varied in size from just twenty students (Sarajevo) to over 200 in Belgrade. The average rate of acceptance was one in ten. At most schools, the major courses were given in acting, speech, movement, musical education, history of the national theatre and literature, dramatic theory, psychology, makeup and costume history among others.

Education was always free, and many theatres gave grants for living expenses to individual students or even groups of students in order to rejuvenate their ensembles. After graduation the students had the right to work in any professional theatres in the country that would hire them. Graduates were not officially assigned to specific theatres or to regions of the country, nor did they have the right to choose the theatre where they would be engaged. The relationship was based exclusively on individual agreement. After two years of even occasional work, they could apply for membership of the theatre workers' union, which included certain social benefits such as medical insurance and a pension plan.

Criticism, Scholarship and Publishing

Theatre research has traditionally been carried on at universities, usually within literature, history or philology departments. By the late 1980s, it was also being done within the comparative literature departments of philosophical faculties as well as in dramaturgy courses at theatre academies. Major university theatre arts departments were located in Belgrade, Ljubljana, Sarajevo and Zagreb.

The Muzej pozorišne umetnosti SR Srbije (Serbian Museum of Theatre Art) in Belgrade, the Slovenski gledališki in filmski muzej (Slovenian Theatre and Film Museum) in Ljubljana, the Centar za pozorišnu dokumentaciju Sterijinog pozorja (Centre for Theatre Documentation of the Sterija Stage) in Novi Sad, the Muzej književnosti i pozorišne umjetnosti Bosne i Hercegovine (Museum of Literature and Theatre Art of Bosnia-Herzegovina) in Sarajevo, and Zavod za književnost i teatrologiju JAZU (Institute for Literature and Theatre Science of the Yugoslav Academy for Science and Art) in Zagreb all collected a wide range of theatre materials.

Among the country's key monthly and bimonthly theatre magazines and journals were *Pozorište* (*Theatre*) founded in 1959, *Scena* (*Stage*) founded in 1965, and *Prolog* (*Prologue*) and *Novi Prolog* (*New Prologue*) founded in 1968. Among the specialized magazines which published articles on theatre history as well as documents from theatre archives were *Dokumenti slovenskega gledališkega in filmskega muzeja* (*Documents of the Slovenian Theatre and Film Museum*) founded in 1964, *Teatron* founded in 1974 and *Kronika Zavoda za književnost i teatrologiju JAZU* (*Chronicle of the Institute for Literature and Theatre Science*). Important materials were also printed in yearbooks which most Yugoslav theatres published annually.

A range of leading publishers produced books on theatrical subjects, although there were no specialized theatrical publishers as such. Certain of the national theatres as well as critics' associations sometimes acted as publishing companies as well. Sterijino pozorje, for instance, was also an important publisher. Among smaller organizations of theatrical note were Knjižnica Mestnog gledališča ljubljanskog (Library of the Ljubljana City Theatre), which published more than a hundred volumes, and Hrvatsko društvo kazališnih kritičara i teatrologa (Croatian Association of Theatre Critics and Theatre Theoreticians) in Zagreb, which published more than twenty volumes.

Field researchers and staff
Translated by Aranka Legyel-Bosiljevac
and Irene Pauzer

(See also BOSNIA-HERZEGOVINA, CROATIA, MACEDONIA, SERBIA-MONTENEGRO and SLOVENIA)

Further Reading

'Atelje 212'. *Teatron* 33–34–35 (1982).

Batušić, Nikola. *Drama i pozornica: deset godina hrvatske drame na zagrebačkim pozornicama, 1964–1974*. [Drama and stage: ten years of Croatian drama on the stages of Zagreb 1964–74]. Novi Sad: Sterijino pozorje, 1975. 237 pp.

Hecimović, Branko. *Dramaturški triptihon*. [Dramaturgical triptych]. Zagreb: Hrvatsko društvo kazališnih kritičara i teatrologa, 1979. 188 pp.

Histoire des spectacles: *Encyclopédie de la Pléiade*. Paris: 1965. S.v. 'Yugoslavia' by Marijan Matković.

Karahasan, Dževad. *Kazalište i kritika*. [Theatre and criticism]. Sarajevo: Svjetlost, 1980. 241 pp.

Matković, Marijan, ed. *Le Théâtre yougoslave d'aujourd'hui/Yugoslav Theatre Today*. Zagreb–Belgrade–Dubrovnik: Yugoslavian Centre of the ITI, 1955.

Miletíc, Stjepan. *Hrvatsko Glumište: Dramaturški Zapisci*. [Croatian theatre: dramaturgical notes]. Zagreb: Centar za kulturnu djelatnost Saveza socijalističke omladine Zagreba, 1978. 509 pp.

Mrkšić, Borislav: *Drveni osmjesi. Eseji iz teorije i povijesti lutkarstva*. [Wooden smiles. Essays on the theory and history of puppetry]. Zagreb, 1976. 322 pp.

Pervić, Muharem. *Premijera: naša drama u našem pozorištu*. [Première: our drama in our theatre]. Belgrade: Nolit, 1978. 337 pp.

Popovic, Žorž: *Istorija arhitekture, pozorišta, kazališta gledališča i teatara Jugoslavije i Evrope*. [History of architecture and theatre of Yugoslavia and Europe]. Belgrade, 1986, 1977. 722 pp.

Šovagović, Fabijan. *Glumčevi zapisi*. [Actor's notes]. Zagreb: Centar za kulturnu djelatnost Saveza socijalističke omladine. Zagreba, 1977. 214 pp.

Stamenković, Vladimir. *Kraljevstvo ekperimenta*. [The kingdom of experimentation]. Belgrade: Prosveta pozorište u dramatizovanom društvu, 1987. 282 pp.

Theatre in Yugoslavia. Belgrade: Museum of Theatre Art in Belgrade, 1955. 86 pp.

FURTHER READING

Allen, John. *A History of the Theatre in Europe*. London: Heinemann Educational, and Totowa, NJ: Barnes & Noble, 1983. 314 pp.

——. *Theatre in Europe*. Sussex: John Oxford, 1981. 320 pp.

Allworth, Edward. 'Introduction to the Modern Drama of the Transcaucasus' in *Evil Spirit (Char Voki)* by Alexandre Shirvanzade. Translated by Nishan Parlakian. New York: St Vartan Press, 1980. xi–xxvii.

Berenguer Castellany, Angel. *Teatro europeo de los años 80*. [European theatre of the 1980s]. Colección Divergencias. LAIA, 1984. 208 pp.

Braun, Kazimierz. *Wielka Reforma Teatru w Europie. Luszie-idee-zdarzenia*. [Major theatre reforms in Europe: people, ideas, events]. Wrocław: Zakład Naradowy imienia Ossolińslich, 1984. 416 pp.

Cassidy, Claudia. *Europe on the Aisle*. New York: Random House, 1954. 231 pp.

Dort, Bernard. *Lecture de Brecht*. [Reading Brecht]. Paris: Seuil, 1972. 325 pp.

Duvignaud, Jean. *Sociologie de l'acteur*. [A sociology of the actor]. Paris: Gallimard, 1965. 304 pp.

——. *Sociologie du théâtre: essai sur les ombres collectives*. [A sociology of theatre: an essay on collective shadows]. Paris: Presses universitaires de France, 1965. 585 pp.

——, and Jean Lagoutte. *Le Théâtre contemporain: culture et contre-culture*. [Contemporary theatre: culture and counter-culture]. Séries Larousse Université & Thèmes et textes. Paris: Larousse, 1974. 223 pp.

Elsom, John. *Cold War Theatre*. London: Routledge, 1992. 198 pp.

Fantasia e sovversione. Per una sociologia del teatro politico e dil teatro alternativo in Scandinavia. [Fantasy and subversion: towards a sociology of political and alternative theatre in the Scandinavian countries]. Milan: F. Angeli, 1979.

Fischer-Lichte, Erika, and Harald Xander, eds. *Welttheater – Nationaltheater – Lokaltheater?: Europäisches Theater am Ende des 20. Jahrhunderts*. [World theatre – national theatre – local theatre?: European theatre at the end of the twentieth century]. Tübingen: A. Franke, 1993. 229 pp.

Gaskell, Ronald. *Drama and Reality: European Drama Since Ibsen*. London: Routledge & Kegan Paul, 1972. 171 pp.

Hubert, Marie-Claude. *Histoire de la scène occidentale de l'Antiquité à nos jours*. [A history of western theatre from antiquity to the present]. Paris: Colin, 1992.

——. *Le Théâtre*. [Theatre]. Paris: Colin, 1989.

Innes, Christopher. *Avant Garde Theatre 1892–1992*. London/New York: Routledge, 1993. 261 pp.

Jacquot, Jean, and Denis Bablet. *Le Lieu théâtral dans la société moderne*. [Theatrical space in modern society]. Paris: CNRS, 1963.

Kindermann, Heinz. *Europäische Theatergeschichte*. [History of European theatre]. 10 vols. Salzburg: Otto Müller Verlag, 1957–74.

Larthomas, Pierre. *Le Langage dramatique, sa nature, ses procédés*. [Dramatic language, its nature, its method]. Paris: Colin, 1972.

Marker, Frederick J., and Lise-Lone Marker. *The Scandinavian Theatre: A Short History*. Totowa, NJ: Rowman & Littlefield, 1975. 303 pp.

Marranca, Bonnie, and Gautam Dasgupta, eds. *The New Europe: Marriage of World Cultures*. Special double issue, *Performing Arts Journal* 35/36 (1990).

Mignon, Paul-Louis. *Panorama du théâtre au XXè*

siècle. [An overview of theatre in the twentieth century]. Paris: Gallimard, 1978. 377 pp.

Miller, Anna Irene. *The Independent Theatre in Europe: 1887 to the Present*. New York: B. Blom, 1966. 435 pp.

Palmer, Helen H. *European Drama Criticism 1900–1975*. 2nd ed. Hamden, CT: Shoe String Press, 1977.

Patterson, Michael. *German Theatre Today: Post-War Theatre in West and East Germany, Austria and Northern Switzerland*. London: Pitman, 1976. 129 pp.

Pavis, Patrice. *Voix et images de la scène*. [Voices and images from the stage]. Lille: University of Lille Press, 1985. 260 pp.

Performing Arts Yearbook for Europe. 3rd ed. London: Arts Publishing International, 1993. 472 pp.

Pollieri, Jacques. *Scénographie/sémiographie*. [Scenography/semiography]. Paris: Denoël, 1971. 250 pp.

Salvat, Ricard. *El teatro de los 70*. [Theatre in the 1970s]. Barcelona: Península, 1974. 299 pp.

Sonrel, Pierre. *Traité de scénographie*. [A treatise on scenography]. 2nd ed. Paris: Lib. Théâtrale, 1984.

Souriau, Étienne, ed. *Architecture et dramaturgie*. [Architecture and playwriting]. Paris: Flammarion, 1950.

Staud, Géza, ed. *Revue d'histoire du théâtre*. [Review of theatre history]. Paris: La Société d'Histoire du Théâtre, 1970.

Stephenson, Claude, ed. *Theatre in the Five Scandinavian Countries*. Stockholm: Nordiska Teaterunionen, 1971.

Yarrow, Ralph, ed. *European Theatre 1960–1990: Cross-Cultural Perspectives*. London: Routledge, 1992. 256 pp.

INTERNATIONAL REFERENCE

The following is a list of significant titles that have been published over the last half-century. For a complete listing of world theatre publications, see volume 6 of this encyclopedia, *World Theatre Bibliography/Cumulative Index*. This section was prepared with the collaboration of René Hainaux and the Centre de Recherches et de Formation Théâtrales en Wallonie, with the assistance of collaborators from Europe, North and South America, Africa, the Arab World and Asia.

Reference Works/Dictionaries/ Encyclopedias/Bibliographies

Attisani, Antonio. *Enciclopedia del teatro del '900.* [Theatre encyclopedia of the twentieth century]. Milan: Feltrinelli, 1980.

Bailey, Claudia Jean. *A Guide to Reference and Bibliography for Theatre Research.* 2nd ed. Columbus: Ohio State University Libraries, 1983.

Banham, Martin, ed. *The Cambridge Guide to World Theatre.* Cambridge, England: Cambridge University Press, 1988. 1,104 pp.

Brauneck, Manfred, and Gérard Schneilin, eds. *Theaterlexikon: Begriffe und Epoche. Bühnen und Ensembles.* [Theatre lexicon: terms and periods. Stages and ensembles]. Hamburg: Rowohlt, 1986. 1,120 pp.

Cao, Yu, and Wang, Zuo Ling, eds. *China's Great Encyclopedia of World Theatre and Drama.* Beijing/Shanghai: China's Great Encyclopedia Press, 1989. 583 pp.

Cohen, Selma Jeanne, ed. *International Encyclopedia of Dance.* Oxford: Oxford University Press, 1994.

Corvin, Michel. *Dictionnaire encyclopédique du théâtre.* [Encyclopedic dictionary of theatre]. Paris: Bordas, 1991.

Couty, Daniel, and Alan Rey, eds. *Le Théâtre.* [Theatre]. Paris: Borduas, 1980.

D'Amico, Silvio, ed. *Enciclopedia dello spettacolo.* [Encyclopedia of the performing arts]. 11 vols. Rome: Le Maschere, 1954–66.

Dalhaus, Carl. *Pipers Enzyklopädia des Musiktheaters.* [Piper's encyclopedia of music theatre].

Esslin, Martin, ed. *The Encyclopedia of World Theater.* New York: Scribner, 1977.

Fielding, Eric, gen. ed. *Theatre Words: An International Vocabulary in Nine Languages.* Prague Publication and Information Exchange Commission of OISTAT, 1993.

Gassner, John, and Edward Quinn, eds. *The Readers' Encyclopedia of World Drama.* New York: Thomas Y. Crowell, 1969. 1,030 pp.

Giteau, Cécile. *Dictionnaire des arts du spectacle: Théâtre-Cinéma-Cirque-Danse-Radio-Marionettes-Télévision-Documentologie.* [Dictionary of the performing arts: Theatre-Film-Circus-Dance-Radio-Puppetry-Television-Documentation]. Paris: Dunod, 1970. 430 pp. In French, English and German.

Gregor, Josef, and Margret Dietrich. *Der*

Schauspielführer: Der Inhalt der wichtigsten Theaterstücke aus aller Welt. [The play guide: Synopses of the most important plays from the whole world]. 14 vols. Stuttgart: Anton Hierseman, 1953–89.

Hainaux, René, ed. *Stage Design Throughout the World.* 4 vols. Harrap, London and New York: Theatre Arts Books, 1956–75.

Hartnoll, Phyllis, ed. *The Concise Companion to the Theatre.* New York: Oxford University Press, 1972.

——. *The Oxford Companion to the Theatre.* 3rd ed. London: Oxford University Press, 1967.

Hochman, Stanley, ed. *McGraw-Hill Encyclopedia of World Drama.* 2nd ed. 5 vols. New York: McGraw-Hill, 1984.

Hoffmann, Christel, ed. *Kinder- und Jugendtheater der Welt.* [Children's and youth theatre of the world]. 2nd ed. Berlin: Henschelverlag, 1984. 276 pp.

Kienzle, Siegfried. *Schauspielführer der Gegenwart. Interpretation zum Schauspiel ab 1945.* [A guide to contemporary plays: an interpretation of plays since 1945]. Stuttgart: Alfred Kröner Verlag, 1978. 659 pp.

Koegler, Horst, ed. *The Concise Oxford Dictionary of Ballet.* Oxford: Oxford University Press, 1987.

Matlaw, Myron. *Modern World Drama: An Encyclopedia.* London: Secker & Warburg, 1972. 960 pp.

Mikotowicz, Thomas J., ed. *Theatrical Designers: An International Biographical Dictionary.* Westport, CT: Greenwood Press, 1992. 365 pp.

Mokulski, S.S., and P.A. Markov, eds. *Teatralnaia Entsiklopedia.* [Theatre encyclopedia]. 6 vols. Moscow: Sovietskaia Entsiklopedia, 1961–7.

Ortolani, Benito, ed. *International Bibliography of Theatre.* 7 vols. New York: Theatre Research Data Center, 1985–93.

Pavis, Patrice. *Dictionnaire du théâtre. Termes et concepts de l'analyse théâtrale.* [Dictionary of the theatre: terms and concepts of theatrical analysis]. 2nd ed. Paris: Éditions Sociales, 1987.

Philpott, A.R. *Dictionary of Puppetry.* London: MacDonald, 1969. 291 pp.

Quéant, G., ed. *Encyclopédie du théâtre contemporain.* [Encyclopedia of contemporary theatre]. Paris: Olivier Perrin. 211 pp.

Rischbieter, Henning. *Theater-Lexikon.* [Theatre lexicon]. Rev. Zurich-Schwäbisch Hall: Orell Füssli, 1983. 484 pp.

Sadie, Stanley, ed. *The New Grove Dictionary of Opera.* 4 vols. London: Macmillan, 1992.

Schindler, Otto G. *Theaterliteratur. Ein bibliographischer Behelf für das Studium der Theaterwissenschaft.* [A bibliographic guide for theatre studies]. 3 vols. Vienna: Institut für Theaterwissenschaft, 1973.

Shigetoshi, Kawatake, ed. *Engeki Hyakka Daijiten.* [Encyclopedia of world theatre]. 6 vols. Tokyo: Heibonsha, 1960–2.

Swortzell, Lowell, ed. *International Guide to Children's Theatre and Educational Theatre. A Historical and Geographical Source Book.* Westport, CT: Greenwood Press, 1990. 360 pp.

Trapido, Joel, ed. *An International Dictionary of Theatre Language.* Westport, CT: Greenwood Press, 1985. 1,032 pp.

Veinstein, André, and Alfred Golding, eds. *Performing Arts Libraries and Museums of the World/Bibliothèques et Musées des Arts du Spectacle dans le monde.* 4th ed. Paris: Centre National de la Recherche Scientifique, 1992. 773 pp.

Wilcox, R. Turner. *The Dictionary of Costume.* New York: Scribner, 1969.

Theatre History

Anderson, Jack. *Ballet and Modern Dance.* Princeton, NJ: Princeton Book Company, 1987.

Arnott, Peter. *The Theatre in its Time.* Boston, MA: Little, Brown, 1981. 566 pp.

Aslan, Odette. *L'Art du théâtre.* [The art of theatre]. Verviers: Marabout, 1963. 672 pp.

Awad, Louis. *Al masrah al âlami.* [World theatre]. Egypt: 1964.

Brockett, Oscar G. *History of the Theatre.* 6th ed. Boston, MA: Allyn & Bacon, 1990. 680 pp.

Calendoli, G. *Storia universale della danza.* [Dance world history]. Milan: Mondadori, 1985.

Dumur, Guy, ed. *Histoire des spectacles.* [History of the performing arts]. Coll. Encyclopédie de la Pléiade. Paris: Gallimard, 1965. 2,010 pp.

Jurkowski, Henryk. *Dzieje teatru lalek. Od wielkiej reformy do współczesności.* [History of the puppet theatre. From theatre's reform to today]. Warsaw: 1984.

——. *Écrivains et marionettes. Quatre siècles de littérature dramatique.* [Writers and puppets:

four centuries of dramatic literature]. Charleville-Mézières: Institut National de la Marionnette, 1991.

Kuritz, Paul. *The Making of Theatre History*. Englewood Cliffs, NJ: Prentice-Hall, 1988. 468 pp.

Kybalova, Ludmila, Olga Herbenova, and Milena Lamarova. *The Pictorial Encyclopedia of Fashion*. New York: Crown, 1968.

Londré, Felicia Hardison. *The History of World Theater*. 2 vols. New York: Continuum, 1991.

Molinari, Cesare. *Teatro*. [Theatre]. Milan: Mondadori, 1972.

——. *Theatre Through the Ages*. New York: McGraw-Hill, 1975. 324 pp.

Mordden, Ethan. *The Fireside Companion to the Theatre*. New York: Simon & Schuster, 1988. 313 pp.

Nagler, A.M. *A Sourcebook in Theatrical History*. New York: Dover, 1952. 611 pp.

Nicoll, Allardyce. *The Development of the Theatre: A Study of Theatrical Art from the Beginnings to the Present Day*. 5th ed. London: George G. Harrap, 1966. 318 pp.

Niculescu, Margareta. *Teatrul de păpuşi în lume*. [Puppet theatre in the world]. Berlin: Henschelverlag, and Bucharest: Meridiane, 1966. 230 pp.

Nutku, Őzdemir. *Dünya Tiyatrosu Tarihi*. [A history of world theatre]. 2 vols. Ankara: Ankara Universitesi dil ve Tarih Coğrafya Fakültesi Yayınları, 1973.

Ottai, Antonella, ed. *Teatro Oriente/Occidente*. [Oriental/occidental theatre]. Biblioteca Teatrale 47. Rome: Bulzoni, 1986. 565 pp.

Pandolfi, Vito. *Storia universale del teatro drammatico*. [World history of dramatic art]. 2 vols. Turin: Unione Typografico-Editrice, 1964. 1,626 pp.

Pérez Coterillo, Moisés, ed. *Escenarios de dos mundos: Inventario teatral de Iberoamérica*. [Stages of two worlds: A theatre inventory of Latin America]. 4 vols. Madrid: Centro de Documentación Teatral, 1988.

Pronko, Leonard C. *Theater East and West: Perspectives Toward a Total Theater*. Berkeley: University of California Press, 1967. 280 pp.

Roose-Evans, James. *Experimental Theatre: From Stanislavski to Peter Brook*. 2nd ed. London: Routledge, 1989.

Zamora Guerrero, Juan. *Historia del teatro contemporáneo*. [History of contemporary theatre]. 4 vols. Barcelona: Juan Flors, 1961–2.

Criticism and Aesthetics

Appia, Adolphe. *Oeuvres complètes*. [Complete works]. 3 vols. Edited by Marie L. Bablet-Hahn. Lausanne: L'Age d'Homme, 1983–8.

Artaud, Antonin. *Oeuvres complètes*. [Complete works]. 25 vols. Paris: Gallimard, 1961–90.

Barba, Eugenio. *Beyond the Floating Islands*. New York: PAJ Publications, 1986. 282 pp.

——. *The Floating Islands*. Holstebro, Denmark: Thomsens Bogtrykkeri, 1979. 224 pp.

——, and Nicola Savarese. *The Secret Art of the Performer. A Dictionary of Theatre Anthropology*. Edited and compiled by Richard Gough. London: Routledge, 1991. 272 pp.

Bawtree, Michael. *The New Singing Theatre*. Bristol Classical Press, Bristol, UK and New York: Oxford University Press, 1991.

Beckerman, Bernard. *Dynamics of Drama*. New York: Drama Book Specialists, 1979. 272 pp.

Bentley, Eric. *The Dramatic Event*. New York: Horizon, 1954.

——. *The Life of the Drama*. New York: Atheneum, 1964.

——. *The Playwright as Thinker*. New York: Harcourt, Brace, 1946.

Birringer, Johannes. *Theatre, History and Post-Modernism*. Bloomington: Indiana University Press, 1991. 240 pp.

Boal, Augusto. *Theatre of the Oppressed*. New York: Theatre Communications Group, 1985. 197 pp.

Brecht, Bertolt. *Kleines Organon für das Theater*. [A little organon for the theatre]. Frankfurt: Suhrkamp Verlag, 1958.

——. *Schriften zum Theater*. [Writings on the theatre]. 7 vols. Werner Hecht, ed. Berlin: Aufbau Verlag, 1963–4.

Brook, Peter. *The Empty Space*. London: MacGibbon & Kee, 1969. 141 pp.

Brustein, Robert. *The Theatre of Revolt*. Boston, MA: Little, Brown, 1964.

Clark, Barrett H. *European Theories of the Drama*. New York: Crown, 1965. 628 pp.

Craig, Edward Gordon. *On the Art of Theatre*. London: Heinemann, 1911, 1968. 295 pp.

——. *Towards a New Theatre*. London: J.M. Dent, 1913.

Dort, Bernard. *Théâtre en jeu*. [Drama in performance]. Paris: Seuil, 1979. 334 pp.

——. *Théâtre réel*. [Real theatre]. Paris: Seuil, 1971. 300 pp.

Epskamp, Kees P. *Theatre in of Search for Social Change: The Relative Significance of Different Theatrical Approaches.* The Hague: Centre for the Study of Education in Developing Countries, 1989.

Esslin, Martin. *The Field of Drama.* London: Methuen, 1987. 190 pp.

———. *The Theatre of the Absurd.* New York: Anchor, Doubleday, 1961.

Frye, Northrop. *Anatomy of Criticism.* Princeton, NJ: Princeton University Press, 1957. 383 pp.

Goodman, Lizbeth. *Contemporary Feminist Theatres.* London: Routledge, 1992.

Grotowski, Jerzy. *Towards a Poor Theatre.* New York: Simon & Schuster, 1968. 262 pp.

Ionesco, Eugène. *Notes et contrenotes.* [Notes and counternotes]. Paris: Gallimard, 1962.

Kidd, Ross. *The Performing Arts, Non-Formal Education and Social Change in the Third World: A Bibliography and Review Essay.* The Hague: Centre for the Study of Education in Developing Countries, 1981.

Kott, Jan. *Shakespeare Our Contemporary.* New York: Anchor, Doubleday, 1966.

Pavis, Patrice. *Theatre at the Crossroads of Culture.* London: Routledge, 1991. 256 pp.

Schechner, Richard. *Between Theatre and Anthropology.* Philadelphia: University of Pennsylvania Press, 1985. 342 pp.

———. *Environmental Theatre.* New York: Hawthorne, 1973.

———. *Performance Theory.* London: Routledge, 1988.

Seltzer, Daniel. *The Modern Theatre: Readings and Documents.* Boston, MA: Little, Brown, 1967. 495 pp.

Stanislavski, Konstantin. *The Collected Works of Konstantin Stanislavsky.* Sharon Marie Carnicke, gen. ed. 10 vols. London: Routledge, 1993–.

———. *Sobraniye Sochinenii.* [Collected works]. 7 vols. Moscow: Iskusstvo, 1954–60.

Strehler, Giorgio. *Per un teatro umano. Pensieri, scritti e parlati ed attuali.* [For a humanized theatre: contemporary thinking, writing and talking]. Milan: Feltrinelli, 1974.

Turner, Victor. *From Ritual to Theatre: The Human Seriousness of Play.* New York: PAJ Publications, 1982. 127 pp.

Ubersfeld, Anne. *L'École du spectateur.* [The school for theatregoers]. Paris: Éditions Sociales, 1981. 352 pp.

———. *Lire le théâtre.* [Reading performance]. Paris: Éditions Sociales, 1977. 280 pp.

Wandor, Michelene. *Carry On, Understudies: Theatre and Sexual Politics.* London: Routledge, 1986. 224 pp.

Theatre Arts

Bablet, Denis. *Les Révolutions scéniques du XXe siècle.* [The scenic revolutions of the twentieth century]. Paris: Société Internationale d'Art XXe siècle, 1975. 388 pp.

Barton, Lucy. *Historic Costume for the Stage.* Boston, MA: W.H. Baker, 1961.

Bellman, Williard F. *Scenography and Stage Technology.* New York: Thomas Crowell, 1977. 639 pp.

Braun, Edward. *The Director and the Stage: From Naturalism to Grotowski.* London: Methuen, 1982. 218 pp.

Cole, Toby, and Helen K. Chinoy. *Actors on Acting: The Theories, Techniques and Practices of the Great Actors of all Times as Told in Their Own Words.* New York: Crown, 1970. 715 pp.

Duerr, Edwin, ed. *The Length and Depth of Acting.* New York: Holt-Rinehart & Winston, 1962. 590 pp.

Gorelik, Mordecai. *New Theatres for Old.* New York: Dutton, 1962.

Grebanier, Bernard. *Playwriting.* New York: Thomas Crowell, 1961. 386 pp.

Izenour, George C. *Theater Design.* New York: McGraw-Hill, 1977. 631 pp.

Malkin, Michael R. *Traditional and Folk Puppets of the World.* New York: A.S. Barnes, 1977. 194 pp.

Mello, Bruno. *Trattato di scenotecnica.* [A treatise on scene design]. Novara: G.G. Gorlich, Instituto Geografico de Agostini, 1979.

Niccoli, A. *Lo spazio scenico: Storia dell'arte teatrale.* [Scenic space: a history of theatre art]. Rome: Bulzoni, 1971.

Pilbrow, Richard. *Stage Lighting.* New York: Van Nostrand Reinhold, 1971.

Saint-Denis, Michel. *The Rediscovery of Style.* New York: Theatre Arts Books, 1960.

———. *Training for the Theatre.* New York: Theatre Arts Books, 1982. 242 pp.

Spolin, Viola. *Improvisation for the Theatre. A Handbook of Teaching and Directing*

Techniques. Evanston, IL: Northwestern University Press, 1963. 397 pp.

Tidworth, Simon. *Theatres: An Architectural and Cultural History*. New York: Praeger, 1973. 224 pp.

Watson, Lee. *Lighting Design Handbook*. New York: McGraw-Hill, 1990. 458 pp.

WRITERS
AND NATIONAL
EDITORIAL COMMITTEES

ALBANIA

Writers: Josif Papagjoni (Qendra e Studimit të Artit, Tirana), Pandi Bello (Qendra e Studimit të Artit, Tirana).

ARMENIA

Writers: Sargis Aroutchian, Artashes Emin (Canadian Mission, Yerevan), Levon Hakhverdian (Theatre Historian, Yerevan), Emmanuel Manoukian, Nishan Parlakian (Professor of Armenian Studies, John Jay College, New York).
Editorial Committee: Kevork Abadjian, Arthur Elbakian, Silva Kharshafdjian, Roseanne Sahakian, Ratik Sharoyan.

AUSTRIA

Writers: Ulf Birbaumer (Institut für Theaterwissenschaft, University of Vienna), Klaus Behrendt (Österreichisches Theatermuseum, Vienna), Evelyn Deutsch-Schreiner, Wolfgang Greisenegger (Institut für Theaterwissenschaft, University of Vienna), Klemens Gruber (Institut für Theaterwissenschaft, University of Vienna), Ursula Kneiss (Institut für Theaterwissenschaft, University of Vienna), Rainer Maria Köppl (Institut für Theaterwissenschaft, University of Vienna), Isolde Schmidt-Reiter (Institut für Theaterwissenschaft, University of Vienna),

Marlene Schneider (Theater der Jugend).
Editorial Committee: Klemens Gruber, Rainer Maria Köppl.

AZERBAIJAN

Writers: Rakhman Badalov (Director of the Department of Aesthetics and Cultural Theory, Azerbaijan Academy of the Sciences), Aidyn Talybov (Senior Lecturer, Guseinzade Art University, Baku).
Editorial Committee: Azer Neymatov (Chair, Theatre Union of Azerbaijan; Producer, National Theatre of Azerbaijan), Illhan Raginli (Assistant Professor, Guseinzade Art University, Baku), Marian Ali-zade (Senior Lecturer, Guseinzade Art University, Baku).

BELARUS

Writer: Vankarem Nikiforovich (Theatre Critic).
Editorial Committee: Sergei Kortes (Artistic Director, State Opera Theatre of Belarus, Minsk), Boris Lutsenka (Artistic Director, State Russian Dramatic Theatre, Minsk), Valery Rayevsky (Artistic Director, Kupala Belorussian State Academic Theatre, Minsk).

BELGIUM

Writers: *Flemish Community*: Werner de Bondt, Toon Brouwers, Alfons Goris, Marc Hermans,

Micheline Heyse, Alfons van Impe, Marianne van Kerkhoven, Patricia Kuypers, Freek Neirynck, Jaak van Schoor; *French Community*: Rina Barbier, Jean-Henri Drèze, Paul Emond, Francis Houtteman, Fernand Leclercq, Marc Quaghebeur, Catherine Simon.
Readers: Marc Maufort (Université Libre de Bruxelles), Carlos Tindemans (Departement Germaanse Filologie, Universitaire Instelling Antwerpen).

BOSNIA-HERZEGOVINA

Writer: Mair Musafija (former Editor and Producer, Television Sarajevo; former Theatre Critic, *Oslobodenje*).

BULGARIA

Writers: Rosalia Bix, Nevyana Injeva, Violetta Konsoulova, Petar Smiicharov, Vassil Stefanov (National Theatre Ivan Vasov), Kalina Stefanova-Peteva, Elena Vladova.

CROATIA

Writer: Nikola Batušić (Professor of Theatre History, Academy of Dramatic Art, Zagreb).

CYPRUS

Writers: Christakis Georgiou (President, Cypriot Centre of the ITI), Nicos Shiafkalis (Director, Cypriot Centre of the ITI).

CZECH REPUBLIC

Writers: Vladimír Adamczyk (Theatre Architecture Consultant, Theatre Institute, Prague), Helena Albertová (Dramatist; Critic; Director, Theatre Institute, Prague), Drahomíra Čeporanová (Theatre Historian; Cabinet Member, Czech Theatre Studium, Prague), Jindřich Černý (Theatre Historian; Director, National Theatre, Prague), Miroslav Česal (Professor of Puppet Theatre History, Academy of Performing Arts, Prague), Nina Malíková (Puppetry Consultant, Theatre Institute, Prague), Jana Patočková (Theatre Critic, Editorial Department, Theatre Institute, Prague), Petr Pavlovský (Aesthetician; Chair of Theatre Science, Charles University, Prague), Ladislava Petišková (Theatre Historian, Theatre Institute,

Prague; Pantomime Consultant, Music Academy, Prague), Věra Ptáčková (Design Consultant, Theatre Institute, Prague and the Janáček Academy of Performing Arts, Brno), Vladimír Vašut (Chair of Dance, Music Academy, Prague), Ivan Vojtěch (Musicologist; Chair of Music Science, Charles University, Prague).
Editorial Committee: Helena Albertová, Jana Patočková, Ladislava Petišková.
Reader: Jarka M. Burian (Professor Emeritus, Department of Theatre, University at Albany, State University of New York).

DENMARK

Writers: Birthe Johansen (Journalist), Mogens Andersen (Head of Music, Denmarks Radio), Heino Byrgesen (Head of Drama Production, Denmarks Radio), Beth Juncker (Journalist, *Politiken*), Elin Rask (Theatre Historian; Journalist, *Kristligt Dagblad*), Bente Scavenius (Art Historian; Journalist, *Politiken*), Jytte Wiingaard (Professor of Theatre History, University of Copenhagen).
Editorial Committee: Heino Byrgesen, Erik Aschengreen (Professor of Aesthetics and Dance History, University of Copenhagen), Jens Kistrup (Theatre and Literature Critic, *Berlingske Tidende*).
Readers: Harry Lane (Drama Department, University of Guelph), Janne Risúm (Institut for Dramaturgi, Århus Universitet).

ESTONIA

Writers: Jaak Rähesoo (Critic and Translator), Reet Neimar (Critic, *Teater. Muusika. Kino*), Kristel Pappel (Music Critic, Tallinn Conservatory), Kustav-Agu Püüman, (Designer), Lea Tormis (Institute of History, Tallinn).
Editorial Committee: Arne Mikk (Artistic Director, Estonia Theatre), Vilma Paalma (Music Critic; Archivist, Estonia Theatre), Priit Pedajas (Director, Estonian Drama Theatre), Lembit Peterson (Director), Jaak Rähesoo, Lea Tormis, Aime Unt (Designer; Professor, Art University Tallinn), Riina Viiding (Secretary, Estonian Theatre Workers' Union).

FINLAND

Writers: Timo Koho (Theatre Architecture Writer), Raija Ojala (Editor-in-Chief, *Teatteri*), Auli Räsänen (Music and Dance Theatre Critic, *Uusi Suomi* and *Helsingin Sanomat*), Heta

Reitala (Writer; Professor of Theatre, Helsinki University), Riitta Seppälä (Director, Central Organization of Finnish Theatre and the Finnish Centre of the ITI), Anneli Suur-Kujala (Assistant Director, Finnish Centre of the ITI; Editor, *News from the Finnish Theatre*), Maiju Tawast (Producer, Green Apple Puppet Theatre).
Readers: Harry Lane (Drama Department, University of Guelph), Soila Lehtonen (Journalist; Critic).

FRANCE

Writers: Philippe Rouyer (Director, CERT, Université de Bordeaux III), Marie-Claude Hubert (Centres des Lettres et Sciences Humaines, Université de Provence Aix-Marsaille).
Reader: Felicia Londré (Curator's Professor of Theatre, Department of Theatre, University of Missouri, Kansas City).

GEORGIA

Writer: Eteri Gougoushvili (Dean, Georgian State Shota Rustaveli Theatrical College).

GERMANY

Writers: Günther Erken (FRG), Rolf Rohmer (GDR), Werner Gommlich, Gunter Kaiser, Joachim Näther, Horst Seeger (Editor, *Musik-Lexikon* and *Opern-Lexikon*), Käthe Seelig, Peter Ullrich, Wolfgang Wöhlert (Literary Advisor, Carousel Theater an der Parkaue, Berlin).
Reader: Erika Fischer-Lichte (Institut für Theaterwissenschaft, Johannes Gutenberg-Universität Mainz).

GREECE

Writer: Aliki Bacopoulou-Halls (Associate Professor, Athens University; Secretary-General, Hellenic Centre of the ITI).
Editorial Committee: Nicos Hourmouziadis (Professor, University of Thessaloniki), Costas Georgousopoulos (Theatre Critic; Lecturer, University of Athens), Eleni Varopoulou (Theatre Critic; Lecturer, University of Patras), John Stefanellis (Designer).
Reader: Anne Fletcher (World Civilization Programme, Tufts University, Medford).

HUNGARY

Writer: György Székely (Committee for Theatre Research, Hungarian Academy of Sciences).
Editorial Committee: Péter Nagy (Hungarian Academy of Sciences), Tamás Bécsy (Professor, ELTE University of Philology), Anna Földes (Theatre Critic, Association of Hungarian Journalists), György Lengyel (President, Hungarian Centre of the ITI), György Székely, Dezső Szilágyi (President, UNIMA Publications Committee), László Vámos (Hungarian Centre of the ITI).
Readers: Georges Baal (Centre National de la Recherche Scientifique, IMESCO), Andreas Kotte (Institut für Theaterwissenschaft, Universität Bern), Péter Szaffkó (English Department, Lionel Kossuth University, Debrecen).

ICELAND

Writers: Árni Ibsen (National Theatre, Reykjavík), Sveinn Einarsson (Icelandic National Broadcasting Service), Thorsteinn Gunnarsson, Helga Hjörvar, Sigurdur Pálsson, Hallveig Thorlacius, Sigrún Valbergsdóttir.
Editorial Committee: Árni Ibsen, Sveinn Einarsson, Sigrún Valbergsdóttir.
Reader: Harry Lane (Drama Department, University of Guelph).

IRELAND

Writers: Christopher Morash (Lecturer, St Patrick's College, Maynooth), John McCormick (Senior Lecturer, Samuel Beckett Centre for Drama and Theatre Studies, Trinity College, Dublin), Carolyn Swift (Founding Member, Pike Theatre; Dance Critic, *The Irish Times*).
Readers: Richard Allen Cave (Department of Drama and Theatre Studies, Royal Holloway University of London), Stephen Wilmer (Samuel Beckett Centre for Drama and Theatre Studies, Trinity College, Dublin).

ISRAEL

Writer: Haim Nagid. **Reader:** Freddie Rokem (Department of Theatre Arts, Yolanda and David Katz Faculty of Fine Arts, Tel Aviv University).

ITALY

Writer: Carlo Vallauri (Theatre Critic; Editor, *Ridotto*; University of Sienna).

LATVIA

Writers: Livija Akurātere, Ija Bite, Viktors Hausmanis, Irēna Lagzdiņa, Aldis Linē, Edite Tišheizere, Antra Torgāne, Guna Zeltiņa.
Reader: Veneranda Kreipans (Drama Teacher, CECM English Sector, Montreal).

LITHUANIA

Writers: Antanas Vengris (Professor Emeritus, Philology, Vilnius), Elona Bundzaitė-Bajorinienė (Theatre Critic, *Kultūros barai*), Edmundas Gedgaudas (Music Critic, Lithuanian Culture and Education Ministry), Audronė Girdzijauskaitė (Institute of Culture and Art, Vilnius), Eugenijus Gūzas (Architect; Board Member of Lithuanian Architects Union), Audronis Imbrasas (Dance Critic, *Mūzu malunas*), Gražina Mareckaitė (Researcher, Institute of Culture and Art, Vilnius).

LUXEMBOURG

Writer: Marc Olinger.
Reader: Marc Turpel (Luxembourg UNESCO Commission).

MACEDONIA

Writers: Aleksandar Aleksiev (Professor; Theatre Historian; Critic), Emilija Džipunova (Ballet Critic; Dancer) Vladimir Georgievski (Professor; Designer), Ivan Ivanovski (Journalist; Critic; Theatre Historian), Dragoslav Ortakov (Professor; Musicologist; Composer), Risto Stefanovski (Director, Drama Theatre; Director, National Theatre of Macedonia).
Editorial Committee: Risto Stefanovski, Slavomir Marinkovik (Editor; Publisher).

MALTA

Writers: Vicki Ann Cremona (Mediterranean Institute Theatre Programme, University of Malta), John J. Schranz (Mediterranean Institute Theatre Programme, University of Malta), Cecilia Xuereb, Paul Xuereb.

MOLDOVA

Writer: Constantin Cheianu (Secretary, Moldovan Theatre Union).
Editor: Veniamin Apostol (Chair, Moldovan Theatre Union).

NETHERLANDS

Writers: Hanny Alkema (Critic), Tom Blokdijk (Dramaturge, Theatergroep Hallandia, Zaandam), Jackelien van Deursen (Journalist), Janny Donker (Editor, *Notes*), Pol Eggermont (Dramaturge, Toneelgroep Amsterdam), Lia Gieling (Design Scholar).
Reader: Robert L. Erenstein (Instituut voor Theaterwetenschap, Universiteit van Amsterdam).

NORWAY

Writers: Knut Ove Arntzen (Associate Professor, Drama and Theatre Department, University of Bergen), Kirsten Broch (Dramaturge, Den Nationale Scene, Bergen), Harriet Eide (*Dagbladet*), Halldis Hoaas, Trine Næss (Head of the Theatre Collection, Royal University Library, Oslo), Steinar Vestlie (Nationaltheatret, Oslo).
Editorial Committee: Kirsten Broch, Margrethe Aaby (Nationaltheatret, Oslo), Janken Varden (Oslo Nye Teater).
Readers: Harry Lane (Drama Department, University of Guelph), Willmar Sauter (Institutionen for Teater och Filmvetenskap, Stockholms Universitet).

POLAND

Writers: Paweł Chynowski (Literary Manager, Teatr Wielki, Warsaw;), Marta Fik (Theatre and Literary Critic; Researcher, Institute of the Arts, Polish Academy of Sciences), Henryk Jurkowski (Professor, State Theatre Academy, Warsaw), Jan Kłossowicz (Theatre Critic and Historian), Małgorzata Komorowska (Assistant Professor, Chopin Academy of Music, Warsaw), Paweł Konic (Foreign Section Editor, *Dialog*), Edward Krasiński (Professor, Insitute of the Arts, Polish Academy of Sciences), Paweł Obracaj (Stage Designer; Researcher, Technical University, Opole), Juliusz Tyszka (Theatre Critic; Researcher, Institute of Culture, Poznań University), Elżbieta Wysińska (Editor-in-Chief, *Le Théâtre en Pologne/Theatre in Poland*).

Editor: Małgorzata Semil (Deputy Editor, *Dialog*; Lecturer, State Theatre Academy, Warsaw).
Readers: Tamara Trojanowska, Zbigniew Wilski.

PORTUGAL

Writers: Luiz Francisco Rebello (Sociedade Portuguesa de Autores), Carlos Porto, Maria Helena Serôdio (Portuguese Centre of AICT), Mário Vieira de Carvalho.
Reader: Erminio G. Neglia (Department of Spanish and Portuguese, University of Toronto).

ROMANIA

Writers: Ileana Berlogea, Petre Codreanu, Mihai Crişan, Mircea Ghiţulescu, Ion Lucian, Traian Niţescu.
Editorial Committee: Margareta Barbutza, Radu Beligan.
Reader: Valentin Silvestru.

RUSSIA

Writer: Mikhail Shvidkoi (Editor, *Teatr*).
Editorial Committee: Valery Khasanov (Secretary General, Russian Centre of the ITI), the late Melitina Kotovskaia (Professor of Theatre, GITIS, Moscow).

SERBIA-MONTENEGRO

Writers: Petar Marjanović (Professor of Yugoslav Theatre History, Faculty of Dramatic Arts, Belgrade), Raško Jovanović, Radoslav Lazić, Aleksandar Milosavljević, Milenko Misailović, Svetozar Rapajić, Mira Santini.

SLOVAK REPUBLIC

Writers: Jaroslav Blaho (Director, National Theatre Centre, Bratislava), Andrej Maťašík (Head, Contemporary Theatre Department, National Theatre Centre, Bratislava).
Editorial Committee: Dana Sliuková (Theatre Critic; Associate Director, National Theatre Centre, Bratislava), Jaroslav Blaho, Oleg Dlouhý (Head, Theatre Documentation Department, National Theatre Centre, Bratislava).
Reader: Jarka M. Burian (Professor Emeritus, Department of Theatre, University at Albany, State University of New York).

SLOVENIA

Writers: Simon Kardum (Theatre Critic), Lado Kralj (Associate Professor), Andrej Inkret (Theatre Professor), Albert Kos (Senior Advisor, Ministry of Culture), Edi Majaron, Viktor Molka (Theatre Architect), Henrik Neubauer (President, Slovenian Centre of the ITI), Denis Poniž (Associate Professor), Vasja Predan (Theatre Critic), Rapa Šuklje.
Editorial Committee: Lado Kralj, Simon Kardum, Albert Kos, Henrik Neubauer, Vasja Predan.

SPAIN

Writers: Eduardo Huertas Vázquez, María Francisca Vilches de Frutos (Consejo Superior de Investigaciones Científicas, Madrid), Elena Santos Deulofeu (Consejo Superior de Investigaciones Científicas, Madrid).
Reader: Erminio G. Neglia (Department of Spanish and Portuguese, University of Toronto).

SWEDEN

Writers: Claes Englund (Editor, *Entre*), Leif Janzon, Peter Bohlin.
Readers: Harry Lane (Drama Department, University of Guelph), Willmar Sauter (Institutionen for Teater och Filmvetenskap, Stockholms Universitet).

SWITZERLAND

Writers: Christoph Reichenau (Publicist), Martin Dreier (Director, Swiss Theatre Collection, Bern), Bibi Gessner (Secretary, Swiss Centre of the ITI).
Editor: Walter Boris Fischer (President, Swiss Centre of the ITI).
Reader: Béatrice Perregaux (Département de langue et littérature françaises modernes, Université de Genève).

TURKEY

Writers: Özdemir Nutku (Professor of Drama, G. Eyül University, İzmír), Sevda Şener (Professor of Drama, Ankara University), Ayşegül Yüksel (Professor of Drama and English, Ankara University).
Editorial Committee: Sevda Şener, Özdemir Nutku, the late Irfan Şahinbaş (Professor of

Drama and English, Ankara University), Ayşegül Yüksel.
Readers: Turgut Akter (Director; Historian), Zeynep Oral (Editor-in-Chief, *Milliyet Art Review*; Writer; Theatre Critic).

UKRAINE

Writers: Nelli Kornienko (Candidate of Theatre Arts History), Maryna Cherkashyna (Doctor of Theatre Arts).
Readers: Romana Bahry (Department of

Languages and Literatures, York University, Toronto), Natalie Rewa (Department of Drama, Queen's University, Kingston), Virlana Tkacz (Director, New York).

UNITED KINGDOM

Writers: John Elsom, Caroline Astles, Peter Brinson, Olivia Eisinger, John Keefe, Carl Miller, David Prosser.
Reader: Michael Anderson (Professor of Drama, University of Kent at Canterbury).

INDEX